THE OFFICIAL

1988 PRICE GUIDE TO

BASEBALL
CARDS

THE OFFICIAL®

1988 PRICE GUIDE TO

BASEBALL CARDS

BY DR. JAMES BECKETT

SEVENTH EDITION

THE HOUSE OF COLLECTIBLES
NEW YORK, NEW YORK 10022

Published by: The House of Collectibles
            201 East 50th Street
            New York, New York 10022

Distributed by Ballantine Books, a division of Random House, Inc., New York and simulta-
neously in Canada by Random House of Canada Limited, Toronto.

Manufactured in the United States of America

Library of Congress Catalog Card Number: 84-645496

ISBN: 0-876-37737-1

10 9 8 7 6 5 4 3 2

TABLE OF CONTENTS

ABOUT THE AUTHOR

Jim Beckett, the leading authority on sport card values in the United States, maintains a wide range of activities in the world of sports. He possesses one of the finest collections of sports cards and autographs in the world, has made numerous appearances on radio and television, and has been frequently cited in many national publications. He was awarded the first "Special Achievement Award" for Contributions to the Hobby by the National Sports Collectors Convention in 1980 and the "Jock-Jasperson Award" for Hobby Dedication in 1983.

Dr. Beckett is the author of *The Sport Americana Football, Hockey, Basketball and Boxing Price Guide*, *The Official Price Guide to Football Cards*, *The Sport Americana Baseball Card Price Guide*, *The Official Price Guide to Baseball Cards*, *The Sport Americana Price Guide to Baseball Collectibles*, *The Sport Americana Baseball Memorabilia and Autograph Price Guide*, and *The Sport Americana Alphabetical Baseball Card Checklist*. In addition, he is the founder, author, and editor of *Beckett Baseball Card Monthly*, a magazine dedicated to advancing the card collecting hobby.

Jim Beckett received his Ph.D. in Statistics from Southern Methodist University in 1975. He resides in Dallas with his wife Patti and their daughters, Christina and Rebecca, while actively pursuing his writing and consultancy careers.

PREFACE

Isn't it great? Every year this book gets bigger and bigger with all the new sets coming out. But even more exciting is that every year there are more collectors, more shows, more stores, and ... more interest in the cards we love so much. This edition has been enhanced and expanded from the previous edition. The cards you collect—who they are of, what they look like, where they are from, and (most important to many of you) what their current values are—are enumerated within. Many of the features contained in the other *Beckett Price Guides* have been incorporated into this volume since condition grading, nomenclature, and many other aspects of collecting are common to the card hobby in general. We hope you find the book both interesting and useful in your collecting pursuits.

The Beckett Guide has been successful where other attempts have failed because it is complete, current, and valid. This price guide contains not just one, but three, prices by condition for all the baseball cards in the issues listed. These account for almost all the baseball cards in existence. The prices were added to the card lists just prior to printing and reflect not the author's opinions or desires but the going retail prices for each card, based on the marketplace (sports memorabilia conventions and shows, hobby papers, current mail order catalogs, local club meetings, auction results, and other firsthand reportings of actually realized prices).

To facilitate your use of this book, read the complete introductory section in the pages following before going to the pricing pages. Every collectible field has its own terminology; we've tried to capture most of these terms and definitions in our glossary. Please read carefully the section on grading and the condition of your cards as you will not be able to determine which price column is appropriate for a given card without first knowing its condition.

Welcome to the world of baseball cards.

ACKNOWLEDGMENTS

This edition of the *Price Guide* contains new sets and, of course, completely revised prices on all the cards. A great deal of hard work went into this volume, and it could not have been done without a considerable amount of help from many people. Our thanks are extended to each and every one of you.

First, we owe a special acknowledgment to Dennis W. Eckes, "Mr. Sport Americana," who had the vision to see where the hobby was going and the perseverance and drive to help it get there. The success of the *Beckett Price Guides* has been the result of a team effort. Although Denny has chosen no longer to be a co-author on price guides—in order to devote more time to his business, Den's Collector's Den—he is still on board as a special consultant.

Those who have worked closely with us on this and many other books have again proven themselves invaluable—Frank and Vivian Barning (Baseball Hobby News), Cartophilium (Andrew Pywowarczuk), Mike Cramer (Pacific Trading Cards), Bill and Diane Dodge, Gervise Ford, Larry and Jeff Fritsch, Tony Galovich, Mike and Howard Gordon, John Greenwald, Wayne Grove, Bill Haber, Bill Henderson, Danny Hitt, Alan Kaye (Baseball Card News), Ralph Nozaki, Jack Pollard, Gavin Riley, Alan Rosen (Mr. Mint), John Rumierz, San Diego Sport Collectibles (Bill Goepner and Nacho Arredondo), John Spalding, Frank Steele, Murvin Sterling, Ed Twombly (New England Bullpen), and Kit Young.

Special mention goes to three people this year. Brian Morris, who has broad collecting and dealing interests, put his experience in writing by marking up and sending us his old (last year's) copy of the *Price Guide*. This is my favorite way to receive a maximum amount of input from a very knowledgeable person. Others have done this besides Brian—but Brian did the best job this year.

Lew Lipset has done much to further the knowledge of cards and collecting; most advanced collectors are familiar with his three encyclopedic volumes covering N, T, and E cards. However, we thank him this year for the development of his "Old Judge" newsletter and the popularization of the "break factor." Lew, with help from his son Rob, has analyzed the relationship between the sum of the individual prices and the complete set price. The resulting ratio is the "break factor." This year's edition herein shows that knowledgeable collectors and dealers are increasingly aware of the "break factor" as set prices have risen markedly on most older issues.

Knowledge of the "who, what, where, when, and how much" of Press Pins has been advanced this year based on the extensive and laborious contributions of Jim Johnston, one of the top collector/dealers in those attractive and valuable items. We thank him for his labor of love.

All three of the above have my thanks as well as a lifetime subscription to *Beckett Monthly*.

Special thanks are extended to the Donruss Company, the Fleer Corporation,

Sportflics, and the Topps Chewing Gum Company, who have consistently provided checklists and visual materials in order that the *Price Guide* could be complete.

Many other people have provided price input, illustrative material, checklist verifications, errata, and/or background information. At the risk of inadvertently overlooking or omitting these many contributors, we should like to individually thank Ab D Cards (Dale Wesolewski), Jerry Adamic, A.J.'s Sport Stop, Bob Alexander, Dennis Anderson, Eric Anderson, Lee Anderson, Thomas D. Anderson, Mark Angle, Rick Apter, Mark Argo (Olde South Cards), Jerry Baldwin, Ball Four Cards, Ed Barry (Ed's Collectibles), Bob Bartosz, Baseball Card Shop, Bay State Cards (Lenny DeAngelico), Chris Benjamin, Eric Bechtel, Beulah Sports, Big Andy's, John Blank, Levi Bleam, Bob Boffa, Tim Bond, Gary Borofsky, Joe Borte, Bill Bossert (Mid-Atlantic Coin Exchange), Major Charles Botello, Scott Bowery, Jeffery Brandon, Greg Brown, Kevin Brown, Shanan Brown, Larry Calder, Murray Calder, California Card Co., Cards and Comics, Louis Centolanza, Ira Cetron, Charles Champ, Sandy Chan, Don Chandler, Dwight Chapin, Chriss Christiansen, Barry Colla, Collection de Sport AZ, Ben Contorno, Kenny Conyers, Ron Coons, Paul Cords, Kevin Cormier, Taylor Crane, William Craven, James Critzer, John Curtis, Alan Custer, Dave Dame, Donna Davis, James Dickson, Greg Diehl, Dixie Dugout, George Dolence, Serge Donikian, Bill Downes, John Dorsey, Charles Dugre, Ruston Eastman, Larry Eccles, Jason Egge, Doak Ewing, David and Mark Federman, John Ferer, David Festberg, Bill Finneran, Stewart Flate, Leo Font Jr., Frank Fox (The Card Shop), Steve Freedman, Jeff Freyer, Hank Friedman, Jason Galla, Willie George, Bob Gilbert (Brewer Sports Collectibles), Dick Goddard, Steve Gold (AU Sports), Greg Goldstein (Dragon's Den), Jeff Goldstein, Rich Gove (Central Coast Baseball Cards), Todd Grady, Grand Slam Sports Collectibles, Ron Gulledge, Dave Hadeler, Dean Haley, Ronald Haley, Charley Hall, Hall's Nostalgia, John Halpin, Ernie Hammond, Hershell Hanks, Phil Haseltine, P. Hawkins, Joel Hellman (JJ's Budget Baseball Cards), Jeffrey Hewitt, Janet Hock, Eric Hook, Paul Hundrieser, Ryan Hurba, Tom Hutchinson, Chad Irwin, Richard L. Johnson, Rosie Jones, Stewart Jones, Dave Jurgensmeier, John Kagawa, Dr. Neil Katz, Jim Kelley, Rick Keplinger, Ted Kern, Ray Kessler, Tom Kiecker, Robert Lee King, Jim Knowler, John Kolodziej, Thomas Kunnecke, Wayne Larned, Dan Lavin, Leo LeClair, Morley Leeking, Charles Leinberry, Irv Lerner, Kathie Liles, LNW Sports, Chris Lockwood, Mike London, Chad Long, Jeff Long, Steve Ludwiski, John Machacek, Jim Macie, Paul Marchant, Bob May, Raymond May, Dr. William McAvoy, Mike McDonald (Sports Page), Gail McEldowney, J. McElroy, Brian McNeil, Dan McReynolds, Mendal Mearkle (Chariots Inc.), John Mehlin, Blake Meyer (Lone Star Sportscards), Joe Michalowicz, Sean Millar, David "Otis" Miller, Wayne Miller, Dick Millerd, Ashby Milstead, Ilan Mochari, Mike Moloney, Matthew Morgan, Dick Mueller, Ray Murphy, Gary Nagle, Edward Nazzaro (The Collector), Chip Nelson, Eddie Nelson, Murry Nelson, Tony Niemann (ADC Sports), Mike Nolde, North Conway Baseball Card Shop, Mike O'Brien, Keith Olbermann, Carl Olsen (Baseball Card Express), Bruce Parker, Jack Parsons, Clay Pasternack, Bill Pekarik (Pastime Hobbies), Michael Perrotta, Gerald Perry, Tom Pfirrmann, Pine Tree Stamps, Charles M. Placek, Michael Poynter, Mickey Rabinowitz, Michael Raduenz, Troy Rambo, Rick Rapa and Barry Sanders (Atlanta Sports Cards), Steve Rateike, Trey Rees, Gordon Reid, Tom Reid, Pat Reiter, Paul Richman, Owen Ricker, Rick's Coin Shop, Ken Rinehart, Dave Ring, Nathan Roach, Norman Rodriguez, Clifton Rouse, George Rusnak, Terry Sack, Steve St.Peter, Jennifer Salems, Ang Savelli, Robert Scagnelli, Matt Schindler, Don Schlaff, F.C. Schlauch, Shawn Schuetz, Michele Scott, David Shannon, Gerry Shebib, Scott Shepherd, Chris and Kelly Shore, Barry Sloate, Darren Smith, Stuart Smith, Robert Sochacki, Southern Sports (Roy Young), State Video and Comics, Dave Steckling, Don Steinbach, Mark Stewart (Blue Chip), Rick Stineman, Raymond Strawn, Strikeout Sports Cards, Richard Strobino, Barrie Sullivan, Hugh Sullivan, Fred Suzman, Swamp Fox Collectibles, David Taylor, Ian Taylor, Lyle Telfer, Lee Temanson, Scott Thompson, Charles Thorpe, Richard Thurman, Triple Play Cards, Ralph Triplette, 20th Century Collectibles, Rich Unruh, Charles Usher, John Vanden Beek, John Vangen, Trent Vich, Pokie Villalon, Tom Wamble, Christopher Waters, Bill Wesslund, Richard West, Bob Wilke (The Shoe Box), Jeff Williams, Joe Willis, World Series Cards (Neil Armstrong), Steve Wozniak, Kit Young, Ted Zanidakis, and Robert Zanze.

We have appreciated all of the help we have received over the years from collectors across the country and, indeed, throughout the world. Hopefully we haven't missed you in the list above if you have contributed input in the past year. Every year we make active solicitations to individuals and groups for input to that year's edition and we are particularly appreciative of help (large and small) provided for this volume. While we receive many inquiries, comments, and questions regarding material within this book—and, in fact, each and every one is read and digested—time constraints prevent us from personally replying to all but a few such letters. We hope that the letters will continue, and that even though no reply is received, you will feel that you are making significant contributions to the hobby through your interest and comments.

Special thanks go the staff of *Beckett Publications* for their help on many of the little things that added up to making this book possible. Assistant editors, Fred Reed and Pepper Hastings, were most helpful with the introduction and advertising, respectively. Lou Cather and Edna Harless cheerfully helped with the paste-up and layout. The overall operations of our ongoing commitment to the hobby through *Beckett Monthly* were skillfully directed by Claire Backus, my sister. Thanks also go to Dale Backus, my new brother-in-law, who was very understanding about Claire's overtime during this period as well as his contributing directly to our success in the past year on the magazine; Claire has been ably assisted by Anne Lowe (our subscription manager), Mary Gregory, Lily Windus, Julie Grove, and Nancy Paterson. Thanks also go to Jim and Sandy Beane, who performed several major system programming jobs for us this year, in order to help us accomplish our work faster and more accurately. The whole *Beckett Publications* team has my thanks for jobs well done. Thank you, everyone.

Last year I acknowledged my loving family by saying, "Writing this book would have been a very unpleasant experience without the understanding and cooperation of my wife, Patti, and daughters, Christina and Rebecca. I thank them and promise them that I will pay them back for all those hours." This year I must admit that their patience is wearing thin and I don't blame them as they have not been paid back for those many hundreds of missing hours. Writing this book *IS* an unpleasant experience for someone who really wants to be a good husband and father. My daughters do not understand why Daddy comes home when they are waking up . . . Patti isn't too keen on that either. At any rate I am committed to correcting my priorities in the next year, without jeopardizing the high standards my readers have come to expect.

ERRATA

There are thousands of names, more than 100,000 prices, and untold other words in this book. There are going to be a few typographical errors, a few misspellings, and possibly, a number or two out of place. If you catch a blooper, drop me a note directly or in care of the publisher, and we will fix it up in the next year's edition.

INTRODUCTION

Welcome to the exciting world of baseball card collecting, America's fastest-growing avocation. You have made a good choice in buying this book, since it will open up to you the entire panorama of this field in the simplest, most concise way.

It is estimated that nearly a quarter of a million different baseball cards have been issued during the past century. And the number of total cards put out by all manufacturers last year has been estimated at over two billion. With all that cardboard available in the marketplace, it should be no surprise that several million sports fans like you collect baseball cards today, and that number is growing by hundreds of thousands each year.

The growth of *Beckett Baseball Card Monthly* is another indication of this rising crescendo of popularity for baseball cards. Founded less than three years ago by Dr. James Beckett, the author of this price guide, *Beckett Monthly* has grown to the pinnacle of the baseball card hobby with more than a quarter of a million readers anxiously awaiting each enjoyable issue.

So collecting baseball cards—while still pursued as a hobby with youthful exuberance by kids in the neighborhood—has also taken on the trappings of an industry, with thousands of full- and part-time card dealers, as well as vendors of supplies, clubs and conventions. Each year since 1980, in fact, thousands of hobbyists have assembled for a National Sports Collectors Convention, at which hundreds of dealers have displayed their wares, seminars have been conducted, autographs penned by sports notables, and millions of cards changed hands. These colossal affairs have been staged in Los Angeles, Detroit, St. Louis, Chicago, New York, Anaheim, Arlington, TX, and this year in San Francisco. So baseball card collecting is really national in scope!

This increasing interest has been reflected in card values. As more collectors compete for available supplies, card prices rise. A national publication indicated a "very strong advance" in baseball card prices during the past decade, and a quick perusal of prices in this book compared to the figures in earlier editions of this price guide will quickly confirm this. Which brings us back around again to the book you have in your hands. It is the best annual guide available to this exciting world of baseball cards. Read it and use it. May your enjoyment and your card collection increase in the coming months and years.

HOW TO COLLECT

Each collection is personal and reflects the individuality of its owner. There are no set rules on how to collect cards. Since card collecting is a hobby or leisure pastime, what you collect, how much you collect, and how much time and money you spend collecting are entirely up to you. The funds you have available for collecting and your own personal taste should determine how you collect. Information and ideas presented here are intended to help you get the most enjoyment from this hobby.

It is impossible to collect every card ever produced. Therefore, beginners as well as intermediate and advanced collectors usually specialize in some way. One of the reasons this hobby is popular is that individual collectors can define and tailor their collecting methods to match their own tastes. To give you some ideas of the various approaches to collecting, we will list some of the more popular areas of specialization.

Many collectors select complete sets from particular years. For example, they may concentrate on assembling complete sets from all the years since their birth or since they became avid sports fans. They may try to collect a card for every player during that specified period of time.

Many others wish to acquire only certain players. Usually such players are the superstars of the sport, but occasionally collectors will specialize in all the cards of players who attended certain colleges or came from certain towns. Some collectors are only interested in the first cards or rookie cards of certain players.

Another fun way to collect cards is by team. Most fans have a favorite team, and it is natural for that loyalty to be translated into a desire for cards of the players on that favorite team. For most of the recent years, team sets (all the cards from a given team for that year) are readily available at a reasonable price.

OBTAINING CARDS

Several avenues are open to card collectors. Cards can be purchased in the traditional way at the local candy, grocery, or drug stores, with the bubble gum or other products included. In recent years, it has also become possible to purchase complete sets of baseball cards through mail order advertisers found in traditional sports media publications, such as *The Sporting News, Baseball Digest, Street & Smith's Yearbooks,* and others. These sets are also advertised in the card collecting periodicals. Many collectors will begin by subscribing to at least one of the monthly hobby publications, all with good up-to-date information. In fact, subscription offers can be found in the advertising section of this book.

Most serious card collectors obtain old (and new) cards from one or more of several main sources: (1) trading or buying from other collectors or dealers; (2) responding to sale or auction ads in the monthly hobby publications; and/or (3) attending sports collectibles shows or conventions. We advise that you try all three methods since each has its own distinct advantages: (1) trading is a great way to make new friends; (2) monthly hobby periodicals help you keep up with what's going on in the hobby (including when and where the conventions are happening); and (3) shows provide enjoyment and the opportunity to view millions of collectibles under one roof, in addition to meeting some of the hundreds or even thousands of other collectors with similar interests who also attend the shows.

PRESERVING YOUR CARDS

Cards are fragile. They must be handled properly in order to retain their value. Careless handling can easily result in creased or bent cards. It is, however, not recommended that tweezers or tongs be used to pick up your cards since such utensils might mar or indent card surfaces and thus reduce those cards' conditions and values. In general, your cards should be handled directly as little as possible. This is sometimes easier to say than to do. Although there are still many who use custom boxes, storage trays, or even shoe boxes, plastic sheets are the preferred method of storing cards. A collection stored in plastic pages in a three-ring album allows you to view your collection at any time without the need to touch the card itself. For a large collection, some collectors may use a combination of the above methods.

When purchasing plastic sheets for your cards, be sure that you find the pocket size that fits the cards snugly. Don't put your 1951 Bowmans in a sheet designed to fit 1981 Topps. Most hobby and collectibles shops and virtually all collectors' conventions will have these plastic pages available in quantity for the various sizes offered or you can purchase them directly from the advertisers in this book.

Damp, sunny and/or hot conditions—no, this is not a weather forecast—are three elements to avoid in extremes if you are interested in preserving your collection. Too much (or too little) humidity can cause gradual deterioration of a card. Direct, bright sun (or fluorescent light) over time will bleach out the color of a card. Extreme heat accelerates the decomposition of the card. On the other hand, many cards have lasted more than 50 years without much scientific intervention. So be cautious, even if the above factors typically present a problem only when present in the extreme. It never hurts to be prudent.

COLLECTING/INVESTING

Collecting individual players and collecting complete sets are both popular vehicles for investment and speculation. Most investors and speculators stock up on complete sets or on quantities of players they think have good investment potential. There is obviously no guarantee in this book, or anywhere else for that matter, that cards will outperform the stock market or other investment alternatives in the future.

After all, baseball cards do not pay quarterly dividends. Nevertheless, investors have noticed a favorable trend in the past performance of baseball and other sports collectibles, and certain cards and sets have outperformed just about any other investment in some years.

Some of the obvious questions are: Which cards? When to buy? When to sell? The best investment you can make is in your own education. The more you know about your collection and the hobby, the more informed the decisions you will be able to make. We're not selling investment tips. We're selling information about the current value of baseball cards. It's up to you to use that information to your best advantage.

NOMENCLATURE

Each hobby has its own language to describe its area of interest. The nomenclature traditionally used for trading cards is derived from the *American Card Catalog*, published in 1960 by Nostalgia Press. That catalog, written by Jefferson Burdick (who is called the "Father of Card Collecting" for his pioneering work), uses letter and number designations for each separate set of cards.

The letter used in the ACC designation refers to the generic type of card. While both sport and non-sport issues are classified in the ACC, we shall confine ourselves to the sport issues. The following list defines the letters and their meanings as used by the *American Card Catalog*.

(none) or N—19th Century U.S. Tobacco
B—Blankets
D—Bakery Inserts Including Bread
E—Early Candy and Gum
F—Food Inserts
H—Advertising
M—Periodicals

PC—Postcards
R—Candy and Gum Cards 1930 to Present
T—20th Century U.S. Tobacco
UO—Gas and Oil Inserts
V—Canadian Candy
W—Exhibits, Strip Cards, Team Issues

Following the letter prefix and an optional hyphen are one-, two-, or three-digit numbers, 1-999. These typically represent the company or entity issuing the cards. In several cases, the ACC number is extended by an additional hyphen and another one- or two-digit numerical suffix. For example, the 1957 Topps regular series baseball card issue carries an ACC designation of R414-11. The "R" indicates a Candy or Gum Card produced since 1930. The "414" is the ACC designation for Topps Chewing Gum baseball card issues, and the "11" is the ACC designation for the 1957 regular issue (Topps' eleventh baseball set).

Like other traditional methods of identification, this system provides order to the process of cataloging cards; however, most serious collectors learn the ACC designation of the popular sets by repetition and familiarity, rather than by attempting to "figure out" what they might or should be.

From 1948 forward, collectors and dealers commonly refer to all sets by their year, maker, type of issue, and any other distinguishing characteristic. For example, such a characteristic could be an unusual issue or one of several regular issues put out by a specific maker in a single year. Regional issues are usually referred to by year, maker, and sometimes by title or theme of the set.

GLOSSARY/LEGEND

Our glossary defines terms frequently used in the card collecting hobby. Many of these terms are also common to other types of sports memorabilia collecting. Some terms may have several meanings depending on use.

AAS. Action All Stars, a postcard-size set issued by the Donruss Company.

ACC. Acronym for *American Card Catalog*.

AD CARD. See Display Card.

AL. Abbreviation for American League or American Leaguer.

ALL STAR CARD. A card portraying an All Star Player of the previous year that says "All Star" on its face.

ALPH. Alphabetical.

AS. Abbreviation for All Star (card).

ATG. All Time Great card.

AUTOGRAPHED CARD. A card that has been signed (usually on its face) by the player(s) portrayed on the card with a fountain pen, felt tip, magic marker, or ball-point pen. This term does not include stamped or facsimile signature cards.

BLANKET. A felt square (normally 5" to 6") portraying a baseball player.

BOX. Card issued on a box or a card depicting a Boxer.

BRICK. A group of cards, usually 50 or more having common characteristics, that is intended to be bought, sold, or traded as a unit.

C. Abbreviation for Catcher.

CABINETS. Very popular and highly valuable photographs on thick card stock produced in the 19th and early 20th century.

CF. Abbreviation for Center Fielder.

CHECKLIST. A list of the cards contained in a particular set. The list is always in numerical order if the cards are numbered. Some unnumbered sets are artificially numbered in alphabetical order, or by team and alphabetically within the team for convenience.

CHECKLIST CARD. A card that lists in order the cards and players in the set or series. Older checklist cards in mint condition that have not been checked off are very desirable.

CL. Abbreviation for Checklist.

COA. Abbreviation for Coach.

COIN. A small disc of metal or plastic portraying a player in its center.

COLLECTOR. A person who engages in the hobby of collecting cards primarily for his own enjoyment, with any profit motive being secondary.

COLLECTOR ISSUE. A set produced for the sake of the card itself with no product or service sponsor. It derives its name from the fact that most of these sets are produced for sale directly to the hobby market.

COMBINATION CARD. A single card depicting two or more players (but not a team card).

COMMON CARD. The typical card of any set; it has no premium value accruing from subject matter, numerical scarcity, popular demand, or anomaly.

COMP. Card issued by the Post Cereal Company through their mail-in offer.

CONVENTION. A large weekend gathering of dealers and collectors at a single location for the purpose of buying, selling, and sometimes trading sports memorabilia items. Conventions are open to the public and sometimes feature celebrities, door prizes, films, contests, etc.

CONVENTION ISSUE. A set produced in conjunction with a sports collectibles convention to commemorate or promote the show.

COR. Correct or corrected card.

COUPON. See Tab.

CREASE. A wrinkle on the card, usually caused by bending the card. Creases are a common defect from careless handling.

CY. Cy Young Award.

DEALER. A person who engages in buying, selling, and trading sports collectibles or supplies. A dealer may also be a collector, but as a dealer, he anticipates a profit.

DH. Double Header (1955 Topps) or Designated Hitter.

DIE-CUT. A card with part of its stock partially cut, allowing one or more parts to be folded or removed. After removal or appropriate folding, the remaining part of the card can frequently be made to stand up.

DISC. A circular-shaped card.

DISPLAY CARD. A sheet, usually containing three to nine cards, that is printed and used by the manufacturer to advertise and/or display the packages containing his products and cards. The backs of display cards are blank or contain advertisements.

DK. Diamond King (artwork produced by Perez-Steele for Donruss).

DP. Double Print (a card that was printed in double the quantity compared to the other cards in the same series).

E CARD. A candy or gum card produced and issued prior to 1930.

ERA. Earned Run Average.

ERR. Error card (see also COR).

ERROR CARD. A card with erroneous information, spelling, or depiction on either side of the card. Note that not all errors are corrected by the producing card company.

EXHIBIT. The generic name given to thick stock, postcard-size cards with single color obverse pictures. The name is derived from the Exhibit Supply Co. of Chicago, the principal manufacturer of this type of card. These are also known as Arcade cards since they were found in many arcades.

FDP. First Draft Pick (see 1985 Topps Baseball).

FULL SHEET. A complete sheet of cards that has not been cut up into individual cards by the manufacturer. Also called an uncut sheet.

HALL OF FAMER. (HOF'er) A card that portrays a player who has been inducted into the Hall of Fame.

HIGH NUMBER. The cards in the last series of numbers in a year in which such higher-numbered cards were printed or distributed in significantly lesser amounts than the lower-numbered cards. The high-number designation refers to a scarcity of the high-numbered cards. Not all years have high numbers in terms of this definition.

HL. Highlight card.

HOC. House of Collectibles.

HOF. Acronym for Hall of Fame.

HOR. Horizontal pose on card as opposed to the standard vertical orientation found on most cards.

HR. Abbreviation for Home Run.

IA. In Action (type of card).

INF. Abbreviation for Infielder.

INSERT. A card of a different type, e.g., a poster, or any other sports collectible contained and sold in the same package along with a card or cards of a major set.

ISSUE. Synonymous with set, but usually used in conjunction with a manufacturer, e.g., a Topps issue.

KP. Kid Picture (a sub-series issued in the Topps Baseball sets of 1972 and 1973).

LAYERING. The separation or peeling of one or more layers of the card stock, usually at the corner of the card.

LEGITIMATE ISSUE. A set produced to promote or boost sales of a product or service, e.g., bubble gum, cereal, cigarettes, etc. Most collector issues are not legitimate issues in this sense.

LHP. Left-Handed Pitcher.

LID. A circular-shaped card (possibly with tab) that forms the top of the container for the product being promoted.

LL. Living Legends (Donruss 1984) or large letters.

MAJOR SET. A set produced by a national manufacturer of cards containing a large number of cards. Usually 100 or more different cards comprise the set.

MGR. Abbreviation for Manager.

MINI. A small card; specifically, a Topps baseball card of identical design but smaller dimensions than the regular Topps issue of 1975.

MISCUT. A card that has been cut particularly unevenly at the manufacturer's cutting stage.

ML. Major League.

MVP. Most Valuable Player.

N CARD. A tobacco card produced and issued during the 19th Century.

NL. National League.

NNOF. No Name on Front (see 1949 Bowman).

NOF. Name on Front (see 1949 Bowman).

NON-SPORT CARD. A card from a set whose major theme is a subject other than a sports subject. A card of a sports figure or event that is part of a non-sport set is still a non-sport card, e.g., while the "Look 'N' See" non-sport card set contains a card of Babe Ruth, a sports figure, that card is a non-sport card.

NOTCHING. The grooving of the card, usually caused by fingernails, rubber bands, or bumping card edges against other objects.

NY. New York.

OBVERSE. The front, face, or pictured side of the card.

OF. Outfielder.

OLY. Olympics (see 1985 Topps Baseball; the members of the 1984 U.S. Olympic Baseball team were a featured sub-series).

OPT. Option.

P. Pitcher or Pitching pose.

P1. First Printing.

P2. Second Printing.

P3. Third Printing.

PANEL. An extended card that is composed of two or more individual cards. Often the panel forms the back part of the container for the product being promoted, e.g., a Hostess panel, a Bazooka panel, an Esskay Meat panel.

PCL. Pacific Coast League.

PG. Price Guide.

PLASTIC SHEET. A clear, plastic page that is punched for insertion into a binder (with standard three-ring spacing) containing pockets for displaying cards. Many different styles of sheets exist with pockets of varying sizes to hold the many differing card formats.

PREMIUM. A card, sometimes on photographic stock, that is purchased or obtained in conjunction with/or redemption for another card or product. The premium is not packaged in the same unit as the primary item.

PUZZLE CARD. A card whose back contains a part of a picture which, when joined correctly with other puzzle cards, forms the completed picture.

PUZZLE PIECE. An actual die-cut piece designed to interlock with similar pieces.

R CARD. A candy or gum card produced and issued since 1930.

RARE. A card or series of cards of very limited availability. Unfortunately, "rare" is a subjective term sometimes used indiscriminately. Rare cards are harder to obtain than scarce cards.

RB. Record Breaker card.

RBI. Abbreviation for Runs Batted In.

REGIONAL. A card issued and distributed only in a limited geographical area of the country. The producer is not a major, national producer of trading cards.

REPRINT. A reproduction of an original card, usually produced by a maker other than the original manufacturer from a source other than the original artwork or negative.

REVERSE. The back or narrative side of the card.

RHP. Right-Handed Pitcher.

ROOKIE CARD. The first regular card of a particular player or a card which portrays one or more players with the notation on the card that those players are Rookies.

ROY. Acronym for Rookie of the Year.

RR. Rated Rookies (a subset featured in the Donruss Baseball sets).

SA. Super Action or Sport Americana.

SASE. Self-Addressed, Stamped Envelope.

SB. Stolen Bases.

SCARCE. A card or series of cards of limited availability. This subjective term is sometimes used indiscriminately to promote or hype value. Scarce cards are not as difficult to obtain as rare cards.

SCR. Script name on back (see 1949 Bowman Baseball).

SEMI-HIGH. A card from the next to last series of a sequentially issued set. It has more value than an average card and generally less value than a high number. A card is not called a semi-high unless the next to last series in which it exists has an additional premium attached to it.

SERIES. The entire set of cards issued by a particular producer in a particular year, e.g., the 1971 Topps series. Also, within a particular set, series can refer to a group of (consecutively numbered) cards printed at the same time, e.g., the first series of the 1957 Topps issue (numbers 1 through 88).

SET. One each of the entire run of cards of the same type produced by a particular manufacturer during a single year. In other words, if you have a (complete) set of 1976 Topps then you have every card from number 1 up through and including number 660, i.e., all the different cards that were produced.

SF. San Francisco.

SKIP-NUMBERED. A set that has many unissued card numbers between the lowest number in the set and the highest number in the set, e.g., the 1948 Leaf baseball set contains 98 cards skip-numbered from number 1 to number 168. A major set in which a few numbers were not printed is not considered to be skip-numbered.

SO. Strikeouts.

SP. Single or Short Print (a card which was printed in lesser quantity compared to the other cards in the same series; see also DP and TP).

SPECIAL CARD. A card that portrays something other than a single player or team, for example, a card that portrays the previous year's statistical leaders or the results from the previous year's post-season action.

SS. Abbreviation for Shortstop.

STAMP. Adhesive-backed papers depicting a player. The stamp may be individual or in a sheet of many stamps. Moisture must be applied to the adhesive in order for the stamp to be attached to another surface.

STAR CARD. A card that portrays a player of some repute, usually determined by his ability; however, sometimes referring to sheer popularity.

STICKER. A card with a removable layer that can be affixed to (stuck onto) another surface.

STOCK. The cardboard or paper on which the card is printed.

STRIP CARDS. A sheet or strip of cards, particularly popular in the 1920s and 1930s, with the individual cards usually separated by broken or dotted lines.

SUPERSTAR CARD. A card that portrays a superstar, e.g., a Hall of Fame member or a Hall of Fame prospect.

SV. Super Veteran.

T CARD. A tobacco card produced and issued during the 20th century.

TAB. A card portion set off from the rest of the card, usually with perforations, that may be removed without damaging the central character or event depicted by the card.

TBC. Turn Back the Clock cards.

TEAM CARD. A card that depicts an entire team.

TEST SET. A set, usually containing a small number of cards, issued by a national card producer and distributed in a limited section or sections of the country. Presumably, the purpose of a test set is to test market appeal for a particular type of card.

TL. Team Leader card.

TP. Triple Print (a card that was printed in triple the quantity compared to the other cards in the same series).

TR. Trade or Traded.

TRIMMED. A card cut down from its original size. Trimmed cards are undesirable to most collectors.

UMP. Umpire (see 1955 Bowman Baseball last series).

VARIATION. One of two or more cards from the same series with the same number (or player with identical pose if the series is unnumbered) differing from one another by some aspect, the different feature stemming from the printing or stock of the card. This can be caused when the manufacturer of the cards notices an error in one (or more) of the cards, makes the changes, and then resumes the print run. In this case there will be two versions or variations of the same card. Sometimes one of the variations is relatively scarce.

VERT. Vertical pose on card.

W CARD. A card grouped within a general miscellaneous category by the ACC. Included in this category are Exhibits, strip cards, team issues, and those issues that do not conveniently fall into other established categories.

WASH. Washington.

WL. White Letters (see 1969 Topps Baseball).

WS. World Series card.

YL. Yellow Letters (see 1958 Topps Baseball).

YT. Yellow Team (see 1958 Topps Baseball).

1B. First Base or First Baseman.

2B. Second Base or Second Baseman.

3B. Third Base or Third Baseman.

HISTORY OF BASEBALL CARDS

Today's version of the baseball card, with its colorful front and statistical back, is a far cry from its earliest predecessors. The issue remains cloudy as to which was the very first baseball card ever produced, but the institution of baseball cards dates from the latter half of the 19th century, more than 100 years ago. Early issues, generally printed on heavy cardboard, were of poor quality, with photographs, drawings and printing far short of today's standards.

Goodwin & Co., of New York, makers of Gypsy Queen, Old Judge, and other cigarette brands, is considered by many to be the first issuer of baseball and other sports cards. Their issues, predominantly in the 1½" by 2½" size, generally consisted of photographs of baseball players, boxers, wrestlers, and other subjects mounted on stiff cardboard. More than 2,000 different photos of baseball players alone have been identified. These "Old Judges," a collective name commonly used for the Goodwin & Co. cards, were issued from 1886 to 1890 and are treasured parts of many collections today.

Among the other cigarette companies which issued baseball cards that still attract attention today are Allen & Ginter, D. Buchner & Co. (Gold Coin Chewing Tobacco), and P.H. Mayo & Brother. Cards from the first two companies bore colored line drawings, while the Mayos are sepia photographs on black cardboard.

In addition to the small-size cards from this era, several tobacco companies issued cabinet-size baseball cards. These "cabinets" were considerably larger than the small cards, usually about 4¼" by 6½", and were printed on heavy stock. Goodwin & Co.'s Old Judge cabinets and the National Tobacco Works' "Newsboy" baseball photos are two that remain popular today.

By 1895 the American Tobacco Company began to dominate its competition. They discontinued baseball card inserts in their cigarette packages (actually slide boxes in those days). The lack of competition in the cigarette market had made these inserts unnecessary. This marked the end of the first era of the baseball card.

At the dawn of the 20th century, few baseball cards were being issued. But once again it was the cigarette companies—particularly, the American Tobacco Company—followed to a lesser extent by the candy and gum makers that revived the practice of including baseball cards with their products. The bulk of these cards, identified in the *American Card Catalog* (designated hereafter as ACC) as T or E cards for 20th century "Tobacco" or "Early Candy and Gum" issues respectively, were released from 1909 to 1915.

This romantic and popular era of baseball card collecting produced many desirable items. The most outstanding is the fabled T-206 Honus Wagner card. Other perennial favorites among collectors are the T-206 Eddie Plank card, and the T-206 Magee error card. The former was once the second most valuable card and only recently relinquished that position to a more distinctive and aesthetically pleasing Napoleon Lajoie card from the 1933/34 Goudey Gum series. The latter misspells the player's name as "Magie," the most famous and valuable blooper card.

The ingenuity and distinctiveness of this era has yet to be surpassed. Highlights include the T-202 Hassan triple-folders, one of the best looking and the most distinctive cards ever issued; the durable T-201 Mecca double-folders, one of the first sets with players' records on the reverse; the T-3 Turkey Reds, the hobby's most popular cabinet card; the E-145 Cracker Jacks, the only major set containing Federal League player cards; and the T-204 Ramlys, with their distinctive black and white oval photos and ornate gold borders. These are but a few of the varieties issued during this period.

While the American Tobacco Company dominated the field, several other tobacco companies, as well as clothing manufacturers, newspapers and periodicals, game makers, and companies whose identities remain anonymous, also issued cards during this period. In fact, the Collins-McCarthy Candy Company, makers of Zeenuts Pacific Coast League baseball cards, issued cards yearly from 1911 to 1938. Their record for continuous annual card production has been exceeded only by the Topps Chewing Gum Company. The era of the tobacco card issues closed with the onset of World War I, with the exception of the Red Man chewing tobacco sets produced from 1952 to 1955.

The next flurry of card issues broke out in the roaring and prosperous 1920s, the era of the E card. The caramel companies (National Caramel, American Caramel, York Caramel) were the leading distributors of these E cards. In addition, the strip card, a continous strip with several cards divided by dotted lines or other sectioning features, flourished during this time. While the E cards and the strip cards are generally considered less imaginative than the T cards or the recent candy and gum issues, they are still sought after by many advanced collectors.

Another significant event of the 1920s was the introduction of the arcade card. Taking its designation from its issuer, the Exhibit Supply Company of Chicago, it is usually known as the "Exhibit" card. Once a trademark of the penny arcades, amusement parks, and county fairs across the country, Exhibit machines dispensed nearly postcard-size photos on thick stock for one penny. These picture cards bore likenesses of a favorite cowboy, actor, actress or baseball player. Exhibit Supply and its associated companies produced baseball cards during a longer time span, although discontinuous, than any other manufacturer. Its first cards appeared in 1921, while its last issue was in 1966. In 1979, the Exhibit Supply Company was bought and somewhat revived by a collector/dealer who has since reprinted Exhibit photos of the past.

If the T card period, from 1909 to 1915, can be said to be the "Golden Age" of baseball card collecting, then perhaps the "Silver Age" commenced with the introduction of the Big League Gum series of 239 cards in 1933 (a 240th card was added in 1934). These are the forerunners of today's baseball gum cards, and the Goudey Gum Company of Boston is responsible for their success. This era spanned the period from the Depression days of 1933 to America's formal involvement in World War II in 1941.

Goudey's attractive designs, with full color line drawings on thick card stock, influenced greatly other cards being issued at that time. As a result, the most attractive and popular cards in collecting history were produced in this "Silver Age." The 1933 Goudey Big League Gum series also owes its popularity to the more than 40 Hall of Fame players in the set. These include four cards of Babe Ruth and two of Lou Gehrig. Goudey's reign continued in 1934 when it issued a 96-card set in color, together with the single remaining card from the 1933 series, #106, the Napoleon Lajoie card.

In addition to Goudey, several other bubble gum manufacturers issued baseball cards during this era. DeLong Gum Company issued an extremely attractive set in 1933. National Chicle Company's 192-card "Batter-Up" series of 1934-1936 became the largest die-cut set in card history. In addition, that company offered the popular "Diamond Stars" series during the same period. Other popular sets included the "Tattoo Orbit" set of 60 color cards issued in 1933 and Gum Products' 75-card "Double Play" set, featuring sepia depictions of two players per card.

In 1939 Gum Inc., which later became Bowman Gum, replaced Goudey Gum as the leading baseball card producer. In 1939 and the following year, it issued two important sets of black and white cards. In 1939 its "Play Ball America" set consisted of 162 cards. The larger, 240-card "Play Ball" set of 1940 is still considered by many to be the most attractive black and white cards ever produced. That firm introduced its only color set in 1941, consisting of 72 cards entitled "Play Ball Sports Hall of Fame." Many of these were colored repeats of poses from the black and white 1940 series.

In addition to regular gum cards, many manufacturers distributed premium issues during the 1930s. These premiums were printed on paper or photographic stock, rather than card stock. They were much larger than the regular cards and were sold for a penny across the counter with gum (which was packaged separately from the premium). They were often redeemed at the store or through the mail in exchange for the wrappers of previously purchased gum cards, a proof-of-purchase box-top premiums today. The gum premiums are scarcer than the card issues of the 1930s and in most cases no manufacturer's name is present.

World War II brought an end to this popular era of card collecting when paper and rubber shortages curtailed the production of bubble gum baseball cards. They were resurrected again in 1948 by the Bowman Gum Company (the direct descendant of Gum, Inc.). This marked the beginning of the modern era of card collecting.

In 1948, Bowman Gum issued a 48-card set in black and white consisting of one card and one slab of gum in every one-cent pack. That same year, the Leaf Gum Company also issued a set of cards. Although rather poor in quality, these cards were issued in color. A squabble over the rights to use players' pictures developed between Bowman and Leaf. Eventually Leaf dropped out of the card market, but not before it had left a lasting heritage to the hobby by issuing some of the rarest cards now in existence. Leaf's baseball card series of 1948-49 contained 98 cards, skip numbered to #168 (not all numbers were printed). Of these 98 cards, 49 are relatively plentiful; however, the other 49 are rare and quite valuable.

Bowman continued its production of cards in 1949 with a color series of 240 cards. Because there are many scarce "high numbers" this series remains the most difficult Bowman regular issue to complete. Although the set was printed in color and commands great interest due to its scarcity, it is considered aesthetically inferior to the Goudey and National Chicle issues of the 1930s. In addition to the regular issue of 1949, Bowman also produced a set of 36 Pacific Coast League players. While this was not a regular issue, it is still prized by collectors. In fact, it has become the most valuable Bowman series.

In 1950 (Bowman's one-year monopoly of the baseball card market), the company began a string of top quality cards which continued until its demise in 1955. The 1950 series was itself something of an oddity because the "low" numbers, rather than the traditional high numbers, were the more difficult cards to obtain.

The year 1951 marked the beginning of the most competitive and perhaps the highest quality period of baseball card production. In that year that Topps Chewing Gum Company of Brooklyn entered the market. Topps' 1951 series consisted of two sets of 52 cards each, one set with red backs and the other with blue backs. In addition, Topps also issued 31 insert cards, three of which remain the rarest Topps cards ("Current All-Stars" Konstanty, Roberts, and Stanky). The 1951 Topps cards were unattractive and paled in comparison to the 1951 Bowman issues. However, they were successful, and Topps has continued to produce cards ever since.

Topps issued a larger and much more attractive card in 1952. This larger size became standard for the next five years. (Bowman followed with larger-size baseball cards in 1953.) This 1952 Topps set has become, like the 1933 Goudey series and the T-206 white border series, the classic set of its era. The 407-card set is a collector's dream of scarcities, rarities, errors, and variations. It also contains the first Topps issues of Mickey Mantle and Willie Mays.

As with Bowman and Leaf in the late 1940s, competition over player rights arose. Ensuing court battles occurred between Topps and Bowman. The market split due to stiff competition, and in January, 1956, Topps bought out Bowman. Topps remained relatively unchallenged as the primary producer of baseball cards through 1980. So, the story of major baseball card sets from 1956 through 1980 is by and large the story of Topps' issues with few exceptions. Fleer Gum produced small sets in 1959, 1960,

1961, and 1963, and several cartoon sets in the 1970s, and more recently Kelloggs Cereal and Hostess Cakes issued baseball cards to promote their products.

A court decision in 1980 paved the way for two other large gum companies to enter, or reenter, the baseball card arena. The Fleer Corporation, which had last made photo cards in 1963, and the Donruss Company (a division of General Mills) secured rights to produce baseball cards of current players, breaking Topps' monopoly. Each company issued major card sets in 1981 with bubble gum products. Then a higher court decision in that year overturned the lower court ruling against Topps. It appeared that Topps had regained its sole position as a producer of baseball cards. Undaunted by the revocation ruling, Fleer and Donruss continued to issue cards in 1982 but without bubble gum or any other edible product. Fleer issued its current player baseball cards with "team logo stickers," while Donruss issued its cards with a piece of a baseball jigsaw puzzle.

Since 1981, these three major baseball card producers have all thrived, sharing relatively equal recognition. Each has steadily increased its involvement in terms of numbers of issues per year. To the delight of collectors, their competition has generated novel, and in some cases exceptional, issues of current major league baseball players. These major producers have become increasingly aware of the organized collecting market. While the corner candy store remains the major marketplace for card sales, an increasing number of issues have been directed to this organized hobby marketplace. In fact, many of these issues have been distributed exclusively through hobby channels. Although no one can ever say what the future will bring, one can only surmise that the hobby market will play a significant role in future plans of all the major baseball card producers.

The above has been a thumbnail sketch of card collecting from its inception in the 1880s to the present. It is difficult to tell the whole story in just a few pages—there are several other good sources of information. Serious collectors should subscribe to at least one of the excellent hobby periodicals. We also suggest that collectors attend a sports collectibles convention in their area. Card collecting is still a young and informal hobby. Chances are good that you will run into one or more of the "experts" at such a show. They are usually more than happy to share their knowledge with you.

BUSINESS OF BASEBALL CARD COLLECTING

DETERMINING VALUE

Why are some cards more valuable than others? Obviously, the economic law of supply and demand is applicable to card collecting just as it is to any other field where a commodity is bought, sold, or traded.

Supply (the number of cards available on the market) is less than the total number of cards originally produced since attrition diminishes that original quantity. Each year a percentage of cards are typically thrown away, destroyed, or otherwise lost to collectors. This percentage is smaller today than it was in the past because more and more people have become increasingly aware of the value of their cards. For those who collect only "Mint" condition cards, the supply of older cards can be quite small indeed. Until recently, collectors were not so conscious of the need to preserve the condition of their cards. For this reason, it is difficult to know exactly how many 1953 Topps are currently available, Mint or otherwise. It is generally accepted that there are fewer 1953 Topps available than 1963, 1973, or 1983 Topps cards. If demand were equal for each of these sets, the law of supply and demand would increase the price for the least available sets. Demand, however, is not equal for all sets, so price correlations can be complicated.

The demand for a card is influenced by many factors. These include: (1) the age of the card; (2) the number of cards printed; (3) the player(s) portrayed on the card; (4) the attractiveness and popularity of the set; and perhaps most important, (5) the physical condition of the card.

In general, (1) the older the card, (2) the fewer the number of the cards printed, (3) the more famous the player, (4) the more attractive and popular the set, or (5) the better the condition of the card, the higher the value of the card will be. There are exceptions to all but one of these factors: the condition of the card. Given two cards similar in all respects except condition, the one in the best condition will always be valued higher.

While there are certain guidelines that help to establish the value of a card, the exceptions and peculiarities make any simple, direct mathematical formula to determine card values impossible.

REGIONAL VARIATION

Two types of price variations exist among the sections of the country where a card is bought or sold. The first is the general price variation on all cards bought and sold in one geographical area as compared to another. Card prices are slightly higher on the East and West coasts, and slightly lower in the middle of the country. Although prices may vary from the East to the West, or from the Southwest to the Midwest, the prices listed in this guide are nonetheless presented as a consensus of all sections of this large and diverse country.

Still, prices for a particular player's cards may well be higher in his home team's area than in other regions. This exhibits the second type of regional price variation in which local players are favored over those from distant areas. For example, an Al Kaline card would be valued higher in Detroit than in Cincinnati because Kaline played in Detroit; therefore, the demand there for Al Kaline cards is higher than it is in

Cincinnati. On the other hand, a Johnny Bench card would be priced higher in Cincinnati where he played than in Detroit for similar reasons. Sometimes even common player cards command such a premium from hometown collectors.

SET PRICES

A somewhat paradoxical situation exists in the price of a complete set versus the combined cost of the individual cards in the set. In nearly every case, the sum of the prices for the individual cards is higher than the cost for the complete set. This is especially prevalent in the cards of the past few years. The reasons for this apparent anomaly stem from the habits of collectors and from the carrying costs to dealers. Today each card in a set is normally produced in the same quantity as all others in its set. However, many collectors pick up only stars, superstars, and particular teams. As a result, the dealer is left with a shortage of certain player cards and an abundance of others. He therefore incurs an expense in simply "carrying" these less desirable cards in stock. On the other hand, if he sells a complete set, he gets rid of large numbers of cards at one time. For this reason, he is often willing to receive less money for a complete set. By doing this, he recovers all of his costs and also receives some profit.

The disparity between the price of the complete set and that for the sum of the individual cards has also been influenced by the fact that the major manufacturers are now pre-collating card sets. Since "pulling" individual cards from the sets of all three manufacturers involves a specific type of labor (and cost), the singles or star card market is not affected significantly by pre-collation.

Set prices also do not include rare card varieties, unless specifically stated. Of course, the prices for sets do include one example of each type for the given set, but this is the least expensive variety.

SCARCE SERIES

Scarce series occur because cards issued before 1974 were made available to the public each year in several series of finite numbers of cards, rather than all cards of the set being available for purchase at one time. At some point during the year, usually toward the end of the baseball season, interest in current year baseball cards waned. Consequently, the manufacturers produced smaller numbers of these later series of cards. Nearly all nationwide issues from post-World War II manufacturers (1948 to 1973) exhibit these series variations. Topps, for example, issued series composed of many different numbers of cards, including 55, 66, 80, 88, and others. Recently Topps has settled on what is now their standard sheet size of 132 cards.

While the number of cards within a given series is usually the same as the number of cards on one printed sheet, this is not always the case. For example, Bowman used 36 cards on its standard printed sheets, but in 1948 substituted 12 cards during later print runs of that year's baseball cards. Twelve of the cards from the initial sheet of 36 cards were removed and replaced by 12 different cards giving, in effect, a first series of 36 cards and a second series of 12 new cards. This replacement produced a scarcity of 24 cards—the 12 cards removed from the original sheet and the 12 new cards added to the sheet. A full sheet of 1948 Bowman cards (second printing) shows that card numbers 37 through 48 have replaced 12 of the cards on the first printing sheet.

The Topps Gum Company has also created scarcities and/or excesses of certain cards in many of their sets. Topps, however, has most frequently gone the other direction by double printing some of the cards. Double printing causes an abundance of cards of the players who are on the same sheet more than one time. During the years from 1978 to 1981, Topps double-printed 66 cards out of their large 726-card set. The Topps practice of double printing cards in earlier years is the most logical explanation for the known scarcities of particular cards in some of these Topps sets.

GRADING YOUR CARDS

Each hobby has its own grading terminology—stamps, coins, comic books, beer cans, right down the line. Collectors of sports cards are no exception. The one invariable criterion for determining the value of a card is its condition: the better the condition of the card, the more valuable it is. However, condition grading is very subjective. Individual card dealers and collectors differ in the strictness of their grading, but the stated condition of a card should be determined without regard to whether it is being bought or sold.

The physical defects which lower the condition of a card are usually quite apparent, but each individual places his own estimation (negative value in this case) on these defects. We present the condition guide for use in determining values listed in this price guide.

The defects listed in the condition guide below are those either placed in the card at the time of printing—uneven borders, focus—or those defects that occur to a card under normal handling—corner sharpness, gloss, edge wear—and finally, environmental conditions—browning. Other defects to cards are caused by human carelessness and in all cases should be noted separately and in addition to the condition grade. Among the more common alterations are tape, tape stains, rubber band marks, water damage, smoke damage, trimming, paste, tears, writing, pin or tack holes, any back damage, and missing parts (tabs, tops, coupons, backgrounds).

CONDITION GUIDE

MINT (M OR MT). A card with no defects. The card has sharp corners, even borders, original gloss or shine on the surface, sharp focus of the picture, smooth edges, no signs of wear, and white borders. There is no allowance made for the age of the card.

EXCELLENT (EX OR E). A card with very minor defects. Any of the following would be sufficient to lower the grade of a card from mint to the excellent category: very slight rounding or layering at some of the corners, a very small amount of the original gloss lost, minor wear on the edges, slight unevenness of the borders, slight wear visible only on close inspection; slight off-whiteness of the borders.

VERY GOOD (VG). A card that has been handled but not abused. Some rounding at all corners, slight layering or scuffing at one or two corners, slight notching on edges, gloss lost from the surface but not scuffed, borders might be somewhat uneven but some white is visible on all borders, noticeable yellowing or browning of borders, pictures may be slightly off focus.

GOOD (G). A well-handled card, rounding and some layering at the corners, scuffing at the corners and minor scuffing on the face, borders noticeably uneven and browning, loss of gloss on the face, notching on the edges.

FAIR (F) Round and layering corners, brown and dirty borders, frayed edges, noticeable scuffing on the face, white not visible on one or more borders, cloudy focus.

POOR (P) An abused card, the lowest grade of card, frequently some major physical alteration has been performed on the card, collectible only as a filler until a better-condition replacement can be obtained.

Categories between these major condition grades are frequently used, such as very good to excellent (VG-E), fair to good (F-G), etc. Such grades indicate a card with all qualities at least in the lower of the two categories, but with several qualities in the higher of the two categories.

The most common physical defect in a trading card is the crease or wrinkle. The crease may vary from a slight crease barely noticeable at one corner of the card to a major crease across the entire card. Therefore, the degree that creasing lowers the value of the card depends on the type and number of creases. On giving the condition of a card, creases should be noted separately. If the crease is noticeable only upon close inspection under bright light, an otherwise mint card could be called excellent; whereas noticeable but light creases would lower most otherwise mint cards into the VG category. A heavily creased card could be classified as fair at best.

SELLING YOUR CARDS

Just about every collector sells cards or will sell cards eventually. Someday you may be interested in selling your duplicates or maybe even your whole collection. You may sell to other collectors, friends, or dealers. You may even sell cards you purchased from a certain dealer back to that same dealer. In any event, it helps to know some of the mechanics of the typical transaction between buyer and seller.

Dealers will buy cards in order to resell them to other collectors who are interested in the cards. Dealers will always pay a higher percentage for items which (in their opinion) can be resold quickly, and a much lower percentage for those items which are perceived as having low demand and hence are slow moving. In either case, dealers must buy at a price that allows for the expense of doing business and a fair margin for profit. Virtually all dealers are interested in older complete sets and superstar cards in excellent condition.

If you have cards for sale, the best advice we can give is that you get three offers for your cards and take the best offer, all things considered. Note, the "best" offer may not be the one for the highest amount. And remember, if a dealer really wants your cards, he won't let you get away without making his best competitive offer. Another alternative is to take your cards to a nearby convention and either auction them off in the show auction or offer them for sale to some of the dealers present.

Many people think nothing of going into a department store and paying $15 for an item of clothing for which the store paid $5. But, if you were selling your $15 card to a dealer and he offered you only $5 for it, you might think his mark-up unreasonable. To complete the analogy: most department stores (and card dealers) that pay $10 for $15 items eventually go out of business. An exception to this is when the dealer knows that a willing buyer for the merchandise you are attempting to sell is only a phone call away. Then an offer of ⅔ or maybe 70% of the book value will still allow him to make a reasonable profit due to the short time he will need to hold the merchandise. Nevertheless, most cards and collections will bring offers in the range of 25% to 50% of retail price. Material from the past five to ten years or so is very plentiful. Don't be surprised if your best offer is only 20% of the book value for these recent years.

INTERESTING NOTES

The numerically first card of an issue is the single card most likely to obtain excessive wear. Consequently, you will typically find the price on the number one card (in Mint condition) somewhat higher than might otherwise be the case. Similarly, but to a lesser extent (because normally the less important, reverse side of the card is the one exposed), the numerically last card in an issue is also prone to abnormal wear. This extra wear and tear occurs because the first and last cards are exposed to the elements (human element included) more than any other cards. They are generally end cards in any brick formations, rubber bandings, stackings on wet surfaces, and like activities.

Sports cards have no intrinsic value. The value of a card, like the value of other collectibles, can only be determined by you and your enjoyment in viewing and possessing these cardboard swatches.

Remember, the buyer ultimately determines the price of each baseball card. You are the determining price factor because you have the ability to say NO to the price of any card by not exchanging your hard-earned money for a given card. When the cost of a trading card exceeds the enjoyment you will receive from it, your answer should be NO. We assess and report the prices. You set them!

We are always interested in receiving the price input of collectors and dealers from around the country. We happily credit major contributors. We welcome your opinions, since your contributions assist us in ensuring a better guide each year. If you would like to join our survey list for the next editions of this book and others authored by Dr. Beckett, please send your name and address to Dr. James Beckett, 3410 MidCourt, Suite 110, Carrollton, Texas 75006.

ADVERTISING

Within this price guide you will find advertisements for sports memorabilia material, mail order, and retail sports collectibles establishments. All advertisements were accepted in good faith based on the reputation of the advertiser; however, neither the author, the publisher, the distributors, nor the other advertisers in the price guide accept any responsibility for any particular advertiser not complying with the terms of his or her ad.

Readers should also be aware that prices in advertisements are subject to change over the annual period before a new edition of this volume is issued each spring. When replying to an advertisement late in the baseball year, the reader should take this into account, and contact the dealer by phone or in writing for up-to-date price information. Should you come into contact with any of the advertisers in this guide as a result of their advertisement herein, please mention to them this source as your contact.

ADDITIONAL READING

Other literature on the collecting hobby can be divided into two principal categories: books and periodicals. We have furnished a listing for both that we feel would further advance your knowledge and enjoyment.

BOOKS AVAILABLE

The Sport Americana Price Guide to Baseball Collectibles.
By Dr. James Beckett (First Edition, $9.95, released 1986, published by Edgewater Book Company)—the complete guide/checklist with up to date values for box cards, coins, decals, labels, Canadian cards, stamps, stickers, pins, etc.

The Sport Americana Football, Hockey, Basketball and Boxing Card Price Guide.
By Dr. James Beckett (Fourth Edition, $11.95, released 1985, published by Edgewater Book Company)—the most comprehensive price guide/checklist ever issued on football and other non-baseball sports cards. No serious hobbyist should be without it.

The Official Price Guide to Football Cards.
By Dr. James Beckett (Sixth Edition, $4.95, released 1986, published by The House of Collectibles)—an abridgement of the *Sport Americana Price Guide* listed above in a convenient and economical pocket-size format providing Dr. Beckett's pricing of the major football sets since 1948.

The Sport Americana Baseball Memorabilia and Autograph Price Guide.
By Dr. James Beckett and Dennis W. Eckes (First Edition, $9.95, released 1982, co-published by Den's Collectors Den and Edgewater Book Company)—the most complete book ever produced on baseball memorabilia other than baseball cards. This book presents in an illustrated, logical fashion information on baseball memorabilia and autographs which had been heretofore unavailable to the collector.

The Sport Americana Alphabetical Baseball Card Checklist.
By Dr. James Beckett and Dennis W. Eckes (Second Edition, $8.95, released 1983, co-published by Den's Collectors Den and Edgewater Book Company)—an illustrated, alphabetical listing, by the last name of the player portrayed on the card, of virtually all baseball cards produced up to 1983.

The Sport Americana Price Guide to the Non-Sports Cards.
By Christopher Benjamin and Dennis W. Eckes (Second Edition, $8.95, released 1983, co-published by Den's Collector's Den and Edgewater Book Company)—the definitive guide to all popular non-sports American tobacco and bubble gum cards. In addition to cards, illustrations and prices for wrappers are also included.

The Sport Americana Baseball Address List.
By Jack Smalling and Dennis W. Eckes (Fourth Edition, $9.95, released 1986, co-

published by Den's Collector's Den and Edgewater Book Company)—the definitive guide for autograph hunters giving addresses and deceased information for virtually all major league baseball players past and present.

The Sport Americana Baseball Card Team Checklist.
By Jeff Fritsch and Dennis W. Eckes (Second Edition, $8.95, released 1985, co-published by Den's Collectors Den and Edgewater Book Company)—includes all Topps, Bowman, Fleer, Play Ball, Goudey, and Donruss cards, with the players portrayed on the cards listed with the teams for whom they played. The book is invaluable to the collector who specializes in an individual team because it is the most complete baseball card team checklist available.

Hockey Card Checklist and Price Guide.
By Andrew Pywowarczuk (Sixth Edition, publisher: Cartophilium)—contains the most complete list of hockey card checklists ever assembled including a listing of Bee Hive photos.

The Encyclopedia of Baseball Cards, Volume I: 19th Century Cards.
By Lew Lipset ($9.95, released 1983, published by the author)—everything you ever wanted to know about 19th century cards.

The Encyclopedia of Baseball Cards, Volume II: Early Gum and Candy Cards.
By Lew Lipset ($10.95, released 1984, published by the author)—everything you ever wanted to know about Early Candy and Gum cards.

The Encyclopedia of Baseball Cards, Volume III: 20th Century Tobacco Cards, 1909-1932.
By Lew Lipset ($12.95, released 1986, published by the author)—everything you ever wanted to know about old tobacco cards.

PERIODICALS

Several magazines and periodicals about the card collecting hobby are published on monthly, bimonthly, or weekly bases. One (or more) of those listed below should be just right for you.

Beckett Baseball Card Monthly.
Authored and edited by Dr. James Beckett—contains the most extensive and accepted monthly price guide, feature articles, "who's hot and who's not" section, convention calendar, and numerous letters to and responses from the editor. Published

10 times annually, it is the hobby's largest circulation periodical.

Baseball Hobby News.
Published by Frank and Vivian Barning—monthly tabloid newspaper format with good mix of news, editorials, features, and ads.

The Old Judge.
Published by Lew Lipset—bimonthly newsletter with in-depth information about older card issues and memorabilia.

Sports Collectors Digest.
Published by Krause Publications—weekly tabloid issues loaded with ads.

Baseball Card News.
Published by Krause Publications—monthly tabloid format with good mix of editorials, features, and ads.

Baseball Cards.
Published by Krause Publications—monthly magazine with interior color and mix of features and ads.

PRICES IN THIS GUIDE

   Prices found in this guide reflect current retail rates just prior to the printing of this book. They do not reflect the FOR SALE prices of the author, the publisher, the distributors, the advertisers, or any card dealers associated with this guide. No one is obligated in any way to buy, sell, or trade his or her cards based on these prices. The price listings were compiled by the author from actual buy/sell transactions at sports conventions, buy/sell advertisements in the hobby papers, for sale prices from dealer catalogs and price lists, and discussions with leading hobbyists in the U.S. and Canada. All prices are in U.S. dollars.

1952 Topps

The cards in this 407-card set measure 2⅝" by 3¾". The 1952 Topps set is Topps' first truly major set. Card numbers 1 to 80 were issued with red or black backs, both of which are less plentiful than card numbers 81 to 250. Card number 48 (Joe Page) and number 49 (Johnny Sain) can be found with each other's write-up on their back. Card numbers 251 to 310 are somewhat scarce and numbers 311 to 407 are quite scarce. Cards 281-300 were single printed compared to the other cards in the next to last series. Cards 311-313 were double printed on the last high number printing sheet. The key card in the set is obviously Mickey Mantle #311, Mickey's first of many Topps cards.

	MINT	VG-E	F-G
Complete Set	18000.00	7500.00	2000.
Common Player (1-80)	14.00	6.50	1.60
Common Player (81-250)	8.00	3.25	.80
Common Player (251-280)	16.00	6.50	1.60
Common Player (281-300)	20.00	8.00	2.00
Common Player (301-310)	16.00	6.50	1.60
Common Player (311-407)	75.00	30.00	7.50

		MINT	VG-E	F-G
☐ 1	Andy Pafko	350.00	15.00	3.00
☐ 2	James Pete Runnels	17.00	7.25	1.80
☐ 3	Henry Thompson	17.00	7.25	1.80
☐ 4	Don Lenhardt	14.00	6.50	1.60
☐ 5	Larry Jansen	14.00	6.50	1.60
☐ 6	Grady Hatton	14.00	6.50	1.60

		MINT	VG-E	F-G
☐ 7	Wayne Terwilliger	14.00	6.50	1.60
☐ 8	Fred Marsh	14.00	6.50	1.60
☐ 9	Robert Hogue	14.00	6.50	1.60
☐ 10	Al Rosen	24.00	10.00	2.50
☐ 11	Phil Rizzuto	60.00	24.00	6.00
☐ 12	Romanus Basgall	14.00	6.50	1.60
☐ 13	Johnny Wyrostek	14.00	6.50	1.60
☐ 14	Bob Elliott	17.00	7.25	1.80
☐ 15	Johnny Pesky	17.00	7.25	1.80
☐ 16	Gene Hermanski	14.00	6.50	1.60
☐ 17	Jim Hegan	17.00	6.50	1.60
☐ 18	Merrill Combs	14.00	6.50	1.60
☐ 19	Johnny Bucha	14.00	6.50	1.60
☐ 20	Billy Loes	24.00	10.00	2.50
☐ 21	Ferris Fain	17.00	7.25	1.80
☐ 22	Dom DiMaggio	24.00	10.00	2.50
☐ 23	Billy Goodman	17.00	7.25	1.80
☐ 24	Luke Easter	17.00	7.25	1.80
☐ 25	John Groth	14.00	6.50	1.60
☐ 26	Monte Irvin	30.00	13.00	3.20
☐ 27	Sam Jethroe	17.00	7.25	1.80
☐ 28	Jerry Priddy	14.00	6.50	1.60
☐ 29	Ted Kluszewski	24.00	10.00	2.50
☐ 30	Mel Parnell	17.00	7.25	1.80
☐ 31	Gus Zernial	17.00	7.25	1.80
☐ 32	Eddie Robinson	14.00	6.50	1.60
☐ 33	Warren Spahn	70.00	30.00	7.50
☐ 34	Elmer Valo	14.00	6.50	1.60
☐ 35	Hank Sauer	17.00	7.25	1.80
☐ 36	Gil Hodges	50.00	20.00	5.00
☐ 37	Duke Snider	90.00	36.00	9.00
☐ 38	Wally Westlake	14.00	6.50	1.60
☐ 39	Dizzy Trout	14.00	6.50	1.60
☐ 40	Irv Noren	14.00	6.50	1.60
☐ 41	Bob Wellman	14.00	6.50	1.60
☐ 42	Lou Kretlow	14.00	6.50	1.60
☐ 43	Ray Scarborough	14.00	6.50	1.60
☐ 44	Con Dempsey	14.00	6.50	1.60
☐ 45	Eddie Joost	14.00	6.50	1.60
☐ 46	Gordon Goldsberry	14.00	6.50	1.60
☐ 47	Willie Jones	14.00	6.50	1.60
☐ 48 A	Joe Page COR	20.00	8.00	2.00
☐ 48 B	Joe Page ERR	150.00	60.00	15.00
☐ 49 A	Johnny Sain COR	20.00	8.00	2.00
☐ 49 B	Johnny Sain ERR	150.00	60.00	15.00
☐ 50	Marv Rickert	14.00	6.50	1.60
☐ 51	Jim Russell	14.00	6.50	1.60
☐ 52	Don Mueller	17.00	7.25	1.80
☐ 53	Chris Van Cuyk	14.00	6.50	1.60
☐ 54	Leo Kiely	14.00	6.50	1.60
☐ 55	Ray Boone	17.00	7.25	1.80
☐ 56	Thomas Glaviano	14.00	6.50	1.60
☐ 57	Ed Lopat	24.00	10.00	2.50

		MINT	VG-E	F-G
☐ 58	Bob Mahoney	14.00	6.50	1.60
☐ 59	Robin Roberts	45.00	18.00	4.50
☐ 60	Sid Hudson	14.00	6.50	1.60
☐ 61	Tookie Gilbert	14.00	6.50	1.60
☐ 62	Chuck Stobbs	14.00	6.50	1.60
☐ 63	Howie Pollet	14.00	6.50	1.60
☐ 64	Roy Sievers	17.00	7.25	1.80
☐ 65	Enos Slaughter	40.00	16.00	4.00
☐ 66	Preacher Roe	24.00	10.00	2.50
☐ 67	Allie Reynolds	24.00	10.00	2.50
☐ 68	Cliff Chambers	14.00	6.50	1.60
☐ 69	Virgil Stallcup	14.00	6.50	1.60
☐ 70	Al Zarilla	14.00	6.50	1.60
☐ 71	Tom Upton	14.00	6.50	1.60
☐ 72	Karl Olson	14.00	6.50	1.60
☐ 73	William Werle	14.00	6.50	1.60
☐ 74	Andy Hansen	14.00	6.50	1.60
☐ 75	Wes Westrum	14.00	6.50	1.60
☐ 76	Eddie Stanky	17.00	7.25	1.80
☐ 77	Bob Kennedy	14.00	6.50	1.60
☐ 78	Ellis Kinder	14.00	6.50	1.60
☐ 79	Gerald Staley	14.00	6.50	1.60
☐ 80	Herman Wehmeier	14.00	6.50	1.60
☐ 81	Vernon Law	10.00	4.00	1.00
☐ 82	Duane Pillette	8.00	3.25	.80
☐ 83	Billy Johnson	8.00	3.25	.80
☐ 84	Vern Stephens	9.00	3.75	.90
☐ 85	Bob Kuzava	8.00	3.25	.80
☐ 86	Ted Gray	8.00	3.25	.80
☐ 87	Dale Coogan	8.00	3.25	.80
☐ 88	Bob Feller	50.00	20.00	5.00
☐ 89	Johnny Lipon	8.00	3.25	.80
☐ 90	Mickey Grasso	8.00	3.25	.80
☐ 91	Red Schoendienst	12.00	5.00	1.20
☐ 92	Dale Mitchell	9.00	3.75	.90
☐ 93	Al Sima	8.00	3.25	.80
☐ 94	Sam Mele	8.00	3.25	.80
☐ 95	Ken Holcombe	8.00	3.25	.80
☐ 96	Willard Marshall	8.00	3.25	.80
☐ 97	Earl Torgeson	8.00	3.25	.80
☐ 98	Billy Pierce	10.00	4.00	1.00
☐ 99	Gene Woodling	10.00	4.00	1.00
☐ 100	Del Rice	8.00	3.25	.80
☐ 101	Max Lanier	8.00	3.25	.80
☐ 102	Bill Kennedy	8.00	3.25	.80
☐ 103	Cliff Mapes	8.00	3.25	.80
☐ 104	Don Kolloway	8.00	3.25	.80
☐ 105	John Pramesa	8.00	3.25	.80
☐ 106	Mickey Vernon	10.00	4.00	1.00
☐ 107	Connie Ryan	8.00	3.25	.80
☐ 108	Jim Konstanty	10.00	4.00	1.00
☐ 109	Ted Wilks	8.00	3.25	.80
☐ 110	Dutch Leonard	8.00	3.25	.80

		MINT	VG-E	F-G
☐ 111	Peanuts Lowrey	8.00	3.25	.80
☐ 112	Henry Majeski	8.00	3.25	.80
☐ 113	Dick Sisler	8.00	3.25	.80
☐ 114	Willard Ramsdell	8.00	3.25	.80
☐ 115	Red Munger	8.00	3.25	.80
☐ 116	Carl Scheib	8.00	3.25	.80
☐ 117	Sherman Lollar	9.00	3.75	.90
☐ 118	Ken Raffensberger	8.00	3.25	.80
☐ 119	Mickey McDermott	8.00	3.25	.80
☐ 120	Bob Chakales	8.00	3.25	.80
☐ 121	Gus Niarhos	8.00	3.25	.80
☐ 122	Jackie Jensen	18.00	7.25	1.80
☐ 123	Eddie Yost	9.00	3.75	.90
☐ 124	Monte Kennedy	8.00	3.25	.80
☐ 125	Bill Rigney	8.00	3.25	.80
☐ 126	Fred Hutchinson	10.00	4.00	1.00
☐ 127	Paul Minner	8.00	3.25	.80
☐ 128	Don Bollweg	8.00	3.25	.80
☐ 129	Johnny Mize	25.00	10.00	2.50
☐ 130	Sheldon Jones	8.00	3.25	.80
☐ 131	Morris Martin	8.00	3.25	.80
☐ 132	Clyde Klutz	8.00	3.25	.80
☐ 133	Al Widmar	8.00	3.25	.80
☐ 134	Joe Tipton	8.00	3.25	.80
☐ 135	Dixie Howell	8.00	3.25	.80
☐ 136	Johnny Schmitz	8.00	3.25	.80
☐ 137	Roy McMillan	8.00	3.25	.80
☐ 138	Bill MacDonald	8.00	3.25	.80
☐ 139	Ken Wood	8.00	3.25	.80
☐ 140	Johnny Antonelli	10.00	4.00	1.00
☐ 141	Clint Hartung	8.00	3.25	.80
☐ 142	Harry Perkowski	8.00	3.25	.80
☐ 143	Les Moss	8.00	3.25	.80
☐ 144	Ed Blake	8.00	3.25	.80
☐ 145	Joe Haynes	8.00	3.25	.80
☐ 146	Frank House	8.00	3.25	.80
☐ 147	Bob Young	8.00	3.25	.80
☐ 148	Johnny Klippstein	8.00	3.25	.80
☐ 149	Dick Kryhoski	8.00	3.25	.80
☐ 150	Ted Beard	8.00	3.25	.80
☐ 151	Wally Post	8.00	3.25	.80
☐ 152	Al Evans	8.00	3.25	.80
☐ 153	Bob Rush	8.00	3.25	.80
☐ 154	Joe Muir	8.00	3.25	.80
☐ 155	Frank Overmire	8.00	3.25	.80
☐ 156	Frank Hiller	8.00	3.25	.80
☐ 157	Bob Usher	8.00	3.25	.80
☐ 158	Eddie Waitkus	8.00	3.25	.80
☐ 159	Saul Rogovin	8.00	3.25	.80
☐ 160	Owen Friend	8.00	3.25	.80
☐ 161	Bud Byerly	8.00	3.25	.80
☐ 162	Del Crandall	10.00	4.00	1.00
☐ 163	Stan Rojek	8.00	3.25	.80

		MINT	VG-E	F-G			MINT	VG-E	F-G
☐ 164	Walt Dubiel	8.00	3.25	.80	☐ 217	Snuffy Stirnweiss	9.00	3.75	.90
☐ 165	Eddie Kazak	8.00	3.25	.80	☐ 218	Clyde McCullough	8.00	3.25	.80
☐ 166	Paul LaPalme	8.00	3.25	.80	☐ 219	Bobby Shantz	12.00	5.00	1.20
☐ 167	Bill Howerton	8.00	3.25	.80	☐ 220	Joe Presko	8.00	3.25	.80
☐ 168	Charlie Silvera	8.00	3.25	.80	☐ 221	Granny Hamner	8.00	3.25	.80
☐ 169	Howie Judson	8.00	3.25	.80	☐ 222	Hoot Evers	8.00	3.25	.80
☐ 170	Gus Bell	9.00	3.75	.90	☐ 223	Del Ennis	10.00	4.00	1.00
☐ 171	Ed Erautt	8.00	3.25	.80	☐ 224	Bruce Edwards	8.00	3.25	.80
☐ 172	Eddie Miksis	8.00	3.25	.80	☐ 225	Frank Baumholtz	8.00	3.25	.80
☐ 173	Roy Smalley	8.00	3.25	.80	☐ 226	Dave Philley	8.00	3.25	.80
☐ 174	Clarence Marshall	8.00	3.25	.80	☐ 227	Joe Garagiola	25.00	10.00	2.50
☐ 175	Billy Martin	75.00	30.00	7.50	☐ 228	Al Brazle	8.00	3.25	.80
☐ 176	Hank Edwards	8.00	3.25	.80	☐ 229	Gene Bearden	8.00	3.25	.80
☐ 177	Bill Wight	8.00	3.25	.80	☐ 230	Matt Batts	8.00	3.25	.80
☐ 178	Cass Michaels	8.00	3.25	.80	☐ 231	Sam Zoldak	8.00	3.25	.80
☐ 179	Frank Smith	8.00	3.25	.80	☐ 232	Billy Cox	10.00	4.00	1.00
☐ 180	Charley Maxwell	8.00	3.25	.80	☐ 233	Bob Friend	10.00	4.00	1.00
☐ 181	Bob Swift	8.00	3.25	.80	☐ 234	Steve Souchock	8.00	3.25	.80
☐ 182	Billy Hitchcock	8.00	3.25	.80	☐ 235	Walt Dropo	8.00	3.25	.80
☐ 183	Erv Dusak	8.00	3.25	.80	☐ 236	Ed Fitzgerald	8.00	3.25	.80
☐ 184	Bob Ramazotti	8.00	3.25	.80	☐ 237	Jerry Coleman	10.00	4.00	1.00
☐ 185	Bill Nicholson	8.00	3.25	.80	☐ 238	Art Houtteman	8.00	3.25	.80
☐ 186	Walt Masterson	8.00	3.25	.80	☐ 239	Rocky Bridges	8.00	3.25	.80
☐ 187	Bob Miller	8.00	3.25	.80	☐ 240	Jack Phillips	8.00	3.25	.80
☐ 188	Clarence Podbielan	8.00	3.25	.80	☐ 241	Tommy Byrne	9.00	3.75	.90
☐ 189	Pete Reiser	10.00	4.00	1.00	☐ 242	Tom Poholsky	8.00	3.25	.80
☐ 190	Don Johnson	8.00	3.25	.80	☐ 243	Larry Doby	15.00	6.00	1.50
☐ 191	Yogi Berra	90.00	36.00	9.00	☐ 244	Vic Wertz	10.00	4.00	1.00
☐ 192	Myron Ginsberg	8.00	3.25	.80	☐ 245	Sherry Robertson	8.00	3.25	.80
☐ 193	Harry Simpson	8.00	3.25	.80	☐ 246	George Kell	25.00	10.00	2.50
☐ 194	Joe Hatton	8.00	3.25	.80	☐ 247	Randy Gumpert	8.00	3.25	.80
☐ 195	Minnie Minoso	18.00	7.25	1.80	☐ 248	Frank Shea	8.00	3.25	.80
☐ 196	Solly Hemus	8.00	3.25	.80	☐ 249	Bobby Adams	8.00	3.25	.80
☐ 197	George Strickland	8.00	3.25	.80	☐ 250	Carl Erskine	16.00	6.50	1.60
☐ 198	Phil Haugstad	8.00	3.25	.80	☐ 251	Chico Carrasquel	16.00	6.50	1.60
☐ 199	George Zuverink	8.00	3.25	.80	☐ 252	Vern Bickford	16.00	6.50	1.60
☐ 200	Ralph Houk	18.00	7.25	1.80	☐ 253	Johnny Berardino	18.00	7.25	1.80
☐ 201	Alex Kellner	8.00	3.25	.80	☐ 254	Joe Dobson	16.00	6.50	1.60
☐ 202	Joe Collins	9.00	3.75	.90	☐ 255	Clyde Vollmer	16.00	6.50	1.60
☐ 203	Curt Simmons	10.00	4.00	1.00	☐ 256	Pete Suder	16.00	6.50	1.60
☐ 204	Ron Northey	8.00	3.25	.80	☐ 257	Bobby Avila	18.00	7.25	1.80
☐ 205	Clyde King	9.00	3.75	.90	☐ 258	Steve Gromek	16.00	6.50	1.60
☐ 206	Joe Ostrowski	8.00	3.25	.80	☐ 259	Bob Addis	16.00	6.50	1.60
☐ 207	Mickey Harris	8.00	3.25	.80	☐ 260	Pete Castiglione	16.00	6.50	1.60
☐ 208	Marlin Stuart	8.00	3.25	.80	☐ 261	Willie Mays	500.00	200.00	50.00
☐ 209	Howie Fox	8.00	3.25	.80	☐ 262	Virgil Trucks	18.00	7.25	1.80
☐ 210	Dick Fowler	8.00	3.25	.80	☐ 263	Harry Brecheen	18.00	7.25	1.80
☐ 211	Ray Coleman	8.00	3.25	.80	☐ 264	Roy Hartsfield	16.00	6.50	1.60
☐ 212	Ned Garver	8.00	3.25	.80	☐ 265	Chuck Diering	16.00	6.50	1.60
☐ 213	Nippy Jones	8.00	3.25	.80	☐ 266	Murry Dickson	16.00	6.50	1.60
☐ 214	Johnny Hopp	9.00	3.75	.90	☐ 267	Sid Gordon	16.00	6.50	1.60
☐ 215	Hank Bauer	16.00	6.50	1.60	☐ 268	Bob Lemon	75.00	30.00	7.50
☐ 216	Richie Ashburn	21.00	8.50	2.10	☐ 269	Willard Nixon	16.00	6.50	1.60

		MINT	VG-E	F-G
☐ 270	Lou Brissie	16.00	6.50	1.60
☐ 271	Jim Delsing	16.00	6.50	1.60
☐ 272	Mike Garcia	18.00	7.25	1.80
☐ 273	Erv Palica	16.00	6.50	1.60
☐ 274	Ralph Branca	18.00	7.25	1.80
☐ 275	Pat Mullin	16.00	6.50	1.60
☐ 276	Jim Wilson	16.00	6.50	1.60
☐ 277	Early Wynn	75.00	30.00	7.50
☐ 278	Al Clark	16.00	6.50	1.60
☐ 279	Ed Stewart	16.00	6.50	1.60
☐ 280	Cloyd Boyer	18.00	7.25	1.80
☐ 281	Tommy Brown SP	20.00	8.00	2.00
☐ 282	Birdie Tebbetts SP	20.00	8.00	2.00
☐ 283	Philip Masi SP	20.00	8.00	2.00
☐ 284	Hank Arft SP	20.00	8.00	2.00
☐ 285	Cliff Fannin SP	20.00	8.00	2.00
☐ 286	Joe DeMaestri SP	20.00	8.00	2.00
☐ 287	Steve Bilko SP	20.00	8.00	2.00
☐ 288	Chet Nichols SP	20.00	8.00	2.00
☐ 289	Tommy Holmes SP	20.00	8.00	2.00
☐ 290	Joe Astroth SP	20.00	8.00	2.00
☐ 291	Gil Coan SP	20.00	8.00	2.00
☐ 292	Floyd Baker SP	20.00	8.00	2.00
☐ 293	Sibby Sisti SP	20.00	8.00	2.00
☐ 294	Walker Cooper SP	20.00	8.00	2.00
☐ 295	Phil Cavarretta SP	20.00	8.00	2.00
☐ 296	Red Rolfe SP	20.00	8.00	2.00
☐ 297	Andy Seminick SP	20.00	8.00	2.00
☐ 298	Bob Ross SP	20.00	8.00	2.00
☐ 299	Ray Murray SP	20.00	8.00	2.00
☐ 300	Barney McCosky SP	20.00	8.00	2.00
☐ 301	Bob Porterfield	16.00	6.50	1.60
☐ 302	Max Surkont	16.00	6.50	1.60
☐ 303	Harry Dorish	16.00	6.50	1.60
☐ 304	Sam Dente	16.00	6.50	1.60
☐ 305	Paul Richards	18.00	7.25	1.80
☐ 306	Lou Sleater	16.00	6.50	1.60
☐ 307	Frank Campos	16.00	6.50	1.60
☐ 308	Luis Aloma	16.00	6.50	1.60
☐ 309	Jim Busby	16.00	6.50	1.60
☐ 310	George Metkovich	16.00	6.50	1.60
☐ 311	Mickey Mantle DP	3300.00	1100.00	200.00
☐ 312	Jackie Robinson DP	450.00	180.00	45.00
☐ 313	Bobby Thomson DP	90.00	36.00	9.00
☐ 314	Roy Campanella	650.00	260.00	65.00
☐ 315	Leo Durocher	150.00	60.00	15.00
☐ 316	Dave Williams	90.00	36.00	9.00
☐ 317	Conrado Marrerro	75.00	30.00	7.50
☐ 318	Harold Gregg	75.00	30.00	7.50
☐ 319	Al Walker	75.00	30.00	7.50
☐ 320	John Rutherford	75.00	30.00	7.50
☐ 321	Joe Black	90.00	36.00	9.00
☐ 322	Randy Jackson	75.00	30.00	7.50
☐ 323	Bubba Church	75.00	30.00	7.50
☐ 324	Warren Hacker	75.00	30.00	7.50
☐ 325	Bill Serena	75.00	30.00	7.50
☐ 326	George Shuba	75.00	30.00	7.50
☐ 327	Al Wilson	75.00	30.00	7.50
☐ 328	Bob Borkowski	75.00	30.00	7.50
☐ 329	Ike Delock	75.00	30.00	7.50
☐ 330	Turk Lown	75.00	30.00	7.50
☐ 331	Tom Morgan	75.00	30.00	7.50
☐ 332	Anthony Bartirome	75.00	30.00	7.50
☐ 333	Pee Wee Reese	350.00	140.00	35.00
☐ 334	Wilmer Mizell	75.00	30.00	7.50
☐ 335	Ted Lepcio	75.00	30.00	7.50
☐ 336	Dave Koslo	75.00	30.00	7.50
☐ 337	Jim Hearn	75.00	30.00	7.50
☐ 338	Sal Yvars	75.00	30.00	7.50
☐ 339	Russ Meyer	75.00	30.00	7.50
☐ 340	Bob Hooper	75.00	30.00	7.50
☐ 341	Hal Jeffcoat	75.00	30.00	7.50
☐ 342	Clem Labine	90.00	36.00	9.00
☐ 343	Dick Gernert	75.00	30.00	7.50
☐ 344	Ewell Blackwell	90.00	36.00	9.00
☐ 345	Sammy White	75.00	30.00	7.50
☐ 346	George Spencer	75.00	30.00	7.50
☐ 347	Joe Adcock	90.00	36.00	9.00
☐ 348	Robert Kelly	75.00	30.00	7.50
☐ 349	Bob Cain	75.00	30.00	7.50
☐ 350	Cal Abrams	75.00	30.00	7.50
☐ 351	Alvin Dark	90.00	36.00	9.00
☐ 352	Karl Drews	75.00	30.00	7.50
☐ 353	Bobby Del Greco	75.00	30.00	7.50
☐ 354	Fred Hatfield	75.00	30.00	7.50
☐ 355	Bobby Morgan	75.00	30.00	7.50
☐ 356	Toby Atwell	75.00	30.00	7.50
☐ 357	Smoky Burgess	90.00	36.00	9.00
☐ 358	John Kucab	75.00	30.00	7.50
☐ 359	Dee Fondy	75.00	30.00	7.50
☐ 360	George Crowe	75.00	30.00	7.50
☐ 361	William Posedel	75.00	30.00	7.50
☐ 362	Ken Heintzelman	75.00	30.00	7.50
☐ 363	Dick Rozek	75.00	30.00	7.50
☐ 364	Clyde Sukeforth	75.00	30.00	7.50
☐ 365	Cookie Lavagetto	75.00	30.00	7.50
☐ 366	Dave Madison	75.00	30.00	7.50
☐ 367	Ben Thorpe	75.00	30.00	7.50
☐ 368	Ed Wright	75.00	30.00	7.50
☐ 369	Dick Groat	150.00	60.00	15.00
☐ 370	Billy Hoeft	75.00	30.00	7.50
☐ 371	Bobby Hofman	75.00	30.00	7.50
☐ 372	Gil McDougald	150.00	60.00	15.00
☐ 373	Jim Turner COA	75.00	30.00	7.50
☐ 374	John Benton	75.00	30.00	7.50
☐ 375	John Merson	75.00	30.00	7.50

		MINT	VG-E	F-G
☐ 376	Faye Throneberry	75.00	30.00	7.50
☐ 377	Chuck Dressen MGR	90.00	36.00	9.00
☐ 378	Leroy Fusselman	75.00	30.00	7.50
☐ 379	Joseph Rossi	75.00	30.00	7.50
☐ 380	Clem Koshorek	75.00	30.00	7.50
☐ 381	Milton Stock	75.00	30.00	7.50
☐ 382	Sam Jones	75.00	30.00	7.50
☐ 383	Del Wilber	75.00	30.00	7.50
☐ 384	Frank Crosetti COA	150.00	60.00	15.00
☐ 385	Herman Franks	75.00	30.00	7.50
☐ 386	John Yuhas	75.00	30.00	7.50
☐ 387	William Meyer	75.00	30.00	7.50
☐ 388	Bob Chipman	75.00	30.00	7.50
☐ 389	Ben Wade	75.00	30.00	7.50
☐ 390	Glenn Nelson	75.00	30.00	7.50
☐ 391	Ben Chapman (photo actually Sam Chapman)	75.00	30.00	7.50
☐ 392	Hoyt Wilhelm	250.00	100.00	25.00
☐ 393	Ebba St.Claire	75.00	30.00	7.50
☐ 394	Billy Herman COA	120.00	50.00	12.00
☐ 395	Jake Pitler COA	75.00	30.00	7.50
☐ 396	Dick Williams	90.00	36.00	9.00
☐ 397	Forrest Main	75.00	30.00	7.50
☐ 398	Hal Rice	75.00	30.00	7.50
☐ 399	Jim Fridley	75.00	30.00	7.50
☐ 400	Bill Dickey COA	300.00	120.00	30.00
☐ 401	Bob Schultz	75.00	30.00	7.50
☐ 402	Earl Harrist	75.00	30.00	7.50
☐ 403	Bill Miller	75.00	30.00	7.50
☐ 404	Dick Brodowski	75.00	30.00	7.50
☐ 405	Ed Pellagrini	75.00	30.00	7.50
☐ 406	Joe Nuxhall	90.00	36.00	9.00
☐ 407	Eddie Mathews	750.00	150.00	30.00

1953 Topps

*The cards in this 274-card set measure 2⅝"
by 3¾". Although the last card is numbered
280, there are only 274 cards in the set since
numbers 253, 261, 267, 268, 271, and 275
were never issued. The 1953 Topps series
contains line drawings of players in full color.
The name and team panel at the card base is
easily damaged, making it very difficult to
complete a mint set. The high number series,
221 to 280, was produced in shorter supply
late in the year and hence is more difficult to
complete than the lower numbers. The key
cards in the set are Mickey Mantle #82 and
Willie Mays #244.*

		MINT	VG-E	F-G
	Complete Set	3000.00	1000.00	300.00
	Common Player (1-165)	5.00	2.00	.50
	Common Player (166-220)	3.50	1.40	.35
	Common Player (221-280)	17.00	7.00	1.70
☐ 1	Jackie Robinson	150.00	30.00	6.00
☐ 2	Luke Easter	5.00	2.00	.50
☐ 3	George Crowe	5.00	2.00	.50
☐ 4	Ben Wade	5.00	2.00	.50
☐ 5	Joe Dobson	5.00	2.00	.50
☐ 6	Sam Jones	5.00	2.00	.50
☐ 7	Bob Borkowski	5.00	2.00	.50
☐ 8	Clem Koshorek	5.00	2.00	.50
☐ 9	Joe Collins	5.00	2.00	.50
☐ 10	Smoky Burgess	6.00	2.40	.60
☐ 11	Sal Yvars	5.00	2.00	.50
☐ 12	Howie Judson	5.00	2.00	.50
☐ 13	Connie Marrero	5.00	2.00	.50
☐ 14	Clem Labine	6.00	2.40	.60
☐ 15	Bobo Newsom	6.00	2.40	.60
☐ 16	Peanuts Lowrey	5.00	2.00	.50
☐ 17	Billy Hitchcock	5.00	2.00	.50
☐ 18	Ted Lepcio	5.00	2.00	.50
☐ 19	Mel Parnell	6.00	2.40	.60
☐ 20	Hank Thompson	5.00	2.00	.50
☐ 21	Billy Johnson	5.00	2.00	.50
☐ 22	Howie Fox	5.00	2.00	.50
☐ 23	Toby Atwell	5.00	2.00	.50
☐ 24	Ferris Fain	6.00	2.40	.60
☐ 25	Ray Boone	5.00	2.00	.50
☐ 26	Dale Mitchell	6.00	2.40	.60
☐ 27	Roy Campanella	60.00	24.00	6.00
☐ 28	Eddie Pellagrini	5.00	2.00	.50
☐ 29	Hal Jeffcoat	5.00	2.00	.50

		MINT	VG-E	F-G				MINT	VG-E	F-G
☐	30 Willard Nixon	5.00	2.00	.50	☐	83 Howie Pollet	5.00	2.00	.50
☐	31 Ewell Blackwell	6.00	2.40	.60	☐	84 Bob Hooper	5.00	2.00	.50
☐	32 Clyde Vollmer	5.00	2.00	.50	☐	85 Bobby Morgan	5.00	2.00	.50
☐	33 Bob Kennedy	5.00	2.00	.50	☐	86 Billy Martin	27.00	11.00	2.70
☐	34 George Shuba	6.00	2.40	.60	☐	87 Ed Lopat	9.00	3.75	.90
☐	35 Irv Noren	5.00	2.00	.50	☐	88 Willie Jones	5.00	2.00	.50
☐	36 Johnny Groth	5.00	2.00	.50	☐	89 Chuck Stobbs	5.00	2.00	.50
☐	37 Ed Mathews	21.00	8.50	2.10	☐	90 Hank Edwards	5.00	2.00	.50
☐	38 Jim Hearn	5.00	2.00	.50	☐	91 Ebba St.Claire	5.00	2.00	.50
☐	39 Eddie Miksis	5.00	2.00	.50	☐	92 Paul Minner	5.00	2.00	.50
☐	40 John Lipon	5.00	2.00	.50	☐	93 Hal Rice	5.00	2.00	.50
☐	41 Enos Slaughter	12.50	5.00	1.25	☐	94 Bill Kennedy	5.00	2.00	.50
☐	42 Gus Zernial	5.00	2.00	.50	☐	95 Willard Marshall	5.00	2.00	.50
☐	43 Gil McDougald	7.50	3.00	.75	☐	96 Virgil Trucks	6.00	2.40	.60
☐	44 Ellis Kinder	5.00	2.00	.50	☐	97 Don Kolloway	5.00	2.00	.50
☐	45 Grady Hatton	5.00	2.00	.50	☐	98 Cal Abrams	5.00	2.00	.50
☐	46 Johnny Klippstein	5.00	2.00	.50	☐	99 Dave Madison	5.00	2.00	.50
☐	47 Bubba Church	5.00	2.00	.50	☐	100 Bill Miller	5.00	2.00	.50
☐	48 Bob Del Greco	5.00	2.00	.50	☐	101 Ted Wilks	5.00	2.00	.50
☐	49 Faye Throneberry	5.00	2.00	.50	☐	102 Connie Ryan	5.00	2.00	.50
☐	50 Chuck Dressen MGR	6.00	2.40	.60	☐	103 Joe Astroth	5.00	2.00	.50
☐	51 Frank Campos	5.00	2.00	.50	☐	104 Yogi Berra	50.00	20.00	5.00
☐	52 Ted Gray	5.00	2.00	.50	☐	105 Joe Nuxhall	6.00	2.40	.60
☐	53 Sherman Lollar	6.00	2.40	.60	☐	106 Johnny Antonelli	6.00	2.40	.60
☐	54 Bob Feller	32.00	13.00	3.20	☐	107 Danny O'Connell	5.00	2.00	.50
☐	55 Maurice McDermott	5.00	2.00	.50	☐	108 Bob Porterfield	5.00	2.00	.50
☐	56 Gerry Staley	5.00	2.00	.50	☐	109 Alvin Dark	7.50	3.00	.75
☐	57 Carl Scheib	5.00	2.00	.50	☐	110 Herman Wehmeier	5.00	2.00	.50
☐	58 George Metkovich	5.00	2.00	.50	☐	111 Hank Sauer	6.00	2.40	.60
☐	59 Karl Drews	5.00	2.00	.50	☐	112 Ned Garver	5.00	2.00	.50
☐	60 Cloyd Boyer	5.00	2.00	.50	☐	113 Jerry Priddy	5.00	2.00	.50
☐	61 Early Wynn	12.50	5.00	1.25	☐	114 Phil Rizzuto	27.00	11.00	2.70
☐	62 Monte Irvin	10.00	4.00	1.00	☐	115 George Spencer	5.00	2.00	.50
☐	63 Gus Niarhos	5.00	2.00	.50	☐	116 Frank Smith	5.00	2.00	.50
☐	64 Dave Philley	5.00	2.00	.50	☐	117 Sid Gordon	5.00	2.00	.50
☐	65 Earl Harrist	5.00	2.00	.50	☐	118 Gus Bell	6.00	2.40	.60
☐	66 Minnie Minoso	7.50	3.00	.75	☐	119 John Sain	9.00	3.75	.90
☐	67 Roy Sievers	6.00	2.40	.60	☐	120 Davey Williams	6.00	2.40	.60
☐	68 Del Rice	5.00	2.00	.50	☐	121 Walter Dropo	5.00	2.00	.50
☐	69 Dick Brodowski	5.00	2.00	.50	☐	122 Elmer Valo	5.00	2.00	.50
☐	70 Ed Yuhas	5.00	2.00	.50	☐	123 Tommy Byrne	5.00	2.00	.50
☐	71 Tony Bartirome	5.00	2.00	.50	☐	124 Sibby Sisti	5.00	2.00	.50
☐	72 Fred Hutchinson	6.00	2.40	.60	☐	125 Dick Williams	7.50	3.00	.75
☐	73 Eddie Robinson	5.00	2.00	.50	☐	126 Bill Connelly	5.00	2.00	.50
☐	74 Joe Rossi	5.00	2.00	.50	☐	127 Clint Courtney	5.00	2.00	.50
☐	75 Mike Garcia	6.00	2.40	.60	☐	128 Wilmer Mizell	6.00	2.40	.60
☐	76 Pee Wee Reese	27.00	11.00	2.70	☐	129 Keith Thomas	5.00	2.00	.50
☐	77 Johnny Mize	14.00	5.75	1.40	☐	130 Turk Lown	5.00	2.00	.50
☐	78 Al (Red) Schoendienst	7.50	3.00	.75	☐	131 Harry Byrd	5.00	2.00	.50
☐	79 Johnny Wyrostek	5.00	2.00	.50	☐	132 Tom Morgan	5.00	2.00	.50
☐	80 Jim Hegan	6.00	2.40	.60	☐	133 Gil Coan	5.00	2.00	.50
☐	81 Joe Black	6.00	2.40	.60	☐	134 Rube Walker	6.00	2.40	.60
☐	82 Mickey Mantle	600.00	240.00	60.00	☐	135 Al Rosen	10.00	4.00	1.00

		MINT	VG-E	F-G
☐ 136	Ken Heintzelman	5.00	2.00	.50
☐ 137	John Rutherford	5.00	2.00	.50
☐ 138	George Kell	12.50	5.00	1.25
☐ 139	Sammy White	5.00	2.00	.50
☐ 140	Tommy Glaviano	5.00	2.00	.50
☐ 141	Allie Reynolds	9.00	3.75	.90
☐ 142	Vic Wertz	5.00	2.00	.50
☐ 143	Billy Pierce	7.50	3.00	.75
☐ 144	Bob Schultz	5.00	2.00	.50
☐ 145	Harry Dorish	5.00	2.00	.50
☐ 146	Granny Hamner	5.00	2.00	.50
☐ 147	Warren Spahn	30.00	12.00	3.00
☐ 148	Mickey Grasso	5.00	2.00	.50
☐ 149	Dom DiMaggio	10.00	4.00	1.00
☐ 150	Harry Simpson	5.00	2.00	.50
☐ 151	Hoyt Wilhelm	18.00	7.25	1.80
☐ 152	Bob Adams	5.00	2.00	.50
☐ 153	Andy Seminick	5.00	2.00	.50
☐ 154	Dick Groat	7.50	3.00	.75
☐ 155	Dutch Leonard	5.00	2.00	.50
☐ 156	Jim Rivera	5.00	2.00	.50
☐ 157	Bob Addis	5.00	2.00	.50
☐ 158	John Logan	6.00	2.40	.60
☐ 159	Wayne Terwilliger	5.00	2.00	.50
☐ 160	Bob Young	5.00	2.00	.50
☐ 161	Vern Bickford	5.00	2.00	.50
☐ 162	Ted Kluszewski	9.00	3.75	.90
☐ 163	Fred Hatfield	5.00	2.00	.50
☐ 164	Frank Shea	5.00	2.00	.50
☐ 165	Billy Hoeft	5.00	2.00	.50
☐ 166	Bill Hunter	3.50	1.40	.35
☐ 167	Art Schult	3.50	1.40	.35
☐ 168	Willard Schmidt	3.50	1.40	.35
☐ 169	Dizzy Trout	3.50	1.40	.35
☐ 170	Bill Werle	3.50	1.40	.35
☐ 171	Bill Glynn	3.50	1.40	.35
☐ 172	Rip Repulski	3.50	1.40	.35
☐ 173	Preston Ward	3.50	1.40	.35
☐ 174	Billy Loes	3.50	1.40	.35
☐ 175	Ronnie Kline	3.50	1.40	.35
☐ 176	Don Hoak	4.50	1.80	.45
☐ 177	Jim Dyck	3.50	1.40	.35
☐ 178	Jim Waugh	3.50	1.40	.35
☐ 179	Gene Hermanski	3.50	1.40	.35
☐ 180	Virgil Stallcup	3.50	1.40	.35
☐ 181	Al Zarilla	3.50	1.40	.35
☐ 182	Bobby Hofman	3.50	1.40	.35
☐ 183	Stu Miller	3.50	1.40	.35
☐ 184	Hal Brown	3.50	1.40	.35
☐ 185	Jim Pendleton	3.50	1.40	.35
☐ 186	Charlie Bishop	3.50	1.40	.35
☐ 187	Jim Fridley	3.50	1.40	.35
☐ 188	Andy Carey	4.50	1.80	.45

		MINT	VG-E	F-G
☐ 189	Ray Jablonski	3.50	1.40	.35
☐ 190	Dixie Walker	3.50	1.40	.35
☐ 191	Ralph Kiner	15.00	6.00	1.50
☐ 192	Wally Westlake	3.50	1.40	.35
☐ 193	Mike Clark	3.50	1.40	.35
☐ 194	Eddie Kazak	3.50	1.40	.35
☐ 195	Ed McGhee	3.50	1.40	.35
☐ 196	Bob Keegan	3.50	1.40	.35
☐ 197	Del Crandall	4.50	1.80	.45
☐ 198	Forrest Main	3.50	1.40	.35
☐ 199	Marion Fricano	3.50	1.40	.35
☐ 200	Gordon Goldsberry	3.50	1.40	.35
☐ 201	Paul LaPalme	3.50	1.40	.35
☐ 202	Carl Sawatski	3.50	1.40	.35
☐ 203	Cliff Fannin	3.50	1.40	.35
☐ 204	Dick Bokelman	3.50	1.40	.35
☐ 205	Vern Benson	3.50	1.40	.35
☐ 206	Ed Bailey	4.50	1.80	.45
☐ 207	Whitey Ford	25.00	10.00	2.50
☐ 208	Jim Wilson	3.50	1.40	.35
☐ 209	Jim Greengrass	3.50	1.40	.35
☐ 210	Bob Cerv	4.50	1.80	.45
☐ 211	J.W. Porter	3.50	1.40	.35
☐ 212	Jack Dittmer	3.50	1.40	.35
☐ 213	Ray Scarborough	3.50	1.40	.35
☐ 214	Bill Bruton	4.50	1.80	.45
☐ 215	Gene Conley	4.50	1.80	.45
☐ 216	Jim Hughes	3.50	1.40	.35
☐ 217	Murray Wall	3.50	1.40	.35
☐ 218	Les Fusselman	3.50	1.40	.35
☐ 219	Pete Runnels	4.50	1.80	.45
	(photo actually			
	Don Johnson)			
☐ 220	Satchel Paige	90.00	36.00	9.00
☐ 221	Bob Milliken	17.00	7.00	1.70
☐ 222	Vic Janowicz	20.00	8.00	2.00
☐ 223	Johnny O'Brien	17.00	7.00	1.70
☐ 224	Lou Sleater	17.00	7.00	1.70
☐ 225	Bobby Shantz	24.00	10.00	2.40
☐ 226	Ed Erautt	17.00	7.00	1.70
☐ 227	Morris Martin	17.00	7.00	1.70
☐ 228	Hal Newhouser	32.00	13.00	3.20
☐ 229	Rockey Krsnich	17.00	7.00	1.70
☐ 230	Johnny Lindell	17.00	7.00	1.70
☐ 231	Solly Hemus	17.00	7.00	1.70
☐ 232	Dick Kokos	17.00	7.00	1.70
☐ 233	Al Aber	17.00	7.00	1.70
☐ 234	Ray Murray	17.00	7.00	1.70
☐ 235	John Hetki	17.00	7.00	1.70
☐ 236	Harry Perkowski	17.00	7.00	1.70
☐ 237	Bud Podbielan	17.00	7.00	1.70
☐ 238	Cal Hogue	17.00	7.00	1.70
☐ 239	Jim Delsing	17.00	7.00	1.70

		MINT	VG-E	F-G
☐ 240	Freddie Marsh	17.00	7.00	1.70
☐ 241	Al Sima	17.00	7.00	1.70
☐ 242	Charlie Silvera	17.00	7.00	1.70
☐ 243	Carlos Bernier	17.00	7.00	1.70
☐ 244	Willie Mays	600.00	240.00	60.00
☐ 245	Bill Norman	17.00	7.00	1.70
☐ 246	Roy Face	32.00	13.00	3.20
☐ 247	Mike Sandlock	17.00	7.00	1.70
☐ 248	Gene Stephens	17.00	7.00	1.70
☐ 249	Eddie O'Brien	17.00	7.00	1.70
☐ 250	Bob Wilson	17.00	7.00	1.70
☐ 251	Sid Hudson	17.00	7.00	1.70
☐ 252	Henry Foiles	17.00	7.00	1.70
☐ 253	Does not exist	0.00	0.00	0.00
☐ 254	Preacher Roe	32.00	13.00	3.20
☐ 255	Dixie Howell	17.00	7.00	1.70
☐ 256	Les Peden	17.00	7.00	1.70
☐ 257	Bob Boyd	17.00	7.00	1.70
☐ 258	Jim Gilliam	90.00	36.00	9.00
☐ 259	Roy McMillan	17.00	7.00	1.70
☐ 260	Sam Calderone	17.00	7.00	1.70
☐ 261	Does not exist	0.00	0.00	0.00
☐ 262	Bob Oldis	17.00	7.00	1.70
☐ 263	Johnny Podres	75.00	30.00	7.50
☐ 264	Gene Woodling	32.00	13.00	3.20
☐ 265	Jackie Jensen	40.00	16.00	4.00
☐ 266	Bob Cain	17.00	7.00	1.70
☐ 267	Does not exist	0.00	0.00	0.00
☐ 268	Does not exist	0.00	0.00	0.00
☐ 269	Duane Pillette	17.00	7.00	1.70
☐ 270	Vern Stephens	20.00	8.00	2.00
☐ 271	Does not exist	0.00	0.00	0.00
☐ 272	Bill Antonello	17.00	7.00	1.70
☐ 273	Harvey Haddix	24.00	10.00	2.40
☐ 274	John Riddle	17.00	7.00	1.70
☐ 275	Does not exist	0.00	0.00	0.00
☐ 276	Ken Raffensberger	17.00	7.00	1.70
☐ 277	Don Lund	17.00	7.00	1.70
☐ 278	Willie Miranda	17.00	7.00	1.70
☐ 279	Joe Coleman	17.00	7.00	1.70
☐ 280	Milt Bolling	90.00	12.00	2.00

1954 Topps

The cards in this 250-card set measure 2⅝"
by 3¾". Each of the cards in the 1954 Topps
set contains a large "head" shot of the player
in color plus a smaller full-length photo in
black and white set against a color background. This series contains the rookie cards
of Hank Aaron, Ernie Banks, and Al Kaline
and two separate cards of Ted Williams
(number 1 and number 250). Conspicuous
by his absence is Mickey Mantle who apparently was the exclusive property of Bowman
during 1954 (and 1955).

		MINT	VG-E	F-G
	Complete Set	1500.00	650.00	175.00
	Common Player (1-50)	1.50	.60	.15
	Common Player (51-75)	3.50	1.40	.35
	Common Player (76-250)	2.00	.80	.20
☐ 1	Ted Williams	125.00	25.00	5.00
☐ 2	Gus Zernial	1.50	.60	.15
☐ 3	Monte Irvin	6.50	2.60	.65
☐ 4	Hank Sauer	2.00	.80	.20
☐ 5	Ed Lopat	4.00	1.60	.40
☐ 6	Pete Runnels	2.00	.80	.20
☐ 7	Ted Kluszewski	4.00	1.60	.40
☐ 8	Bob Young	1.50	.60	.15
☐ 9	Harvey Haddix	2.00	.80	.20
☐ 10	Jackie Robinson	60.00	24.00	6.00
☐ 11	Paul Leslie Smith	1.50	.60	.15
☐ 12	Del Crandall	2.00	.80	.20
☐ 13	Billy Martin	20.00	8.00	2.00
☐ 14	Preacher Roe	4.00	1.60	.40
☐ 15	Al Rosen	5.00	2.00	.50
☐ 16	Vic Janowicz	2.00	.80	.20
☐ 17	Phil Rizzuto	18.00	7.25	1.80

		MINT	VG-E	F-G			MINT	VG-E	F-G
☐	18 Walt Dropo	1.50	.60	.15	☐ 71 Frank Smith	3.50	1.40	.35
☐	19 Johnny Lipon	1.50	.60	.15	☐ 72 Preston Ward	3.50	1.40	.35
☐	20 Warren Spahn	20.00	8.00	2.00	☐ 73 Wayne Terwilliger	3.50	1.40	.35
☐	21 Bobby Shantz	2.00	.80	.20	☐ 74 Bill Taylor	3.50	1.40	.35
☐	22 Jim Greengrass	1.50	.60	.15	☐ 75 Fred Haney	3.50	1.40	.35
☐	23 Luke Easter	2.00	.80	.20	☐ 76 Bob Scheffing	2.00	.80	.20
☐	24 Granny Hamner	1.50	.60	.15	☐ 77 Ray Boone	2.50	1.00	.25
☐	25 Harvey Kuenn	6.00	2.40	.60	☐ 78 Ted Kazanski	2.00	.80	.20
☐	26 Ray Jablonski	1.50	.60	.15	☐ 79 Andy Pafko	2.00	.80	.20
☐	27 Ferris Fain	2.00	.80	.20	☐ 80 Jackie Jensen	3.50	1.40	.35
☐	28 Paul Minner	1.50	.60	.15	☐ 81 Dave Hoskins	2.00	.80	.20
☐	29 Jim Hegan	1.50	.60	.15	☐ 82 Milt Bolling	2.00	.80	.20
☐	30 Ed Mathews	16.00	6.50	1.60	☐ 83 Joe Collins	2.50	1.00	.25
☐	31 Johnny Klippstein	1.50	.60	.15	☐ 84 Dick Cole	2.00	.80	.20
☐	32 Duke Snider	40.00	16.00	4.00	☐ 85 Bob Turley	4.50	1.80	.45
☐	33 Johnny Schmitz	1.50	.60	.15	☐ 86 Billy Herman	3.50	1.40	.35
☐	34 Jim Rivera	1.50	.60	.15	☐ 87 Roy Face	2.50	1.00	.25
☐	35 Jim Gilliam	4.00	1.60	.40	☐ 88 Matt Batts	2.00	.80	.20
☐	36 Hoyt Wilhelm	9.00	3.75	.90	☐ 89 Howie Pollet	2.00	.80	.20
☐	37 Whitey Ford	18.00	7.25	1.80	☐ 90 Willie Mays	150.00	60.00	15.00
☐	38 Eddie Stanky	2.00	.80	.20	☐ 91 Bob Oldis	2.00	.80	.20
☐	39 Sherm Lollar	2.00	.80	.20	☐ 92 Wally Westlake	2.00	.80	.20
☐	40 Mel Parnell	2.00	.80	.20	☐ 93 Sid Hudson	2.00	.80	.20
☐	41 Willie Jones	1.50	.60	.15	☐ 94 Ernie Banks	100.00	40.00	10.00
☐	42 Don Mueller	2.00	.80	.20	☐ 95 Hal Rice	2.00	.80	.20
☐	43 Dick Groat	3.50	1.40	.35	☐ 96 Charlie Silvera	2.00	.80	.20
☐	44 Ned Garver	1.50	.60	.15	☐ 97 Jerald Hal Lane	2.00	.80	.20
☐	45 Richie Ashburn	5.00	2.00	.50	☐ 98 Joe Black	2.50	1.00	.25
☐	46 Ken Raffensberger	1.50	.60	.15	☐ 99 Bobby Hofman	2.00	.80	.20
☐	47 Ellis Kinder	1.50	.60	.15	☐ 100 Bob Keegan	2.00	.80	.20
☐	48 William Hunter	1.50	.60	.15	☐ 101 Gene Woodling	2.50	1.00	.25
☐	49 Ray Murray	1.50	.60	.15	☐ 102 Gil Hodges	18.00	7.25	1.80
☐	50 Yogi Berra	35.00	14.00	3.50	☐ 103 Jim Lemon	2.50	1.00	.25
☐	51 Johnny Lindell	3.50	1.40	.35	☐ 104 Mike Sandlock	2.00	.80	.20
☐	52 Vic Power	3.50	1.40	.35	☐ 105 Andy Carey	2.50	1.00	.25
☐	53 Jack Dittmer	3.50	1.40	.35	☐ 106 Dick Kokos	2.00	.80	.20
☐	54 Vern Stephens	4.00	1.60	.40	☐ 107 Duane Pillette	2.00	.80	.20
☐	55 Phil Cavarretta	4.00	1.60	.40	☐ 108 Thornton Kipper	2.00	.80	.20
☐	56 Willie Miranda	3.50	1.40	.35	☐ 109 Bill Bruton	2.00	.80	.20
☐	57 Luis Aloma	3.50	1.40	.35	☐ 110 Harry Dorish	2.00	.80	.20
☐	58 Bob Wilson	3.50	1.40	.35	☐ 111 Jim Delsing	2.00	.80	.20
☐	59 Gene Conley	3.50	1.40	.35	☐ 112 Bill Renna	2.00	.80	.20
☐	60 Frank Baumholtz	3.50	1.40	.35	☐ 113 Bob Boyd	2.00	.80	.20
☐	61 Bob Cain	3.50	1.40	.35	☐ 114 Dean Stone	2.00	.80	.20
☐	62 Eddie Robinson	3.50	1.40	.35	☐ 115 Rip Repulski	2.00	.80	.20
☐	63 Johnny Pesky	4.00	1.60	.40	☐ 116 Steve Bilko	2.00	.80	.20
☐	64 Hank Thompson	4.00	1.60	.40	☐ 117 Solly Hemus	2.00	.80	.20
☐	65 Bob Swift	3.50	1.40	.35	☐ 118 Carl Scheib	2.00	.80	.20
☐	66 Ted Lepcio	3.50	1.40	.35	☐ 119 Johnny Antonelli	2.50	1.00	.25
☐	67 Jim Willis	3.50	1.40	.35	☐ 120 Roy McMillan	2.50	1.00	.25
☐	68 Sam Calderone	3.50	1.40	.35	☐ 121 Clem Labine	2.50	1.00	.25
☐	69 Bud Podbielan	3.50	1.40	.35	☐ 122 Johnny Logan	2.50	1.00	.25
☐	70 Larry Doby	7.50	3.00	.75	☐ 123 Bobby Adams	2.00	.80	.20

		MINT	VG-E	F-G
☐ 124	Marion Fricano	2.00	.80	.20
☐ 125	Harry Perkowski	2.00	.80	.20
☐ 126	Ben Wade	2.00	.80	.20
☐ 127	Steve O'Neill	2.00	.80	.20
☐ 128	Hank Aaron	325.00	130.00	32.00
☐ 129	Forrest Jacobs	2.00	.80	.20
☐ 130	Hank Bauer	4.00	1.60	.40
☐ 131	Reno Bertoia	2.00	.80	.20
☐ 132	Tom Lasorda	25.00	10.00	2.50
☐ 133	Dave Baker	2.00	.80	.20
☐ 134	Cal Hogue	2.00	.80	.20
☐ 135	Joe Presko	2.00	.80	.20
☐ 136	Connie Ryan	2.00	.80	.20
☐ 137	Wally Moon	4.00	1.60	.40
☐ 138	Bob Borkowski	2.00	.80	.20
☐ 139	The O'Briens	3.50	1.40	.35
	Johnny O'Brien			
	Eddie O'Brien			
☐ 140	Tom Wright	2.00	.80	.20
☐ 141	Joe Jay	2.50	1.00	.25
☐ 142	Tom Poholsky	2.00	.80	.20
☐ 143	Ralston Hemsley	2.00	.80	.20
☐ 144	Bill Werle	2.00	.80	.20
☐ 145	Elmer Valo	2.00	.80	.20
☐ 146	Don Johnson	2.00	.80	.20
☐ 147	Johnny Riddle	2.00	.80	.20
☐ 148	Bob Trice	2.00	.80	.20
☐ 149	Al Robertson	2.00	.80	.20
☐ 150	Dick Kryhoski	2.00	.80	.20
☐ 151	Alex Grammas	2.00	.80	.20
☐ 152	Michael Blyzka	2.00	.80	.20
☐ 153	Al Walker	2.00	.80	.20
☐ 154	Mike Fornieles	2.00	.80	.20
☐ 155	Bob Kennedy	2.00	.80	.20
☐ 156	Joe Coleman	2.00	.80	.20
☐ 157	Don Lenhardt	2.00	.80	.20
☐ 158	Peanuts Lowrey	2.00	.80	.20
☐ 159	Dave Philley	2.00	.80	.20
☐ 160	Ralph Kress	2.00	.80	.20
☐ 161	John Hetki	2.00	.80	.20
☐ 162	Herman Wehmeier	2.00	.80	.20
☐ 163	Frank House	2.00	.80	.20
☐ 164	Stu Miller	2.00	.80	.20
☐ 165	Jim Pendleton	2.00	.80	.20
☐ 166	Johnny Podres	4.00	1.60	.40
☐ 167	Don Lund	2.00	.80	.20
☐ 168	Morrie Martin	2.00	.80	.20
☐ 169	Jim Hughes	2.00	.80	.20
☐ 170	James (Dusty) Rhodes	2.50	1.00	.25
☐ 171	Leo Kiely	2.00	.80	.20
☐ 172	Harold Brown	2.00	.80	.20
☐ 173	Jack Harshman	2.00	.80	.20
☐ 174	Tom Qualters	2.00	.80	.20

		MINT	VG-E	F-G
☐ 175	Frank Leja	2.00	.80	.20
☐ 176	Robert Keeley	2.00	.80	.20
☐ 177	Bob Milliken	2.00	.80	.20
☐ 178	Bill Glynn	2.00	.80	.20
☐ 179	Gair Allie	2.00	.80	.20
☐ 180	Wes Westrum	2.00	.80	.20
☐ 181	Mel Roach	2.00	.80	.20
☐ 182	Chuck Harmon	2.00	.80	.20
☐ 183	Earle Combs	3.00	1.20	.30
☐ 184	Ed Bailey	2.00	.80	.20
☐ 185	Chuck Stobbs	2.00	.80	.20
☐ 186	Karl Olson	2.00	.80	.20
☐ 187	Henry Manush	3.00	1.20	.30
☐ 188	Dave Jolly	2.00	.80	.20
☐ 189	Floyd Ross	2.00	.80	.20
☐ 190	Ray Herbert	2.00	.80	.20
☐ 191	John (Dick) Schofield	2.50	1.00	.25
☐ 192	Ellis Deal	2.00	.80	.20
☐ 193	Johnny Hopp	2.50	1.00	.25
☐ 194	Bill Sarni	2.00	.80	.20
☐ 195	Bill Consolo	2.00	.80	.20
☐ 196	Stanley Jok	2.00	.80	.20
☐ 197	Lynwood Rowe	2.50	1.00	.25
☐ 198	Carl Sawatski	2.00	.80	.20
☐ 199	Glenn (Rocky) Nelson	2.00	.80	.20
☐ 200	Larry Jansen	2.00	.80	.20
☐ 201	Al Kaline	120.00	50.00	12.00
☐ 202	Bob Purkey	2.00	.80	.20
☐ 203	Harry Brecheen	2.00	.80	.20
☐ 204	Angel Scull	2.00	.80	.20
☐ 205	Johnny Sain	4.50	1.80	.45
☐ 206	Ray Crone	2.00	.80	.20
☐ 207	Tom Oliver	2.00	.80	.20
☐ 208	Grady Hatton	2.00	.80	.20
☐ 209	Chuck Thompson	2.00	.80	.20
☐ 210	Bob Buhl	2.50	1.00	.25
☐ 211	Don Hoak	2.00	.80	.20
☐ 212	Bob Micelotta	2.00	.80	.20
☐ 213	Johnny Fitzpatrick	2.00	.80	.20
☐ 214	Arnie Portocarrero	2.00	.80	.20
☐ 215	Warren McGhee	2.00	.80	.20
☐ 216	Al Sima	2.00	.80	.20
☐ 217	Paul Schreiber	2.00	.80	.20
☐ 218	Fred Marsh	2.00	.80	.20
☐ 219	Chuck Kress	2.00	.80	.20
☐ 220	Ruben Gomez	2.00	.80	.20
☐ 221	Dick Brodowski	2.00	.80	.20
☐ 222	Bill Wilson	2.00	.80	.20
☐ 223	Joe Haynes	2.00	.80	.20
☐ 224	Dick Weik	2.00	.80	.20
☐ 225	Don Liddle	2.00	.80	.20
☐ 226	Jehosie Heard	2.00	.80	.20
☐ 227	Colonel Mills	2.00	.80	.20

		MINT	VG-E	F-G
☐ 228	Gene Hermanski	2.00	.80	.20
☐ 229	Robert Talbot	2.00	.80	.20
☐ 230	Bob Kuzava	2.00	.80	.20
☐ 231	Roy Smalley	2.00	.80	.20
☐ 232	Lou Limmer	2.00	.80	.20
☐ 233	Augie Galan	2.00	.80	.20
☐ 234	Jerry Lynch	2.50	1.00	.25
☐ 235	Vernon Law	2.50	1.00	.25
☐ 236	Paul Penson	2.00	.80	.20
☐ 237	Dominic Ryba	2.00	.80	.20
☐ 238	Al Aber	2.00	.80	.20
☐ 239	Bill Skowron	6.00	2.40	.60
☐ 240	Sam Mele	2.00	.80	.20
☐ 241	Robert Miller	2.00	.80	.20
☐ 242	Curt Roberts	2.00	.80	.20
☐ 243	Ray Blades	2.00	.80	.20
☐ 244	Leroy Wheat	2.00	.80	.20
☐ 245	Roy Sievers	2.50	1.00	.25
☐ 246	Howie Fox	2.00	.80	.20
☐ 247	Ed Mayo	2.00	.80	.20
☐ 248	Alphonse Smith	2.50	1.00	.25
☐ 249	Wilmer Mizell	2.00	.80	.20
☐ 250	Ted Williams	125.00	25.00	5.00

1955 Topps

The cards in this 206-card set measure 2⅝" by 3¾". Both the large "head" shot and the smaller full-length photos used on each card of the 1955 Topps set are in color. The card fronts were designed horizontally for the first time in Topps' history. The first card features Dusty Rhodes, hitting star for the Giants 1954 World Series sweep over the Indians. A "high" series, 161 to 210, is more difficult to find than cards 1 to 160. Numbers 175, 186, 203, and 209 were never issued. To fill in for the four cards not issued in the high number series, Topps double printed four players, those appearing on cards 170, 172, 184, and 188.

		MINT	VG-E	F-G
	Complete Set	1200.00	500.00	150.00
	Common Player (1-150)	1.50	.60	.15
	Common Player (151-160)	3.00	1.20	.30
	Common Player (161-210)	4.25	1.70	.42
☐ 1	Dusty Rhodes	6.00	1.00	.20
☐ 2	Ted Williams	60.00	24.00	6.00
☐ 3	Art Fowler	1.50	.60	.15
☐ 4	Al Kaline	22.00	9.00	2.20
☐ 5	Jim Gilliam	3.00	1.20	.30
☐ 6	Stan Hack	1.50	.60	.15
☐ 7	Jim Hegan	1.50	.60	.15
☐ 8	Harold Smith	1.50	.60	.15
☐ 9	Robert Miller	1.50	.60	.15
☐ 10	Bob Keegan	1.50	.60	.15
☐ 11	Ferris Fain	1.50	.60	.15
☐ 12	Vernon Thies	1.50	.60	.15
☐ 13	Fred Marsh	1.50	.60	.15
☐ 14	Jim Finigan	1.50	.60	.15
☐ 15	Jim Pendleton	1.50	.60	.15
☐ 16	Roy Sievers	1.50	.60	.15
☐ 17	Bobby Hofman	1.50	.60	.15
☐ 18	Russ Kemmerer	1.50	.60	.15
☐ 19	Billy Herman	2.50	1.00	.25
☐ 20	Andy Carey	1.50	.60	.15
☐ 21	Alex Grammas	1.50	.60	.15
☐ 22	Bill Skowron	3.00	1.20	.30
☐ 23	Jack Parks	1.50	.60	.15
☐ 24	Hal Newhouser	3.00	1.20	.30
☐ 25	John Podres	3.00	1.20	.30
☐ 26	Dick Groat	2.50	1.00	.25
☐ 27	Bill Gardner	1.50	.60	.15
☐ 28	Ernie Banks	18.00	7.25	1.80
☐ 29	Herman Wehmeier	1.50	.60	.15
☐ 30	Vic Power	1.50	.60	.15
☐ 31	Warren Spahn	14.00	5.75	1.40
☐ 32	Warren McGhee	1.50	.60	.15
☐ 33	Tom Qualters	1.50	.60	.15
☐ 34	Wayne Terwilliger	1.50	.60	.15
☐ 35	Dave Jolly	1.50	.60	.15
☐ 36	Leo Kiely	1.50	.60	.15
☐ 37	Joe Cunningham	2.00	.80	.20
☐ 38	Bob Turley	2.50	1.00	.25
☐ 39	Bill Glynn	1.50	.60	.15
☐ 40	Don Hoak	1.50	.60	.15
☐ 41	Chuck Stobbs	1.50	.60	.15
☐ 42	John (Windy) McCall	1.50	.60	.15
☐ 43	Harvey Haddix	2.00	.80	.20
☐ 44	Harold Valentine	1.50	.60	.15
☐ 45	Hank Sauer	2.00	.80	.20
☐ 46	Ted Kazanski	1.50	.60	.15

	MINT	VG-E	F-G		MINT	VG-E	F-G
☐ 47 Hank Aaron	60.00	24.00	6.00	☐ 100 Monte Irvin	5.00	2.00	.50
☐ 48 Bob Kennedy	1.50	.60	.15	☐ 101 Johnny Gray	1.50	.60	.15
☐ 49 J.W. Porter	1.50	.60	.15	☐ 102 Wally Westlake	1.50	.60	.15
☐ 50 Jackie Robinson	50.00	20.00	5.00	☐ 103 Chuck White	1.50	.60	.15
☐ 51 Jim Hughes	1.50	.60	.15	☐ 104 Jack Harshman	1.50	.60	.15
☐ 52 Bill Tremel	1.50	.60	.15	☐ 105 Chuck Diering	1.50	.60	.15
☐ 53 Bill Taylor	1.50	.60	.15	☐ 106 Frank Sullivan	1.50	.60	.15
☐ 54 Lou Limmer	1.50	.60	.15	☐ 107 Curt Roberts	1.50	.60	.15
☐ 55 Rip Repulski	1.50	.60	.15	☐ 108 Al Walker	1.50	.60	.15
☐ 56 Ray Jablonski	1.50	.60	.15	☐ 109 Ed Lopat	3.00	1.20	.30
☐ 57 Billy O'Dell	1.50	.60	.15	☐ 110 Gus Zernial	1.50	.60	.15
☐ 58 Jim Rivera	1.50	.60	.15	☐ 111 Bob Milliken	1.50	.60	.15
☐ 59 Gair Allie	1.50	.60	.15	☐ 112 Nelson King	1.50	.60	.15
☐ 60 Dean Stone	1.50	.60	.15	☐ 113 Harry Brecheen	1.50	.60	.15
☐ 61 Forrest Jacobs	1.50	.60	.15	☐ 114 Louis Ortiz	1.50	.60	.15
☐ 62 Thornton Kipper	1.50	.60	.15	☐ 115 Ellis Kinder	1.50	.60	.15
☐ 63 Joe Collins	1.50	.60	.15	☐ 116 Tom Hurd	1.50	.60	.15
☐ 64 Gus Triandos	1.50	.60	.15	☐ 117 Mel Roach	1.50	.60	.15
☐ 65 Ray Boone	1.50	.60	.15	☐ 118 Bob Purkey	1.50	.60	.15
☐ 66 Ron Jackson	1.50	.60	.15	☐ 119 Bob Lennon	1.50	.60	.15
☐ 67 Wally Moon	2.00	.80	.20	☐ 120 Ted Kluszewski	3.00	1.20	.30
☐ 68 Jim Davis	1.50	.60	.15	☐ 121 Bill Renna	1.50	.60	.15
☐ 69 Ed Bailey	1.50	.60	.15	☐ 122 Carl Sawatski	1.50	.60	.15
☐ 70 Al Rosen	3.50	1.40	.35	☐ 123 Sandy Koufax	125.00	50.00	12.50
☐ 71 Ruben Gomez	1.50	.60	.15	☐ 124 Harmon Killebrew	60.00	24.00	6.00
☐ 72 Karl Olson	1.50	.60	.15	☐ 125 Ken Boyer	6.00	2.40	.60
☐ 73 Jack Shepard	1.50	.60	.15	☐ 126 Dick Hall	1.50	.60	.15
☐ 74 Robert Borkowski	1.50	.60	.15	☐ 127 Dale Long	1.50	.60	.15
☐ 75 Sandy Amoros	2.00	.80	.20	☐ 128 Ted Lepcio	1.50	.60	.15
☐ 76 Howie Pollet	1.50	.60	.15	☐ 129 Elvin Tappe	1.50	.60	.15
☐ 77 Arnold Portocarrero	1.50	.60	.15	☐ 130 Mayo Smith MGR	1.50	.60	.15
☐ 78 Gordon Jones	1.50	.60	.15	☐ 131 Grady Hatton	1.50	.60	.15
☐ 79 Clyde Schell	1.50	.60	.15	☐ 132 Bob Trice	1.50	.60	.15
☐ 80 Bob Grim	2.00	.80	.20	☐ 133 Dave Hoskins	1.50	.60	.15
☐ 81 Gene Conley	1.50	.60	.15	☐ 134 Joe Jay	1.50	.60	.15
☐ 82 Chuck Harmon	1.50	.60	.15	☐ 135 Johnny O'Brien	1.50	.60	.15
☐ 83 Tom Brewer	1.50	.60	.15	☐ 136 Vernon Stewart	1.50	.60	.15
☐ 84 Camilo Pascual	2.00	.80	.20	☐ 137 Harry Elliott	1.50	.60	.15
☐ 85 Don Mossi	2.00	.80	.20	☐ 138 Ray Herbert	1.50	.60	.15
☐ 86 Bill Wilson	1.50	.60	.15	☐ 139 Steve Kraly	1.50	.60	.15
☐ 87 Frank House	1.50	.60	.15	☐ 140 Mel Parnell	2.00	.80	.20
☐ 88 Bob Skinner	2.00	.80	.20	☐ 141 Tom Wright	1.50	.60	.15
☐ 89 Joe Frazier	1.50	.60	.15	☐ 142 Gerry Lynch	1.50	.60	.15
☐ 90 Karl Spooner	1.50	.60	.15	☐ 143 John (Dick) Schofield	1.50	.60	.15
☐ 91 Milt Bolling	1.50	.60	.15	☐ 144 John (Joe) Amalfitano	1.50	.60	.15
☐ 92 Don Zimmer	3.00	1.20	.30	☐ 145 Elmer Valo	1.50	.60	.15
☐ 93 Steve Bilko	1.50	.60	.15	☐ 146 Dick Donovan	1.50	.60	.15
☐ 94 Reno Bertoia	1.50	.60	.15	☐ 147 Hugh Pepper	1.50	.60	.15
☐ 95 Preston Ward	1.50	.60	.15	☐ 148 Hector Brown	1.50	.60	.15
☐ 96 Chuck Bishop	1.50	.60	.15	☐ 149 Ray Crone	1.50	.60	.15
☐ 97 Carlos Paula	1.50	.60	.15	☐ 150 Michael Higgins	1.50	.60	.15
☐ 98 John Riddle	1.50	.60	.15	☐ 151 Ralph Kress	3.00	1.20	.30
☐ 99 Frank Leja	1.50	.60	.15	☐ 152 Harry Agganis	4.50	1.80	.45

		MINT	VG-E	F-G
☐ 153	Bud Podbielian	3.00	1.20	.30
☐ 154	Willie Miranda	3.00	1.20	.30
☐ 155	Eddie Mathews	16.00	6.50	1.60
☐ 156	Joe Black	4.50	1.80	.45
☐ 157	Robert Miller	3.00	1.20	.30
☐ 158	Tommy Carroll	4.50	1.80	.45
☐ 159	Johnny Schmitz	3.00	1.20	.30
☐ 160	Ray Narleski	3.00	1.20	.30
☐ 161	Chuck Tanner	5.00	2.00	.50
☐ 162	Joe Coleman	4.25	1.70	.42
☐ 163	Faye Throneberry	4.25	1.70	.42
☐ 164	Roberto Clemente	200.00	80.00	20.00
☐ 165	Don Johnson	4.25	1.70	.42
☐ 166	Hank Bauer	9.00	3.75	.90
☐ 167	Thomas Casagrande	4.25	1.70	.42
☐ 168	Duane Pillette	4.25	1.70	.42
☐ 169	Bob Oldis	4.25	1.70	.42
☐ 170	Jim Pearce DP	2.00	.80	.20
☐ 171	Dick Brodowski	4.25	1.70	.42
☐ 172	Frank Baumholtz DP	2.00	.80	.20
☐ 173	Johnny Kline	4.25	1.70	.42
☐ 174	Rudy Minarcin	4.25	1.70	.42
☐ 175	Does not exist	0.00	.00	.00
☐ 176	Norm Zauchin	4.25	1.70	.42
☐ 177	Al Robertson	4.25	1.70	.42
☐ 178	Bobby Adams	4.25	1.70	.42
☐ 179	Jim Bolger	4.25	1.70	.42
☐ 180	Clem Labine	5.00	2.00	.50
☐ 181	Roy McMillan	4.25	1.70	.42
☐ 182	Humberto Robinson	4.25	1.70	.42
☐ 183	Anthony Jacobs	4.25	1.70	.42
☐ 184	Harry Perkowski DP	2.00	.80	.20
☐ 185	Don Ferrarese	4.25	1.70	.42
☐ 186	Does not exist	0.00	.00	.00
☐ 187	Gil Hodges	40.00	16.00	4.00
☐ 188	Charlie Silvera DP	2.00	.80	.20
☐ 189	Phil Rizzuto	35.00	14.00	3.50
☐ 190	Gene Woodling	5.00	2.00	.50
☐ 191	Eddie Stanky	5.00	2.00	.50
☐ 192	Jim Delsing	4.25	1.70	.42
☐ 193	Johnny Sain	6.00	2.40	.60
☐ 194	Willie Mays	200.00	80.00	20.00
☐ 195	Ed Roebuck	5.00	2.00	.50
☐ 196	Gale Wade	4.25	1.70	.42
☐ 197	Al Smith	4.25	1.70	.42
☐ 198	Yogi Berra	60.00	24.00	6.00
☐ 199	Odbert Hamric	4.25	1.70	.42
☐ 200	Jackie Jensen	7.00	2.80	.70
☐ 201	Sherman Lollar	5.00	2.00	.50
☐ 202	Jim Owens	4.25	1.70	.42
☐ 203	Does not exist	0.00	.00	.00
☐ 204	Frank Smith	4.25	1.70	.42
☐ 205	Gene Freese	4.25	1.70	.42

		MINT	VG-E	F-G
☐ 206	Pete Daley	4.25	1.70	.42
☐ 207	Bill Consolo	4.25	1.70	.42
☐ 208	Ray Moore	4.25	1.70	.42
☐ 209	Does not exist	0.00	.00	.00
☐ 210	Duke Snider	175.00	50.00	10.00

1956 Topps

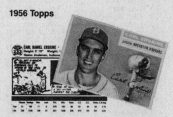

The cards in this 340-card set measure 2⅝″ by 3¾″. Following up with another horizontally oriented card in 1956, Topps improved the format by layering the color ''head'' shot onto an actual action sequence involving the player. Cards 1 to 180 come with either white or gray backs: in the 1 to 100 sequence, gray backs are less common (worth about 10% more) and in the 101 to 180 sequence, white backs are less common (worth 30% more). The team cards used for the first time in a regular set by Topps, are found dated 1955, or undated, with the team name appearing on either side. The two unnumbered checklist cards are highly prized (must be unmarked to qualify as excellent or mint). The complete set price below does not include the unnumbered checklist cards or any of the variations.

	MINT	VG-E	F-G
Complete Set (340)	1250.00	550.00	150.00
Common Player (1-100)	1.00	.40	.10
Common Player (101-180)	1.50	.60	.15
Common Player (181-260)	2.50	1.00	.25
Common Player (261-340)	1.50	.60	.15

			MINT	VG-E	F-G
☐	1	William Harridge (AL President)	10.00	2.00	.40
☐	2	Warren Giles (NL President)	2.50	1.00	.25
☐	3	Elmer Valo	1.00	.40	.10
☐	4	Carlos Paula	2.00	.80	.20
☐	5	Ted Williams	50.00	20.00	5.00
☐	6	Ray Boone	1.00	.40	.10
☐	7	Ron Negray	1.00	.40	.10
☐	8	Walter Alston MGR	7.50	3.00	.75
☐	9	Ruben Gomez	1.00	.40	.10
☐	10	Warren Spahn	12.50	5.00	1.25
☐	11 A	Chicago Cubs (centered)	3.00	1.20	.30
☐	11 B	Cubs Team (dated 1955)	15.00	6.00	1.50
☐	11 C	Cubs Team (name at far left)	3.00	1.20	.30
☐	12	Andy Carey	1.25	.50	.12
☐	13	Roy Face	1.50	.60	.15
☐	14	Ken Boyer	2.50	1.00	.25
☐	15	Ernie Banks	14.00	5.75	1.40
☐	16	Hector Lopez	1.00	.40	.10
☐	17	Gene Conley	1.00	.40	.10
☐	18	Dick Donovan	1.00	.40	.10
☐	19	Chuck Diering	1.00	.40	.10
☐	20	Al Kaline	16.00	6.50	1.60
☐	21	Joe Collins	1.25	.50	.12
☐	22	Jim Finigan	1.00	.40	.10
☐	23	Freddie Marsh	1.00	.40	.10
☐	24	Dick Groat	2.00	.80	.20
☐	25	Ted Kluszewski	3.00	1.20	.30
☐	26	Grady Hatton	1.00	.40	.10
☐	27	Nelson Burbrink	1.00	.40	.10
☐	28	Bobby Hofman	1.00	.40	.10
☐	29	Jack Harshman	1.00	.40	.10
☐	30	Jackie Robinson	45.00	18.00	4.50
☐	31	Hank Aaron (small photo actually W.Mays)	50.00	20.00	5.00
☐	32	Frank House	1.00	.40	.10
☐	33	Roberto Clemente	45.00	18.00	4.50
☐	34	Tom Brewer	1.00	.40	.10
☐	35	Al Rosen	3.00	1.20	.30
☐	36	Rudy Minarcin	1.00	.40	.10
☐	37	Alex Grammas	1.00	.40	.10
☐	38	Bob Kennedy	1.00	.40	.10
☐	39	Don Mossi	1.50	.60	.15
☐	40	Bob Turley	2.00	.80	.20
☐	41	Hank Sauer	1.25	.50	.12
☐	42	Sandy Amoros	1.25	.50	.12
☐	43	Ray Moore	1.00	.40	.10
☐	44	Windy McCall	1.00	.40	.10
☐	45	Gus Zernial	1.00	.40	.10
☐	46	Gene Freese	1.00	.40	.10
☐	47	Art Fowler	1.00	.40	.10
☐	48	Jim Hegan	1.00	.40	.10
☐	49	Pedro Ramos	1.00	.40	.10
☐	50	Dusty Rhodes	1.25	.50	.12
☐	51	Ernie Oravetz	1.00	.40	.10
☐	52	Bob Grim	1.25	.50	.12
☐	53	Arnie Portocarrero	1.00	.40	.10
☐	54	Bob Keegan	1.00	.40	.10
☐	55	Wally Moon	1.25	.50	.12
☐	56	Dale Long	1.00	.40	.10
☐	57	Duke Maas	1.00	.40	.10
☐	58	Ed Roebuck	1.00	.40	.10
☐	59	Jose Santiago	1.00	.40	.10
☐	60	Mayo Smith MGR	1.00	.40	.10
☐	61	Bill Skowron	3.00	1.20	.30
☐	62	Hal Smith	1.00	.40	.10
☐	63	Roger Craig	3.00	1.20	.30
☐	64	Luis Arroyo	1.25	.50	.12
☐	65	Johnny O'Brien	1.00	.40	.10
☐	66	Bob Speake	1.00	.40	.10
☐	67	Vic Power	1.00	.40	.10
☐	68	Chuck Stobbs	1.00	.40	.10
☐	69	Chuck Tanner	1.25	.50	.12
☐	70	Jim Rivera	1.00	.40	.10
☐	71	Frank Sullivan	1.00	.40	.10
☐	72 A	Phillies Team (centered)	3.00	1.20	.30
☐	72 B	Phillies Team (dated 1955)	15.00	6.00	1.50
☐	72 C	Phillies Team (name at far left)	3.00	1.20	.30
☐	73	Wayne Terwilliger	1.00	.40	.10
☐	74	Jim King	1.00	.40	.10
☐	75	Roy Sievers	1.25	.50	.12
☐	76	Ray Crone	1.00	.40	.10
☐	77	Harvey Haddix	1.25	.50	.12
☐	78	Herman Wehmeier	1.00	.40	.10
☐	79	Sandy Koufax	45.00	18.00	4.50
☐	80	Gus Triandos	1.25	.50	.12
☐	81	Wally Westlake	1.00	.40	.10
☐	82	Bill Renna	1.00	.40	.10
☐	83	Karl Spooner	1.25	.50	.12
☐	84	Babe Birrer	1.00	.40	.10
☐	85 A	Cleveland Indians (centered)	3.00	1.20	.30
☐	85 B	Indians Team (dated 1955)	15.00	6.00	1.50
☐	85 C	Indians Team (name at far left)	3.00	1.20	.30
☐	86	Ray Jablonski	1.00	.40	.10
☐	87	Dean Stone	1.00	.40	.10

		MINT	VG-E	F-G
☐ 88	Johnny Kucks	1.25	.50	.12
☐ 89	Norm Zauchin	1.00	.40	.10
☐ 90 A	Cincinnati Redlegs Team (centered)	3.00	1.20	.30
☐ 90 B	Reds Team (dated 1955)	15.00	6.00	1.50
☐ 90 C	Reds Team (name at far left)	3.00	1.20	.30
☐ 91	Gail Harris	1.00	.40	.10
☐ 92	Bob (Red) Wilson	1.00	.40	.10
☐ 93	George Susce	1.00	.40	.10
☐ 94	Ronnie Kline	1.00	.40	.10
☐ 95 A	Milwaukee Braves Team (centered)	3.00	1.20	.30
☐ 95 B	Braves Team (dated 1955)	15.00	6.00	1.50
☐ 95 C	Braves Team (name at far left)	3.00	1.20	.30
☐ 96	Bill Tremel	1.00	.40	.10
☐ 97	Jerry Lynch	1.00	.40	.10
☐ 98	Camilo Pascual	1.25	.50	.12
☐ 99	Don Zimmer	1.50	.60	.15
☐ 100 A	Baltimore Orioles Team (centered)	3.00	1.20	.30
☐ 100 B	Orioles Team (dated 1955)	15.00	6.00	1.50
☐ 100 C	Orioles Team (name at far left)	3.00	1.20	.30
☐ 101	Roy Campanella	36.00	15.00	3.60
☐ 102	Jim Davis	1.50	.60	.15
☐ 103	Willie Miranda	1.50	.60	.15
☐ 104	Bob Lennon	1.50	.60	.15
☐ 105	Al Smith	1.50	.60	.15
☐ 106	Joe Astroth	1.50	.60	.15
☐ 107	Ed Mathews	11.00	4.50	1.10
☐ 108	Laurin Pepper	1.50	.60	.15
☐ 109	Enos Slaughter	7.00	2.80	.70
☐ 110	Yogi Berra	27.00	11.00	2.70
☐ 111	Boston Red Sox Team	4.50	1.80	.45
☐ 112	Dee Fondy	1.50	.60	.15
☐ 113	Phil Rizzuto	14.00	5.75	1.40
☐ 114	Jim Owens	1.50	.60	.15
☐ 115	Jackie Jensen	2.50	1.00	.25
☐ 116	Eddie O'Brien	1.50	.60	.15
☐ 117	Virgil Trucks	1.50	.60	.15
☐ 118	Nelson Fox	3.50	1.40	.35
☐ 119	Larry Jackson	1.50	.60	.15
☐ 120	Richie Ashburn	4.00	1.60	.40
☐ 121	Pirates Team	3.50	1.40	.35
☐ 122	Willard Nixon	1.50	.60	.15
☐ 123	Roy McMillan	1.50	.60	.15
☐ 124	Don Kaiser	1.50	.60	.15
☐ 125	Minnie Minoso	3.00	1.20	.30

		MINT	VG-E	F-G
☐ 126	Jim Brady	1.50	.60	.15
☐ 127	Willie Jones	1.50	.60	.15
☐ 128	Eddie Yost	1.50	.60	.15
☐ 129	Jake Martin	1.50	.60	.15
☐ 130	Willie Mays	60.00	24.00	6.00
☐ 131	Bob Roselli	1.50	.60	.15
☐ 132	Bobby Avila	1.50	.60	.15
☐ 133	Ray Narleski	1.50	.60	.15
☐ 134	Cardinals Team	4.00	1.60	.40
☐ 135	Mickey Mantle	200.00	80.00	20.00
☐ 136	Johnny Logan	2.00	.80	.20
☐ 137	Al Silvera	1.50	.60	.15
☐ 138	Johnny Antonelli	2.00	.80	.20
☐ 139	Tommy Carroll	1.50	.60	.15
☐ 140	Herb Score	3.50	1.40	.35
☐ 141	Joe Frazier	1.50	.60	.15
☐ 142	Gene Baker	1.50	.60	.15
☐ 143	Jim Piersall	2.50	1.00	.25
☐ 144	Leroy Powell	1.50	.60	.15
☐ 145	Gil Hodges	12.50	5.00	1.25
☐ 146	Washington Team	3.00	1.20	.30
☐ 147	Earl Torgeson	1.50	.60	.15
☐ 148	Al Dark	2.00	.80	.20
☐ 149	Dixie Howell	1.50	.60	.15
☐ 150	Duke Snider	40.00	16.00	4.00
☐ 151	Spook Jacobs	1.50		.15
☐ 152	Billy Hoeft	1.50	.60	.15
☐ 153	Frank Thomas	1.50	.60	.15
☐ 154	Dave Pope	1.50	.60	.15
☐ 155	Harvey Kuenn	2.50	1.00	.25
☐ 156	Wes Westrum	1.50	.60	.15
☐ 157	Dick Brodowski	1.50	.60	.15
☐ 158	Wally Post	1.50	.60	.15
☐ 159	Clint Courtney	1.50	.60	.15
☐ 160	Billy Pierce	2.00	.80	.20
☐ 161	Joe DeMaestri	1.50	.60	.15
☐ 162	Dave (Gus) Bell	2.00	.80	.20
☐ 163	Gene Woodling	2.00	.80	.20
☐ 164	Harmon Killebrew	18.00	7.25	1.80
☐ 165	Red Schoendienst	2.50	1.00	.25
☐ 166	Brooklyn Dodgers Team Card	24.00	10.00	2.40
☐ 167	Harry Dorish	1.50	.60	.15
☐ 168	Sammy White	1.50	.60	.15
☐ 169	Bob Nelson	1.50	.60	.15
☐ 170	Bill Virdon	2.50	1.00	.25
☐ 171	Jim Wilson	1.50	.60	.15
☐ 172	Frank Torre	1.50	.60	.15
☐ 173	Johnny Podres	2.50	1.00	.25
☐ 174	Glen Gorbous	1.50	.60	.15
☐ 175	Del Crandall	2.00	.80	.20
☐ 176	Alex Kellner	1.50	.60	.15
☐ 177	Hank Bauer	2.50	1.00	.25

		MINT	VG-E	F-G
☐ 178	Joe Black	2.00	.80	.20
☐ 179	Harry Chiti	1.50	.60	.15
☐ 180	Robin Roberts	9.00	3.75	.90
☐ 181	Billy Martin	16.00	6.50	1.60
☐ 182	Paul Minner	2.50	1.00	.25
☐ 183	Stan Lopata	2.50	1.00	.25
☐ 184	Don Bessent	2.50	1.00	.25
☐ 185	Bill Bruton	2.50	1.00	.25
☐ 186	Ron Jackson	2.50	1.00	.25
☐ 187	Early Wynn	11.00	4.50	1.10
☐ 188	White Sox Team	4.50	1.80	.45
☐ 189	Ned Garver	2.50	1.00	.25
☐ 190	Carl Furillo	5.00	2.00	.50
☐ 191	Frank Lary	3.00	1.20	.30
☐ 192	Smoky Burgess	3.00	1.20	.30
☐ 193	Wilmer Mizell	2.50	1.00	.25
☐ 194	Monte Irvin	9.00	3.75	.90
☐ 195	George Kell	10.00	4.00	1.00
☐ 196	Tom Poholsky	2.50	1.00	.25
☐ 197	Granny Hamner	2.50	1.00	.25
☐ 198	Ed Fitzgerald	2.50	1.00	.25
☐ 199	Hank Thompson	3.00	1.20	.30
☐ 200	Bob Feller	25.00	10.00	2.50
☐ 201	Rip Repulski	2.50	1.00	.25
☐ 202	Jim Hearn	2.50	1.00	.25
☐ 203	Bill Tuttle	2.50	1.00	.25
☐ 204	Art Swanson	2.50	1.00	.25
☐ 205	Whitey Lockman	2.50	1.00	.25
☐ 206	Erv Palica	2.50	1.00	.25
☐ 207	Jim Small	2.50	1.00	.25
☐ 208	Elston Howard	7.00	2.80	.70
☐ 209	Max Surkont	2.50	1.00	.25
☐ 210	Mike Garcia	3.00	1.20	.30
☐ 211	Murry Dickson	2.50	1.00	.25
☐ 212	Johnny Temple	3.00	1.20	.30
☐ 213	Detroit Tigers Team	7.50	3.00	.75
☐ 214	Bob Rush	2.50	1.00	.25
☐ 215	Tommy Byrne	2.50	1.00	.25
☐ 216	Jerry Schoonmaker	2.50	1.00	.25
☐ 217	Billy Klaus	2.50	1.00	.25
☐ 218	Joe Nuxall	3.00	1.20	.30
	(sic, Nuxhall)			
☐ 219	Lew Burdette	4.50	1.80	.45
☐ 220	Del Ennis	3.00	1.20	.30
☐ 221	Bob Friend	3.00	1.20	.30
☐ 222	Dave Philley	2.50	1.00	.25
☐ 223	Randy Jackson	2.50	1.00	.25
☐ 224	Bud Podbielan	2.50	1.00	.25
☐ 225	Gil McDougald	6.00	2.40	.60
☐ 226	Giants Team	10.00	4.00	1.00
☐ 227	Russ Meyer	2.50	1.00	.25
☐ 228	Mickey Vernon	3.00	1.20	.30
☐ 229	Harry Brecheen	2.50	1.00	.25

		MINT	VG-E	F-G
☐ 230	Chico Carrasquel	2.50	1.00	.25
☐ 231	Bob Hale	2.50	1.00	.25
☐ 232	Toby Atwell	2.50	1.00	.25
☐ 233	Carl Erskine	6.00	2.40	.60
☐ 234	Pete Runnels	3.00	1.20	.30
☐ 235	Don Newcombe	10.00	4.00	1.00
☐ 236	Athletics Team	4.50	1.80	.45
☐ 237	Jose Valdivielso	2.50	1.00	.25
☐ 238	Walt Dropo	2.50	1.00	.25
☐ 239	Harry Simpson	2.50	1.00	.25
☐ 240	Whitey Ford	20.00	8.00	2.00
☐ 241	Don Mueller	3.00	1.20	.30
☐ 242	Hershell Freeman	2.50	1.00	.25
☐ 243	Sherm Lollar	3.00	1.20	.30
☐ 244	Bob Buhl	2.50	1.00	.25
☐ 245	Billy Goodman	3.00	1.20	.30
☐ 246	Tom Gorman	2.50	1.00	.25
☐ 247	Bill Sarni	2.50	1.00	.25
☐ 248	Bob Porterfield	2.50	1.00	.25
☐ 249	Johnny Klippstein	2.50	1.00	.25
☐ 250	Larry Doby	5.00	2.00	.50
☐ 251	New York Yankees	32.00	13.00	3.20
	Team Card			
☐ 252	Vernon Law	3.00	1.20	.30
☐ 253	Irv Noren	2.50	1.00	.25
☐ 254	George Crowe	2.50	1.00	.25
☐ 255	Bob Lemon	11.00	4.50	1.10
☐ 256	Tom Hurd	2.50	1.00	.25
☐ 257	Bobby Thomson	4.50	1.80	.45
☐ 258	Art Ditmar	2.50	1.00	.25
☐ 259	Sam Jones	3.00	1.20	.30
☐ 260	Pee Wee Reese	20.00	8.00	2.00
☐ 261	Bobby Shantz	2.00	.80	.20
☐ 262	Howie Pollet	1.50	.60	.15
☐ 263	Bob Miller	1.50	.60	.15
☐ 264	Ray Monzant	1.50	.60	.15
☐ 265	Sandy Consuegra	1.50	.60	.15
☐ 266	Don Ferrarese	1.50	.60	.15
☐ 267	Bob Nieman	1.50	.60	.15
☐ 268	Dale Mitchell	2.00	.80	.20
☐ 269	Jack Meyer	1.50	.60	.15
☐ 270	Billy Loes	2.00	.80	.20
☐ 271	Foster Castleman	1.50	.60	.15
☐ 272	Danny O'Connell	1.50	.60	.15
☐ 273	Walker Cooper	1.50	.60	.15
☐ 274	Frank Baumholtz	1.50	.60	.15
☐ 275	Jim Greengrass	1.50	.60	.15
☐ 276	George Zuverink	1.50	.60	.15
☐ 277	Daryl Spencer	1.50	.60	.15
☐ 278	Chet Nichols	1.50	.60	.15
☐ 279	Johnny Groth	1.50	.60	.15
☐ 280	Jim Gilliam	3.50	1.40	.35
☐ 281	Art Houtteman	1.50	.60	.15

		MINT	VG-E	F-G
☐ 282	Warren Hacker	1.50	.60	.15
☐ 283	Hal Smith	1.50	.60	.15
☐ 284	Ike Delock	1.50	.60	.15
☐ 285	Eddie Miksis	1.50	.60	.15
☐ 286	Bill Wight	1.50	.60	.15
☐ 287	Bobby Adams	1.50	.60	.15
☐ 288	Bob Cerv	2.00	.80	.20
☐ 289	Hal Jeffcoat	1.50	.60	.15
☐ 290	Curt Simmons	2.00	.80	.20
☐ 291	Frank Kellert	1.50	.60	.15
☐ 292	Luis Aparicio	24.00	10.00	2.40
☐ 293	Stu Miller	1.50	.60	.15
☐ 294	Ernie Johnson	1.50	.60	.15
☐ 295	Clem Labine	2.00	.80	.20
☐ 296	Andy Seminick	1.50	.60	.15
☐ 297	Bob Skinner	2.00	.80	.20
☐ 298	Johnny Schmitz	1.50	.60	.15
☐ 299	Charley Neal	2.00	.80	.20
☐ 300	Vic Wertz	2.00	.80	.20
☐ 301	Marv Grissom	1.50	.60	.15
☐ 302	Eddie Robinson	1.50	.60	.15
☐ 303	Jim Dyck	1.50	.60	.15
☐ 304	Frank Malzone	2.00	.80	.20
☐ 305	Brooks Lawrence	1.50	.60	.15
☐ 306	Curt Roberts	1.50	.60	.15
☐ 307	Hoyt Wilhelm	10.00	4.00	1.00
☐ 308	Chuck Harmon	1.50	.60	.15
☐ 309	Don Blasingame	2.00	.80	.20
☐ 310	Steve Gromek	1.50	.60	.15
☐ 311	Hal Naragon	1.50	.60	.15
☐ 312	Andy Pafko	1.50	.60	.15
☐ 313	Gene Stephens	1.50	.60	.15
☐ 314	Hobie Landrith	1.50	.60	.15
☐ 315	Milt Bolling	1.50	.60	.15
☐ 316	Jerry Coleman	2.00	.80	.20
☐ 317	Al Aber	1.50	.60	.15
☐ 318	Fred Hatfield	1.50	.60	.15
☐ 319	Jack Crimian	1.50	.60	.15
☐ 320	Joe Adcock	2.50	1.00	.25
☐ 321	Jim Konstanty	2.00	.80	.20
☐ 322	Karl Olson	1.50	.60	.15
☐ 323	Willard Schmidt	1.50	.60	.15
☐ 324	Rocky Bridges	1.50	.60	.15
☐ 325	Don Liddle	1.50	.60	.15
☐ 326	Connie Johnson	1.50	.60	.15
☐ 327	Bob Wiesler	1.50	.60	.15
☐ 328	Preston Ward	1.50	.60	.15
☐ 329	Lou Berberet	1.50	.60	.15
☐ 330	Jim Busby	1.50	.60	.15
☐ 331	Dick Hall	1.50	.60	.15
☐ 332	Don Larsen	4.00	1.60	.40
☐ 333	Rube Walker	2.00	.80	.20
☐ 334	Bob Miller	1.50	.60	.15

		MINT	VG-E	F-G
☐ 335	Don Hoak	1.50	.60	.15
☐ 336	Ellis Kinder	1.50	.60	.15
☐ 337	Bobby Morgan	1.50	.60	.15
☐ 338	Jim Delsing	1.50	.60	.15
☐ 339	Rance Pless	1.50	.60	.15
☐ 340	Mickey McDermott	4.00	1.00	.20
☐ 341	Checklist 1/3 (unnumbered)	90.00	15.00	3.00
☐ 342	Checklist 2/4 (unnumbered)	90.00	15.00	3.00

1957 Topps

The cards in this 407-card set measure 2½"
by 3½". In 1957, Topps returned to the vertical obverse, adopted what we now call the
standard card size, and used a large, unclut-
tered color photo for the first time since 1952.
Cards in the series 265 to 352 and the unnumbered checklist cards are scarcer than
other cards in the set. The first star combination cards, #400 and #407, are quite popular
with collectors. They feature the big stars of
the previous season's World Series teams,
the Dodgers (Furillo, Hodges, Campanella,
and Snider) and Yankees (Berra and Mantle). The complete set price below does not
include the unnumbered checklist cards.

	MINT	VG-E	F-G
Complete Set (407)	1600.00	700.00	175.00
Common Player (1-264)	.90	.36	.09
Common Player (265-352)	5.00	2.00	.50
Common Player (353-407)	1.00	.40	.10

		MINT	VG-E	F-G
☐ 1	Ted Williams	125.00	25.00	5.00
☐ 2	Yogi Berra	25.00	10.00	2.50
☐ 3	Dale Long	.90	.36	.09
☐ 4	Johnny Logan	1.00	.40	.10
☐ 5	Sal Maglie	2.50	1.00	.25
☐ 6	Hector Lopez	.90	.36	.09
☐ 7	Luis Aparicio	6.00	2.40	.60
☐ 8	Don Mossi	1.00	.40	.10
☐ 9	Johnny Temple	1.00	.40	.10
☐ 10	Willie Mays	45.00	18.00	4.50
☐ 11	George Zuverink	.90	.36	.09
☐ 12	Dick Groat	1.50	.60	.15
☐ 13	Wally Burnette	.90	.36	.09
☐ 14	Bob Nieman	.90	.36	.09
☐ 15	Robin Roberts	7.00	2.80	.70
☐ 16	Walt Moryn	.90	.36	.09
☐ 17	Billy Gardner	.90	.36	.09
☐ 18	Don Drysdale	40.00	16.00	4.00
☐ 19	Bob Wilson	.90	.36	.09
☐ 20	Hank Aaron	50.00	20.00	5.00
	(reverse negative photo on front)			
☐ 21	Frank Sullivan	.90	.36	.09
☐ 22	Jerry Snyder	.90	.36	.09
	(photo actually Ed Fitzgerald)			
☐ 23	Sherm Lollar	1.00	.40	.10
☐ 24	Bill Mazeroski	6.00	2.40	.60
☐ 25	Whitey Ford	12.00	5.00	1.20
☐ 26	Bob Boyd	.90	.36	.09
☐ 27	Ted Kazanski	.90	.36	.09
☐ 28	Gene Conley	.90	.36	.09
☐ 29	Whitey Herzog	3.00	1.20	.30
☐ 30	Pee Wee Reese	12.50	5.00	1.25
☐ 31	Ron Northey	.90	.36	.09
☐ 32	Hershell Freeman	.90	.36	.09
☐ 33	Jim Small	.90	.36	.09
☐ 34	Tom Sturdivant	.90	.36	.09
☐ 35	Frank Robinson	45.00	18.00	4.50
☐ 36	Bob Grim	1.00	.40	.10
☐ 37	Frank Torre	1.00	.40	.10
☐ 38	Nelson Fox	3.00	1.20	.30
☐ 39	Al Worthington	.90	.36	.09
☐ 40	Early Wynn	6.50	2.60	.65
☐ 41	Hal W. Smith	.90	.36	.09
☐ 42	Dee Fondy	.90	.36	.09
☐ 43	Connie Johnson	.90	.36	.09
☐ 44	Joe DeMaestri	.90	.36	.09
☐ 45	Carl Furillo	3.00	1.20	.30
☐ 46	Robert J. Miller	.90	.36	.09
☐ 47	Don Blasingame	.90	.36	.09
☐ 48	Bill Bruton	1.00	.40	.10
☐ 49	Daryl Spencer	.90	.36	.09
☐ 50	Herb Score	1.50	.60	.15
☐ 51	Clint Courtney	.90	.36	.09
☐ 52	Lee Walls	.90	.36	.09
☐ 53	Clem Labine	1.25	.50	.12
☐ 54	Elmer Valo	.90	.36	.09
☐ 55	Ernie Banks	13.00	5.25	1.30
☐ 56	Dave Sisler	.90	.36	.09
☐ 57	Jim Lemon	1.00	.40	.10
☐ 58	Ruben Gomez	.90	.36	.09
☐ 59	Dick Williams	1.25	.50	.12
☐ 60	Billy Hoeft	.90	.36	.09
☐ 61	James Rhodes	1.00	.40	.10
☐ 62	Billy Martin	10.00	4.00	1.00
☐ 63	Ike Delock	.90	.36	.09
☐ 64	Pete Runnels	1.00	.40	.10
☐ 65	Wally Moon	1.25	.50	.12
☐ 66	Brooks Lawrence	.90	.36	.09
☐ 67	Chico Carrasquel	.90	.36	.09
☐ 68	Ray Crone	.90	.36	.09
☐ 69	Roy McMillan	.90	.36	.09
☐ 70	Richie Ashburn	3.50	1.40	.35
☐ 71	Murry Dickson	.90	.36	.09
☐ 72	Bill Tuttle	.90	.36	.09
☐ 73	George Crowe	.90	.36	.09
☐ 74	Vito Valentinetti	.90	.36	.09
☐ 75	Jim Piersall	1.75	.70	.17
☐ 76	Roberto Clemente	27.00	11.00	2.70
☐ 77	Paul Foytack	.90	.36	.09
☐ 78	Vic Wertz	1.00	.40	.10
☐ 79	Lindy McDaniel	1.00	.40	.10
☐ 80	Gil Hodges	10.00	4.00	1.00
☐ 81	Herman Wehmeier	.90	.36	.09
☐ 82	Elston Howard	3.00	1.20	.30
☐ 83	Lou Skizas	.90	.36	.09
☐ 84	Moe Drabowsky	1.00	.40	.10
☐ 85	Larry Doby	2.00	.80	.20
☐ 86	Bill Sarni	.90	.36	.09
☐ 87	Tom Gorman	.90	.36	.09
☐ 88	Harvey Kuenn	2.00	.80	.20
☐ 89	Roy Sievers	1.00	.40	.10
☐ 90	Warren Spahn	12.00	5.00	1.20
☐ 91	Mack Burk	.90	.36	.09
☐ 92	Mickey Vernon	1.00	.40	.10
☐ 93	Hal Jeffcoat	.90	.36	.09
☐ 94	Bobby Del Greco	.90	.36	.09
☐ 95	Mickey Mantle	200.00	80.00	20.00
☐ 96	Hank Aguirre	.90	.36	.09
☐ 97	New York Yankees Team Card	7.50	3.00	.75
☐ 98	Alvin Dark	1.50	.60	.15
☐ 99	Bob Keegan	.90	.36	.09
☐ 100	Giles and Harridge League Presidents	2.00	.80	.20

	MINT	VG-E	F-G
☐ 101 Chuck Stobbs	.90	.36	.09
☐ 102 Ray Boone	1.00	.40	.10
☐ 103 Joe Nuxhall	1.00	.40	.10
☐ 104 Hank Foiles	.90	.36	.09
☐ 105 Johnny Antonelli	1.25	.50	.12
☐ 106 Ray Moore	.90	.36	.09
☐ 107 Jim Rivera	.90	.36	.09
☐ 108 Tommy Byrne	1.00	.40	.10
☐ 109 Hank Thompson	1.00	.40	.10
☐ 110 Bill Virdon	1.75	.70	.17
☐ 111 Hal R. Smith	.90	.36	.09
☐ 112 Tom Brewer	.90	.36	.09
☐ 113 Wilmer Mizell	.90	.36	.09
☐ 114 Milwaukee Braves Team Card	3.00	1.20	.30
☐ 115 Jim Gilliam	2.50	1.00	.25
☐ 116 Mike Fornieles	.90	.36	.09
☐ 117 Joe Adcock	1.50	.60	.15
☐ 118 Bob Porterfield	.90	.36	.09
☐ 119 Stan Lopata	.90	.36	.09
☐ 120 Bob Lemon	6.00	2.40	.60
☐ 121 Cletis Boyer	2.00	.80	.20
☐ 122 Ken Boyer	2.50	1.00	.25
☐ 123 Steve Ridzik	.90	.36	.09
☐ 124 Dave Philley	.90	.36	.09
☐ 125 Al Kaline	12.50	5.00	1.25
☐ 126 Bob Wiesler	.90	.36	.09
☐ 127 Bob Buhl	.90	.36	.09
☐ 128 Ed Bailey	.90	.36	.09
☐ 129 Saul Rogovin	.90	.36	.09
☐ 130 Don Newcombe	3.00	1.20	.30
☐ 131 Milt Bolling	.90	.36	.09
☐ 132 Art Ditmar	.90	.36	.09
☐ 133 Del Crandall	1.00	.40	.10
☐ 134 Don Kaiser	.90	.36	.09
☐ 135 Bill Skowron	2.50	1.00	.25
☐ 136 Jim Hegan	1.00	.40	.10
☐ 137 Bob Rush	.90	.36	.09
☐ 138 Minnie Minoso	2.50	1.00	.25
☐ 139 Lou Kretlow	.90	.36	.09
☐ 140 Frank Thomas	1.00	.40	.10
☐ 141 Al Aber	.90	.36	.09
☐ 142 Charley Thompson	.90	.36	.09
☐ 143 Andy Pafko	.90	.36	.09
☐ 144 Ray Narleski	.90	.36	.09
☐ 145 Al Smith	.90	.36	.09
☐ 146 Don Ferrarese	.90	.36	.09
☐ 147 Al Walker	.90	.36	.09
☐ 148 Don Mueller	1.00	.40	.10
☐ 149 Bob Kennedy	1.00	.40	.10
☐ 150 Bob Friend	1.25	.50	.12
☐ 151 Willie Miranda	.90	.36	.09
☐ 152 Jack Harshman	.90	.36	.09

	MINT	VG-E	F-G
☐ 153 Karl Olson	.90	.36	.09
☐ 154 Red Schoendienst	1.75	.70	.17
☐ 155 Jim Brosnan	1.00	.40	.10
☐ 156 Gus Triandos	1.00	.40	.10
☐ 157 Wally Post	.90	.36	.09
☐ 158 Curt Simmons	1.25	.50	.12
☐ 159 Solly Drake	.90	.36	.09
☐ 160 Billy Pierce	1.50	.60	.15
☐ 161 Pirates Team	2.00	.80	.20
☐ 162 Jack Meyer	.90	.36	.09
☐ 163 Sammy White	.90	.36	.09
☐ 164 Tommy Carroll	.90	.36	.09
☐ 165 Ted Kluszewski	2.50	1.00	.25
☐ 166 Elroy Face	1.50	.60	.15
☐ 167 Vic Power	1.00	.40	.10
☐ 168 Frank Lary	1.00	.40	.10
☐ 169 Herb Plews	.90	.36	.09
☐ 170 Duke Snider	27.00	11.00	2.70
☐ 171 Boston Red Sox Team Card	2.00	.80	.20
☐ 172 Gene Woodling	1.25	.50	.12
☐ 173 Roger Craig	1.50	.60	.15
☐ 174 Willie Jones	.90	.36	.09
☐ 175 Don Larsen	2.50	1.00	.25
☐ 176 Gene Baker	.90	.36	.09
☐ 177 Eddie Yost	1.00	.40	.10
☐ 178 Don Bessent	.90	.36	.09
☐ 179 Ernie Oravetz	.90	.36	.09
☐ 180 Dave (Gus) Bell	1.00	.40	.10
☐ 181 Dick Donovan	.90	.36	.09
☐ 182 Hobie Landrith	.90	.36	.09
☐ 183 Chicago Cubs Team	2.00	.80	.20
☐ 184 Tito Francona	1.00	.40	.10
☐ 185 Johnny Kucks	1.00	.40	.10
☐ 186 Jim King	.90	.36	.09
☐ 187 Virgil Trucks	1.00	.40	.10
☐ 188 Felix Mantilla	.90	.36	.09
☐ 189 Willard Nixon	.90	.36	.09
☐ 190 Randy Jackson	.90	.36	.09
☐ 191 Joe Margoneri	.90	.36	.09
☐ 192 Gerry Coleman	1.00	.40	.10
☐ 193 Del Rice	.90	.36	.09
☐ 194 Hal Brown	.90	.36	.09
☐ 195 Bobby Avila	.90	.36	.09
☐ 196 Larry Jackson	.90	.36	.09
☐ 197 Hank Sauer	1.25	.50	.12
☐ 198 Detroit Tigers Team	3.00	1.20	.30
☐ 199 Vern Law	1.25	.50	.12
☐ 200 Gil McDougald	2.50	1.00	.25
☐ 201 Sandy Amoros	1.25	.50	.12
☐ 202 Dick Gernert	.90	.36	.09
☐ 203 Hoyt Wilhelm	6.00	2.40	.60
☐ 204 Athletics Team	2.00	.80	.20

	MINT	VG-E	F-G		MINT	VG-E	F-G
☐ 205 Charlie Maxwell	.90	.36	.09	☐ 258 Steve Gromek	.90	.36	.09
☐ 206 Willard Schmidt	.90	.36	.09	☐ 259 Eddie O'Brien	.90	.36	.09
☐ 207 Gordon (Billy) Hunter	.90	.36	.09	☐ 260 Del Ennis	1.00	.40	.10
☐ 208 Lou Burdette	2.50	1.00	.25	☐ 261 Bob Chakales	.90	.36	.09
☐ 209 Bob Skinner	1.00	.40	.10	☐ 262 Bobby Thomson	2.00	.80	.20
☐ 210 Roy Campanella	27.00	11.00	2.70	☐ 263 George Strickland	.90	.36	.09
☐ 211 Camilo Pascual	1.00	.40	.10	☐ 264 Bob Turley	2.00	.80	.20
☐ 212 Rocco Colavito	5.00	2.00	.50	☐ 265 Harvey Haddix	6.00	2.40	.60
☐ 213 Les Moss	.90	.36	.09	☐ 266 Ken Kuhn	5.00	2.00	.50
☐ 214 Phillies Team	2.00	.80	.20	☐ 267 Danny Kravitz	5.00	2.00	.50
☐ 215 Enos Slaughter	6.00	2.40	.60	☐ 268 Joe Collum	5.00	2.00	.50
☐ 216 Marv Grissom	.90	.36	.09	☐ 269 Bob Cerv	6.00	2.40	.60
☐ 217 Gene Stephens	.90	.36	.09	☐ 270 Washington Team	8.00	3.25	.80
☐ 218 Ray Jablonski	.90	.36	.09	☐ 271 Danny O'Connell	5.00	2.00	.50
☐ 219 Tom Acker	.90	.36	.09	☐ 272 Bobby Shantz	11.00	4.50	1.10
☐ 220 Jackie Jensen	1.75	.70	.17	☐ 273 Jim Davis	5.00	2.00	.50
☐ 221 Dixie Howell	.90	.36	.09	☐ 274 Don Hoak	5.00	2.00	.50
☐ 222 Alex Grammas	.90	.36	.09	☐ 275 Indians Team	8.00	3.25	.80
☐ 223 Frank House	.90	.36	.09	☐ 276 Jim Pyburn	5.00	2.00	.50
☐ 224 Marv Blaylock	.90	.36	.09	☐ 277 Johnny Podres	25.00	10.00	2.50
☐ 225 Harry Simpson	.90	.36	.09	☐ 278 Fred Hatfield	5.00	2.00	.50
☐ 226 Preston Ward	.90	.36	.09	☐ 279 Bob Thurman	5.00	2.00	.50
☐ 227 Gerry Staley	.90	.36	.09	☐ 280 Alex Kellner	5.00	2.00	.50
☐ 228 Smoky Burgess	1.00	.40	.10	☐ 281 Gail Harris	5.00	2.00	.50
☐ 229 George Susce	.90	.36	.09	☐ 282 Jack Dittmer	5.00	2.00	.50
☐ 230 George Kell	6.00	2.40	.60	☐ 283 Wes Covington	6.00	2.40	.60
☐ 231 Solly Hemus	.90	.36	.09	☐ 284 Don Zimmer	7.00	2.80	.70
☐ 232 Whitey Lockman	1.00	.40	.10	☐ 285 Ned Garver	5.00	2.00	.50
☐ 233 Art Fowler	.90	.36	.09	☐ 286 Bobby Richardson	27.00	11.00	2.70
☐ 234 Dick Cole	.90	.36	.09	☐ 287 Sam Jones	6.00	2.40	.60
☐ 235 Tom Poholsky	.90	.36	.09	☐ 288 Ted Lepcio	5.00	2.00	.50
☐ 236 Joe Ginsberg	.90	.36	.09	☐ 289 Jim Bolger	5.00	2.00	.50
☐ 237 Foster Castleman	.90	.36	.09	☐ 290 Andy Carey	6.00	2.40	.60
☐ 238 Eddie Robinson	.90	.36	.09	☐ 291 Windy McCall	5.00	2.00	.50
☐ 239 Tom Morgan	.90	.36	.09	☐ 292 Billy Klaus	5.00	2.00	.50
☐ 240 Hank Bauer	2.50	1.00	.25	☐ 293 Ted Abernathy	5.00	2.00	.50
☐ 241 Joe Lonnett	.90	.36	.09	☐ 294 Rocky Bridges	5.00	2.00	.50
☐ 242 Charlie Neal	1.00	.40	.10	☐ 295 Joe Collins	6.00	2.40	.60
☐ 243 Cardinals Team	2.50	1.00	.25	☐ 296 Johnny Klippstein	5.00	2.00	.50
☐ 244 Billy Loes	1.00	.40	.10	☐ 297 Jack Crimian	5.00	2.00	.50
☐ 245 Rip Repulski	.90	.36	.09	☐ 298 Irv Noren	5.00	2.00	.50
☐ 246 Jose Valdivielso	.90	.36	.09	☐ 299 Chuck Harmon	5.00	2.00	.50
☐ 247 Turk Lown	.90	.36	.09	☐ 300 Mike Garcia	7.00	2.80	.70
☐ 248 Jim Finigan	.90	.36	.09	☐ 301 Sammy Esposito	5.00	2.00	.50
☐ 249 Dave Pope	.90	.36	.09	☐ 302 Sandy Koufax	125.00	50.00	12.50
☐ 250 Ed Mathews	8.00	3.25	.80	☐ 303 Billy Goodman	6.00	2.40	.60
☐ 251 Orioles Team	2.50	1.00	.25	☐ 304 Joe Cunningham	6.00	2.40	.60
☐ 252 Carl Erskine	2.50	1.00	.25	☐ 305 Chico Fernandez	5.00	2.00	.50
☐ 253 Gus Zernial	1.00	.40	.10	☐ 306 Darrell Johnson	5.00	2.00	.50
☐ 254 Ron Negray	.90	.36	.09	☐ 307 J.D. (Bubba) Phillips	5.00	2.00	.50
☐ 255 Charlie Silvera	.90	.36	.09	☐ 308 Richard Hall	5.00	2.00	.50
☐ 256 Ron Kline	.90	.36	.09	☐ 309 Jim Busby	5.00	2.00	.50
☐ 257 Walt Dropo	.90	.36	.09	☐ 310 Max Surkont	5.00	2.00	.50

		MINT	VG-E	F-G
☐ 311	Al Pilarcik	5.00	2.00	.50
☐ 312	Tony Kubek	35.00	14.00	3.50
☐ 313	Mel Parnell	6.00	2.40	.60
☐ 314	Ed Bouchee	5.00	2.00	.50
☐ 315	Lou Berberet	5.00	2.00	.50
☐ 316	Billy O'Dell	5.00	2.00	.50
☐ 317	New York Giants Team Card	21.00	8.50	2.10
☐ 318	Mickey McDermott	5.00	2.00	.50
☐ 319	Gino Cimoli	5.00	2.00	.50
☐ 320	Neil Chrisley	5.00	2.00	.50
☐ 321	John (Red) Murff	5.00	2.00	.50
☐ 322	Cincinnati Team	18.00	7.25	1.80
☐ 323	Wes Westrum	5.00	2.00	.50
☐ 324	Brooklyn Dodgers Team Card	32.00	13.00	3.20
☐ 325	Frank Bolling	5.00	2.00	.50
☐ 326	Pedro Ramos	5.00	2.00	.50
☐ 327	Jim Pendleton	5.00	2.00	.50
☐ 328	Brooks Robinson	125.00	50.00	12.50
☐ 329	White Sox Team	12.00	5.00	1.20
☐ 330	Jim Wilson	5.00	2.00	.50
☐ 331	Ray Katt	5.00	2.00	.50
☐ 332	Bob Bowman	5.00	2.00	.50
☐ 333	Ernie Johnson	5.00	2.00	.50
☐ 334	Jerry Schoonmaker	5.00	2.00	.50
☐ 335	Granny Hamner	5.00	2.00	.50
☐ 336	Haywood Sullivan	6.00	2.40	.60
☐ 337	Rene Valdes	5.00	2.00	.50
☐ 338	Jim Bunning	30.00	12.00	3.00
☐ 339	Bob Speake	5.00	2.00	.50
☐ 340	Bill Wight	5.00	2.00	.50
☐ 341	Don Gross	5.00	2.00	.50
☐ 342	Gene Mauch	8.00	3.25	.80
☐ 343	Taylor Phillips	5.00	2.00	.50
☐ 344	Paul LaPalme	5.00	2.00	.50
☐ 345	Paul Smith	5.00	2.00	.50
☐ 346	Dick Littlefield	5.00	2.00	.50
☐ 347	Hal Naragon	5.00	2.00	.50
☐ 348	Jim Hearn	5.00	2.00	.50
☐ 349	Nellie King	5.00	2.00	.50
☐ 350	Eddie Miksis	5.00	2.00	.50
☐ 351	Dave Hillman	5.00	2.00	.50
☐ 352	Ellis Kinder	5.00	2.00	.50
☐ 353	Cal Neeman	1.00	.40	.10
☐ 354	W. (Rip) Coleman	1.00	.40	.10
☐ 355	Frank Malzone	1.50	.60	.15
☐ 356	Faye Throneberry	1.00	.40	.10
☐ 357	Earl Torgeson	1.00	.40	.10
☐ 358	Gerry Lynch	1.25	.50	.12
☐ 359	Tom Cheney	1.00	.40	.10
☐ 360	Johnny Groth	1.00	.40	.10
☐ 361	Curt Barclay	1.00	.40	.10
☐ 362	Roman Mejias	1.00	.40	.10
☐ 363	Eddie Kasko	1.00	.40	.10
☐ 364	Cal McLish	1.00	.40	.10
☐ 365	Ozzie Virgil	1.00	.40	.10
☐ 366	Ken Lehman	1.00	.40	.10
☐ 367	Ed Fitzgerald	1.00	.40	.10
☐ 368	Bob Purkey	1.00	.40	.10
☐ 369	Milt Graff	1.00	.40	.10
☐ 370	Warren Hacker	1.00	.40	.10
☐ 371	Bob Lennon	1.00	.40	.10
☐ 372	Norm Zauchin	1.00	.40	.10
☐ 373	Pete Whisenant	1.00	.40	.10
☐ 374	Don Cardwell	1.00	.40	.10
☐ 375	Jim Landis	1.00	.40	.10
☐ 376	Don Elston	1.00	.40	.10
☐ 377	Andre Rodgers	1.00	.40	.10
☐ 378	Elmer Singleton	1.00	.40	.10
☐ 379	Don Lee	1.00	.40	.10
☐ 380	Walker Cooper	1.00	.40	.10
☐ 381	Dean Stone	1.00	.40	.10
☐ 382	Jim Brideweser	1.00	.40	.10
☐ 383	Juan Pizarro	1.00	.40	.10
☐ 384	Bobby G. Smith	1.00	.40	.10
☐ 385	Art Houtteman	1.00	.40	.10
☐ 386	Lyle Luttrell	1.00	.40	.10
☐ 387	Jack Sanford	2.00	.80	.20
☐ 388	Pete Daley	1.00	.40	.10
☐ 389	Dave Jolly	1.00	.40	.10
☐ 390	Reno Bertoia	1.00	.40	.10
☐ 391	Ralph Terry	2.00	.80	.20
☐ 392	Chuck Tanner	1.50	.60	.15
☐ 393	Raul Sanchez	1.00	.40	.10
☐ 394	Luis Arroyo	1.25	.50	.12
☐ 395	J.M. (Bubba) Phillips	1.00	.40	.10
☐ 396	K. (Casey) Wise	1.00	.40	.10
☐ 397	Roy Smalley	1.00	.40	.10
☐ 398	Al Cicotte	1.00	.40	.10
☐ 399	Bill Consolo	1.00	.40	.10
☐ 400	Dodgers' Sluggers Carl Furillo Gil Hodges Roy Campanella Duke Snider	45.00	18.00	4.50
☐ 401	Earl Battey	1.25	.50	.12
☐ 402	Jim Pisani	1.00	.40	.10
☐ 403	Richard Hyde	1.00	.40	.10
☐ 404	Harry Anderson	1.00	.40	.10
☐ 405	Duke Maas	1.00	.40	.10
☐ 406	Bob Hale	1.00	.40	.10
☐ 407	Yankee Power Hitters Mickey Mantle Yogi Berra	75.00	30.00	7.50

		MINT	VG-E	F-G
☐ 408	Checklist ½ (unnumbered)	35.00	6.00	1.00
☐ 409	Checklist ⅔ (unnumbered)	50.00	8.00	1.50
☐ 410	Checklist ¾ (unnumbered)	100.00	18.00	3.00
☐ 411	Checklist ⅘ (unnumbered)	150.00	25.00	5.00

1958 Topps

The cards in this 494-card set measure 2½" by 3½". Although the last card is numbered 495, number 145 was not issued, bringing the set total to 494 cards. The 1958 Topps set contains the first Sport Magazine All-Star Selection series (475-495) and expanded use of combination cards. The team cards carried series checklists on back (Milwaukee, Detroit, Baltimore, and Cincinnati are also found with players listed alphabetically). Cards with the scarce yellow name (YL) or team (YT) lettering as opposed to the common white lettering are noted in the checklist. In the last series cards of Stan Musial and Mickey Mantle were triple printed; the cards they replaced (443, 446, 450, and 462) on the printing sheet were hence printed in shorter supply than other cards in the last series and are marked with an SP in the list below.

	MINT	VG-E	F-G
Complete Set (494)	1000.00	400.00	125.00
Common Player (1-110)	.90	.36	.09
Common Player (111-198)	.70	.28	.07

		MINT	VG-E	F-G
	Common Player (199-440)	.60	.24	.06
	Common Player (441-474)	.50	.20	.05
	Common Player (475-495)	.60	.24	.06
☐ 1	Ted Williams	100.00	20.00	4.00
☐ 2 A	Bob Lemon	5.00	2.00	.50
☐ 2 B	Bob Lemon YT	15.00	6.00	1.50
☐ 3	Alex Kellner	.90	.36	.09
☐ 4	Hank Foiles	.90	.36	.09
☐ 5	Willie Mays	36.00	15.00	3.60
☐ 6	George Zuverink	.90	.36	.09
☐ 7	Dale Long	.90	.36	.09
☐ 8 A	Eddie Kasko	.90	.36	.09
☐ 8 B	Eddie Kasko YL	11.00	4.50	1.10
☐ 9	Hank Bauer	2.00	.80	.20
☐ 10	Lou Burdette	2.00	.80	.20
☐ 11 A	Jim Rivera	.90	.36	.09
☐ 11 B	Jim Rivera YT	7.50	3.00	.75
☐ 12	George Crowe	.90	.36	.09
☐ 13 A	Billy Hoeft	.90	.36	.09
☐ 13 B	Billy Hoeft YL	11.00	4.50	1.10
☐ 14	Rip Repulski	.90	.36	.09
☐ 15	Jim Lemon	1.00	.40	.10
☐ 16	Charley Neal	1.00	.40	.10
☐ 17	Felix Mantilla	.90	.36	.09
☐ 18	Frank Sullivan	.90	.36	.09
☐ 19	New York Giants Team Card	4.50	.75	.15
☐ 20 A	Gil McDougald	2.50	1.00	.25
☐ 20 B	Gil McDougald YL	15.00	6.00	1.50
☐ 21	Curt Barclay	.90	.36	.09
☐ 22	Hal Naragon	.90	.36	.09
☐ 23 A	Bill Tuttle	.90	.36	.09
☐ 23 B	Bill Tuttle YL	11.00	4.50	1.10
☐ 24 A	Hobie Landrith	.90	.36	.09
☐ 24 B	Hobie Landrith YL	11.00	4.50	1.10
☐ 25	Don Drysdale	9.00	3.75	.90
☐ 26	Ron Jackson	.90	.36	.09
☐ 27	Bud Freeman	.90	.36	.09
☐ 28	Jim Busby	.90	.36	.09
☐ 29	Ted Lepcio	.90	.36	.09
☐ 30 A	Hank Aaron	36.00	15.00	3.60
☐ 30 B	Hank Aaron YL	90.00	36.00	9.00
☐ 31	Tex Clevenger	.90	.36	.09
☐ 32 A	J.W. Porter	.90	.36	.09
☐ 32 B	J.W. Porter YL	11.00	4.50	1.10
☐ 33 A	Cal Neeman	.90	.36	.09
☐ 33 B	Cal Neeman YT	7.50	3.00	.75
☐ 34	Bob Thurman	.90	.36	.09
☐ 35 A	Don Mossi	1.00	.40	.10

		MINT	VG-E	F-G
☐ 35	B Don Mossi YT	8.50	3.50	.85
☐ 36	Ted Kazanski	.90	.36	.09
☐ 37	Mike McCormick	1.50	.60	.15
	(photo actually			
	Ray Monzant)			
☐ 38	Dick Gernert	.90	.36	.09
☐ 39	Bob Martyn	.90	.36	.09
☐ 40	George Kell	5.00	2.00	.50
☐ 41	Dave Hillman	.90	.36	.09
☐ 42	John Roseboro	2.00	.80	.20
☐ 43	Sal Maglie	1.75	.70	.17
☐ 44	Washington Senators	2.50	.50	.10
	Team Card			
☐ 45	Dick Groat	1.50	.60	.15
☐ 46	A Lou Sleater	.90	.36	.09
☐ 46	B Lou Sleater YL	11.00	4.50	1.10
☐ 47	Roger Maris	50.00	20.00	5.00
☐ 48	Chuck Harmon	.90	.36	.09
☐ 49	Smoky Burgess	1.00	.40	.10
☐ 50	A Billy Pierce	1.50	.60	.15
☐ 50	B Billy Pierce YT	11.00	4.50	1.10
☐ 51	Del Rice	.90	.36	.09
☐ 52	A Bob Clemente	18.00	7.25	1.80
☐ 52	B Bob Clemente YT	45.00	18.00	4.50
☐ 53	A Morrie Martin	.90	.36	.09
☐ 53	B Morrie Martin YL	11.00	4.50	1.10
☐ 54	Norm Siebern	.90	.36	.09
☐ 55	Chico Carrasquel	.90	.36	.09
☐ 56	Bill Fischer	.90	.36	.09
☐ 57	A Tim Thompson	.90	.36	.09
☐ 57	B Tim Thompson YL	11.00	4.50	1.10
☐ 58	A Art Schult	.90	.36	.09
☐ 58	B Art Schult YT	7.50	3.00	.75
☐ 59	Dave Sisler	.90	.36	.09
☐ 60	A Del Ennis	1.00	.40	.10
☐ 60	B Del Ennis YL	11.00	4.50	1.10
☐ 61	A Darrell Johnson	1.00	.40	.10
☐ 61	B Darrell Johnson YL	11.00	4.50	1.10
☐ 62	Joe DeMaestri	.90	.36	.09
☐ 63	Joe Nuxhall	1.00	.40	.10
☐ 64	Joe Lonnett	.90	.36	.09
☐ 65	A Von McDaniel	.90	.36	.09
☐ 65	B Von McDaniel YL	11.00	4.50	1.10
☐ 66	Lee Walls	.90	.36	.09
☐ 67	Joe Ginsberg	.90	.36	.09
☐ 68	Daryl Spencer	.90	.36	.09
☐ 69	Wally Burnette	.90	.36	.09
☐ 70	A Al Kaline	11.00	4.50	1.10
☐ 70	B Al Kaline YL	40.00	16.00	4.00
☐ 71	Dodgers Team	6.50	1.00	.20
☐ 72	Bud Byerly	.90	.36	.09
☐ 73	Pete Daley	.90	.36	.09
☐ 74	Roy Face	1.25	.50	.12
☐ 75	Gus Bell	1.00	.40	.10
☐ 76	A Dick Farrell	1.00	.40	.10
☐ 76	B Dick Farrell YT	7.50	3.00	.75
☐ 77	A Don Zimmer	1.25	.50	.12
☐ 77	B Don Zimmer YT	8.50	3.50	.85
☐ 78	A Ernie Johnson	.90	.36	.09
☐ 78	B Ernie Johnson YL	11.00	4.50	1.10
☐ 79	A Dick Williams	1.25	.50	.12
☐ 79	B Dick Williams YT	8.50	3.50	.85
☐ 80	Dick Drott	.90	.36	.09
☐ 81	A Steve Boros	1.00	.40	.10
☐ 81	B Steve Boros YT	8.50	3.50	.85
☐ 82	Ronnie Kline	.90	.36	.09
☐ 83	Bob Hazle	.90	.36	.09
☐ 84	Billy O'Dell	.90	.36	.09
☐ 85	A Luis Aparicio	5.00	2.00	.50
☐ 85	B Luis Aparicio YT	18.00	7.25	1.80
☐ 86	Valmy Thomas	.90	.36	.09
☐ 87	Johnny Kucks	.90	.36	.09
☐ 88	Duke Snider	18.00	7.25	1.80
☐ 89	Billy Klaus	.90	.36	.09
☐ 90	Robin Roberts	6.00	2.40	.60
☐ 91	Chuck Tanner	1.25	.50	.12
☐ 92	A Clint Courtney	.90	.36	.09
☐ 92	B Clint Courtney YL	11.00	4.50	1.10
☐ 93	Sandy Amoros	1.25	.50	.12
☐ 94	Bob Skinner	1.00	.40	.10
☐ 95	Frank Bolling	.90	.36	.09
☐ 96	Joe Durham	.90	.36	.09
☐ 97	A Larry Jackson	.90	.36	.09
☐ 97	B Larry Jackson YL	11.00	4.50	1.10
☐ 98	A Billy Hunter	.90	.36	.09
☐ 98	B Billy Hunter YL	11.00	4.50	1.10
☐ 99	Bobby Adams	.90	.36	.09
☐ 100	A Early Wynn	5.00	2.00	.50
☐ 100	B Early Wynn YT	15.00	6.00	1.50
☐ 101	A Bobby Richardson	3.00	1.20	.30
☐ 101	B Bobby Richardson YL	15.00	6.00	1.50
☐ 102	George Strickland	.90	.36	.09
☐ 103	Jerry Lynch	1.00	.40	.10
☐ 104	Jim Pendleton	.90	.36	.09
☐ 105	Billy Gardner	1.00	.40	.10
☐ 106	Dick Schofield	.90	.36	.09
☐ 107	Ossie Virgil	.90	.36	.09
☐ 108	A Jim Landis	.90	.36	.09
☐ 108	B Jim Landis YT	7.50	3.00	.75
☐ 109	Herb Plews	.90	.36	.09
☐ 110	Johnny Logan	1.00	.40	.10
☐ 111	Stu Miller	.70	.28	.07
☐ 112	Gus Zernial	.80	.32	.08
☐ 113	Jerry Walker	.70	.28	.07
☐ 114	Irv Noren	.70	.28	.07
☐ 115	Jim Bunning	3.00	1.20	.30

		MINT	VG-E	F-G			MINT	VG-E	F-G
☐ 116	Dave Philley	.70	.28	.07	☐ 169	Ralph Terry	1.00	.40	.10
☐ 117	Frank Torre	.80	.32	.08	☐ 170	Vic Wertz	.80	.32	.08
☐ 118	Harvey Haddix	1.00	.40	.10	☐ 171	Harry Anderson	.70	.28	.07
☐ 119	Harry Chiti	.70	.28	.07	☐ 172	Don Gross	.70	.28	.07
☐ 120	Johnny Podres	2.00	.80	.20	☐ 173	Eddie Yost	.70	.28	.07
☐ 121	Eddie Miksis	.70	.28	.07	☐ 174	Athletics Team	2.50	.50	.10
☐ 122	Walt Moryn	.70	.28	.07	☐ 175	Marv Throneberry	3.00	1.20	.30
☐ 123	Dick Tomanek	.70	.28	.07	☐ 176	Bob Buhl	.70	.28	.07
☐ 124	Bobby Usher	.70	.28	.07	☐ 177	Al Smith	.70	.28	.07
☐ 125	Al Dark	1.25	.50	.12	☐ 178	Ted Kluszewski	2.00	.80	.20
☐ 126	Stan Palys	.70	.28	.07	☐ 179	Willie Miranda	.70	.28	.07
☐ 127	Tom Sturdivant	.80	.32	.08	☐ 180	Lindy McDaniel	.80	.32	.08
☐ 128	Willie Kirkland	.80	.32	.08	☐ 181	Willie Jones	.70	.28	.07
☐ 129	Jim Derrington	.70	.28	.07	☐ 182	Joe Caffie	.70	.28	.07
☐ 130	Jackie Jensen	2.50	1.00	.25	☐ 183	Dave Jolly	.70	.28	.07
☐ 131	Bob Henrich	.70	.28	.07	☐ 184	Elvin Tappe	.70	.28	.07
☐ 132	Vernon Law	.90	.36	.09	☐ 185	Ray Boone	.80	.32	.08
☐ 133	Russ Nixon	.70	.28	.07	☐ 186	Jack Meyer	.70	.28	.07
☐ 134	Phillies Team	2.50	.50	.10	☐ 187	Sandy Koufax	27.00	11.00	2.70
☐ 135	Mike (Moe) Drabowsky	.70	.28	.07	☐ 188	Milt Bolling	.70	.28	.07
☐ 136	Jim Finigan	.70	.28	.07		(photo actually			
☐ 137	Russ Kemmerer	.70	.28	.07		Lou Berberet)			
☐ 138	Earl Torgeson	.70	.28	.07	☐ 189	George Susce	.70	.28	.07
☐ 139	George Brunet	.70	.28	.07	☐ 190	Red Schoendienst	1.25	.50	.12
☐ 140	Wes Covington	.80	.32	.08	☐ 191	Art Ceccarelli	.70	.28	.07
☐ 141	Ken Lehman	.70	.28	.07	☐ 192	Milt Graff	.70	.28	.07
☐ 142	Enos Slaughter	4.50	1.80	.45	☐ 193	Jerry Lumpe	.80	.32	.08
☐ 143	Billy Muffett	.70	.28	.07	☐ 194	Roger Craig	1.25	.50	.12
☐ 144	Bobby Morgan	.70	.28	.07	☐ 195	Whitey Lockman	.80	.32	.08
☐ 145	Never issued	.00	.00	.00	☐ 196	Mike Garcia	.90	.36	.09
☐ 146	Dick Gray	.70	.28	.07	☐ 197	Haywood Sullivan	.80	.32	.08
☐ 147	Don McMahon	.80	.32	.08	☐ 198	Bill Virdon	1.25	.50	.12
☐ 148	Billy Consolo	.70	.28	.07	☐ 199	Don Blasingame	.60	.24	.06
☐ 149	Tom Acker	.70	.28	.07	☐ 200	Bob Keegan	.60	.24	.06
☐ 150	Mickey Mantle	120.00	50.00	12.00	☐ 201	Jim Bolger	.60	.24	.06
☐ 151	Buddy Pritchard	.70	.28	.07	☐ 202	Woody Held	.60	.24	.06
☐ 152	Johnny Antonelli	.90	.36	.09	☐ 203	Al Walker	.60	.24	.06
☐ 153	Les Moss	.70	.28	.07	☐ 204	Leo Kiely	.60	.24	.06
☐ 154	Harry Byrd	.70	.28	.07	☐ 205	Johnny Temple	.70	.28	.07
☐ 155	Hector Lopez	.70	.28	.07	☐ 206	Bob Shaw	.60	.24	.06
☐ 156	Dick Hyde	.70	.28	.07	☐ 207	Solly Hemus	.60	.24	.06
☐ 157	Dee Fondy	.70	.28	.07	☐ 208	Cal McLish	.60	.24	.06
☐ 158	Indians Team	2.50	.50	.10	☐ 209	Bob Anderson	.60	.24	.06
☐ 159	Taylor Phillips	.70	.28	.07	☐ 210	Wally Moon	.80	.32	.08
☐ 160	Don Hoak	.70	.28	.07	☐ 211	Pete Burnside	.60	.24	.06
☐ 161	Don Larsen	2.00	.80	.20	☐ 212	Bubba Phillips	.60	.24	.06
☐ 162	Gil Hodges	8.00	3.25	.80	☐ 213	Red Wilson	.60	.24	.06
☐ 163	Jim Wilson	.70	.28	.07	☐ 214	Willard Schmidt	.60	.24	.06
☐ 164	Bob Taylor	.70	.28	.07	☐ 215	Jim Gilliam	2.00	.80	.20
☐ 165	Bob Nieman	.70	.28	.07	☐ 216	Cardinals Team	2.50	.50	.10
☐ 166	Danny O'Connell	.70	.28	.07	☐ 217	Jack Harshman	.60	.24	.06
☐ 167	Frank Baumann	.70	.28	.07	☐ 218	Dick Rand	.60	.24	.06
☐ 168	Joe Cunningham	.80	.32	.08	☐ 219	Camilo Pascual	.70	.28	.07

		MINT	VG-E	F-G
☐ 220	Tom Brewer	.60	.24	.06
☐ 221	Jerry Kindall	.60	.24	.06
☐ 222	Bud Daley	.60	.24	.06
☐ 223	Andy Pafko	.60	.24	.06
☐ 224	Bob Grim	.80	.32	.08
☐ 225	Billy Goodman	.70	.28	.07
☐ 226	Bob Smith	.60	.24	.06
☐ 227	Gene Stephens	.60	.24	.06
☐ 228	Duke Maas	.60	.24	.06
☐ 229	Frank Zupo	.60	.24	.06
☐ 230	Richie Ashburn	3.00	1.20	.30
☐ 231	Lloyd Merritt	.60	.24	.06
☐ 232	Reno Bertoia	.60	.24	.06
☐ 233	Mickey Vernon	.80	.32	.08
☐ 234	Carl Sawatski	.60	.24	.06
☐ 235	Tom Gorman	.60	.24	.06
☐ 236	Ed Fitzgerald	.60	.24	.06
☐ 237	Bill Wight	.60	.24	.06
☐ 238	Bill Mazeroski	2.50	1.00	.25
☐ 239	Chuck Stobbs	.60	.24	.06
☐ 240	Moose Skowron	2.50	1.00	.25
☐ 241	Dick Littlefield	.60	.24	.06
☐ 242	Johnny Klippstein	.60	.24	.06
☐ 243	Larry Raines	.60	.24	.06
☐ 244	Don Demeter	.60	.24	.06
☐ 245	Frank Lary	.80	.32	.08
☐ 246	Yankees Team	9.00	1.50	.30
☐ 247	Casey Wise	.60	.24	.06
☐ 248	Herm Wehmeier	.60	.24	.06
☐ 249	Ray Moore	.60	.24	.06
☐ 250	Roy Sievers	.80	.32	.08
☐ 251	Warren Hacker	.60	.24	.06
☐ 252	Bob Trowbridge	.60	.24	.06
☐ 253	Don Mueller	.70	.28	.07
☐ 254	Alex Grammas	.60	.24	.06
☐ 255	Bob Turley	2.25	.90	.22
☐ 256	White Sox Team	2.50	.50	.10
☐ 257	Hal Smith	.60	.24	.06
☐ 258	Carl Erskine	2.00	.80	.20
☐ 259	Al Pilarcik	.60	.24	.06
☐ 260	Frank Malzone	.80	.32	.08
☐ 261	Turk Lown	.60	.24	.06
☐ 262	Johnny Groth	.60	.24	.06
☐ 263	Eddie Bressoud	.60	.24	.06
☐ 264	Jack Sanford	.70	.28	.07
☐ 265	Pete Runnels	.70	.28	.07
☐ 266	Connie Johnson	.60	.24	.06
☐ 267	Sherm Lollar	.70	.28	.07
☐ 268	Granny Hamner	.60	.24	.06
☐ 269	Paul Smith	.60	.24	.06
☐ 270	Warren Spahn	8.00	3.25	.80
☐ 271	Billy Martin	3.25	1.30	.32
☐ 272	Ray Crone	.60	.24	.06

		MINT	VG-E	F-G
☐ 273	Hal Smith	.60	.24	.06
☐ 274	Rocky Bridges	.60	.24	.06
☐ 275	Elston Howard	2.50	1.00	.25
☐ 276	Bobby Avila	.70	.28	.07
☐ 277	Virgil Trucks	.70	.28	.07
☐ 278	Mack Burk	.60	.24	.06
☐ 279	Bob Boyd	.60	.24	.06
☐ 280	Jim Piersall	1.75	.70	.17
☐ 281	Sam Taylor	.60	.24	.06
☐ 282	Paul Foytack	.60	.24	.06
☐ 283	Ray Shearer	.60	.24	.06
☐ 284	Ray Katt	.60	.24	.06
☐ 285	Frank Robinson	11.00	4.50	1.10
☐ 286	Gino Cimoli	.60	.24	.06
☐ 287	Sam Jones	.70	.28	.07
☐ 288	Harmon Killebrew	11.00	4.50	1.10
☐ 289	Series Hurling Rivals	1.50	.60	.15
	Lou Burdette			
	Bobby Shantz			
☐ 290	Dick Donovan	.60	.24	.06
☐ 291	Don Landrum	.60	.24	.06
☐ 292	Ned Garver	.60	.24	.06
☐ 293	Gene Freese	.60	.24	.06
☐ 294	Hal Jeffcoat	.60	.24	.06
☐ 295	Minnie Minoso	2.00	.80	.20
☐ 296	Ryne Duren	1.50	.60	.15
☐ 297	Don Buddin	.60	.24	.06
☐ 298	Jim Hearn	.60	.24	.06
☐ 299	Harry Simpson	.60	.24	.06
☐ 300	Harridge and Giles	2.00	.80	.20
	League Presidents			
☐ 301	Randy Jackson	.60	.24	.06
☐ 302	Mike Baxes	.60	.24	.06
☐ 303	Neil Chrisley	.60	.24	.06
☐ 304	Tigers' Big Bats	3.50	1.40	.35
	Harvey Kuenn			
	Al Kaline			
☐ 305	Clem Labine	.80	.32	.08
☐ 306	Whammy Douglas	.60	.24	.06
☐ 307	Brooks Robinson	20.00	8.00	2.00
☐ 308	Paul Giel	.60	.24	.06
☐ 309	Gail Harris	.60	.24	.06
☐ 310	Ernie Banks	14.00	5.75	1.40
☐ 311	Bob Purkey	.60	.24	.06
☐ 312	Boston Red Sox Team	3.00	.60	.10
☐ 313	Bob Rush	.60	.24	.06
☐ 314	Dodgers' Boss and	7.00	2.80	.70
	Power: Duke Snider			
	Walt Alston			
☐ 315	Bob Friend	.80	.32	.08
☐ 316	Tito Francona	.70	.28	.07
☐ 317	Albie Pearson	.80	.32	.08
☐ 318	Frank House	.60	.24	.06

	MINT	VG-E	F-G
☐ 319 Lou Skizas	.60	.24	.06
☐ 320 Whitey Ford	10.00	4.00	1.00
☐ 321 Sluggers Supreme	9.00	3.75	.90
Ted Kluszewski			
Ted Williams			
☐ 322 Harding Peterson	.70	.28	.07
☐ 323 Elmer Valo	.60	.24	.06
☐ 324 Hoyt Wilhelm	4.50	1.80	.45
☐ 325 Joe Adcock	1.25	.50	.12
☐ 326 Bob Miller	.60	.24	.06
☐ 327 Chicago Cubs Team	2.50	.50	.10
☐ 328 Ike Delock	.60	.24	.06
☐ 329 Bob Cerv	.70	.28	.07
☐ 330 Ed Bailey	.70	.28	.07
☐ 331 Pedro Ramos	.60	.24	.06
☐ 332 Jim King	.60	.24	.06
☐ 333 Andy Carey	.70	.28	.07
☐ 334 Mound Aces:	1.00	.40	.10
Bob Friend			
Billy Pierce			
☐ 335 Ruben Gomez	.60	.24	.06
☐ 336 Bert Hamric	.60	.24	.06
☐ 337 Hank Aguirre	.60	.24	.06
☐ 338 Walt Dropo	.60	.24	.06
☐ 339 Fred Hatfield	.60	.24	.06
☐ 340 Don Newcombe	2.25	.90	.22
☐ 341 Pirates Team	2.50	.50	.10
☐ 342 Jim Brosnan	.70	.28	.07
☐ 343 Orlando Cepeda	10.00	4.00	1.00
☐ 344 Bob Porterfield	.60	.24	.06
☐ 345 Jim Hegan	.70	.28	.07
☐ 346 Steve Bilko	.60	.24	.06
☐ 347 Don Rudolph	.60	.24	.06
☐ 348 Chico Fernandez	.60	.24	.06
☐ 349 Murry Dickson	.60	.24	.06
☐ 350 Ken Boyer	2.00	.80	.20
☐ 351 Braves Fence Busters	9.00	3.75	.90
Del Crandall			
Eddie Mathews			
Hank Aaron			
Joe Adcock			
☐ 352 Herb Score	1.25	.50	.12
☐ 353 Stan Lopata	.60	.24	.06
☐ 354 Art Ditmar	.70	.28	.07
☐ 355 Bill Bruton	.70	.28	.07
☐ 356 Bob Malkmus	.60	.24	.06
☐ 357 Danny McDevitt	.60	.24	.06
☐ 358 Gene Baker	.60	.24	.06
☐ 359 Billy Loes	.70	.28	.07
☐ 360 Roy McMillan	.60	.24	.06
☐ 361 Mike Fornieles	.60	.24	.06
☐ 362 Ray Jablonski	.60	.24	.06
☐ 363 Don Elston	.60	.24	.06

	MINT	VG-E	F-G
☐ 364 Earl Battey	.70	.28	.07
☐ 365 Tom Morgan	.60	.24	.06
☐ 366 Gene Green	.60	.24	.06
☐ 367 Jack Urban	.60	.24	.06
☐ 368 Rocky Colavito	2.50	1.00	.25
☐ 369 Ralph Lumenti	.60	.24	.06
☐ 370 Yogi Berra	12.00	5.00	1.20
☐ 371 Marty Keough	.60	.24	.06
☐ 372 Don Cardwell	.60	.24	.06
☐ 373 Joe Pignatano	.70	.28	.07
☐ 374 Brooks Lawrence	.60	.24	.06
☐ 375 Pee Wee Reese	9.00	3.75	.90
☐ 376 Charley Rabe	.60	.24	.06
☐ 377 A Milwaukee Team	3.00	1.20	.30
alphabetical			
☐ 377 B Milwaukee Team	20.00	3.00	.50
numerical			
☐ 378 Hank Sauer	.80	.32	.08
☐ 379 Ray Herbert	.60	.24	.06
☐ 380 Charley Maxwell	.60	.24	.06
☐ 381 Hal Brown	.60	.24	.06
☐ 382 Al Cicotte	.70	.28	.07
☐ 383 Lou Berberet	.60	.24	.06
☐ 384 John Goryl	.60	.24	.06
☐ 385 Wilmer Mizell	.60	.24	.06
☐ 386 Birdie's Sluggers	2.00	.80	.20
Ed Bailey			
Birdie Tebbetts			
Frank Robinson			
☐ 387 Wally Post	.60	.24	.06
☐ 388 Billy Moran	.60	.24	.06
☐ 389 Bill Taylor	.60	.24	.06
☐ 390 Del Crandall	.80	.32	.08
☐ 391 Dave Melton	.60	.24	.06
☐ 392 Bennie Daniels	.60	.24	.06
☐ 393 Tony Kubek	3.50	1.40	.35
☐ 394 Jim Grant	.60	.24	.06
☐ 395 Willard Nixon	.60	.24	.06
☐ 396 Dutch Dotterer	.60	.24	.06
☐ 397 A Detroit Team	3.00	1.20	.30
alphabetical			
☐ 397 B Detroit Team	20.00	3.00	.50
numerical			
☐ 398 Gene Woodling	.80	.32	.08
☐ 399 Marv Grissom	.60	.24	.06
☐ 400 Nellie Fox	2.50	1.00	.25
☐ 401 Don Bessent	.70	.28	.07
☐ 402 Bobby Gene Smith	.60	.24	.06
☐ 403 Steve Korcheck	.60	.24	.06
☐ 404 Curt Simmons	.80	.32	.08
☐ 405 Ken Aspromonte	.60	.24	.06
☐ 406 Vic Power	.70	.28	.07
☐ 407 Carlton Willey	.60	.24	.06

		MINT	VG-E	F-G
☐ 408	A Baltimore Team alphabetical	3.00	1.20	.30
☐ 408	B Baltimore Team numerical	20.00	3.00	.50
☐ 409	Frank Thomas	.70	.28	.07
☐ 410	Murray Wall	.60	.24	.06
☐ 411	Tony Taylor	.60	.24	.06
☐ 412	Jerry Staley	.60	.24	.06
☐ 413	Jim Davenport	.80	.32	.08
☐ 414	Sammy White	.60	.24	.06
☐ 415	Bob Bowman	.60	.24	.06
☐ 416	Foster Castleman	.60	.24	.06
☐ 417	Carl Furillo	2.25	.90	.22
☐ 418	World Series Batting Foes: Mickey Mantle Hank Aaron	30.00	12.00	3.00
☐ 419	Bobby Shantz	1.25	.50	.12
☐ 420	Vada Pinson	4.00	1.60	.40
☐ 421	Dixie Howell	.60	.24	.06
☐ 422	Norm Zauchin	.60	.24	.06
☐ 423	Phil Clark	.60	.24	.06
☐ 424	Larry Doby	1.75	.70	.17
☐ 425	Sam Esposito	.60	.24	.06
☐ 426	Johnny O'Brien	.60	.24	.06
☐ 427	Al Worthington	.60	.24	.06
☐ 428	A Cincinnati Team alphabetical	3.00	1.20	.30
☐ 428	B Cincinnati Team numerical	20.00	3.00	.50
☐ 429	Gus Triandos	.80	.32	.08
☐ 430	Bobby Thomson	1.25	.50	.12
☐ 431	Gene Conley	.70	.28	.07
☐ 432	John Powers	.60	.24	.06
☐ 433	A Pancho Herrera COR	.70	.28	.07
☐ 433	B Pancho Herrer ERR	20.00	8.00	2.00
☐ 434	Harvey Kuenn	1.75	.70	.17
☐ 435	Ed Roebuck	.70	.28	.07
☐ 436	Rival Fence Busters Willie Mays Duke Snider	18.00	7.25	1.80
☐ 437	Bob Speake	.60	.24	.06
☐ 438	Whitey Herzog	1.25	.50	.12
☐ 439	Ray Narleski	.60	.24	.06
☐ 440	Ed Mathews	7.50	3.00	.75
☐ 441	Jim Marshall	.50	.20	.05
☐ 442	Phil Paine	.50	.20	.05
☐ 443	Billy Harrell SP	4.50	1.80	.45
☐ 444	Danny Kravitz	.50	.20	.05
☐ 445	Bob Smith	.50	.20	.05
☐ 446	Carroll Hardy SP	4.50	1.80	.45
☐ 447	Ray Monzant	.50	.20	.05
☐ 448	Charlie Lau	1.00	.40	.10
☐ 449	Gene Fodge	.50	.20	.05

		MINT	VG-E	F-G
☐ 450	Preston Ward SP	4.50	1.80	.45
☐ 451	Joe Taylor	.50	.20	.05
☐ 452	Roman Mejias	.50	.20	.05
☐ 453	Tom Qualters	.50	.20	.05
☐ 454	Harry Hanebrink	.50	.20	.05
☐ 455	Hal Griggs	.50	.20	.05
☐ 456	Dick Brown	.50	.20	.05
☐ 457	Milt Pappas	1.25	.50	.12
☐ 458	Julio Becquer	.50	.20	.05
☐ 459	Ron Blackburn	.50	.20	.05
☐ 460	Chuck Essegian	.50	.20	.05
☐ 461	Ed Mayer	.50	.20	.05
☐ 462	Gary Geiger SP	4.50	1.80	.45
☐ 463	Vito Valentinetti	.50	.20	.05
☐ 464	Curt Flood	3.00	1.20	.30
☐ 465	Arnie Portocarrero	.50	.20	.05
☐ 466	Pete Whisenant	.50	.20	.05
☐ 467	Glen Hobbie	.50	.20	.05
☐ 468	Bob Schmidt	.50	.20	.05
☐ 469	Don Ferrarese	.50	.20	.05
☐ 470	R.C. Stevens	.50	.20	.05
☐ 471	Lenny Green	.50	.20	.05
☐ 472	Joe Jay	.50	.20	.05
☐ 473	Bill Renna	.50	.20	.05
☐ 474	Roman Semproch	.50	.20	.05
☐ 475	Haney/Stengel AS (checklist back)	4.00	1.00	.20
☐ 476	Stan Musial AS TP	6.00	2.40	.45
☐ 477	Bill Skowron AS	.80	.32	.08
☐ 478	Johnny Temple AS	.60	.24	.06
☐ 479	Nellie Fox AS	1.50	.60	.15
☐ 480	Eddie Mathews AS	3.50	1.40	.35
☐ 481	Frank Malzone AS	.60	.24	.06
☐ 482	Ernie Banks AS	4.00	1.60	.40
☐ 483	Luis Aparicio AS	3.00	1.20	.30
☐ 484	Frank Robinson AS	3.50	1.40	.35
☐ 485	Ted Williams AS	12.00	5.00	1.20
☐ 486	Willie Mays AS	9.00	3.75	.90
☐ 487	Mickey Mantle AS TP	10.00	4.00	1.00
☐ 488	Hank Aaron AS	9.00	3.75	.90
☐ 489	Jackie Jensen AS	.70	.28	.07
☐ 490	Ed Bailey AS	.60	.24	.06
☐ 491	Sherm Lollar AS	.60	.24	.06
☐ 492	Bob Friend AS	.60	.24	.06
☐ 493	Bob Turley AS	.70	.28	.07
☐ 494	Warren Spahn AS	3.00	1.20	.30
☐ 495	Herb Score AS	1.00	.40	.10

1959 Topps

The cards in this 572-card set measure 2½" by 3½". The 1959 Topps set contains bust pictures of the players in a colored circle. Card numbers 551 to 572 are the Sporting News All-Star Selections. High numbers 507 to 572 have the card number in a black background on the reverse rather than a green background as in the lower numbers. The high numbers are more difficult to obtain. Several cards in the 300's exist with or without an extra traded or option line on the back of the card. Cards 199 to 286 exist with either white or gray backs. Cards 461 to 470 contain "Highlights" while cards 116 to 146 give an alphabetically ordered listing of "Rookie Prospects." These Rookie Prospects (RP) were Topps' first organized inclusion of untested "Rookie" cards. Card 440 features Lew Burdette erroneously posing as a left-handed pitcher.

	MINT	VG-E	F-G
Complete Set	850.00	340.00	85.00
Common Player (1-110)	.60	.24	.06
Common Player (111-506)	.50	.20	.05
Common Player (507-550)	2.50	1.00	.25
Common Player (551-572)	3.00	1.20	.30

		MINT	VG-E	F-G
☐ 1	Ford Frick	4.00	1.00	.20
☐ 2	Eddie Yost	.60	.24	.06
☐ 3	Don McMahon	.60	.24	.06
☐ 4	Albie Pearson	.60	.24	.06
☐ 5	Dick Donovan	.60	.24	.06
☐ 6	Alex Grammas	.60	.24	.06

		MINT	VG-E	F-G
☐ 7	Al Pilarcik	.60	.24	.06
☐ 8	Phillies Team	2.25	.50	.10
☐ 9	Paul Giel	.60	.24	.06
☐ 10	Mickey Mantle	90.00	36.00	9.00
☐ 11	Billy Hunter	.60	.24	.06
☐ 12	Vern Law	.75	.30	.07
☐ 13	Dick Gernert	.60	.24	.06
☐ 14	Pete Whisenant	.60	.24	.06
☐ 15	Dick Drott	.60	.24	.06
☐ 16	Joe Pignatano	.60	.24	.06
☐ 17	Danny's Stars	.90	.36	.09
	Frank Thomas			
	Danny Murtaugh			
	Ted Kluszewski			
☐ 18	Jack Urban	.60	.24	.06
☐ 19	Eddie Bressoud	.60	.24	.06
☐ 20	Duke Snider	12.50	5.00	1.25
☐ 21	Connie Johnson	.60	.24	.06
☐ 22	Al Smith	.60	.24	.06
☐ 23	Murry Dickson	.60	.24	.06
☐ 24	Red Wilson	.60	.24	.06
☐ 25	Don Hoak	.60	.24	.06
☐ 26	Chuck Stobbs	.60	.24	.06
☐ 27	Andy Pafko	.60	.24	.06
☐ 28	Ray Worthington	.60	.24	.06
☐ 29	Jim Bolger	.60	.24	.06
☐ 30	Nellie Fox	2.50	1.00	.25
☐ 31	Ken Lehman	.60	.24	.06
☐ 32	Don Buddin	.60	.24	.06
☐ 33	Ed Fitzgerald	.60	.24	.06
☐ 34	Pitchers Beware	2.25	.90	.22
	Al Kaline			
	Charley Maxwell			
☐ 35	Ted Kluszewski	1.50	.60	.15
☐ 36	Hank Aguirre	.60	.24	.06
☐ 37	Gene Green	.60	.24	.06
☐ 38	Morrie Martin	.60	.24	.06
☐ 39	Ed Bouchee	.60	.24	.06
☐ 40	Warren Spahn	8.50	3.50	.85
☐ 41	Bob Martyn	.60	.24	.06
☐ 42	Murray Wall	.60	.24	.06
☐ 43	Steve Bilko	.60	.24	.06
☐ 44	Vito Valentinetti	.60	.24	.06
☐ 45	Andy Carey	.75	.30	.07
☐ 46	R. Henry	.60	.24	.06
☐ 47	Jim Finigan	.60	.24	.06
☐ 48	Orioles Team	2.25	.50	.10
☐ 49	Bill Hall	.60	.24	.06
☐ 50	Willie Mays	32.00	13.00	3.20
☐ 51	Rip Coleman	.60	.24	.06
☐ 52	Coot Veal	.60	.24	.06
☐ 53	Stan Williams	.60	.24	.06
☐ 54	Mel Roach	.60	.24	.06

		MINT	VG-E	F-G
☐ 55	Tom Brewer	.60	.24	.06
☐ 56	Carl Sawatski	.60	.24	.06
☐ 57	Al Cicotte	.60	.24	.06
☐ 58	Eddie Miksis	.60	.24	.06
☐ 59	Irv Noren	.60	.24	.06
☐ 60	Bob Turley	1.50	.60	.15
☐ 61	Dick Brown	.60	.24	.06
☐ 62	Tony Taylor	.60	.24	.06
☐ 63	Jim Hearn	.60	.24	.06
☐ 64	Joe DeMaestri	.60	.24	.06
☐ 65	Frank Torre	.60	.24	.06
☐ 66	Joe Ginsberg	.60	.24	.06
☐ 67	Brooks Lawrence	.60	.24	.06
☐ 68	Dick Schofield	.60	.24	.06
☐ 69	Giants Team	2.25	.50	.10
☐ 70	Harvey Kuenn	1.50	.60	.15
☐ 71	Don Bessent	.60	.24	.06
☐ 72	Bill Renna	.60	.24	.06
☐ 73	Ron Jackson	.60	.24	.06
☐ 74	Directing Power	.75	.30	.07
	Jim Lemon			
	Cookie Lavagetto			
	Roy Sievers			
☐ 75	Sam Jones	.75	.30	.07
☐ 76	Bobby Richardson	2.50	1.00	.25
☐ 77	John Goryl	.60	.24	.06
☐ 78	Pedro Ramos	.60	.24	.06
☐ 79	Harry Chiti	.60	.24	.06
☐ 80	Minnie Minoso	2.00	.80	.20
☐ 81	Hal Jeffcoat	.60	.24	.06
☐ 82	Bob Boyd	.60	.24	.06
☐ 83	Bob Smith	.60	.24	.06
☐ 84	Reno Bertoia	.60	.24	.06
☐ 85	Harry Anderson	.60	.24	.06
☐ 86	Bob Keegan	.60	.24	.06
☐ 87	Danny O'Connell	.60	.24	.06
☐ 88	Herb Score	1.25	.50	.12
☐ 89	Billy Gardner	.75	.30	.07
☐ 90	Bill Skowron	2.25	.90	.22
☐ 91	Herb Moford	.60	.24	.06
☐ 92	Dave Philley	.60	.24	.06
☐ 93	Julio Becquer	.60	.24	.06
☐ 94	White Sox Team	2.50	.50	.10
☐ 95	Carl Willey	.60	.24	.06
☐ 96	Lou Berberet	.60	.24	.06
☐ 97	Jerry Lynch	.60	.24	.06
☐ 98	Arnie Portocarrero	.60	.24	.06
☐ 99	Ted Kazanski	.60	.24	.06
☐ 100	Bob Cerv	.75	.30	.07
☐ 101	Alex Kellner	.60	.24	.06
☐ 102	Felipe Alou	2.00	.80	.20
☐ 103	Billy Goodman	.75	.30	.07
☐ 104	Del Rice	.60	.24	.06
☐ 105	Lee Walls	.60	.24	.06
☐ 106	Hal Woodeshick	.60	.24	.06
☐ 107	Norm Larker	.60	.24	.06
☐ 108	Zack Monroe	.60	.24	.06
☐ 109	Bob Schmidt	.60	.24	.06
☐ 110	George Witt	.60	.24	.06
☐ 111	Redlegs Team	2.50	.50	.10
☐ 112	Billy Consolo	.50	.20	.05
☐ 113	Taylor Phillips	.50	.20	.05
☐ 114	Earl Battey	.60	.24	.06
☐ 115	Mickey Vernon	.60	.24	.06
☐ 116	Bob Allison RP	2.50	1.00	.25
☐ 117	John Blanchard RP	.75	.30	.07
☐ 118	John Buzhardt RP	.50	.20	.05
☐ 119	John Callison RP	1.75	.70	.17
☐ 120	Chuck Coles RP	.50	.20	.05
☐ 121	Bob Conley RP	.50	.20	.05
☐ 122	Bennie Daniels RP	.50	.20	.05
☐ 123	Don Dillard RP	.50	.20	.05
☐ 124	Dan Dobbek RP	.50	.20	.05
☐ 125	Ron Fairly RP	1.50	.60	.15
☐ 126	Ed Haas RP	.60	.24	.06
☐ 127	Kent Hadley RP	.50	.20	.05
☐ 128	Bob Hartman RP	.50	.20	.05
☐ 129	Frank Herrera RP	.50	.20	.05
☐ 130	Lou Jackson RP	.50	.20	.05
☐ 131	Deron Johnson RP	.60	.24	.06
☐ 132	Don Lee RP	.50	.20	.05
☐ 133	Bob Lillis RP	.75	.30	.07
☐ 134	Jim McDaniel RP	.50	.20	.05
☐ 135	Gene Oliver RP	.50	.20	.05
☐ 136	Jim O'Toole RP	.75	.30	.07
☐ 137	Dick Ricketts RP	.50	.20	.05
☐ 138	John Romano RP	.50	.20	.05
☐ 139	Ed Sadowski RP	.50	.20	.05
☐ 140	Charlie Secrest RP	.50	.20	.05
☐ 141	Joe Shipley RP	.50	.20	.05
☐ 142	Dick Stigman RP	.50	.20	.05
☐ 143	Willie Tasby RP	.50	.20	.05
☐ 144	Jerry Walker RP	.50	.20	.05
☐ 145	Dom Zanni RP	.50	.20	.05
☐ 146	Jerry Zimmerman RP	.50	.20	.05
☐ 147	Cubs Clubbers	2.00	.80	.20
	Dale Long			
	Ernie Banks			
	Walt Moryn			
☐ 148	Mike McCormick	.75	.30	.07
☐ 149	Jim Bunning	2.50	1.00	.25
☐ 150	Stan Musial	30.00	12.00	3.00
☐ 151	Bob Malkmus	.50	.20	.05
☐ 152	John Klippstein	.50	.20	.05
☐ 153	Jim Marshall	.50	.20	.05
☐ 154	Ray Herbert	.50	.20	.05

		MINT	VG-E	F-G
☐ 155	Enos Slaughter	4.00	1.60	.40
☐ 156	Ace Hurlers	1.50	.60	.15
	Billy Pierce			
	Robin Roberts			
☐ 157	Felix Mantilla	.50	.20	.05
☐ 158	Walt Dropo	.50	.20	.05
☐ 159	Bob Shaw	.50	.20	.05
☐ 160	Dick Groat	1.25	.50	.12
☐ 161	Frank Baumann	.50	.20	.05
☐ 162	Bobby G. Smith	.50	.20	.05
☐ 163	Sandy Koufax	22.00	9.00	2.20
☐ 164	Johnny Groth	.50	.20	.05
☐ 165	Bill Bruton	.50	.20	.05
☐ 166	Destruction Crew	1.00	.40	.10
	Minnie Minoso			
	Rocky Colavito			
	Larry Doby			
☐ 167	Duke Maas	.50	.20	.05
☐ 168	Carroll Hardy	.50	.20	.05
☐ 169	Ted Abernathy	.50	.20	.05
☐ 170	Gene Woodling	.75	.30	.07
☐ 171	Willard Schmidt	.50	.20	.05
☐ 172	Athletics Team	2.25	.50	.10
☐ 173	Bill Monbouquette	.50	.20	.05
☐ 174	Jim Pendleton	.50	.20	.05
☐ 175	Dick Farrell	.50	.20	.05
☐ 176	Preston Ward	.50	.20	.05
☐ 177	John Briggs	.50	.20	.05
☐ 178	Ruben Amaro	.50	.20	.05
☐ 179	Don Rudolph	.50	.20	.05
☐ 180	Yogi Berra	11.00	4.50	1.10
☐ 181	Bob Porterfield	.50	.20	.05
☐ 182	Milt Graff	.50	.20	.05
☐ 183	Stu Miller	.50	.20	.05
☐ 184	Harvey Haddix	.75	.30	.07
☐ 185	Jim Busby	.50	.20	.05
☐ 186	Mudcat Grant	.50	.20	.05
☐ 187	Bubba Phillips	.50	.20	.05
☐ 188	Juan Pizarro	.50	.20	.05
☐ 189	Neil Chrisley	.50	.20	.05
☐ 190	Bill Virdon	1.00	.40	.10
☐ 191	Russ Kemmerer	.50	.20	.05
☐ 192	Charlie Beamon	.50	.20	.05
☐ 193	Sammy Taylor	.50	.20	.05
☐ 194	Jim Brosnan	.60	.24	.06
☐ 195	Rip Repulski	.50	.20	.05
☐ 196	Billy Moran	.50	.20	.05
☐ 197	Ray Semproch	.50	.20	.05
☐ 198	Jim Davenport	.60	.24	.06
☐ 199	Leo Kiely	.50	.20	.05
☐ 200	Warren Giles	1.50	.60	.15
	(NL President)			
☐ 201	Tom Acker	.50	.20	.05

		MINT	VG-E	F-G
☐ 202	Roger Maris	9.00	3.75	.90
☐ 203	Ossie Virgil	.50	.20	.05
☐ 204	Casey Wise	.50	.20	.05
☐ 205	Don Larsen	1.75	.70	.17
☐ 206	Carl Furillo	1.75	.70	.17
☐ 207	George Strickland	.50	.20	.05
☐ 208	Willie Jones	.50	.20	.05
☐ 209	Lenny Green	.50	.20	.05
☐ 210	Ed Bailey	.50	.20	.05
☐ 211	Bob Blaylock	.50	.20	.05
☐ 212	Fence Busters	6.00	2.40	.60
	Hank Aaron			
	Eddie Mathews			
☐ 213	Jim Rivera	.50	.20	.05
☐ 214	Marcelino Solis	.50	.20	.05
☐ 215	Jim Lemon	.60	.24	.06
☐ 216	Andre Rodgers	.50	.20	.05
☐ 217	Carl Erskine	1.50	.60	.15
☐ 218	Roman Mejias	.50	.20	.05
☐ 219	George Zuverink	.50	.20	.05
☐ 220	Frank Malzone	.60	.24	.06
☐ 221	Bob Bowman	.50	.20	.05
☐ 222	Bobby Shantz	.75	.30	.07
☐ 223	Cardinals Team	2.25	.50	.10
☐ 224	Claude Osteen	1.00	.40	.10
☐ 225	Johnny Logan	.60	.24	.06
☐ 226	Art Ceccarelli	.50	.20	.05
☐ 227	Hal W. Smith	.50	.20	.05
☐ 228	Don Gross	.50	.20	.05
☐ 229	Vic Power	.50	.20	.05
☐ 230	Bill Fischer	.50	.20	.05
☐ 231	Ellis Burton	.50	.20	.05
☐ 232	Eddie Kasko	.50	.20	.05
☐ 233	Paul Foytack	.50	.20	.05
☐ 234	Chuck Tanner	.75	.30	.07
☐ 235	Valmy Thomas	.50	.20	.05
☐ 236	Ted Bowsfield	.50	.20	.05
☐ 237	Run Preventers	1.25	.50	.12
	Gil McDougald			
	Bob Turley			
	Bobby Richardson			
☐ 238	Gene Baker	.50	.20	.05
☐ 239	Bob Trowbridge	.50	.20	.05
☐ 240	Hank Bauer	1.25	.50	.12
☐ 241	Billy Muffett	.50	.20	.05
☐ 242	Ron Samford	.50	.20	.05
☐ 243	Marv Grissom	.50	.20	.05
☐ 244	Ted Gray	.50	.20	.05
☐ 245	Ned Garver	.50	.20	.05
☐ 246	J.W. Porter	.50	.20	.05
☐ 247	Don Ferrarese	.50	.20	.05
☐ 248	Red Sox Team	2.50	.50	.10
☐ 249	Bobby Adams	.50	.20	.05

		MINT	VG-E	F-G
☐ 250	Billy O'Dell	.50	.20	.05
☐ 251	Cletis Boyer	1.00	.40	.10
☐ 252	Ray Boone	.60	.24	.06
☐ 253	Seth Morehead	.50	.20	.05
☐ 254	Zeke Bella	.50	.20	.05
☐ 255	Del Ennis	.60	.24	.06
☐ 256	Jerry Davie	.50	.20	.05
☐ 257	Leon Wagner	.50	.20	.05
☐ 258	Fred Kipp	.50	.20	.05
☐ 259	Jim Pisoni	.50	.20	.05
☐ 260	Early Wynn	4.00	1.60	.40
☐ 261	Gene Stephens	.50	.20	.05
☐ 262	Hitters' Foes	2.00	.80	.20
	Johnny Podres			
	Clem Labine			
	Don Drysdale			
☐ 263	B. Daley	.50	.20	.05
☐ 264	Chico Carrasquel	.50	.20	.05
☐ 265	Ron Kline	.50	.20	.05
☐ 266	Woody Held	.50	.20	.05
☐ 267	John Romonosky	.50	.20	.05
☐ 268	Tito Francona	.60	.24	.06
☐ 269	Jack Mayer	.50	.20	.05
☐ 270	Gil Hodges	4.50	1.80	.45
☐ 271	Orlando Pena	.50	.20	.05
☐ 272	Jerry Lumpe	.50	.20	.05
☐ 273	Joey Jay	.60	.24	.06
☐ 274	Jerry Kindall	.50	.20	.05
☐ 275	Jack Sanford	.60	.24	.06
☐ 276	Pete Daley	.50	.20	.05
☐ 277	Turk Lown	.50	.20	.05
☐ 278	Chuck Essegian	.50	.20	.05
☐ 279	Ernie Johnson	.50	.20	.05
☐ 280	Frank Bolling	.50	.20	.05
☐ 281	Walt Craddock	.50	.20	.05
☐ 282	R.C. Stevens	.50	.20	.05
☐ 283	Russ Heman	.50	.20	.05
☐ 284	Steve Korcheck	.50	.20	.05
☐ 285	Joe Cunningham	.60	.24	.06
☐ 286	Dean Stone	.50	.20	.05
☐ 287	Don Zimmer	.75	.30	.07
☐ 288	Dutch Dotterer	.50	.20	.05
☐ 289	Johnny Kucks	.60	.24	.06
☐ 290	Wes Covington	.60	.24	.06
☐ 291	Pitching Partners	.60	.24	.06
	Pedro Ramos			
	Camilo Pascual			
☐ 292	Dick Williams	.60	.24	.06
☐ 293	Ray Moore	.50	.20	.05
☐ 294	Hank Foiles	.50	.20	.05
☐ 295	Billy Martin	2.50	1.00	.25
☐ 296	Ernie Broglio	.60	.24	.06
☐ 297	Jackie Brandt	.50	.20	.05

		MINT	VG-E	F-G
☐ 298	Tex Clevenger	.50	.20	.05
☐ 299	Billy Klaus	.50	.20	.05
☐ 300	Richie Ashburn	2.50	1.00	.25
☐ 301	Earl Averill	.50	.20	.05
☐ 302	Don Mossi	.60	.24	.06
☐ 303	Marty Keough	.50	.20	.05
☐ 304	Cubs Team	2.25	.50	.10
☐ 305	Curt Raydon	.50	.20	.05
☐ 306	Jim Gilliam	1.75	.70	.17
☐ 307	Curt Barclay	.50	.20	.05
☐ 308	Norm Siebern	.50	.20	.05
☐ 309	Sal Maglie	1.25	.50	.12
☐ 310	Luis Aparicio	4.00	1.60	.40
☐ 311	Norm Zauchin	.50	.20	.05
☐ 312	Don Newcombe	1.25	.50	.12
☐ 313	Frank House	.50	.20	.05
☐ 314	Don Cardwell	.50	.20	.05
☐ 315	Joe Adcock	1.00	.40	.10
☐ 316 A	Ralph Lumenti (opt.)	.60	.24	.06
	(photo actually			
	Camilo Pascual)			
☐ 316 B	Ralph Lumenti	40.00	16.00	4.00
	(no option)			
	(photo actually			
	Camilo Pascual)			
☐ 317	Hitting Kings	5.00	2.00	.50
	Willie Mays			
	Richie Ashburn			
☐ 318	Rocky Bridges	.50	.20	.05
☐ 319	Dave Hillmann	.50	.20	.05
☐ 320	Bob Skinner	.60	.24	.06
☐ 321 A	Bob Giallombardo	.60	.24	.06
	(option)			
☐ 321 B	Bob Giallombardo	40.00	16.00	4.00
	(no option)			
☐ 322 A	Harry Hanebrink	.60	.24	.06
	(traded)			
☐ 322 B	Harry Hanebrink	40.00	16.00	4.00
	(no trade)			
☐ 323	Frank Sullivan	.50	.20	.05
☐ 324	Don Demeter	.50	.20	.05
☐ 325	Ken Boyer	1.50	.60	.15
☐ 326	Marv Throneberry	1.50	.60	.15
☐ 327	Gary Bell	.50	.20	.05
☐ 328	Lou Skizas	.50	.20	.05
☐ 329	Tigers Team	2.50	.50	.10
☐ 330	Gus Triandos	.60	.24	.06
☐ 331	Steve Boros	.60	.24	.06
☐ 332	Ray Monzant	.50	.20	.05
☐ 333	Harry Simpson	.50	.20	.05
☐ 334	Glen Hobbie	.50	.20	.05
☐ 335	Johnny Temple	.60	.24	.06

	MINT	VG-E	F-G			MINT	VG-E	F-G
☐ 336 A Billy Loes (with traded line)	.60	.24	.06	☐ 381 Mike Baxes		.50	.20	.05
☐ 336 B Billy Loes (no trade)	40.00	16.00	4.00	☐ 382 Curt Simmons		.60	.24	.06
☐ 337 George Crowe	.50	.20	.05	☐ 383 Words of Wisdom Don Larsen Casey Stengel	2.00	.80	.20
☐ 338 Sparky Anderson	3.00	1.20	.30	☐ 384 Dave Sisler	.50	.20	.05
☐ 339 Roy Face	1.00	.40	.10	☐ 385 Sherm Lollar	.60	.24	.06
☐ 340 Roy Sievers	.60	.24	.06	☐ 386 Jim Delsing	.50	.20	.05
☐ 341 Tom Qualters	.50	.20	.05	☐ 387 Don Drysdale	6.50	2.60	.65
☐ 342 Ray Jablonski	.60	.24	.06	☐ 388 Bob Will	.50	.20	.05
☐ 343 Bill Hoeft	.50	.20	.05	☐ 389 Joe Nuxhall	.60	.24	.06
☐ 344 Russ Nixon	.50	.20	.05	☐ 390 Orlando Cepeda	2.25	.90	.22
☐ 345 Gil McDougald	1.50	.60	.15	☐ 391 Milt Pappas	.60	.24	.06
☐ 346 Batter Bafflers Dave Sisler Tom Brewer	.60	.24	.06	☐ 392 Whitey Herzog	1.00	.40	.10
				☐ 393 Frank Lary	.60	.24	.06
				☐ 394 Randy Jackson	.50	.20	.05
☐ 347 Bob Buhl	.50	.20	.05	☐ 395 Elston Howard	2.00	.80	.20
☐ 348 Ted Lepcio	.50	.20	.05	☐ 396 Bob Rush	.50	.20	.05
☐ 349 Hoyt Wilhelm	4.00	1.60	.40	☐ 397 Senators Team	2.25	.50	.10
☐ 350 Ernie Banks	11.00	4.50	1.10	☐ 398 Wally Post	.50	.20	.05
☐ 351 Earl Torgeson	.50	.20	.05	☐ 399 Larry Jackson	.50	.20	.05
☐ 352 Robin Roberts	4.00	1.60	.40	☐ 400 Jackie Jensen	1.00	.40	.10
☐ 353 Curt Flood	1.25	.50	.12	☐ 401 Ron Blackburn	.50	.20	.05
☐ 354 Pete Burnside	.50	.20	.05	☐ 402 Hector Lopez	.50	.20	.05
☐ 355 Jim Piersall	1.25	.50	.12	☐ 403 Clem Labine	.60	.24	.06
☐ 356 Bob Mabe	.50	.20	.05	☐ 404 Hank Sauer	.60	.24	.06
☐ 357 Dick Stuart	1.00	.40	.10	☐ 405 Roy McMillan	.50	.20	.05
☐ 358 Ralph Terry	.75	.30	.07	☐ 406 Solly Drake	.50	.20	.05
☐ 359 Bill White	2.00	.80	.20	☐ 407 Moe Drabowsky	.60	.24	.06
☐ 360 Al Kaline	9.00	3.75	.90	☐ 408 Keystone Combo Nellie Fox Luis Aparicio	2.00	.80	.20
☐ 361 Willard Nixon	.50	.20	.05				
☐ 362 A Dolan Nichols (with option line)	.60	.24	.06	☐ 409 Gus Zernial	.60	.24	.06
☐ 362 B Dolan Nichols (no option)	40.00	16.00	4.00	☐ 410 Billy Pierce	.75	.30	.07
				☐ 411 Whitey Lockman	.60	.24	.06
☐ 363 Bobby Avila	.50	.20	.05	☐ 412 Stan Lopata	.50	.20	.05
☐ 364 Danny McDevitt	.50	.20	.05	☐ 413 Camilo Pascual (listed as Camillo on front)	.60	.24	.06
☐ 365 Gus Bell	.60	.24	.06				
☐ 366 Humberto Robinson	.50	.20	.05				
☐ 367 Cal Neeman	.50	.20	.05	☐ 414 Dale Long	.50	.20	.05
☐ 368 Don Mueller	.60	.24	.06	☐ 415 Bill Mazeroski	1.75	.70	.17
☐ 369 Dick Tomanek	.50	.20	.05	☐ 416 Haywood Sullivan	.60	.24	.06
☐ 370 Pete Runnels	.60	.24	.06	☐ 417 Virgil Trucks	.60	.24	.06
☐ 371 Dick Brodowski	.50	.20	.05	☐ 418 Gino Cimoli	.50	.20	.05
☐ 372 Jim Hegan	.60	.24	.06	☐ 419 Braves Team	2.50	.50	.10
☐ 373 Herb Plews	.50	.20	.05	☐ 420 Rocky Colavito	1.75	.70	.17
☐ 374 Art Ditmar	.60	.24	.06	☐ 421 Herm Wehmeier	.50	.20	.05
☐ 375 Bob Nieman	.50	.20	.05	☐ 422 Hobie Landrith	.50	.20	.05
☐ 376 Hal Naragon	.50	.20	.05	☐ 423 Bob Grim	.60	.24	.06
☐ 377 John Antonelli	.75	.30	.07	☐ 424 Ken Aspromonte	.50	.20	.05
☐ 378 Gail Harris	.50	.20	.05	☐ 425 Del Crandall	.60	.24	.06
☐ 379 Bob Miller	.50	.20	.05	☐ 426 Jerry Staley	.50	.20	.05
☐ 380 Hank Aaron	27.00	11.00	2.70	☐ 427 Charlie Neal	.60	.24	.06

	MINT	VG-E	F-G
☐ 428 Buc Hill Aces	.75	.30	.07
Ron Kline			
Bob Friend			
Vernon Law			
Roy Face			
☐ 429 Bobby Thomson	1.00	.40	.10
☐ 430 Whitey Ford	9.00	3.75	.90
☐ 431 Whammy Douglas	.50	.20	.05
☐ 432 Smoky Burgess	.60	.24	.06
☐ 433 Billy Harrell	.50	.20	.05
☐ 434 Hal Griggs	.50	.20	.05
☐ 435 Frank Robinson	9.00	3.75	.90
☐ 436 Granny Hamner	.50	.20	.05
☐ 437 Ike Delock	.50	.20	.05
☐ 438 Sam Esposito	.50	.20	.05
☐ 439 Brooks Robinson	11.00	4.50	1.10
☐ 440 Lou Burdette	2.25	.90	.22
(posing as if			
lefthanded)			
☐ 441 John Roseboro	.75	.30	.07
☐ 442 Ray Narleski	.50	.20	.05
☐ 443 Daryl Spencer	.50	.20	.05
☐ 444 Ron Hansen	.75	.30	.07
☐ 445 Cal McLish	.50	.20	.05
☐ 446 Rocky Nelson	.50	.20	.05
☐ 447 Bob Anderson	.50	.20	.05
☐ 448 Vada Pinson	1.50	.60	.15
☐ 449 Tom Gorman	.50	.20	.05
☐ 450 Ed Mathews	5.00	2.00	.50
☐ 451 Jimmy Constable	.50	.20	.05
☐ 452 Chico Fernandez	.50	.20	.05
☐ 453 Les Moss	.50	.20	.05
☐ 454 Phil Clark	.50	.20	.05
☐ 455 Larry Doby	1.25	.50	.12
☐ 456 Jerry Casale	.50	.20	.05
☐ 457 Dodgers Team	5.00	1.00	.20
☐ 458 Gordon Jones	.50	.20	.05
☐ 459 Bill Tuttle	.50	.20	.05
☐ 460 Bob Friend	.60	.24	.06
☐ 461 Mantle Hits Homer	7.50	3.00	.75
☐ 462 Colavito's Catch	.90	.36	.09
☐ 463 Kaline Batting Champ	2.00	.80	.20
☐ 464 Mays' Series Catch	5.00	2.00	.50
☐ 465 Sievers Sets Mark	.60	.24	.06
☐ 466 Pierce All-Star	.60	.24	.06
☐ 467 Aaron Clubs Homer	4.00	1.60	.40
☐ 468 Snider's Play	3.00	1.20	.30
☐ 469 Hustler Banks	2.00	.80	.20
☐ 470 Musial's 3000 Hit	3.50	1.40	.35
☐ 471 Tom Sturdivant	.50	.20	.05
☐ 472 Gene Freese	.50	.20	.05
☐ 473 Mike Fornieles	.50	.20	.05
☐ 474 Moe Thacker	.50	.20	.05
☐ 475 Jack Harshman	.50	.20	.05
☐ 476 Indians Team	2.25	.50	.10
☐ 477 Barry Latman	.50	.20	.05
☐ 478 Bob Clemente	15.00	6.00	1.50
☐ 479 Lindy McDaniel	.60	.24	.06
☐ 480 Red Schoendienst	1.25	.50	.12
☐ 481 Charlie Maxwell	.50	.20	.05
☐ 482 Russ Meyer	.50	.20	.05
☐ 483 Clint Courtney	.50	.20	.05
☐ 484 Willie Kirkland	.50	.20	.05
☐ 485 Ryne Duren	.75	.30	.07
☐ 486 Sammy White	.50	.20	.05
☐ 487 Hal Brown	.50	.20	.05
☐ 488 Walt Moryn	.50	.20	.05
☐ 489 John Powers	.50	.20	.05
☐ 490 Frank Thomas	.60	.24	.06
☐ 491 Don Blasingame	.50	.20	.05
☐ 492 Gene Conley	.50	.20	.05
☐ 493 Jim Landis	.50	.20	.05
☐ 494 Don Pavletich	.50	.20	.05
☐ 495 John Podres	1.25	.50	.12
☐ 496 Wayne Terwilliger	.50	.20	.05
☐ 497 Hal R. Smith	.50	.20	.05
☐ 498 Dick Hyde	.50	.20	.05
☐ 499 John O'Brien	.50	.20	.05
☐ 500 Vic Wertz	.60	.24	.06
☐ 501 Bob Tiefenauer	.50	.20	.05
☐ 502 Alvin Dark	.75	.30	.07
☐ 503 Jim Owens	.50	.20	.05
☐ 504 Ossie Alvarez	.50	.20	.05
☐ 505 Tony Kubek	2.00	.80	.20
☐ 506 Bob Purkey	.50	.20	.05
☐ 507 Bob Hale	2.50	1.00	.25
☐ 508 Art Fowler	2.50	1.00	.25
☐ 509 Norm Cash	5.00	2.00	.50
☐ 510 Yankees Team	10.00	2.00	.40
☐ 511 George Susce	2.50	1.00	.25
☐ 512 George Altman	2.50	1.00	.25
☐ 513 Tommy Carroll	2.50	1.00	.25
☐ 514 Bob Gibson	50.00	20.00	5.00
☐ 515 Harmon Killebrew	20.00	8.00	2.00
☐ 516 Mike Garcia	3.00	1.20	.30
☐ 517 Joe Koppe	2.50	1.00	.25
☐ 518 Mike Cueller	3.50	1.40	.35
(sic, *Cuellar*)			
☐ 519 Infield Power	3.00	1.20	.30
Pete Runnels			
Dick Gernert			
Frank Malzone			
☐ 520 Don Elston	2.50	1.00	.25
☐ 521 Gary Geiger	2.50	1.00	.25
☐ 522 Gene Snyder	2.50	1.00	.25
☐ 523 Harry Bright	2.50	1.00	.25

		MINT	VG-E	F-G
☐ 524	Larry Osborne	2.50	1.00	.25
☐ 525	Jim Coates	2.50	1.00	.25
☐ 526	Bob Speake	2.50	1.00	.25
☐ 527	Solly Hemus	2.50	1.00	.25
☐ 528	Pirates Team	5.00	1.00	.20
☐ 529	George Bamberger	4.50	1.80	.45
☐ 530	Wally Moon	3.00	1.00	.25
☐ 531	Ray Webster	2.50	1.00	.25
☐ 532	Mark Freeman	2.50	1.00	.25
☐ 533	Darrell Johnson	2.50	1.00	.25
☐ 534	Faye Throneberry	2.50	1.00	.25
☐ 535	Ruben Gomez	2.50	1.00	.25
☐ 536	Danny Kravitz	2.50	1.00	.25
☐ 537	Rudolph Arias	2.50	1.00	.25
☐ 538	Chick King	2.50	1.00	.25
☐ 539	Gary Blaylock	2.50	1.00	.25
☐ 540	Willie Miranda	2.50	1.00	.25
☐ 541	Bob Thurman	2.50	1.00	.25
☐ 542	Jim Perry	5.00	2.00	.50
☐ 543	Corsair Trio	12.50	5.00	1.25
	Bob Skinner			
	Bill Virdon			
	Roberto Clemente			
☐ 544	Lee Tate	2.50	1.00	.25
☐ 545	Tom Morgan	2.50	1.00	.25
☐ 546	Al Schroll	2.50	1.00	.25
☐ 547	Jim Baxes	2.50	1.00	.25
☐ 548	Elmer Singleton	2.50	1.00	.25
☐ 549	Howie Nunn	2.50	1.00	.25
☐ 550	Roy Campanella	30.00	12.00	3.00
	(Symbol of Courage)			
☐ 551	Fred Haney MGR AS	3.00	1.20	.30
☐ 552	Casey Stengel MGR AS	4.50	1.80	.45
☐ 553	Orlando Cepeda AS	3.00	1.20	.30
☐ 554	Bill Skowron AS	3.00	1.20	.30
☐ 555	Bill Mazeroski AS	3.00	1.20	.30
☐ 556	Nellie Fox AS	3.50	1.40	.35
☐ 557	Ken Boyer AS	3.00	1.20	.30
☐ 558	Frank Malzone AS	3.00	1.20	.30
☐ 559	Ernie Banks AS	9.00	3.75	.90
☐ 560	Luis Aparicio AS	6.00	2.40	.60
☐ 561	Hank Aaron AS	20.00	8.00	2.00
☐ 562	Al Kaline AS	9.00	3.75	.90
☐ 563	Willie Mays AS	20.00	8.00	2.00
☐ 564	Mickey Mantle AS	45.00	18.00	4.50
☐ 565	Wes Covington AS	3.00	1.20	.30
☐ 566	Roy Sievers AS	3.00	1.20	.30
☐ 567	Del Crandall AS	3.00	1.20	.30
☐ 568	Gus Triandos AS	3.00	1.20	.30
☐ 569	Bob Friend AS	3.00	1.20	.30
☐ 570	Bob Turley AS	3.00	1.20	.30
☐ 571	Warren Spahn AS	8.00	3.25	.80
☐ 572	Billy Pierce AS	3.00	1.20	.30

1960 Topps

The cards in this 572-card set measure 2½" by 3½". The 1960 Topps set is the only Topps standard size issue to use a horizontally oriented front. World Series cards appeared for the first time (385 to 391), and there is a Rookie Prospect (RP) series (117-148), the most famous of which is Carl Yastrzemski, and a Sport Magazine All-Star Selection (AS) series (553-572). There are 16 manager cards listed alphabetically from 212 through 227. The coaching staff of each team was also afforded their own card in 16-card subset (455-470). Cards 375 to 440 come with either gray or white backs, and the high series (507-572) were printed on a more limited basis than the rest of the set. The team cards have series checklists on the reverse.

	MINT	VG-E	F-G
Complete Set	800.00	320.00	80.00
Common Player (1-286)	.40	.16	.04
Common Player (287-440)	.50	.20	.05
Common Player (441-506)	.75	.30	.07
Common Player (507-552)	2.25	.90	.22
Common Player (553-572)	2.75	1.10	.27

		MINT	VG-E	F-G
☐ 1	Early Wynn	5.00	1.50	.30
☐ 2	Roman Mejias	.40	.16	.04
☐ 3	Joe Adcock	.80	.32	.08
☐ 4	Bob Purkey	.40	.16	.04
☐ 5	Wally Moon	.50	.20	.05

		MINT	VG-E	F-G
☐ 6	Lou Berberet	.40	.16	.04
☐ 7	Master and Mentor	4.00	1.60	.40
	Willie Mays			
	Bill Rigney			
☐ 8	Bud Daley	.40	.16	.04
☐ 9	Faye Throneberry	.40	.16	.04
☐ 10	Ernie Banks	6.50	2.60	.65
☐ 11	Norm Siebern	.40	.16	.04
☐ 12	Milt Pappas	.50	.20	.05
☐ 13	Wally Post	.40	.16	.04
☐ 14	Jim Grant	.40	.16	.04
☐ 15	Pete Runnels	.50	.20	.05
☐ 16	Ernie Broglio	.50	.20	.05
☐ 17	Johnny Callison	.60	.24	.06
☐ 18	Dodgers Team	3.50	.75	.15
☐ 19	Felix Mantilla	.40	.16	.04
☐ 20	Roy Face	.80	.32	.08
☐ 21	Dutch Dotterer	.40	.16	.04
☐ 22	Rocky Bridges	.40	.16	.04
☐ 23	Eddie Fisher	.40	.16	.04
☐ 24	Dick Gray	.40	.16	.04
☐ 25	Roy Sievers	.50	.20	.05
☐ 26	Wayne Terwilliger	.40	.16	.04
☐ 27	Dick Drott	.40	.16	.04
☐ 28	Brooks Robinson	10.00	4.00	1.00
☐ 29	Clem Labine	.50	.20	.05
☐ 30	Tito Francona	.50	.20	.05
☐ 31	Sammy Esposito	.40	.16	.04
☐ 32	Sophomore Stalwarts	.60	.24	.06
	Jim O'Toole			
	Vada Pinson			
☐ 33	Tom Morgan	.40	.16	.04
☐ 34	George Anderson	1.25	.50	.12
☐ 35	Whitey Ford	6.50	2.60	.65
☐ 36	Russ Nixon	.40	.16	.04
☐ 37	Bill Bruton	.40	.16	.04
☐ 38	Jerry Casale	.40	.16	.04
☐ 39	Earl Averill	.40	.16	.04
☐ 40	Joe Cunningham	.50	.20	.05
☐ 41	Barry Latman	.40	.16	.04
☐ 42	Hobie Landrith	.40	.16	.04
☐ 43	Senators Team	2.00	.40	.08
☐ 44	Bob Locke	.40	.16	.04
☐ 45	Roy McMillan	.40	.16	.04
☐ 46	Jerry Fisher	.40	.16	.04
☐ 47	Don Zimmer	.60	.24	.06
☐ 48	Hal W. Smith	.40	.16	.04
☐ 49	Curt Raydon	.40	.16	.04
☐ 50	Al Kaline	7.00	2.80	.70
☐ 51	Jim Coates	.40	.16	.04
☐ 52	Dave Philley	.40	.16	.04
☐ 53	Jackie Brandt	.40	.16	.04
☐ 54	Mike Fornieles	.40	.16	.04

		MINT	VG-E	F-G
☐ 55	Bill Mazeroski	1.50	.60	.15
☐ 56	Steve Korcheck	.40	.16	.04
☐ 57	Win Savers	.50	.20	.05
	Turk Lown			
	Jerry Staley			
☐ 58	Gino Cimoli	.40	.16	.04
☐ 59	Juan Pizarro	.40	.16	.04
☐ 60	Gus Triandos	.50	.20	.05
☐ 61	Eddie Kasko	.40	.16	.04
☐ 62	Roger Craig	.80	.32	.08
☐ 63	George Strickland	.40	.16	.04
☐ 64	Jack Meyer	.40	.16	.04
☐ 65	Elston Howard	1.75	.70	.17
☐ 66	Bob Trowbridge	.40	.16	.04
☐ 67	Jose Pagan	.40	.16	.04
☐ 68	Dave Hillman	.40	.16	.04
☐ 69	Billy Goodman	.50	.20	.05
☐ 70	Lew Burdette	1.25	.50	.12
☐ 71	Marty Keough	.40	.16	.04
☐ 72	Tigers Team	2.25	.50	.10
☐ 73	Bob Gibson	7.50	3.00	.75
☐ 74	Walt Moryn	.40	.16	.04
☐ 75	Vic Power	.40	.16	.04
☐ 76	Bill Fischer	.40	.16	.04
☐ 77	Hank Foiles	.40	.16	.04
☐ 78	Bob Grim	.40	.16	.04
☐ 79	Walt Dropo	.40	.16	.04
☐ 80	Johnny Antonelli	.60	.24	.06
☐ 81	Russ Snyder	.40	.16	.04
☐ 82	Ruben Gomez	.40	.16	.04
☐ 83	Tony Kubek	1.75	.70	.17
☐ 84	Hal R. Smith	.40	.16	.04
☐ 85	Frank Lary	.50	.20	.05
☐ 86	Dick Gernert	.40	.16	.04
☐ 87	John Romonosky	.40	.16	.04
☐ 88	John Roseboro	.50	.20	.05
☐ 89	Hal Brown	.40	.16	.04
☐ 90	Bobby Avila	.40	.16	.04
☐ 91	Bennie Daniels	.40	.16	.04
☐ 92	Whitey Herzog	1.00	.40	.10
☐ 93	Art Schult	.40	.16	.04
☐ 94	Leo Kiely	.40	.16	.04
☐ 95	Frank Thomas	.50	.20	.05
☐ 96	Ralph Terry	.60	.24	.06
☐ 97	Ted Lepcio	.40	.16	.04
☐ 91	Gordon Jones	.40	.16	.04
☐ 99	Lenny Green	.40	.16	.04
☐ 100	Nellie Fox	1.75	.70	.17
☐ 101	Bob Miller	.40	.16	.04
☐ 102	Kent Hadley	.40	.16	.04
☐ 103	Dick Farrell	.40	.16	.04
☐ 104	Dick Schofield	.40	.16	.04
☐ 105	Larry Sherry	.75	.30	.07

	MINT	VG-E	F-G
☐ 106 Billy Gardner	.50	.20	.05
☐ 107 Carlton Willey	.40	.16	.04
☐ 108 Pete Daley	.40	.16	.04
☐ 109 Clete Boyer	.75	.30	.07
☐ 110 Cal McLish	.40	.16	.04
☐ 111 Vic Wertz	.50	.20	.05
☐ 112 Jack Harshman	.40	.16	.04
☐ 113 Bob Skinner	.50	.20	.05
☐ 114 Ken Aspromonte	.40	.16	.04
☐ 115 Fork and Knuckler	1.50	.60	.15
Roy Face			
Hoyt Wilhelm			
☐ 116 Jim Rivera	.40	.16	.04
☐ 117 Tom Borland RP	.40	.16	.04
☐ 118 Bob Bruce RP	.40	.16	.04
☐ 119 Chico Cardenas RP	.50	.20	.05
☐ 120 Duke Carmel RP	.40	.16	.04
☐ 121 Camilo Carreon RP	.40	.16	.04
☐ 122 Don Dillard RP	.40	.16	.04
☐ 123 Dan Dobbek RP	.40	.16	.04
☐ 124 Jim Donohue RP	.40	.16	.04
☐ 125 Dick Ellsworth RP	.60	.24	.06
☐ 126 Chuck Estrada RP	.75	.30	.07
☐ 127 Ron Hansen RP	.50	.20	.05
☐ 128 Bill Harris RP	.40	.16	.04
☐ 129 Bob Hartman RP	.40	.16	.04
☐ 130 Frank Herrera RP	.40	.16	.04
☐ 131 Ed Hobaugh RP	.40	.16	.04
☐ 132 Frank Howard RP	3.00	1.20	.30
☐ 133 Manuel Javier RP	.50	.20	.05
(sic, *Julian*)			
☐ 134 Deron Johnson RP	.50	.20	.05
☐ 135 Ken Johnson RP	.40	.16	.04
☐ 136 Jim Kaat RP	10.00	4.00	1.00
☐ 137 Lou Klimchock RP	.40	.16	.04
☐ 138 Art Mahaffey RP	.50	.20	.05
☐ 139 Carl Mathias RP	.40	.16	.04
☐ 140 Julio Navarro RP	.40	.16	.04
☐ 141 Jim Proctor RP	.40	.16	.04
☐ 142 Bill Short RP	.40	.16	.04
☐ 143 Al Spangler RP	.40	.16	.04
☐ 144 Al Stieglitz RP	.40	.16	.04
☐ 145 Jim Umbricht RP	.40	.16	.04
☐ 146 Ted Wieand RP	.40	.16	.04
☐ 147 Bob Will RP	.40	.16	.04
☐ 148 Carl Yastrzemski RP	110.00	45.00	11.00
☐ 149 Bob Nieman	.40	.16	.04
☐ 150 Billy Pierce	.75	.30	.07
☐ 151 Giants Team	2.25	.50	.10
☐ 152 Gail Harris	.40	.16	.04
☐ 153 Bobby Thomson	.80	.32	.08
☐ 154 Jim Davenport	.60	.24	.06
☐ 155 Charlie Neal	.50	.20	.05

	MINT	VG-E	F-G
☐ 156 Art Ceccarelli	.40	.16	.04
☐ 157 Rocky Nelson	.40	.16	.04
☐ 158 Wes Covington	.50	.20	.05
☐ 159 Jim Piersall	1.00	.40	.10
☐ 160 Rival All-Stars	7.00	2.80	.70
Mickey Mantle			
Ken Boyer			
☐ 161 Ray Narleski	.40	.16	.04
☐ 162 Sammy Taylor	.40	.16	.04
☐ 163 Hector Lopez	.40	.16	.04
☐ 164 Reds Team	2.25	.50	.10
☐ 165 Jack Sanford	.50	.20	.05
☐ 166 Chuck Essegian	.40	.16	.04
☐ 167 Valmy Thomas	.40	.16	.04
☐ 168 Alex Grammas	.40	.16	.04
☐ 169 Jake Striker	.40	.16	.04
☐ 170 Del Crandall	.50	.20	.05
☐ 171 Johnny Groth	.40	.16	.04
☐ 172 Willie Kirkland	.40	.16	.04
☐ 173 Billy Martin	2.00	.80	.20
☐ 174 Indians Team	2.00	.40	.08
☐ 175 Pete Ramos	.40	.16	.04
☐ 176 Vada Pinson	1.25	.50	.12
☐ 177 Johnny Kucks	.40	.16	.04
☐ 178 Woody Held	.40	.16	.04
☐ 179 Rip Coleman	.40	.16	.04
☐ 180 Harry Simpson	.40	.16	.04
☐ 181 Billy Loes	.40	.16	.04
☐ 182 Glen Hobbie	.40	.16	.04
☐ 183 Eli Grba	.40	.16	.04
☐ 184 Gary Geiger	.40	.16	.04
☐ 185 Jim Owens	.40	.16	.04
☐ 186 Dave Sisler	.40	.16	.04
☐ 187 Jay Hook	.40	.16	.04
☐ 188 Dick Williams	.60	.24	.06
☐ 189 Don McMahon	.40	.16	.04
☐ 190 Gene Woodling	.60	.24	.06
☐ 191 John Klippstein	.40	.16	.04
☐ 192 Danny O'Connell	.40	.16	.04
☐ 193 Dick Hyde	.40	.16	.04
☐ 194 Bobby Gene Smith	.40	.16	.04
☐ 195 Lindy McDaniel	.50	.20	.05
☐ 196 Andy Carey	.50	.20	.05
☐ 197 Ron Kline	.40	.16	.04
☐ 198 Jerry Lynch	.40	.16	.04
☐ 199 Dick Donovan	.40	.16	.04
☐ 200 Willie Mays	27.00	11.00	2.70
☐ 201 Larry Osborne	.40	.16	.04
☐ 202 Fred Kipp	.40	.16	.04
☐ 203 Sammy White	.40	.16	.04
☐ 204 Ryne Duren	.75	.30	.07
☐ 205 John Logan	.50	.20	.05
☐ 206 Claude Osteen	.50	.20	.05

		MINT	VG-E	F-G
☐ 207	Bob Boyd	.40	.16	.04
☐ 208	White Sox Team	2.00	.40	.08
☐ 209	Ron Blackburn	.40	.16	.04
☐ 210	Harmon Killebrew	5.50	2.20	.55
☐ 211	Taylor Phillips	.40	.16	.04
☐ 212	Walt Alston MGR	1.75	.70	.17
☐ 213	Chuck Dressen MGR	.50	.20	.05
☐ 214	Jimmy Dykes MGR	.50	.20	.05
☐ 215	Bob Elliott MGR	.40	.16	.04
☐ 216	Joe Gordon MGR	.50	.20	.05
☐ 217	Charlie Grimm MGR	.50	.20	.05
☐ 218	Solly Hemus MGR	.40	.16	.04
☐ 219	Fred Hutchinson MGR	.60	.24	.06
☐ 220	Billy Jurges MGR	.40	.16	.04
☐ 221	Cookie Lavagetto MGR	.40	.16	.04
☐ 222	Al Lopez MGR	1.50	.60	.15
☐ 223	Danny Murtaugh MGR	.50	.20	.05
☐ 224	Paul Richards MGR	.50	.20	.05
☐ 225	Bill Rigney MGR	.40	.16	.04
☐ 226	Eddie Sawyer MGR	.40	.16	.04
☐ 227	Casey Stengel MGR	4.50	1.80	.45
☐ 228	Ernie Johnson	.40	.16	.04
☐ 229	Joe M. Morgan	.40	.16	.04
☐ 230	Mound Magicians	2.25	.90	.22
	Lou Burdette			
	Warren Spahn			
	Bob Buhl			
☐ 231	Hal Naragon	.40	.16	.04
☐ 232	Jim Busby	.40	.16	.04
☐ 233	Don Elston	.40	.16	.04
☐ 234	Don Demeter	.40	.16	.04
☐ 235	Gus Bell	.50	.20	.05
☐ 236	Dick Ricketts	.40	.16	.04
☐ 237	Elmer Valo	.40	.16	.04
☐ 238	Danny Kravitz	.40	.16	.04
☐ 239	Joe Shipley	.40	.16	.04
☐ 240	Luis Aparicio	3.50	1.40	.35
☐ 241	Albie Pearson	.40	.16	.04
☐ 242	Cardinals Team	2.00	.40	.08
☐ 243	Bubba Phillips	.40	.16	.04
☐ 244	Hal Griggs	.40	.16	.04
☐ 245	Ed Yost	.40	.16	.04
☐ 246	Lee Maye	.40	.16	.04
☐ 247	Gil McDougald	1.50	.60	.15
☐ 248	Del Rice	.40	.16	.04
☐ 249	Earl Wilson	.50	.20	.05
☐ 250	Stan Musial	21.00	8.50	2.10
☐ 251	Bob Malkmus	.40	.16	.04
☐ 252	Ray Herbert	.40	.16	.04
☐ 253	Eddie Bressoud	.40	.16	.04
☐ 254	Arnie Portocarrero	.40	.16	.04
☐ 255	Jim Gilliam	1.50	.60	.15
☐ 256	Dick Brown	.40	.16	.04
☐ 257	Gordy Coleman	.50	.20	.05
☐ 258	Dick Groat	1.75	.70	.17
☐ 259	George Altman	.40	.16	.04
☐ 260	Power Plus	.50	.20	.05
	Rocky Colavito			
	Tito Francona			
☐ 261	Pete Burnside	.40	.16	.04
☐ 262	Hank Bauer	.75	.30	.07
☐ 263	Darrell Johnson	.50	.20	.05
☐ 264	Robin Roberts	3.50	1.40	.35
☐ 265	Rip Repulski	.40	.16	.04
☐ 266	Joe Jay	.40	.16	.04
☐ 267	Jim Marshall	.40	.16	.04
☐ 268	Al Worthington	.40	.16	.04
☐ 269	Gene Green	.40	.16	.04
☐ 270	Bob Turley	1.00	.40	.10
☐ 271	Julio Becquer	.40	.16	.04
☐ 272	Fred Green	.40	.16	.04
☐ 273	Neil Chrisley	.40	.16	.04
☐ 274	Tom Acker	.40	.16	.04
☐ 275	Curt Flood	1.00	.40	.10
☐ 276	Ken McBride	.40	.16	.04
☐ 277	Harry Bright	.40	.16	.04
☐ 278	Stan Williams	.50	.20	.05
☐ 279	Chuck Tanner	.60	.24	.06
☐ 280	Frank Sullivan	.40	.16	.04
☐ 281	Ray Boone	.50	.20	.05
☐ 282	Joe Nuxhall	.50	.20	.05
☐ 283	John Blanchard	.50	.20	.05
☐ 284	Don Gross	.40	.16	.04
☐ 285	Harry Anderson	.40	.16	.04
☐ 286	Ray Semproch	.40	.16	.04
☐ 287	Felipe Alou	.75	.30	.07
☐ 288	Bob Mabe	.50	.20	.05
☐ 289	Willie Jones	.50	.20	.05
☐ 290	Jerry Lumpe	.50	.20	.05
☐ 291	Bob Keegan	.50	.20	.05
☐ 292	Dodger Backstops	.60	.24	.06
	Joe Pignatano			
	John Roseboro			
☐ 293	Gene Conley	.50	.20	.05
☐ 294	Tony Taylor	.50	.20	.05
☐ 295	Gil Hodges	4.00	1.60	.40
☐ 296	Nelson Chittum	.50	.20	.05
☐ 297	Reno Bertoia	.50	.20	.05
☐ 298	George Witt	.50	.20	.05
☐ 299	Earl Torgeson	.50	.20	.05
☐ 300	Hank Aaron	27.00	11.00	2.70
☐ 301	Jerry Davie	.50	.20	.05
☐ 302	Phillies Team	2.00	.40	.08
☐ 303	Billy O'Dell	.50	.20	.05
☐ 304	Joe Ginsberg	.50	.20	.05
☐ 305	Richie Ashburn	2.00	.80	.20

	MINT	VG-E	F-G		MINT	VG-E	F-G
☐ 306 Frank Baumann	.50	.20	.05	☐ 354 Bob Lillis	.60	.24	.06
☐ 307 Gene Oliver	.50	.20	.05.	☐ 355 Bill White	.80	.32	.08
☐ 308 Dick Hall	.50	.20	.05	☐ 356 Joe Amalfitano	.50	.20	.05
☐ 309 Bob Hale	.50	.20	.05	☐ 357 Al Schroll	.50	.20	.05
☐ 310 Frank Malzone	.60	.24	.06	☐ 358 Joe DeMaestri	.50	.20	.05
☐ 311 Raul Sanchez	.50	.20	.05	☐ 359 Buddy Gilbert	.50	.20	.05
☐ 312 Charley Lau	.60	.24	.06	☐ 360 Herb Score	.80	.32	.08
☐ 313 Turk Lown	.50	.20	.05	☐ 361 Bob Oldis	.50	.20	.05
☐ 314 Chico Fernandez	.50	.20	.05	☐ 362 Russ Kemmerer	.50	.20	.05
☐ 315 Bobby Shantz	.80	.32	.08	☐ 363 Gene Stephens	.50	.20	.05
☐ 316 Willie McCovey	45.00	18.00	4.50	☐ 364 Paul Foytack	.50	.20	.05
☐ 317 Pumpsie Green	.50	.20	.05	☐ 365 Minnie Minoso	1.25	.50	.12
☐ 318 Jim Baxes	.50	.20	.05	☐ 366 Dallas Green	1.50	.60	.15
☐ 319 Joe Koppe	.50	.20	.05	☐ 367 Bill Tuttle	.50	.20	.05
☐ 320 Bob Allison	.75	.30	.07	☐ 368 Daryl Spencer	.50	.20	.05
☐ 321 Ron Fairly	.60	.24	.06	☐ 369 Billy Hoeft	.50	.20	.05
☐ 322 Willie Tasby	.50	.20	.05	☐ 370 Bill Skowron	1.50	.60	.15
☐ 323 John Romano	.50	.20	.05	☐ 371 Bud Byerly	.50	.20	.05
☐ 324 Jim Perry	.80	.32	.08	☐ 372 Frank House	.50	.20	.05
☐ 325 Jim O'Toole	.60	.24	.06	☐ 373 Don Hoak	.50	.20	.05
☐ 326 Bob Clemente	16.00	6.50	1.60	☐ 374 Bob Buhl	.50	.20	.05
☐ 327 Ray Sadecki	.50	.20	.05	☐ 375 Dale Long	.50	.20	.05
☐ 328 Earl Battey	.60	.24	.06	☐ 376 John Briggs	.50	.20	.05
☐ 329 Zack Monroe	.50	.20	.05	☐ 377 Roger Maris	16.00	6.50	1.60
☐ 330 Harvey Kuenn	1.25	.50	.12	☐ 378 Stu Miller	.50	.20	.05
☐ 331 Henry Mason	.50	.20	.05	☐ 379 Red Wilson	.50	.20	.05
☐ 332 Yankees Team	6.50	1.00	.20	☐ 380 Bob Shaw	.50	.20	.05
☐ 333 Danny McDevitt	.50	.20	.05	☐ 381 Braves Team	2.00	.40	.08
☐ 334 Ted Abernathy	.50	.20	.05	☐ 382 Ted Bowsfield	.50	.20	.05
☐ 335 Red Schoendienst	1.00	.40	.10	☐ 383 Leon Wagner	.50	.20	.05
☐ 336 Ike Delock	.50	.20	.05	☐ 384 Don Cardwell	.50	.20	.05
☐ 337 Cal Neeman	.50	.20	.05	☐ 385 World Series Game 1	1.50	.60	.15
☐ 338 Ray Monzant	.50	.20	.05	Neal Steals Second			
☐ 339 Harry Chiti	.50	.20	.05	☐ 386 World Series Game 2	1.50	.60	.15
☐ 340 Harvey Haddix	.75	.30	.07	Neal Belts 2nd Homer			
☐ 341 Carroll Hardy	.50	.20	.05	☐ 387 World Series Game 3	1.50	.60	.15
☐ 342 Casey Wise	.50	.20	.05	Furillo Breaks Game			
☐ 343 Sandy Koufax	15.00	6.00	1.50	☐ 388 World Series Game 4	2.00	.80	.20
☐ 344 Clint Courtney	.50	.20	.05	Hodges' Homer			
☐ 345 Don Newcombe	.80	.32	.08	☐ 389 World Series Game 5	2.00	.80	.20
☐ 346 J.C. Martin	.60	.24	.06	Luis Swipes Base			
(face actually				☐ 390 World Series Game 6	1.50	.60	.15
Gary Peters)				Scrambling After Ball			
☐ 347 Ed Bouchee	.50	.20	.05	☐ 391 World Series Summary	1.50	.60	.15
☐ 348 Barry Shetrone	.50	.20	.05	The Champs Celebrate			
☐ 349 Moe Drabowsky	.50	.20	.05	☐ 392 Tex Clevenger	.50	.20	.05
☐ 350 Mickey Mantle	75.00	30.00	7.50	☐ 393 Smoky Burgess	.60	.24	.06
☐ 351 Don Nottebart	.50	.20	.05	☐ 394 Norm Larker	.50	.20	.05
☐ 352 Cincy Clouters	1.75	.70	.17	☐ 395 Hoyt Wilhelm	3.50	1.40	.35
Gus Bell				☐ 396 Steve Bilko	.50	.20	.05
Frank Robinson				☐ 397 Don Blasingame	.50	.20	.05
Jerry Lynch				☐ 398 Mike Cuellar	.60	.24	.06
☐ 353 Don Larsen	.80	.32	.08				

		MINT	VG-E	F-G
☐ 399	Young Hill Stars	.60	.24	.06
	Milt Pappas			
	Jack Fisher			
	Jerry Walker			
☐ 400	Rocky Colavito	1.25	.50	.12
☐ 401	Bob Duliba	.50	.20	.05
☐ 402	Dick Stuart	.60	.24	.06
☐ 403	Ed Sadowski	.50	.20	.05
☐ 404	Bob Rush	.50	.20	.05
☐ 405	Bobby Richardson	1.75	.70	.17
☐ 406	Billy Klaus	.50	.20	.05
☐ 407	Gary Peters	.80	.32	.08
	(face actually			
	J.C. Martin)			
☐ 408	Carl Furillo	1.50	.60	.15
☐ 409	Ron Samford	.50	.20	.05
☐ 410	Sam Jones	.60	.24	.06
☐ 411	Ed Bailey	.50	.20	.05
☐ 412	Bob Anderson	.50	.20	.05
☐ 413	Athletics Team	2.00	.00	.00
☐ 414	Don Williams	.50	.20	.05
☐ 415	Bob Cerv	.60	.24	.06
☐ 416	Humberto Robinson	.50	.20	.05
☐ 417	Chuck Cottier	.75	.30	.07
☐ 418	Don Mossi	.60	.24	.06
☐ 419	George Crowe	.50	.20	.05
☐ 420	Ed Mathews	4.50	1.80	.45
☐ 421	Duke Maas	.50	.20	.05
☐ 422	John Powers	.50	.20	.05
☐ 423	Ed Fitzgerald	.50	.20	.05
☐ 424	Pete Whisenant	.50	.20	.05
☐ 425	John Podres	1.25	.50	.12
☐ 426	Ron Jackson	.50	.20	.05
☐ 427	Al Grunwald	.50	.20	.05
☐ 428	Al Smith	.50	.20	.05
☐ 429	AL Kings	1.25	.50	.12
	Nellie Fox			
	Harvey Kuenn			
☐ 430	Art Ditmar	.60	.24	.06
☐ 431	Andre Rodgers	.50	.20	.05
☐ 432	Chuck Stobbs	.50	.20	.05
☐ 433	Irv Noren	.50	.20	.05
☐ 434	Brooks Lawrence	.50	.20	.05
☐ 435	Gene Freese	.50	.20	.05
☐ 436	Marv Throneberry	1.25	.50	.12
☐ 437	Bob Friend	.60	.24	.06
☐ 438	Jim Coker	.50	.20	.05
☐ 439	Tom Brewer	.50	.20	.05
☐ 440	Jim Lemon	.60	.24	.06
☐ 441	Gary Bell	.75	.30	.07
☐ 442	Joe Pignatano	.75	.30	.07
☐ 443	Charley Maxwell	.75	.30	.07
☐ 444	Jerry Kindall	.75	.30	.07

		MINT	VG-E	F-G
☐ 445	Warren Spahn	7.00	2.80	.70
☐ 446	Ellis Burton	.75	.30	.07
☐ 447	Ray Moore	.75	.30	.07
☐ 448	Jim Gentile	1.00	.40	.10
☐ 449	Jim Brosnan	.90	.36	.09
☐ 450	Orlando Cepeda	2.25	.90	.22
☐ 451	Curt Simmons	1.00	.40	.10
☐ 452	Ray Webster	.75	.30	.07
☐ 453	Vern Law	1.25	.50	.12
☐ 454	Hal Woodeshick	.75	.30	.07
☐ 455	Baltimore Coaches	1.00	.40	.10
	Eddie Robinson			
	Harry Brecheen			
	Luman Harris			
☐ 456	Red Sox Coaches	1.25	.50	.12
	Rudy York			
	Billy Herman			
	Sal Maglie			
	Del Baker			
☐ 457	Cubs Coaches	1.00	.40	.10
	Charlie Root			
	Lou Klein			
	Elvin Tappe			
☐ 458	White Sox Coaches	1.00	.40	.10
	Johnny Cooney			
	Don Gutteridge			
	Tony Cuccinello			
	Ray Berres			
☐ 459	Reds Coaches	1.00	.40	.10
	Reggie Otero			
	Cot Deal			
	Wally Moses			
☐ 460	Indians Coaches	1.25	.50	.12
	Mel Harder			
	Jo-Jo White			
	Bob Lemon			
	Ralph (Red) Kress			
☐ 461	Tigers Coaches	1.25	.50	.12
	Tom Ferrick			
	Luke Appling			
	Billy Hitchcock			
☐ 462	Athletics Coaches	1.00	.40	.10
	Fred Fitzsimmons			
	Don Heffner			
	Walker Cooper			
☐ 463	Dodgers Coaches	1.25	.50	.12
	Bobby Bragan			
	Pete Reiser			
	Joe Becker			
	Greg Mulleavy			

	MINT	VG-E	F-G
☐ 464 Braves Coaches	1.00	.40	.10
Bob Scheffing			
Whitlow Wyatt			
Andy Pafko			
George Myatt			
☐ 465 Yankees Coaches	2.50	1.00	.25
Bill Dickey			
Ralph Houk			
Frank Crosetti			
Ed Lopat			
☐ 466 Phillies Coaches	1.00	.40	.10
Ken Silvestri			
Dick Carter			
Andy Cohen			
☐ 467 Pirates Coaches	1.00	.40	.10
Mickey Vernon			
Frank Oceak			
Sam Narron			
Bill Burwell			
☐ 468 Cardinals Coaches	1.00	.40	.10
Johnny Keane			
Howie Pollet			
Ray Katt			
Harry Walker			
☐ 469 Giants Coaches	1.00	.40	.10
Wes Westrum			
Salty Parker			
Bill Posedel			
☐ 470 Senators Coaches	1.00	.40	.10
Bob Swift			
Ellis Clary			
Sam Mele			
☐ 471 Ned Garver	.75	.30	.07
☐ 472 Al Dark	1.00	.40	.10
☐ 473 Al Cicotte	.75	.30	.07
☐ 474 Haywood Sullivan	.90	.36	.09
☐ 475 Don Drysdale	6.50	2.60	.65
☐ 476 Lou Johnson	.75	.30	.07
☐ 477 Don Ferrarese	.75	.30	.07
☐ 478 Frank Torre	.75	.30	.07
☐ 479 Georges Maranda	.75	.30	.07
☐ 480 Yogi Berra	11.00	4.50	1.10
☐ 481 Wes Stock	.90	.36	.09
☐ 482 Frank Bolling	.75	.30	.07
☐ 483 Camilo Pascual	1.00	.40	.10
☐ 484 Pirates Team	5.00	1.00	.20
☐ 485 Ken Boyer	1.75	.70	.17
☐ 486 Bobby Del Greco	.75	.30	.07
☐ 487 Tom Sturdivant	.75	.30	.07
☐ 488 Norm Cash	2.00	.80	.20
☐ 489 Steve Ridzik	.75	.30	.07
☐ 490 Frank Robinson	8.50	3.50	.85
☐ 491 Mel Roach	.75	.30	.07

	MINT	VG-E	F-G
☐ 492 Larry Jackson	.75	.30	.07
☐ 493 Duke Snider	11.00	4.50	1.10
☐ 494 Orioles Team	3.00	.60	.10
☐ 495 Sherm Lollar	.90	.36	.09
☐ 496 Bill Virdon	1.25	.50	.12
☐ 497 John Tsitouris	.75	.30	.07
☐ 498 Al Pilarcik	.75	.30	.07
☐ 499 Johnny James	.75	.30	.07
☐ 500 Johnny Temple	.90	.36	.09
☐ 501 Bob Schmidt	.75	.30	.07
☐ 502 Jim Bunning	2.50	1.00	.25
☐ 503 Don Lee	.75	.30	.07
☐ 504 Seth Morehead	.75	.30	.07
☐ 505 Ted Kluszewski	1.50	.60	.15
☐ 506 Lee Walls	.75	.30	.07
☐ 507 Dick Stigman	2.25	.90	.22
☐ 508 Bill Consolo	2.25	.90	.22
☐ 509 Tommy Davis	5.00	2.00	.50
☐ 510 Jerry Staley	2.25	.90	.22
☐ 511 Ken Walters	2.25	.90	.22
☐ 512 Joe Gibbon	2.25	.90	.22
☐ 513 Cubs Team	5.00	1.00	.20
☐ 514 Steve Barber	2.50	1.00	.25
☐ 515 Stan Lopata	2.25	.90	.22
☐ 516 Marty Kutyna	2.25	.90	.22
☐ 517 Charlie James	2.25	.90	.22
☐ 518 Tony Gonzales	2.25	.90	.22
☐ 519 Ed Roebuck	2.25	.90	.22
☐ 520 Don Buddin	2.25	.90	.22
☐ 521 Mike Lee	2.25	.90	.22
☐ 522 Ken Hunt	2.25	.90	.22
☐ 523 Clay Dalrymple	2.25	.90	.22
☐ 524 Bill Henry	2.25	.90	.22
☐ 525 Marv Breeding	2.25	.90	.22
☐ 526 Paul Giel	2.25	.90	.22
☐ 527 Jose Valdivielso	2.25	.90	.22
☐ 528 Ben Johnson	2.25	.90	.22
☐ 529 Norm Sherry	2.50	1.00	.25
☐ 530 Mike McCormick	2.50	1.00	.25
☐ 531 Sandy Amoros	2.50	1.00	.25
☐ 532 Mike Garcia	2.50	1.00	.25
☐ 533 Lou Clinton	2.25	.90	.22
☐ 534 Ken Mackenzie	2.25	.90	.22
☐ 535 Whitey Lockman	2.50	1.00	.25
☐ 536 Wynn Hawkins	2.25	.90	.22
☐ 537 Red Sox Team	5.00	1.00	.20
☐ 538 Frank Barnes	2.25	.90	.22
☐ 539 Gene Baker	2.25	.90	.22
☐ 540 Jerry Walker	2.25	.90	.22
☐ 541 Tony Curry	2.25	.90	.22
☐ 542 Ken Hamlin	2.25	.90	.22
☐ 543 Elio Chacon	2.25	.90	.22
☐ 544 Bill Monbouquette	2.25	.90	.22

		MINT	VG-E	F-G
☐ 545	Carl Sawatski	2.25	.90	.22
☐ 546	Hank Aguirre	2.25	.90	.22
☐ 547	Bob Aspromonte	2.25	.90	.22
☐ 548	Don Mincher	3.00	1.20	.30
☐ 549	John Buzhardt	2.25	.90	.22
☐ 550	Jim Landis	2.25	.90	.22
☐ 551	Ed Rakow	2.25	.90	.22
☐ 552	Walt Bond	2.25	.90	.22
☐ 553	Bill Skowron AS	2.75	1.10	.27
☐ 554	Willie McCovey AS	11.00	4.50	1.10
☐ 555	Nellie Fox AS	3.00	1.20	.30
☐ 556	Charlie Neal AS	2.75	1.10	.27
☐ 557	Frank Malzone AS	2.75	1.10	.27
☐ 558	Eddie Mathews AS	7.00	2.80	.70
☐ 559	Luis Aparicio AS	6.00	2.40	.60
☐ 560	Ernie Banks AS	9.00	3.75	.90
☐ 561	Al Kaline AS	9.00	3.75	.90
☐ 562	Joe Cunningham AS	2.75	1.10	.27
☐ 563	Mickey Mantle AS	45.00	18.00	4.50
☐ 564	Willie Mays AS	20.00	8.00	2.00
☐ 565	Roger Maris AS	9.00	3.75	.90
☐ 566	Hank Aaron AS	20.00	8.00	2.00
☐ 567	Sherm Lollar AS	2.75	1.10	.27
☐ 568	Del Crandall AS	2.75	1.10	.27
☐ 569	Camilo Pascual AS	2.75	1.10	.27
☐ 570	Don Drysdale AS	7.00	2.80	.70
☐ 571	Billy Pierce AS	2.75	1.10	.27
☐ 572	Johnny Antonelli AS	3.00	1.20	.30

1961 Topps

*The cards in this 587-card set measure 2½"
by 3½". In 1961, Topps returned to the vertical obverse format. Introduced for the first
time were "League Leaders" (41 to 50) and
separate, numbered checklist cards. Two*

*number 463's exist: the Braves team card
carrying that number was meant to be number 426. There are three versions of the second series checklist card #98; the variations
are distinguished by the color of the
"CHECKLIST" headline on the front of the
card, the color of the printing of the card number on the bottom of the reverse, and the
presence of the copyright notice running ver-
tically on the card back. There are two
groups of managers (131-139 and 219-226)
as well as separate series of World Series
cards (306-313), Baseball Thrills (401 to
410), previous MVP's (AL 471-478 and NL
479-486) and Sporting News All-Stars (566
to 589). The usual last series scarcity (523 to
589) exists. The set actually totals 587 cards
since numbers 587 and 588 were never
issued.*

	MINT	VG-E	F-G
Complete Set	1400.00	600.00	150.00
Common Player (1-370)	.35	.14	.03
Common Player (371-522)	.50	.20	.05
Common Player (523-565)	7.00	2.80	.70
Common Player (566-589)	8.00	3.25	.80

		MINT	VG-E	F-G
☐ 1	Dick Groat	3.00	.50	.10
☐ 2	Roger Maris	16.00	6.50	1.60
☐ 3	John Buzhardt	.35	.14	.03
☐ 4	Lenny Green	.35	.14	.03
☐ 5	John Romano	.35	.14	.03
☐ 6	Ed Roebuck	.35	.14	.03
☐ 7	White Sox Team	1.00	.40	.10
☐ 8	Dick Williams	.50	.20	.05
☐ 9	Bob Purkey	.35	.14	.03
☐ 10	Brooks Robinson	7.50	3.00	.75
☐ 11	Curt Simmons	.50	.20	.05
☐ 12	Moe Thacker	.35	.14	.03
☐ 13	Chuck Cottier	.50	.20	.05
☐ 14	Don Mossi	.50	.20	.05
☐ 15	Willie Kirkland	.35	.14	.03
☐ 16	Billy Muffett	.35	.14	.03
☐ 17	Checklist 1	3.00	.30	.06
☐ 18	Jim Grant	.35	.14	.03
☐ 19	Cletis Boyer	.75	.30	.07
☐ 20	Robin Roberts	3.50	1.40	.35
☐ 21	Zorro Versalles	.50	.20	.05

		MINT	VG-E	F-G
☐ 22	Clem Labine	.50	.20	.05
☐ 23	Don Demeter	.35	.14	.03
☐ 24	Ken Johnson	.35	.14	.03
☐ 25	Reds' Heavy Artillery	1.50	.60	.15
	Vada Pinson			
	Gus Bell			
	Frank Robinson			
☐ 26	Wes Stock	.35	.14	.03
☐ 27	Jerry Kindall	.35	.14	.03
☐ 28	Hector Lopez	.35	.14	.03
☐ 29	Don Nottebart	.35	.14	.03
☐ 30	Nellie Fox	1.75	.70	.17
☐ 31	Bob Schmidt	.35	.14	.03
☐ 32	Ray Sadecki	.35	.14	.03
☐ 33	Gary Geiger	.35	.14	.03
☐ 34	Wynn Hawkins	.35	.14	.03
☐ 35	Ron Santo	2.50	1.00	.25
☐ 36	Jack Kralick	.35	.14	.03
☐ 37	Charley Maxwell	.35	.14	.03
☐ 38	Bob Lillis	.50	.20	.05
☐ 39	Leo Posada	.35	.14	.03
☐ 40	Bob Turley	.75	.30	.07
☐ 41	NL Batting Leaders	1.50	.60	.15
	Dick Groat			
	Norm Larker			
	Willie Mays			
	Roberto Clemente			
☐ 42	AL Batting Leaders	1.00	.40	.10
	Pete Runnels			
	Al Smith			
	Minnie Minoso			
	Bill Skowron			
☐ 43	NL Home Run Leaders	2.00	.80	.20
	Ernie Banks			
	Hank Aaron			
	Ed Mathews			
	Ken Boyer			
☐ 44	AL Home Run Leaders	3.00	1.20	.30
	Mickey Mantle			
	Roger Maris			
	Jim Lemon			
	Rocky Colavito			
☐ 45	NL ERA Leaders	1.00	.40	.10
	Mike McCormick			
	Ernie Broglio			
	Don Drysdale			
	Bob Friend			
	Stan Williams			
☐ 46	AL ERA Leaders	1.00	.40	.10
	Frank Baumann			
	Jim Bunning			
	Art Ditmar			
	H. Brown			

		MINT	VG-E	F-G
☐ 47	NL Pitching Leaders	1.00	.40	.10
	Ernie Broglio			
	Warren Spahn			
	Vern Law			
	Lou Burdette			
☐ 48	AL Pitching Leaders	1.00	.40	.10
	Chuck Estrada			
	Jim Perry			
	Bud Daley			
	Art Ditmar			
	Frank Lary			
	Milt Pappas			
☐ 49	NL Strikeout Leaders	1.50	.60	.15
	Don Drysdale			
	Sandy Koufax			
	Sam Jones			
	Ernie Broglio			
☐ 50	AL Strikeout Leaders	1.00	.40	.10
	Jim Bunning			
	Pedro Ramos			
	Early Wynn			
	Frank Lary			
☐ 51	Tigers Team	1.00	.40	.10
☐ 52	George Crowe	.35	.14	.03
☐ 53	Russ Nixon	.35	.14	.03
☐ 54	Earl Francis	.35	.14	.03
☐ 55	Jim Davenport	.50	.20	.05
☐ 56	Russ Kemmerer	.35	.14	.03
☐ 57	Marv Throneberry	1.00	.40	.10
☐ 58	Joe Schaffernoth	.35	.14	.03
☐ 59	Jim Woods	.35	.14	.03
☐ 60	Woodie Held	.35	.14	.03
☐ 61	Ron Piche	.35	.14	.03
☐ 62	Al Pilarcik	.35	.14	.03
☐ 63	Jim Kaat	2.50	1.00	.25
☐ 64	Alex Grammas	.35	.14	.03
☐ 65	Ted Kluszewski	1.25	.50	.12
☐ 66	Billy Henry	.35	.14	.03
☐ 67	Ossie Virgil	.35	.14	.03
☐ 68	Deron Johnson	.35	.14	.03
☐ 69	Earl Wilson	.35	.14	.03
☐ 70	Bill Virdon	.75	.30	.07
☐ 71	Jerry Adair	.35	.14	.03
☐ 72	Stu Miller	.35	.14	.03
☐ 73	Al Spangler	.35	.14	.03
☐ 74	Joe Pignatano	.35	.14	.03
☐ 75	Lindy Shows Larry	.50	.20	.05
	Lindy McDaniel			
	Larry Jackson			
☐ 76	Harry Anderson	.35	.14	.03
☐ 77	Dick Stigman	.35	.14	.03
☐ 78	Lee Walls	.35	.14	.03
☐ 79	Joe Ginsberg	.35	.14	.03

		MINT	VG-E	F-G
☐ 80	Harmon Killebrew	4.50	1.80	.45
☐ 81	Tracy Stallard	.35	.14	.03
☐ 82	Joe Christopher	.35	.14	.03
☐ 83	Bob Bruce	.35	.14	.03
☐ 84	Lee Maye	.35	.14	.03
☐ 85	Jerry Walker	.35	.14	.03
☐ 86	Dodgers Team	1.50	.60	.15
☐ 87	Joe Amalfitano	.35	.14	.03
☐ 88	Richie Ashburn	1.75	.70	.17
☐ 89	Billy Martin	2.00	.80	.20
☐ 90	Jerry Staley	.35	.14	.03
☐ 91	Walt Moryn	.35	.14	.03
☐ 92	Hal Naragon	.35	.14	.03
☐ 93	Tony Gonzalez	.35	.14	.03
☐ 94	John Kucks	.35	.14	.03
☐ 95	Norm Cash	1.25	.50	.12
☐ 96	Bill O'Dell	.35	.14	.03
☐ 97	Jerry Lynch	.35	.14	.03
☐ 98 A	Checklist 2 (red "Checklist," 98 black on white)	3.00	.30	.06
☐ 98 B	Checklist 2 (yellow "Checklist," 98 black on white)	3.00	.30	.06
☐ 98 C	Checklist 2 (yellow "Checklist," 98 white on black, no copyright)	3.00	.30	.06
☐ 99	Don Buddin	.35	.14	.03
☐ 100	Harvey Haddix	.60	.24	.06
☐ 101	Bubba Phillips	.35	.14	.03
☐ 102	Gene Stephens	.35	.14	.03
☐ 103	Ruben Amaro	.35	.14	.03
☐ 104	John Blanchard	.50	.20	.05
☐ 105	Carl Willey	.35	.14	.03
☐ 106	Whitey Herzog	1.00	.40	.10
☐ 107	Seth Morehead	.35	.14	.03
☐ 108	Dan Dobbek	.35	.14	.03
☐ 109	John Podres	1.25	.50	.12
☐ 110	Vada Pinson	1.25	.50	.12
☐ 111	Jack Meyer	.35	.14	.03
☐ 112	Chico Fernandez	.35	.14	.03
☐ 113	Mike Fornieles	.35	.14	.03
☐ 114	Hobie Landrith	.35	.14	.03
☐ 115	Johnny Antonelli	.50	.20	.05
☐ 116	Joe DeMaestri	.35	.14	.03
☐ 117	Dale Long	.35	.14	.03
☐ 118	Chris Cannizzaro	.35	.14	.03
☐ 119	A's Big Armor Norm Siebern Hank Bauer Jerry Lumpe	.50	.20	.05
☐ 120	Ed Mathews	4.00	1.60	.40

		MINT	VG-E	F-G
☐ 121	Eli Grba	.35	.14	.03
☐ 122	Cubs Team	1.00	.40	.10
☐ 123	Billy Gardner	.50	.20	.05
☐ 124	J.C. Martin	.35	.14	.03
☐ 125	Steve Barber	.35	.14	.03
☐ 126	Dick Stuart	.50	.20	.05
☐ 127	Ron Kline	.35	.14	.03
☐ 128	Rip Repulski	.35	.14	.03
☐ 129	Ed Hobaugh	.35	.14	.03
☐ 130	Norm Larker	.35	.14	.03
☐ 131	Paul Richards MGR	.50	.20	.05
☐ 132	Al Lopez MGR	1.25	.50	.12
☐ 133	Ralph Houk MGR	.75	.30	.07
☐ 134	Mickey Vernon MGR	.50	.20	.05
☐ 135	Fred Hutchinson MGR	.50	.20	.05
☐ 136	Walt Alston MGR	1.50	.60	.15
☐ 137	Chuck Dressen MGR	.50	.20	.05
☐ 138	Danny Murtaugh MGR	.50	.20	.05
☐ 139	Solly Hemus MGR	.35	.14	.03
☐ 140	Gus Triandos	.50	.20	.05
☐ 141	Billy Williams	18.00	7.25	1.80
☐ 142	Luis Arroyo	.50	.20	.05
☐ 143	Russ Snyder	.35	.14	.03
☐ 144	Jim Coker	.35	.14	.03
☐ 145	Bob Buhl	.35	.14	.03
☐ 146	Marty Keough	.35	.14	.03
☐ 147	Ed Rakow	.35	.14	.03
☐ 148	Julian Javier	.35	.14	.03
☐ 149	Bob Oldis	.35	.14	.03
☐ 150	Willie Mays	25.00	10.00	2.50
☐ 151	Jim Donohue	.35	.14	.03
☐ 152	Earl Torgeson	.35	.14	.03
☐ 153	Don Lee	.35	.14	.03
☐ 154	Bobby Del Greco	.35	.14	.03
☐ 155	John Temple	.35	.14	.03
☐ 156	Ken Hunt	.35	.14	.03
☐ 157	Cal McLish	.35	.14	.03
☐ 158	Pete Daley	.35	.14	.03
☐ 159	Orioles Team	1.00	.40	.10
☐ 160	Whitey Ford	8.00	3.25	.80
☐ 161	Sherman Jones (photo actually Eddie Fisher)	.50	.20	.05
☐ 162	Jay Hook	.35	.14	.03
☐ 163	Ed Sadowski	.35	.14	.03
☐ 164	Felix Mantilla	.35	.14	.03
☐ 165	Gino Cimoli	.35	.14	.03
☐ 166	Danny Kravitz	.35	.14	.03
☐ 167	Giants Team	1.00	.40	.10
☐ 168	Tommy Davis	1.25	.50	.12
☐ 169	Don Elston	.35	.14	.03
☐ 170	Al Smith	.35	.14	.03
☐ 171	Paul Foytack	.35	.14	.03

	MINT	VG-E	F-G			MINT	VG-E	F-G
☐ 172 Don Dillard	.35	.14	.03	☐ 220 Al Dark MGR		.50	.20	.05
☐ 173 Beantown Bombers	.50	.20	.05	☐ 221 Mike Higgins MGR		.35	.14	.03
Frank Malzone				☐ 222 Jimmie Dykes MGR		.35	.14	.03
Vic Wertz				☐ 223 Bob Scheffing MGR		.35	.14	.03
Jackie Jensen				☐ 224 Joe Gordon MGR		.35	.14	.03
☐ 174 Ray Semproch	.35	.14	.03	☐ 225 Bill Rigney MGR		.35	.14	.03
☐ 175 Gene Freese	.35	.14	.03	☐ 226 Harry Lavagetto MGR		.35	.14	.03
☐ 176 Ken Aspromonte	.35	.14	.03	☐ 227 Juan Pizarro		.35	.14	.03
☐ 177 Don Larsen	.50	.20	.05	☐ 228 Yankees Team		5.00	2.00	.50
☐ 178 Bob Nieman	.35	.14	.03	☐ 229 Rudy Hernandez		.35	.14	.03
☐ 179 Joe Koppe	.35	.14	.03	☐ 230 Don Hoak		.35	.14	.03
☐ 180 Bobby Richardson	1.75	.70	.17	☐ 231 Dick Drott		.35	.14	.03
☐ 181 Fred Green	.35	.14	.03	☐ 232 Bill White		.60	.24	.06
☐ 182 Dave Nicholson	.35	.14	.03	☐ 233 Joe Jay		.35	.14	.03
☐ 183 Andre Rodgers	.35	.14	.03	☐ 234 Ted Lepcio		.35	.14	.03
☐ 184 Steve Bilko	.35	.14	.03	☐ 235 Camilo Pascual		.50	.20	.05
☐ 185 Herb Score	.60	.24	.06	☐ 236 Don Gile		.35	.14	.03
☐ 186 Elmer Valo	.35	.14	.03	☐ 237 Billy Loes		.35	.14	.03
☐ 187 Billy Klaus	.35	.14	.03	☐ 238 Jim Gilliam		1.50	.60	.15
☐ 188 Jim Marshall	.35	.14	.03	☐ 239 Dave Sisler		.35	.14	.03
☐ 189 Checklist 3	3.00	.30	.06	☐ 240 Ron Hansen		.35	.14	.03
☐ 190 Stan Williams	.35	.14	.03	☐ 241 Al Cicotte		.35	.14	.03
☐ 191 Mike De La Hoz	.35	.14	.03	☐ 242 Hal Smith		.35	.14	.03
☐ 192 Dick Brown	.35	.14	.03	☐ 243 Frank Lary		.50	.20	.05
☐ 193 Gene Conley	.35	.14	.03	☐ 244 Chico Cardenas		.35	.14	.03
☐ 194 Gordy Coleman	.35	.14	.03	☐ 245 Joe Adcock		.80	.32	.08
☐ 195 Jerry Casale	.35	.14	.03	☐ 246 Bob Davis		.35	.14	.03
☐ 196 Ed Bouchee	.35	.14	.03	☐ 247 Billy Goodman		.50	.20	.05
☐ 197 Dick Hall	.35	.14	.03	☐ 248 Ed Keegan		.35	.14	.03
☐ 198 Carl Sawatski	.35	.14	.03	☐ 249 Reds Team		1.25	.50	.12
☐ 199 Bob Boyd	.35	.14	.03	☐ 250 Buc Hill Aces		.60	.24	.06
☐ 200 Warren Spahn	5.50	2.20	.55	Vern Law				
☐ 201 Pete Whisenant	.35	.14	.03	Roy Face				
☐ 202 Al Neiger	.35	.14	.03	☐ 251 Bill Bruton		.35	.14	.03
☐ 203 Eddie Bressoud	.35	.14	.03	☐ 252 Bill Short		.35	.14	.03
☐ 204 Bob Skinner	.50	.20	.05	☐ 253 Sammy Taylor		.35	.14	.03
☐ 205 Bill Pierce	.75	.30	.07	☐ 254 Ted Sadowski		.35	.14	.03
☐ 206 Gene Green	.35	.14	.03	☐ 255 Vic Power		.35	.14	.03
☐ 207 Dodger Southpaws	2.50	1.00	.25	☐ 256 Billy Hoeft		.35	.14	.03
Sandy Koufax				☐ 257 Carroll Hardy		.35	.14	.03
Johnny Podres				☐ 258 Jack Sanford		.35	.14	.03
☐ 208 Larry Osborne	.35	.14	.03	☐ 259 John Schaive		.35	.14	.03
☐ 209 Ken McBride	.35	.14	.03	☐ 260 Don Drysdale		4.50	1.80	.45
☐ 210 Pete Runnels	.50	.20	.05	☐ 261 Charlie Lau		.60	.24	.06
☐ 211 Bob Gibson	5.50	2.20	.55	☐ 262 Tony Curry		.35	.14	.03
☐ 212 Haywood Sullivan	.50	.20	.05	☐ 263 Ken Hamlin		.35	.14	.03
☐ 213 Billy Stafford	.50	.20	.05	☐ 264 Glen Hobbie		.35	.14	.03
☐ 214 Danny Murphy	.35	.14	.03	☐ 265 Tony Kubek		2.25	.90	.22
☐ 215 Gus Bell	.50	.20	.05	☐ 266 Lindy McDaniel		.35	.14	.03
☐ 216 Ted Bowsfield	.35	.14	.03	☐ 267 Norm Siebern		.35	.14	.03
☐ 217 Mel Roach	.35	.14	.03	☐ 268 Ike Delock		.35	.14	.03
☐ 218 Hal Brown	.35	.14	.03	☐ 269 Harry Chiti		.35	.14	.03
☐ 219 Gene Mauch MGR	.50	.20	.05	☐ 270 Bob Friend		.50	.20	.05

		MINT	VG-E	F-G
☐ 271	Jim Landis	.35	.14	.03
☐ 272	Tom Morgan	.35	.14	.03
☐ 273	Checklist 4	3.00	.30	.06
☐ 274	Gary Bell	.35	.14	.03
☐ 275	Gene Woodling	.50	.20	.05
☐ 276	Ray Rippelmeyer	.35	.14	.03
☐ 277	Hank Foiles	.35	.14	.03
☐ 278	Don McMahon	.35	.14	.03
☐ 279	Jose Pagan	.35	.14	.03
☐ 280	Frank Howard	1.25	.50	.12
☐ 281	Frank Sullivan	.35	.14	.03
☐ 282	Faye Throneberry	.35	.14	.03
☐ 283	Bob Anderson	.35	.14	.03
☐ 284	Dick Gernert	.35	.14	.03
☐ 285	Sherm Lollar	.50	.20	.05
☐ 286	George Witt	.35	.14	.03
☐ 287	Carl Yastrzemski	65.00	26.00	6.50
☐ 288	Albie Pearson	.35	.14	.03
☐ 289	Ray Moore	.35	.14	.03
☐ 290	Stan Musial	20.00	8.00	2.00
☐ 291	Tex Clevenger	.35	.14	.03
☐ 292	Jim Baumer	.50	.20	.05
☐ 293	Tom Sturdivant	.35	.14	.03
☐ 294	Don Blasingame	.35	.14	.03
☐ 295	Milt Pappas	.60	.24	.06
☐ 296	Wes Covington	.50	.20	.05
☐ 297	Athletics Team	1.00	.40	.10
☐ 298	Jim Golden	.35	.14	.03
☐ 299	Clay Dalrymple	.35	.14	.03
☐ 300	Mickey Mantle	75.00	30.00	7.50
☐ 301	Chet Nichols	.35	.14	.03
☐ 302	Al Heist	.35	.14	.03
☐ 303	Gary Peters	.50	.20	.05
☐ 304	Rocky Nelson	.35	.14	.03
☐ 305	Mike McCormick	.50	.20	.05
☐ 306	World Series Game 1 ... Virdon Saves Game	1.50	.60	.15
☐ 307	World Series Game 2 ... Mantle 2 Homers	5.00	2.00	.50
☐ 308	World Series Game 3 ... Richardson is Hero	1.50	.60	.15
☐ 309	World Series Game 4 ... Cimoli Safe	1.50	.60	.15
☐ 310	World Series Game 5 ... Face Saves the Day	1.50	.60	.15
☐ 311	World Series Game 6 ... Ford Second Shutout	2.00	.80	.20
☐ 312	World Series Game 7 ... Mazeroski's Homer	2.00	.80	.20
☐ 313	World Series Summary . Pirates Celebrate	1.50	.60	.15
☐ 314	Bob Miller	.35	.14	.03
☐ 315	Earl Battey	.35	.14	.03

		MINT	VG-E	F-G
☐ 316	Bobby Gene Smith	.35	.14	.03
☐ 317	Jim Brewer	.35	.14	.0?
☐ 318	Danny O'Connell	.35	.14	.03
☐ 319	Valmy Thomas	.35	.14	.03
☐ 320	Lou Burdette	1.25	.50	.12
☐ 321	Marv Breeding	.35	.14	.03
☐ 322	Bill Kunkel	.50	.20	.05
☐ 323	Sammy Esposito	.35	.14	.03
☐ 324	Hank Aguirre	.35	.14	.03
☐ 325	Wally Moon	.50	.20	.05
☐ 326	Dave Hillman	.35	.14	.03
☐ 327	Matty Alou	1.25	.50	.12
☐ 328	Jim O'Toole	.50	.20	.05
☐ 329	Julio Becquer	.35	.14	.03
☐ 330	Rocky Colavito	1.25	.50	.12
☐ 331	Ned Garver	.35	.14	.03
☐ 332	Dutch Dotterer (photo actually Tommy Dotterer, Dutch's brother)	.50	.20	.05
☐ 333	Fritz Brickell	.35	.14	.03
☐ 334	Walt Bond	.35	.14	.03
☐ 335	Frank Bolling	.35	.14	.03
☐ 336	Don Mincher	.50	.20	.05
☐ 337	Al's Aces Early Wynn Al Lopez Herb Score	1.50	.60	.15
☐ 338	Don Landrum	.35	.14	.03
☐ 339	Gene Baker	.35	.14	.03
☐ 340	Vic Wertz	.50	.20	.05
☐ 341	Jim Owens	.35	.14	.03
☐ 342	Clint Courtney	.35	.14	.03
☐ 343	Earl Robinson	.35	.14	.03
☐ 344	Sandy Koufax	15.00	6.00	1.50
☐ 345	Jim Piersall	.80	.32	.08
☐ 346	Howie Nunn	.35	.14	.03
☐ 347	Cardinals Team	1.00	.40	.10
☐ 348	Steve Boros	.50	.20	.05
☐ 349	Danny McDevitt	.35	.14	.03
☐ 350	Ernie Banks	6.00	2.40	.60
☐ 351	Jim King	.35	.14	.03
☐ 352	Bob Shaw	.35	.14	.03
☐ 353	Howie Bedell	.35	.14	.03
☐ 354	Billy Harrell	.35	.14	.03
☐ 355	Bob Allison	.60	.24	.06
☐ 356	Ryne Duren	.75	.30	.07
☐ 357	Daryl Spencer	.35	.14	.03
☐ 358	Earl Averill	.35	.14	.03
☐ 359	Dallas Green	.75	.30	.07
☐ 360	Frank Robinson	10.00	4.00	1.00
☐ 361	A Checklist 5 (no ad on back)	3.00	.30	.06

	MINT	VG-E	F-G
☐ 361 **B** Checklist 5	6.00	.60	.10
(Special Feature			
ad on back)			
☐ 362 Frank Funk	.35	.14	.03
☐ 363 John Roseboro	.50	.20	.05
☐ 364 Moe Drabowsky	.35	.14	.03
☐ 365 Jerry Lumpe	.35	.14	.03
☐ 366 Eddie Fisher	.35	.14	.03
☐ 367 Jim Rivera	.35	.14	.03
☐ 368 Bennie Daniels	.35	.14	.03
☐ 369 Dave Philley	.35	.14	.03
☐ 370 Roy Face	.80	.32	.08
☐ 371 Bill Skowron	2.00	.80	.20
☐ 372 Bob Hendley	.50	.20	.05
☐ 373 Red Sox Team	1.25	.50	.12
☐ 374 Paul Giel	.50	.20	.05
☐ 375 Ken Boyer	2.00	.80	.20
☐ 376 Mike Roarke	.50	.20	.05
☐ 377 Ruben Gomez	.50	.20	.05
☐ 378 Wally Post	.50	.20	.05
☐ 379 Bobby Shantz	1.00	.40	.10
☐ 380 Minnie Minoso	1.25	.50	.12
☐ 381 Dave Wickersham	.50	.20	.05
☐ 382 Frank Thomas	.60	.24	.06
☐ 383 Frisco First Liners	.60	.24	.06
Mike McCormick			
Jack Sanford			
Billy O'Dell			
☐ 384 Chuck Essegian	.50	.20	.05
☐ 385 Jim Perry	.80	.32	.08
☐ 386 Joe Hicks	.50	.20	.05
☐ 387 Duke Maas	.50	.20	.05
☐ 388 Bob Clemente	15.00	6.00	1.50
☐ 389 Ralph Terry	.80	.32	.08
☐ 390 Del Crandall	.60	.24	.06
☐ 391 Winston Brown	.50	.20	.05
☐ 392 Reno Bertoia	.50	.20	.05
☐ 393 Batter Bafflers	.60	.24	.06
Don Cardwell			
Glen Hobbie			
☐ 394 Ken Walters	.50	.20	.05
☐ 395 Chuck Estrada	.60	.24	.06
☐ 396 Bob Aspromonte	.50	.20	.05
☐ 397 Hal Woodeshick	.50	.20	.05
☐ 398 Hank Bauer	.80	.32	.08
☐ 399 Cliff Cook	.50	.20	.05
☐ 400 Vern Law	.80	.32	.08
☐ 401 Ruth 60th Homer	6.00	2.40	.60
☐ 402 Perfect Game (Larsen)	2.00	.80	.20
☐ 403 26 Inning Tie	.80	.32	.08
☐ 404 Hornsby .424 Average	1.50	.60	.15
☐ 405 Gehrig's Streak	4.00	1.60	.40
☐ 406 Mantle 565 Ft. Homer	6.00	2.40	.60

	MINT	VG-E	F-G
☐ 407 Chesbro Wins 41	.80	.32	.08
☐ 408 Mathewson Fans 267	2.00	.80	.20
☐ 409 Johnson Shutouts	2.00	.80	.20
☐ 410 Haddix 12 Perfect			
Innings	1.00	.40	.10
☐ 411 Tony Taylor	.50	.20	.05
☐ 412 Larry Sherry	.75	.30	.07
☐ 413 Eddie Yost	.50	.20	.05
☐ 414 Dick Donovan	.50	.20	.05
☐ 415 Hank Aaron	30.00	12.00	3.00
☐ 416 Dick Howser	2.00	.80	.20
☐ 417 Juan Marichal	36.00	15.00	3.60
☐ 418 Ed Bailey	.50	.20	.05
☐ 419 Tom Borland	.50	.20	.05
☐ 420 Ernie Broglio	.60	.24	.06
☐ 421 Ty Cline	.50	.20	.05
☐ 422 Bud Daley	.50	.20	.05
☐ 423 Charlie Neal	.60	.24	.06
☐ 424 Turk Lown	.50	.20	.05
☐ 425 Yogi Berra	10.00	4.00	1.00
☐ 426 Braves Team	4.00	1.60	.40
(back numbered 463)			
☐ 427 Dick Ellsworth	.75	.30	.07
☐ 428 Ray Barker	.50	.20	.05
☐ 429 Al Kaline	8.00	3.25	.80
☐ 430 Bill Mazeroski	1.75	.70	.17
☐ 431 Chuck Stobbs	.50	.20	.05
☐ 432 Coot Veal	.50	.20	.05
☐ 433 Art Mahaffey	.50	.20	.05
☐ 434 Tom Brewer	.50	.20	.05
☐ 435 Orlando Cepeda	2.00	.80	.20
☐ 436 Jim Maloney	1.25	.50	.12
☐ 437 Checklist 6	3.00	.60	.10
☐ 438 Curt Flood	1.00	.40	.10
☐ 439 Phil Regan	.60	.24	.06
☐ 440 Luis Aparicio	3.50	1.40	.35
☐ 441 Dick Bertell	.50	.20	.05
☐ 442 Gordon Jones	.50	.20	.05
☐ 443 Duke Snider	9.00	3.75	.90
☐ 444 Joe Nuxhall	.60	.24	.06
☐ 445 Frank Malzone	.60	.24	.06
☐ 446 Bob Taylor	.50	.20	.05
☐ 447 Harry Bright	.50	.20	.05
☐ 448 Del Rice	.50	.20	.05
☐ 449 Bob Bolin	.50	.20	.05
☐ 450 Jim Lemon	.60	.24	.06
☐ 451 Power for Ernie	.60	.24	.06
Daryl Spencer			
Bill White			
Ernie Broglio			
☐ 452 Bob Allen	.50	.20	.05
☐ 453 Dick Schofield	.50	.20	.05
☐ 454 Pumpsie Green	.50	.20	.05

		MINT	VG-E	F-G
☐ 455	Early Wynn	3.50	1.40	.35
☐ 456	Hal Bevan	.50	.20	.05
☐ 457	John James	.50	.20	.05
☐ 458	Willie Tasby	.50	.20	.05
☐ 459	Terry Fox	.50	.20	.05
☐ 460	Gil Hodges	4.00	1.60	.40
☐ 461	Smoky Burgess	.60	.24	.06
☐ 462	Lou Klimchock	.50	.20	.05
☐ 463	Jack Fisher	.60	.24	.06
	(See also 426)			
☐ 464	Leroy Thomas	.50	.20	.05
☐ 465	Roy McMillan	.50	.20	.05
☐ 466	Ron Moeller	.50	.20	.05
☐ 467	Indians Team	1.00	.40	.10
☐ 468	John Callison	.60	.24	.06
☐ 469	Ralph Lumenti	.50	.20	.05
☐ 470	Roy Sievers	.60	.24	.06
☐ 471	Phil Rizzuto MVP	4.00	1.60	.40
☐ 472	Yogi Berra MVP	5.00	2.00	.50
☐ 473	Bob Shantz MVP	.80	.32	.08
☐ 474	Al Rosen MVP	1.00	.40	.10
☐ 475	Mickey Mantle MVP	15.00	6.00	1.50
☐ 476	Jackie Jensen MVP	.80	.32	.08
☐ 477	Nellie Fox MVP	1.25	.50	.12
☐ 478	Roger Maris MVP	5.00	2.00	.50
☐ 479	Jim Konstanty MVP	.80	.32	.08
☐ 480	Roy Campanella MVP	8.00	3.25	.80
☐ 481	Hank Sauer MVP	.80	.32	.08
☐ 482	Willie Mays MVP	8.00	3.25	.80
☐ 483	Don Newcombe MVP	.80	.32	.08
☐ 484	Hank Aaron MVP	8.00	3.25	.80
☐ 485	Ernie Banks MVP	4.00	1.60	.40
☐ 486	Dick Groat MVP	.80	.32	.08
☐ 487	Gene Oliver	.50	.20	.05
☐ 488	Joe McClain	.50	.20	.05
☐ 489	Walt Dropo	.50	.20	.05
☐ 490	Jim Bunning	2.00	.80	.20
☐ 491	Phillies Team	1.00	.40	.10
☐ 492	Ron Fairly	.60	.24	.06
☐ 493	Don Zimmer	.75	.30	.07
☐ 494	Tom Cheney	.50	.20	.05
☐ 495	Elston Howard	2.00	.80	.20
☐ 496	Ken Mackenzie	.50	.20	.05
☐ 497	Willie Jones	.50	.20	.05
☐ 498	Ray Herbert	.50	.20	.05
☐ 499	Chuck Schilling	.50	.20	.05
☐ 500	Harvey Kuenn	1.25	.50	.12
☐ 501	John DeMerit	.50	.20	.05
☐ 502	Clarence Coleman	.50	.20	.05
☐ 503	Tito Francona	.60	.24	.06
☐ 504	Billy Consolo	.50	.20	.05
☐ 505	Red Schoendienst	1.25	.50	.12
☐ 506	Willie Davis	2.00	.80	.20

		MINT	VG-E	F-G
☐ 507	Pete Burnside	.50	.20	.05
☐ 508	Rocky Bridges	.50	.20	.05
☐ 509	Camilo Carreon	.50	.20	.05
☐ 510	Art Ditmar	.50	.20	.05
☐ 511	Joe Morgan	.50	.20	.05
☐ 512	Bob Will	.50	.20	.05
☐ 513	Jim Brosnan	.60	.24	.06
☐ 514	Jake Wood	.50	.20	.05
☐ 515	Jackie Brandt	.50	.20	.05
☐ 516	Checklist 7	4.00	.80	.15
☐ 517	Willie McCovey	10.00	4.00	1.00
☐ 518	Andy Carey	.50	.20	.05
☐ 519	Jim Pagliaroni	.50	.20	.05
☐ 520	Joe Cunningham	.60	.24	.06
☐ 521	Brother Battery	.60	.24	.06
	Norm Sherry			
	Larry Sherry			
☐ 522	Dick Farrell	.50	.20	.05
☐ 523	Joe Gibbon	7.00	2.80	.70
☐ 524	John Logan	8.00	3.25	.80
☐ 525	Ron Perranoski	8.00	3.25	.80
☐ 526	R.C. Stevens	7.00	2.80	.70
☐ 527	Gene Leek	7.00	2.80	.70
☐ 528	Pedro Ramos	7.00	2.80	.70
☐ 529	Bob Roselli	7.00	2.80	.70
☐ 530	Bob Malkmus	7.00	2.80	.70
☐ 531	Jim Coates	7.00	2.80	.70
☐ 532	Bob Hale	7.00	2.80	.70
☐ 533	Jack Curtis	7.00	2.80	.70
☐ 534	Eddie Kasko	7.00	2.80	.70
☐ 535	Larry Jackson	7.00	2.80	.70
☐ 536	Bill Tuttle	7.00	2.80	.70
☐ 537	Bobby Locke	7.00	2.80	.70
☐ 538	Chuck Hiller	7.00	2.80	.70
☐ 539	John Klippstein	7.00	2.80	.70
☐ 540	Jackie Jensen	9.00	3.75	.90
☐ 541	Roland Sheldon	7.00	2.80	.70
☐ 542	Minnesota Twins	12.00	5.00	1.20
	Team Card			
☐ 543	Roger Craig	10.00	4.00	1.00
☐ 544	George Thomas	7.00	2.80	.70
☐ 545	Hoyt Wilhelm	20.00	8.00	2.00
☐ 546	Marty Kutyna	7.00	2.80	.70
☐ 547	Leon Wagner	7.00	2.80	.70
☐ 548	Ted Wills	7.00	2.80	.70
☐ 549	Hal R. Smith	7.00	2.80	.70
☐ 550	Frank Baumann	7.00	2.80	.70
☐ 551	George Altman	7.00	2.80	.70
☐ 552	Jim Archer	7.00	2.80	.70
☐ 553	Bill Fischer	7.00	2.80	.70
☐ 554	Pirates Team	10.00	4.00	1.00
☐ 555	Sam Jones	8.00	3.25	.80
☐ 556	Ken R. Hunt	7.00	2.80	.70

		MINT	VG-E	F-G
☐ 557	Jose Valdivielso	7.00	2.80	.70
☐ 558	Don Ferrarese	7.00	2.80	.70
☐ 559	Jim Gentile	8.00	3.25	.80
☐ 560	Barry Latman	7.00	2.80	.70
☐ 561	Charley James	7.00	2.80	.70
☐ 562	Bill Monbouquette	7.00	2.80	.70
☐ 563	Bob Cerv	8.00	3.25	.80
☐ 564	Don Cardwell	7.00	2.80	.70
☐ 565	Felipe Alou	8.00	3.25	.80
☐ 566	Paul Richards MGR AS	8.00	3.25	.80
☐ 567	Danny Murtaugh MGR AS	8.00	3.25	.80
☐ 568	Bill Skowron AS	8.00	3.25	.80
☐ 569	Frank Herrera AS	8.00	3.25	.80
☐ 570	Nellie Fox AS	10.00	4.00	1.00
☐ 571	Bill Mazeroski AS	9.00	3.75	.90
☐ 572	Brooks Robinson AS	24.00	10.00	2.40
☐ 573	Ken Boyer AS	9.00	3.75	.90
☐ 574	Luis Aparicio AS	18.00	7.25	1.80
☐ 575	Ernie Banks AS	24.00	10.00	2.40
☐ 576	Roger Maris AS	24.00	10.00	2.40
☐ 577	Hank Aaron AS	60.00	24.00	6.00
☐ 578	Mickey Mantle AS	120.00	50.00	12.00
☐ 579	Willie Mays AS	60.00	24.00	6.00
☐ 580	Al Kaline AS	24.00	10.00	2.40
☐ 581	Frank Robinson AS	24.00	10.00	2.40
☐ 582	Earl Battey AS	8.00	3.25	.80
☐ 583	Del Crandall AS	8.00	3.25	.80
☐ 584	Jim Perry AS	8.00	3.25	.80
☐ 585	Bob Friend AS	8.00	3.25	.80
☐ 586	Whitey Ford AS	24.00	10.00	2.40
☐ 587	Does not exist	0.00	0.00	.00
☐ 588	Does not exist	0.00	0.00	.00
☐ 589	Warren Spahn AS	24.00	10.00	2.40

*The cards in this 598-card set measure 2½"
by 3½". The 1962 Topps set contains a mini-
series spotlighting Babe Ruth (135 to 144).
Other subsets in the set include League
Leaders (51-60), World Series cards (232-
237), In Action cards (311-319), NL All Stars
(390-399), AL All Stars (466-475), and Rookie Prospects (591-598). The second series
had two distinct printings which are distin-
guishable by numberous color and pose variations. Card number 139 exists as A: Babe
Ruth Special card, B: Hal Reniff with arms
over head, or C: Hal Reniff in the same pose
as card number 159. In addition, two poses
exist for players depicted on card numbers
129, 132, 134, 147, 174, 176, and 190. The
high number series, 523 to 598, is somewhat
more difficult to obtain than other cards in the
set. The set price listed does not include the
pose variations (see checklist below for individual values).*

	MINT	VG-E	F-G
Complete Set	950.00	400.00	120.00
Common Player (1-370)	.35	.14	.03
Common Player (371-522)	.55	.22	.05
Common Player (523-590)	2.50	1.00	.25
Common Player (591-598)	5.00	2.00	.50

1962 Topps

		MINT	VG-E	F-G
☐ 1	Roger Maris	35.00	5.00	1.00
☐ 2	Jim Brosnan	.50	.20	.05
☐ 3	Pete Runnels	.50	.20	.05
☐ 4	John DeMerit	.35	.14	.03
☐ 5	Sandy Koufax	15.00	6.00	1.50
☐ 6	Marv Breeding	.35	.14	.03
☐ 7	Frank Thomas	.50	.20	.05
☐ 8	Ray Herbert	.35	.14	.03
☐ 9	Jim Davenport	.50	.20	.05
☐ 10	Bob Clemente	15.00	6.00	1.50
☐ 11	Tom Morgan	.35	.14	.03
☐ 12	Harry Craft MGR	.35	.14	.03
☐ 13	Dick Howser	.60	.24	.06
☐ 14	Bill White	.60	.24	.06
☐ 15	Dick Donovan	.35	.14	.03
☐ 16	Darrell Johnson	.35	.14	.03
☐ 17	John Callison	.50	.20	.05

			MINT	VG-E	F-G
☐	18	Managers' Dream	20.00	8.00	2.00
		Mickey Mantle			
		Willie Mays			
☐	19	Ray Washburn	.35	.14	.03
☐	20	Rocky Colavito	1.00	.40	.10
☐	21	Jim Kaat	1.50	.60	.15
☐	22	A Checklist 1 COR	2.50	.25	.05
☐	22	B Checklist 1 ERR	3.50	.35	.07
		(121-176 on back)			
☐	23	Norm Larker	.35	.14	.03
☐	24	Tigers Team	1.00	.40	.10
☐	25	Ernie Banks	5.00	2.00	.50
☐	26	Chris Cannizzaro	.35	.14	.03
☐	27	Chuck Cottier	.50	.20	.05
☐	28	Minnie Minoso	1.00	.40	.10
☐	29	Casey Stengel MGR	4.00	1.60	.40
☐	30	Ed Mathews	4.00	1.60	.40
☐	31	Tom Tresh	2.50	1.00	.25
☐	32	John Roseboro	.50	.20	.05
☐	33	Don Larsen	.60	.24	.06
☐	34	Johnny Temple	.35	.14	.03
☐	35	Don Schwall	.35	.14	.03
☐	36	Don Leppert	.35	.14	.03
☐	37	Tribe Hill Trio	.50	.20	.05
		Barry Latman			
		Dick Stigman			
		Jim Perry			
☐	38	Gene Stephens	.35	.14	.03
☐	39	Joe Koppe	.35	.14	.03
☐	40	Orlando Cepeda	1.50	.60	.15
☐	41	Cliff Cook	.35	.14	.03
☐	42	Jim King	.35	.14	.03
☐	43	Dodgers Team	1.25	.50	.12
☐	44	Don Taussig	.35	.14	.03
☐	45	Brooks Robinson	7.50	3.00	.75
☐	46	Jack Baldschun	.35	.14	.03
☐	47	Bob Will	.35	.14	.03
☐	48	Ralph Terry	.60	.24	.06
☐	49	Hal Jones	.35	.14	.03
☐	50	Stan Musial	18.00	7.25	1.80
☐	51	AL Batting Leaders	.80	.32	.08
		Norm Cash			
		Jim Piersall			
		Al Kaline			
		Elston Howard			
☐	52	NL Batting Leaders	1.00	.40	.10
		Bob Clemente			
		Vada Pinson			
		Ken Boyer			
		Wally Moon			
☐	53	AL Home Run Leaders	3.50	1.40	.35
		Roger Maris			
		Mickey Mantle			
		Jim Gentile			
		Harmon Killebrew			
☐	54	NL Home Run Leaders	1.25	.50	.12
		Orlando Cepeda			
		Willie Mays			
		Frank Robinson			
☐	55	AL ERA Leaders	.80	.32	.08
		Dick Donovan			
		Bill Stafford			
		Don Mossi			
		Milt Pappas			
☐	56	NL ERA Leaders	1.00	.40	.10
		Warren Spahn			
		Jim O'Toole			
		Curt Simmons			
		Mike McCormick			
☐	57	AL Wins Leaders	1.00	.40	.10
		Whitey Ford			
		Frank Lary			
		Steve Barber			
		Jim Bunning			
☐	58	NL Wins Leaders	1.00	.40	.10
		Warren Spahn			
		Joe Jay			
		Jim O'Toole			
☐	59	AL Strikeout Leaders	.80	.32	.08
		Camilo Pascual			
		Whitey Ford			
		Jim Bunning			
		Juan Pizarro			
☐	60	NL Strikeout Leaders	1.50	.60	.15
		Sandy Koufax			
		Stan Williams			
		Don Drysdale			
		Jim O'Toole			
☐	61	Cardinals Team	1.00	.40	.10
☐	62	Steve Boros	.50	.20	.05
☐	63	Tony Cloninger	.35	.14	.03
☐	64	Russ Snyder	.35	.14	.03
☐	65	Bobby Richardson	1.50	.60	.15
☐	66	Cuno Barragan	.35	.14	.03
☐	67	Harvey Haddix	.50	.20	.05
☐	68	Ken Hunt	.35	.14	.03
☐	69	Phil Ortega	.35	.14	.03
☐	70	Harmon Killebrew	4.00	1.60	.40
☐	71	Dick LeMay	.35	.14	.03
☐	72	Bob's Pupils	.50	.20	.05
		Steve Boros			
		Bob Scheffing			
		Jake Wood			

		MINT	VG-E	F-G
☐ 73	Nellie Fox	1.50	.60	.15
☐ 74	Bob Lillis	.50	.20	.05
☐ 75	Milt Pappas	.50	.20	.05
☐ 76	Howie Bedell	.35	.14	.03
☐ 77	Tony Taylor	.35	.14	.03
☐ 78	Gene Green	.35	.14	.03
☐ 79	Ed Hobaugh	.35	.14	.03
☐ 80	Vada Pinson	1.00	.40	.10
☐ 81	Jim Pagliaroni	.35	.14	.03
☐ 82	Deron Johnson	.35	.14	.03
☐ 83	Larry Jackson	.35	.14	.03
☐ 84	Lenny Green	.35	.14	.03
☐ 85	Gil Hodges	3.50	1.40	.35
☐ 86	Donn Clendenon	.75	.30	.07
☐ 87	Mike Roarke	.35	.14	.03
☐ 88	Ralph Houk MGR	.75	.30	.07
☐ 89	Barney Schultz	.35	.14	.03
☐ 90	Jim Piersall	.75	.30	.07
☐ 91	J.C. Martin	.35	.14	.03
☐ 92	Sam Jones	.35	.14	.03
☐ 93	John Blanchard	.50	.20	.05
☐ 94	Jay Hook	.35	.14	.03
☐ 95	Don Hoak	.35	.14	.03
☐ 96	Eli Grba	.35	.14	.03
☐ 97	Tito Francona	.50	.20	.05
☐ 98	Checklist 2	2.50	.50	.10
☐ 99	John (Boog) Powell	3.00	1.20	.30
☐ 100	Warren Spahn	5.00	2.00	.50
☐ 101	Carroll Hardy	.35	.14	.03
☐ 102	Al Schroll	.35	.14	.03
☐ 103	Don Blasingame	.35	.14	.03
☐ 104	Ted Savage	.35	.14	.03
☐ 105	Don Mossi	.50	.20	.05
☐ 106	Carl Sawatski	.35	.14	.03
☐ 107	Mike McCormick	.50	.20	.05
☐ 108	Willie Davis	.75	.30	.07
☐ 109	Bob Shaw	.35	.14	.03
☐ 110	Bill Skowron	1.50	.60	.15
☐ 111	Dallas Green	.50	.20	.05
☐ 112	Hank Foiles	.35	.14	.03
☐ 113	White Sox Team	1.00	.40	.10
☐ 114	Howie Koplitz	.35	.14	.03
☐ 115	Bob Skinner	.50	.20	.05
☐ 116	Herb Score	.60	.24	.06
☐ 117	Gary Geiger	.35	.14	.03
☐ 118	Julian Javier	.35	.14	.03
☐ 119	Danny Murphy	.35	.14	.03
☐ 120	Bob Purkey	.35	.14	.03
☐ 121	Billy Hitchcock MGR	.35	.14	.03
☐ 122	Norm Bass	.35	.14	.03
☐ 123	Mike De La Hoz	.35	.14	.03
☐ 124	Bill Pleis	.35	.14	.03
☐ 125	Gene Woodling	.50	.20	.05

		MINT	VG-E	F-G
☐ 126	Al Cicotte	.35	.14	.03
☐ 127	Pride of A's	.50	.20	.05
	Norm Siebern			
	Hank Bauer			
	Jerry Lumpe			
☐ 128	Art Fowler	.35	.14	.03
☐ 129 A	Lee Walls	.60	.24	.06
	(facing right)			
☐ 129 B	Lee Walls	6.00	2.40	.60
	(face left)			
☐ 130	Frank Bolling	.35	.14	.03
☐ 131	Pete Richert	.35	.14	.03
☐ 132 A	Angels Team	1.00	.40	.10
	(without photo)			
☐ 132 B	Angels Team	6.00	2.40	.60
	(with photo)			
☐ 133	Felipe Alou	.60	.24	.06
☐ 134 A	Billy Hoeft	.60	.24	.06
	(facing right)			
☐ 134 B	Billy Hoeft	6.00	2.40	.60
	(facing straight)			
☐ 135	Babe Ruth Special 1	4.00	1.60	.40
	Babe as a boy			
☐ 136	Babe Ruth Special 2	4.00	1.60	.40
	Babe Joins Yanks			
☐ 137	Babe Ruth Special 3	4.00	1.60	.40
	Babe with Huggins			
☐ 138	Babe Ruth Special 4	4.00	1.60	.40
	Famous Slugger			
☐ 139 A	Babe Ruth Special 5	6.00	2.40	.60
☐ 139 B	Hal Reniff PORT	7.50	3.00	.75
☐ 139 C	Hal Reniff	25.00	10.00	2.50
	(pitching)			
☐ 140	Babe Ruth Special 6	5.00	2.00	.50
	Gehrig and Ruth			
☐ 141	Babe Ruth Special 7	4.00	1.60	.40
	Twilight Years			
☐ 142	Babe Ruth Special 8	4.00	1.60	.40
	Coaching Dodgers			
☐ 143	Babe Ruth Special 9	4.00	1.60	.40
	Greatest Sports Hero			
☐ 144	Babe Ruth Special 10	4.00	1.60	.40
	Farewell Speech			
☐ 145	Barry Latman	.35	.14	.03
☐ 146	Don Demeter	.35	.14	.03
☐ 147 A	Bill Kunkel PORT	.60	.24	.06
☐ 147 B	Bill Kunkel	6.00	2.40	.60
	(pitching pose)			
☐ 148	Wally Post	.35	.14	.03
☐ 149	Bob Duliba	.35	.14	.03
☐ 150	Al Kaline	5.50	2.20	.55
☐ 151	Johnny Klippstein	.35	.14	.03
☐ 152	Mickey Vernon	.50	.20	.05

		MINT	VG-E	F-G
☐ 153	Pumpsie Green	.35	.14	.03
☐ 154	Lee Thomas	.35	.14	.03
☐ 155	Stu Miller	.35	.14	.03
☐ 156	Merritt Ranew	.35	.14	.03
☐ 157	Wes Covington	.35	.14	.03
☐ 158	Braves Team	1.00	.40	.10
☐ 159	Hal Reniff	.60	.24	.06
☐ 160	Dick Stuart	.60	.24	.06
☐ 161	Frank Baumann	.35	.14	.03
☐ 162	Sammy Drake	.35	.14	.03
☐ 163	Hot Corner Guard	.60	.24	.06
	Billy Gardner			
	Cletis Boyer			
☐ 164	Hal Naragon	.35	.14	.03
☐ 165	Jackie Brandt	.35	.14	.03
☐ 166	Don Lee	.35	.14	.03
☐ 167	Tim McCarver	2.50	1.00	.25
☐ 168	Leo Posada	.35	.14	.03
☐ 169	Bob Cerv	.50	.20	.05
☐ 170	Ron Santo	1.25	.50	.12
☐ 171	Dave Sisler	.35	.14	.03
☐ 172	Fred Hutchinson MGR	.50	.20	.05
☐ 173	Chico Fernandez	.35	.14	.03
☐ 174 A	Carl Willey (capless)	.60	.24	.06
☐ 174 B	Carl Willey (with cap)	6.00	2.40	.60
☐ 175	Frank Howard	1.00	.40	.10
☐ 176 A	Eddie Yost PORT	.60	.24	.06
☐ 176 B	Eddie Yost BATTING	6.00	2.40	.60
☐ 177	Bobby Shantz	.60	.24	.06
☐ 178	Camilo Carreon	.35	.14	.03
☐ 179	Tom Sturdivant	.35	.14	.03
☐ 180	Bob Allison	.50	.20	.05
☐ 181	Paul Brown	.35	.14	.03
☐ 182	Bob Nieman	.35	.14	.03
☐ 183	Roger Craig	.60	.24	.06
☐ 184	Haywood Sullivan	.50	.20	.05
☐ 185	Roland Sheldon	.35	.14	.03
☐ 186	Mack Jones	.35	.14	.03
☐ 187	Gene Conley	.35	.14	.03
☐ 188	Chuck Hiller	.35	.14	.03
☐ 189	Dick Hall	.35	.14	.03
☐ 190 A	Wally Moon PORT	.60	.24	.06
☐ 190 B	Wally Moon BATTING	6.00	2.40	.60
☐ 191	Jim Brewer	.35	.14	.03
☐ 192 A	Checklist 3 (without comma)	2.50	.25	.05
☐ 192 B	Checklist 3 (comma after Checklist)	3.50	.35	.07
☐ 193	Eddie Kasko	.35	.14	.03
☐ 194	Dean Chance	.75	.30	.07
☐ 195	Joe Cunningham	.35	.14	.03
☐ 196	Terry Fox	.35	.14	.03
☐ 197	Daryl Spencer	.35	.14	.03
☐ 198	Johnny Keane MGR	.50	.20	.05
☐ 199	Gaylord Perry	30.00	12.00	3.00
☐ 200	Mickey Mantle	90.00	36.00	9.00
☐ 201	Ike Delock	.35	.14	.03
☐ 202	Carl Warwick	.35	.14	.03
☐ 203	Jack Fisher	.35	.14	.03
☐ 204	Johnny Weekly	.35	.14	.03
☐ 205	Gene Freese	.35	.14	.03
☐ 206	Senators Team	.90	.36	.09
☐ 207	Pete Burnside	.35	.14	.03
☐ 208	Billy Martin	2.00	.80	.20
☐ 209	Jim Fregosi	2.50	1.00	.25
☐ 210	Roy Face	.75	.30	.07
☐ 211	Midway Masters	.50	.20	.05
	Frank Bolling			
	Roy McMillan			
☐ 212	Jim Owens	.35	.14	.03
☐ 213	Richie Ashburn	1.25	.50	.12
☐ 214	Dom Zanni	.35	.14	.03
☐ 215	Woody Held	.35	.14	.03
☐ 216	Ron Kline	.35	.14	.03
☐ 217	Walt Alston MGR	1.25	.50	.12
☐ 218	Joe Torre	5.00	2.00	.50
☐ 219	Al Downing	.60	.24	.06
☐ 220	Roy Sievers	.50	.20	.05
☐ 221	Bill Short	.35	.14	.03
☐ 222	Jerry Zimmerman	.35	.14	.03
☐ 223	Alex Grammas	.35	.14	.03
☐ 224	Don Rudolph	.35	.14	.03
☐ 225	Frank Malzone	.50	.20	.05
☐ 226	Giants Team	1.00	.40	.10
☐ 227	Bob Tiefenauer	.35	.14	.03
☐ 228	Dale Long	.35	.14	.03
☐ 229	Jesus McFarlane	.35	.14	.03
☐ 230	Camilo Pascual	.50	.20	.05
☐ 231	Ernie Bowman	.35	.14	.03
☐ 232	World Series Game 1 Yanks win opener	1.25	.50	.12
☐ 233	World Series Game 2 Jay ties it up	1.25	.50	.12
☐ 234	World Series Game 3 Maris wins in 9th	2.50	1.00	.25
☐ 235	World Series Game 4 Ford sets new mark	2.50	1.00	.25
☐ 236	World Series Game 5 Yanks crush Reds	1.25	.50	.12
☐ 237	World Series Summary Yanks celebrate	1.25	.50	.12
☐ 238	Norm Sherry	.50	.20	.05
☐ 239	Cecil Butler	.35	.14	.03

	MINT	VG-E	F-G
☐ 240 George Altman	.35	.14	.03
☐ 241 Johnny Kucks	.35	.14	.03
☐ 242 Mel McGaha	.35	.14	.03
☐ 243 Robin Roberts	3.00	1.20	.30
☐ 244 Don Gile	.35	.14	.03
☐ 245 Ron Hansen	.35	.14	.03
☐ 246 Art Ditmar	.35	.14	.03
☐ 247 Joe Pignatano	.35	.14	.03
☐ 248 Bob Aspromonte	.35	.14	.03
☐ 249 Ed Keegan	.35	.14	.03
☐ 250 Norm Cash	1.00	.40	.10
☐ 251 New York Yankees	4.00	1.60	.40
Team Card			
☐ 252 Earl Francis	.35	.14	.03
☐ 253 Harry Chiti	.35	.14	.03
☐ 254 Gordon Windhorn	.35	.14	.03
☐ 255 Juan Pizarro	.35	.14	.03
☐ 256 Elio Chacon	.35	.14	.03
☐ 257 Jack Spring	.35	.14	.03
☐ 258 Marty Keough	.35	.14	.03
☐ 259 Lou Klimchock	.35	.14	.03
☐ 260 Bill Pierce	.75	.30	.07
☐ 261 George Alusik	.35	.14	.03
☐ 262 Bob Schmidt	.35	.14	.03
☐ 263 The Right Pitch	.50	.20	.05
Bob Purkey			
Jim Turner			
Joe Jay			
☐ 264 Dick Ellsworth	.50	.20	.05
☐ 265 Joe Adcock	.75	.30	.07
☐ 266 John Anderson	.35	.14	.03
☐ 267 Dan Dobbek	.35	.14	.03
☐ 268 Ken McBride	.35	.14	.03
☐ 269 Bob Oldis	.35	.14	.03
☐ 270 Dick Groat	.90	.36	.09
☐ 271 Ray Rippelmeyer	.35	.14	.03
☐ 272 Earl Robinson	.35	.14	.03
☐ 273 Gary Bell	.35	.14	.03
☐ 274 Sammy Taylor	.35	.14	.03
☐ 275 Norm Siebern	.35	.14	.03
☐ 276 Hal Kolstad	.35	.14	.03
☐ 277 Checklist 4	2.50	.25	.05
☐ 278 Ken Johnson	.35	.14	.03
☐ 279 Hobie Landrith	.35	.14	.03
☐ 280 Johnny Podres	1.00	.40	.10
☐ 281 Jake Gibbs	.50	.20	.05
☐ 282 Dave Hillman	.35	.14	.03
☐ 283 Charlie Smith	.35	.14	.03
☐ 284 Ruben Amaro	.35	.14	.03
☐ 285 Curt Simmons	.50	.20	.05
☐ 286 Al Lopez MGR	1.00	.40	.10
☐ 287 George Witt	.35	.14	.03
☐ 288 Billy Williams	5.00	2.00	.50

	MINT	VG-E	F-G
☐ 289 Mike Krsnich	.35	.14	.03
☐ 290 Jim Gentile	.50	.20	.05
☐ 291 Hal Stowe	.35	.14	.03
☐ 292 Jerry Kindall	.35	.14	.03
☐ 293 Bob Miller	.35	.14	.03
☐ 294 Phillies Team	1.00	.40	.10
☐ 295 Vern Law	.60	.24	.06
☐ 296 Ken Hamlin	.35	.14	.03
☐ 297 Ron Perranoski	.50	.20	.05
☐ 298 Bill Tuttle	.35	.14	.03
☐ 299 Don Wert	.35	.14	.03
☐ 300 Willie Mays	35.00	14.00	3.50
☐ 301 Galen Cisco	.35	.14	.03
☐ 302 John Edwards	.35	.14	.03
☐ 303 Frank Torre	.35	.14	.03
☐ 304 Dick Farrell	.35	.14	.03
☐ 305 Jerry Lumpe	.35	.14	.03
☐ 306 Redbird Rippers	.50	.20	.05
Lindy McDaniel			
Larry Jackson			
☐ 307 Jim Grant	.35	.14	.03
☐ 308 Neil Chrisley	.35	.14	.03
☐ 309 Moe Morhardt	.35	.14	.03
☐ 310 Whitey Ford	6.00	2.40	.60
☐ 311 Tony Kubek IA	.90	.36	.09
☐ 312 Warren Spahn IA	2.00	.80	.20
☐ 313 Roger Maris IA	2.50	1.00	.25
☐ 314 Rocky Colavito IA	.90	.36	.09
☐ 315 Whitey Ford IA	2.00	.80	.20
☐ 316 Harmon Killebrew IA	2.00	.80	.20
☐ 317 Stan Musial IA	3.50	1.40	.35
☐ 318 Mickey Mantle IA	7.00	2.80	.70
☐ 319 Mike McCormick IA	.60	.24	.06
☐ 320 Hank Aaron	35.00	14.00	3.50
☐ 321 Lee Stange	.35	.14	.03
☐ 322 Al Dark	.50	.20	.05
☐ 323 Don Landrum	.35	.14	.03
☐ 324 Joe McClain	.35	.14	.03
☐ 325 Luis Aparicio	3.50	1.40	.35
☐ 326 Tom Parsons	.35	.14	.03
☐ 327 Ozzie Virgil	.35	.14	.03
☐ 328 Ken Walters	.35	.14	.03
☐ 329 Bob Bolin	.35	.14	.03
☐ 330 John Romano	.35	.14	.03
☐ 331 Moe Drabowsky	.35	.14	.03
☐ 332 Don Buddin	.35	.14	.03
☐ 333 Frank Cipriani	.35	.14	.03
☐ 334 Red Sox Team	1.00	.40	.10
☐ 335 Bill Bruton	.35	.14	.03
☐ 336 Billy Muffett	.35	.14	.03
☐ 337 Jim Marshall	.35	.14	.03
☐ 338 Billy Gardner	.35	.14	.03
☐ 339 Jose Valdivielso	.35	.14	.03

		MINT	VG-E	F-G
☐ 340	Don Drysdale	6.50	2.60	.65
☐ 341	Mike Hershberger	.35	.14	.03
☐ 342	Ed Rakow	.35	.14	.03
☐ 343	Albie Pearson	.35	.14	.03
☐ 344	Ed Bauta	.35	.14	.03
☐ 345	Chuck Schilling	.35	.14	.03
☐ 346	Jack Kralick	.35	.14	.03
☐ 347	Chuck Hinton	.35	.14	.03
☐ 348	Larry Burright	.35	.14	.03
☐ 349	Paul Foytack	.35	.14	.03
☐ 350	Frank Robinson	7.00	2.80	.70
☐ 351	Braves' Backstops	.60	.24	.06
	Joe Torre			
	Del Crandall			
☐ 352	Frank Sullivan	.35	.14	.03
☐ 353	Bill Mazeroski	1.00	.40	.10
☐ 354	Roman Mejias	.35	.14	.03
☐ 355	Steve Barber	.35	.14	.03
☐ 356	Tom Haller	.35	.14	.03
☐ 357	Jerry Walker	.35	.14	.03
☐ 358	Tommy Davis	1.00	.40	.10
☐ 359	Bobby Locke	.35	.14	.03
☐ 360	Yogi Berra	9.00	3.75	.90
☐ 361	Bob Hendley	.35	.14	.03
☐ 362	Ty Cline	.35	.14	.03
☐ 363	Bob Roselli	.35	.14	.03
☐ 364	Ken Hunt	.35	.14	.03
☐ 365	Charley Neal	.50	.20	.05
☐ 366	Phil Regan	.50	.20	.05
☐ 367	Checklist 5	2.50	.25	.05
☐ 368	Bob Tillman	.35	.14	.03
☐ 369	Ted Bowsfield	.35	.14	.03
☐ 370	Ken Boyer	1.50	.60	.15
☐ 371	Earl Battey	.55	.22	.05
☐ 372	Jack Curtis	.55	.22	.05
☐ 373	Al Heist	.55	.22	.05
☐ 374	Gene Mauch	.75	.30	.07
☐ 375	Ron Fairly	.75	.30	.07
☐ 376	Bud Daley	.55	.22	.05
☐ 377	John Orsino	.55	.22	.05
☐ 378	Bennie Daniels	.55	.22	.05
☐ 379	Chuck Essegian	.55	.22	.05
☐ 380	Lou Burdette	1.00	.40	.10
☐ 381	Chico Cardenas	.55	.22	.05
☐ 382	Dick Williams	.75	.30	.07
☐ 383	Ray Sadecki	.55	.22	.05
☐ 384	K.C. Athletics	1.00	.40	.10
	Team Card			
☐ 385	Early Wynn	3.50	1.40	.35
☐ 386	Don Mincher	.55	.22	.05
☐ 387	Lou Brock	45.00	18.00	4.50
☐ 388	Ryne Duren	.75	.30	.07
☐ 389	Smoky Burgess	.75	.30	.07
☐ 390	Orlando Cepeda AS	1.00	.40	.10
☐ 391	Bill Mazeroski AS	.75	.30	.07
☐ 392	Ken Boyer AS	.75	.30	.07
☐ 393	Roy McMillan AS	.55	.22	.05
☐ 394	Hank Aaron AS	8.00	3.25	.80
☐ 395	Willie Mays AS	8.00	3.25	.80
☐ 396	Frank Robinson AS	3.50	1.40	.35
☐ 397	John Roseboro AS	.55	.22	.05
☐ 398	Don Drysdale AS	3.00	1.20	.30
☐ 399	Warren Spahn AS	3.00	1.20	.30
☐ 400	Elston Howard	1.75	.70	.17
☐ 401	AL/NL Homer Kings	6.00	2.40	.60
	Roger Maris			
	Orlando Cepeda			
☐ 402	Gino Cimoli	.55	.22	.05
☐ 403	Chet Nichols	.55	.22	.05
☐ 404	Tim Harkness	.55	.22	.05
☐ 405	Jim Perry	.90	.36	.09
☐ 406	Bob Taylor	.55	.22	.05
☐ 407	Hank Aguirre	.55	.22	.05
☐ 408	Gus Bell	.75	.30	.07
☐ 409	Pirates Team	1.00	.40	.10
☐ 410	Al Smith	.55	.22	.05
☐ 411	Danny O'Connell	.55	.22	.05
☐ 412	Charlie James	.55	.22	.05
☐ 413	Matty Alou	.75	.30	.07
☐ 414	Joe Gaines	.55	.22	.05
☐ 415	Bill Virdon	.90	.36	.09
☐ 416	Bob Scheffing MGR	.55	.22	.05
☐ 417	Joe Azcue	.55	.22	.05
☐ 418	Andy Carey	.55	.22	.05
☐ 419	Bob Bruce	.55	.22	.05
☐ 420	Gus Triandos	.55	.22	.05
☐ 421	Ken Mackenzie	.55	.22	.05
☐ 422	Steve Bilko	.55	.22	.05
☐ 423	Rival League			
	Relief Aces	1.50	.60	.15
	Roy Face			
	Hoyt Wilhelm			
☐ 424	Al McBean	.55	.22	.05
☐ 425	Carl Yastrzemski	80.00	32.00	8.00
☐ 426	Bob Farley	.55	.22	.05
☐ 427	Jake Wood	.55	.22	.05
☐ 428	Joe Hicks	.55	.22	.05
☐ 429	Billy O'Dell	.55	.22	.05
☐ 430	Tony Kubek	3.00	1.20	.30
☐ 431	Bob Rodgers	.55	.22	.05
☐ 432	Jim Pendleton	.55	.22	.05
☐ 433	Jim Archer	.55	.22	.05
☐ 434	Clay Dalrymple	.55	.22	.05
☐ 435	Larry Sherry	.75	.30	.07
☐ 436	Felix Mantilla	.55	.22	.05
☐ 437	Ray Moore	.55	.22	.05

		MINT	VG-E	F-G
☐ 438	Dick Brown	.55	.22	.05
☐ 439	Jerry Buchek	.55	.22	.05
☐ 440	Joe Jay	.55	.22	.05
☐ 441	Checklist 6	3.00	.30	.06
☐ 442	Wes Stock	.55	.22	.05
☐ 443	Del Crandall	.75	.30	.07
☐ 444	Ted Wills	.55	.22	.05
☐ 445	Vic Power	.55	.22	.05
☐ 446	Don Elston	.55	.22	.05
☐ 447	Willie Kirkland	.55	.22	.05
☐ 448	Joe Gibbon	.55	.22	.05
☐ 449	Jerry Adair	.55	.22	.05
☐ 450	Jim O'Toole	.55	.22	.05
☐ 451	Jose Tartabull	.55	.22	.05
☐ 452	Earl Averill	.55	.22	.05
☐ 453	Cal McLish	.55	.22	.05
☐ 454	Floyd Robinson	.55	.22	.05
☐ 455	Luis Arroyo	.55	.22	.05
☐ 456	Joe Amalfitano	.55	.22	.05
☐ 457	Lou Clinton	.55	.22	.05
☐ 458 A	Bob Buhl	.75	.30	.07
	(Braves cap emblem)			
☐ 458 B	Bob Buhl	15.00	6.00	1.50
	(no emblem on cap)			
☐ 459	Ed Bailey	.55	.22	.05
☐ 460	Jim Bunning	2.50	1.00	.25
☐ 461	Ken Hubbs	2.50	1.00	.25
☐ 462 A	Willie Tasby	.75	.30	.07
	(Senators cap emblem)			
☐ 462 B	Willie Tasby	15.00	6.00	1.50
	(no emblem on cap)			
☐ 463	Hank Bauer	.75	.30	.07
☐ 464	Al Jackson	.55	.22	.05
☐ 465	Reds Team	1.25	.50	.12
☐ 466	Norm Cash AS	.75	.30	.07
☐ 467	Chuck Schilling AS	.55	.22	.05
☐ 468	Brooks Robinson AS	4.50	1.80	.45
☐ 469	Luis Aparicio AS	2.00	.80	.20
☐ 470	Al Kaline AS	4.50	1.80	.45
☐ 471	Mickey Mantle AS	20.00	8.00	2.00
☐ 472	Rocky Colavito AS	.90	.36	.09
☐ 473	Elston Howard AS	.90	.36	.09
☐ 474	Frank Lary AS	.55	.22	.05
☐ 475	Whitey Ford AS	4.00	1.60	.40
☐ 476	Orioles Team	1.25	.50	.12
☐ 477	Andre Rodgers	.55	.22	.05
☐ 478	Don Zimmer	.75	.30	.07
☐ 479	Joel Horlen	.75	.30	.07
☐ 480	Harvey Kuenn	1.00	.40	.10
☐ 481	Vic Wertz	.75	.30	.07
☐ 482	Sam Mele MGR	.55	.22	.05
☐ 483	Don McMahon	.55	.22	.05
☐ 484	Dick Schofield	.55	.22	.05
☐ 485	Pedro Ramos	.55	.22	.05
☐ 486	Jim Gilliam	2.50	1.00	.25
☐ 487	Jerry Lynch	.55	.22	.05
☐ 488	Hal Brown	.55	.22	.05
☐ 489	Julio Gotay	.55	.22	.05
☐ 490	Clete Boyer	1.75	.70	.17
☐ 491	Leon Wagner	.55	.22	.05
☐ 492	Hal W. Smith	.55	.22	.05
☐ 493	Danny McDevitt	.55	.22	.05
☐ 494	Sammy White	.55	.22	.05
☐ 495	Don Cardwell	.55	.22	.05
☐ 496	Wayne Causey	.55	.22	.05
☐ 497	Ed Bouchee	.55	.22	.05
☐ 498	Jim Donohue	.55	.22	.05
☐ 499	Zoilo Versalles	.55	.22	.05
☐ 500	Duke Snider	12.00	5.00	1.20
☐ 501	Claude Osteen	.75	.30	.07
☐ 502	Hector Lopez	.55	.22	.05
☐ 503	Danny Murtaugh MGR	.55	.22	.05
☐ 504	Eddie Bressoud	.55	.22	.05
☐ 505	Juan Marichal	10.00	4.00	1.00
☐ 506	Charlie Maxwell	.55	.22	.05
☐ 507	Ernie Broglio	.55	.22	.05
☐ 508	Gordy Coleman	.55	.22	.05
☐ 509	Dave Giusti	.75	.30	.07
☐ 510	Jim Lemon	.55	.22	.05
☐ 511	Bubba Phillips	.55	.22	.05
☐ 512	Mike Fornieles	.55	.22	.05
☐ 513	Whitey Herzog	1.00	.40	.10
☐ 514	Sherm Lollar	.55	.22	.05
☐ 515	Stan Williams	.55	.22	.05
☐ 516	Checklist 7	5.00	.50	.10
☐ 517	Dave Wickersham	.55	.22	.05
☐ 518	Lee Maye	.55	.22	.05
☐ 519	Bob Johnson	.55	.22	.05
☐ 520	Bob Friend	.75	.30	.07
☐ 521	Jacke Davis	.55	.22	.05
☐ 522	Lindy McDaniel	.55	.22	.05
☐ 523	Russ Nixon	2.50	1.00	.25
☐ 524	Howie Nunn	2.50	1.00	.25
☐ 525	George Thomas	2.50	1.00	.25
☐ 526	Hal Woodeshick	2.50	1.00	.25
☐ 527	Dick McAuliffe	3.00	1.20	.30
☐ 528	Turk Lown	2.50	1.00	.25
☐ 529	John Schaive	2.50	1.00	.25
☐ 530	Bob Gibson	35.00	14.00	3.50
☐ 531	Bobby G. Smith	2.50	1.00	.25
☐ 532	Dick Stigman	2.50	1.00	.25
☐ 533	Charley Lau	2.50	1.00	.25
☐ 534	Tony Gonzalez	2.50	1.00	.25
☐ 535	Ed Roebuck	2.50	1.00	.25
☐ 536	Dick Gernert	2.50	1.00	.25
☐ 537	Indians Team	4.50	1.80	.45

		MINT	VG-E	F-G
☐ 538	Jack Sanford	2.50	1.00	.25
☐ 539	Billy Moran	2.50	1.00	.25
☐ 540	Jim Landis	2.50	1.00	.25
☐ 541	Don Nottebart	2.50	1.00	.25
☐ 542	Dave Philley	2.50	1.00	.25
☐ 543	Bob Allen	2.50	1.00	.25
☐ 544	Willie McCovey	35.00	14.00	3.50
☐ 545	Hoyt Wilhelm	15.00	6.00	1.50
☐ 546	Moe Thacker	2.50	1.00	.25
☐ 547	Don Ferrarese	2.50	1.00	.25
☐ 548	Bobby Del Greco	2.50	1.00	.25
☐ 549	Bill Rigney MGR	2.50	1.00	.25
☐ 550	Art Mahaffey	2.50	1.00	.25
☐ 551	Harry Bright	2.50	1.00	.25
☐ 552	Chicago Cubs Team	4.50	1.80	.45
☐ 553	Jim Coates	2.50	1.00	.25
☐ 554	Bubba Morton	2.50	1.00	.25
☐ 555	John Buzhardt	2.50	1.00	.25
☐ 556	Al Spangler	2.50	1.00	.25
☐ 557	Bob Anderson	2.50	1.00	.25
☐ 558	John Goryl	2.50	1.00	.25
☐ 559	Mike Higgins MGR	2.50	1.00	.25
☐ 560	Chuck Estrada	2.50	1.00	.25
☐ 561	Gene Oliver	2.50	1.00	.25
☐ 562	Bill Henry	2.50	1.00	.25
☐ 563	Ken Aspromonte	2.50	1.00	.25
☐ 564	Bob Grim	2.50	1.00	.25
☐ 565	Jose Pagan	2.50	1.00	.25
☐ 566	Marty Kutyna	2.50	1.00	.25
☐ 567	Tracy Stallard	2.50	1.00	.25
☐ 568	Jim Golden	2.50	1.00	.25
☐ 569	Ed Sadowski	2.50	1.00	.25
☐ 570	Bill Stafford	2.50	1.00	.25
☐ 571	Billy Klaus	2.50	1.00	.25
☐ 572	Bob G. Miller	2.50	1.00	.25
☐ 573	Johnny Logan	2.50	1.00	.25
☐ 574	Dean Stone	2.50	1.00	.25
☐ 575	Red Schoendienst	3.00	1.20	.30
☐ 576	Russ Kemmerer	2.50	1.00	.25
☐ 577	Dave Nicholson	2.50	1.00	.25
☐ 578	Jim Duffalo	2.50	1.00	.25
☐ 579	Jim Schaffer	2.50	1.00	.25
☐ 580	Bill Monbouquette	2.50	1.00	.25
☐ 581	Mel Roach	2.50	1.00	.25
☐ 582	Ron Piche	2.50	1.00	.25
☐ 583	Larry Osborne	2.50	1.00	.25
☐ 584	Minnesota Twins Team Card	4.50	1.80	.45
☐ 585	Glen Hobbie	2.50	1.00	.25
☐ 586	Sam Esposito	2.50	1.00	.25
☐ 587	Frank Funk	2.50	1.00	.25
☐ 588	Birdie Tebbetts MGR	2.50	1.00	.25
☐ 589	Bob Turley	3.00	1.20	.30

		MINT	VG-E	F-G
☐ 590	Curt Flood	3.50	1.40	.35
☐ 591	Rookie Pitchers	9.00	3.75	.90
	Sam McDowell			
	Ron Taylor			
	Ron Nischwitz			
	Art Quirk			
	Dick Radatz			
☐ 592	Rookie Pitchers	12.00	5.00	1.20
	Dan Pfister			
	Bo Belinsky			
	Dave Stenhouse			
	Jim Bouton			
	Joe Bonikowski			
☐ 593	Rookie Pitchers	6.00	2.40	.60
	Jack Lamabe			
	Craig Anderson			
	Jack Hamilton			
	Bob Moorhead			
	Bob Veale			
☐ 594	Rookie Catchers	35.00	14.00	3.50
	Doc Edwards			
	Ken Retzer			
	Bob Uecker			
	Doug Camilli			
	Don Pavletich			
☐ 595	Rookie Catchers	5.00	2.00	.50
	Bob Sadowski			
	Felix Torres			
	Marlan Coughtry			
	Ed Charles			
☐ 596	Rookie Infielders	9.00	3.75	.90
	Bernie Allen			
	Joe Pepitone			
	Phil Linz			
	Rich Rollins			
☐ 597	Rookie Infielders	5.00	2.00	.50
	Jim McKnight			
	Rod Kanehl			
	Amado Samuel			
	Denis Menke			
☐ 598	Rookie Outfielders	6.00	2.40	.60
	Al Luplow			
	Manny Jimenez			
	Howie Goss			
	Jim Hickman			
	Ed Olivares			

1963 Topps

*The cards in this 576-card set measure 2½"
by 3½". The sharp color photographs of the
1963 set are a vivid contrast to the drab pictures of 1962. In addition to the "Leaders"
series (1-10) and the World Series cards
(142-148), the seventh and last series of
cards (507-576) contains seven rookie cards
(each depicting four players). This set has
gained special prominence in recent years
since it contains the rookie card of Pete Rose,
#537.*

	MINT	VG-E	F-G
Complete Set	1350.00	600.00	150.00
Common Player (1-196)	.25	.10	.02
Common Player (197-446)	.35	.14	.03
Common Player (447-506)	2.50	1.00	.25
Common Player (507-576)	2.00	.80	.20

			MINT	VG-E	F-G
☐	1	NL Batting Leaders Tommy Davis Frank Robinson Stan Musial Hank Aaron Bill White	3.00	.60	.12
☐	2	AL Batting Leaders Pete Runnels Mickey Mantle Floyd Robinson Norm Siebern Chuck Hinton	2.00	.80	.20
☐	3	NL Home Run Leaders Willie Mays Hank Aaron Frank Robinson Orlando Cepeda Ernie Banks	3.00	1.20	.30
☐	4	AL Home Run Leaders Harmon Killebrew Norm Cash Rocky Colavito Roger Maris Jim Gentile Leon Wagner	1.25	.50	.12
☐	5	NL ERA Leaders Sandy Koufax Bob Shaw Bob Purkey Bob Gibson Don Drysdale	1.50	.60	.15
☐	6	AL ERA Leaders Hank Aguirre Robin Roberts Whitey Ford Eddie Fisher Dean Chance	1.00	.40	.10
☐	7	AL Pitching Leaders Don Drysdale Jack Sanford Bob Purkey Billy O'Dell Art Mahaffey Joe Jay	1.00	.40	.10
☐	8	AL Pitching Leaders Ralph Terry Dick Donovan Ray Herbert Jim Bunning Camilo Pascual	.80	.32	.08
☐	9	NL Strikeout Leaders Don Drysdale Sandy Koufax Bob Gibson Billy O'Dell Dick Farrell	2.00	.80	.20
☐	10	AL Strikeout Leaders Camilo Pascual Jim Bunning Ralph Terry Juan Pizarro Jim Kaat	.80	.32	.08
☐	11	Lee Walls	.25	.10	.02
☐	12	Steve Barber	.25	.10	.02
☐	13	Phillies Team	.70	.28	.07

			MINT	VG-E	F-G
☐	14	Pedro Ramos	.25	.10	.02
☐	15	Ken Hubbs	1.00	.40	.10
☐	16	Al Smith	.25	.10	.02
☐	17	Ryne Duren	.35	.14	.03
☐	18	Buc Blasters	2.00	.80	.20
		Smoky Burgess			
		Dick Stuart			
		Bob Clemente			
		Bob Skinner			
☐	19	Pete Burnside	.25	.10	.02
☐	20	Tony Kubek	1.50	.60	.15
☐	21	Marty Keough	.25	.10	.02
☐	22	Curt Simmons	.35	.14	.06
☐	23	Ed Lopat MGR	.60	.24	.06
☐	24	Bob Bruce	.25	.10	.02
☐	25	Al Kaline	5.00	2.00	.50
☐	26	Ray Moore	.25	.10	.02
☐	27	Choo Choo Coleman	.25	.10	.02
☐	28	Mike Fornieles	.25	.10	.02
☐	29	A 1963 Rookie Stars	.35	.14	.03
		Sammy Ellis			
		Ray Culp			
		John Boozer			
		Jesse Gonder			
☐	29	B 1962 Rookie Stars	2.00	.80	.20
		Sammy Ellis			
		Ray Culp			
		John Boozer			
		Jesse Gonder			
☐	30	Harvey Kuenn	.70	.28	.07
☐	31	Cal Koonce	.25	.10	.02
☐	32	Tony Gonzalez	.25	.10	.02
☐	33	Bo Belinsky	.35	.14	.03
☐	34	Dick Schofield	.25	.10	.02
☐	35	John Buzhardt	.25	.10	.02
☐	36	Jerry Kindall	.25	.10	.02
☐	37	Jerry Lynch	.25	.10	.02
☐	38	Bud Daley	.25	.10	.02
☐	39	Angels Team	.70	.28	.07
☐	40	Vic Power	.25	.10	.02
☐	41	Charley Lau	.35	.14	.03
☐	42	Stan Williams	.25	.10	.02
☐	43	Veteran Masters	1.25	.50	.12
		Casey Stengel			
		Gene Woodling			
☐	44	Terry Fox	.25	.10	.02
☐	45	Bob Aspromonte	.25	.10	.02
☐	46	Tommy Aaron	.35	.14	.03
☐	47	Don Lock	.25	.10	.02
☐	48	Birdie Tebbetts MGR	.25	.10	.02
☐	49	Dal Maxvill	.25	.10	.02
☐	50	Billy Pierce	.60	.24	.06
☐	51	George Alusik	.25	.10	.02

			MINT	VG-E	F-G
☐	52	Chuck Schilling	.25	.10	.02
☐	53	Joe Moeller	.25	.10	.02
☐	54	A 1963 Rookie Stars	2.50	1.00	.25
		Nelson Mathews			
		Harry Fanok			
		Jack Cullen			
		Dave DeBusschere			
☐	54	B 1962 Rookie Stars	4.00	1.60	.40
		Nelson Mathews			
		Harry Fanok			
		Jack Cullen			
		Dave DeBusschere			
☐	55	Bill Virdon	.80	.32	.08
☐	56	Dennis Bennett	.25	.10	.02
☐	57	Billy Moran	.25	.10	.02
☐	58	Bob Will	.25	.10	.02
☐	59	Craig Anderson	.25	.10	.02
☐	60	Elston Howard	2.00	.80	.20
☐	61	Ernie Bowman	.25	.10	.02
☐	62	Bob Hendley	.25	.10	.02
☐	63	Reds Team	.70	.28	.07
☐	64	Dick McAuliffe	.25	.10	.02
☐	65	Jackie Brandt	.25	.10	.02
☐	66	Mike Joyce	.25	.10	.02
☐	67	Ed Charles	.25	.10	.02
☐	68	Friendly Foes	3.00	1.20	.30
		Duke Snider			
		Gil Hodges			
☐	69	Bud Zipfel	.25	.10	.02
☐	70	Jim O'Toole	.25	.10	.02
☐	71	Bobby Wine	.25	.10	.02
☐	72	Johnny Romano	.25	.10	.02
☐	73	Bob Bragan MGR	.25	.10	.02
☐	74	Denny Lemaster	.25	.10	.02
☐	75	Bob Allison	.35	.14	.03
☐	76	Earl Wilson	.25	.10	.02
☐	77	Al Spangler	.25	.10	.02
☐	78	Marv Throneberry	.80	.32	.08
☐	79	Checklist 1	2.50	.25	.05
☐	80	Jim Gilliam	1.50	.60	.15
☐	81	Jim Schaffer	.25	.10	.02
☐	82	Ed Rakow	.25	.10	.02
☐	83	Charley James	.25	.10	.02
☐	84	Ron Kline	.25	.10	.02
☐	85	Tom Haller	.25	.10	.02
☐	86	Charley Maxwell	.25	.10	.02
☐	87	Bob Veale	.35	.14	.03
☐	88	Ron Hansen	.25	.10	.02
☐	89	Dick Stigman	.25	.10	.02
☐	90	Gordy Coleman	.25	.10	.02
☐	91	Dallas Green	.35	.14	.03
☐	92	Hector Lopez	.25	.10	.02
☐	93	Galen Cisco	.25	.10	.02

		MINT	VG-E	F-G
☐ 94	Bob Schmidt	.25	.10	.02
☐ 95	Larry Jackson	.25	.10	.02
☐ 96	Lou Clinton	.25	.10	.02
☐ 97	Bob Duliba	.25	.10	.02
☐ 98	George Thomas	.25	.10	.02
☐ 99	Jim Umbricht	.25	.10	.02
☐ 100	Joe Cunningham	.35	.14	.03
☐ 101	Joe Gibbon	.25	.10	.02
☐ 102 A	Checklist 2 (red on yellow)	2.50	.25	.05
☐ 102 B	Checklist 2 (white on red)	3.50	.35	.07
☐ 103	Chuck Essegian	.25	.10	.02
☐ 104	Lew Krausse	.25	.10	.02
☐ 105	Ron Fairly	.35	.14	.03
☐ 106	Bobby Bolin	.25	.10	.02
☐ 107	Jim Hickman	.25	.10	.02
☐ 108	Hoyt Wilhelm	3.00	1.20	.30
☐ 109	Lee Maye	.25	.10	.02
☐ 110	Rich Rollins	.25	.10	.02
☐ 111	Al Jackson	.25	.10	.02
☐ 112	Dick Brown	.25	.10	.02
☐ 113	Don Landrum (photo actually Ron Santo)	.35	.14	.03
☐ 114	Dan Osinski	.25	.10	.02
☐ 115	Carl Yastrzemski	35.00	14.00	3.50
☐ 116	Jim Brosnan	.35	.14	.03
☐ 117	Jacke Davis	.25	.10	.02
☐ 118	Sherm Lollar	.35	.14	.03
☐ 119	Bob Lillis	.35	.14	.03
☐ 120	Roger Maris	6.50	2.60	.65
☐ 121	Jim Hannan	.25	.10	.02
☐ 122	Julio Gotay	.25	.10	.02
☐ 123	Frank Howard	1.00	.40	.10
☐ 124	Dick Howser	.50	.20	.05
☐ 125	Robin Roberts	3.00	1.20	.30
☐ 126	Bob Uecker	5.00	2.00	.50
☐ 127	Bill Tuttle	.25	.10	.02
☐ 128	Matty Alou	.35	.14	.03
☐ 129	Gary Bell	.25	.10	.02
☐ 130	Dick Groat	.60	.24	.06
☐ 131	Senators Team	.70	.28	.07
☐ 132	Jack Hamilton	.25	.10	.02
☐ 133	Gene Freese	.25	.10	.02
☐ 134	Bob Scheffing MGR	.25	.10	.02
☐ 135	Richie Ashburn	1.50	.60	.15
☐ 136	Ike Delock	.25	.10	.02
☐ 137	Mack Jones	.25	.10	.02
☐ 138	Pride of NL Willie Mays Stan Musial	7.50	3.00	.75
☐ 139	Earl Averill	.25	.10	.02

		MINT	VG-E	F-G
☐ 140	Frank Lary	.35	.14	.03
☐ 141	Manny Mota	1.50	.60	.15
☐ 142	World Series Game 1 ... Ford wins series opener	2.25	.90	.22
☐ 143	World Series Game 2 ... Sanford flashes shutout magic	1.50	.60	.15
☐ 144	World Series Game 3 ... Maris sparks Yankee rally	2.25	.90	.22
☐ 145	World Series Game 4 ... Hiller blasts grand slammer	1.50	.60	.15
☐ 146	World Series Game 5 ... Tresh's homer defeats Giants	1.50	.60	.15
☐ 147	World Series Game 6 ... Pierce stars in 3 hit victory	1.50	.60	.15
☐ 148	World Series Game 7 ... Yanks celebrate as Terry wins	1.50	.60	.15
☐ 149	Marv Breeding	.25	.10	.02
☐ 150	John Podres	.90	.36	.09
☐ 151	Pirates Team	.70	.28	.07
☐ 152	Ron Nischwitz	.25	.10	.02
☐ 153	Hal Smith	.25	.10	.02
☐ 154	Walt Alston MGR	1.00	.40	.10
☐ 155	Bill Stafford	.25	.10	.02
☐ 156	Roy McMillan	.25	.10	.02
☐ 157	Diego Segui	.25	.10	.02
☐ 158	Rookie Stars Rogelio Alvares Dave Roberts Tommy Harper Bob Saverine	.35	.14	.03
☐ 159	Jim Pagliaroni	.25	.10	.02
☐ 160	Juan Pizarro	.25	.10	.02
☐ 161	Frank Torre	.25	.10	.02
☐ 162	Twins Team	.70	.28	.07
☐ 163	Don Larsen	.50	.20	.05
☐ 164	Bubba Morton	.25	.10	.02
☐ 165	Jim Kaat	1.75	.70	.17
☐ 166	Johnny Keane MGR	.35	.14	.03
☐ 167	Jim Fregosi	.80	.32	.08
☐ 168	Russ Nixon	.25	.10	.02
☐ 169	Rookie Stars Dick Egan Julio Navarro Tommie Sisk Gaylord Perry	6.50	2.60	.65
☐ 170	Joe Adcock	.50	.20	.05

		MINT	VG-E	F-G			MINT	VG-E	F-G
☐ 171	Steve Hamilton	.25	.10	.02	☐ 217	Joe Christopher	.35	.14	.03
☐ 172	Gene Oliver	.25	.10	.02	☐ 218	Tiger Twirlers	.75	.30	.07
☐ 173	Bombers' Best	9.00	3.75	.90		Frank Lary			
	Tom Tresh					Don Mossi			
	Mickey Mantle					Jim Bunning			
	Bobby Richardson				☐ 219	Chuck Cottier	.35	.14	.03
☐ 174	Larry Burright	.25	.10	.02	☐ 220	Camilo Pascual	.35	.14	.03
☐ 175	Bob Buhl	.25	.10	.02	☐ 221	Cookie Rojas	.35	.14	.03
☐ 176	Jim King	.25	.10	.02	☐ 222	Cubs Team	1.00	.40	.10
☐ 177	Bubba Phillips	.25	.10	.02	☐ 223	Eddie Fisher	.35	.14	.03
☐ 178	Johnny Edwards	.25	.10	.02	☐ 224	Mike Roarke	.35	.14	.03
☐ 179	Ron Piche	.25	.10	.02	☐ 225	Joe Jay	.35	.14	.03
☐ 180	Bill Skowron	.80	.32	.08	☐ 226	Julian Javier	.35	.14	.03
☐ 181	Sammy Esposito	.25	.10	.02	☐ 227	Jim Grant	.35	.14	.03
☐ 182	Albie Pearson	.25	.10	.02	☐ 228	Rookie Stars	6.50	2.60	.65
☐ 183	Joe Pepitone	.60	.24	.06		Max Alvis			
☐ 184	Vern Law	.35	.14	.03		Bob Bailey			
☐ 185	Chuck Hiller	.25	.10	.02		Pedro Oliva			
☐ 186	Jerry Zimmerman	.25	.10	.02		Ed Kranepool			
☐ 187	Willie Kirkland	.25	.10	.02	☐ 229	Willie Davis	.75	.30	.07
☐ 188	Eddie Bressoud	.25	.10	.02	☐ 230	Pete Runnels	.50	.20	.05
☐ 189	Dave Giusti	.25	.10	.02	☐ 231	Eli Grba	.50	.20	.05
☐ 190	Minnie Minoso	1.00	.40	.10		(large photo is			
☐ 191	Checklist 3	2.50	.25	.05		Ryne Duren)			
☐ 192	Clay Dalrymple	.25	.10	.02	☐ 232	Frank Malzone	.50	.20	.05
☐ 193	Andre Rodgers	.25	.10	.02	☐ 233	Casey Stengel MGR	4.00	1.60	.40
☐ 194	Joe Nuxhall	.35	.14	.03	☐ 234	Dave Nicholson	.35	.14	.03
☐ 195	Manny Jimenez	.25	.10	.02	☐ 235	Billy O'Dell	.35	.14	.03
☐ 196	Doug Camilli	.25	.10	.02	☐ 236	Bill Bryan	.35	.14	.03
☐ 197	Roger Craig	.75	.30	.07	☐ 237	Jim Coates	.35	.14	.03
☐ 198	Lenny Green	.35	.14	.03	☐ 238	Lou Johnson	.35	.14	.03
☐ 199	Joe Amalfitano	.35	.14	.03	☐ 239	Harvey Haddix	.50	.20	.05
☐ 200	Mickey Mantle	75.00	30.00	7.50	☐ 240	Rocky Colavito	1.25	.50	.12
☐ 201	Cecil Butler	.35	.14	.03	☐ 241	Bob Smith	.35	.14	.03
☐ 202	Red Sox Team	1.00	.40	.10	☐ 242	Power Plus	4.50	1.80	.45
☐ 203	Chico Cardenas	.35	.14	.03		Ernie Banks			
☐ 204	Don Nottebart	.35	.14	.03		Hank Aaron			
☐ 205	Luis Aparicio	3.50	1.40	.35	☐ 243	Don Leppert	.35	.14	.03
☐ 206	Ray Washburn	.35	.14	.03	☐ 244	John Tsitouris	.35	.14	.03
☐ 207	Ken Hunt	.35	.14	.03	☐ 245	Gil Hodges	3.50	1.40	.35
☐ 208	Rookie Stars	.35	.14	.03	☐ 246	Lee Stange	.35	.14	.03
	Ron Herbel				☐ 247	Yankees Team	3.50	1.40	.35
	John Miller				☐ 248	Tito Francona	.35	.14	.03
	Wally Wolf				☐ 249	Leo Burke	.35	.14	.03
	Ron Taylor				☐ 250	Stan Musial	20.00	8.00	2.00
☐ 209	Hobie Landrith	.35	.14	.03	☐ 251	Jack Lamabe	.35	.14	.03
☐ 210	Sandy Koufax	27.00	11.00	2.70	☐ 252	Ron Santo	1.25	.50	.12
☐ 211	Fred Whitfield	.35	.14	.03	☐ 253	Rookie Stars	.35	.14	.03
☐ 212	Glen Hobbie	.35	.14	.03		Len Gabrielson			
☐ 213	Billy Hitchcock MGR	.35	.14	.03		Pete Jernigan			
☐ 214	Orlando Pena	.35	.14	.03		John Wojcik			
☐ 215	Bob Skinner	.35	.14	.03		Deacon Jones			
☐ 216	Gene Conley	.35	.14	.03	☐ 254	Mike Hershberger	.35	.14	.03

	MINT	VG-E	F-G
☐ 255 Bob Shaw	.35	.14	.03
☐ 256 Jerry Lumpe	.35	.14	.03
☐ 257 Hank Aguirre	.35	.14	.03
☐ 258 Al Dark MGR	.60	.24	.06
☐ 259 John Logan	.50	.20	.05
☐ 260 Jim Gentile	.50	.20	.05
☐ 261 Bob Miller	.35	.14	.03
☐ 262 Ellis Burton	.35	.14	.03
☐ 263 Dave Stenhouse	.35	.14	.03
☐ 264 Phil Linz	.35	.14	.03
☐ 265 Vada Pinson	1.25	.50	.12
☐ 266 Bob Allen	.35	.14	.03
☐ 267 Carl Sawatski	.35	.14	.03
☐ 268 Don Demeter	.35	.14	.03
☐ 269 Don Mincher	.50	.20	.05
☐ 270 Felipe Alou	.75	.30	.07
☐ 271 Dean Stone	.35	.14	.03
☐ 272 Danny Murphy	.35	.14	.03
☐ 273 Sammy Taylor	.35	.14	.03
☐ 274 Checklist 4	2.50	.25	.05
☐ 275 Eddie Mathews	4.50	1.80	.45
☐ 276 Barry Shetrone	.35	.14	.03
☐ 277 Dick Farrell	.35	.14	.03
☐ 278 Chico Fernandez	.35	.14	.03
☐ 279 Wally Moon	.50	.20	.05
☐ 280 Bob Rodgers	.35	.14	.03
☐ 281 Tom Sturdivant	.35	.14	.03
☐ 282 Bobby Del Greco	.35	.14	.03
☐ 283 Roy Sievers	.50	.20	.05
☐ 284 Dave Sisler	.35	.14	.03
☐ 285 Dick Stuart	.50	.20	.05
☐ 286 Stu Miller	.35	.14	.03
☐ 287 Dick Bertell	.35	.14	.03
☐ 288 White Sox Team	1.00	.40	.10
☐ 289 Hal Brown	.35	.14	.03
☐ 290 Bill White	.50	.20	.05
☐ 291 Don Rudolph	.35	.14	.03
☐ 292 Pumpsie Green	.35	.14	.03
☐ 293 Bill Pleis	.35	.14	.03
☐ 294 Bill Rigney MGR	.35	.14	.03
☐ 295 Ed Roebuck	.35	.14	.03
☐ 296 Doc Edwards	.35	.14	.03
☐ 297 Jim Golden	.35	.14	.03
☐ 298 Don Dillard	.35	.14	.03
☐ 299 Rookie Stars	.35	.14	.03
Dave Morehead			
Bob Dustal			
Tom Butters			
Dan Schneider			
☐ 300 Willie Mays	35.00	14.00	3.50
☐ 301 Bill Fischer	.35	.14	.03
☐ 302 Whitey Herzog	.75	.30	.07
☐ 303 Earl Francis	.35	.14	.03

	MINT	VG-E	F-G
☐ 304 Harry Bright	.35	.14	.03
☐ 305 Don Hoak	.35	.14	.03
☐ 306 Star Receivers	.80	.32	.08
Earl Battey			
Elston Howard			
☐ 307 Chet Nichols	.35	.14	.03
☐ 308 Camilo Carreon	.35	.14	.03
☐ 309 Jim Brewer	.35	.14	.03
☐ 310 Tommy Davis	1.00	.40	.10
☐ 311 Joe McClain	.35	.14	.03
☐ 312 Houston Colts Team	3.00	1.20	.30
☐ 313 Ernie Broglio	.50	.20	.05
☐ 314 John Goryl	.35	.14	.03
☐ 315 Ralph Terry	.50	.20	.05
☐ 316 Norm Sherry	.50	.20	.05
☐ 317 Sam McDowell	.75	.30	.07
☐ 318 Gene Mauch MGR	.75	.30	.07
☐ 319 Joe Gaines	.35	.14	.03
☐ 320 Warren Spahn	6.50	2.60	.65
☐ 321 Gino Cimoli	.35	.14	.03
☐ 322 Bob Turley	.75	.30	.07
☐ 323 Bill Mazeroski	1.00	.40	.10
☐ 324 Rookie Stars	.75	.30	.07
George Williams			
Pete Ward			
Phil Ward			
Vic Davalillo			
☐ 325 Jack Sanford	.35	.14	.03
☐ 326 Hank Foiles	.35	.14	.03
☐ 327 Paul Foytack	.35	.14	.03
☐ 328 Dick Williams MGR	.75	.30	.07
☐ 329 Lindy McDaniel	.35	.14	.03
☐ 330 Chuck Hinton	.35	.14	.03
☐ 331 Series Foes	.50	.20	.05
Bill Stafford			
Bill Pierce			
☐ 332 Joel Horlen	.50	.20	.05
☐ 333 Carl Warwick	.35	.14	.03
☐ 334 Wynn Hawkins	.35	.14	.03
☐ 335 Leon Wagner	.35	.14	.03
☐ 336 Ed Bauta	.35	.14	.03
☐ 337 Dodgers Team	3.00	1.20	.30
☐ 338 Russ Kemmerer	.35	.14	.03
☐ 339 Ted Bowsfield	.35	.14	.03
☐ 340 Yogi Berra	12.00	5.00	1.20
☐ 341 Jack Baldschun	.35	.14	.03
☐ 342 Gene Woodling	.50	.20	.05
☐ 343 Johnny Pesky MGR	.50	.20	.05
☐ 344 Don Schwall	.35	.14	.03
☐ 345 Brooks Robinson	12.00	5.00	1.20
☐ 346 Billy Hoeft	.35	.14	.03
☐ 347 Joe Torre	1.75	.70	.17
☐ 348 Vic Wertz	.50	.20	.05

		MINT	VG-E	F-G
349	Zoilo Versailles	.35	.14	.03
350	Bob Purkey	.35	.14	.03
351	Al Luplow	.35	.14	.03
352	Ken Johnson	.35	.14	.03
353	Billy Williams	4.00	1.60	.40
354	Dom Zanni	.35	.14	.03
355	Dean Chance	.50	.20	.05
356	John Schaive	.35	.14	.03
357	George Altman	.35	.14	.03
358	Milt Pappas	.50	.20	.05
359	Haywood Sullivan	.50	.20	.05
360	Don Drysdale	5.50	2.20	.55
361	Cletis Boyer	.75	.30	.07
362	Checklist 5	2.50	.25	.05
363	Dick Radatz	.50	.20	.05
364	Howie Goss	.35	.14	.03
365	Jim Bunning	2.25	.90	.22
366	Tony Taylor	.35	.14	.03
367	Tony Cloninger	.35	.14	.03
368	Ed Bailey	.35	.14	.03
369	Jim Lemon MGR	.35	.14	.03
370	Dick Donovan	.35	.14	.03
371	Rod Kanehl	.35	.14	.03
372	Don Lee	.35	.14	.03
373	Jim Campbell	.35	.14	.03
374	Claude Osteen	.50	.20	.05
375	Ken Boyer	1.50	.60	.15
376	John Wyatt	.35	.14	.03
377	Orioles Team	1.00	.40	.10
378	Bill Henry	.35	.14	.03
379	Bob Anderson	.35	.14	.03
380	Ernie Banks	12.50	5.00	1.25
381	Frank Baumann	.35	.14	.03
382	Ralph Houk MGR	.75	.30	.07
383	Pete Richert	.35	.14	.03
384	Bob Tillman	.35	.14	.03
385	Art Mahaffey	.35	.14	.03
386	Rookie Stars	.60	.24	.06
	Ed Kirkpatrick			
	John Bateman			
	Larry Bearnarth			
	Garry Roggenburk			
387	Al McBean	.35	.14	.03
388	Jim Davenport	.50	.20	.05
389	Frank Sullivan	.35	.14	.03
390	Hank Aaron	35.00	14.00	3.50
391	B. Dailey	.35	.14	.03
392	Tribe Thumpers	.50	.20	.05
	Johnny Romano			
	Tito Francona			
393	Ken MacKenzie	.35	.14	.03
394	Tim McCarver	1.00	.40	.10
395	Don McMahon	.35	.14	.03
396	Joe Koppe	.35	.14	.03
397	K.C. Athletics Team	.90	.36	.09
398	Boog Powell	1.75	.70	.17
399	Dick Ellsworth	.35	.14	.03
400	Frank Robinson	12.00	5.00	1.20
401	Jim Bouton	1.50	.60	.15
402	Mickey Vernon	.50	.20	.05
403	Ron Perranoski	.50	.20	.05
404	Bob Oldis	.35	.14	.03
405	Floyd Robinson	.35	.14	.03
406	Howie Koplitz	.35	.14	.03
407	Rookie Stars	.35	.14	.03
	Frank Kostro			
	Chico Ruiz			
	Larry Elliot			
	Dick Simpson			
408	Billy Gardner	.35	.14	.03
409	Roy Face	.75	.30	.07
410	Earl Battey	.50	.20	.05
411	Jim Constable	.35	.14	.03
412	Dodger Big Three	7.00	2.80	.70
	Johnny Podres			
	Don Drysdale			
	Sandy Koufax			
413	Jerry Walker	.35	.14	.03
414	Ty Cline	.35	.14	.03
415	Bob Gibson	12.00	5.00	1.20
416	Alex Grammas	.35	.14	.03
417	Giants Team	1.00	.40	.10
418	John Orsino	.35	.14	.03
419	Tracy Stallard	.35	.14	.03
420	Bobby Richardson	1.75	.70	.17
421	Tom Morgan	.35	.14	.03
422	Fred Hutchinson MGR	.60	.24	.06
423	Ed Hobaugh	.35	.14	.03
424	Charley Smith	.35	.14	.03
425	Smoky Burgess	.50	.20	.05
426	Barry Latman	.35	.14	.03
427	Bernie Allen	.35	.14	.03
428	Carl Boles	.35	.14	.03
429	Lou Burdette	1.00	.40	.10
430	Norm Siebern	.35	.14	.03
431	A Checklist 6 (white on red)	2.50	.25	.05
431	B Checklist 6 (black on orange)	5.00	.50	.10
432	Roman Mejias	.35	.14	.03
433	Denis Menke	.35	.14	.03
434	John Callison	.50	.20	.05
435	Woody Held	.35	.14	.03
436	Tim Harkness	.35	.14	.03
437	Bill Bruton	.35	.14	.03
438	Wes Stock	.35	.14	.03

		MINT	VG-E	F-G
☐ 439	Don Zimmer	.50	.20	.05
☐ 440	Juan Marichal	7.50	3.00	.75
☐ 441	Lee Thomas	.35	.14	.03
☐ 442	J.C. Hartman	.35	.14	.03
☐ 443	Jim Piersall	.90	.36	.09
☐ 444	Jim Maloney	.75	.30	.07
☐ 445	Norm Cash	1.50	.60	.15
☐ 446	Whitey Ford	12.00	5.00	1.20
☐ 447	Felix Mantilla	2.50	1.00	.25
☐ 448	Jack Kralick	2.50	1.00	.25
☐ 449	Jose Tartabull	2.50	1.00	.25
☐ 450	Bob Friend	3.00	1.20	.30
☐ 451	Indians Team	4.00	1.60	.40
☐ 452	Buddy Schultz	2.50	1.00	.25
☐ 453	Jake Wood	2.50	1.00	.25
☐ 454 A	Art Fowler	2.50	1.00	.25
	(card number on			
	white background)			
☐ 454 B	Art Fowler	5.00	2.00	.50
	(card number on			
	orange background)			
☐ 455	Ruben Amaro	2.50	1.00	.25
☐ 456	Jim Coker	2.50	1.00	.25
☐ 457	Tex Clevenger	2.50	1.00	.25
☐ 458	Al Lopez MGR	4.00	1.60	.40
☐ 459	Dick LeMay	2.50	1.00	.25
☐ 460	Del Crandall	3.00	1.20	.30
☐ 461	Norm Bass	2.50	1.00	.25
☐ 462	Wally Post	2.50	1.00	.25
☐ 463	Joe Schaffernoth	2.50	1.00	.25
☐ 464	Ken Aspromonte	2.50	1.00	.25
☐ 465	Chuck Estrada	2.50	1.00	.25
☐ 466	Rookie Stars	4.00	1.60	.40
	Nate Oliver			
	Tony Martinez			
	Bill Freehan			
	Jerry Robinson			
☐ 467	Phil Ortega	2.50	1.00	.25
☐ 468	Carroll Hardy	2.50	1.00	.25
☐ 469	Jay Hook	2.50	1.00	.25
☐ 470	Tom Tresh	10.00	4.00	1.00
☐ 471	Ken Retzer	2.50	1.00	.25
☐ 472	Lou Brock	50.00	20.00	5.00
☐ 473	Mets Team	5.00	2.00	.50
☐ 474	Jack Fisher	2.50	1.00	.25
☐ 475	Gus Triandos	2.50	1.00	.25
☐ 476	Frank Funk	2.50	1.00	.25
☐ 477	Donn Clendenon	3.00	1.20	.30
☐ 478	Paul Brown	2.50	1.00	.25
☐ 479	Ed Brinkman	2.50	1.00	.25
☐ 480	Bill Monbouquette	2.50	1.00	.25
☐ 481	Bill Taylor	2.50	1.00	.25
☐ 482	Frank Torre	2.50	1.00	.25
☐ 483	Jim Owens	2.50	1.00	.25
☐ 484	Dale Long	2.50	1.00	.25
☐ 485	Jim Landis	2.50	1.00	.25
☐ 486	Ray Sadecki	2.50	1.00	.25
☐ 487	John Roseboro	2.50	1.00	.25
☐ 488	Jerry Adair	2.50	1.00	.25
☐ 489	Paul Toth	2.50	1.00	.25
☐ 490	Willie McCovey	35.00	14.00	3.50
☐ 491	Harry Craft MGR	2.50	1.00	.25
☐ 492	Dave Wickersham	2.50	1.00	.25
☐ 493	Walt Bond	2.50	1.00	.25
☐ 494	Phil Regan	2.50	1.00	.25
☐ 495	Frank Thomas	2.50	1.00	.25
☐ 496	Rookie Stars	2.50	1.00	.25
	Steve Dalkowski			
	Fred Newman			
	Jack Smith			
	Carl Bouldin			
☐ 497	Bennie Daniels	2.50	1.00	.25
☐ 498	Ed Kasko	2.50	1.00	.25
☐ 499	J.C. Martin	2.50	1.00	.25
☐ 500	Harmon Killebrew	21.00	8.50	2.10
☐ 501	Joe Azcue	2.50	1.00	.25
☐ 502	Daryl Spencer	2.50	1.00	.25
☐ 503	Braves Team	4.00	1.60	.40
☐ 504	Bob Johnson	2.50	1.00	.25
☐ 505	Curt Flood	5.00	2.00	.50
☐ 506	Gene Green	2.50	1.00	.25
☐ 507	Rollie Sheldon	2.00	.80	.20
☐ 508	Ted Savage	2.00	.80	.20
☐ 509	Checklist 7	7.50	.75	.15
☐ 510	Ken McBride	2.00	.80	.20
☐ 511	Charlie Neal	2.00	.80	.20
☐ 512	Cal McLish	2.00	.80	.20
☐ 513	Gary Geiger	2.00	.80	.20
☐ 514	Larry Osborne	2.00	.80	.20
☐ 515	Don Elston	2.00	.80	.20
☐ 516	Purnell Goldy	2.00	.80	.20
☐ 517	Hal Woodeshick	2.00	.80	.20
☐ 518	Don Blasingame	2.00	.80	.20
☐ 519	Claude Raymond	2.00	.80	.20
☐ 520	Orlando Cepeda	5.00	2.00	.50
☐ 521	Dan Pfister	2.00	.80	.20
☐ 522	Rookie Stars	2.50	1.00	.25
	Mel Nelson			
	Gary Peters			
	Jim Roland			
	Art Quirk			
☐ 523	Bill Kunkel	2.00	.80	.20
☐ 524	Cardinals Team	4.00	1.60	.40
☐ 525	Nellie Fox	4.00	1.60	.40
☐ 526	Dick Hall	2.00	.80	.20
☐ 527	Ed Sadowski	2.00	.80	.20

		MINT	VG-E	F-G
☐ 528	Carl Willey	2.00	.80	.20
☐ 529	Wes Covington	2.00	.80	.20
☐ 530	Don Mossi	2.50	1.00	.25
☐ 531	Sam Mele MGR	2.00	.80	.20
☐ 532	Steve Boros	2.00	.80	.20
☐ 533	Bobby Shantz	2.50	1.00	.25
☐ 534	Ken Walters	2.00	.80	.20
☐ 535	Jim Perry	3.00	1.20	.30
☐ 536	Norm Larker	2.00	.80	.20
☐ 537	Rookie Stars	500.00	200.00	50.00
	Pedro Gonzales			
	Ken McMullen			
	Al Weis			
	Pete Rose			
☐ 538	George Brunet	2.00	.80	.20
☐ 539	Wayne Causey	2.00	.80	.20
☐ 540	Bob Clemente	60.00	24.00	6.00
☐ 541	Ron Moeller	2.00	.80	.20
☐ 542	Lou Klimchock	2.00	.80	.20
☐ 543	Russ Snyder	2.00	.80	.20
☐ 544	Rookie Stars	12.00	5.00	1.20
	Duke Carmel			
	Bill Haas			
	Rusty Staub			
	Dick Phillips			
☐ 545	Jose Pagan	2.00	.80	.20
☐ 546	Hal Reniff	2.00	.80	.20
☐ 547	Gus Bell	2.00	.80	.20
☐ 548	Tom Satriano	2.00	.80	.20
☐ 549	Rookie Stars	2.00	.80	.20
	Marcelino Lopez			
	Pete Lovrich			
	Paul Ratliff			
	Elmo Plaskett			
☐ 550	Duke Snider	25.00	10.00	2.50
☐ 551	Billy Klaus	2.00	.80	.20
☐ 552	Tigers Team	6.00	2.40	.60
☐ 553	Rookie Stars	60.00	24.00	6.00
	Brock Davis			
	Jim Gosger			
	Willie Stargell			
	John Hermstein			
☐ 554	Hank Fischer	2.00	.80	.20
☐ 555	John Blanchard	2.00	.80	.20
☐ 556	Al Worthington	2.00	.80	.20
☐ 557	Cuno Barragan	2.00	.80	.20
☐ 558	Rookie Stars	2.00	.80	.20
	Bill Faul			
	Ron Hunt			
	Al Moran			
	Bob Lipski			
☐ 559	Danny Murtaugh MGR	2.00	.80	.20
☐ 560	Ray Herbert	2.00	.80	.20

		MINT	VG-E	F-G
☐ 561	Mike De La Hoz	2.00	.80	.20
☐ 562	Rookie Stars	4.00	1.60	.40
	Randy Cardinal			
	Dave McNally			
	Ken Rowe			
	Don Rowe			
☐ 563	Mike McCormick	2.50	1.00	.25
☐ 564	George Banks	2.00	.80	.20
☐ 565	Larry Sherry	2.50	1.00	.25
☐ 566	Cliff Cook	2.00	.80	.20
☐ 567	Jim Duffalo	2.00	.80	.20
☐ 568	Bob Sadowski	2.00	.80	.20
☐ 569	Luis Arroyo	2.00	.80	.20
☐ 570	Frank Bolling	2.00	.80	.20
☐ 571	John Klippstein	2.00	.80	.20
☐ 572	Jack Spring	2.00	.80	.20
☐ 573	Coot Veal	2.00	.80	.20
☐ 574	Hal Kolstad	2.00	.80	.20
☐ 575	Don Cardwell	2.00	.80	.20
☐ 576	Johnny Temple	3.50	1.40	.35

1964 Topps

*The cards in this 587-card set measure 2½"
by 3½". Players in the 1964 Topps baseball
series were easy to sort by team due to the
giant block lettering found at the top of each
card. The name and position of the player are
found underneath the picture and the card is
numbered in a ball design on the orange-col-
ored back. The usual last series scarcity
holds for this set (523 to 587). Subsets within
this set include League Leaders (1-12) and
World Series cards (136-140).*

			MINT	VG-E	F-G
	Complete Set		725.00	325.00	80.00
	Common Player (1-370)		.25	.10	.02
	Common Player (371-522)		.40	.16	.04
	Common Player (523-587)		.90	.36	.09
☐	1	NL ERA Leaders	3.00	.75	.15
		Sandy Koufax			
		Dick Ellsworth			
		Bob Friend			
☐	2	AL ERA Leaders	.80	.32	.08
		Gary Peters			
		Juan Pizarro			
		Camilo Pascual			
☐	3	NL Pitching Leaders	2.50	1.00	.25
		Sandy Koufax			
		Juan Marichal			
		Warren Spahn			
		Jim Maloney			
☐	4	AL Pitching Leaders	1.25	.50	.12
		Whitey Ford			
		Camilo Pascual			
		Jim Bouton			
☐	5	NL Strikeout Leaders ...	2.00	.80	.20
		Sandy Koufax			
		Jim Maloney			
		Don Drysdale			
☐	6	AL Strikeout Leaders ...	.80	.32	.08
		Camilo Pascual			
		Jim Bunning			
		Dick Stigman			
☐	7	NL Batting Leaders	1.50	.60	.15
		Tommy Davis			
		Bob Clemente			
		Dick Groat			
		Hank Aaron			
☐	8	AL Batting Leaders	2.00	.80	.20
		Carl Yastrzemski			
		Al Kaline			
		Rich Rollins			
☐	9	NL Home Run Leaders .	3.00	1.20	.30
		Hank Aaron			
		Willie McCovey			
		Willie Mays			
		Orlando Cepeda			
☐	10	AL Home Run Leaders .	1.00	.40	.10
		Harmon Killebrew			
		Dick Stuart			
		Bob Allison			

			MINT	VG-E	F-G
☐	11	NL RBI Leaders	1.00	.40	.10
		Hank Aaron			
		Ken Boyer			
		Bill White			
☐	12	AL RBI Leaders	1.00	.40	.10
		Dick Stuart			
		Al Kaline			
		Harmon Killebrew			
☐	13	Hoyt Wilhelm	3.00	1.20	.30
☐	14	Dodgers Rookies	.25	.10	.02
		Dick Nen			
		Nick Willhite			
☐	15	Zoilo Versalles	.25	.10	.02
☐	16	John Boozer	.25	.10	.02
☐	17	Willie Kirkland	.25	.10	.02
☐	18	Billy O'Dell	.25	.10	.02
☐	19	Don Wert	.25	.10	.02
☐	20	Bob Friend	.35	.14	.03
☐	21	Yogi Berra	8.00	3.25	.80
☐	22	Jerry Adair	.25	.10	.02
☐	23	Chris Zachary	.25	.10	.02
☐	24	Carl Sawatski	.25	.10	.02
☐	25	Bill Monbouquette	.25	.10	.02
☐	26	Gino Cimoli	.25	.10	.02
☐	27	Mets Team	1.00	.40	.10
☐	28	Claude Osteen	.35	.14	.03
☐	29	Lou Brock	10.00	4.00	1.00
☐	30	Ron Perranoski	.35	.14	.03
☐	31	Dave Nicholson	.25	.10	.02
☐	32	Dean Chance	.35	.14	.03
☐	33	Reds Rookies	.35	.14	.03
		Sammy Ellis			
		Mel Queen			
☐	34	Jim Perry	.35	.14	.03
☐	35	Ed Mathews	3.50	1.40	.35
☐	36	Hal Reniff	.25	.10	.02
☐	37	Smoky Burgess	.35	.14	.03
☐	38	Jim Wynn	.75	.30	.07
☐	39	Hank Aguirre	.25	.10	.02
☐	40	Dick Groat	.60	.24	.06
☐	41	Friendly Foes	1.25	.50	.12
		Willie McCovey			
		Leon Wagner			
☐	42	Moe Drabowsky	.25	.10	.02
☐	43	Roy Sievers	.35	.14	.03
☐	44	Duke Carmel	.25	.10	.02
☐	45	Milt Pappas	.35	.14	.03
☐	46	Ed Brinkman	.25	.10	.02
☐	47	Giants Rookies	.50	.20	.05
		Jesus Alou			
		Ron Herbel			
☐	48	Bob Perry	.25	.10	.02
☐	49	Bill Henry	.25	.10	.02

			MINT	VG-E	F-G
☐	50	Mickey Mantle	60.00	24.00	6.00
☐	51	Pete Richert	.25	.10	.02
☐	52	Chuck Hinton	.25	.10	.02
☐	53	Denis Menke	.25	.10	.02
☐	54	Sam Mele MGR	.25	.10	.02
☐	55	Ernie Banks	5.00	2.00	.50
☐	56	Hal Brown	.25	.10	.02
☐	57	Tim Harkness	.25	.10	.02
☐	58	Don Demeter	.25	.10	.02
☐	59	Ernie Broglio	.35	.14	.03
☐	60	Frank Malzone	.35	.14	.03
☐	61	Angel Backstops	.35	.14	.03
		Bob Rodgers			
		Ed Sadowski			
☐	62	Ted Savage	.25	.10	.02
☐	63	Johnny Orsino	.25	.10	.02
☐	64	Ted Abernathy	.25	.10	.02
☐	65	Felipe Alou	.50	.20	.05
☐	66	Eddie Fisher	.25	.10	.02
☐	67	Tigers Team	.85	.34	.08
☐	68	Willie Davis	.60	.24	.06
☐	69	Clete Boyer	.35	.14	.03
☐	70	Joe Torre	1.00	.40	.10
☐	71	Jack Spring	.25	.10	.02
☐	72	Chico Cardenas	.25	.10	.02
☐	73	Jimmie Hall	.25	.10	.02
☐	74	Pirates Rookies	.25	.10	.02
		Bob Priddy			
		Tom Butters			
☐	75	Wayne Causey	.25	.10	.02
☐	76	Checklist 1	2.25	.20	.04
☐	77	Jerry Walker	.25	.10	.02
☐	78	Merritt Ranew	.25	.10	.02
☐	79	Bob Heffner	.25	.10	.02
☐	80	Vada Pinson	1.00	.40	.10
☐	81	All-Star Vets	2.50	1.00	.25
		Nellie Fox			
		Harmon Killebrew			
☐	82	Jim Davenport	.35	.14	.03
☐	83	Gus Triandos	.35	.14	.03
☐	84	Carl Willey	.25	.10	.02
☐	85	Pete Ward	.25	.10	.02
☐	86	Al Downing	.35	.14	.03
☐	87	Cardinals Team	1.00	.40	.10
☐	88	John Roseboro	.35	.14	.03
☐	89	Boog Powell	1.25	.50	.12
☐	90	Earl Battey	.35	.14	.03
☐	91	Bob Bailey	.25	.10	.02
☐	92	Steve Ridzik	.25	.10	.02
☐	93	Gary Geiger	.25	.10	.02
☐	94	Braves Rookies	.25	.10	.02
		Jim Britton			
		Larry Maxie			
☐	95	George Altman	.25	.10	.02
☐	96	Bob Buhl	.25	.10	.02
☐	97	Jim Fregosi	.50	.20	.05
☐	98	Bill Bruton	.25	.10	.02
☐	99	Al Stanek	.25	.10	.02
☐	100	Elston Howard	1.25	.50	.12
☐	101	Walt Alston MGR	1.00	.40	.10
☐	102	Checklist 2	2.25	.20	.04
☐	103	Curt Flood	.80	.32	.08
☐	104	Art Mahaffey	.25	.10	.02
☐	105	Woody Held	.25	.10	.02
☐	106	Joe Nuxhall	.35	.14	.03
☐	107	White Sox Rookies	.25	.10	.02
		Bruce Howard			
		Frank Kreutzer			
☐	108	John Wyatt	.25	.10	.02
☐	109	Rusty Staub	2.00	.80	.20
☐	110	Albie Pearson	.25	.10	.02
☐	111	Don Elston	.25	.10	.02
☐	112	Bob Tillman	.25	.10	.02
☐	113	Grover Powell	.25	.10	.02
☐	114	Don Lock	.25	.10	.02
☐	115	Frank Bolling	.25	.10	.02
☐	116	Twins Rookies	3.00	1.20	.30
		Jay Ward			
		Tony Oliva			
☐	117	Earl Francis	.25	.10	.02
☐	118	John Blanchard	.25	.10	.02
☐	119	Gary Kolb	.25	.10	.02
☐	120	Don Drysdale	4.50	1.80	.45
☐	121	Pete Runnels	.35	.14	.03
☐	122	Don McMahon	.25	.10	.02
☐	123	Jose Pagan	.25	.10	.02
☐	124	Orlando Pena	.25	.10	.02
☐	125	Pete Rose	120.00	50.00	12.00
☐	126	Russ Snyder	.25	.10	.02
☐	127	Angels Rookies	.25	.10	.02
		Aubrey Gatewood			
		Dick Simpson			
☐	128	Mickey Lolich	3.00	1.20	.30
☐	129	Amado Samuel	.25	.10	.02
☐	130	Gary Peters	.35	.14	.03
☐	131	Steve Boros	.35	.14	.03
☐	132	Braves Team	.85	.34	.08
☐	133	Jim Grant	.25	.10	.02
☐	134	Don Zimmer	.50	.20	.05
☐	135	Johnny Callison	.35	.14	.03
☐	136	World Series Game 1	3.00	1.20	.30
		Koufax strikes out 15			
☐	137	World Series Game 2	1.50	.60	.15
		Davis sparks rally			
☐	138	World Series Game 3	1.50	.60	.15
		LA 3 straight			

		MINT	VG-E	F-G
☐ 139	World Series Game 4 ... Sealing Yanks doom	1.50	.60	.15
☐ 140	World Series Summary . Dodgers celebrate	1.50	.60	.15
☐ 141	Danny Murtaugh MGR .	.25	.10	.02
☐ 142	John Bateman	.25	.10	.02
☐ 143	Bubba Phillips	.25	.10	.02
☐ 144	Al Worthington	.25	.10	.02
☐ 145	Norm Siebern	.25	.10	.02
☐ 146	Indians Rookies Tommy John Bob Chance	8.00	3.25	.80
☐ 147	Ray Sadecki	.25	.10	.02
☐ 148	J.C. Martin	.25	.10	.02
☐ 149	Paul Foytack	.25	.10	.02
☐ 150	Willie Mays	22.00	9.00	2.20
☐ 151	Athletics Team	.80	.32	.08
☐ 152	Denver Lemaster	.25	.10	.02
☐ 153	Dick Williams MGR	.35	.14	.03
☐ 154	Dick Tracewski	.25	.10	.02
☐ 155	Duke Snider	6.50	2.60	.65
☐ 156	Bill Dailey	.25	.10	.02
☐ 157	Gene Mauch MGR	.35	.14	.03
☐ 158	Ken Johnson	.25	.10	.02
☐ 159	Charlie Dees	.25	.10	.02
☐ 160	Ken Boyer	2.00	.80	.20
☐ 161	Dave McNally	.75	.30	.07
☐ 162	Hitting Area Dick Sisler Vada Pinson	.35	.14	.03
☐ 163	Donn Clendenon	.35	.14	.03
☐ 164	Bud Daley	.25	.10	.02
☐ 165	Jerry Lumpe	.25	.10	.02
☐ 166	Marty Keough	.25	.10	.02
☐ 167	Senators Rookies Mike Brumley Lou Piniella	7.50	3.00	.75
☐ 168	Al Weis	.25	.10	.02
☐ 169	Del Crandall	.35	.14	.03
☐ 170	Dick Radatz	.35	.14	.03
☐ 171	Ty Cline	.25	.10	.02
☐ 172	Indians Team	.85	.34	.08
☐ 173	Ryne Duren	.35	.14	.03
☐ 174	Doc Edwards	.25	.10	.02
☐ 175	Billy Williams	3.50	1.40	.35
☐ 176	Tracy Stallard	.25	.10	.02
☐ 177	Harmon Killebrew	4.50	1.80	.45
☐ 178	Hank Bauer MGR	.35	.14	.03
☐ 179	Carl Warwick	.25	.10	.02
☐ 180	Tommy Davis	.65	.26	.06
☐ 181	Dave Wickersham	.25	.10	.02

		MINT	VG-E	F-G
☐ 182	Sox Sockers Carl Yastrzemski Chuck Schilling	3.00	1.20	.30
☐ 183	Ron Taylor	.25	.10	.02
☐ 184	Al Luplow	.25	.10	.02
☐ 185	Jim O'Toole	.25	.10	.02
☐ 186	Roman Mejias	.25	.10	.02
☐ 187	Ed Roebuck	.25	.10	.02
☐ 188	Checklist 3	2.25	.20	.04
☐ 189	Bob Hendley	.25	.10	.02
☐ 190	Bobby Richardson	1.25	.50	.12
☐ 191	Clay Dalrymple	.25	.10	.02
☐ 192	Cubs Rookies: John Boccabella Billy Cowan	.25	.10	.02
☐ 193	Jerry Lynch	.25	.10	.02
☐ 194	John Goryl	.25	.10	.02
☐ 195	Floyd Robinson	.25	.10	.02
☐ 196	Jim Gentile	.35	.14	.03
☐ 197	Frank Lary	.35	.14	.03
☐ 198	Len Gabrielson	.25	.10	.02
☐ 199	Joe Azcue	.25	.10	.02
☐ 200	Sandy Koufax	16.00	6.50	1.60
☐ 201	Orioles Rookies: Sam Bowens Wally Bunker	.35	.14	.03
☐ 202	Galen Cisco	.25	.10	.02
☐ 203	John Kennedy	.25	.10	.02
☐ 204	Matty Alou	.35	.14	.03
☐ 205	Nellie Fox	1.50	.60	.15
☐ 206	Steve Hamilton	.25	.10	.02
☐ 207	Fred Hutchinson MGR	.35	.14	.03
☐ 208	Wes Covington	.35	.14	.03
☐ 209	Bob Allen	.25	.10	.02
☐ 210	Carl Yastrzemski	32.00	13.00	3.20
☐ 211	Jim Coker	.25	.10	.02
☐ 212	Pete Lovrich	.25	.10	.02
☐ 213	Angels Team	.80	.32	.08
☐ 214	Ken McMullen	.35	.14	.03
☐ 215	Ray Herbert	.25	.10	.02
☐ 216	Mike De La Hoz	.25	.10	.02
☐ 217	Jim King	.25	.10	.02
☐ 218	Hank Fischer	.25	.10	.02
☐ 219	Young Aces Al Downing Jim Bouton	.75	.30	.07
☐ 220	Dick Ellsworth	.35	.14	.03
☐ 221	Bob Saverine	.25	.10	.02
☐ 222	Billy Pierce	.60	.24	.06
☐ 223	George Banks	.25	.10	.02
☐ 224	Tommie Sisk	.25	.10	.02
☐ 225	Roger Maris	6.00	2.40	.60

		MINT	VG-E	F-G
☐ 226	Colts Rookies	.35	.14	.03
	Gerald Grote			
	Larry Yellen			
☐ 227	Barry Latman	.25	.10	.02
☐ 228	Felix Mantilla	.25	.10	.02
☐ 229	Charley Lau	.35	.14	.03
☐ 230	Brooks Robinson	9.00	3.75	.90
☐ 231	Dick Calmus	.25	.10	.02
☐ 232	Al Lopez MGR	1.25	.50	.12
☐ 233	Hal Smith	.25	.10	.02
☐ 234	Gary Bell	.25	.10	.02
☐ 235	Ron Hunt	.25	.10	.02
☐ 236	Bill Faul	.25	.10	.02
☐ 237	Cubs Team	.80	.32	.08
☐ 238	Roy McMillan	.25	.10	.02
☐ 239	Herm Starrette	.25	.10	.02
☐ 240	Bill White	.35	.14	.03
☐ 241	Jim Owens	.25	.10	.02
☐ 242	Harvey Kuenn	.65	.26	.06
☐ 243	Phillies Rookies	4.50	1.80	.45
	Richie Allen			
	John Herrnstein			
☐ 244	Tony LaRussa	1.25	.50	.12
☐ 245	Dick Stigman	.25	.10	.02
☐ 246	Manny Mota	.60	.24	.06
☐ 247	Dave DeBusschere	1.50	.60	.15
☐ 248	Johnny Pesky MGR	.35	.14	.03
☐ 249	Doug Camilli	.25	.10	.02
☐ 250	Al Kaline	5.50	2.20	.55
☐ 251	Choo Choo Coleman	.25	.10	.02
☐ 252	Ken Aspromonte	.25	.10	.02
☐ 253	Wally Post	.25	.10	.02
☐ 254	Don Hoak	.25	.10	.02
☐ 255	Lee Thomas	.25	.10	.02
☐ 256	Johnny Weekly	.25	.10	.02
☐ 257	Giants Team	.80	.32	.08
☐ 258	Garry Roggenburk	.25	.10	.02
☐ 259	Harry Bright	.25	.10	.02
☐ 260	Frank Robinson	4.50	1.80	.45
☐ 261	Jim Hannan	.25	.10	.02
☐ 262	Cards Rookies	1.00	.40	.10
	Mike Shannon			
	Harry Fanok			
☐ 263	Chuck Estrada	.35	.14	.03
☐ 264	Jim Landis	.25	.10	.02
☐ 265	Jim Bunning	1.50	.60	.15
☐ 266	Gene Freese	.25	.10	.02
☐ 267	Wilbur Wood	.60	.24	.06
☐ 268	Bill's Got It	.35	.14	.03
	Danny Murtaugh			
	Bill Virdon			
☐ 269	Ellis Burton	.25	.10	.02
☐ 270	Rich Rollins	.25	.10	.02

		MINT	VG-E	F-G
☐ 271	Bob Sadowski	.25	.10	.02
☐ 272	Jake Wood	.25	.10	.02
☐ 273	Mel Nelson	.25	.10	.02
☐ 274	Checklist 4	2.25	.20	.04
☐ 275	John Tsitouris	.25	.10	.02
☐ 276	Jose Tartabull	.25	.10	.02
☐ 277	Ken Retzer	.25	.10	.02
☐ 278	Bobby Shantz	.35	.14	.03
☐ 279	Joe Koppe (glove			
	on wrong hand)	.35	.14	.03
☐ 280	Juan Marichal	4.00	1.60	.40
☐ 281	Yankees Rookies	.35	.14	.03
	Jake Gibbs			
	Tom Metcalf			
☐ 282	Bob Bruce	.25	.10	.02
☐ 283	Tommy McCraw	.25	.10	.02
☐ 284	Dick Schofield	.25	.10	.02
☐ 285	Robin Roberts	3.00	1.20	.30
☐ 286	Don Landrum	.25	.10	.02
☐ 287	Red Sox Rookies	2.50	1.00	.25
	Tony Conigliaro			
	Bill Spanswick			
☐ 288	Al Moran	.25	.10	.02
☐ 289	Frank Funk	.25	.10	.02
☐ 290	Bob Allison	.35	.14	.03
☐ 291	Phil Ortega	.25	.10	.02
☐ 292	Mike Roarke	.25	.10	.02
☐ 293	Phillies Team	.80	.32	.08
☐ 294	Kent Hunt	.25	.10	.02
☐ 295	Roger Craig	.60	.24	.06
☐ 296	Ed Kirkpatrick	.25	.10	.02
☐ 297	Ken MacKenzie	.25	.10	.02
☐ 298	Harry Craft	.25	.10	.02
☐ 299	Bill Stafford	.25	.10	.02
☐ 300	Hank Aaron	22.00	9.00	2.20
☐ 301	Larry Brown	.25	.10	.02
☐ 302	Dan Pfister	.25	.10	.02
☐ 303	Jim Campbell	.25	.10	.02
☐ 304	Bob Johnson	.25	.10	.02
☐ 305	Jack Lamabe	.25	.10	.02
☐ 306	Giant Gunners	5.00	2.00	.50
	Willie Mays			
	Orlando Cepeda			
☐ 307	Joe Gibbon	.25	.10	.02
☐ 308	Gene Stephens	.25	.10	.02
☐ 309	Paul Toth	.25	.10	.02
☐ 310	Jim Gilliam	1.25	.50	.12
☐ 311	Tom Brown	.25	.10	.02
☐ 312	Tigers Rookies	.25	.10	.02
	Fritz Fisher			
	Fred Gladding			
☐ 313	Chuck Hiller	.25	.10	.02
☐ 314	Jerry Buchek	.25	.10	.02

		MINT	VG-E	F-G
☐ 315	Bo Belinsky	.35	.14	.03
☐ 316	Gene Oliver	.25	.10	.02
☐ 317	Al Smith	.25	.10	.02
☐ 318	Twins Team	.80	.32	.08
☐ 319	Paul Brown	.25	.10	.02
☐ 320	Rocky Colavito	1.25	.50	.12
☐ 321	Bob Lillis	.35	.14	.03
☐ 322	George Brunet	.25	.10	.02
☐ 323	John Buzhardt	.25	.10	.02
☐ 324	Casey Stengel MGR	4.00	1.60	.40
☐ 325	Hector Lopez	.25	.10	.02
☐ 326	Ron Brand	.25	.10	.02
☐ 327	Don Blasingame	.25	.10	.02
☐ 328	Bob Shaw	.25	.10	.02
☐ 329	Russ Nixon	.25	.10	.02
☐ 330	Tommy Harper	.35	.14	.03
☐ 331	AL Bombers	15.00	6.00	1.50
	Roger Maris			
	Norm Cash			
	Mickey Mantle			
	Al Kaline			
☐ 332	Ray Washburn	.25	.10	.02
☐ 333	Billy Moran	.25	.10	.02
☐ 334	Lew Krausse	.25	.10	.02
☐ 335	Don Mossi	.35	.14	.03
☐ 336	Andre Rodgers	.25	.10	.02
☐ 337	Dodgers Rookies	.50	.20	.05
	Al Ferrara			
	Jeff Torborg			
☐ 338	Jack Kralick	.25	.10	.02
☐ 339	Walt Bond	.25	.10	.02
☐ 340	Joe Cunningham	.25	.10	.02
☐ 341	Jim Roland	.25	.10	.02
☐ 342	Willie Stargell	7.50	3.00	.75
☐ 343	Senators Team	.80	.32	.08
☐ 344	Phil Linz	.25	.10	.02
☐ 345	Frank Thomas	.25	.10	.02
☐ 346	Joe Jay	.25	.10	.02
☐ 347	Bobby Wine	.25	.10	.02
☐ 348	Ed Lopat MGR	.50	.20	.05
☐ 349	Art Fowler	.25	.10	.02
☐ 350	Willie McCovey	6.50	2.60	.65
☐ 351	Dan Schneider	.25	.10	.02
☐ 352	Eddie Bressoud	.25	.10	.02
☐ 353	Wally Moon	.35	.14	.03
☐ 354	Dave Giusti	.35	.14	.03
☐ 355	Vic Power	.25	.10	.02
☐ 356	Reds Rookies	.35	.14	.03
	Bill McCool			
	Chico Ruiz			
☐ 357	Charley James	.25	.10	.02
☐ 358	Ron Kline	.25	.10	.02
☐ 359	Jim Schaffer	.25	.10	.02

		MINT	VG-E	F-G
☐ 360	Joe Pepitone	.60	.24	.06
☐ 361	Jay Hook	.25	.10	.02
☐ 362	Checklist 5	2.25	.20	.04
☐ 363	Dick McAuliffe	.25	.10	.02
☐ 364	Joe Gaines	.25	.10	.02
☐ 365	Cal McLish	.25	.10	.02
☐ 366	Nelson Mathews	.25	.10	.02
☐ 367	Fred Whitfield	.25	.10	.02
☐ 368	White Sox Rookies	.35	.14	.03
	Fritz Ackley			
	Don Buford			
☐ 369	Jerry Zimmerman	.25	.10	.02
☐ 370	Hal Woodeshick	.25	.10	.02
☐ 371	Frank Howard	1.25	.50	.12
☐ 372	Howie Koplitz	.40	.16	.04
☐ 373	Pirates Team	1.00	.40	.10
☐ 374	Bobby Bolin	.40	.16	.04
☐ 375	Ron Santo	1.00	.40	.10
☐ 376	Dave Morehead	.40	.16	.04
☐ 377	Bob Skinner	.50	.20	.05
☐ 378	Braves Rookies	.50	.20	.05
	Woody Woodward			
	Jack Smith			
☐ 379	Tony Gonzalez	.40	.16	.04
☐ 380	Whitey Ford	7.00	2.80	.70
☐ 381	Bob Taylor	.40	.16	.04
☐ 382	Wes Stock	.40	.16	.04
☐ 383	Bill Rigney MGR	.40	.16	.04
☐ 384	Ron Hansen	.40	.16	.04
☐ 385	Curt Simmons	.50	.20	.05
☐ 386	Lenny Green	.40	.16	.04
☐ 387	Terry Fox	.40	.16	.04
☐ 388	A's Rookies	.40	.16	.04
	John O'Donoghue			
	George Williams			
☐ 389	Jim Umbricht	.40	.16	.04
☐ 390	Orlando Cepeda	2.00	.80	.20
☐ 391	Sam McDowell	.75	.30	.07
☐ 392	Jim Pagliaroni	.40	.16	.04
☐ 393	Casey Teaches	2.00	.80	.20
	Casey Stengel			
	Ed Kranepool			
☐ 394	Bob Miller	.40	.16	.04
☐ 395	Tom Tresh	1.00	.40	.10
☐ 396	Dennis Bennett	.40	.16	.04
☐ 397	Chuck Cottier	.50	.20	.05
☐ 398	Mets Rookies	.40	.16	.04
	Bill Haas			
	Dick Smith			
☐ 399	Jackie Brandt	.40	.16	.04
☐ 400	Warren Spahn	7.00	2.80	.70
☐ 401	Charlie Maxwell	.40	.16	.04
☐ 402	Tom Sturdivant	.40	.16	.04

	MINT	VG-E	F-G
☐ 403 Reds Team	1.00	.40	.10
☐ 404 Tony Martinez	.40	.16	.04
☐ 405 Ken McBride	.40	.16	.04
☐ 406 Al Spangler	.40	.16	.04
☐ 407 Bill Freehan	1.50	.60	.15
☐ 408 Cubs Rookies	.40	.16	.04
Jim Stewart			
Fred Burdette			
☐ 409 Bill Fischer	.40	.16	.04
☐ 410 Dick Stuart	.60	.24	.06
☐ 411 Lee Walls	.40	.16	.04
☐ 412 Ray Culp	.40	.16	.04
☐ 413 Johnny Keane MGR	.50	.20	.05
☐ 414 Jack Sanford	.50	.20	.05
☐ 415 Tony Kubek	2.25	.90	.22
☐ 416 Lee Maye	.40	.16	.04
☐ 417 Don Cardwell	.40	.16	.04
☐ 418 Orioles Rookies	.60	.24	.06
Darold Knowles			
Les Narum			
☐ 419 Ken Harrelson	2.50	1.00	.25
☐ 420 Jim Maloney	.75	.30	.07
☐ 421 Camilo Carreon	.40	.16	.04
☐ 422 Jack Fisher	.40	.16	.04
☐ 423 Tops in NL	12.00	5.00	1.20
Hank Aaron			
Willie Mays			
☐ 424 Dick Bertell	.40	.16	.04
☐ 425 Norm Cash	1.00	.40	.10
☐ 426 Bob Rodgers	.40	.16	.04
☐ 427 Don Rudolph	.40	.16	.04
☐ 428 Red Sox Rookies	.40	.16	.04
Archie Skeen			
Pete Smith			
☐ 429 Tim McCarver	1.00	.40	.10
☐ 430 Juan Pizarro	.40	.16	.04
☐ 431 George Alusik	.40	.16	.04
☐ 432 Ruben Amaro	.40	.16	.04
☐ 433 Yankees Team	2.50	1.00	.25
☐ 434 Don Nottebart	.40	.16	.04
☐ 435 Vic Davalillo	.50	.20	.05
☐ 436 Charlie Neal	.50	.20	.05
☐ 437 Ed Bailey	.40	.16	.04
☐ 438 Checklist 6	2.50	.25	.05
☐ 439 Harvey Haddix	.60	.24	.06
☐ 440 Bob Clemente	16.00	6.50	1.60
☐ 441 Bob Duliba	.40	.16	.04
☐ 442 Pumpsie Green	.40	.16	.04
☐ 443 Chuck Dressen MGR	.40	.16	.04
☐ 444 Larry Jackson	.40	.16	.04
☐ 445 Bill Skowron	1.00	.40	.10
☐ 446 Julian Javier	.40	.16	.04
☐ 447 Ted Bowsfield	.40	.16	.04

	MINT	VG-E	F-G
☐ 448 Cookie Rojas	.40	.16	.04
☐ 449 Deron Johnson	.40	.16	.04
☐ 450 Steve Barber	.40	.16	.04
☐ 451 Joe Amalfitano	.40	.16	.04
☐ 452 Giants Rookies	1.00	.40	.10
Gil Garrido			
Jim Ray Hart			
☐ 453 Frank Baumann	.40	.16	.04
☐ 454 Tommie Aaron	.60	.24	.06
☐ 455 Bernie Allen	.40	.16	.04
☐ 456 Dodgers Rookies	1.25	.50	.12
Wes Parker			
John Werhas			
☐ 457 Jesse Gonder	.40	.16	.04
☐ 458 Ralph Terry	.60	.24	.06
☐ 459 Red Sox Rookies	.40	.16	.04
Pete Charton			
Dalton Jones			
☐ 460 Bob Gibson	7.50	3.00	.75
☐ 461 George Thomas	.40	.16	.04
☐ 462 Birdie Tebbetts MGR	.40	.16	.04
☐ 463 Don Leppert	.40	.16	.04
☐ 464 Dallas Green	.75	.30	.07
☐ 465 Mike Hershberger	.40	.16	.04
☐ 466 A's Rookies	.40	.16	.04
Dick Green			
Aurelio Monteagudo			
☐ 467 Bob Aspromonte	.40	.16	.04
☐ 468 Gaylord Perry	7.00	2.80	.70
☐ 469 Cubs Rookies	.60	.24	.06
Fred Norman			
Sterling Slaughter			
☐ 470 Jim Bouton	1.25	.50	.12
☐ 471 Gates Brown	1.00	.40	.10
☐ 472 Vern Law	.65	.26	.06
☐ 473 Orioles Team	1.00	.40	.10
☐ 474 Larry Sherry	.50	.20	.05
☐ 475 Ed Charles	.40	.16	.04
☐ 476 Braves Rookies	2.25	.90	.22
Rico Carty			
Dick Kelley			
☐ 477 Mike Joyce	.40	.16	.04
☐ 478 Dick Howser	.75	.30	.07
☐ 479 Cardinals Rookies	.40	.16	.04
Dave Bakenhaster			
Johnny Lewis			
☐ 480 Bob Purkey	.40	.16	.04
☐ 481 Chuck Schilling	.40	.16	.04
☐ 482 Phillies Rookies	.60	.24	.06
John Briggs			
Danny Cater			
☐ 483 Fred Valentine	.40	.16	.04
☐ 484 Bill Pleis	.40	.16	.04

	MINT	VG-E	F-G
☐ 485 Tom Haller	.40	.16	.04
☐ 486 Bob Kennedy MGR	.40	.16	.04
☐ 487 Mike McCormick	.50	.20	.05
☐ 488 Yankees Rookies	.40	.16	.04
Pete Mikkelsen			
Bob Meyer			
☐ 489 Julio Navarro	.40	.16	.04
☐ 490 Ron Fairly	.50	.20	.05
☐ 491 Ed Rakow	.40	.16	.04
☐ 492 Colts Rookies	.40	.16	.04
Jim Beauchamp			
Mike White			
☐ 493 Don Lee	.40	.16	.04
☐ 494 Al Jackson	.40	.16	.04
☐ 495 Bill Virdon	1.00	.40	.10
☐ 496 White Sox Team	1.00	.40	.10
☐ 497 Jeoff Long	.40	.16	.04
☐ 498 Dave Stenhouse	.40	.16	.04
☐ 499 Indians Rookies	.40	.16	.04
Chico Salmon			
Gordon Seyfried			
☐ 500 Camilo Pascual	.50	.20	.05
☐ 501 Bob Veale	.50	.20	.05
☐ 502 Angels Rookies	.50	.20	.05
Bobby Knoop			
Bob Lee			
☐ 503 Earl Wilson	.40	.16	.04
☐ 504 Claude Raymond	.40	.16	.04
☐ 505 Stan Williams	.40	.16	.04
☐ 506 Bobby Bragan MGR	.40	.16	.04
☐ 507 John Edwards	.40	.16	.04
☐ 508 Diego Segui	.40	.16	.04
☐ 509 Pirates Rookies	.80	.32	.08
Gene Alley			
Orlando McFarlane			
☐ 510 Lindy McDaniel	.50	.20	.05
☐ 511 Lou Jackson	.40	.16	.04
☐ 512 Tigers Rookies	2.25	.90	.22
Willie Horton			
Joe Sparma			
☐ 513 Don Larsen	.60	.24	.06
☐ 514 Jim Hickman	.40	.16	.04
☐ 515 Johnny Romano	.40	.16	.04
☐ 516 Twins Rookies	.40	.16	.04
Jerry Arrigo			
Dwight Siebler			
☐ 517 A Checklist 7 COR	3.00	.30	.06
(correct numbering			
on back)			
☐ 517 B Checklist 7 ERR	6.00	.60	.10
(incorrect numbering			
sequence on back)			
☐ 518 Carl Bouldin	.40	.16	.04

	MINT	VG-E	F-G
☐ 519 Charlie Smith	.40	.16	.04
☐ 520 Jack Baldschun	.40	.16	.04
☐ 521 Tom Satriano	.40	.16	.04
☐ 522 Bob Tiefenauer	.40	.16	.04
☐ 523 Lou Burdette	2.00	.80	.20
(pitching lefty)			
☐ 524 Reds Rookies	.90	.36	.09
Jim Dickson			
Bobby Klaus			
☐ 525 Al McBean	.90	.36	.09
☐ 526 Lou Clinton	.90	.36	.09
☐ 527 Larry Bearnarth	.90	.36	.09
☐ 528 A's Rookies	1.00	.40	.10
Dave Duncan			
Tom Reynolds			
☐ 529 Al Dark MGR	1.00	.40	.10
☐ 530 Leon Wagner	.90	.36	.09
☐ 531 Dodgers Team	2.50	1.00	.25
☐ 532 Twins Rookies	.90	.36	.09
Bud Bloomfield			
(Bloomfield photo			
actually Jay Ward)			
Joe Nossek			
☐ 533 John Klippstein	.90	.36	.09
☐ 534 Gus Bell	1.00	.40	.10
☐ 535 Phil Regan	1.00	.40	.10
☐ 536 Mets Rookies	.90	.36	.09
Larry Elliot			
John Stephenson			
☐ 537 Dan Osinski	.90	.36	.09
☐ 538 Minnie Minoso	2.00	.80	.20
☐ 539 Roy Face	1.50	.60	.15
☐ 540 Luis Aparicio	5.50	2.20	.55
☐ 541 Braves Rookies	35.00	14.00	3.50
Phil Roof			
Phil Niekro			
☐ 542 Don Mincher	1.00	.40	.10
☐ 543 Bob Uecker	9.00	3.75	.90
☐ 544 Colts Rookies	.90	.36	.09
Steve Hertz			
Joe Hoerner			
☐ 545 Max Alvis	.90	.36	.09
☐ 546 Joe Christopher	.90	.36	.09
☐ 547 Gil Hodges	4.00	1.60	.40
☐ 548 NL Rookies	.90	.36	.09
Wayne Schurr			
Paul Speckenbach			
☐ 549 Joe Moeller	.90	.36	.09
☐ 550 Ken Hubbs	3.00	1.20	.30
(in memoriam)			
☐ 551 Billy Hoeft	.90	.36	.09

		MINT	VG-E	F-G
☐ 552	Indians Rookies	1.00	.40	.10
	Tom Kelley			
	Sonny Siebert			
☐ 553	Jim Brewer	.90	.36	.09
☐ 554	Hank Foiles	.90	.36	.09
☐ 555	Lee Stange	.90	.36	.09
☐ 556	Mets Rookies	.90	.36	.09
	Steve Dillon			
	Ron Locke			
☐ 557	Leo Burke	.90	.36	.09
☐ 558	Don Schwall	.90	.36	.09
☐ 559	Dick Phillips	.90	.36	.09
☐ 560	Dick Farrell	.90	.36	.09
☐ 561	Phillies Rookies	2.00	.80	.20
	Dave Bennett			
	(19 ... is 18)			
	Rick Wise			
☐ 562	Pedro Ramos	.90	.36	.09
☐ 563	Dal Maxvill	.90	.36	.09
☐ 564	AL Rookies	.90	.36	.09
	Joe McCabe			
	Jerry McNertney			
☐ 565	Stu Miller	.90	.36	.09
☐ 566	Ed Kranepool	1.25	.50	.12
☐ 567	Jim Kaat	4.00	1.60	.40
☐ 568	NL Rookies	.90	.36	.09
	Phil Gagliano			
	Cap Peterson			
☐ 569	Fred Newman	.90	.36	.09
☐ 570	Bill Mazeroski	2.00	.80	.20
☐ 571	Gene Conley	.90	.36	.09
☐ 572	AL Rookies	.90	.36	.09
	Dave Gray			
	Dick Egan			
☐ 573	Jim Duffalo	.90	.36	.09
☐ 574	Manny Jimenez	.90	.36	.09
☐ 575	Tony Cloninger	.90	.36	.09
☐ 576	Mets Rookies	.90	.36	.09
	Jerry Hinsley			
	Bill Wakefield			
☐ 577	Gordy Coleman	.90	.36	.09
☐ 578	Glen Hobbie	.90	.36	.09
☐ 579	Red Sox Team	2.00	.80	.20
☐ 580	Johnny Podres	1.75	.70	.17
☐ 581	Yankees Rookies	.90	.36	.09
	Pedro Gonzales			
	Archie Moore			
☐ 582	Rod Kanehl	.90	.36	.09
☐ 583	Tito Francona	1.00	.40	.10
☐ 584	Joel Horlen	1.00	.40	.10
☐ 585	Tony Taylor	.90	.36	.09
☐ 586	Jim Piersall	1.50	.60	.15
☐ 587	Bennie Daniels	1.50	.50	.10

1965 Topps

*The cards in this 598-card set measure 2½"
by 3½". The cards comprising the 1965
Topps set have team names located within a
distinctive pennant design below the picture.
The cards have blue borders on the reverse
and were issued by series. Cards 523 to 598
are more difficult to obtain than all other series. In addition, the sixth series (447-522) is
more difficult to obtain than series one
through five. Featured subsets within this set
include League Leaders (1-12) and World
Series cards (132-139). Key cards in this set
include Steve Carlton's rookie and Pete
Rose.*

	MINT	VG-E	F-G
Complete Set	750.00	300.00	75.00
Common Player (1-198)	.21	.09	.02
Common Player (199-446)	.30	.12	.03
Common Player (447-522)	.55	.22	.05
Common Player (523-598)	.85	.34	.08

		MINT	VG-E	F-G
☐ 1	AL Batting Leaders	2.25	.50	.10
	Tony Oliva			
	Elston Howard			
	Brooks Robinson			
☐ 2	NL Batting Leaders	2.00	.80	.20
	Bob Clemente			
	Hank Aaron			
	Rico Carty			

		MINT	VG-E	F-G
☐ 3	AL Home Run Leaders .	2.00	.80	.20
	Harmon Killebrew			
	Mickey Mantle			
	Boog Powell			
☐ 4	NL Home Run Leaders .	2.00	.80	.20
	Willie Mays			
	Billy Williams			
	Jim Ray Hart			
	Orlando Cepeda			
	Johnny Callison			
☐ 5	AL RBI Leaders	2.00	.80	.20
	Brooks Robinson			
	Harmon Killebrew			
	Mickey Mantle			
	Dick Stuart			
☐ 6	NL RBI Leaders	1.00	.40	.10
	Ken Boyer			
	Willie Mays			
	Ron Santo			
☐ 7	AL ERA Leaders	.75	.30	.07
	Dean Chance			
	Joel Horlen			
☐ 8	NL ERA Leaders	3.00	1.20	.30
	Sandy Koufax			
	Don Drysdale			
☐ 9	AL Pitching Leaders	.75	.30	.07
	Dean Chance			
	Gary Peters			
	Dave Wickersham			
	Juan Pizarro			
	Wally Bunker			
☐ 10	NL Pitching Leaders	.75	.30	.07
	Larry Jackson			
	Ray Sadecki			
	Juan Marichal			
☐ 11	AL Strikeout Leaders	.75	.30	.07
	Al Downing			
	Dean Chance			
	Camilo Pascual			
☐ 12	NL Strikeout Leaders	1.00	.40	.10
	Bob Veale			
	Don Drysdale			
	Bob Gibson			
☐ 13	Pedro Ramos	.21	.09	.02
☐ 14	Len Gabrielson	.21	.09	.02
☐ 15	Robin Roberts	3.00	1.20	.30
☐ 16	Houston Rookies	18.00	7.25	1.80
	Joe Morgan			
	Sonny Jackson			
☐ 17	John Romano	.21	.09	.02
☐ 18	Bill McCool	.21	.09	.02
☐ 19	Gates Brown	.30	.12	.03
☐ 20	Jim Bunning	1.50	.60	.15

		MINT	VG-E	F-G
☐ 21	Don Blasingame	.21	.09	.02
☐ 22	Charlie Smith	.21	.09	.02
☐ 23	Bob Tiefenauer	.21	.09	.02
☐ 24	Twins Team	1.00	.40	.10
☐ 25	Al McBean	.21	.09	.02
☐ 26	Bob Knoop	.21	.09	.02
☐ 27	Dick Bertell	.21	.09	.02
☐ 28	Barney Schultz	.21	.09	.02
☐ 29	Felix Mantilla	.21	.09	.02
☐ 30	Jim Bouton	.75	.30	.07
☐ 31	Mike White	.21	.09	.02
☐ 32	Herman Franks MGR	.21	.09	.02
☐ 33	Jackie Brandt	.21	.09	.02
☐ 34	Cal Koonce	.21	.09	.02
☐ 35	Ed Charles	.21	.09	.02
☐ 36	Bob Wine	.21	.09	.02
☐ 37	Fred Gladding	.21	.09	.02
☐ 38	Jim King	.21	.09	.02
☐ 39	Gerry Arrigo	.21	.09	.02
☐ 40	Frank Howard	.90	.36	.09
☐ 41	White Sox Rookies	.21	.09	.02
	Bruce Howard			
	Marv Staehle			
☐ 42	Earl Wilson	.21	.09	.02
☐ 43	Mike Shannon	.40	.16	.04
☐ 44	Wade Blasingame	.21	.09	.02
☐ 45	Roy McMillan	.21	.09	.02
☐ 46	Bob Lee	.21	.09	.02
☐ 47	Tom Harper	.30	.12	.03
☐ 48	Claude Raymond	.21	.09	.02
☐ 49	Orioles Rookies	.50	.20	.05
	Curt Blefary			
	John Miller			
☐ 50	Juan Marichal	3.50	1.40	.35
☐ 51	Bill Bryan	.21	.09	.02
☐ 52	Ed Roebuck	.21	.09	.02
☐ 53	Dick McAuliffe	.21	.09	.02
☐ 54	Joe Gibbon	.21	.09	.02
☐ 55	Tony Conigliaro	.90	.36	.09
☐ 56	Ron Kline	.21	.09	.02
☐ 57	Cardinals Team	.80	.32	.08
☐ 58	Fred Talbot	.21	.09	.02
☐ 59	Nate Oliver	.21	.09	.02
☐ 60	Jim O'Toole	.21	.09	.02
☐ 61	Chris Cannizzaro	.21	.09	.02
☐ 62	Jim Katt (sic, Kaat)	2.00	.80	.20
☐ 63	Ty Cline	.21	.09	.02
☐ 64	Lou Burdette	.65	.26	.06
☐ 65	Tony Kubek	1.25	.50	.12
☐ 66	Bill Rigney MGR	.21	.09	.02
☐ 67	Harvey Haddix	.35	.14	.03
☐ 68	Del Crandall	.30	.12	.03
☐ 69	Bill Virdon	.60	.24	.06

		MINT	VG-E	F-G
☐ 70	Bill Skowron	.60	.24	.06
☐ 71	John O'Donoghue	.21	.09	.02
☐ 72	Tony Gonzalez	.21	.09	.02
☐ 73	Dennis Ribant	.21	.09	.02
☐ 74	Red Sox Rookies	1.00	.40	.10
	Rico Petrocelli			
	Jerry Stephenson			
☐ 75	Deron Johnson	.25	.10	.02
☐ 76	Sam McDowell	.35	.14	.03
☐ 77	Doug Camilli	.21	.09	.02
☐ 78	Dal Maxvill	.21	.09	.02
☐ 79	Checklist 1	2.00	.20	.04
☐ 80	Turk Farrell	.21	.09	.02
☐ 81	Don Buford	.21	.09	.02
☐ 82	Braves Rookies	.30	.12	.03
	Santos Alomar			
	John Braun			
☐ 83	George Thomas	.21	.09	.02
☐ 84	Ron Herbel	.21	.09	.02
☐ 85	Willie Smith	.21	.09	.02
☐ 86	Les Narum	.21	.09	.02
☐ 87	Nelson Mathews	.21	.09	.02
☐ 88	Jack Lamabe	.21	.09	.02
☐ 89	Mike Hershberger	.21	.09	.02
☐ 90	Rich Rollins	.21	.09	.02
☐ 91	Cubs Team	.75	.30	.07
☐ 92	Dick Howser	.50	.20	.05
☐ 93	Jack Fisher	.21	.09	.02
☐ 94	Charlie Lau	.30	.12	.03
☐ 95	Bill Mazeroski	1.00	.40	.10
☐ 96	Sonny Siebert	.25	.10	.02
☐ 97	Pedro Gonzalez	.21	.09	.02
☐ 98	Bob Miller	.21	.09	.02
☐ 99	Gil Hodges MGR	3.00	1.20	.30
☐ 100	Ken Boyer	1.25	.50	.12
☐ 101	Fred Newman	.21	.09	.02
☐ 102	Steve Boros	.30	.12	.03
☐ 103	Harvey Kuenn	.55	.22	.05
☐ 104	Checklist 2	2.00	.20	.04
☐ 105	Chico Salmon	.21	.09	.02
☐ 106	Gene Oliver	.21	.09	.02
☐ 107	Phillies Rookies	.75	.30	.07
	Pat Corrales			
	Costen Shockley			
☐ 108	Don Mincher	.25	.10	.02
☐ 109	Walt Bond	.21	.09	.02
☐ 110	Ron Santo	.80	.32	.08
☐ 111	Lee Thomas	.21	.09	.02
☐ 112	Derrell Griffith	.21	.09	.02
☐ 113	Steve Barber	.21	.09	.02
☐ 114	Jim Hickman	.21	.09	.02
☐ 115	Bobby Richardson	1.00	.40	.10

		MINT	VG-E	F-G
☐ 116	Cardinals Rookies	.40	.16	.04
	Dave Dowling			
	Bob Tolan			
☐ 117	Wes Stock	.25	.10	.02
☐ 118	Hal Lanier	.50	.20	.05
☐ 119	John Kennedy	.21	.09	.02
☐ 120	Frank Robinson	4.50	1.80	.45
☐ 121	Gene Alley	.25	.10	.02
☐ 122	Bill Pleis	.21	.09	.02
☐ 123	Frank Thomas	.21	.09	.02
☐ 124	Tom Satriano	.21	.09	.02
☐ 125	Juan Pizarro	.21	.09	.02
☐ 126	Dodgers Team	1.50	.60	.15
☐ 127	Frank Lary	.25	.10	.02
☐ 128	Vic Davalillo	.25	.10	.02
☐ 129	Bennie Daniels	.21	.09	.02
☐ 130	Al Kaline	4.50	1.80	.45
☐ 131	Johnny Keane MGR	.30	.12	.03
☐ 132	World Series Game 1	1.00	.40	.10
	Cards take opener			
☐ 133	World Series Game 2	1.00	.40	.10
	Stottlemyre wins			
☐ 134	World Series Game 3	4.50	1.80	.45
	Mantle's homer			
☐ 135	World Series Game 4	1.25	.50	.12
	Boyer's grand-slam			
☐ 136	World Series Game 5	1.00	.40	.10
	10th inning triumph			
☐ 137	World Series Game 6	1.25	.50	.12
	Bouton wins again			
☐ 138	World Series Game 7	2.25	.90	.22
	Gibson wins finale			
☐ 139	World Series Summary	1.00	.40	.10
	Cards celebrate			
☐ 140	Dean Chance	.25	.10	.02
☐ 141	Charlie James	.21	.09	.02
☐ 142	Bill Monbouquette	.21	.09	.02
☐ 143	Pirates Rookies	.21	.09	.02
	John Gelnar			
	Jerry May			
☐ 144	Ed Kranepool	.30	.12	.03
☐ 145	Luis Tiant	2.50	1.00	.25
☐ 146	Ron Hansen	.21	.09	.02
☐ 147	Dennis Bennett	.21	.09	.02
☐ 148	Willie Kirkland	.21	.09	.02
☐ 149	Wayne Schurr	.21	.09	.02
☐ 150	Brooks Robinson	5.00	2.00	.50
☐ 151	Athletics Team	.75	.30	.07
☐ 152	Phil Ortega	.21	.09	.02
☐ 153	Norm Cash	.90	.36	.09
☐ 154	Bob Humphreys	.21	.09	.02
☐ 155	Roger Maris	5.00	2.00	.50
☐ 156	Bob Sadowski	.21	.09	.02

		MINT	VG-E	F-G
☐ 157	Zoilo Versalles	.50	.20	.05
☐ 158	Dick Sisler	.21	.09	.02
☐ 159	Jim Duffalo	.21	.09	.02
☐ 160	Bob Clemente	12.00	5.00	1.20
☐ 161	Frank Baumann	.21	.09	.02
☐ 162	Russ Nixon	.21	.09	.02
☐ 163	John Briggs	.21	.09	.02
☐ 164	Al Spangler	.21	.09	.02
☐ 165	Dick Ellsworth	.25	.10	.02
☐ 166	Indians Rookies	.50	.20	.05
	George Culver			
	Tommie Agee			
☐ 167	Bill Wakefield	.21	.09	.02
☐ 168	Dick Green	.21	.09	.02
☐ 169	Dave Vineyard	.21	.09	.02
☐ 170	Hank Aaron	20.00	8.00	2.00
☐ 171	Jim Roland	.21	.09	.02
☐ 172	Jim Piersall	.65	.26	.06
☐ 173	Tigers Team	.85	.34	.08
☐ 174	Joe Jay	.21	.09	.02
☐ 175	Bob Aspromonte	.21	.09	.02
☐ 176	Willie McCovey	5.00	2.00	.50
☐ 177	Pete Mikkelsen	.21	.09	.02
☐ 178	Dalton Jones	.21	.09	.02
☐ 179	Hal Woodeshick	.21	.09	.02
☐ 180	Bob Allison	.35	.14	.03
☐ 181	Senators Rookies	.21	.09	.02
	Don Loun			
	Joe McCabe			
☐ 182	Mike De La Hoz	.21	.09	.02
☐ 183	Dave Nicholson	.21	.09	.02
☐ 184	John Boozer	.21	.09	.02
☐ 185	Max Alvis	.21	.09	.02
☐ 186	Bill Cowan	.21	.09	.02
☐ 187	Casey Stengel MGR	3.50	1.40	.35
☐ 188	Sam Bowens	.21	.09	.02
☐ 189	Checklist 3	2.00	.20	.04
☐ 190	Bill White	.40	.16	.04
☐ 191	Phil Regan	.25	.10	.02
☐ 192	Jim Coker	.21	.09	.02
☐ 193	Gaylord Perry	3.50	1.40	.35
☐ 194	Rookie Stars	.25	.10	.02
	Bill Kelso			
	Rick Reichardt			
☐ 195	Bob Veale	.30	.12	.03
☐ 196	Ron Fairly	.30	.12	.03
☐ 197	Diego Segui	.21	.09	.02
☐ 198	Smoky Burgess	.30	.12	.03
☐ 199	Bob Heffner	.30	.12	.03
☐ 200	Joe Torre	1.00	.40	.10
☐ 201	Twins Rookies	.40	.16	.04
	Sandy Valdespino			
	Cesar Tovar			
☐ 202	Leo Burke	.30	.12	.03
☐ 203	Dallas Green	.40	.16	.04
☐ 204	Russ Snyder	.30	.12	.03
☐ 205	Warren Spahn	4.50	1.80	.45
☐ 206	Willie Horton	.75	.30	.07
☐ 207	Pete Rose	110.00	45.00	11.00
☐ 208	Tommy John	2.25	.90	.22
☐ 209	Pirates Team	.85	.34	.08
☐ 210	Jim Fregosi	.50	.20	.05
☐ 211	Steve Ridzik	.30	.12	.03
☐ 212	Ron Brand	.30	.12	.03
☐ 213	Jim Davenport	.40	.16	.04
☐ 214	Bob Purkey	.30	.12	.03
☐ 215	Pete Ward	.30	.12	.03
☐ 216	Al Worthington	.30	.12	.03
☐ 217	Walt Alston MGR	1.00	.40	.10
☐ 218	Dick Schofield	.30	.12	.03
☐ 219	Bob Meyer	.30	.12	.03
☐ 220	Billy Williams	3.50	1.40	.35
☐ 221	John Tsitouris	.30	.12	.03
☐ 222	Bob Tillman	.30	.12	.03
☐ 223	Dan Osinski	.30	.12	.03
☐ 224	Bob Chance	.30	.12	.03
☐ 225	Bo Belinsky	.40	.16	.04
☐ 226	Yankees Rookies	.40	.16	.04
	Elvio Jimenez			
	Jake Gibbs			
☐ 227	Bob Klaus	.30	.12	.03
☐ 228	Jack Sanford	.40	.16	.04
☐ 229	Lou Clinton	.30	.12	.03
☐ 230	Ray Sadecki	.30	.12	.03
☐ 231	Jerry Adair	.30	.12	.03
☐ 232	Steve Blass	.60	.24	.06
☐ 233	Don Zimmer	.50	.20	.05
☐ 234	White Sox Team	.85	.34	.08
☐ 235	Chuck Hinton	.30	.12	.03
☐ 236	Dennis McLain	2.50	1.00	.25
☐ 237	Bernie Allen	.30	.12	.03
☐ 238	Joe Moeller	.30	.12	.03
☐ 239	Doc Edwards	.30	.12	.03
☐ 240	Bob Bruce	.30	.12	.03
☐ 241	Mack Jones	.30	.12	.03
☐ 242	George Brunet	.30	.12	.03
☐ 243	Reds Rookies	.50	.20	.05
	Ted Davidson			
	Tommy Helms			
☐ 244	Lindy McDaniel	.30	.12	.03
☐ 245	Joe Pepitone	.50	.20	.05
☐ 246	Tom Butters	.30	.12	.03
☐ 247	Wally Moon	.40	.16	.04
☐ 248	Gus Triandos	.40	.16	.04
☐ 249	Dave McNally	.75	.30	.07
☐ 250	Willie Mays	22.00	9.00	2.20

		MINT	VG-E	F-G
☐ 251	Billy Herman MGR	1.00	.40	.10
☐ 252	Pete Richert	.30	.12	.03
☐ 253	Danny Cater	.30	.12	.03
☐ 254	Roland Sheldon	.30	.12	.03
☐ 255	Camilo Pascual	.40	.16	.04
☐ 256	Tito Francona	.40	.16	.04
☐ 257	Jim Wynn	.60	.24	.06
☐ 258	Larry Bearnarth	.30	.12	.03
☐ 259	Tigers Rookies	.50	.20	.05
	Jim Northrup			
	Ray Oyler			
☐ 260	Don Drysdale	4.00	1.60	.40
☐ 261	Duke Carmel	.30	.12	.03
☐ 262	Bud Daley	.30	.12	.03
☐ 263	Marty Keough	.30	.12	.03
☐ 264	Bob Buhl	.30	.12	.03
☐ 265	Jim Pagliaroni	.30	.12	.03
☐ 266	Bert Campaneris	1.25	.50	.12
☐ 267	Senators Team	.75	.30	.07
☐ 268	Ken McBride	.30	.12	.03
☐ 269	Frank Bolling	.30	.12	.03
☐ 270	Milt Pappas	.40	.16	.04
☐ 271	Don Wert	.30	.12	.03
☐ 272	Chuck Schilling	.30	.12	.03
☐ 273	Checklist 4	2.00	.20	.04
☐ 274	Lum Harris MGR	.30	.12	.03
☐ 275	Dick Groat	.60	.24	.06
☐ 276	Hoyt Wilhelm	3.00	1.20	.30
☐ 277	John Lewis	.30	.12	.03
☐ 278	Ken Retzer	.30	.12	.03
☐ 279	Dick Tracewski	.30	.12	.03
☐ 280	Dick Stuart	.40	.16	.04
☐ 281	Bill Stafford	.30	.12	.03
☐ 282	Giants Rookies	.60	.24	.06
	Dick Estelle			
	Masanori Murakami			
☐ 283	Fred Whitfield	.30	.12	.03
☐ 284	Nick Willhite	.30	.12	.03
☐ 285	Ron Hunt	.30	.12	.03
☐ 286	Athletics Rookies	.30	.12	.03
	Jim Dickson			
	Aurelio Monteagudo			
☐ 287	Gary Kolb	.30	.12	.03
☐ 288	Jack Hamilton	.30	.12	.03
☐ 289	Gordy Coleman	.30	.12	.03
☐ 290	Wally Bunker	.30	.12	.03
☐ 291	Jerry Lynch	.30	.12	.03
☐ 292	Larry Yellen	.30	.12	.03
☐ 293	Angels Team	.75	.30	.07
☐ 294	Tim McCarver	.85	.34	.08
☐ 295	Dick Radatz	.40	.16	.04
☐ 296	Tony Taylor	.30	.12	.03
☐ 297	Dave Debusschere	1.50	.60	.15

		MINT	VG-E	F-G
☐ 298	Jim Stewart	.30	.12	.03
☐ 299	Jerry Zimmerman	.30	.12	.03
☐ 300	Sandy Koufax	20.00	8.00	2.00
☐ 301	Birdie Tebbetts MGR	.30	.12	.03
☐ 302	Al Stanek	.30	.12	.03
☐ 303	John Orsino	.30	.12	.03
☐ 304	Dave Stenhouse	.30	.12	.03
☐ 305	Rico Carty	.75	.30	.07
☐ 306	Bubba Phillips	.30	.12	.03
☐ 307	Barry Latman	.30	.12	.03
☐ 308	Mets Rookies	.40	.16	.04
	Cleon Jones			
	Tom Parsons			
☐ 309	Steve Hamilton	.30	.12	.03
☐ 310	John Callison	.40	.16	.04
☐ 311	Orlando Pena	.30	.12	.03
☐ 312	Joe Nuxhall	.40	.16	.04
☐ 313	Jim Schaffer	.30	.12	.03
☐ 314	Sterling Slaughter	.30	.12	.03
☐ 315	Frank Malzone	.40	.16	.04
☐ 316	Reds Team	.85	.34	.08
☐ 317	Don McMahon	.30	.12	.03
☐ 318	Matty Alou	.40	.16	.04
☐ 319	Ken McMullen	.30	.12	.03
☐ 320	Bob Gibson	4.00	1.60	.40
☐ 321	Rusty Staub	1.75	.70	.17
☐ 322	Rick Wise	.50	.20	.05
☐ 323	Hank Bauer MGR	.40	.16	.04
☐ 324	Bob Locke	.30	.12	.03
☐ 325	Donn Clendenon	.40	.16	.04
☐ 326	Dwight Siebler	.30	.12	.03
☐ 327	Denis Menke	.30	.12	.03
☐ 328	Eddie Fisher	.30	.12	.03
☐ 329	Hawk Taylor	.30	.12	.03
☐ 330	Whitey Ford	5.50	2.20	.55
☐ 331	Dodgers Rookies	.40	.16	.04
	Al Ferrara			
	John Purdin			
☐ 332	Ted Abernathy	.30	.12	.03
☐ 333	Tom Reynolds	.30	.12	.03
☐ 334	Vic Roznovsky	.30	.12	.03
☐ 335	Mickey Lolich	1.50	.60	.15
☐ 336	Woody Held	.30	.12	.03
☐ 337	Mike Cuellar	.50	.20	.05
☐ 338	Phillies Team	.80	.32	.08
☐ 339	Ryne Duren	.40	.16	.04
☐ 340	Tony Oliva	2.00	.80	.20
☐ 341	Bob Bolin	.30	.12	.03
☐ 342	Bob Rodgers	.30	.12	.03
☐ 343	Mike McCormick	.40	.16	.04
☐ 344	Wes Parker	.50	.20	.05
☐ 345	Floyd Robinson	.30	.12	.03
☐ 346	Bob Bragan MGR	.30	.12	.03

		MINT	VG-E	F-G
☐ 347	Roy Face	.60	.24	.06
☐ 348	George Banks	.30	.12	.03
☐ 349	Larry Miller	.30	.12	.03
☐ 350	Mickey Mantle	75.00	30.00	7.50
☐ 351	Jim Perry	.50	.20	.05
☐ 352	Alex Johnson	.40	.16	.04
☐ 353	Jerry Lumpe	.30	.12	.03
☐ 354	Cubs Rookies	.30	.12	.03
	Billy Ott			
	Jack Warner			
☐ 355	Vada Pinson	1.00	.40	.10
☐ 356	Bill Spanswick	.30	.12	.03
☐ 357	Carl Warwick	.30	.12	.03
☐ 358	Albie Pearson	.30	.12	.03
☐ 359	Ken Johnson	.30	.12	.03
☐ 360	Orlando Cepeda	1.75	.70	.17
☐ 361	Checklist 5	2.00	.20	.04
☐ 362	Don Schwall	.30	.12	.03
☐ 363	Bob Johnson	.30	.12	.03
☐ 364	Galen Cisco	.30	.12	.03
☐ 365	Jim Gentile	.40	.16	.04
☐ 366	Dan Schneider	.30	.12	.03
☐ 367	Leon Wagner	.30	.12	.03
☐ 368	White Sox Rookies	.40	.16	.04
	Ken Berry			
	Joel Gibson			
☐ 369	Phil Linz	.40	.16	.04
☐ 370	Tommy Davis	.65	.26	.06
☐ 371	Frank Kreutzer	.30	.12	.03
☐ 372	Clay Dalrymple	.30	.12	.03
☐ 373	Curt Simmons	.40	.16	.04
☐ 374	Angels Rookies	.50	.20	.05
	Jose Cardenal			
	Dick Simpson			
☐ 375	Dave Wickersham	.30	.12	.03
☐ 376	Jim Landis	.30	.12	.03
☐ 377	Willie Stargell	4.50	1.80	.45
☐ 378	Chuck Estrada	.40	.16	.04
☐ 379	Giants Team	.85	.34	.08
☐ 380	Rocky Colavito	1.25	.50	.12
☐ 381	Al Jackson	.30	.12	.03
☐ 382	J.C. Martin	.30	.12	.03
☐ 383	Felipe Alou	.40	.16	.04
☐ 384	John Klippstein	.30	.12	.03
☐ 385	Carl Yastrzemski	35.00	14.00	3.50
☐ 386	Cubs Rookies	.40	.16	.04
	Paul Jaeckel			
	Fred Norman			
☐ 387	John Podres	.90	.36	.09
☐ 388	John Blanchard	.40	.16	.04
☐ 389	Don Larsen	.50	.20	.05
☐ 390	Bill Freehan	.90	.36	.09
☐ 391	Mel McGaha MGR	.30	.12	.03

		MINT	VG-E	F-G
☐ 392	Bob Friend	.40	.16	.04
☐ 393	Ed Kirkpatrick	.30	.12	.03
☐ 394	Jim Hannan	.30	.12	.03
☐ 395	Jim Ray Hart	.40	.16	.04
☐ 396	Frank Bertaina	.30	.12	.03
☐ 397	Jerry Buchek	.30	.12	.03
☐ 398	Reds Rookies	.30	.12	.03
	Dan Neville			
	Art Shamsky			
☐ 399	Ray Herbert	.30	.12	.03
☐ 400	Harmon Killebrew	4.50	1.80	.45
☐ 401	Carl Willey	.30	.12	.03
☐ 402	Joe Amalfitano	.30	.12	.03
☐ 403	Red Sox Team	.85	.34	.08
☐ 404	Stan Williams	.30	.12	.03
☐ 405	John Roseboro	.40	.16	.04
☐ 406	Ralph Terry	.40	.16	.04
☐ 407	Lee Maye	.30	.12	.03
☐ 408	Larry Sherry	.40	.16	.04
☐ 409	Astros Rookies	.50	.20	.05
	Jim Beauchamp			
	Larry Dierker			
☐ 410	Luis Aparicio	3.00	1.20	.30
☐ 411	Roger Craig	.50	.20	.05
☐ 412	Bob Bailey	.30	.12	.03
☐ 413	Hal Reniff	.30	.12	.03
☐ 414	Al Lopez MGR	1.25	.50	.12
☐ 415	Curt Flood	.75	.30	.07
☐ 416	Jim Brewer	.30	.12	.03
☐ 417	Ed Brinkman	.30	.12	.03
☐ 418	John Edwards	.30	.12	.03
☐ 419	Ruben Amaro	.30	.12	.03
☐ 420	Larry Jackson	.30	.12	.03
☐ 421	Twins Rookies	.30	.12	.03
	Gary Dotter			
	Jay Ward			
☐ 422	Aubrey Gatewood	.30	.12	.03
☐ 423	Jesse Gonder	.30	.12	.03
☐ 424	Gary Bell	.30	.12	.03
☐ 425	Wayne Causey	.30	.12	.03
☐ 426	Braves Team	.85	.34	.08
☐ 427	Bob Saverine	.30	.12	.03
☐ 428	Bob Shaw	.30	.12	.03
☐ 429	Don Demeter	.30	.12	.03
☐ 430	Gary Peters	.40	.16	.04
☐ 431	Cards Rookies	.50	.20	.05
	Nelson Briles			
	Wayne Spiezio			
☐ 432	Jim Grant	.30	.12	.03
☐ 433	John Bateman	.30	.12	.03
☐ 434	Dave Morehead	.30	.12	.03
☐ 435	Willie Davis	.60	.24	.06
☐ 436	Don Elston	.30	.12	.03

		MINT	VG-E	F-G
☐ 437	Chico Cardenas	.30	.12	.03
☐ 438	Harry Walker MGR	.30	.12	.03
☐ 439	Moe Drabowsky	.30	.12	.03
☐ 440	Tom Tresh	.70	.28	.07
☐ 441	Denny Lemaster	.30	.12	.03
☐ 442	Vic Power	.30	.12	.03
☐ 443	Checklist 6	2.25	.20	.04
☐ 444	Bob Hendley	.30	.12	.03
☐ 445	Don Lock	.30	.12	.03
☐ 446	Art Mahaffey	.30	.12	.03
☐ 447	Julian Javier	.55	.22	.05
☐ 448	Lee Stange	.55	.22	.05
☐ 449	Mets Rookies	.55	.22	.05
	Gary Kroll			
	Jerry Hinsley			
☐ 450	Elston Howard	1.75	.70	.17
☐ 451	Jim Owens	.55	.22	.05
☐ 452	Gary Geiger	.55	.22	.05
☐ 453	Dodgers Rookies	.65	.26	.06
	Willie Crawford			
	John Werhas			
☐ 454	Ed Rakow	.55	.22	.05
☐ 455	Norm Siebern	.55	.22	.05
☐ 456	Bill Henry	.55	.22	.05
☐ 457	Bob Kennedy MGR	.55	.22	.05
☐ 458	John Buzhardt	.55	.22	.05
☐ 459	Frank Kostro	.55	.22	.05
☐ 460	Richie Allen	2.00	.80	.20
☐ 461	Braves Rookies	9.00	3.75	.90
	Clay Carroll			
	Phil Niekro			
☐ 462	Lew Krausse	.55	.22	.05
	(photo actually			
	Pete Lovrich)			
☐ 463	Manny Mota	.75	.30	.07
☐ 464	Ron Piche	.55	.22	.05
☐ 465	Tom Haller	.55	.22	.05
☐ 466	Senators Rookies	.55	.22	.05
	Pete Craig			
	Dick Nen			
☐ 467	Ray Washburn	.55	.22	.05
☐ 468	Larry Brown	.55	.22	.05
☐ 469	Don Nottebart	.55	.22	.05
☐ 470	Yogi Berra MGR	10.00	4.00	1.00
☐ 471	Bill Hoeft	.55	.22	.05
☐ 472	Don Pavletich	.55	.22	.05
☐ 473	Orioles Rookies	4.00	1.60	.40
	Paul Blair			
	Dave Johnson			
☐ 474	Cookie Rojas	.55	.22	.05
☐ 475	Clete Boyer	1.00	.40	.10
☐ 476	Billy O'Dell	.55	.22	.05

		MINT	VG-E	F-G
☐ 477	Cards Rookies	110.00	45.00	11.00
	Fritz Ackley			
	Steve Carlton			
☐ 478	Wilbur Wood	.75	.30	.07
☐ 479	Ken Harrelson	1.50	.60	.15
☐ 480	Joel Horlen	.65	.26	.06
☐ 481	Indians Team	1.25	.50	.12
☐ 482	Bob Priddy	.55	.22	.05
☐ 483	George Smith	.55	.22	.05
☐ 484	Ron Perranoski	.75	.30	.07
☐ 485	Nellie Fox	1.75	.70	.17
☐ 486	Angels Rookies	.55	.22	.05
	Tom Egan			
	Pat Rogan			
☐ 487	Woody Woodward	.55	.22	.05
☐ 488	Ted Wills	.55	.22	.05
☐ 489	Gene Mauch MGR	.75	.30	.07
☐ 490	Earl Battey	.55	.22	.05
☐ 491	Tracy Stallard	.55	.22	.05
☐ 492	Gene Freese	.55	.22	.05
☐ 493	Tigers Rookies	.55	.22	.05
	Bill Roman			
	Bruce Brubaker			
☐ 494	Jay Ritchie	.55	.22	.05
☐ 495	Joe Christopher	.55	.22	.05
☐ 496	Joe Cunningham	.55	.22	.05
☐ 497	Giants Rookies	.65	.26	.06
	Ken Henderson			
	Jack Hiatt			
☐ 498	Gene Stephens	.55	.22	.05
☐ 499	Stu Miller	.55	.22	.05
☐ 500	Ed Mathews	6.00	2.40	.60
☐ 501	Indians Rookies	.55	.22	.05
	Ralph Gagliano			
	Jim Rittwage			
☐ 502	Don Cardwell	.55	.22	.05
☐ 503	Phil Gagliano	.55	.22	.05
☐ 504	Jerry Grote	.55	.22	.05
☐ 505	Ray Culp	.55	.22	.05
☐ 506	Sam Mele MGR	.55	.22	.05
☐ 507	Sam Ellis	.55	.22	.05
☐ 508	Checklist 7	3.50	.35	.07
☐ 509	Red Sox Rookies	.55	.22	.05
	Bob Guindon			
	Gerry Vezendy			
☐ 510	Ernie Banks	14.00	5.75	1.40
☐ 511	Ron Locke	.55	.22	.05
☐ 512	Cap Peterson	.55	.22	.05
☐ 513	Yankees Team	2.50	1.00	.25
☐ 514	Joe Azcue	.55	.22	.05
☐ 515	Vern Law	.75	.30	.07
☐ 516	Al Weis	.55	.22	.05

		MINT	VG-E	F-G
☐ 517	Angels Rookies	.55	.22	.05
	Paul Schaal			
	Jack Warner			
☐ 518	Ken Rowe	.55	.22	.05
☐ 519	Bob Uecker	8.00	3.25	.80
☐ 520	Tony Cloninger	.55	.22	.05
☐ 521	Phillies Rookies	.55	.22	.05
	Dave Bennett			
	Morrie Stevens			
☐ 522	Hank Aguirre	.55	.22	.05
☐ 523	Mike Brumley	.85	.34	.08
☐ 524	Dave Giusti	.85	.34	.08
☐ 525	Ed Bressoud	.85	.34	.08
☐ 526	Athletics Rookies	25.00	10.00	2.50
	Rene Lachemann			
	Johnny Odom			
	Jim Hunter			
	Skip Lockwood			
☐ 527	Jeff Torborg	1.00	.40	.10
☐ 528	George Altman	.85	.34	.08
☐ 529	Jerry Fosnow	.85	.34	.08
☐ 530	Jim Maloney	1.00	.40	.10
☐ 531	Chuck Hiller	.85	.34	.08
☐ 532	Hector Lopez	.85	.34	.08
☐ 533	Mets Rookies	4.50	1.80	.45
	Dan Napoleon			
	Ron Swoboda			
	Tug McGraw			
	Jim Bethke			
☐ 534	John Herrnstein	.85	.34	.08
☐ 535	Jack Kralick	.85	.34	.08
☐ 536	Andre Rodgers	.85	.34	.08
☐ 537	Angels Rookies	1.00	.40	.10
	Marcelino Lopes			
	Phil Roof			
	Rudy May			
☐ 538	Chuck Dressen MGR	.85	.34	.08
☐ 539	Herm Starrette	.85	.34	.08
☐ 540	Lou Brock	14.00	5.75	1.40
☐ 541	White Sox Rookies	.85	.34	.08
	Greg Bollo			
	Bob Locker			
☐ 542	Lou Klimchock	.85	.34	.08
☐ 543	Ed Connolly	.85	.34	.08
☐ 544	Howie Reed	.85	.34	.08
☐ 545	Jesus Alou	.85	.34	.08
☐ 546	Indians Rookies	.85	.34	.08
	Bill Davis			
	Mike Hedlund			
	Ray Barker			
	Floyd Weaver			
☐ 547	Jake Wood	.85	.34	.08
☐ 548	Dick Stigman	.85	.34	.08

		MINT	VG-E	F-G
☐ 549	Cubs Rookies	1.50	.60	.15
	Roberto Pena			
	Glenn Beckert			
☐ 550	Mel Stottlemyre	4.00	1.60	.40
☐ 551	Mets Team	2.50	1.00	.25
☐ 552	Julio Gotay	.85	.34	.08
☐ 553	Astros Rookies	.85	.34	.08
	Gene Ratliff			
	Jack McClure			
☐ 554	Chico Ruiz	.85	.34	.08
☐ 555	Jack Baldschun	.85	.34	.08
☐ 556	Red Schoendienst MGR	1.50	.60	.15
☐ 557	Jose Santiago	.85	.34	.08
☐ 558	Tom Sisk	.85	.34	.08
☐ 559	Ed Bailey	.85	.34	.08
☐ 560	Boog Powell	1.75	.70	.17
☐ 561	Dodgers Rookies	1.75	.70	.17
	Dennis Daboll			
	Mike Kekich			
	Hector Valle			
	Jim Lefebvre			
☐ 562	Bill Moran	.85	.34	.08
☐ 563	Julio Navarro	.85	.34	.08
☐ 564	Mel Nelson	.85	.34	.08
☐ 565	Ernie Broglio	.85	.34	.08
☐ 566	Yankees Rookies	.85	.34	.08
	Gil Blanco			
	Ross Moschitto			
	Art Lopez			
☐ 567	Tommie Aaron	1.00	.40	.10
☐ 568	Ron Taylor	.85	.34	.08
☐ 569	Gino Cimoli	.85	.34	.08
☐ 570	Claude Osteen	1.00	.40	.10
☐ 571	Ossie Virgil	.85	.34	.08
☐ 572	Orioles Team	1.75	.70	.17
☐ 573	Red Sox Rookies	2.00	.80	.20
	Jim Lonborg			
	Gerry Moses			
	Bill Schlesinger			
	Mike Ryan			
☐ 574	Roy Sievers	1.00	.40	.10
☐ 575	Jose Pagan	.85	.34	.08
☐ 576	Terry Fox	.85	.34	.08
☐ 577	AL Rookie Stars	.85	.34	.08
	Darold Knowles			
	Don Buschhorn			
	Richie Scheinblum			
☐ 578	Camilo Carreon	.85	.34	.08
☐ 579	Dick Smith	.85	.34	.08
☐ 580	Jim Hall	.85	.34	.08

		MINT	VG-E	F-G
☐ 581	NL Rookie Stars	18.00	7.25	1.80
	Tony Perez			
	Dave Ricketts			
	Kevin Collins			
☐ 582	Bob Schmidt	.85	.34	.08
☐ 583	Wes Covington	.85	.34	.08
☐ 584	Harry Bright	.85	.34	.08
☐ 585	Hank Fischer	.85	.34	.08
☐ 586	Tom McCraw	.85	.34	.08
☐ 587	Joe Sparma	.85	.34	.08
☐ 588	Len Green	.85	.34	.08
☐ 589	Giants Rookies	.85	.34	.08
	Frank Linzy			
	B. Schroder			
☐ 590	John Wyatt	.85	.34	.08
☐ 591	Bob Skinner	1.00	.40	.10
☐ 592	Frank Bork	.85	.34	.08
☐ 593	Tigers Rookies	1.00	.40	.10
	Jackie Moore			
	John Sullivan			
☐ 594	Joe Gaines	.85	.34	.08
☐ 595	Don Lee	.85	.34	.08
☐ 596	Don Landrum	.85	.34	.08
☐ 597	Twins Rookies	.85	.34	.08
	Joe Nossek			
	John Sevcik			
	Dick Reese			
☐ 598	Al Downing	1.50	.50	.10

1966 Topps

*The cards in this 598-card set measure 2½"
by 3½". There are the same number of cards
as in the 1965 set. Once again, the seventh
series cards (523 to 598) are considered
more difficult to obtain than any other series'*

*cards in the set. The only featured subset
within this set is League Leaders (215-226).
Noteworthy rookie cards in the set include
Jim Palmer (126) and Don Sutton (288).*

		MINT	VG-E	F-G
	Complete Set	950.00	400.00	100.00
	Common Player (1-110)	.21	.09	.02
	Common Player (111-446)	.27	.11	.03
	Common Player (447-522)	.65	.26	.06
	Common Player (523-598)	4.25	1.70	.42
☐ 1	Willie Mays	40.00	12.00	2.00
☐ 2	Ted Abernathy	.21	.09	.02
☐ 3	Sam Mele MGR	.21	.09	.02
☐ 4	Ray Culp	.21	.09	.02
☐ 5	Jim Fregosi	.40	.16	.04
☐ 6	Chuck Schilling	.21	.09	.02
☐ 7	Tracy Stallard	.21	.09	.02
☐ 8	Floyd Robinson	.21	.09	.02
☐ 9	Clete Boyer	.35	.14	.03
☐ 10	Tony Cloninger	.21	.09	.02
☐ 11	Senators Rookies	.21	.09	.02
	Brant Alyea			
	Pete Craig			
☐ 12	John Tsitouris	.21	.09	.02
☐ 13	Lou Johnson	.21	.09	.02
☐ 14	Norm Siebern	.21	.09	.02
☐ 15	Vern Law	.30	.12	.03
☐ 16	Larry Brown	.21	.09	.02
☐ 17	John Stephenson	.21	.09	.02
☐ 18	Roland Sheldon	.21	.09	.02
☐ 19	Giants Team	.65	.26	.06
☐ 20	Willie Horton	.50	.20	.05
☐ 21	Don Nottebart	.21	.09	.02
☐ 22	Joe Nossek	.21	.09	.02
☐ 23	Jack Sanford	.21	.09	.02
☐ 24	Don Kessinger	.65	.26	.06
☐ 25	Pete Ward	.21	.09	.02
☐ 26	Ray Sadecki	.21	.09	.02
☐ 27	Orioles Rookies	.30	.12	.03
	Darold Knowles			
	Andy Etchebarren			
☐ 28	Phil Niekro	5.00	2.00	.50
☐ 29	Mike Brumley	.21	.09	.02
☐ 30	Pete Rose	40.00	16.00	4.00
☐ 31	Jack Cullen	.21	.09	.02
☐ 32	Adolfo Phillips	.21	.09	.02
☐ 33	Jim Pagliaroni	.21	.09	.02
☐ 34	Checklist 1	2.00	.20	.04

		MINT	VG-E	F-G			MINT	VG-E	F-G
☐ 35	Ron Swoboda	.21	.09	.02	☐ 79	Joe Pepitone	.50	.20	.05
☐ 36	Jim Hunter	5.00	2.00	.50	☐ 80	Richie Allen	1.25	.50	.12
☐ 37	Billy Herman MGR	.80	.32	.08	☐ 81	Ray Oyler	.21	.09	.02
☐ 38	Ron Nischwitz	.21	.09	.02	☐ 82	Bob Hendley	.21	.09	.02
☐ 39	Ken Henderson	.21	.09	.02	☐ 83	Albie Pearson	.21	.09	.02
☐ 40	Jim Grant	.21	.09	.02	☐ 84	Braves Rookies	.21	.09	.02
☐ 41	Don LeJohn	.21	.09	.02		Jim Beauchamp			
☐ 42	Aubrey Gatewood	.21	.09	.02		Dick Kelley			
☐ 43	Don Landrum	.21	.09	.02	☐ 85	Eddie Fisher	.21	.09	.02
☐ 44	Indians Rookies	.21	.09	.02	☐ 86	John Bateman	.21	.09	.02
	Bill Davis				☐ 87	Dan Napoleon	.21	.09	.02
	Tom Kelley				☐ 88	Fred Whitfield	.21	.09	.02
☐ 45	Jim Gentile	.30	.12	.03	☐ 89	Ted Davidson	.21	.09	.02
☐ 46	Howie Koplitz	.21	.09	.02	☐ 90	Luis Aparicio	3.00	1.20	.30
☐ 47	J.C. Martin	.21	.09	.02	☐ 91 A	Bob Uecker	4.00	1.60	.40
☐ 48	Paul Blair	.30	.12	.03		(with traded line)			
☐ 49	Woody Woodward	.21	.09	.02	☐ 91 B	Bob Uecker	20.00	8.00	2.00
☐ 50	Mickey Mantle	50.00	20.00	5.00		(no traded line)			
☐ 51	Gordon Richardson	.21	.09	.02	☐ 92	Yankees Team	1.25	.50	.12
☐ 52	Power Plus	.25	.10	.02	☐ 93	Jim Lonborg	.50	.20	.05
	Wes Covington				☐ 94	Matty Alou	.30	.12	.03
	Johnny Callison				☐ 95	Pete Richert	.21	.09	.02
☐ 53	Bob Duliba	.21	.09	.02	☐ 96	Felipe Alou	.30	.12	.03
☐ 54	Jose Pagan	.21	.09	.02	☐ 97	Jim Merritt	.21	.09	.02
☐ 55	Ken Harrelson	.80	.32	.08	☐ 98	Don Demeter	.21	.09	.02
☐ 56	Sandy Valdespino	.21	.09	.02	☐ 99	Buc Belters	1.25	.50	.12
☐ 57	Jim Lefebvre	.30	.12	.03		Willie Stargell			
☐ 58	Dave Wickersham	.21	.09	.02		Donn Clendenon			
☐ 59	Reds Team	.75	.30	.07	☐ 100	Sandy Koufax	14.00	5.75	1.40
☐ 60	Curt Flood	.60	.24	.06	☐ 101 A	Checklist 2	2.50	.25	.05
☐ 61	Bob Bolin	.21	.09	.02		(115 Bill Henry)			
☐ 62 A	Merritt Ranew	.25	.09	.02	☐ 101 B	Checklist 2	6.00	.60	.10
	(with sold line)					(115 W. Spahn)			
☐ 62 B	Merritt Ranew	12.00	5.00	1.20	☐ 102	Ed Kirkpatrick	.21	.09	.02
	(without sold line)				☐ 103 A	Dick Groat	.50	.20	.05
☐ 63	Jim Stewart	.21	.09	.02		(with traded line)			
☐ 64	Bob Bruce	.21	.09	.02	☐ 103 B	Dick Groat	15.00	6.00	1.50
☐ 65	Leon Wagner	.21	.09	.02		(no traded line)			
☐ 66	Al Weis	.21	.09	.02	☐ 104 A	Alex Johnson	.40	.16	.04
☐ 67	Mets Rookies	.30	.12	.03		(with traded line)			
	Cleon Jones				☐ 104 B	Alex Johnson	15.00	6.00	1.50
	Dick Selma					(no traded line)			
☐ 68	Hal Reniff	.21	.09	.02	☐ 105	Milt Pappas	.30	.12	.03
☐ 69	Ken Hamlin	.21	.09	.02	☐ 106	Rusty Staub	1.25	.50	.12
☐ 70	Carl Yastrzemski	27.00	11.00	2.70	☐ 107	A's Rookies	.21	.09	.02
☐ 71	Frank Carpin	.21	.09	.02		Larry Stahl			
☐ 72	Tony Perez	3.50	1.40	.35		Ron Tompkins			
☐ 73	Jerry Zimmerman	.21	.09	.02	☐ 108	Bobby Klaus	.21	.09	.02
☐ 74	Don Mossi	.30	.12	.03	☐ 109	Ralph Terry	.30	.12	.03
☐ 75	Tommy Davis	.50	.20	.05	☐ 110	Ernie Banks	4.00	1.60	.40
☐ 76	Red Schoendienst MGR	.50	.20	.05	☐ 111	Gary Peters	.35	.14	.03
☐ 77	Johnny Orsino	.21	.09	.02	☐ 112	Manny Mota	.35	.14	.03
☐ 78	Frank Linzy	.21	.09	.02	☐ 113	Hank Aguirre	.27	.11	.03

	MINT	VG-E	F-G
☐ 114 Jim Gosger	.27	.11	.03
☐ 115 Bill Henry	.27	.11	.03
☐ 116 Walt Alston MGR	.90	.36	.09
☐ 117 Jake Gibbs	.27	.11	.03
☐ 118 Mike McCormick	.35	.14	.03
☐ 119 Art Shamsky	.27	.11	.03
☐ 120 Harmon Killebrew	4.00	1.60	.40
☐ 121 Ray Herbert	.27	.11	.03
☐ 122 Joe Gaines	.27	.11	.03
☐ 123 Pirates Rookies	.27	.11	.03
Frank Bork			
Jerry May			
☐ 124 Tug McGraw	1.25	.50	.12
☐ 125 Lou Brock	5.50	2.20	.55
☐ 126 Jim Palmer	36.00	15.00	3.60
☐ 127 Ken Berry	.27	.11	.03
☐ 128 Jim Landis	.27	.11	.03
☐ 129 Jack Kralick	.27	.11	.03
☐ 130 Joe Torre	.80	.32	.08
☐ 131 Angels Team	.75	.30	.07
☐ 132 Orlando Cepeda	1.50	.60	.15
☐ 133 Don McMahon	.27	.11	.03
☐ 134 Wes Parker	.40	.16	.04
☐ 135 Dave Morehead	.27	.11	.03
☐ 136 Woody Held	.27	.11	.03
☐ 137 Pat Corrales	.40	.16	.04
☐ 138 Roger Repoz	.27	.11	.03
☐ 139 Cubs Rookies	.27	.11	.03
Byron Browne			
Don Young			
☐ 140 Jim Maloney	.35	.14	.03
☐ 141 Tom McCraw	.27	.11	.03
☐ 142 Don Dennis	.27	.11	.03
☐ 143 Jose Tartabull	.27	.11	.03
☐ 144 Don Schwall	.27	.11	.03
☐ 145 Bill Freehan	.60	.24	.06
☐ 146 George Altman	.27	.11	.03
☐ 147 Lum Harris MGR	.27	.11	.03
☐ 148 Bob Johnson	.27	.11	.03
☐ 149 Dick Nen	.27	.11	.03
☐ 150 Rocky Colavito	1.00	.40	.10
☐ 151 Gary Wagner	.27	.11	.03
☐ 152 Frank Malzone	.35	.14	.03
☐ 153 Rico Carty	.65	.26	.06
☐ 154 Chuck Hiller	.27	.11	.03
☐ 155 Marcelino Lopez	.27	.11	.03
☐ 156 Double Play Combo	.40	.16	.04
Dick Schofield			
Hal Lanier			
☐ 157 Rene Lachemann	.40	.16	.04
☐ 158 Jim Brewer	.27	.11	.03
☐ 159 Chico Ruiz	.27	.11	.03
☐ 160 Whitey Ford	5.00	2.00	.50

	MINT	VG-E	F-G
☐ 161 Jerry Lumpe	.27	.11	.03
☐ 162 Lee Maye	.27	.11	.03
☐ 163 Tito Francona	.35	.14	.03
☐ 164 White Sox Rookies	.45	.18	.04
Tommie Agee			
Marv Staehle			
☐ 165 Don Lock	.27	.11	.03
☐ 166 Chris Krug	.27	.11	.03
☐ 167 Boog Powell	1.00	.40	.10
☐ 168 Dan Osinski	.27	.11	.03
☐ 169 Duke Sims	.27	.11	.03
☐ 170 Cookie Rojas	.27	.11	.03
☐ 171 Nick Willhite	.27	.11	.03
☐ 172 Mets Team	.85	.34	.08
☐ 173 Al Spangler	.27	.11	.03
☐ 174 Ron Taylor	.27	.11	.03
☐ 175 Bert Campaneris	.60	.24	.06
☐ 176 Jim Davenport	.35	.14	.03
☐ 177 Hector Lopez	.27	.11	.03
☐ 178 Bob Tillman	.27	.11	.03
☐ 179 Cards Rookies	.35	.14	.03
Dennis Aust			
Bob Tolan			
☐ 180 Vada Pinson	.90	.36	.09
☐ 181 Al Worthington	.27	.11	.03
☐ 182 Jerry Lynch	.27	.11	.03
☐ 183 Checklist 3	2.00	.20	.04
☐ 184 Denis Menke	.27	.11	.03
☐ 185 Bob Buhl	.27	.11	.03
☐ 186 Ruben Amaro	.27	.11	.03
☐ 187 Chuck Dressen MGR	.27	.11	.03
☐ 188 Al Luplow	.27	.11	.03
☐ 189 John Roseboro	.35	.14	.03
☐ 190 Jimmie Hall	.27	.11	.03
☐ 191 Darrell Sutherland	.27	.11	.03
☐ 192 Vic Power	.27	.11	.03
☐ 193 Dave McNally	.50	.20	.05
☐ 194 Senators Team	.75	.30	.07
☐ 195 Joe Morgan	5.00	2.00	.50
☐ 196 Don Pavletich	.27	.11	.03
☐ 197 Sonny Siebert	.35	.14	.03
☐ 198 Mickey Stanley	.60	.24	.06
☐ 199 Chisox Clubbers	.35	.14	.03
Bill Skowron			
Johnny Romano			
Floyd Robinson			
☐ 200 Eddie Mathews	3.50	1.40	.35
☐ 201 Jim Dickson	.27	.11	.03
☐ 202 Clay Dalrymple	.27	.11	.03
☐ 203 Jose Santiago	.27	.11	.03
☐ 204 Cubs Team	.75	.30	.07
☐ 205 Tom Tresh	.65	.26	.06
☐ 206 Alvin Jackson	.27	.11	.03

		MINT	VG-E	F-G
☐ 207	Frank Quilici	.27	.11	.03
☐ 208	Bob Miller	.27	.11	.03
☐ 209	Tigers Rookies	.75	.30	.07
	Fritz Fisher			
	John Hiller			
☐ 210	Bill Mazeroski	.90	.36	.09
☐ 211	Frank Kreutzer	.27	.11	.03
☐ 212	Ed Kranepool	.40	.16	.04
☐ 213	Fred Newman	.27	.11	.03
☐ 214	Tommy Harper	.35	.14	.03
☐ 215	NL Batting Leaders	5.00	2.00	.50
	Bob Clemente			
	Hank Aaron			
	Willie Mays			
☐ 216	AL Batting Leaders	1.50	.60	.15
	Tony Oliva			
	Carl Yastrzemski			
	Vic Davalillo			
☐ 217	NL Home Run Leaders	3.50	1.40	.35
	Willie Mays			
	Willie McCovey			
	Billy Williams			
☐ 218	AL Home Run Leaders	.80	.32	.08
	Tony Conigliaro			
	Norm Cash			
	Willie Horton			
☐ 219	NL RBI Leaders	1.50	.60	.15
	Deron Johnson			
	Frank Robinson			
	Willie Mays			
☐ 220	AL RBI Leaders	.80	.32	.08
	Rocky Colavito			
	Willie Horton			
	Tony Oliva			
☐ 221	NL ERA Leaders	1.75	.70	.17
	Sandy Koufax			
	Juan Marichal			
	Vern Law			
☐ 222	AL ERA Leaders	.80	.32	.08
	Sam McDowell			
	Eddie Fisher			
	Sonny Siebert			
☐ 223	NL Pitching Leaders	1.75	.70	.17
	Sandy Koufax			
	Tony Cloninger			
	Don Drysdale			
☐ 224	AL Pitching Leaders	.80	.32	.08
	Jim Grant			
	Mel Stottlemyre			
	Jim Kaat			

		MINT	VG-E	F-G
☐ 225	NL Strikeout Leaders	1.75	.70	.17
	Sandy Koufax			
	Bob Veale			
	Bob Gibson			
☐ 226	AL Strikeout Leaders	.80	.32	.08
	Sam McDowell			
	Mickey Lolich			
	Dennis McLain			
	Sonny Siebert			
☐ 227	Russ Nixon	.27	.11	.03
☐ 228	Larry Dierker	.27	.11	.03
☐ 229	Hank Bauer MGR	.35	.14	.03
☐ 230	John Callison	.35	.14	.03
☐ 231	Floyd Weaver	.27	.11	.03
☐ 232	Glenn Beckert	.35	.14	.03
☐ 233	Dom Zanni	.27	.11	.03
☐ 234	Yankees Rookies	1.50	.60	.15
	Rich Beck			
	Roy White			
☐ 235	Don Cardwell	.27	.11	.03
☐ 236	Mike Hershberger	.27	.11	.03
☐ 237	Billy O'Dell	.27	.11	.03
☐ 238	Dodgers Team	1.00	.40	.10
☐ 239	Orlando Pena	.27	.11	.03
☐ 240	Earl Battey	.27	.11	.03
☐ 241	Dennis Ribant	.27	.11	.03
☐ 242	Jesus Alou	.27	.11	.03
☐ 243	Nelson Briles	.35	.14	.03
☐ 244	Astros Rookies	.27	.11	.03
	Chuck Harrison			
	Sonny Jackson			
☐ 245	John Buzhardt	.27	.11	.03
☐ 246	Ed Bailey	.27	.11	.03
☐ 247	Carl Warwick	.27	.11	.03
☐ 248	Pete Mikkelsen	.27	.11	.03
☐ 249	Bill Rigney MGR	.27	.11	.03
☐ 250	Sam Ellis	.27	.11	.03
☐ 251	Ed Brinkman	.27	.11	.03
☐ 252	Denny Lemaster	.27	.11	.03
☐ 253	Don Wert	.27	.11	.03
☐ 254	Phillies Rookies	12.00	5.00	1.20
	Ferguson Jenkins			
	Bill Sorrell			
☐ 255	Willie Stargell	4.50	1.80	.45
☐ 256	Lew Krausse	.27	.11	.03
☐ 257	Jeff Torborg	.35	.14	.03
☐ 258	Dave Giusti	.27	.11	.03
☐ 259	Red Sox Team	.75	.30	.07
☐ 260	Bob Shaw	.27	.11	.03
☐ 261	Ron Hansen	.27	.11	.03
☐ 262	Jack Hamilton	.27	.11	.03
☐ 263	Tom Egan	.27	.11	.03

		MINT	VG-E	F-G
☐ 264	Twins Rookies	.27	.11	.03
	Andy Kosco			
	Ted Uhlaender			
☐ 265	Stu Miller	.27	.11	.03
☐ 266	Pedro Gonzalez	.27	.11	.03
☐ 267	Joe Sparma	.27	.11	.03
☐ 268	John Blanchard	.27	.11	.03
☐ 269	Don Heffner MGR	.27	.11	.03
☐ 270	Claude Osteen	.35	.14	.03
☐ 271	Hal Lanier	.50	.20	.05
☐ 272	Jack Baldschun	.27	.11	.03
☐ 273	Astro Aces	.50	.20	.05
	Bob Aspromonte			
	Rusty Staub			
☐ 274	Buster Narum	.27	.11	.03
☐ 275	Tim McCarver	.75	.30	.07
☐ 276	Jim Bouton	.75	.30	.07
☐ 277	George Thomas	.27	.11	.03
☐ 278	Calvin Koonce	.27	.11	.03
☐ 279	Checklist 4	2.00	.20	.04
☐ 280	Bobby Knoop	.27	.11	.03
☐ 281	Bruce Howard	.27	.11	.03
☐ 282	Johnny Lewis	.27	.11	.03
☐ 283	Jim Perry	.40	.16	.04
☐ 284	Bobby Wine	.27	.11	.03
☐ 285	Luis Tiant	1.00	.40	.10
☐ 286	Gary Geiger	.27	.11	.03
☐ 287	Jack Aker	.27	.11	.03
☐ 288	Dodgers Rookies	27.00	11.00	2.70
	Bill Singer			
	Don Sutton			
☐ 289	Larry Sherry	.35	.14	.03
☐ 290	Ron Santo	.75	.30	.07
☐ 291	Moe Drabowsky	.27	.11	.03
☐ 292	Jim Coker	.27	.11	.03
☐ 293	Mike Shannon	.50	.20	.05
☐ 294	Steve Ridzik	.27	.11	.03
☐ 295	Jim Ray Hart	.35	.14	.03
☐ 296	Johnny Keane MGR	.35	.14	.03
☐ 297	Jim Owens	.27	.11	.03
☐ 298	Rico Petrocelli	.35	.14	.03
☐ 299	Lou Burdette	.55	.22	.05
☐ 300	Bob Clemente	20.00	8.00	2.00
☐ 301	Greg Bollo	.27	.11	.03
☐ 302	Ernie Bowman	.27	.11	.03
☐ 303	Indians Team	.75	.30	.07
☐ 304	John Herrnstein	.27	.11	.03
☐ 305	Camilo Pascual	.35	.14	.03
☐ 306	Ty Cline	.27	.11	.03
☐ 307	Clay Carroll	.27	.11	.03
☐ 308	Tom Haller	.27	.11	.03
☐ 309	Diego Segui	.27	.11	.03
☐ 310	Frank Robinson	10.00	4.00	1.00

		MINT	VG-E	F-G
☐ 311	Reds Rookies	.40	.16	.04
	Tommy Helms			
	Dick Simpson			
☐ 312	Bob Saverine	.27	.11	.03
☐ 313	Chris Zachary	.27	.11	.03
☐ 314	Hector Valle	.27	.11	.03
☐ 315	Norm Cash	.90	.36	.09
☐ 316	Jack Fisher	.27	.11	.03
☐ 317	Dalton Jones	.27	.11	.03
☐ 318	Harry Walker MGR	.27	.11	.03
☐ 319	Gene Freese	.27	.11	.03
☐ 320	Bob Gibson	4.50	1.80	.45
☐ 321	Rick Reichardt	.27	.11	.03
☐ 322	Bill Faul	.27	.11	.03
☐ 323	Ray Barker	.27	.11	.03
☐ 324	John Boozer	.27	.11	.03
☐ 325	Vic Davalillo	.27	.11	.03
☐ 326	Braves Team	.75	.30	.07
☐ 327	Bernie Allen	.27	.11	.03
☐ 328	Jerry Grote	.27	.11	.03
☐ 329	Pete Charton	.27	.11	.03
☐ 330	Ron Fairly	.35	.14	.03
☐ 331	Ron Herbel	.27	.11	.03
☐ 332	Billy Bryan	.27	.11	.03
☐ 333	Senators Rookies	.27	.11	.03
	Joe Coleman			
	Jim French			
☐ 334	Marty Keough	.27	.11	.03
☐ 335	Juan Pizarro	.27	.11	.03
☐ 336	Gene Alley	.40	.16	.04
☐ 337	Fred Gladding	.27	.11	.03
☐ 338	Dal Maxvill	.27	.11	.03
☐ 339	Del Crandall	.35	.14	.03
☐ 340	Dean Chance	.35	.14	.03
☐ 341	Wes Westrum MGR	.27	.11	.03
☐ 342	Bob Humphreys	.27	.11	.03
☐ 343	Joe Christopher	.27	.11	.03
☐ 344	Steve Blass	.35	.14	.03
☐ 345	Bob Allison	.35	.14	.03
☐ 346	Mike De La Hoz	.27	.11	.03
☐ 347	Phil Regan	.35	.14	.03
☐ 348	Orioles Team	.75	.30	.07
☐ 349	Cap Peterson	.27	.11	.03
☐ 350	Mel Stottlemyre	.75	.30	.07
☐ 351	Fred Valentine	.27	.11	.03
☐ 352	Bob Aspromonte	.27	.11	.03
☐ 353	Al McBean	.27	.11	.03
☐ 354	Smoky Burgess	.35	.14	.03
☐ 355	Wade Blasingame	.27	.11	.03
☐ 356	Red Sox Rookies	.27	.11	.03
	Owen Johnson			
	Ken Sanders			
☐ 357	Gerry Arrigo	.27	.11	.03

		MINT	VG-E	F-G			MINT	VG-E	F-G
☐ 358	Charlie Smith	.27	.11	.03	☐ 407	John Kennedy	.27	.11	.03
☐ 359	Johnny Briggs	.27	.11	.03	☐ 408	Lee Thomas	.27	.11	.03
☐ 360	Ron Hunt	.27	.11	.03	☐ 409	Billy Hoeft	.27	.11	.03
☐ 361	Tom Satriano	.27	.11	.03	☐ 410	Al Kaline	4.50	1.80	.45
☐ 362	Gates Brown	.35	.14	.03	☐ 411	Gene Mauch MGR	.40	.16	.04
☐ 363	Checklist 5	2.00	.20	.04	☐ 412	Sam Bowens	.27	.11	.03
☐ 364	Nate Oliver	.27	.11	.03	☐ 413	John Romano	.27	.11	.03
☐ 365	Roger Maris	5.00	2.00	.50	☐ 414	Dan Coombs	.27	.11	.03
☐ 366	Wayne Causey	.27	.11	.03	☐ 415	Max Alvis	.27	.11	.03
☐ 367	Mel Nelson	.27	.11	.03	☐ 416	Phil Ortega	.27	.11	.03
☐ 368	Charlie Lau	.35	.14	.03	☐ 417	Angels Rookies	.35	.14	.03
☐ 369	Jim King	.27	.11	.03		Jim McGlothlin			
☐ 370	Chico Cardenas	.27	.11	.03		Ed Sukla			
☐ 371	Lee Stange	.27	.11	.03	☐ 418	Phil Gagliano	.27	.11	.03
☐ 372	Harvey Kuenn	.50	.20	.05	☐ 419	Mike Ryan	.27	.11	.03
☐ 373	Giants Rookies	.27	.11	.03	☐ 420	Juan Marichal	3.50	1.40	.35
	Jack Hiatt				☐ 421	Roy McMillan	.27	.11	.03
	Dick Estelle				☐ 422	Ed Charles	.27	.11	.03
☐ 374	Bob Locker	.27	.11	.03	☐ 423	Ernie Broglio	.27	.11	.03
☐ 375	Donn Clendenon	.35	.14	.03	☐ 424	Reds Rookies	1.25	.50	.12
☐ 376	Paul Schaal	.27	.11	.03		Lee May			
☐ 377	Turk Farrell	.27	.11	.03		Darrell Osteen			
☐ 378	Dick Tracewski	.27	.11	.03	☐ 425	Bob Veale	.35	.14	.03
☐ 379	Cardinal Team	.75	.30	.07	☐ 426	White Sox Team	.75	.30	.07
☐ 380	Tony Conigliaro	.80	.32	.08	☐ 427	John Miller	.27	.11	.03
☐ 381	Hank Fischer	.27	.11	.03	☐ 428	Sandy Alomar	.27	.11	.03
☐ 382	Phil Roof	.27	.11	.03	☐ 429	Bill Monbouquette	.27	.11	.03
☐ 383	Jack Brandt	.27	.11	.03	☐ 430	Don Drysdale	4.00	1.60	.40
☐ 384	Al Downing	.35	.14	.03	☐ 431	Walt Bond	.27	.11	.03
☐ 385	Ken Boyer	1.25	.50	.12	☐ 432	Bob Heffner	.27	.11	.03
☐ 386	Gil Hodges MGR	2.50	1.00	.25	☐ 433	Alvin Dark MGR	.35	.14	.03
☐ 387	Howie Reed	.27	.11	.03	☐ 434	Willie Kirkland	.27	.11	.03
☐ 388	Don Mincher	.35	.14	.03	☐ 435	Jim Bunning	1.50	.60	.15
☐ 389	Jim O'Toole	.27	.11	.03	☐ 436	Julian Javier	.35	.14	.03
☐ 390	Brooks Robinson	5.00	2.00	.50	☐ 437	Al Stanek	.27	.11	.03
☐ 391	Chuck Hinton	.27	.11	.03	☐ 438	Willie Smith	.27	.11	.03
☐ 392	Cubs Rookies	.40	.16	.04	☐ 439	Pedro Ramos	.27	.11	.03
	Bill Hands				☐ 440	Deron Johnson	.27	.11	.03
	Randy Hundley				☐ 441	Tommie Sisk	.27	.11	.03
☐ 393	George Brunet	.27	.11	.03	☐ 442	Orioles Rookies	.27	.11	.03
☐ 394	Ron Brand	.27	.11	.03		Ed Barnowski			
☐ 395	Len Gabrielson	.27	.11	.03		Eddie Watt			
☐ 396	J. Stephenson	.27	.11	.03	☐ 443	Bill Wakefield	.27	.11	.03
☐ 397	Bill White	.40	.16	.04	☐ 444	Checklist 6	2.50	.25	.05
☐ 398	Danny Cater	.27	.11	.03	☐ 445	Jim Kaat	2.00	.80	.20
☐ 399	Ray Washburn	.27	.11	.03	☐ 446	Mack Jones	.27	.11	.03
☐ 400	Zoilo Versalles	.35	.14	.03	☐ 447	Dick Ellsworth	.75	.30	.07
☐ 401	Ken McMullen	.27	.11	.03		(photo actually			
☐ 402	Jim Hickman	.27	.11	.03		Ken Hubbs)			
☐ 403	Fred Talbot	.27	.11	.03	☐ 448	Eddie Stanky MGR	.75	.30	.07
☐ 404	Pirates Team	.75	.30	.07	☐ 449	Joe Moeller	.65	.26	.06
☐ 405	Elston Howard	1.25	.50	.12	☐ 450	Tony Oliva	1.75	.70	.17
☐ 406	Joe Jay	.27	.11	.03	☐ 451	Barry Latman	.65	.26	.06

		MINT	VG-E	F-G
☐ 452	Joe Azcue	.65	.26	.06
☐ 453	Ron Kline	.65	.26	.06
☐ 454	Jerry Buchek	.65	.26	.06
☐ 455	Mickey Lolich	1.25	.50	.12
☐ 456	Red Sox Rookies	.65	.26	.06
	Darrell Brandon			
	Joe Foy			
☐ 457	Joe Gibbon	.65	.26	.06
☐ 458	Manny Jiminez	.65	.26	.06
☐ 459	Bill McCool	.65	.26	.06
☐ 460	Curt Blefary	.75	.30	.07
☐ 461	Roy Face	.90	.36	.09
☐ 462	Bob Rodgers	.65	.26	.06
☐ 463	Phillies Team	1.00	.40	.10
☐ 464	Larry Bearnarth	.65	.26	.06
☐ 465	Don Buford	.65	.26	.06
☐ 466	Ken Johnson	.65	.26	.06
☐ 467	Vic Roznovsky	.65	.26	.06
☐ 468	Johnny Podres	1.25	.50	.12
☐ 469	Yankees Rookies	4.50	1.80	.45
	Bobby Murcer			
	Dooley Womack			
☐ 470	Sam McDowell	.75	.30	.07
☐ 471	Bob Skinner	.75	.30	.07
☐ 472	Terry Fox	.65	.26	.06
☐ 473	Rich Rollins	.65	.26	.06
☐ 474	Dick Schofield	.65	.26	.06
☐ 475	Dick Radatz	.75	.30	.07
☐ 476	Bobby Bragan MGR	.65	.26	.06
☐ 477	Steve Barber	.65	.26	.06
☐ 478	Tony Gonzalez	.65	.26	.06
☐ 479	Jim Hannan	.65	.26	.06
☐ 480	Dick Stuart	.75	.30	.07
☐ 481	Bob Lee	.65	.26	.06
☐ 482	Cubs Rookies	.65	.26	.06
	John Boccabella			
	Dave Dowling			
☐ 483	Joe Nuxhall	.75	.30	.07
☐ 484	Wes Covington	.75	.30	.07
☐ 485	Bob Bailey	.65	.26	.06
☐ 486	Tommy John	2.50	1.00	.25
☐ 487	Al Ferrara	.65	.26	.06
☐ 488	George Banks	.65	.26	.06
☐ 489	Curt Simmons	.75	.30	.07
☐ 490	Bobby Richardson	2.50	1.00	.25
☐ 491	Dennis Bennett	.65	.26	.06
☐ 492	Athletics Team	1.00	.40	.10
☐ 493	John Klippstein	.65	.26	.06
☐ 494	Gordon Coleman	.65	.26	.06
☐ 495	Dick McAuliffe	.75	.30	.07
☐ 496	Lindy McDaniel	.75	.30	.07
☐ 497	Chris Cannizzaro	.65	.26	.06

		MINT	VG-E	F-G
☐ 498	Pirates Rookies	.75	.30	.07
	Luke Walker			
	Woody Fryman			
☐ 499	Wally Bunker	.65	.26	.06
☐ 500	Hank Aaron	25.00	10.00	2.50
☐ 501	John O'Donoghue	.65	.26	.06
☐ 502	Lenny Green	.65	.26	.06
☐ 503	Steve Hamilton	.65	.26	.06
☐ 504	Grady Hatton MGR	.65	.26	.06
☐ 505	Jose Cardenal	.65	.26	.06
☐ 506	Bo Belinsky	.75	.30	.07
☐ 507	John Edwards	.65	.26	.06
☐ 508	Steve Hargan	.65	.26	.06
☐ 509	Jake Wood	.65	.26	.06
☐ 510	Hoyt Wilhelm	4.00	1.60	.40
☐ 511	Giants Rookies	.65	.26	.06
	Bob Barton			
	Tito Fuentes			
☐ 512	Dick Stigman	.65	.26	.06
☐ 513	Camilo Carreon	.65	.26	.06
☐ 514	Hal Woodeshick	.65	.26	.06
☐ 515	Frank Howard	1.50	.60	.15
☐ 516	Eddie Bressoud	.65	.26	.06
☐ 517	Checklist 7	5.00	.50	.10
☐ 518	Braves Rookies	.65	.26	.06
	Herb Hippauf			
	Arnie Umbach			
☐ 519	Bob Friend	.75	.30	.07
☐ 520	Jim Wynn	.75	.30	.07
☐ 521	John Wyatt	.65	.26	.06
☐ 522	Phil Linz	.75	.30	.07
☐ 523	Bob Sadowski	4.25	1.70	.42
☐ 524	Giants Rookies	4.25	1.70	.42
	Ollie Brown			
	Don Mason			
☐ 525	Gary Bell	4.25	1.70	.42
☐ 526	Twins Team	8.00	3.25	.80
☐ 527	Julio Navarro	4.25	1.70	.42
☐ 528	Jesse Gonder	4.25	1.70	.42
☐ 529	White Sox Rookies	5.00	2.00	.50
	Lee Elia			
	Dennis Higgins			
	Bill Voss			
☐ 530	Robin Roberts	14.00	5.75	1.40
☐ 531	Joe Cunningham	4.25	1.70	.42
☐ 532	Aurelio Monteagudo	4.25	1.70	.42
☐ 533	Jerry Adair	4.25	1.70	.42
☐ 534	Mets Rookies	4.25	1.70	.42
	Dave Eilers			
	Rob Gardner			
☐ 535	Willie Davis	6.00	2.40	.60
☐ 536	Dick Egan	4.25	1.70	.42
☐ 537	Herman Franks MGR	4.25	1.70	.42

		MINT	VG-E	F-G
☐ 538	Bob Allen	4.25	1.70	.42
☐ 539	Astros Rookies	4.25	1.70	.42
	Bill Heath			
	Carroll Sembera			
☐ 540	Denny McLain	12.00	5.00	1.20
☐ 541	Gene Oliver	4.25	1.70	.42
☐ 542	George Smith	4.25	1.70	.42
☐ 543	Roger Craig	6.00	2.40	.60
☐ 544	Cardinals Rookies	4.25	1.70	.42
	Joe Hoerner			
	George Kernek			
	Jimmy Williams			
☐ 545	Dick Green	4.25	1.70	.42
☐ 546	Dwight Siebler	4.25	1.70	.42
☐ 547	Horace Clarke	5.00	2.00	.50
☐ 548	Gary Kroll	4.25	1.70	.42
☐ 549	Senators Rookies	4.25	1.70	.42
	Al Closter			
	Casey Cox			
☐ 550	Willie McCovey	50.00	20.00	5.00
☐ 551	Bob Purkey	4.25	1.70	.42
☐ 552	Birdie Tebbetts MGR	4.25	1.70	.42
☐ 553	Rookie Stars	4.25	1.70	.42
	Pat Garrett			
	Jackie Warner			
☐ 554	Jim Northrup	5.00	2.00	.50
☐ 555	Ron Perranoski	5.00	2.00	.50
☐ 556	Mel Queen	4.25	1.70	.42
☐ 557	Felix Mantilla	4.25	1.70	.42
☐ 558	Red Sox Rookies	7.50	3.00	.75
	Guido Grilli			
	Pete Magrini			
	George Scott			
☐ 559	Roberto Pena	4.25	1.70	.42
☐ 560	Joel Horlen	5.00	2.00	.50
☐ 561	Choo Choo Coleman	4.25	1.70	.42
☐ 562	Russ Snyder	4.25	1.70	.42
☐ 563	Twins Rookies	5.00	2.00	.50
	Pete Cimino			
	Cesar Tovar			
☐ 564	Bob Chance	4.25	1.70	.42
☐ 565	Jimmy Piersall	6.50	2.60	.65
☐ 566	Mike Cuellar	5.00	2.00	.50
☐ 567	Dick Howser	6.00	2.40	.60
☐ 568	Athletics Rookies	5.00	2.00	.50
	Paul Lindblad			
	Rod Stone			
☐ 569	Orlando McFarlane	4.25	1.70	.42
☐ 570	Art Mahaffey	4.25	1.70	.42
☐ 571	Dave Roberts	4.25	1.70	.42
☐ 572	Bob Priddy	4.25	1.70	.42
☐ 573	Derrell Griffith	4.25	1.70	.42

		MINT	VG-E	F-G
☐ 574	Mets Rookies	4.25	1.70	.42
	Bill Hepler			
	Bill Murphy			
☐ 575	Earl Wilson	4.25	1.70	.42
☐ 576	Dave Nicholson	4.25	1.70	.42
☐ 577	Jack Lamabe	4.25	1.70	.42
☐ 578	Chi Chi Olivo	4.25	1.70	.42
☐ 579	Orioles Rookies	6.00	2.40	.60
	Frank Bertaina			
	Gene Brabender			
	Dave Johnson			
☐ 580	Billy Williams	20.00	8.00	2.00
☐ 581	Tony Martinez	4.25	1.70	.42
☐ 582	Garry Roggenburk	4.25	1.70	.42
☐ 583	Tigers Team	12.00	5.00	1.20
☐ 584	Yankees Rookies	5.00	2.00	.50
	Frank Fernandez			
	Fritz Peterson			
☐ 585	Tony Taylor	4.25	1.70	.42
☐ 586	Claude Raymond	4.25	1.70	.42
☐ 587	Dick Bertell	4.25	1.70	.42
☐ 588	Athletics Rookies	4.25	1.70	.42
	Chuck Dobson			
	Ken Suarez			
☐ 589	Lou Klimchock	4.25	1.70	.42
☐ 590	Bill Skowron	6.00	2.40	.60
☐ 591	NL Rookies	5.00	2.00	.50
	Bart Shirley			
	Grant Jackson			
☐ 592	Andre Rodgers	4.25	1.70	.42
☐ 593	Doug Camilli	4.25	1.70	.42
☐ 594	Chico Salmon	4.25	1.70	.42
☐ 595	Larry Jackson	4.25	1.70	.42
☐ 596	Astros Rookies	5.00	2.00	.50
	Nate Colbert			
	Greg Sims			
☐ 597	John Sullivan	4.25	1.70	.42
☐ 598	Gaylord Perry	90.00	25.00	5.00

1967 Topps

BOB UECKER · CATCHER

The cards in this 609-card set measure 2½"
by 3½". The 1967 Topps series is considered
by some collectors to be one of the company's finest accomplishments in baseball
card production. Excellent color photographs are combined with easy to read
backs. Cards 458 to 533 are slightly harder to
find than numbers 1 to 457, and the inevitable
(difficult to find) high series (534 to 609) exists. Each checklist card features a small cir-
cular picture of a popular player included in
that series. Printing discrepancies resulted in
some high series cards being in short supply.
Featured subsets within this set include
World Series cards (151-155) and League
Leaders (233-244). Although there are several relatively expensive cards in this popular
set, the key cards in the set are undoubtedly
the Tom Seaver rookie card (581) and the
Rod Carew rookie card (569).

	MINT	VG-E	F-G
Complete Set	1250.00	550.00	150.00
Common Player (1-370)	.25	.10	.02
Common Player (371-457)	.35	.14	.03
Common Player (458-533)	.75	.30	.07
Common Player (534-609)	2.25	.90	.22

		MINT	VG-E	F-G
☐	1 The Champs	3.50	1.40	.35
	Frank Robinson			
	Hank Bauer			
	Brooks Robinson			

		MINT	VG-E	F-G
☐	2 Jack Hamilton	.25	.10	.02
☐	3 Duke Sims	.25	.10	.02
☐	4 Hal Lanier	.40	.16	.04
☐	5 Whitey Ford	4.50	1.80	.45
☐	6 Dick Simpson	.25	.10	.02
☐	7 Don McMahon	.25	.10	.02
☐	8 Chuck Harrison	.25	.10	.02
☐	9 Ron Hansen	.25	.10	.02
☐	10 Matty Alou	.35	.14	.03
☐	11 Barry Moore	.25	.10	.02
☐	12 Dodgers Rookies	.35	.14	.03
	Jim Campanis			
	Bill Singer			
☐	13 Joe Sparma	.25	.10	.02
☐	14 Phil Linz	.25	.10	.02
☐	15 Earl Battey	.25	.10	.02
☐	16 Bill Hands	.25	.10	.02
☐	17 Jim Gosger	.25	.10	.02
☐	18 Gene Oliver	.25	.10	.02
☐	19 Jim McGlothlin	.25	.10	.02
☐	20 Orlando Cepeda	2.00	.80	.20
☐	21 Dave Bristol MGR	.25	.10	.02
☐	22 Gene Brabender	.25	.10	.02
☐	23 Larry Elliot	.25	.10	.02
☐	24 Bob Allen	.25	.10	.02
☐	25 Elston Howard	1.25	.50	.12
☐	26 A Bob Priddy	.25	.10	.02
	(with traded line)			
☐	26 B Bob Priddy	10.00	4.00	1.00
	(no traded line)			
☐	27 Bob Saverine	.25	.10	.02
☐	28 Barry Latman	.25	.10	.02
☐	29 Tommy McCraw	.25	.10	.02
☐	30 Al Kaline	4.00	1.60	.40
☐	31 Jim Brewer	.25	.10	.02
☐	32 Bob Bailey	.25	.10	.02
☐	33 Athletic Rookies	1.00	.40	.10
	Sal Bando			
	Randy Schwartz			
☐	34 Pete Cimino	.25	.10	.02
☐	35 Rico Carty	.55	.22	.05
☐	36 Bob Tillman	.25	.10	.02
☐	37 Rick Wise	.35	.14	.03
☐	38 Bob Johnson	.25	.10	.02
☐	39 Curt Simmons	.35	.14	.03
☐	40 Rick Reichardt	.25	.10	.02
☐	41 Joe Hoerner	.25	.10	.02
☐	42 Mets Team	.85	.34	.08
☐	43 Chico Salmon	.25	.10	.02
☐	44 Joe Nuxhall	.35	.14	.03
☐	45 Roger Maris	4.50	1.80	.45
☐	46 Lindy McDaniel	.25	.10	.02
☐	47 Ken McMullen	.25	.10	.02

		MINT	VG-E	F-G
☐ 48	Bill Freehan	.60	.24	.06
☐ 49	Roy Face	.45	.18	.04
☐ 50	Tony Oliva	1.25	.50	.12
☐ 51	Astros Rookies	.25	.10	.02
	Dave Adlesh			
	Wes Bales			
☐ 52	Dennis Higgins	.25	.10	.02
☐ 53	Clay Dalrymple	.25	.10	.02
☐ 54	Dick Green	.25	.10	.02
☐ 55	Don Drysdale	3.50	1.40	.35
☐ 56	Jose Tartabull	.25	.10	.02
☐ 57	Pat Jarvis	.25	.10	.02
☐ 58	Paul Schaal	.25	.10	.02
☐ 59	Ralph Terry	.35	.14	.03
☐ 60	Luis Aparicio	2.75	1.10	.27
☐ 61	Gordy Coleman	.25	.10	.02
☐ 62	Checklist 1	1.75	.15	.03
	Frank Robinson			
☐ 63	Cards' Clubbers	1.50	.60	.15
	Lou Brock			
	Curt Flood			
☐ 64	Fred Valentine	.25	.10	.02
☐ 65	Tom Haller	.25	.10	.02
☐ 66	Manny Mota	.35	.14	.03
☐ 67	Ken Berry	.25	.10	.02
☐ 68	Bob Buhl	.25	.10	.02
☐ 69	Vic Davalillo	.25	.10	.02
☐ 70	Ron Santo	.65	.26	.06
☐ 71	Camilo Pascual	.35	.14	.03
☐ 72	Tigers Rookies	.35	.14	.03
	George Korince (photo			
	actually John Brown)			
	John (Tom) Matchick			
☐ 73	Rusty Staub	1.25	.50	.12
☐ 74	Wes Stock	.25	.10	.02
☐ 75	George Scott	.35	.14	.03
☐ 76	Jim Barbieri	.25	.10	.02
☐ 77	Dooley Womack	.25	.10	.02
☐ 78	Pat Corrales	.35	.14	.03
☐ 79	Bubba Morton	.25	.10	.02
☐ 80	Jim Maloney	.35	.14	.03
☐ 81	Eddie Stanky MGR	.35	.14	.03
☐ 82	Steve Barber	.25	.10	.02
☐ 83	Ollie Brown	.25	.10	.02
☐ 84	Tommie Sisk	.25	.10	.02
☐ 85	Johnny Callison	.35	.14	.03
☐ 86 A	Mike McCormick	.35	.14	.03
	(with traded line)			
☐ 86 B	Mike McCormick	10.00	4.00	1.00
	(no traded line)			
☐ 87	George Altman	.25	.10	.02
☐ 88	Mickey Lolich	.80	.32	.08
☐ 89	Felix Millan	.35	.14	.03
☐ 90	Jim Nash	.25	.10	.02
☐ 91	Johnny Lewis	.25	.10	.02
☐ 92	Ray Washburn	.25	.10	.02
☐ 93	Yankees Rookies	1.25	.50	.12
	Stan Bahnsen			
	Bobby Murcer			
☐ 94	Ron Fairly	.35	.14	.03
☐ 95	Sonny Siebert	.35	.14	.03
☐ 96	Art Shamsky	.25	.10	.02
☐ 97	Mike Cuellar	.35	.14	.03
☐ 98	Rich Rollins	.25	.10	.02
☐ 99	Lee Stange	.25	.10	.02
☐ 100	Frank Robinson	3.75	1.50	.37
☐ 101	Ken Johnson	.25	.10	.02
☐ 102	Phillies Team	.75	.30	.07
☐ 103	Checklist 2	2.50	.25	.05
	Mickey Mantle			
☐ 104	Minnie Rojas	.25	.10	.02
☐ 105	Ken Boyer	.80	.32	.08
☐ 106	Randy Hundley	.35	.14	.03
☐ 107	Joel Horlen	.35	.14	.03
☐ 108	Alex Johnson	.35	.14	.03
☐ 109	Tribe Thumpers	.40	.16	.04
	Rocky Colavito			
	Leon Wagner			
☐ 110	Jack Aker	.25	.10	.02
☐ 111	John Kennedy	.25	.10	.02
☐ 112	Dave Wickersham	.25	.10	.02
☐ 113	Dave Nicholson	.25	.10	.02
☐ 114	Jack Baldschun	.25	.10	.02
☐ 115	Paul Casanova	.25	.10	.02
☐ 116	Herman Franks MGR	.25	.10	.02
☐ 117	Darrell Brandon	.25	.10	.02
☐ 118	Bernie Allen	.25	.10	.02
☐ 119	Wade Blasingame	.25	.10	.02
☐ 120	Floyd Robinson	.25	.10	.02
☐ 121	Ed Bressoud	.25	.10	.02
☐ 122	George Brunet	.25	.10	.02
☐ 123	Pirates Rookies	.25	.10	.02
	Jim Price			
	Luke Walker			
☐ 124	Jim Stewart	.25	.10	.02
☐ 125	Moe Drabowsky	.25	.10	.02
☐ 126	Tony Taylor	.25	.10	.02
☐ 127	John O'Donoghue	.25	.10	.02
☐ 128	Ed Spiezio	.25	.10	.02
☐ 129	Phil Roof	.25	.10	.02
☐ 130	Phil Regan	.35	.14	.03
☐ 131	Yankees Team	.90	.36	.09
☐ 132	Ozzie Virgil	.25	.10	.02
☐ 133	Ron Kline	.25	.10	.02
☐ 134	Gates Brown	.35	.14	.03
☐ 135	Deron Johnson	.25	.10	.02

		MINT	VG-E	F-G
☐ 136	Carroll Sembera	.25	.10	.02
☐ 137	Twins Rookies	.25	.10	.02
	Ron Clark			
	Jim Ollum			
☐ 138	Dick Kelley	.25	.10	.02
☐ 139	Dalton Jones	.25	.10	.02
☐ 140	Willie Stargell	4.00	1.60	.40
☐ 141	John Miller	.25	.10	.02
☐ 142	Jackie Brandt	.25	.10	.02
☐ 143	Sox Sockers	.35	.14	.03
	Pete Ward			
	Don Buford			
☐ 144	Bill Hepler	.25	.10	.02
☐ 145	Larry Brown	.25	.10	.02
☐ 146	Steve Carlton	36.00	15.00	3.60
☐ 147	Tom Egan	.25	.10	.02
☐ 148	Adolfo Phillips	.25	.10	.02
☐ 149	Joe Moeller	.25	.10	.02
☐ 150	Mickey Mantle	50.00	20.00	5.00
☐ 151	World Series Game 1	1.00	.40	.10
	Moe mows down 11			
☐ 152	World Series Game 2	2.00	.80	.20
	Palmer blanks Dodgers			
☐ 153	World Series Game 3	1.00	.40	.10
	Blair's homer			
	defeats L.A.			
☐ 154	World Series Game 4	1.00	.40	.10
	Orioles 4 straight			
☐ 155	World Series Summary	1.25	.50	.12
	Winners celebrate			
☐ 156	Ron Herbel	.25	.10	.02
☐ 157	Danny Cater	.25	.10	.02
☐ 158	Jimmie Coker	.25	.10	.02
☐ 159	Bruce Howard	.25	.10	.02
☐ 160	Willie Davis	.50	.20	.05
☐ 161	Dick Williams MGR	.35	.14	.03
☐ 162	Billy O'Dell	.25	.10	.02
☐ 163	Vic Roznovsky	.25	.10	.02
☐ 164	Dwight Siebler	.25	.10	.02
☐ 165	Cleon Jones	.25	.10	.02
☐ 166	Ed Mathews	3.00	1.20	.30
☐ 167	Senators Rookies	.25	.10	.02
	Joe Coleman			
	Tim Cullen			
☐ 168	Ray Culp	.25	.10	.02
☐ 169	Horace Clarke	.25	.10	.02
☐ 170	Dick McAuliffe	.35	.14	.03
☐ 171	Calvin Koonce	.25	.10	.02
☐ 172	Bill Heath	.25	.10	.02
☐ 173	Cardinals Team	.85	.34	.08
☐ 174	Dick Radatz	.35	.14	.03
☐ 175	Bobby Knoop	.25	.10	.02
☐ 176	Sammy Ellis	.25	.10	.02

		MINT	VG-E	F-G
☐ 177	Tito Fuentes	.25	.10	.02
☐ 178	John Buzhardt	.25	.10	.02
☐ 179	Braves Rookies	.25	.10	.02
	Charles Vaughan			
	Cecil Upshaw			
☐ 180	Curt Blefary	.35	.14	.03
☐ 181	Terry Fox	.25	.10	.02
☐ 182	Ed Charles	.25	.10	.02
☐ 183	Jim Pagliaroni	.25	.10	.02
☐ 184	George Thomas	.25	.10	.02
☐ 185	Ken Holtzman	.75	.30	.07
☐ 186	Mets Maulers	.40	.16	.04
	Ed Kranepool			
	Ron Swoboda			
☐ 187	Pedro Ramos	.25	.10	.02
☐ 188	Ken Harrelson	.75	.30	.07
☐ 189	Chuck Hinton	.25	.10	.02
☐ 190	Turk Farrell	.25	.10	.02
☐ 191 A	Checklist 3	2.00	.20	.04
	(214 Tom Kelley)			
	(Willie Mays)			
☐ 191 B	Checklist 3	5.00	.50	.10
	(214 Dick Kelley)			
	(Willie Mays)			
☐ 192	Fred Gladding	.25	.10	.02
☐ 193	Jose Cardenal	.25	.10	.02
☐ 194	Bob Allison	.35	.14	.03
☐ 195	Al Jackson	.25	.10	.02
☐ 196	Johnny Romano	.25	.10	.02
☐ 197	Ron Perranoski	.35	.14	.03
☐ 198	Chuck Hiller	.25	.10	.02
☐ 199	Billy Hitchcock MGR	.25	.10	.02
☐ 200	Willie Mays	21.00	8.50	2.10
☐ 201	Hal Reniff	.25	.10	.02
☐ 202	Johnny Edwards	.25	.10	.02
☐ 203	Al McBean	.25	.10	.02
☐ 204	Orioles Rookies	.35	.14	.03
	Mike Epstein			
	Tom Phoebus			
☐ 205	Dick Groat	.50	.20	.05
☐ 206	Dennis Bennett	.25	.10	.02
☐ 207	John Orsino	.25	.10	.02
☐ 208	Jack Lamabe	.25	.10	.02
☐ 209	Joe Nossek	.25	.10	.02
☐ 210	Bob Gibson	3.75	1.50	.37
☐ 211	Twins Team	.75	.30	.07
☐ 212	Chris Zachary	.25	.10	.02
☐ 213	Jay Johnstone	.35	.14	.03
☐ 214	Dick Kelley	.25	.10	.02
☐ 215	Ernie Banks	3.75	1.50	.37
☐ 216	Bengal Belters	1.75	.70	.17
	Norm Cash			
	Al Kaline			

		MINT	VG-E	F-G
☐ 217	Rob Gardner	.25	.10	.02
☐ 218	Wes Parker	.35	.14	.03
☐ 219	Clay Carroll	.25	.10	.02
☐ 220	Jim Ray Hart	.35	.14	.03
☐ 221	Woody Fryman	.25	.10	.02
☐ 222	Reds Rookies	.45	.18	.04
	Darrell Osteen			
	Lee May			
☐ 223	Mike Ryan	.25	.10	.02
☐ 224	Walt Bond	.25	.10	.02
☐ 225	Mel Stottlemyre	.65	.26	.06
☐ 226	Julian Javier	.35	.14	.03
☐ 227	Paul Lindblad	.25	.10	.02
☐ 228	Gil Hodges MGR	2.25	.90	.22
☐ 229	Larry Jackson	.25	.10	.02
☐ 230	Boog Powell	1.00	.40	.10
☐ 231	John Bateman	.25	.10	.02
☐ 232	Don Buford	.25	.10	.02
☐ 233	AL ERA Leaders	.80	.32	.08
	Gary Peters			
	Joel Horlen			
	Steve Hargan			
☐ 234	NL ERA Leaders	2.50	1.00	.25
	Sandy Koufax			
	Mike Cuellar			
	Juan Marichal			
☐ 235	AL Pitching Leaders	.80	.32	.08
	Jim Kaat			
	Denny McLain			
	Earl Wilson			
☐ 236	NL Pitching Leaders	3.50	1.40	.35
	Sandy Koufax			
	Juan Marichal			
	Bob Gibson			
	Gaylord Perry			
☐ 237	AL Strikeout Leaders	.80	.32	.08
	Sam McDowell			
	Jim Kaat			
	Earl Wilson			
☐ 238	NL Strikeout Leaders	1.50	.60	.15
	Sandy Koufax			
	Jim Bunning			
	Bob Veale			
☐ 239	AL Batting Leaders	1.75	.70	.17
	Frank Robinson			
	Tony Oliva			
	Al Kaline			
☐ 240	NL Batting Leaders	.80	.32	.08
	Matty Alou			
	Felipe Alou			
	Rico Carty			

		MINT	VG-E	F-G
☐ 241	AL RBI Leaders	1.50	.60	.15
	Frank Robinson			
	Harmon Killebrew			
	Boog Powell			
☐ 242	NL RBI Leaders	2.00	.80	.20
	Hank Aaron			
	Bob Clementè			
	Richie Allen			
☐ 243	AL Home Run Leaders	1.50	.60	.15
	Frank Robinson			
	Harmon Killebrew			
	Boog Powell			
☐ 244	NL Home Run Leaders	2.00	.80	.20
	Hank Aaron			
	Richie Allen			
	Willie Mays			
☐ 245	Curt Flood	.55	.22	.05
☐ 246	Jim Perry	.45	.18	.04
☐ 247	Jerry Lumpe	.25	.10	.02
☐ 248	Gene Mauch MGR	.35	.14	.03
☐ 249	Nick Willhite	.25	.10	.02
☐ 250	Hank Aaron	21.00	8.50	2.10
☐ 251	Woody Held	.25	.10	.02
☐ 252	Bob Bolin	.25	.10	.02
☐ 253	Indians Rookies	.25	.10	.02
	Bill Davis			
	Gus Gil			
☐ 254	Milt Pappas	.35	.14	.03
☐ 255	Frank Howard	.80	.32	.08
☐ 256	Bob Hendley	.25	.10	.02
☐ 257	Charlie Smith	.25	.10	.02
☐ 258	Lee Maye	.25	.10	.02
☐ 259	Don Dennis	.25	.10	.02
☐ 260	Jim Lefebvre	.35	.14	.03
☐ 261	John Wyatt	.25	.10	.02
☐ 262	Athletics Team	.75	.30	.07
☐ 263	Hank Aguirre	.25	.10	.02
☐ 264	Ron Swoboda	.35	.14	.03
☐ 265	Lou Burdette	.60	.24	.06
☐ 266	Pitt Power	1.25	.50	.12
	Willie Stargell			
	Donn Clendenon			
☐ 267	Don Schwall	.25	.10	.02
☐ 268	John Briggs	.25	.10	.02
☐ 269	Don Nottebart	.25	.10	.02
☐ 270	Zoilo Versalles	.25	.10	.02
☐ 271	Eddie Watt	.25	.10	.02
☐ 272	Cubs Rookies	.25	.10	.02
	Bill Connors			
	Dave Dowling			
☐ 273	Dick Lines	.25	.10	.02
☐ 274	Bob Aspromonte	.25	.10	.02
☐ 275	Fred Whitfield	.25	.10	.02

		MINT	VG-E	F-G
☐ 276	Bruce Brubaker	.25	.10	.02
☐ 277	Steve Whitaker	.25	.10	.02
☐ 278	Checklist 4	1.75	.15	.03
	Jim Kaat			
☐ 279	Frank Linzy	.25	.10	.02
☐ 280	Tony Conigliaro	.75	.30	.07
☐ 281	Bob Rodgers	.25	.10	.02
☐ 282	Johnny Odom	.25	.10	.02
☐ 283	Gene Alley	.35	.14	.03
☐ 284	Johnny Podres	.60	.24	.06
☐ 285	Lou Brock	5.00	2.00	.50
☐ 286	Wayne Causey	.25	.10	.02
☐ 287	Mets Rookies	.25	.10	.02
	Greg Goossen			
	Bart Shirley			
☐ 288	Denny Lemaster	.25	.10	.02
☐ 289	Tom Tresh	.45	.18	.04
☐ 290	Bill White	.45	.18	.04
☐ 291	Jim Hannan	.25	.10	.02
☐ 292	Don Pavletich	.25	.10	.02
☐ 293	Ed Kirkpatrick	.25	.10	.02
☐ 294	Walt Alston MGR	.90	.36	.09
☐ 295	Sam McDowell	.45	.18	.04
☐ 296	Glenn Beckert	.40	.16	.04
☐ 297	Dave Morehead	.25	.10	.02
☐ 298	Ron Davis	.25	.10	.02
☐ 299	Norm Siebern	.25	.10	.02
☐ 300	Jim Kaat	1.25	.50	.12
☐ 301	Jesse Gonder	.25	.10	.02
☐ 302	Orioles Team	.75	.30	.07
☐ 303	Gil Blanco	.25	.10	.02
☐ 304	Phil Gagliano	.25	.10	.02
☐ 305	Earl Wilson	.25	.10	.02
☐ 306	Bud Harrelson	.35	.14	.03
☐ 307	Jim Beauchamp	.25	.10	.02
☐ 308	Al Downing	.35	.14	.03
☐ 309	Hurlers Beware	.45	.18	.04
	Johnny Callison			
	Richie Allen			
☐ 310	Gary Peters	.35	.14	.03
☐ 311	Ed Brinkman	.25	.10	.02
☐ 312	Don Mincher	.25	.10	.02
☐ 313	Bob Lee	.25	.10	.02
☐ 314	Red Sox Rookies	1.50	.60	.15
	Mike Andrews			
	Reggie Smith			
☐ 315	Billy Williams	3.50	1.40	.35
☐ 316	Jack Kralick	.25	.10	.02
☐ 317	Cesar Tovar	.25	.10	.02
☐ 318	Dave Giusti	.25	.10	.02
☐ 319	Paul Blair	.35	.14	.03
☐ 320	Gaylord Perry	3.00	1.20	.30
☐ 321	Mayo Smith MGR	.25	.10	.02
☐ 322	Jose Pagan	.25	.10	.02
☐ 323	Mike Hershberger	.25	.10	.02
☐ 324	Hal Woodeshick	.25	.10	.02
☐ 325	Chico Cardenas	.25	.10	.02
☐ 326	Bob Uecker	3.50	1.40	.35
☐ 327	Angels Team	.75	.30	.07
☐ 328	Clete Boyer	.45	.18	.04
☐ 329	Charlie Lau	.35	.14	.03
☐ 330	Claude Osteen	.35	.14	.03
☐ 331	Joe Foy	.25	.10	.02
☐ 332	Jesus Alou	.25	.10	.02
☐ 333	Fergie Jenkins	2.00	.80	.20
☐ 334	Twin Terrors	1.75	.70	.17
	Bob Allison			
	Harmon Killebrew			
☐ 335	Bob Veale	.35	.14	.03
☐ 336	Joe Azcue	.25	.10	.02
☐ 337	Joe Morgan	3.00	1.20	.30
☐ 338	Bob Locker	.25	.10	.02
☐ 339	Chico Ruiz	.25	.10	.02
☐ 340	Joe Pepitone	.45	.18	.04
☐ 341	Giants Rookies	.25	.10	.02
	Dick Dietz			
	Bill Sorrell			
☐ 342	Hank Fischer	.25	.10	.02
☐ 343	Tom Satriano	.25	.10	.02
☐ 344	Ossie Chavarria	.25	.10	.02
☐ 345	Stu Miller	.25	.10	.02
☐ 346	Jim Hickman	.25	.10	.02
☐ 347	Grady Hatton MGR	.25	.10	.02
☐ 348	Tug McGraw	.75	.30	.07
☐ 349	Bob Chance	.25	.10	.02
☐ 350	Joe Torre	.75	.30	.07
☐ 351	Vern Law	.35	.14	.03
☐ 352	Ray Oyler	.25	.10	.02
☐ 353	Bill McCool	.25	.10	.02
☐ 354	Cubs Team	.75	.30	.07
☐ 355	Carl Yastrzemski	45.00	18.00	4.50
☐ 356	Larry Jaster	.25	.10	.02
☐ 357	Bill Skowron	.50	.20	.05
☐ 358	Ruben Amaro	.25	.10	.02
☐ 359	Dick Ellsworth	.35	.14	.03
☐ 360	Leon Wagner	.25	.10	.02
☐ 361	Checklist 5	2.00	.20	.04
	Roberto Clemente			
☐ 362	Darold Knowles	.25	.10	.02
☐ 363	Dave Johnson	.75	.30	.07
☐ 364	Claude Raymond	.25	.10	.02
☐ 365	John Roseboro	.35	.14	.03
☐ 366	Andy Kosco	.25	.10	.02
☐ 367	Angels Rookies	.25	.10	.02
	Bill Kelso			
	Don Wallace			

	MINT	VG-E	F-G
☐ 368 Jack Hiatt	.25	.10	.02
☐ 369 Jim Hunter	3.50	1.40	.35
☐ 370 Tommy Davis	.50	.20	.05
☐ 371 Jim Lonborg	.80	.32	.08
☐ 372 Mike De La Hoz	.35	.14	.03
☐ 373 White Sox Rookies	.35	.14	.03
Duane Josephson			
Fred Klages			
☐ 374 Mel Queen	.35	.14	.03
☐ 375 Jake Gibbs	.35	.14	.03
☐ 376 Don Lock	.35	.14	.03
☐ 377 Luis Tiant	.90	.36	.09
☐ 378 Tigers Team	.90	.36	.09
☐ 379 Jerry May	.35	.14	.03
☐ 380 Dean Chance	.35	.14	.03
☐ 381 Dick Schofield	.35	.14	.03
☐ 382 Dave McNally	.75	.30	.07
☐ 383 Ken Henderson	.35	.14	.03
☐ 384 Cardinals Rookies	.35	.14	.03
Jim Cosman			
Dick Hughes			
☐ 385 Jim Fregosi	.65	.26	.06
(batting wrong)			
☐ 386 Dick Selma	.35	.14	.03
☐ 387 Cap Peterson	.35	.14	.03
☐ 388 Arnold Earley	.35	.14	.03
☐ 389 Al Dark MGR	.45	.18	.04
☐ 390 Jim Wynn	.60	.24	.06
☐ 391 Wilbur Wood	.50	.20	.05
☐ 392 Tommy Harper	.45	.18	.04
☐ 393 Jim Bouton	.90	.36	.09
☐ 394 Jake Wood	.35	.14	.03
☐ 395 Chris Short	.35	.14	.03
☐ 396 Atlanta Aces	.40	.16	.04
Denis Menke			
Tony Cloninger			
☐ 397 Willie Smith	.35	.14	.03
☐ 398 Jeff Torborg	.40	.16	.04
☐ 399 Al Worthington	.35	.14	.03
☐ 400 Bob Clemente	15.00	6.00	1.50
☐ 401 Jim Coates	.35	.14	.03
☐ 402 Phillies Rookies	.40	.16	.04
Grant Jackson			
Billy Wilson			
☐ 403 Dick Nen	.35	.14	.03
☐ 404 Nelson Briles	.45	.18	.04
☐ 405 Russ Snyder	.35	.14	.03
☐ 406 Lee Elia	.35	.14	.03
☐ 407 Reds Team	.90	.36	.09
☐ 408 Jim Northrup	.45	.18	.04
☐ 409 Ray Sadecki	.35	.14	.03
☐ 410 Lou Johnson	.35	.14	.03
☐ 411 Dick Howser	.60	.24	.06

	MINT	VG-E	F-G
☐ 412 Astros Rookies	.75	.30	.07
Norm Miller			
Doug Rader			
☐ 413 Jerry Grote	.35	.14	.03
☐ 414 Casey Cox	.35	.14	.03
☐ 415 Sonny Jackson	.35	.14	.03
☐ 416 Roger Repoz	.35	.14	.03
☐ 417 Bob Bruce	.35	.14	.03
☐ 418 Sam Mele MGR	.35	.14	.03
☐ 419 Don Kessinger	.50	.20	.05
☐ 420 Denny McLain	1.25	.50	.12
☐ 421 Dal Maxvill	.35	.14	.03
☐ 422 Hoyt Wilhelm	3.00	1.20	.30
☐ 423 Fence Busters	5.00	2.00	.50
Willie Mays			
Willie McCovey			
☐ 424 Pedro Gonzales	.35	.14	.03
☐ 425 Pete Mikkelsen	.35	.14	.03
☐ 426 Lou Clinton	.35	.14	.03
☐ 427 Ruben Gomez	.35	.14	.03
☐ 428 Dodgers Rookies	.60	.24	.06
Tom Hutton			
Gene Michael			
☐ 429 Garry Roggenburk	.35	.14	.03
☐ 430 Pete Rose	50.00	20.00	5.00
☐ 431 Ted Uhlaender	.35	.14	.03
☐ 432 Jimmie Hall	.35	.14	.03
☐ 433 Al Luplow	.35	.14	.03
☐ 434 Eddie Fisher	.35	.14	.03
☐ 435 Mack Jones	.35	.14	.03
☐ 436 Pete Ward	.35	.14	.03
☐ 437 Senators Team	.75	.30	.07
☐ 438 Chuck Dobson	.35	.14	.03
☐ 439 Byron Browne	.35	.14	.03
☐ 440 Steve Hargan	.35	.14	.03
☐ 441 Jim Davenport	.50	.20	.05
☐ 442 Yankees Rookies	.50	.20	.05
Bill Robinson			
Joe Verbanic			
☐ 443 Tito Francona	.40	.16	.04
☐ 444 George Smith	.35	.14	.03
☐ 445 Don Sutton	4.50	1.80	.45
☐ 446 Russ Nixon	.35	.14	.03
☐ 447 Bo Belinsky	.40	.16	.04
☐ 448 Harry Walker MGR	.35	.14	.03
☐ 449 Orlando Pena	.35	.14	.03
☐ 450 Richie Allen	1.25	.50	.12
☐ 451 Fred Newman	.35	.14	.03
☐ 452 Ed Kranepool	.50	.20	.05
☐ 453 Aurelio Monteagudo	.35	.14	.03
☐ 454 A Checklist 6	2.50	.25	.05
Juan Marichal			
(missing left ear)			

	MINT	VG-E	F-G
☐ 454 **B Checklist 6**	5.00	.50	.10
Juan Marichal			
(left ear showing)			
☐ 455 Tommy Agee	.40	.16	.04
☐ 456 Phil Niekro	3.50	1.40	.35
☐ 457 Andy Etchebarren	.35	.14	.03
☐ 458 Lee Thomas	.75	.30	.07
☐ 459 Senators Rookies	.75	.30	.07
Dick Bosman			
Pete Craig			
☐ 460 Harmon Killebrew	6.00	2.40	.60
☐ 461 Bob Miller	.75	.30	.07
☐ 462 Bob Barton	.75	.30	.07
☐ 463 Hill Aces	.90	.36	.09
Sam McDowell			
Sonny Siebert			
☐ 464 Dan Coombs	.75	.30	.07
☐ 465 Willie Horton	.90	.36	.09
☐ 466 Bobby Wine	.75	.30	.07
☐ 467 Jim O'Toole	.75	.30	.07
☐ 468 Ralph Houk MGR	.90	.36	.09
☐ 469 Len Gabrielson	.75	.30	.07
☐ 470 Bob Shaw	.75	.30	.07
☐ 471 Rene Lachemann	.90	.36	.09
☐ 472 Rookies Pirates	.75	.30	.07
John Gelnar			
George Spriggs			
☐ 473 Jose Santiago	.75	.30	.07
☐ 474 Bob Tolan	.90	.36	.09
☐ 475 Jim Palmer	11.00	4.50	1.10
☐ 476 Tony Perez SP	12.50	5.00	1.25
☐ 477 Braves Team	1.25	.50	.12
☐ 478 Bob Humphreys	.75	.30	.07
☐ 479 Gary Bell	.75	.30	.07
☐ 480 Willie McCovey	7.50	3.00	.75
☐ 481 Leo Durocher MGR	1.25	.50	.12
☐ 482 Bill Monbouquette	.75	.30	.07
☐ 483 Jim Landis	.75	.30	.07
☐ 484 Jerry Adair	.75	.30	.07
☐ 485 Tim McCarver	1.25	.50	.12
☐ 486 Twins Rookies	.75	.30	.07
Rich Reese			
Bill Whitby			
☐ 487 Tommie Reynolds	.75	.30	.07
☐ 488 Gerry Arrigo	.75	.30	.07
☐ 489 Doug Clemens	.75	.30	.07
☐ 490 Tony Cloninger	.75	.30	.07
☐ 491 Sam Bowens	.75	.30	.07
☐ 492 Pirates Team	1.25	.50	.12
☐ 493 Phil Ortega	.75	.30	.07
☐ 494 Bill Rigney MGR	.75	.30	.07
☐ 495 Fritz Peterson	.75	.30	.07
☐ 496 Orlando McFarlane	.75	.30	.07

	MINT	VG-E	F-G
☐ 497 Ron Campbell	.75	.30	.07
☐ 498 Larry Dierker	.90	.36	.09
☐ 499 Indians Rookies	.75	.30	.07
George Culver			
Jose Vidal			
☐ 500 Juan Marichal	5.00	2.00	.50
☐ 501 Jerry Zimmerman	.75	.30	.07
☐ 502 Derrell Griffith	.75	.30	.07
☐ 503 Dodgers Team	2.00	.80	.20
☐ 504 Orlando Martinez	.75	.30	.07
☐ 505 Tommy Helms	.90	.36	.09
☐ 506 Smoky Burgess	.90	.36	.09
☐ 507 Orioles Rookies	.75	.30	.07
Ed Barnowski			
Larry Haney			
☐ 508 Dick Hall	.75	.30	.07
☐ 509 Jim King	.75	.30	.07
☐ 510 Bill Mazeroski	1.50	.60	.15
☐ 511 Don Wert	.75	.30	.07
☐ 512 Red Schoendienst MGR .	1.00	.40	.10
☐ 513 Marcelino Lopez	.75	.30	.07
☐ 514 John Werhas	.75	.30	.07
☐ 515 Bert Campaneris	1.00	.40	.10
☐ 516 Giants Team	1.25	.50	.12
☐ 517 Fred Talbot	.75	.30	.07
☐ 518 Denis Menke	.75	.30	.07
☐ 519 Ted Davidson	.75	.30	.07
☐ 520 Max Alvis	.75	.30	.07
☐ 521 Bird Bombers	.90	.36	.09
Boog Powell			
Curt Blefary			
☐ 522 John Stephenson	.75	.30	.07
☐ 523 Jim Merritt	.75	.30	.07
☐ 524 Felix Mantilla	.75	.30	.07
☐ 525 Ron Hunt	.75	.30	.07
☐ 526 Tigers Rookies	1.25	.50	.12
Pat Dobson			
George Korince			
(See 67T-72)			
☐ 527 Dennis Ribant	.75	.30	.07
☐ 528 Rico Petrocelli	1.00	.40	.10
☐ 529 Gary Wagner	.75	.30	.07
☐ 530 Felipe Alou	1.00	.40	.10
☐ 531 Checklist 7	3.50	.35	
Brooks Robinson			
☐ 532 Jim Hicks	.75	.30	.07
☐ 533 Jack Fisher	.75	.30	.07
☐ 534 Hank Bauer	3.00	1.20	.30
☐ 535 Donn Clendenon	3.00	1.20	.30
☐ 536 Cubs Rookies	4.50	1.80	.45
Joe Niekro			
Paul Popovich			
☐ 537 Chuck Estrada	2.25	.90	.22

	MINT	VG-E	F-G
538 J.C. Martin	2.25	.90	.22
539 Dick Egan	2.25	.90	.22
540 Norm Cash	8.00	3.25	.80
541 Joe Gibbon	2.25	.90	.22
542 Athletics Rookies	3.50	1.40	.35
Rick Monday			
Tony Pierce			
543 Dan Schneider	2.25	.90	.22
544 Indians Team	4.50	1.80	.45
545 Jim Grant	2.25	.90	.22
546 Woody Woodward	2.25	.90	.22
547 Red Sox Rookies	2.25	.90	.22
Russ Gibson			
Bill Rohr			
548 Tony Gonzalez	2.25	.90	.22
549 Jack Sanford	2.25	.90	.22
550 Vada Pinson	3.00	1.20	.30
551 Doug Camilli	2.25	.90	.22
552 Ted Savage	2.25	.90	.22
553 Yankees Rookies	4.50	1.80	.45
Mike Hegan			
Thad Tillotson			
554 Andre Rodgers	2.25	.90	.22
555 Don Cardwell	2.25	.90	.22
556 Al Weis	2.25	.90	.22
557 Al Ferrara	2.25	.90	.22
558 Orioles Rookies	7.50	3.00	.75
Mark Belanger			
Bill Dillman			
559 Dick Tracewski	2.25	.90	.22
560 Jim Bunning	12.50	5.00	1.25
561 Sandy Alomar	2.25	.90	.22
562 Steve Blass	2.25	.90	.22
563 Joe Adcock	7.50	3.00	.75
564 Astros Rookies	2.25	.90	.22
Alonzo Harris			
Aaron Pointer			
565 Lew Krausse	2.25	.90	.22
566 Gary Geiger	2.25	.90	.22
567 Steve Hamilton	2.25	.90	.22
568 John Sullivan	2.25	.90	.22
569 AL Rookies	120.00	50.00	12.00
Rod Carew			
Hank Allen			
570 Maury Wills	50.00	20.00	5.00
571 Larry Sherry	2.25	.90	.22
572 Don Demeter	2.25	.90	.22
573 White Sox Team	4.50	1.80	.45
574 Jerry Buchek	2.25	.90	.22
575 Dave Boswell	2.25	.90	.22
576 NL Rookies	2.25	.90	.22
Ramon Hernandez			
Norm Gigon			
577 Bill Short	2.25	.90	.22
578 John Boccabella	2.25	.90	.22
579 Bill Henry	2.25	.90	.22
580 Rocky Colavito	9.00	3.75	.90
581 Mets Rookies	250.00	100.00	25.00
Bill Denehy			
Tom Seaver			
582 Jim Owens	2.25	.90	.22
583 Ray Barker	2.25	.90	.22
584 Jim Piersall	6.00	2.40	.60
585 Wally Bunker	2.25	.90	.22
586 Manny Jimenez	2.25	.90	.22
587 NL Rookies	2.25	.90	.22
Don Shaw			
Gary Sutherland			
588 Johnny Klippstein	2.25	.90	.22
589 Dave Ricketts	2.25	.90	.22
590 Pete Richert	2.25	.90	.22
591 Ty Cline	2.25	.90	.22
592 NL Rookies	2.25	.90	.22
Jim Shellenback			
Ron Willis			
593 Wes Westrum MGR	2.25	.90	.22
594 Dan Osinski	2.25	.90	.22
595 Cookie Rojas	2.25	.90	.22
596 Galen Cisco	2.25	.90	.22
597 Ted Abernathy	2.25	.90	.22
598 White Sox Rookies	2.25	.90	.22
Walt Williams			
Ed Stroud			
599 Bob Duliba	2.25	.90	.22
600 Brooks Robinson	100.00	40.00	10.00
601 Bill Bryan	2.25	.90	.22
602 Juan Pizarro	2.25	.90	.22
603 Athletics Rookies	2.25	.90	.22
Tim Talton			
Ramon Webster			
604 Red Sox Team	8.00	3.25	.80
605 Mike Shannon	3.00	1.20	.30
606 Ron Taylor	2.25	.90	.22
607 Mickey Stanley	3.00	1.20	.30
608 Cubs Rookies	2.25	.90	.22
Rich Nye			
John Upham			
609 Tommy John	30.00	12.00	3.00

1968 Topps

The cards in this 598-card set measure 2½"
by 3½". The 1968 Topps set includes the
Sporting News All-Star Selections as card
numbers 361 to 380. Other subsets in the set
include League Leaders (1-12) and World
Series cards (151-158). The front of each
checklist card features a picture of a popular
player inside a circle. High numbers 534 to
598 are slightly more difficult to obtain. The
first series looks different from the other series as it has a lighter, wider mesh background on the card front. The later series all
had a much darker, finer mesh pattern. Key
cards in the set are the rookie cards of Johnny Bench (247) and Nolan Ryan (177).

	MINT	VG-E	F-G
Complete Set	600.00	240.00	60.00
Common Player (1-457)	.21	.09	.02
Common Player (458-533)	.30	.12	.03
Common Player (534-598)	.30	.12	.03

		MINT	VG-E	F-G
☐ 1	NL Batting Leaders ..... Bob Clemente Tony Gonzales Matty Alou	2.50	.60	.12
☐ 2	AL Batting Leaders .... Carl Yastrzemski Frank Robinson Al Kaline	2.50	1.00	.25
☐ 3	NL RBI Leaders .... Orlando Cepeda Bob Clemente Hank Aaron	2.00	.80	.20
☐ 4	AL RBI Leaders .... Carl Yastrzemski Harmon Killebrew Frank Robinson	2.50	1.00	.25
☐ 5	NL Home Run Leaders . Hank Aaron Jim Wynn Ron Santo Willie McCovey	1.50	.60	.15
☐ 6	NL Home Run Leaders . Carl Yastrzemski Harmon Killebrew Frank Howard	2.00	.80	.20
☐ 7	NL ERA Leaders .... Phil Niekro Jim Bunning Chris Short	.80	.32	.08
☐ 8	AL ERA Leaders .... Joe Horlen Gary Peters Sonny Siebert	.60	.24	.06
☐ 9	NL Pitching Leaders .... Mike McCormick Ferguson Jenkins Jim Bunning Claude Osteen	.80	.32	.08
☐ 10	AL Pitching Leaders .... Jim Lonborg Earl Wilson Dean Chance	.60	.24	.06
☐ 11	NL Strikeout Leaders ... Jim Bunning Ferguson Jenkins Gaylord Perry	1.25	.50	.12
☐ 12	AL Strikeout Leaders ... Jim Lonborg Sam McDowell Dean Chance	.60	.24	.06
☐ 13	Chuck Hartenstein	.21	.09	.02
☐ 14	Jerry McNertney	.21	.09	.02
☐ 15	Ron Hunt	.21	.09	.02
☐ 16	Indians Rookies .... Lou Piniella Richie Scheinblum	1.00	.40	.10
☐ 17	Dick Hall	.21	.09	.02
☐ 18	Mike Hershberger	.21	.09	.02
☐ 19	Juan Pizarro	.21	.09	.02
☐ 20	Brooks Robinson	4.25	1.70	.42
☐ 21	Ron Davis	.21	.09	.02
☐ 22	Pat Dobson	.30	.12	.03
☐ 23	Chico Cardenas	.21	.09	.02
☐ 24	Bobby Locke	.21	.09	.02
☐ 25	Julian Javier	.21	.09	.02

		MINT	VG-E	F-G
☐	26 Darrell Brandon	.21	.09	.02
☐	27 Gil Hodges MGR	2.00	.80	.20
☐	28 Ted Uhlaender	.21	.09	.02
☐	29 Joe Verbanic	.21	.09	.02
☐	30 Joe Torre	.75	.30	.07
☐	31 Ed Stroud	.21	.09	.02
☐	32 Joe Gibbon	.21	.09	.02
☐	33 Pete Ward	.21	.09	.02
☐	34 Al Ferrara	.21	.09	.02
☐	35 Steve Hargan	.21	.09	.02
☐	36 Pirates Rookies	.30	.12	.03
	Bob Moose			
	Bob Robertson			
☐	37 Billy Williams	3.00	1.20	.30
☐	38 Tony Pierce	.21	.09	.02
☐	39 Cookie Rojas	.21	.09	.02
☐	40 Denny McLain	1.50	.60	.15
☐	41 Julio Gotay	.21	.09	.02
☐	42 Larry Haney	.21	.09	.02
☐	43 Gary Bell	.21	.09	.02
☐	44 Frank Kostro	.21	.09	.02
☐	45 Tom Seaver	30.00	12.00	3.00
☐	46 Dave Ricketts	.21	.09	.02
☐	47 Ralph Houk MGR	.35	.14	.03
☐	48 Ted Davidson	.21	.09	.02
☐	49 A Eddie Brinkman	.30	.12	.03
	(white team name)			
☐	49 B Eddie Brinkman	10.00	4.00	1.00
	(yellow team name)			
☐	50 Willie Mays	15.00	6.00	1.50
☐	51 Bob Locker	.21	.09	.02
☐	52 Hawk Taylor	.21	.09	.02
☐	53 Gene Alley	.30	.12	.03
☐	54 Stan Williams	.21	.09	.02
☐	55 Felipe Alou	.30	.12	.03
☐	56 Orioles Rookies	.21	.09	.02
	Dave Leonhard			
	Dave May			
☐	57 Dan Schneider	.21	.09	.02
☐	58 Eddie Mathews	3.00	1.20	.30
☐	59 Don Lock	.21	.09	.02
☐	60 Ken Holtzman	.35	.14	.03
☐	61 Reggie Smith	.75	.30	.07
☐	62 Chuck Dobson	.21	.09	.02
☐	63 Dick Kenworthy	.21	.09	.02
☐	64 Jim Merritt	.21	.09	.02
☐	65 John Roseboro	.30	.12	.03
☐	66 A Casey Cox	.30	.12	.03
	(white team name)			
☐	66 B Casey Cox	10.00	4.00	1.00
	(yellow team name)			
☐	67 Checklist 1	1.50	.15	.03
	Jim Kaat			

		MINT	VG-E	F-G
☐	68 Ron Willis	.21	.09	.02
☐	69 Tom Tresh	.40	.16	.04
☐	70 Bob Veale	.30	.12	.03
☐	71 Vern Fuller	.21	.09	.02
☐	72 Tommy John	1.50	.60	.15
☐	73 Jim Ray Hart	.30	.12	.03
☐	74 Milt Pappas	.30	.12	.03
☐	75 Don Mincher	.21	.09	.02
☐	76 Braves Rookies	.30	.12	.03
	Jim Britton			
	Ron Reed			
☐	77 Don Wilson	.21	.09	.02
☐	78 Jim Northrup	.30	.12	.03
☐	79 Ted Kubiak	.21	.09	.02
☐	80 Rod Carew	21.00	8.50	2.10
☐	81 Larry Jackson	.21	.09	.02
☐	82 Sam Bowens	.21	.09	.02
☐	83 John Stephenson	.21	.09	.02
☐	84 Bob Tolan	.21	.09	.02
☐	85 Gaylord Perry	2.50	1.00	.25
☐	86 Willie Stargell	3.50	1.40	.35
☐	87 Dick Williams MGR	.30	.12	.03
☐	88 Phil Regan	.30	.12	.03
☐	89 Jake Gibbs	.21	.09	.02
☐	90 Vada Pinson	.75	.30	.07
☐	91 Jim Ollom	.21	.09	.02
☐	92 Ed Kranepool	.30	.12	.03
☐	93 Tony Cloninger	.21	.09	.02
☐	94 Lee Maye	.21	.09	.02
☐	95 Bob Aspromonte	.21	.09	.02
☐	96 Senator Rookies	.21	.09	.02
	Frank Coggins			
	Dick Nold			
☐	97 Tom Phoebus	.21	.09	.02
☐	98 Gary Sutherland	.21	.09	.02
☐	99 Rocky Colavito	.75	.30	.07
☐	100 Bob Gibson	4.00	1.60	.40
☐	101 Glenn Beckert	.30	.12	.03
☐	102 Jose Cardenal	.21	.09	.02
☐	103 Don Sutton	2.50	1.00	.25
☐	104 Dick Dietz	.21	.09	.02
☐	105 Al Downing	.21	.09	.02
☐	106 Dalton Jones	.21	.09	.02
☐	107 A Checklist 2	1.50	.15	.03
	Juan Marichal			
	(tan wide mesh)			
☐	107 B Checklist 2	2.00	.20	.04
	Juan Marichal			
	(brown fine mesh)			
☐	108 Don Pavletich	.21	.09	.02
☐	109 Bert Campaneris	.35	.14	.03
☐	110 Hank Aaron	15.00	6.00	1.50
☐	111 Rich Reese	.21	.09	.02

		MINT	VG-E	F-G
☐ 112	Woody Fryman	.21	.09	.02
☐ 113	Tigers Rookies	.21	.09	.02
	Tom Matchick			
	Daryl Patterson			
☐ 114	Ron Swoboda	.30	.12	.03
☐ 115	Sam McDowell	.35	.14	.03
☐ 116	Ken McMullen	.21	.09	.02
☐ 117	Larry Jaster	.21	.09	.02
☐ 118	Mark Belanger	.50	.20	.05
☐ 119	Ted Savage	.21	.09	.02
☐ 120	Mel Stottlemyre	.35	.14	.03
☐ 121	Jimmie Hall	.21	.09	.02
☐ 122	Gene Mauch MGR	.30	.12	.03
☐ 123	Jose Santiago	.21	.09	.02
☐ 124	Nate Oliver	.21	.09	.02
☐ 125	Joe Horlen	.30	.12	.03
☐ 126	Bob Etheridge	.21	.09	.02
☐ 127	Paul Lindblad	.21	.09	.02
☐ 128	Astros Rookies	.21	.09	.02
	Tom Dukes			
	Alonzo Harris			
☐ 129	Mickey Stanley	.30	.12	.03
☐ 130	Tony Perez	2.00	.80	.20
☐ 131	Frank Bertaina	.21	.09	.02
☐ 132	Bud Harrelson	.30	.12	.03
☐ 133	Fred Whitfield	.21	.09	.02
☐ 134	Pat Jarvis	.21	.09	.02
☐ 135	Paul Blair	.30	.12	.03
☐ 136	Randy Hundley	.21	.09	.02
☐ 137	Twins Team	.55	.22	.05
☐ 138	Ruben Amaro	.21	.09	.02
☐ 139	Chris Short	.21	.09	.02
☐ 140	Tony Conigliaro	.65	.26	.06
☐ 141	Dal Maxvill	.21	.09	.02
☐ 142	White Sox Rookies	.21	.09	.02
	Buddy Bradford			
	Bill Voss			
☐ 143	Pete Cimino	.21	.09	.02
☐ 144	Joe Morgan	2.50	1.00	.25
☐ 145	Don Drysdale	3.00	1.20	.30
☐ 146	Sal Bando	.50	.20	.05
☐ 147	Frank Linzy	.21	.09	.02
☐ 148	Dave Bristol MGR	.21	.09	.02
☐ 149	Bob Saverine	.21	.09	.02
☐ 150	Bob Clemente	11.00	4.50	1.10
☐ 151	World Series Game 1 ...	2.00	.80	.20
	Brock socks 4 hits			
	in opener			
☐ 152	World Series Game 2 ...	2.50	1.00	.25
	Yaz smashes 2 homers			
☐ 153	World Series Game 3 ...	1.00	.40	.10
	Briles cools			
	off Boston			
☐ 154	World Series Game 4 ...	2.00	.80	.20
	Gibson hurls shutout			
☐ 155	World Series Game 5 ...	1.00	.40	.10
	Lonborg wins again			
☐ 156	World Series Game 6 ...	1.00	.40	.10
	Petrocelli 2 homers			
☐ 157	World Series Game 7 ...	1.00	.40	.10
	St. Louis wins it			
☐ 158	World Series Summary .	1.00	.40	.10
	Cardinals celebrate			
☐ 159	Don Kessinger	.35	.14	.03
☐ 160	Earl Wilson	.21	.09	.02
☐ 161	Norm Miller	.21	.09	.02
☐ 162	Cards Rookies	.60	.24	.06
	Hal Gilson			
	Mike Torrez			
☐ 163	Gene Brabender	.21	.09	.02
☐ 164	Ramon Webster	.21	.09	.02
☐ 165	Tony Oliva	1.00	.40	.10
☐ 166	Claude Raymond	.21	.09	.02
☐ 167	Elston Howard	1.00	.40	.10
☐ 168	Dodgers Team	.80	.32	.08
☐ 169	Bob Bolin	.21	.09	.02
☐ 170	Jim Fregosi	.40	.16	.04
☐ 171	Don Nottebart	.21	.09	.02
☐ 172	Walt Williams	.21	.09	.02
☐ 173	John Boozer	.21	.09	.02
☐ 174	Bob Tillman	.21	.09	.02
☐ 175	Maury Wills	1.25	.50	.12
☐ 176	Bob Allen	.21	.09	.02
☐ 177	Mets Rookies	80.00	32.00	8.00
	Jerry Koosman			
	Nolan Ryan			
☐ 178	Don Wert	.21	.09	.02
☐ 179	Bill Stoneman	.21	.09	.02
☐ 180	Curt Flood	.55	.22	.05
☐ 181	Jerry Zimmerman	.21	.09	.02
☐ 182	Dave Giusti	.21	.09	.02
☐ 183	Bob Kennedy MGR	.21	.09	.02
☐ 184	Lou Johnson	.21	.09	.02
☐ 185	Tom Haller	.21	.09	.02
☐ 186	Eddie Watt	.21	.09	.02
☐ 187	Sonny Jackson	.21	.09	.02
☐ 188	Cap Peterson	.21	.09	.02
☐ 189	Bill Landis	.21	.09	.02
☐ 190	Bill White	.35	.14	.03
☐ 191	Dan Frisella	.21	.09	.02
☐ 192	Checklist 3	1.75	.15	.03
	Carl Yastrzemski			
☐ 193	Jack Hamilton	.21	.09	.02
☐ 194	Don Buford	.21	.09	.02
☐ 195	Joe Pepitone	.35	.14	.03
☐ 196	Gary Nolan	.21	.09	.02

		MINT	VG-E	F-G
☐ 197	Larry Brown	.21	.09	.02
☐ 198	Roy Face	.40	.16	.04
☐ 199	A's Rookies	.21	.09	.02
	Roberto Rodriquez			
	Darrell Osteen			
☐ 200	Orlando Cepeda	1.50	.60	.15
☐ 201	Mike Marshall	.75	.30	.07
☐ 202	Adolfo Phillips	.21	.09	.02
☐ 203	Dick Kelley	.21	.09	.02
☐ 204	Andy Etchebarren	.21	.09	.02
☐ 205	Juan Marichal	3.00	1.20	.30
☐ 206	Cal Ermer MGR	.21	.09	.02
☐ 207	Carroll Sembera	.21	.09	.02
☐ 208	Willie Davis	.45	.18	.04
☐ 209	Tim Cullen	.21	.09	.02
☐ 210	Gary Peters	.30	.12	.03
☐ 211	J.C. Martin	.21	.09	.02
☐ 212	Dave Morehead	.21	.09	.02
☐ 213	Chico Ruiz	.21	.09	.02
☐ 214	Yankees Rookies	.40	.16	.04
	Stan Bahnsen			
	Frank Fernandez			
☐ 215	Jim Bunning	1.50	.60	.15
☐ 216	Bubba Morton	.21	.09	.02
☐ 217	Turk Farrell	.21	.09	.02
☐ 218	Ken Suarez	.21	.09	.02
☐ 219	Rob Gardner	.21	.09	.02
☐ 220	Harmon Killebrew	3.50	1.40	.35
☐ 221	Braves Team	.60	.24	.06
☐ 222	Jim Hardin	.21	.09	.02
☐ 223	Ollie Brown	.21	.09	.02
☐ 224	Jack Aker	.21	.09	.02
☐ 225	Richie Allen	.80	.32	.08
☐ 226	Jimmie Price	.21	.09	.02
☐ 227	Joe Hoerner	.21	.09	.02
☐ 228	Dodgers Rookies	.30	.12	.03
	Jack Billingham			
	Jim Fairey			
☐ 229	Fred Klages	.21	.09	.02
☐ 230	Pete Rose	36.00	15.00	3.60
☐ 231	Dave Baldwin	.21	.09	.02
☐ 232	Denis Menke	.21	.09	.02
☐ 233	George Scott	.30	.12	.03
☐ 234	Bill Monbouquette	.21	.09	.02
☐ 235	Ron Santo	.60	.24	.06
☐ 236	Tug McGraw	.75	.30	.07
☐ 237	Alvin Dark MGR	.30	.12	.03
☐ 238	Tom Satriano	.21	.09	.02
☐ 239	Bill Henry	.21	.09	.02
☐ 240	Al Kaline	4.00	1.60	.40
☐ 241	Felix Millan	.21	.09	.02
☐ 242	Moe Drabowsky	.21	.09	.02
☐ 243	Rich Rollins	.21	.09	.02

		MINT	VG-E	F-G
☐ 244	John Donaldson	.21	.09	.02
☐ 245	Tony Gonzalez	.21	.09	.02
☐ 246	Fritz Peterson	.21	.09	.02
☐ 247	Reds Rookies	70.00	28.00	7.00
	Johnny Bench			
	Ron Tompkins			
☐ 248	Fred Valentine	.21	.09	.02
☐ 249	Bill Singer	.21	.09	.02
☐ 250	Carl Yastrzemski	18.00	7.25	1.80
☐ 251	Manny Sanguillen	.75	.30	.07
☐ 252	Angels Team	.55	.22	.05
☐ 253	Dick Hughes	.21	.09	.02
☐ 254	Cleon Jones	.21	.09	.02
☐ 255	Dean Chance	.30	.12	.03
☐ 256	Norm Cash	.75	.30	.07
☐ 257	Phil Niekro	2.50	1.00	.25
☐ 258	Cubs Rookies	.21	.09	.02
	Jose Arcia			
	Bill Schlesinger			
☐ 259	Ken Boyer	.75	.30	.07
☐ 260	Jim Wynn	.50	.20	.05
☐ 261	Dave Duncan	.21	.09	.02
☐ 262	Rick Wise	.30	.12	.03
☐ 263	Horace Clarke	.21	.09	.02
☐ 264	Ted Abernathy	.21	.09	.02
☐ 265	Tommy Davis	.40	.16	.04
☐ 266	Paul Popovich	.21	.09	.02
☐ 267	Herman Franks MGR	.21	.09	.02
☐ 268	Bob Humphreys	.21	.09	.02
☐ 269	Bob Tiefenauer	.21	.09	.02
☐ 270	Matty Alou	.30	.12	.03
☐ 271	Bobby Knoop	.21	.09	.02
☐ 272	Ray Culp	.21	.09	.02
☐ 273	Dave Johnson	.50	.20	.05
☐ 274	Mike Cuellar	.35	.14	.03
☐ 275	Tim McCarver	.50	.20	.05
☐ 276	Jim Roland	.21	.09	.02
☐ 277	Jerry Buchek	.21	.09	.02
☐ 278	Checklist 4	1.50	.15	.03
	Orlando Cepeda			
☐ 279	Bill Hands	.21	.09	.02
☐ 280	Mickey Mantle	45.00	18.00	4.50
☐ 281	Jim Campanis	.21	.09	.02
☐ 282	Rick Monday	.40	.16	.04
☐ 283	Mel Queen	.21	.09	.02
☐ 284	John Briggs	.21	.09	.02
☐ 285	Dick McAuliffe	.21	.09	.02
☐ 286	Cecil Upshaw	.21	.09	.02
☐ 287	White Sox Rookies	.21	.09	.02
	Mickey Abarbanel			
	Cisco Carlos			
☐ 288	Dave Wickersham	.21	.09	.02
☐ 289	Woody Held	.21	.09	.02

		MINT	VG-E	F-G
☐ 290	Willie McCovey	3.50	1.40	.35
☐ 291	Dick Lines	.21	.09	.02
☐ 292	Art Shamsky	.21	.09	.02
☐ 293	Bruce Howard	.21	.09	.02
☐ 294	Red Schoendienst MGR	.40	.16	.04
☐ 295	Sonny Siebert	.30	.12	.03
☐ 296	Byron Browne	.21	.09	.02
☐ 297	Russ Gibson	.21	.09	.02
☐ 298	Jim Brewer	.21	.09	.02
☐ 299	Gene Michael	.35	.14	.03
☐ 300	Rusty Staub	.75	.30	.07
☐ 301	Twins Rookies	.21	.09	.02
	George Mitterwald			
	Rick Renick			
☐ 302	Gerry Arrigo	.21	.09	.02
☐ 303	Dick Green	.21	.09	.02
☐ 304	Sandy Valdespino	.21	.09	.02
☐ 305	Minnie Rojas	.21	.09	.02
☐ 306	Mike Ryan	.21	.09	.02
☐ 307	John Hiller	.35	.14	.03
☐ 308	Pirates Team	.55	.22	.05
☐ 309	Ken Henderson	.21	.09	.02
☐ 310	Luis Aparicio	2.50	1.00	.25
☐ 311	Jack Lamabe	.21	.09	.02
☐ 312	Curt Blefary	.30	.12	.03
☐ 313	Al Weis	.21	.09	.02
☐ 314	Red Sox Rookies	.21	.09	.02
	Bill Rohr			
	George Spriggs			
☐ 315	Zoilo Versalles	.21	.09	.02
☐ 316	Steve Barber	.21	.09	.02
☐ 317	Ron Brand	.21	.09	.02
☐ 318	Chico Salmon	.21	.09	.02
☐ 319	George Culver	.21	.09	.02
☐ 320	Frank Howard	.75	.30	.07
☐ 321	Leo Durocher MGR	.75	.30	.07
☐ 322	Dave Boswell	.21	.09	.02
☐ 323	Deron Johnson	.21	.09	.02
☐ 324	Jim Nash	.21	.09	.02
☐ 325	Manny Mota	.30	.12	.03
☐ 326	Denny Ribant	.21	.09	.02
☐ 327	Tony Taylor	.21	.09	.02
☐ 328	Angels Rookies	.21	.09	.02
	Chuck Vinson			
	Jim Weaver			
☐ 329	Duane Josephson	.21	.09	.02
☐ 330	Roger Maris	3.50	1.40	.35
☐ 331	Dan Osinski	.21	.09	.02
☐ 332	Doug Rader	.30	.12	.03
☐ 333	Ron Herbel	.21	.09	.02
☐ 334	Orioles Team	.55	.22	.05
☐ 335	Bob Allison	.35	.14	.03
☐ 336	John Purdin	.21	.09	.02

		MINT	VG-E	F-G
☐ 337	Bill Robinson	.21	.09	.02
☐ 338	Bob Johnson	.21	.09	.02
☐ 339	Rich Nye	.21	.09	.02
☐ 340	Max Alvis	.21	.09	.02
☐ 341	Jim Lemon MGR	.21	.09	.02
☐ 342	Ken Johnson	.21	.09	.02
☐ 343	Jim Gosger	.21	.09	.02
☐ 344	Donn Clendenon	.30	.12	.03
☐ 345	Bob Hendley	.21	.09	.02
☐ 346	Jerry Adair	.21	.09	.02
☐ 347	George Brunet	.21	.09	.02
☐ 348	Phillies Rookies	.21	.09	.02
	Larry Colton			
	Dick Thoenen			
☐ 349	Ed Spiezio	.21	.09	.02
☐ 350	Hoyt Wilhelm	2.50	1.00	.25
☐ 351	Bob Barton	.21	.09	.02
☐ 352	Jackie Hernandez	.21	.09	.02
☐ 353	Mack Jones	.21	.09	.02
☐ 354	Pete Richert	.21	.09	.02
☐ 355	Ernie Banks	3.50	1.40	.35
☐ 356 A	Checklist 5	1.50	.15	.03
	Ken Holtzman			
	(head centered			
	within circle)			
☐ 356 B	Checklist 5	1.50	.15	.03
	Ken Holtzman			
	(head shifted right			
	within circle)			
☐ 357	Len Gabrielson	.21	.09	.02
☐ 358	Mike Epstein	.21	.09	.02
☐ 359	Joe Moeller	.21	.09	.02
☐ 360	Willie Horton	.45	.18	.04
☐ 361	Harmon Killebrew AS	1.75	.70	.17
☐ 362	Orlando Cepeda AS	.75	.30	.07
☐ 363	Rod Carew AS	3.50	1.40	.35
☐ 364	Joe Morgan AS	1.50	.60	.15
☐ 365	Brooks Robinson AS	2.50	1.00	.25
☐ 366	Ron Santo AS	.40	.16	.04
☐ 367	Jim Fregosi AS	.35	.14	.03
☐ 368	Gene Alley AS	.35	.14	.03
☐ 369	Carl Yastrzemski AS	3.75	1.50	.37
☐ 370	Hank Aaron AS	3.75	1.50	.37
☐ 371	Tony Oliva AS	.45	.18	.04
☐ 372	Lou Brock AS	2.50	1.00	.25
☐ 373	Frank Robinson AS	2.50	1.00	.25
☐ 374	Bob Clemente AS	3.25	1.30	.32
☐ 375	Bill Freehan AS	.35	.14	.03
☐ 376	Tim McCarver AS	.35	.14	.03
☐ 377	Joe Horlen AS	.35	.14	.03
☐ 378	Bob Gibson AS	2.25	.90	.22
☐ 379	Gary Peters AS	.35	.14	.03
☐ 380	Ken Holtzman AS	.35	.14	.03

	MINT	VG-E	F-G
☐ 381 Boog Powell	.75	.30	.07
☐ 382 Ramon Hernandez	.21	.09	.02
☐ 383 Steve Whitaker	.21	.09	.02
☐ 384 Reds Rookies	2.00	.80	.20
Bill Henry			
Hal McRae			
☐ 385 Jim Hunter	2.75	1.10	.27
☐ 386 Greg Goossen	.21	.09	.02
☐ 387 Joe Foy	.21	.09	.02
☐ 388 Ray Washburn	.21	.09	.02
☐ 389 Jay Johnstone	.30	.12	.03
☐ 390 Bill Mazeroski	.60	.24	.06
☐ 391 Bob Priddy	.21	.09	.02
☐ 392 Grady Hatton MGR	.21	.09	.02
☐ 393 Jim Perry	.40	.16	.04
☐ 394 Tommie Aaron	.30	.12	.03
☐ 395 Camilo Pascual	.30	.12	.03
☐ 396 Bobby Wine	.21	.09	.02
☐ 397 Vic Davalillo	.21	.09	.02
☐ 398 Jim Grant	.21	.09	.02
☐ 399 Ray Oyler	.21	.09	.02
☐ 400 Mike McCormick	.30	.12	.03
☐ 401 Mets Team	.75	.30	.07
☐ 402 Mike Hegan	.21	.09	.02
☐ 403 John Buzhardt	.21	.09	.02
☐ 404 Floyd Robinson	.21	.09	.02
☐ 405 Tommy Helms	.30	.12	.03
☐ 406 Dick Ellsworth	.30	.12	.03
☐ 407 Gary Kolb	.21	.09	.02
☐ 408 Steve Carlton	25.00	10.00	2.50
☐ 409 Orioles Rookies	.21	.09	.02
Frank Peters			
Don Stone			
☐ 410 Ferguson Jenkins	1.50	.60	.15
☐ 411 Ron Hansen	.21	.09	.02
☐ 412 Clay Carroll	.21	.09	.02
☐ 413 Tommy McCraw	.21	.09	.02
☐ 414 Mickey Lolich	1.00	.40	.10
☐ 415 Johnny Callison	.30	.12	.03
☐ 416 Bill Rigney MGR	.21	.09	.02
☐ 417 Willie Crawford	.21	.09	.02
☐ 418 Eddie Fisher	.21	.09	.02
☐ 419 Jack Hiatt	.21	.09	.02
☐ 420 Cesar Tovar	.21	.09	.02
☐ 421 Ron Taylor	.21	.09	.02
☐ 422 Rene Lachemann	.30	.12	.03
☐ 423 Fred Gladding	.21	.09	.02
☐ 424 White Sox Team	.55	.22	.05
☐ 425 Jim Maloney	.35	.14	.03
☐ 426 Hank Allen	.21	.09	.02
☐ 427 Dick Calmus	.21	.09	.02
☐ 428 Vic Roznovsky	.21	.09	.02
☐ 429 Tommie Sisk	.21	.09	.02

	MINT	VG-E	F-G
☐ 430 Rico Petrocelli	.35	.14	.03
☐ 431 Dooley Womack	.21	.09	.02
☐ 432 Indians Rookies	.21	.09	.02
Bill Davis			
Jose Vidal			
☐ 433 Bob Rodgers	.21	.09	.02
☐ 434 Ricardo Joseph	.21	.09	.02
☐ 435 Ron Perranoski	.30	.12	.03
☐ 436 Hal Lanier	.40	.16	.04
☐ 437 Don Cardwell	.21	.09	.02
☐ 438 Lee Thomas	.21	.09	.02
☐ 439 Luman Harris MGR	.21	.09	.02
☐ 440 Claude Osteen	.35	.14	.03
☐ 441 Alex Johnson	.30	.12	.03
☐ 442 Dick Bosman	.21	.09	.02
☐ 443 Joe Azcue	.21	.09	.02
☐ 444 Jack Fisher	.21	.09	.02
☐ 445 Mike Shannon	.35	.14	.03
☐ 446 Ron Kline	.21	.09	.02
☐ 447 Tigers Rookies	.21	.09	.02
George Korince			
Fred Lasher			
☐ 448 Gary Wagner	.21	.09	.02
☐ 449 Gene Oliver	.21	.09	.02
☐ 450 Jim Kaat	1.25	.50	.12
☐ 451 Al Spangler	.21	.09	.02
☐ 452 Jesus Alou	.21	.09	.02
☐ 453 Sammy Ellis	.21	.09	.02
☐ 454 A Checklist 6	1.50	.15	.03
Frank Robinson			
(cap complete			
within circle)			
☐ 454 B Checklist 6	1.50	.15	.03
Frank Robinson			
(cap partially			
within circle)			
☐ 455 Rico Carty	.50	.20	.05
☐ 456 John O'Donoghue	.21	.09	.02
☐ 457 Jim Lefebvre	.30	.12	.03
☐ 458 Lew Krausse	.30	.12	.03
☐ 459 Dick Simpson	.30	.12	.03
☐ 460 Jim Lonborg	.50	.20	.05
☐ 461 Chuck Hiller	.30	.12	.03
☐ 462 Barry Moore	.30	.12	.03
☐ 463 Jim Schaffer	.30	.12	.03
☐ 464 Don McMahon	.30	.12	.03
☐ 465 Tommie Agee	.40	.16	.04
☐ 466 Bill Dillman	.30	.12	.03
☐ 467 Dick Howser	.50	.20	.05
☐ 468 Larry Sherry	.40	.16	.04
☐ 469 Ty Cline	.30	.12	.03
☐ 470 Bill Freehan	.60	.24	.06
☐ 471 Orlando Pena	.30	.12	.03

	MINT	VG-E	F-G		MINT	VG-E	F-G
☐ 472 Walt Alston MGR	.90	.36	.09	☐ 518 A Checklist 7	1.50	.15	.03
☐ 473 Al Worthington	.30	.12	.03	(539 ML Rookies)			
☐ 474 Paul Schaal	.30	.12	.03	(Clete Boyer)			
☐ 475 Joe Niekro	1.00	.40	.10	☐ 518 B Checklist 7	5.00	.50	.10
☐ 476 Woody Woodward	.30	.12	.03	(539 AL Rookies)			
☐ 477 Phillies Team	.65	.26	.06	(Clete Boyer)			
☐ 478 Dave McNally	.65	.26	.06	☐ 519 Jerry Stephenson	.30	.12	.03
☐ 479 Phil Gagliano	.30	.12	.03	☐ 520 Lou Brock	5.50	2.20	.55
☐ 480 Manager's Dream	5.00	2.00	.50	☐ 521 Don Shaw	.30	.12	.03
Tony Oliva				☐ 522 Wayne Causey	.30	.12	.03
Chico Cardenas				☐ 523 John Tsitouris	.30	.12	.03
Bob Clemente				☐ 524 Andy Kosco	.30	.12	.03
☐ 481 John Wyatt	.30	.12	.03	☐ 525 Jim Davenport	.40	.16	.04
☐ 482 Jose Pagan	.30	.12	.03	☐ 526 Bill Denehy	.30	.12	.03
☐ 483 Darold Knowles	.30	.12	.03	☐ 527 Tito Francona	.40	.16	.04
☐ 484 Phil Roof	.30	.12	.03	☐ 528 Tigers Team	2.50	1.00	.25
☐ 485 Ken Berry	.30	.12	.03	☐ 529 Bruce Von Hoff	.30	.12	.03
☐ 486 Cal Koonce	.30	.12	.03	☐ 530 Bird Belters	3.50	1.40	.35
☐ 487 Lee May	.50	.20	.05	Brooks Robinson			
☐ 488 Dick Tracewski	.30	.12	.03	Frank Robinson			
☐ 489 Wally Bunker	.40	.16	.04	☐ 531 Chuck Hinton	.30	.12	.03
☐ 490 Super Stars	12.50	5.00	1.25	☐ 532 Luis Tiant	.75	.30	.07
Harmon Killebrew				☐ 533 Wes Parker	.45	.18	.04
Willie Mays				☐ 534 Bob Miller	.30	.12	.03
Mickey Mantle				☐ 535 Danny Cater	.30	.12	.03
☐ 491 Denny Lemaster	.30	.12	.03	☐ 536 Bill Short	.30	.12	.03
☐ 492 Jeff Torborg	.30	.12	.03	☐ 537 Norm Siebern	.30	.12	.03
☐ 493 Jim McGlothlin	.30	.12	.03	☐ 538 Manny Jimenez	.30	.12	.03
☐ 494 Ray Sadecki	.30	.12	.03	☐ 539 Major League Rookies	.60	.24	.06
☐ 495 Leon Wagner	.30	.12	.03	Jim Ray			
☐ 496 Steve Hamilton	.30	.12	.03	Mike Ferraro			
☐ 497 Cards Team	.85	.34	.08	☐ 540 Nelson Briles	.40	.16	.04
☐ 498 Bill Bryan	.30	.12	.03	☐ 541 Sandy Alomar	.30	.12	.03
☐ 499 Steve Blass	.40	.16	.04	☐ 542 John Boccabella	.30	.12	.03
☐ 500 Frank Robinson	4.50	1.80	.45	☐ 543 Bob Lee	.30	.12	.03
☐ 501 John Odom	.30	.12	.03	☐ 544 Mayo Smith MGR	.30	.12	.03
☐ 502 Mike Andrews	.30	.12	.03	☐ 545 Lindy McDaniel	.30	.12	.03
☐ 503 Al Jackson	.30	.12	.03	☐ 546 Roy White	.45	.18	.04
☐ 504 Russ Snyder	.30	.12	.03	☐ 547 Dan Coombs	.30	.12	.03
☐ 505 Joe Sparma	.30	.12	.03	☐ 548 Bernie Allen	.30	.12	.03
☐ 506 Clarence Jones	.30	.12	.03	☐ 549 Orioles Rookies	.30	.12	.03
☐ 507 Wade Blasingame	.30	.12	.03	Curt Motton			
☐ 508 Duke Sims	.30	.12	.03	Roger Nelson			
☐ 509 Dennis Higgins	.30	.12	.03	☐ 550 Clete Boyer	.50	.20	.05
☐ 510 Ron Fairly	.40	.16	.04	☐ 551 Darrell Sutherland	.30	.12	.03
☐ 511 Bill Kelso	.30	.12	.03	☐ 552 Ed Kirkpatrick	.30	.12	.03
☐ 512 Grant Jackson	.30	.12	.03	☐ 553 Hank Aguirre	.30	.12	.03
☐ 513 Hank Bauer MGR	.40	.16	.04	☐ 554 A's Team	.85	.34	.08
☐ 514 Al McBean	.30	.12	.03	☐ 555 Jose Tartabull	.30	.12	.03
☐ 515 Russ Nixon	.30	.12	.03	☐ 556 Dick Selma	.30	.12	.03
☐ 516 Pete Mikkelsen	.30	.12	.03	☐ 557 Frank Quilici	.30	.12	.03
☐ 517 Diego Segui	.30	.12	.03	☐ 558 John Edwards	.30	.12	.03

		MINT	VG-E	F-G
☐ 559	Pirates Rookies .... Carl Taylor Luke Walker	.30	.12	.03
☐ 560	Paul Casanova	.30	.12	.03
☐ 561	Lee Elia	.30	.12	.03
☐ 562	Jim Bouton	.80	.32	.08
☐ 563	Ed Charles	.30	.12	.03
☐ 564	Ed Stanky MGR	.40	.16	.04
☐ 565	Larry Dierker	.40	.16	.04
☐ 566	Ken Harrelson	.75	.30	.07
☐ 567	Clay Dalrymple	.30	.12	.03
☐ 568	Willie Smith	.30	.12	.03
☐ 569	NL Rookies .... Ivan Murrell Les Rohr	.30	.12	.03
☐ 570	Rick Reichardt	.30	.12	.03
☐ 571	Tony LaRussa	.50	.20	.05
☐ 572	Don Bosch	.30	.12	.03
☐ 573	Joe Coleman	.30	.12	.03
☐ 574	Reds Team	.85	.34	.08
☐ 575	Jim Palmer	7.00	2.80	.70
☐ 576	Dave Adlesh	.30	.12	.03
☐ 577	Fred Talbot	.30	.12	.03
☐ 578	Orlando Martinez	.30	.12	.03
☐ 579	NL Rookies .... Larry Hisle Mike Lum	.70	.28	.07
☐ 580	Bob Bailey	.30	.12	.03
☐ 581	Garry Roggenburk	.30	.12	.03
☐ 582	Jerry Grote	.30	.12	.03
☐ 583	Gates Brown	.45	.18	.04
☐ 584	Larry Shepard MGR	.30	.12	.03
☐ 585	Wilbur Wood	.40	.16	.04
☐ 586	Jim Pagliaroni	.30	.12	.03
☐ 587	Roger Repoz	.30	.12	.03
☐ 588	Dick Schofield	.30	.12	.03
☐ 589	Twins Rookies .... Ron Clark Moe Ogier	.30	.12	.03
☐ 590	Tommy Harper	.40	.16	.04
☐ 591	Dick Nen	.30	.12	.03
☐ 592	John Bateman	.30	.12	.03
☐ 593	Lee Stange	.30	.12	.03
☐ 594	Phil Linz	.30	.12	.03
☐ 595	Phil Ortega	.30	.12	.03
☐ 596	Charlie Smith	.30	.12	.03
☐ 597	Bill McCool	.30	.12	.03
☐ 598	Jerry May	.75	.15	.03

1969 Topps

The cards in this 664-card set measure 2½" by 3½". The 1969 Topps set includes the Sporting News All-Star Selections as card numbers 416 to 435. Other popular subsets within this set include League Leaders (1-12) and World Series cards (162-169). The fifth series contains several variations; the more difficult variety consists of cards with the player's whole name in white letters, which are designated in the checklist below by WL. Each checklist card features a different popular player's picture inside a circle on the front of the checklist card. Two different poses of Clay Dalrymple and Donn Clendenon exist as indicated in the checklist.

	MINT	VG-E	F-G
Complete Set	600.00	240.00	60.00
Common Player (1-218)	.21	.09	.02
Common Player (219-327)	.35	.14	.03
Common Player (328-512)	.21	.09	.02
Common Player (513-664)	.25	.10	.02

		MINT	VG-E	F-G
☐ 1	AL Batting Leaders ..... Carl Yastrzemski Danny Cater Tony Oliva	2.50	.60	.10
☐ 2	NL Batting Leaders ..... Pete Rose Matty Alou Felipe Alou	2.00	.80	.20

		MINT	VG-E	F-G
☐ 3	AL RBI Leaders	.70	.28	.07
	Ken Harrelson			
	Frank Howard			
	Jim Northrup			
☐ 4	NL RBI Leaders	1.00	.40	.10
	Willie McCovey			
	Ron Santo			
	Billy Williams			
☐ 5	AL Home Run Leaders .	.70	.28	.07
	Frank Howard			
	Willie Horton			
	Ken Harrelson			
☐ 6	NL Home Run Leaders .	1.25	.50	.12
	Willie McCovey			
	Richie Allen			
	Ernie Banks			
☐ 7	AL ERA Leaders	.60	.24	.06
	Luis Tiant			
	Sam McDowell			
	Dave McNally			
☐ 8	NL ERA Leaders	.75	.30	.07
	Bob Gibson			
	Bobby Bolin			
	Bob Veale			
☐ 9	AL Pitching Leaders .	.60	.24	.06
	Denny McLain			
	Dave McNally			
	Luis Tiant			
	Mel Stottlemyre			
☐ 10	NL Pitching Leaders	1.50	.60	.15
	Juan Marichal			
	Bob Gibson			
	Fergie Jenkins			
☐ 11	AL Strikeout Leaders ...	.60	.24	.06
	Sam McDowell			
	Denny McLain			
	Luis Tiant			
☐ 12	NL Strikeout Leaders ...	.80	.32	.08
	Bob Gibson			
	Fergie Jenkins			
	Bill Singer			
☐ 13	Mickey Stanley	.30	.12	.03
☐ 14	Al McBean	.21	.09	.02
☐ 15	Boog Powell	.75	.30	.07
☐ 16	Giants Rookies	.21	.09	.02
	Cesar Gutierrez			
	Rich Robertson			
☐ 17	Mike Marshall	.45	.18	.04
☐ 18	Dick Schofield	.21	.09	.02
☐ 19	Ken Suarez	.21	.09	.02
☐ 20	Ernie Banks	3.25	1.30	.32
☐ 21	Jose Santiago	.21	.09	.02
☐ 22	Jesus Alou	.21	.09	.02

		MINT	VG-E	F-G
☐ 23	Lew Krausse	.21	.09	.02
☐ 24	Walt Alston MGR	.80	.32	.08
☐ 25	Roy White	.30	.12	.03
☐ 26	Clay Carroll	.21	.09	.02
☐ 27	Bernie Allen	.21	.09	.02
☐ 28	Mike Ryan	.21	.09	.02
☐ 29	Dave Morehead	.21	.09	.02
☐ 30	Bob Allison	.35	.14	.03
☐ 31	Mets Rookies	.85	.34	.08
	Gary Gentry			
	Amos Otis			
☐ 32	Sammy Ellis	.21	.09	.02
☐ 33	Wayne Causey	.21	.09	.02
☐ 34	Gary Peters	.30	.12	.03
☐ 35	Joe Morgan	2.50	1.00	.25
☐ 36	Luke Walker	.21	.09	.02
☐ 37	Curt Motton	.21	.09	.02
☐ 38	Zoilo Versalles	.21	.09	.02
☐ 39	Dick Hughes	.21	.09	.02
☐ 40	Mayo Smith MGR	.21	.09	.02
☐ 41	Bob Barton	.21	.09	.02
☐ 42	Tommy Harper	.30	.12	.03
☐ 43	Joe Niekro	.60	.24	.06
☐ 44	Danny Cater	.21	.09	.02
☐ 45	Maury Wills	1.00	.40	.10
☐ 46	Fritz Peterson	.21	.09	.02
☐ 47 A	Paul Popovich	.30	.12	.03
	(no helmet emblem)			
☐ 47 B	Paul Popovich	10.00	4.00	1.00
	(C emblem on helmet)			
☐ 48	Brant Alyea	.21	.09	.02
☐ 49 A	Royals Rookies	.30	.12	.03
	Steve Jones			
	E. Rodriguez "g"			
☐ 49 B	Royals Rookies	10.00	4.00	1.00
	Steve Jones			
	E. Rodriguez "q"			
☐ 50	Bob Clemente	9.00	3.75	.90
☐ 51	Woody Fryman	.21	.09	.02
☐ 52	Mike Andrews	.21	.09	.02
☐ 53	Sonny Jackson	.21	.09	.02
☐ 54	Cisco Carlos	.21	.09	.02
☐ 55	Jerry Grote	.21	.09	.02
☐ 56	Rich Reese	.21	.09	.02
☐ 57	Checklist 1	1.50	.15	.03
	Denny McLain			
☐ 58	Fred Gladding	.21	.09	.02
☐ 59	Jay Johnstone	.30	.12	.03
☐ 60	Nelson Briles	.30	.12	.03
☐ 61	Jimmie Hall	.21	.09	.02
☐ 62	Chico Salmon	.30	.12	.03
☐ 63	Jim Hickman	.21	.09	.02
☐ 64	Bill Monbouquette	.21	.09	.02

		MINT	VG-E	F-G
☐ 65	Willie Davis	.45	.18	.04
☐ 66	Orioles Rookies	.30	.12	.03
	Mike Adamson			
	Merv Rettenmund			
☐ 67	Bill Stoneman	.21	.09	.02
☐ 68	Dave Duncan	.21	.09	.02
☐ 69	Steve Hamilton	.21	.09	.02
☐ 70	Tommy Helms	.30	.12	.03
☐ 71	Steve Whitaker	.21	.09	.02
☐ 72	Ron Taylor	.21	.09	.02
☐ 73	Johnny Briggs	.21	.09	.02
☐ 74	Preston Gomez MGR	.21	.09	.02
☐ 75	Luis Aparicio	2.50	1.00	.25
☐ 76	Norm Miller	.21	.09	.02
☐ 77 A	Ron Perranoski	.30	.12	.03
	(no emblem on cap)			
☐ 77 B	Ron Perranoski	10.00	4.00	1.00
	(LA on cap)			
☐ 78	Tom Satriano	.21	.09	.02
☐ 79	Milt Pappas	.30	.12	.03
☐ 80	Norm Cash	.75	.30	.07
☐ 81	Mel Queen	.21	.09	.02
☐ 82	Pirates Rookies	7.00	2.80	.70
	Rich Hebner			
	Al Oliver			
☐ 83	Mike Ferraro	.35	.14	.03
☐ 84	Bob Humphreys	.21	.09	.02
☐ 85	Lou Brock	4.00	1.60	.40
☐ 86	Pete Richert	.21	.09	.02
☐ 87	Horace Clarke	.21	.09	.02
☐ 88	Rich Nye	.21	.09	.02
☐ 89	Russ Gibson	.21	.09	.02
☐ 90	Jerry Koosman	.90	.36	.09
☐ 91	Al Dark MGR	.30	.12	.03
☐ 92	Jack Billingham	.21	.09	.02
☐ 93	Joe Foy	.21	.09	.02
☐ 94	Hank Aguirre	.21	.09	.02
☐ 95	Johnny Bench	30.00	12.00	3.00
☐ 96	Denver Lemaster	.21	.09	.02
☐ 97	Buddy Bradford	.21	.09	.02
☐ 98	Dave Giusti	.21	.09	.02
☐ 99 A	Twins Rookies	8.00	3.25	.80
	Danny Morris			
	Graig Nettles			
	(no loop)			
☐ 99 B	Twins Rookies	16.00	6.50	1.60
	Danny Morris			
	Graig Nettles			
	(errant loop in			
	upper left corner			
	of obverse)			
☐ 100	Hank Aaron	12.50	5.00	1.25
☐ 101	Daryl Patterson	.21	.09	.02

		MINT	VG-E	F-G
☐ 102	Jim Davenport	.30	.12	.03
☐ 103	Roger Repoz	.21	.09	.02
☐ 104	Steve Blass	.30	.12	.03
☐ 105	Rick Monday	.30	.12	.03
☐ 106	Jim Hannan	.21	.09	.02
☐ 107 A	Checklist 2	1.50	.15	.03
	(161 Jim Purdin)			
	(Bob Gibson)			
☐ 107 B	Checklist 2	4.00	.40	.08
	(161 John Purdin)			
	(Bob Gibson)			
☐ 108	Tony Taylor	.21	.09	.02
☐ 109	Jim Lonborg	.35	.14	.03
☐ 110	Mike Shannon	.35	.14	.03
☐ 111	Johnny Morris	.30	.12	.03
☐ 112	J.C. Martin	.21	.09	.02
☐ 113	Dave May	.21	.09	.02
☐ 114	Yankees Rookies	.21	.09	.02
	Alan Closter			
	John Cumberland			
☐ 115	Bill Hands	.21	.09	.02
☐ 116	Chuck Harrison	.21	.09	.02
☐ 117	Jim Fairey	.21	.09	.02
☐ 118	Stan Williams	.21	.09	.02
☐ 119	Doug Rader	.30	.12	.03
☐ 120	Pete Rose	25.00	10.00	2.50
☐ 121	Joe Grzenda	.21	.09	.02
☐ 122	Ron Fairly	.30	.12	.03
☐ 123	Wilbur Wood	.30	.12	.03
☐ 124	Hank Bauer MGR	.30	.12	.03
☐ 125	Ray Sadecki	.21	.09	.02
☐ 126	Dick Tracewski	.21	.09	.02
☐ 127	Kevin Collins	.21	.09	.02
☐ 128	Tommie Aaron	.30	.12	.03
☐ 129	Bill McCool	.21	.09	.02
☐ 130	Carl Yastrzemski	16.00	6.50	1.60
☐ 131	Chris Cannizzaro	.21	.09	.02
☐ 132	Dave Baldwin	.21	.09	.02
☐ 133	Johnny Callison	.30	.12	.03
☐ 134	Jim Weaver	.21	.09	.02
☐ 135	Tommy Davis	.45	.18	.04
☐ 136	Cards Rookies	.30	.12	.03
	Steve Huntz			
	Mike Torrez			
☐ 137	Wally Bunker	.21	.09	.02
☐ 138	John Bateman	.21	.09	.02
☐ 139	Andy Kosco	.21	.09	.02
☐ 140	Jim Lefebvre	.21	.09	.02
☐ 141	Bill Dillman	.21	.09	.02
☐ 142	Woody Woodward	.21	.09	.02
☐ 143	Joe Nossek	.21	.09	.02
☐ 144	Bob Hendley	.21	.09	.02
☐ 145	Max Alvis	.21	.09	.02

	MINT	VG-E	F-G
☐ 146 Jim Perry	.40	.16	.04
☐ 147 Leo Durocher MGR	.75	.30	.07
☐ 148 Lee Stange	.21	.09	.02
☐ 149 Ollie Brown	.21	.09	.02
☐ 150 Denny McLain	1.00	.40	.10
☐ 151 A Clay Dalrymple (Portrait) (Orioles)	.30	.12	.03
☐ 151 B Clay Dalrymple (Catching) (Phillies)	10.00	4.00	1.00
☐ 152 Tommie Sisk	.21	.09	.02
☐ 153 Ed Brinkman	.21	.09	.02
☐ 154 Jim Britton	.21	.09	.02
☐ 155 Pete Ward	.21	.09	.02
☐ 156 Houston Rookies Hal Gilson Leon McFadden	.21	.09	.02
☐ 157 Bob Rodgers	.21	.09	.02
☐ 158 Joe Gibbon	.21	.09	.02
☐ 159 Jerry Adair	.21	.09	.02
☐ 160 Vada Pinson	.75	.30	.07
☐ 161 John Purdin	.21	.09	.02
☐ 162 World Series Game 1 Gibson fans 17	2.25	.90	.22
☐ 163 World Series Game 2 Tiger homers deck the Cards	1.00	.40	.10
☐ 164 World Series Game 3 McCarver's homer	1.25	.50	.12
☐ 165 World Series Game 4 Brock lead-off homer	2.25	.90	.22
☐ 166 World Series Game 5 Kaline's key hit	2.50	1.00	.25
☐ 167 World Series Game 6 Northrup grandslam	1.00	.40	.10
☐ 168 World Series Game 7 Lolich outduels Bob Gibson	2.00	.80	.20
☐ 169 World Series Summary Tigers celebrate	1.00	.40	.10
☐ 170 Frank Howard	.70	.28	.07
☐ 171 Glenn Beckert	.30	.12	.03
☐ 172 Jerry Stephenson	.21	.09	.02
☐ 173 White Sox Rookies Bob Christian Gerry Nyman	.21	.09	.02
☐ 174 Grant Jackson	.21	.09	.02
☐ 175 Jim Bunning	1.00	.40	.10
☐ 176 Joe Azcue	.21	.09	.02
☐ 177 Ron Reed	.21	.09	.02
☐ 178 Ray Oyler	.21	.09	.02
☐ 179 Don Pavletich	.21	.09	.02
☐ 180 Willie Horton	.35	.14	.03
☐ 181 Mel Nelson	.21	.09	.02

	MINT	VG-E	F-G
☐ 182 Bill Rigney MGR	.21	.09	.02
☐ 183 Don Shaw	.21	.09	.02
☐ 184 Roberto Pena	.21	.09	.02
☐ 185 Tom Phoebus	.21	.09	.02
☐ 186 John Edwards	.21	.09	.02
☐ 187 Leon Wagner	.21	.09	.02
☐ 188 Rick Wise	.30	.12	.03
☐ 189 Red Sox Rookies Joe Lahoud John Thibodeau	.21	.09	.02
☐ 190 Willie Mays	12.50	5.00	1.25
☐ 191 Lindy McDaniel	.21	.09	.02
☐ 192 Jose Pagan	.21	.09	.02
☐ 193 Don Cardwell	.21	.09	.02
☐ 194 Ted Uhlaender	.21	.09	.02
☐ 195 John Odom	.21	.09	.02
☐ 196 Lum Harris MGR	.21	.09	.02
☐ 197 Dick Selma	.21	.09	.02
☐ 198 Willie Smith	.21	.09	.02
☐ 199 Jim French	.21	.09	.02
☐ 200 Bob Gibson	3.00	1.20	.30
☐ 201 Russ Snyder	.21	.09	.02
☐ 202 Don Wilson	.21	.09	.02
☐ 203 Dave Johnson	.50	.20	.05
☐ 204 Jack Hiatt	.21	.09	.02
☐ 205 Rick Reichardt	.21	.09	.02
☐ 206 Phillies Rookies Larry Hisle Barry Lersch	.30	.12	.03
☐ 207 Roy Face	.35	.14	.03
☐ 208 A Donn Clendenon (Houston)	.30	.12	.03
☐ 208 B Donn Clendenon (Expos)	10.00	4.00	1.00
☐ 209 Larry Haney (reverse negative)	.30	.12	.03
☐ 210 Felix Millan	.21	.09	.02
☐ 211 Galen Cisco	.21	.09	.02
☐ 212 Tom Tresh	.35	.14	.03
☐ 213 Gerry Arrigo	.21	.09	.02
☐ 214 Checklist 3 With 69T deckle CL on back (no player)	1.50	.15	.03
☐ 215 Rico Petrocelli	.30	.12	.03
☐ 216 Don Sutton	2.00	.80	.20
☐ 217 John Donaldson	.21	.09	.02
☐ 218 John Roseboro	.30	.12	.03
☐ 219 Freddie Patek	.35	.14	.03
☐ 220 Sam McDowell	.50	.20	.05
☐ 221 Art Shamsky	.35	.14	.03
☐ 222 Duane Josephson	.35	.14	.03
☐ 223 Tom Dukes	.35	.14	.03

		MINT	VG-E	F-G
☐ 224	Angels Rookies	.35	.14	.03
	Bill Harrelson			
	Steve Kealey			
☐ 225	Don Kessinger	.50	.20	.05
☐ 226	Bruce Howard	.35	.14	.03
☐ 227	Frank Johnson	.35	.14	.03
☐ 228	Dave Leonhard	.35	.14	.03
☐ 229	Don Lock	.35	.14	.03
☐ 230	Rusty Staub	.80	.32	.08
☐ 231	Pat Dobson	.50	.20	.05
☐ 232	Dave Ricketts	.35	.14	.03
☐ 233	Steve Barber	.35	.14	.03
☐ 234	Dave Bristol MGR	.35	.14	.03
☐ 235	Jim Hunter	3.00	1.20	.30
☐ 236	Manny Mota	.50	.20	.05
☐ 237	Bobby Cox MGR	.50	.20	.05
☐ 238	Ken Johnson	.35	.14	.03
☐ 239	Bob Taylor	.35	.14	.03
☐ 240	Ken Harrelson	.75	.30	.07
☐ 241	Jim Brewer	.35	.14	.03
☐ 242	Frank Kostro	.35	.14	.03
☐ 243	Ron Kline	.35	.14	.03
☐ 244	Indians Rookies	.50	.20	.05
	Ray Fosse			
	George Woodson			
☐ 245	Ed Charles	.35	.14	.03
☐ 246	Joe Coleman	.35	.14	.03
☐ 247	Gene Oliver	.35	.14	.03
☐ 248	Bob Priddy	.35	.14	.03
☐ 249	Ed Spiezio	.35	.14	.03
☐ 250	Frank Robinson	6.50	2.60	.65
☐ 251	Ron Herbel	.35	.14	.03
☐ 252	Chuck Cottier	.35	.14	.03
☐ 253	Jerry Johnson	.35	.14	.03
☐ 254	Joe Schultz	.35	.14	.03
☐ 255	Steve Carlton	25.00	10.00	2.50
☐ 256	Gates Brown	.45	.18	.04
☐ 257	Jim Ray	.35	.14	.03
☐ 258	Jackie Hernandez	.35	.14	.03
☐ 259	Bill Short	.35	.14	.03
☐ 260	Reggie Jackson	100.00	40.00	10.00
☐ 261	Bob Johnson	.35	.14	.03
☐ 262	Mike Kekich	.35	.14	.03
☐ 263	Jerry May	.35	.14	.03
☐ 264	Bill Landis	.35	.14	.03
☐ 265	Chico Cardenas	.35	.14	.03
☐ 266	Dodger Rookies	.35	.14	.03
	Tom Hutton			
	Alan Foster			
☐ 267	Vicente Romo	.35	.14	.03
☐ 268	Al Spangler	.35	.14	.03
☐ 269	Al Weis	.35	.14	.03
☐ 270	Mickey Lolich	1.00	.40	.10
☐ 271	Larry Stahl	.35	.14	.03
☐ 272	Ed Stroud	.35	.14	.03
☐ 273	Ron Willis	.35	.14	.03
☐ 274	Clyde King MGR	.35	.14	.03
☐ 275	Vic Davalillo	.35	.14	.03
☐ 276	Gary Wagner	.35	.14	.03
☐ 277	Rod Hendricks	.35	.14	.03
☐ 278	Gary Geiger	.45	.18	.04
	(Batting wrong)			
☐ 279	Roger Nelson	.35	.14	.03
☐ 280	Alex Johnson	.45	.18	.04
☐ 281	Ted Kubiak	.35	.14	.03
☐ 282	Pat Jarvis	.35	.14	.03
☐ 283	Sandy Alomar	.35	.14	.03
☐ 284	Expos Rookies	.35	.14	.03
	Jerry Robertson			
	Mike Wegener			
☐ 285	Don Mincher	.45	.18	.04
☐ 286	Dock Ellis	.35	.14	.03
☐ 287	Jose Tartabull	.35	.14	.03
☐ 288	Ken Holtzman	.55	.22	.05
☐ 289	Bart Shirley	.35	.14	.03
☐ 290	Jim Kaat	1.75	.70	.17
☐ 291	Vern Fuller	.35	.14	.03
☐ 292	Al Downing	.35	.14	.03
☐ 293	Dick Dietz	.35	.14	.03
☐ 294	Jim Lemon MGR	.35	.14	.03
☐ 295	Tony Perez	2.25	.90	.22
☐ 296	Andy Messersmith	.75	.30	.07
☐ 297	Deron Johnson	.35	.14	.03
☐ 298	Dave Nicholson	.35	.14	.03
☐ 299	Mark Belanger	.50	.20	.05
☐ 300	Felipe Alou	.50	.20	.05
☐ 301	Darrell Brandon	.45	.18	.04
☐ 302	Jim Pagliaroni	.35	.14	.03
☐ 303	Cal Koonce	.35	.14	.03
☐ 304	Padres Rookies	.35	.14	.03
	Bill Davis			
	Clarence Gaston			
☐ 305	Dick McAuliffe	.35	.14	.03
☐ 306	Jim Grant	.35	.14	.03
☐ 307	Gary Kolb	.35	.14	.03
☐ 308	Wade Blasingame	.35	.14	.03
☐ 309	Walt Williams	.35	.14	.03
☐ 310	Tom Haller	.35	.14	.03
☐ 311	Sparky Lyle	1.50	.60	.15
☐ 312	Lee Elia	.45	.18	.04
☐ 313	Bill Robinson	.35	.14	.03
☐ 314	Checklist 4	1.50	.15	.03
	Don Drysdale			
☐ 315	Eddie Fisher	.35	.14	.03
☐ 316	Hal Lanier	.50	.20	.05
☐ 317	Bruce Look	.35	.14	.03

		MINT	VG-E	F-G
☐ 318	Jack Fisher	.35	.14	.03
☐ 319	Ken McMullen	.35	.14	.03
☐ 320	Dal Maxvill	.35	.14	.03
☐ 321	Jim McAndrew	.35	.14	.03
☐ 322	Jose Vidal	.45	.18	.04
☐ 323	Larry Miller	.35	.14	.03
☐ 324	Tiger Rookies	.35	.14	.03
	Les Cain			
	Dave Campbell			
☐ 325	Jose Cardenal	.35	.14	.03
☐ 326	Gary Sutherland	.35	.14	.03
☐ 327	Willie Crawford	.35	.14	.03
☐ 328	Joe Horlen	.30	.12	.03
☐ 329	Rick Joseph	.21	.09	.02
☐ 330	Tony Conigliaro	.60	.24	.06
☐ 331	Braves Rookies	.35	.14	.03
	Gil Garrido			
	Tom House			
☐ 332	Fred Talbot	.21	.09	.02
☐ 333	Ivan Murrell	.21	.09	.02
☐ 334	Phil Roof	.21	.09	.02
☐ 335	Bill Mazeroski	.60	.24	.06
☐ 336	Jim Roland	.21	.09	.02
☐ 337	Marty Martinez	.21	.09	.02
☐ 338	Del Unser	.21	.09	.02
☐ 339	Reds Rookies	.21	.09	.02
	Steve Mingori			
	Jose Pena			
☐ 340	Dave McNally	.40	.16	.04
☐ 341	Dave Adlesh	.21	.09	.02
☐ 342	Bubba Morton	.21	.09	.02
☐ 343	Dan Frisella	.21	.09	.02
☐ 344	Tom Matchick	.21	.09	.02
☐ 345	Frank Linzy	.21	.09	.02
☐ 346	Wayne Comer	.30	.12	.03
☐ 347	Randy Hundley	.21	.09	.02
☐ 348	Steve Hargan	.21	.09	.02
☐ 349	Dick Williams MGR	.30	.12	.03
☐ 350	Richie Allen	.75	.30	.07
☐ 351	Carroll Sembera	.21	.09	.02
☐ 352	Paul Schaal	.21	.09	.02
☐ 353	Jeff Torborg	.21	.09	.02
☐ 354	Nate Oliver	.21	.09	.02
☐ 355	Phil Niekro	2.50	1.00	.25
☐ 356	Frank Quilici MGR	.21	.09	.02
☐ 357	Carl Taylor	.21	.09	.02
☐ 358	Athletics Rookies	.21	.09	.02
	George Lauzerique			
	Roberto Rodriquez			
☐ 359	Dick Kelley	.21	.09	.02
☐ 360	Jim Wynn	.35	.14	.03
☐ 361	Gary Holman	.21	.09	.02
☐ 362	Jim Maloney	.30	.12	.03
☐ 363	Russ Nixon	.21	.09	.02
☐ 364	Tommie Agee	.30	.12	.03
☐ 365	Jim Fregosi	.40	.16	.04
☐ 366	Bo Belinsky	.30	.12	.03
☐ 367	Lou Johnson	.21	.09	.02
☐ 368	Vic Roznovsky	.21	.09	.02
☐ 369	Bob Skinner	.30	.12	.03
☐ 370	Juan Marichal	2.75	1.10	.27
☐ 371	Sal Bando	.50	.20	.05
☐ 372	Adolfo Phillips	.21	.09	.02
☐ 373	Fred Lasher	.21	.09	.02
☐ 374	Bob Tillman	.21	.09	.02
☐ 375	Harmon Killebrew	5.00	2.00	.50
☐ 376	Royals Rookies	.21	.09	.02
	Mike Fiore			
	Jim Rooker			
☐ 377	Gary Bell	.30	.12	.03
☐ 378	Jose Herrera	.21	.09	.02
☐ 379	Ken Boyer	.75	.30	.07
☐ 380	Stan Bahnsen	.21	.09	.02
☐ 381	Ed Kranepool	.30	.12	.03
☐ 382	Pat Corrales	.30	.12	.03
☐ 383	Casey Cox	.21	.09	.02
☐ 384	Larry Shepard MGR	.21	.09	.02
☐ 385	Orlando Cepeda	1.25	.50	.12
☐ 386	Jim McGlothlin	.21	.09	.02
☐ 387	Bobby Klaus	.21	.09	.02
☐ 388	Tom McCraw	.21	.09	.02
☐ 389	Dan Coombs	.21	.09	.02
☐ 390	Bill Freehan	.50	.20	.05
☐ 391	Ray Culp	.21	.09	.02
☐ 392	Bob Burda	.21	.09	.02
☐ 393	Gene Brabender	.21	.09	.02
☐ 394	Pilots Rookies	1.25	.50	.12
	Lou Piniella			
	Marv Staehle			
☐ 395	Chris Short	.21	.09	.02
☐ 396	Jim Campanis	.21	.09	.02
☐ 397	Chuck Dobson	.21	.09	.02
☐ 398	Tito Francona	.21	.09	.02
☐ 399	Bob Bailey	.21	.09	.02
☐ 400	Don Drysdale	3.00	1.20	.30
☐ 401	Jake Gibbs	.21	.09	.02
☐ 402	Ken Boswell	.21	.09	.02
☐ 403	Bob Miller	.21	.09	.02
☐ 404	Cubs Rookies	.21	.09	.02
	Vic LaRose			
	Gary Ross			
☐ 405	Lee May	.40	.16	.04
☐ 406	Phil Ortega	.21	.09	.02
☐ 407	Tom Egan	.21	.09	.02
☐ 408	Nate Colbert	.21	.09	.02
☐ 409	Bob Moose	.21	.09	.02

	MINT	VG-E	F-G
☐ 410 Al Kaline	3.50	1.40	.35
☐ 411 Larry Dierker	.30	.12	.03
☐ 412 Checklist 5	2.50	.25	.05
Mickey Mantle			
☐ 413 Roland Sheldon	.30	.12	.03
☐ 414 Duke Sims	.21	.09	.02
☐ 415 Ray Washburn	.21	.09	.02
☐ 416 Willie McCovey AS	2.00	.80	.20
☐ 417 Ken Harrelson AS	.30	.12	.03
☐ 418 Tommy Helms AS	.30	.12	.03
☐ 419 Rod Carew AS	3.00	1.20	.30
☐ 420 Ron Santo AS	.30	.12	.03
☐ 421 Brooks Robinson AS	2.50	1.00	.25
☐ 422 Don Kessinger AS	.30	.12	.03
☐ 423 Bert Campaneris AS	.30	.12	.03
☐ 424 Pete Rose AS	6.50	2.60	.65
☐ 425 Carl Yastrzemski AS	4.00	1.60	.40
☐ 426 Curt Flood AS	.30	.12	.03
☐ 427 Tony Oliva AS	.45	.18	.04
☐ 428 Lou Brock AS	2.25	.90	.22
☐ 429 Willie Horton AS	.30	.12	.03
☐ 430 Johnny Bench AS	4.00	1.60	.40
☐ 431 Bill Freehan AS	.30	.12	.03
☐ 432 Bob Gibson AS	2.00	.80	.20
☐ 433 Denny McLain AS	.40	.16	.04
☐ 434 Jerry Koosman AS	.30	.12	.03
☐ 435 Sam McDowell AS	.30	.12	.03
☐ 436 Gene Alley	.30	.12	.03
☐ 437 Luis Alcaraz	.21	.09	.02
☐ 438 Gary Waslewski	.21	.09	.02
☐ 439 White Sox Rookies	.21	.09	.02
Ed Herrmann			
Dan Lazar			
☐ 440 A Willie McCovey	7.50	3.00	.75
☐ 440 B Willie McCovey WL	50.00	20.00	5.00
☐ 441 A Dennis Higgins	.25	.10	.02
☐ 441 B Dennis Higgins WL	6.50	2.40	.60
☐ 442 Ty Cline	.21	.09	.02
☐ 443 Don Wert	.21	.09	.02
☐ 444 A Joe Moeller	.25	.10	.02
☐ 444 B Joe Moeller WL	6.50	2.40	.60
☐ 445 Bobby Knoop	.21	.09	.02
☐ 446 Claude Raymond	.21	.09	.02
☐ 447 A Ralph Houk MGR	.40	.16	.04
☐ 447 B Ralph Houk WL MGR	7.50	2.80	.70
☐ 448 Bob Tolan	.21	.09	.02
☐ 449 Paul Lindblad	.21	.09	.02
☐ 450 Billy Williams	3.00	1.20	.30
☐ 451 A Rich Rollins	.25	.10	.02
☐ 451 B Rich Rollins WL	6.50	2.40	.60
☐ 452 A Al Ferrara	.25	.10	.02
☐ 452 B Al Ferrara WL	6.50	2.40	.60
☐ 453 Mike Cuellar	.50	.20	.05

	MINT	VG-E	F-G
☐ 454 A Phillies Rookies	.35	.14	.03
Larry Colton			
Don Money			
☐ 454 B Phillies Rookies WL	7.50	2.80	.70
Larry Colton			
Don Money			
☐ 455 Sonny Siebert	.30	.12	.03
☐ 456 Bud Harrelson	.30	.12	.03
☐ 457 Dalton Jones	.21	.09	.02
☐ 458 Curt Blefary	.21	.09	.02
☐ 459 Dave Boswell	.21	.09	.02
☐ 460 Joe Torre	.70	.28	.07
☐ 461 A Mike Epstein	.25	.10	.02
☐ 461 B Mike Epstein WL	6.50	2.40	.60
☐ 462 Red Schoendienst MGR	.45	.18	.04
☐ 463 Dennis Ribant	.21	.09	.02
☐ 464 A Dave Marshall	.25	.10	.02
☐ 464 B Dave Marshall WL	6.50	2.40	.60
☐ 465 Tommy John	1.25	.50	.12
☐ 466 John Boccabella	.21	.09	.02
☐ 467 Tom Reynolds	.21	.09	.02
☐ 468 A Pirates Rookies	.25	.10	.02
Bruce Dal Canton			
Bob Robertson			
☐ 468 B Pirates Rookies WL	6.50	2.40	.60
Bruce Dal Canton			
Bob Robertson			
☐ 469 Chico Ruiz	.21	.09	.02
☐ 470 A Mel Stottlemyre	.50	.20	.05
☐ 470 B Mel Stottlemyre WL	7.50	2.80	.70
☐ 471 A Ted Savage	.25	.10	.02
☐ 471 B Ted Savage WL	6.50	2.40	.60
☐ 472 Jim Price	.21	.09	.02
☐ 473 A Jose Arcia	.25	.10	.02
☐ 473 B Jose Arcia WL	6.50	2.40	.60
☐ 474 Tom Murphy	.21	.09	.02
☐ 475 Tim McCarver	.35	.14	.03
☐ 476 A Boston Rookies	.30	.12	.03
Ken Brett			
Gerry Moses			
☐ 476 B Boston Rookies WL	6.50	2.40	.60
Ken Brett			
Gerry Moses			
☐ 477 Jeff James	.21	.09	.02
☐ 478 Don Buford	.21	.09	.02
☐ 479 Richie Scheinblum	.21	.09	.02
☐ 480 Tom Seaver	25.00	10.00	2.50
☐ 481 Bill Melton	.21	.09	.02
☐ 482 A Jim Gosger	.25	.10	.02
☐ 482 B Jim Gosger WL	6.50	2.40	.60
☐ 483 Ted Abernathy	.21	.09	.02
☐ 484 Joe Gordon MGR	.30	.12	.03
☐ 485 A Gaylord Perry	3.00	1.20	.30

	MINT	VG-E	F-G			MINT	VG-E	F-G
□ 485 B Gaylord Perry WL	25.00	10.00	2.50	□ 522 Joe Hoerner	.25	.10	.02
□ 486 A Paul Casanova	.25	.10	.02	□ 523 Bob Chance	.25	.10	.02
□ 486 B Paul Casanova WL ...	6.50	2.40	.60	□ 524 Expos Rookies	.25	.10	.02
□ 487 Denis Menke	.30	.12	.03	Jose Laboy			
□ 488 Joe Sparma	.21	.09	.02	Floyd Wicker			
□ 489 Clete Boyer	.40	.16	.04	□ 525 Earl Wilson	.25	.10	.02
□ 490 Matty Alou	.30	.12	.03	□ 526 Hector Torres	.25	.10	.02
□ 491 A Twins Rookies	.30	.12	.03	□ 527 Al Lopez MGR	1.00	.40	.10
Jerry Crider				□ 528 Claude Osteen	.35	.14	.03
George Mitterwald				□ 529 Ed Kirkpatrick	.25	.10	.02
□ 491 B Twins Rookies WL ...	6.50	2.40	.60	□ 530 Cesar Tovar	.25	.10	.02
Jerry Crider				□ 531 Dick Farrell	.25	.10	.02
George Mitterwald				□ 532 Bird Hill Aces	.45	.18	.04
□ 492 Tony Cloninger	.21	.09	.02	Tom Phoebus			
□ 493 A Wes Parker	.40	.16	.04	Jim Hardin			
□ 493 B Wes Parker WL	7.50	2.80	.70	Dave McNally			
□ 494 Ken Berry	.21	.09	.02	Mike Cuellar			
□ 495 Bert Campaneris	.40	.16	.04	□ 533 Nolan Ryan	25.00	10.00	2.50
□ 496 Larry Jaster	.21	.09	.02	□ 534 Jerry McNertney	.30	.12	.03
□ 497 Julian Javier	.30	.12	.03	□ 535 Phil Regan	.35	.14	.03
□ 498 Juan Pizarro	.21	.09	.02	□ 536 Padres Rookies	.25	.10	.02
□ 499 Astro Rookies	.21	.09	.02	Danny Breeden			
Don Bryant				Dave Roberts			
Steve Shea				□ 537 Mike Paul	.25	.10	.02
□ 500 A Mickey Mantle	50.00	20.00	5.00	□ 538 Charlie Smith	.25	.10	.02
□ 500 B Mickey Mantle WL	125.00	50.00	12.50	□ 539 Ted Shows How	2.00	.80	.20
□ 501 A Tony Gonzalez	.30	.12	.03	Mike Epstein			
□ 501 B Tony Gonzalez WL	6.50	2.40	.60	Ted Williams			
□ 502 Minnie Rojas	.21	.09	.02	□ 540 Curt Flood	.50	.20	.05
□ 503 Larry Brown	.21	.09	.02	□ 541 Joe Verbanic	.25	.10	.02
□ 504 Checklist 6	1.50	.15	.03	□ 542 Bob Aspromonte	.25	.10	.02
Brooks Robinson				□ 543 Fred Newman	.25	.10	.02
□ 505 A Bobby Bolin	.25	.10	.02	□ 544 Tigers Rookies	.25	.10	.02
□ 505 B Bobby Bolin WL	6.50	2.40	.60	Mike Kilkenny			
□ 506 Paul Blair	.30	.12	.03	Ron Woods			
□ 507 Cookie Rojas	.21	.09	.02	□ 545 Willie Stargell	3.50	1.40	.35
□ 508 Moe Drabowsky	.21	.09	.02	□ 546 Jim Nash	.25	.10	.02
□ 509 Manny Sanguillen	.35	.14	.03	□ 547 Billy Martin MGR	1.00	.40	.10
□ 510 Rod Carew	20.00	8.00	2.00	□ 548 Bob Locker	.25	.10	.02
□ 511 A Diego Segui	.35	.14	.03	□ 549 Ron Brand	.25	.10	.02
□ 511 B Diego Segui WL	6.50	2.40	.60	□ 550 Brooks Robinson	6.50	2.60	.65
□ 512 Cleon Jones	.21	.09	.02	□ 551 Wayne Granger	.25	.10	.02
□ 513 Camilo Pascual	.30	.12	.03	□ 552 Dodgers Rookies	.40	.16	.04
□ 514 Mike Lum	.25	.10	.02	Ted Sizemore			
□ 515 Dick Green	.25	.10	.02	Bill Sudakis			
□ 516 Earl Weaver MGR	2.00	.80	.20	□ 553 Ron Davis	.25	.10	.02
□ 517 Mike McCormick	.35	.14	.03	□ 554 Frank Bertaina	.25	.10	.02
□ 518 Fred Whitfield	.25	.10	.02	□ 555 Jim Ray Hart	.35	.14	.03
□ 519 Yankees Rookies	.25	.10	.02	□ 556 A's Stars	.45	.18	.04
Gerry Kenney				Sal Bando			
Len Boehmer				Bert Campaneris			
□ 520 Bob Veale	.35	.14	.03	Danny Cater			
□ 521 George Thomas	.25	.10	.02	□ 557 Frank Fernandez	.25	.10	.02

		MINT	VG-E	F-G
☐ 558	Tom Burgmeier	.35	.14	.03
☐ 559	Cardinals Rookies	.25	.10	.02
	Joe Hague			
	Jim Hicks			
☐ 560	Luis Tiant	.75	.30	.07
☐ 561	Ron Clark	.25	.10	.02
☐ 562	Bob Watson	1.00	.40	.10
☐ 563	Martin Pattin	.35	.14	.03
☐ 564	Gil Hodges MGR	2.50	1.00	.25
☐ 565	Hoyt Wilhelm	3.00	1.20	.30
☐ 566	Ron Hansen	.25	.10	.02
☐ 567	Pirates Rookies	.25	.10	.02
	Elvio Jimenez			
	Jim Shellenback			
☐ 568	Cecil Upshaw	.25	.10	.02
☐ 569	Billy Harris	.25	.10	.02
☐ 570	Ron Santo	.65	.26	.06
☐ 571	Cap Peterson	.25	.10	.02
☐ 572	Giants Heroes	4.00	1.60	.40
	Willie McCovey			
	Juan Marichal			
☐ 573	Jim Palmer	6.50	2.60	.65
☐ 574	George Scott	.35	.14	.03
☐ 575	Bill Singer	.25	.10	.02
☐ 576	Phillies Rookies	.25	.10	.02
	Ron Stone			
	Bill Wilson			
☐ 577	Mike Hegan	.30	.12	.03
☐ 578	Don Bosch	.25	.10	.02
☐ 579	Dave Nelson	.25	.10	.02
☐ 580	Jim Northrup	.35	.14	.03
☐ 581	Gary Nolan	.25	.10	.02
☐ 582 A	Checklist 7	1.75	.15	.03
	(white circle on back)			
	(Tony Oliva)			
☐ 582 B	Checklist 7	3.50	.35	.07
	(red circle on back)			
	(Tony Oliva)			
☐ 583	Clyde Wright	.25	.10	.02
☐ 584	Don Mason	.25	.10	.02
☐ 585	Ron Swoboda	.35	.14	.03
☐ 586	Tim Cullen	.25	.10	.02
☐ 587	Joe Rudi	.75	.30	.07
☐ 588	Bill White	.45	.18	.04
☐ 589	Joe Pepitone	.45	.18	.04
☐ 590	Rico Carty	.45	.18	.04
☐ 591	Mike Hedlund	.25	.10	.02
☐ 592	Padres Rookies	.25	.10	.02
	Rafael Robles			
	Al Santorini			
☐ 593	Don Nottebart	.25	.10	.02
☐ 594	Dooley Womack	.25	.10	.02
☐ 595	Lee Maye	.25	.10	.02

		MINT	VG-E	F-G
☐ 596	Chuck Hartenstein	.25	.10	.02
☐ 597	AL Rookies	10.00	4.00	1.00
	Bob Floyd			
	Larry Burchart			
	Rollie Fingers			
☐ 598	Ruben Amaro	.25	.10	.02
☐ 599	John Boozer	.25	.10	.02
☐ 600	Tony Oliva	1.00	.40	.10
☐ 601	Tug McGraw	1.00	.40	.10
☐ 602	Cubs Rookies	.25	.10	.02
	Alec Distaso			
	Don Young			
	Jim Qualls			
☐ 603	Joe Keough	.25	.10	.02
☐ 604	Bobby Etheridge	.25	.10	.02
☐ 605	Dick Ellsworth	.25	.10	.02
☐ 606	Gene Mauch MGR	.35	.14	.03
☐ 607	Dick Bosman	.25	.10	.02
☐ 608	Dick Simpson	.25	.10	.02
☐ 609	Phil Gagliano	.25	.10	.02
☐ 610	Jim Hardin	.25	.10	.02
☐ 611	Braves Rookies	.25	.10	.02
	Bob Didier			
	Walt Hriniak			
	Gary Neibauer			
☐ 612	Jack Aker	.35	.14	.03
☐ 613	Jim Beauchamp	.25	.10	.02
☐ 614	Houston Rookies	.25	.10	.02
	Tom Griffin			
	Skip Guinn			
☐ 615	Len Gabrielson	.25	.10	.02
☐ 616	Don McMahon	.25	.10	.02
☐ 617	Jesse Gonder	.25	.10	.02
☐ 618	Ramon Webster	.25	.10	.02
☐ 619	Royals Rookies	.40	.16	.04
	Bill Butler			
	Pat Kelly			
	Juan Rios			
☐ 620	Dean Chance	.35	.14	.03
☐ 621	Bill Voss	.25	.10	.02
☐ 622	Dan Osinski	.25	.10	.02
☐ 623	Hank Allen	.25	.10	.02
☐ 624	NL Rookies	.35	.14	.03
	Darrel Chaney			
	Duffy Dyer			
	Terry Harmon			
☐ 625	Mack Jones	.35	.14	.03
	(Batting wrong)			
☐ 626	Gene Michael	.35	.14	.03
☐ 627	George Stone	.25	.10	.02

		MINT	VG-E	F-G
☐ 628	Red Sox Rookies	.35	.14	.03
	Bill Conigliaro			
	Syd O'Brien			
	Fred Wenz			
☐ 629	Jack Hamilton	.25	.10	.02
☐ 630	Bobby Bonds	2.00	.80	.20
☐ 631	John Kennedy	.30	.12	.03
☐ 632	Jon Warden	.25	.10	.02
☐ 633	Harry Walker MGR	.25	.10	.02
☐ 634	Andy Etchebarren	.25	.10	.02
☐ 635	George Culver	.25	.10	.02
☐ 636	Woodie Held	.25	.10	.02
☐ 637	Padres Rookies	.25	.10	.02
	Jerry DaVanon			
	Frank Reberger			
	Clay Kirby			
☐ 638	Ed Sprague	.25	.10	.02
☐ 639	Barry Moore	.25	.10	.02
☐ 640	Fergie Jenkins	1.50	.60	.15
☐ 641	NL Rookies	.25	.10	.02
	Bobby Darwin			
	John Miller			
	Tommy Dean			
☐ 642	John Hiller	.35	.14	.03
☐ 643	Billy Cowan	.25	.10	.02
☐ 644	Chuck Hinton	.25	.10	.02
☐ 645	George Brunet	.25	.10	.02
☐ 646	Expos Rookies	.25	.10	.02
	Dan McGinn			
	Carl Morton			
☐ 647	Dave Wickersham	.25	.10	.02
☐ 648	Bobby Wine	.25	.10	.02
☐ 649	Al Jackson	.25	.10	.02
☐ 650	Ted Williams MGR	3.50	1.40	.35
☐ 651	Gus Gil	.30	.12	.03
☐ 652	Eddie Watt	.25	.10	.02
☐ 653	Aurelio Rodriguez	1.25	.50	.12
	(photo actually			
	Angels' batboy)			
☐ 654	White Sox Rookies	.45	.18	.04
	Carlos May			
	Don Secrist			
	Rich Morales			
☐ 655	Mike Hershberger	.25	.10	.02
☐ 656	Dan Schneider	.25	.10	.02
☐ 657	Bobby Murcer	.80	.32	.08
☐ 658	AL Rookies	.25	.10	.02
	Tom Hall			
	Bill Burbach			
	Jim Miles			
☐ 659	Johnny Podres	.55	.22	.05
☐ 660	Reggie Smith	.85	.34	.08
☐ 661	Jim Merritt	.25	.10	.02

		MINT	VG-E	F-G
☐ 662	Royals Rookies	.35	.14	.03
	Dick Drago			
	George Spriggs			
	Bob Oliver			
☐ 663	Dick Radatz	.35	.14	.03
☐ 664	Ron Hunt	.60	.24	.06

1970 Topps

The cards in this 720-card set measure 2½" by 3½". The Topps set for 1970 has color photos surrounded by white frame lines and gray borders. The backs have a blue biographical section and a yellow record section. All-Star selections are featured on cards 450 to 469. Other topical subsets within this set include League Leaders (61-72), Playoffs cards (195-202), and World Series cards (305-310). There are graduations of scarcity, terminating in the high series (634-720), which are outlined in the value summary.

	MINT	VG-E	F-G
Complete Set	600.00	240.00	60.00
Common Player (1-132)	.16	.07	.01
Common Player (133-459)	.20	.08	.02
Common Player (460-546)	.25	.10	.02
Common Player (547-633)	.40	.16	.04
Common Player (634-720)	1.00	.40	.10

		MINT	VG-E	F-G
☐ 1	New York Mets	2.50	.50	.10
	Team Card			
☐ 2	Diego Segui	.20	.08	.02

		MINT	VG-E	F-G
☐	3 Darrel Chaney	.16	.07	.01
☐	4 Tom Egan	.16	.07	.01
☐	5 Wes Parker	.25	.10	.02
☐	6 Grant Jackson	.16	.07	.01
☐	7 Indians Rookies	.16	.07	.01
	Gary Boyd			
	Russ Nagelson			
☐	8 Jose Martinez	.16	.07	.01
☐	9 Checklist 1	1.25	.12	.02
☐	10 Carl Yastrzemski	15.00	6.00	1.50
☐	11 Nate Colbert	.16	.07	.01
☐	12 John Hiller	.20	.08	.02
☐	13 Jack Hiatt	.16	.07	.01
☐	14 Hank Allen	.16	.07	.01
☐	15 Larry Dierker	.20	.08	.02
☐	16 Charlie Metro MGR	.16	.07	.01
☐	17 Hoyt Wilhelm	2.25	.90	.22
☐	18 Carlos May	.20	.08	.02
☐	19 John Boccabella	.16	.07	.01
☐	20 Dave McNally	.30	.12	.03
☐	21 A's Rookies	1.75	.70	.17
	Vida Blue			
	Gene Tenace			
☐	22 Ray Washburn	.16	.07	.01
☐	23 Bill Robinson	.16	.07	.01
☐	24 Dick Selma	.16	.07	.01
☐	25 Cesar Tovar	.16	.07	.01
☐	26 Tug McGraw	.60	.24	.06
☐	27 Chuck Hinton	.16	.07	.01
☐	28 Billy Wilson	.16	.07	.01
☐	29 Sandy Alomar	.16	.07	.01
☐	30 Matty Alou	.25	.10	.02
☐	31 Marty Pattin	.20	.08	.02
☐	32 Harry Walker MGR	.16	.07	.01
☐	33 Don Wert	.16	.07	.01
☐	34 Willie Crawford	.16	.07	.01
☐	35 Joe Horlen	.16	.07	.01
☐	36 Red Rookies	.16	.07	.01
	Danny Breeden			
	Bernie Carbo			
☐	37 Dick Drago	.16	.07	.01
☐	38 Mack Jones	.16	.07	.01
☐	39 Mike Nagy	.16	.07	.01
☐	40 Rich Allen	.60	.24	.06
☐	41 George Lauzerique	.16	.07	.01
☐	42 Tito Fuentes	.16	.07	.01
☐	43 Jack Aker	.16	.07	.01
☐	44 Roberto Pena	.16	.07	.01
☐	45 Dave Johnson	.35	.14	.03
☐	46 Ken Rudolph	.16	.07	.01
☐	47 Bob Miller	.16	.07	.01
☐	48 Gil Garrido	.16	.07	.01
☐	49 Tim Cullen	.16	.07	.01

		MINT	VG-E	F-G
☐	50 Tommie Agee	.20	.08	.02
☐	51 Bob Christian	.16	.07	.01
☐	52 Bruce Dal Canton	.16	.07	.01
☐	53 John Kennedy	.20	.08	.02
☐	54 Jeff Torborg	.16	.07	.01
☐	55 John Odom	.16	.07	.01
☐	56 Phillies Rookies	.16	.07	.01
	Joe Lis			
	Scott Reid			
☐	57 Pat Kelly	.16	.07	.01
☐	58 Dave Marshall	.16	.07	.01
☐	59 Dick Ellsworth	.16	.07	.01
☐	60 Jim Wynn	.25	.10	.02
☐	61 NL Batting Leaders	2.00	.80	.20
	Pete Rose			
	Bob Clemente			
	Cleon Jones			
☐	62 AL Batting Leaders	1.00	.40	.10
	Rod Carew			
	Reggie Smith			
	Tony Oliva			
☐	63 NL RBI Leaders	.80	.32	.08
	Willie McCovey			
	Ron Santo			
	Tony Perez			
☐	64 AL RBI Leaders	1.00	.40	.10
	Harmon Killebrew			
	Boog Powell			
	Reggie Jackson			
☐	65 NL Home Run Leaders	1.25	.50	.12
	Willie McCovey			
	Hank Aaron			
	Lee May			
☐	66 AL Home Run Leaders	1.25	.50	.12
	Harmon Killebrew			
	Frank Howard			
	Reggie Jackson			
☐	67 NL ERA Leaders	2.00	.80	.20
	Juan Marichal			
	Steve Carlton			
	Bob Gibson			
☐	68 AL ERA Leaders	.70	.28	.07
	Dick Bosman			
	Jim Palmer			
	Mike Cuellar			
☐	69 NL Pitching Leaders	2.00	.80	.20
	Tom Seaver			
	Phil Niekro			
	Fergie Jenkins			
	Juan Marichal			

			MINT	VG-E	F-G
☐	70	AL Pitching Leaders	.50	.20	.05
		Dennis McLain			
		Mike Cuellar			
		Dave Boswell			
		Dave McNally			
		Jim Perry			
		Mel Stottlemyre			
☐	71	NL Strikeout Leaders ...	.75	.30	.07
		Fergie Jenkins			
		Bob Gibson			
		Bill Singer			
☐	72	AL Strikeout Leaders ...	.50	.20	.05
		Sam McDowell			
		Mickey Lolich			
		Andy Messersmith			
☐	73	Wayne Granger	.16	.07	.01
☐	74	Angels Rookies	.16	.07	.01
		Greg Washburn			
		Wally Wolf			
☐	75	Jim Kaat	1.00	.40	.10
☐	76	Carl Taylor	.16	.07	.01
☐	77	Frank Linzy	.16	.07	.01
☐	78	Joe Lahoud	.16	.07	.01
☐	79	Clay Kirby	.16	.07	.01
☐	80	Don Kessinger	.25	.10	.02
☐	81	Dave May	.16	.07	.01
☐	82	Frank Fernandez	.16	.07	.01
☐	83	Don Cardwell	.16	.07	.01
☐	84	Paul Casanova	.16	.07	.01
☐	85	Max Alvis	.16	.07	.01
☐	86	Lum Harris MGR	.16	.07	.01
☐	87	Steve Renko	.16	.07	.01
☐	88	Pilots Rookies	.20	.08	.02
		Miguel Fuentes			
		Dick Baney			
☐	89	Juan Rios	.16	.07	.01
☐	90	Tim McCarver	.35	.14	.03
☐	91	Rich Morales	.16	.07	.01
☐	92	George Culver	.16	.07	.01
☐	93	Rick Renick	.16	.07	.01
☐	94	Fred Patek	.20	.08	.02
☐	95	Earl Wilson	.16	.07	.01
☐	96	Cardinals Rookies	1.50	.60	.15
		Leron Lee			
		Jerry Reuss			
☐	97	Joe Moeller	.16	.07	.01
☐	98	Gates Brown	.20	.08	.02
☐	99	Bobby Pfeil	.16	.07	.01
☐	100	Mel Stottlemyre	.25	.10	.02
☐	101	Bobby Floyd	.16	.07	.01
☐	102	Joe Rudi	.30	.12	.03
☐	103	Frank Reberger	.16	.07	.01
☐	104	Gerry Moses	.16	.07	.01

			MINT	VG-E	F-G
☐	105	Tony Gonzalez	.16	.07	.01
☐	106	Darold Knowles	.16	.07	.01
☐	107	Bobby Etheridge	.16	.07	.01
☐	108	Tom Burgmeier	.20	.08	.02
☐	109	Expos Rookies	.25	.10	.02
		Garry Jestadt			
		Carl Morton			
☐	110	Bob Moose	.16	.07	.01
☐	111	Mike Hegan	.20	.08	.02
☐	112	Dave Nelson	.16	.07	.01
☐	113	Jim Ray	.16	.07	.01
☐	114	Gene Michael	.25	.10	.02
☐	115	Alex Johnson	.20	.08	.02
☐	116	Sparky Lyle	.55	.22	.05
☐	117	Don Young	.16	.07	.01
☐	118	George Mitterwald	.16	.07	.01
☐	119	Chuck Taylor	.16	.07	.01
☐	120	Sal Bando	.40	.16	.04
☐	121	Orioles Rookies	.20	.08	.02
		Fred Beene			
		Terry Crowley			
☐	122	George Stone	.16	.07	.01
☐	123	Don Gutteridge	.16	.07	.01
☐	124	Larry Jaster	.16	.07	.01
☐	125	Deron Johnson	.16	.07	.01
☐	126	Marty Martinez	.16	.07	.01
☐	127	Joe Coleman	.16	.07	.01
☐	128	Checklist 2	1.25	.12	.02
☐	129	Jimmie Price	.16	.07	.01
☐	130	Ollie Brown	.16	.07	.01
☐	131	Dodgers Rookies	.16	.07	.01
		Ray Lamb			
		Bob Stinson			
☐	132	Jim McGlothlin	.16	.07	.01
☐	133	Clay Carroll	.20	.08	.02
☐	134	Danny Walton	.25	.10	.02
☐	135	Dick Dietz	.20	.08	.02
☐	136	Steve Hargan	.20	.08	.02
☐	137	Art Shamsky	.20	.08	.02
☐	138	Joe Foy	.20	.08	.02
☐	139	Rich Nye	.20	.08	.02
☐	140	Reggie Jackson	25.00	10.00	2.50
☐	141	Pirates Rookies	.30	.12	.03
		Dave Cash			
		Johnny Jeter			
☐	142	Fritz Peterson	.20	.08	.02
☐	143	Phil Gagliano	.20	.08	.02
☐	144	Ray Culp	.20	.08	.02
☐	145	Rico Carty	.40	.16	.04
☐	146	Danny Murphy	.20	.08	.02
☐	147	Angel Hermoso	.20	.08	.02
☐	148	Earl Weaver MGR	.75	.30	.07
☐	149	Billy Champion	.20	.08	.02

	MINT	VG-E	F-G
☐ 150 Harmon Killebrew	3.25	1.30	.32
☐ 151 Dave Roberts	.20	.08	.02
☐ 152 Ike Brown	.20	.08	.02
☐ 153 Gary Gentry	.20	.08	.02
☐ 154 Senators Rookies	.20	.08	.02
Jim Miles			
Jan Dukes			
☐ 155 Denis Menke	.20	.08	.02
☐ 156 Eddie Fisher	.20	.08	.02
☐ 157 Manny Mota	.30	.12	.03
☐ 158 Jerry McNertney	.25	.10	.02
☐ 159 Tommy Helms	.25	.10	.02
☐ 160 Phil Niekro	2.00	.80	.20
☐ 161 Richie Scheinblum	.20	.08	.02
☐ 162 Jerry Johnson	.20	.08	.02
☐ 163 Syd O'Brien	.20	.08	.02
☐ 164 Ty Cline	.20	.08	.02
☐ 165 Ed Kirkpatrick	.20	.08	.02
☐ 166 Al Oliver	1.50	.60	.15
☐ 167 Bill Burbach	.20	.08	.02
☐ 168 Dave Watkins	.20	.08	.02
☐ 169 Tom Hall	.20	.08	.02
☐ 170 Billy Williams	2.50	1.00	.25
☐ 171 Jim Nash	.20	.08	.02
☐ 172 Braves Rookies	.75	.30	.07
Garry Hill			
Ralph Garr			
☐ 173 Jim Hicks	.20	.08	.02
☐ 174 Ted Sizemore	.20	.08	.02
☐ 175 Dick Bosman	.20	.08	.02
☐ 176 Jim Ray Hart	.25	.10	.02
☐ 177 Jim Northrup	.25	.10	.02
☐ 178 Denny Lemaster	.20	.08	.02
☐ 179 Ivan Murrell	.20	.08	.02
☐ 180 Tommy John	1.25	.50	.12
☐ 181 Sparky Anderson MGR	.50	.20	.05
☐ 182 Dick Hall	.20	.08	.02
☐ 183 Jerry Grote	.20	.08	.02
☐ 184 Ray Fosse	.20	.08	.02
☐ 185 Don Mincher	.25	.10	.02
☐ 186 Rick Joseph	.20	.08	.02
☐ 187 Mike Hedlund	.20	.08	.02
☐ 188 Manny Sanguillen	.35	.14	.03
☐ 189 Yankees Rookies	21.00	8.50	2.10
Thurman Munson			
Dave McDonald			
☐ 190 Joe Torre	.60	.24	.06
☐ 191 Vicente Romo	.20	.08	.02
☐ 192 Jim Qualls	.20	.08	.02
☐ 193 Mike Wegener	.20	.08	.02
☐ 194 Chuck Manuel	.20	.08	.02
☐ 195 NL Playoff Game 1	1.50	.60	.15
Seaver wins opener			
☐ 196 NL Playoff Game 2	.75	.30	.07
Mets show muscle			
☐ 197 NL Playoff Game 3	1.50	.60	.15
Ryan saves the day			
☐ 198 NL Playoff Summary	.75	.30	.07
Mets celebrate			
☐ 199 AL Playoff Game 1	.75	.30	.07
Orioles win			
squeaker (Cuellar)			
☐ 200 AL Playoff Game 2	.75	.30	.07
Powell scores			
winning run			
☐ 201 AL Playoff Game 3	.75	.30	.07
Birds wrap it up			
☐ 202 AL Playoff Summary	.75	.30	.07
Orioles celebrate			
☐ 203 Rudy May	.20	.08	.02
☐ 204 Len Gabrielson	.20	.08	.02
☐ 205 Bert Campaneris	.35	.14	.03
☐ 206 Clete Boyer	.35	.14	.03
☐ 207 Tigers Rookies	.20	.08	.02
Norman McRae			
Bob Reed			
☐ 208 Fred Gladding	.20	.08	.02
☐ 209 Ken Suarez	.20	.08	.02
☐ 210 Juan Marichal	2.50	1.00	.25
☐ 211 Ted Williams MGR	3.00	1.20	.30
☐ 212 Al Santorini	.20	.08	.02
☐ 213 Andy Etchebarren	.20	.08	.02
☐ 214 Ken Boswell	.20	.08	.02
☐ 215 Reggie Smith	.75	.30	.07
☐ 216 Chuck Hartenstein	.20	.08	.02
☐ 217 Ron Hansen	.20	.08	.02
☐ 218 Ron Stone	.20	.08	.02
☐ 219 Jerry Kenney	.20	.08	.02
☐ 220 Steve Carlton	10.00	4.00	1.00
☐ 221 Ron Brand	.20	.08	.02
☐ 222 Jim Rooker	.20	.08	.02
☐ 223 Nate Oliver	.20	.08	.02
☐ 224 Steve Barber	.25	.10	.02
☐ 225 Lee May	.35	.14	.03
☐ 226 Ron Perranoski	.30	.12	.03
☐ 227 Astros Rookies	.60	.24	.06
John Mayberry			
Bob Watkins			
☐ 228 Aurelio Rodriguez	.25	.10	.02
☐ 229 Rich Robertson	.20	.08	.02
☐ 230 Brooks Robinson	4.00	1.60	.40
☐ 231 Luis Tiant	.55	.22	.05
☐ 232 Bob Didier	.20	.08	.02
☐ 233 Lew Krausse	.20	.08	.02
☐ 234 Tommy Dean	.20	.08	.02

	MINT	VG-E	F-G
☐ 235 Mike Epstein	.20	.08	.02
☐ 236 Bob Veale	.25	.10	.02
☐ 237 Russ Gibson	.20	.08	.02
☐ 238 Jose Laboy	.20	.08	.02
☐ 239 Ken Berry	.20	.08	.02
☐ 240 Fergie Jenkins	1.00	.40	.10
☐ 241 Royals Rookies	.20	.08	.02
Al Fitzmorris			
Scott Northey			
☐ 242 Walter Alston MGR	.75	.30	.07
☐ 243 Joe Sparma	.20	.08	.02
☐ 244 A Checklist 3	1.25	.12	.02
(red bat on front)			
☐ 244 B Checklist 3	1.50	.15	.03
(brown bat on front)			
☐ 245 Leo Cardenas	.20	.08	.02
☐ 246 Jim McAndrew	.20	.08	.02
☐ 247 Lou Klimchock	.20	.08	.02
☐ 248 Jesus Alou	.20	.08	.02
☐ 249 Bob Locker	.25	.10	.02
☐ 250 Willie McCovey	3.50	1.40	.35
☐ 251 Dick Schofield	.20	.08	.02
☐ 252 Lowell Palmer	.20	.08	.02
☐ 253 Ron Woods	.20	.08	.02
☐ 254 Camilo Pascual	.25	.10	.02
☐ 255 Jim Spencer	.20	.08	.02
☐ 256 Vic Davalillo	.20	.08	.02
☐ 257 Dennis Higgins	.20	.08	.02
☐ 258 Paul Popovich	.20	.08	.02
☐ 259 Tommie Reynolds	.20	.08	.02
☐ 260 Claude Osteen	.25	.10	.02
☐ 261 Curt Motton	.20	.08	.02
☐ 262 Twins Rookies	.20	.08	.02
Jerry Morales			
Jim Williams			
☐ 263 Duane Josephson	.20	.08	.02
☐ 264 Rich Hebner	.25	.10	.02
☐ 265 Randy Hundley	.25	.10	.02
☐ 266 Wally Bunker	.20	.08	.02
☐ 267 Twins Rookies	.20	.08	.02
Herman Hill			
Paul Ratliff			
☐ 268 Claude Raymond	.20	.08	.02
☐ 269 Cesar Gutierrez	.20	.08	.02
☐ 270 Chris Short	.20	.08	.02
☐ 271 Greg Goossen	.25	.10	.02
☐ 272 Hector Torres	.20	.08	.02
☐ 273 Ralph Houk MGR	.35	.14	.03
☐ 274 Gerry Arrigo	.20	.08	.02
☐ 275 Duke Sims	.20	.08	.02
☐ 276 Ron Hunt	.20	.08	.02
☐ 277 Paul Doyle	.20	.08	.02
☐ 278 Tommie Aaron	.30	.12	.03
☐ 279 Bill Lee	.30	.12	.03
☐ 280 Donn Clendenon	.30	.12	.03
☐ 281 Casey Cox	.20	.08	.02
☐ 282 Steve Huntz	.20	.08	.02
☐ 283 Angel Bravo	.20	.08	.02
☐ 284 Jack Baldschun	.20	.08	.02
☐ 285 Paul Blair	.25	.10	.02
☐ 286 Dodgers Rookies	5.00	2.00	.50
Jack Jenkins			
Bill Buckner			
☐ 287 Fred Talbot	.20	.08	.02
☐ 288 Larry Hisle	.30	.12	.03
☐ 289 Gene Brabender	.25	.10	.02
☐ 290 Rod Carew	11.00	4.50	1.10
☐ 291 Leo Durocher MGR	.60	.24	.06
☐ 292 Eddie Leon	.20	.08	.02
☐ 293 Bob Bailey	.20	.08	.02
☐ 294 Jose Azcue	.20	.08	.02
☐ 295 Cecil Upshaw	.20	.08	.02
☐ 296 Woody Woodward	.20	.08	.02
☐ 297 Curt Blefary	.20	.08	.02
☐ 298 Ken Henderson	.20	.08	.02
☐ 299 Buddy Bradford	.20	.08	.02
☐ 300 Tom Seaver	15.00	6.00	1.50
☐ 301 Chico Salmon	.20	.08	.02
☐ 302 Jeff James	.20	.08	.02
☐ 303 Brant Alyea	.20	.08	.02
☐ 304 Bill Russell	1.50	.60	.15
☐ 305 World Series Game 1	.75	.30	.07
Buford leadoff homer			
☐ 306 World Series Game 2	.75	.30	.07
Clendenon's homer			
breaks ice			
☐ 307 World Series Game 3	.75	.30	.07
Agee's catch			
saves the day			
☐ 308 World Series Game 4	.75	.30	.07
Martin's bunt			
ends deadlock			
☐ 309 World Series Game 5	.75	.30	.07
Koosman shuts door			
☐ 310 World Series Summary	.75	.30	.07
Mets whoop it up			
☐ 311 Dick Green	.20	.08	.02
☐ 312 Mike Torrez	.35	.14	.03
☐ 313 Mayo Smith MGR	.20	.08	.02
☐ 314 Bill McCool	.20	.08	.02
☐ 315 Luis Aparicio	2.25	.90	.22
☐ 316 Skip Guinn	.20	.08	.02
☐ 317 Red Sox Rookies	.30	.12	.03
Billy Conigliaro			
Luis Alvarado			
☐ 318 Willie Smith	.20	.08	.02

		MINT	VG-E	F-G			MINT	VG-E	F-G
☐ 319	Clay Dalrymple	.20	.08	.02	☐ 367	Mike Lum	.20	.08	.02
☐ 320	Jim Maloney	.25	.10	.02	☐ 368	Ed Herrmann	.20	.08	.02
☐ 321	Lou Piniella	.80	.32	.08	☐ 369	Alan Foster	.20	.08	.02
☐ 322	Luke Walker	.20	.08	.02	☐ 370	Tommy Harper	.25	.10	.02
☐ 323	Wayne Comer	.25	.10	.02	☐ 371	Rod Gaspar	.20	.08	.02
☐ 324	Tony Taylor	.20	.08	.02	☐ 372	Dave Giusti	.20	.08	.02
☐ 325	Dave Boswell	.20	.08	.02	☐ 373	Roy White	.30	.12	.03
☐ 326	Bill Voss	.20	.08	.02	☐ 374	Tommie Sisk	.20	.08	.02
☐ 327	Hal King	.20	.08	.02	☐ 375	Johnny Callison	.25	.10	.02
☐ 328	George Brunet	.20	.08	.02	☐ 376	Lefty Phillips MGR	.20	.08	.02
☐ 329	Chris Cannizzaro	.20	.08	.02	☐ 377	Bill Butler	.20	.08	.02
☐ 330	Lou Brock	3.50	1.40	.35	☐ 378	Jim Davenport	.30	.12	.03
☐ 331	Chuck Dobson	.20	.08	.02	☐ 379	Tom Tischinski	.20	.08	.02
☐ 332	Bobby Wine	.20	.08	.02	☐ 380	Tony Perez	1.25	.50	.12
☐ 333	Bobby Murcer	.70	.28	.07	☐ 381	Athletics Rookies	.20	.08	.02
☐ 334	Phil Regan	.25	.10	.02		Bobby Brooks			
☐ 335	Bill Freehan	.40	.16	.04		Mike Olivo			
☐ 336	Del Unser	.20	.08	.02	☐ 382	Jack DiLauro	.20	.08	.02
☐ 337	Mike McCormick	.30	.12	.03	☐ 383	Mickey Stanley	.25	.10	.02
☐ 338	Paul Schaal	.20	.08	.02	☐ 384	Gary Neibauer	.20	.08	.02
☐ 339	Johnny Edwards	.20	.08	.02	☐ 385	George Scott	.25	.10	.02
☐ 340	Tony Conigliaro	.45	.18	.04	☐ 386	Bill Dillman	.20	.08	.02
☐ 341	Bill Sudakis	.20	.08	.02	☐ 387	Orioles Team	.70	.28	.07
☐ 342	Wilbur Wood	.25	.10	.02	☐ 388	Byron Browne	.20	.08	.02
☐ 343 A	Checklist 4	1.25	.12	.02	☐ 389	Jim Shellenback	.20	.08	.02
	(red bat on front)				☐ 390	Willie Davis	.40	.16	.04
☐ 343 B	Checklist 4	1.50	.15	.03	☐ 391	Larry Brown	.20	.08	.02
	(brown bat on front)				☐ 392	Walt Hriniak	.20	.08	.02
☐ 344	Marcelino Lopez	.20	.08	.02	☐ 393	John Gelnar	.25	.10	.02
☐ 345	Al Ferrara	.20	.08	.02	☐ 394	Gil Hodges MGR	2.00	.80	.20
☐ 346	Red Schoendienst MGR	.40	.16	.04	☐ 395	Walt Williams	.20	.08	.02
☐ 347	Russ Snyder	.20	.08	.02	☐ 396	Steve Blass	.25	.10	.02
☐ 348	Mets Rookies	.25	.10	.02	☐ 397	Roger Repoz	.20	.08	.02
	Mike Jorgensen				☐ 398	Bill Stoneman	.20	.08	.02
	Jesse Hudson				☐ 399	Yankees Team	.75	.30	.07
☐ 349	Steve Hamilton	.20	.08	.02	☐ 400	Denny McLain	.65	.26	.06
☐ 350	Roberto Clemente	12.00	5.00	1.20	☐ 401	Giants Rookies	.20	.08	.02
☐ 351	Tom Murphy	.20	.08	.02		John Harrell			
☐ 352	Bob Barton	.20	.08	.02		Bernie Williams			
☐ 353	Stan Williams	.20	.08	.02	☐ 402	Ellie Rodriguez	.20	.08	.02
☐ 354	Amos Otis	.35	.14	.03	☐ 403	Jim Bunning	1.00	.40	.10
☐ 355	Doug Rader	.30	.12	.03	☐ 404	Rich Reese	.20	.08	.02
☐ 356	Fred Lasher	.20	.08	.02	☐ 405	Bill Hands	.20	.08	.02
☐ 357	Bob Burda	.20	.08	.02	☐ 406	Mike Andrews	.20	.08	.02
☐ 358	Pedro Borbon	.20	.08	.02	☐ 407	Bob Watson	.40	.16	.04
☐ 359	Phil Roof	.25	.10	.02	☐ 408	Paul Lindblad	.20	.08	.02
☐ 360	Curt Flood	.40	.16	.04	☐ 409	Bob Tolan	.20	.08	.02
☐ 361	Ray Jarvis	.20	.08	.02	☐ 410	Boog Powell	1.25	.50	.12
☐ 362	Joe Hague	.20	.08	.02	☐ 411	Dodgers Team	.75	.30	.07
☐ 363	Tom Shopay	.20	.08	.02	☐ 412	Larry Burchart	.20	.08	.02
☐ 364	Dan McGinn	.20	.08	.02	☐ 413	Sonny Jackson	.20	.08	.02
☐ 365	Zoilo Versalles	.20	.08	.02	☐ 414	Paul Edmondson	.20	.08	.02
☐ 366	Barry Moore	.20	.08	.02	☐ 415	Julian Javier	.20	.08	.02

		MINT	VG-E	F-G
☐ 416	Joe Verbanic	.20	.08	.02
☐ 417	John Bateman	.20	.08	.02
☐ 418	John Donaldson	.25	.10	.02
☐ 419	Ron Taylor	.20	.08	.02
☐ 420	Ken McMullen	.20	.08	.02
☐ 421	Pat Dobson	.25	.10	.02
☐ 422	Royals Team	.55	.22	.05
☐ 423	Jerry May	.20	.08	.02
☐ 424	Mike Kilkenny	.20	.08	.02
☐ 425	Bobby Bonds	.75	.30	.07
☐ 426	Bill Rigney MGR	.20	.08	.02
☐ 427	Fred Norman	.20	.08	.02
☐ 428	Don Buford	.20	.08	.02
☐ 429	Cubs Rookies	.20	.08	.02
	Randy Bobb			
	Jim Cosman			
☐ 430	Andy Messersmith	.45	.18	.04
☐ 431	Ron Swoboda	.25	.10	.02
☐ 432	A Checklist 5	1.25	.12	.02
	("*Baseball*" in			
	yellow letters)			
☐ 432	B Checklist 5	1.50	.15	.03
	("*Baseball*" in			
	white letters)			
☐ 433	Ron Bryant	.20	.08	.02
☐ 434	Felipe Alou	.25	.10	.02
☐ 435	Nelson Briles	.25	.10	.02
☐ 436	Phillies Team	.55	.22	.05
☐ 437	Danny Cater	.20	.08	.02
☐ 438	Pat Jarvis	.20	.08	.02
☐ 439	Lee Maye	.20	.08	.02
☐ 440	Bill Mazeroski	.50	.20	.05
☐ 441	John O'Donoghue	.25	.10	.02
☐ 442	Gene Mauch MGR	.30	.12	.03
☐ 443	Al Jackson	.20	.08	.02
☐ 444	White Sox Rookies	.20	.08	.02
	Billy Farmer			
	John Matias			
☐ 445	Vada Pinson	.60	.24	.06
☐ 446	Billy Grabarkewitz	.20	.08	.02
☐ 447	Lee Stange	.20	.08	.02
☐ 448	Astros Team	.55	.22	.05
☐ 449	Jim Palmer	6.00	2.40	.60
☐ 450	Willie McCovey AS	2.00	.80	.20
☐ 451	Boog Powell AS	.45	.18	.04
☐ 452	Felix Millan AS	.25	.10	.02
☐ 453	Rod Carew AS	3.00	1.20	.30
☐ 454	Ron Santo AS	.25	.10	.02
☐ 455	Brooks Robinson AS	2.25	.90	.22
☐ 456	Don Kessinger AS	.25	.10	.02
☐ 457	Rico Petrocelli AS	.25	.10	.02
☐ 458	Pete Rose AS	6.50	2.60	.65
☐ 459	Reggie Jackson AS	4.50	1.80	.45

		MINT	VG-E	F-G
☐ 460	Matty Alou AS	.25	.10	.02
☐ 461	Carl Yastrzemski AS	3.50	1.40	.35
☐ 462	Hank Aaron AS	3.50	1.40	.35
☐ 463	Frank Robinson AS	2.00	.80	.20
☐ 464	Johnny Bench AS	3.25	1.30	.32
☐ 465	Bill Freehan AS	.25	.10	.02
☐ 466	Juan Marichal AS	1.75	.70	.17
☐ 467	Denny McLain AS	.35	.14	.03
☐ 468	Jerry Koosman AS	.25	.10	.02
☐ 469	Sam McDowell AS	.25	.10	.02
☐ 470	Willie Stargell	3.00	1.20	.30
☐ 471	Chris Zachary	.45	.18	.04
☐ 472	Braves Team	.60	.24	.06
☐ 473	Don Bryant	.25	.10	.02
☐ 474	Dick Kelley	.25	.10	.02
☐ 475	Dick McAuliffe	.25	.10	.02
☐ 476	Don Shaw	.25	.10	.02
☐ 477	Orioles Rookies	.25	.10	.02
	Al Severinsen			
	Roger Freed			
☐ 478	Bob Heise	.25	.10	.02
☐ 479	Dick Woodson	.25	.10	.02
☐ 480	Glen Beckert	.35	.14	.03
☐ 481	Jose Tartabull	.25	.10	.02
☐ 482	Tom Hilgendorf	.25	.10	.02
☐ 483	Gail Hopkins	.25	.10	.02
☐ 484	Gary Nolan	.25	.10	.02
☐ 485	Jay Johnstone	.35	.14	.03
☐ 486	Terry Harmon	.25	.10	.02
☐ 487	Cisco Carlos	.25	.10	.02
☐ 488	J.C. Martin	.25	.10	.02
☐ 489	Eddie Kasko MGR	.25	.10	.02
☐ 490	Bill Singer	.25	.10	.02
☐ 491	Graig Nettles	2.25	.90	.22
☐ 492	Astros Rookies	.25	.10	.02
	Keith Lampard			
	Scipio Spinks			
☐ 493	Lindy McDaniel	.25	.10	.02
☐ 494	Larry Stahl	.25	.10	.02
☐ 495	Dave Morehead	.25	.10	.02
☐ 496	Steve Whitaker	.25	.10	.02
☐ 497	Eddie Watt	.25	.10	.02
☐ 498	Al Weis	.25	.10	.02
☐ 499	Skip Lockwood	.25	.10	.02
☐ 500	Hank Aaron	14.00	5.75	1.40
☐ 501	White Sox Team	.60	.24	.06
☐ 502	Rollie Fingers	2.50	1.00	.25
☐ 503	Dal Maxvill	.25	.10	.02
☐ 504	Don Pavletich	.25	.10	.02
☐ 505	Ken Holtzman	.35	.14	.03
☐ 506	Ed Stroud	.25	.10	.02
☐ 507	Pat Corrales	.35	.14	.03
☐ 508	Joe Niekro	.45	.18	.04

		MINT	VG-E	F-G
☐ 509	Expos Team	.60	.24	.06
☐ 510	Tony Oliva	1.00	.40	.10
☐ 511	Joe Hoerner	.25	.10	.02
☐ 512	Billy Harris	.25	.10	.02
☐ 513	Preston Gomez MGR	.25	.10	.02
☐ 514	Steve Hovley	.25	.10	.02
☐ 515	Don Wilson	.25	.10	.02
☐ 516	Yankees Rookies	.25	.10	.02
	John Ellis			
	Jim Lyttle			
☐ 517	Joe Gibbon	.25	.10	.02
☐ 518	Bill Melton	.25	.10	.02
☐ 519	Don McMahon	.25	.10	.02
☐ 520	Willie Horton	.50	.20	.05
☐ 521	Cal Koonce	.25	.10	.02
☐ 522	Angels Team	.60	.24	.06
☐ 523	Jose Pena	.25	.10	.02
☐ 524	Alvin Dark MGR	.25	.10	.02
☐ 525	Jerry Adair	.25	.10	.02
☐ 526	Ron Herbel	.25	.10	.02
☐ 527	Don Bosch	.25	.10	.02
☐ 528	Elrod Hendricks	.25	.10	.02
☐ 529	Bob Aspromonte	.25	.10	.02
☐ 530	Bob Gibson	3.50	1.40	.35
☐ 531	Ron Clark	.25	.10	.02
☐ 532	Danny Murtaugh MGR	.25	.10	.02
☐ 533	Buzz Stephen	.25	.10	.02
☐ 534	Twins Team	.60	.24	.06
☐ 535	Andy Kosco	.25	.10	.02
☐ 536	Mike Kekich	.25	.10	.02
☐ 537	Joe Morgan	2.25	.90	.22
☐ 538	Bob Humphreys	.25	.10	.02
☐ 539	Phillies Rookies	2.50	1.00	.25
	Dennis Doyle			
	Larry Bowa			
☐ 540	Gary Peters	.35	.14	.03
☐ 541	Bill Heath	.25	.10	.02
☐ 542	Checklist 6	1.50	.15	.03
☐ 543	Clyde Wright	.25	.10	.02
☐ 544	Reds Team	.80	.32	.08
☐ 545	Ken Harrelson	.75	.30	.07
☐ 546	Ron Reed	.25	.10	.02
☐ 547	Rick Monday	.60	.24	.06
☐ 548	Howie Reed	.40	.16	.04
☐ 549	Cardinals Team	.90	.36	.09
☐ 550	Frank Howard	.85	.34	.08
☐ 551	Dock Ellis	.40	.16	.04
☐ 552	Royals Rookies	.40	.16	.04
	Don O'Riley			
	Dennis Paepke			
	Fred Rico			
☐ 553	Jim Lefebvre	.40	.16	.04
☐ 554	Tom Timmermann	.40	.16	.04

		MINT	VG-E	F-G
☐ 555	Orlando Cepeda	1.75	.70	.17
☐ 556	Dave Bristol MGR	.40	.16	.04
☐ 557	Ed Kranepool	.50	.20	.05
☐ 558	Vern Fuller	.40	.16	.04
☐ 559	Tommy Davis	.60	.24	.06
☐ 560	Gaylord Perry	3.50	1.40	.35
☐ 561	Tom McCraw	.40	.16	.04
☐ 562	Ted Abernathy	.40	.16	.04
☐ 563	Red Sox Team	.80	.32	.08
☐ 564	Johnny Briggs	.40	.16	.04
☐ 565	Jim Hunter	3.50	1.40	.35
☐ 566	Gene Alley	.50	.20	.05
☐ 567	Bob Oliver	.40	.16	.04
☐ 568	Stan Bahnsen	.40	.16	.04
☐ 569	Cookie Rojas	.40	.16	.04
☐ 570	Jim Fregosi	.60	.24	.06
☐ 571	Jim Brewer	.40	.16	.04
☐ 572	Frank Quilici MGR	.40	.16	.04
☐ 573	Padres Rookies	.40	.16	.04
	Mike Corkins			
	Rafael Robles			
	Ron Slocum			
☐ 574	Bobby Bolin	.40	.16	.04
☐ 575	Cleon Jones	.40	.16	.04
☐ 576	Milt Pappas	.50	.20	.05
☐ 577	Bernie Allen	.40	.16	.04
☐ 578	Tom Griffin	.40	.16	.04
☐ 579	Tigers Team	.90	.36	.09
☐ 580	Pete Rose	55.00	22.00	5.50
☐ 581	Tom Satriano	.40	.16	.04
☐ 582	Mike Paul	.40	.16	.04
☐ 583	Hal Lanier	.60	.24	.06
☐ 584	Al Downing	.50	.20	.05
☐ 585	Rusty Staub	1.00	.40	.10
☐ 586	Rickey Clark	.40	.16	.04
☐ 587	Jose Arcia	.40	.16	.04
☐ 588	A Checklist 7	1.75	.15	.03
	(666 Adolpho)			
☐ 588	B Checklist 7	3.50	.35	.07
	(666 Adolfo)			
☐ 589	Joe Keough	.40	.16	.04
☐ 590	Mike Cuellar	.60	.24	.06
☐ 591	Mike Ryan	.40	.16	.04
☐ 592	Daryl Patterson	.40	.16	.04
☐ 593	Cubs Team	.80	.32	.08
☐ 594	Jake Gibbs	.40	.16	.04
☐ 595	Maury Wills	1.00	.40	.10
☐ 596	Mike Hershberger	.40	.16	.04
☐ 597	Sonny Siebert	.50	.20	.05
☐ 598	Joe Pepitone	.50	.20	.05

		MINT	VG-E	F-G
☐ 599	Senators Rookies	.40	.16	.04
	Dick Stelmaszek			
	Gene Martin			
	Dick Such			
☐ 600	Willie Mays	15.00	6.00	1.50
☐ 601	Pete Richert	.40	.16	.04
☐ 602	Ted Savage	.40	.16	.04
☐ 603	Ray Oyler	.40	.16	.04
☐ 604	Clarence Gaston	.40	.16	.04
☐ 605	Rick Wise	.50	.20	.05
☐ 606	Chico Ruiz	.40	.16	.04
☐ 607	Gary Waslewski	.40	.16	.04
☐ 608	Pirates Team	.80	.32	.08
☐ 609	Buck Martinez	.40	.16	.04
☐ 610	Jerry Koosman	.80	.32	.08
☐ 611	Norm Cash	.80	.32	.08
☐ 612	Jim Hickman	.40	.16	.04
☐ 613	Dave Baldwin...........	.40	.16	.04
☐ 614	Mike Shannon	.60	.24	.06
☐ 615	Mark Belanger	.60	.24	.06
☐ 616	Jim Merritt	.40	.16	.04
☐ 617	Jim French	.40	.16	.04
☐ 618	Billy Wynne	.40	.16	.04
☐ 619	Norm Miller	.40	.16	.04
☐ 620	Jim Perry	.90	.36	.09
☐ 621	Braves Rookies	3.50	1.40	.35
	Mike McQueen			
	Darrell Evans			
	Rick Kester			
☐ 622	Don Sutton	2.50	1.00	.25
☐ 623	Horace Clarke	.40	.16	.04
☐ 624	Clyde King MGR	.40	.16	.04
☐ 625	Dean Chance	.50	.20	.05
☐ 626	Dave Ricketts	.40	.16	.04
☐ 627	Gary Wagner	.40	.16	.04
☐ 628	Wayne Garrett	.40	.16	.04
☐ 629	Merv Rettenmund	.40	.16	.04
☐ 630	Ernie Banks	8.00	3.25	.80
☐ 631	Athletics Team	.80	.32	.08
☐ 632	Gary Sutherland	.40	.16	.04
☐ 633	Roger Nelson	.35	.14	.03
☐ 634	Bud Harrelson	1.25	.50	.12
☐ 635	Bob Allison	1.25	.50	.12
☐ 636	Jim Stewart	1.00	.40	.10
☐ 637	Indians Team	1.75	.70	.17
☐ 638	Frank Bertaina	1.00	.40	.10
☐ 639	Dave Campbell	1.00	.40	.10
☐ 640	Al Kaline	12.00	5.00	1.20
☐ 641	Al McBean	1.00	.40	.10
☐ 642	Angels Rookies..........	1.00	.40	.10
	Greg Garrett			
	Gordon Lund			
	Jarvis Tatum			

		MINT	VG-E	F-G
☐ 643	Jose Pagan	1.00	.40	.10
☐ 644	Gerry Nyman	1.00	.40	.10
☐ 645	Don Money	1.25	.50	.12
☐ 646	Jim Britton	1.00	.40	.10
☐ 647	Tom Matchick	1.00	.40	.10
☐ 648	Larry Haney	1.00	.40	.10
☐ 649	Jimmie Hall	1.00	.40	.10
☐ 650	Sam McDowell	1.25	.50	.12
☐ 651	Jim Gosger	1.00	.40	.10
☐ 652	Rich Rollins	1.00	.40	.10
☐ 653	Moe Drabowsky	1.00	.40	.10
☐ 654	NL Rookies	2.00	.80	.20
	Oscar Gamble			
	Boots Day			
	Angel Mangual			
☐ 655	John Roseboro	1.25	.50	.12
☐ 656	Jim Hardin	1.00	.40	.10
☐ 657	Padres Team	2.50	1.00	.25
☐ 658	Ken Tatum	1.00	.40	.10
☐ 659	Pete Ward	1.00	.40	.10
☐ 660	Johnny Bench	60.00	24.00	6.00
☐ 661	Jerry Robertson	1.00	.40	.10
☐ 662	Frank Lucchesi MGR	1.00	.40	.10
☐ 663	Tito Francona	1.00	.40	.10
☐ 664	Bob Robertson	1.00	.40	.10
☐ 665	Jim Lonborg	1.25	.50	.12
☐ 666	Adolpho Phillips	1.00	.40	.10
☐ 667	Bob Meyer	1.00	.40	.10
☐ 668	Bob Tillman	1.00	.40	.10
☐ 669	White Sox Rookies	1.00	.40	.10
	Bart Johnson			
	Dan Lazar			
	Mickey Scott			
☐ 670	Ron Santo	1.75	.70	.17
☐ 671	Jim Campanis	1.00	.40	.10
☐ 672	Leon McFadden	1.00	.40	.10
☐ 673	Ted Uhlaender	1.00	.40	.10
☐ 674	Dave Leonhard	1.00	.40	.10
☐ 675	Jose Cardenal	1.25	.50	.12
☐ 676	Senators Team	1.75	.70	.17
☐ 677	Woodie Fryman	1.25	.50	.12
☐ 678	Dave Duncan	1.00	.40	.10
☐ 679	Ray Sadecki	1.00	.40	.10
☐ 680	Rico Petrocelli	1.25	.50	.12
☐ 681	Bob Garibaldi	1.00	.40	.10
☐ 682	Dalton Jones	1.00	.40	.10
☐ 683	Reds Rookies	2.00	.80	.20
	Vern Geishert			
	Hal McRae			
	Wayne Simpson			
☐ 684	Jack Fisher	1.00	.40	.10
☐ 685	Tom Haller	1.00	.40	.10
☐ 686	Jackie Hernandez	1.00	.40	.10

		MINT	VG-E	F-G
☐ 687	Bob Priddy	1.00	.40	.10
☐ 688	Ted Kubiak	1.00	.40	.10
☐ 689	Frank Tepedino	1.00	.40	.10
☐ 690	Ron Fairly	1.25	.50	.12
☐ 691	Joe Grzenda	1.00	.40	.10
☐ 692	Duffy Dyer	1.00	.40	.10
☐ 693	Bob Johnson	1.00	.40	.10
☐ 694	Gary Ross	1.00	.40	.10
☐ 695	Bobby Knoop	1.00	.40	.10
☐ 696	Giants Team	1.75	.70	.17
☐ 697	Jim Hannan	1.00	.40	.10
☐ 698	Tom Tresh	1.50	.60	.15
☐ 699	Hank Aguirre	1.00	.40	.10
☐ 700	Frank Robinson	12.00	5.00	1.20
☐ 701	Jack Billingham	1.00	.40	.10
☐ 702	AL Rookies	1.00	.40	.10
	Bob Johnson			
	Ron Klimkowski			
	Bill Zepp			
☐ 703	Lou Marone	1.00	.40	.10
☐ 704	Frank Baker	1.00	.40	.10
☐ 705	Tony Cloninger	1.00	.40	.10
☐ 706	John McNamara MGR	2.25	.90	.22
☐ 707	Kevin Collins	1.00	.40	.10
☐ 708	Jose Santiago	1.00	.40	.10
☐ 709	Jack Fiore	1.00	.40	.10
☐ 710	Felix Millan	1.00	.40	.10
☐ 711	Ed Brinkman	1.00	.40	.10
☐ 712	Nolan Ryan	25.00	10.00	2.50
☐ 713	Pilots Team	6.00	2.40	.60
☐ 714	Al Spengler	1.00	.40	.10
☐ 715	Mickey Lolich	2.00	.80	.20
☐ 716	Cardinals Rookies	1.00	.40	.10
	Sal Campisi			
	Reggie Cleveland			
	Santiago Guzman			
☐ 717	Tom Phoebus	1.00	.40	.10
☐ 718	Ed Spiezio	1.00	.40	.10
☐ 719	Jim Roland	1.00	.40	.10
☐ 720	Rick Reichardt	1.50	.50	.10

1971 Topps

The cards in this 752-card set measure 2½"
by 3½". The 1971 Topps set is a challenge to
complete in mint condition because the black
obverse border is easily scratched and damaged. An unusual feature of this set is that
the player is also pictured in black and white
on the back of the card. Featured subsets
within this set include League Leaders (61-
72), Playoffs cards (195-202), and World Series cards (327-332). Cards 524-643 and the
last series (644-752) are somewhat scarce.

	MINT	VG-E	F-G
Complete Set	650.00	260.00	65.00
Common Player (1-523)	.23	.10	.02
Common Player (524-643)	.45	.18	.04
Common Player (644-752)	1.00	.40	.10

		MINT	VG-E	F-G
☐ 1	Orioles Team	2.00	.80	.20
☐ 2	Dock Ellis	.23	.10	.02
☐ 3	Dick McAuliffe	.23	.10	.02
☐ 4	Vic Davalillo	.23	.10	.02
☐ 5	Thurman Munson	10.00	4.00	1.00
☐ 6	Ed Spiezio	.23	.10	.02
☐ 7	Jim Holt	.23	.10	.02
☐ 8	Mike McQueen	.23	.10	.02
☐ 9	George Scott	.30	.12	.03
☐ 10	Claude Osteen	.30	.12	.03
☐ 11	Elliott Maddox	.23	.10	.02
☐ 12	Johnny Callison	.30	.12	.03
☐ 13	White Sox Rookies	.23	.10	.02
	Charlie Brinkman			
	Dick Moloney			

		MINT	VG-E	F-G
☐ 14	Dave Concepcion	4.00	1.60	.40
☐ 15	Andy Messersmith	.35	.14	.03
☐ 16	Ken Singleton	1.50	.60	.15
☐ 17	Billy Sorrell	.23	.10	.02
☐ 18	Norm Miller	.23	.10	.02
☐ 19	Skip Pitlock	.23	.10	.02
☐ 20	Reggie Jackson	14.00	5.75	1.40
☐ 21	Dan McGinn	.23	.10	.02
☐ 22	Phil Roof	.23	.10	.02
☐ 23	Oscar Gamble	.40	.16	.04
☐ 24	Rich Hand	.23	.10	.02
☐ 25	Clarence Gaston	.23	.10	.02
☐ 26	Bert Blyleven	8.00	3.25	.80
☐ 27	Pirates Rookies	.23	.10	.02
	Fred Cambria			
	Gene Clines			
☐ 28	Ron Klimkowski	.23	.10	.02
☐ 29	Don Buford	.23	.10	.02
☐ 30	Phil Niekro	2.00	.80	.20
☐ 31	Eddie Kasko MGR	.23	.10	.02
☐ 32	Jerry DaVanon	.23	.10	.02
☐ 33	Del Unser	.23	.10	.02
☐ 34	Sandy Vance	.23	.10	.02
☐ 35	Lou Piniella	.65	.26	.06
☐ 36	Dean Chance	.30	.12	.03
☐ 37	Rich McKinney	.23	.10	.02
☐ 38	Jim Colborn	.23	.10	.02
☐ 39	Tiger Rookies	.23	.10	.02
	Lerrin LaGrow			
	Gene Lamont			
☐ 40	Lee May	.35	.14	.03
☐ 41	Rick Austin	.23	.10	.02
☐ 42	Boots Day	.23	.10	.02
☐ 43	Steve Kealey	.23	.10	.02
☐ 44	Johnny Edwards	.23	.10	.02
☐ 45	Jim Hunter	2.50	1.00	.25
☐ 46	Dave Campbell	.23	.10	.02
☐ 47	Johnny Jeter	.23	.10	.02
☐ 48	Dave Baldwin	.23	.10	.02
☐ 49	Don Money	.30	.12	.03
☐ 50	Willie McCovey	3.00	1.20	.30
☐ 51	Steve Kline	.23	.10	.02
☐ 52	Braves Rookies	.35	.14	.03
	Oscar Brown			
	Earl Williams			
☐ 53	Paul Blair	.30	.12	.03
☐ 54	Checklist 1	1.00	.10	.02
☐ 55	Steve Carlton	10.00	4.00	1.00
☐ 56	Duane Josephson	.23	.10	.02
☐ 57	Von Joshua	.23	.10	.02
☐ 58	Bill Lee	.30	.12	.03
☐ 59	Gene Mauch MGR	.30	.12	.03
☐ 60	Dick Bosman	.23	.10	.02

		MINT	VG-E	F-G
☐ 61	AL Batting Leaders	1.00	.40	.10
	Alex Johnson			
	Carl Yastrzemski			
	Tony Oliva			
☐ 62	NL Batting Leaders	.50	.20	.05
	Rico Carty			
	Joe Torre			
	Manny Sanguillen			
☐ 63	AL RBI Leaders	.75	.30	.07
	Frank Robinson			
	Tony Conigliaro			
	Boog Powell			
☐ 64	NL RBI Leaders	1.00	.40	.10
	Johnny Bench			
	Tony Perez			
	Billy Williams			
☐ 65	AL HR Leaders	1.00	.40	.10
	Frank Howard			
	Harmon Killebrew			
	Carl Yastrzemski			
☐ 66	NL HR Leaders	1.00	.40	.10
	Johnny Bench			
	Billy Williams			
	Tony Perez			
☐ 67	AL ERA Leaders	.50	.20	.05
	Diego Segui			
	Jim Palmer			
	Clyde Wright			
☐ 68	NL ERA Leaders	.75	.30	.07
	Tom Seaver			
	Wayne Simpson			
	Luke Walker			
☐ 69	AL Pitching Leaders	.50	.20	.05
	Mike Cuellar			
	Dave McNally			
	Jim Perry			
☐ 70	NL Pitching Leaders	1.25	.50	.12
	Bob Gibson			
	Gaylord Perry			
	Fergie Jenkins			
☐ 71	AL Strikeout Leaders	.50	.20	.05
	Sam McDowell			
	Mickey Lolich			
	Bob Johnson			
☐ 72	NL Strikeout Leaders	1.25	.50	.12
	Tom Seaver			
	Bob Gibson			
	Fergie Jenkins			
☐ 73	George Brunet	.23	.10	.02
☐ 74	Twins Rookies	.23	.10	.02
	Pete Hamm			
	Jim Nettles			
☐ 75	Gary Nolan	.23	.10	.02

		MINT	VG-E	F-G
☐ 76	Ted Savage	.23	.10	.02
☐ 77	Mike Compton	.23	.10	.02
☐ 78	Jim Spencer	.23	.10	.02
☐ 79	Wade Blasingame	.23	.10	.02
☐ 80	Bill Melton	.23	.10	.02
☐ 81	Felix Millan	.23	.10	.02
☐ 82	Casey Cox	.23	.10	.02
☐ 83	Met Rookies	.35	.14	.03
	Tim Foli			
	Randy Bobb			
☐ 84	Marcel Lachemann	.23	.10	.02
☐ 85	Bill Grabarkewitz	.23	.10	.02
☐ 86	Mike Kilkenny	.23	.10	.02
☐ 87	Jack Heidemann	.23	.10	.02
☐ 88	Hal King	.23	.10	.02
☐ 89	Ken Brett	.23	.10	.02
☐ 90	Joe Pepitone	.35	.14	.03
☐ 91	Bob Lemon MGR	.75	.30	.07
☐ 92	Fred Wenz	.23	.10	.02
☐ 93	Senators Rookies	.23	.10	.02
	Norm McRae			
	Denny Riddleberger			
☐ 94	Don Hahn	.23	.10	.02
☐ 95	Luis Tiant	.60	.24	.06
☐ 96	Joe Hague	.23	.10	.02
☐ 97	Floyd Wicker	.23	.10	.02
☐ 98	Joe Decker	.23	.10	.02
☐ 99	Mark Belanger	.35	.14	.03
☐ 100	Pete Rose	33.00	12.50	3.00
☐ 101	Les Cain	.23	.10	.02
☐ 102	Astros Rookies	.40	.16	.04
	Ken Forsch			
	Larry Howard			
☐ 103	Rich Severinson	.23	.10	.02
☐ 104	Dan Frisella	.23	.10	.02
☐ 105	Tony Conigliaro	.40	.16	.04
☐ 106	Tom Dukes	.23	.10	.02
☐ 107	Roy Foster	.23	.10	.02
☐ 108	John Cumberland	.23	.10	.02
☐ 109	Steve Hovley	.23	.10	.02
☐ 110	Bill Mazeroski	.50	.20	.05
☐ 111	Yankee Rookies	.23	.10	.02
	Loyd Colson			
	Bobby Mitchell			
☐ 112	Manny Mota	.35	.14	.03
☐ 113	Jerry Crider	.23	.10	.02
☐ 114	Billy Conigliaro	.23	.10	.02
☐ 115	Donn Clendenon	.30	.12	.03
☐ 116	Ken Sanders	.23	.10	.02
☐ 117	Ted Simmons	5.00	2.00	.50
☐ 118	Cookie Rojas	.23	.10	.02
☐ 119	Frank Lucchesi MGR	.23	.10	.02
☐ 120	Willie Horton	.35	.14	.03

		MINT	VG-E	F-G
☐ 121	Cubs Rookies	.23	.10	.02
	Jim Dunegan			
	Roe Skidmore			
☐ 122	Eddie Watt	.23	.10	.02
☐ 123	A Checklist 2	1.25	.12	.02
	(card number			
	at bottom right)			
☐ 123	B Checklist 2	1.50	.15	.03
	(card number			
	centered)			
☐ 124	Don Gullett	.35	.14	.03
☐ 125	Ray Fosse	.23	.10	.02
☐ 126	Danny Coombs	.23	.10	.02
☐ 127	Danny Thompson	.23	.10	.02
☐ 128	Frank Johnson	.23	.10	.02
☐ 129	Aurelio Monteagudo	.23	.10	.02
☐ 130	Denis Menke	.23	.10	.02
☐ 131	Curt Blefary	.23	.10	.02
☐ 132	Jose Laboy	.23	.10	.02
☐ 133	Mickey Lolich	.60	.24	.06
☐ 134	Jose Arcia	.23	.10	.02
☐ 135	Rick Monday	.35	.14	.03
☐ 136	Duffy Dyer	.23	.10	.02
☐ 137	Marcelino Lopez	.23	.10	.02
☐ 138	Phillies Rookies	.35	.14	.03
	Joe Lis			
	Willie Montanez			
☐ 139	Paul Casanova	.23	.10	.02
☐ 140	Gaylord Perry	3.00	1.20	.30
☐ 141	Frank Quilici MGR	.23	.10	.02
☐ 142	Mack Jones	.23	.10	.02
☐ 143	Steve Blass	.30	.12	.03
☐ 144	Jackie Hernandez	.23	.10	.02
☐ 145	Bill Singer	.23	.10	.02
☐ 146	Ralph Houk MGR	.30	.12	.03
☐ 147	Bob Priddy	.23	.10	.02
☐ 148	John Mayberry	.30	.12	.03
☐ 149	Mike Hershberger	.23	.10	.02
☐ 150	Sam McDowell	.35	.14	.03
☐ 151	Tommy Davis	.40	.16	.04
☐ 152	Angels Rookies	.23	.10	.02
	Lloyd Allen			
	Winston Llenas			
☐ 153	Gary Ross	.23	.10	.02
☐ 154	Cesar Gutierrez	.23	.10	.02
☐ 155	Ken Henderson	.23	.10	.02
☐ 156	Bart Johnson	.23	.10	.02
☐ 157	Bob Bailey	.23	.10	.02
☐ 158	Jerry Reuss	.60	.24	.06
☐ 159	Jarvis Tatum	.23	.10	.02
☐ 160	Tom Seaver	11.00	4.50	1.10
☐ 161	Coin Checklist	1.00	.10	.02
☐ 162	Jack Billingham	.23	.10	.02

		MINT	VG-E	F-G
☐ 163	Buck Martinez	.23	.10	.02
☐ 164	Reds Rookies	.45	.18	.04
	Frank Duffy			
	Milt Wilcox			
☐ 165	Cesar Tovar	.23	.10	.02
☐ 166	Joe Hoerner	.23	.10	.02
☐ 167	Tom Grieve	.35	.14	.03
☐ 168	Bruce Dal Canton	.23	.10	.02
☐ 169	Ed Herrmann	.23	.10	.02
☐ 170	Mike Cuellar	.35	.14	.03
☐ 171	Bobby Wine	.23	.10	.02
☐ 172	Duke Sims	.23	.10	.02
☐ 173	Gil Garrido	.23	.10	.02
☐ 174	Dave LaRoche	.23	.10	.02
☐ 175	Jim Hickman	.23	.10	.02
☐ 176	Red Sox Rookies	.23	.10	.02
	Bob Montgomery			
	Doug Griffin			
☐ 177	Hal McRae	.40	.16	.04
☐ 178	Dave Duncan	.23	.10	.02
☐ 179	Mike Corkins	.23	.10	.02
☐ 180	Al Kaline	3.25	1.30	.32
☐ 181	Hal Lanier	.40	.16	.04
☐ 182	Al Downing	.23	.10	.02
☐ 183	Gil Hodges MGR	1.75	.70	.17
☐ 184	Stan Bahnsen	.23	.10	.02
☐ 185	Julian Javier	.23	.10	.02
☐ 186	Bob Spence	.23	.10	.02
☐ 187	Ted Abernathy	.23	.10	.02
☐ 188	Dodgers Rookies	1.00	.40	.10
	Bob Valentine			
	Mike Strahler			
☐ 189	George Mitterwald	.23	.10	.02
☐ 190	Bob Tolan	.23	.10	.02
☐ 191	Mike Andrews	.23	.10	.02
☐ 192	Billy Wilson	.23	.10	.02
☐ 193	Bob Grich	1.50	.60	.15
☐ 194	Mike Lum	.23	.10	.02
☐ 195	AL Playoff Game 1	.75	.30	.07
	Powell muscles Twins			
☐ 196	AL Playoff Game 2	.75	.30	.07
	McNally makes it			
	two straight			
☐ 197	AL Playoff Game 3	1.25	.50	.12
	Palmer mows'em down			
☐ 198	AL Playoff Summary	.75	.30	.07
	Orioles celebrate			
☐ 199	NL Playoff Game 1	.75	.30	.07
	Cline pinch-triple			
	decides it			
☐ 200	NL Playoff Game 2	.75	.30	.07
	Tolan scores for			
	third time			

		MINT	VG-E	F-G
☐ 201	NL Playoff Game 3	.75	.30	.07
	Cline scores			
	winning run			
☐ 202	NL Playoff Summary	.75	.30	.07
	Reds celebrate			
☐ 203	Larry Gura	.75	.30	.07
☐ 204	Brewers Rookies	.23	.10	.02
	Bernie Smith			
	George Kopacz			
☐ 205	Gerry Moses	.23	.10	.02
☐ 206	Checklist 3	1.00	.10	.02
☐ 207	Alan Foster	.23	.10	.02
☐ 208	Billy Martin MGR	1.00	.40	.10
☐ 209	Steve Renko	.23	.10	.02
☐ 210	Rod Carew	10.00	4.00	1.00
☐ 211	Phil Hennigan	.23	.10	.02
☐ 212	Rich Hebner	.30	.12	.03
☐ 213	Frank Baker	.23	.10	.02
☐ 214	Al Ferrara	.23	.10	.02
☐ 215	Diego Segui	.23	.10	.02
☐ 216	Cards Rookies	.23	.10	.02
	Reggie Cleveland			
	Luis Melendez			
☐ 217	Ed Stroud	.23	.10	.02
☐ 218	Tony Cloninger	.23	.10	.02
☐ 219	Elrod Hendricks	.23	.10	.02
☐ 220	Ron Santo	.50	.20	.05
☐ 221	Dave Morehead	.23	.10	.02
☐ 222	Bob Watson	.40	.16	.04
☐ 223	Cecil Upshaw	.23	.10	.02
☐ 224	Alan Gallagher	.23	.10	.02
☐ 225	Gary Peters	.30	.12	.03
☐ 226	Bill Russell	.35	.14	.03
☐ 227	Floyd Weaver	.23	.10	.02
☐ 228	Wayne Garrett	.23	.10	.02
☐ 229	Jim Hannan	.23	.10	.02
☐ 230	Willie Stargell	3.00	1.20	.30
☐ 231	Indians Rookies	.35	.14	.03
	Vince Colbert			
	John Lowenstein			
☐ 232	John Strohmayer	.23	.10	.02
☐ 233	Larry Bowa	1.00	.40	.10
☐ 234	Jim Lyttle	.23	.10	.02
☐ 235	Nate Colbert	.23	.10	.02
☐ 236	Bob Humphreys	.23	.10	.02
☐ 237	Cesar Cedeno	1.25	.50	.12
☐ 238	Chuck Dobson	.23	.10	.02
☐ 239	Red Schoendienst MGR	.40	.16	.04
☐ 240	Clyde Wright	.23	.10	.02
☐ 241	Dave Nelson	.23	.10	.02
☐ 242	Jim Ray	.23	.10	.02
☐ 243	Carlos May	.30	.12	.03
☐ 244	Bob Tillman	.23	.10	.02

		MINT	VG-E	F-G
☐ 245	Jim Kaat	1.00	.40	.10
☐ 246	Tony Taylor	.23	.10	.02
☐ 247	Royals Rookies	.40	.16	.04
	Jerry Cram			
	Paul Splittorff			
☐ 248	Hoyt Wilhelm	2.00	.80	.20
☐ 249	Chico Salmon	.23	.10	.02
☐ 250	Johnny Bench	11.00	4.50	1.10
☐ 251	Frank Reberger	.23	.10	.02
☐ 252	Eddie Leon	.23	.10	.02
☐ 253	Bill Sudakis	.23	.10	.02
☐ 254	Cal Koonce	.23	.10	.02
☐ 255	Bob Robertson	.23	.10	.02
☐ 256	Tony Gonzalez	.23	.10	.02
☐ 257	Nelson Briles	.30	.12	.03
☐ 258	Dick Green	.23	.10	.02
☐ 259	Dave Marshall	.23	.10	.02
☐ 260	Tommy Harper	.30	.12	.03
☐ 261	Darold Knowles	.23	.10	.02
☐ 262	Padres Rookies	.23	.10	.02
	Jim Williams			
	Dave Robinson			
☐ 263	John Ellis	.23	.10	.02
☐ 264	Joe Morgan	2.25	.90	.22
☐ 265	Jim Northrup	.30	.12	.03
☐ 266	Bill Stoneman	.23	.10	.02
☐ 267	Rich Morales	.23	.10	.02
☐ 268	Phillies Team	.55	.22	.05
☐ 269	Gail Hopkins	.23	.10	.02
☐ 270	Rico Carty	.45	.18	.04
☐ 271	Bill Zepp	.23	.10	.02
☐ 272	Tommy Helms	.30	.12	.03
☐ 273	Pete Richert	.23	.10	.02
☐ 274	Ron Slocum	.23	.10	.02
☐ 275	Vada Pinson	.60	.24	.06
☐ 276	Giants Rookies	4.50	1.80	.45
	Mike Davison			
	George Foster			
☐ 277	Gary Waslewski	.23	.10	.02
☐ 278	Jerry Grote	.23	.10	.02
☐ 279	Lefty Phillips MGR	.23	.10	.02
☐ 280	Fergie Jenkins	1.25	.50	.12
☐ 281	Danny Walton	.23	.10	.02
☐ 282	Jose Pagan	.23	.10	.02
☐ 283	Dick Such	.23	.10	.02
☐ 284	Jim Gosger	.23	.10	.02
☐ 285	Sal Bando	.35	.14	.03
☐ 286	Jerry McNertney	.23	.10	.02
☐ 287	Mike Fiore	.23	.10	.02
☐ 288	Joe Moeller	.23	.10	.02
☐ 289	White Sox Team	.55	.22	.05
☐ 290	Tony Oliva	.90	.36	.09
☐ 291	George Culver	.23	.10	.02

		MINT	VG-E	F-G
☐ 292	Jay Johnstone	.35	.14	.03
☐ 293	Pat Corrales	.35	.14	.03
☐ 294	Steve Dunning	.23	.10	.02
☐ 295	Bobby Bonds	.65	.26	.06
☐ 296	Tom Timmermann	.23	.10	.02
☐ 297	Johnny Briggs	.23	.10	.02
☐ 298	Jim Nelson	.23	.10	.02
☐ 299	Ed Kirkpatrick	.23	.10	.02
☐ 300	Brooks Robinson	4.50	1.80	.45
☐ 301	Earl Wilson	.23	.10	.02
☐ 302	Phil Gagliano	.23	.10	.02
☐ 303	Lindy McDaniel	.23	.10	.02
☐ 304	Ron Brand	.23	.10	.02
☐ 305	Reggie Smith	.60	.24	.06
☐ 306	Jim Nash	.23	.10	.02
☐ 307	Don Wert	.23	.10	.02
☐ 308	Cardinals Team	.55	.22	.05
☐ 309	Dick Ellsworth	.23	.10	.02
☐ 310	Tommie Agee	.30	.12	.03
☐ 311	Lee Stange	.23	.10	.02
☐ 312	Harry Walker MGR	.23	.10	.02
☐ 313	Tom Hall	.23	.10	.02
☐ 314	Jeff Torborg	.23	.10	.02
☐ 315	Ron Fairly	.30	.12	.03
☐ 316	Fred Scherman	.23	.10	.02
☐ 317	Athletic Rookies	.23	.10	.02
	Jim Driscoll			
	Angel Mangual			
☐ 318	Rudy May	.23	.10	.02
☐ 319	Ty Cline	.23	.10	.02
☐ 320	Dave McNally	.35	.14	.03
☐ 321	Tom Matchick	.23	.10	.02
☐ 322	Jim Beauchamp	.23	.10	.02
☐ 323	Billy Champion	.23	.10	.02
☐ 324	Graig Nettles	2.00	.80	.20
☐ 325	Juan Marichal	2.50	1.00	.25
☐ 326	Richie Scheinblum	.23	.10	.02
☐ 327	World Series Game 1	.75	.30	.07
	Powell homers to			
	opposite field			
☐ 328	World Series Game 2	.75	.30	.07
	Don Buford			
☐ 329	World Series Game 3	1.50	.60	.15
	Frank Robinson			
	shows muscle			
☐ 330	World Series Game 4	.75	.30	.07
	Reds stay alive			
☐ 331	World Series Game 5	1.50	.60	.15
	Brooks Robinson			
	commits robbery			
☐ 332	World Series Summary	.75	.30	.07
	Orioles celebrate			
☐ 333	Clay Kirby	.23	.10	.02

		MINT	VG-E	F-G
☐ 334	Roberto Pena	.23	.10	.02
☐ 335	Jerry Koosman	.50	.20	.05
☐ 336	Tigers Team	.60	.24	.06
☐ 337	Jesus Alou	.23	.10	.02
☐ 338	Gene Tenace	.35	.14	.03
☐ 339	Wayne Simpson	.23	.10	.02
☐ 340	Rico Petrocelli	.35	.14	.03
☐ 341	Steve Garvey	45.00	18.00	4.50
☐ 342	Frank Tepedino	.23	.10	.02
☐ 343	Pirates Rookies	.23	.10	.02
	Ed Acosta			
	Milt May			
☐ 344	Ellie Rodriguez	.23	.10	.02
☐ 345	Joe Horlen	.30	.12	.03
☐ 346	Lum Harris MGR	.23	.10	.02
☐ 347	Ted Uhlaender	.23	.10	.02
☐ 348	Fred Norman	.23	.10	.02
☐ 349	Rich Reese	.23	.10	.02
☐ 350	Billy Williams	2.50	1.00	.25
☐ 351	Jim Shellenback	.23	.10	.02
☐ 352	Denny Doyle	.23	.10	.02
☐ 353	Carl Taylor	.23	.10	.02
☐ 354	Don McMahon	.23	.10	.02
☐ 355	Bud Harrelson	.30	.12	.03
☐ 356	Bob Locker	.23	.10	.02
☐ 357	Reds Team	.75	.30	.07
☐ 358	Danny Cater	.23	.10	.02
☐ 359	Ron Reed	.23	.10	.02
☐ 360	Jim Fregosi	.40	.16	.04
☐ 361	Don Sutton	1.75	.70	.17
☐ 362	Orioles Rookies	.23	.10	.02
	Mike Adamson			
	Roger Freed			
☐ 363	Mike Nagy	.23	.10	.02
☐ 364	Tommy Dean	.23	.10	.02
☐ 365	Bob Johnson	.23	.10	.02
☐ 366	Ron Stone	.23	.10	.02
☐ 367	Dalton Jones	.23	.10	.02
☐ 368	Bob Veale	.30	.12	.03
☐ 369	Checklist 4	1.00	.10	.02
☐ 370	Joe Torre	1.25	.50	.12
☐ 371	Jack Hiatt	.23	.10	.02
☐ 372	Lew Krausse	.23	.10	.02
☐ 373	Tom McCraw	.23	.10	.02
☐ 374	Clete Boyer	.35	.14	.03
☐ 375	Steve Hargan	.23	.10	.02
☐ 376	Expos Rookies	.23	.10	.02
	Clyde Mashore			
	Ernie McAnally			
☐ 377	Greg Garrett	.23	.10	.02
☐ 378	Tito Fuentes	.23	.10	.02
☐ 379	Wayne Granger	.23	.10	.02
☐ 380	Ted Williams MGR	3.00	1.20	.30

		MINT	VG-E	F-G
☐ 381	Fred Gladding	.23	.10	.02
☐ 382	Jake Gibbs	.23	.10	.02
☐ 383	Rod Gaspar	.23	.10	.02
☐ 384	Rollie Fingers	2.00	.80	.20
☐ 385	Maury Wills	.90	.36	.09
☐ 386	Red Sox Team	.75	.30	.07
☐ 387	Ron Herbel	.23	.10	.02
☐ 388	Al Oliver	1.75	.70	.17
☐ 389	Ed Brinkman	.23	.10	.02
☐ 390	Glenn Beckert	.35	.14	.03
☐ 391	Twins Rookies	.35	.14	.03
	Steve Brye			
	Cotton Nash			
☐ 392	Grant Jackson	.23	.10	.02
☐ 393	Merv Rettenmund	.23	.10	.02
☐ 394	Clay Carroll	.23	.10	.02
☐ 395	Roy White	.35	.14	.03
☐ 396	Dick Schofield	.23	.10	.02
☐ 397	Alvin Dark MGR	.35	.14	.03
☐ 398	Howie Reed	.23	.10	.02
☐ 399	Jim French	.23	.10	.02
☐ 400	Hank Aaron	12.00	5.00	1.20
☐ 401	Tom Murphy	.23	.10	.02
☐ 402	Dodgers Team	.75	.30	.07
☐ 403	Joe Coleman	.23	.10	.02
☐ 404	Astros Rookies	.23	.10	.02
	Buddy Harris			
	Roger Metzger			
☐ 405	Leo Cardenas	.23	.10	.02
☐ 406	Ray Sadecki	.23	.10	.02
☐ 407	Joe Rudi	.35	.14	.03
☐ 408	Rafael Robles	.23	.10	.02
☐ 409	Don Pavletich	.23	.10	.02
☐ 410	Ken Holtzman	.35	.14	.03
☐ 411	George Spriggs	.23	.10	.02
☐ 412	Jerry Johnson	.23	.10	.02
☐ 413	Pat Kelly	.23	.10	.02
☐ 414	Woodie Fryman	.23	.10	.02
☐ 415	Mike Hegan	.23	.10	.02
☐ 416	Gene Alley	.30	.12	.03
☐ 417	Dick Hall	.23	.10	.02
☐ 418	Adolfo Phillips	.23	.10	.02
☐ 419	Ron Hansen	.23	.10	.02
☐ 420	Jim Merritt	.23	.10	.02
☐ 421	John Stephenson	.23	.10	.02
☐ 422	Frank Bertaina	.23	.10	.02
☐ 423	Tigers Rookies	.23	.10	.02
	Dennis Saunders			
	Tim Marting			
☐ 424	R. Rodriguez	.23	.10	.02
☐ 425	Doug Rader	.35	.14	.03
☐ 426	Chris Cannizzaro	.23	.10	.02
☐ 427	Bernie Allen	.23	.10	.02

		MINT	VG-E	F-G
☐ 428	Jim McAndrew	.23	.10	.02
☐ 429	Chuck Hinton	.23	.10	.02
☐ 430	Wes Parker	.35	.14	.03
☐ 431	Tom Burgmeier	.23	.10	.02
☐ 432	Bob Didier	.23	.10	.02
☐ 433	Skip Lockwood	.23	.10	.02
☐ 434	Gary Sutherland	.23	.10	.02
☐ 435	Jose Cardenal	.23	.10	.02
☐ 436	Wilbur Wood	.35	.14	.03
☐ 437	Danny Murtaugh MGR	.23	.10	.02
☐ 438	Mike McCormick	.35	.14	.03
☐ 439	Phillies Rookies	1.75	.70	.17
	Greg Luzinski			
	Scott Reid			
☐ 440	Bert Campaneris	.35	.14	.03
☐ 441	Milt Pappas	.35	.14	.03
☐ 442	Angels Team	.55	.22	.05
☐ 443	Rich Robertson	.23	.10	.02
☐ 444	Jimmie Price	.23	.10	.02
☐ 445	Art Shamsky	.23	.10	.02
☐ 446	Bobby Bolin	.23	.10	.02
☐ 447	Cesar Geronimo	.23	.10	.02
☐ 448	Dave Roberts	.23	.10	.02
☐ 449	Brant Alyea	.23	.10	.02
☐ 450	Bob Gibson	3.50	1.40	.35
☐ 451	Joe Keough	.23	.10	.02
☐ 452	John Boccabella	.23	.10	.02
☐ 453	Terry Crowley	.23	.10	.02
☐ 454	Mike Paul	.23	.10	.02
☐ 455	Don Kessinger	.35	.14	.03
☐ 456	Bob Meyer	.23	.10	.02
☐ 457	Willie Smith	.23	.10	.02
☐ 458	White Sox Rookies	.23	.10	.02
	Ron Lolich			
	Dave Lemonds			
☐ 459	Jim Lefebvre	.23	.10	.02
☐ 460	Fritz Peterson	.23	.10	.02
☐ 461	Jim Ray Hart	.35	.14	.03
☐ 462	Senators Team	.55	.22	.05
☐ 463	Tom Kelley	.23	.10	.02
☐ 464	Aurelio Rodriguez	.23	.10	.02
☐ 465	Tim McCarver	.45	.18	.04
☐ 466	Ken Berry	.23	.10	.02
☐ 467	Al Santorini	.23	.10	.02
☐ 468	Frank Fernandez	.23	.10	.02
☐ 469	Bob Aspromonte	.23	.10	.02
☐ 470	Bob Oliver	.23	.10	.02
☐ 471	Tom Griffin	.23	.10	.02
☐ 472	Ken Rudolph	.23	.10	.02
☐ 473	Gary Wagner	.23	.10	.02
☐ 474	Jim Fairey	.23	.10	.02
☐ 475	Ron Perranoski	.35	.14	.03
☐ 476	Dal Maxvill	.23	.10	.02

		MINT	VG-E	F-G
☐ 477	Earl Weaver MGR	.75	.30	.07
☐ 478	Bernie Carbo	.23	.10	.02
☐ 479	Dennis Higgins	.23	.10	.02
☐ 480	Manny Sanguillen	.35	.14	.03
☐ 481	Daryl Patterson	.23	.10	.02
☐ 482	Padres Team	.55	.22	.05
☐ 483	Gene Michael	.35	.14	.03
☐ 484	Don Wilson	.23	.10	.02
☐ 485	Ken McMullen	.23	.10	.02
☐ 486	Steve Huntz	.23	.10	.02
☐ 487	Paul Schaal	.23	.10	.02
☐ 488	Jerry Stephenson	.23	.10	.02
☐ 489	Luis Alvarado	.23	.10	.02
☐ 490	Deron Johnson	.23	.10	.02
☐ 491	Jim Hardin	.23	.10	.02
☐ 492	Ken Boswell	.23	.10	.02
☐ 493	Dave May	.23	.10	.02
☐ 494	Braves Rookies	.35	.14	.03
	Ralph Garr			
	Rick Kester			
☐ 495	Felipe Alou	.35	.14	.03
☐ 496	Woody Woodward	.23	.10	.02
☐ 497	Horacio Pina	.23	.10	.02
☐ 498	John Kennedy	.23	.10	.02
☐ 499	Checklist 5	1.00	.10	.02
☐ 500	Jim Perry	.50	.20	.05
☐ 501	Andy Etchebarren	.23	.10	.02
☐ 502	Cubs Team	.55	.22	.05
☐ 503	Gates Brown	.30	.12	.03
☐ 504	Ken Wright	.23	.10	.02
☐ 505	Ollie Brown	.23	.10	.02
☐ 506	Bobby Knoop	.23	.10	.02
☐ 507	George Stone	.23	.10	.02
☐ 508	Roger Repoz	.23	.10	.02
☐ 509	Jim Grant	.23	.10	.02
☐ 510	Ken Harrelson	.65	.26	.06
☐ 511	Chris Short	.23	.10	.02
☐ 512	Red Sox Rookies	.23	.10	.02
	Dick Mills			
	Mike Garman			
☐ 513	Nolan Ryan	11.00	4.50	1.10
☐ 514	Ron Woods	.23	.10	.02
☐ 515	Carl Morton	.23	.10	.02
☐ 516	Ted Kubiak	.23	.10	.02
☐ 517	Charlie Fox MGR	.23	.10	.02
☐ 518	Joe Grzenda	.23	.10	.02
☐ 519	Willie Crawford	.23	.10	.02
☐ 520	Tommy John	1.50	.60	.15
☐ 521	Leron Lee	.23	.10	.02
☐ 522	Twins Team	.55	.22	.05
☐ 523	John Odom	.23	.10	.02
☐ 524	Mickey Stanley	.60	.24	.06
☐ 525	Ernie Banks	5.50	2.20	.55

	MINT	VG-E	F-G		MINT	VG-E	F-G
526 Ray Jarvis	.45	.18	.04	573 Ed Kranepool	.60	.24	.06
527 Cleon Jones	.45	.18	.04	574 Jim Bunning	1.25	.50	.12
528 Wally Bunker	.45	.18	.04	575 Bill Freehan	.75	.30	.07
529 NL Rookie Infielders	2.50	1.00	.25	576 Cubs Rookies	.45	.18	.04
Enzo Hernandez				Adrian Garrett			
Bill Buckner				Brock Davis			
Marty Perez				Garry Jestadt			
530 Carl Yastrzemski	15.00	6.00	1.50	577 Jim Lonborg	.60	.24	.06
531 Mike Torrez	.60	.24	.06	578 Ron Hunt	.45	.18	.04
532 Bill Rigney MGR	.45	.18	.04	579 Marty Pattin	.45	.18	.04
533 Mike Ryan	.45	.18	.04	580 Tony Perez	1.50	.60	.15
534 Luke Walker	.45	.18	.04	581 Roger Nelson	.45	.18	.04
535 Curt Flood	.65	.26	.06	582 Dave Cash	.60	.24	.06
536 Claude Raymond	.45	.18	.04	583 Ron Cook	.45	.18	.04
537 Tom Egan	.45	.18	.04	584 Indians Team	1.00	.40	.10
538 Angel Bravo	.45	.18	.04	585 Willie Davis	.65	.26	.06
539 Larry Brown	.45	.18	.04	586 Dick Woodson	.45	.18	.04
540 Larry Dierker	.60	.24	.06	587 Sonny Jackson	.45	.18	.04
541 Bob Burda	.45	.18	.04	588 Tom Bradley	.45	.18	.04
542 Bob Miller	.45	.18	.04	589 Bob Barton	.45	.18	.04
543 Yankees Team	1.00	.40	.10	590 Alex Johnson	.60	.24	.06
544 Vida Blue	2.25	.90	.22	591 Jackie Brown	.60	.24	.06
545 Dick Dietz	.45	.18	.04	592 Randy Hundley	.45	.18	.04
546 John Matias	.45	.18	.04	593 Jack Aker	.45	.18	.04
547 Pat Dobson	.60	.24	.06	594 Cards Rookies	.90	.36	.09
548 Don Mason	.45	.18	.04	Bob Chlupsa			
549 Jim Brewer	.45	.18	.04	Bob Stinson			
550 Harmon Killebrew	4.50	1.80	.45	Al Hrabosky			
551 Frank Linzy	.45	.18	.04	595 Dave Johnson	1.25	.50	.12
552 Buddy Bradford	.45	.18	.04	596 Mike Jorgensen	.45	.18	.04
553 Kevin Collins	.45	.18	.04	597 Ken Suarez	.45	.18	.04
554 Lowell Palmer	.45	.18	.04	598 Rick Wise	.60	.24	.06
555 Walt Williams	.45	.18	.04	599 Norm Cash	1.00	.40	.10
556 Jim McGlothlin	.45	.18	.04	600 Willie Mays	16.00	6.50	1.60
557 Tom Satriano	.45	.18	.04	601 Ken Tatum	.45	.18	.04
558 Hector Torres	.45	.18	.04	602 Marty Martinez	.45	.18	.04
559 AL Rookie Pitchers	.45	.18	.04	603 Pirates Team	1.00	.40	.10
Terry Cox				604 John Gelnar	.45	.18	.04
Bill Gogolewski				605 Orlando Cepeda	1.50	.60	.15
Gary Jones				606 Chuck Taylor	.45	.18	.04
560 Rusty Staub	1.00	.40	.10	607 Paul Ratliff	.45	.18	.04
561 Syd O'Brien	.45	.18	.04	608 Mike Wegener	.45	.18	.04
562 Dave Giusti	.45	.18	.04	609 Leo Durocher MGR	.80	.32	.08
563 Giants Team	1.00	.40	.10	610 Amos Otis	.75	.30	.07
564 Al Fitzmorris	.45	.18	.04	611 Tom Phoebus	.45	.18	.04
565 Jim Wynn	.65	.26	.06	612 Indians Rookies	.45	.18	.04
566 Tim Cullen	.45	.18	.04	Lou Camilli			
567 Walt Alston MGR	1.25	.50	.12	Ted Ford			
568 Sal Campisi	.45	.18	.04	Steve Mingori			
569 Ivan Murrell	.45	.18	.04	613 Pedro Borbon	.45	.18	.04
570 Jim Palmer	6.00	2.40	.60	614 Billy Cowan	.45	.18	.04
571 Ted Sizemore	.45	.18	.04	615 Mel Stottlemyre	.75	.30	.07
572 Jerry Kenney	.45	.18	.04	616 Larry Hisle	.60	.24	.06

	MINT	VG-E	F-G
☐ 617 Clay Dalrymple	.45	.18	.04
☐ 618 Tug McGraw	1.00	.40	.10
☐ 619 A Checklist 6 (copyright on back)	1.50	.15	.03
☐ 619 B Checklist 6 (no copyright)	2.00	.20	.04
☐ 620 Frank Howard	1.00	.40	.10
☐ 621 Ron Bryant	.45	.18	.04
☐ 622 Joe Lahoud	.45	.18	.04
☐ 623 Pat Jarvis	.45	.18	.04
☐ 624 Athletics Team	1.00	.40	.10
☐ 625 Lou Brock	6.50	2.60	.65
☐ 626 Freddie Patek	.60	.24	.06
☐ 627 Steve Hamilton	.45	.18	.04
☐ 628 John Bateman	.45	.18	.04
☐ 629 John Hiller	.60	.24	.06
☐ 630 Roberto Clemente	15.00	6.00	1.50
☐ 631 Eddie Fisher	.45	.18	.04
☐ 632 Darrel Chaney	.45	.18	.04
☐ 633 AL Rookie Outfielders Bobby Brooks Pete Koegel Scott Northey	.45	.18	.04
☐ 634 Phil Regan	.60	.24	.06
☐ 635 Bobby Murcer	1.00	.40	.10
☐ 636 Denny Lemaster	.45	.18	.04
☐ 637 Dave Bristol MGR	.45	.18	.04
☐ 638 Stan Williams	.45	.18	.04
☐ 639 Tom Haller	.45	.18	.04
☐ 640 Frank Robinson	7.50	3.00	.75
☐ 641 Mets Team	1.50	.60	.15
☐ 642 Jim Roland	.45	.18	.04
☐ 643 Rick Reichardt	.45	.18	.04
☐ 644 Jim Stewart	1.00	.40	.10
☐ 645 Jim Maloney	1.25	.50	.12
☐ 646 Bobby Floyd	1.00	.40	.10
☐ 647 Juan Pizarro	1.00	.40	.10
☐ 648 Mets Rookies Rich Folkers Ted Martinez John Matlack	3.00	1.20	.30
☐ 649 Sparky Lyle	2.00	.80	.20
☐ 650 Rich Allen	5.00	2.00	.50
☐ 651 Jerry Robertson	1.00	.40	.10
☐ 652 Braves Team	2.00	.80	.20
☐ 653 Russ Snyder	1.00	.40	.10
☐ 654 Don Shaw	1.00	.40	.10
☐ 655 Mike Epstein	1.00	.40	.10
☐ 656 Gerry Nyman	1.00	.40	.10
☐ 657 Jose Azcue	1.00	.40	.10
☐ 658 Paul Lindblad	1.00	.40	.10
☐ 659 Byron Browne	1.00	.40	.10
☐ 660 Ray Culp	1.00	.40	.10

	MINT	VG-E	F-G
☐ 661 Chuck Tanner MGR	1.75	.70	.17
☐ 662 Mike Hedlund	1.00	.40	.10
☐ 663 Marv Staehle	1.00	.40	.10
☐ 664 Rookie Pitchers Archie Reynolds Bob Reynolds Ken Reynolds	1.25	.50	.12
☐ 665 Ron Swoboda	1.25	.50	.12
☐ 666 Gene Brabender	1.00	.40	.10
☐ 667 Pete Ward	1.00	.40	.10
☐ 668 Gary Neibauer	1.00	.40	.10
☐ 669 Ike Brown	1.00	.40	.10
☐ 670 Bill Hands	1.00	.40	.10
☐ 671 Bill Voss	1.00	.40	.10
☐ 672 Ed Crosby	1.00	.40	.10
☐ 673 Gerry Janeski	1.00	.40	.10
☐ 674 Expos Team	2.25	.90	.22
☐ 675 Dave Boswell	1.00	.40	.10
☐ 676 Tommie Reynolds	1.00	.40	.10
☐ 677 Jack DiLauro	1.00	.40	.10
☐ 678 George Thomas	1.00	.40	.10
☐ 679 Don O'Riley	1.00	.40	.10
☐ 680 Don Mincher	1.25	.50	.12
☐ 681 Bill Butler	1.00	.40	.10
☐ 682 Terry Harmon	1.00	.40	.10
☐ 683 Bill Burbach	1.00	.40	.10
☐ 684 Curt Motton	1.00	.40	.10
☐ 685 Moe Drabowsky	1.00	.40	.10
☐ 686 Chico Ruiz	1.00	.40	.10
☐ 687 Ron Taylor	1.00	.40	.10
☐ 688 Sparky Anderson MGR	2.25	.90	.22
☐ 689 Frank Baker	1.00	.40	.10
☐ 690 Bob Moose	1.00	.40	.10
☐ 691 Bob Heise	1.00	.40	.10
☐ 692 AL Rookie Pitchers Hal Haydel Rogelio Moret Wayne Twitchell	1.00	.40	.10
☐ 693 Jose Pena	1.00	.40	.10
☐ 694 Rick Renick	1.00	.40	.10
☐ 695 Joe Niekro	2.00	.80	.20
☐ 696 Jerry Morales	1.00	.40	.10
☐ 697 Rickey Clark	1.00	.40	.10
☐ 698 Brewers Team	2.25	.90	.22
☐ 699 Jim Britton	1.00	.40	.10
☐ 700 Boog Powell	2.25	.90	.22
☐ 701 Bob Garibaldi	1.00	.40	.10
☐ 702 Milt Ramirez	1.00	.40	.10
☐ 703 Mike Kekich	1.00	.40	.10
☐ 704 J.C. Martin	1.00	.40	.10
☐ 705 Dick Selma	1.00	.40	.10
☐ 706 Joe Foy	1.00	.40	.10
☐ 707 Fred Lasher	1.00	.40	.10

		MINT	VG-E	F-G
☐ 708	Russ Nagelson	1.00	.40	.10
☐ 709	Rookie Outfielders	18.00	7.25	1.80
	Dusty Baker			
	Don Baylor			
	Tom Paciorek			
☐ 710	Sonny Siebert	1.25	.50	.12
☐ 711	Larry Stahl	1.00	.40	.10
☐ 712	Jose Martinez	1.00	.40	.10
☐ 713	Mike Marshall	1.50	.60	.15
☐ 714	Dick Williams MGR	1.25	.50	.12
☐ 715	Horace Clarke	1.00	.40	.10
☐ 716	Dave Leonhard	1.00	.40	.10
☐ 717	Tommie Aaron	1.25	.50	.12
☐ 718	Billy Wynne	1.00	.40	.10
☐ 719	Jerry May	1.00	.40	.10
☐ 720	Matty Alou	1.25	.50	.12
☐ 721	John Morris	1.00	.40	.10
☐ 722	Astros Team	2.00	.80	.20
☐ 723	Vicente Romo	1.00	.40	.10
☐ 724	Tom Tischinski	1.00	.40	.10
☐ 725	Gary Gentry	1.00	.40	.10
☐ 726	Paul Popovich	1.00	.40	.10
☐ 727	Ray Lamb	1.00	.40	.10
☐ 728	NL Rookie Outfielders	1.00	.40	.10
	Wayne Redmond			
	Keith Lampard			
	Bernie Williams			
☐ 729	Dick Billings	1.00	.40	.10
☐ 730	Jim Rooker	1.00	.40	.10
☐ 731	Jim Qualls	1.00	.40	.10
☐ 732	Bob Reed	1.00	.40	.10
☐ 733	Lee Maye	1.00	.40	.10
☐ 734	Rob Gardner	1.00	.40	.10
☐ 735	Mike Shannon	1.50	.60	.15
☐ 736	Mel Queen	1.00	.40	.10
☐ 737	Preston Gomez MGR	1.00	.40	.10
☐ 738	Russ Gibson	1.00	.40	.10
☐ 739	Barry Lersch	1.00	.40	.10
☐ 740	Luis Aparicio	6.00	2.40	.60
☐ 741	Skip Guinn	1.00	.40	.10
☐ 742	Royals Team	2.25	.90	.22
☐ 743	John O'Donoghue	1.00	.40	.10
☐ 744	Chuck Manuel	1.00	.40	.10
☐ 745	Sandy Alomar	1.00	.40	.10
☐ 746	Andy Kosco	1.00	.40	.10
☐ 747	NL Rookie Pitchers	1.00	.40	.10
	Al Severinsen			
	Scipio Spinks			
	Balor Moore			
☐ 748	John Purdin	1.00	.40	.10
☐ 749	Ken Szotkiewicz	1.00	.40	.10
☐ 750	Denny McLain	2.25	.90	.22
☐ 751	Al Weis	1.50	.60	.15

		MINT	VG-E	F-G
☐ 752	Dick Drago	1.50	.50	.10

1972 Topps

The cards in this 787-card set measure 2½"
by 3½". The 1972 Topps set contained the
most cards ever for a Topps set to that point
in time. Features appearing for the first time
were "Boyhood Photos" (KP: 341-348 and
491-498), Awards and Trophy cards (621-
626), "In Action" (distributed throughout the
set) and "Traded Cards" (TR: 751-757). Other subsets included League Leaders (85-96),
Playoffs cards (221-222), and World Series
cards (223-230). The curved lines of the color
picture are a departure from the rectangular
designs of other years. There is a series of
intermediate scarcity (526-656) and the usual high numbers (657-787).

	MINT	VG-E	F-G
Complete Set	675.00	300.00	75.00
Common Player (1-132)	.15	.06	.01
Common Player (133-394)	.18	.08	.01
Common Player (395-525)	.22	.10	.02
Common Player (526-656)	.40	.16	.04
Common Player (657-787)	1.20	.50	.12

		MINT	VG-E	F-G
☐ 1	Pirates Team	1.75	.35	.05
☐ 2	Ray Culp	.15	.06	.01
☐ 3	Bob Tolan	.15	.06	.01
☐ 4	Checklist 1	.90	.10	.02

		MINT	VG-E	F-G
☐	5 John Bateman	.15	.06	.01
☐	6 Fred Scherman	.15	.06	.01
☐	7 Enzo Hernandez	.15	.06	.01
☐	8 Ron Swoboda	.20	.08	.02
☐	9 Stan Williams	.15	.06	.01
☐	10 Amos Otis	.30	.12	.03
☐	11 Bobby Valentine	.50	.20	.05
☐	12 Jose Cardenal	.15	.06	.01
☐	13 Joe Grzenda	.15	.06	.01
☐	14 Phillies Rookies	.15	.06	.01
	Pete Koegel			
	Mike Anderson			
	Wayne Twitchell			
☐	15 Walt Williams	.15	.06	.01
☐	16 Mike Jorgensen	.15	.06	.01
☐	17 Dave Duncan	.15	.06	.01
☐	18 A Juan Pizarro	.20	.08	.02
	(yellow underline			
	C and S of Cubs)			
☐	18 B Juan Pizarro	4.00	1.60	.40
	(green underline			
	C and S of Cubs)			
☐	19 Billy Cowan	.15	.06	.01
☐	20 Don Wilson	.15	.06	.01
☐	21 Braves Team	.50	.20	.05
☐	22 Rob Gardner	.15	.06	.01
☐	23 Ted Kubiak	.15	.06	.01
☐	24 Ted Ford	.15	.06	.01
☐	25 Bill Singer	.15	.06	.01
☐	26 Andy Etchebarren	.15	.06	.01
☐	27 Bob Johnson	.15	.06	.01
☐	28 Twins Rookies	.15	.06	.01
	Bob Gebhard			
	Steve Brye			
	Hal Haydel			
☐	29 A Bill Bonham	.20	.08	.02
	(yellow underline			
	C and S of Cubs)			
☐	29 B Bill Bonham	4.00	1.60	.40
	(green underline			
	C and S of Cubs)			
☐	30 Rico Petrocelli	.25	.10	.02
☐	31 Cleon Jones	.15	.06	.01
☐	32 Jones In Action	.15	.06	.01
☐	33 Billy Martin MGR	.90	.36	.09
☐	34 Martin In Action	.50	.20	.05
☐	35 Jerry Johnson	.15	.06	.01
☐	36 Johnson In Action	.15	.06	.01
☐	37 Carl Yastrzemski	9.00	3.75	.90
☐	38 Yastrzemski In Action	4.50	1.80	.45
☐	39 Bob Barton	.15	.06	.01
☐	40 Barton In Action	.15	.06	.01
☐	41 Tommy Davis	.25	.10	.02

		MINT	VG-E	F-G
☐	42 Davis In Action	.20	.08	.02
☐	43 Rick Wise	.15	.06	.01
☐	44 Wise In Action	.15	.06	.01
☐	45 A Glenn Beckert	.30	.12	.03
	(yellow underline			
	C and S of Cubs)			
☐	45 B Glenn Beckert	4.50	1.80	.45
	(green underline			
	C and S of Cubs)			
☐	46 Beckert In Action	.20	.08	.02
☐	47 John Ellis	.15	.06	.01
☐	48 Ellis In Action	.15	.06	.01
☐	49 Willie Mays	9.00	3.75	.90
☐	50 Mays In Action	4.50	1.80	.45
☐	51 Harmon Killebrew	2.00	.80	.20
☐	52 Killebrew In Action	1.00	.40	.10
☐	53 Bud Harrelson	.15	.06	.01
☐	54 Harrelson In Action	.15	.06	.01
☐	55 Clyde Wright	.15	.06	.01
☐	56 Rich Chiles	.15	.06	.01
☐	57 Bob Oliver	.15	.06	.01
☐	58 Ernie McAnally	.15	.06	.01
☐	59 Fred Stanley	.15	.06	.01
☐	60 Manny Sanguillen	.25	.10	.02
☐	61 Cubs Rookies	.60	.24	.06
	Burt Hooton			
	Gene Hiser			
	Earl Stephenson			
☐	62 Angel Mangual	.15	.06	.01
☐	63 Duke Sims	.15	.06	.01
☐	64 Pete Broberg	.15	.06	.01
☐	65 Cesar Cedeno	.60	.24	.06
☐	66 Ray Corbin	.15	.06	.01
☐	67 Red Schoendienst MGR	.30	.12	.03
☐	68 Jim York	.15	.06	.01
☐	69 Roger Freed	.15	.06	.01
☐	70 Mike Cuellar	.25	.10	.02
☐	71 Angels Team	.45	.18	.04
☐	72 Bruce Kison	.50	.20	.05
☐	73 Steve Huntz	.15	.06	.01
☐	74 Cecil Upshaw	.15	.06	.01
☐	75 Bert Campaneris	.30	.12	.03
☐	76 Don Carrithers	.15	.06	.01
☐	77 Ron Theobald	.15	.06	.01
☐	78 Steve Arlin	.15	.06	.01
☐	79 Red Sox Rookies	18.00	7.25	1.80
	Mike Garman			
	Cecil Cooper			
	Carlton Fisk			
☐	80 Tony Perez	1.00	.40	.10
☐	81 Mike Hedlund	.15	.06	.01
☐	82 Ron Woods	.15	.06	.01
☐	83 Dalton Jones	.15	.06	.01

		MINT	VG-E	F-G
☐ 84	Vince Colbert	.15	.06	.01
☐ 85	NL Batting Leaders	.50	.20	.05
	Joe Torre			
	Ralph Garr			
	Glenn Beckert			
☐ 86	AL Batting Leaders	.50	.20	.05
	Tony Oliva			
	Bobby Murcer			
	Merv Rettenmund			
☐ 87	NL RBI Leaders	1.00	.40	.10
	Joe Torre			
	Willie Stargell			
	Hank Aaron			
☐ 88	AL RBI Leaders	.75	.30	.07
	Harmon Killebrew			
	Frank Robinson			
	Reggie Smith			
☐ 89	NL Home Run Leaders	1.00	.40	.10
	Willie Stargell			
	Hank Aaron			
	Lee May			
☐ 90	AL Home Run Leaders	.75	.30	.07
	Bill Melton			
	Norm Cash			
	Reggie Jackson			
☐ 91	NL ERA Leaders	.75	.30	.07
	Tom Seaver			
	Dave Roberts			
	(photo actually			
	Danny Coombs)			
	Don Wilson			
☐ 92	AL ERA Leaders	.65	.26	.06
	Vida Blue			
	Wilbur Wood			
	Jim Palmer			
☐ 93	NL Pitching Leaders	1.00	.40	.10
	Fergie Jenkins			
	Steve Carlton			
	Al Downing			
	Tom Seaver			
☐ 94	AL Pitching Leaders	.50	.20	.05
	Mickey Lolich			
	Vida Blue			
	Wilbur Wood			
☐ 95	NL Strikeout Leaders	.75	.30	.07
	Tom Seaver			
	Fergie Jenkins			
	Bill Stoneman			
☐ 96	AL Strikeout Leaders	.50	.20	.05
	Mickey Lolich			
	Vida Blue			
	Joe Coleman			
☐ 97	Tom Kelley	.15	.06	.01

		MINT	VG-E	F-G
☐ 98	Chuck Tanner MGR	.25	.10	.02
☐ 99	Ross Grimsley	.15	.06	.01
☐ 100	Frank Robinson	2.50	1.00	.25
☐ 101	Astros Rookies	1.25	.50	.12
	Bill Greif			
	J.R. Richard			
	Ray Busse			
☐ 102	Lloyd Allen	.15	.06	.01
☐ 103	Checklist 2	.90	.10	.02
☐ 104	Toby Harrah	1.50	.60	.15
☐ 105	Gary Gentry	.15	.06	.01
☐ 106	Brewers Team	.50	.20	.05
☐ 107	Jose Cruz	2.50	1.00	.25
☐ 108	Gary Waslewski	.15	.06	.01
☐ 109	Jerry May	.15	.06	.01
☐ 110	Ron Hunt	.15	.06	.01
☐ 111	Jim Grant	.15	.06	.01
☐ 112	Greg Luzinski	.85	.34	.08
☐ 113	Rogelio Moret	.15	.06	.01
☐ 114	Bill Buckner	1.50	.60	.15
☐ 115	Jim Fregosi	.30	.12	.03
☐ 116	Ed Farmer	.25	.10	.02
☐ 117 A	Cleo James	.20	.08	.02
	(yellow underline			
	C and S of Cubs)			
☐ 117 B	Cleo James	4.00	1.60	.40
	(green underline			
	C and S of Cubs)			
☐ 118	Skip Lockwood	.15	.06	.01
☐ 119	Marty Perez	.15	.06	.01
☐ 120	Bill Freehan	.30	.12	.03
☐ 121	Ed Sprague	.15	.06	.01
☐ 122	Larry Biittner	.15	.06	.01
☐ 123	Ed Acosta	.15	.06	.01
☐ 124	Yankees Rookies	.15	.06	.01
	Alan Closter			
	Rusty Torres			
	Roger Hambright			
☐ 125	Dave Cash	.15	.06	.01
☐ 126	Bart Johnson	.15	.06	.01
☐ 127	Duffy Dyer	.15	.06	.01
☐ 128	Eddie Watt	.15	.06	.01
☐ 129	Charlie Fox MGR	.15	.06	.01
☐ 130	Bob Gibson	2.50	1.00	.25
☐ 131	Jim Nettles	.15	.06	.01
☐ 132	Joe Morgan	2.00	.80	.20
☐ 133	Joe Keough	.18	.08	.01
☐ 134	Carl Morton	.18	.08	.01
☐ 135	Vada Pinson	.35	.14	.03
☐ 136	Darrell Chaney	.18	.08	.01
☐ 137	Dick Williams MGR	.25	.10	.02
☐ 138	Mike Kekich	.18	.08	.01
☐ 139	Tim McCarver	.35	.14	.03

		MINT	VG-E	F-G
☐ 140	Pat Dobson	.25	.10	.02
☐ 141	Mets Rookies	.40	.16	.04
	Buzz Capra			
	Leroy Stanton			
	Jon Matlack			
☐ 142	Chris Chambliss	1.75	.70	.17
☐ 143	Garry Jestadt	.18	.08	.01
☐ 144	Marty Pattin	.18	.08	.01
☐ 145	Don Kessinger	.25	.10	.02
☐ 146	Steve Kealey	.18	.08	.01
☐ 147	Dave Kingman	4.00	1.60	.40
☐ 148	Dick Billings	.18	.08	.01
☐ 149	Gary Neibauer	.18	.08	.01
☐ 150	Norm Cash	.40	.16	.04
☐ 151	Jim Brewer	.18	.08	.01
☐ 152	Gene Clines	.18	.08	.01
☐ 153	Rick Auerbach	.18	.08	.01
☐ 154	Ted Simmons	1.25	.50	.12
☐ 155	Larry Dierker	.25	.10	.02
☐ 156	Twins Team	.45	.18	.04
☐ 157	Don Gullett	.25	.10	.02
☐ 158	Jerry Kenney	.18	.08	.01
☐ 159	John Boccabella	.18	.08	.01
☐ 160	Andy Messersmith	.35	.14	.03
☐ 161	Brock Davis	.18	.08	.01
☐ 162	Brewers Rookies	1.00	.40	.10
	Jerry Bell			
	Darrell Porter			
	Bob Reynolds			
	(Porter and Bell			
	photos switched)			
☐ 163	Tug McGraw	.50	.20	.05
☐ 164	McGraw In Action	.25	.10	.02
☐ 165	Chris Speier	.18	.08	.01
☐ 166	Speier In Action	.18	.08	.01
☐ 167	Deron Johnson	.18	.08	.01
☐ 168	Johnson In Action	.18	.08	.01
☐ 169	Vida Blue	.65	.26	.06
☐ 170	Blue In Action	.35	.14	.03
☐ 171	Darrell Evans	.65	.26	.06
☐ 172	Evans In Action	.35	.14	.03
☐ 173	Clay Kirby	.18	.08	.01
☐ 174	Kirby In Action	.18	.08	.01
☐ 175	Tom Haller	.18	.08	.01
☐ 176	Haller In Action	.18	.08	.01
☐ 177	Paul Schaal	.18	.08	.01
☐ 178	Schaal In Action	.18	.08	.01
☐ 179	Dock Ellis	.18	.08	.01
☐ 180	Ellis In Action	.18	.08	.01
☐ 181	Ed Kranepool	.25	.10	.02
☐ 182	Kranepool In Action	.25	.10	.02
☐ 183	Bill Melton	.18	.08	.01
☐ 184	Melton In Action	.18	.08	.01

		MINT	VG-E	F-G
☐ 185	Ron Bryant	.18	.08	.01
☐ 186	Bryant In Action	.18	.08	.01
☐ 187	Gates Brown	.25	.10	.02
☐ 188	Frank Lucchesi MGR	.18	.08	.01
☐ 189	Gene Tenace	.25	.10	.02
☐ 190	Dave Giusti	.18	.08	.01
☐ 191	Jeff Burroughs	.50	.20	.05
☐ 192	Cubs Team	.50	.20	.05
☐ 193	Kurt Bevacqua	.18	.08	.01
☐ 194	Fred Norman	.18	.08	.01
☐ 195	Orlando Cepeda	1.00	.40	.10
☐ 196	Mel Queen	.18	.08	.01
☐ 197	Johnny Briggs	.18	.08	.01
☐ 198	Dodgers Rookies	.75	.30	.07
	Charlie Hough			
	Bob O'Brien			
	Mike Strahler			
☐ 199	Mike Fiore	.18	.08	.01
☐ 200	Lou Brock	2.75	1.10	.27
☐ 201	Phil Roof	.18	.08	.01
☐ 202	Scipio Spinks	.18	.08	.01
☐ 203	Ron Blomberg	.18	.08	.01
☐ 204	Tommy Helms	.25	.10	.02
☐ 205	Dick Drago	.18	.08	.01
☐ 206	Dal Maxvill	.18	.08	.01
☐ 207	Tom Egan	.18	.08	.01
☐ 208	Milt Pappas	.25	.10	.02
☐ 209	Joe Rudi	.30	.12	.03
☐ 210	Denny McLain	.60	.24	.06
☐ 211	Gary Sutherland	.18	.08	.01
☐ 212	Grant Jackson	.18	.08	.01
☐ 213	Angels Rookies	.18	.08	.01
	Billy Parker			
	Art Kusnyer			
	Tom Silverio			
☐ 214	Mike McQueen	.18	.08	.01
☐ 215	Alex Johnson	.25	.10	.02
☐ 216	Joe Niekro	.35	.14	.03
☐ 217	Roger Metzger	.18	.08	.01
☐ 218	Eddie Kasko MGR	.18	.08	.01
☐ 219	Rennie Stennett	.25	.10	.02
☐ 220	Jim Perry	.30	.12	.03
☐ 221	NL Playoffs	.60	.24	.06
	Bucs champs			
☐ 222	AL Playoffs	.90	.36	.09
	Orioles champs			
	(Brooks Robinson)			
☐ 223	World Series Game 1	.60	.24	.06
	(McNally pitching)			
☐ 224	World Series Game 2	.60	.24	.06
	(B. Robinson and			
	Belanger)			

	MINT	VG-E	F-G
☐ 225 World Series Game 3 ... (Sanguillen scoring)	.60	.24	.06
☐ 226 World Series Game 4 ... (Clemente on 2nd)	1.50	.60	.15
☐ 227 World Series Game 5 ... (Briles pitching)	.60	.24	.06
☐ 228 World Series Game 6 ... (Frank Robinson and Manny Sanguillen)	.75	.30	.07
☐ 229 World Series Game 7 ... (Blass pitching)	.60	.24	.06
☐ 230 World Series Summary . Pirates celebrate	.60	.24	.06
☐ 231 Casey Cox	.18	.08	.01
☐ 232 Giants Rookies	.18	.08	.01
Chris Arnold			
Jim Barr			
Dave Rader			
☐ 233 Jay Johnstone	.25	.10	.02
☐ 234 Ron Taylor	.18	.08	.01
☐ 235 Merv Rettenmund	.18	.08	.01
☐ 236 Jim McGlothlin	.18	.08	.01
☐ 237 Yankees Team	.65	.26	.06
☐ 238 Leron Lee	.18	.08	.01
☐ 239 Tom Timmermann	.18	.08	.01
☐ 240 Rich Allen	1.00	.40	.10
☐ 241 Rollie Fingers	1.50	.60	.15
☐ 242 Don Mincher	.18	.08	.01
☐ 243 Frank Linzy	.18	.08	.01
☐ 244 Steve Braun	.18	.08	.01
☐ 245 Tommie Agee	.18	.08	.01
☐ 246 Tom Burgmeier	.18	.08	.01
☐ 247 Milt May	.18	.08	.01
☐ 248 Tom Bradley	.18	.08	.01
☐ 249 Harry Walker MGR	.18	.08	.01
☐ 250 Boog Powell	.60	.24	.06
☐ 251 Checklist 3	.90	.10	.02
☐ 252 Ken Reynolds	.18	.08	.01
☐ 253 Sandy Alomar	.18	.08	.01
☐ 254 Boots Day	.18	.08	.01
☐ 255 Jim Lonborg	.25	.10	.02
☐ 256 George Foster	1.50	.60	.15
☐ 257 Tigers Rookies	.18	.08	.01
Jim Foor			
Tim Hosley			
Paul Jata			
☐ 258 Randy Hundley	.18	.08	.01
☐ 259 Sparky Lyle	.35	.14	.03
☐ 260 Ralph Garr	.25	.10	.02
☐ 261 Steve Mingori	.18	.08	.01
☐ 262 Padres Team	.45	.18	.04
☐ 263 Felipe Alou	.25	.10	.02
☐ 264 Tommy John	1.25	.50	.12

	MINT	VG-E	F-G
☐ 265 Wes Parker	.25	.10	.02
☐ 266 Bobby Bolin	.18	.08	.01
☐ 267 Dave Concepcion	1.25	.50	.12
☐ 268 A's Rookies	.18	.08	.01
Dwain Anderson			
Chris Floethe			
☐ 269 Don Hahn	.18	.08	.01
☐ 270 Jim Palmer	3.25	1.30	.32
☐ 271 Ken Rudolph	.18	.08	.01
☐ 272 Mickey Rivers	.90	.36	.09
☐ 273 Bobby Floyd	.18	.08	.01
☐ 274 Al Severinsen	.18	.08	.01
☐ 275 Cesar Tovar	.18	.08	.01
☐ 276 Gene Mauch MGR	.25	.10	.02
☐ 277 Elliot Maddox	.18	.08	.01
☐ 278 Dennis Higgins	.18	.08	.01
☐ 279 Larry Brown	.18	.08	.01
☐ 280 Willie McCovey	3.00	1.20	.30
☐ 281 Bill Parsons	.18	.08	.01
☐ 282 Astros Team	.45	.18	.04
☐ 283 Darrell Brandon	.18	.08	.01
☐ 284 Ike Brown	.18	.08	.01
☐ 285 Gaylord Perry	2.75	1.10	.27
☐ 286 Gene Alley	.25	.10	.02
☐ 287 Jim Hardin	.18	.08	.01
☐ 288 Johnny Jeter	.18	.08	.01
☐ 289 Syd O'Brien	.18	.08	.01
☐ 290 Sonny Siebert	.25	.10	.02
☐ 291 Hal McRae	.35	.14	.03
☐ 292 McRae In Action	.18	.08	.01
☐ 293 Danny Frisella	.18	.08	.01
☐ 294 Frisella In Action	.18	.08	.01
☐ 295 Dick Dietz	.18	.08	.01
☐ 296 Dietz In Action	.18	.08	.01
☐ 297 Claude Osteen	.25	.10	.02
☐ 298 Osteen In Action	.18	.08	.01
☐ 299 Hank Aaron	9.00	3.75	.90
☐ 300 Aaron in Action	4.50	1.80	.45
☐ 301 George Mitterwald	.18	.08	.01
☐ 302 Mitterwald In Action	.18	.08	.01
☐ 303 Joe Pepitone	.25	.10	.02
☐ 304 Pepitone In Action	.18	.08	.01
☐ 305 Ken Boswell	.18	.08	.01
☐ 306 Boswell In Action	.18	.08	.01
☐ 307 Steve Renko	.18	.08	.01
☐ 308 Renko In Action	.18	.08	.01
☐ 309 Roberto Clemente	7.50	3.00	.75
☐ 310 Clemente In Action	3.75	1.50	.37
☐ 311 Clay Carroll	.18	.08	.01
☐ 312 Carroll In Action	.18	.08	.01
☐ 313 Luis Aparicio	2.00	.80	.20
☐ 314 Aparicio In Action	1.00	.40	.10
☐ 315 Paul Splittorff	.25	.10	.02

		MINT	VG-E	F-G			MINT	VG-E	F-G
☐ 316	Cardinals Rookies	.30	.12	.03	☐ 360	Dave Roberts	.18	.08	.01
	Jim Bibby				☐ 361	Mike Andrews	.18	.08	.01
	Jorge Roque				☐ 362	Mets Team	.60	.24	.06
	Santiago Guzman				☐ 363	Ron Klimkowski	.18	.08	.01
☐ 317	Rich Hand	.18	.08	.01	☐ 364	Johnny Callison	.25	.10	.02
☐ 318	Sonny Jackson	.18	.08	.01	☐ 365	Dick Bosman	.18	.08	.01
☐ 319	Aurelio Rodriguez	.18	.08	.01	☐ 366	Jimmy Rosario	.18	.08	.01
☐ 320	Steve Blass	.25	.10	.02	☐ 367	Ron Perranoski	.25	.10	.02
☐ 321	Joe Lahoud	.18	.08	.01	☐ 368	Danny Thompson	.18	.08	.01
☐ 322	Jose Pena	.18	.08	.01	☐ 369	Jim Lefebvre	.18	.08	.01
☐ 323	Earl Weaver MGR	.35	.14	.03	☐ 370	Don Buford	.18	.08	.01
☐ 324	Mike Ryan	.18	.08	.01	☐ 371	Denny Lemaster	.18	.08	.01
☐ 325	Mel Stottlemyre	.25	.10	.02	☐ 372	Royals Rookies	.18	.08	.01
☐ 326	Pat Kelly	.18	.08	.01		Lance Clemons			
☐ 327	Steve Stone	.65	.26	.06		Monty Montgomery			
☐ 328	Red Sox Team	.60	.24	.06	☐ 373	John Mayberry	.25	.10	.02
☐ 329	Roy Foster	.18	.08	.01	☐ 374	Jack Heidemann	.18	.08	.01
☐ 330	Jim Hunter	2.50	1.00	.25	☐ 375	Reggie Cleveland	.18	.08	.01
☐ 331	Stan Swanson	.18	.08	.01	☐ 376	Andy Kosco	.18	.08	.01
☐ 332	Buck Martinez	.18	.08	.01	☐ 377	Terry Harmon	.18	.08	.01
☐ 333	Steve Barber	.18	.08	.01	☐ 378	Checklist 4	.90	.10	.02
☐ 334	Rangers Rookies	.18	.08	.01	☐ 379	Ken Berry	.18	.08	.01
	Bill Fahey				☐ 380	Earl Williams	.18	.08	.01
	Jim Mason				☐ 381	White Sox Team	.50	.20	.05
	Tom Ragland				☐ 382	Joe Gibbon	.18	.08	.01
☐ 335	Bill Hands	.18	.08	.01	☐ 383	Brant Alyea	.18	.08	.01
☐ 336	Marty Martinez	.18	.08	.01	☐ 384	Dave Campbell	.18	.08	.01
☐ 337	Mike Kilkenny	.18	.08	.01	☐ 385	Mickey Stanley	.25	.10	.02
☐ 338	Bob Grich	.50	.20	.05	☐ 386	Jim Colborn	.18	.08	.01
☐ 339	Ron Cook	.18	.08	.01	☐ 387	Horace Clarke	.18	.08	.01
☐ 340	Roy White	.25	.10	.02	☐ 388	Charlie Williams	.18	.08	.01
☐ 341	KP: Joe Torre	.30	.12	.03	☐ 389	Bill Rigney MGR	.18	.08	.01
☐ 342	KP: Wilbur Wood	.18	.08	.01	☐ 390	Willie Davis	.30	.12	.03
☐ 343	KP: Willie Stargell	.50	.20	.05	☐ 391	Ken Sanders	.18	.08	.01
☐ 344	KP: Dave McNally	.18	.08	.01	☐ 392	Pirates Rookies	.75	.30	.07
☐ 345	KP: Rick Wise	.18	.08	.01		Fred Cambria			
☐ 346	KP: Jim Fregosi	.25	.10	.02		Richie Zisk			
☐ 347	KP: Tom Seaver	1.00	.40	.10	☐ 393	Curt Motton	.18	.08	.01
☐ 348	KP: Sal Bando	.18	.08	.01	☐ 394	Ken Forsch	.25	.10	.02
☐ 349	Al Fitzmorris	.18	.08	.01	☐ 395	Matty Alou	.30	.12	.03
☐ 350	Frank Howard	.50	.20	.05	☐ 396	Paul Lindblad	.22	.10	.02
☐ 351	Braves Rookies	.25	.10	.02	☐ 397	Phillies Team	.60	.24	.06
	Tom House				☐ 398	Larry Hisle	.35	.14	.03
	Rick Kester				☐ 399	Milt Wilcox	.30	.12	.03
	Jimmy Britton				☐ 400	Tony Oliva	1.00	.40	.10
☐ 352	Dave LaRoche	.18	.08	.01	☐ 401	Jim Nash	.22	.10	.02
☐ 353	Art Shamsky	.18	.08	.01	☐ 402	Bobby Heise	.22	.10	.02
☐ 354	Tom Murphy	.18	.08	.01	☐ 403	John Cumberland	.22	.10	.02
☐ 355	Bob Watson	.30	.12	.03	☐ 404	Jeff Torborg	.22	.10	.02
☐ 356	Gerry Moses	.18	.08	.01	☐ 405	Ron Fairly	.30	.12	.03
☐ 357	Woodie Fryman	.18	.08	.01	☐ 406	George Hendrick	1.00	.40	.10
☐ 358	Sparky Anderson MGR	.35	.14	.03	☐ 407	Chuck Taylor	.22	.10	.02
☐ 359	Don Pavletich	.18	.08	.01	☐ 408	Jim Northrup	.30	.12	.03

	MINT	VG-E	F-G
☐ 409 Frank Baker	.22	.10	.02
☐ 410 Fergie Jenkins	1.00	.40	.10
☐ 411 Bob Montgomery	.22	.10	.02
☐ 412 Dick Kelley	.22	.10	.02
☐ 413 White Sox Rookies	.22	.10	.02
Don Eddy			
Dave Lemonds			
☐ 414 Bob Miller	.22	.10	.02
☐ 415 Cookie Rojas	.22	.10	.02
☐ 416 Johnny Edwards	.22	.10	.02
☐ 417 Tom Hall	.22	.10	.02
☐ 418 Tom Shopay	.22	.10	.02
☐ 419 Jim Spencer	.22	.10	.02
☐ 420 Steve Carlton	10.00	4.00	1.00
☐ 421 Ellie Rodriguez	.22	.10	.02
☐ 422 Ray Lamb	.22	.10	.02
☐ 423 Oscar Gamble	.30	.12	.03
☐ 424 Bill Gogolewski	.22	.10	.02
☐ 425 Ken Singleton	.60	.24	.06
☐ 426 Singleton In Action	.30	.12	.03
☐ 427 Tito Fuentes	.22	.10	.02
☐ 428 Fuentes In Action	.22	.10	.02
☐ 429 Bob Robertson	.22	.10	.02
☐ 430 Robertson In Action	.22	.10	.02
☐ 431 Clarence Gaston	.22	.10	.02
☐ 432 Gaston In Action	.22	.10	.02
☐ 433 Johnny Bench	11.00	4.50	1.10
☐ 434 Bench In Action	5.50	2.20	.55
☐ 435 Reggie Jackson	11.00	4.50	1.10
☐ 436 Jackson In Action	5.50	2.20	.55
☐ 437 Maury Wills	.90	.36	.09
☐ 438 Wills In Action	.50	.20	.05
☐ 439 Billy Williams	2.00	.80	.20
☐ 440 Williams In Action	1.00	.40	.10
☐ 441 Thurman Munson	6.50	2.60	.65
☐ 442 Munson In Action	3.25	1.30	.32
☐ 443 Ken Henderson	.22	.10	.02
☐ 444 Henderson In Action	.22	.10	.02
☐ 445 Tom Seaver	9.00	3.75	.90
☐ 446 Seaver In Action	4.50	1.80	.45
☐ 447 Willie Stargell	2.50	1.00	.25
☐ 448 Stargell In Action	1.25	.50	.12
☐ 449 Bob Lemon MGR	.60	.24	.06
☐ 450 Mickey Lolich	.60	.24	.06
☐ 451 Tony LaRussa	.35	.14	.03
☐ 452 Ed Herrmann	.22	.10	.02
☐ 453 Barry Lerch	.22	.10	.02
☐ 454 A's Team	.70	.28	.07
☐ 455 Tommy Harper	.30	.12	.03
☐ 456 Mark Belanger	.35	.14	.03

	MINT	VG-E	F-G
☐ 457 Padres Rookies	.30	.12	.03
Darcy Fast			
Derrel Thomas			
Mike Ivie			
☐ 458 Aurelio Monteagudo	.22	.10	.02
☐ 459 Rick Renick	.22	.10	.02
☐ 460 Al Downing	.30	.12	.03
☐ 461 Tim Cullen	.22	.10	.02
☐ 462 Rickey Clark	.22	.10	.02
☐ 463 Bernie Carbo	.22	.10	.02
☐ 464 Jim Roland	.22	.10	.02
☐ 465 Gil Hodges MGR	1.50	.60	.15
☐ 466 Norm Miller	.22	.10	.02
☐ 467 Steve Kline	.22	.10	.02
☐ 468 Richie Scheinblum	.22	.10	.02
☐ 469 Ron Herbel	.22	.10	.02
☐ 470 Ray Fosse	.22	.10	.02
☐ 471 Luke Walker	.22	.10	.02
☐ 472 Phil Gagliano	.22	.10	.02
☐ 473 Dan McGinn	.22	.10	.02
☐ 474 Orioles Rookies	2.00	.80	.20
Don Baylor			
Roric Harrison			
Johnny Oates			
☐ 475 Gary Nolan	.22	.10	.02
☐ 476 Lee Richard	.22	.10	.02
☐ 477 Tom Phoebus	.22	.10	.02
☐ 478 Checklist 5	.90	.10	.02
☐ 479 Don Shaw	.22	.10	.02
☐ 480 Lee May	.35	.14	.03
☐ 481 Billy Conigliaro	.30	.12	.03
☐ 482 Joe Hoerner	.22	.10	.02
☐ 483 Ken Suarez	.22	.10	.02
☐ 484 Lum Harris MGR	.22	.10	.02
☐ 485 Phil Regan	.30	.12	.03
☐ 486 John Lowenstein	.30	.12	.03
☐ 487 Tigers Team	.75	.30	.07
☐ 488 Mike Nagy	.22	.10	.02
☐ 489 Expos Rookies	.22	.10	.02
Terry Humphrey			
Keith Lampard			
☐ 490 Dave McNally	.35	.14	.03
☐ 491 KP: Lou Piniella	.35	.14	.03
☐ 492 KP: Mel Stottlemyre	.30	.12	.03
☐ 493 KP: Bob Bailey	.22	.10	.02
☐ 494 KP: Willie Horton	.30	.12	.03
☐ 495 KP: Bill Melton	.22	.10	.02
☐ 496 KP: Bud Harrelson	.22	.10	.02
☐ 497 KP: Jim Perry	.30	.12	.03
☐ 498 KP: Brooks Robinson	1.00	.40	.10
☐ 499 Vicente Romo	.22	.10	.02
☐ 500 Joe Torre	.60	.24	.06
☐ 501 Pete Hamm	.22	.10	.02

		MINT	VG-E	F-G
☐ 502	Jackie Hernandez	.22	.10	.02
☐ 503	Gary Peters	.30	.12	.03
☐ 504	Ed Spiezio	.22	.10	.02
☐ 505	Mike Marshall	.35	.14	.03
☐ 506	Indians Rookies	.35	.14	.03
	Terry Ley			
	Jim Moyer			
	Dick Tidrow			
☐ 507	Fred Gladding	.22	.10	.02
☐ 508	Ellie Hendricks	.22	.10	.02
☐ 509	Don McMahon	.22	.10	.02
☐ 510	Ted Williams MGR	3.50	1.40	.35
☐ 511	Tony Taylor	.22	.10	.02
☐ 512	Paul Popovich	.22	.10	.02
☐ 513	Lindy McDaniel	.22	.10	.02
☐ 514	Ted Sizemore	.22	.10	.02
☐ 515	Bert Blyleven	2.00	.80	.20
☐ 516	Oscar Brown	.22	.10	.02
☐ 517	Ken Brett	.22	.10	.02
☐ 518	Wayne Garrett	.22	.10	.02
☐ 519	Ted Abernathy	.22	.10	.02
☐ 520	Larry Bowa	1.00	.40	.10
☐ 521	Alan Foster	.22	.10	.02
☐ 522	Dodgers Team	.90	.36	.09
☐ 523	Chuck Dobson	.22	.10	.02
☐ 524	Reds Rookies	.22	.10	.02
	Ed Armbrister			
	Mel Behney			
☐ 525	Carlos May	.22	.10	.02
☐ 526	Bob Bailey	.40	.16	.04
☐ 527	Dave Leonhard	.40	.16	.04
☐ 528	Ron Stone	.40	.16	.04
☐ 529	Dave Nelson	.40	.16	.04
☐ 530	Don Sutton	2.25	.90	.22
☐ 531	Freddie Patek	.50	.20	.05
☐ 532	Fred Kendall	.40	.16	.04
☐ 533	Ralph Houk MGR	.60	.24	.06
☐ 534	Jim Hickman	.40	.16	.04
☐ 535	Ed Brinkman	.40	.16	.04
☐ 536	Doug Rader	.50	.20	.05
☐ 537	Bob Locker	.40	.16	.04
☐ 538	Charlie Sands	.40	.16	.04
☐ 539	Terry Forster	1.50	.60	.15
☐ 540	Felix Millan	.40	.16	.04
☐ 541	Roger Repoz	.40	.16	.04
☐ 542	Jack Billingham	.40	.16	.04
☐ 543	Duane Josephson	.40	.16	.04
☐ 544	Ted Martinez	.40	.16	.04
☐ 545	Wayne Granger	.40	.16	.04
☐ 546	Joe Hague	.40	.16	.04
☐ 547	Indians Team	.75	.30	.07
☐ 548	Frank Reberger	.40	.16	.04
☐ 549	Dave May	.40	.16	.04

		MINT	VG-E	F-G
☐ 550	Brooks Robinson	5.50	2.20	.55
☐ 551	Ollie Brown	.40	.16	.04
☐ 552	Brown In Action	.40	.16	.04
☐ 553	Wilbur Wood	.50	.20	.05
☐ 554	Wood In Action	.40	.16	.04
☐ 555	Ron Santo	.75	.30	.07
☐ 556	Santo In Action	.50	.20	.05
☐ 557	John Odom	.40	.16	.04
☐ 558	Odom In Action	.40	.16	.04
☐ 559	Pete Rose	45.00	18.00	4.50
☐ 560	Rose In Action	15.00	6.00	1.50
☐ 561	Leo Cardenas	.40	.16	.04
☐ 562	Cardenas In Action	.40	.16	.04
☐ 563	Ray Sadecki	.40	.16	.04
☐ 564	Sadecki In Action	.40	.16	.04
☐ 565	Reggie Smith	.75	.30	.07
☐ 566	Smith In Action	.50	.20	.05
☐ 567	Juan Marichal	2.50	1.00	.25
☐ 568	Marichal In Action	1.25	.50	.12
☐ 569	Ed Kirkpatrick	.40	.16	.04
☐ 570	Kirkpatrick In Action	.40	.16	.04
☐ 571	Nate Colbert	.40	.16	.04
☐ 572	Colbert In Action	.40	.16	.04
☐ 573	Fritz Peterson	.40	.16	.04
☐ 574	Peterson In Action	.40	.16	.04
☐ 575	Al Oliver	1.50	.60	.15
☐ 576	Leo Durocher MGR	.75	.30	.07
☐ 577	Mike Paul	.40	.16	.04
☐ 578	Billy Grabarkewitz	.40	.16	.04
☐ 579	Doyle Alexander	1.00	.40	.10
☐ 580	Lou Piniella	1.50	.60	.15
☐ 581	Wade Blasingame	.40	.16	.04
☐ 582	Expos Team	.75	.30	.07
☐ 583	Darold Knowles	.40	.16	.04
☐ 584	Jerry McNertney	.40	.16	.04
☐ 585	George Scott	.50	.20	.05
☐ 586	Denis Menke	.40	.16	.04
☐ 587	Billy Wilson	.40	.16	.04
☐ 588	Jim Holt	.40	.16	.04
☐ 589	Hal Lanier	.60	.24	.06
☐ 590	Graig Nettles	1.75	.70	.17
☐ 591	Paul Casanova	.40	.16	.04
☐ 592	Lew Krausse	.40	.16	.04
☐ 593	Rich Morales	.40	.16	.04
☐ 594	Jim Beauchamp	.40	.16	.04
☐ 595	Nolan Ryan	11.00	4.50	1.10
☐ 596	Manny Mota	.60	.24	.06
☐ 597	Jim Magnuson	.40	.16	.04
☐ 598	Hal King	.40	.16	.04
☐ 599	Billy Champion	.40	.16	.04
☐ 600	Al Kaline	6.00	2.40	.60
☐ 601	George Stone	.40	.16	.04
☐ 602	Dave Bristol MGR	.40	.16	.04

		MINT	VG-E	F-G
☐ 603	Jim Ray	.40	.16	.04
☐ 604	**A** Checklist 6 (copyright on back bottom right)	2.00	.20	.04
☐ 604	**B** Checklist 6 (copyright on back bottom left)	4.00	.40	.08
☐ 605	Nelson Briles	.50	.20	.05
☐ 606	Luis Melendez	.40	.16	.04
☐ 607	Frank Duffy	.40	.16	.04
☐ 608	Mike Corkins	.40	.16	.04
☐ 609	Tom Grieve	.60	.24	.06
☐ 610	Bill Stoneman	.40	.16	.04
☐ 611	Rich Reese	.40	.16	.04
☐ 612	Joe Decker	.40	.16	.04
☐ 613	Mike Ferraro	.50	.20	.05
☐ 614	Ted Uhlaender	.40	.16	.04
☐ 615	Steve Hargan	.40	.16	.04
☐ 616	Joe Ferguson	.60	.24	.06
☐ 617	Royals Team	.75	.30	.07
☐ 618	Rich Robertson	.40	.16	.04
☐ 619	Rich McKinney	.40	.16	.04
☐ 620	Phil Niekro	2.00	.80	.20
☐ 621	Commissioners Award	.60	.24	.06
☐ 622	MVP Award	.60	.24	.06
☐ 623	Cy Young Award	.60	.24	.06
☐ 624	Minor League Player	.60	.24	.06
☐ 625	Rookie of the Year	.60	.24	.06
☐ 626	Babe Ruth Award	.90	.36	.09
☐ 627	Moe Drabowsky	.40	.16	.04
☐ 628	Terry Crowley	.40	.16	.04
☐ 629	Paul Doyle	.40	.16	.04
☐ 630	Rich Hebner	.40	.16	.04
☐ 631	John Strohmayer	.40	.16	.04
☐ 632	Mike Hegan	.40	.16	.04
☐ 633	Jack Hiatt	.40	.16	.04
☐ 634	Dick Woodson	.40	.16	.04
☐ 635	Don Money	.50	.20	.05
☐ 636	Bill Lee	.50	.20	.05
☐ 637	Preston Gomez MGR	.40	.16	.04
☐ 638	Ken Wright	.40	.16	.04
☐ 639	J.C. Martin	.40	.16	.04
☐ 640	Joe Coleman	.40	.16	.04
☐ 641	Mike Lum	.40	.16	.04
☐ 642	Dennis Riddleberger	.40	.16	.04
☐ 643	Russ Gibson	.40	.16	.04
☐ 644	Bernie Allen	.40	.16	.04
☐ 645	Jim Maloney	.50	.20	.05
☐ 646	Chico Salmon	.40	.16	.04
☐ 647	Bob Moose	.40	.16	.04
☐ 648	Jim Lyttle	.40	.16	.04
☐ 649	Pete Richert	.40	.16	.04
☐ 650	Sal Bando	.60	.24	.06

		MINT	VG-E	F-G
☐ 651	Reds Team	.90	.36	.09
☐ 652	Marcelino Lopez	.40	.16	.04
☐ 653	Jim Fairey	.40	.16	.04
☐ 654	Horacio Pina	.40	.16	.04
☐ 655	Jerry Grote	.40	.16	.04
☐ 656	Rudy May	.40	.16	.04
☐ 657	Bobby Wine	1.20	.50	.12
☐ 658	Steve Dunning	1.20	.50	.12
☐ 659	Bob Aspromonte	1.20	.50	.12
☐ 660	Paul Blair	1.50	.60	.15
☐ 661	Bill Virdon	1.75	.70	.17
☐ 662	Stan Bahnsen	1.20	.50	.12
☐ 663	Fran Healy	1.20	.50	.12
☐ 664	Bobby Knoop	1.20	.50	.12
☐ 665	Chris Short	1.20	.50	.12
☐ 666	Hector Torres	1.20	.50	.12
☐ 667	Ray Newman	1.20	.50	.12
☐ 668	Rangers Team	3.00	1.20	.30
☐ 669	Willie Crawford	1.20	.50	.12
☐ 670	Ken Holtzman	1.50	.60	.15
☐ 671	Donn Clendenon	1.50	.60	.15
☐ 672	Archie Reynolds	1.20	.50	.12
☐ 673	Dave Marshall	1.20	.50	.12
☐ 674	John Kennedy	1.20	.50	.12
☐ 675	Pat Jarvis	1.20	.50	.12
☐ 676	Danny Cater	1.20	.50	.12
☐ 677	Ivan Murrell	1.20	.50	.12
☐ 678	Steve Luebber	1.20	.50	.12
☐ 679	Astros Rookies Bob Fenwick Bob Stinson	1.20	.50	.12
☐ 680	Dave Johnson	2.50	1.00	.25
☐ 681	Bobby Pfeil	1.20	.50	.12
☐ 682	Mike McCormick	1.50	.60	.15
☐ 683	Steve Hovley	1.20	.50	.12
☐ 684	Hal Breeden	1.20	.50	.12
☐ 685	Joe Horlen	1.50	.60	.15
☐ 686	Steve Garvey	55.00	22.00	5.50
☐ 687	Del Unser	1.20	.50	.12
☐ 688	Cardinals Team	2.25	.90	.22
☐ 689	Eddie Fisher	1.20	.50	.12
☐ 690	Willie Montanez	1.20	.50	.12
☐ 691	Curt Blefary	1.20	.50	.12
☐ 692	Blefary In Action	1.20	.50	.12
☐ 693	Alan Gallagher	1.20	.50	.12
☐ 694	Gallagher In Action	1.20	.50	.12
☐ 695	Rod Carew	55.00	22.00	5.50
☐ 696	Carew In Action	20.00	8.00	2.00
☐ 697	Jerry Koosman	4.00	1.60	.40
☐ 698	Koosman In Action	2.00	.80	.20
☐ 699	Bobby Murcer	4.00	1.60	.40
☐ 700	Murcer In Action	2.00	.80	.20
☐ 701	Jose Pagan	1.20	.50	.12

	MINT	VG-E	F-G
☐ 702 Pagan In Action	1.20	.50	.12
☐ 703 Doug Griffin	1.20	.50	.12
☐ 704 Griffin In Action	1.20	.50	.12
☐ 705 Pat Corrales	1.75	.70	.17
☐ 706 Corrales In Action	1.50	.60	.15
☐ 707 Tim Foli	1.20	.50	.12
☐ 708 Foli In Action	1.20	.50	.12
☐ 709 Jim Kaat	4.00	1.60	.40
☐ 710 Kaat In Action	2.00	.80	.20
☐ 711 Bobby Bonds	3.50	1.40	.35
☐ 712 Bonds In Action	1.75	.70	.17
☐ 713 Gene Michael	1.75	.70	.17
☐ 714 Michael In Action	1.50	.60	.15
☐ 715 Mike Epstein	1.20	.50	.12
☐ 716 Jesus Alou	1.20	.50	.12
☐ 717 Bruce Dal Canton	1.20	.50	.12
☐ 718 Del Rice MGR	1.20	.50	.12
☐ 719 Cesar Geronimo	1.20	.50	.12
☐ 720 Sam McDowell	1.50	.60	.15
☐ 721 Eddie Leon	1.20	.50	.12
☐ 722 Bill Sudakis	1.20	.50	.12
☐ 723 Al Santorini	1.20	.50	.12
☐ 724 AL Rookie Pitchers	1.50	.60	.15
John Curtis			
Rich Hinton			
Mickey Scott			
☐ 725 Dick McAuliffe	1.20	.50	.12
☐ 726 Dick Selma	1.20	.50	.12
☐ 727 Jose LaBoy	1.20	.50	.12
☐ 728 Gail Hopkins	1.20	.50	.12
☐ 729 Bob Veale	1.50	.60	.15
☐ 730 Rick Monday	1.75	.70	.17
☐ 731 Orioles Team	2.25	.90	.22
☐ 732 George Culver	1.20	.50	.12
☐ 733 Jim Ray Hart	1.50	.60	.15
☐ 734 Bob Burda	1.20	.50	.12
☐ 735 Diego Segui	1.20	.50	.12
☐ 736 Bill Russell	2.50	1.00	.25
☐ 737 Lenny Randle	1.20	.50	.12
☐ 738 Jim Merritt	1.20	.50	.12
☐ 739 Don Mason	1.20	.50	.12
☐ 740 Rico Carty	1.75	.70	.17
☐ 741 Rookie First Basemen	1.75	.70	.17
Tom Hutton			
John Milner			
Rick Miller			
☐ 742 Jim Rooker	1.50	.60	.15
☐ 743 Cesar Gutierrez	1.20	.50	.12
☐ 744 Jim Slaton	1.50	.60	.15
☐ 745 Julian Javier	1.20	.50	.12
☐ 746 Lowell Palmer	1.20	.50	.12
☐ 747 Jim Stewart	1.20	.50	.12
☐ 748 Phil Hennigan	1.20	.50	.12

	MINT	VG-E	F-G
☐ 749 Walter Alston MGR	3.00	1.20	.30
☐ 750 Willie Horton	1.75	.70	.17
☐ 751 Steve Carlton TR	30.00	12.00	3.00
☐ 752 Joe Morgan TR	9.00	3.75	.90
☐ 753 Denny McLain TR	2.50	1.00	.25
☐ 754 Frank Robinson TR	9.00	3.75	.90
☐ 755 Jim Fregosi TR	2.00	.80	.20
☐ 756 Rick Wise TR	1.50	.60	.15
☐ 757 Jose Cardenal TR	1.50	.60	.15
☐ 758 Gil Garrido	1.20	.50	.12
☐ 759 Chris Cannizzaro	1.20	.50	.12
☐ 760 Bill Mazeroski	2.00	.80	.20
☐ 761 Rookie Outfielders	10.00	4.00	1.00
Ben Oglivie			
Ron Cey			
Bernie Williams			
☐ 762 Wayne Simpson	1.20	.50	.12
☐ 763 Ron Hansen	1.20	.50	.12
☐ 764 Dusty Baker	3.00	1.20	.30
☐ 765 Ken McMullen	1.20	.50	.12
☐ 766 Steve Hamilton	1.20	.50	.12
☐ 767 Tom McCraw	1.20	.50	.12
☐ 768 Denny Doyle	1.20	.50	.12
☐ 769 Jack Aker	1.20	.50	.12
☐ 770 Jim Wynn	1.75	.70	.17
☐ 771 Giants Team	2.25	.90	.22
☐ 772 Ken Tatum	1.20	.50	.12
☐ 773 Ron Brand	1.20	.50	.12
☐ 774 Luis Alvarado	1.20	.50	.12
☐ 775 Jerry Reuss	2.25	.90	.22
☐ 776 Bill Voss	1.20	.50	.12
☐ 777 Hoyt Wilhelm	6.00	2.40	.60
☐ 778 Twins Rookies	2.00	.80	.20
Vic Albury			
Rick Dempsey			
Jim Strickland			
☐ 779 Tony Cloninger	1.20	.50	.12
☐ 780 Dick Green	1.20	.50	.12
☐ 781 Jim McAndrew	1.20	.50	.12
☐ 782 Larry Stahl	1.20	.50	.12
☐ 783 Les Cain	1.20	.50	.12
☐ 784 Ken Aspromonte	1.20	.50	.12
☐ 785 Vic Davalillo	1.50	.60	.15
☐ 786 Chuck Brinkman	1.20	.50	.12
☐ 787 Ron Reed	1.50	.60	.15

1973 Topps

The cards in this 660-card set measure 2½"
by 3½". The 1973 Topps set marked the last
year in which Topps marketed baseball
cards in consecutive series. The last series
(529-660) is more difficult to obtain. Beginning in 1974, all Topps cards were printed at
the same time, thus eliminating the "high
number" factor. The set features team leader
cards featuring small individual pictures of
the coaching staff members with a larger picture of the manager. The "background" variations below, with respect to these leader
cards, are subtle and are best understood
after a side-by-side comparison of the two
varieties. An "All-Time Leaders" series (471-
478) appeared for the first time in this set. Kid
Pictures appeared again for the second year
in a row (341-346). Other topical subsets
within the set included League Leaders (61-
68), Playoffs cards (201-202), World Series
cards (203-210), and Rookie Prospects
(601-616).

	MINT	VG-E	F-G
Complete Set	350.00	140.00	35.00
Common Player (1-264)	.14	.06	.01
Common Player (265-396)	.17	.07	.01
Common Player (397-528)	.22	.10	.02
Common Player (529-660)	.75	.30	.07

		MINT	VG-E	F-G
☐	1 All-Time HR Leaders .. 714 Babe Ruth 673 Hank Aaron 654 Willie Mays	6.00	2.40	.60
☐	2 Rich Hebner	.14	.06	.01
☐	3 Jim Lonborg	.20	.08	.02
☐	4 John Milner	.14	.06	.01
☐	5 Ed Brinkman	.14	.06	.01
☐	6 Mac Scarce	.14	.06	.01
☐	7 Texas Rangers Team	.40	.16	.04
☐	8 Tom Hall	.14	.06	.01
☐	9 Johnny Oates	.14	.06	.01
☐	10 Don Sutton	1.50	.60	.15
☐	11 Chris Chambliss	.35	.14	.03
☐	12 A Padres Leaders Don Zimmer MGR Dave Garcia CO Johnny Podres CO Bob Skinner CO Whitey Wietelmann CO (Padres no right ear)	.30	.12	.03
☐	12 B Padres Leaders (Padres has right ear)	.60	.24	.06
☐	13 George Hendrick	.50	.20	.05
☐	14 Sonny Siebert	.20	.08	.02
☐	15 Ralph Garr	.20	.08	.02
☐	16 Steve Braun	.14	.06	.01
☐	17 Fred Gladding	.14	.06	.01
☐	18 Leroy Stanton	.14	.06	.01
☐	19 Tim Foli	.14	.06	.01
☐	20 Stan Bahnsen	.14	.06	.01
☐	21 Randy Hundley	.14	.06	.01
☐	22 Ted Abernathy	.14	.06	.01
☐	23 Dave Kingman	1.25	.50	.12
☐	24 Al Santorini	.14	.06	.01
☐	25 Roy White	.20	.08	.02
☐	26 Pirates Team	.40	.16	.04
☐	27 Bill Gogolewski	.14	.06	.01
☐	28 Hal McRae	.35	.14	.03
☐	29 Tony Taylor	.14	.06	.01
☐	30 Tug McGraw	.50	.20	.05
☐	31 Buddy Bell	3.00	1.20	.30
☐	32 Fred Norman	.14	.06	.01
☐	33 Jim Breazeale	.14	.06	.01
☐	34 Pat Dobson	.20	.08	.02
☐	35 Willie Davis	.30	.12	.03
☐	36 Steve Barber	.14	.06	.01
☐	37 Bill Robinson	.14	.06	.01
☐	38 Mike Epstein	.14	.06	.01
☐	39 Dave Roberts	.14	.06	.01
☐	40 Reggie Smith	.50	.20	.05
☐	41 Tom Walker	.14	.06	.01
☐	42 Mike Andrews	.14	.06	.01

			MINT	VG-E	F-G
☐	43	Randy Moffitt	.14	.06	.01
☐	44	Rick Monday	.25	.10	.02
☐	45	Ellie Rodriguez	.20	.08	.02
		(photo actually			
		John Felske)			
☐	46	Lindy McDaniel	.14	.06	.01
☐	47	Luis Melendez	.14	.06	.01
☐	48	Paul Splittorff	.25	.10	.02
☐	49	A Twins Leaders	.30	.12	.03
		Frank Quilici MGR			
		Vern Morgan CO			
		Bob Rodgers CO			
		Ralph Rowe CO			
		Al Worthington CO			
		(solid backgrounds)			
☐	49	B Twins Leaders	.60	.24	.06
		(natural backgrounds)			
☐	50	Roberto Clemente	8.00	3.25	.80
☐	51	Chuck Seelbach	.14	.06	.01
☐	52	Denis Menke	.14	.06	.01
☐	53	Steve Dunning	.14	.06	.01
☐	54	Checklist 1	.80	.08	.01
☐	55	Jon Matlack	.25	.10	.02
☐	56	Merv Rettenmund	.14	.06	.01
☐	57	Derrel Thomas	.14	.06	.01
☐	58	Mike Paul	.14	.06	.01
☐	59	Steve Yeager	.45	.18	.04
☐	60	Ken Holtzman	.25	.10	.02
☐	61	Batting Leaders	1.00	.40	.10
		Billy Williams			
		Rod Carew			
☐	62	Home Run Leaders	.90	.36	.09
		Johnny Bench			
		Dick Allen			
☐	63	RBI Leaders	.90	.36	.09
		Johnny Bench			
		Dick Allen			
☐	64	Stolen Base Leaders	.60	.24	.06
		Lou Brock			
		Bert Campaneris			
☐	65	ERA Leaders	.75	.30	.07
		Steve Carlton			
		Luis Tiant			
☐	66	Victory Leaders	.90	.36	.09
		Steve Carlton			
		Gaylord Perry			
		Wilbur Wood			
☐	67	Strikeout Leaders	2.00	.80	.20
		Steve Carlton			
		Nolan Ryan			
☐	68	Leading Firemen	.30	.12	.03
		Clay Carroll			
		Sparky Lyle			

			MINT	VG-E	F-G
☐	69	Phil Gagliano	.14	.06	.01
☐	70	Milt Pappas	.20	.08	.02
☐	71	Johnny Briggs	.14	.06	.01
☐	72	Ron Reed	.14	.06	.01
☐	73	Ed Herrmann	.14	.06	.01
☐	74	Billy Champion	.14	.06	.01
☐	75	Vada Pinson	.35	.14	.03
☐	76	Doug Rader	.25	.10	.02
☐	77	Mike Torrez	.25	.10	.02
☐	78	Richie Scheinblum	.14	.06	.01
☐	79	Jim Willoughby	.14	.06	.01
☐	80	Tony Oliva	.65	.26	.06
☐	81	A Cubs Leaders	.35	.14	.03
		Whitey Lockman MGR			
		Hank Aguirre CO			
		Ernie Banks CO			
		Larry Jansen CO			
		Pete Reiser CO			
		(solid backgrounds)			
☐	81	B Cubs Leaders	.70	.28	.07
		(natural backgrounds)			
☐	82	Fritz Peterson	.14	.06	.01
☐	83	Leron Lee	.14	.06	.01
☐	84	Rollie Fingers	1.25	.50	.12
☐	85	Ted Simmons	1.00	.40	.10
☐	86	Tom McCraw	.14	.06	.01
☐	87	Ken Boswell	.14	.06	.01
☐	88	Mickey Stanley	.20	.08	.02
☐	89	Jack Billingham	.14	.06	.01
☐	90	Brooks Robinson	3.00	1.20	.30
☐	91	Dodgers Team	.60	.24	.06
☐	92	Jerry Bell	.14	.06	.01
☐	93	Jesus Alou	.14	.06	.01
☐	94	Dick Billings	.14	.06	.01
☐	95	Steve Blass	.14	.06	.01
☐	96	Doug Griffin	.14	.06	.01
☐	97	Willie Montanez	.14	.06	.01
☐	98	Dick Woodson	.14	.06	.01
☐	99	Carl Taylor	.14	.06	.01
☐	100	Hank Aaron	9.00	3.75	.90
☐	101	Ken Henderson	.14	.06	.01
☐	102	Rudy May	.14	.06	.01
☐	103	Celerino Sanchez	.14	.06	.01
☐	104	Reggie Cleveland	.14	.06	.01
☐	105	Carlos May	.14	.06	.01
☐	106	Terry Humphrey	.14	.06	.01
☐	107	Phil Hennigan	.14	.06	.01
☐	108	Bill Russell	.25	.10	.02
☐	109	Doyle Alexander	.25	.10	.02
☐	110	Bob Watson	.25	.10	.02
☐	111	Dave Nelson	.14	.06	.01
☐	112	Gary Ross	.14	.06	.01
☐	113	Jerry Grote	.14	.06	.01

	MINT	VG-E	F-G
☐ 114 Lynn McGlothen	.14	.06	.01
☐ 115 Ron Santo	.35	.14	.03
☐ 116 A Yankees Leaders	.40	.16	.04
Ralph Houk MGR			
Jim Hegan CO			
Elston Howard CO			
Dick Howser CO			
Jim Turner CO			
(solid backgrounds)			
☐ 116 B Yankees Leaders	.75	.30	.07
(natural backgrounds)			
☐ 117 Ramon Hernandez	.14	.06	.01
☐ 118 John Mayberry	.25	.10	.02
☐ 119 Larry Bowa	.60	.24	.06
☐ 120 Joe Coleman	.14	.06	.01
☐ 121 Dave Rader	.14	.06	.01
☐ 122 Jim Strickland	.14	.06	.01
☐ 123 Sandy Alomar	.14	.06	.01
☐ 124 Jim Hardin	.14	.06	.01
☐ 125 Ron Fairly	.20	.08	.02
☐ 126 Jim Brewer	.14	.06	.01
☐ 127 Brewers Team	.40	.16	.04
☐ 128 Ted Sizemore	.14	.06	.01
☐ 129 Terry Forster	.35	.14	.03
☐ 130 Pete Rose	15.00	6.00	1.50
☐ 131 A Red Sox Leaders	.25	.10	.02
Eddie Kasko MGR			
Doug Camilli CO			
Don Lenhardt CO			
Eddie Popowski CO			
Lee Stange CO			
(Popowski no right ear)			
☐ 131 B Red Sox Leaders	.50	.20	.05
(Popowski has right ear)			
☐ 132 Matty Alou	.20	.08	.02
☐ 133 Dave Roberts	.14	.06	.01
☐ 134 Milt Wilcox	.20	.08	.02
☐ 135 Lee May	.25	.10	.02
☐ 136 A Orioles Leaders	.50	.20	.05
Earl Weaver MGR			
George Bamberger CO			
Jim Frey CO			
Billy Hunter CO			
George Staller CO			
(orange backgrounds)			
☐ 136 B Orioles Leaders	.90	.36	.09
(dark pale backgrounds)			
☐ 137 Jim Beauchamp	.14	.06	.01
☐ 138 Horacio Pina	.14	.06	.01
☐ 139 Carmen Fanzone	.14	.06	.01
☐ 140 Lou Piniella	.50	.20	.05
☐ 141 Bruce Kison	.25	.10	.02
☐ 142 Thurman Munson	4.00	1.60	.40

	MINT	VG-E	F-G
☐ 143 John Curtis	.14	.06	.01
☐ 144 Marty Perez	.14	.06	.01
☐ 145 Bobby Bonds	.35	.14	.03
☐ 146 Woodie Fryman	.14	.06	.01
☐ 147 Mike Anderson	.14	.06	.01
☐ 148 Dave Goltz	.20	.08	.02
☐ 149 Ron Hunt	.14	.06	.01
☐ 150 Wilbur Wood	.20	.08	.02
☐ 151 Wes Parker	.25	.10	.02
☐ 152 Dave May	.14	.06	.01
☐ 153 Al Hrabosky	.25	.10	.02
☐ 154 Jeff Torborg	.14	.06	.01
☐ 155 Sal Bando	.30	.12	.03
☐ 156 Cesar Geronimo	.14	.06	.01
☐ 157 Denny Riddleberger	.14	.06	.01
☐ 158 Astros Team	.40	.16	.04
☐ 159 Clarence Gaston	.14	.06	.01
☐ 160 Jim Palmer	3.00	1.20	.30
☐ 161 Ted Martinez	.14	.06	.01
☐ 162 Pete Broberg	.14	.06	.01
☐ 163 Vic Davalillo	.14	.06	.01
☐ 164 Monty Montgomery	.14	.06	.01
☐ 165 Luis Aparicio	1.75	.70	.17
☐ 166 Terry Harmon	.14	.06	.01
☐ 167 Steve Stone	.30	.12	.03
☐ 168 Jim Northrup	.20	.08	.02
☐ 169 Ron Schueler	.14	.06	.01
☐ 170 Harmon Killebrew	2.25	.90	.22
☐ 171 Bernie Carbo	.14	.06	.01
☐ 172 Steve Kline	.14	.06	.01
☐ 173 Hal Breeden	.14	.06	.01
☐ 174 Rich Gossage	6.00	2.40	.60
☐ 175 Frank Robinson	2.75	1.10	.27
☐ 176 Chuck Taylor	.14	.06	.01
☐ 177 Bill Plummer	.14	.06	.01
☐ 178 Don Rose	.14	.06	.01
☐ 179 A A's Leaders	.30	.12	.03
Dick Williams MGR			
Jerry Adair CO			
Vern Hoscheit CO			
Irv Noren CO			
Wes Stock CO			
(orange backgrounds)			
☐ 179 B A's Leaders	.60	.24	.06
(dark pale backgrounds)			
☐ 180 Fergie Jenkins	.90	.36	.09
☐ 181 Jack Brohamer	.14	.06	.01
☐ 182 Mike Caldwell	.45	.18	.04
☐ 183 Don Buford	.14	.06	.01
☐ 184 Jerry Koosman	.35	.14	.03
☐ 185 Jim Wynn	.30	.12	.03
☐ 186 Bill Fahey	.14	.06	.01
☐ 187 Luke Walker	.14	.06	.01

		MINT	VG-E	F-G
☐ 188	Cookie Rojas	.14	.06	.01
☐ 189	Greg Luzinski	.75	.30	.07
☐ 190	Bob Gibson	2.50	1.00	.25
☐ 191	Tigers Team	.50	.20	.05
☐ 192	Pat Jarvis	.14	.06	.01
☐ 193	Carlton Fisk	2.50	1.00	.25
☐ 194	Jorge Orta	.14	.06	.01
☐ 195	Clay Carroll	.14	.06	.01
☐ 196	Ken McMullen	.14	.06	.01
☐ 197	Ed Goodson	.14	.06	.01
☐ 198	Horace Clarke	.14	.06	.01
☐ 199	Bert Blyleven	.80	.32	.08
☐ 200	Billy Williams	1.75	.70	.17
☐ 201	A.L. Playoffs	.60	.24	.06
	A's over Tigers; Hendrick scores winning run			
☐ 202	N.L. Playoffs	.60	.24	.06
	Reds over Pirates Foster's run decides			
☐ 203	World Series Game 1	.60	.24	.06
	Tenace the Menace			
☐ 204	World Series Game 2	.60	.24	.06
	A's two straight			
☐ 205	World Series Game 3	.60	.24	.06
	Reds win squeeker			
☐ 206	World Series Game 4	.60	.24	.06
	Tenace singles in ninth			
☐ 207	World Series Game 5	.60	.24	.06
	Odom out at plate			
☐ 208	World Series Game 6	.60	.24	.06
	Red's slugging ties series			
☐ 209	World Series Game 7	.60	.24	.06
	Campy stars winning rally			
☐ 210	World Series Summary	.60	.24	.06
	World champions: A's Win			
☐ 211	Balor Moore	.14	.06	.01
☐ 212	Joe Lahoud	.14	.06	.01
☐ 213	Steve Garvey	8.00	3.25	.80
☐ 214	Steve Hamilton	.14	.06	.01
☐ 215	Dusty Baker	.70	.28	.07
☐ 216	Toby Harrah	.35	.14	.03
☐ 217	Don Wilson	.14	.06	.01
☐ 218	Aurelio Rodriguez	.14	.06	.01
☐ 219	Cardinals Team	.40	.16	.04
☐ 220	Nolan Ryan	5.00	2.00	.50
☐ 221	Fred Kendall	.14	.06	.01
☐ 222	Rob Gardner	.14	.06	.01
☐ 223	Bud Harrelson	.20	.08	.02

		MINT	VG-E	F-G
☐ 224	Bill Lee	.20	.08	.02
☐ 225	Al Oliver	1.00	.40	.10
☐ 226	Ray Fosse	.14	.06	.01
☐ 227	Wayne Twitchell	.14	.06	.01
☐ 228	Bobby Darwin	.14	.06	.01
☐ 229	Roric Harrison	.14	.06	.01
☐ 230	Joe Morgan	2.00	.80	.20
☐ 231	Bill Parsons	.14	.06	.01
☐ 232	Ken Singleton	.35	.14	.03
☐ 233	Ed Kirkpatrick	.14	.06	.01
☐ 234	Bill North	.20	.08	.02
☐ 235	Jim Hunter	1.75	.70	.17
☐ 236	Tito Fuentes	.14	.06	.01
☐ 237	A Braves Leaders	.50	.20	.05
	Eddie Mathews MGR Lew Burdette CO Jim Busby CO Roy Hartsfield CO Ken Silvestri CO (orange backgrounds)			
☐ 237	B Braves Leaders	.90	.36	.09
	(dark pale backgrounds)			
☐ 238	Tony Muser	.14	.06	.01
☐ 239	Pete Richert	.14	.06	.01
☐ 240	Bobby Murcer	.50	.20	.05
☐ 241	Dwain Anderson	.14	.06	.01
☐ 242	George Culver	.14	.06	.01
☐ 243	Angels Team	.40	.16	.04
☐ 244	Ed Acosta	.14	.06	.01
☐ 245	Carl Yastrzemski	8.00	3.25	.80
☐ 246	Ken Sanders	.14	.06	.01
☐ 247	Del Unser	.14	.06	.01
☐ 248	Jerry Johnson	.14	.06	.01
☐ 249	Larry Biittner	.14	.06	.01
☐ 250	Manny Sanguillen	.25	.10	.02
☐ 251	Roger Nelson	.14	.06	.01
☐ 252	A Giants Leaders	.25	.10	.02
	Charlie Fox MGR Joe Amalfitano CO Andy Gilbert CO Don McMahon CO John McNamara CO (orange backgrounds)			
☐ 252	B Giants Leaders	.50	.20	.05
	(dark pale backgrounds)			
☐ 253	Mark Belanger	.25	.10	.02
☐ 254	Bill Stoneman	.14	.06	.01
☐ 255	Reggie Jackson	10.00	4.00	1.00
☐ 256	Chris Zachary	.14	.06	.01

	MINT	VG-E	F-G
☐ 257 **A** Mets Leaders	.50	.20	.05
Yogi Berra MGR			
Roy McMillan CO			
Joe Pignatano CO			
Rube Walker CO			
Eddie Yost CO			
(orange backgrounds)			
☐ 257 **B** Mets Leaders	.90	.36	.09
(dark pale backgrounds)			
☐ 258 Tommy John	.90	.36	.09
☐ 259 Jim Holt	.14	.06	.01
☐ 260 Gary Nolan	.14	.06	.01
☐ 261 Pat Kelly	.14	.06	.01
☐ 262 Jack Aker	.14	.06	.01
☐ 263 George Scott	.20	.08	.02
☐ 264 Checklist 2	.80	.08	.01
☐ 265 Gene Michael	.25	.10	.02
☐ 266 Mike Lum	.17	.07	.01
☐ 267 Lloyd Allen	.17	.07	.01
☐ 268 Jerry Morales	.17	.07	.01
☐ 269 Tim McCarver	.30	.12	.03
☐ 270 Luis Tiant	.35	.14	.03
☐ 271 Tom Hutton	.17	.07	.01
☐ 272 Ed Farmer	.17	.07	.01
☐ 273 Chris Speier	.17	.07	.01
☐ 274 Darold Knowles	.17	.07	.01
☐ 275 Tony Perez	.75	.30	.07
☐ 276 Joe Lovitto	.17	.07	.01
☐ 277 Bob Miller	.17	.07	.01
☐ 278 Orioles Team	.45	.18	.04
☐ 279 Mike Strahler	.17	.07	.01
☐ 280 Al Kaline	2.75	1.10	.27
☐ 281 Mike Jorgensen	.17	.07	.01
☐ 282 Steve Hovley	.17	.07	.01
☐ 283 Ray Sadecki	.17	.07	.01
☐ 284 Glenn Borgmann	.17	.07	.01
☐ 285 Don Kessinger	.25	.10	.02
☐ 286 Frank Linzy	.17	.07	.01
☐ 287 Eddie Leon	.17	.07	.01
☐ 288 Gary Gentry	.17	.07	.01
☐ 289 Bob Oliver	.17	.07	.01
☐ 290 Cesar Cedeno	.35	.14	.03
☐ 291 Rogelio Moret	.17	.07	.01
☐ 292 Jose Cruz	.65	.26	.06
☐ 293 Bernie Allen	.17	.07	.01
☐ 294 Steve Arlin	.17	.07	.01
☐ 295 Bert Campaneris	.30	.12	.03
☐ 296 Reds Leaders	.35	.14	.03
Sparky Anderson MGR			
Alex Grammas CO			
Ted Kluszewski CO			
George Scherger CO			
Larry Shepard CO			

	MINT	VG-E	F-G
☐ 297 Walt Williams	.17	.07	.01
☐ 298 Ron Bryant	.17	.07	.01
☐ 299 Ted Ford	.17	.07	.01
☐ 300 Steve Carlton	6.50	2.60	.65
☐ 301 Billy Grabarkewitz	.17	.07	.01
☐ 302 Terry Crowley	.17	.07	.01
☐ 303 Nelson Briles	.25	.10	.02
☐ 304 Duke Sims	.17	.07	.01
☐ 305 Willie Mays	9.00	3.75	.90
☐ 306 Tom Burgmeier	.17	.07	.01
☐ 307 Boots Day	.17	.07	.01
☐ 308 Skip Lockwood	.17	.07	.01
☐ 309 Paul Popovich	.17	.07	.01
☐ 310 Dick Allen	.40	.16	.04
☐ 311 Joe Decker	.17	.07	.01
☐ 312 Oscar Brown	.17	.07	.01
☐ 313 Jim Ray	.17	.07	.01
☐ 314 Ron Swoboda	.25	.10	.02
☐ 315 John Odom	.17	.07	.01
☐ 316 Padres Team	.45	.18	.04
☐ 317 Danny Cater	.17	.07	.01
☐ 318 Jim McGlothlin	.17	.07	.01
☐ 319 Jim Spencer	.17	.07	.01
☐ 320 Lou Brock	2.50	1.00	.25
☐ 321 Rich Hinton	.17	.07	.01
☐ 322 Garry Maddox	.50	.20	*.05
☐ 323 Tigers Leaders	.50	.20	.05
Billy Martin MGR			
Art Fowler CO			
Charlie Silvera CO			
Dick Tracewski CO			
☐ 324 Al Downing	.17	.07	.01
☐ 325 Boog Powell	.50	.20	.05
☐ 326 Darrell Brandon	.17	.07	.01
☐ 327 John Lowenstein	.17	.07	.01
☐ 328 Bill Bonham	.17	.07	.01
☐ 329 Ed Kranepool	.17	.07	.01
☐ 330 Rod Carew	6.00	2.40	.60
☐ 331 Carl Morton	.17	.07	.01
☐ 332 John Felske	.17	.07	.01
☐ 333 Gene Clines	.17	.07	.01
☐ 334 Freddie Patek	.17	.07	.01
☐ 335 Bob Tolan	.17	.07	.01
☐ 336 Tom Bradley	.17	.07	.01
☐ 337 Dave Duncan	.17	.07	.01
☐ 338 Checklist 3	.80	.08	.01
☐ 339 Dick Tidrow	.17	.07	.01
☐ 340 Nate Colbert	.17	.07	.01
☐ 341 KP: Jim Palmer	.90	.36	.09
☐ 342 KP: Sam McDowell ...	.17	.07	.01
☐ 343 KP: Bobby Murcer	.25	.10	.02
☐ 344 KP: Jim Hunter	.75	.30	.07
☐ 345 KP: Chris Speier	.17	.07	.01

	MINT	VG-E	F-G
☐ 346 KP: Gaylord Perry	.60	.24	.06
☐ 347 Royals Team	.45	.18	.04
☐ 348 Rennie Stennett	.17	.07	.01
☐ 349 Dick McAuliffe	.17	.07	.01
☐ 350 Tom Seaver	6.00	2.40	.60
☐ 351 Jimmy Stewart	.17	.07	.01
☐ 352 Don Stanhouse	.17	.07	.01
☐ 353 Steve Brye	.17	.07	.01
☐ 354 Billy Parker	.17	.07	.01
☐ 355 Mike Marshall	.35	.14	.03
☐ 356 White Sox Leaders	.30	.12	.03
Chuck Tanner MGR			
Joe Lonnett CO			
Jim Mahoney CO			
Al Monchak CO			
Johnny Sain CO			
☐ 357 Ross Grimsley	.17	.07	.01
☐ 358 Jim Nettles	.17	.07	.01
☐ 359 Cecil Upshaw	.17	.07	.01
☐ 360 Joe Rudi	.35	.14	.03
(photo actually			
Gene Tenace)			
☐ 361 Fran Healy	.17	.07	.01
☐ 362 Eddie Watt	.17	.07	.01
☐ 363 Jackie Hernandez	.17	.07	.01
☐ 364 Rick Wise	.17	.07	.01
☐ 365 Rico Petrocelli	.25	.10	.02
☐ 366 Brock Davis	.17	.07	.01
☐ 367 Burt Hooton	.25	.10	.02
☐ 368 Bill Buckner	.70	.28	.07
☐ 369 Lerrin LaGrow	.17	.07	.01
☐ 370 Willie Stargell	2.25	.90	.22
☐ 371 Mike Kekich	.17	.07	.01
☐ 372 Oscar Gamble	.25	.10	.02
☐ 373 Clyde Wright	.17	.07	.01
☐ 374 Darrell Evans	.50	.20	.05
☐ 375 Larry Dierker	.17	.07	.01
☐ 376 Frank Duffy	.17	.07	.01
☐ 377 Expos Leaders	.30	.12	.03
Gene Mauch MGR			
Dave Bristol CO			
Larry Doby CO			
Cal McLish CO			
Jerry Zimmerman CO			
☐ 378 Lenny Randle	.17	.07	.01
☐ 379 Cy Acosta	.17	.07	.01
☐ 380 Johnny Bench	6.50	2.60	.65
☐ 381 Vicente Romo	.17	.07	.01
☐ 382 Mike Hegan	.17	.07	.01
☐ 383 Diego Segui	.17	.07	.01
☐ 384 Don Baylor	1.00	.40	.10
☐ 385 Jim Perry	.35	.14	.03
☐ 386 Don Money	.17	.07	.01

	MINT	VG-E	F-G
☐ 387 Jim Barr	.17	.07	.01
☐ 388 Ben Oglivie	.50	.20	.05
☐ 389 Mets Team	.90	.36	.09
☐ 390 Mickey Lolich	.50	.20	.05
☐ 391 Lee Lacy	.80	.32	.08
☐ 392 Dick Drago	.17	.07	.01
☐ 393 Jose Cardenal	.17	.07	.01
☐ 394 Sparky Lyle	.40	.16	.04
☐ 395 Roger Metzger	.17	.07	.01
☐ 396 Grant Jackson	.17	.07	.01
☐ 397 Dave Cash	.22	.10	.02
☐ 398 Rich Hand	.22	.10	.02
☐ 399 George Foster	1.25	.50	.12
☐ 400 Gaylord Perry	1.75	.70	.17
☐ 401 Clyde Mashore	.22	.10	.02
☐ 402 Jack Hiatt	.22	.10	.02
☐ 403 Sonny Jackson	.22	.10	.02
☐ 404 Chuck Brinkman	.22	.10	.02
☐ 405 Cesar Tovar	.22	.10	.02
☐ 406 Paul Lindblad	.22	.10	.02
☐ 407 Felix Millan	.22	.10	.02
☐ 408 Jim Colborn	.22	.10	.02
☐ 409 Ivan Murrell	.22	.10	.02
☐ 410 Willie McCovey	2.50	1.00	.25
☐ 411 Ray Corbin	.22	.10	.02
☐ 412 Manny Mota	.30	.12	.03
☐ 413 Tom Timmerman	.22	.10	.02
☐ 414 Ken Rudolph	.22	.10	.02
☐ 415 Marty Pattin	.22	.10	.02
☐ 416 Paul Schaal	.22	.10	.02
☐ 417 Scipio Spinks	.22	.10	.02
☐ 418 Bobby Grich	.40	.16	.04
☐ 419 Casey Cox	.22	.10	.02
☐ 420 Tommie Agee	.22	.10	.02
☐ 421 A Angels Leaders	.30	.12	.03
Bobby Winkles MGR			
Tom Morgan CO			
Salty Parker CO			
Jimmie Reese CO			
John Roseboro CO			
(orange backgrounds)			
☐ 421 B Angels Leaders	.60	.24	.06
(dark pale backgrounds)			
☐ 422 Bob Robertson	.22	.10	.02
☐ 423 Johnny Jeter	.22	.10	.02
☐ 424 Denny Doyle	.22	.10	.02
☐ 425 Alex Johnson	.30	.12	.03
☐ 426 Dave LaRoche	.22	.10	.02
☐ 427 Rick Auerbach	.22	.10	.02
☐ 428 Wayne Simpson	.22	.10	.02
☐ 429 Jim Fairey	.22	.10	.02
☐ 430 Vida Blue	.45	.18	.04
☐ 431 Gerry Moses	.22	.10	.02

	MINT	VG-E	F-G
☐ 432 Dan Frisella	.22	.10	.02
☐ 433 Willie Horton	.30	.12	.03
☐ 434 Giants Team	.50	.20	.05
☐ 435 Rico Carty	.40	.16	.04
☐ 436 Jim McAndrew	.22	.10	.02
☐ 437 John Kennedy	.22	.10	.02
☐ 438 Enzo Hernandez	.22	.10	.02
☐ 439 Eddie Fisher	.22	.10	.02
☐ 440 Glenn Beckert	.22	.10	.02
☐ 441 Gail Hopkins	.22	.10	.02
☐ 442 Dick Dietz	.22	.10	.02
☐ 443 Danny Thompson	.22	.10	.02
☐ 444 Ken Brett	.22	.10	.02
☐ 445 Ken Berry	.22	.10	.02
☐ 446 Jerry Reuss	.40	.16	.04
☐ 447 Joe Hague	.22	.10	.02
☐ 448 John Hiller	.30	.12	.03
☐ 449 A Indians Leaders	.35	.14	.03
Ken Aspromonte MGR			
Rocky Colavito CO			
Joe Lutz CO			
Warren Spahn CO			
(Spahn's right			
ear pointed)			
☐ 449 B Indians Leaders	.75	.30	.07
(Spahn's right			
ear round)			
☐ 450 Joe Torre	.60	.24	.06
☐ 451 John Vuckovich	.22	.10	.02
☐ 452 Paul Casanova	.22	.10	.02
☐ 453 Checklist 4	1.00	.10	.02
☐ 454 Tom Haller	.22	.10	.02
☐ 455 Bill Melton	.22	.10	.02
☐ 456 Dick Green	.22	.10	.02
☐ 457 John Strohmayer	.22	.10	.02
☐ 458 Jim Mason	.22	.10	.02
☐ 459 Jimmy Howarth	.22	.10	.02
☐ 460 Bill Freehan	.35	.14	.03
☐ 461 Mike Corkins	.22	.10	.02
☐ 462 Ron Blomberg	.22	.10	.02
☐ 463 Ken Tatum	.22	.10	.02
☐ 464 Chicago Cubs Team	.50	.20	.05
☐ 465 Dave Giusti	.22	.10	.02
☐ 466 Jose Arcia	.22	.10	.02
☐ 467 Mike Ryan	.22	.10	.02
☐ 468 Tom Griffin	.22	.10	.02
☐ 469 Dan Monzon	.22	.10	.02
☐ 470 Mike Cuellar	.35	.14	.03
☐ 471 Hits Leaders	2.00	.80	.20
Ty Cobb 4191			
☐ 472 Grand Slam Leaders	2.00	.80	.20
Lou Gehrig 23			

	MINT	VG-E	F-G
☐ 473 Total Bases Leaders	2.00	.80	.20
Hank Aaron 6172			
☐ 474 RBI Leaders	3.00	1.20	.30
Babe Ruth 2209			
☐ 475 Batting Leaders	2.00	.80	.20
Ty Cobb .367			
☐ 476 Shutout Leaders	1.00	.40	.10
Walter Johnson 113			
☐ 477 Victory Leaders	1.00	.40	.10
Cy Young 511			
☐ 478 Strikeout Leaders	1.00	.40	.10
Walter Johnson 3508			
☐ 479 Hal Lanier	.40	.16	.04
☐ 480 Juan Marichal	2.25	.90	.22
☐ 481 White Sox Team	.45	.18	.04
☐ 482 Rick Reuschel	.75	.30	.07
☐ 483 Dal Maxvill	.22	.10	.02
☐ 484 Ernie McAnally	.22	.10	.02
☐ 485 Norm Cash	.40	.16	.04
☐ 486 A Phillies Leaders	.35	.14	.03
Danny Ozark MGR			
Carroll Beringer CO			
Billy DeMars CO			
Ray Rippelmeyer CO			
Bobby Wine CO			
(orange backgrounds)			
☐ 486 B Phillies Leaders	.70	.28	.07
(dark pale backgrounds)			
☐ 487 Bruce Dal Canton	.22	.10	.02
☐ 488 Dave Campbell	.22	.10	.02
☐ 489 Jeff Burroughs	.35	.14	.03
☐ 490 Claude Osteen	.30	.12	.03
☐ 491 Bob Montgomery	.22	.10	.02
☐ 492 Pedro Borbon	.22	.10	.02
☐ 493 Duffy Dyer	.22	.10	.02
☐ 494 Rich Morales	.22	.10	.02
☐ 495 Tommy Helms	.30	.12	.03
☐ 496 Ray Lamb	.22	.10	.02
☐ 497 A Cardinals Leaders	.35	.14	.03
Red Schoendienst MGR			
Vern Benson CO			
George Kissell CO			
Barney Schultz CO			
(orange backgrounds)			
☐ 497 B Cardinals Leaders	.70	.28	.07
(dark pale backgrounds)			
☐ 498 Graig Nettles	1.75	.70	.17
☐ 499 Bob Moose	.22	.10	.02
☐ 500 Oakland A's Team	.65	.26	.06
☐ 501 Larry Gura	.35	.14	.03
☐ 502 Bobby Valentine	.45	.18	.04
☐ 503 Phil Niekro	1.75	.70	.17
☐ 504 Earl Williams	.22	.10	.02

	MINT	VG-E	F-G		MINT	VG-E	F-G
☐ 505 Bob Bailey	.22	.10	.02	☐ 548 Don Durham	.75	.30	.07
☐ 506 Bart Johnson	.22	.10	.02	☐ 549 Rangers Leaders	1.50	.60	.15
☐ 507 Darrel Chaney	.22	.10	.02	Whitey Herzog MGR			
☐ 508 Gates Brown	.30	.12	.03	Chuck Estrada CO			
☐ 509 Jim Nash	.22	.10	.02	Chuck Hiller CO			
☐ 510 Amos Otis	.35	.14	.03	Jackie Moore CO			
☐ 511 Sam McDowell	.30	.12	.03	☐ 550 Dave Johnson	2.25	.90	.22
☐ 512 Dalton Jones	.22	.10	.02	☐ 551 Mike Kilkenny	.75	.30	.07
☐ 513 Dave Marshall	.22	.10	.02	☐ 552 J.C. Martin	.75	.30	.07
☐ 514 Jerry Kenney	.22	.10	.02	☐ 553 Mickey Scott	.75	.30	.07
☐ 515 Andy Messersmith	.35	.14	.03	☐ 554 Dave Concepcion	2.00	.80	.20
☐ 516 Danny Walton	.22	.10	.02	☐ 555 Bill Hands	.75	.30	.07
☐ 517 A Pirates Leaders	.30	.12	.03	☐ 556 Yankees Team	2.00	.80	.20
Bill Virdon MGR				☐ 557 Bernie Williams	.75	.30	.07
Don Leppert CO				☐ 558 Jerry May	.75	.30	.07
Bill Mazeroski CO				☐ 559 Barry Lersch	.75	.30	.07
Dave Ricketts CO				☐ 560 Frank Howard	1.75	.70	.17
Mel Wright CO				☐ 561 Jim Geddes	.75	.30	.07
(Mazeroski has				☐ 562 Wayne Garrett	.75	.30	.07
no right ear)				☐ 563 Larry Haney	.75	.30	.07
				☐ 564 Mike Thompson	.75	.30	.07
☐ 517 B Pirates Leaders	.60	.24	.06	☐ 565 Jim Hickman	.75	.30	.07
(Mazeroski has				☐ 566 Lew Krausse	.75	.30	.07
right ear)				☐ 567 Bob Fenwick	.75	.30	.07
☐ 518 Bob Veale	.30	.12	.03	☐ 568 Ray Newman	.75	.30	.07
☐ 519 John Edwards	.22	.10	.02	☐ 569 Dodgers Leaders	1.75	.70	.17
☐ 520 Mel Stottlemyre	.35	.14	.03	Walt Alston MGR			
☐ 521 Atlanta Braves Team	.45	.18	.04	Red Adams CO			
☐ 522 Leo Cardenas	.22	.10	.02	Monty Basgall CO			
☐ 523 Wayne Granger	.22	.10	.02	Jim Gilliam CO			
☐ 524 Gene Tenace	.30	.12	.03	Tom Lasorda CO			
☐ 525 Jim Fregosi	.40	.16	.04				
☐ 526 Ollie Brown	.22	.10	.02	☐ 570 Bill Singer	.75	.30	.07
☐ 527 Dan McGinn	.22	.10	.02	☐ 571 Rusty Torres	.75	.30	.07
☐ 528 Paul Blair	.30	.12	.03	☐ 572 Gary Sutherland	.75	.30	.07
☐ 529 Milt May	.75	.30	.07	☐ 573 Fred Beene	.75	.30	.07
☐ 530 Jim Kaat	2.00	.80	.20	☐ 574 Bob Didier	.75	.30	.07
☐ 531 Ron Woods	.75	.30	.07	☐ 575 Dock Ellis	.75	.30	.07
☐ 532 Steve Mingori	.75	.30	.07	☐ 576 Expos Team	1.50	.60	.15
☐ 533 Larry Stahl	.75	.30	.07	☐ 577 Eric Soderholm	.75	.30	.07
☐ 534 Dave Lemonds	.75	.30	.07	☐ 578 Ken Wright	.75	.30	.07
☐ 535 John Callison	.90	.36	.09	☐ 579 Tom Grieve	1.00	.40	.10
☐ 536 Phillies Team	1.25	.50	.12	☐ 580 Joe Pepitone	1.00	.40	.10
☐ 537 Bill Slayback	.75	.30	.07	☐ 581 Steve Kealey	.75	.30	.07
☐ 538 Jim Ray Hart	.90	.36	.09	☐ 582 Darrell Porter	1.25	.50	.12
☐ 539 Tom Murphy	.75	.30	.07	☐ 583 Bill Grief	.75	.30	.07
☐ 540 Cleon Jones	.75	.30	.07	☐ 584 Chris Arnold	.75	.30	.07
☐ 541 Bob Bolin	.75	.30	.07	☐ 585 Joe Niekro	1.50	.60	.15
☐ 542 Pat Corrales	.90	.36	.09	☐ 586 Bill Sudakis	.75	.30	.07
☐ 543 Alan Foster	.75	.30	.07	☐ 587 Rich McKinney	.75	.30	.07
☐ 544 Von Joshua	.75	.30	.07	☐ 588 Checklist 5	10.00	1.00	.20
☐ 545 Orlando Cepeda	2.00	.80	.20	☐ 589 Ken Forsch	.90	.36	.09
☐ 546 Jim York	.75	.30	.07	☐ 590 Deron Johnson	.75	.30	.07
☐ 547 Bobby Heise	.75	.30	.07	☐ 591 Mike Hedlund	.75	.30	.07

		MINT	VG-E	F-G
☐ 592	John Boccabella	.75	.30	.07
☐ 593	Royals Leaders	1.00	.40	.10
	Jack McKeon MGR			
	Galen Cisco CO			
	Harry Dunlop CO			
	Charlie Lau CO			
☐ 594	Vic Harris	.75	.30	.07
☐ 595	Don Gullett	.90	.36	.09
☐ 596	Red Sox Team	1.50	.60	.15
☐ 597	Mickey Rivers	1.50	.60	.15
☐ 598	Phil Roof	.75	.30	.07
☐ 599	Ed Crosby	.75	.30	.07
☐ 600	Dave McNally	1.25	.50	.12
☐ 601	Rookie Catchers	.75	.30	.07
	Sergio Robles			
	George Pena			
	Rick Stelmaszek			
☐ 602	Rookie Pitchers	.75	.30	.07
	Mel Behney			
	Ralph Garcia			
	Doug Rau			
☐ 603	Rookie 3rd Basemen	.75	.30	.07
	Terry Hughes			
	Bill McNulty			
	Ken Reitz			
☐ 604	Rookie Pitchers	.75	.30	.07
	Jesse Jefferson			
	Dennis O'Toole			
	Bob Strampe			
☐ 605	Rookie 1st Basemen	1.00	.40	.10
	Enos Cabell			
	Pat Bourque			
	Gonzalo Marquez			
☐ 606	Rookie Outfielders	2.50	1.00	.25
	Gary Matthews			
	Tom Paciorek			
	Jorge Roque			
☐ 607	Rookie Shortstops	.75	.30	.07
	Pepe Frias			
	Ray Busse			
	Mario Guerrero			
☐ 608	Rookie Pitchers	1.00	.40	.10
	Steve Busby			
	Dick Colpaert			
	George Medich			
☐ 609	Rookie 2nd Basemen	2.50	1.00	.25
	Larvell Blanks			
	Pedro Garcia			
	Dave Lopes			
☐ 610	Rookie Pitchers	1.50	.60	.15
	Jimmy Freeman			
	Charlie Hough			
	Hank Webb			

		MINT	VG-E	F-G
☐ 611	Rookie Outfielders	1.50	.60	.15
	Rich Coggins			
	Jim Wohlford			
	Richie Zisk			
☐ 612	Rookie Pitchers	.75	.30	.07
	Steve Lawson			
	Bob Reynolds			
	Brent Strom			
☐ 613	Rookie Catchers	2.00	.80	.20
	Bob Boone			
	Skip Jutze			
	Mike Ivie			
☐ 614	Rookie Outfielders	7.50	3.00	.75
	Alonza Bumbry			
	Dwight Evans			
	Charlie Spikes			
☐ 615	Rookie 3rd Basemen	125.00	50.00	12.50
	Ron Cey			
	John Hilton			
	Mike Schmidt			
☐ 616	Rookie Pitchers	.75	.30	.07
	Norm Angelini			
	Steve Blateric			
	Mike Garman			
☐ 617	Rich Chiles	.75	.30	.07
☐ 618	Andy Etchebarren	.75	.30	.07
☐ 619	Billy Wilson	.75	.30	.07
☐ 620	Tommy Harper	.90	.36	.09
☐ 621	Joe Ferguson	.90	.36	.09
☐ 622	Larry Hisle	.90	.36	.09
☐ 623	Steve Renko	.75	.30	.07
☐ 624	Astros Leaders	1.50	.60	.15
	Leo Durocher MGR			
	Preston Gomez CO			
	Grady Hatton CO			
	Hub Kittle CO			
	Jim Owens CO			
☐ 625	Angel Mangual	.75	.30	.07
☐ 626	Bob Barton	.75	.30	.07
☐ 627	Luis Alvarado	.75	.30	.07
☐ 628	Jim Slaton	.90	.36	.09
☐ 629	Indians Team	1.50	.60	.15
☐ 630	Denny McLain	1.75	.70	.17
☐ 631	Tom Matchick	.75	.30	.07
☐ 632	Dick Selma	.75	.30	.07
☐ 633	Ike Brown	.75	.30	.07
☐ 634	Alan Closter	.75	.30	.07
☐ 635	Gene Alley	.90	.36	.09
☐ 636	Rickey Clark	.75	.30	.07
☐ 637	Norm Miller	.75	.30	.07
☐ 638	Ken Reynolds	.75	.30	.07
☐ 639	Willie Crawford	.75	.30	.07
☐ 640	Dick Bosman	.75	.30	.07

	MINT	VG-E	F-G
☐ 641 Reds Team	1.75	.70	.17
☐ 642 Jose LaBoy	.75	.30	.07
☐ 643 Al Fitzmorris	.75	.30	.07
☐ 644 Jack Heidemann	.75	.30	.07
☐ 645 Bob Locker	.75	.30	.07
☐ 646 Brewers Leaders	1.25	.50	.12
Del Crandall MGR			
Harvey Kuenn CO			
Joe Nossek CO			
Bob Shaw CO			
Jim Walton CO			
☐ 647 George Stone	.75	.30	.07
☐ 648 Tom Egan	.75	.30	.07
☐ 649 Rich Folkers	.75	.30	.07
☐ 650 Felipe Alou	.90	.36	.09
☐ 651 Don Carrithers	.75	.30	.07
☐ 652 Ted Kubiak	.75	.30	.07
☐ 653 Joe Hoerner	.75	.30	.07
☐ 654 Twins Team	1.50	.60	.15
☐ 655 Clay Kirby	.75	.30	.07
☐ 656 John Ellis	.75	.30	.07
☐ 657 Bob Johnson	.75	.30	.07
☐ 658 Elliott Maddox	.75	.30	.07
☐ 659 Jose Pagan	.75	.30	.07
☐ 660 Fred Scherman	1.25	.50	.12

1974 Topps

The cards in this 660-card set measure 2½" by 3½". This year marked the first time Topps issued all the cards of its baseball set at the same time rather than in series. Some interesting variations were created by the rumored move of the San Diego Padres to Washington. Fifteen cards (13 players, the team card, and the rookie card #599) of the Padres were printed either as "San Diego"

(SD) or "Washington." The latter are the scarcer variety and are denoted in the checklist below by WASH. Each team's manager and his coaches again have a combined card with small pictures of each coach below the larger photo of the team's manager. The first six cards in the set (1-6) feature Hank Aaron and his illustrious career. Other topical subsets included in the set are League Leaders (201-208), All-Star selections (331-339), Playoffs cards (470-471), World Series cards (472-479), and Rookie Prospects (596-608).

		MINT	VG-E	F-G
	Complete Set	250.00	100.00	25.00
	Common Player (1-660)	.15	.06	.01
☐ 1	Hank Aaron	9.00	3.75	.90
	Complete ML record			
☐ 2	Aaron Special 54-57	2.25	.90	.22
	Records on back			
☐ 3	Aaron Special 58-61	2.25	.90	.22
	Memorable homers			
☐ 4	Aaron Special 62-65	2.25	.90	.22
	Life in ML's 1954-63			
☐ 5	Aaron Special 66-69	2.25	.90	.22
	Life in ML's 1964-73			
☐ 6	Aaron Special 70-73	2.25	.90	.22
	Milestone homers			
☐ 7	Jim Hunter	1.75	.70	.17
☐ 8	George Theodore	.15	.06	.01
☐ 9	Mickey Lolich	.35	.14	.03
☐ 10	Johnny Bench	5.00	2.00	.50
☐ 11	Jim Bibby	.20	.08	.02
☐ 12	Dave May	.15	.06	.01
☐ 13	Tom Hilgendorf	.15	.06	.01
☐ 14	Paul Popovich	.15	.06	.01
☐ 15	Joe Torre	.50	.20	.05
☐ 16	Orioles Team	.40	.16	.04
☐ 17	Doug Bird	.15	.06	.01
☐ 18	Gary Thomasson	.15	.06	.01
☐ 19	Gerry Moses	.15	.06	.01
☐ 20	Nolan Ryan	4.50	1.80	.45
☐ 21	Bob Gallagher	.15	.06	.01
☐ 22	Cy Acosta	.15	.06	.01
☐ 23	Craig Robinson	.15	.06	.01
☐ 24	John Hiller	.20	.08	.02
☐ 25	Ken Singleton	.30	.12	.03
☐ 26	Bill Campbell	.25	.10	.02
☐ 27	George Scott	.20	.08	.02
☐ 28	Manny Sanguillen	.20	.08	.02

	MINT	VG-E	F-G
☐ 29 Phil Niekro	1.25	.50	.12
☐ 30 Bobby Bonds	.30	.12	.03
☐ 31 Astros Leaders	.25	.10	.02
Preston Gomez MGR			
Roger Craig CO			
Hub Kittle CO			
Grady Hatton CO			
Bob Lillis CO			
☐ 32 A Johnny Grubb SD	.30	.12	.03
☐ 32 B Johnny Grubb WASH	3.00	1.20	.30
☐ 33 Don Newhauser	.15	.06	.01
☐ 34 Andy Kosco	.15	.06	.01
☐ 35 Gaylord Perry	1.75	.70	.17
☐ 36 Cardinals Team	.40	.16	.04
☐ 37 Dave Sells	.15	.06	.01
☐ 38 Don Kessinger	.20	.08	.02
☐ 39 Ken Suarez	.15	.06	.01
☐ 40 Jim Palmer	2.75	1.10	.27
☐ 41 Bobby Floyd	.15	.06	.01
☐ 42 Claude Osteen	.20	.08	.02
☐ 43 Jim Wynn	.25	.10	.02
☐ 44 Mel Stottlemyre	.25	.10	.02
☐ 45 Dave Johnson	.35	.14	.03
☐ 46 Pat Kelly	.15	.06	.01
☐ 47 Dick Ruthven	.15	.06	.01
☐ 48 Dick Sharon	.15	.06	.01
☐ 49 Steve Renko	.15	.06	.01
☐ 50 Rod Carew	4.50	1.80	.45
☐ 51 Bob Heise	.15	.06	.01
☐ 52 Al Oliver	.90	.36	.09
☐ 53 A Fred Kendall SD	.30	.12	.03
☐ 53 B Fred Kendall WASH	3.00	1.20	.30
☐ 54 Elias Sosa	.15	.06	.01
☐ 55 Frank Robinson	2.25	.90	.22
☐ 56 New York Mets Team	.60	.24	.06
☐ 57 Darold Knowles	.15	.06	.01
☐ 58 Charlie Spikes	.15	.06	.01
☐ 59 Ross Grimsley	.15	.06	.01
☐ 60 Lou Brock	2.25	.90	.22
☐ 61 Luis Aparicio	1.75	.70	.17
☐ 62 Bob Locker	.15	.06	.01
☐ 63 Bill Sudakis	.15	.06	.01
☐ 64 Doug Rau	.15	.06	.01
☐ 65 Amos Otis	.30	.12	.03
☐ 66 Sparky Lyle	.30	.12	.03
☐ 67 Tommy Helms	.20	.08	.02
☐ 68 Grant Jackson	.15	.06	.01
☐ 69 Del Unser	.15	.06	.01
☐ 70 Dick Allen	.40	.16	.04
☐ 71 Dan Frisella	.15	.06	.01
☐ 72 Aurelio Rodriguez	.15	.06	.01
☐ 73 Mike Marshall	.45	.18	.04
☐ 74 Twins Team	.40	.16	.04

	MINT	VG-E	F-G
☐ 75 Jim Colborn	.15	.06	.01
☐ 76 Mickey Rivers	.30	.12	.03
☐ 77 A Rich Troedson SD	.30	.12	.03
☐ 77 B Rich Troedson WASH	3.00	1.20	.30
☐ 78 Giants Leaders	.25	.10	.02
Charlie Fox MGR			
John McNamara CO			
Joe Amalfitano CO			
Andy Gilbert CO			
Don McMahon CO			
☐ 79 Gene Tenace	.20	.08	.02
☐ 80 Tom Seaver	5.00	2.00	.50
☐ 81 Frank Duffy	.15	.06	.01
☐ 82 Dave Giusti	.15	.06	.01
☐ 83 Orlando Cepeda	.55	.22	.05
☐ 84 Rick Wise	.20	.08	.02
☐ 85 Joe Morgan	1.75	.70	.17
☐ 86 Joe Ferguson	.20	.06	.02
☐ 87 Fergie Jenkins	.80	.32	.08
☐ 88 Fred Patek	.15	.06	.01
☐ 89 Jackie Brown	.15	.06	.01
☐ 90 Bobby Murcer	.45	.18	.04
☐ 91 Ken Forsch	.20	.08	.02
☐ 92 Paul Blair	.20	.08	.02
☐ 93 Rod Gilbreath	.15	.06	.01
☐ 94 Tigers Team	.40	.16	.04
☐ 95 Steve Carlton	5.00	2.00	.50
☐ 96 Jerry Hairston	.15	.06	.01
☐ 97 Bob Bailey	.15	.06	.01
☐ 98 Bert Blyleven	.60	.24	.06
☐ 99 Brewers Leaders	.30	.12	.03
Del Crandall MGR			
Harvey Kuenn CO			
Joe Nossek CO			
Jim Walton CO			
Al Widmar CO			
☐ 100 Willie Stargell	2.00	.80	.20
☐ 101 Bobby Valentine	.35	.14	.03
☐ 102 A Bill Greif SD	.30	.12	.03
☐ 102 B Bill Greif WASH	3.00	1.20	.30
☐ 103 Sal Bando	.30	.12	.03
☐ 104 Ron Bryant	.15	.06	.01
☐ 105 Carlton Fisk	1.25	.50	.12
☐ 106 Harry Parker	.15	.06	.01
☐ 107 Alex Johnson	.20	.08	.02
☐ 108 Al Hrabosky	.20	.08	.02
☐ 109 Bobby Grich	.30	.12	.03
☐ 110 Billy Williams	1.50	.60	.15
☐ 111 Clay Carroll	.15	.06	.01
☐ 112 Dave Lopes	.30	.12	.03
☐ 113 Dick Drago	.15	.06	.01
☐ 114 Angels Team	.40	.16	.04
☐ 115 Willie Horton	.25	.10	.02

	MINT	VG-E	F-G
☐ 116 Jerry Reuss	.30	.12	.03
☐ 117 Ron Blomberg	.15	.06	.01
☐ 118 Bill Lee	.20	.08	.02
☐ 119 Phillies Leaders	.25	.10	.02
Danny Ozark MGR			
Ray Ripplemeyer CO			
Bobby Wine CO			
Carroll Beringer CO			
Billy DeMars CO			
☐ 120 Wilbur Wood	.20	.08	.02
☐ 121 Larry Lintz	.15	.06	.01
☐ 122 Jim Holt	.15	.06	.01
☐ 123 Nellie Briles	.20	.08	.02
☐ 124 Bobby Coluccio	.15	.06	.01
☐ 125 A Nate Colbert SD	.30	.12	.03
☐ 125 B Nate Colbert WASH	3.00	1.20	.30
☐ 126 Checklist 1	.75	.07	.01
☐ 127 Tom Paciorek	.20	.08	.02
☐ 128 John Ellis	.15	.06	.01
☐ 129 Chris Speier	.15	.06	.01
☐ 130 Reggie Jackson	6.00	2.40	.60
☐ 131 Bob Boone	.35	.14	.03
☐ 132 Felix Millan	.15	.06	.01
☐ 133 David Clyde	.20	.08	.02
☐ 134 Denis Menke	.15	.06	.01
☐ 135 Roy White	.20	.08	.02
☐ 136 Rick Reuschel	.25	.10	.02
☐ 137 Al Bumbry	.15	.06	.01
☐ 138 Eddie Brinkman	.15	.06	.01
☐ 139 Aurelio Monteagudo	.15	.06	.01
☐ 140 Darrell Evans	.35	.14	.03
☐ 141 Pat Bourque	.15	.06	.01
☐ 142 Pedro Garcia	.15	.06	.01
☐ 143 Dick Woodson	.15	.06	.01
☐ 144 Dodgers Leaders	.55	.22	.05
Walter Alston MGR			
Tom Lasorda CO			
Jim Gilliam CO			
Red Adams CO			
Monty Basgall CO			
☐ 145 Dock Ellis	.15	.06	.01
☐ 146 Ron Fairly	.20	.08	.02
☐ 147 Bart Johnson	.15	.06	.01
☐ 148 A Dave Hilton SD	.30	.12	.03
☐ 148 B Dave Hilton WASH	3.00	1.20	.30
☐ 149 Mac Scarce	.15	.06	.01
☐ 150 John Mayberry	.20	.08	.02
☐ 151 Diego Segui	.15	.06	.01
☐ 152 Oscar Gamble	.25	.10	.02
☐ 153 Jon Matlack	.25	.10	.02
☐ 154 Astros Team	.40	.16	.04
☐ 155 Bert Campaneris	.30	.12	.03
☐ 156 Randy Moffitt	.15	.06	.01

	MINT	VG-E	F-G
☐ 157 Vic Harris	.15	.06	.01
☐ 158 Jack Billingham	.15	.06	.01
☐ 159 Jim Ray Hart	.20	.08	.02
☐ 160 Brooks Robinson	2.50	1.00	.25
☐ 161 Ray Burris	.50	.20	.05
☐ 162 Bill Freehan	.30	.12	.03
☐ 163 Ken Berry	.15	.06	.01
☐ 164 Tom House	.20	.08	.02
☐ 165 Willie Davis	.25	.10	.02
☐ 166 Royals Leaders	.25	.10	.02
Jack McKeon MGR			
Charlie Lau CO			
Harry Dunlop CO			
Galen Cisco CO			
☐ 167 Luis Tiant	.35	.14	.03
☐ 168 Danny Thompson	.15	.06	.01
☐ 169 Steve Rogers	.90	.36	.09
☐ 170 Bill Melton	.15	.06	.01
☐ 171 Eduardo Rodriguez	.15	.06	.01
☐ 172 Gene Clines	.15	.06	.01
☐ 173 A Randy Jones SD	.45	.18	.04
☐ 173 B Randy Jones WASH	3.50	1.40	.35
☐ 174 Bill Robinson	.15	.06	.01
☐ 175 Reggie Cleveland	.15	.06	.01
☐ 176 John Lowenstein	.15	.06	.01
☐ 177 Dave Roberts	.15	.06	.01
☐ 178 Garry Maddox	.20	.08	.02
☐ 179 Mets Leaders	.65	.26	.06
Yogi Berra MGR			
Rube Walker CO			
Eddie Yost CO			
Roy McMillan CO			
Joe Pignatano CO			
☐ 180 Ken Holtzman	.25	.10	.02
☐ 181 Cesar Geronimo	.15	.06	.01
☐ 182 Lindy McDaniel	.15	.06	.01
☐ 183 Johnny Oates	.15	.06	.01
☐ 184 Rangers Team	.40	.16	.04
☐ 185 Jose Cardenal	.15	.06	.01
☐ 186 Fred Scherman	.15	.06	.01
☐ 187 Don Baylor	.70	.28	.07
☐ 188 Rudy Meoli	.15	.06	.01
☐ 189 Jim Brewer	.15	.06	.01
☐ 190 Tony Oliva	.50	.20	.05
☐ 191 Al Fitzmorris	.15	.06	.01
☐ 192 Mario Guerrero	.15	.06	.01
☐ 193 Tom Walker	.15	.06	.01
☐ 194 Darrell Porter	.25	.10	.02
☐ 195 Carlos May	.15	.06	.01
☐ 196 Jim Fregosi	.30	.12	.03
☐ 197 A Vicente Romo SD	.30	.12	.03
☐ 197 B Vicente Romo WASH	3.00	1.20	.30
☐ 198 Dave Cash	.20	.08	.02

		MINT	VG-E	F-G
☐ 199	Mike Kekich	.15	.06	.01
☐ 200	Cesar Cedeno	.30	.12	.03
☐ 201	Batting Leaders	2.50	1.00	.25
	Rod Carew			
	Pete Rose			
☐ 202	Home Run Leaders	1.25	.50	.12
	Reggie Jackson			
	Willie Stargell			
☐ 203	RBI Leaders	1.25	.50	.12
	Reggie Jackson			
	Willie Stargell			
☐ 204	Stolen Base Leaders	.60	.24	.06
	Tommy Harper			
	Lou Brock			
☐ 205	Victory Leaders	.30	.12	.03
	Wilbur Wood			
	Ron Bryant			
☐ 206	ERA Leaders	1.50	.60	.15
	Jim Palmer			
	Tom Seaver			
☐ 207	Strikeout Leaders	1.50	.60	.15
	Nolan Ryan			
	Tom Seaver			
☐ 208	Leading Firemen	.30	.12	.03
	John Hiller			
	Mike Marshall			
☐ 209	Ted Sizemore	.15	.06	.01
☐ 210	Bill Singer	.15	.06	.01
☐ 211	Chicago Cubs Team	.40	.16	.04
☐ 212	Rollie Fingers	1.00	.40	.10
☐ 213	Dave Rader	.15	.06	.01
☐ 214	Bill Grabarkewitz	.15	.06	.01
☐ 215	Al Kaline	2.25	.90	.22
☐ 216	Ray Sadecki	.15	.06	.01
☐ 217	Tim Foli	.15	.06	.01
☐ 218	John Briggs	.15	.06	.01
☐ 219	Doug Griffin	.15	.06	.01
☐ 220	Don Sutton	1.50	.60	.15
☐ 221	White Sox Leaders	.25	.10	.02
	Chuck Tanner MGR			
	Jim Mahoney CO			
	Alex Monchak CO			
	Johnny Sain CO			
	Joe Lonnett CO			
☐ 222	Ramon Hernandez	.15	.06	.01
☐ 223	Jeff Burroughs	.40	.16	.04
☐ 224	Roger Metzger	.15	.06	.01
☐ 225	Paul Splittorff	.20	.08	.02
☐ 226 A	Padres Team SD	.60	.24	.06
☐ 226 B	Padres Team WASH	5.00	2.00	.50
☐ 227	Mike Lum	.15	.06	.01
☐ 228	Ted Kubiak	.15	.06	.01
☐ 229	Fritz Peterson	.15	.06	.01

		MINT	VG-E	F-G
☐ 230	Tony Perez	.65	.26	.06
☐ 231	Dick Tidrow	.15	.06	.01
☐ 232	Steve Brye	.15	.06	.01
☐ 233	Jim Barr	.15	.06	.01
☐ 234	John Milner	.15	.06	.01
☐ 235	Dave McNally	.25	.10	.02
☐ 236	Cardinals Leaders	.30	.12	.03
	Red Schoendienst MGR			
	Barney Schultz CO			
	George Kissell CO			
	Johnny Lewis CO			
	Vern Benson CO			
☐ 237	Ken Brett	.15	.06	.01
☐ 238	Fran Healy	.15	.06	.01
☐ 239	Bill Russell	.25	.10	.02
☐ 240	Joe Coleman	.15	.06	.01
☐ 241 A	Glenn Beckert SD	.30	.12	.03
☐ 241 B	Glenn Beckert WASH	3.00	1.20	.30
☐ 242	Bill Gogolewski	.15	.06	.01
☐ 243	Bob Oliver	.15	.06	.01
☐ 244	Carl Morton	.15	.06	.01
☐ 245	Cleon Jones	.15	.06	.01
☐ 246	Athletics Team	.45	.18	.04
☐ 247	Rick Miller	.15	.06	.01
☐ 248	Tom Hall	.15	.06	.01
☐ 249	George Mitterwald	.15	.06	.01
☐ 250 A	Willie McCovey SD	3.00	1.20	.30
☐ 250 B	Willie McCovey WASH	16.00	6.50	1.60
☐ 251	Graig Nettles	1.50	.60	.15
☐ 252	Dave Parker	14.00	5.75	1.40
☐ 253	John Boccabella	.15	.06	.01
☐ 254	Stan Bahnsen	.15	.06	.01
☐ 255	Larry Bowa	.45	.18	.04
☐ 256	Tom Griffin	.15	.06	.01
☐ 257	Buddy Bell	.80	.32	.08
☐ 258	Jerry Morales	.15	.06	.01
☐ 259	Bob Reynolds	.15	.06	.01
☐ 260	Ted Simmons	.80	.32	.08
☐ 261	Jerry Bell	.15	.06	.01
☐ 262	Ed Kirkpatrick	.15	.06	.01
☐ 263	Checklist 2	.75	.07	.01
☐ 264	Joe Rudi	.25	.10	.02
☐ 265	Tug McGraw	.35	.14	.03
☐ 266	Jim Northrup	.20	.08	.02
☐ 267	Andy Messersmith	.25	.10	.02
☐ 268	Tom Grieve	.25	.10	.02
☐ 269	Bob Johnson	.15	.06	.01
☐ 270	Ron Santo	.35	.14	.03
☐ 271	Bill Hands	.15	.06	.01
☐ 272	Paul Casanova	.15	.06	.01
☐ 273	Checklist 3	.75	.07	.01
☐ 274	Fred Beene	.15	.06	.01
☐ 275	Ron Hunt	.15	.06	.01

	MINT	VG-E	F-G			MINT	VG-E	F-G
☐ 276 Angels Leaders	.25	.10	.02	☐ 318 Jim Merritt		.15	.06	.01
Bobby Winkles MGR				☐ 319 Randy Hundley		.15	.06	.01
John Roseboro CO				☐ 320 Dusty Baker		.40	.16	.04
Tom Morgan CO				☐ 321 Steve Braun		.15	.06	.01
Jimmie Reese CO				☐ 322 Ernie McAnally		.15	.06	.01
Salty Parker CO				☐ 323 Richie Scheinblum		.15	.06	.01
☐ 277 Gary Nolan	.15	.06	.01	☐ 324 Steve Kline		.15	.06	.01
☐ 278 Cookie Rojas	.15	.06	.01	☐ 325 Tommy Harper		.20	.08	.02
☐ 279 Jim Crawford	.15	.06	.01	☐ 326 Reds Leaders		.30	.12	.03
☐ 280 Carl Yastrzemski	6.50	2.60	.65	Sparky Anderson MGR				
☐ 281 Giants Team	.40	.16	.04	Larry Shephard CO				
☐ 282 Doyle Alexander	.20	.08	.02	George Scherger CO				
☐ 283 Mike Schmidt	20.00	8.00	2.00	Alex Grammas CO				
☐ 284 Dave Duncan	.15	.06	.01	Ted Kluszewski CO				
☐ 285 Reggie Smith	.35	.14	.03	☐ 327 Tom Timmermann		.15	.06	.01
☐ 286 Tony Muser	.15	.06	.01	☐ 328 Skip Jutze		.15	.06	.01
☐ 287 Clay Kirby	.15	.06	.01	☐ 329 Mark Belanger		.25	.10	.02
☐ 288 Gorman Thomas	1.50	.60	.15	☐ 330 Juan Marichal		2.00	.80	.20
☐ 289 Rick Auerbach	.15	.06	.01	☐ 331 All-Star Catchers		1.25	.50	.12
☐ 290 Vida Blue	.35	.14	.03	Carlton Fisk				
☐ 291 Don Hahn	.15	.06	.01	Johnny Bench				
☐ 292 Chuck Seelbach	.15	.06	.01	☐ 332 All-Star 1B		1.25	.50	.12
☐ 293 Milt May	.15	.06	.01	Dick Allen				
☐ 294 Steve Foucault	.15	.06	.01	Hank Aaron				
☐ 295 Rick Monday	.20	.08	.02	☐ 333 All-Star 2B		1.25	.50	.12
☐ 296 Ray Corbin	.15	.06	.01	Rod Carew				
☐ 297 Hal Breeden	.15	.06	.01	Joe Morgan				
☐ 298 Roric Harrison	.15	.06	.01	☐ 334 All-Star 3B		.90	.36	.09
☐ 299 Gene Michael	.25	.10	.02	Brooks Robinson				
☐ 300 Pete Rose	13.00	5.25	1.30	Ron Santo				
☐ 301 Bob Montgomery	.15	.06	.01	☐ 335 All-Star SS		.25	.10	.02
☐ 302 Rudy May	.15	.06	.01	Bert Campaneris				
☐ 303 George Hendrick	.35	.14	.03	Chris Speier				
☐ 304 Don Wilson	.15	.06	.01	☐ 336 All-Star LF		2.25	.90	.22
☐ 305 Tito Fuentes	.15	.06	.01	Bobby Murcer				
☐ 306 Orioles Leaders	.45	.18	.04	Pete Rose				
Earl Weaver MGR				☐ 337 All-Star CF		.25	.10	.02
Jim Frey CO				Amos Otis				
George Bamberger CO				Cesar Cedeno				
Billy Hunter CO				☐ 338 All-Star RF		1.50	.60	.15
George Staller CO				Reggie Jackson				
☐ 307 Luis Melendez	.15	.06	.01	Billy Williams				
☐ 308 Bruce Dal Canton	.15	.06	.01	☐ 339 All-Star Pitchers		.40	.16	.04
☐ 309 A Dave Roberts SD	.30	.12	.03	Jim Hunter				
☐ 309 B Dave Roberts WASH	3.75	1.50	.37	Rick Wise				
☐ 310 Terry Forster	.30	.12	.03	☐ 340 Thurman Munson		3.50	1.40	.35
☐ 311 Jerry Grote	.15	.06	.01	☐ 341 Dan Driessen		.35	.14	.03
☐ 312 Deron Johnson	.15	.06	.01	☐ 342 Jim Lonborg		.20	.08	.02
☐ 313 Barry Lersch	.15	.06	.01	☐ 343 Royals Team		.40	.16	.04
☐ 314 Brewers Team	.40	.16	.04	☐ 344 Mike Caldwell		.20	.08	.02
☐ 315 Ron Cey	1.00	.40	.10	☐ 345 Bill North		.15	.06	.01
☐ 316 Jim Perry	.25	.10	.02	☐ 346 Ron Reed		.15	.06	.01
☐ 317 Richie Zisk	.25	.10	.02	☐ 347 Sandy Alomar		.15	.06	.01

		MINT	VG-E	F-G
☐ 348	Pete Richert	.15	.06	.01
☐ 349	John Vukovich	.15	.06	.01
☐ 350	Bob Gibson	2.25	.90	.22
☐ 351	Dwight Evans	1.25	.50	.12
☐ 352	Bill Stoneman	.15	.06	.01
☐ 353	Rich Coggins	.15	.06	.01
☐ 354	Cubs Leaders	.25	.10	.02
	Whitey Lockman MGR			
	J.C. Martin CO			
	Hank Aguirre CO			
	Al Spangler CO			
	Jim Marshall CO			
☐ 355	Dave Nelson	.15	.06	.01
☐ 356	Jerry Koosman	.30	.12	.03
☐ 357	Buddy Bradford	.15	.06	.01
☐ 358	Dal Maxvill	.15	.06	.01
☐ 359	Brent Strom	.15	.06	.01
☐ 360	Greg Luzinski	.70	.28	.07
☐ 361	Don Carrithers	.15	.06	.01
☐ 362	Hal King	.15	.06	.01
☐ 363	Yankees Team	.55	.22	.05
☐ 364 A	Cito Gaston SD	.30	.12	.03
☐ 364 B	Cito Gaston WASH	3.75	1.50	.37
☐ 365	Steve Busby	.25	.10	.02
☐ 366	Larry Hisle	.25	.10	.02
☐ 367	Norm Cash	.35	.14	.03
☐ 368	Manny Mota	.25	.10	.02
☐ 369	Paul Lindblad	.15	.06	.01
☐ 370	Bob Watson	.30	.12	.03
☐ 371	Jim Slaton	.15	.06	.01
☐ 372	Ken Reitz	.15	.06	.01
☐ 373	John Curtis	.15	.06	.01
☐ 374	Marty Perez	.15	.06	.01
☐ 375	Earl Williams	.15	.06	.01
☐ 376	Jorge Orta	.15	.06	.01
☐ 377	Ron Woods	.15	.06	.01
☐ 378	Burt Hooton	.20	.08	.02
☐ 379	Rangers Leaders	.55	.22	.05
	Billy Martin MGR			
	Frank Lucchesi CO			
	Art Fowler CO			
	Charlie Silvera CO			
	Jackie Moore CO			
☐ 380	Bud Harrelson	.15	.06	.01
☐ 381	Charlie Sands	.15	.06	.01
☐ 382	Bob Moose	.15	.06	.01
☐ 383	Phillies Team	.40	.16	.04
☐ 384	Chris Chambliss	.30	.12	.03
☐ 385	Don Gullett	.20	.08	.02
☐ 386	Gary Matthews	.45	.18	.04
☐ 387 A	Rich Morales SD	.30	.12	.03
☐ 387 B	Rich Morales WASH	3.75	1.50	.37
☐ 388	Phil Roof	.15	.06	.01
☐ 389	Gates Brown	.20	.08	.02
☐ 390	Lou Piniella	.45	.18	.04
☐ 391	Billy Champion	.15	.06	.01
☐ 392	Dick Green	.15	.06	.01
☐ 393	Orlando Pena	.15	.06	.01
☐ 394	Ken Henderson	.15	.06	.01
☐ 395	Doug Rader	.20	.08	.02
☐ 396	Tommy Davis	.25	.10	.02
☐ 397	George Stone	.15	.06	.01
☐ 398	Duke Sims	.15	.06	.01
☐ 399	Mike Paul	.15	.06	.01
☐ 400	Harmon Killebrew	2.25	.90	.22
☐ 401	Elliott Maddox	.15	.06	.01
☐ 402	Jim Rooker	.15	.06	.01
☐ 403	Red Sox Leaders	.25	.10	.02
	Darrell Johnson MGR			
	Eddie Popowski CO			
	Lee Stange CO			
	Don Zimmer CO			
	Don Bryant CO			
☐ 404	Jim Howarth	.15	.06	.01
☐ 405	Ellie Rodriguez	.15	.06	.01
☐ 406	Steve Arlin	.15	.06	.01
☐ 407	Jim Wohlford	.15	.06	.01
☐ 408	Charlie Hough	.30	.12	.03
☐ 409	Ike Brown	.15	.06	.01
☐ 410	Pedro Borbon	.15	.06	.01
☐ 411	Frank Baker	.15	.06	.01
☐ 412	Chuck Taylor	.15	.06	.01
☐ 413	Don Money	.20	.08	.02
☐ 414	Checklist 4	.75	.07	.01
☐ 415	Gary Gentry	.15	.06	.01
☐ 416	White Sox Team	.40	.16	.04
☐ 417	Rich Folkers	.15	.06	.01
☐ 418	Walt Williams	.15	.06	.01
☐ 419	Wayne Twitchell	.15	.06	.01
☐ 420	Ray Fosse	.15	.06	.01
☐ 421	Dan Fife	.15	.06	.01
☐ 422	Gonzalo Marquez	.15	.06	.01
☐ 423	Fred Stanley	.15	.06	.01
☐ 424	Jim Beauchamp	.15	.06	.01
☐ 425	Pete Broberg	.15	.06	.01
☐ 426	Rennie Stennett	.15	.06	.01
☐ 427	Bobby Bolin	.15	.06	.01
☐ 428	Gary Sutherland	.15	.06	.01
☐ 429	Dick Lange	.15	.06	.01
☐ 430	Matty Alou	.20	.08	.02
☐ 431	Gene Garber	.20	.08	.02
☐ 432	Chris Arnold	.15	.06	.01
☐ 433	Lerrin LaGrow	.15	.06	.01
☐ 434	Ken McMullen	.15	.06	.01
☐ 435	Dave Concepcion	.50	.20	.05
☐ 436	Don Hood	.15	.06	.01

	MINT	VG-E	F-G
☐ 437 Jim Lyttle	.15	.06	.01
☐ 438 Ed Herrmann	.15	.06	.01
☐ 439 Norm Miller	.15	.06	.01
☐ 440 Jim Kaat	.75	.30	.07
☐ 441 Tom Ragland	.15	.06	.01
☐ 442 Alan Foster	.15	.06	.01
☐ 443 Tom Hutton	.15	.06	.01
☐ 444 Vic Davalillo	.15	.06	.01
☐ 445 George Medich	.20	.08	.02
☐ 446 Len Randle	.15	.06	.01
☐ 447 Twins Leaders	.25	.10	.02
Frank Quilici MGR			
Ralph Rowe CO			
Bob Rodgers CO			
Vern Morgan CO			
☐ 448 Ron Hodges	.15	.06	.01
☐ 449 Tom McCraw	.15	.06	.01
☐ 450 Rich Hebner	.15	.06	.01
☐ 451 Tommy John	.85	.34	.08
☐ 452 Gene Hiser	.15	.06	.01
☐ 453 Balor Moore	.15	.06	.01
☐ 454 Kurt Bevacqua	.15	.06	.01
☐ 455 Tom Bradley	.15	.06	.01
☐ 456 Dave Winfield	18.00	7.25	1.80
☐ 457 Chuck Goggin	.15	.06	.01
☐ 458 Jim Ray	.15	.06	.01
☐ 459 Reds Team	.45	.18	.04
☐ 460 Boog Powell	.50	.20	.05
☐ 461 John Odom	.15	.06	.01
☐ 462 Luis Alvarado	.15	.06	.01
☐ 463 Pat Dobson	.20	.08	.02
☐ 464 Jose Cruz	.50	.20	.05
☐ 465 Dick Bosman	.15	.06	.01
☐ 466 Dick Billings	.15	.06	.01
☐ 467 Winston Llenas	.15	.06	.01
☐ 468 Pepe Frias	.15	.06	.01
☐ 469 Joe Decker	.15	.06	.01
☐ 470 AL Playoffs	1.50	.60	.15
A's over Orioles			
(Reggie Jackson)			
☐ 471 NL Playoffs	.50	.20	.05
Mets over Reds			
(Matlack pitching)			
☐ 472 World Series Game 1	.50	.20	.05
(Knowles pitching)			
☐ 473 World Series Game 2	1.50	.60	.15
(Willie Mays batting)			
☐ 474 World Series Game 3	.50	.20	.05
(Campaneris stealing)			
☐ 475 World Series Game 4	.50	.20	.05
(Staub batting)			
☐ 476 World Series Game 5	.50	.20	.05
Cleon Jones scoring)			

	MINT	VG-E	F-G
☐ 477 World Series Game 6	1.50	.60	.15
(Reggie Jackson)			
☐ 478 World Series Game 7	.50	.20	.05
(Campaneris batting)			
☐ 479 World Series Summary	.50	.20	.05
A's celebrate; Win			
2nd Consecutive			
Championship			
☐ 480 Willie Crawford	.15	.06	.01
☐ 481 Jerry Terrell	.15	.06	.01
☐ 482 Bob Didier	.15	.06	.01
☐ 483 Braves Team	.40	.16	.04
☐ 484 Carmen Fanzone	.15	.06	.01
☐ 485 Felipe Alou	.25	.10	.02
☐ 486 Steve Stone	.25	.10	.02
☐ 487 Ted Martinez	.15	.06	.01
☐ 488 Andy Etchebarren	.15	.06	.01
☐ 489 Pirates Leaders	.25	.10	.02
Danny Murtaugh MGR			
Don Osborn CO			
Don Leppert CO			
Bill Mazeroski CO			
Bob Skinner CO			
☐ 490 Vada Pinson	.35	.14	.03
☐ 491 Roger Nelson	.15	.06	.01
☐ 492 Mike Rogodzinski	.15	.06	.01
☐ 493 Joe Hoerner	.15	.06	.01
☐ 494 Ed Goodson	.15	.06	.01
☐ 495 Dick McAuliffe	.15	.06	.01
☐ 496 Tom Murphy	.15	.06	.01
☐ 497 Bobby Mitchell	.15	.06	.01
☐ 498 Pat Corrales	.25	.10	.02
☐ 499 Rusty Torres	.15	.06	.01
☐ 500 Lee May	.25	.10	.02
☐ 501 Eddie Leon	.15	.06	.01
☐ 502 Dave LaRoche	.15	.06	.01
☐ 503 Eric Soderholm	.15	.06	.01
☐ 504 Joe Niekro	.30	.12	.03
☐ 505 Bill Buckner	.50	.20	.05
☐ 506 Ed Farmer	.15	.06	.01
☐ 507 Larry Stahl	.15	.06	.01
☐ 508 Expos Team	.40	.16	.04
☐ 509 Jesse Jefferson	.15	.06	.01
☐ 510 Wayne Garrett	.15	.06	.01
☐ 511 Toby Harrah	.25	.10	.02
☐ 512 Joe Lahoud	.15	.06	.01
☐ 513 Jim Campanis	.15	.06	.01
☐ 514 Paul Schaal	.15	.06	.01
☐ 515 Willie Montanez	.15	.06	.01
☐ 516 Horacio Pina	.15	.06	.01
☐ 517 Mike Hegan	.15	.06	.01
☐ 518 Derrel Thomas	.15	.06	.01
☐ 519 Bill Sharp	.15	.06	.01

		MINT	VG-E	F-G
☐ 520	Tim McCarver	.30	.12	.03
☐ 521	Indians Leaders	.25	.10	.02
	Ken Aspromonte MGR			
	Clay Bryant CO			
	Tony Pacheco CO			
☐ 522	J.R. Richard	.40	.16	.04
☐ 523	Cecil Cooper	1.50	.60	.15
☐ 524	Bill Plummer	.15	.06	.01
☐ 525	Clyde Wright	.15	.06	.01
☐ 526	Frank Tepedino	.15	.06	.01
☐ 527	Bobby Darwin	.15	.06	.01
☐ 528	Bill Bonham	.15	.06	.01
☐ 529	Horace Clarke	.15	.06	.01
☐ 530	Mickey Stanley	.15	.06	.01
☐ 531	Expos Leaders	.25	.10	.02
	Gene Mauch MGR			
	Dave Bristol CO			
	Cal McLish CO			
	Larry Doby CO			
	Jerry Zimmerman CO			
☐ 532	Skip Lockwood	.15	.06	.01
☐ 533	Mike Phillips	.15	.06	.01
☐ 534	Eddie Watt	.15	.06	.01
☐ 535	Bob Tolan	.15	.06	.01
☐ 536	Duffy Dyer	.15	.06	.01
☐ 537	Steve Mingori	.15	.06	.01
☐ 538	Cesar Tovar	.15	.06	.01
☐ 539	Lloyd Allen	.15	.06	.01
☐ 540	Bob Robertson	.15	.06	.01
☐ 541	Indians Team	.40	.16	.04
☐ 542	Rich Gossage	1.50	.60	.15
☐ 543	Danny Cater	.15	.06	.01
☐ 544	Ron Schueler	.15	.06	.01
☐ 545	Billy Conigliaro	.15	.06	.01
☐ 546	Mike Corkins	.15	.06	.01
☐ 547	Glenn Borgmann	.15	.06	.01
☐ 548	Sonny Siebert	.20	.08	.02
☐ 549	Mike Jorgensen	.15	.06	.01
☐ 550	Sam McDowell	.20	.08	.02
☐ 551	Von Joshua	.15	.06	.01
☐ 552	Denny Doyle	.15	.06	.01
☐ 553	Jim Willoughby	.15	.06	.01
☐ 554	Tim Johnson	.15	.06	.01
☐ 555	Woody Fryman	.15	.06	.01
☐ 556	Dave Campbell	.15	.06	.01
☐ 557	Jim McGlothlin	.15	.06	.01
☐ 558	Bill Fahey	.15	.06	.01
☐ 559	Darrell Chaney	.15	.06	.01
☐ 560	Mike Cuellar	.25	.10	.02
☐ 561	Ed Kranepool	.20	.08	.02
☐ 562	Jack Aker	.15	.06	.01
☐ 563	Hal McRae	.30	.12	.03
☐ 564	Mike Ryan	.15	.06	.01

		MINT	VG-E	F-G
☐ 565	Milt Wilcox	.20	.08	.02
☐ 566	Jackie Hernandez	.15	.06	.01
☐ 567	Red Sox Team	.40	.16	.04
☐ 568	Mike Torrez	.25	.10	.02
☐ 569	Rick Dempsey	.25	.10	.02
☐ 570	Ralph Garr	.25	.10	.02
☐ 571	Rich Hand	.15	.06	.01
☐ 572	Enzo Hernandez	.15	.06	.01
☐ 573	Mike Adams	.15	.06	.01
☐ 574	Bill Parsons	.15	.06	.01
☐ 575	Steve Garvey	6.50	2.60	.65
☐ 576	Scipio Spinks	.15	.06	.01
☐ 577	Mike Sadek	.15	.06	.01
☐ 578	Ralph Houk MGR	.25	.10	.02
☐ 579	Cecil Upshaw	.15	.06	.01
☐ 580	Jim Spencer	.15	.06	.01
☐ 581	Fred Norman	.15	.06	.01
☐ 582	Bucky Dent	.50	.20	.05
☐ 583	Marty Pattin	.15	.06	.01
☐ 584	Ken Rudolph	.15	.06	.01
☐ 585	Merv Rettenmund	.15	.06	.01
☐ 586	Jack Brohamer	.15	.06	.01
☐ 587	Larry Christenson	.15	.06	.01
☐ 588	Hal Lanier	.30	.12	.03
☐ 589	Boots Day	.15	.06	.01
☐ 590	Roger Moret	.15	.06	.01
☐ 591	Sonny Jackson	.15	.06	.01
☐ 592	Ed Bane	.15	.06	.01
☐ 593	Steve Yeager	.20	.08	.02
☐ 594	Lee Stanton	.15	.06	.01
☐ 595	Steve Blass	.15	.06	.01
☐ 596	Rookie Pitchers	.30	.12	.03
	Wayne Garland			
	Fred Holdsworth			
	Mark Littell			
	Dick Pole			
☐ 597	Rookie Shortstops	.75	.30	.07
	Dave Chalk			
	John Gamble			
	Pete MacKanin			
	Manny Trillo			
☐ 598	Rookie Outfielders	1.75	.70	.17
	Dave Augustine			
	Ken Griffey			
	Steve Ontiveros			
	Jim Tyrone			
☐ 599	A Rookie Pitchers			
	WASH	.75	.30	.07
	Ron Diorio			
	Dave Freisleben			
	Frank Riccelli			
	Greg Shanahan			

	MINT	VG-E	F-G
☐ 599 B Rookie Pitchers SD .. (SD in large print)	2.50	1.00	.25
☐ 599 C Rookie Pitchers SD .. (SD in small print)	6.00	2.40	.60
☐ 600 Rookie Infielders	6.00	2.40	.60
Ron Cash			
Jim Cox			
Bill Madlock			
Reggie Sanders			
☐ 601 Rookie Outfielders	1.00	.40	.10
Ed Armbrister			
Rich Bladt			
Brian Downing			
Bake McBride			
☐ 602 Rookie Pitchers	.40	.16	.04
Glen Abbott			
Rick Henninger			
Craig Swan			
Dan Vossler			
☐ 603 Rookie Catchers	.30	.12	.03
Barry Foote			
Tom Lundstedt			
Charlie Moore			
Sergio Robles			
☐ 604 Rookie Infielders	2.25	.90	.22
Terry Hughes			
John Knox			
Andy Thornton			
Frank White			
☐ 605 Rookie Pitchers	.60	.24	.06
Vic Albury			
Ken Frailing			
Kevin Kobel			
Frank Tanana			
☐ 606 Rookie Outfielders	.20	.08	.02
Jim Fuller			
Wilbur Howard			
Tommy Smith			
Otto Velez			
☐ 607 Rookie Shortstops	.20	.08	.02
Leo Foster			
Tom Heintzelman			
Dave Rosello			
Frank Taveras			
☐ 608 A Rookie Pitchers ERR	2.25	.90	.22
Bob Apodaco (sic)			
Dick Baney			
John D'Acquisto			
Mike Wallace			

	MINT	VG-E	F-G
☐ 608 B Rookie Pitchers COR	.30	.12	.03
Bob Apodaca			
Dick Baney			
John D'Acquisto			
Mike Wallace			
☐ 609 Rico Petrocelli	.25	.10	.02
☐ 610 Dave Kingman	.80	.32	.08
☐ 611 Rich Stelmaszek	.15	.06	.01
☐ 612 Luke Walker	.15	.06	.01
☐ 613 Dan Monzon	.15	.06	.01
☐ 614 Adrian Devine	.15	.06	.01
☐ 615 John Jeter	.15	.06	.01
☐ 616 Larry Gura	.25	.10	.02
☐ 617 Ted Ford	.15	.06	.01
☐ 618 Jim Mason	.15	.06	.01
☐ 619 Mike Anderson	.15	.06	.01
☐ 620 Al Downing	.15	.06	.01
☐ 621 Bernie Carbo	.15	.06	.01
☐ 622 Phil Gagliano	.15	.06	.01
☐ 623 Celerino Sanchez	.15	.06	.01
☐ 624 Bob Miller	.15	.06	.01
☐ 625 Ollie Brown	.15	.06	.01
☐ 626 Pirates Team	.40	.16	.04
☐ 627 Carl Taylor	.15	.06	.01
☐ 628 Ivan Murrell	.15	.06	.01
☐ 629 Rusty Staub	.50	.20	.05
☐ 630 Tommy Agee	.15	.06	.01
☐ 631 Steve Barber	.15	.06	.01
☐ 632 George Culver	.15	.06	.01
☐ 633 Dave Hamilton	.15	.06	.01
☐ 634 Braves Leaders	.55	.22	.05
Eddie Mathews MGR			
Herm Starrette CO			
Connie Ryan CO			
Jim Busby CO			
Ken Silvestri CO			
☐ 635 John Edwards	.15	.06	.01
☐ 636 Dave Goltz	.20	.08	.02
☐ 637 Checklist 5	.75	.07	.01
☐ 638 Ken Sanders	.15	.06	.01
☐ 639 Joe Lovitto	.15	.06	.01
☐ 640 Milt Pappas	.25	.10	.02
☐ 641 Chuck Brinkman	.15	.06	.01
☐ 642 Terry Harmon	.15	.06	.01
☐ 643 Dodgers Team	.60	.24	.06
☐ 644 Wayne Granger	.15	.06	.01
☐ 645 Ken Boswell	.15	.06	.01
☐ 646 George Foster	.90	.36	.09
☐ 647 Juan Beniquez	.60	.24	.06
☐ 648 Terry Crowley	.15	.06	.01
☐ 649 Fernando Gonzalez	.15	.06	.01
☐ 650 Mike Epstein	.15	.06	.01
☐ 651 Leron Lee	.15	.06	.01

		MINT	VG-E	F-G
☐ 652	Gail Hopkins	.15	.06	.01
☐ 653	Bob Stinson	.15	.06	.01
☐ 654 A	Jesus Alou (outfield)	.35	.14	.03
☐ 654 B	Jesus Alou (no position)	6.00	2.40	.60
☐ 655	Mike Tyson	.15	.06	.01
☐ 656	Adrian Garrett	.15	.06	.01
☐ 657	Jim Shellenback	.15	.06	.01
☐ 658	Lee Lacy	.25	.10	.02
☐ 659	Joe Lis	.15	.06	.01
☐ 660	Larry Dierker	.30	.12	.03

1974 Topps Traded

The cards in this 44-card set measure 2½ by 3½. The 1974 Topps Traded set contains 43 player cards and one unnumbered checklist card. The obverses have the word "traded" in block letters and the backs are designed in newspaper style. Card numbers are the same as in the regular set except they are followed by a "T." No known scarcities exist for this set.

		MINT	VG-E	F-G
	Complete Set	5.50	2.20	.55
	Common Player	.10	.04	.01
☐ 23 T	Craig Robinson	.10	.04	.01
☐ 42 T	Claude Osteen	.15	.06	.01
☐ 43 T	Jim Wynn	.20	.08	.02
☐ 51 T	Bobby Heise	.10	.04	.01
☐ 59 T	Ross Grimsley	.10	.04	.01
☐ 62 T	Bob Locker	.10	.04	.01
☐ 63 T	Bill Sudakis	.10	.04	.01
☐ 73 T	Mike Marshall	.25	.10	.02
☐ 123 T	Nelson Briles	.15	.06	.01

		MINT	VG-E	F-G
☐ 139 T	Aurelio Monteagudo	.10	.04	.01
☐ 151 T	Diego Segui	.10	.04	.01
☐ 165 T	Willie Davis	.25	.10	.02
☐ 175 T	Reggie Cleveland	.10	.04	.01
☐ 182 T	Lindy McDaniel	.15	.06	.01
☐ 186 T	Fred Scherman	.10	.04	.01
☐ 249 T	George Mitterwald	.10	.04	.01
☐ 262 T	Ed Kirkpatrick	.10	.04	.01
☐ 269 T	Bob Johnson	.10	.04	.01
☐ 270 T	Ron Santo	.35	.14	.03
☐ 313 T	Barry Lersch	.10	.04	.01
☐ 319 T	Randy Hundley	.15	.06	.01
☐ 330 T	Juan Marichal	1.50	.60	.15
☐ 348 T	Pete Richert	.10	.04	.01
☐ 373 T	John Curtis	.10	.04	.01
☐ 390 T	Lou Piniella	.35	.14	.03
☐ 428 T	Gary Sutherland	.10	.04	.01
☐ 454 T	Kurt Bevacqua	.10	.04	.01
☐ 458 T	Jim Ray	.10	.04	.01
☐ 485 T	Felipe Alou	.15	.06	.01
☐ 486 T	Steve Stone	.15	.06	.01
☐ 496 T	Tom Murphy	.10	.04	.01
☐ 516 T	Horacio Pina	.10	.04	.01
☐ 534 T	Eddie Watt	.10	.04	.01
☐ 538 T	Cesar Tovar	.10	.04	.01
☐ 544 T	Ron Schueler	.10	.04	.01
☐ 579 T	Cecil Upshaw	.10	.04	.01
☐ 585 T	Merv Rettenmund	.10	.04	.01
☐ 612 T	Luke Walker	.10	.04	.01
☐ 616 T	Larry Gura	.20	.08	.02
☐ 618 T	Jim Mason	.10	.04	.01
☐ 630 T	Tommie Agee	.15	.06	.01
☐ 648 T	Terry Crowley	.10	.04	.01
☐ 649 T	Fernando Gonzalez	.10	.04	.01
☐ xxx	Traded Checklist (unnumbered)	.50	.05	.01

1975 Topps

The cards in the 1975 Topps set were issued in two different sizes: a regular standard size and a mini size which was issued as a test in certain areas of the country. The standard-size cards measure 2½" by 3½" versus 2¼" by 3⅛" for the minis. The 660-card Topps baseball set for 1975 was radically different in appearance from sets of the preceding years. The most prominent change was the use of a two-color frame surrounding the picture area rather than a single, subdued color. A facsimile autograph appears on the picture, and the backs are printed in red and green on gray. Cards 189-212 depict the MVP's of both leagues from 1951 through 1974. The first seven cards (1-7) feature players breaking records or achieving milestones during the previous season. Cards 306-313 picture league leaders in various statistical categories. Cards 459-466 depict the results of post-season action. Team cards feature a checklist back for players on that team and show a small inset photo of the manager on the front. This set is quite popular with collectors, at least in part due to the fact that the rookie cards of Robin Yount, George Brett, Jim Rice, Gary Carter, Fred Lynn, and Keith Hernandez are all in the set. Topps minis have the same checklist and are worth approximately double the prices listed below.

	MINT	VG-E	F-G
Complete Set	350.00	140.00	35.00
Common Player (1-132)	.18	.08	.01
Common Player (133-660)	.15	.06	.01

		MINT	VG-E	F-G
☐ 1	RB: Hank Aaron Sets Homer Mark	6.50	2.00	.40
☐ 2	RB: Lou Brock 118 Stolen Bases	1.25	.50	.12
☐ 3	RB: Bob Gibson 3000th Strikeout	1.25	.50	.12
☐ 4	RB: Al Kaline 3000 Hit Club	1.25	.50	.12
☐ 5	RB: Nolan Ryan Fans 300 for 3rd Year in a Row	1.50	.60	.15
☐ 6	RB: Mike Marshall Hurls 106 Games	.30	.12	.03

		MINT	VG-E	F-G
☐ 7	No Hitters Steve Busby Dick Bosman Nolan Ryan	.50	.20	.05
☐ 8	Rogelio Moret	.18	.08	.01
☐ 9	Frank Tepedino	.18	.08	.01
☐ 10	Willie Davis	.25	.10	.02
☐ 11	Bill Melton	.18	.08	.01
☐ 12	David Clyde	.18	.08	.01
☐ 13	Gene Locklear	.18	.08	.01
☐ 14	Milt Wilcox	.18	.08	.01
☐ 15	Jose Cardenal	.18	.08	.01
☐ 16	Frank Tanana	.30	.12	.03
☐ 17	Dave Concepcion	.50	.20	.05
☐ 18	Tigers: Team/Mgr. Ralph Houk (checklist back)	.40	.08	.01
☐ 19	Jerry Koosman	.30	.12	.03
☐ 20	Thurman Munson	3.50	1.40	.35
☐ 21	Rollie Fingers	.90	.36	.09
☐ 22	Dave Cash	.18	.08	.01
☐ 23	Bill Russell	.25	.10	.02
☐ 24	Al Fitzmorris	.18	.08	.01
☐ 25	Lee May	.25	.10	.02
☐ 26	Dave McNally	.25	.10	.02
☐ 27	Ken Reitz	.18	.08	.01
☐ 28	Tom Murphy	.18	.08	.01
☐ 29	Dave Parker	3.50	1.40	.35
☐ 30	Bert Blyleven	.60	.24	.06
☐ 31	Dave Rader	.18	.08	.01
☐ 32	Reggie Cleveland	.18	.08	.01
☐ 33	Dusty Baker	.40	.16	.04
☐ 34	Steve Renko	.18	.08	.01
☐ 35	Ron Santo	.35	.14	.03
☐ 36	Joe Lovitto	.18	.08	.01
☐ 37	Dave Freisleben	.18	.08	.01
☐ 38	Buddy Bell	.75	.30	.07
☐ 39	Andy Thornton	.60	.24	.06
☐ 40	Bill Singer	.18	.08	.01
☐ 41	Cesar Geronimo	.18	.08	.01
☐ 42	Joe Coleman	.18	.08	.01
☐ 43	Cleon Jones	.18	.08	.01
☐ 44	Pat Dobson	.18	.08	.01
☐ 45	Joe Rudi	.25	.10	.02
☐ 46	Phillies: Team/Mgr. Danny Ozark (checklist back)	.40	.08	.01
☐ 47	Tommy John	.80	.32	.08
☐ 48	Freddie Patek	.18	.08	.01
☐ 49	Larry Dierker	.25	.10	.02
☐ 50	Brooks Robinson	2.50	1.00	.25
☐ 51	Bob Forsch	.75	.30	.07
☐ 52	Darrell Porter	.25	.10	.02

		MINT	VG-E	F-G
☐ 53	Dave Giusti	.18	.08	.01
☐ 54	Eric Soderholm	.18	.08	.01
☐ 55	Bobby Bonds	.35	.14	.03
☐ 56	Rick Wise	.25	.10	.02
☐ 57	Dave Johnson	.35	.14	.03
☐ 58	Chuck Taylor	.18	.08	.01
☐ 59	Ken Henderson	.18	.08	.01
☐ 60	Fergie Jenkins	.75	.30	.07
☐ 61	Dave Winfield	5.00	2.00	.50
☐ 62	Fritz Peterson	.18	.08	.01
☐ 63	Steve Swisher	.18	.08	.01
☐ 64	Dave Chalk	.18	.08	.01
☐ 65	Don Gullett	.25	.10	.02
☐ 66	Willie Horton	.25	.10	.02
☐ 67	Tug McGraw	.35	.14	.03
☐ 68	Ron Blomberg	.18	.08	.01
☐ 69	John Odom	.18	.08	.01
☐ 70	Mike Schmidt	15.00	6.00	1.50
☐ 71	Charlie Hough	.30	.12	.03
☐ 72	Royals: Team/Mgr.	.40	.08	.01
	Jack McKeon			
	(checklist back)			
☐ 73	J.R. Richard	.30	.12	.03
☐ 74	Mark Belanger	.25	.10	.02
☐ 75	Ted Simmons	.75	.30	.07
☐ 76	Ed Sprague	.18	.08	.01
☐ 77	Richie Zisk	.25	.10	.02
☐ 78	Ray Corbin	.18	.08	.01
☐ 79	Gary Matthews	.35	.14	.03
☐ 80	Carlton Fisk	1.00	.40	.10
☐ 81	Ron Reed	.18	.08	.01
☐ 82	Pat Kelly	.18	.08	.01
☐ 83	Jim Merritt	.18	.08	.01
☐ 84	Enzo Hernandez	.18	.08	.01
☐ 85	Bill Bonham	.18	.08	.01
☐ 86	Joe Lis	.18	.08	.01
☐ 87	George Foster	.90	.36	.09
☐ 88	Tom Egan	.18	.08	.01
☐ 89	Jim Ray	.18	.08	.01
☐ 90	Rusty Staub	.35	.14	.03
☐ 91	Dick Green	.18	.08	.01
☐ 92	Cecil Upshaw	.18	.08	.01
☐ 93	Dave Lopes	.35	.14	.03
☐ 94	Jim Lonborg	.25	.10	.02
☐ 95	John Mayberry	.25	.10	.02
☐ 96	Mike Cosgrove	.18	.08	.01
☐ 97	Earl Williams	.18	.08	.01
☐ 98	Rich Folkers	.18	.08	.01
☐ 99	Mike Hegan	.18	.08	.01
☐ 100	Willie Stargell	2.00	.80	.20
☐ 101	Expos: Team/Mgr.	.40	.08	.01
	Gene Mauch			
	(checklist back)			
☐ 102	Joe Decker	.18	.08	.01
☐ 103	Rick Miller	.18	.08	.01
☐ 104	Bill Madlock	1.50	.60	.15
☐ 105	Buzz Capra	.18	.08	.01
☐ 106	Mike Hargrove	.50	.20	.05
☐ 107	Jim Barr	.18	.08	.01
☐ 108	Tom Hall	.18	.08	.01
☐ 109	George Hendrick	.30	.12	.03
☐ 110	Wilbur Wood	.25	.10	.02
☐ 111	Wayne Garrett	.18	.08	.01
☐ 112	Larry Hardy	.18	.08	.01
☐ 113	Elliott Maddox	.18	.08	.01
☐ 114	Dick Lange	.18	.08	.01
☐ 115	Joe Ferguson	.25	.10	.02
☐ 116	Lerrin LaGrow	.18	.08	.01
☐ 117	Orioles: Team/Mgr.	.50	.10	.02
	Earl Weaver			
	(checklist back)			
☐ 118	Mike Anderson	.18	.08	.01
☐ 119	Tommy Helms	.18	.08	.01
☐ 120	Steve Busby	.25	.10	.02
	(photo actually			
	Fran Healy)			
☐ 121	Bill North	.18	.08	.01
☐ 122	Al Hrabosky	.25	.10	.02
☐ 123	Johnny Briggs	.18	.08	.01
☐ 124	Jerry Reuss	.35	.14	.03
☐ 125	Ken Singleton	.35	.14	.03
☐ 126	Checklist 1-132	.75	.07	.01
☐ 127	Glenn Borgmann	.18	.08	.01
☐ 128	Bill Lee	.25	.10	.02
☐ 129	Rick Monday	.25	.10	.02
☐ 130	Phil Niekro	1.25	.50	.12
☐ 131	Toby Harrah	.25	.10	.02
☐ 132	Randy Moffitt	.18	.08	.01
☐ 133	Dan Driessen	.20	.08	.02
☐ 134	Ron Hodges	.15	.06	.01
☐ 135	Charlie Spikes	.15	.06	.01
☐ 136	Jim Mason	.15	.06	.01
☐ 137	Terry Forster	.25	.10	.02
☐ 138	Del Unser	.15	.06	.01
☐ 139	Horacio Pina	.15	.06	.01
☐ 140	Steve Garvey	4.50	1.80	.45
☐ 141	Mickey Stanley	.15	.06	.01
☐ 142	Bob Reynolds	.15	.06	.01
☐ 143	Cliff Johnson	.20	.08	.02
☐ 144	Jim Wohlford	.15	.06	.01
☐ 145	Ken Holtzman	.20	.08	.02
☐ 146	Padres: Team/Mgr.	.40	.08	.01
	John McNamara			
	(checklist back)			
☐ 147	Pedro Garcia	.15	.06	.01
☐ 148	Jim Rooker	.15	.06	.01

		MINT	VG-E	F-G
☐ 149	Tim Foli	.15	.06	.01
☐ 150	Bob Gibson	1.75	.70	.17
☐ 151	Steve Brye	.15	.06	.01
☐ 152	Mario Guerrero	.15	.06	.01
☐ 153	Rick Reuschel	.25	.10	.02
☐ 154	Mike Lum	.15	.06	.01
☐ 155	Jim Bibby	.20	.08	.02
☐ 156	Dave Kingman	.90	.36	.09
☐ 157	Pedro Borbon	.15	.06	.01
☐ 158	Jerry Grote	.15	.06	.01
☐ 159	Steve Arlin	.15	.06	.01
☐ 160	Graig Nettles	1.25	.50	.12
☐ 161	Stan Bahnsen	.15	.06	.01
☐ 162	Willie Montanez	.15	.06	.01
☐ 163	Jim Brewer	.15	.06	.01
☐ 164	Mickey Rivers	.20	.08	.02
☐ 165	Doug Rader	.20	.08	.02
☐ 166	Woodie Fryman	.15	.06	.01
☐ 167	Rich Coggins	.15	.06	.01
☐ 168	Bill Greif	.15	.06	.01
☐ 169	Cookie Rojas	.15	.06	.01
☐ 170	Bert Campaneris	.25	.10	.02
☐ 171	Ed Kirkpatrick	.15	.06	.01
☐ 172	Red Sox: Team/Mgr.	.40	.08	.01
	Darrell Johnson			
	(checklist back)			
☐ 173	Steve Rogers	.30	.12	.03
☐ 174	Bake McBride	.20	.08	.02
☐ 175	Don Money	.20	.08	.02
☐ 176	Burt Hooton	.20	.08	.02
☐ 177	Vic Correll	.15	.06	.01
☐ 178	Cesar Tovar	.15	.06	.01
☐ 179	Tom Bradley	.15	.06	.01
☐ 180	Joe Morgan	2.25	.90	.22
☐ 181	Fred Beene	.15	.06	.01
☐ 182	Don Hahn	.15	.06	.01
☐ 183	Mel Stottlemyre	.25	.10	.02
☐ 184	Jorge Orta	.15	.06	.01
☐ 185	Steve Carlton	4.50	1.80	.45
☐ 186	Willie Crawford	.15	.06	.01
☐ 187	Denny Doyle	.15	.06	.01
☐ 188	Tom Griffin	.15	.06	.01
☐ 189	1951 MVP's	1.00	.40	.10
	Larry (Yogi) Berra			
	Roy Campanella			
	(Campy never issued)			
☐ 190	1952 MVP's	.30	.12	.03
	Bobby Shantz			
	Hank Bauer			
☐ 191	1953 MVP's	.55	.22	.05
	Al Rosen			
	Roy Campanella			

		MINT	VG-E	F-G
☐ 192	1954 MVP's	1.00	.40	.10
	Yogi Berra			
	Willie Mays			
☐ 193	1955 MVP's	1.25	.50	.12
	Yogi Berra			
	Roy Campanella			
	(Campy never issued)			
☐ 194	1956 MVP's	1.25	.50	.12
	Mickey Mantle			
	Don Newcombe			
☐ 195	1957 MVP's	2.25	.90	.22
	Mickey Mantle			
	Hank Aaron			
☐ 196	1958 MVP's	.55	.22	.05
	Jackie Jensen			
	Ernie Banks			
☐ 197	1959 MVP's	.55	.22	.05
	Nellie Fox			
	Ernie Banks			
☐ 198	1960 MVP's	.55	.22	.05
	Roger Maris			
	Dick Groat			
☐ 199	1961 MVP's	.75	.30	.07
	Roger Maris			
	Frank Robinson			
☐ 200	1962 MVP's	1.75	.70	.17
	Mickey Mantle			
	Maury Wills			
	(Wills never issued)			
☐ 201	1963 MVP's	.55	.22	.05
	Elston Howard			
	Sandy Koufax			
☐ 202	1964 MVP's	.55	.22	.05
	Brooks Robinson			
	Ken Boyer			
☐ 203	1965 MVP's	.55	.22	.05
	Zoilo Versalles			
	Willie Mays			
☐ 204	1966 MVP's	.75	.30	.07
	Frank Robinson			
	Bob Clemente			
☐ 205	1967 MVP's	.75	.30	.07
	Carl Yastrzemski			
	Orlando Cepeda			
☐ 206	1968 MVP's	.55	.22	.05
	Denny McLain			
	Bob Gibson			
☐ 207	1969 MVP's	.65	.26	.06
	Harmon Killebrew			
	Willie McCovey			
☐ 208	1970 MVP's	.55	.22	.05
	Boog Powell			
	Johnny Bench			

		MINT	VG-E	F-G
☐ 209	1971 MVP's	.45	.18	.04
	Vida Blue			
	Joe Torre			
☐ 210	1972 MVP's	.55	.22	.05
	Rich Allen			
	Johnny Bench			
☐ 211	1973 MVP's	2.25	.90	.22
	Reggie Jackson			
	Pete Rose			
☐ 212	1974 MVP's	.55	.22	.05
	Jeff Burroughs			
	Steve Garvey			
☐ 213	Oscar Gamble	.25	.10	.02
☐ 214	Harry Parker	.15	.06	.01
☐ 215	Bobby Valentine	.30	.12	.03
☐ 216	Giants: Team/Mgr.	.40	.08	.01
	Wes Westrum			
	(checklist back)			
☐ 217	Lou Piniella	.35	.14	.03
☐ 218	Jerry Johnson	.15	.06	.01
☐ 219	Ed Herrmann	.15	.06	.01
☐ 220	Don Sutton	1.25	.50	.12
☐ 221	Aurelio Rodriguez	.15	.06	.01
☐ 222	Dan Spillner	.25	.10	.02
☐ 223	Robin Yount	25.00	10.00	2.50
☐ 224	Ramon Hernandez	.15	.06	.01
☐ 225	Bob Grich	.30	.12	.03
☐ 226	Bill Campbell	.20	.08	.02
☐ 227	Bob Watson	.25	.10	.02
☐ 228	George Brett	37.50	14.00	2.50
☐ 229	Barry Foote	.15	.06	.01
☐ 230	Jim Hunter	1.50	.60	.15
☐ 231	Mike Tyson	.15	.06	.01
☐ 232	Diego Segui	.15	.06	.01
☐ 233	Billy Grabarkewitz	.15	.06	.01
☐ 234	Tom Grieve	.25	.10	.02
☐ 235	Jack Billingham	.15	.06	.01
☐ 236	Angels: Team/Mgr.	.40	.08	.01
	Dick Williams			
	(checklist back)			
☐ 237	Carl Morton	.15	.06	.01
☐ 238	Dave Duncan	.15	.06	.01
☐ 239	George Stone	.15	.06	.01
☐ 240	Garry Maddox	.20	.08	.02
☐ 241	Dick Tidrow	.15	.06	.01
☐ 242	Jay Johnstone	.25	.10	.02
☐ 243	Jim Kaat	.65	.26	.06
☐ 244	Bill Buckner	.50	.20	.05
☐ 245	Mickey Lolich	.30	.12	.03
☐ 246	Cardinals: Team/Mgr.	.40	.08	.01
	Red Schoendienst			
	(checklist back)			
☐ 247	Enos Cabell	.20	.08	.02

		MINT	VG-E	F-G
☐ 248	Randy Jones	.20	.08	.02
☐ 249	Danny Thompson	.15	.06	.01
☐ 250	Ken Brett	.15	.06	.01
☐ 251	Fran Healy	.15	.06	.01
☐ 252	Fred Scherman	.15	.06	.01
☐ 253	Jesus Alou	.15	.06	.01
☐ 254	Mike Torrez	.20	.08	.02
☐ 255	Dwight Evans	.75	.30	.07
☐ 256	Billy Champion	.15	.06	.01
☐ 257	Checklist: 133-264	.60	.06	.01
☐ 258	Dave LaRoche	.15	.06	.01
☐ 259	Len Randle	.15	.06	.01
☐ 260	Johnny Bench	4.50	1.80	.45
☐ 261	Andy Hassler	.15	.06	.01
☐ 262	Rowland Office	.15	.06	.01
☐ 263	Jim Perry	.25	.10	.02
☐ 264	John Milner	.15	.06	.01
☐ 265	Ron Bryant	.15	.06	.01
☐ 266	Sandy Alomar	.15	.06	.01
☐ 267	Dick Ruthven	.15	.06	.01
☐ 268	Hal McRae	.30	.12	.03
☐ 269	Doug Rau	.15	.06	.01
☐ 270	Ron Fairly	.20	.08	.02
☐ 271	Jerry Moses	.15	.06	.01
☐ 272	Lynn McGlothen	.15	.06	.01
☐ 273	Steve Braun	.15	.06	.01
☐ 274	Vincente Romo	.15	.06	.01
☐ 275	Paul Blair	.20	.08	.02
☐ 276	White Sox Team/Mgr.	.40	.08	.01
	Chuck Tanner			
	(checklist back)			
☐ 277	Frank Taveras	.15	.06	.01
☐ 278	Paul Lindblad	.15	.06	.01
☐ 279	Milt May	.15	.06	.01
☐ 280	Carl Yastrzemski	5.50	2.20	.55
☐ 281	Jim Slaton	.15	.06	.01
☐ 282	Jerry Morales	.15	.06	.01
☐ 283	Steve Foucault	.15	.06	.01
☐ 284	Ken Griffey	.55	.22	.05
☐ 285	Ellie Rodriguez	.15	.06	.01
☐ 286	Mike Jorgensen	.15	.06	.01
☐ 287	Roric Harrison	.15	.06	.01
☐ 288	Bruce Ellingsen	.15	.06	.01
☐ 289	Ken Rudolph	.15	.06	.01
☐ 290	Jon Matlack	.25	.10	.02
☐ 291	Bill Sudakis	.15	.06	.01
☐ 292	Ron Schueler	.15	.06	.01
☐ 293	Dick Sharon	.15	.06	.01
☐ 294	Geoff Zahn	.25	.10	.02
☐ 295	Vada Pinson	.35	.14	.03
☐ 296	Alan Foster	.15	.06	.01
☐ 297	Craig Kusick	.15	.06	.01
☐ 298	Johnny Grubb	.15	.06	.01

	MINT	VG-E	F-G
☐ 299 Bucky Dent	.30	.12	.03
☐ 300 Reggie Jackson	6.00	2.40	.60
☐ 301 Dave Roberts	.15	.06	.01
☐ 302 Rick Burleson	.75	.30	.07
☐ 303 Grant Jackson	.15	.06	.01
☐ 304 Pirates: Team/Mgr.	.40	.08	.01
Danny Murtaugh			
(checklist back)			
☐ 305 Jim Colborn	.15	.06	.01
☐ 306 Batting Leaders	.55	.22	.05
Rod Carew			
Ralph Garr			
☐ 307 Home Run Leaders	.75	.30	.07
Dick Allen			
Mike Schmidt			
☐ 308 RBI Leaders	.55	.22	.05
Jeff Burroughs			
Johnny Bench			
☐ 309 Stolen Base Leaders	.55	.22	.05
Bill North			
Lou Brock			
☐ 310 Victory Leaders	.65	.26	.06
Jim Hunter			
Fergie Jenkins			
Andy Messersmith			
Phil Niekro			
☐ 311 ERA Leaders	.35	.14	.03
Jim Hunter			
Buzz Capra			
☐ 312 Strikeout Leaders	1.75	.70	.17
Nolan Ryan			
Steve Carlton			
☐ 313 Leading Firemen	.30	.12	.03
Terry Forster			
Mike Marshall			
☐ 314 Buck Martinez	.15	.06	.01
☐ 315 Don Kessinger	.20	.08	.02
☐ 316 Jackie Brown	.15	.06	.01
☐ 317 Joe Lahoud	.15	.06	.01
☐ 318 Ernie McAnally	.15	.06	.01
☐ 319 Johnny Oates	.15	.06	.01
☐ 320 Pete Rose	13.00	5.25	1.30
☐ 321 Rudy May	.15	.06	.01
☐ 322 Ed Goodson	.15	.06	.01
☐ 323 Fred Holdsworth	.15	.06	.01
☐ 324 Ed Kranepool	.20	.08	.02
☐ 325 Tony Oliva	.50	.20	.05
☐ 326 Wayne Twitchell	.15	.06	.01
☐ 327 Jerry Hairston	.15	.06	.01
☐ 328 Sonny Siebert	.20	.08	.02
☐ 329 Ted Kubiak	.15	.06	.01
☐ 330 Mike Marshall	.25	.10	.02

	MINT	VG-E	F-G
☐ 331 Indians: Team/Mgr.	.50	.10	.02
Frank Robinson			
(checklist back)			
☐ 332 Fred Kendall	.15	.06	.01
☐ 333 Dick Drago	.15	.06	.01
☐ 334 Greg Gross	.15	.06	.01
☐ 335 Jim Palmer	2.75	1.10	.27
☐ 336 Rennie Stennett	.15	.06	.01
☐ 337 Kevin Kobel	.15	.06	.01
☐ 338 Rick Stelmaszek	.15	.06	.01
☐ 339 Jim Fregosi	.30	.12	.03
☐ 340 Paul Splittorff	.20	.08	.02
☐ 341 Hal Breeden	.15	.06	.01
☐ 342 Leroy Stanton	.15	.06	.01
☐ 343 Danny Frisella	.15	.06	.01
☐ 344 Ben Oglivie	.30	.12	.03
☐ 345 Clay Carroll	.15	.06	.01
☐ 346 Bobby Darwin	.15	.06	.01
☐ 347 Mike Caldwell	.20	.08	.02
☐ 348 Tony Muser	.15	.06	.01
☐ 349 Ray Sadecki	.15	.06	.01
☐ 350 Bobby Murcer	.45	.18	.04
☐ 351 Bob Boone	.25	.10	.02
☐ 352 Darold Knowles	.15	.06	.01
☐ 353 Luis Melendez	.15	.06	.01
☐ 354 Dick Bosman	.15	.06	.01
☐ 355 Chris Cannizzaro	.15	.06	.01
☐ 356 Rico Petrocelli	.20	.08	.02
☐ 357 Ken Forsch	.20	.08	.02
☐ 358 Al Bumbry	.15	.06	.01
☐ 359 Paul Popovich	.15	.06	.01
☐ 360 George Scott	.20	.08	.02
☐ 361 Dodgers: Team/Mgr.	.50	.10	.02
Walter Alston			
(checklist back)			
☐ 362 Steve Hargan	.15	.06	.01
☐ 363 Carmen Fanzone	.15	.06	.01
☐ 364 Doug Bird	.15	.06	.01
☐ 365 Bob Bailey	.15	.06	.01
☐ 366 Ken Sanders	.15	.06	.01
☐ 367 Craig Robinson	.15	.06	.01
☐ 368 Vic Albury	.15	.06	.01
☐ 369 Merv Rettenmund	.15	.06	.01
☐ 370 Tom Seaver	4.50	1.80	.45
☐ 371 Gates Brown	.20	.08	.02
☐ 372 John D'Acquisto	.15	.06	.01
☐ 373 Bill Sharp	.15	.06	.01
☐ 374 Eddie Watt	.15	.06	.01
☐ 375 Roy White	.20	.08	.02
☐ 376 Steve Yeager	.20	.08	.02
☐ 377 Tom Hilgendorf	.15	.06	.01
☐ 378 Derrel Thomas	.15	.06	.01
☐ 379 Bernie Carbo	.15	.06	.01

		MINT	VG-E	F-G
☐ 380	Sal Bando	.25	.10	.02
☐ 381	John Curtis	.15	.06	.01
☐ 382	Don Baylor	.80	.32	.08
☐ 383	Jim York	.15	.06	.01
☐ 384	Brewers: Team/Mgr. Del Crandall (checklist back)	.40	.08	.01
☐ 385	Dock Ellis	.15	.06	.01
☐ 386	Checklist: 265-396	.60	.06	.01
☐ 387	Jim Spencer	.15	.06	.01
☐ 388	Steve Stone	.25	.10	.02
☐ 389	Tony Solaita	.15	.06	.01
☐ 390	Ron Cey	.70	.28	.07
☐ 391	Don DeMola	.15	.06	.01
☐ 392	Bruce Bochte	.55	.22	.05
☐ 393	Gary Gentry	.15	.06	.01
☐ 394	Larvell Blanks	.15	.06	.01
☐ 395	Bud Harrelson	.20	.08	.02
☐ 396	Fred Norman	.15	.06	.01
☐ 397	Bill Freehan	.25	.10	.02
☐ 398	Elias Sosa	.15	.06	.01
☐ 399	Terry Harmon	.15	.06	.01
☐ 400	Dick Allen	.40	.16	.04
☐ 401	Mike Wallace	.15	.06	.01
☐ 402	Bob Tolan	.15	.06	.01
☐ 403	Tom Buskey	.15	.06	.01
☐ 404	Ted Sizemore	.15	.06	.01
☐ 405	John Montague	.15	.06	.01
☐ 406	Bob Gallagher	.15	.06	.01
☐ 407	Herb Washington	.15	.06	.01
☐ 408	Clyde Wright	.15	.06	.01
☐ 409	Bob Robertson	.15	.06	.01
☐ 410	Mike Cueller (sic, Cuellar)	.25	.10	.02
☐ 411	George Mitterwald	.15	.06	.01
☐ 412	Bill Hands	.15	.06	.01
☐ 413	Marty Pattin	.15	.06	.01
☐ 414	Manny Mota	.25	.10	.02
☐ 415	John Hiller	.25	.10	.02
☐ 416	Larry Lintz	.15	.06	.01
☐ 417	Skip Lockwood	.15	.06	.01
☐ 418	Leo Foster	.15	.06	.01
☐ 419	Dave Goltz	.20	.08	.02
☐ 420	Larry Bowa	.35	.14	.03
☐ 421	Mets: Team/Mgr. Yogi Berra (checklist back)	.50	.10	.02
☐ 422	Brian Downing	.25	.10	.02
☐ 423	Clay Kirby	.15	.06	.01
☐ 424	John Lowenstein	.15	.06	.01
☐ 425	Tito Fuentes	.15	.06	.01
☐ 426	George Medich	.20	.08	.02
☐ 427	Clarence Gaston	.15	.06	.01

		MINT	VG-E	F-G
☐ 428	Dave Hamilton	.15	.06	.01
☐ 429	Jim Dwyer	.15	.06	.01
☐ 430	Luis Tiant	.35	.14	.03
☐ 431	Rod Gilbreath	.15	.06	.01
☐ 432	Ken Berry	.15	.06	.01
☐ 433	Larry Demery	.15	.06	.01
☐ 434	Bob Locker	.15	.06	.01
☐ 435	Dave Nelson	.15	.06	.01
☐ 436	Ken Frailing	.15	.06	.01
☐ 437	Al Cowens	.40	.16	.04
☐ 438	Don Carrithers	.15	.06	.01
☐ 439	Ed Brinkman	.15	.06	.01
☐ 440	Andy Messersmith	.25	.10	.02
☐ 441	Bobby Heise	.15	.06	.01
☐ 442	Maximino Leon	.15	.06	.01
☐ 443	Twins: Team/Mgr. Frank Quilici (checklist back)	.40	.08	.01
☐ 444	Gene Garber	.20	.08	.02
☐ 445	Felix Millan	.15	.06	.01
☐ 446	Bart Johnson	.15	.06	.01
☐ 447	Terry Crowley	.15	.06	.01
☐ 448	Frank Duffy	.15	.06	.01
☐ 449	Charlie Williams	.15	.06	.01
☐ 450	Willie McCovey	2.50	1.00	.25
☐ 451	Rick Dempsey	.25	.10	.02
☐ 452	Angel Mangual	.15	.06	.01
☐ 453	Claude Osteen	.25	.10	.02
☐ 454	Doug Griffin	.15	.06	.01
☐ 455	Don Wilson	.15	.06	.01
☐ 456	Bob Coluccio	.15	.06	.01
☐ 457	Mario Mendoza	.15	.06	.01
☐ 458	Ross Grimsley	.15	.06	.01
☐ 459	1974 AL Champs: A's over Orioles (Second base action pictured)	.30	.12	.03
☐ 460	1974 NL Champs: Dodgers over Pirates (Taveras and Garvey at second base)	.50	.20	.05
☐ 461	World Series Game 1 (Reggie Jackson)	1.25	.50	.12
☐ 462	World Series Game 2 (Dodger dugout)	.30	.12	.03
☐ 463	World Series Game 3 (Fingers pitching)	.50	.20	.05
☐ 464	World Series Game 4 (A's batter)	.30	.12	.03
☐ 465	World Series Game 5 (Rudi rounding third)	.30	.12	.03

		MINT	VG-E	F-G
☐ 466	World Series Summary A's do it again Win 3rd straight (A's group)	.30	.12	.03
☐ 467	Ed Halicki	.15	.06	.01
☐ 468	Bobby Mitchell	.15	.06	.01
☐ 469	Tom Dettore	.15	.06	.01
☐ 470	Jeff Burroughs	.20	.08	.02
☐ 471	Bob Stinson	.15	.06	.01
☐ 472	Bruce Dal Canton	.15	.06	.01
☐ 473	Ken McMullen	.15	.06	.01
☐ 474	Luke Walker	.15	.06	.01
☐ 475	Darrell Evans	.40	.16	.04
☐ 476	Eduardo Figueroa	.20	.08	.02
☐ 477	Tom Hutton	.15	.06	.01
☐ 478	Tom Burgmeier	.15	.06	.01
☐ 479	Ken Boswell	.15	.06	.01
☐ 480	Carlos May	.20	.08	.02
☐ 481	Will McEnaney	.15	.06	.01
☐ 482	Tom McCraw	.15	.06	.01
☐ 483	Steve Ontiveros	.15	.06	.01
☐ 484	Glenn Beckert	.20	.08	.02
☐ 485	Sparky Lyle	.35	.14	.03
☐ 486	Ray Fosse	.15	.06	.01
☐ 487	Astros: Team/Mgr. Preston Gomez (checklist back)	.40	.08	.01
☐ 488	Bill Travers	.15	.06	.01
☐ 489	Cecil Cooper	1.00	.40	.10
☐ 490	Reggie Smith	.30	.12	.03
☐ 491	Doyle Alexander	.25	.10	.02
☐ 492	Rich Hebner	.15	.06	.01
☐ 493	Don Stanhouse	.15	.06	.01
☐ 494	Pete LaCock	.20	.08	.02
☐ 495	Nelson Briles	.20	.08	.02
☐ 496	Pepe Frias	.15	.06	.01
☐ 497	Jim Nettles	.15	.06	.01
☐ 498	Al Downing	.15	.06	.01
☐ 499	Marty Perez	.15	.06	.01
☐ 500	Nolan Ryan	4.25	1.70	.42
☐ 501	Bill Robinson	.15	.06	.01
☐ 502	Pat Bourque	.15	.06	.01
☐ 503	Fred Stanley	.15	.06	.01
☐ 504	Buddy Bradford	.15	.06	.01
☐ 505	Chris Speier	.15	.06	.01
☐ 506	Leron Lee	.15	.06	.01
☐ 507	Tom Carroll	.15	.06	.01
☐ 508	Bob Hansen	.15	.06	.01
☐ 509	Dave Hilton	.15	.06	.01
☐ 510	Vida Blue	.35	.14	.03
☐ 511	Rangers: Team/Mgr. Billy Martin (checklist back)	.50	.10	.02

		MINT	VG-E	F-G
☐ 512	Larry Milbourne	.15	.06	.01
☐ 513	Dick Pole	.15	.06	.01
☐ 514	Jose Cruz	.50	.20	.05
☐ 515	Manny Sanguillen	.25	.10	.02
☐ 516	Don Hood	.15	.06	.01
☐ 517	Checklist: 397-528	.60	.06	.01
☐ 518	Leo Cardenas	.15	.06	.01
☐ 519	Jim Todd	.15	.06	.01
☐ 520	Amos Otis	.30	.12	.03
☐ 521	Dennis Blair	.15	.06	.01
☐ 522	Gary Sutherland	.15	.06	.01
☐ 523	Tom Paciorek	.15	.06	.01
☐ 524	John Doherty	.15	.06	.01
☐ 525	Tom House	.15	.06	.01
☐ 526	Larry Hisle	.20	.08	.02
☐ 527	Mac Scarce	.15	.06	.01
☐ 528	Eddie Leon	.15	.06	.01
☐ 529	Gary Thomasson	.15	.06	.01
☐ 530	Gaylord Perry	1.75	.70	.17
☐ 531	Reds: Team/Mgr. Sparky Anderson (checklist back)	.50	.10	.02
☐ 532	Gorman Thomas	.75	.30	.07
☐ 533	Rudy Meoli	.15	.06	.01
☐ 534	Alex Johnson	.20	.08	.02
☐ 535	Gene Tenace	.20	.08	.02
☐ 536	Bob Moose	.15	.06	.01
☐ 537	Tommy Harper	.20	.08	.02
☐ 538	Duffy Dyer	.15	.06	.01
☐ 539	Jesse Jefferson	.15	.06	.01
☐ 540	Lou Brock	2.00	.80	.20
☐ 541	Roger Metzger	.15	.06	.01
☐ 542	Pete Broberg	.15	.06	.01
☐ 543	Larry Biittner	.15	.06	.01
☐ 544	Steve Mingori	.15	.06	.01
☐ 545	Billy Williams	1.25	.50	.12
☐ 546	John Knox	.15	.06	.01
☐ 547	Von Joshua	.15	.06	.01
☐ 548	Charlie Sands	.15	.06	.01
☐ 549	Bill Butler	.15	.06	.01
☐ 550	Ralph Garr	.20	.08	.02
☐ 551	Larry Christenson	.15	.06	.01
☐ 552	Jack Brohamer	.15	.06	.01
☐ 553	John Boccabella	.15	.06	.01
☐ 554	Rich Gossage	1.00	.40	.10
☐ 555	Al Oliver	.75	.30	.07
☐ 556	Tim Johnson	.15	.06	.01
☐ 557	Larry Gura	.25	.10	.02
☐ 558	Dave Roberts	.15	.06	.01
☐ 559	Bob Montgomery	.15	.06	.01
☐ 560	Tony Perez	.75	.30	.07

	MINT	VG-E	F-G
☐ 561 A's: Team/Mgr.	.40	.08	.01
Alvin Dark			
(checklist back)			
☐ 562 Gary Nolan	.15	.06	.01
☐ 563 Wilbur Howard	.15	.06	.01
☐ 564 Tommy Davis	.25	.10	.02
☐ 565 Joe Torre	.50	.20	.05
☐ 566 Ray Burris	.20	.08	.02
☐ 567 Jim Sundberg	.75	.30	.07
☐ 568 Dale Murray	.15	.06	.01
☐ 569 Frank White	.50	.20	.05
☐ 570 Jim Wynn	.25	.10	.02
☐ 571 Dave Lemanczyk	.15	.06	.01
☐ 572 Roger Nelson	.15	.06	.01
☐ 573 Orlando Pena	.15	.06	.01
☐ 574 Tony Taylor	.15	.06	.01
☐ 575 Gene Clines	.15	.06	.01
☐ 576 Phil Roof	.15	.06	.01
☐ 577 John Morris	.15	.06	.01
☐ 578 Dave Tomlin	.15	.06	.01
☐ 579 Skip Pitlock	.15	.06	.01
☐ 580 Frank Robinson	2.00	.80	.20
☐ 581 Darrel Chaney	.15	.06	.01
☐ 582 Eduardo Rodriguez	.15	.06	.01
☐ 583 Andy Etchebarren	.15	.06	.01
☐ 584 Mike Garman	.15	.06	.01
☐ 585 Chris Chambliss	.30	.12	.03
☐ 586 Tim McCarver	.30	.12	.03
☐ 587 Chris Ward	.15	.06	.01
☐ 588 Rick Auerbach	.15	.06	.01
☐ 589 Braves: Team/Mgr.	.40	.08	.01
Clyde King			
(checklist back)			
☐ 590 Cesar Cedeno	.30	.12	.03
☐ 591 Glenn Abbott	.15	.06	.01
☐ 592 Balor Moore	.15	.06	.01
☐ 593 Gene Lamont	.15	.06	.01
☐ 594 Jim Fuller	.15	.06	.01
☐ 595 Joe Niekro	.30	.12	.03
☐ 596 Ollie Brown	.15	.06	.01
☐ 597 Winston Llenas	.15	.06	.01
☐ 598 Bruce Kison	.15	.06	.01
☐ 599 Nate Colbert	.15	.06	.01
☐ 600 Rod Carew	4.50	1.80	.45
☐ 601 Juan Beniquez	.25	.10	.02
☐ 602 John Vukovich	.15	.06	.01
☐ 603 Lew Krausse	.15	.06	.01
☐ 604 Oscar Zamora	.15	.06	.01
☐ 605 John Ellis	.15	.06	.01
☐ 606 Bruce Miller	.15	.06	.01
☐ 607 Jim Holt	.15	.06	.01
☐ 608 Gene Michael	.20	.08	.02
☐ 609 Ellie Hendricks	.15	.06	.01

	MINT	VG-E	F-G
☐ 610 Ron Hunt	.15	.06	.01
☐ 611 Yankees: Team/Mgr.	.50	.10	.02
Bill Virdon			
(checklist back)			
☐ 612 Terry Hughes	.15	.06	.01
☐ 613 Bill Parsons	.15	.06	.01
☐ 614 Rookie Pitchers	.25	.10	.02
Jack Kucek			
Dyar Miller			
Vern Ruhle			
Paul Siebert			
☐ 615 Rookie Pitchers	1.00	.40	.10
Pat Darcy			
Dennis Leonard			
Tom Underwood			
Hank Webb			
☐ 616 Rookie Outfielders	35.00	14.00	3.50
Dave Augustine			
Pepe Mangual			
Jim Rice			
John Scott			
☐ 617 Rookie Infielders	2.50	1.00	.25
Mike Cubbage			
Doug DeCinces			
Reggie Sanders			
Manny Trillo			
☐ 618 Rookie Pitchers	2.00	.80	.20
Jamie Easterly			
Tom Johnson			
Scott McGregor			
Rick Rhoden			
☐ 619 Rookie Outfielders	.25	.10	.02
Benny Ayala			
Nyls Nyman			
Tommy Smith			
Jerry Turner			
☐ 620 Rookie Catcher/OF	35.00	14.00	3.50
Gary Carter			
Marc Hill			
Danny Meyer			
Leon Roberts			
☐ 621 Rookie Pitchers	1.50	.60	.15
John Denny			
Rawly Eastwick			
Jim Kern			
Juan Veintidos			
☐ 622 Rookie Outfielders	10.00	4.00	1.00
Ed Armbrister			
Fred Lynn			
Tom Poquette			
Terry Whitfield			

		MINT	VG-E	F-G
☐ 623	Rookie Infielders	20.00	8.00	2.00
	Phil Garner			
	Keith Hernandez			
	Bob Sheldon			
	Tom Veryzer			
☐ 624	Rookie Pitchers	.30	.12	.03
	Doug Konieczny			
	Gary Lavelle			
	Jim Otten			
	Eddie Solomon			
☐ 625	Boog Powell	.45	.18	.04
☐ 626	Larry Haney	.25	.10	.02
	(photo actually			
	Dave Duncan)			
☐ 627	Tom Walker	.15	.06	.01
☐ 628	Ron LeFlore	.50	.20	.05
☐ 629	Joe Hoerner	.15	.06	.01
☐ 630	Greg Luzinski	.60	.24	.06
☐ 631	Lee Lacy	.25	.10	.02
☐ 632	Morris Nettles	.15	.06	.01
☐ 633	Paul Casanova	.15	.06	.01
☐ 634	Cy Acosta	.15	.06	.01
☐ 635	Chuck Dobson	.15	.06	.01
☐ 636	Charlie Moore	.15	.06	.01
☐ 637	Ted Martinez	.15	.06	.01
☐ 638	Cubs: Team/Mgr.	.40	.08	.01
	Jim Marshall			
	(checklist back)			
☐ 639	Steve Kline	.15	.06	.01
☐ 640	Harmon Killebrew	1.75	.70	.17
☐ 641	Jim Northrup	.20	.08	.02
☐ 642	Mike Phillips	.15	.06	.01
☐ 643	Brent Strom	.15	.06	.01
☐ 644	Bill Fahey	.15	.06	.01
☐ 645	Danny Cater	.15	.06	.01
☐ 646	Checklist: 529-660	.60	.06	.01
☐ 647	Claudell Washington ...	1.00	.40	.10
☐ 648	Dave Pagan	.15	.06	.01
☐ 649	Jack Heidemann	.15	.06	.01
☐ 650	Dave May	.15	.06	.01
☐ 651	John Morlan	.15	.06	.01
☐ 652	Lindy McDaniel	.15	.06	.01
☐ 653	Lee Richard	.15	.06	.01
☐ 654	Jerry Terrell	.15	.06	.01
☐ 655	Rico Carty	.25	.10	.02
☐ 656	Bill Plummer	.15	.06	.01
☐ 657	Bob Oliver	.15	.06	.01
☐ 658	Vic Harris	.15	.06	.01
☐ 659	Bob Apodaca	.15	.06	.01
☐ 660	Hank Aaron	7.50	3.00	.75

1976 Topps

The 1976 Topps set of 660 cards (measuring 2½" by 3½") is known for its sharp color photographs and interesting presentation of subjects. Team cards feature a checklist back for players on that team and show a small inset photo of the manager on the front. A "Father and Son" series (66-70) spotlights five Major Leaguers whose fathers also made the "Big Show." Other subseries include "All Time All Stars" (341-350), "Record Breakers" from the previous season (1-6), League Leaders (191-205), Post-season cards (461-462), and Rookie Prospects (589-599).

		MINT	VG-E	F-G
	Complete Set	180.00	75.00	18.00
	Common Player (1-660)	.13	.05	.01
☐ 1	RB: Hank Aaron	5.00	1.50	.30
	Most RBI's 2262			
☐ 2	RB: Bobby Bonds	.25	.10	.02
	Most leadoff HR's 32;			
	plus 3 seasons of			
	30 HR's and 30 SB's			
☐ 3	RB: Mickey Lolich	.25	.10	.02
	Lefthander most			
	strikeouts 2679			
☐ 4	RB: Dave Lopes	.25	.10	.02
	Most consecutive			
	SB attempts, 38			
☐ 5	RB: Tom Seaver	1.25	.50	.12
	Most cons. seasons			
	with 200 SO's, 8			
☐ 6	RB: Rennie Stennett ...	.20	.08	.02
	Most hits in a 9			
	inning game, 7			

		MINT	VG-E	F-G
☐	7 Jim Umbarger	.13	.05	.01
☐	8 Tito Fuentes	.13	.05	.01
☐	9 Paul Lindblad	.13	.05	.01
☐	10 Lou Brock	1.75	.70	.17
☐	11 Jim Hughes	.13	.05	.01
☐	12 Richie Zisk	.20	.08	.02
☐	13 John Wockenfuss	.13	.05	.01
☐	14 Gene Garber	.13	.05	.01
☐	15 George Scott	.20	.08	.02
☐	16 Bob Apodaca	.13	.05	.01
☐	17 New York Yankees	.50	.10	.02
	Team Card			
	(checklist back)			
☐	18 Dale Murray	.13	.05	.01
☐	19 George Brett	10.00	4.00	1.00
☐	20 Bob Watson	.20	.08	.02
☐	21 Dave LaRoche	.13	.05	.01
☐	22 Bill Russell	.20	.08	.02
☐	23 Brian Downing	.20	.08	.02
☐	24 Cesar Geronimo	.13	.05	.01
☐	25 Mike Torrez	.20	.08	.02
☐	26 Andy Thornton	.25	.10	.02
☐	27 Ed Figueroa	.13	.05	.01
☐	28 Dusty Baker	.30	.12	.03
☐	29 Rick Burleson	.25	.10	.02
☐	30 John Montefusco	.30	.12	.03
☐	31 Len Randle	.13	.05	.01
☐	32 Danny Frisella	.13	.05	.01
☐	33 Bill North	.13	.05	.01
☐	34 Mike Garman	.13	.05	.01
☐	35 Tony Oliva	.40	.16	.04
☐	36 Frank Taveras	.13	.05	.01
☐	37 John Hiller	.20	.08	.02
☐	38 Garry Maddox	.20	.08	.02
☐	39 Pete Broberg	.13	.05	.01
☐	40 Dave Kingman	.60	.24	.06
☐	41 Tippy Martinez	.50	.20	.05
☐	42 Barry Foote	.13	.05	.01
☐	43 Paul Splittorff	.13	.05	.01
☐	44 Doug Rader	.20	.08	.02
☐	45 Boog Powell	.35	.14	.03
☐	46 Dodgers Team	.50	.10	.02
	(checklist back)			
☐	47 Jesse Jefferson	.13	.05	.01
☐	48 Dave Concepcion	.35	.14	.03
☐	49 Dave Duncan	.13	.05	.01
☐	50 Fred Lynn	2.00	.80	.20
☐	51 Ray Burris	.13	.05	.01
☐	52 Dave Chalk	.13	.05	.01
☐	53 Mike Beard	.13	.05	.01
☐	54 Dave Radar	.13	.05	.01
☐	55 Gaylord Perry	1.25	.50	.12
☐	56 Bob Tolan	.13	.05	.01

		MINT	VG-E	F-G
	57 Phil Garner	.25	.10	.02
	58 Ron Reed	.13	.05	.01
	59 Larry Hisle	.20	.08	.02
	60 Jerry Reuss	.25	.10	.02
	61 Ron LeFlore	.25	.10	.02
	62 Johnny Oates	.13	.05	.01
	63 Bobby Darwin	.13	.05	.01
	64 Jerry Koosman	.30	.12	.03
	65 Chris Chambliss	.25	.10	.02
	66 Father and Son	.35	.14	.03
	Gus Bell			
	Buddy Bell			
☐	67 Father and Son	.20	.08	.02
	Ray Boone			
	Bob Boone			
☐	68 Father and Son	.20	.08	.02
	Joe Coleman			
	Joe Coleman Jr.			
☐	69 Father and Son	.20	.08	.02
	Jim Hegan			
	Mike Hegan			
☐	70 Father and Son	.20	.08	.02
	Roy Smalley			
	Roy Smalley Jr.			
☐	71 Steve Rogers	.25	.10	.02
☐	72 Hal McRae	.25	.10	.02
☐	73 Orioles Team	.50	.10	.02
	(checklist back)			
☐	74 Oscar Gamble	.20	.08	.02
☐	75 Larry Dierker	.20	.08	.02
☐	76 Willie Crawford	.13	.05	.01
☐	77 Pedro Borbon	.13	.05	.01
☐	78 Cecil Cooper	.75	.30	.07
☐	79 Jerry Morales	.13	.05	.01
☐	80 Jim Kaat	.50	.20	.05
☐	81 Darrell Evans	.35	.14	.03
☐	82 Von Joshua	.13	.05	.01
☐	83 Jim Spencer	.13	.05	.01
☐	84 Brent Strom	.13	.05	.01
☐	85 Mickey Rivers	.25	.10	.02
☐	86 Mike Tyson	.13	.05	.01
☐	87 Tom Burgmeier	.13	.05	.01
☐	88 Duffy Dyer	.13	.05	.01
☐	89 Vern Ruhle	.13	.05	.01
☐	90 Sal Bando	.25	.10	.02
☐	91 Tom Hutton	.13	.05	.01
☐	92 Eduardo Rodriguez	.13	.05	.01
☐	93 Mike Phillips	.13	.05	.01
☐	94 Jim Dwyer	.13	.05	.01
☐	95 Brooks Robinson	1.75	.70	.17
☐	96 Doug Bird	.13	.05	.01
☐	97 Wilbur Howard	.13	.05	.01
☐	98 Dennis Eckersley	1.00	.40	

		MINT	VG-E	F-G
☐ 99	Lee Lacy	.25	.10	.02
☐ 100	Jim Hunter	1.25	.50	.12
☐ 101	Pete LaCock	.13	.05	.01
☐ 102	Jim Willoughby	.13	.05	.01
☐ 103	Biff Pocoroba	.13	.05	.01
☐ 104	Reds Team	.50	.10	.02
	(checklist back)			
☐ 105	Gary Lavelle	.20	.08	.02
☐ 106	Tom Grieve	.20	.08	.02
☐ 107	Dave Roberts	.13	.05	.01
☐ 108	Don Kirkwood	.13	.05	.01
☐ 109	Larry Lintz	.13	.05	.01
☐ 110	Carlos May	.13	.05	.01
☐ 111	Danny Thompson	.13	.05	.01
☐ 112	Kent Tekulve	.75	.30	.07
☐ 113	Gary Sutherland	.13	.05	.01
☐ 114	Jay Johnstone	.20	.08	.02
☐ 115	Ken Holtzman	.20	.08	.02
☐ 116	Charlie Moore	.13	.05	.01
☐ 117	Mike Jorgensen	.13	.05	.01
☐ 118	Red Sox Team	.50	.10	.02
	(checklist back)			
☐ 119	Checklist 1-132	.50	.05	.01
☐ 120	Rusty Staub	.35	.14	.03
☐ 121	Tony Solaita	.13	.05	.01
☐ 122	Mike Cosgrove	.13	.05	.01
☐ 123	Walt Williams	.13	.05	.01
☐ 124	Doug Rau	.13	.05	.01
☐ 125	Don Baylor	.65	.26	.06
☐ 126	Tom Dettore	.13	.05	.01
☐ 127	Larvell Blanks	.13	.05	.01
☐ 128	Ken Griffey	.35	.14	.03
☐ 129	Andy Etchebarren	.13	.05	.01
☐ 130	Luis Tiant	.30	.12	.03
☐ 131	Bill Stein	.13	.05	.01
☐ 132	Don Hood	.13	.05	.01
☐ 133	Gary Matthews	.30	.12	.03
☐ 134	Mike Ivie	.13	.05	.01
☐ 135	Bake McBride	.20	.08	.02
☐ 136	Dave Goltz	.20	.08	.02
☐ 137	Bill Robinson	.13	.05	.01
☐ 138	Lerrin LaGrow	.13	.05	.01
☐ 139	Gorman Thomas	.45	.18	.04
☐ 140	Vida Blue	.30	.12	.03
☐ 141	Larry Parrish	1.25	.50	.12
☐ 142	Dick Drago	.13	.05	.01
☐ 143	Jerry Grote	.13	.05	.01
☐ 144	Al Fitzmorris	.13	.05	.01
☐ 145	Larry Bowa	.40	.16	.04
☐ 146	George Medich	.20	.08	.02
☐ 147	Astros Team	.40	.08	.01
	(checklist back)			
☐ 148	Stan Thomas	.13	.05	.01

		MINT	VG-E	F-G
☐ 149	Tommy Davis	.20	.08	.02
☐ 150	Steve Garvey	3.75	1.50	.37
☐ 151	Bill Bonham	.13	.05	.01
☐ 152	Leroy Stanton	.13	.05	.01
☐ 153	Buzz Capra	.13	.05	.01
☐ 154	Bucky Dent	.25	.10	.02
☐ 155	Jack Billingham	.13	.05	.01
☐ 156	Rico Carty	.25	.10	.02
☐ 157	Mike Caldwell	.20	.08	.02
☐ 158	Ken Reitz	.13	.05	.01
☐ 159	Jerry Terrell	.13	.05	.01
☐ 160	Dave Winfield	3.50	1.40	.35
☐ 161	Bruce Kison	.13	.05	.01
☐ 162	Jack Pierce	.13	.05	.01
☐ 163	Jim Slaton	.13	.05	.01
☐ 164	Pepe Mangual	.13	.05	.01
☐ 165	Gene Tenace	.13	.05	.01
☐ 166	Skip Lockwood	.13	.05	.01
☐ 167	Freddie Patek	.13	.05	.01
☐ 168	Tom Hilgendorf	.13	.05	.01
☐ 169	Graig Nettles	1.00	.40	.10
☐ 170	Rick Wise	.20	.08	.02
☐ 171	Greg Gross	.13	.05	.01
☐ 172	Rangers Team	.40	.08	.01
	(checklist back)			
☐ 173	Steve Swisher	.13	.05	.01
☐ 174	Charlie Hough	.25	.10	.02
☐ 175	Ken Singleton	.35	.14	.03
☐ 176	Dick Lange	.13	.05	.01
☐ 177	Marty Perez	.13	.05	.01
☐ 178	Tom Buskey	.13	.05	.01
☐ 179	George Foster	.85	.34	.08
☐ 180	Rich Gossage	1.00	.40	.10
☐ 181	Willie Montanez	.13	.05	.01
☐ 182	Harry Rasmussen	.13	.05	.01
☐ 183	Steve Braun	.13	.05	.01
☐ 184	Bill Greif	.13	.05	.01
☐ 185	Dave Parker	2.25	.90	.22
☐ 186	Tom Walker	.13	.05	.01
☐ 187	Pedro Garcia	.13	.05	.01
☐ 188	Fred Scherman	.13	.05	.01
☐ 189	Claudell Washington	.35	.14	.03
☐ 190	Jon Matlack	.20	.08	.02
☐ 191	NL Batting Leaders	.40	.16	.04
	Bill Madlock			
	Ted Simmons			
	Manny Sanguillen			
☐ 192	AL Batting Leaders	1.25	.50	.12
	Rod Carew			
	Fred Lynn			
	Thurman Munson			

		MINT	VG-E	F-G
☐ 193	NL Home Run Leaders	.65	.26	.06
	Mike Schmidt			
	Dave Kingman			
	Greg Luzinski			
☐ 194	AL Home Run Leaders	.65	.26	.06
	Reggie Jackson			
	George Scott			
	John Mayberry			
☐ 195	NL RBI Leaders	.45	.18	.04
	Greg Luzinski			
	Johnny Bench			
	Tony Perez			
☐ 196	AL RBI Leaders	.40	.16	.04
	George Scott			
	John Mayberry			
	Fred Lynn			
☐ 197	NL Steals Leaders	.75	.30	.07
	Dave Lopes			
	Joe Morgan			
	Lou Brock			
☐ 198	AL Steals Leaders	.25	.10	.02
	Mickey Rivers			
	Claudell Washington			
	Amos Otis			
☐ 199	NL Victory Leaders	.45	.18	.04
	Tom Seaver			
	Randy Jones			
	Andy Messersmith			
☐ 200	AL Victory Leaders	.65	.26	.06
	Jim Hunter			
	Jim Palmer			
	Vida Blue			
☐ 201	NL ERA Leaders	.45	.18	.04
	Randy Jones			
	Andy Messersmith			
	Tom Seaver			
☐ 202	AL ERA Leaders	.55	.22	.05
	Jim Palmer			
	Jim Hunter			
	Dennis Eckersley			
☐ 203	NL Strikeout Leaders	.45	.18	.04
	Tom Seaver			
	John Montefusco			
	Andy Messersmith			
☐ 204	AL Strikeout Leaders	.40	.16	.04
	Frank Tanana			
	Bert Blyleven			
	Gaylord Perry			
☐ 205	Leading Firemen	.25	.10	.02
	Al Hrabosky			
	Rich Gossage			

		MINT	VG-E	F-G
☐ 206	Manny Trillo	.25	.10	.02
☐ 207	Andy Hassler	.13	.05	.01
☐ 208	Mike Lum	.13	.05	.01
☐ 209	Alan Ashby	.25	.10	.02
☐ 210	Lee May	.25	.10	.02
☐ 211	Clay Carroll	.13	.05	.01
☐ 212	Pat Kelly	.13	.05	.01
☐ 213	Dave Heaverlo	.13	.05	.01
☐ 214	Eric Soderholm	.13	.05	.01
☐ 215	Reggie Smith	.35	.14	.03
☐ 216	Expos Team	.40	.08	.01
	(checklist back)			
☐ 217	Dave Freisleben	.13	.05	.01
☐ 218	John Knox	.13	.05	.01
☐ 219	Tom Murphy	.13	.05	.01
☐ 220	Manny Sanguillen	.20	.08	.02
☐ 221	Jim Todd	.13	.05	.01
☐ 222	Wayne Garrett	.13	.05	.01
☐ 223	Ollie Brown	.13	.05	.01
☐ 224	Jim York	.13	.05	.01
☐ 225	Roy White	.20	.08	.02
☐ 226	Jim Sundberg	.20	.08	.02
☐ 227	Oscar Zamora	.13	.05	.01
☐ 228	John Hale	.13	.05	.01
☐ 229	Jerry Remy	.30	.12	.03
☐ 230	Carl Yastrzemski	4.50	1.80	.45
☐ 231	Tom House	.20	.08	.02
☐ 232	Frank Duffy	.13	.05	.01
☐ 233	Grant Jackson	.13	.05	.01
☐ 234	Mike Sadek	.13	.05	.01
☐ 235	Bert Blyleven	.50	.20	.05
☐ 236	Royals Team	.40	.08	.01
	(checklist back)			
☐ 237	Dave Hamilton	.13	.05	.01
☐ 238	Larry Biittner	.13	.05	.01
☐ 239	John Curtis	.13	.05	.01
☐ 240	Pete Rose	12.00	5.00	1.20
☐ 241	Hector Torres	.13	.05	.01
☐ 242	Dan Meyer	.13	.05	.01
☐ 243	Jim Rooker	.13	.05	.01
☐ 244	Bill Sharp	.13	.05	.01
☐ 245	Felix Millan	.13	.05	.01
☐ 246	Cesar Tovar	.13	.05	.01
☐ 247	Terry Harmon	.13	.05	.01
☐ 248	Dick Tidrow	.13	.05	.01
☐ 249	Cliff Johnson	.13	.05	.01
☐ 250	Fergie Jenkins	.45	.18	.04
☐ 251	Rick Monday	.20	.08	.02
☐ 252	Tim Nordbrook	.13	.05	.01
☐ 253	Bill Buckner	.45	.18	.04
☐ 254	Rudy Meoli	.13	.05	.01
☐ 255	Fritz Peterson	.13	.05	.01
☐ 256	Rowland Office	.13	.05	.01

	MINT	VG-E	F-G		MINT	VG-E	F-G
☐ 257 Ross Grimsley	.13	.05	.01	☐ 308 Jim Barr	.13	.05	.01
☐ 258 Nyls Nyman	.13	.05	.01	☐ 309 Bill Melton	.13	.05	.01
☐ 259 Darrel Chaney	.13	.05	.01	☐ 310 Randy Jones	.25	.10	.02
☐ 260 Steve Busby	.20	.08	.02	☐ 311 Cookie Rojas	.13	.05	.01
☐ 261 Gary Thomasson	.13	.05	.01	☐ 312 Don Carrithers	.13	.05	.01
☐ 262 Checklist 133-264	.50	.05	.01	☐ 313 Dan Ford	.25	.10	.02
☐ 263 Lyman Bostock	.60	.24	.06	☐ 314 Ed Kranepool	.20	.08	.02
☐ 264 Steve Renko	.13	.05	.01	☐ 315 Al Hrabosky	.20	.08	.02
☐ 265 Willie Davis	.20	.08	.02	☐ 316 Robin Yount	5.00	2.00	.50
☐ 266 Alan Foster	.13	.05	.01	☐ 317 John Candelaria	2.00	.80	.20
☐ 267 Aurelio Rodriguez	.13	.05	.01	☐ 318 Bob Boone	.25	.10	.02
☐ 268 Del Unser	.13	.05	.01	☐ 319 Larry Gura	.20	.08	.02
☐ 269 Rick Austin	.13	.05	.01	☐ 320 Willie Horton	.20	.08	.02
☐ 270 Willie Stargell	1.75	.70	.17	☐ 321 Jose Cruz	.40	.16	.04
☐ 271 Jim Lonborg	.20	.08	.02	☐ 322 Glenn Abbott	.13	.05	.01
☐ 272 Rick Dempsey	.20	.08	.02	☐ 323 Rob Sperring	.13	.05	.01
☐ 273 Joe Niekro	.25	.10	.02	☐ 324 Jim Bibby	.20	.08	.02
☐ 274 Tommy Harper	.20	.08	.02	☐ 325 Tony Perez	.50	.20	.05
☐ 275 Rick Manning	.25	.10	.02	☐ 326 Dick Pole	.13	.05	.01
☐ 276 Mickey Scott	.13	.05	.01	☐ 327 Dave Moates	.13	.05	.01
☐ 277 Cubs Team	.40	.08	.01	☐ 328 Carl Morton	.13	.05	.01
(checklist back)				☐ 329 Joe Ferguson	.20	.08	.02
☐ 278 Bernie Carbo	.13	.05	.01	☐ 330 Nolan Ryan	3.50	1.40	.35
☐ 279 Roy Howell	.13	.05	.01	☐ 331 Padres Team	.40	.08	.01
☐ 280 Burt Hooton	.20	.08	.02	(checklist back)			
☐ 281 Dave May	.13	.05	.01	☐ 332 Charlie Williams	.13	.05	.01
☐ 282 Dan Osborn	.13	.05	.01	☐ 333 Bob Coluccio	.13	.05	.01
☐ 283 Merv Rettenmund	.13	.05	.01	☐ 334 Dennis Leonard	.30	.12	.03
☐ 284 Steve Ontiveros	.13	.05	.01	☐ 335 Bob Grich	.25	.10	.02
☐ 285 Mike Cuellar	.20	.08	.02	☐ 336 Vic Albury	.13	.05	.01
☐ 286 Jim Wohlford	.13	.05	.01	☐ 337 Bud Harrelson	.20	.08	.02
☐ 287 Pete Mackanin	.13	.05	.01	☐ 338 Bob Bailey	.13	.05	.01
☐ 288 Bill Campbell	.13	.05	.01	☐ 339 John Denny	.40	.16	.04
☐ 289 Enzo Hernandez	.13	.05	.01	☐ 340 Jim Rice	10.00	4.00	1.00
☐ 290 Ted Simmons	.65	.26	.06	☐ 341 All-Time 1B	1.75	.70	.17
☐ 291 Ken Sanders	.13	.05	.01	Lou Gehrig			
☐ 292 Leon Roberts	.13	.05	.01	☐ 342 All-Time 2B	1.00	.40	.10
☐ 293 Bill Castro	.13	.05	.01	Rogers Hornsby			
☐ 294 Ed Kirkpatrick	.13	.05	.01	☐ 343 All-Time 3B	.60	.24	.06
☐ 295 Dave Cash	.13	.05	.01	Pie Traynor			
☐ 296 Pat Dobson	.20	.08	.02	☐ 344 All-Time SS	1.00	.40	.10
☐ 297 Roger Metzger	.13	.05	.01	Honus Wagner			
☐ 298 Dick Bosman	.13	.05	.01	☐ 345 All-Time OF	2.75	1.10	.27
☐ 299 Champ Summers	.13	.05	.01	Babe Ruth			
☐ 300 Johnny Bench	3.50	1.40	.35	☐ 346 All-Time OF	1.75	.70	.17
☐ 301 Jackie Brown	.13	.05	.01	Ty Cobb			
☐ 302 Rick Miller	.13	.05	.01	☐ 347 All-Time OF	1.75	.70	.17
☐ 303 Steve Foucault	.13	.05	.01	Ted Williams			
☐ 304 Angels Team	.40	.08	.01	☐ 348 All-Time C	.60	.24	.06
(checklist back)				Mickey Cochrane			
☐ 305 Andy Messersmith	.25	.10	.02	☐ 349 All-Time RHP	1.00	.40	.10
☐ 306 Rod Gilbreath	.13	.05	.01	Walter Johnson			
☐ 307 Al Bumbry	.13	.05	.01				

	MINT	VG-E	F-G
☐ 350 All-Time LHP Lefty Grove	.75	.30	.07
☐ 351 Randy Hundley	.13	.05	.01
☐ 352 Dave Giusti	.13	.05	.01
☐ 353 Sixto Lezcano	.25	.10	.02
☐ 354 Ron Blomberg	.13	.05	.01
☐ 355 Steve Carlton	4.00	1.60	.40
☐ 356 Ted Martinez	.13	.05	.01
☐ 357 Ken Forsch	.20	.08	.02
☐ 358 Buddy Bell	.35	.14	.03
☐ 359 Rick Reuschel	.20	.08	.02
☐ 360 Jeff Burroughs	.20	.08	.02
☐ 361 Tigers Team (checklist back)	.50	.10	.02
☐ 362 Will McEnaney	.13	.05	.01
☐ 363 Dave Collins	.90	.36	.09
☐ 364 Elias Sosa	.13	.05	.01
☐ 365 Carlton Fisk	.90	.36	.09
☐ 366 Bobby Valentine	.30	.12	.03
☐ 367 Bruce Miller	.13	.05	.01
☐ 368 Wilbur Wood	.20	.08	.02
☐ 369 Frank White	.40	.16	.04
☐ 370 Ron Cey	.60	.24	.06
☐ 371 Ellie Hendricks	.13	.05	.01
☐ 372 Rick Baldwin	.13	.05	.01
☐ 373 Johnny Briggs	.13	.05	.01
☐ 374 Dan Warthen	.13	.05	.01
☐ 375 Ron Fairly	.20	.08	.02
☐ 376 Rich Hebner	.13	.05	.01
☐ 377 Mike Hegan	.13	.05	.01
☐ 378 Steve Stone	.20	.08	.02
☐ 379 Ken Boswell	.13	.05	.01
☐ 380 Bobby Bonds	.30	.12	.03
☐ 381 Denny Doyle	.13	.05	.01
☐ 382 Matt Alexander	.13	.05	.01
☐ 383 John Ellis	.13	.05	.01
☐ 384 Phillies Team (checklist back)	.40	.08	.01
☐ 385 Mickey Lolich	.30	.12	.03
☐ 386 Ed Goodson	.13	.05	.01
☐ 387 Mike Miley	.13	.05	.01
☐ 388 Stan Perzanowski	.13	.05	.01
☐ 389 Glenn Adams	.13	.05	.01
☐ 390 Don Gullett	.20	.08	.02
☐ 391 Jerry Hairston	.13	.05	.01
☐ 392 Checklist 265-396	.50	.05	.01
☐ 393 Paul Mitchell	.13	.05	.01
☐ 394 Fran Healy	.13	.05	.01
☐ 395 Jim Wynn	.20	.08	.02
☐ 396 Bill Lee	.20	.08	.02
☐ 397 Tim Foli	.13	.05	.01
☐ 398 Dave Tomlin	.13	.05	.01
☐ 399 Luis Melendez	.13	.05	.01

	MINT	VG-E	F-G
☐ 400 Rod Carew	3.50	1.40	.35
☐ 401 Ken Brett	.13	.05	.01
☐ 402 Don Money	.13	.05	.01
☐ 403 Geoff Zahn	.13	.05	.01
☐ 404 Enos Cabell	.13	.05	.01
☐ 405 Rollie Fingers	.75	.30	.07
☐ 406 Ed Herrmann	.13	.05	.01
☐ 407 Tom Underwood	.13	.05	.01
☐ 408 Charlie Spikes	.13	.05	.01
☐ 409 Dave Lemanczyk	.13	.05	.01
☐ 410 Ralph Garr	.20	.08	.02
☐ 411 Bill Singer	.13	.05	.01
☐ 412 Toby Harrah	.20	.08	.02
☐ 413 Pete Varney	.13	.05	.01
☐ 414 Wayne Garland	.13	.05	.01
☐ 415 Vada Pinson	.25	.10	.02
☐ 416 Tommy John	.65	.26	.06
☐ 417 Gene Clines	.13	.05	.01
☐ 418 Jose Morales	.13	.05	.01
☐ 419 Reggie Cleveland	.13	.05	.01
☐ 420 Joe Morgan	2.25	.90	.22
☐ 421 A's Team (checklist back)	.40	.08	.01
☐ 422 Johnny Grubb	.13	.05	.01
☐ 423 Ed Halicki	.13	.05	.01
☐ 424 Phil Roof	.13	.05	.01
☐ 425 Rennie Stennett	.13	.05	.01
☐ 426 Bob Forsch	.25	.10	.02
☐ 427 Kurt Bevacqua	.13	.05	.01
☐ 428 Jim Crawford	.13	.05	.01
☐ 429 Fred Stanley	.13	.05	.01
☐ 430 Jose Cardenal	.13	.05	.01
☐ 431 Dick Ruthven	.13	.05	.01
☐ 432 Tom Veryzer	.13	.05	.01
☐ 433 Rick Waits	.20	.08	.02
☐ 434 Morris Nettles	.13	.05	.01
☐ 435 Phil Niekro	1.25	.50	.12
☐ 436 Bill Fahey	.13	.05	.01
☐ 437 Terry Forster	.25	.10	.02
☐ 438 Doug DeCinces	.65	.26	.06
☐ 439 Rick Rhoden	.50	.20	.05
☐ 440 John Mayberry	.20	.08	.02
☐ 441 Gary Carter	10.00	4.00	1.00
☐ 442 Hank Webb	.13	.05	.01
☐ 443 Giants Team (checklist back)	.40	.08	.01
☐ 444 Gary Nolan	.13	.05	.01
☐ 445 Rico Petrocelli	.20	.08	.02
☐ 446 Larry Haney	.13	.05	.01
☐ 447 Gene Locklear	.13	.05	.01
☐ 448 Tom Johnson	.13	.05	.01
☐ 449 Bob Robertson	.13	.05	.01
☐ 450 Jim Palmer	2.50	1.00	.25

		MINT	VG-E	F-G
☐ 451	Buddy Bradford	.13	.05	.01
☐ 452	Tom Hausman	.13	.05	.01
☐ 453	Lou Piniella	.30	.12	.03
☐ 454	Tom Griffin	.13	.05	.01
☐ 455	Dick Allen	.35	.14	.03
☐ 456	Joe Coleman	.13	.05	.01
☐ 457	Ed Crosby	.13	.05	.01
☐ 458	Earl Williams	.13	.05	.01
☐ 459	Jim Brewer	.13	.05	.01
☐ 460	Cesar Cedeno	.25	.10	.02
☐ 461	NL and AL Champs	.40	.16	.04
	Reds sweep Bucs			
	Bosox surprise A's			
☐ 462	'75 World Series	.40	.16	.04
	Reds Champs			
☐ 463	Steve Hargan	.13	.05	.01
☐ 464	Ken Henderson	.13	.05	.01
☐ 465	Mike Marshall	.20	.08	.02
☐ 466	Bob Stinson	.13	.05	.01
☐ 467	Woodie Fryman	.13	.05	.01
☐ 468	Jesus Alou	.13	.05	.01
☐ 469	Rawley Eastwick	.13	.05	.01
☐ 470	Bobby Murcer	.35	.14	.03
☐ 471	Jim Burton	.13	.05	.01
☐ 472	Bob Davis	.13	.05	.01
☐ 473	Paul Blair	.20	.08	.02
☐ 474	Ray Corbin	.13	.05	.01
☐ 475	Joe Rudi	.20	.08	.02
☐ 476	Bob Moose	.13	.05	.01
☐ 477	Indians Team	.40	.08	.01
	(checklist back)			
☐ 478	Lynn McGlothen	.13	.05	.01
☐ 479	Bobby Mitchell	.13	.05	.01
☐ 480	Mike Schmidt	9.00	3.75	.90
☐ 481	Rudy May	.13	.05	.01
☐ 482	Tim Hosley	.13	.05	.01
☐ 483	Mickey Stanley	.13	.05	.01
☐ 484	Eric Raich	.13	.05	.01
☐ 485	Mike Hargrove	.20	.08	.02
☐ 486	Bruce Dal Canton	.13	.05	.01
☐ 487	Leron Lee	.13	.05	.01
☐ 488	Claude Osteen	.20	.08	.02
☐ 489	Skip Jutze	.13	.05	.01
☐ 490	Frank Tanana	.25	.10	.02
☐ 491	Terry Crowley	.13	.05	.01
☐ 492	Martin Pattin	.13	.05	.01
☐ 493	Derrel Thomas	.13	.05	.01
☐ 494	Craig Swan	.20	.08	.02
☐ 495	Nate Colbert	.13	.05	.01
☐ 496	Juan Beniquez	.20	.08	.02
☐ 497	Joe McIntosh	.13	.05	.01
☐ 498	Glenn Borgmann	.13	.05	.01
☐ 499	Mario Guerrero	.13	.05	.01

		MINT	VG-E	F-G
☐ 500	Reggie Jackson	6.00	2.40	.60
☐ 501	Billy Champion	.13	.05	.01
☐ 502	Tim McCarver	.25	.10	.02
☐ 503	Elliott Maddox	.13	.05	.01
☐ 504	Pirates Team	.40	.08	.01
	(checklist back)			
☐ 505	Mark Belanger	.25	.10	.02
☐ 506	George Mitterwald	.13	.05	.01
☐ 507	Ray Bare	.13	.05	.01
☐ 508	Duane Kuiper	.13	.05	.01
☐ 509	Bill Hands	.13	.05	.01
☐ 510	Amos Otis	.25	.10	.02
☐ 511	Jamie Easterley	.13	.05	.01
☐ 512	Ellie Rodriguez	.13	.05	.01
☐ 513	Bart Johnson	.13	.05	.01
☐ 514	Dan Driessen	.20	.08	.02
☐ 515	Steve Yeager	.20	.08	.02
☐ 516	Wayne Granger	.13	.05	.01
☐ 517	John Milner	.13	.05	.01
☐ 518	Doug Flynn	.13	.05	.01
☐ 519	Steve Brye	.13	.05	.01
☐ 520	Willie McCovey	1.75	.70	.17
☐ 521	Jim Colborn	.13	.05	.01
☐ 522	Ted Sizemore	.13	.05	.01
☐ 523	Bob Montgomery	.13	.05	.01
☐ 524	Pete Falcone	.13	.05	.01
☐ 525	Billy Williams	1.25	.50	.12
☐ 526	Checklist 397-528	.50	.05	.01
☐ 527	Mike Anderson	.13	.05	.01
☐ 528	Dock Ellis	.13	.05	.01
☐ 529	Deron Johnson	.13	.05	.01
☐ 530	Don Sutton	1.25	.50	.12
☐ 531	New York Mets Team	.50	.10	.02
	(checklist back)			
☐ 532	Milt May	.13	.05	.01
☐ 533	Lee Richard	.13	.05	.01
☐ 534	Stan Bahnsen	.13	.05	.01
☐ 535	Dave Nelson	.13	.05	.01
☐ 536	Mike Thompson	.13	.05	.01
☐ 537	Tony Muser	.13	.05	.01
☐ 538	Pat Darcy	.13	.05	.01
☐ 539	John Balaz	.13	.05	.01
☐ 540	Bill Freehan	.25	.10	.02
☐ 541	Steve Mingori	.13	.05	.01
☐ 542	Keith Hernandez	5.00	2.00	.50
☐ 543	Wayne Twitchell	.13	.05	.01
☐ 544	Pepe Frias	.13	.05	.01
☐ 545	Sparky Lyle	.30	.12	.03
☐ 546	Dave Rosello	.13	.05	.01
☐ 547	Roric Harrison	.13	.05	.01
☐ 548	Manny Mota	.20	.08	.02
☐ 549	Randy Tate	.13	.05	.01
☐ 550	Hank Aaron	5.00	2.00	.50

		MINT	VG-E	F-G
☐ 551	Jerry DaVanon	.13	.05	.01
☐ 552	Terry Humphrey	.13	.05	.01
☐ 553	Randy Moffitt	.13	.05	.01
☐ 554	Ray Fosse	.13	.05	.01
☐ 555	Dyar Miller	.13	.05	.01
☐ 556	Twins Team	.40	.08	.01
	(checklist back)			
☐ 557	Dan Spillner	.13	.05	.01
☐ 558	Clarence Gaston	.13	.05	.01
☐ 559	Clyde Wright	.13	.05	.01
☐ 560	Jorge Orta	.13	.05	.01
☐ 561	Tom Carroll	.13	.05	.01
☐ 562	Adrian Garrett	.13	.05	.01
☐ 563	Larry Demery	.13	.05	.01
☐ 564	Bubble Gum Champ:	.20	.08	.02
	Kurt Bevacqua			
☐ 565	Tug McGraw	.30	.12	.03
☐ 566	Ken McMullen	.13	.05	.01
☐ 567	George Stone	.13	.05	.01
☐ 568	Rob Andrews	.13	.05	.01
☐ 569	Nelson Briles	.20	.08	.02
☐ 570	George Hendrick	.25	.10	.02
☐ 571	Don DeMola	.13	.05	.01
☐ 572	Rich Coggins	.13	.05	.01
☐ 573	Bill Travers	.13	.05	.01
☐ 574	Don Kessinger	.20	.08	.02
☐ 575	Dwight Evans	.50	.20	.05
☐ 576	Maximino Leon	.13	.05	.01
☐ 577	Marc Hill	.13	.05	.01
☐ 578	Ted Kubiak	.13	.05	.01
☐ 579	Clay Kirby	.13	.05	.01
☐ 580	Bert Campaneris	.25	.10	.02
☐ 581	Cardinals Team	.50	.10	.02
	(checklist back)			
☐ 582	Mike Kekich	.13	.05	.01
☐ 583	Tommy Helms	.13	.05	.01
☐ 584	Stan Wall	.13	.05	.01
☐ 585	Joe Torre	.40	.16	.04
☐ 586	Ron Schueler	.13	.05	.01
☐ 587	Leo Cardenas	.13	.05	.01
☐ 588	Kevin Kobel	.13	.05	.01
☐ 589	Rookie Pitchers	1.25	.50	.12
	Santo Alcala			
	Mike Flanagan			
	Joe Pactwa			
	Pablo Torrealba			
☐ 590	Rookie Outfielders	1.25	.50	.12
	Henry Cruz			
	Chet Lemon			
	Ellis Valentine			
	Terry Whitfield			

		MINT	VG-E	F-G
☐ 591	Rookie Pitchers	.20	.08	.02
	Steve Grilli			
	Craig Mitchell			
	Jose Sosa			
	George Throop			
☐ 592	Rookie Infielders	1.25	.50	.12
	Willie Randolph			
	Dave McKay			
	Jerry Royster			
	Roy Staiger			
☐ 593	Rookie Pitchers	.25	.10	.02
	Larry Anderson			
	Ken Crosby			
	Mark Littell			
	Butch Metzger			
☐ 594	Rookie Catchers/OF	.20	.08	.02
	Andy Merchant			
	Ed Ott			
	Royle Stillman			
	Jerry White			
☐ 595	Rookie Pitchers	.20	.08	.02
	Art DeFilipis			
	Randy Lerch			
	Sid Monge			
	Steve Barr			
☐ 596	Rookie Infielders	.35	.14	.03
	Craig Reynolds			
	Lamar Johnson			
	Johnnie LeMaster			
	Jerry Manuel			
☐ 597	Rookie Pitchers	.75	.30	.07
	Don Aase			
	Jack Kucek			
	Frank LaCorte			
	Mike Pazik			
☐ 598	Rookie Outfielders	.20	.08	.02
	Hector Cruz			
	Jamie Quirk			
	Jerry Turner			
	Joe Wallis			
☐ 599	Rookie Pitchers	10.00	4.00	1.00
	Rob Dressler			
	Ron Guidry			
	Bob McClure			
	Pat Zachry			
☐ 600	Tom Seaver	3.50	1.40	.35
☐ 601	Ken Rudolph	.13	.05	.01
☐ 602	Doug Konieczny	.13	.05	.01
☐ 603	Jim Holt	.13	.05	.01
☐ 604	Joe Lovitto	.13	.05	.01
☐ 605	Al Downing	.13	.05	.01
☐ 606	Brewers Team	.40	.08	.01
	(checklist back)			

		MINT	VG-E	F-G
☐ 607	Rich Hinton	.13	.05	.01
☐ 608	Vic Correll	.13	.05	.01
☐ 609	Fred Norman	.13	.05	.01
☐ 610	Greg Luzinski	.40	.16	.04
☐ 611	Rich Folkers	.13	.05	.01
☐ 612	Joe Lahoud	.13	.05	.01
☐ 613	Tim Johnson	.13	.05	.01
☐ 614	Fernando Arroyo	.13	.05	.01
☐ 615	Mike Cubbage	.13	.05	.01
☐ 616	Buck Martinez	.13	.05	.01
☐ 617	Darold Knowles	.13	.05	.01
☐ 618	Jack Brohamer	.13	.05	.01
☐ 619	Bill Butler	.13	.05	.01
☐ 620	Al Oliver	.60	.24	.06
☐ 621	Tom Hall	.13	.05	.01
☐ 622	Rick Auerbach	.13	.05	.01
☐ 623	Bob Allietta	.13	.05	.01
☐ 624	Tony Taylor	.13	.05	.01
☐ 625	J.R. Richard	.25	.10	.02
☐ 626	Bob Sheldon	.13	.05	.01
☐ 627	Bill Plummer	.13	.05	.01
☐ 628	John D'Acquisto	.13	.05	.01
☐ 629	Sandy Alomar	.13	.05	.01
☐ 630	Chris Speier	.13	.05	.01
☐ 631	Braves Team	.40	.08	.01
	(checklist back)			
☐ 632	Rogelio Moret	.13	.05	.01
☐ 633	John Stearns	.25	.10	.02
☐ 634	Larry Christenson	.13	.05	.01
☐ 635	Jim Fregosi	.25	.10	.02
☐ 636	Joe Decker	.13	.05	.01
☐ 637	Bruce Bochte	.20	.08	.02
☐ 638	Doyle Alexander	.20	.08	.02
☐ 639	Fred Kendall	.13	.05	.01
☐ 640	Bill Madlock	.75	.30	.07
☐ 641	Tom Paciorek	.13	.05	.01
☐ 642	Dennis Blair	.13	.05	.01
☐ 643	Checklist 529-660	.50	.05	.01
☐ 644	Tom Bradley	.13	.05	.01
☐ 645	Darrell Porter	.20	.08	.02
☐ 646	John Lowenstein	.13	.05	.01
☐ 647	Ramon Hernandez	.13	.05	.01
☐ 648	Al Cowens	.20	.08	.02
☐ 649	Dave Roberts	.13	.05	.01
☐ 650	Thurman Munson	3.50	1.40	.35
☐ 651	John Odom	.13	.05	.01
☐ 652	Ed Armbrister	.13	.05	.01
☐ 653	Mike Norris	.25	.10	.02
☐ 654	Doug Griffin	.13	.05	.01
☐ 655	Mike Vail	.13	.05	.01
☐ 656	White Sox Team	.40	.08	.01
	(checklist back)			
☐ 657	Roy Smalley	.45	.18	.04

		MINT	VG-E	F-G
☐ 658	Jerry Johnson	.13	.05	.01
☐ 659	Ben Oglivie	.25	.10	.02
☐ 660	Dave Lopes	.60	.24	.06

1976 Topps Traded

The cards in this 44-card set measure 2½" by 3½". The 1976 Topps Traded set contains 43 players and one unnumbered checklist card. The individuals pictured were traded after the Topps regular set was printed. A "Sports Extra" heading design is found on each picture and is also used to introduce the biographical section of the reverse. Each card is numbered according to the player's regular 1976 card with the addition of "T" to indicate his new status.

		MINT	VG-E	F-G
	Complete Set	5.00	2.00	.50
	Common Player	.10	.04	.01
☐ 27	T Ed Figueroa	.10	.04	.01
☐ 28	T Dusty Baker	.30	.12	.03
☐ 44	T Doug Rader	.15	.06	.01
☐ 58	T Ron Reed	.15	.06	.01
☐ 74	T Oscar Gamble	.20	.08	.02
☐ 80	T Jim Kaat	.50	.20	.05
☐ 83	T Jim Spencer	.10	.04	.01
☐ 85	T Mickey Rivers	.15	.06	.01
☐ 99	T Lee Lacy	.20	.08	.02
☐ 120	T Rusty Staub	.35	.14	.03
☐ 127	T Larvell Blanks	.10	.04	.01
☐ 146	T George Medich	.15	.06	.01
☐ 158	T Ken Reitz	.10	.04	.01
☐ 208	T Mike Lum	.10	.04	.01

		MINT	VG-E	F-G
☐ 211	T Clay Carroll	.10	.04	.01
☐ 231	T Tom House	.15	.06	.01
☐ 250	T Fergie Jenkins	.50	.20	.05
☐ 259	T Darrel Chaney	.10	.04	.01
☐ 292	T Leon Roberts	.10	.04	.01
☐ 296	T Pat Dobson	.15	.06	.01
☐ 309	T Bill Melton	.10	.04	.01
☐ 338	T Bob Bailey	.10	.04	.01
☐ 380	T Bobby Bonds	.25	.10	.02
☐ 383	T John Ellis	.10	.04	.01
☐ 385	T Mickey Lolich	.25	.10	.02
☐ 401	T Ken Brett	.15	.06	.01
☐ 410	T Ralph Garr	.15	.06	.01
☐ 411	T Bill Singer	.10	.04	.01
☐ 428	T Jim Crawford	.10	.04	.01
☐ 434	T Morris Nettles	.10	.04	.01
☐ 464	T Ken Henderson	.10	.04	.01
☐ 497	T Joe McIntosh	.10	.04	.01
☐ 524	T Pete Falcone	.10	.04	.01
☐ 527	T Mike Anderson	.10	.04	.01
☐ 528	T Dock Ellis	.10	.04	.01
☐ 532	T Milt May	.10	.04	.01
☐ 554	T Ray Fosse	.10	.04	.01
☐ 579	T Clay Kirby	.10	.04	.01
☐ 583	T Tommy Helms	.10	.04	.01
☐ 592	T Willie Randolph	.50	.20	.05
☐ 618	T Jack Brohamer	.10	.04	.01
☐ 632	T Rogelio Moret	.10	.04	.01
☐ 649	T Dave Roberts	.10	.04	.01
☐ xxxx	Traded Checklist	.40	.04	.00
	(unnumbered)			

1977 Topps

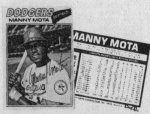

*The cards in this 660-card set measure 2½"
by 3½". In 1977, for the fifth consecutive year,
Topps produced a 660-card baseball set.*

The player's name, team affiliation, and his
position are compactly arranged over the
picture area and a facsimile autograph
appears on the photo. Team cards feature a
checklist of that team's players in the set and
a small picture of the manager on the front of
the card. Appearing for the first time are the
series "Brothers" (631-634) and "Turn Back
The Clock" (433-437). Other subseries in the
set are League Leaders (1-8), Record Breakers (231-234), Playoffs cards (276-277),
World Series cards (411-413), and Rookie
Prospects (472-479 and 487-494). The key
card in the set is the rookie card of Dale Murphy (476).

		MINT	VG-E	F-G
	Complete Set	180.00	75.00	18.00
	Common Player (1-660)	.11	.05	.01
☐ 1	Batting Leaders	1.25	.25	.05
	George Brett			
	Bill Madlock			
☐ 2	Home Run Leaders	.60	.24	.06
	Graig Nettles			
	Mike Schmidt			
☐ 3	RBI Leaders	.30	.12	.03
	Lee May			
	George Foster			
☐ 4	Stolen Base Leaders	.20	.08	.02
	Bill North			
	Dave Lopes			
☐ 5	Victory Leaders	.35	.14	.03
	Jim Palmer			
	Randy Jones			
☐ 6	Strikeout Leaders	1.25	.50	.12
	Nolan Ryan			
	Tom Seaver			
☐ 7	ERA Leaders	.20	.08	.02
	Mark Fidrych			
	John Denny			
☐ 8	Leading Firemen	.15	.06	.01
	Bill Campbell			
	Rawly Eastwick			
☐ 9	Doug Rader	.15	.06	.01
☐ 10	Reggie Jackson	5.50	2.20	.55
☐ 11	Rob Dressler	.11	.05	.01
☐ 12	Larry Haney	.11	.05	.01
☐ 13	Luis Gomez	.11	.05	.01
☐ 14	Tommy Smith	.11	.05	.01
☐ 15	Don Gullett	.15	.06	.01
☐ 16	Bob Jones	.11	.05	.01

		MINT	VG-E	F-G
☐ 17	Steve Stone	.15	.06	.01
☐ 18	Indians Team/Mgr.	.50	.10	.02
	Frank Robinson			
	(checklist back)			
☐ 19	John D'Acquisto	.11	.05	.01
☐ 20	Graig Nettles	.80	.32	.08
☐ 21	Ken Forsch	.15	.06	.01
☐ 22	Bill Freehan	.20	.08	.02
☐ 23	Dan Driessen	.15	.06	.01
☐ 24	Carl Morton	.11	.05	.01
☐ 25	Dwight Evans	.40	.16	.04
☐ 26	Ray Sadecki	.11	.05	.01
☐ 27	Bill Buckner	.35	.14	.03
☐ 28	Woodie Fryman	.11	.05	.01
☐ 29	Bucky Dent	.20	.08	.02
☐ 30	Greg Luzinski	.35	.14	.03
☐ 31	Jim Todd	.11	.05	.01
☐ 32	Checklist 1	.50	.05	.01
☐ 33	Wayne Garland	.11	.05	.01
☐ 34	Angels Team/Mgr.	.40	.08	.01
	Norm Sherry			
	(checklist back)			
☐ 35	Rennie Stennett	.11	.05	.01
☐ 36	John Ellis	.11	.05	.01
☐ 37	Steve Hargan	.11	.05	.01
☐ 38	Craig Kusick	.11	.05	.01
☐ 39	Tom Griffin	.11	.05	.01
☐ 40	Bobby Murcer	.30	.12	.03
☐ 41	Jim Kern	.11	.05	.01
☐ 42	Jose Cruz	.35	.14	.03
☐ 43	Ray Bare	.11	.05	.01
☐ 44	Bud Harrelson	.15	.06	.01
☐ 45	Rawly Eastwick	.11	.05	.01
☐ 46	Buck Martinez	.11	.05	.01
☐ 47	Lynn McGlothen	.11	.05	.01
☐ 48	Tom Paciorek	.11	.05	.01
☐ 49	Grant Jackson	.11	.05	.01
☐ 50	Ron Cey	.40	.16	.04
☐ 51	Brewers Team/Mgr.	.40	.08	.01
	Alex Grammas			
	(checklist back)			
☐ 52	Ellis Valentine	.15	.06	.01
☐ 53	Paul Mitchell	.11	.05	.01
☐ 54	Sandy Alomar	.11	.05	.01
☐ 55	Jeff Burroughs	.15	.06	.01
☐ 56	Rudy May	.11	.05	.01
☐ 57	Marc Hill	.11	.05	.01
☐ 58	Chet Lemon	.30	.12	.03
☐ 59	Larry Christenson	.11	.05	.01
☐ 60	Jim Rice	6.00	2.40	.60
☐ 61	Manny Sanguillen	.15	.06	.01
☐ 62	Eric Raich	.11	.05	.01
☐ 63	Tito Fuentes	.11	.05	.01

		MINT	VG-E	F-G
☐ 64	Larry Biittner	.11	.05	.01
☐ 65	Skip Lockwood	.11	.05	.01
☐ 66	Roy Smalley	.15	.06	.01
☐ 67	Joaquin Andujar	1.25	.50	.12
☐ 68	Bruce Bochte	.15	.06	.01
☐ 69	Jim Crawford	.11	.05	.01
☐ 70	Johnny Bench	2.75	1.10	.27
☐ 71	Dock Ellis	.11	.05	.01
☐ 72	Mike Anderson	.11	.05	.01
☐ 73	Charles Williams	.11	.05	.01
☐ 74	A's Team/Mgr.	.40	.08	.01
	Jack McKeon			
	(checklist back)			
☐ 75	Dennis Leonard	.20	.08	.02
☐ 76	Tim Foli	.11	.05	.01
☐ 77	Dyar Miller	.11	.05	.01
☐ 78	Bob Davis	.11	.05	.01
☐ 79	Don Money	.11	.05	.01
☐ 80	Andy Messersmith	.15	.06	.01
☐ 81	Juan Beniquez	.15	.06	.01
☐ 82	Jim Rooker	.11	.05	.01
☐ 83	Kevin Bell	.11	.05	.01
☐ 84	Ollie Brown	.11	.05	.01
☐ 85	Duane Kuiper	.11	.05	.01
☐ 86	Pat Zachry	.11	.05	.01
☐ 87	Glenn Borgmann	.11	.05	.01
☐ 88	Stan Wall	.11	.05	.01
☐ 89	Butch Hobson	.11	.05	.01
☐ 90	Cesar Cedeno	.20	.08	.02
☐ 91	John Verhoeven	.11	.05	.01
☐ 92	Dave Rosello	.11	.05	.01
☐ 93	Tom Poquette	.11	.05	.01
☐ 94	Craig Swan	.15	.06	.01
☐ 95	Keith Hernandez	2.50	1.00	.25
☐ 96	Lou Piniella	.25	.10	.02
☐ 97	Dave Heaverlo	.11	.05	.01
☐ 98	Milt May	.11	.05	.01
☐ 99	Tom Hausman	.11	.05	.01
☐ 100	Joe Morgan	1.25	.50	.12
☐ 101	Dick Bosman	.11	.05	.01
☐ 102	Jose Morales	.11	.05	.01
☐ 103	Mike Bacsik	.11	.05	.01
☐ 104	Omar Moreno	.25	.10	.02
☐ 105	Steve Yeager	.15	.06	.01
☐ 106	Mike Flanagan	.25	.10	.02
☐ 107	Bill Melton	.11	.05	.01
☐ 108	Alan Foster	.11	.05	.01
☐ 109	Jorge Orta	.11	.05	.01
☐ 110	Steve Carlton	3.50	1.40	.35
☐ 111	Rico Petrocelli	.15	.06	.01
☐ 112	Bill Greif	.11	.05	.01

		MINT	VG-E	F-G
☐ 113	Blue Jays Leaders	.30	.06	.01
	Roy Hartsfield MGR			
	Don Leppert CO			
	Bob Miller CO			
	Jackie Moore CO			
	Harry Warner CO			
	(checklist back)			
☐ 114	Bruce Dal Canton	.11	.05	.01
☐ 115	Rick Manning	.15	.06	.01
☐ 116	Joe Niekro	.25	.10	.02
☐ 117	Frank White	.10	.02	
☐ 118	Rick Jones	.11	.05	.01
☐ 119	John Stearns	.15	.06	.01
☐ 120	Rod Carew	3.50	1.40	.35
☐ 121	Gary Nolan	.11	.05	.01
☐ 122	Ben Oglivie	.20	.08	.02
☐ 123	Fred Stanley	.11	.05	.01
☐ 124	George Mitterwald	.11	.05	.01
☐ 125	Bill Travers	.11	.05	.01
☐ 126	Rod Gilbreath	.11	.05	.01
☐ 127	Ron Fairly	.15	.06	.01
☐ 128	Tommy John	.55	.22	.05
☐ 129	Mike Sadek	.11	.05	.01
☐ 130	Al Oliver	.55	.22	.05
☐ 131	Orlando Ramirez	.11	.05	.01
☐ 132	Chip Lang	.11	.05	.01
☐ 133	Ralph Garr	.15	.06	.01
☐ 134	Padres Team/Mgr.	.40	.08	.01
	John McNamara			
	(checklist back)			
☐ 135	Mark Belanger	.15	.06	.01
☐ 136	Jerry Mumphrey	.35	.14	.03
☐ 137	Jeff Terpko	.11	.05	.01
☐ 138	Bob Stinson	.11	.05	.01
☐ 139	Fred Norman	.11	.05	.01
☐ 140	Mike Schmidt	7.00	2.80	.70
☐ 141	Mark Littell	.11	.05	.01
☐ 142	Steve Dillard	.11	.05	.01
☐ 143	Ed Herrmann	.11	.05	.01
☐ 144	Bruce Sutter	3.00	1.20	.30
☐ 145	Tom Veryzer	.11	.05	.01
☐ 146	Dusty Baker	.25	.10	.02
☐ 147	Jackie Brown	.11	.05	.01
☐ 148	Fran Healy	.11	.05	.01
☐ 149	Mike Cubbage	.11	.05	.01
☐ 150	Tom Seaver	3.00	1.20	.30
☐ 151	Johnny LeMaster	.11	.05	.01
☐ 152	Gaylord Perry	1.25	.50	.12
☐ 153	Ron Jackson	.11	.05	.01
☐ 154	Dave Giusti	.11	.05	.01
☐ 155	Joe Rudi	.15	.06	.01
☐ 156	Pete Mackanin	.11	.05	.01
☐ 157	Ken Brett	.11	.05	.01
☐ 158	Ted Kubiak	.11	.05	.01
☐ 159	Bernie Carbo	.11	.05	.01
☐ 160	Will McEnaney	.11	.05	.01
☐ 161	Garry Templeton	1.25	.50	.12
☐ 162	Mike Cuellar	.15	.06	.01
☐ 163	Dave Hilton	.11	.05	.01
☐ 164	Tug McGraw	.25	.10	.02
☐ 165	Jim Wynn	.15	.06	.01
☐ 166	Bill Campbell	.15	.06	.01
☐ 167	Rich Hebner	.11	.05	.01
☐ 168	Charlie Spikes	.11	.05	.01
☐ 169	Darold Knowles	.11	.05	.01
☐ 170	Thurman Munson	2.75	1.10	.27
☐ 171	Ken Sanders	.11	.05	.01
☐ 172	John Milner	.11	.05	.01
☐ 173	Chuck Scrivener	.11	.05	.01
☐ 174	Nelson Briles	.15	.06	.01
☐ 175	Butch Wynegar	.65	.26	.06
☐ 176	Bob Robertson	.11	.05	.01
☐ 177	Bart Johnson	.11	.05	.01
☐ 178	Bombo Rivera	.11	.05	.01
☐ 179	Paul Hartzell	.11	.05	.01
☐ 180	Dave Lopes	.25	.10	.02
☐ 181	Ken McMullen	.11	.05	.01
☐ 182	Dan Spillner	.11	.05	.01
☐ 183	Cardinals Team/Mgr.	.40	.08	.01
	Vern Rapp			
	(checklist back)			
☐ 184	Bo McLaughlin	.11	.05	.01
☐ 185	Sixto Lezcano	.15	.06	.01
☐ 186	Doug Flynn	.11	.05	.01
☐ 187	Dick Pole	.11	.05	.01
☐ 188	Bob Tolan	.11	.05	.01
☐ 189	Rick Dempsey	.15	.06	.01
☐ 190	Ray Burris	.11	.05	.01
☐ 191	Doug Griffin	.11	.05	.01
☐ 192	Clarence Gaston	.11	.05	.01
☐ 193	Larry Gura	.15	.06	.01
☐ 194	Gary Matthews	.25	.10	.02
☐ 195	Ed Figueroa	.11	.05	.01
☐ 196	Len Randle	.11	.05	.01
☐ 197	Ed Ott	.11	.05	.01
☐ 198	Wilbur Wood	.15	.06	.01
☐ 199	Pepe Frias	.11	.05	.01
☐ 200	Frank Tanana	.20	.08	.02
☐ 201	Ed Kranepool	.15	.06	.01
☐ 202	Tom Johnson	.11	.05	.01
☐ 203	Ed Armbrister	.11	.05	.01
☐ 204	Jeff Newman	.11	.05	.01
☐ 205	Pete Falcone	.11	.05	.01
☐ 206	Boog Powell	.30	.12	.03
☐ 207	Glenn Abbott	.11	.05	.01
☐ 208	Checklist 2	.50	.05	.01

	MINT	VG-E	F-G
☐ 209 Rob Andrews	.11	.05	.01
☐ 210 Fred Lynn	1.50	.60	.15
☐ 211 Giants Team/Mgr.	.40	.08	.01
Joe Altobelli			
(checklist back)			
☐ 212 Jim Mason	.11	.05	.01
☐ 213 Maximino Leon	.11	.05	.01
☐ 214 Darrell Porter	.15	.06	.01
☐ 215 Butch Metzger	.11	.05	.01
☐ 216 Doug DeCinces	.35	.14	.03
☐ 217 Tom Underwood	.11	.05	.01
☐ 218 John Wathan	.25	.10	.02
☐ 219 Joe Coleman	.11	.05	.01
☐ 220 Chris Chambliss	.20	.08	.02
☐ 221 Bob Bailey	.11	.05	.01
☐ 222 Fran Barrios	.11	.05	.01
☐ 223 Earl Williams	.11	.05	.01
☐ 224 Rusty Torres	.11	.05	.01
☐ 225 Bob Apodaca	.11	.05	.01
☐ 226 Leroy Stanton	.11	.05	.01
☐ 227 Joe Sambito	.30	.12	.03
☐ 228 Twins Team/Mgr.	.40	.08	.01
Gene Mauch			
(checklist back)			
☐ 229 Don Kessinger	.15	.06	.01
☐ 230 Vida Blue	.25	.10	.02
☐ 231 RB: George Brett	1.50	.60	.15
Most cons. games			
with 3 or more hits			
☐ 232 RB: Minnie Minoso	.20	.08	.02
Oldest to hit safely			
☐ 233 RB: Jose Morales	.15	.06	.01
Most pinch-hits, season			
☐ 234 RB: Nolan Ryan	1.00	.40	.10
Most seasons 300			
or more strikeouts			
☐ 235 Cecil Cooper	.65	.26	.06
☐ 236 Tom Buskey	.11	.05	.01
☐ 237 Gene Clines	.11	.05	.01
☐ 238 Tippy Martinez	.15	.06	.01
☐ 239 Bill Plummer	.11	.05	.01
☐ 240 Ron LeFlore	.20	.08	.02
☐ 241 Dave Tomlin	.11	.05	.01
☐ 242 Ken Henderson	.11	.05	.01
☐ 243 Ron Reed	.11	.05	.01
☐ 244 John Mayberry	.25	.10	.02
(cartoon mentions			
T206 Wagner)			
☐ 245 Rick Rhoden	.25	.10	.02
☐ 246 Mike Vail	.11	.05	.01
☐ 247 Chris Knapp	.11	.05	.01
☐ 248 Wilbur Howard	.11	.05	.01
☐ 249 Pete Redfern	.11	.05	.01

	MINT	VG-E	F-G
☐ 250 Bill Madlock	.75	.30	.07
☐ 251 Tony Muser	.11	.05	.01
☐ 252 Dale Murray	.11	.05	.01
☐ 253 John Hale	.11	.05	.01
☐ 254 Doyle Alexander	.15	.06	.01
☐ 255 George Scott	.15	.06	.01
☐ 256 Joe Hoerner	.11	.05	.01
☐ 257 Mike Miley	.11	.05	.01
☐ 258 Luis Tiant	.25	.10	.02
☐ 259 Mets Team/Mgr.	.50	.10	.02
Joe Frazier			
(checklist back)			
☐ 260 J.R. Richard	.25	.10	.02
☐ 261 Phil Garner	.15	.06	.01
☐ 262 Al Cowens	.15	.06	.01
☐ 263 Mike Marshall	.15	.06	.01
☐ 264 Tom Hutton	.11	.05	.01
☐ 265 Mark Fidrych	.50	.20	.05
☐ 266 Derrel Thomas	.11	.05	.01
☐ 267 Ray Fosse	.11	.05	.01
☐ 268 Rick Sawyer	.11	.05	.01
☐ 269 Joe Lis	.11	.05	.01
☐ 270 Dave Parker	1.75	.70	.17
☐ 271 Terry Forster	.25	.10	.02
☐ 272 Lee Lacy	.20	.08	.02
☐ 273 Eric Soderholm	.11	.05	.01
☐ 274 Don Stanhouse	.11	.05	.01
☐ 275 Mike Hargrove	.15	.06	.01
☐ 276 AL Champs	.35	.14	.03
Chambliss' homer			
decides it			
☐ 277 NL Champs	.35	.14	.03
Reds sweep Phillies			
☐ 278 Danny Frisella	.11	.05	.01
☐ 279 Joe Wallis	.11	.05	.01
☐ 280 Jim Hunter	1.00	.40	.10
☐ 281 Roy Staiger	.11	.05	.01
☐ 282 Sid Monge	.11	.05	.01
☐ 283 Jerry DaVanon	.11	.05	.01
☐ 284 Mike Norris	.15	.06	.01
☐ 285 Brooks Robinson	1.75	.70	.17
☐ 286 Johnny Grubb	.11	.05	.01
☐ 287 Reds Team/Mgr.	.50	.10	.02
Sparky Anderson			
(checklist back)			
☐ 288 Bob Montgomery	.11	.05	.01
☐ 289 Gene Garber	.15	.06	.01
☐ 290 Amos Otis	.20	.08	.02
☐ 291 Jason Thompson	.60	.24	.06
☐ 292 Rogelio Moret	.11	.05	.01
☐ 293 Jack Brohamer	.11	.05	.01
☐ 294 George Medich	.15	.06	.01
☐ 295 Gary Carter	6.00	2.40	.60

		MINT	VG-E	F-G
☐ 296	Don Hood	.11	.05	.01
☐ 297	Ken Reitz	.11	.05	.01
☐ 298	Charlie Hough	.25	.10	.02
☐ 299	Otto Velez	.11	.05	.01
☐ 300	Jerry Koosman	.25	.10	.02
☐ 301	Toby Harrah	.15	.06	.01
☐ 302	Mike Garman	.11	.05	.01
☐ 303	Gene Tenace	.15	.06	.01
☐ 304	Jim Hughes	.11	.05	.01
☐ 305	Mickey Rivers	.15	.06	.01
☐ 306	Rick Waits	.11	.05	.01
☐ 307	Gary Sutherland	.11	.05	.01
☐ 308	Gene Pentz	.11	.05	.01
☐ 309	Red Sox Team/Mgr.	.40	.08	.01
	Don Zimmer			
	(checklist back)			
☐ 310	Larry Bowa	.35	.14	.03
☐ 311	Vern Ruhle	.11	.05	.01
☐ 312	Rob Belloir	.11	.05	.01
☐ 313	Paul Blair	.15	.06	.01
☐ 314	Steve Mingori	.11	.05	.01
☐ 315	Dave Chalk	.11	.05	.01
☐ 316	Steve Rogers	.20	.08	.02
☐ 317	Kurt Bevacqua	.11	.05	.01
☐ 318	Duffy Dyer	.11	.05	.01
☐ 319	Rich Gossage	.70	.28	.07
☐ 320	Ken Griffey	.25	.10	.02
☐ 321	Dave Goltz	.15	.06	.01
☐ 322	Bill Russell	.15	.06	.01
☐ 323	Larry Lintz	.11	.05	.01
☐ 324	John Curtis	.11	.05	.01
☐ 325	Mike Ivie	.11	.05	.01
☐ 326	Jesse Jefferson	.11	.05	.01
☐ 327	Astros Team/Mgr.	.40	.08	.01
	Bill Virdon			
	(checklist back)			
☐ 328	Tommy Boggs	.11	.05	.01
☐ 329	Ron Hodges	.11	.05	.01
☐ 330	George Hendrick	.25	.10	.02
☐ 331	Jim Colborn	.11	.05	.01
☐ 332	Elliott Maddox	.11	.05	.01
☐ 333	Paul Reuschel	.11	.05	.01
☐ 334	Bill Stein	.11	.05	.01
☐ 335	Bill Robinson	.11	.05	.01
☐ 336	Denny Doyle	.11	.05	.01
☐ 337	Ron Schueler	.11	.05	.01
☐ 338	Dave Duncan	.11	.05	.01
☐ 339	Adrian Devine	.11	.05	.01
☐ 340	Hal McRae	.20	.08	.02
☐ 341	Joe Kerrigan	.11	.05	.01
☐ 342	Jerry Remy	.15	.06	.01
☐ 343	Ed Halicki	.11	.05	.01
☐ 344	Brian Downing	.15	.06	.01
☐ 345	Reggie Smith	.25	.10	.02
☐ 346	Bill Singer	.11	.05	.01
☐ 347	George Foster	.90	.36	.09
☐ 348	Brent Strom	.11	.05	.01
☐ 349	Jim Holt	.11	.05	.01
☐ 350	Larry Dierker	.15	.06	.01
☐ 351	Jim Sundberg	.15	.06	.01
☐ 352	Mike Phillips	.11	.05	.01
☐ 353	Stan Thomas	.11	.05	.01
☐ 354	Pirates Team/Mgr.	.40	.08	.01
	Chuck Tanner			
	(checklist back)			
☐ 355	Lou Brock	1.50	.60	.15
☐ 356	Checklist 3	.50	.05	.01
☐ 357	Tim McCarver	.20	.08	.02
☐ 358	Tom House	.15	.06	.01
☐ 359	Willie Randolph	.35	.14	.03
☐ 360	Rick Monday	.15	.06	.01
☐ 361	Ed Rodriguez	.11	.05	.01
☐ 362	Tommy Davis	.20	.08	.02
☐ 363	Dave Roberts	.11	.05	.01
☐ 364	Vic Correll	.11	.05	.01
☐ 365	Mike Torrez	.15	.06	.01
☐ 366	Ted Sizemore	.11	.05	.01
☐ 367	Dave Hamilton	.11	.05	.01
☐ 368	Mike Jorgensen	.11	.05	.01
☐ 369	Terry Humphrey	.11	.05	.01
☐ 370	John Montefusco	.15	.06	.01
☐ 371	Royals Team/Mgr.	.40	.08	.01
	Whitey Herzog			
	(checklist back)			
☐ 372	Rich Folkers	.11	.05	.01
☐ 373	Bert Campaneris	.20	.08	.02
☐ 374	Kent Tekulve	.20	.08	.02
☐ 375	Larry Hisle	.15	.06	.01
☐ 376	Nino Espinosa	.11	.05	.01
☐ 377	Dave McKay	.11	.05	.01
☐ 378	Jim Umbarger	.11	.05	.01
☐ 379	Larry Cox	.11	.05	.01
☐ 380	Lee May	.20	.08	.02
☐ 381	Bob Forsch	.20	.08	.02
☐ 382	Charlie Moore	.11	.05	.01
☐ 383	Stan Bahnsen	.11	.05	.01
☐ 384	Darrel Chaney	.11	.05	.01
☐ 385	Dave LaRoche	.11	.05	.01
☐ 386	Manny Mota	.15	.06	.01
☐ 387	Yankees Team	.50	.20	.05
☐ 388	Terry Harmon	.11	.05	.01
☐ 389	Ken Kravec	.11	.05	.01
☐ 390	Dave Winfield	2.75	1.10	.27
☐ 391	Dan Warthen	.11	.05	.01
☐ 392	Phil Roof	.11	.05	.01
☐ 393	John Lowenstein	.11	.05	.01

	MINT	VG-E	F-G
☐ 394 Bill Laxton	.11	.05	.01
☐ 395 Manny Trillo	.15	.06	.01
☐ 396 Tom Murphy	.11	.05	.01
☐ 397 Larry Herndon	.45	.18	.04
☐ 398 Tom Burgmeier	.11	.05	.01
☐ 399 Bruce Boisclair	.11	.05	.01
☐ 400 Steve Garvey	3.00	1.20	.30
☐ 401 Mickey Scott	.11	.05	.01
☐ 402 Tommy Helms	.11	.05	.01
☐ 403 Tom Grieve	.15	.06	.01
☐ 404 Eric Rasmussen	.11	.05	.01
☐ 405 Claudell Washington	.20	.08	.02
☐ 406 Tim Johnson	.11	.05	.01
☐ 407 Dave Freisleben	.11	.05	.01
☐ 408 Cesar Tovar	.11	.05	.01
☐ 409 Pete Broberg	.11	.05	.01
☐ 410 Willie Montanez	.11	.05	.01
☐ 411 W.S. Games 1 and 2	.40	.16	.04
Morgan homers opener;			
Bench stars as			
Reds take 2nd game			
☐ 412 W.S. Games 3 and 4	.40	.16	.04
Reds' stop Yankees;			
Bench's two homers			
wrap it up			
☐ 413 World Series Summary	.40	.16	.04
Cincy wins 2nd			
straight series			
☐ 414 Tommy Harper	.15	.06	.01
☐ 415 Jay Johnstone	.15	.06	.01
☐ 416 Chuck Hartenstein	.11	.05	.01
☐ 417 Wayne Garrett	.11	.05	.01
☐ 418 White Sox Team/Mgr.	.50	.10	.02
Bob Lemon			
(checklist back)			
☐ 419 Steve Swisher	.11	.05	.01
☐ 420 Rusty Staub	.25	.10	.02
☐ 421 Doug Rau	.11	.05	.01
☐ 422 Freddie Patek	.11	.05	.01
☐ 423 Gary Lavelle	.15	.06	.01
☐ 424 Steve Brye	.11	.05	.01
☐ 425 Joe Torre	.35	.14	.03
☐ 426 Dick Drago	.11	.05	.01
☐ 427 Dave Rader	.11	.05	.01
☐ 428 Rangers Team/Mgr.	.40	.08	.01
Frank Lucchesi			
(checklist back)			
☐ 429 Ken Boswell	.11	.05	.01
☐ 430 Fergie Jenkins	.40	.16	.04
☐ 431 Dave Collins	.25	.10	.02
(photo actually			
Bobby Jones)			
☐ 432 Buzz Capra	.11	.05	.01
☐ 433 Turn Back Clock 1972	.15	.06	.01
Nate Colbert			
☐ 434 Turn Back Clock 1967	1.50	.60	.15
Yaz Triple Crown			
☐ 435 Turn Back Clock 1962	.40	.16	.04
Wills 104 steals			
☐ 436 Turn Back Clock 1957	.15	.06	.01
Keegan hurls Majors'			
only no-hitter			
☐ 437 Turn Back Clock 1952	.40	.16	.04
Kiner leads NL HR's			
7th straight year			
☐ 438 Marty Perez	.11	.05	.01
☐ 439 Gorman Thomas	.35	.14	.03
☐ 440 Jon Matlack	.15	.06	.01
☐ 441 Larvell Blanks	.11	.05	.01
☐ 442 Braves Team/Mgr.	.40	.08	.01
Dave Bristol			
(checklist back)			
☐ 443 Lamar Johnson	.11	.05	.01
☐ 444 Wayne Twitchell	.11	.05	.01
☐ 445 Ken Singleton	.30	.12	.03
☐ 446 Bill Bonham	.11	.05	.01
☐ 447 Jerry Turner	.11	.05	.01
☐ 448 Ellie Rodriguez	.11	.05	.01
☐ 449 Al Fitzmorris	.11	.05	.01
☐ 450 Pete Rose	7.50	3.00	.75
☐ 451 Checklist 4	.50		
☐ 452 Mike Caldwell	.15	.06	.01
☐ 453 Pedro Garcia	.11	.05	.01
☐ 454 Andy Etchebarren	.11	.05	.01
☐ 455 Rick Wise	.15	.06	.01
☐ 456 Leon Roberts	.11	.05	.01
☐ 457 Steve Luebber	.11	.05	.01
☐ 458 Leo Foster	.11	.05	.01
☐ 459 Steve Foucault	.11	.05	.01
☐ 460 Willie Stargell	1.50	.60	.15
☐ 461 Dick Tidrow	.11	.05	.01
☐ 462 Don Baylor	.55	.22	.05
☐ 463 Jamie Quirk	.11	.05	.01
☐ 464 Randy Moffitt	.11	.05	.01
☐ 465 Rico Carty	.20	.08	.02
☐ 466 Fred Holdsworth	.11	.05	.01
☐ 467 Phillies Team/Mgr.	.40	.08	.01
Danny Ozark			
(checklist back)			
☐ 468 Ramon Hernandez	.11	.05	.01
☐ 469 Pat Kelly	.11	.05	.01
☐ 470 Ted Simmons	.45	.18	.04
☐ 471 Del Unser	.11	.05	.01

		MINT	VG-E	F-G
☐ 472	Rookie Pitchers	.50	.20	.05
	Don Aase			
	Bob McClure			
	Gil Patterson			
	Dave Wehrmeister			
☐ 473	Rookie Outfielders	6.00	2.40	.60
	Andre Dawson			
	Gene Richards			
	John Scott			
	Denny Walling			
☐ 474	Rookie Shortstops	.20	.08	.02
	Bob Bailor			
	Kiko Garcia			
	Craig Reynolds			
	Alex Taveras			
☐ 475	Rookie Pitchers	.45	.18	.04
	Chris Batton			
	Rick Camp			
	Scott McGregor			
	Manny Sarmiento			
☐ 476	Rookie Catchers	48.00	18.00	4.00
	Gary Alexander			
	Rick Cerone			
	Dale Murphy			
	Kevin Pasley			
☐ 477	Rookie Infielders	.20	.08	.02
	Doug Ault			
	Rich Dauer			
	Orlando Gonzalez			
	Phil Mankowski			
☐ 478	Rookie Pitchers	.20	.08	.02
	Jim Gideon			
	Leon Hooten			
	Dave Johnson			
	Mark Lemongello			
☐ 479	Rookie Outfielders	.20	.08	.02
	Brian Asselstine			
	Wayne Gross			
	Sam Mejias			
	Alvis Woods			
☐ 480	Carl Yastrzemski	3.50	1.40	.35
☐ 481	Roger Metzger	.11	.05	.01
☐ 482	Tony Solaita	.11	.05	.01
☐ 483	Richie Zisk	.15	.06	.01
☐ 484	Burt Hooton	.15	.06	.01
☐ 485	Roy White	.15	.06	.01
☐ 486	Ed Bane	.11	.05	.01
☐ 487	Rookie Pitchers	.20	.08	.02
	Larry Anderson			
	Ed Glynn			
	Joe Henderson			
	Greg Terlecky			

		MINT	VG-E	F-G
☐ 488	Rookie Outfielders	5.00	2.00	.50
	Jack Clark			
	Ruppert Jones			
	Lee Mazzilli			
	Dan Thomas			
☐ 489	Rookie Pitchers	.60	.24	.06
	Len Barker			
	Randy Lerch			
	Greg Minton			
	Mike Overy			
☐ 490	Rookie Shortstops	.30	.12	.03
	Billy Almon			
	Mickey Klutts			
	Tommy McMillan			
	Mark Wagner			
☐ 491	Rookie Pitchers	.30	.12	.03
	Mike Dupree			
	Denny Martinez			
	Craig Mitchell			
	Bob Sykes			
☐ 492	Rookie Outfielders	2.50	1.00	.25
	Tony Armas			
	Steve Kemp			
	Carlos Lopez			
	Gary Woods			
☐ 493	Rookie Pitchers	1.25	.50	.12
	Mike Krukow			
	Jim Otten			
	Gary Wheelock			
	Mike Willis			
☐ 494	Rookie Infielders	.50	.20	.05
	Juan Bernhardt			
	Mike Champion			
	Jim Gantner			
	Bump Wills			
☐ 495	Al Hrabosky	.15	.06	.01
☐ 496	Gary Thomasson	.11	.05	.01
☐ 497	Clay Carroll	.11	.05	.01
☐ 498	Sal Bando	.20	.08	.02
☐ 499	Pablo Torrealba	.11	.05	.01
☐ 500	Dave Kingman	.50	.20	.05
☐ 501	Jim Bibby	.15	.06	.01
☐ 502	Randy Hundley	.11	.05	.01
☐ 503	Bill Lee	.15	.06	.01
☐ 504	Dodgers Team/Mgr.	.50	.10	.02
	Tom Lasorda			
	(checklist back)			
☐ 505	Oscar Gamble	.20	.08	.02
☐ 506	Steve Grilli	.11	.05	.01
☐ 507	Mike Hegan	.11	.05	.01
☐ 508	Dave Pagan	.11	.05	.01
☐ 509	Cookie Rojas	.11	.05	.01
☐ 510	John Candelaria	.25	.10	.02

	MINT	VG-E	F-G
☐ 511 Bill Fahey	.11	.05	.01
☐ 512 Jack Billingham	.11	.05	.01
☐ 513 Jerry Terrell	.11	.05	.01
☐ 514 Cliff Johnson	.11	.05	.01
☐ 515 Chris Speier	.11	.05	.01
☐ 516 Bake McBride	.15	.06	.01
☐ 517 Pete Vuckovich	.50	.20	.05
☐ 518 Cubs Team/Mgr.	.40	.08	.01
Herman Franks			
(checklist back)			
☐ 519 Don Kirkwood	.11	.05	.01
☐ 520 Garry Maddox	.15	.06	.01
☐ 521 Bob Grich	.20	.08	.02
☐ 522 Enzo Hernandez	.11	.05	.01
☐ 523 Rollie Fingers	.60	.24	.06
☐ 524 Rowland Office	.11	.05	.01
☐ 525 Dennis Eckersley	.20	.08	.02
☐ 526 Larry Parrish	.25	.10	.02
☐ 527 Dan Meyer	.11	.05	.01
☐ 528 Bill Castro	.11	.05	.01
☐ 529 Jim Essian	.11	.05	.01
☐ 530 Rick Reuschel	.20	.08	.02
☐ 531 Lyman Bostock	.25	.10	.02
☐ 532 Jim Willoughby	.11	.05	.01
☐ 533 Mickey Stanley	.11	.05	.01
☐ 534 Paul Splittorff	.15	.06	.01
☐ 535 Cesar Geronimo	.11	.05	.01
☐ 536 Vic Albury	.11	.05	.01
☐ 537 Dave Roberts	.11	.05	.01
☐ 538 Frank Taveras	.11	.05	.01
☐ 539 Mike Wallace	.11	.05	.01
☐ 540 Bob Watson	.15	.06	.01
☐ 541 John Denny	.25	.10	.02
☐ 542 Frank Duffy	.11	.05	.01
☐ 543 Ron Blomberg	.11	.05	.01
☐ 544 Gary Ross	.11	.05	.01
☐ 545 Bob Boone	.20	.08	.02
☐ 546 Orioles Team/Mgr.	.50	.10	.02
Earl Weaver			
(checklist back)			
☐ 547 Willie McCovey	1.50	.60	.15
☐ 548 Joel Youngblood	.11	.05	.01
☐ 549 Jerry Royster	.11	.05	.01
☐ 550 Randy Jones	.15	.06	.01
☐ 551 Bill North	.11	.05	.01
☐ 552 Pepe Mangual	.11	.05	.01
☐ 553 Jack Heidemann	.11	.05	.01
☐ 554 Bruce Kimm	.11	.05	.01
☐ 555 Dan Ford	.15	.06	.01
☐ 556 Doug Bird	.11	.05	.01
☐ 557 Jerry White	.11	.05	.01
☐ 558 Elias Sosa	.11	.05	.01
☐ 559 Alan Bannister	.11	.05	.01

	MINT	VG-E	F-G
☐ 560 Dave Concepcion	.35	.14	.03
☐ 561 Pete LaCock	.11	.05	.01
☐ 562 Checklist 5	.50	.05	.01
☐ 563 Bruce Kison	.11	.05	.01
☐ 564 Alan Ashby	.15	.06	.01
☐ 565 Mickey Lolich	.25	.10	.02
☐ 566 Rick Miller	.11	.05	.01
☐ 567 Enos Cabell	.11	.05	.01
☐ 568 Carlos May	.11	.05	.01
☐ 569 Jim Lonborg	.15	.06	.01
☐ 570 Bobby Bonds	.25	.10	.02
☐ 571 Darrell Evans	.30	.12	.03
☐ 572 Ross Grimsley	.11	.05	.01
☐ 573 Joe Ferguson	.15	.06	.01
☐ 574 Aurelio Rodriguez	.11	.05	.01
☐ 575 Dick Ruthven	.11	.05	.01
☐ 576 Fred Kendall	.11	.05	.01
☐ 577 Jerry Augustine	.11	.05	.01
☐ 578 Bob Randall	.11	.05	.01
☐ 579 Don Carrithers	.11	.05	.01
☐ 580 George Brett	6.00	2.40	.60
☐ 581 Pedro Borbon	.11	.05	.01
☐ 582 Ed Kirkpatrick	.11	.05	.01
☐ 583 Paul Lindblad	.11	.05	.01
☐ 584 Ed Goodson	.11	.05	.01
☐ 585 Rick Burleson	.15	.06	.01
☐ 586 Steve Renko	.11	.05	.01
☐ 587 Rick Baldwin	.11	.05	.01
☐ 588 Dave Moates	.11	.05	.01
☐ 589 Mike Cosgrove	.11	.05	.01
☐ 590 Buddy Bell	.35	.14	.03
☐ 591 Chris Arnold	.11	.05	.01
☐ 592 Dan Briggs	.11	.05	.01
☐ 593 Dennis Blair	.11	.05	.01
☐ 594 Biff Pocoroba	.11	.05	.01
☐ 595 John Hiller	.15	.06	.01
☐ 596 Jerry Martin	.11	.05	.01
☐ 597 Mariners Leaders	.30	.06	.01
Darrell Johnson MGR			
Don Bryant CO			
Jim Busby CO			
Vada Pinson CO			
Wes Stock CO			
(checklist back)			
☐ 598 Sparky Lyle	.35	.14	.03
☐ 599 Mike Tyson	.11	.05	.01
☐ 600 Jim Palmer	1.75	.70	.17
☐ 601 Mike Lum	.11	.05	.01
☐ 602 Andy Hassler	.11	.05	.01
☐ 603 Willie Davis	.15	.06	.01
☐ 604 Jim Slaton	.11	.05	.01
☐ 605 Felix Millan	.11	.05	.01
☐ 606 Steve Braun	.11	.05	.01

	MINT	VG-E	F-G
☐ 607 Larry Demery	.11	.05	.01
☐ 608 Roy Howell	.11	.05	.01
☐ 609 Jim Barr	.11	.05	.01
☐ 610 Jose Cardenal	.11	.05	.01
☐ 611 Dave Lemanczyk	.11	.05	.01
☐ 612 Barry Foote	.11	.05	.01
☐ 613 Reggie Cleveland	.11	.05	.01
☐ 614 Greg Gross	.11	.05	.01
☐ 615 Phil Niekro	1.00	.40	.10
☐ 616 Tommy Sandt	.11	.05	.01
☐ 617 Bobby Darwin	.11	.05	.01
☐ 618 Pat Dobson	.15	.06	.01
☐ 619 Johnny Oates	.11	.05	.01
☐ 620 Don Sutton	1.00	.40	.10
☐ 621 Tigers Team/Mgr.	.50	.10	.02
Ralph Houk			
(checklist back)			
☐ 622 Jim Wohlford	.11	.05	.01
☐ 623 Jack Kucek	.11	.05	.01
☐ 624 Hector Cruz	.11	.05	.01
☐ 625 Ken Holtzman	.15	.06	.01
☐ 626 Al Bumbry	.11	.05	.01
☐ 627 Bob Myrick	.11	.05	.01
☐ 628 Mario Guerrero	.11	.05	.01
☐ 629 Bob Valentine	.25	.10	.02
☐ 630 Bert Blyleven	.40	.16	.04
☐ 631 Big League Brothers	1.25	.50	.12
George Brett			
Ken Brett			
☐ 632 Big League Brothers	.25	.10	.02
Bob Forsch			
Ken Forsch			
☐ 633 Big League Brothers	.25	.10	.02
Lee May			
Carlos May			
☐ 634 Big League Brothers	.25	.10	.02
Paul Reuschel			
Rick Reuschel			
(photos switched)			
☐ 635 Robin Yount	3.50	1.40	.35
☐ 636 Santo Alcala	.11	.05	.01
☐ 637 Alex Johnson	.15	.06	.01
☐ 638 Jim Kaat	.40	.16	.04
☐ 639 Jerry Morales	.11	.05	.01
☐ 640 Carlton Fisk	.65	.26	.06
☐ 641 Dan Larson	.11	.05	.01
☐ 642 Willie Crawford	.11	.05	.01
☐ 643 Mike Pazik	.11	.05	.01
☐ 644 Matt Alexander	.11	.05	.01
☐ 645 Jerry Reuss	.20	.08	.02
☐ 646 Andres Mora	.11	.05	.01

	MINT	VG-E	F-G
☐ 647 Expos Team/Mgr.	.40	.08	.01
Dick Williams			
(checklist back)			
☐ 648 Jim Spencer	.11	.05	.01
☐ 649 Dave Cash	.11	.05	.01
☐ 650 Nolan Ryan	2.75	1.10	.27
☐ 651 Von Joshua	.11	.05	.01
☐ 652 Tom Walker	.11	.05	.01
☐ 653 Diego Segui	.11	.05	.01
☐ 654 Ron Pruitt	.11	.05	.01
☐ 655 Tony Perez	.45	.18	.04
☐ 656 Ron Guidry	2.25	.90	.22
☐ 657 Mick Kelleher	.11	.05	.01
☐ 658 Marty Pattin	.11	.05	.01
☐ 659 Merv Rettenmund	.11	.05	.01
☐ 660 Willie Horton	.20	.08	.02

1978 Topps

The cards in this 726-card set measure 2½" by 3½". The 1978 Topps set experienced an increase in number of cards from the previous five regular issue sets of 660. Cards 1 through 7 feature Record Breakers (RB) of the 1977 season. Other subsets within this set include League Leaders (201-208), Post-season cards (411-413), and Rookie Prospects (701-711). While no scarcities exist, 66 of the cards are more abundant in supply as they were "double printed." These 66 double printed cards are noted in the checklist by DP. Team cards again feature a checklist of that team's players in the set on the back.

	MINT	VG-E	F-G
Complete Set	140.00	55.00	15.00
Common Player (1-726)	.09	.04	.01
Common DP's (1-726)	.04	.02	.00

		MINT	VG-E	F-G
☐ 1	RB: Lou Brock .... Most steals, lifetime	1.25	.50	.12
☐ 2	RB: Sparky Lyle .... Most games pure relief, lifetime	.15	.06	.01
☐ 3	RB: Willie McCovey .. Most times 2 HR's inning, lifetime	.50	.20	.05
☐ 4	RB: Brooks Robinson .. Most consecutive seasons with one club	.75	.30	.07
☐ 5	RB: Pete Rose .... Most hits switch hitter, lifetime	1.75	.70	.17
☐ 6	RB: Nolan Ryan .... Most games with 10 or more strikeouts, lifetime	.90	.36	.09
☐ 7	RB: Reggie Jackson ... Most homers one World Series	1.25	.50	.12
☐ 8	Mike Sadek	.09	.04	.01
☐ 9	Doug DeCinces	.25	.10	.02
☐ 10	Phil Niekro	.85	.34	.08
☐ 11	Rick Manning	.09	.04	.01
☐ 12	Don Aase	.15	.06	.01
☐ 13	Art Howe	.09	.04	.01
☐ 14	Lerrin LaGrow	.09	.04	.01
☐ 15	Tony Perez DP	.15	.06	.01
☐ 16	Roy White	.12	.05	.01
☐ 17	Mike Krukow	.25	.10	.02
☐ 18	Bob Grich	.15	.06	.01
☐ 19	Darrell Porter	.15	.06	.01
☐ 20	Pete Rose DP	3.25	1.30	.32
☐ 21	Steve Kemp	.25	.10	.02
☐ 22	Charlie Hough	.15	.06	.01
☐ 23	Bump Wills	.09	.04	.01
☐ 24	Don Money DP	.04	.02	.00
☐ 25	Jon Matlack	.12	.05	.01
☐ 26	Rich Hebner	.09	.04	.01
☐ 27	Geoff Zahn	.09	.04	.01
☐ 28	Ed Ott	.09	.04	.01
☐ 29	Bob Lacey	.09	.04	.01
☐ 30	George Hendrick	.15	.06	.01
☐ 31	Glenn Abbott	.09	.04	.01
☐ 32	Garry Templeton	.35	.14	.03
☐ 33	Dave Lemanczyk	.09	.04	.01
☐ 34	Willie McCovey	1.50	.60	.15
☐ 35	Sparky Lyle	.20	.08	.02
☐ 36	Eddie Murray	27.00	11.00	2.70
☐ 37	Rick Waits	.09	.04	.01
☐ 38	Willie Montanez	.09	.04	.01
☐ 39	Floyd Bannister	.75	.30	.07

		MINT	VG-E	F-G
☐ 40	Carl Yastrzemski	2.25	.90	.22
☐ 41	Burt Hooton	.09	.04	.01
☐ 42	Jorge Orta	.09	.04	.01
☐ 43	Bill Atkinson	.09	.04	.01
☐ 44	Toby Harrah	.12	.05	.01
☐ 45	Mark Fidrych	.20	.08	.02
☐ 46	Al Cowens	.12	.05	.01
☐ 47	Jack Billingham	.09	.04	.01
☐ 48	Don Baylor	.45	.18	.04
☐ 49	Ed Kranepool	.12	.05	.01
☐ 50	Rick Reuschel	.15	.06	.01
☐ 51	Charlie Moore DP	.04	.02	.00
☐ 52	Jim Lonborg	.12	.05	.01
☐ 53	Phil Garner DP	.04	.02	.00
☐ 54	Tom Johnson	.09	.04	.01
☐ 55	Mitchell Page	.12	.05	.01
☐ 56	Randy Jones	.12	.05	.01
☐ 57	Dan Meyer	.09	.04	.01
☐ 58	Bob Forsch	.15	.06	.01
☐ 59	Otto Velez	.09	.04	.01
☐ 60	Thurman Munson	1.75	.70	.17
☐ 61	Larvell Blanks	.09	.04	.01
☐ 62	Jim Barr	.09	.04	.01
☐ 63	Don Zimmer	.09	.04	.01
☐ 64	Gene Pentz	.09	.04	.01
☐ 65	Ken Singleton	.20	.08	.02
☐ 66	White Sox Team ...... (checklist back)	.35	.07	.01
☐ 67	Claudell Washington ...	.15	.06	.01
☐ 68	Steve Foucault DP	.04	.02	.00
☐ 69	Mike Vail	.09	.04	.01
☐ 70	Rich Gossage	.60	.24	.06
☐ 71	Terry Humphrey	.09	.04	.01
☐ 72	Andre Dawson	1.00	.40	.10
☐ 73	Andy Hassler	.09	.04	.01
☐ 74	Checklist 1	.30	.03	.00
☐ 75	Dick Ruthven	.09	.04	.01
☐ 76	Steve Ontiveros	.09	.04	.01
☐ 77	Ed Kirkpatrick	.09	.04	.01
☐ 78	Pablo Torrealba	.09	.04	.01
☐ 79	Darrell Johnson DP ...	.04	.02	.00
☐ 80	Ken Griffey	.20	.08	.02
☐ 81	Pete Redfern	.09	.04	.01
☐ 82	Giants Team .... (checklist back)	.35	.07	.01
☐ 83	Bob Montgomery	.09	.04	.01
☐ 84	Kent Tekulve	.15	.06	.01
☐ 85	Ron Fairly	.12	.05	.01
☐ 86	Dave Tomlin	.09	.04	.01
☐ 87	John Lowenstein	.09	.04	.01
☐ 88	Mike Phillips	.09	.04	.01
☐ 89	Ken Clay	.09	.04	.01
☐ 90	Larry Bowa	.25	.10	.02

		MINT	VG-E	F-G
☐ 91	Oscar Zamora	.09	.04	.01
☐ 92	Adrian Devine	.09	.04	.01
☐ 93	Bobby Cox DP	.04	.02	.00
☐ 94	Chuck Scrivener	.09	.04	.01
☐ 95	Jamie Quirk	.09	.04	.01
☐ 96	Orioles Team	.35	.07	.01
	(checklist back)			
☐ 97	Stan Bahnsen	.09	.04	.01
☐ 98	Jim Essian	.09	.04	.01
☐ 99	Willie Hernandez	1.25	.50	.12
☐ 100	George Brett	3.50	1.40	.35
☐ 101	Sid Monge	.09	.04	.01
☐ 102	Matt Alexander	.09	.04	.01
☐ 103	Tom Murphy	.09	.04	.01
☐ 104	Lee Lacy	.15	.06	.01
☐ 105	Reggie Cleveland	.09	.04	.01
☐ 106	Bill Plummer	.09	.04	.01
☐ 107	Ed Halicki	.09	.04	.01
☐ 108	Von Joshua	.09	.04	.01
☐ 109	Joe Torre	.20	.08	.02
☐ 110	Richie Zisk	.12	.05	.01
☐ 111	Mike Tyson	.09	.04	.01
☐ 112	Astros Team	.35	.07	.01
	(checklist back)			
☐ 113	Don Carrithers	.09	.04	.01
☐ 114	Paul Blair	.12	.05	.01
☐ 115	Gary Nolan	.09	.04	.01
☐ 116	Tucker Ashford	.09	.04	.01
☐ 117	John Montague	.09	.04	.01
☐ 118	Terry Harmon	.09	.04	.01
☐ 119	Denny Martinez	.12	.05	.01
☐ 120	Gary Carter	3.00	1.20	.30
☐ 121	Alvis Woods	.09	.04	.01
☐ 122	Dennis Eckersley	.12	.05	.01
☐ 123	Manny Trillo	.12	.05	.01
☐ 124	Dave Rozema	.12	.05	.01
☐ 125	George Scott	.12	.05	.01
☐ 126	Paul Moskau	.09	.04	.01
☐ 127	Chet Lemon	.15	.06	.01
☐ 128	Bill Russell	.12	.05	.01
☐ 129	Jim Colborn	.09	.04	.01
☐ 130	Jeff Burroughs	.12	.05	.01
☐ 131	Bert Blyleven	.30	.12	.03
☐ 132	Enos Cabell	.09	.04	.01
☐ 133	Jerry Augustine	.09	.04	.01
☐ 134	Steve Henderson	.12	.05	.01
☐ 135	Ron Guidry DP	.70	.28	.07
☐ 136	Ted Sizemore	.09	.04	.01
☐ 137	Craig Kusick	.09	.04	.01
☐ 138	Larry Demery	.09	.04	.01
☐ 139	Wayne Gross	.09	.04	.01
☐ 140	Rollie Fingers	.50	.20	.05
☐ 141	Ruppert Jones	.15	.06	.01
☐ 142	John Montefusco	.12	.05	.01
☐ 143	Keith Hernandez	2.00	.80	.20
☐ 144	Jesse Jefferson	.09	.04	.01
☐ 145	Rick Monday	.12	.05	.01
☐ 146	Doyle Alexander	.12	.05	.01
☐ 147	Lee Mazzilli	.15	.06	.01
☐ 148	Andre Thornton	.20	.08	.02
☐ 149	Dale Murray	.09	.04	.01
☐ 150	Bobby Bonds	.20	.08	.02
☐ 151	Milt Wilcox	.12	.05	.01
☐ 152	Ivan DeJesus	.09	.04	.01
☐ 153	Steve Stone	.12	.05	.01
☐ 154	Cecil Cooper DP	.20	.08	.02
☐ 155	Butch Hobson	.09	.04	.01
☐ 156	Andy Messersmith	.15	.06	.00
☐ 157	Pete LaCock DP	.04	.02	.00
☐ 158	Joaquin Andujar	.30	.12	.03
☐ 159	Lou Piniella	.25	.10	.02
☐ 160	Jim Palmer	1.50	.60	.15
☐ 161	Bob Boone	.15	.06	.01
☐ 162	Paul Thormodsgard	.09	.04	.01
☐ 163	Bill North	.09	.04	.01
☐ 164	Bob Owchinko	.09	.04	.01
☐ 165	Rennie Stennett	.09	.04	.01
☐ 166	Carlos Lopez	.09	.04	.01
☐ 167	Tim Foli	.09	.04	.01
☐ 168	Reggie Smith	.25	.10	.02
☐ 169	Jerry Johnson	.09	.04	.01
☐ 170	Lou Brock	1.50	.60	.15
☐ 171	Pat Zachry	.09	.04	.01
☐ 172	Mike Hargrove	.12	.05	.01
☐ 173	Robin Yount	2.25	.90	.22
☐ 174	Wayne Garland	.09	.04	.01
☐ 175	Jerry Morales	.09	.04	.01
☐ 176	Milt May	.09	.04	.01
☐ 177	Gene Garber DP	.04	.02	.00
☐ 178	Dave Chalk	.09	.04	.01
☐ 179	Dick Tidrow	.09	.04	.01
☐ 180	Dave Concepcion	.25	.10	.02
☐ 181	Ken Forsch	.12	.05	.01
☐ 182	Jim Spencer	.09	.04	.01
☐ 183	Doug Bird	.09	.04	.01
☐ 184	Checklist 2	.30	.03	.00
☐ 185	Ellis Valentine	.12	.05	.01
☐ 186	Bob Stanley DP	.25	.10	.02
☐ 187	Jerry Royster DP	.04	.02	.00
☐ 188	Al Bumbry	.09	.04	.01
☐ 189	Tom Lasorda MGR	.15	.06	.01
☐ 190	John Candelaria	.18	.08	.01
☐ 191	Rodney Scott	.09	.04	.01
☐ 192	Padres Team	.35	.07	.01
	(checklist back)			
☐ 193	Rich Chiles	.09	.04	.01

		MINT	VG-E	F-G
☐ 194	Derrel Thomas	.09	.04	.01
☐ 195	Larry Dierker	.12	.05	.01
☐ 196	Bob Bailor	.09	.04	.01
☐ 197	Nino Espinosa	.09	.04	.01
☐ 198	Ron Pruitt	.09	.04	.01
☐ 199	Craig Reynolds	.09	.04	.01
☐ 200	Reggie Jackson	2.50	1.00	.25
☐ 201	Batting Leaders	.50	.20	.05
	Dave Parker			
	Rod Carew			
☐ 202	Home Run Leaders DP	.12	.05	.01
	George Foster			
	Jim Rice			
☐ 203	RBI Leaders	.20	.08	.02
	George Foster			
	Larry Hisle			
☐ 204	Steals Leaders DP	.09	.04	.01
	Frank Taveras			
	Freddie Patek			
☐ 205	Victory Leaders	.45	.18	.04
	Steve Carlton			
	Dave Goltz			
	Dennis Leonard			
	Jim Palmer			
☐ 206	Strikeout Leaders DP	.12	.05	.01
	Phil Niekro			
	Nolan Ryan			
☐ 207	ERA Leaders DP	.09	.04	.01
	John Candelaria			
	Frank Tanana			
☐ 208	Top Firemen	.18	.08	.01
	Rollie Fingers			
	Bill Campbell			
☐ 209	Dock Ellis	.09	.04	.01
☐ 210	Jose Cardenal	.09	.04	.01
☐ 211	Earl Weaver MGR DP	.09	.04	.01
☐ 212	Mike Caldwell	.12	.05	.01
☐ 213	Alan Bannister	.09	.04	.01
☐ 214	Angels Team	.35	.07	.01
	(checklist back)			
☐ 215	Darrell Evans	.25	.10	.02
☐ 216	Mike Paxton	.09	.04	.01
☐ 217	Rod Gilbreath	.09	.04	.01
☐ 218	Marty Pattin	.09	.04	.01
☐ 219	Mike Cubbage	.09	.04	.01
☐ 220	Pedro Borbon	.09	.04	.01
☐ 221	Chris Speier	.09	.04	.01
☐ 222	Jerry Martin	.09	.04	.01
☐ 223	Bruce Kison	.09	.04	.01
☐ 224	Jerry Tabb	.09	.04	.01
☐ 225	Don Gullett DP	.04	.02	.00
☐ 226	Joe Ferguson	.12	.05	.01
☐ 227	Al Fitzmorris	.09	.04	.01

		MINT	VG-E	F-G
☐ 228	Manny Mota DP	.09	.04	.01
☐ 229	Leo Foster	.09	.04	.01
☐ 230	Al Hrabosky	.12	.05	.01
☐ 231	Wayne Nordhagen	.09	.04	.01
☐ 232	Mickey Stanley	.09	.04	.01
☐ 233	Dick Pole	.09	.04	.01
☐ 234	Herman Franks MGR	.09	.04	.01
☐ 235	Tim McCarver	.15	.06	.01
☐ 236	Terry Whitfield	.09	.04	.01
☐ 237	Rich Dauer	.09	.04	.01
☐ 238	Juan Beniquez	.12	.05	.01
☐ 239	Dyar Miller	.09	.04	.01
☐ 240	Gene Tenace	.09	.04	.01
☐ 241	Pete Vuckovich	.18	.08	.01
☐ 242	Barry Bonnell DP	.09	.04	.01
☐ 243	Bob McClure	.09	.04	.01
☐ 244	Expos Team DP	.15	.03	.00
	(checklist back)			
☐ 245	Rick Burleson	.15	.06	.01
☐ 246	Dan Driessen	.12	.05	.01
☐ 247	Larry Christenson	.09	.04	.01
☐ 248	Frank White DP	.09	.04	.01
☐ 249	Dave Goltz DP	.04	.02	.00
☐ 250	Graig Nettles DP	.18	.08	.01
☐ 251	Don Kirkwood	.09	.04	.01
☐ 252	Steve Swisher DP	.04	.02	.00
☐ 253	Jim Kern	.09	.04	.01
☐ 254	Dave Collins	.15	.06	.01
☐ 255	Jerry Reuss	.18	.08	.01
☐ 256	Joe Altobelli MGR	.09	.04	.01
☐ 257	Hector Cruz	.09	.04	.01
☐ 258	John Hiller	.12	.05	.01
☐ 259	Dodgers Team	.40	.08	.01
	(checklist back)			
☐ 260	Bert Campaneris	.15	.06	.01
☐ 261	Tim Hosley	.09	.04	.01
☐ 262	Rudy May	.09	.04	.01
☐ 263	Danny Walton	.09	.04	.01
☐ 264	Jamie Easterly	.09	.04	.01
☐ 265	Sal Bando DP	.09	.04	.01
☐ 266	Bob Shirley	.09	.04	.01
☐ 267	Doug Ault	.09	.04	.01
☐ 268	Gil Flores	.09	.04	.01
☐ 269	Wayne Twitchell	.09	.04	.01
☐ 270	Carlton Fisk	.60	.24	.06
☐ 271	Randy Lerch DP	.04	.02	.00
☐ 272	Royle Stillman	.09	.04	.01
☐ 273	Fred Norman	.09	.04	.01
☐ 274	Freddie Patek	.09	.04	.01
☐ 275	Dan Ford	.12	.05	.01
☐ 276	Bill Bonham DP	.04	.02	.00
☐ 277	Bruce Boisclair	.09	.04	.01
☐ 278	Enrique Romo	.09	.04	.01

		MINT	VG-E	F-G
☐ 279	Bill Virdon MGR	.12	.05	.01
☐ 280	Buddy Bell	.25	.10	.02
☐ 281	Eric Rasmussen DP	.04	.02	.00
☐ 282	Yankees Team	.50	.10	.02
	(checklist back)			
☐ 283	Omar Moreno	.12	.05	.01
☐ 284	Randy Moffitt	.09	.04	.01
☐ 285	Steve Yeager DP	.04	.02	.00
☐ 286	Ben Oglivie	.15	.06	.01
☐ 287	Kiko Garcia	.09	.04	.01
☐ 288	Dave Hamilton	.09	.04	.01
☐ 289	Checklist 3	.30	.03	.00
☐ 290	Willie Horton	.12	.05	.01
☐ 291	Gary Ross	.09	.04	.01
☐ 292	Gene Richards	.09	.04	.01
☐ 293	Mike Willis	.09	.04	.01
☐ 294	Larry Parrish	.20	.08	.02
☐ 295	Bill Lee	.12	.05	.01
☐ 296	Biff Pocoroba	.09	.04	.01
☐ 297	Warren Brusstar DP	.04	.02	.00
☐ 298	Tony Armas	.40	.16	.04
☐ 299	Whitey Herzog MGR	.12	.05	.01
☐ 300	Joe Morgan	1.00	.40	.10
☐ 301	Buddy Schultz	.09	.04	.01
☐ 302	Cubs Team	.35	.07	.01
	(checklist back)			
☐ 303	Sam Hinds	.09	.04	.01
☐ 304	John Milner	.09	.04	.01
☐ 305	Rico Carty	.15	.06	.01
☐ 306	Joe Niekro	.20	.08	.02
☐ 307	Glenn Borgmann	.09	.04	.01
☐ 308	Jim Rooker	.09	.04	.01
☐ 309	Cliff Johnson	.09	.04	.01
☐ 310	Don Sutton	.85	.34	.08
☐ 311	Jose Baez DP	.04	.02	.00
☐ 312	Greg Minton	.18	.08	.01
☐ 313	Andy Etchebarren	.09	.04	.01
☐ 314	Paul Lindblad	.09	.04	.01
☐ 315	Mark Belanger	.15	.06	.01
☐ 316	Henry Cruz DP	.04	.02	.00
☐ 317	Dave Johnson	.20	.08	.02
☐ 318	Tom Griffin	.09	.04	.01
☐ 319	Alan Ashby	.09	.04	.01
☐ 320	Fred Lynn	.90	.36	.09
☐ 321	Santo Alcala	.09	.04	.01
☐ 322	Tom Paciorek	.09	.04	.01
☐ 323	Jim Fregosi DP	.09	.04	.01
☐ 324	Vern Rapp MGR	.09	.04	.01
☐ 325	Bruce Sutter	.80	.32	.08
☐ 326	Mike Lum DP	.04	.02	.00
☐ 327	Rick Langford DP	.04	.02	.00

		MINT	VG-E	F-G
☐ 328	Milwaukee Brewers	.35	.07	.01
	Team Card			
	(checklist back)			
☐ 329	John Verhoeven	.09	.04	.01
☐ 330	Bob Watson	.12	.05	.01
☐ 331	Mark Littell	.09	.04	.01
☐ 332	Duane Kuiper	.09	.04	.01
☐ 333	Jim Todd	.09	.04	.01
☐ 334	John Stearns	.09	.04	.01
☐ 335	Bucky Dent	.18	.08	.01
☐ 336	Steve Busby	.12	.05	.01
☐ 337	Tom Grieve	.12	.05	.01
☐ 338	Dave Heaverlo	.09	.04	.01
☐ 339	Mario Guerrero	.09	.04	.01
☐ 340	Bake McBride	.12	.05	.01
☐ 341	Mike Flanagan	.18	.08	.01
☐ 342	Aurelio Rodriguez	.09	.04	.01
☐ 343	John Wathan DP	.04	.02	.00
☐ 344	Sam Ewing	.09	.04	.01
☐ 345	Luis Tiant	.18	.08	.01
☐ 346	Larry Biittner	.09	.04	.01
☐ 347	Terry Forster	.18	.08	.01
☐ 348	Del Unser	.09	.04	.01
☐ 349	Rick Camp DP	.09	.04	.01
☐ 350	Steve Garvey	2.50	1.00	.25
☐ 351	Jeff Torborg	.09	.04	.01
☐ 352	Tony Scott	.09	.04	.01
☐ 353	Doug Bair	.12	.05	.01
☐ 354	Cesar Geronimo	.09	.04	.01
☐ 355	Bill Travers	.09	.04	.01
☐ 356	Mets Team	.40	.08	.01
	(checklist back)			
☐ 357	Tom Poquette	.09	.04	.01
☐ 358	Mark Lemongello	.09	.04	.01
☐ 359	Marc Hill	.09	.04	.01
☐ 360	Mike Schmidt	4.00	1.60	.40
☐ 361	Chris Knapp	.09	.04	.01
☐ 362	Dave May	.09	.04	.01
☐ 363	Bob Randall	.09	.04	.01
☐ 364	Jerry Turner	.09	.04	.01
☐ 365	Ed Figueroa	.09	.04	.01
☐ 366	Larry Milbourne DP	.04	.02	.00
☐ 367	Rick Dempsey	.12	.05	.01
☐ 368	Balor Moore	.09	.04	.01
☐ 369	Tim Nordbrook	.09	.04	.01
☐ 370	Rusty Staub	.20	.08	.02
☐ 371	Ray Burris	.09	.04	.01
☐ 372	Brian Asselstine	.09	.04	.01
☐ 373	Jim Willoughby	.09	.04	.01
☐ 374	Jose Morales	.09	.04	.01
☐ 375	Tommy John	.45	.18	.04
☐ 376	Jim Wohlford	.09	.04	.01
☐ 377	Manny Sarmiento	.09	.04	.01

		MINT	VG-E	F-G
☐ 378	Bobby Winkles MGR	.09	.04	.01
☐ 379	Skip Lockwood	.09	.04	.01
☐ 380	Ted Simmons	.35	.14	.03
☐ 381	Phillies Team	.35	.07	.01
	(checklist back)			
☐ 382	Joe Lahoud	.09	.04	.01
☐ 383	Mario Mendoza	.09	.04	.01
☐ 384	Jack Clark	.90	.36	.09
☐ 385	Tito Fuentes	.09	.04	.01
☐ 386	Bob Gorinski	.09	.04	.01
☐ 387	Ken Holtzman	.12	.05	.01
☐ 388	Bill Fahey DP	.04	.02	.00
☐ 389	Julio Gonzalez	.09	.04	.01
☐ 390	Oscar Gamble	.12	.05	.01
☐ 391	Larry Haney	.09	.04	.01
☐ 392	Billy Almon	.12	.05	.01
☐ 393	Tippy Martinez	.12	.05	.01
☐ 394	Roy Howell DP	.04	.02	.00
☐ 395	Jim Hughes	.09	.04	.01
☐ 396	Bob Stinson DP	.04	.02	.00
☐ 397	Greg Gross	.09	.04	.01
☐ 398	Don Hood	.09	.04	.01
☐ 399	Pete Mackanin	.09	.04	.01
☐ 400	Nolan Ryan	2.00	.80	.20
☐ 401	Sparky Anderson MGR ..	.15	.06	.01
☐ 402	Dave Campbell	.09	.04	.01
☐ 403	Bud Harrelson	.12	.05	.01
☐ 404	Tigers Team	.40	.08	.01
	(checklist back)			
☐ 405	Rawly Eastwick	.09	.04	.01
☐ 406	Mike Jorgensen	.09	.04	.01
☐ 407	Odell Jones	.09	.04	.01
☐ 408	Joe Zdeb	.09	.04	.01
☐ 409	Ron Schueler	.09	.04	.01
☐ 410	Bill Madlock	.50	.20	.05
☐ 411	AL Champs	.45	.18	.04
	Yankees rally to			
	defeat Royals			
☐ 412	NL Champs	.45	.18	.04
	Dodgers overpower			
	Phillies in four			
☐ 413	World Series	1.00	.40	.10
	Reggie and Yankees			
	reign supreme			
☐ 414	Darold Knowles DP	.04	.02	.00
☐ 415	Ray Fosse	.09	.04	.01
☐ 416	Jack Brohamer	.09	.04	.01
☐ 417	Mike Garman DP	.04	.02	.00
☐ 418	Tony Muser	.09	.04	.01
☐ 419	Jerry Garvin	.09	.04	.01
☐ 420	Greg Luzinski	.25	.10	.02
☐ 421	Junior Moore	.09	.04	.01
☐ 422	Steve Braun	.09	.04	.01

		MINT	VG-E	F-G
☐ 423	Dave Rosello	.09	.04	.01
☐ 424	Red Sox Team	.35	.07	.01
	(checklist back)			
☐ 425	Steve Rogers DP	.09	.04	.01
☐ 426	Fred Kendall	.09	.04	.01
☐ 427	Mario Soto	1.00	.40	.10
☐ 428	Joel Youngblood	.09	.04	.01
☐ 429	Mike Barlow	.09	.04	.01
☐ 430	Al Oliver	.40	.16	.04
☐ 431	Butch Metzger	.12	.05	.01
☐ 432	Terry Bulling	.09	.04	.01
☐ 433	Fernando Gonzalez	.09	.04	.01
☐ 434	Mike Norris	.12	.05	.01
☐ 435	Checklist 4	.30	.03	.00
☐ 436	Vic Harris DP	.04	.02	.00
☐ 437	Bo McLaughlin	.09	.04	.01
☐ 438	John Ellis	.09	.04	.01
☐ 439	Ken Kravec	.09	.04	.01
☐ 440	Dave Lopes	.20	.08	.02
☐ 441	Larry Gura	.15	.06	.01
☐ 442	Elliott Maddox	.09	.04	.01
☐ 443	Darrel Chaney	.09	.04	.01
☐ 444	Roy Hartsfield MGR	.09	.04	.01
☐ 445	Mike Ivie	.09	.04	.01
☐ 446	Tug McGraw	.20	.08	.02
☐ 447	Leroy Stanton	.09	.04	.01
☐ 448	Bill Castro	.09	.04	.01
☐ 449	Tim Blackwell DP	.04	.02	.00
☐ 450	Tom Seaver	2.00	.80	.20
☐ 451	Twins Team	.35	.07	.01
	(checklist back)			
☐ 452	Jerry Mumphrey	.15	.06	.01
☐ 453	Doug Flynn	.09	.04	.01
☐ 454	Dave LaRoche	.09	.04	.01
☐ 455	Bill Robinson	.09	.04	.01
☐ 456	Vern Ruhle	.09	.04	.01
☐ 457	Bob Bailey	.09	.04	.01
☐ 458	Jeff Newman	.09	.04	.01
☐ 459	Charlie Spikes	.09	.04	.01
☐ 460	Jim Hunter	.90	.36	.09
☐ 461	Rob Andrews DP	.04	.02	.00
☐ 462	Rogelio Moret	.09	.04	.01
☐ 463	Kevin Bell	.09	.04	.01
☐ 464	Jerry Grote	.09	.04	.01
☐ 465	Hal McRae	.18	.08	.01
☐ 466	Dennis Blair	.09	.04	.01
☐ 467	Alvin Dark MGR	.12	.05	.01
☐ 468	Warren Cromartie	.15	.06	.01
☐ 469	Rick Cerone	.12	.05	.01
☐ 470	J.R. Richard	.18	.08	.01
☐ 471	Roy Smalley	.12	.05	.01
☐ 472	Ron Reed	.09	.04	.01
☐ 473	Bill Buckner	.25	.10	.02

	MINT	VG-E	F-G
☐ 474 Jim Slaton	.09	.04	.01
☐ 475 Gary Matthews	.18	.08	.01
☐ 476 Bill Stein	.09	.04	.01
☐ 477 Doug Capilla	.09	.04	.01
☐ 478 Jerry Remy	.12	.05	.01
☐ 479 Cardinals Team (checklist back)	.35	.07	.01
☐ 480 Ron LeFlore	.15	.06	.01
☐ 481 Jackson Todd	.09	.04	.01
☐ 482 Rick Miller	.09	.04	.01
☐ 483 Ken Macha	.09	.04	.01
☐ 484 Jim Norris	.09	.04	.01
☐ 485 Chris Chambliss	.15	.06	.01
☐ 486 John Curtis	.09	.04	.01
☐ 487 Jim Tyrone	.09	.04	.01
☐ 488 Dan Spillner	.09	.04	.01
☐ 489 Rudy Meoli	.09	.04	.01
☐ 490 Amos Otis	.18	.08	.01
☐ 491 Scott McGregor	.18	.08	.01
☐ 492 Jim Sundberg	.12	.05	.01
☐ 493 Steve Renko	.09	.04	.01
☐ 494 Chuck Tanner MGR	.12	.05	.01
☐ 495 Dave Cash	.09	.04	.01
☐ 496 Jim Clancy DP	.12	.05	.01
☐ 497 Glenn Adams	.09	.04	.01
☐ 498 Joe Sambito	.12	.05	.01
☐ 499 Seattle Mariners Team (checklist back)	.30	.06	.01
☐ 500 George Foster	.70	.28	.07
☐ 501 Dave Roberts	.09	.04	.01
☐ 502 Pat Rockett	.09	.04	.01
☐ 503 Ike Hampton	.09	.04	.01
☐ 504 Roger Freed	.09	.04	.01
☐ 505 Felix Millan	.09	.04	.01
☐ 506 Ron Blomberg	.09	.04	.01
☐ 507 Willie Crawford	.09	.04	.01
☐ 508 Johnny Oates	.09	.04	.01
☐ 509 Brent Strom	.09	.04	.01
☐ 510 Willie Stargell	1.25	.50	.12
☐ 511 Frank Duffy	.09	.04	.01
☐ 512 Larry Herndon	.15	.06	.01
☐ 513 Barry Foote	.09	.04	.01
☐ 514 Rob Sperring	.09	.04	.01
☐ 515 Tim Corcoran	.09	.04	.01
☐ 516 Gary Beare	.09	.04	.01
☐ 517 Andres Mora	.09	.04	.01
☐ 518 Tommy Boggs DP	.04	.02	.00
☐ 519 Brian Downing	.12	.05	.01
☐ 520 Larry Hisle	.12	.05	.01
☐ 521 Steve Staggs	.09	.04	.01
☐ 522 Dick Williams MGR	.12	.05	.01
☐ 523 Donnie Moore	.50	.20	.05
☐ 524 Bernie Carbo	.09	.04	.01
☐ 525 Jerry Terrell	.09	.04	.01
☐ 526 Reds Team (checklist back)	.40	.08	.01
☐ 527 Vic Correll	.09	.04	.01
☐ 528 Rob Picciolo	.09	.04	.01
☐ 529 Paul Hartzell	.09	.04	.01
☐ 530 Dave Winfield	1.75	.70	.17
☐ 531 Tom Underwood	.09	.04	.01
☐ 532 Skip Jutze	.09	.04	.01
☐ 533 Sandy Alomar	.09	.04	.01
☐ 534 Wilbur Howard	.09	.04	.01
☐ 535 Checklist 5	.30	.03	.00
☐ 536 Roric Harrison	.09	.04	.01
☐ 537 Bruce Bochte	.12	.05	.01
☐ 538 Johnny LeMaster	.09	.04	.01
☐ 539 Vic Davalillo DP	.04	.02	.00
☐ 540 Steve Carlton	2.00	.80	.20
☐ 541 Larry Cox	.09	.04	.01
☐ 542 Tim Johnson	.09	.04	.01
☐ 543 Larry Harlow DP	.04	.02	.00
☐ 544 Len Randle DP	.04	.02	.00
☐ 545 Bill Campbell	.12	.05	.01
☐ 546 Ted Martinez	.09	.04	.01
☐ 547 John Scott	.09	.04	.01
☐ 548 Billy Hunter MGR DP	.04	.02	.00
☐ 549 Joe Kerrigan	.09	.04	.01
☐ 550 John Mayberry	.12	.05	.01
☐ 551 Atlanta Braves Team (checklist back)	.35	.07	.01
☐ 552 Francisco Barrios	.09	.04	.01
☐ 553 Terry Puhl	.35	.14	.03
☐ 554 Joe Coleman	.09	.04	.01
☐ 555 Butch Wynegar	.15	.06	.01
☐ 556 Ed Armbrister	.09	.04	.01
☐ 557 Tony Solaita	.09	.04	.01
☐ 558 Paul Mitchell	.09	.04	.01
☐ 559 Phil Mankowski	.09	.04	.01
☐ 560 Dave Parker	1.50	.60	.15
☐ 561 Charlie Williams	.09	.04	.01
☐ 562 Glenn Burke	.09	.04	.01
☐ 563 Dave Rader	.09	.04	.01
☐ 564 Mick Kelleher	.09	.04	.01
☐ 565 Jerry Koosman	.20	.08	.02
☐ 566 Merv Rettenmund	.09	.04	.01
☐ 567 Dick Drago	.09	.04	.01
☐ 568 Tom Hutton	.09	.04	.01
☐ 569 Lary Sorensen	.09	.04	.01
☐ 570 Dave Kingman	.50	.20	.05
☐ 571 Buck Martinez	.09	.04	.01
☐ 572 Rick Wise	.12	.05	.01
☐ 573 Luis Gomez	.09	.04	.01
☐ 574 Bob Lemon MGR	.18	.08	.01
☐ 575 Pat Dobson	.12	.05	.01

	MINT	VG-E	F-G
☐ 576 Sam Mejias	.09	.04	.01
☐ 577 Oakland A's Team	.35	.07	.01
(checklist back)			
☐ 578 Buzz Capra	.09	.04	.01
☐ 579 Rance Mulliniks	.15	.06	.01
☐ 580 Rod Carew	1.75	.70	.17
☐ 581 Lynn McGlothen	.09	.04	.01
☐ 582 Fran Healy	.09	.04	.01
☐ 583 George Medich	.12	.05	.01
☐ 584 John Hale	.09	.04	.01
☐ 585 Woodie Fryman DP	.04	.02	.00
☐ 586 Ed Goodson	.09	.04	.01
☐ 587 John Urrea	.09	.04	.01
☐ 588 Jim Mason	.09	.04	.01
☐ 589 Bob Knepper	1.50	.60	.15
☐ 590 Bobby Murcer	.25	.10	.02
☐ 591 George Zeber	.09	.04	.01
☐ 592 Bob Apodaca	.09	.04	.01
☐ 593 Dave Skaggs	.09	.04	.01
☐ 594 Dave Freisleben	.09	.04	.01
☐ 595 Sixto Lezcano	.12	.05	.01
☐ 596 Gary Wheelock	.09	.04	.01
☐ 597 Steve Dillard	.09	.04	.01
☐ 598 Eddie Solomon	.09	.04	.01
☐ 599 Gary Woods	.09	.04	.01
☐ 600 Frank Tanana	.15	.06	.01
☐ 601 Gene Mauch MGR	.12	.05	.01
☐ 602 Eric Soderholm	.09	.04	.01
☐ 603 Will McEnaney	.09	.04	.01
☐ 604 Earl Williams	.09	.04	.01
☐ 605 Rick Rhoden	.20	.08	.02
☐ 606 Pirates Team	.35	.07	.01
(checklist back)			
☐ 607 Fernando Arroyo	.09	.04	.01
☐ 608 Johnny Grubb	.09	.04	.01
☐ 609 John Denny	.20	.08	.02
☐ 610 Garry Maddox	.12	.05	.01
☐ 611 Pat Scanlon	.09	.04	.01
☐ 612 Ken Henderson	.09	.04	.01
☐ 613 Marty Perez	.09	.04	.01
☐ 614 Joe Wallis	.09	.04	.01
☐ 615 Clay Carroll	.09	.04	.01
☐ 616 Pat Kelly	.09	.04	.01
☐ 617 Joe Nolan	.09	.04	.01
☐ 618 Tommy Helms	.09	.04	.01
☐ 619 Thad Bosley DP	.09	.04	.01
☐ 620 Willie Randolph	.20	.08	.02
☐ 621 Craig Swan DP	.09	.04	.01
☐ 622 Champ Summers	.09	.04	.01
☐ 623 Ed Rodriquez	.09	.04	.01
☐ 624 Gary Alexander DP	.04	.02	.00
☐ 625 Jose Cruz	.30	.12	.03

	MINT	VG-E	F-G
☐ 626 Blue Jays Team DP	.15	.03	.00
(checklist back)			
☐ 627 David Johnson	.09	.04	.01
☐ 628 Ralph Garr	.12	.05	.01
☐ 629 Don Stanhouse	.09	.04	.01
☐ 630 Ron Cey	.30	.12	.03
☐ 631 Danny Ozark MGR	.09	.04	.01
☐ 632 Rowland Office	.09	.04	.01
☐ 633 Tom Veryzer	.09	.04	.01
☐ 634 Len Barker	.15	.06	.01
☐ 635 Joe Rudi	.12	.05	.01
☐ 636 Jim Bibby	.12	.05	.01
☐ 637 Duffy Dyer	.09	.04	.01
☐ 638 Paul Splittorff	.12	.05	.01
☐ 639 Gene Clines	.09	.04	.01
☐ 640 Lee May DP	.09	.04	.01
☐ 641 Doug Rau	.09	.04	.01
☐ 642 Denny Doyle	.09	.04	.01
☐ 643 Tom House	.09	.04	.01
☐ 644 Jim Dwyer	.09	.04	.01
☐ 645 Mike Torrez	.12	.05	.01
☐ 646 Rick Auerbach DP	.04	.02	.00
☐ 647 Steve Dunning	.09	.04	.01
☐ 648 Gary Thomasson	.09	.04	.01
☐ 649 Moose Haas	.45	.18	.04
☐ 650 Cesar Cedeno	.20	.08	.02
☐ 651 Doug Rader	.12	.05	.01
☐ 652 Checklist 6	.30	.03	.00
☐ 653 Ron Hodges DP	.04	.02	.00
☐ 654 Pepe Frias	.09	.04	.01
☐ 655 Lyman Bostock	.18	.08	.01
☐ 656 Dave Garcia MGR	.09	.04	.01
☐ 657 Bombo Rivera	.09	.04	.01
☐ 658 Manny Sanguillen	.12	.05	.01
☐ 659 Rangers Team	.35	.07	.01
(checklist back)			
☐ 660 Jason Thompson	.18	.08	.01
☐ 661 Grant Jackson	.09	.04	.01
☐ 662 Paul Dade	.09	.04	.01
☐ 663 Paul Reuschel	.09	.04	.01
☐ 664 Fred Stanley	.09	.04	.01
☐ 665 Dennis Leonard	.15	.06	.01
☐ 666 Billy Smith	.09	.04	.01
☐ 667 Jeff Byrd	.09	.04	.01
☐ 668 Dusty Baker	.18	.08	.01
☐ 669 Pete Falcone	.09	.04	.01
☐ 670 Jim Rice	3.50	1.40	.35
☐ 671 Gary Lavelle	.12	.05	.01
☐ 672 Don Kessinger	.12	.05	.01
☐ 673 Steve Brye	.09	.04	.01
☐ 674 Ray Knight	1.00	.40	.10
☐ 675 Jay Johnstone	.12	.05	.01
☐ 676 Bob Myrick	.09	.04	.01

		MINT	VG-E	F-G
☐ 677	Ed Herrmann	.09	.04	.01
☐ 678	Tom Burgmeier	.09	.04	.01
☐ 679	Wayne Garrett	.09	.04	.01
☐ 680	Vida Blue	.18	.08	.01
☐ 681	Rob Belloir	.09	.04	.01
☐ 682	Ken Brett	.12	.05	.01
☐ 683	Mike Champion	.09	.04	.01
☐ 684	Ralph Houk MGR	.12	.05	.01
☐ 685	Frank Taveras	.09	.04	.01
☐ 686	Gaylord Perry	1.25	.50	.12
☐ 687	Julio Cruz	.25	.10	.02
☐ 688	George Mitterwald	.09	.04	.01
☐ 689	Indians Team	.35	.07	.01
	(checklist back)			
☐ 690	Mickey Rivers	.15	.06	.01
☐ 691	Ross Grimsley	.09	.04	.01
☐ 692	Ken Reitz	.09	.04	.01
☐ 693	Lamar Johnson	.09	.04	.01
☐ 694	Elias Sosa	.09	.04	.01
☐ 695	Dwight Evans	.35	.14	.03
☐ 696	Steve Mingori	.09	.04	.01
☐ 697	Roger Metzger	.09	.04	.01
☐ 698	Juan Bernhardt	.09	.04	.01
☐ 699	Jackie Brown	.09	.04	.01
☐ 700	Johnny Bench	1.75	.70	.17
☐ 701	Rookie Pitchers	.30	.12	.03
	Tom Hume			
	Larry Landreth			
	Steve McCatty			
	Bruce Taylor			
☐ 702	Rookie Catchers	.12	.05	.01
	Bill Nahorodny			
	Kevin Pasley			
	Rick Sweet			
	Don Werner			
☐ 703	Rookie Pitchers DP	4.50	1.80	.45
	Larry Andersen			
	Tim Jones			
	Mickey Mahler			
	Jack Morris			
☐ 704	Rookie 2nd Basemen	6.00	2.40	.60
	Garth Iorg			
	Dave Oliver			
	Sam Perlozzo			
	Lou Whitaker			
☐ 705	Rookie Outfielders	.30	.12	.03
	Dave Bergman			
	Miguel Dilone			
	Clint Hurdle			
	Willie Norwood			

		MINT	VG-E	F-G
☐ 706	Rookie 1st Basemen	.20	.08	.02
	Wayne Cage			
	Ted Cox			
	Pat Putnam			
	Dave Revering			
☐ 707	Rookie Shortstops	9.00	3.75	.90
	Mickey Klutts			
	Paul Molitor			
	Alan Trammell			
	U.L. Washington			
☐ 708	Rookie Catchers	24.00	10.00	2.40
	Bo Diaz			
	Dale Murphy			
	Lance Parrish			
	Ernie Whitt			
☐ 709	Rookie Pitchers	.20	.08	.02
	Steve Burke			
	Matt Keough			
	Lance Rautzhan			
	Dan Schatzeder			
☐ 710	Rookie Outfielders	1.50	.60	.15
	Dell Alston			
	Rick Bosetti			
	Mike Easler			
	Keith Smith			
☐ 711	Rookie Pitchers DP	.12	.05	.01
	Cardell Camper			
	Dennis Lamp			
	Craig Mitchell			
	Roy Thomas			
☐ 712	Bobby Valentine	.18	.08	.01
☐ 713	Bob Davis	.09	.04	.01
☐ 714	Mike Anderson	.09	.04	.01
☐ 715	Jim Kaat	.30	.12	.03
☐ 716	Clarence Gaston	.09	.04	.01
☐ 717	Nelson Briles	.12	.05	.01
☐ 718	Ron Jackson	.09	.04	.01
☐ 719	Randy Elliott	.09	.04	.01
☐ 720	Fergie Jenkins	.30	.12	.03
☐ 721	Billy Martin MGR	.25	.10	.02
☐ 722	Pete Broberg	.09	.04	.01
☐ 723	John Wockenfuss	.09	.04	.01
☐ 724	K.C. Royals Team	.35	.07	.01
	(checklist back)			
☐ 725	Kurt Bevacqua	.09	.04	.01
☐ 726	Wilbur Wood	.15	.06	.01

1979 Topps

*The cards in this 726-card set measure 2½"
by 3½". Topps continued with the same number
of cards as in 1978. Various series spot-
light League Leaders (1-8), "Season and
Career Record Holders" (411-418), "Record
Breakers of 1978" (201-206) and one "Prospects" card for each team (701-726). Team
cards feature a checklist on back of that
team's players in the set and a small picture
of the manager on the front of the card. There
are 66 cards that were double printed and
these are noted in the checklist by the abbreviation DP. Bump Wills was initially depicted
in a Ranger uniform but with a Blue Jays affiliation; later printings correctly labeled him
with Texas. The set price listed does not include the scarcer Wills (Rangers) card.*

	MINT	VG-E	F-G
Complete Set	100.00	40.00	10.00
Common Player (1-726)	.08	.03	.01
Common DP's (1-726)	.03	.01	.00

			MINT	VG-E	F-G
☐	1	Batting Leaders	.75	.15	.03
		Rod Carew			
		Dave Parker			
☐	2	Home Run Leaders	.35	.14	.03
		Jim Rice			
		George Foster			
☐	3	RBI Leaders	.35	.14	.03
		Jim Rice			
		George Foster			
☐	4	Stolen Base Leaders	.12	.05	.01
		Ron LeFlore			
		Omar Moreno			
☐	5	Victory Leaders	.25	.10	.02
		Ron Guidry			
		Gaylord Perry			
☐	6	Strikeout Leaders	.25	.10	.02
		Nolan Ryan			
		J.R. Richard			
☐	7	ERA Leaders	.15	.06	.01
		Ron Guidry			
		Craig Swan			
☐	8	Leading Firemen	.20	.08	.02
		Rich Gossage			
		Rollie Fingers			
☐	9	Dave Campbell	.08	.03	.01
☐	10	Lee May	.12	.05	.01
☐	11	Marc Hill	.08	.03	.01
☐	12	Dick Drago	.08	.03	.01
☐	13	Paul Dade	.08	.03	.01
☐	14	Rafael Landestoy	.08	.03	.01
☐	15	Ross Grimsley	.08	.03	.01
☐	16	Fred Stanley	.08	.03	.01
☐	17	Donnie Moore	.12	.05	.01
☐	18	Tony Solaita	.08	.03	.01
☐	19	Larry Gura DP	.08	.03	.01
☐	20	Joe Morgan DP	.20	.08	.02
☐	21	Kevin Kobel	.08	.03	.01
☐	22	Mike Jorgensen	.08	.03	.01
☐	23	Terry Forster	.15	.06	.01
☐	24	Paul Molitor	.65	.26	.06
☐	25	Steve Carlton	1.75	.70	.17
☐	26	Jamie Quirk	.08	.03	.01
☐	27	Dave Goltz	.12	.05	.01
☐	28	Steve Brye	.08	.03	.01
☐	29	Rick Langford	.08	.03	.01
☐	30	Dave Winfield	1.75	.70	.17
☐	31	Tom House DP	.03	.01	.00
☐	32	Jerry Mumphrey	.12	.05	.01
☐	33	Dave Rozema	.08	.03	.01
☐	34	Rob Andrews	.08	.03	.01
☐	35	Ed Figueroa	.08	.03	.01
☐	36	Alan Ashby	.08	.03	.01
☐	37	Joe Kerrigan DP	.03	.01	.00
☐	38	Bernie Carbo	.08	.03	.01
☐	39	Dale Murphy	6.00	2.40	.60
☐	40	Dennis Eckersley	.12	.05	.01
☐	41	Twins Team/Mgr.	.30	.06	.01
		Gene Mauch			
		(checklist back)			
☐	42	Ron Blomberg	.08	.03	.01
☐	43	Wayne Twitchell	.08	.03	.01
☐	44	Kurt Bevacqua	.08	.03	.01
☐	45	Al Hrabosky	.12	.05	.01
☐	46	Ron Hodges	.08	.03	.01
☐	47	Fred Norman	.08	.03	.01

			MINT	VG-E	F-G
☐	48	Merv Rettenmund	.08	.03	.01
☐	49	Vern Ruhle	.08	.03	.01
☐	50	Steve Garvey DP	.80	.32	.08
☐	51	Ray Fosse DP	.03	.01	.00
☐	52	Randy Lerch	.08	.03	.01
☐	53	Mick Kelleher	.08	.03	.01
☐	54	Dell Alston DP	.03	.01	.00
☐	55	Willie Stargell	1.25	.50	.12
☐	56	John Hale	.08	.03	.01
☐	57	Eric Rasmussen	.08	.03	.01
☐	58	Bob Randall DP	.03	.01	.00
☐	59	John Denny DP	.08	.03	.01
☐	60	Mickey Rivers	.12	.05	.01
☐	61	Bo Diaz	.20	.08	.02
☐	62	Randy Moffitt	.08	.03	.01
☐	63	Jack Brohamer	.08	.03	.01
☐	64	Tom Underwood	.08	.03	.01
☐	65	Mark Belanger	.15	.06	.01
☐	66	Tigers Team/Mgr.	.30	.06	.01
		Les Moss			
		(checklist back)			
☐	67	Jim Mason DP	.03	.01	.00
☐	68	Joe Niekro DP	.08	.03	.01
☐	69	Elliott Maddox	.08	.03	.01
☐	70	John Candelaria	.15	.06	.01
☐	71	Brian Downing	.12	.05	.01
☐	72	Steve Mingori	.08	.03	.01
☐	73	Ken Henderson	.08	.03	.01
☐	74	Shane Rawley	.75	.30	.07
☐	75	Steve Yeager	.12	.05	.01
☐	76	Warren Cromartie	.08	.03	.01
☐	77	Dan Briggs DP	.03	.01	.00
☐	78	Elias Sosa	.08	.03	.01
☐	79	Ted Cox	.08	.03	.01
☐	80	Jason Thompson	.12	.05	.01
☐	81	Roger Erickson	.12	.05	.01
☐	82	Mets Team/Mgr.	.30	.06	.01
		Joe Torre			
		(checklist back)			
☐	83	Fred Kendall	.08	.03	.01
☐	84	Greg Minton	.12	.05	.01
☐	85	Gary Matthews	.18	.08	.01
☐	86	Rodney Scott	.08	.03	.01
☐	87	Pete Falcone	.08	.03	.01
☐	88	Bob Molinaro	.08	.03	.01
☐	89	Dick Tidrow	.08	.03	.01
☐	90	Bob Boone	.12	.05	.01
☐	91	Terry Crowley	.08	.03	.01
☐	92	Jim Bibby	.12	.05	.01
☐	93	Phil Mankowski	.08	.03	.01
☐	94	Len Barker	.15	.06	.01
☐	95	Robin Yount	1.75	.70	.17

			MINT	VG-E	F-G
☐	96	Indians Team/Mgr.	.30	.06	.01
		Jeff Torborg			
		(checklist back)			
☐	97	Sam Mejias	.08	.03	.01
☐	98	Ray Burris	.08	.03	.01
☐	99	John Wathan	.08	.03	.01
☐	100	Tom Seaver DP	.80	.32	.08
☐	101	Roy Howell	.08	.03	.01
☐	102	Mike Anderson	.08	.03	.01
☐	103	Jim Todd	.08	.03	.01
☐	104	Johnny Oates DP	.03	.01	.00
☐	105	Rick Camp DP	.03	.01	.00
☐	106	Frank Duffy	.08	.03	.01
☐	107	Jesus Alou DP	.03	.01	.00
☐	108	Eduardo Rodriguez	.08	.03	.01
☐	109	Joel Youngblood	.08	.03	.01
☐	110	Vida Blue	.15	.06	.01
☐	111	Roger Freed	.08	.03	.01
☐	112	Phillies Team/Mgr.	.30	.06	.01
		Danny Ozark			
		(checklist back)			
☐	113	Pete Redfern	.08	.03	.01
☐	114	Cliff Johnson	.08	.03	.01
☐	115	Nolan Ryan	1.75	.70	.17
☐	116	Ozzie Smith	4.50	1.80	.45
☐	117	Grant Jackson	.08	.03	.01
☐	118	Bud Harrelson	.12	.05	.01
☐	119	Don Stanhouse	.08	.03	.01
☐	120	Jim Sundberg	.12	.05	.01
☐	121	Checklist 1 DP	.10	.01	.00
☐	122	Mike Paxton	.08	.03	.01
☐	123	Lou Whitaker	1.50	.60	.15
☐	124	Dan Schatzeder	.08	.03	.01
☐	125	Rick Burleson	.12	.05	.01
☐	126	Doug Bair	.08	.03	.01
☐	127	Thad Bosley	.08	.03	.01
☐	128	Ted Martinez	.08	.03	.01
☐	129	Marty Pattin DP	.03	.01	.00
☐	130	Bob Watson DP	.08	.03	.01
☐	131	Jim Clancy	.12	.05	.01
☐	132	Rowland Office	.08	.03	.01
☐	133	Bill Castro	.08	.03	.01
☐	134	Alan Bannister	.08	.03	.01
☐	135	Bobby Murcer	.18	.08	.01
☐	136	Jim Kaat	.30	.12	.03
☐	137	Larry Wolfe DP	.03	.01	.00
☐	138	Mark Lee	.08	.03	.01
☐	139	Luis Pujols	.08	.03	.01
☐	140	Don Gullett	.12	.05	.01
☐	141	Tom Paciorek	.08	.03	.01
☐	142	Charlie Williams	.08	.03	.01
☐	143	Tony Scott	.08	.03	.01
☐	144	Sandy Alomar	.08	.03	.01

	MINT	VG-E	F-G
☐ 145 Rick Rhoden	.18	.08	.01
☐ 146 Duane Kuiper	.08	.03	.01
☐ 147 Dave Hamilton	.08	.03	.01
☐ 148 Bruce Boisclair	.08	.03	.01
☐ 149 Manny Sarmiento	.08	.03	.01
☐ 150 Wayne Cage	.08	.03	.01
☐ 151 John Hiller	.12	.05	.01
☐ 152 Rick Cerone	.12	.05	.01
☐ 153 Dennis Lamp	.08	.03	.01
☐ 154 Jim Gantner DP	.08	.03	.01
☐ 155 Dwight Evans	.30	.12	.03
☐ 156 Buddy Solomon	.08	.03	.01
☐ 157 U.L. Washington	.08	.03	.01
☐ 158 Joe Sambito	.12	.05	.01
☐ 159 Roy White	.12	.05	.01
☐ 160 Mike Flanagan	.18	.08	.01
☐ 161 Barry Foote	.08	.03	.01
☐ 162 Tom Johnson	.08	.03	.01
☐ 163 Glenn Burke	.08	.03	.01
☐ 164 Mickey Lolich	.18	.08	.01
☐ 165 Frank Taveras	.08	.03	.01
☐ 166 Leon Roberts	.08	.03	.01
☐ 167 Roger Metzger DP	.03	.01	.00
☐ 168 Dave Freisleben	.08	.03	.01
☐ 169 Bill Nahorodny	.08	.03	.01
☐ 170 Don Sutton	.75	.30	.07
☐ 171 Gene Clines	.08	.03	.01
☐ 172 Mike Bruhert	.08	.03	.01
☐ 173 John Lowenstein	.08	.03	.01
☐ 174 Rick Auerbach	.08	.03	.01
☐ 175 George Hendrick	.15	.06	.01
☐ 176 Aurelio Rodriguez	.08	.03	.01
☐ 177 Ron Reed	.08	.03	.01
☐ 178 Alvis Woods	.08	.03	.01
☐ 179 Jim Beattie DP	.08	.03	.01
☐ 180 Larry Hisle	.12	.05	.01
☐ 181 Mike Garman	.08	.03	.01
☐ 182 Tim Johnson	.08	.03	.01
☐ 183 Paul Splittorff	.12	.05	.01
☐ 184 Darrel Chaney	.08	.03	.01
☐ 185 Mike Torrez	.12	.05	.01
☐ 186 Eric Soderholm	.08	.03	.01
☐ 187 Mark Lemongello	.08	.03	.01
☐ 188 Pat Kelly	.08	.03	.01
☐ 189 Eddie Whitson	.35	.14	.03
☐ 190 Ron Cey	.30	.12	.03
☐ 191 Mike Norris	.12	.05	.01
☐ 192 Cardinals Team/Mgr.	.30	.06	.01
Ken Boyer			
(checklist back)			
☐ 193 Glenn Adams	.08	.03	.01
☐ 194 Randy Jones	.12	.05	.01
☐ 195 Bill Madlock	.35	.14	.03

	MINT	VG-E	F-G
☐ 196 Steve Kemp DP	.08	.03	.01
☐ 197 Bob Apodaca	.08	.03	.01
☐ 198 Johnny Grubb	.08	.03	.01
☐ 199 Larry Milbourne	.08	.03	.01
☐ 200 Johnny Bench DP	.75	.30	.07
☐ 201 RB: Mike Edwards	.08	.03	.01
Most unassisted			
2nd basemen DP's			
☐ 202 RB: Ron Guidry	.30	.12	.03
Most strikeouts,			
lefthander			
9 inning game			
☐ 203 RB: J.R. Richard	.15	.06	.01
Most strikeouts			
season, righthander			
☐ 204 RB: Pete Rose	1.25	.50	.12
Most consecutive			
games batting safe			
☐ 205 RB: John Stearns	.08	.03	.01
Most SB's by			
catcher, season			
☐ 206 RB: Sammy Stewart	.12	.05	.01
7 straight SO's			
First ML game			
☐ 207 Dave Lemanczyk	.08	.03	.01
☐ 208 Clarence Gaston	.08	.03	.01
☐ 209 Reggie Cleveland	.08	.03	.01
☐ 210 Larry Bowa	.20	.08	.02
☐ 211 Denny Martinez	.12	.05	.01
☐ 212 Carney Lansford	1.50	.60	.15
☐ 213 Bill Travers	.08	.03	.01
☐ 214 Red Sox Team/Mgr.	.30	.06	.01
Don Zimmer			
(checklist back)			
☐ 215 Willie McCovey	1.25	.50	.12
☐ 216 Wilbur Wood	.12	.05	.01
☐ 217 Steve Dillard	.08	.03	.01
☐ 218 Dennis Leonard	.15	.06	.01
☐ 219 Roy Smalley	.12	.05	.01
☐ 220 Cesar Geronimo	.08	.03	.01
☐ 221 Jesse Jefferson	.08	.03	.01
☐ 222 Bob Beall	.08	.03	.01
☐ 223 Kent Tekulve	.15	.06	.01
☐ 224 Dave Revering	.08	.03	.01
☐ 225 Rich Gossage	.50	.20	.05
☐ 226 Ron Pruitt	.08	.03	.01
☐ 227 Steve Stone	.12	.05	.01
☐ 228 Vic Davalillo	.08	.03	.01
☐ 229 Doug Flynn	.08	.03	.01
☐ 230 Bob Forsch	.15	.06	.01
☐ 231 Johnny Wockenfuss	.08	.03	.01
☐ 232 Jimmy Sexton	.08	.03	.01
☐ 233 Paul Mitchell	.08	.03	.01

	MINT	VG-E	F-G
☐ 234 Toby Harrah	.12	.05	.01
☐ 235 Steve Rogers	.15	.06	.01
☐ 236 Jim Dwyer	.08	.03	.01
☐ 237 Billy Smith	.08	.03	.01
☐ 238 Balor Moore	.08	.03	.01
☐ 239 Willie Horton	.12	.05	.01
☐ 240 Rick Reuschel	.12	.05	.01
☐ 241 Checklist 2 DP	.10	.01	.00
☐ 242 Pablo Torrealba	.08	.03	.01
☐ 243 Buck Martinez DP	.03	.01	.00
☐ 244 Pirates Team/Mgr.	.30	.06	.01
Chuck Tanner			
(checklist back)			
☐ 245 Jeff Burroughs	.12	.05	.01
☐ 246 Darrell Jackson	.08	.03	.01
☐ 247 Tucker Ashford DP	.03	.01	.00
☐ 248 Pete LaCock	.08	.03	.01
☐ 249 Paul Thormodsgard	.08	.03	.01
☐ 250 Willie Randolph	.15	.06	.01
☐ 251 Jack Morris	1.50	.60	.15
☐ 252 Bob Stinson	.08	.03	.01
☐ 253 Rick Wise	.12	.05	.01
☐ 254 Luis Gomez	.08	.03	.01
☐ 255 Tommy John	.35	.14	.03
☐ 256 Mike Sadek	.08	.03	.01
☐ 257 Adrian Devine	.08	.03	.01
☐ 258 Mike Phillips	.08	.03	.01
☐ 259 Reds Team/Mgr.	.30	.06	.01
Sparky Anderson			
(checklist back)			
☐ 260 Richie Zisk	.12	.05	.01
☐ 261 Mario Guerrero	.08	.03	.01
☐ 262 Nelson Briles	.12	.05	.01
☐ 263 Oscar Gamble	.12	.05	.01
☐ 264 Don Robinson	.35	.14	.03
☐ 265 Don Money	.12	.05	.01
☐ 266 Jim Willoughby	.08	.03	.01
☐ 267 Joe Rudi	.12	.05	.01
☐ 268 Julio Gonzalez	.08	.03	.01
☐ 269 Woodie Fryman	.08	.03	.01
☐ 270 Butch Hobson	.08	.03	.01
☐ 271 Rawly Eastwick	.08	.03	.01
☐ 272 Tim Corcoran	.08	.03	.01
☐ 273 Jerry Terrell	.08	.03	.01
☐ 274 Willie Norwood	.08	.03	.01
☐ 275 Junior Moore	.08	.03	.01
☐ 276 Jim Colborn	.08	.03	.01
☐ 277 Tom Grieve	.12	.05	.01
☐ 278 Andy Messersmith	.15	.06	.01
☐ 279 Jerry Grote DP	.03	.01	.00
☐ 280 Andre Thornton	.15	.06	.01
☐ 281 Vic Correll DP	.03	.01	.00

	MINT	VG-E	F-G
☐ 282 Blue Jays Team/Mgr.	.25	.05	.01
Roy Hartsfield			
(checklist back)			
☐ 283 Ken Kravec	.08	.03	.01
☐ 284 Johnnie LeMaster	.08	.03	.01
☐ 285 Bobby Bonds	.18	.08	.01
☐ 286 Duffy Dyer	.08	.03	.01
☐ 287 Andres Mora	.08	.03	.01
☐ 288 Milt Wilcox	.12	.05	.01
☐ 289 Jose Cruz	.25	.10	.02
☐ 290 Dave Lopes	.20	.08	.02
☐ 291 Tom Griffin	.08	.03	.01
☐ 292 Don Reynolds	.08	.03	.01
☐ 293 Jerry Garvin	.08	.03	.01
☐ 294 Pepe Frias	.08	.03	.01
☐ 295 Mitchell Page	.08	.03	.01
☐ 296 Preston Hanna	.08	.03	.01
☐ 297 Ted Sizemore	.08	.03	.01
☐ 298 Rich Gale	.08	.03	.01
☐ 299 Steve Ontiveros	.08	.03	.01
☐ 300 Rod Carew	1.50	.60	.15
☐ 301 Tom Hume	.08	.03	.01
☐ 302 Braves Team/Mgr.	.30	.06	.01
Bobby Cox			
(checklist back)			
☐ 303 Lary Sorensen	.08	.03	.01
☐ 304 Steve Swisher	.08	.03	.01
☐ 305 Willie Montanez	.08	.03	.01
☐ 306 Floyd Bannister	.15	.06	.01
☐ 307 Larvell Blanks	.08	.03	.01
☐ 308 Bert Blyleven	.30	.12	.03
☐ 309 Ralph Garr	.12	.05	.01
☐ 310 Thurman Munson	1.50	.60	.15
☐ 311 Gary Lavelle	.12	.05	.01
☐ 312 Bob Robertson	.08	.03	.01
☐ 313 Dyar Miller	.08	.03	.01
☐ 314 Larry Harlow	.08	.03	.01
☐ 315 Jon Matlack	.12	.05	.01
☐ 316 Milt May	.08	.03	.01
☐ 317 Jose Cardenal	.08	.03	.01
☐ 318 Bob Welch	1.00	.40	.10
☐ 319 Wayne Garrett	.08	.03	.01
☐ 320 Carl Yastrzemski	2.00	.80	.20
☐ 321 Gaylord Perry	.85	.34	.08
☐ 322 Danny Goodwin	.08	.03	.01
☐ 323 Lynn McGlothen	.08	.03	.01
☐ 324 Mike Tyson	.08	.03	.01
☐ 325 Cecil Cooper	.40	.16	.04
☐ 326 Pedro Borbon	.08	.03	.01
☐ 327 Art Howe	.08	.03	.01
☐ 328 Oakland A's Team/Mgr.	.25	.05	.01
Jack McKeon			
(checklist back)			

		MINT	VG-E	F-G
☐ 329	Joe Coleman	.08	.03	.01
☐ 330	George Brett	2.50	1.00	.25
☐ 331	Mickey Mahler	.08	.03	.01
☐ 332	Gary Alexander	.08	.03	.01
☐ 333	Chet Lemon	.15	.06	.01
☐ 334	Craig Swan	.12	.05	.01
☐ 335	Chris Chambliss	.15	.06	.01
☐ 336	Bobby Thompson	.08	.03	.01
☐ 337	John Montague	.08	.03	.01
☐ 338	Vic Harris	.08	.03	.01
☐ 339	Ron Jackson	.08	.03	.01
☐ 340	Jim Palmer	1.00	.40	.10
☐ 341	Willie Upshaw	1.00	.40	.10
☐ 342	Dave Roberts	.08	.03	.01
☐ 343	Ed Glynn	.08	.03	.01
☐ 344	Jerry Royster	.08	.03	.01
☐ 345	Tug McGraw	.18	.08	.01
☐ 346	Bill Buckner	.20	.08	.02
☐ 347	Doug Rau	.08	.03	.01
☐ 348	Andre Dawson	.85	.34	.08
☐ 349	Jim Wright	.08	.03	.01
☐ 350	Garry Templeton	.25	.10	.02
☐ 351	Wayne Nordhagen	.08	.03	.01
☐ 352	Steve Renko	.08	.03	.01
☐ 353	Checklist 3	.30	.03	.00
☐ 354	Bill Bonham	.08	.03	.01
☐ 355	Lee Mazzilli	.12	.05	.01
☐ 356	Giants Team/Mgr.	.30	.06	.01
	Joe Altobelli			
	(checklist back)			
☐ 357	Jerry Augustine	.08	.03	.01
☐ 358	Alan Trammell	1.50	.60	.15
☐ 359	Dan Spillner DP	.08	.03	.01
☐ 360	Amos Otis	.15	.06	.01
☐ 361	Tom Dixon	.08	.03	.01
☐ 362	Mike Cubbage	.08	.03	.01
☐ 363	Craig Skok	.08	.03	.01
☐ 364	Gene Richards	.08	.03	.01
☐ 365	Sparky Lyle	.18	.08	.01
☐ 366	Juan Bernhardt	.08	.03	.01
☐ 367	Dave Skaggs	.08	.03	.01
☐ 368	Don Aase	.15	.06	.01
☐ 369	A Bump Wills ERR	3.00	1.20	.30
	(Blue Jays)			
☐ 369	B Bump Wills COR	4.00	1.60	.40
	(Rangers)			
☐ 370	Dave Kingman	.40	.16	.04
☐ 371	Jeff Holly	.08	.03	.01
☐ 372	Lamar Johnson	.08	.03	.01
☐ 373	Lance Rautzhan	.08	.03	.01
☐ 374	Ed Herrmann	.08	.03	.01
☐ 375	Bill Campbell	.12	.05	.01
☐ 376	Gorman Thomas	.25	.10	.02

		MINT	VG-E	F-G
☐ 377	Paul Moskau	.08	.03	.01
☐ 378	Rob Picciolo DP	.03	.01	.00
☐ 379	Dale Murray	.08	.03	.01
☐ 380	John Mayberry	.12	.05	.01
☐ 381	Astros Team/Mgr.	.30	.06	.01
	Bill Virdon			
	(checklist back)			
☐ 382	Jerry Martin	.08	.03	.01
☐ 383	Phil Garner	.12	.05	.01
☐ 384	Tommy Boggs	.08	.03	.01
☐ 385	Dan Ford	.12	.05	.01
☐ 386	Francisco Barrios	.08	.03	.01
☐ 387	Gary Thomasson	.08	.03	.01
☐ 388	Jack Billingham	.08	.03	.01
☐ 389	Joe Zdeb	.08	.03	.01
☐ 390	Rollie Fingers	.35	.14	.03
☐ 391	Al Oliver	.30	.12	.03
☐ 392	Doug Ault	.08	.03	.01
☐ 393	Scott McGregor	.15	.06	.01
☐ 394	Randy Stein	.08	.03	.01
☐ 395	Dave Cash	.08	.03	.01
☐ 396	Bill Plummer	.08	.03	.01
☐ 397	Sergio Ferrer	.08	.03	.01
☐ 398	Ivan DeJesus	.08	.03	.01
☐ 399	David Clyde	.08	.03	.01
☐ 400	Jim Rice	2.50	1.00	.25
☐ 401	Ray Knight	.25	.10	.02
☐ 402	Paul Hartzell	.08	.03	.01
☐ 403	Tim Foli	.08	.03	.01
☐ 404	White Sox Team/Mgr	.30	.06	.01
	Don Kessinger			
	(checklist back)			
☐ 405	Butch Wynegar DP	.08	.03	.01
☐ 406	Joe Wallis DP	.03	.01	.00
☐ 407	Pete Vuckovich	.12	.05	.01
☐ 408	Charlie Moore DP	.03	.01	.00
☐ 409	Willie Wilson	1.50	.60	.15
☐ 410	Darrell Evans	.25	.10	.02
☐ 411	Hits Record	.40	.16	.04
	Season: George Sisler			
	Career: Ty Cobb			
☐ 412	RBI Record	.40	.16	.04
	Season: Hack Wilson			
	Career: Hank Aaron			
☐ 413	Home Run Record	.40	.16	.04
	Season: Roger Maris			
	Career: Hank Aaron			
☐ 414	Batting Record	.40	.16	.04
	Season: R.Hornsby			
	Career: Ty Cobb			
☐ 415	Steals Record	.40	.16	.04
	Season: Lou Brock			
	Career: Lou Brock			

	MINT	VG-E	F-G
☐ 416 Wins Record	.20	.08	.02
Season: Jack Chesbro			
Career: Cy Young			
☐ 417 Strikeout Record DP ...	.10	.04	.01
Season: Nolan Ryan			
Career: Walter Johnson			
☐ 418 ERA Record DP	.08	.03	.01
Season: Dutch Leonard			
Career: Walter Johnson			
☐ 419 Dick Ruthven	.08	.03	.01
☐ 420 Ken Griffey	.15	.06	.01
☐ 421 Doug DeCinces	.18	.08	.01
☐ 422 Ruppert Jones	.12	.05	.01
☐ 423 Bob Montgomery	.08	.03	.01
☐ 424 Angels Team/Mgr.	.30	.06	.01
Jim Fregosi			
(checklist back)			
☐ 425 Rick Manning	.08	.03	.01
☐ 426 Chris Speier	.08	.03	.01
☐ 427 Andy Replogle	.08	.03	.01
☐ 428 Bobby Valentine	.18	.08	.01
☐ 429 John Urrea DP	.03	.01	.00
☐ 430 Dave Parker	1.00	.40	.10
☐ 431 Glenn Borgmann	.08	.03	.01
☐ 432 Dave Heaverlo	.08	.03	.01
☐ 433 Larry Biittner	.08	.03	.01
☐ 434 Ken Clay	.08	.03	.01
☐ 435 Gene Tenace	.12	.05	.01
☐ 436 Hector Cruz	.08	.03	.01
☐ 437 Rick Williams	.08	.03	.01
☐ 438 Horace Speed	.08	.03	.01
☐ 439 Frank White	.20	.08	.02
☐ 440 Rusty Staub	.20	.08	.02
☐ 441 Lee Lacy	.15	.06	.01
☐ 442 Doyle Alexander	.12	.05	.01
☐ 443 Bruce Bochte	.12	.05	.01
☐ 444 Aurelio Lopez	.25	.10	.02
☐ 445 Steve Henderson	.12	.05	.01
☐ 446 Jim Lonborg	.12	.05	.01
☐ 447 Manny Sanguillen	.12	.05	.01
☐ 448 Moose Haas	.12	.05	.01
☐ 449 Bombo Rivera	.08	.03	.01
☐ 450 Dave Concepcion	.20	.08	.02
☐ 451 Royals Team/Mgr.	.30	.06	.01
Whitey Herzog			
(checklist back)			
☐ 452 Jerry Morales	.08	.03	.01
☐ 453 Chris Knapp	.08	.03	.01
☐ 454 Len Randle	.08	.03	.01
☐ 455 Bill Lee DP	.08	.03	.01
☐ 456 Chuck Baker	.08	.03	.01
☐ 457 Bruce Sutter	.65	.26	.06
☐ 458 Jim Essian	.08	.03	.01

	MINT	VG-E	F-G
☐ 459 Sid Monge	.08	.03	.01
☐ 460 Graig Nettles	.35	.14	.03
☐ 461 Jim Barr DP	.03	.01	.00
☐ 462 Otto Velez	.08	.03	.01
☐ 463 Steve Comer	.08	.03	.01
☐ 464 Joe Nolan	.08	.03	.01
☐ 465 Reggie Smith	.18	.08	.01
☐ 466 Mark Littell	.08	.03	.01
☐ 467 Don Kessinger DP	.08	.03	.01
☐ 468 Stan Bahnsen DP	.03	.01	.00
☐ 469 Lance Parrish	3.50	1.40	.35
☐ 470 Garry Maddox DP	.08	.03	.01
☐ 471 Joaquin Andujar	.25	.10	.02
☐ 472 Craig Kusick	.08	.03	.01
☐ 473 Dave Roberts	.08	.03	.01
☐ 474 Dick Davis	.08	.03	.01
☐ 475 Dan Driessen	.12	.05	.01
☐ 476 Tom Poquette	.08	.03	.01
☐ 477 Bob Grich	.15	.06	.01
☐ 478 Juan Beniquez	.12	.05	.01
☐ 479 Padres Team/Mgr.	.30	.06	.01
Roger Craig			
(checklist back)			
☐ 480 Fred Lynn	.75	.30	.07
☐ 481 Skip Lockwood	.08	.03	.01
☐ 482 Craig Reynolds	.08	.03	.01
☐ 483 Checklist 4 DP	.10	.01	.00
☐ 484 Rick Waits	.08	.03	.01
☐ 485 Bucky Dent	.15	.06	.01
☐ 486 Bob Knepper	.40	.16	.04
☐ 487 Miguel Dilone	.12	.05	.01
☐ 488 Bob Owchinko	.08	.03	.01
☐ 489 Larry Cox	.12	.05	.01
(photo actually			
Dave Rader)			
☐ 490 Al Cowens	.12	.05	.01
☐ 491 Tippy Martinez	.12	.05	.01
☐ 492 Bob Bailor	.08	.03	.01
☐ 493 Larry Christenson	.08	.03	.01
☐ 494 Jerry White	.08	.03	.01
☐ 495 Tony Perez	.35	.14	.03
☐ 496 Barry Bonnell DP	.03	.01	.00
☐ 497 Glenn Abbott	.08	.03	.01
☐ 498 Rich Chiles	.08	.03	.01
☐ 499 Rangers Team/Mgr.	.30	.06	.01
Pat Corrales			
(checklist back)			
☐ 500 Ron Guidry	.90	.36	.09
☐ 501 Junior Kennedy	.08	.03	.01
☐ 502 Steve Braun	.08	.03	.01
☐ 503 Terry Humphrey	.08	.03	.01
☐ 504 Larry McWilliams	.40	.16	.04
☐ 505 Ed Kranepool	.12	.05	.01

	MINT	VG-E	F-G
☐ 506 John D'Acquisto	.08	.03	.01
☐ 507 Tony Armas	.30	.12	.03
☐ 508 Charlie Hough	.15	.06	.01
☐ 509 Mario Mendoza	.08	.03	.01
☐ 510 Ted Simmons	.35	.14	.03
☐ 511 Paul Reuschel DP	.03	.01	.00
☐ 512 Jack Clark	.50	.20	.05
☐ 513 Dave Johnson	.18	.08	.01
☐ 514 Mike Proly	.08	.03	.01
☐ 515 Enos Cabell	.08	.03	.01
☐ 516 Champ Summers DP	.03	.01	.00
☐ 517 Al Bumbry	.08	.03	.01
☐ 518 Jim Umbarger	.08	.03	.01
☐ 519 Ben Oglivie	.15	.06	.01
☐ 520 Gary Carter	2.50	1.00	.25
☐ 521 Sam Ewing	.08	.03	.01
☐ 522 Ken Holtzman	.12	.05	.01
☐ 523 John Milner	.08	.03	.01
☐ 524 Tom Burgmeier	.08	.03	.01
☐ 525 Freddie Patek	.08	.03	.01
☐ 526 Dodgers Team/Mgr.	.35	.07	.01
Tom Lasorda			
(checklist back)			
☐ 527 Lerrin LaGrow	.08	.03	.01
☐ 528 Wayne Gross DP	.03	.01	.00
☐ 529 Brian Asselstine	.08	.03	.01
☐ 530 Frank Tanana	.15	.06	.01
☐ 531 Fernando Gonzalez	.08	.03	.01
☐ 532 Buddy Schultz	.08	.03	.01
☐ 533 Leroy Stanton	.08	.03	.01
☐ 534 Ken Forsch	.08	.03	.01
☐ 535 Ellis Valentine	.12	.05	.01
☐ 536 Jerry Reuss	.15	.06	.01
☐ 537 Tom Veryzer	.08	.03	.01
☐ 538 Mike Ivie DP	.03	.01	.00
☐ 539 John Ellis	.08	.03	.01
☐ 540 Greg Luzinski	.20	.08	.02
☐ 541 Jim Slaton	.08	.03	.01
☐ 542 Rick Bosetti	.08	.03	.01
☐ 543 Kiko Garcia	.08	.03	.01
☐ 544 Fergie Jenkins	.30	.12	.03
☐ 545 John Stearns	.08	.03	.01
☐ 546 Bill Russell	.12	.05	.01
☐ 547 Clint Hurdle	.08	.03	.01
☐ 548 Enrique Romo	.08	.03	.01
☐ 549 Bob Bailey	.08	.03	.01
☐ 550 Sal Bando	.15	.06	.01
☐ 551 Cubs Team/Mgr.	.30	.06	.01
Herman Franks			
(checklist back)			
☐ 552 Jose Morales	.08	.03	.01
☐ 553 Denny Walling	.08	.03	.01
☐ 554 Matt Keough	.12	.05	.01

	MINT	VG-E	F-G
☐ 555 Biff Pocoroba	.08	.03	.01
☐ 556 Mike Lum	.08	.03	.01
☐ 557 Ken Brett	.12	.05	.01
☐ 558 Jay Johnstone	.12	.05	.01
☐ 559 Greg Pryor	.08	.03	.01
☐ 560 John Montefusco	.12	.05	.01
☐ 561 Ed Ott	.08	.03	.01
☐ 562 Dusty Baker	.18	.08	.01
☐ 563 Roy Thomas	.08	.03	.01
☐ 564 Jerry Turner	.08	.03	.01
☐ 565 Rico Carty	.15	.06	.01
☐ 566 Nino Espinosa	.08	.03	.01
☐ 567 Rich Hebner	.08	.03	.01
☐ 568 Carlos Lopez	.08	.03	.01
☐ 569 Bob Sykes	.08	.03	.01
☐ 570 Cesar Cedeno	.18	.08	.01
☐ 571 Darrell Porter	.12	.05	.01
☐ 572 Rod Gilbreath	.08	.03	.01
☐ 573 Jim Kern	.08	.03	.01
☐ 574 Claudell Washington	.15	.06	.01
☐ 575 Luis Tiant	.18	.08	.01
☐ 576 Mike Parrott	.08	.03	.01
☐ 577 Brewers Team/Mgr.	.30	.06	.01
George Bamberger			
(checklist back)			
☐ 578 Pete Broberg	.08	.03	.01
☐ 579 Greg Gross	.08	.03	.01
☐ 580 Ron Fairly	.12	.05	.01
☐ 581 Darold Knowles	.08	.03	.01
☐ 582 Paul Blair	.12	.05	.01
☐ 583 Julio Cruz	.12	.05	.01
☐ 584 Jim Rooker	.08	.03	.01
☐ 585 Hal McRae	.15	.06	.01
☐ 586 Bob Horner	4.00	1.60	.40
☐ 587 Ken Reitz	.08	.03	.01
☐ 588 Tom Murphy	.08	.03	.01
☐ 589 Terry Whitfield	.08	.03	.01
☐ 590 J.R. Richard	.18	.08	.01
☐ 591 Mike Hargrove	.12	.05	.01
☐ 592 Mike Krukow	.20	.08	.02
☐ 593 Rick Dempsey	.12	.05	.01
☐ 594 Bob Shirley	.08	.03	.01
☐ 595 Phil Niekro	.75	.30	.07
☐ 596 Jim Wohlford	.08	.03	.01
☐ 597 Bob Stanley	.15	.06	.01
☐ 598 Mark Wagner	.08	.03	.01
☐ 599 Jim Spencer	.08	.03	.01
☐ 600 George Foster	.65	.26	.06
☐ 601 Dave LaRoche	.08	.03	.01
☐ 602 Checklist 5	.30	.03	.00
☐ 603 Rudy May	.08	.03	.01
☐ 604 Jeff Newman	.08	.03	.01
☐ 605 Rick Monday DP	.08	.03	.01

		MINT	VG-E	F-G
☐ 606	Expos Team/Mgr. Dick Williams (checklist back)	.30	.06	.01
☐ 607	Omar Moreno	.12	.05	.01
☐ 608	Dave McKay	.08	.03	.01
☐ 609	Silvio Martinez	.08	.03	.01
☐ 610	Mike Schmidt	2.75	1.10	.27
☐ 611	Jim Norris	.08	.03	.01
☐ 612	Rick Honeycutt	.75	.30	.07
☐ 613	Mike Edwards	.08	.03	.01
☐ 614	Willie Hernandez	.50	.20	.05
☐ 615	Ken Singleton	.20	.08	.02
☐ 616	Billy Almon	.08	.03	.01
☐ 617	Terry Puhl	.12	.05	.01
☐ 618	Jerry Remy	.12	.05	.01
☐ 619	Ken Landreaux	.30	.12	.03
☐ 620	Bert Campaneris	.12	.05	.01
☐ 621	Pat Zachry	.08	.03	.01
☐ 622	Dave Collins	.15	.06	.01
☐ 623	Bob McClure	.08	.03	.01
☐ 624	Larry Herndon	.12	.05	.01
☐ 625	Mark Fidrych	.15	.06	.01
☐ 626	Yankees Team/Mgr. Bob Lemon (checklist back)	.35	.07	.01
☐ 627	Gary Serum	.08	.03	.01
☐ 628	Del Unser	.08	.03	.01
☐ 629	Gene Garber	.12	.05	.01
☐ 630	Bake McBride	.12	.05	.01
☐ 631	Jorge Orta	.08	.03	.01
☐ 632	Don Kirkwood	.08	.03	.01
☐ 633	Rob Wilfong DP	.03	.01	.00
☐ 634	Paul Lindblad	.08	.03	.01
☐ 635	Don Baylor	.75	.30	.07
☐ 636	Wayne Garland	.08	.03	.01
☐ 637	Bill Robinson	.08	.03	.01
☐ 638	Al Fitzmorris	.08	.03	.01
☐ 639	Manny Trillo	.12	.05	.01
☐ 640	Eddie Murray	4.50	1.80	.45
☐ 641	Bobby Castillo	.08	.03	.01
☐ 642	Wilbur Howard DP	.03	.01	.00
☐ 643	Tom Hausman	.08	.03	.01
☐ 644	Manny Mota	.12	.05	.01
☐ 645	George Scott DP	.08	.03	.01
☐ 646	Rick Sweet	.08	.03	.01
☐ 647	Bob Lacey	.08	.03	.01
☐ 648	Lou Piniella	.20	.08	.02
☐ 649	John Curtis	.08	.03	.01
☐ 650	Pete Rose	4.00	1.60	.40
☐ 651	Mike Caldwell	.12	.05	.01
☐ 652	Stan Papi	.08	.03	.01
☐ 653	Warren Brusstar DP	.03	.01	.00
☐ 654	Rick Miller	.08	.03	.01
☐ 655	Jerry Koosman	.15	.06	.01
☐ 656	Hosken Powell	.08	.03	.01
☐ 657	George Medich	.12	.05	.01
☐ 658	Taylor Duncan	.08	.03	.01
☐ 659	Mariners Team/Mgr. Darrell Johnson (checklist back)	.25	.05	.01
☐ 660	Ron LeFlore DP	.08	.03	.01
☐ 661	Bruce Kison	.08	.03	.01
☐ 662	Kevin Bell	.08	.03	.01
☐ 663	Mike Vail	.08	.03	.01
☐ 664	Doug Bird	.08	.03	.01
☐ 665	Lou Brock	1.25	.50	.12
☐ 666	Rich Dauer	.08	.03	.01
☐ 667	Don Hood	.08	.03	.01
☐ 668	Bill North	.08	.03	.01
☐ 669	Checklist 6	.30	.03	.00
☐ 670	Jim Hunter DP	.25	.10	.02
☐ 671	Joe Ferguson DP	.03	.01	.00
☐ 672	Ed Halicki	.08	.03	.01
☐ 673	Tom Hutton	.08	.03	.01
☐ 674	Dave Tomlin	.08	.03	.01
☐ 675	Tim McCarver	.15	.06	.01
☐ 676	Johnny Sutton	.08	.03	.01
☐ 677	Larry Parrish	.15	.06	.01
☐ 678	Geoff Zahn	.08	.03	.01
☐ 679	Derrel Thomas	.08	.03	.01
☐ 680	Carlton Fisk	.50	.20	.05
☐ 681	John Henry Johnson	.08	.03	.01
☐ 682	Dave Chalk	.08	.03	.01
☐ 683	Dan Meyer DP	.03	.01	.00
☐ 684	Jamie Easterly DP	.03	.01	.00
☐ 685	Sixto Lezcano	.12	.05	.01
☐ 686	Ron Schueler DP	.03	.01	.00
☐ 687	Rennie Stennett	.08	.03	.01
☐ 688	Mike Willis	.08	.03	.01
☐ 689	Orioles Team/Mgr. Earl Weaver (checklist back)	.35	.07	.01
☐ 690	Buddy Bell DP	.10	.04	.01
☐ 691	Dock Ellis DP	.03	.01	.00
☐ 692	Mickey Stanley	.08	.03	.01
☐ 693	Dave Rader	.08	.03	.01
☐ 694	Burt Hooton	.12	.05	.01
☐ 695	Keith Hernandez	1.50	.60	.15
☐ 696	Andy Hassler	.08	.03	.01
☐ 697	Dave Bergman	.08	.03	.01
☐ 698	Bill Stein	.08	.03	.01
☐ 699	Hal Dues	.08	.03	.01
☐ 700	Reggie Jackson DP	.90	.36	.09

	MINT	VG-E	F-G		MINT	VG-E	F-G
☐ 701 Orioles Prospects .... Mark Corey John Flinn Sammy Stewart	.25	.10	.02	☐ 714 Blue Jays Prospects ... Victor Cruz Pat Kelly Ernie Whitt	.12	.05	.01
☐ 702 Red Sox Prospects ..... Joel Finch Garry Hancock Allen Ripley	.12	.05	.01	☐ 715 Braves Prospects .... Bruce Benedict Glenn Hubbard Larry Whisenton	.40	.16	.04
☐ 703 Angels Prospects .... Jim Anderson Dave Frost Bob Slater	.12	.05	.01	☐ 716 Cubs Prospects .... Dave Geisel Karl Pagel Scot Thompson	.12	.05	.01
☐ 704 White Sox Prospects ... Ross Baumgarten Mike Colbern Mike Squires	.12	.05	.01	☐ 717 Reds Prospects .... Mike LaCoss Ron Oester Harry Spilman	.40	.16	.04
☐ 705 Indians Prospects .... Alfredo Griffin Tim Norrid Dave Oliver	.60	.24	.06	☐ 718 Astros Prospects .... Bruce Bochy Mike Fischlin Don Pisker	.12	.05	.01
☐ 706 Tigers Prospects .... Dave Stegman Dave Tobik Kip Young	.12	.05	.01	☐ 719 Dodgers Prospects ..... Pedro Guerrero Rudy Law Joe Simpson	4.00	1.60	.40
☐ 707 Royals Prospects .... Randy Bass Jim Gaudet Randy McGilberry	.12	.05	.01	☐ 720 Expos Prospects .... Jerry Fry Jerry Pirtle Scott Sanderson	.25	.10	.02
☐ 708 Brewers Prospects ...... Kevin Bass Eddie Romero Ned Yost	1.25	.50	.12	☐ 721 Mets Prospects .... Juan Berenguer Dwight Bernard Dan Norman	.15	.06	.01
☐ 709 Twins Prospects .... Sam Perlozzo Rick Sofield Kevin Stanfield	.12	.05	.01	☐ 722 Phillies Prospects .... Jim Morrison Lonnie Smith Jim Wright	.90	.36	.09
☐ 710 Yankees Prospects ..... Brian Doyle Mike Heath Dave Rajsich	.25	.10	.02	☐ 723 Pirates Prospects .... Dale Berra Eugenio Cotes Ben Wiltbank	.30	.12	.03
☐ 711 A's Prospects .... Dwayne Murphy Bruce Robinson Alan Wirth	.80	.32	.08	☐ 724 Cardinals Prospects .... Tom Bruno George Frazier Terry Kennedy	.90	.36	.09
☐ 712 Mariners Prospects ..... Bud Anderson Greg Biercevicz Byron McLaughlin	.12	.05	.01	☐ 725 Padres Prospects .... Jim Beswick Steve Mura Broderick Perkins	.12	.05	.01
☐ 713 Rangers Prospects ..... Danny Darwin Pat Putnam Billy Sample	.40	.16	.04	☐ 726 Giants Prospects .... Greg Johnston Joe Strain John Tamargo	.12	.05	.01

1980 Topps

The cards in this 726-card set measure 2½" by 3½". In 1980 Topps released another set of the same size and number of cards as the previous two years. As with those sets, Topps again has produced 66 double printed cards in the set; they are noted by DP in the checklist below. The player's name appears over the picture and his position and team are found in pennant design. Every card carries a facsimile autograph. Team cards feature a team checklist of players in the set on the back and the manager's name on the front. Cards 1-6 show Highlights (HL) of the 1979 season, cards 201-207 are League Leaders, and cards 661-686 feature American and National League rookie "Future Stars," one card for each team showing three young prospects.

	MINT	VG-E	F-G
Complete Set	90.00	36.00	9.00
Common Player (1-726)	.07	.03	.01
Common DP's (1-726)	.03	.01	.00

			MINT	VG-E	F-G
☐	1	HL: Brock and Yaz, Enter 3000 hit circle	1.00	.20	.04
☐	2	HL: Willie McCovey, 512th homer sets new mark for NL lefties	.50	.20	.05
☐	3	HL: Manny Mota, All-time pinch-hits, 145	.12	.05	.01
☐	4	HL: Pete Rose, Career Record 10th season with 200 or more hits	1.50	.60	.15
☐	5	HL: Garry Templeton 1st with 100 hits from each side of plate	.18	.08	.01
☐	6	HL: Del Unser, 3rd cons. pinch homer sets new ML standard	.10	.04	.01
☐	7	Mike Lum	.07	.03	.01
☐	8	Craig Swan	.10	.04	.01
☐	9	Steve Braun	.07	.03	.01
☐	10	Denny Martinez	.10	.04	.01
☐	11	Jimmy Sexton	.07	.03	.01
☐	12	John Curtis DP	.03	.01	.00
☐	13	Ron Pruitt	.07	.03	.01
☐	14	Dave Cash	.10	.04	.01
☐	15	Bill Campbell	.10	.04	.01
☐	16	Jerry Narron	.07	.03	.01
☐	17	Bruce Sutter	.40	.16	.04
☐	18	Ron Jackson	.07	.03	.01
☐	19	Balor Moore	.07	.03	.01
☐	20	Dan Ford	.07	.03	.01
☐	21	Manny Sarmiento	.07	.03	.01
☐	22	Pat Putnam	.07	.03	.01
☐	23	Derrel Thomas	.07	.03	.01
☐	24	Jim Slaton	.10	.04	.01
☐	25	Lee Mazzilli	.12	.05	.01
☐	26	Marty Pattin	.07	.03	.01
☐	27	Del Unser	.07	.03	.01
☐	28	Bruce Kison	.07	.03	.01
☐	29	Mark Wagner	.07	.03	.01
☐	30	Vida Blue	.18	.08	.01
☐	31	Jay Johnstone	.10	.04	.01
☐	32	Julio Cruz DP	.07	.03	.01
☐	33	Tony Scott	.07	.03	.01
☐	34	Jeff Newman DP	.03	.01	.00
☐	35	Luis Tiant	.18	.08	.01
☐	36	Rusty Torres	.07	.03	.01
☐	37	Kiko Garcia	.07	.03	.01
☐	38	Dan Spillner DP	.03	.01	.00
☐	39	Rowland Office	.07	.03	.01
☐	40	Carlton Fisk	.35	.14	.03
☐	41	Rangers Team/Mgr. Pat Corrales (checklist back)	.25	.05	.01
☐	42	David Palmer	.45	.18	.04
☐	43	Bombo Rivera	.07	.03	.01
☐	44	Bill Fahey	.07	.03	.01
☐	45	Frank White	.15	.06	.01
☐	46	Rico Carty	.10	.04	.01
☐	47	Bill Bonham DP	.03	.01	.00
☐	48	Rick Miller	.07	.03	.01
☐	49	Mario Guerrero	.07	.03	.01
☐	50	J.R. Richard	.18	.08	.01
☐	51	Joe Ferguson DP	.03	.01	.00

		MINT	VG-E	F-G
☐ 52	Warren Brusstar	.07	.03	.01
☐ 53	Ben Oglivie	.15	.06	.01
☐ 54	Dennis Lamp	.07	.03	.01
☐ 55	Bill Madlock	.35	.14	.03
☐ 56	Bobby Valentine	.15	.06	.01
☐ 57	Pete Vuckovich	.12	.05	.01
☐ 58	Doug Flynn	.07	.03	.01
☐ 59	Eddy Putman	.07	.03	.01
☐ 60	Bucky Dent	.12	.05	.01
☐ 61	Gary Serum	.07	.03	.01
☐ 62	Mike Ivie	.07	.03	.01
☐ 63	Bob Stanley	.12	.05	.01
☐ 64	Joe Nolan	.07	.03	.01
☐ 65	Al Bumbry	.07	.03	.01
☐ 66	Royals Team/Mgr.	.25	.05	.01
	Jim Frey			
	(checklist back)			
☐ 67	Doyle Alexander	.10	.04	.01
☐ 68	Larry Harlow	.07	.03	.01
☐ 69	Rick Williams	.07	.03	.01
☐ 70	Gary Carter	2.00	.80	.20
☐ 71	John Milner DP	.03	.01	.00
☐ 72	Fred Howard DP	.03	.01	.00
☐ 73	Dave Collins	.10	.04	.01
☐ 74	Sid Monge	.07	.03	.01
☐ 75	Bill Russell	.10	.04	.01
☐ 76	John Stearns	.07	.03	.01
☐ 77	Dave Stieb	1.50	.60	.15
☐ 78	Ruppert Jones	.10	.04	.01
☐ 79	Bob Owchinko	.07	.03	.01
☐ 80	Ron LeFlore	.10	.04	.01
☐ 81	Ted Sizemore	.07	.03	.01
☐ 82	Astros Team/Mgr.	.25	.05	.01
	Bill Virdon			
	(checklist back)			
☐ 83	Steve Trout	.35	.14	.03
☐ 84	Gary Lavelle	.10	.04	.01
☐ 85	Ted Simmons	.35	.14	.03
☐ 86	Dave Hamilton	.07	.03	.01
☐ 87	Pepe Frias	.07	.03	.01
☐ 88	Ken Landreaux	.10	.04	.01
☐ 89	Don Hood	.07	.03	.01
☐ 90	Manny Trillo	.10	.04	.01
☐ 91	Rick Dempsey	.10	.04	.01
☐ 92	Rick Rhoden	.15	.06	.01
☐ 93	Dave Roberts DP	.03	.01	.00
☐ 94	Neil Allen	.35	.14	.03
☐ 95	Cecil Cooper	.30	.12	.03
☐ 96	A's Team/Mgr.	.25	.05	.01
	Jim Marshall			
	(checklist back)			
☐ 97	Bill Lee	.10	.04	.01
☐ 98	Jerry Terrell	.07	.03	.01

		MINT	VG-E	F-G
☐ 99	Victor Cruz	.07	.03	.01
☐ 100	Johnny Bench	1.50	.60	.15
☐ 101	Aurelio Lopez	.07	.03	.01
☐ 102	Rich Dauer	.07	.03	.01
☐ 103	Bill Caudill	.35	.14	.03
☐ 104	Manny Mota	.10	.04	.01
☐ 105	Frank Tanana	.12	.05	.01
☐ 106	Jeff Leonard	.75	.30	.07
☐ 107	Francisco Barrios	.07	.03	.01
☐ 108	Bob Horner	1.00	.40	.10
☐ 109	Bill Travers	.07	.03	.01
☐ 110	Fred Lynn DP	.25	.10	.02
☐ 111	Bob Knepper	.20	.08	.02
☐ 112	White Sox Team/Mgr.	.25	.05	.01
	Tony LaRussa			
	(checklist back)			
☐ 113	Geoff Zahn	.07	.03	.01
☐ 114	Juan Beniquez	.10	.04	.01
☐ 115	Sparky Lyle	.15	.06	.01
☐ 116	Larry Cox	.07	.03	.01
☐ 117	Dock Ellis	.07	.03	.01
☐ 118	Phil Garner	.10	.04	.01
☐ 119	Sammy Stewart	.10	.04	.01
☐ 120	Greg Luzinski	.20	.08	.02
☐ 121	Checklist 1	.20	.02	.00
☐ 122	Dave Rosello DP	.03	.01	.00
☐ 123	Lynn Jones	.07	.03	.01
☐ 124	Dave Lemanczyk	.07	.03	.01
☐ 125	Tony Perez	.25	.10	.02
☐ 126	Dave Tomlin	.07	.03	.01
☐ 127	Gary Thomasson	.07	.03	.01
☐ 128	Tom Burgmeier	.07	.03	.01
☐ 129	Craig Reynolds	.07	.03	.01
☐ 130	Amos Otis	.12	.05	.01
☐ 131	Paul Mitchell	.07	.03	.01
☐ 132	Biff Pocoroba	.07	.03	.01
☐ 133	Jerry Turner	.07	.03	.01
☐ 134	Matt Keough	.07	.03	.01
☐ 135	Bill Buckner	.20	.08	.02
☐ 136	Dick Ruthven	.07	.03	.01
☐ 137	John Castino	.20	.08	.02
☐ 138	Ross Baumgarten	.07	.03	.01
☐ 139	Dane Iorg	.15	.06	.01
☐ 140	Rich Gossage	.40	.16	.04
☐ 141	Gary Alexander	.07	.03	.01
☐ 142	Phil Huffman	.07	.03	.01
☐ 143	Bruce Bochte DP	.03	.01	.00
☐ 144	Steve Comer	.07	.03	.01
☐ 145	Darrell Evans	.18	.08	.01
☐ 146	Bob Welch	.18	.08	.01
☐ 147	Terry Puhl	.10	.04	.01
☐ 148	Manny Sanguillen	.10	.04	.01
☐ 149	Tom Hume	.07	.03	.01

	MINT	VG-E	F-G
☐ 150 Jason Thompson	.15	.06	.01
☐ 151 Tom Hausman DP	.03	.01	.00
☐ 152 John Fulgham	.07	.03	.01
☐ 153 Tim Blackwell	.07	.03	.01
☐ 154 Lary Sorensen	.07	.03	.01
☐ 155 Jerry Remy	.10	.04	.01
☐ 156 Tony Brizzolara	.07	.03	.01
☐ 157 Willie Wilson DP	.18	.08	.01
☐ 158 Rob Picciolo DP	.03	.01	.00
☐ 159 Ken Clay	.07	.03	.01
☐ 160 Eddie Murray	2.75	1.10	.27
☐ 161 Larry Christenson	.07	.03	.01
☐ 162 Bob Randall	.07	.03	.01
☐ 163 Steve Swisher	.07	.03	.01
☐ 164 Greg Pryor	.07	.03	.01
☐ 165 Omar Moreno	.07	.03	.01
☐ 166 Glenn Abbott	.07	.03	.01
☐ 167 Jack Clark	.40	.16	.04
☐ 168 Rick Waits	.07	.03	.01
☐ 169 Luis Gomez	.07	.03	.01
☐ 170 Burt Hooton	.07	.03	.01
☐ 171 Fernando Gonzalez	.07	.03	.01
☐ 172 Ron Hodges	.07	.03	.01
☐ 173 John Henry Johnson	.07	.03	.01
☐ 174 Ray Knight	.15	.06	.01
☐ 175 Rick Reuschel	.12	.05	.01
☐ 176 Champ Summers	.07	.03	.01
☐ 177 Dave Heaverlo	.07	.03	.01
☐ 178 Tim McCarver	.15	.06	.01
☐ 179 Ron Davis	.25	.10	.02
☐ 180 Warren Cromartie	.07	.03	.01
☐ 181 Moose Haas	.10	.04	.01
☐ 182 Ken Reitz	.07	.03	.01
☐ 183 Jim Anderson DP	.03	.01	.00
☐ 184 Steve Renko DP	.03	.01	.00
☐ 185 Hal McRae	.12	.05	.01
☐ 186 Junior Moore	.07	.03	.01
☐ 187 Alan Ashby	.07	.03	.01
☐ 188 Terry Crowley	.07	.03	.01
☐ 189 Kevin Kobel	.07	.03	.01
☐ 190 Buddy Bell	.18	.08	.01
☐ 191 Ted Martinez	.07	.03	.01
☐ 192 Braves Team/Mgr.	.25	.05	.01
Bobby Cox (checklist back)			
☐ 193 Dave Goltz	.10	.04	.01
☐ 194 Mike Easler	.20	.08	.02
☐ 195 John Montefusco	.10	.04	.01
☐ 196 Lance Parrish	1.50	.60	.15
☐ 197 Byron McLaughlin	.07	.03	.01
☐ 198 Dell Alston DP	.03	.01	.00
☐ 199 Mike LaCoss	.07	.03	.01
☐ 200 Jim Rice	2.00	.80	.20

	MINT	VG-E	F-G
☐ 201 Batting Leaders	.20	.08	.02
Keith Hernandez			
Fred Lynn			
☐ 202 Home Run Leaders	.15	.06	.01
Dave Kingman			
Gorman Thomas			
☐ 203 RBI Leaders	.20	.08	.02
Dave Winfield			
Don Baylor			
☐ 204 Stolen Base Leaders	.12	.05	.01
Omar Moreno			
Willie Wilson			
☐ 205 Victory Leaders	.20	.08	.02
Joe Niekro			
Phil Niekro			
Mike Flanagan			
☐ 206 Strikeout Leaders	.20	.08	.02
J.R. Richard			
Nolan Ryan			
☐ 207 ERA Leaders	.15	.06	.01
J.R. Richard			
Ron Guidry			
☐ 208 Wayne Cage	.07	.03	.01
☐ 209 Von Joshua	.07	.03	.01
☐ 210 Steve Carlton	1.75	.70	.17
☐ 211 Dave Skaggs DP	.03	.01	.00
☐ 212 Dave Roberts	.07	.03	.01
☐ 213 Mike Jorgensen DP	.03	.01	.00
☐ 214 Angels Team/Mgr.	.25	.05	.01
Jim Fregosi (checklist back)			
☐ 215 Sixto Lezcano	.07	.03	.01
☐ 216 Phil Mankowski	.07	.03	.01
☐ 217 Ed Halicki	.07	.03	.01
☐ 218 Jose Morales	.07	.03	.01
☐ 219 Steve Mingori	.07	.03	.01
☐ 220 Dave Concepcion	.20	.08	.02
☐ 221 Joe Cannon	.07	.03	.01
☐ 222 Ron Hassey	.10	.04	.01
☐ 223 Bob Sykes	.07	.03	.01
☐ 224 Willie Montanez	.10	.04	.01
☐ 225 Lou Piniella	.18	.08	.01
☐ 226 Bill Stein	.07	.03	.01
☐ 227 Len Barker	.12	.05	.01
☐ 228 Johnny Oates	.07	.03	.01
☐ 229 Jim Bibby	.10	.04	.01
☐ 230 Dave Winfield	1.50	.60	.15
☐ 231 Steve McCatty	.07	.03	.01
☐ 232 Alan Trammell	.90	.36	.09
☐ 233 LaRue Washington	.07	.03	.01
☐ 234 Vern Ruhle	.07	.03	.01
☐ 235 Andre Dawson	.90	.36	.09
☐ 236 Marc Hill	.07	.03	.01

		MINT	VG-E	F-G
☐ 237	Scott McGregor	.12	.05	.01
☐ 238	Rob Wilfong	.07	.03	.01
☐ 239	Don Aase	.12	.05	.01
☐ 240	Dave Kingman	.35	.14	.03
☐ 241	Checklist 2	.20	.02	.00
☐ 242	Lamar Johnson	.07	.03	.01
☐ 243	Jerry Augustine	.07	.03	.01
☐ 244	Cardinals Team/Mgr.	.25	.05	.01
	Ken Boyer			
	(checklist back)			
☐ 245	Phil Niekro	.50	.20	.05
☐ 246	Tim Foli DP	.03	.01	.00
☐ 247	Frank Riccelli	.07	.03	.01
☐ 248	Jamie Quirk	.07	.03	.01
☐ 249	Jim Clancy	.10	.04	.01
☐ 250	Jim Kaat	.30	.12	.03
☐ 251	Kip Young	.07	.03	.01
☐ 252	Ted Cox	.07	.03	.01
☐ 253	John Montague	.07	.03	.01
☐ 254	Paul Dade DP	.03	.01	.00
☐ 255	Dusty Baker DP	.07	.03	.01
☐ 256	Roger Erickson	.07	.03	.01
☐ 257	Larry Herndon	.10	.04	.01
☐ 258	Paul Moskau	.07	.03	.01
☐ 259	Mets Team/Mgr.	.30	.06	.01
	Joe Torre			
	(checklist back)			
☐ 260	Al Oliver	.25	.10	.02
☐ 261	Dave Chalk	.07	.03	.01
☐ 262	Benny Ayala	.07	.03	.01
☐ 263	Dave LaRoche DP	.03	.01	.00
☐ 264	Bill Robinson	.07	.03	.01
☐ 265	Robin Yount	1.50	.60	.15
☐ 266	Bernie Carbo	.07	.03	.01
☐ 267	Dan Schatzeder	.07	.03	.01
☐ 268	Rafael Landestoy	.07	.03	.01
☐ 269	Dave Tobik	.07	.03	.01
☐ 270	Mike Schmidt DP	1.00	.40	.10
☐ 271	Dick Drago DP	.03	.01	.00
☐ 272	Ralph Garr	.10	.04	.01
☐ 273	Eduardo Rodriguez	.07	.03	.01
☐ 274	Dale Murphy	4.00	1.60	.40
☐ 275	Jerry Koosman	.15	.06	.01
☐ 276	Tom Veryzer	.07	.03	.01
☐ 277	Rick Bosetti	.07	.03	.01
☐ 278	Jim Spencer	.07	.03	.01
☐ 279	Rob Andrews	.07	.03	.01
☐ 280	Gaylord Perry	.55	.22	.05
☐ 281	Paul Blair	.10	.04	.01
☐ 282	Mariners Team/Mgr.	.20	.04	.01
	Darrell Johnson			
	(checklist back)			
☐ 283	John Ellis	.07	.03	.01
☐ 284	Larry Murray DP	.03	.01	.00
☐ 285	Don Baylor	.35	.14	.03
☐ 286	Darold Knowles DP	.03	.01	.00
☐ 287	John Lowenstein	.07	.03	.01
☐ 288	Dave Rozema	.07	.03	.01
☐ 289	Bruce Bochy	.07	.03	.01
☐ 290	Steve Garvey	1.50	.60	.15
☐ 291	Randy Scarberry	.07	.03	.01
☐ 292	Dale Berra	.10	.04	.01
☐ 293	Elias Sosa	.07	.03	.01
☐ 294	Charlie Spikes	.07	.03	.01
☐ 295	Larry Gura	.10	.04	.01
☐ 296	Dave Rader	.07	.03	.01
☐ 297	Tim Johnson	.07	.03	.01
☐ 298	Ken Holtzman	.10	.04	.01
☐ 299	Steve Henderson	.07	.03	.01
☐ 300	Ron Guidry	.75	.30	.07
☐ 301	Mike Edwards	.07	.03	.01
☐ 302	Dodgers Team/Mgr.	.30	.06	.01
	Tom Lasorda			
	(checklist back)			
☐ 303	Bill Castro	.07	.03	.01
☐ 304	Butch Wynegar	.10	.04	.01
☐ 305	Randy Jones	.10	.04	.01
☐ 306	Denny Walling	.07	.03	.01
☐ 307	Rick Honeycutt	.15	.06	.01
☐ 308	Mike Hargrove	.10	.04	.01
☐ 309	Larry McWilliams	.10	.04	.01
☐ 310	Dave Parker	.85	.34	.08
☐ 311	Roger Metzger	.07	.03	.01
☐ 312	Mike Barlow	.07	.03	.01
☐ 313	Johnny Grubb	.07	.03	.01
☐ 314	Tim Stoddard	.20	.08	.02
☐ 315	Steve Kemp	.15	.06	.01
☐ 316	Bob Lacey	.07	.03	.01
☐ 317	Mike Anderson DP	.03	.01	.00
☐ 318	Jerry Reuss	.12	.05	.01
☐ 319	Chris Speier	.07	.03	.01
☐ 320	Dennis Eckersley	.10	.04	.01
☐ 321	Keith Hernandez	1.00	.40	.10
☐ 322	Claudell Washington	.12	.05	.01
☐ 323	Mick Kelleher	.07	.03	.01
☐ 324	Tom Underwood	.07	.03	.01
☐ 325	Dan Driessen	.10	.04	.01
☐ 326	Bo McLaughlin	.07	.03	.01
☐ 327	Ray Fosse DP	.03	.01	.00
☐ 328	Twins Team/Mgr.	.25	.05	.01
	Gene Mauch			
	(checklist back)			
☐ 329	Bert Roberge	.07	.03	.01
☐ 330	Al Cowens	.10	.04	.01
☐ 331	Rich Hebner	.07	.03	.01
☐ 332	Enrique Romo	.07	.03	.01

	MINT	VG-E	F-G
333 Jim Norris DP	.03	.01	.00
334 Jim Beattie	.07	.03	.01
335 Willie McCovey	1.25	.50	.12
336 George Medich	.07	.03	.01
337 Carney Lansford	.35	.14	.03
338 Johnny Wockenfuss	.07	.03	.01
339 John D'Acquisto	.07	.03	.01
340 Ken Singleton	.18	.08	.01
341 Jim Essian	.07	.03	.01
342 Odell Jones	.07	.03	.01
343 Mike Vail	.07	.03	.01
344 Randy Lerch	.07	.03	.01
345 Larry Parrish	.12	.05	.01
346 Buddy Solomon	.07	.03	.01
347 Harry Chappas	.07	.03	.01
348 Checklist 3	.20	.02	.00
349 Jack Brohamer	.07	.03	.01
350 George Hendrick	.15	.06	.01
351 Bob Davis	.07	.03	.01
352 Dan Briggs	.07	.03	.01
353 Andy Hassler	.07	.03	.01
354 Rick Auerbach	.07	.03	.01
355 Gary Matthews	.18	.08	.01
356 Padres Team/Mgr.	.25	.05	.01
Jerry Coleman			
(checklist back)			
357 Bob McClure	.10	.04	.01
358 Lou Whitaker	.90	.36	.09
359 Randy Moffitt	.07	.03	.01
360 Darrell Porter DP	.07	.03	.01
361 Wayne Garland	.07	.03	.01
362 Danny Goodwin	.07	.03	.01
363 Wayne Gross	.07	.03	.01
364 Ray Burris	.07	.03	.01
365 Bobby Murcer	.18	.08	.01
366 Rob Dressler	.07	.03	.01
367 Billy Smith	.07	.03	.01
368 Willie Aikens	.20	.08	.02
369 Jim Kern	.07	.03	.01
370 Cesar Cedeno	.15	.06	.01
371 Jack Morris	1.25	.50	.12
372 Joel Youngblood	.07	.03	.01
373 Dan Petry DP	1.00	.40	.10
374 Jim Gantner	.10	.04	.01
375 Ross Grimsley	.07	.03	.01
376 Gary Allenson	.10	.04	.01
377 Junior Kennedy	.07	.03	.01
378 Jerry Mumphrey	.10	.04	.01
379 Kevin Bell	.07	.03	.01
380 Garry Maddox	.10	.04	.01
381 Cubs Team/Mgr.	.25	.05	.01
Preston Gomez			
(checklist back)			

	MINT	VG-E	F-G
382 Dave Freisleben	.07	.03	.01
383 Ed Ott	.07	.03	.01
384 Joey McLaughlin	.07	.03	.01
385 Enos Cabell	.07	.03	.01
386 Darrell Jackson	.07	.03	.01
387 Fred Stanley	.07	.03	.01
388 Mike Paxton	.07	.03	.01
389 Pete LaCock	.07	.03	.01
390 Fergie Jenkins	.35	.14	.03
391 Tony Armas DP	.10	.04	.01
392 Milt Wilcox	.10	.04	.01
393 Ozzie Smith	.80	.32	.08
394 Reggie Cleveland	.07	.03	.01
395 Ellis Valentine	.10	.04	.01
396 Dan Meyer	.07	.03	.01
397 Roy Thomas DP	.03	.01	.00
398 Barry Foote	.07	.03	.01
399 Mike Proly DP	.03	.01	.00
400 George Foster	.40	.16	.04
401 Pete Falcone	.07	.03	.01
402 Merv Rettenmund	.07	.03	.01
403 Pete Redfern DP	.03	.01	.00
404 Orioles Team/Mgr.	.30	.06	.01
Earl Weaver			
(checklist back)			
405 Dwight Evans	.35	.14	.03
406 Paul Molitor	.35	.14	.03
407 Tony Solaita	.07	.03	.01
408 Bill North	.07	.03	.01
409 Paul Splittorff	.10	.04	.01
410 Bobby Bonds	.18	.08	.01
411 Frank LaCorte	.07	.03	.01
412 Thad Bosley	.07	.03	.01
413 Allen Ripley	.07	.03	.01
414 George Scott	.10	.04	.01
415 Bill Atkinson	.07	.03	.01
416 Tom Brookens	.07	.03	.01
417 Craig Chamberlain DP	.03	.01	.00
418 Roger Freed DP	.03	.01	.00
419 Vic Correll	.07	.03	.01
420 Butch Hobson	.07	.03	.01
421 Doug Bird	.07	.03	.01
422 Larry Milbourne	.07	.03	.01
423 Dave Frost	.07	.03	.01
424 Yankees Team/Mgr.	.30	.06	.01
Dick Howser			
(checklist back)			
425 Mark Belanger	.12	.05	.01
426 Grant Jackson	.07	.03	.01
427 Tom Hutton DP	.03	.01	.00
428 Pat Zachry	.07	.03	.01
429 Duane Kuiper	.07	.03	.01
430 Larry Hisle DP	.07	.03	.01

	MINT	VG-E	F-G		MINT	VG-E	F-G
☐ 431 Mike Krukow	.15	.06	.01	☐ 480 Bob Watson	.10	.04	.01
☐ 432 Willie Norwood	.07	.03	.01	☐ 481 Tom Paciorek	.07	.03	.01
☐ 433 Rich Gale	.07	.03	.01	☐ 482 Rickey Henderson	22.00	9.00	2.00
☐ 434 Johnnie LeMaster	.07	.03	.01	☐ 483 Bo Diaz	.10	.04	.01
☐ 435 Don Gullett	.10	.04	.01	☐ 484 Checklist 4	.20	.02	.00
☐ 436 Billy Almon	.07	.03	.01	☐ 485 Mickey Rivers	.10	.04	.01
☐ 437 Joe Niekro	.15	.06	.01	☐ 486 Mike Tyson DP	.03	.01	.00
☐ 438 Dave Revering	.07	.03	.01	☐ 487 Wayne Nordhagen	.07	.03	.01
☐ 439 Mike Phillips	.07	.03	.01	☐ 488 Roy Howell	.07	.03	.01
☐ 440 Don Sutton	.60	.24	.06	☐ 489 Preston Hanna DP	.03	.01	.00
☐ 441 Eric Soderholm	.07	.03	.01	☐ 490 Lee May	.10	.04	.01
☐ 442 Jorge Orta	.07	.03	.01	☐ 491 Steve Mura DP	.03	.01	.00
☐ 443 Mike Parrott	.07	.03	.01	☐ 492 Todd Cruz	.10	.04	.01
☐ 444 Alvis Woods	.07	.03	.01	☐ 493 Jerry Martin	.07	.03	.01
☐ 445 Mark Fidrych	.15	.06	.01	☐ 494 Craig Minetto	.07	.03	.01
☐ 446 Duffy Dyer	.07	.03	.01	☐ 495 Bake McBride	.10	.04	.01
☐ 447 Nino Espinosa	.07	.03	.01	☐ 496 Silvio Martinez	.07	.03	.01
☐ 448 Jim Wohlford	.07	.03	.01	☐ 497 Jim Mason	.07	.03	.01
☐ 449 Doug Bair	.07	.03	.01	☐ 498 Danny Darwin	.10	.04	.01
☐ 450 George Brett	2.75	1.10	.27	☐ 499 Giants Team/Mgr.	.25	.05	.01
☐ 451 Indians Team/Mgr.	.25	.05	.01	Dave Bristol			
Dave Garcia				☐ 500 Tom Seaver	1.25	.50	.12
(checklist back)				☐ 501 Rennie Stennett	.07	.03	.01
☐ 452 Steve Dillard	.07	.03	.01	☐ 502 Rich Wortham DP	.03	.01	.00
☐ 453 Mike Bacsik	.07	.03	.01	☐ 503 Mike Cubbage	.07	.03	.01
☐ 454 Tom Donohue	.07	.03	.01	☐ 504 Gene Garber	.07	.03	.01
☐ 455 Mike Torrez	.10	.04	.01	☐ 505 Bert Campaneris	.12	.05	.01
☐ 456 Frank Taveras	.07	.03	.01	☐ 506 Tom Buskey	.07	.03	.01
☐ 457 Bert Blyleven	.30	.12	.03	☐ 507 Leon Roberts	.07	.03	.01
☐ 458 Billy Sample	.07	.03	.01	☐ 508 U.L. Washington	.07	.03	.01
☐ 459 Mickey Lolich DP	.07	.03	.01	☐ 509 Ed Glynn	.07	.03	.01
☐ 460 Willie Randolph	.12	.05	.01	☐ 510 Ron Cey	.30	.12	.03
☐ 461 Dwayne Murphy	.15	.06	.01	☐ 511 Eric Wilkins	.07	.03	.01
☐ 462 Mike Sadek DP	.03	.01	.00	☐ 512 Jose Cardenal	.07	.03	.01
☐ 463 Jerry Royster	.07	.03	.01	☐ 513 Tom Dixon DP	.03	.01	.00
☐ 464 John Denny	.15	.06	.01	☐ 514 Steve Ontiveros	.07	.03	.01
☐ 465 Rick Monday	.10	.04	.01	☐ 515 Mike Caldwell	.10	.04	.01
☐ 466 Mike Squires	.07	.03	.01	☐ 516 Hector Cruz	.07	.03	.01
☐ 467 Jesse Jefferson	.07	.03	.01	☐ 517 Don Stanhouse	.07	.03	.01
☐ 468 Aurelio Rodriguez	.07	.03	.01	☐ 518 Nelson Norman	.07	.03	.01
☐ 469 Randy Niemann DP	.03	.01	.00	☐ 519 Steve Nicosia	.07	.03	.01
☐ 470 Bob Boone	.10	.04	.01	☐ 520 Steve Rogers	.15	.06	.01
☐ 471 Hosken Powell DP	.03	.01	.00	☐ 521 Ken Brett	.10	.04	.01
☐ 472 Willie Hernandez	.40	.16	.04	☐ 522 Jim Morrison	.10	.04	.01
☐ 473 Bump Wills	.07	.03	.01	☐ 523 Ken Henderson	.07	.03	.01
☐ 474 Steve Busby	.10	.04	.01	☐ 524 Jim Wright DP	.03	.01	.00
☐ 475 Cesar Geronimo	.07	.03	.01	☐ 525 Clint Hurdle	.07	.03	.01
☐ 476 Bob Shirley	.07	.03	.01	☐ 526 Phillies Team/Mgr.	.25	.05	.01
☐ 477 Buck Martinez	.07	.03	.01	Dallas Green			
☐ 478 Gil Flores	.07	.03	.01	(checklist back)			
☐ 479 Expos Team/Mgr.	.25	.05	.01	☐ 527 Doug Rau DP	.03	.01	.00
Dick Williams				☐ 528 Adrian Devine	.07	.03	.01
(checklist back)				☐ 529 Jim Barr	.07	.03	.01

		MINT	VG-E	F-G
☐ 530	Jim Sundberg DP	.07	.03	.01
☐ 531	Eric Rasmussen	.07	.03	.01
☐ 532	Willie Horton	.10	.04	.01
☐ 533	Checklist 5	.20	.02	.00
☐ 534	Andre Thornton	.18	.08	.01
☐ 535	Bob Forsch	.12	.05	.01
☐ 536	Lee Lacy	.15	.06	.01
☐ 537	Alex Trevino	.12	.05	.01
☐ 538	Joe Strain	.07	.03	.01
☐ 539	Rudy May	.07	.03	.01
☐ 540	Pete Rose	3.50	1.40	.35
☐ 541	Miguel Dilone	.07	.03	.01
☐ 542	Joe Coleman	.07	.03	.01
☐ 543	Pat Kelly	.07	.03	.01
☐ 544	Rick Sutcliffe	1.25	.50	.12
☐ 545	Jeff Burroughs	.10	.04	.01
☐ 546	Rick Langford	.07	.03	.01
☐ 547	John Wathan	.07	.03	.01
☐ 548	Dave Rajsich	.07	.03	.01
☐ 549	Larry Wolfe	.07	.03	.01
☐ 550	Ken Griffey	.12	.05	.01
☐ 551	Pirates Team/Mgr. Chuck Tanner (checklist back)	.25	.05	.01
☐ 552	Bill Nahorodny	.07	.03	.01
☐ 553	Dick Davis	.07	.03	.01
☐ 554	Art Howe	.07	.03	.01
☐ 555	Ed Figueroa	.07	.03	.01
☐ 556	Joe Rudi	.10	.04	.01
☐ 557	Mark Lee	.07	.03	.01
☐ 558	Alfredo Griffin	.15	.06	.01
☐ 559	Dale Murray	.07	.03	.01
☐ 560	Dave Lopes	.15	.06	.01
☐ 561	Eddie Whitson	.12	.05	.01
☐ 562	Joe Wallis	.07	.03	.01
☐ 563	Will McEnaney	.07	.03	.01
☐ 564	Rick Manning	.07	.03	.01
☐ 565	Dennis Leonard	.12	.05	.01
☐ 566	Bud Harrelson	.10	.04	.01
☐ 567	Skip Lockwood	.07	.03	.01
☐ 568	Gary Roenicke	.30	.12	.03
☐ 569	Terry Kennedy	.25	.10	.02
☐ 570	Roy Smalley	.10	.04	.01
☐ 571	Joe Sambito	.10	.04	.01
☐ 572	Jerry Morales DP	.03	.01	.00
☐ 573	Kent Tekulve	.12	.05	.01
☐ 574	Scot Thompson	.07	.03	.01
☐ 575	Ken Kravec	.07	.03	.01
☐ 576	Jim Dwyer	.07	.03	.01
☐ 577	Blue Jays Team/Mgr. Bobby Mattick (checklist back)	.20	.04	.01
☐ 578	Scott Sanderson	.10	.04	.01
☐ 579	Charlie Moore	.07	.03	.01
☐ 580	Nolan Ryan	1.25	.50	.12
☐ 581	Bob Bailor	.07	.03	.01
☐ 582	Brian Doyle	.07	.03	.01
☐ 583	Bob Stinson	.07	.03	.01
☐ 584	Kurt Bevacqua	.07	.03	.01
☐ 585	Al Hrabosky	.10	.04	.01
☐ 586	Mitchell Page	.07	.03	.01
☐ 587	Garry Templeton	.18	.08	.01
☐ 588	Greg Minton	.10	.04	.01
☐ 589	Chet Lemon	.12	.05	.01
☐ 590	Jim Palmer	1.00	.40	.10
☐ 591	Rick Cerone	.10	.04	.01
☐ 592	Jon Matlack	.10	.04	.01
☐ 593	Jesus Alou	.07	.03	.01
☐ 594	Dick Tidrow	.07	.03	.01
☐ 595	Don Money	.07	.03	.01
☐ 596	Rick Matula	.07	.03	.01
☐ 597	Tom Poquette	.07	.03	.01
☐ 598	Fred Kendall DP	.03	.01	.00
☐ 599	Mike Norris	.10	.04	.01
☐ 600	Reggie Jackson	1.75	.70	.17
☐ 601	Buddy Schultz	.07	.03	.01
☐ 602	Brian Downing	.10	.04	.01
☐ 603	Jack Billingham DP	.03	.01	.00
☐ 604	Glenn Adams	.07	.03	.01
☐ 605	Terry Forster	.15	.06	.01
☐ 606	Reds Team/Mgr. John McNamara (checklist back)	.25	.05	.01
☐ 607	Woodie Fryman	.07	.03	.01
☐ 608	Alan Bannister	.07	.03	.01
☐ 609	Ron Reed	.07	.03	.01
☐ 610	Willie Stargell	.90	.36	.09
☐ 611	Jerry Garvin DP	.03	.01	.00
☐ 612	Cliff Johnson	.07	.03	.01
☐ 613	Randy Stein	.07	.03	.01
☐ 614	John Hiller	.10	.04	.01
☐ 615	Doug DeCinces	.18	.08	.01
☐ 616	Gene Richards	.07	.03	.01
☐ 617	Joaquin Andujar	.18	.08	.01
☐ 618	Bob Montgomery DP	.03	.01	.00
☐ 619	Sergio Ferrer	.07	.03	.01
☐ 620	Richie Zisk	.10	.04	.01
☐ 621	Bob Grich	.15	.06	.01
☐ 622	Mario Soto	.15	.06	.01
☐ 623	Gorman Thomas	.18	.08	.01
☐ 624	Lerrin LaGrow	.07	.03	.01
☐ 625	Chris Chambliss	.12	.05	.01
☐ 626	Tigers Team/Mgr. Sparky Anderson (checklist back)	.30	.06	.01
☐ 627	Pedro Borbon	.07	.03	.01

	MINT	VG-E	F-G
☐ 628 Doug Capilla	.07	.03	.01
☐ 629 Jim Todd	.07	.03	.01
☐ 630 Larry Bowa	.20	.08	.02
☐ 631 Mark Littell	.07	.03	.01
☐ 632 Barry Bonnell	.10	.04	.01
☐ 633 Bob Apodaca	.07	.03	.01
☐ 634 Glenn Borgmann DP	.03	.01	.00
☐ 635 John Candelaria	.15	.06	.01
☐ 636 Toby Harrah	.10	.04	.01
☐ 637 Joe Simpson	.07	.03	.01
☐ 638 Mark Clear	.35	.14	.03
☐ 639 Larry Biittner	.07	.03	.01
☐ 640 Mike Flanagan	.12	.05	.01
☐ 641 Ed Kranepool	.10	.04	.01
☐ 642 Ken Forsch DP	.07	.03	.01
☐ 643 John Mayberry	.10	.04	.01
☐ 644 Charlie Hough	.15	.06	.01
☐ 645 Rick Burleson	.12	.05	.01
☐ 646 Checklist 6	.20	.02	.00
☐ 647 Milt May	.07	.03	.01
☐ 648 Roy White	.10	.04	.01
☐ 649 Tom Griffin	.07	.03	.01
☐ 650 Joe Morgan	.75	.30	.07
☐ 651 Rollie Fingers	.35	.14	.03
☐ 652 Mario Mendoza	.07	.03	.01
☐ 653 Stan Bahnsen	.07	.03	.01
☐ 654 Bruce Boisclair DP	.03	.01	.00
☐ 655 Tug McGraw	.18	.08	.01
☐ 656 Larvell Blanks	.07	.03	.01
☐ 657 Dave Edwards	.07	.03	.01
☐ 658 Chris Knapp	.07	.03	.01
☐ 659 Brewers Team/Mgr.	.25	.05	.01
George Bamberger			
(checklist back)			
☐ 660 Rusty Staub	.18	.08	.01
☐ 661 Orioles Rookies	.12	.05	.01
Mark Corey			
Dave Ford			
Wayne Krenchicki			
☐ 662 Red Sox Rookies	.12	.05	.01
Joel Finch			
Mike O'Berry			
Chuck Rainey			
☐ 663 Angels Rookies	.50	.20	.05
Ralph Botting			
Bob Clark			
Dickie Thon			
☐ 664 White Sox Rookies	.12	.05	.01
Mike Colbern			
Guy Hoffman			
Dewey Robinson			

	MINT	VG-E	F-G
☐ 665 Indians Rookies	.12	.05	.01
Larry Anderson			
Bobby Cuellar			
Randy Wihtol			
☐ 666 Tigers Rookies	.12	.05	.01
Mike Chris			
Al Greene			
Bruce Robbins			
☐ 667 Royals Rookies	2.50	1.00	.25
Renie Martin			
Bill Paschall			
Dan Quisenberry			
☐ 668 Brewers Rookies	.12	.05	.01
Danny Boitano			
Willie Mueller			
Lenn Sakata			
☐ 669 Twins Rookies	.75	.30	.07
Dan Graham			
Rick Sofield			
Gary Ward			
☐ 670 Yankees Rookies	.12	.05	.01
Bobby Brown			
Brad Gulden			
Darryl Jones			
☐ 671 A's Rookies	.25	.10	.02
Derek Bryant			
Brian Kingman			
Mike Morgan			
☐ 672 Mariners Rookies	.12	.05	.01
Charlie Beamon			
Rodney Craig			
Rafael Vasquez			
☐ 673 Rangers Rookies	.12	.05	.01
Brian Allard			
Jerry Don Gleaton			
Greg Mahlberg			
☐ 674 Blue Jays Rookies	.12	.05	.01
Butch Edge			
Pat Kelly			
Ted Wilborn			
☐ 675 Braves Rookies	.20	.08	.02
Bruce Benedict			
Larry Bradford			
Eddie Miller			
☐ 676 Cubs Rookies	.12	.05	.01
Dave Geisel			
Steve Macko			
Karl Pagel			
☐ 677 Reds Rookies	.12	.05	.01
Art DeFreites			
Frank Pastore			
Harry Spilman			

		MINT	VG-E	F-G
☐ 678	Astros Rookies	.20	.08	.02
	Reggie Baldwin			
	Alan Knicely			
	Pete Ladd			
☐ 679	Dodgers Rookies	.30	.12	.03
	Joe Beckwith			
	Mickey Hatcher			
	Dave Patterson			
☐ 680	Expos Rookies	.60	.24	.06
	Tony Bernazard			
	Randy Miller			
	John Tamargo			
☐ 681	Mets Rookies	5.00	2.00	.50
	Dan Norman			
	Jesse Orosco			
	Mike Scott			
☐ 682	Phillies Rookies	.20	.08	.02
	Ramon Aviles			
	Dickie Noles			
	Kevin Saucier			
☐ 683	Pirates Rookies	.12	.05	.01
	Dorian Boyland			
	Alberto Lois			
	Harry Saferight			
☐ 684	Cardinals Rookies	.75	.30	.07
	George Frazier			
	Tom Herr			
	Dan O'Brien			
☐ 685	Padres Rookies	.12	.05	.01
	Tim Flannery			
	Brian Greer			
	Jim Wilhelm			
☐ 686	Giants Rookies	.12	.05	.01
	Greg Johnston			
	Dennis Littlejohn			
	Phil Nastu			
☐ 687	Mike Heath DP	.03	.01	.00
☐ 688	Steve Stone	.12	.05	.01
☐ 689	Red Sox Team/Mgr.	.25	.05	.01
	Don Zimmer			
	(checklist back)			
☐ 690	Tommy John	.25	.10	.02
☐ 691	Ivan DeJesus	.07	.03	.01
☐ 692	Rawly Eastwick DP	.03	.01	.00
☐ 693	Craig Kusick	.07	.03	.01
☐ 694	Jim Rooker	.07	.03	.01
☐ 695	Reggie Smith	.15	.06	.01
☐ 696	Julio Gonzalez	.07	.03	.01
☐ 697	David Clyde	.07	.03	.01
☐ 698	Oscar Gamble	.10	.04	.01
☐ 699	Floyd Bannister	.10	.04	.01
☐ 700	Rod Carew DP	.65	.26	.06
☐ 701	Ken Oberkfell	.35	.14	.03

		MINT	VG-E	F-G
☐ 702	Ed Farmer	.07	.03	.01
☐ 703	Otto Velez	.07	.03	.01
☐ 704	Gene Tenace	.07	.03	.01
☐ 705	Freddie Patek	.07	.03	.01
☐ 706	Tippy Martinez	.10	.04	.01
☐ 707	Elliott Maddox	.07	.03	.01
☐ 708	Bob Tolan	.07	.03	.01
☐ 709	Pat Underwood	.07	.03	.01
☐ 710	Graig Nettles	.30	.12	.03
☐ 711	Bob Galasso	.07	.03	.01
☐ 712	Rodney Scott	.07	.03	.01
☐ 713	Terry Whitfield	.07	.03	.01
☐ 714	Fred Norman	.07	.03	.01
☐ 715	Sal Bando	.10	.04	.01
☐ 716	Lynn McGlothen	.07	.03	.01
☐ 717	Mickey Klutts DP	.03	.01	.00
☐ 718	Greg Gross	.07	.03	.01
☐ 719	Don Robinson	.10	.04	.01
☐ 720	Carl Yastrzemski DP	.85	.34	.08
☐ 721	Paul Hartzell	.07	.03	.01
☐ 722	Jose Cruz	.20	.08	.02
☐ 723	Shane Rawley	.15	.06	.01
☐ 724	Jerry White	.07	.03	.01
☐ 725	Rick Wise	.10	.04	.01
☐ 726	Steve Yeager	.15	.06	.01

1981 Topps

The cards in this 726-card set measure 2½" by 3½". League Leaders (1-8), Record Breakers (201-208), and Post-season cards (401-404) are topical subsets found in this set marketed by Topps in 1981. The team cards are all grouped together (661-686) and feature team checklist backs and a very small photo of the team's manager in the upper right corner of the obverse. The obverses *carry the player's position and team in a baseball cap design, and the company name is printed in a small baseball. The backs are red and gray. The 66 double printed cards are noted in the checklist by DP. The set is quite popular with collectors partly due to the presence of rookie cards of Fernando Valenzuela, Tim Raines, Kirk Gibson, Harold Baines, John Tudor, Lloyd Moseby, Hubie Brooks, Mike Boddicker, and Tony Pena.*

	MINT	VG-E	F-G
Complete Set	60.00	24.00	6.00
Common Player (1-726)	.05	.02	.00
Common DP's (1-726)	.02	.01	.00

		MINT	VG-E	F-G
☐ 1	Batting Leaders	.50	.20	.05
	George Brett			
	Bill Buckner			
☐ 2	Home Run Leaders	.30	.12	.03
	Reggie Jackson			
	Ben Oglivie			
	Mike Schmidt			
☐ 3	RBI Leaders	.20	.08	.02
	Cecil Cooper			
	Mike Schmidt			
☐ 4	Stolen Base Leaders	.18	.08	.01
	Rickey Henderson			
	Ron LeFlore			
☐ 5	Victory Leaders	.15	.06	.01
	Steve Stone			
	Steve Carlton			
☐ 6	Strikeout Leaders	.15	.06	.01
	Len Barker			
	Steve Carlton			
☐ 7	ERA Leaders	.10	.04	.01
	Rudy May			
	Don Sutton			
☐ 8	Leading Firemen	.15	.06	.01
	Dan Quisenberry			
	Rollie Fingers			
	Tom Hume			
☐ 9	Pete LaCock DP	.02	.01	.00
☐ 10	Mike Flanagan	.10	.04	.01
☐ 11	Jim Wohlford DP	.02	.01	.00
☐ 12	Mark Clear	.05	.02	.00
☐ 13	Joe Charboneau	.15	.06	.01
☐ 14	John Tudor	1.50	.60	.15
☐ 15	Larry Parrish	.10	.04	.01
☐ 16	Ron Davis	.10	.04	.01
☐ 17	Cliff Johnson	.05	.02	.00
☐ 18	Glenn Adams	.05	.02	.00

		MINT	VG-E	F-G
☐ 19	Jim Clancy	.08	.03	.01
☐ 20	Jeff Burroughs	.08	.03	.01
☐ 21	Ron Oester	.08	.03	.01
☐ 22	Danny Darwin	.05	.02	.00
☐ 23	Alex Trevino	.05	.02	.00
☐ 24	Don Stanhouse	.05	.02	.00
☐ 25	Sixto Lezcano	.05	.02	.00
☐ 26	U.L. Washington	.05	.02	.00
☐ 27	Champ Summers DP	.02	.01	.00
☐ 28	Enrique Romo	.05	.02	.00
☐ 29	Gene Tenace	.05	.02	.00
☐ 30	Jack Clark	.25	.10	.02
☐ 31	Checklist 1-121 DP	.07	.01	.00
☐ 32	Ken Oberkfell	.05	.02	.00
☐ 33	Rick Honeycutt	.08	.03	.01
☐ 34	Aurelio Rodriguez	.05	.02	.00
☐ 35	Mitchell Page	.05	.02	.00
☐ 36	Ed Farmer	.05	.02	.00
☐ 37	Gary Roenicke	.08	.03	.01
☐ 38	Win Remmerswaal	.05	.02	.00
☐ 39	Tom Veryzer	.05	.02	.00
☐ 40	Tug McGraw	.15	.06	.01
☐ 41	Ranger Rookies	.20	.08	.02
	Bob Babcock			
	John Butcher			
	Jerry Don Gleaton			
☐ 42	Jerry White DP	.02	.01	.00
☐ 43	Jose Morales	.05	.02	.00
☐ 44	Larry McWilliams	.08	.03	.00
☐ 45	Enos Cabell	.05	.02	.00
☐ 46	Rick Bosetti	.05	.02	.00
☐ 47	Ken Brett	.08	.03	.01
☐ 48	Dave Skaggs	.05	.02	.00
☐ 49	Bob Shirley	.05	.02	.00
☐ 50	Dave Lopes	.12	.05	.01
☐ 51	Bill Robinson DP	.02	.01	.00
☐ 52	Hector Cruz	.05	.02	.00
☐ 53	Kevin Saucier	.05	.02	.00
☐ 54	Ivan DeJesus	.05	.02	.00
☐ 55	Mike Norris	.08	.03	.01
☐ 56	Buck Martinez	.05	.02	.00
☐ 57	Dave Roberts	.05	.02	.00
☐ 58	Joel Youngblood	.05	.02	.00
☐ 59	Dan Petry	.35	.14	.03
☐ 60	Willie Randolph	.12	.05	.01
☐ 61	Butch Wynegar	.08	.03	.01
☐ 62	Joe Pettini	.05	.02	.00
☐ 63	Steve Renko DP	.02	.01	.00
☐ 64	Brian Asselstine	.05	.02	.00
☐ 65	Scott McGregor	.12	.05	.01

		MINT	VG-E	F-G
☐ 66	Royals Rookies	.10	.04	.01
	Manny Castillo			
	Tim Ireland			
	Mike Jones			
☐ 67	Ken Kravec	.05	.02	.00
☐ 68	Matt Alexander DP	.02	.01	.00
☐ 69	Ed Halicki	.05	.02	.00
☐ 70	Al Oliver DP	.10	.04	.01
☐ 71	Hal Dues	.05	.02	.00
☐ 72	Barry Evans DP	.02	.01	.00
☐ 73	Doug Bair	.05	.02	.00
☐ 74	Mike Hargrove	.08	.03	.01
☐ 75	Reggie Smith	.12	.05	.01
☐ 76	Mario Mendoza	.05	.02	.00
☐ 77	Mike Barlow	.05	.02	.00
☐ 78	Steve Dillard	.05	.02	.00
☐ 79	Bruce Robbins	.05	.02	.00
☐ 80	Rusty Staub	.15	.06	.01
☐ 81	Dave Stapleton	.10	.04	.01
☐ 82	Astros Rookies DP	.10	.04	.01
	Danny Heep			
	Alan Knicely			
	Bobby Sprowl			
☐ 83	Mike Proly	.05	.02	.00
☐ 84	Johnnie LeMaster	.05	.02	.00
☐ 85	Mike Caldwell	.08	.03	.01
☐ 86	Wayne Gross	.05	.02	.00
☐ 87	Rick Camp	.05	.02	.00
☐ 88	Joe LeFebvre	.10	.04	.01
☐ 89	Darrell Jackson	.05	.02	.00
☐ 90	Bake McBride	.08	.03	.01
☐ 91	Tim Stoddard DP	.05	.02	.00
☐ 92	Mike Easler	.12	.05	.01
☐ 93	Ed Glynn DP	.02	.01	.00
☐ 94	Harry Spilman DP	.02	.01	.00
☐ 95	Jim Sundberg	.08	.03	.01
☐ 96	A's Rookies	.12	.05	.01
	Dave Beard			
	Ernie Camacho			
	Pat Dempsey			
☐ 97	Chris Speier	.05	.02	.00
☐ 98	Clint Hurdle	.05	.02	.00
☐ 99	Eric Wilkins	.05	.02	.00
☐ 100	Rod Carew	1.25	.50	.12
☐ 101	Benny Ayala	.05	.02	.00
☐ 102	Dave Tobik	.05	.02	.00
☐ 103	Jerry Martin	.05	.02	.00
☐ 104	Terry Forster	.12	.05	.01
☐ 105	Jose Cruz	.20	.08	.02
☐ 106	Don Money	.05	.02	.00
☐ 107	Rich Wortham	.05	.02	.00
☐ 108	Bruce Benedict	.08	.03	.01
☐ 109	Mike Scott	.75	.30	.07

		MINT	VG-E	F-G
☐ 110	Carl Yastrzemski	1.25	.50	.12
☐ 111	Greg Minton	.08	.03	.01
☐ 112	White Sox Rookies	.10	.04	.01
	Rusty Kuntz			
	Fran Mullin			
	Leo Sutherland			
☐ 113	Mike Phillips	.05	.02	.00
☐ 114	Tom Underwood	.05	.02	.00
☐ 115	Roy Smalley	.08	.03	.01
☐ 116	Joe Simpson	.05	.02	.00
☐ 117	Pete Falcone	.05	.02	.00
☐ 118	Kurt Bevacqua	.05	.02	.00
☐ 119	Tippy Martinez	.08	.03	.01
☐ 120	Larry Bowa	.15	.06	.01
☐ 121	Larry Harlow	.05	.02	.00
☐ 122	John Denny	.12	.05	.01
☐ 123	Al Cowens	.08	.03	.01
☐ 124	Jerry Garvin	.05	.02	.00
☐ 125	Andre Dawson	.50	.20	.05
☐ 126	Charlie Leibrandt	.50	.20	.05
☐ 127	Rudy Law	.05	.02	.00
☐ 128	Garry Allenson DP	.02	.01	.00
☐ 129	Art Howe	.05	.02	.00
☐ 130	Larry Gura	.08	.03	.01
☐ 131	Keith Moreland	.75	.30	.07
☐ 132	Tommy Boggs	.05	.02	.00
☐ 133	Jeff Cox	.05	.02	.00
☐ 134	Steve Mura	.05	.02	.00
☐ 135	Gorman Thomas	.18	.08	.01
☐ 136	Doug Capilla	.05	.02	.00
☐ 137	Hosken Powell	.05	.02	.00
☐ 138	Rich Dotson DP	.30	.12	.03
☐ 139	Oscar Gamble	.10	.04	.01
☐ 140	Bob Forsch	.10	.04	.01
☐ 141	Miguel Dilone	.05	.02	.00
☐ 142	Jackson Todd	.05	.02	.00
☐ 143	Dan Meyer	.05	.02	.00
☐ 144	Allen Ripley	.05	.02	.00
☐ 145	Mickey Rivers	.10	.04	.01
☐ 146	Bobby Castillo	.05	.02	.00
☐ 147	Dale Berra	.08	.03	.01
☐ 148	Randy Niemann	.05	.02	.00
☐ 149	Joe Nolan	.05	.02	.00
☐ 150	Mark Fidrych	.10	.04	.01
☐ 151	Claudell Washington	.12	.05	.01
☐ 152	John Urrea	.05	.02	.00
☐ 153	Tom Poquette	.05	.02	.00
☐ 154	Rick Langford	.05	.02	.00
☐ 155	Chris Chambliss	.10	.04	.01
☐ 156	Bob McClure	.05	.02	.00
☐ 157	John Wathan	.05	.02	.00
☐ 158	Fergie Jenkins	.25	.10	.02
☐ 159	Brian Doyle	.05	.02	.00

		MINT	VG-E	F-G
☐ 160	Garry Maddox	.08	.03	.01
☐ 161	Dan Graham	.05	.02	.00
☐ 162	Doug Corbett	.15	.06	.01
☐ 163	Billy Almon	.05	.02	.00
☐ 164	LaMarr Hoyt	.50	.20	.05
☐ 165	Tony Scott	.05	.02	.00
☐ 166	Floyd Bannister	.10	.04	.01
☐ 167	Terry Whitfield	.05	.02	.00
☐ 168	Don Robinson DP	.02	.01	.00
☐ 169	John Mayberry	.08	.03	.01
☐ 170	Ross Grimsley	.05	.02	.00
☐ 171	Gene Richards	.05	.02	.00
☐ 172	Gary Woods	.05	.02	.00
☐ 173	Bump Wills	.05	.02	.00
☐ 174	Doug Rau	.05	.02	.00
☐ 175	Dave Collins	.08	.03	.01
☐ 176	Mike Krukow	.15	.06	.01
☐ 177	Rick Peters	.05	.02	.00
☐ 178	Jim Essian DP	.02	.01	.00
☐ 179	Rudy May	.05	.02	.00
☐ 180	Pete Rose	3.25	1.30	.32
☐ 181	Elias Sosa	.05	.02	.00
☐ 182	Bob Grich	.12	.05	.01
☐ 183	Dick Davis DP	.02	.01	.00
☐ 184	Jim Dwyer	.05	.02	.00
☐ 185	Dennis Leonard	.10	.04	.01
☐ 186	Wayne Nordhagen	.05	.02	.00
☐ 187	Mike Parrott	.05	.02	.00
☐ 188	Doug DeCinces	.15	.06	.01
☐ 189	Craig Swan	.08	.03	.01
☐ 190	Cesar Cedeno	.12	.05	.01
☐ 191	Rick Sutcliffe	.35	.14	.03
☐ 192	Braves Rookies	.25	.10	.02
	Terry Harper			
	Ed Miller			
	Rafael Ramirez			
☐ 193	Pete Vuckovich	.12	.05	.01
☐ 194	Rod Scurry	.12	.05	.01
☐ 195	Rich Murray	.05	.02	.00
☐ 196	Duffy Dyer	.05	.02	.00
☐ 197	Jim Kern	.05	.02	.00
☐ 198	Jerry Dybzinski	.05	.02	.00
☐ 199	Chuck Rainey	.05	.02	.00
☐ 200	George Foster	.25	.10	.02
☐ 201	RB: Johnny Bench	.30	.12	.03
	Most HR's			
	lifetime catcher			
☐ 202	RB: Steve Carlton	.30	.12	.03
	Most strikeouts,			
	lefthander, lifetime			

		MINT	VG-E	F-G
☐ 203	RB: Bill Gullickson	.10	.04	.01
	Most strikeouts			
	game, rookie			
☐ 204	RB: Ron LeFlore and	.08	.03	.01
	Rodney Scott			
	Most stolen bases			
	teammates, season			
☐ 205	RB: Pete Rose	.75	.30	.07
	Most cons. seasons			
	600 or more at-bats			
☐ 206	RB: Mike Schmidt	.40	.16	.04
	Most homers, third			
	baseman, season			
☐ 207	RB: Ozzie Smith	.12	.05	.01
	Most assists			
	season, SS			
☐ 208	RB: Willie Wilson	.12	.05	.01
	Most at-bats, season			
☐ 209	Dickie Thon DP	.08	.03	.01
☐ 210	Jim Palmer	.75	.30	.07
☐ 211	Derrel Thomas	.05	.02	.00
☐ 212	Steve Nicosia	.05	.02	.00
☐ 213	Al Holland	.25	.10	.02
☐ 214	Angels Rookies	.10	.04	.01
	Ralph Botting			
	Jim Dorsey			
	John Harris			
☐ 215	Larry Hisle	.08	.03	.01
☐ 216	John Henry Johnson	.05	.02	.00
☐ 217	Rich Hebner	.05	.02	.00
☐ 218	Paul Splittorff	.08	.03	.01
☐ 219	Ken Landreaux	.08	.03	.01
☐ 220	Tom Seaver	1.25	.50	.12
☐ 221	Bob Davis	.05	.02	.00
☐ 222	Jorge Orta	.05	.02	.00
☐ 223	Roy Lee Jackson	.08	.03	.01
☐ 224	Pat Zachry	.05	.02	.00
☐ 225	Ruppert Jones	.08	.03	.01
☐ 226	Manny Sanguillen DP	.05	.02	.00
☐ 227	Fred Martinez	.05	.02	.00
☐ 228	Tom Paciorek	.05	.02	.00
☐ 229	Rollie Fingers	.40	.16	.04
☐ 230	George Hendrick	.12	.05	.01
☐ 231	Joe Beckwith	.05	.02	.00
☐ 232	Mickey Klutts	.05	.02	.00
☐ 233	Skip Lockwood	.05	.02	.00
☐ 234	Lou Whitaker	.50	.20	.05
☐ 235	Scott Sanderson	.08	.03	.01
☐ 236	Mike Ivie	.05	.02	.00
☐ 237	Charlie Moore	.05	.02	.00
☐ 238	Willie Hernandez	.25	.10	.02
☐ 239	Rick Miller DP	.02	.01	.00
☐ 240	Nolan Ryan	1.25	.50	.12

	MINT	VG-E	F-G
☐ 241 Checklist 122-242 DP	.07	.01	.00
☐ 242 Chet Lemon	.10	.04	.01
☐ 243 Sal Butera	.05	.02	.00
☐ 244 Cardinals Rookies	.15	.06	.01
Tito Landrum			
Al Olmsted			
Andy Rincon			
☐ 245 Ed Figueroa	.05	.02	.00
☐ 246 Ed Ott DP	.02	.01	.00
☐ 247 Glen Hubbard DP	.02	.01	.00
☐ 248 Joey McLaughlin	.05	.02	.00
☐ 249 Larry Cox	.05	.02	.00
☐ 250 Ron Guidry	.45	.18	.04
☐ 251 Tom Brookens	.05	.02	.00
☐ 252 Victor Cruz	.05	.02	.00
☐ 253 Dave Bergman	.05	.02	.00
☐ 254 Ozzie Smith	.50	.20	.05
☐ 255 Mark Littell	.05	.02	.00
☐ 256 Bombo Rivera	.05	.02	.00
☐ 257 Rennie Stennett	.05	.02	.00
☐ 258 Joe Price	.08	.03	.01
☐ 259 Mets Rookies	2.25	.90	.22
Juan Berenguer			
Hubie Brooks			
Mookie Wilson			
☐ 260 Ron Cey	.20	.08	.02
☐ 261 Rickey Henderson	3.00	1.20	.30
☐ 262 Sammy Stewart	.05	.02	.00
☐ 263 Brian Downing	.08	.03	.01
☐ 264 Jim Norris	.05	.02	.00
☐ 265 John Candelaria	.12	.05	.01
☐ 266 Tom Herr	.20	.08	.02
☐ 267 Stan Bahnsen	.05	.02	.00
☐ 268 Jerry Royster	.05	.02	.00
☐ 269 Ken Forsch	.08	.03	.01
☐ 270 Greg Luzinski	.15	.06	.01
☐ 271 Bill Castro	.05	.02	.00
☐ 272 Bruce Kimm	.05	.02	.00
☐ 273 Stan Papi	.05	.02	.00
☐ 274 Craig Chamberlain	.05	.02	.00
☐ 275 Dwight Evans	.25	.10	.02
☐ 276 Dan Spillner	.05	.02	.00
☐ 277 Alfredo Griffin	.10	.04	.01
☐ 278 Rick Sofield	.05	.02	.00
☐ 279 Bob Knepper	.15	.06	.01
☐ 280 Ken Griffey	.12	.05	.01
☐ 281 Fred Stanley	.05	.02	.00
☐ 282 Mariners Rookies	.08	.03	.01
Rick Anderson			
Greg Biercevicz			
Rodney Craig			
☐ 283 Billy Sample	.05	.02	.00
☐ 284 Brian Kingman	.05	.02	.00

	MINT	VG-E	F-G
☐ 285 Jerry Turner	.05	.02	.00
☐ 286 Dave Frost	.05	.02	.00
☐ 287 Lenn Sakata	.05	.02	.00
☐ 288 Bob Clark	.05	.02	.00
☐ 289 Mickey Hatcher	.08	.03	.01
☐ 290 Bob Boone DP	.05	.02	.00
☐ 291 Aurelio Lopez	.05	.02	.00
☐ 292 Mike Squires	.05	.02	.00
☐ 293 Charlie Lea	.25	.10	.02
☐ 294 Mike Tyson DP	.02	.01	.00
☐ 295 Hal McRae	.10	.04	.01
☐ 296 Bill Nahorodny DP	.02	.01	.00
☐ 297 Bob Bailor	.05	.02	.00
☐ 298 Buddy Solomon	.05	.02	.00
☐ 299 Elliott Maddox	.05	.02	.00
☐ 300 Paul Molitor	.20	.08	.02
☐ 301 Matt Keough	.05	.02	.00
☐ 302 Dodgers Rookies	7.50	3.00	.75
Jack Perconte			
Mike Scioscia			
Fernando Valenzuela			
☐ 303 Johnny Oates	.05	.02	.00
☐ 304 John Castino	.05	.02	.00
☐ 305 Ken Clay	.05	.02	.00
☐ 306 Juan Beniquez DP	.05	.02	.00
☐ 307 Gene Garber	.05	.02	.00
☐ 308 Rick Manning	.05	.02	.00
☐ 309 Luis Salazar	.10	.04	.01
☐ 310 Vida Blue DP	.08	.03	.01
☐ 311 Freddie Patek	.05	.02	.00
☐ 312 Rick Rhoden	.15	.06	.01
☐ 313 Luis Pujols	.05	.02	.00
☐ 314 Rich Dauer	.05	.02	.00
☐ 315 Kirk Gibson	4.00	1.60	.40
☐ 316 Craig Minetto	.05	.02	.00
☐ 317 Lonnie Smith	.12	.05	.01
☐ 318 Steve Yeager	.08	.03	.01
☐ 319 Rowland Office	.05	.02	.00
☐ 320 Tom Burgmeier	.05	.02	.00
☐ 321 Leon Durham	.90	.36	.09
☐ 322 Neil Allen	.08	.03	.01
☐ 323 Jim Morrison DP	.05	.02	.00
☐ 324 Mike Willis	.05	.02	.00
☐ 325 Ray Knight	.15	.06	.01
☐ 326 Biff Pocoroba	.05	.02	.00
☐ 327 Moose Haas	.08	.03	.01
☐ 328 Twins Rookies	.30	.12	.03
Dave Engle			
Greg Johnston			
Gary Ward			
☐ 329 Joaquin Andujar	.18	.08	.01
☐ 330 Frank White	.15	.06	.01
☐ 331 Dennis Lamp	.05	.02	.00

	MINT	VG-E	F-G
☐ 332 Lee Lacy DP	.05	.02	.00
☐ 333 Sid Monge	.05	.02	.00
☐ 334 Dane Iorg	.05	.02	.00
☐ 335 Rick Cerone	.08	.03	.01
☐ 336 Eddie Whitson	.10	.04	.01
☐ 337 Lynn Jones	.05	.02	.00
☐ 338 Checklist 243-363	.15	.02	.00
☐ 339 John Ellis	.05	.02	.00
☐ 340 Bruce Kison	.05	.02	.00
☐ 341 Dwayne Murphy	.12	.05	.01
☐ 342 Eric Rasmussen DP	.02	.01	.00
☐ 343 Frank Taveras	.05	.02	.00
☐ 344 Byron McLaughlin	.05	.02	.00
☐ 345 Warren Cromartie	.05	.02	.00
☐ 346 Larry Christenson DP	.02	.01	.00
☐ 347 Harold Baines	4.50	1.80	.45
☐ 348 Bob Sykes	.05	.02	.00
☐ 349 Glenn Hoffman	.10	.04	.01
☐ 350 J.R. Richard	.15	.06	.01
☐ 351 Otto Velez	.05	.02	.00
☐ 352 Dick Tidrow DP	.02	.01	.00
☐ 353 Terry Kennedy	.15	.06	.01
☐ 354 Mario Soto	.12	.05	.01
☐ 355 Bob Horner	.40	.16	.04
☐ 356 Padres Rookies	.10	.04	.01
George Stablein			
Craig Stimac			
Tom Tellmann			
☐ 357 Jim Slaton	.05	.02	.00
☐ 358 Mark Wagner	.05	.02	.00
☐ 359 Tom Hausman	.05	.02	.00
☐ 360 Willie Wilson	.25	.10	.02
☐ 361 Joe Strain	.05	.02	.00
☐ 362 Bo Diaz	.08	.03	.01
☐ 363 Geoff Zahn	.08	.03	.01
☐ 364 Mike Davis	.50	.20	.05
☐ 365 Graig Nettles DP	.08	.03	.01
☐ 366 Mike Ramsey	.05	.02	.00
☐ 367 Denny Martinez	.08	.03	.01
☐ 368 Leon Roberts	.05	.02	.00
☐ 369 Frank Tanana	.10	.04	.01
☐ 370 Dave Winfield	.80	.32	.08
☐ 371 Charlie Hough	.12	.05	.01
☐ 372 Jay Johnstone	.08	.03	.01
☐ 373 Pat Underwood	.05	.02	.00
☐ 374 Tom Hutton	.05	.02	.00
☐ 375 Dave Concepcion	.15	.06	.01
☐ 376 Ron Reed	.05	.02	.00
☐ 377 Jerry Morales	.05	.02	.00
☐ 378 Dave Rader	.05	.02	.00
☐ 379 Lary Sorensen	.05	.02	.00
☐ 380 Willie Stargell	.80	.32	.08

	MINT	VG-E	F-G
☐ 381 Cubs Rookies	.10	.04	.01
Carlos Lezcano			
Steve Macko			
Randy Martz			
☐ 382 Paul Mirabella	.05	.02	.00
☐ 383 Eric Soderholm DP	.02	.01	.00
☐ 384 Mike Sadek	.05	.02	.00
☐ 385 Joe Sambito	.08	.03	.01
☐ 386 Dave Edwards	.05	.02	.00
☐ 387 Phil Niekro	.65	.26	.06
☐ 388 Andre Thornton	.15	.06	.01
☐ 389 Marty Pattin	.05	.02	.00
☐ 390 Cesar Geronimo	.05	.02	.00
☐ 391 Dave Lemanczyk DP	.02	.01	.00
☐ 392 Lance Parrish	.80	.32	.08
☐ 393 Broderick Perkins	.05	.02	.00
☐ 394 Woodie Fryman	.05	.02	.00
☐ 395 Scot Thompson	.05	.02	.00
☐ 396 Bill Campbell	.08	.03	.01
☐ 397 Julio Cruz	.05	.02	.00
☐ 398 Ross Baumgarten	.05	.02	.00
☐ 399 Orioles Rookies	2.00	.80	.20
Mike Boddicker			
Mark Corey			
Floyd Rayford			
☐ 400 Reggie Jackson	1.50	.60	.15
☐ 401 AL Champs	.40	.16	.04
Royals sweep Yanks			
(Brett swinging)			
☐ 402 NL Champs	.20	.08	.02
Phillies squeak			
past Astros			
☐ 403 1980 World Series	.20	.08	.02
Phillies beat			
Royals in 6			
☐ 404 1980 World Series	.20	.08	.02
Phillies win first			
World Series			
☐ 405 Nino Espinosa	.05	.02	.00
☐ 406 Dickie Noles	.05	.02	.00
☐ 407 Ernie Whitt	.05	.02	.00
☐ 408 Fernando Arroyo	.05	.02	.00
☐ 409 Larry Herndon	.08	.03	.01
☐ 410 Bert Campaneris	.10	.04	.01
☐ 411 Terry Puhl	.08	.03	.01
☐ 412 Britt Burns	.35	.14	.03
☐ 413 Tony Bernazard	.10	.04	.01
☐ 414 John Pacella DP	.02	.01	.00
☐ 415 Ben Oglivie	.12	.05	.01
☐ 416 Gary Alexander	.05	.02	.00
☐ 417 Dan Schatzeder	.05	.02	.00
☐ 418 Bobby Brown	.05	.02	.00
☐ 419 Tom Hume	.05	.02	.00

		MINT	VG-E	F-G
☐ 420	Keith Hernandez	.75	.30	.07
☐ 421	Bob Stanley	.10	.04	.01
☐ 422	Dan Ford	.08	.03	.01
☐ 423	Shane Rawley	.12	.05	.01
☐ 424	Yankees Rookies	.15	.06	.01
	Tim Lollar			
	Bruce Robinson			
	Dennis Werth			
☐ 425	Al Bumbry	.05	.02	.00
☐ 426	Warren Brusstar	.05	.02	.00
☐ 427	John D'Acquisto	.05	.02	.00
☐ 428	John Stearns	.05	.02	.00
☐ 429	Mick Kelleher	.05	.02	.00
☐ 430	Jim Bibby	.08	.03	.01
☐ 431	Dave Roberts	.05	.02	.00
☐ 432	Len Barker	.10	.04	.01
☐ 433	Rance Mulliniks	.08	.03	.01
☐ 434	Roger Erickson	.05	.02	.00
☐ 435	Jim Spencer	.05	.02	.00
☐ 436	Gary Lucas	.10	.04	.01
☐ 437	Mike Heath DP	.02	.01	.00
☐ 438	John Montefusco	.08	.03	.01
☐ 439	Denny Walling	.05	.02	.00
☐ 440	Jerry Reuss	.12	.05	.01
☐ 441	Ken Reitz	.05	.02	.00
☐ 442	Ron Pruitt	.05	.02	.00
☐ 443	Jim Beattie DP	.02	.01	.00
☐ 444	Garth Iorg	.05	.02	.00
☐ 445	Ellis Valentine	.08	.03	.01
☐ 446	Checklist 364-484	.15	.02	.00
☐ 447	Junior Kennedy DP	.02	.01	.00
☐ 448	Tim Corcoran	.05	.02	.00
☐ 449	Paul Mitchell	.05	.02	.00
☐ 450	Dave Kingman DP	.10	.04	.01
☐ 451	Indians Rookies	.15	.06	.01
	Chris Bando			
	Tom Brennan			
	Sandy Wihtol			
☐ 452	Renie Martin	.05	.02	.00
☐ 453	Rob Wilfong DP	.02	.01	.00
☐ 454	Andy Hassler	.05	.02	.00
☐ 455	Rick Burleson	.08	.03	.01
☐ 456	Jeff Reardon	.60	.24	.06
☐ 457	Mike Lum	.05	.02	.00
☐ 458	Randy Jones	.08	.03	.01
☐ 459	Greg Gross	.05	.02	.00
☐ 460	Rich Gossage	.30	.12	.03
☐ 461	Dave McKay	.05	.02	.00
☐ 462	Jack Brohamer	.05	.02	.00
☐ 463	Milt May	.05	.02	.00
☐ 464	Adrian Devine	.05	.02	.00
☐ 465	Bill Russell	.08	.03	.01
☐ 466	Bob Molinaro	.05	.02	.00

		MINT	VG-E	F-G
☐ 467	Dave Stieb	.40	.16	.04
☐ 468	Johnny Wockenfuss	.05	.02	.00
☐ 469	Jeff Leonard	.12	.05	.01
☐ 470	Manny Trillo	.08	.03	.01
☐ 471	Mike Vail	.05	.02	.00
☐ 472	Dyar Miller DP	.02	.01	.00
☐ 473	Jose Cardenal	.05	.02	.00
☐ 474	Mike LaCoss	.05	.02	.00
☐ 475	Buddy Bell	.18	.08	.01
☐ 476	Jerry Koosman	.15	.06	.01
☐ 477	Luis Gomez	.05	.02	.00
☐ 478	Juan Eichelberger	.08	.03	.01
☐ 479	Expos Rookies	6.50	2.60	.65
	Tim Raines			
	Roberto Ramos			
	Bobby Pate			
☐ 480	Carlton Fisk	.30	.12	.03
☐ 481	Bob Lacey DP	.02	.01	.00
☐ 482	Jim Gantner	.08	.03	.01
☐ 483	Mike Griffin	.05	.02	.00
☐ 484	Max Venable DP	.02	.01	.00
☐ 485	Garry Templeton	.15	.06	.01
☐ 486	Marc Hill	.05	.02	.00
☐ 487	Dewey Robinson	.05	.02	.00
☐ 488	Damaso Garcia	.65	.26	.06
☐ 489	John Littlefield	.07	.03	.01
☐ 490	Eddie Murray	1.50	.60	.15
☐ 491	Gordy Pladson	.08	.03	.01
☐ 492	Barry Foote	.05	.02	.00
☐ 493	Dan Quisenberry	.45	.18	.04
☐ 494	Bob Walk	.07	.03	.01
☐ 495	Dusty Baker	.12	.05	.01
☐ 496	Paul Dade	.05	.02	.00
☐ 497	Fred Norman	.05	.02	.00
☐ 498	Pat Putnam	.05	.02	.00
☐ 499	Frank Pastore	.05	.02	.00
☐ 500	Jim Rice	1.25	.50	.12
☐ 501	Tim Foli DP	.02	.01	.00
☐ 502	Giants Rookies	.08	.03	.01
	Chris Bourjos			
	Al Hargesheimer			
	Mike Rowland			
☐ 503	Steve McCatty	.05	.02	.00
☐ 504	Dale Murphy	2.50	1.00	.25
☐ 505	Jason Thompson	.10	.04	.01
☐ 506	Phil Huffman	.05	.02	.00
☐ 507	Jamie Quirk	.05	.02	.00
☐ 508	Rob Dressler	.05	.02	.00
☐ 509	Pete Mackanin	.05	.02	.00
☐ 510	Lee Mazzilli	.08	.03	.01
☐ 511	Wayne Garland	.05	.02	.00
☐ 512	Gary Thomasson	.05	.02	.00
☐ 513	Frank LaCorte	.05	.02	.00

	MINT	VG-E	F-G			MINT	VG-E	F-G
514 George Riley	.08	.03	.01	561 Dennis Littlejohn	.05	.02	.00
515 Robin Yount	1.00	.40	.10	562 Checklist 485-605	.15	.02	.00
516 Doug Bird	.05	.02	.00	563 Jim Kaat	.25	.10	.02
517 Richie Zisk	.08	.03	.01	564 Ron Hassey DP	.02	.01	.00
518 Grant Jackson	.05	.02	.00	565 Burt Hooton	.05	.02	.00
519 John Tamargo DP	.02	.01	.00	566 Del Unser	.05	.02	.00
520 Steve Stone	.10	.04	.01	567 Mark Bomback	.05	.02	.00
521 Sam Mejias	.05	.02	.00	568 Dave Revering	.05	.02	.00
522 Mike Colbern	.05	.02	.00	569 Al Williams DP	.02	.01	.00
523 John Fulgham	.05	.02	.00	570 Ken Singleton	.15	.06	.01
524 Willie Aikens	.10	.04	.01	571 Todd Cruz	.05	.02	.00
525 Mike Torrez	.08	.03	.01	572 Jack Morris	.60	.24	.06
526 Phillies Rookies	.18	.08	.01	573 Phil Garner	.08	.03	.01
Marty Bystrom				574 Bill Caudill	.10	.04	.01
Jay Loviglio				575 Tony Perez	.20	.08	.02
Jim Wright				576 Reggie Cleveland	.05	.02	.00
527 Danny Goodwin	.05	.02	.00	577 Blue Jays Rookies	.20	.08	.02
528 Gary Matthews	.12	.05	.01	Luis Leal			
529 Dave LaRoche	.05	.02	.00	Brian Milner			
530 Steve Garvey	1.25	.50	.12	Ken Schrom			
531 John Curtis	.05	.02	.00	578 Bill Gullickson	.50	.20	.05
532 Bill Stein	.05	.02	.00	579 Tim Flannery	.05	.02	.00
533 Jesus Figueroa	.05	.02	.00	580 Don Baylor	.30	.12	.03
534 Dave Smith	.35	.14	.03	581 Roy Howell	.05	.02	.00
535 Omar Moreno	.08	.03	.01	582 Gaylord Perry	.50	.20	.05
536 Bob Owchinko DP	.02	.01	.00	583 Larry Milbourne	.05	.02	.00
537 Ron Hodges	.05	.02	.00	584 Randy Lerch	.05	.02	.00
538 Tom Griffin	.05	.02	.00	585 Amos Otis	.12	.05	.01
539 Rodney Scott	.05	.02	.00	586 Silvio Martinez	.05	.02	.00
540 Mike Schmidt DP	.85	.34	.08	587 Jeff Newman	.05	.02	.00
541 Steve Swisher	.05	.02	.00	588 Gary Lavelle	.08	.03	.01
542 Larry Bradford DP	.02	.01	.00	589 Lamar Johnson	.05	.02	.00
543 Terry Crowley	.05	.02	.00	590 Bruce Sutter	.35	.14	.03
544 Rich Gale	.05	.02	.00	591 John Lowenstein	.05	.02	.00
545 Johnny Grubb	.05	.02	.00	592 Steve Comer	.05	.02	.00
546 Paul Moskau	.05	.02	.00	593 Steve Kemp	.12	.05	.01
547 Mario Guerrero	.05	.02	.00	594 Preston Hanna DP	.02	.01	.00
548 Dave Goltz	.05	.02	.00	595 Butch Hobson	.05	.02	.00
549 Jerry Remy	.08	.03	.01	596 Jerry Augustine	.05	.02	.00
550 Tommy John	.25	.10	.02	597 Rafael Landestoy	.05	.02	.00
551 Pirates Rookies	1.75	.70	.17	598 George Vukovich DP	.02	.01	.00
Vance Law				599 Dennis Kinney	.05	.02	.00
Tony Pena				600 Johnny Bench	1.25	.50	.12
Pascual Perez				601 Don Aase	.10	.04	.01
552 Steve Trout	.08	.03	.01	602 Bobby Murcer	.15	.06	.01
553 Tim Blackwell	.05	.02	.00	603 John Verhoeven	.05	.02	.00
554 Bert Blyleven	.25	.10	.02	604 Rob Picciolo	.05	.02	.00
555 Cecil Cooper	.25	.10	.02	605 Don Sutton	.60	.24	.06
556 Jerry Mumphrey	.08	.03	.01	606 Reds Rookies DP	.08	.03	.01
557 Chris Knapp	.05	.02	.00	Bruce Berenyi			
558 Barry Bonnell	.08	.03	.01	Geoff Combe			
559 Willie Montanez	.05	.02	.00	Paul Householder			
560 Joe Morgan	.60	.24	.06	607 Dave Palmer	.10	.04	.01

		MINT	VG-E	F-G
☐ 608	Greg Pryor	.05	.02	.00
☐ 609	Lynn McGlothen	.05	.02	.00
☐ 610	Darrell Porter	.08	.03	.01
☐ 611	Rick Matula DP	.02	.01	.00
☐ 612	Duane Kuiper	.05	.02	.00
☐ 613	Jim Anderson	.05	.02	.00
☐ 614	Dave Rozema	.05	.02	.00
☐ 615	Rick Dempsey	.08	.03	.01
☐ 616	Rick Wise	.08	.03	.01
☐ 617	Craig Reynolds	.05	.02	.00
☐ 618	John Milner	.05	.02	.00
☐ 619	Steve Henderson	.08	.03	.01
☐ 620	Dennis Eckersley	.08	.03	.01
☐ 621	Tom Donohue	.05	.02	.00
☐ 622	Randy Moffitt	.05	.02	.00
☐ 623	Sal Bando	.08	.03	.01
☐ 624	Bob Welch	.15	.06	.01
☐ 625	Bill Buckner	.15	.06	.01
☐ 626	Tigers Rookies	.10	.04	.01
	Dave Steffen			
	Jerry Ujdur			
	Roger Weaver			
☐ 627	Luis Tiant	.12	.05	.01
☐ 628	Vic Correll	.05	.02	.00
☐ 629	Tony Armas	.15	.06	.01
☐ 630	Steve Carlton	1.00	.40	.10
☐ 631	Ron Jackson	.05	.02	.00
☐ 632	Alan Bannister	.05	.02	.00
☐ 633	Bill Lee	.08	.03	.01
☐ 634	Doug Flynn	.05	.02	.00
☐ 635	Bobby Bonds	.12	.05	.01
☐ 636	Al Hrabosky	.08	.03	.01
☐ 637	Jerry Narron	.05	.02	.00
☐ 638	Checklist 606-726	.15	.02	.00
☐ 639	Carney Lansford	.20	.08	.02
☐ 640	Dave Parker	.70	.28	.07
☐ 641	Mark Belanger	.08	.03	.01
☐ 642	Vern Ruhle	.05	.02	.00
☐ 643	Lloyd Moseby	1.75	.70	.17
☐ 644	Ramon Aviles DP	.02	.01	.00
☐ 645	Rick Reuschel	.08	.03	.01
☐ 646	Marvis Foley	.05	.02	.00
☐ 647	Dick Drago	.05	.02	.00
☐ 648	Darrell Evans	.18	.08	.01
☐ 649	Manny Sarmiento	.05	.02	.00
☐ 650	Bucky Dent	.12	.05	.01
☐ 651	Pedro Guerrero	1.00	.40	.10
☐ 652	John Montague	.05	.02	.00
☐ 653	Bill Fahey	.05	.02	.00
☐ 654	Ray Burris	.05	.02	.00
☐ 655	Dan Driessen	.08	.03	.01
☐ 656	Jon Matlack	.08	.03	.01
☐ 657	Mike Cubbage DP	.02	.01	.00
☐ 658	Milt Wilcox	.05	.02	.00
☐ 659	Brewers Rookies:	.08	.03	.01
	John Flinn			
	Ed Romero			
	Ned Yost			
☐ 660	Gary Carter	1.50	.60	.15
☐ 661	Orioles Team/Mgr.	.20	.04	.01
	Earl Weaver			
☐ 662	Red Sox Team/Mgr.	.18	.04	.01
	Ralph Houk			
☐ 663	Angels Team/Mgr.	.18	.04	.01
	Jim Fregosi			
☐ 664	White Sox Team/Mgr.	.18	.04	.01
	Tony LaRussa			
☐ 665	Indians Team/Mgr.	.18	.04	.01
	Dave Garcia			
☐ 666	Tigers Team/Mgr.	.20	.04	.01
	Sparky Anderson			
☐ 667	Royals Team/Mgr.	.18	.04	.01
	Jim Frey			
☐ 668	Brewers Team/Mgr.	.18	.04	.01
	Bob Rodgers			
☐ 669	Twins Team/Mgr.	.15	.03	.01
	John Goryl			
☐ 670	Yankees Team/Mgr.	.20	.04	.01
	Gene Michael			
☐ 671	A's Team/Mgr.	.20	.04	.01
	Billy Martin			
☐ 672	Mariners Team/Mgr.	.15	.03	.01
	Maury Wills			
☐ 673	Rangers Team/Mgr.	.15	.03	.01
	Don Zimmer			
☐ 674	Blue Jays Team/Mgr.	.15	.03	.01
	Bobby Mattick			
☐ 675	Braves Team/Mgr.	.18	.04	.01
	Bobby Cox			
☐ 676	Cubs Team/Mgr.	.18	.04	.01
	Joe Amalfitano			
☐ 677	Reds Team/Mgr.	.18	.04	.01
	John McNamara			
☐ 678	Astros Team/Mgr.	.18	.04	.01
	Bill Virdon			
☐ 679	Dodgers Team/Mgr.	.20	.04	.01
	Tom Lasorda			
☐ 680	Expos Team/Mgr.	.18	.04	.01
	Dick Williams			
☐ 681	Mets Team/Mgr.	.20	.04	.01
	Joe Torre			
☐ 682	Phillies Team/Mgr.	.18	.04	.01
	Dallas Green			
☐ 683	Pirates Team/Mgr.	.18	.04	.01
	Chuck Tanner			

		MINT	VG-E	F-G
☐ 684	Cardinals Team/Mgr. .... Whitey Herzog	.18	.04	.01
☐ 685	Padres Team/Mgr. ...... Frank Howard	.15	.03	.01
☐ 686	Giants Team/Mgr. ...... Dave Bristol	.18	.04	.01
☐ 687	Jeff Jones	.10	.04	.01
☐ 688	Kiko Garcia	.05	.02	.00
☐ 689	Red Sox Rookies ...... Bruce Hurst Keith MacWhorter Reid Nichols	1.00	.40	.10
☐ 690	Bob Watson	.08	.03	.01
☐ 691	Dick Ruthven	.05	.02	.00
☐ 692	Lenny Randle	.05	.02	.00
☐ 693	Steve Howe	.20	.08	.02
☐ 694	Bud Harrelson DP	.02	.01	.00
☐ 695	Kent Tekulve	.08	.03	.01
☐ 696	Alan Ashby	.05	.02	.00
☐ 697	Rick Waits	.05	.02	.00
☐ 698	Mike Jorgensen	.05	.02	.00
☐ 699	Glen Abbott	.05	.02	.00
☐ 700	George Brett	1.75	.70	.17
☐ 701	Joe Rudi	.08	.03	.01
☐ 702	George Medich	.05	.02	.00
☐ 703	Alvis Woods	.05	.02	.00
☐ 704	Bill Travers DP	.02	.01	.00
☐ 705	Ted Simmons	.18	.08	.01
☐ 706	Dave Ford	.05	.02	.00
☐ 707	Dave Cash	.05	.02	.00
☐ 708	Doyle Alexander	.08	.03	.01
☐ 709	Alan Trammell DP	.10	.04	.01
☐ 710	Ron LeFlore DP	.05	.02	.00
☐ 711	Joe Ferguson	.08	.03	.01
☐ 712	Bill Bonham	.05	.02	.00
☐ 713	Bill North	.05	.02	.00
☐ 714	Pete Redfern	.05	.02	.00
☐ 715	Bill Madlock	.25	.10	.02
☐ 716	Glenn Borgmann	.05	.02	.00
☐ 717	Jim Barr DP	.02	.01	.00
☐ 718	Larry Biittner	.05	.02	.00
☐ 719	Sparky Lyle	.15	.06	.01
☐ 720	Fred Lynn	.35	.14	.03
☐ 721	Toby Harrah	.08	.03	.01
☐ 722	Joe Niekro	.12	.05	.01
☐ 723	Bruce Bochte	.08	.03	.01
☐ 724	Lou Piniella	.12	.05	.01
☐ 725	Steve Rogers	.12	.05	.01
☐ 726	Rick Monday	.10	.04	.01

1981 Topps Traded

The cards in this 132-card set measure 2½" by 3½". For the first time since 1976, Topps issued a Traded set in 1981. Unlike the small traded sets of 1974 and 1976, this set contains a larger number of cards and was sequentially numbered, alphabetically, from 727 to 858. Thus, this set gives the impression it is a continuation of their regular issue of this year. The sets were issued only through hobby card dealers and were boxed in complete sets of 132 cards.

		MINT	VG-E	F-G
	Complete Set...........	21.00	8.50	2.10
	Common Player	.08	.03	.01
☐ 727	Danny Ainge	.45	.18	.04
☐ 728	Doyle Alexander	.12	.05	.01
☐ 729	Gary Alexander	.08	.03	.01
☐ 730	Billy Almon	.08	.03	.01
☐ 731	Joaquin Andujar	.20	.08	.02
☐ 732	Bob Bailor	.08	.03	.01
☐ 733	Juan Beniquez	.12	.05	.01
☐ 734	Dave Bergman	.08	.03	.01
☐ 735	Tony Bernazard	.12	.05	.01
☐ 736	Larry Biittner	.08	.03	.01
☐ 737	Doug Bird	.08	.03	.01
☐ 738	Bert Blyleven	.40	.16	.04
☐ 739	Mark Bomback	.08	.03	.01
☐ 740	Bobby Bonds	.15	.06	.01
☐ 741	Rick Bosetti	.08	.03	.01
☐ 742	Hubie Brooks	1.50	.60	.15
☐ 743	Rick Burleson	.12	.05	.01
☐ 744	Ray Burris	.08	.03	.01
☐ 745	Jeff Burroughs.............	.12	.05	.01
☐ 746	Enos Cabell	.08	.03	.01

		MINT	VG-E	F-G
☐ 747	Ken Clay	.08	.03	.01
☐ 748	Mark Clear	.12	.05	.01
☐ 749	Larry Cox	.08	.03	.01
☐ 750	Hector Cruz	.08	.03	.01
☐ 751	Victor Cruz	.08	.03	.01
☐ 752	Mike Cubbage	.08	.03	.01
☐ 753	Dick Davis	.08	.03	.01
☐ 754	Brian Doyle	.08	.03	.01
☐ 755	Dick Drago	.08	.03	.01
☐ 756	Leon Durham	.75	.30	.07
☐ 757	Jim Dwyer	.08	.03	.01
☐ 758	Dave Edwards	.08	.03	.01
☐ 759	Jim Essian	.08	.03	.01
☐ 760	Bill Fahey	.08	.03	.01
☐ 761	Rollie Fingers	.75	.30	.07
☐ 762	Carlton Fisk	.60	.24	.06
☐ 763	Barry Foote	.08	.03	.01
☐ 764	Ken Forsch	.12	.05	.01
☐ 765	Kiko Garcia	.08	.03	.01
☐ 766	Cesar Geronimo	.08	.03	.01
☐ 767	Gary Gray	.12	.05	.01
☐ 768	Mickey Hatcher	.12	.05	.01
☐ 769	Steve Henderson	.12	.05	.01
☐ 770	Marc Hill	.08	.03	.01
☐ 771	Butch Hobson	.08	.03	.01
☐ 772	Rick Honeycutt	.12	.05	.01
☐ 773	Roy Howell	.08	.03	.01
☐ 774	Mike Ivie	.08	.03	.01
☐ 775	Roy Lee Jackson	.08	.03	.01
☐ 776	Cliff Johnson	.08	.03	.01
☐ 777	Randy Jones	.12	.05	.01
☐ 778	Ruppert Jones	.12	.05	.01
☐ 779	Mick Kelleher	.08	.03	.01
☐ 780	Terry Kennedy	.20	.08	.02
☐ 781	Dave Kingman	.35	.14	.03
☐ 782	Bob Knepper	.20	.08	.02
☐ 783	Ken Kravec	.08	.03	.01
☐ 784	Bob Lacey	.08	.03	.01
☐ 785	Dennis Lamp	.08	.03	.01
☐ 786	Rafael Landestoy	.08	.03	.01
☐ 787	Ken Landreaux	.12	.05	.01
☐ 788	Carney Lansford	.40	.16	.04
☐ 789	Dave LaRoche	.08	.03	.01
☐ 790	Joe Lefebvre	.08	.03	.01
☐ 791	Ron LeFlore	.12	.05	.01
☐ 792	Randy Lerch	.08	.03	.01
☐ 793	Sixto Lezcano	.12	.05	.01
☐ 794	John Littlefield	.08	.03	.01
☐ 795	Mike Lum	.08	.03	.01
☐ 796	Greg Luzinski	.30	.12	.03
☐ 797	Fred Lynn	.70	.28	.07
☐ 798	Jerry Martin	.08	.03	.01
☐ 799	Buck Martinez	.08	.03	.01
☐ 800	Gary Matthews	.15	.06	.01
☐ 801	Mario Mendoza	.08	.03	.01
☐ 802	Larry Milbourne	.08	.03	.01
☐ 803	Rick Miller	.08	.03	.01
☐ 804	John Montefusco	.12	.05	.01
☐ 805	Jerry Morales	.08	.03	.01
☐ 806	Jose Morales	.08	.03	.01
☐ 807	Joe Morgan	1.25	.50	.12
☐ 808	Jerry Mumphrey	.12	.05	.01
☐ 809	Gene Nelson	.20	.08	.02
☐ 810	Ed Ott	.08	.03	.01
☐ 811	Bob Owchinko	.08	.03	.01
☐ 812	Gaylord Perry	1.25	.50	.12
☐ 813	Mike Phillips	.08	.03	.01
☐ 814	Darrell Porter	.12	.05	.01
☐ 815	Mike Proly	.08	.03	.01
☐ 816	Tim Raines	4.50	1.80	.45
☐ 817	Len Randle	.08	.03	.01
☐ 818	Doug Rau	.08	.03	.01
☐ 819	Jeff Reardon	.35	.14	.03
☐ 820	Ken Reitz	.08	.03	.01
☐ 821	Steve Renko	.08	.03	.01
☐ 822	Rick Reuschel	.15	.06	.01
☐ 823	Dave Revering	.08	.03	.01
☐ 824	Dave Roberts	.08	.03	.01
☐ 825	Leon Roberts	.08	.03	.01
☐ 826	Joe Rudi	.12	.05	.01
☐ 827	Kevin Saucier	.08	.03	.01
☐ 828	Tony Scott	.08	.03	.01
☐ 829	Bob Shirley	.08	.03	.01
☐ 830	Ted Simmons	.40	.16	.04
☐ 831	Lary Sorensen	.08	.03	.01
☐ 832	Jim Spencer	.08	.03	.01
☐ 833	Harry Spilman	.08	.03	.01
☐ 834	Fred Stanley	.08	.03	.01
☐ 835	Rusty Staub	.25	.10	.02
☐ 836	Bill Stein	.08	.03	.01
☐ 837	Joe Strain	.08	.03	.01
☐ 838	Bruce Sutter	.65	.26	.06
☐ 839	Don Sutton	1.00	.40	.10
☐ 840	Steve Swisher	.08	.03	.01
☐ 841	Frank Tanana	.12	.05	.01
☐ 842	Gene Tenace	.08	.03	.01
☐ 843	Jason Thompson	.12	.05	.01
☐ 844	Dickie Thon	.20	.08	.02
☐ 845	Bill Travers	.08	.03	.01
☐ 846	Tom Underwood	.08	.03	.01
☐ 847	John Urrea	.08	.03	.01
☐ 848	Mike Vail	.08	.03	.01
☐ 849	Ellis Valentine	.12	.05	.01
☐ 850	Fernando Valenzuela	5.00	2.00	.50
☐ 851	Pete Vuckovich	.15	.06	.01
☐ 852	Mark Wagner	.08	.03	.01

		MINT	VG-E	F-G
☐ 853	Bob Walk	.08	.03	.01
☐ 854	Claudell Washington	.15	.06	.01
☐ 855	Dave Winfield	1.75	.70	.17
☐ 856	Geoff Zahn	.12	.05	.01
☐ 857	Richie Zisk	.12	.05	.01
☐ 858	Checklist 727-858	.20	.02	.00

1982 Topps

The cards in this 792-card set measure 2½"
by 3½". The 1982 baseball series is the largest set Topps has ever issued at one printing.
The 66-card increase from the previous
year's total eliminated the "double print"
practice which had occurred in every regular
issue since 1978. Cards 1-6 depict Highlights (HL) of the 1981 season, cards 161-168
picture League Leaders, and there are mini-
series of AL (547-557) and NL (337-347) All
Stars (AS). The abbreviation "SA" in the
checklist is given for the 40 "Super Action"
cards introduced in this set. The team cards
are actually Team Leader (TL) cards picturing the batting and pitching leader for that
team with a checklist back.

	MINT	VG-E	F-G
Complete Set	55.00	20.00	5.00
Common Player (1-792)	.04	.02	.00

		MINT	VG-E	F-G
☐ 1	HL: Steve Carlton, sets new NL strikeout record	.40	.10	.02
☐ 2	HL: Ron Davis, rans 8 straight in relief	.06	.02	.00

		MINT	VG-E	F-G
☐ 3	HL: Tim Raines, swipes 71 bases as rookie	.25	.10	.02
☐ 4	HL: Pete Rose, sets NL career hits mark	.75	.30	.07
☐ 5	HL: Nolan Ryan, pitches 5th career no-hitter	.30	.12	.03
☐ 6	HL: Fern. Valenzuela, 8 shutouts as rookie	.30	.12	.03
☐ 7	Scott Sanderson	.04	.02	.00
☐ 8	Rich Dauer	.04	.02	.00
☐ 9	Ron Guidry	.30	.12	.03
☐ 10	SA: Ron Guidry	.15	.06	.01
☐ 11	Gary Alexander	.04	.02	.00
☐ 12	Moose Haas	.06	.02	.00
☐ 13	Lamar Johnson	.04	.02	.00
☐ 14	Steve Howe	.06	.02	.00
☐ 15	Ellis Valentine	.04	.02	.00
☐ 16	Steve Comer	.04	.02	.00
☐ 17	Darrell Evans	.12	.05	.01
☐ 18	Fernando Arroyo	.04	.02	.00
☐ 19	Ernie Whitt	.04	.02	.00
☐ 20	Garry Maddox	.06	.02	.00
☐ 21	Orioles Rookies Bob Bonner Cal Ripken Jeff Schneider	9.00	3.75	.90
☐ 22	Jim Beattie	.04	.02	.00
☐ 23	Willie Hernandez	.20	.08	.02
☐ 24	Dave Frost	.04	.02	.00
☐ 25	Jerry Remy	.04	.02	.00
☐ 26	Jorge Orta	.04	.02	.00
☐ 27	Tom Herr	.12	.05	.01
☐ 28	John Urrea	.04	.02	.00
☐ 29	Dwayne Murphy	.06	.02	.00
☐ 30	Tom Seaver	.65	.26	.06
☐ 31	SA: Tom Seaver	.30	.12	.03
☐ 32	Gene Garber	.04	.02	.00
☐ 33	Jerry Morales	.04	.02	.00
☐ 34	Joe Sambito	.06	.02	.00
☐ 35	Willie Aikens	.06	.02	.00
☐ 36	Rangers TL Mgr. Don Zimmer Batting: Al Oliver Pitching: Doc Medich	.10	.02	.00
☐ 37	Dan Graham	.04	.02	.00
☐ 38	Charlie Lea	.06	.02	.00
☐ 39	Lou Whitaker	.30	.12	.03
☐ 40	Dave Parker	.35	.14	.03
☐ 41	SA: Dave Parker	.15	.06	.01
☐ 42	Rick Sofield	.04	.02	.00
☐ 43	Mike Cubbage	.04	.02	.00
☐ 44	Britt Burns	.08	.03	.01

		MINT	VG-E	F-G
☐ 45	Rick Cerone	.04	.02	.00
☐ 46	Jerry Augustine	.04	.02	.00
☐ 47	Jeff Leonard	.08	.03	.01
☐ 48	Bobby Castillo	.04	.02	.00
☐ 49	Alvis Woods	.04	.02	.00
☐ 50	Buddy Bell	.12	.05	.01
☐ 51	Cubs Rookies	.40	.16	.04
	Jay Howell			
	Carlos Lezcano			
	Ty Waller			
☐ 52	Larry Andersen	.04	.02	.00
☐ 53	Greg Gross	.04	.02	.00
☐ 54	Ron Hassey	.04	.02	.00
☐ 55	Rick Burleson	.06	.02	.00
☐ 56	Mark Littell	.04	.02	.00
☐ 57	Craig Reynolds	.04	.02	.00
☐ 58	John D'Acquisto	.04	.02	.00
☐ 59	Rich Gedman	1.50	.60	.15
☐ 60	Tony Armas	.15	.06	.01
☐ 61	Tommy Boggs	.04	.02	.00
☐ 62	Mike Tyson	.04	.02	.00
☐ 63	Mario Soto	.10	.04	.01
☐ 64	Lynn Jones	.04	.02	.00
☐ 65	Terry Kennedy	.10	.04	.01
☐ 66	Astros TL	.15	.03	.00
	Mgr. Bill Virdon			
	Batting: Art Howe			
	Pitching: Nolan Ryan			
☐ 67	Rich Gale	.04	.02	.00
☐ 68	Roy Howell	.04	.02	.00
☐ 69	Al Williams	.04	.02	.00
☐ 70	Tim Raines	1.25	.50	.12
☐ 71	Roy Lee Jackson	.04	.02	.00
☐ 72	Rick Auerbach	.04	.02	.00
☐ 73	Buddy Solomon	.04	.02	.00
☐ 74	Bob Clark	.04	.02	.00
☐ 75	Tommy John	.20	.08	.02
☐ 76	Greg Pryor	.04	.02	.00
☐ 77	Miguel Dilone	.04	.02	.00
☐ 78	George Medich	.04	.02	.00
☐ 79	Bob Bailor	.04	.02	.00
☐ 80	Jim Palmer	.45	.18	.04
☐ 81	SA: Jim Palmer	.20	.08	.02
☐ 82	Bob Welch	.08	.03	.01
☐ 83	Yankees Rookies	.60	.24	.06
	Steve Balboni			
	Andy McGaffigan			
	Andre Robertson			
☐ 84	Rennie Stennett	.04	.02	.00
☐ 85	Lynn McGlothen	.04	.02	.00
☐ 86	Dane Iorg	.04	.02	.00
☐ 87	Matt Keough	.04	.02	.00
☐ 88	Biff Pocoroba	.04	.02	.00
☐ 89	Steve Henderson	.04	.02	.00
☐ 90	Nolan Ryan	.65	.26	.06
☐ 91	Carney Lansford	.15	.06	.01
☐ 92	Brad Havens	.06	.02	.00
☐ 93	Larry Hisle	.06	.02	.00
☐ 94	Andy Hassler	.04	.02	.00
☐ 95	Ozzie Smith	.25	.10	.02
☐ 96	Royals TL	.15	.03	.00
	Mgr. Jim Frey			
	Batting: George Brett			
	Pitching: Larry Gura			
☐ 97	Paul Moskau	.04	.02	.00
☐ 98	Terry Bulling	.04	.02	.00
☐ 99	Barry Bonnell	.04	.02	.00
☐ 100	Mike Schmidt	1.25	.50	.12
☐ 101	SA: Mike Schmidt	.50	.20	.05
☐ 102	Dan Briggs	.04	.02	.00
☐ 103	Bob Lacey	.04	.02	.00
☐ 104	Rance Mulliniks	.04	.02	.00
☐ 105	Kirk Gibson	.75	.30	.07
☐ 106	Enrique Romo	.04	.02	.00
☐ 107	Wayne Krenchicki	.04	.02	.00
☐ 108	Bob Sykes	.04	.02	.00
☐ 109	Dave Revering	.04	.02	.00
☐ 110	Carlton Fisk	.25	.10	.02
☐ 111	SA: Carlton Fisk	.15	.06	.01
☐ 112	Billy Sample	.04	.02	.00
☐ 113	Steve McCatty	.04	.02	.00
☐ 114	Ken Landreaux	.06	.02	.00
☐ 115	Gaylord Perry	.25	.10	.02
☐ 116	Jim Wohlford	.04	.02	.00
☐ 117	Rawly Eastwick	.04	.02	.00
☐ 118	Expos Rookies	.25	.10	.02
	Terry Francona			
	Brad Mills			
	Bryn Smith			
☐ 119	Joe Pittman	.04	.02	.00
☐ 120	Gary Lucas	.04	.02	.00
☐ 121	Ed Lynch	.12	.05	.01
☐ 122	Jamie Easterly	.06	.02	.00
	(photo actually			
	Reggie Cleveland)			
☐ 123	Danny Goodwin	.04	.02	.00
☐ 124	Reid Nichols	.04	.02	.00
☐ 125	Danny Ainge	.10	.04	.01
☐ 126	Braves TL	.10	.02	.00
	Mgr. Bobby Cox			
	Batting: C. Washington			
	Pitching: Rick Mahler			
☐ 127	Lonnie Smith	.10	.04	.01
☐ 128	Frank Pastore	.04	.02	.00
☐ 129	Checklist 1-132	.10	.01	.00
☐ 130	Julio Cruz	.04	.02	.00

		MINT	VG-E	F-G
☐ 131	Stan Bahnsen	.04	.02	.00
☐ 132	Lee May	.06	.02	.00
☐ 133	Pat Underwood	.04	.02	.00
☐ 134	Dan Ford	.04	.02	.00
☐ 135	Andy Rincon	.04	.02	.00
☐ 136	Lenn Sakata	.04	.02	.00
☐ 137	George Cappuzzello	.04	.02	.00
☐ 138	Tony Pena	.30	.12	.03
☐ 139	Jeff Jones	.04	.02	.00
☐ 140	Ron LeFlore	.06	.02	.00
☐ 141	Indians Rookies	2.00	.80	.20
	Chris Bando			
	Tom Brennan			
	Von Hayes			
☐ 142	Dave LaRoche	.04	.02	.00
☐ 143	Mookie Wilson	.10	.04	.01
☐ 144	Fred Breining	.12	.05	.01
☐ 145	Bob Horner	.35	.14	.03
☐ 146	Mike Griffin	.04	.02	.00
☐ 147	Denny Walling	.04	.02	.00
☐ 148	Mickey Klutts	.04	.02	.00
☐ 149	Pat Putnam	.04	.02	.00
☐ 150	Ted Simmons	.15	.06	.01
☐ 151	Dave Edwards	.04	.02	.00
☐ 152	Ramon Aviles	.04	.02	.00
☐ 153	Roger Erickson	.04	.02	.00
☐ 154	Dennis Werth	.04	.02	.00
☐ 155	Otto Velez	.04	.02	.00
☐ 156	Oakland A's TL	.15	.03	.00
	Mgr. Billy Martin			
	Batting: R.Henderson			
	Pitching: S. McCatty			
☐ 157	Steve Crawford	.08	.03	.01
☐ 158	Brian Downing	.06	.02	.00
☐ 159	Larry Biittner	.04	.02	.00
☐ 160	Luis Tiant	.10	.04	.01
☐ 161	Batting Leaders	.15	.06	.01
	Bill Madlock			
	Carney Lansford			
☐ 162	Home Run Leaders	.20	.08	.02
	Mike Schmidt			
	Tony Armas			
	Dwight Evans			
	Bobby Grich			
	Eddie Murray			
☐ 163	RBI Leaders	.30	.12	.03
	Mike Schmidt			
	Eddie Murray			
☐ 164	Stolen Base Leaders	.30	.12	.03
	Tim Raines			
	Rickey Henderson			
☐ 165	Victory Leaders	.15	.06	.01
	Tom Seaver			
	Denny Martinez			
	Steve McCatty			
	Jack Morris			
	Pete Vuckovich			
☐ 166	Strikeout Leaders	.15	.06	.01
	Fernando Valenzuela			
	Len Barker			
☐ 167	ERA Leaders	.15	.06	.01
	Nolan Ryan			
	Steve McCatty			
☐ 168	Leading Firemen	.15	.06	.01
	Bruce Sutter			
	Rollie Fingers			
☐ 169	Charlie Leibrandt	.08	.03	.01
☐ 170	Jim Bibby	.06	.02	.00
☐ 171	Giants Rookies	1.25	.50	.12
	Bob Brenly			
	Chili Davis			
	Bob Tufts			
☐ 172	Bill Gullickson	.06	.02	.00
☐ 173	Jamie Quirk	.04	.02	.00
☐ 174	Dave Ford	.04	.02	.00
☐ 175	Jerry Mumphrey	.06	.02	.00
☐ 176	Dewey Robinson	.04	.02	.00
☐ 177	John Ellis	.04	.02	.00
☐ 178	Dyar Miller	.04	.02	.00
☐ 179	Steve Garvey	.80	.32	.08
☐ 180	SA: Steve Garvey	.40	.16	.04
☐ 181	Silvio Martinez	.04	.02	.00
☐ 182	Larry Herndon	.06	.02	.00
☐ 183	Mike Proly	.04	.02	.00
☐ 184	Mick Kelleher	.04	.02	.00
☐ 185	Phil Niekro	.40	.16	.04
☐ 186	Cardinals TL	.15	.03	.00
	Mgr. Whitey Herzog			
	Batting K. Hernandez			
	Pitching Bob Forsch			
☐ 187	Jeff Newman	.04	.02	.00
☐ 188	Randy Martz	.04	.02	.00
☐ 189	Glenn Hoffman	.04	.02	.00
☐ 190	J.R. Richard	.10	.04	.01
☐ 191	Tim Wallach	.60	.24	.06
☐ 192	Broderick Perkins	.04	.02	.00
☐ 193	Darrell Jackson	.04	.02	.00
☐ 194	Mike Vail	.04	.02	.00
☐ 195	Paul Molitor	.15	.06	.01
☐ 196	Willie Upshaw	.12	.05	.01
☐ 197	Shane Rawley	.08	.03	.01
☐ 198	Chris Speier	.04	.02	.00
☐ 199	Don Aase	.06	.02	.00
☐ 200	George Brett	1.50	.60	.15

		MINT	VG-E	F-G
☐ 201	SA: George Brett	.60	.24	.06
☐ 202	Rick Manning	.03	.01	.00
☐ 203	Blue Jays Rookies	4.00	1.60	.40
	Jesse Barfield			
	Brian Milner			
	Boomer Wells			
☐ 204	Gary Roenicke	.06	.02	.00
☐ 205	Neil Allen	.06	.02	.00
☐ 206	Tony Bernazard	.06	.02	.00
☐ 207	Rod Scurry	.04	.02	.00
☐ 208	Bobby Murcer	.12	.05	.01
☐ 209	Gary Lavelle	.06	.02	.00
☐ 210	Keith Hernandez	.50	.20	.05
☐ 211	Dan Petry	.20	.08	.02
☐ 212	Mario Mendoza	.04	.02	.00
☐ 213	Dave Stewart	.25	.10	.02
☐ 214	Brian Asselstine	.04	.02	.00
☐ 215	Mike Krukow	.12	.05	.01
☐ 216	White Sox TL	.10	.02	.00
	Mgr. Tony LaRussa			
	Batting: Chet Lemon			
	Pitching: Dennis Lamp			
☐ 217	Bo McLaughlin	.04	.02	.00
☐ 218	Dave Roberts	.04	.02	.00
☐ 219	John Curtis	.04	.02	.00
☐ 220	Manny Trillo	.06	.02	.00
☐ 221	Jim Slaton	.04	.02	.00
☐ 222	Butch Wynegar	.06	.02	.00
☐ 223	Lloyd Moseby	.30	.12	.03
☐ 224	Bruce Bochte	.06	.02	.00
☐ 225	Mike Torrez	.06	.02	.00
☐ 226	Checklist 133-264	.10	.01	.00
☐ 227	Ray Burris	.04	.02	.00
☐ 228	Sam Mejias	.04	.02	.00
☐ 229	Geoff Zahn	.04	.02	.00
☐ 230	Willie Wilson	.25	.10	.02
☐ 231	Phillies Rookies	.40	.16	.04
	Mark Davis			
	Bob Dernier			
	Ozzie Virgil			
☐ 232	Terry Crowley	.04	.02	.00
☐ 233	Duane Kuiper	.04	.02	.00
☐ 234	Ron Hodges	.04	.02	.00
☐ 235	Mike Easler	.10	.04	.01
☐ 236	John Martin	.04	.02	.00
☐ 237	Rusty Kuntz	.04	.02	.00
☐ 238	Kevin Saucier	.04	.02	.00
☐ 239	Jon Matlack	.06	.02	.00
☐ 240	Bucky Dent	.08	.03	.01
☐ 241	SA: Bucky Dent	.06	.02	.00
☐ 242	Milt May	.04	.02	.00
☐ 243	Bob Owchinko	.04	.02	.00
☐ 244	Rufino Linares	.04	.02	.00

		MINT	VG-E	F-G
☐ 245	Ken Reitz	.04	.02	.00
☐ 246	New York Mets TL	.15	.03	.00
	Mgr. Joe Torre			
	Batting: Hubie Brooks			
	Pitching: Mike Scott			
☐ 247	Pedro Guerrero	.60	.24	.06
☐ 248	Frank LaCorte	.04	.02	.00
☐ 249	Tim Flannery	.04	.02	.00
☐ 250	Tug McGraw	.10	.04	.01
☐ 251	Fred Lynn	.30	.12	.03
☐ 252	SA: Fred Lynn	.15	.06	.01
☐ 253	Chuck Baker	.04	.02	.00
☐ 254	Jorge Bell	3.50	1.40	.35
☐ 255	Tony Perez	.20	.08	.02
☐ 256	SA: Tony Perez	.10	.04	.01
☐ 257	Larry Harlow	.04	.02	.00
☐ 258	Bo Diaz	.10	.04	.01
☐ 259	Rodney Scott	.04	.02	.00
☐ 260	Bruce Sutter	.30	.12	.03
☐ 261	Tigers Rookies	.10	.04	.01
	Howard Bailey			
	Marty Castillo			
	Dave Rucker			
☐ 262	Doug Bair	.04	.02	.00
☐ 263	Victor Cruz	.04	.02	.00
☐ 264	Dan Quisenberry	.25	.10	.02
☐ 265	Al Bumbry	.04	.02	.00
☐ 266	Rick Leach	.06	.02	.00
☐ 267	Kurt Bevacqua	.04	.02	.00
☐ 268	Rickey Keeton	.04	.02	.00
☐ 269	Jim Essian	.04	.02	.00
☐ 270	Rusty Staub	.12	.05	.01
☐ 271	Larry Bradford	.04	.02	.00
☐ 272	Bump Wills	.04	.02	.00
☐ 273	Doug Bird	.04	.02	.00
☐ 274	Bob Ojeda	1.25	.50	.12
☐ 275	Bob Watson	.06	.02	.00
☐ 276	Angels TL	.15	.03	.00
	Mgr. Gene Mauch			
	Batting: Rod Carew			
	Pitching: Ken Forsch			
☐ 277	Terry Puhl	.06	.02	.00
☐ 278	John Littlefield	.04	.02	.00
☐ 279	Bill Russell	.06	.02	.00
☐ 280	Ben Oglivie	.08	.03	.01
☐ 281	John Verhoeven	.04	.02	.00
☐ 282	Ken Macha	.04	.02	.00
☐ 283	Brian Allard	.04	.02	.00
☐ 284	Bob Grich	.08	.03	.01
☐ 285	Sparky Lyle	.12	.05	.01
☐ 286	Bill Fahey	.04	.02	.00
☐ 287	Alan Bannister	.04	.02	.00
☐ 288	Garry Templeton	.12	.05	.01

		MINT	VG-E	F-G
☐ 289	Bob Stanley	.06	.02	.00
☐ 290	Ken Singleton	.12	.05	.01
☐ 291	Pirates Rookies	1.25	.50	.12
	Vance Law			
	Bob Long			
	Johnny Ray			
☐ 292	David Palmer	.06	.02	.00
☐ 293	Rob Picciolo	.04	.02	.00
☐ 294	Mike LaCoss	.04	.02	.00
☐ 295	Jason Thompson	.08	.03	.01
☐ 296	Bob Walk	.04	.02	.00
☐ 297	Clint Hurdle	.04	.02	.00
☐ 298	Danny Darwin	.04	.02	.00
☐ 299	Steve Trout	.06	.02	.00
☐ 300	Reggie Jackson	1.25	.50	.12
☐ 301	SA: Reggie Jackson	.50	.20	.05
☐ 302	Doug Flynn	.04	.02	.00
☐ 303	Bill Caudill	.06	.02	.00
☐ 304	Johnnie LeMaster	.04	.02	.00
☐ 305	Don Sutton	.40	.16	.04
☐ 306	SA: Don Sutton	.20	.08	.02
☐ 307	Randy Bass	.04	.02	.00
☐ 308	Charlie Moore	.04	.02	.00
☐ 309	Pete Redfern	.04	.02	.00
☐ 310	Mike Hargrove	.06	.02	.00
☐ 311	Dodgers TL	.10	.02	.00
	Mgr. Tom Lasorda			
	Batting: Dusty Baker			
	Pitching: Burt Hooton			
☐ 312	Lenny Randle	.04	.02	.00
☐ 313	John Harris	.04	.02	.00
☐ 314	Buck Martinez	.04	.02	.00
☐ 315	Burt Hooton	.04	.02	.00
☐ 316	Steve Braun	.04	.02	.00
☐ 317	Dick Ruthven	.04	.02	.00
☐ 318	Mike Heath	.04	.02	.00
☐ 319	Dave Rozema	.04	.02	.00
☐ 320	Chris Chambliss	.06	.02	.00
☐ 321	SA: Chris Chambliss	.06	.02	.00
☐ 322	Garry Hancock	.04	.02	.00
☐ 323	Bill Lee	.06	.02	.00
☐ 324	Steve Dillard	.04	.02	.00
☐ 325	Jose Cruz	.15	.06	.01
☐ 326	Pete Falcone	.04	.02	.00
☐ 327	Joe Nolan	.04	.02	.00
☐ 328	Ed Farmer	.04	.02	.00
☐ 329	U.L. Washington	.04	.02	.00
☐ 330	Rick Wise	.06	.02	.00
☐ 331	Benny Ayala	.04	.02	.00
☐ 332	Don Robinson	.06	.02	.00

		MINT	VG-E	F-G
☐ 333	Brewers Rookies	.15	.06	.01
	Frank DiPino			
	Marshall Edwards			
	Chuck Porter			
☐ 334	Aurelio Rodriguez	.04	.02	.00
☐ 335	Jim Sundberg	.06	.02	.00
☐ 336	Mariners TL	.10	.02	.00
	Mgr. Rene Lachemann			
	Batting: Tom Paciorek			
	Pitching: Glenn Abbott			
☐ 337	Pete Rose AS	.75	.30	.07
☐ 338	Dave Lopes AS	.06	.02	.00
☐ 339	Mike Schmidt AS	.40	.16	.04
☐ 340	Dave Concepcion AS	.08	.03	.01
☐ 341	Andre Dawson AS	.15	.06	.01
☐ 342 A	George Foster AS	.35	.14	.03
	(with autograph)			
☐ 342 B	George Foster AS	2.50	1.00	.25
	(w/o autograph)			
☐ 343	Dave Parker AS	.15	.06	.01
☐ 344	Gary Carter AS	.30	.12	.03
☐ 345	Fern. Valenzuela AS	.25	.10	.02
☐ 346	Tom Seaver AS	.25	.10	.02
☐ 347	Bruce Sutter AS	.15	.06	.01
☐ 348	Derrel Thomas	.04	.02	.00
☐ 349	George Frazier	.04	.02	.00
☐ 350	Thad Bosley	.04	.02	.00
☐ 351	Reds Rookies	.08	.03	.01
	Scott Brown			
	Geoff Coumbe			
	Paul Householder			
☐ 352	Dick Davis	.04	.02	.00
☐ 353	Jack O'Connor	.04	.02	.00
☐ 354	Roberto Ramos	.04	.02	.00
☐ 355	Dwight Evans	.15	.06	.01
☐ 356	Denny Lewallyn	.08	.03	.01
☐ 357	Butch Hobson	.04	.02	.00
☐ 358	Mike Parrott	.04	.02	.00
☐ 359	Jim Dwyer	.04	.02	.00
☐ 360	Len Barker	.08	.03	.01
☐ 361	Rafael Landestoy	.04	.02	.00
☐ 362	Jim Wright	.04	.02	.00
☐ 363	Bob Molinaro	.04	.02	.00
☐ 364	Doyle Alexander	.06	.02	.00
☐ 365	Bill Madlock	.20	.08	.02
☐ 366	Padres TL	.10	.02	.00
	Mgr. Frank Howard			
	Batting: Luis Salazar			
	Pitching: Eichelberger			
☐ 367	Jim Kaat	.15	.06	.01
☐ 368	Alex Trevino	.04	.02	.00
☐ 369	Champ Summers	.04	.02	.00
☐ 370	Mike Norris	.06	.02	.00

		MINT	VG-E	F-G
☐ 371	Jerry Don Gleaton	.04	.02	.00
☐ 372	Luis Gomez	.04	.02	.00
☐ 373	Gene Nelson	.12	.05	.01
☐ 374	Tim Blackwell	.04	.02	.00
☐ 375	Dusty Baker	.08	.03	.01
☐ 376	Chris Welsh	.06	.02	.00
☐ 377	Kiko Garcia	.04	.02	.00
☐ 378	Mike Caldwell	.06	.02	.00
☐ 379	Rob Wilfong	.04	.02	.00
☐ 380	Dave Stieb	.30	.12	.03
☐ 381	Red Sox Rookies	.25	.10	.02
	Bruce Hurst			
	Dave Schmidt			
	Julio Valdez			
☐ 382	Joe Simpson	.04	.02	.00
☐ 383 A	Pascual Perez ERR	35.00	14.00	3.50
	(no position			
	on front)			
☐ 383 B	Pascual Perez COR	.10	.04	.01
☐ 384	Keith Moreland	.08	.03	.01
☐ 385	Ken Forsch	.04	.02	.00
☐ 386	Jerry White	.04	.02	.00
☐ 387	Tom Veryzer	.04	.02	.00
☐ 388	Joe Rudi	.06	.02	.00
☐ 389	George Vukovich	.04	.02	.00
☐ 390	Eddie Murray	1.25	.50	.12
☐ 391	Dave Tobik	.04	.02	.00
☐ 392	Rick Bosetti	.04	.02	.00
☐ 393	Al Hrabosky	.06	.02	.00
☐ 394	Checklist 265-396	.10	.01	.00
☐ 395	Omar Moreno	.04	.02	.00
☐ 396	Twins TL	.10	.04	.01
	Mgr. Billy Gardner			
	Batting: John Castino			
	Pitching: F. Arroyo			
☐ 397	Ken Brett	.04	.02	.00
☐ 398	Mike Squires	.04	.02	.00
☐ 399	Pat Zachry	.04	.02	.00
☐ 400	Johnny Bench	.75	.30	.07
☐ 401	SA: Johnny Bench	.35	.14	.03
☐ 402	Bill Stein	.04	.02	.00
☐ 403	Jim Tracy	.04	.02	.00
☐ 404	Dickie Thon	.10	.04	.01
☐ 405	Rick Reuschel	.06	.02	.00
☐ 406	Al Holland	.06	.02	.00
☐ 407	Danny Boone	.04	.02	.00
☐ 408	Ed Romero	.04	.02	.00
☐ 409	Don Cooper	.04	.02	.00
☐ 410	Ron Cey	.15	.06	.01
☐ 411	SA: Ron Cey	.08	.03	.01
☐ 412	Luis Leal	.04	.02	.00
☐ 413	Dan Meyer	.04	.02	.00
☐ 414	Elias Sosa	.04	.02	.00

		MINT	VG-E	F-G
☐ 415	Don Baylor	.15	.06	.01
☐ 416	Marty Bystrom	.04	.02	.00
☐ 417	Pat Kelly	.04	.02	.00
☐ 418	Rangers Rookies	.08	.03	.01
	John Butcher			
	Bobby Johnson			
	Dave Schmidt			
☐ 419	Steve Stone	.08	.03	.01
☐ 420	George Hendrick	.10	.04	.01
☐ 421	Mark Clear	.04	.02	.00
☐ 422	Cliff Johnson	.04	.02	.00
☐ 423	Stan Papi	.04	.02	.00
☐ 424	Bruce Benedict	.04	.02	.00
☐ 425	John Candelaria	.10	.04	.01
☐ 426	Orioles TL	.15	.03	.00
	Mgr. Earl Weaver			
	Batting: Eddie Murray			
	Pitching: Sam Stewart			
☐ 427	Ron Oester	.06	.02	.00
☐ 428	LaMarr Hoyt	.12	.05	.01
☐ 429	John Wathan	.04	.02	.00
☐ 430	Vida Blue	.10	.04	.01
☐ 431	SA: Vida Blue	.06	.02	.00
☐ 432	Mike Scott	.35	.14	.03
☐ 433	Alan Ashby	.04	.02	.00
☐ 434	Joe Lefebvre	.04	.02	.00
☐ 435	Robin Yount	.75	.30	.07
☐ 436	Joe Strain	.04	.02	.00
☐ 437	Juan Berenguer	.04	.02	.00
☐ 438	Pete Mackanin	.04	.02	.00
☐ 439	Dave Righetti	2.00	.80	.20
☐ 440	Jeff Burroughs	.06	.02	.00
☐ 441	Astros Rookies	.08	.03	.01
	Danny Heep			
	Billy Smith			
	Bobby Sprowl			
☐ 442	Bruce Kison	.04	.02	.00
☐ 443	Mark Wagner	.04	.02	.00
☐ 444	Terry Forster	.10	.04	.01
☐ 445	Larry Parrish	.08	.03	.01
☐ 446	Wayne Garland	.04	.02	.00
☐ 447	Darrell Porter	.08	.03	.01
☐ 448	SA: Darrell Porter	.06	.02	.00
☐ 449	Luis Aguayo	.06	.02	.00
☐ 450	Jack Morris	.50	.20	.05
☐ 451	Ed Miller	.04	.02	.00
☐ 452	Lee Smith	.75	.30	.07
☐ 453	Art Howe	.04	.02	.00
☐ 454	Rick Langford	.04	.02	.00
☐ 455	Tom Burgmeier	.04	.02	.00

	MINT	VG-E	F-G
☐ 456 Chicago Cubs TL	.10	.02	.00
Mgr. Joe Amalfitano			
Batting: Bill Buckner			
Pitching: Randy Martz			
☐ 457 Tim Stoddard	.04	.02	.00
☐ 458 Willie Montanez	.04	.02	.00
☐ 459 Bruce Berenyi	.06	.02	.00
☐ 460 Jack Clark	.25	.10	.02
☐ 461 Rich Dotson	.08	.03	.01
☐ 462 Dave Chalk	.04	.02	.00
☐ 463 Jim Kern	.04	.02	.00
☐ 464 Juan Bonilla	.06	.02	.00
☐ 465 Lee Mazzilli	.06	.02	.00
☐ 466 Randy Lerch	.04	.02	.00
☐ 467 Mickey Hatcher	.04	.02	.00
☐ 468 Floyd Bannister	.08	.03	.01
☐ 469 Ed Ott	.04	.02	.00
☐ 470 John Mayberry	.06	.02	.00
☐ 471 Royals Rookies	.25	.10	.02
Atlee Hammaker			
Mike Jones			
Darryl Motley			
☐ 472 Oscar Gamble	.06	.02	.00
☐ 473 Mike Stanton	.04	.02	.00
☐ 474 Ken Oberkfell	.06	.02	.00
☐ 475 Alan Trammell	.35	.14	.03
☐ 476 Brian Kingman	.04	.02	.00
☐ 477 Steve Yeager	.06	.02	.00
☐ 478 Ray Searage	.12	.05	.01
☐ 479 Rowland Office	.04	.02	.00
☐ 480 Steve Carlton	1.00	.40	.10
☐ 481 SA: Steve Carlton	.40	.16	.04
☐ 482 Glenn Hubbard	.04	.02	.00
☐ 483 Gary Woods	.04	.02	.00
☐ 484 Ivan DeJesus	.04	.02	.00
☐ 485 Kent Tekulve	.08	.03	.01
☐ 486 Yankees TL	.10	.02	.00
Mgr. Bob Lemon			
Batting: J. Mumphrey			
Pitching: Tommy John			
☐ 487 Bob McClure	.04	.02	.00
☐ 488 Ron Jackson	.04	.02	.00
☐ 489 Rick Dempsey	.06	.02	.00
☐ 490 Dennis Eckersley	.06	.02	.00
☐ 491 Checklist 397-528	.10	.01	.00
☐ 492 Joe Price	.04	.02	.00
☐ 493 Chet Lemon	.08	.03	.01
☐ 494 Hubie Brooks	.25	.10	.02
☐ 495 Dennis Leonard	.06	.02	.00
☐ 496 Johnny Grubb	.04	.02	.00
☐ 497 Jim Anderson	.04	.02	.00
☐ 498 Dave Bergman	.04	.02	.00
☐ 499 Paul Mirabella	.04	.02	.00

	MINT	VG-E	F-G
☐ 500 Rod Carew	1.00	.40	.10
☐ 501 SA: Rod Carew	.40	.16	.04
☐ 502 Braves Rookies	1.00	.40	.10
Steve Bedrosian			
Brett Butler			
Larry Owen			
☐ 503 Julio Gonzalez	.04	.02	.00
☐ 504 Rick Peters	.04	.02	.00
☐ 505 Graig Nettles	.20	.08	.02
☐ 506 SA: Graig Nettles	.10	.04	.01
☐ 507 Terry Harper	.04	.02	.00
☐ 508 Jody Davis	.75	.30	.07
☐ 509 Harry Spilman	.04	.02	.00
☐ 510 Fernando Valenzuela	1.50	.60	.15
☐ 511 Ruppert Jones	.04	.02	.00
☐ 512 Jerry Dybzinski	.04	.02	.00
☐ 513 Rick Rhoden	.10	.04	.01
☐ 514 Joe Ferguson	.06	.02	.00
☐ 515 Larry Bowa	.12	.05	.01
☐ 516 SA: Larry Bowa	.06	.02	.00
☐ 517 Mark Brouhard	.06	.02	.00
☐ 518 Garth Iorg	.04	.02	.00
☐ 519 Glenn Adams	.04	.02	.00
☐ 520 Mike Flanagan	.10	.04	.01
☐ 521 Billy Almon	.04	.02	.00
☐ 522 Chuck Rainey	.04	.02	.00
☐ 523 Gary Gray	.06	.02	.00
☐ 524 Tom Hausman	.04	.02	.00
☐ 525 Ray Knight	.10	.04	.01
☐ 526 Expos TL	.10	.02	.00
Mgr. Jim Fanning			
Batting: W.Cromartie			
Pitching: B.Gullickson			
☐ 527 John Henry Johnson	.04	.02	.00
☐ 528 Matt Alexander	.04	.02	.00
☐ 529 Allen Ripley	.04	.02	.00
☐ 530 Dickie Noles	.04	.02	.00
☐ 531 A's Rookies	.08	.03	.01
Rich Bordi			
Mark Budaska			
Kelvin Moore			
☐ 532 Toby Harrah	.06	.02	.00
☐ 533 Joaquin Andujar	.15	.06	.01
☐ 534 Dave McKay	.04	.02	.00
☐ 535 Lance Parrish	.45	.18	.04
☐ 536 Rafael Ramirez	.06	.02	.00
☐ 537 Doug Capilla	.04	.02	.00
☐ 538 Lou Piniella	.10	.04	.01
☐ 539 Vern Ruhle	.04	.02	.00
☐ 540 Andre Dawson	.30	.12	.03
☐ 541 Barry Evans	.04	.02	.00
☐ 542 Ned Yost	.04	.02	.00
☐ 543 Bill Robinson	.04	.02	.00

		MINT	VG-E	F-G
☐ 544	Larry Christenson	.04	.02	.00
☐ 545	Reggie Smith	.10	.04	.01
☐ 546	SA: Reggie Smith	.06	.02	.00
☐ 547	Rod Carew AS	.25	.10	.02
☐ 548	Willie Randolph AS	.06	.02	.00
☐ 549	George Brett AS	.40	.16	.04
☐ 550	Bucky Dent AS	.06	.02	.00
☐ 551	Reggie Jackson AS	.35	.14	.03
☐ 552	Ken Singleton AS	.08	.03	.01
☐ 553	Dave Winfield AS	.30	.12	.03
☐ 554	Carlton Fisk AS	.15	.06	.01
☐ 555	Scott McGregor AS	.06	.02	.00
☐ 556	Jack Morris AS	.15	.06	.01
☐ 557	Rich Gossage AS	.15	.06	.01
☐ 558	John Tudor	.35	.14	.03
☐ 559	Indians TL	.10	.02	.00
	Mgr. Dave Garcia			
	Batting: Mike Hargrove			
	Pitching: Bert Blyleven			
☐ 560	Doug Corbett	.04	.02	.00
☐ 561	Cardinals Rookies	.15	.06	.01
	Glenn Brummer			
	Luis DeLeon			
	Gene Roof			
☐ 562	Mike O'Berry	.04	.02	.00
☐ 563	Ross Baumgarten	.04	.02	.00
☐ 564	Doug DeCinces	.12	.05	.01
☐ 565	Jackson Todd	.04	.02	.00
☐ 566	Mike Jorgensen	.04	.02	.00
☐ 567	Bob Babcock	.04	.02	.00
☐ 568	Joe Pettini	.04	.02	.00
☐ 569	Willie Randolph	.08	.03	.01
☐ 570	SA: Willie Randolph	.06	.02	.00
☐ 571	Glenn Abbott	.04	.02	.00
☐ 572	Juan Beniquez	.04	.02	.00
☐ 573	Rick Waits	.04	.02	.00
☐ 574	Mike Ramsey	.04	.02	.00
☐ 575	Al Cowens	.06	.02	.00
☐ 576	Giants TL	.10	.02	.00
	Mgr. Frank Robinson			
	Batting: Milt May			
	Pitching: Vida Blue			
☐ 577	Rick Monday	.06	.02	.00
☐ 578	Shooty Babitt	.04	.02	.00
☐ 579	Rick Mahler	.25	.10	.02
☐ 580	Bobby Bonds	.10	.04	.01
☐ 581	Ron Reed	.04	.02	.00
☐ 582	Luis Pujols	.04	.02	.00
☐ 583	Tippy Martinez	.04	.02	.00
☐ 584	Hosken Powell	.04	.02	.00
☐ 585	Rollie Fingers	.25	.10	.02
☐ 586	SA: Rollie Fingers	.15	.06	.01
☐ 587	Tim Lollar	.04	.02	.00

		MINT	VG-E	F-G
☐ 588	Dale Berra	.06	.02	.00
☐ 589	Dave Stapleton	.04	.02	.00
☐ 590	Al Oliver	.20	.08	.02
☐ 591	SA: Al Oliver	.10	.04	.01
☐ 592	Craig Swan	.04	.02	.00
☐ 593	Billy Smith	.04	.02	.00
☐ 594	Renie Martin	.04	.02	.00
☐ 595	Dave Collins	.06	.02	.00
☐ 596	Damaso Garcia	.15	.06	.01
☐ 597	Wayne Nordhagen	.04	.02	.00
☐ 598	Bob Galasso	.04	.02	.00
☐ 599	White Sox Rookies	.08	.03	.01
	Jay Loviglio			
	Reggie Patterson			
	Leo Sutherland			
☐ 600	Dave Winfield	.50	.20	.05
☐ 601	Sid Monge	.04	.02	.00
☐ 602	Freddie Patek	.04	.02	.00
☐ 603	Rich Hebner	.04	.02	.00
☐ 604	Orlando Sanchez	.04	.02	.00
☐ 605	Steve Rogers	.08	.03	.01
☐ 606	Blue Jays TL	.10	.02	.00
	Mgr. Bobby Mattick			
	Batting: J.Mayberry			
	Pitching: Dave Stieb			
☐ 607	Leon Durham	.20	.08	.02
☐ 608	Jerry Royster	.04	.02	.00
☐ 609	Rick Sutcliffe	.20	.08	.02
☐ 610	Rickey Henderson	1.50	.60	.15
☐ 611	Joe Niekro	.12	.05	.01
☐ 612	Gary Ward	.06	.02	.00
☐ 613	Jim Gantner	.04	.02	.00
☐ 614	Juan Eichelberger	.04	.02	.00
☐ 615	Bob Boone	.06	.02	.00
☐ 616	SA: Bob Boone	.06	.02	.00
☐ 617	Scott McGregor	.10	.04	.01
☐ 618	Tim Foli	.04	.02	.00
☐ 619	Bill Campbell	.06	.02	.00
☐ 620	Ken Griffey	.10	.04	.01
☐ 621	SA: Ken Griffey	.06	.02	.00
☐ 622	Dennis Lamp	.04	.02	.00
☐ 623	Mets Rookies	.15	.06	.01
	Ron Gardenhire			
	Terry Leach			
	Tim Leary			
☐ 624	Fergie Jenkins	.20	.08	.02
☐ 625	Hal McRae	.08	.03	.01
☐ 626	Randy Jones	.06	.02	.00
☐ 627	Enos Cabell	.04	.02	.00
☐ 628	Bill Travers	.04	.02	.00
☐ 629	Johnny Wockenfuss	.04	.02	.00
☐ 630	Joe Charboneau	.06	.02	.00
☐ 631	Gene Tenace	.04	.02	.00

		MINT	VG-E	F-G
☐ 632	Bryan Clark	.04	.02	.00
☐ 633	Mitchell Page	.04	.02	.00
☐ 634	Checklist 529-660	.10	.01	.00
☐ 635	Ron Davis	.04	.02	.00
☐ 636	Phillies TL	.30	.06	.01
	Mgr. Dallas Green			
	Batting: Pete Rose			
	Pitching: Steve Carlton			
☐ 637	Rick Camp	.04	.02	.00
☐ 638	John Milner	.04	.02	.00
☐ 639	Ken Kravec	.04	.02	.00
☐ 640	Cesar Cedeno	.10	.04	.01
☐ 641	Steve Mura	.04	.02	.00
☐ 642	Mike Scioscia	.08	.03	.01
☐ 643	Pete Vuckovich	.12	.05	.01
☐ 644	John Castino	.04	.02	.00
☐ 645	Frank White	.08	.03	.01
☐ 646	SA: Frank White	.06	.02	.00
☐ 647	Warren Brusstar	.04	.02	.00
☐ 648	Jose Morales	.04	.02	.00
☐ 649	Ken Clay	.04	.02	.00
☐ 650	Carl Yastrzemski	1.25	.50	.12
☐ 651	SA: Carl Yastrzemski	.50	.20	.05
☐ 652	Steve Nicosia	.04	.02	.00
☐ 653	Angels Rookies	2.25	.90	.22
	Tom Brunansky			
	Luis Sanchez			
	Daryl Sconiers			
☐ 654	Jim Morrison	.06	.02	.00
☐ 655	Joel Youngblood	.04	.02	.00
☐ 656	Eddie Whitson	.06	.02	.00
☐ 657	Tom Poquette	.04	.02	.00
☐ 658	Tito Landrum	.04	.02	.00
☐ 659	Fred Martinez	.04	.02	.00
☐ 660	Dave Concepcion	.12	.05	.01
☐ 661	SA: Dave Concepcion	.08	.03	.01
☐ 662	Luis Salazar	.04	.02	.00
☐ 663	Hector Cruz	.04	.02	.00
☐ 664	Dan Spillner	.04	.02	.00
☐ 665	Jim Clancy	.06	.02	.00
☐ 666	Tigers TL	.10	.02	.00
	Mgr. Sparky Anderson			
	Batting: Steve Kemp			
	Pitching: Dan Petry			
☐ 667	Jeff Reardon	.10	.04	.01
☐ 668	Dale Murphy	2.00	.80	.20
☐ 669	Larry Milbourne	.04	.02	.00
☐ 670	Steve Kemp	.08	.03	.01
☐ 671	Mike Davis	.15	.06	.01
☐ 672	Bob Knepper	.10	.04	.01
☐ 673	Keith Drumright	.04	.02	.00
☐ 674	Dave Goltz	.04	.02	.00
☐ 675	Cecil Cooper	.20	.08	.02

		MINT	VG-E	F-G
☐ 676	Sal Butera	.04	.02	.00
☐ 677	Alfredo Griffin	.08	.03	.01
☐ 678	Tom Paciorek	.04	.02	.00
☐ 679	Sammy Stewart	.04	.02	.00
☐ 680	Gary Matthews	.10	.04	.01
☐ 681	Dodgers Rookies	4.00	1.60	.40
	Mike Marshall			
	Ron Roenicke			
	Steve Sax			
☐ 682	Jesse Jefferson	.04	.02	.00
☐ 683	Phil Garner	.06	.02	.00
☐ 684	Harold Baines	.75	.30	.07
☐ 685	Bert Blyleven	.20	.08	.02
☐ 686	Gary Allenson	.04	.02	.00
☐ 687	Greg Minton	.06	.02	.00
☐ 688	Leon Roberts	.04	.02	.00
☐ 689	Lary Sorensen	.04	.02	.00
☐ 690	Dave Kingman	.20	.08	.02
☐ 691	Dan Schatzeder	.04	.02	.00
☐ 692	Wayne Gross	.04	.02	.00
☐ 693	Cesar Geronimo	.04	.02	.00
☐ 694	Dave Wehrmeister	.04	.02	.00
☐ 695	Warren Cromartie	.04	.02	.00
☐ 696	Pirates TL	.10	.02	.00
	Mgr. Chuck Tanner			
	Batting: Bill Madlock			
	Pitching:Eddie Solomon			
☐ 697	John Montefusco	.06	.02	.00
☐ 698	Tony Scott	.04	.02	.00
☐ 699	Dick Tidrow	.04	.02	.00
☐ 700	George Foster	.25	.10	.02
☐ 701	SA: George Foster	.12	.05	.01
☐ 702	Steve Renko	.04	.02	.00
☐ 703	Brewers TL	.10	.02	.00
	Mgr. Bob Rodgers			
	Batting: Cecil Cooper			
	Pitching: P.Vuckovich			
☐ 704	Mickey Rivers	.06	.02	.00
☐ 705	SA: Mickey Rivers	.06	.02	.00
☐ 706	Barry Foote	.04	.02	.00
☐ 707	Mark Bomback	.04	.02	.00
☐ 708	Gene Richards	.04	.02	.00
☐ 709	Don Money	.04	.02	.00
☐ 710	Jerry Reuss	.08	.03	.01
☐ 711	Mariners Rookies	.75	.30	.07
	Dave Edler			
	Dave Henderson			
	Reggie Walton			
☐ 712	Denny Martinez	.04	.02	.00
☐ 713	Del Unser	.04	.02	.00
☐ 714	Jerry Koosman	.10	.04	.01
☐ 715	Willie Stargell	.50	.20	.05
☐ 716	SA: Willie Stargell	.20	.08	.02

	MINT	VG-E	F-G
☐ 717 Rick Miller	.04	.02	.00
☐ 718 Charlie Hough	.08	.03	.01
☐ 719 Jerry Narron	.04	.02	.00
☐ 720 Greg Luzinski	.15	.06	.01
☐ 721 SA: Greg Luzinski	.10	.04	.01
☐ 722 Jerry Martin	.04	.02	.00
☐ 723 Junior Kennedy	.04	.02	.00
☐ 724 Dave Rosello	.04	.02	.00
☐ 725 Amos Otis	.08	.03	.01
☐ 726 SA: Amos Otis	.06	.02	.00
☐ 727 Sixto Lezcano	.04	.02	.00
☐ 728 Aurelio Lopez	.04	.02	.00
☐ 729 Jim Spencer	.04	.02	.00
☐ 730 Gary Carter	1.00	.40	.10
☐ 731 Padres Rookies	.10	.04	.01
Mike Armstrong			
Doug Gwosdz			
Fred Kuhaulua			
☐ 732 Mike Lum	.04	.02	.00
☐ 733 Larry McWilliams	.04	.02	.00
☐ 734 Mike Ivie	.04	.02	.00
☐ 735 Rudy May	.04	.02	.00
☐ 736 Jerry Turner	.04	.02	.00
☐ 737 Reggie Cleveland	.04	.02	.00
☐ 738 Dave Engle	.04	.02	.00
☐ 739 Joey McLaughlin	.04	.02	.00
☐ 740 Dave Lopes	.08	.03	.01
☐ 741 SA: Dave Lopes	.06	.02	.00
☐ 742 Dick Drago	.04	.02	.00
☐ 743 John Stearns	.04	.02	.00
☐ 744 Mike Witt	2.00	.80	.20
☐ 745 Bake McBride	.06	.02	.00
☐ 746 Andre Thornton	.10	.04	.01
☐ 747 John Lowenstein	.04	.02	.00
☐ 748 Marc Hill	.04	.02	.00
☐ 749 Bob Shirley	.04	.02	.00
☐ 750 Jim Rice	1.00	.40	.10
☐ 751 Rick Honeycutt	.06	.02	.00
☐ 752 Lee Lacy	.08	.03	.01
☐ 753 Tom Brookens	.04	.02	.00
☐ 754 Joe Morgan	.40	.16	.04
☐ 755 SA: Joe Morgan	.20	.08	.02
☐ 756 Reds TL	.15	.03	.00
Mgr. John McNamara			
Batting: Ken Griffey			
Pitching: Tom Seaver			
☐ 757 Tom Underwood	.04	.02	.00
☐ 758 Claudell Washington	.10	.04	.01
☐ 759 Paul Splittorff	.06	.02	.00
☐ 760 Bill Buckner	.15	.06	.01
☐ 761 Dave Smith	.10	.04	.01
☐ 762 Mike Phillips	.04	.02	.00
☐ 763 Tom Hume	.04	.02	.00

	MINT	VG-E	F-G
☐ 764 Steve Swisher	.04	.02	.00
☐ 765 Gorman Thomas	.12	.05	.01
☐ 766 Twins Rookies	3.50	1.40	.35
Lenny Faedo			
Kent Hrbek			
Tim Laudner			
☐ 767 Roy Smalley	.06	.02	.00
☐ 768 Jerry Garvin	.04	.02	.00
☐ 769 Richie Zisk	.06	.02	.00
☐ 770 Rich Gossage	.25	.10	.02
☐ 771 SA: Rich Gossage	.15	.06	.01
☐ 772 Bert Campaneris	.08	.03	.01
☐ 773 John Denny	.10	.04	.01
☐ 774 Jay Johnstone	.06	.02	.00
☐ 775 Bob Forsch	.08	.03	.01
☐ 776 Mark Belanger	.06	.02	.00
☐ 777 Tom Griffin	.04	.02	.00
☐ 778 Kevin Hickey	.08	.03	.01
☐ 779 Grant Jackson	.04	.02	.00
☐ 780 Pete Rose	2.25	.90	.22
☐ 781 SA: Pete Rose	.75	.30	.07
☐ 782 Frank Taveras	.04	.02	.00
☐ 783 Greg Harris	.25	.10	.02
☐ 784 Milt Wilcox	.04	.02	.00
☐ 785 Dan Driessen	.06	.02	.00
☐ 786 Red Sox TL	.10	.02	.00
Mgr. Ralph Houk			
Batting: C.Lansford			
Pitching: Mike Torrez			
☐ 787 Fred Stanley	.04	.02	.00
☐ 788 Woodie Fryman	.04	.02	.00
☐ 789 Checklist 661-792	.10	.01	.00
☐ 790 Larry Gura	.06	.02	.00
☐ 791 Bobby Brown	.04	.02	.00
☐ 792 Frank Tanana	.10	.04	.01

1982 Topps Traded

The cards in this 132-card set measure 2½" by 3½". The Topps Traded or extended series for 1982 is distinguished by a "T" printed after the number (located on the reverse). Of the total cards, 70 players represent the American League and 61 represent the National League, with the remaining card a numbered checklist (132T). The Cubs lead the pack with 12 changes while the Red Sox are the only team in either league to have no new additions. All 131 player photos used in the set are completely new. Of this total, 112 individuals are seen in the uniform of their new team, 11 others have been elevated to single card status from "Future Stars" cards, and eight more are entirely new to the 1982 Topps lineup. The backs are almost completely red in color with black print.

	MINT	VG-E	F-G
Complete Set	20.00	8.00	2.00
Common Player	.08	.03	.01

		MINT	VG-E	F-G
☐ 1	T Doyle Alexander	.12	.05	.01
☐ 2	T Jesse Barfield	3.00	1.20	.30
☐ 3	T Ross Baumgarten	.08	.03	.01
☐ 4	T Steve Bedrosian	.20	.08	.02
☐ 5	T Mark Belanger	.12	.05	.01
☐ 6	T Kurt Bevacqua	.08	.03	.01
☐ 7	T Tim Blackwell	.08	.03	.01
☐ 8	T Vida Blue	.16	.07	.01
☐ 9	T Bob Boone	.12	.05	.01
☐ 10	T Larry Bowa	.20	.08	.02
☐ 11	T Dan Briggs	.08	.03	.01
☐ 12	T Bobby Brown	.08	.03	.01
☐ 13	T Tom Brunansky	1.50	.60	.15
☐ 14	T Jeff Burroughs	.12	.05	.01
☐ 15	T Enos Cabell	.08	.03	.01
☐ 16	T Bill Campbell	.08	.03	.01
☐ 17	T Bobby Castillo	.08	.03	.01
☐ 18	T Bill Caudill	.12	.05	.01
☐ 19	T Cesar Cedeno	.15	.06	.01
☐ 20	T Dave Collins	.15	.06	.01
☐ 21	T Doug Corbett	.12	.05	.01
☐ 22	T Al Cowens	.12	.05	.01
☐ 23	T Chili Davis	1.00	.40	.10
☐ 24	T Dick Davis	.08	.03	.01
☐ 25	T Ron Davis	.12	.05	.01
☐ 26	T Doug DeCinces	.25	.10	.02
☐ 27	T Ivan DeJesus	.08	.03	.01
☐ 28	T Bob Dernier	.25	.10	.02
☐ 29	T Bo Diaz	.12	.05	.01
☐ 30	T Roger Erickson	.08	.03	.01
☐ 31	T Jim Essian	.08	.03	.01
☐ 32	T Ed Farmer	.08	.03	.01
☐ 33	T Doug Flynn	.08	.03	.01
☐ 34	T Tim Foli	.08	.03	.01
☐ 35	T Dan Ford	.12	.05	.01
☐ 36	T George Foster	.40	.16	.04
☐ 37	T Dave Frost	.08	.03	.01
☐ 38	T Rich Gale	.08	.03	.01
☐ 39	T Ron Gardenhire	.12	.05	.01
☐ 40	T Ken Griffey	.15	.06	.01
☐ 41	T Greg Harris	.15	.06	.01
☐ 42	T Von Hayes	2.00	.80	.20
☐ 43	T Larry Herndon	.12	.05	.01
☐ 44	T Kent Hrbek	3.00	1.20	.30
☐ 45	T Mike Ivie	.08	.03	.01
☐ 46	T Grant Jackson	.08	.03	.01
☐ 47	T Reggie Jackson	2.50	1.00	.25
☐ 48	T Ron Jackson	.08	.03	.01
☐ 49	T Fergie Jenkins	.35	.14	.03
☐ 50	T Lamar Johnson	.08	.03	.01
☐ 51	T Randy Johnson	.08	.03	.01
☐ 52	T Jay Johnstone	.15	.06	.01
☐ 53	T Mick Kelleher	.08	.03	.01
☐ 54	T Steve Kemp	.15	.06	.01
☐ 55	T Junior Kennedy	.08	.03	.01
☐ 56	T Jim Kern	.08	.03	.01
☐ 57	T Ray Knight	.25	.10	.02
☐ 58	T Wayne Krenchicki	.08	.03	.01
☐ 59	T Mike Krukow	.20	.08	.02
☐ 60	T Duane Kuiper	.08	.03	.01
☐ 61	T Mike LaCoss	.08	.03	.01
☐ 62	T Chet Lemon	.15	.06	.01
☐ 63	T Sixto Lezcano	.12	.05	.01
☐ 64	T Dave Lopes	.15	.06	.01
☐ 65	T Jerry Martin	.08	.03	.01
☐ 66	T Renie Martin	.08	.03	.01
☐ 67	T John Mayberry	.12	.05	.01
☐ 68	T Lee Mazzilli	.12	.05	.01
☐ 69	T Bake McBride	.12	.05	.01
☐ 70	T Dan Meyer	.08	.03	.01
☐ 71	T Larry Milbourne	.08	.03	.01
☐ 72	T Eddie Milner	.25	.10	.02
☐ 73	T Sid Monge	.08	.03	.01
☐ 74	T John Montefusco	.12	.05	.01
☐ 75	T Jose Morales	.08	.03	.01
☐ 76	T Keith Moreland	.25	.10	.02
☐ 77	T Jim Morrison	.12	.05	.01
☐ 78	T Rance Mulliniks	.08	.03	.01
☐ 79	T Steve Mura	.08	.03	.01
☐ 80	T Gene Nelson	.12	.05	.01
☐ 81	T Joe Nolan	.08	.03	.01

			MINT	VG-E	F-G
☐	82	T Dickie Noles	.08	.03	.01
☐	83	T Al Oliver	.40	.16	.04
☐	84	T Jorge Orta	.08	.03	.01
☐	85	T Tom Paciorek	.12	.05	.01
☐	86	T Larry Parrish	.16	.07	.01
☐	87	T Jack Perconte	.08	.03	.01
☐	88	T Gaylord Perry	1.00	.40	.10
☐	89	T Rob Picciolo	.08	.03	.01
☐	90	T Joe Pittman	.08	.03	.01
☐	91	T Hosken Powell	.08	.03	.01
☐	92	T Mike Proly	.08	.03	.01
☐	93	T Greg Pryor	.08	.03	.01
☐	94	T Charlie Puleo	.12	.05	.01
☐	95	T Shane Rawley	.20	.08	.02
☐	96	T Johnny Ray	1.00	.40	.10
☐	97	T Dave Revering	.08	.03	.01
☐	98	T Cal Ripken	7.50	3.00	.75
☐	99	T Allen Ripley	.08	.03	.01
☐	100	T Bill Robinson	.08	.03	.01
☐	101	T Aurelio Rodriguez	.08	.03	.01
☐	102	T Joe Rudi	.12	.05	.01
☐	103	T Steve Sax	2.00	.80	.20
☐	104	T Dan Schatzeder	.08	.03	.01
☐	105	T Bob Shirley	.08	.03	.01
☐	106	T Eric Show	.40	.16	.04
☐	107	T Roy Smalley	.12	.05	.01
☐	108	T Lonnie Smith	.20	.08	.02
☐	109	T Ozzie Smith	.75	.30	.07
☐	110	T Reggie Smith	.20	.08	.02
☐	111	T Lary Sorensen	.08	.03	.01
☐	112	T Elias Sosa	.08	.03	.01
☐	113	T Mike Stanton	.08	.03	.01
☐	114	T Steve Strougther	.12	.05	.01
☐	115	T Champ Summers	.08	.03	.01
☐	116	T Rick Sutcliffe	.40	.16	.04
☐	117	T Frank Tanana	.15	.06	.01
☐	118	T Frank Taveras	.08	.03	.01
☐	119	T Garry Templeton	.20	.08	.02
☐	120	T Alex Trevino	.08	.03	.01
☐	121	T Jerry Turner	.08	.03	.01
☐	122	T Ed VandeBerg	.25	.10	.02
☐	123	T Tom Veryzer	.08	.03	.01
☐	124	T Ron Washington	.12	.05	.01
☐	125	T Bob Watson	.12	.05	.01
☐	126	T Dennis Werth	.08	.03	.01
☐	127	T Eddie Whitson	.12	.05	.01
☐	128	T Rob Wilfong	.08	.03	.01
☐	129	T Bump Wills	.08	.03	.01
☐	130	T Gary Woods	.08	.03	.01
☐	131	T Butch Wynegar	.12	.05	.01
☐	132	T Checklist: 1-132	.20	.02	.00

1983 Topps

*The cards in this 792-card set measure 2½"
by 3½". Each regular card of the Topps set
for 1983 features a large action shot of a player with a small cameo portrait at bottom right.
There are special series for AL and NL All
Stars (386-407), League Leaders (701-708)
and Record Breakers (1-6). In addition, there
are 34 "Super Veteran" (SV) cards and six
numbered checklist cards. The Super Veteran cards are oriented horizontally and show
two pictures of the featured player, a recent
picture and a picture showing the player as a
rookie when he broke in. The cards are numbered on the reverse at the upper left corner.
The team cards are actually Team Leader
(TL) cards picturing the batting and pitching
leader for that team with a checklist back.*

			MINT	VG-E	F-G
		Complete Set	60.00	24.00	6.00
		Common Player (1-792)	.04	.02	.00
☐	1	RB: Tony Armas 11 Putouts by Rightfielder	.12	.04	.01
☐	2	RB: Rickey Henderson Sets modern record for steals, season	.25	.10	.02
☐	3	RB: Greg Minton 269⅓ homerless innings streak	.06	.02	.01
☐	4	RB: Lance Parrish Threw out three Baserunners in All Star game	.15	.06	.01

		MINT	VG-E	F-G
☐	5 RB: Manny Trillo, 479 consecutive errorless chances, second baseman	.06	.02	.00
☐	6 RB: John Wathan, ML steals record for catchers, 31	.06	.02	.00
☐	7 Gene Richards	.04	.02	.00
☐	8 Steve Balboni	.10	.04	.01
☐	9 Joey McLaughlin	.04	.02	.00
☐	10 Gorman Thomas	.12	.05	.01
☐	11 Billy Gardner MGR	.04	.02	.00
☐	12 Paul Mirabella	.04	.02	.00
☐	13 Larry Herndon	.04	.02	.00
☐	14 Frank LaCorte	.04	.02	.00
☐	15 Ron Cey	.15	.06	.01
☐	16 George Vukovich	.04	.02	.00
☐	17 Kent Tekulve	.08	.03	.01
☐	18 SV: Kent Tekulve	.06	.02	.00
☐	19 Oscar Gamble	.06	.02	.00
☐	20 Carlton Fisk	.20	.08	.02
☐	21 Baltimore Orioles TL BA: Eddie Murray ERA: Jim Palmer	.20	.04	.01
☐	22 Randy Martz	.04	.02	.00
☐	23 Mike Heath	.04	.02	.00
☐	24 Steve Mura	.04	.02	.00
☐	25 Hal McRae	.08	.03	.01
☐	26 Jerry Royster	.04	.02	.00
☐	27 Doug Corbett	.04	.02	.00
☐	28 Bruce Bochte	.06	.02	.00
☐	29 Randy Jones	.06	.02	.00
☐	30 Jim Rice	.75	.30	.07
☐	31 Bill Gullickson	.06	.02	.00
☐	32 Dave Bergman	.04	.02	.00
☐	33 Jack O'Connor	.04	.02	.00
☐	34 Paul Householder	.04	.02	.00
☐	35 Rollie Fingers	.25	.10	.02
☐	36 SV: Rollie Fingers	.12	.05	.01
☐	37 Darrell Johnson MGR	.04	.02	.00
☐	38 Tim Flannery	.04	.02	.00
☐	39 Terry Puhl	.06	.02	.00
☐	40 Fernando Valenzuela	.60	.24	.06
☐	41 Jerry Turner	.04	.02	.00
☐	42 Dale Murray	.04	.02	.00
☐	43 Bob Dernier	.08	.03	.01
☐	44 Don Robinson	.06	.02	.00
☐	45 John Mayberry	.06	.02	.00
☐	46 Richard Dotson	.08	.03	.01
☐	47 Dave McKay	.04	.02	.00
☐	48 Lary Sorensen	.04	.02	.00
☐	49 Willie McGee	2.25	.90	.22
☐	50 Bob Horner ('82 RBI total 7)	.35	.14	.03
☐	51 Chicago Cubs TL BA: Leon Durham ERA: Fergie Jenkins	.10	.02	.00
☐	52 Onix Concepcion	.08	.03	.01
☐	53 Mike Witt	.25	.10	.02
☐	54 Jim Maler	.06	.02	.00
☐	55 Mookie Wilson	.08	.03	.01
☐	56 Chuck Rainey	.04	.02	.00
☐	57 Tim Blackwell	.04	.02	.00
☐	58 Al Holland	.04	.02	.00
☐	59 Benny Ayala	.04	.02	.00
☐	60 Johnny Bench	.60	.24	.06
☐	61 SV: Johnny Bench	.25	.10	.02
☐	62 Bob McClure	.04	.02	.00
☐	63 Rick Monday	.06	.02	.00
☐	64 Bill Stein	.04	.02	.00
☐	65 Jack Morris	.30	.12	.03
☐	66 Bob Lillis MGR	.04	.02	.00
☐	67 Sal Butera	.04	.02	.00
☐	68 Eric Show	.20	.08	.02
☐	69 Lee Lacy	.06	.02	.00
☐	70 Steve Carlton	.60	.24	.06
☐	71 SV: Steve Carlton	.25	.10	.02
☐	72 Tom Paciorek	.04	.02	.00
☐	73 Allen Ripley	.04	.02	.00
☐	74 Julio Gonzalez	.04	.02	.00
☐	75 Amos Otis	.08	.03	.01
☐	76 Rick Mahler	.06	.02	.00
☐	77 Hosken Powell	.04	.02	.00
☐	78 Bill Caudill	.06	.02	.00
☐	79 Mick Kelleher	.04	.02	.00
☐	80 George Foster	.20	.08	.02
☐	81 Yankees TL BA: Jerry Mumphrey ERA: Dave Righetti	.10	.02	.00
☐	82 Bruce Hurst	.12	.05	.01
☐	83 Ryne Sandberg	5.00	2.00	.50
☐	84 Milt May	.04	.02	.00
☐	85 Ken Singleton	.10	.04	.01
☐	86 Tom Hume	.04	.02	.00
☐	87 Joe Rudi	.06	.02	.00
☐	88 Jim Gantner	.06	.02	.00
☐	89 Leon Roberts	.04	.02	.00
☐	90 Jerry Reuss	.08	.03	.01
☐	91 Larry Milbourne	.04	.02	.00
☐	92 Mike LaCoss	.04	.02	.00
☐	93 John Castino	.04	.02	.00
☐	94 Dave Edwards	.04	.02	.00
☐	95 Alan Trammell	.30	.12	.03
☐	96 Dick Howser MGR	.06	.02	.00
☐	97 Ross Baumgarten	.04	.02	.00

		MINT	VG-E	F-G
☐ 98	Vance Law	.04	.02	.00
☐ 99	Dickie Noles	.04	.02	.00
☐ 100	Pete Rose	2.00	.80	.20
☐ 101	SV: Pete Rose	.75	.30	.07
☐ 102	Dave Beard	.04	.02	.00
☐ 103	Darrell Porter	.06	.02	.00
☐ 104	Bob Walk	.04	.02	.00
☐ 105	Don Baylor	.15	.06	.01
☐ 106	Gene Nelson	.04	.02	.00
☐ 107	Mike Jorgensen	.04	.02	.00
☐ 108	Glenn Hoffman	.04	.02	.00
☐ 109	Luis Leal	.04	.02	.00
☐ 110	Ken Griffey	.10	.04	.01
☐ 111	Montreal Expos TL	.10	.02	.00
	BA: Al Oliver			
	ERA: Steve Rogers			
☐ 112	Bob Shirley	.04	.02	.00
☐ 113	Ron Roenicke	.04	.02	.00
☐ 114	Jim Slaton	.04	.02	.00
☐ 115	Chili Davis	.15	.06	.01
☐ 116	Dave Schmidt	.04	.02	.00
☐ 117	Alan Knicely	.04	.02	.00
☐ 118	Chris Welsh	.04	.02	.00
☐ 119	Tom Brookens	.04	.02	.00
☐ 120	Len Barker	.06	.02	.00
☐ 121	Mickey Hatcher	.04	.02	.00
☐ 122	Jimmy Smith	.04	.02	.00
☐ 123	George Frazier	.04	.02	.00
☐ 124	Marc Hill	.04	.02	.00
☐ 125	Leon Durham	.12	.05	.01
☐ 126	Joe Torre MGR	.08	.03	.01
☐ 127	Preston Hanna	.04	.02	.00
☐ 128	Mike Ramsey	.04	.02	.00
☐ 129	Checklist: 1-132	.10	.01	.00
☐ 130	Dave Stieb	.20	.08	.02
☐ 131	Ed Ott	.04	.02	.00
☐ 132	Todd Cruz	.04	.02	.00
☐ 133	Jim Barr	.04	.02	.00
☐ 134	Hubie Brooks	.20	.08	.02
☐ 135	Dwight Evans	.15	.06	.01
☐ 136	Willie Aikens	.06	.02	.00
☐ 137	Woodie Fryman	.04	.02	.00
☐ 138	Rick Dempsey	.06	.02	.00
☐ 139	Bruce Berenyi	.04	.02	.00
☐ 140	Willie Randolph	.08	.03	.01
☐ 141	Indians TL	.10	.02	.02
	BA: Toby Harrah			
	ERA: Rick Sutcliffe			
☐ 142	Mike Caldwell	.06	.02	.00
☐ 143	Joe Pettini	.04	.02	.00
☐ 144	Mark Wagner	.04	.02	.00
☐ 145	Don Sutton	.30	.12	.03
☐ 146	SV: Don Sutton	.15	.06	.01
☐ 147	Rick Leach	.04	.02	.00
☐ 148	Dave Roberts	.04	.02	.00
☐ 149	Johnny Ray	.20	.08	.02
☐ 150	Bruce Sutter	.20	.08	.02
☐ 151	SV: Bruce Sutter	.12	.05	.01
☐ 152	Jay Johnstone	.06	.02	.00
☐ 153	Jerry Koosman	.08	.03	.01
☐ 154	Johnnie LeMaster	.04	.02	.00
☐ 155	Dan Quisenberry	.20	.08	.02
☐ 156	Billy Martin MGR	.12	.05	.01
☐ 157	Steve Bedrosian	.08	.03	.01
☐ 158	Rob Wilfong	.04	.02	.00
☐ 159	Mike Stanton	.04	.02	.00
☐ 160	Dave Kingman	.15	.06	.01
☐ 161	SV: Dave Kingman	.10	.04	.01
☐ 162	Mark Clear	.04	.02	.00
☐ 163	Cal Ripken	1.50	.60	.15
☐ 164	David Palmer	.06	.02	.00
☐ 165	Dan Driessen	.04	.02	.00
☐ 166	John Pacella	.04	.02	.00
☐ 167	Mark Brouhard	.04	.02	.00
☐ 168	Juan Eichelberger	.04	.02	.00
☐ 169	Doug Flynn	.04	.02	.00
☐ 170	Steve Howe	.06	.02	.00
☐ 171	Giants TL	.10	.02	.00
	BA: Joe Morgan			
	ERA: Bill Laskey			
☐ 172	Vern Ruhle	.04	.02	.00
☐ 173	Jim Morrison	.06	.02	.00
☐ 174	Jerry Ujdur	.04	.02	.00
☐ 175	Bo Diaz	.06	.02	.00
☐ 176	Dave Righetti	.30	.12	.03
☐ 177	Harold Baines	.30	.12	.03
☐ 178	Luis Tiant	.10	.04	.01
☐ 179	SV: Luis Tiant	.06	.02	.00
☐ 180	Rickey Henderson	.75	.30	.07
☐ 181	Terry Felton	.06	.02	.00
☐ 182	Mike Fischlin	.04	.02	.00
☐ 183	Ed VandeBerg	.15	.06	.01
☐ 184	Bob Clark	.04	.02	.00
☐ 185	Tim Lollar	.04	.02	.00
☐ 186	Whitey Herzog MGR	.06	.02	.00
☐ 187	Terry Leach	.04	.02	.00
☐ 188	Rick Miller	.04	.02	.00
☐ 189	Dan Schatzeder	.04	.02	.00
☐ 190	Cecil Cooper	.15	.06	.01
☐ 191	Joe Price	.04	.02	.00
☐ 192	Floyd Rayford	.04	.02	.00
☐ 193	Harry Spilman	.04	.02	.00
☐ 194	Cesar Geronimo	.04	.02	.00
☐ 195	Bob Stoddard	.06	.02	.00
☐ 196	Bill Fahey	.04	.02	.00
☐ 197	Jim Eisenreich	.08	.03	.01

		MINT	VG-E	F-G
☐ 198	Kiko Garcia	.04	.02	.00
☐ 199	Marty Bystrom	.04	.02	.00
☐ 200	Rod Carew	.75	.30	.07
☐ 201	SV: Rod Carew	.30	.12	.03
☐ 202	Blue Jays TL	.10	.02	.00
	BA: Damaso Garcia			
	ERA: Dave Stieb			
☐ 203	Mike Morgan	.06	.02	.00
☐ 204	Junior Kennedy	.04	.02	.00
☐ 205	Dave Parker	.30	.12	.03
☐ 206	Ken Oberkfell	.04	.02	.00
☐ 207	Rick Camp	.04	.02	.00
☐ 208	Dan Meyer	.04	.02	.00
☐ 209	Mike Moore	.35	.14	.03
☐ 210	Jack Clark	.20	.08	.02
☐ 211	John Denny	.12	.05	.01
☐ 212	John Stearns	.04	.02	.00
☐ 213	Tom Burgmeier	.04	.02	.00
☐ 214	Jerry White	.04	.02	.00
☐ 215	Mario Soto	.10	.04	.01
☐ 216	Tony LaRussa MGR	.06	.02	.00
☐ 217	Tim Stoddard	.04	.02	.00
☐ 218	Roy Howell	.04	.02	.00
☐ 219	Mike Armstrong	.04	.02	.00
☐ 220	Dusty Baker	.08	.03	.01
☐ 221	Joe Niekro	.10	.04	.01
☐ 222	Damaso Garcia	.15	.06	.01
☐ 223	John Montefusco	.06	.02	.00
☐ 224	Mickey Rivers	.06	.02	.00
☐ 225	Enos Cabell	.04	.02	.00
☐ 226	Enrique Romo	.04	.02	.00
☐ 227	Chris Bando	.04	.02	.00
☐ 228	Joaquin Andujar	.15	.06	.01
☐ 229	Phillies TL	.12	.02	.00
	BA: Bo Diaz			
	ERA: Steve Carlton			
☐ 230	Fergie Jenkins	.15	.06	.01
☐ 231	SV: Fergie Jenkins	.10	.04	.01
☐ 232	Tom Brunansky	.25	.10	.02
☐ 233	Wayne Gross	.04	.02	.00
☐ 234	Larry Andersen	.04	.02	.00
☐ 235	Claudell Washington	.08	.03	.01
☐ 236	Steve Renko	.04	.02	.00
☐ 237	Dan Norman	.04	.02	.00
☐ 238	Bud Black	.25	.10	.02
☐ 239	Dave Stapleton	.04	.02	.00
☐ 240	Rich Gossage	.25	.10	.02
☐ 241	SV: Rich Gossage	.12	.05	.01
☐ 242	Joe Nolan	.04	.02	.00
☐ 243	Duane Walker	.08	.03	.01
☐ 244	Dwight Bernard	.04	.02	.00
☐ 245	Steve Sax	.30	.12	.03
☐ 246	George Bamberger MGR	.04	.02	.00

		MINT	VG-E	F-G
☐ 247	Dave Smith	.06	.02	.00
☐ 248	Bake McBride	.06	.02	.00
☐ 249	Checklist: 133-264	.10	.01	.00
☐ 250	Bill Buckner	.15	.06	.01
☐ 251	Alan Wiggins	.25	.10	.02
☐ 252	Luis Aguayo	.04	.02	.00
☐ 253	Larry McWilliams	.06	.02	.00
☐ 254	Rick Cerone	.04	.02	.00
☐ 255	Gene Garber	.04	.02	.00
☐ 256	SV: Gene Garber	.04	.02	.00
☐ 257	Jesse Barfield	.40	.16	.04
☐ 258	Manny Castillo	.04	.02	.00
☐ 259	Jeff Jones	.04	.02	.00
☐ 260	Steve Kemp	.10	.04	.01
☐ 261	Tigers TL	.10	.02	.00
	BA: Larry Herndon			
	ERA: Dan Petry			
☐ 262	Ron Jackson	.04	.02	.00
☐ 263	Renie Martin	.04	.02	.00
☐ 264	Jamie Quirk	.04	.02	.00
☐ 265	Joel Youngblood	.04	.02	.00
☐ 266	Paul Boris	.04	.02	.00
☐ 267	Terry Francona	.04	.02	.00
☐ 268	Storm Davis	.75	.30	.07
☐ 269	Ron Oester	.06	.02	.00
☐ 270	Dennis Eckersley	.06	.02	.00
☐ 271	Ed Romero	.04	.02	.00
☐ 272	Frank Tanana	.06	.02	.00
☐ 273	Mark Belanger	.06	.02	.00
☐ 274	Terry Kennedy	.10	.04	.01
☐ 275	Ray Knight	.10	.04	.01
☐ 276	Gene Mauch MGR	.06	.02	.00
☐ 277	Rance Mulliniks	.04	.02	.00
☐ 278	Kevin Hickey	.04	.02	.00
☐ 279	Greg Gross	.04	.02	.00
☐ 280	Bert Blyleven	.15	.06	.01
☐ 281	Andre Robertson	.04	.02	.00
☐ 282	Reggie Smith	.10	.04	.01
☐ 283	SV: Reggie Smith	.04	.02	.00
☐ 284	Jeff Lahti	.10	.04	.01
☐ 285	Lance Parrish	.35	.14	.03
☐ 286	Rick Langford	.04	.02	.00
☐ 287	Bobby Brown	.04	.02	.00
☐ 288	Joe Cowley	.40	.16	.04
☐ 289	Jerry Dybzinski	.04	.02	.00
☐ 290	Jeff Reardon	.08	.03	.01
☐ 291	Pirates TL	.10	.02	.00
	BA: Bill Madlock			
	ERA: John Candelaria			
☐ 292	Craig Swan	.04	.02	.00
☐ 293	Glenn Gulliver	.04	.02	.00
☐ 294	Dave Engle	.04	.02	.00
☐ 295	Jerry Remy	.04	.02	.00

		MINT	VG-E	F-G
☐ 296	Greg Harris	.06	.02	.00
☐ 297	Ned Yost	.04	.02	.00
☐ 298	Floyd Chiffer	.04	.02	.00
☐ 299	George Wright	.10	.04	.01
☐ 300	Mike Schmidt	.75	.30	.07
☐ 301	SV: Mike Schmidt	.30	.12	.03
☐ 302	Ernie Whitt	.04	.02	.00
☐ 303	Miguel Dilone	.04	.02	.00
☐ 304	Dave Rucker	.04	.02	.00
☐ 305	Larry Bowa	.10	.04	.01
☐ 306	Tom Lasorda MGR	.08	.03	.01
☐ 307	Lou Piniella	.10	.04	.01
☐ 308	Jesus Vega	.04	.02	.00
☐ 309	Jeff Leonard	.06	.02	.00
☐ 310	Greg Luzinski	.12	.05	.01
☐ 311	Glenn Brummer	.04	.02	.00
☐ 312	Brian Kingman	.04	.02	.00
☐ 313	Gary Gray	.04	.02	.00
☐ 314	Ken Dayley	.06	.02	.00
☐ 315	Rick Burleson	.06	.02	.00
☐ 316	Paul Splittorff	.06	.02	.00
☐ 317	Gary Rajsich	.06	.02	.00
☐ 318	John Tudor	.30	.12	.03
☐ 319	Lenn Sakata	.04	.02	.00
☐ 320	Steve Rogers	.08	.03	.01
☐ 321	Brewers TL	.15	.03	.00
	BA: Robin Yount			
	ERA: Pete Vuckovich			
☐ 322	Dave Van Gorder	.04	.02	.00
☐ 323	Luis DeLeon	.04	.02	.00
☐ 324	Mike Marshall	.30	.12	.03
☐ 325	Von Hayes	.30	.12	.03
☐ 326	Garth Iorg	.04	.02	.00
☐ 327	Bobby Castillo	.04	.02	.00
☐ 328	Craig Reynolds	.04	.02	.00
☐ 329	Randy Niemann	.04	.02	.00
☐ 330	Buddy Bell	.15	.06	.01
☐ 331	Mike Krukow	.10	.04	.01
☐ 332	Glenn Wilson	.80	.32	.08
☐ 333	Dave LaRoche	.04	.02	.00
☐ 334	SV: Dave LaRoche	.04	.02	.00
☐ 335	Steve Henderson	.04	.02	.00
☐ 336	Rene Lachemann MGR	.04	.02	.00
☐ 337	Tito Landrum	.04	.02	.00
☐ 338	Bob Owchinko	.04	.02	.00
☐ 339	Terry Harper	.04	.02	.00
☐ 340	Larry Gura	.06	.02	.00
☐ 341	Doug DeCinces	.12	.05	.01
☐ 342	Atlee Hammaker	.08	.03	.01
☐ 343	Bob Bailor	.04	.02	.00
☐ 344	Roger LaFrancois	.04	.02	.00
☐ 345	Jim Clancy	.06	.02	.00
☐ 346	Joe Pittman	.04	.02	.00

		MINT	VG-E	F-G
☐ 347	Sammy Stewart	.04	.02	.00
☐ 348	Alan Bannister	.04	.02	.00
☐ 349	Checklist: 265-396	.10	.01	.00
☐ 350	Robin Yount	.45	.18	.04
☐ 351	Reds TL	.10	.02	.00
	BA: Cesar Cedeno			
	ERA: Mario Soto			
☐ 352	Mike Scioscia	.06	.02	.00
☐ 353	Steve Comer	.04	.02	.00
☐ 354	Randy Johnson	.04	.02	.00
☐ 355	Jim Bibby	.06	.02	.00
☐ 356	Gary Woods	.04	.02	.00
☐ 357	Len Matuszek	.10	.04	.01
☐ 358	Jerry Garvin	.04	.02	.00
☐ 359	Dave Collins	.06	.02	.00
☐ 360	Nolan Ryan	.50	.20	.05
☐ 361	SV: Nolan Ryan	.20	.08	.02
☐ 362	Billy Almon	.04	.02	.00
☐ 363	John Stuper	.10	.04	.01
☐ 364	Bret Butler	.15	.06	.01
☐ 365	Dave Lopes	.08	.03	.01
☐ 366	Dick Williams MGR	.06	.02	.00
☐ 367	Bud Anderson	.04	.02	.00
☐ 368	Richie Zisk	.06	.02	.00
☐ 369	Jesse Orosco	.10	.04	.01
☐ 370	Gary Carter	.60	.24	.06
☐ 371	Mike Richardt	.06	.02	.00
☐ 372	Terry Crowley	.04	.02	.00
☐ 373	Kevin Saucier	.04	.02	.00
☐ 374	Wayne Krenchicki	.04	.02	.00
☐ 375	Pete Vuckovich	.06	.02	.00
☐ 376	Ken Landreaux	.06	.02	.00
☐ 377	Lee May	.06	.02	.00
☐ 378	SV: Lee May	.06	.02	.00
☐ 379	Guy Sularz	.04	.02	.00
☐ 380	Ron Davis	.04	.02	.00
☐ 381	Red Sox TL	.15	.03	.00
	BA: Jim Rice			
	ERA: Bob Stanley			
☐ 382	Bob Knepper	.12	.05	.01
☐ 383	Ozzie Virgil	.08	.03	.01
☐ 384	Dave Dravecky	.50	.20	.05
☐ 385	Mike Easler	.08	.03	.01
☐ 386	Rod Carew AS	.25	.10	.02
☐ 387	Bob Grich AS	.06	.02	.00
☐ 388	George Brett AS	.35	.14	.03
☐ 389	Robin Yount AS	.25	.10	.02
☐ 390	Reggie Jackson AS	.30	.12	.03
☐ 391	Rickey Henderson AS	.35	.14	.03
☐ 392	Fred Lynn AS	.15	.06	.01
☐ 393	Carlton Fisk AS	.12	.05	.01
☐ 394	Pete Vuckovich AS	.06	.02	.00
☐ 395	Larry Gura AS	.06	.02	.00

	MINT	VG-E	F-G
☐ 396 Dan Quisenberry AS	.10	.04	.01
☐ 397 Pete Rose AS	.60	.24	.06
☐ 398 Manny Trillo AS	.06	.02	.00
☐ 399 Mike Schmidt AS	.40	.16	.04
☐ 400 Dave Concepcion AS	.06	.02	.00
☐ 401 Dale Murphy AS	.45	.18	.04
☐ 402 Andre Dawson AS	.15	.06	.01
☐ 403 Tim Raines AS	.20	.08	.02
☐ 404 Gary Carter AS	.30	.12	.03
☐ 405 Steve Rogers AS	.06	.02	.00
☐ 406 Steve Carlton AS	.25	.10	.02
☐ 407 Bruce Sutter AS	.10	.04	.01
☐ 408 Rudy May	.04	.02	.00
☐ 409 Marvis Foley	.04	.02	.00
☐ 410 Phil Niekro	.30	.12	.03
☐ 411 SV: Phil Niekro	.15	.06	.01
☐ 412 Rangers TL	.10	.02	.00
BA: Buddy Bell			
ERA: Charlie Hough			
☐ 413 Matt Keough	.04	.02	.00
☐ 414 Julio Cruz	.04	.02	.00
☐ 415 Bob Forsch	.06	.02	.00
☐ 416 Joe Ferguson	.04	.02	.00
☐ 417 Tom Hausman	.04	.02	.00
☐ 418 Greg Pryor	.04	.02	.00
☐ 419 Steve Crawford	.04	.02	.00
☐ 420 Al Oliver	.15	.06	.01
☐ 421 SV: Al Oliver	.10	.04	.01
☐ 422 George Cappuzello	.04	.02	.00
☐ 423 Tom Lawless	.04	.02	.00
☐ 424 Jerry Augustine	.04	.02	.00
☐ 425 Pedro Guerrero	.45	.18	.04
☐ 426 Earl Weaver MGR	.10	.04	.01
☐ 427 Roy Lee Jackson	.04	.02	.00
☐ 428 Champ Summers	.04	.02	.00
☐ 429 Eddie Whitson	.06	.02	.00
☐ 430 Kirk Gibson	.35	.14	.03
☐ 431 Gary Gaetti	1.00	.40	.10
☐ 432 Porfirio Altamirano	.04	.02	.00
☐ 433 Dale Berra	.06	.02	.00
☐ 434 Dennis Lamp	.04	.02	.00
☐ 435 Tony Armas	.15	.06	.01
☐ 436 Bill Campbell	.06	.02	.00
☐ 437 Rick Sweet	.04	.02	.00
☐ 438 Dave LaPoint	.15	.06	.01
☐ 439 Rafael Ramirez	.04	.02	.00
☐ 440 Ron Guidry	.25	.10	.02
☐ 441 Astros TL	.10	.02	.00
BA: Ray Knight			
ERA: Joe Niekro			
☐ 442 Brian Downing	.06	.02	.00
☐ 443 Don Hood	.04	.02	.00
☐ 444 Wally Backman	.10	.04	.01
☐ 445 Mike Flanagan	.08	.03	.01
☐ 446 Reid Nichols	.04	.02	.00
☐ 447 Bryn Smith	.06	.02	.00
☐ 448 Darrell Evans	.12	.05	.01
☐ 449 Eddie Milner	.15	.06	.01
☐ 450 Ted Simmons	.15	.06	.01
☐ 451 SV: Ted Simmons	.10	.04	.01
☐ 452 Lloyd Moseby	.15	.06	.01
☐ 453 Lamar Johnson	.04	.02	.00
☐ 454 Bob Welch	.08	.03	.01
☐ 455 Sixto Lezcano	.04	.02	.00
☐ 456 Lee Elia MGR	.04	.02	.00
☐ 457 Milt Wilcox	.04	.02	.00
☐ 458 Ron Washington	.06	.02	.00
☐ 459 Ed Farmer	.04	.02	.00
☐ 460 Roy Smalley	.06	.02	.00
☐ 461 Steve Trout	.06	.02	.00
☐ 462 Steve Nicosia	.04	.02	.00
☐ 463 Gaylord Perry	.25	.10	.02
☐ 464 SV: Gaylord Perry	.12	.05	.01
☐ 465 Lonnie Smith	.10	.04	.01
☐ 466 Tom Underwood	.04	.02	.00
☐ 467 Rufino Linares	.04	.02	.00
☐ 468 Dave Goltz	.04	.02	.00
☐ 469 Ron Gardenhire	.04	.02	.00
☐ 470 Greg Minton	.06	.02	.00
☐ 471 K.C. Royals TL	.10	.02	.00
BA: Willie Wilson			
ERA: Vida Blue			
☐ 472 Gary Allenson	.04	.02	.00
☐ 473 John Lowenstein	.04	.02	.00
☐ 474 Ray Burris	.04	.02	.00
☐ 475 Cesar Cedeno	.10	.04	.01
☐ 476 Rob Picciolo	.04	.02	.00
☐ 477 Tom Niedenfuer	.12	.05	.01
☐ 478 Phil Garner	.06	.02	.00
☐ 479 Charlie Hough	.08	.03	.01
☐ 480 Toby Harrah	.06	.02	.00
☐ 481 Scot Thompson	.04	.02	.00
☐ 482 Tony Gwynn	8.00	3.25	.80
☐ 483 Lynn Jones	.04	.02	.00
☐ 484 Dick Ruthven	.04	.02	.00
☐ 485 Omar Moreno	.04	.02	.00
☐ 486 Clyde King MGR	.04	.02	.00
☐ 487 Jerry Hairston	.04	.02	.00
☐ 488 Alfredo Griffin	.04	.02	.00
☐ 489 Tom Herr	.12	.05	.01
☐ 490 Jim Palmer	.35	.14	.03
☐ 491 SV: Jim Palmer	.15	.06	.01
☐ 492 Paul Serna	.04	.02	.00
☐ 493 Steve McCatty	.04	.02	.00
☐ 494 Bob Brenly	.08	.03	.01
☐ 495 Warren Cromartie	.04	.02	.00

	MINT	VG-E	F-G
☐ 496 Tom Veryzer	.04	.02	.00
☐ 497 Rick Sutcliffe	.20	.08	.02
☐ 498 Wade Boggs	22.00	9.00	2.20
☐ 499 Jeff Little	.04	.02	.00
☐ 500 Reggie Jackson	.90	.36	.09
☐ 501 SV: Reggie Jackson	.35	.14	.03
☐ 502 Atlanta Braves TL	.25	.05	.01
BA: Dale Murphy			
ERA: Phil Niekro			
☐ 503 Moose Haas	.06	.02	.00
☐ 504 Don Werner	.04	.02	.00
☐ 505 Garry Templeton	.12	.05	.01
☐ 506 Jim Gott	.10	.04	.01
☐ 507 Tony Scott	.04	.02	.00
☐ 508 Tom Filer	.15	.06	.01
☐ 509 Lou Whitaker	.25	.10	.02
☐ 510 Tug McGraw	.10	.04	.01
☐ 511 SV: Tug McGraw	.06	.02	.00
☐ 512 Doyle Alexander	.06	.02	.00
☐ 513 Fred Stanley	.04	.02	.00
☐ 514 Rudy Law	.04	.02	.00
☐ 515 Gene Tenace	.04	.02	.00
☐ 516 Bill Virdon MGR	.06	.02	.00
☐ 517 Gary Ward	.06	.02	.00
☐ 518 Bill Laskey	.12	.05	.01
☐ 519 Terry Bulling	.04	.02	.00
☐ 520 Fred Lynn	.25	.10	.02
☐ 521 Bruce Benedict	.04	.02	.00
☐ 522 Pat Zachry	.04	.02	.00
☐ 523 Carney Lansford	.12	.05	.01
☐ 524 Tom Brennan	.04	.02	.00
☐ 525 Frank White	.08	.03	.01
☐ 526 Checklist: 397-528	.10	.01	.00
☐ 527 Larry Biittner	.04	.02	.00
☐ 528 Jamie Easterly	.04	.02	.00
☐ 529 Tim Laudner	.04	.02	.00
☐ 530 Eddie Murray	.75	.30	.07
☐ 531 Oakland A's TL	.15	.03	.00
BA: Rickey Henderson			
ERA: Rick Langford			
☐ 532 Dave Stewart	.04	.02	.00
☐ 533 Luis Salazar	.04	.02	.00
☐ 534 John Butcher	.04	.02	.00
☐ 535 Manny Trillo	.06	.02	.00
☐ 536 Johnny Wockenfuss	.04	.02	.00
☐ 537 Rod Scurry	.04	.02	.00
☐ 538 Danny Heep	.04	.02	.00
☐ 539 Roger Erickson	.04	.02	.00
☐ 540 Ozzie Smith	.25	.10	.02
☐ 541 Britt Burns	.08	.03	.01
☐ 542 Jody Davis	.10	.04	.01
☐ 543 Alan Fowlkes	.04	.02	.00
☐ 544 Larry Whisenton	.04	.02	.00
☐ 545 Floyd Bannister	.06	.02	.00
☐ 546 Dave Garcia MGR	.04	.02	.00
☐ 547 Geoff Zahn	.04	.02	.00
☐ 548 Brian Giles	.04	.02	.00
☐ 549 Charlie Puleo	.04	.02	.00
☐ 550 Carl Yastrzemski	1.00	.40	.10
☐ 551 SV: Carl Yastrzemski	.40	.16	.04
☐ 552 Tim Wallach	.10	.04	.01
☐ 553 Denny Martinez	.04	.02	.00
☐ 554 Mike Vail	.04	.02	.00
☐ 555 Steve Yeager	.06	.02	.00
☐ 556 Willie Upshaw	.08	.03	.01
☐ 557 Rick Honeycutt	.06	.02	.00
☐ 558 Dickie Thon	.08	.03	.01
☐ 559 Pete Redfern	.04	.02	.00
☐ 560 Ron LeFlore	.06	.02	.00
☐ 561 Cardinals TL	.10	.02	.00
BA: Lonnie Smith			
ERA: Joaquin Andujar			
☐ 562 Dave Rozema	.04	.02	.00
☐ 563 Juan Bonilla	.04	.02	.00
☐ 564 Sid Monge	.04	.02	.00
☐ 565 Bucky Dent	.06	.02	.00
☐ 566 Manny Sarmiento	.04	.02	.00
☐ 567 Joe Simpson	.04	.02	.00
☐ 568 Willie Hernandez	.15	.06	.01
☐ 569 Jack Perconte	.04	.02	.00
☐ 570 Vida Blue	.10	.04	.01
☐ 571 Mickey Klutts	.04	.02	.00
☐ 572 Bob Watson	.06	.02	.00
☐ 573 Andy Hassler	.04	.02	.00
☐ 574 Glenn Adams	.04	.02	.00
☐ 575 Neil Allen	.06	.02	.00
☐ 576 Frank Robinson MGR	.15	.06	.01
☐ 577 Luis Aponte	.06	.02	.00
☐ 578 David Green	.12	.05	.01
☐ 579 Rich Dauer	.04	.02	.00
☐ 580 Tom Seaver	.60	.24	.06
☐ 581 SV: Tom Seaver	.25	.10	.02
☐ 582 Marshall Edwards	.04	.02	.00
☐ 583 Terry Forster	.08	.03	.01
☐ 584 Dave Hostetler	.06	.02	.00
☐ 585 Jose Cruz	.12	.05	.01
☐ 586 Frank Viola	.90	.36	.09
☐ 587 Ivan DeJesus	.04	.02	.00
☐ 588 Pat Underwood	.04	.02	.00
☐ 589 Alvis Woods	.04	.02	.00
☐ 590 Tony Pena	.20	.08	.02
☐ 591 White Sox TL	.10	.02	.00
BA: Greg Luzinski			
ERA: LaMarr Hoyt			
☐ 592 Shane Rawley	.08	.03	.01
☐ 593 Broderick Perkins	.04	.02	.00

	MINT	VG-E	F-G			MINT	VG-E	F-G
☐ 594 Eric Rasmussen	.04	.02	.00	☐ 645 Bill Madlock		.15	.06	.01
☐ 595 Tim Raines	.40	.16	.04	☐ 646 Jim Essian		.04	.02	.00
☐ 596 Randy Johnson	.04	.02	.00	☐ 647 Bobby Mitchell		.04	.02	.00
☐ 597 Mike Proly	.04	.02	.00	☐ 648 Jeff Burroughs		.06	.02	.00
☐ 598 Dwayne Murphy	.06	.02	.00	☐ 649 Tommy Boggs		.04	.02	.00
☐ 599 Don Aase	.06	.02	.00	☐ 650 George Hendrick		.08	.03	.01
☐ 600 George Brett	1.00	.40	.10	☐ 651 Angels TL		.15	.03	.00
☐ 601 Ed Lynch	.04	.02	.00	BA: Rod Carew				
☐ 602 Rich Gedman	.25	.10	.02	ERA: Mike Witt				
☐ 603 Joe Morgan	.30	.12	.03	☐ 652 Butch Hobson		.04	.02	.00
☐ 604 SV: Joe Morgan	.15	.06	.01	☐ 653 Ellis Valentine		.04	.02	.00
☐ 605 Gary Roenicke	.06	.02	.00	☐ 654 Bob Ojeda		.15	.06	.01
☐ 606 Bobby Cox MGR	.04	.02	.00	☐ 655 Al Bumbry		.04	.02	.00
☐ 607 Charlie Leibrandt	.06	.02	.00	☐ 656 Dave Frost		.04	.02	.00
☐ 608 Don Money	.04	.02	.00	☐ 657 Mike Gates		.04	.02	.00
☐ 609 Danny Darwin	.04	.02	.00	☐ 658 Frank Pastore		.04	.02	.00
☐ 610 Steve Garvey	.75	.30	.07	☐ 659 Charlie Moore		.04	.02	.00
☐ 611 Bert Roberge	.04	.02	.00	☐ 660 Mike Hargrove		.06	.02	.00
☐ 612 Steve Swisher	.04	.02	.00	☐ 661 Bill Russell		.06	.02	.00
☐ 613 Mike Ivie	.04	.02	.00	☐ 662 Joe Sambito		.06	.02	.00
☐ 614 Ed Glynn	.04	.02	.00	☐ 663 Tom O'Malley		.06	.02	.00
☐ 615 Garry Maddox	.06	.02	.00	☐ 664 Bob Molinaro		.04	.02	.00
☐ 616 Bill Nahorodny	.04	.02	.00	☐ 665 Jim Sundberg		.06	.02	.00
☐ 617 Butch Wynegar	.06	.02	.00	☐ 666 Sparky Anderson MGR		.08	.03	.01
☐ 618 LaMarr Hoyt	.10	.04	.01	☐ 667 Dick Davis		.04	.02	.00
☐ 619 Keith Moreland	.10	.04	.01	☐ 668 Larry Christenson		.04	.02	.00
☐ 620 Mike Norris	.06	.02	.00	☐ 669 Mike Squires		.04	.02	.00
☐ 621 New York Mets TL	.10	.02	.00	☐ 670 Jerry Mumphrey		.06	.02	.00
BA: Mookie Wilson				☐ 671 Lenny Faedo		.04	.02	.00
ERA: Craig Swan				☐ 672 Jim Kaat		.15	.06	.01
☐ 622 Dave Edler	.04	.02	.00	☐ 673 SV: Jim Kaat		.08	.03	.01
☐ 623 Luis Sanchez	.04	.02	.00	☐ 674 Kurt Bevacqua		.04	.02	.00
☐ 624 Glenn Hubbard	.04	.02	.00	☐ 675 Jim Beattie		.04	.02	.00
☐ 625 Ken Forsch	.04	.02	.00	☐ 676 Biff Pocoroba		.04	.02	.00
☐ 626 Jerry Martin	.04	.02	.00	☐ 677 Dave Revering		.04	.02	.00
☐ 627 Doug Bair	.04	.02	.00	☐ 678 Juan Beniquez		.06	.02	.00
☐ 628 Julio Valdez	.04	.02	.00	☐ 679 Mike Scott		.30	.12	.03
☐ 629 Charlie Lea	.06	.02	.00	☐ 680 Andre Dawson		.30	.12	.03
☐ 630 Paul Molitor	.15	.06	.01	☐ 681 Dodgers Leaders		.20	.04	.01
☐ 631 Tippy Martinez	.04	.02	.00	BA: Pedro Guerrero				
☐ 632 Alex Trevino	.04	.02	.00	ERA: Fern.Valenzuela				
☐ 633 Vicente Romo	.04	.02	.00	☐ 682 Bob Stanley		.06	.02	.00
☐ 634 Max Venable	.04	.02	.00	☐ 683 Dan Ford		.04	.02	.00
☐ 635 Graig Nettles	.15	.06	.01	☐ 684 Rafael Landestoy		.04	.02	.00
☐ 636 SV: Graig Nettles	.10	.04	.01	☐ 685 Lee Mazzilli		.06	.02	.00
☐ 637 Pat Corrales MGR	.04	.02	.00	☐ 686 Randy Lerch		.04	.02	.00
☐ 638 Dan Petry	.15	.06	.01	☐ 687 U.L. Washington		.04	.02	.00
☐ 639 Art Howe	.04	.02	.00	☐ 688 Jim Wohlford		.04	.02	.00
☐ 640 Andre Thornton	.10	.04	.01	☐ 689 Ron Hassey		.04	.02	.00
☐ 641 Billy Sample	.04	.02	.00	☐ 690 Kent Hrbek		.50	.20	.05
☐ 642 Checklist: 529-660	.10	.01	.00	☐ 691 Dave Tobik		.04	.02	.00
☐ 643 Bump Wills	.04	.02	.00	☐ 692 Denny Walling		.04	.02	.00
☐ 644 Joe Lefebvre	.04	.02	.00	☐ 693 Sparky Lyle		.10	.04	.01

	MINT	VG-E	F-G
☐ 694 SV: Sparky Lyle	.06	.02	.00
☐ 695 Ruppert Jones	.04	.02	.00
☐ 696 Chuck Tanner MGR	.06	.02	.00
☐ 697 Barry Foote	.04	.02	.00
☐ 698 Tony Bernazard	.06	.02	.00
☐ 699 Lee Smith	.12	.05	.01
☐ 700 Keith Hernandez	.45	.18	.04
☐ 701 Batting Leaders	.15	.06	.01
AL: Willie Wilson			
NL: Al Oliver			
☐ 702 Home Run Leaders	.15	.06	.01
AL: Reggie Jackson			
AL: Gorman Thomas			
NL: Dave Kingman			
☐ 703 RBI Leaders	.15	.06	.01
AL: Hal McRae			
NL: Dale Murphy			
NL: Al Oliver			
☐ 704 SB Leaders	.25	.10	.02
AL: Rickey Henderson			
NL: Tim Raines			
☐ 705 Victory Leaders	.15	.06	.01
AL: LaMarr Hoyt			
NL: Steve Carlton			
☐ 706 Strikeout Leaders	.15	.06	.01
AL: Floyd Bannister			
NL: Steve Carlton			
☐ 707 ERA Leaders	.08	.03	.01
AL: Rick Sutcliffe			
NL: Steve Rogers			
☐ 708 Leading Firemen	.10	.04	.01
AL: Dan Quisenberry			
NL: Bruce Sutter			
☐ 709 Jimmy Sexton	.04	.02	.00
☐ 710 Willie Wilson	.25	.10	.02
☐ 711 Mariners TL	.08	.02	.00
BA: Bruce Bochte			
ERA: Jim Beattie			
☐ 712 Bruce Kison	.04	.02	.00
☐ 713 Ron Hodges	.04	.02	.00
☐ 714 Wayne Nordhagen	.04	.02	.00
☐ 715 Tony Perez	.15	.06	.01
☐ 716 SV: Tony Perez	.10	.04	.01
☐ 717 Scott Sanderson	.04	.02	.00
☐ 718 Jim Dwyer	.04	.02	.00
☐ 719 Rich Gale	.04	.02	.00
☐ 720 Dave Concepcion	.10	.04	.01
☐ 721 John Martin	.04	.02	.00
☐ 722 Jorge Orta	.04	.02	.00
☐ 723 Randy Moffitt	.04	.02	.00
☐ 724 Johnny Grubb	.04	.02	.00
☐ 725 Dan Spillner	.04	.02	.00
☐ 726 Harvey Kuenn MGR	.06	.02	.00

	MINT	VG-E	F-G
☐ 727 Chet Lemon	.06	.02	.00
☐ 728 Ron Reed	.04	.02	.00
☐ 729 Jerry Morales	.04	.02	.00
☐ 730 Jason Thompson	.06	.02	.00
☐ 731 Al Williams	.04	.02	.00
☐ 732 Dave Henderson	.10	.04	.01
☐ 733 Buck Martinez	.04	.02	.00
☐ 734 Steve Braun	.04	.02	.00
☐ 735 Tommy John	.15	.06	.01
☐ 736 SV: Tommy John	.10	.04	.01
☐ 737 Mitchell Page	.04	.02	.00
☐ 738 Tim Foli	.04	.02	.00
☐ 739 Rick Ownbey	.06	.02	.00
☐ 740 Rusty Staub	.12	.05	.01
☐ 741 SV: Rusty Staub	.08	.03	.01
☐ 742 Padres TL	.08	.02	.00
BA: Terry Kennedy			
ERA: Tim Lollar			
☐ 743 Mike Torrez	.06	.02	.00
☐ 744 Brad Mills	.04	.02	.00
☐ 745 Scott McGregor	.10	.04	.01
☐ 746 John Wathan	.04	.02	.00
☐ 747 Fred Breining	.04	.02	.00
☐ 748 Derrel Thomas	.04	.02	.00
☐ 749 Jon Matlack	.06	.02	.00
☐ 750 Ben Oglivie	.08	.03	.01
☐ 751 Brad Havens	.04	.02	.00
☐ 752 Luis Pujols	.04	.02	.00
☐ 753 Elias Sosa	.04	.02	.00
☐ 754 Bill Robinson	.04	.02	.00
☐ 755 John Candelaria	.08	.03	.01
☐ 756 Russ Nixon MGR	.04	.02	.00
☐ 757 Rick Manning	.04	.02	.00
☐ 758 Aurelio Rodriguez	.04	.02	.00
☐ 759 Doug Bird	.04	.02	.00
☐ 760 Dale Murphy	1.50	.60	.15
☐ 761 Gary Lucas	.04	.02	.00
☐ 762 Cliff Johnson	.04	.02	.00
☐ 763 Al Cowens	.06	.02	.00
☐ 764 Pete Falcone	.04	.02	.00
☐ 765 Bob Boone	.06	.02	.00
☐ 766 Barry Bonnell	.04	.02	.00
☐ 767 Duane Kuiper	.04	.02	.00
☐ 768 Chris Speier	.04	.02	.00
☐ 769 Checklist: 661-792	.10	.01	.00
☐ 770 Dave Winfield	.45	.18	.04
☐ 771 Twins TL	.10	.02	.00
BA: Kent Hrbek			
ERA: Bobby Castillo			
☐ 772 Jim Kern	.04	.02	.00
☐ 773 Larry Hisle	.06	.02	.00
☐ 774 Alan Ashby	.04	.02	.00
☐ 775 Burt Hooton	.04	.02	.00

		MINT	VG-E	F-G
☐ 776	Larry Parrish	.06	.02	.00
☐ 777	John Curtis	.04	.02	.00
☐ 778	Rich Hebner	.04	.02	.00
☐ 779	Rick Waits	.04	.02	.00
☐ 780	Gary Matthews	.08	.03	.01
☐ 781	Rick Rhoden	.10	.04	.01
☐ 782	Bobby Murcer	.10	.04	.01
☐ 783	SV: Bobby Murcer	.06	.02	.00
☐ 784	Jeff Newman	.04	.02	.00
☐ 785	Dennis Leonard	.06	.02	.00
☐ 786	Ralph Houk MGR	.06	.02	.00
☐ 787	Dick Tidrow	.04	.02	.00
☐ 788	Dane Iorg	.04	.02	.00
☐ 789	Bryan Clark	.04	.02	.00
☐ 790	Bob Grich	.08	.03	.01
☐ 791	Gary Lavelle	.06	.02	.00
☐ 792	Chris Chambliss	.08	.03	.01

1983 Topps Traded

RON KITTLE
OUTFIELD
WHITE SOX

The cards in this 132-card set measure 2½"
by 3½". For the third year in a row, Topps issued a 132-card Traded (or extended) set
featuring some of the year's top rookies and
players who had changed teams during the
year, but were featured with their old team in
the Topps regular issue of 1983. The cards
were available through hobby dealers only
and were printed in Ireland by the Topps affiliate in that country. The set is numbered alphabetically by the last name of the player of
the card.

		MINT	VG-E	F-G
	Complete Set	32.00	13.00	3.20
	Common Player	.08	.03	.01
☐ 1	T Neil Allen	.12	.05	.01
☐ 2	T Bill Almon	.08	.03	.01
☐ 3	T Joe Altobelli MGR	.08	.03	.01
☐ 4	T Tony Armas	.20	.08	.02
☐ 5	T Doug Bair	.08	.03	.01
☐ 6	T Steve Baker	.12	.05	.01
☐ 7	T Floyd Bannister	.12	.05	.01
☐ 8	T Don Baylor	.25	.10	.02
☐ 9	T Tony Bernazard	.12	.05	.01
☐ 10	T Larry Biittner	.08	.03	.01
☐ 11	T Dann Bilardello	.12	.05	.01
☐ 12	T Doug Bird	.08	.03	.01
☐ 13	T Steve Boros MGR	.08	.03	.01
☐ 14	T Greg Brock	.35	.14	.03
☐ 15	T Mike Brown	.15	.06	.01
☐ 16	T Tom Burgmeier	.08	.03	.01
☐ 17	T Randy Bush	.12	.05	.01
☐ 18	T Bert Campaneris	.15	.06	.01
☐ 19	T Ron Cey	.25	.10	.02
☐ 20	T Chris Codiroli	.12	.05	.01
☐ 21	T Dave Collins	.12	.05	.01
☐ 22	T Terry Crowley	.08	.03	.01
☐ 23	T Julio Cruz	.08	.03	.01
☐ 24	T Mike Davis	.25	.10	.02
☐ 25	T Frank DiPino	.12	.05	.01
☐ 26	T Bill Doran	1.25	.50	.12
☐ 27	T Jerry Dybzinski	.08	.03	.01
☐ 28	T Jamie Easterly	.08	.03	.01
☐ 29	T Juan Eichelberger	.08	.03	.01
☐ 30	T Jim Essian	.08	.03	.01
☐ 31	T Pete Falcone	.08	.03	.01
☐ 32	T Mike Ferraro MGR	.08	.03	.01
☐ 33	T Terry Forster	.20	.08	.02
☐ 34	T Julio Franco	1.25	.50	.12
☐ 35	T Rich Gale	.08	.03	.01
☐ 36	T Kiko Garcia	.08	.03	.01
☐ 37	T Steve Garvey	1.25	.50	.12
☐ 38	T Johnny Grubb	.08	.03	.01
☐ 39	T Mel Hall	1.00	.40	.10
☐ 40	T Von Hayes	1.00	.40	.10
☐ 41	T Danny Heep	.12	.05	.01
☐ 42	T Steve Henderson	.08	.03	.01
☐ 43	T Keith Hernandez	1.00	.40	.10
☐ 44	T Leo Hernandez	.15	.06	.01
☐ 45	T Willie Hernandez	.35	.14	.03
☐ 46	T Al Holland	.12	.05	.01
☐ 47	T Frank Howard MGR	.12	.05	.01
☐ 48	T Bobby Johnson	.08	.03	.01
☐ 49	T Cliff Johnson	.08	.03	.01

	MINT	VG-E	F-G
☐ 50 T Odell Jones	.08	.03	.01
☐ 51 T Mike Jorgensen	.08	.03	.01
☐ 52 T Bob Kearney	.08	.03	.01
☐ 53 T Steve Kemp	.15	.06	.01
☐ 54 T Matt Keough	.08	.03	.01
☐ 55 T Ron Kittle	.60	.24	.06
☐ 56 T Mickey Klutts	.08	.03	.01
☐ 57 T Alan Knicely	.08	.03	.01
☐ 58 T Mike Krukow	.20	.08	.02
☐ 59 T Rafael Landestoy	.08	.03	.01
☐ 60 T Carney Lansford	.25	.10	.02
☐ 61 T Joe Lefebvre	.08	.03	.01
☐ 62 T Bryan Little	.12	.05	.01
☐ 63 T Aurelio Lopez	.08	.03	.01
☐ 64 T Mike Madden	.15	.06	.01
☐ 65 T Rick Manning	.08	.03	.01
☐ 66 T Billy Martin MGR	.20	.08	.02
☐ 67 T Lee Mazzilli	.12	.05	.01
☐ 68 T Andy McGaffigan	.08	.03	.01
☐ 69 T Craig McMurtry	.20	.08	.02
☐ 70 T John McNamara MGR	.12	.05	.01
☐ 71 T Orlando Mercado	.12	.05	.01
☐ 72 T Larry Milbourne	.08	.03	.01
☐ 73 T Randy Moffitt	.08	.03	.01
☐ 74 T Sid Monge	.08	.03	.01
☐ 75 T Jose Morales	.08	.03	.01
☐ 76 T Omar Moreno	.12	.05	.01
☐ 77 T Joe Morgan	1.00	.40	.10
☐ 78 T Mike Morgan	.08	.03	.01
☐ 79 T Dale Murray	.08	.03	.01
☐ 80 T Jeff Newman	.08	.03	.01
☐ 81 T Pete O'Brien	1.25	.50	.12
☐ 82 T Jorge Orta	.08	.03	.01
☐ 83 T Alejandro Pena	.40	.16	.04
☐ 84 T Pascual Perez	.12	.05	.01
☐ 85 T Tony Perez	.35	.14	.03
☐ 86 T Broderick Perkins	.08	.03	.01
☐ 87 T Tony Phillips	.12	.05	.01
☐ 88 T Charlie Puleo	.08	.03	.01
☐ 89 T Pat Putnam	.08	.03	.01
☐ 90 T Jamie Quirk	.08	.03	.01
☐ 91 T Doug Rader MGR	.12	.05	.01
☐ 92 T Chuck Rainey	.08	.03	.01
☐ 93 T Bobby Ramos	.08	.03	.01
☐ 94 T Gary Redus	.75	.30	.07
☐ 95 T Steve Renko	.08	.03	.01
☐ 96 T Leon Roberts	.08	.03	.01
☐ 97 T Aurelio Rodriguez	.08	.03	.01
☐ 98 T Dick Ruthven	.08	.03	.01
☐ 99 T Daryl Sconiers	.12	.05	.01
☐ 100 T Mike Scott	1.00	.40	.10
☐ 101 T Tom Seaver	1.25	.50	.12
☐ 102 T John Shelby	.15	.06	.01

	MINT	VG-E	F-G
☐ 103 T Bob Shirley	.08	.03	.01
☐ 104 T Joe Simpson	.08	.03	.01
☐ 105 T Doug Sisk	.15	.06	.01
☐ 106 T Mike Smithson	.20	.08	.02
☐ 107 T Elias Sosa	.08	.03	.01
☐ 108 T Darryl Strawberry	18.00	7.25	1.80
☐ 109 T Tom Tellmann	.08	.03	.01
☐ 110 T Gene Tenace	.08	.03	.01
☐ 111 T Gorman Thomas	.20	.08	.02
☐ 112 T Dick Tidrow	.08	.03	.01
☐ 113 T Dave Tobik	.08	.03	.01
☐ 114 T Wayne Tolleson	.12	.05	.01
☐ 115 T Mike Torrez	.12	.05	.01
☐ 116 T Manny Trillo	.12	.05	.01
☐ 117 T Steve Trout	.12	.05	.01
☐ 118 T Lee Tunnell	.15	.06	.01
☐ 119 T Mike Vail	.08	.03	.01
☐ 120 T Ellis Valentine	.12	.05	.01
☐ 121 T Tom Veryzer	.08	.03	.01
☐ 122 T George Vukovich	.08	.03	.01
☐ 123 T Rick Waits	.08	.03	.01
☐ 124 T Greg Walker	2.00	.80	.20
☐ 125 T Chris Welsh	.08	.03	.01
☐ 126 T Len Whitehouse	.12	.05	.01
☐ 127 T Eddie Whitson	.12	.05	.01
☐ 128 T Jim Wohlford	.08	.03	.01
☐ 129 T Matt Young	.25	.10	.02
☐ 130 T Joel Youngblood	.08	.03	.01
☐ 131 T Pat Zachry	.08	.03	.01
☐ 132 T Checklist 1T-132T	.20	.02	.00

1984 Topps

The cards in this 792-card set measure 2½"
by 3½". For the second year in a row, Topps
utilized a dual picture on the front of the card.
A portrait is shown in a square insert and an

action shot is featured in the main photo. Card numbers 1-6 feature 1983 Highlights (HL), cards 131-138 depict League Leaders, card numbers 386-407 feature All Stars and card numbers 701-718 feature active Major League career leaders in various statistical categories. Each team leader (TL) card features the team's leading hitter and pitcher pictured on the front with a team checklist back. There are six numerical checklist cards in the set. The player cards feature team logos in the upper right corner of the reverse.

	MINT	VG-E	F-G
Complete Set	55.00	22.00	5.50
Common Player (1-792)	.03	.01	.00

		MINT	VG-E	F-G
☐	1 HL: Steve Carlton 300th Win and All Time SO King	.25	.07	.01
☐	2 HL: Rickey Henderson 100 Stolen Bases Three Times	.20	.08	.02
☐	3 HL: Dan Quisenberry Sets Save Record	.10	.04	.01
☐	4 HL: Nolan Ryan, Steve Carlton, and Gaylord Perry (All Surpass Johnson)	.25	.10	.02
☐	5 HL: Dave Righetti, Bob Forsch, and Mike Warren (All Pitch No-Hitters)	.10	.04	.01
☐	6 HL: Johnny Bench Gaylord Perry, and Carl Yastrzemski (Superstars Retire)	.25	.10	.02
☐	7 Gary Lucas	.03	.01	.00
☐	8 Don Mattingly	35.00	14.00	3.50
☐	9 Jim Gott	.03	.01	.00
☐	10 Robin Yount	.35	.14	.03
☐	11 Minnesota Twins TL Kent Hrbek Ken Schrom	.10	.02	.00
☐	12 Billy Sample	.03	.01	.00
☐	13 Scott Holman	.03	.01	.00
☐	14 Tom Brookens	.03	.01	.00
☐	15 Burt Hooton	.03	.01	.00
☐	16 Omar Moreno	.03	.01	.00
☐	17 John Denny	.06	.02	.00
☐	18 Dale Berra	.05	.02	.00
☐	19 Ray Fontenot	.08	.03	.01

		MINT	VG-E	F-G
☐	20 Greg Luzinski	.10	.04	.01
☐	21 Joe Altobelli MGR	.03	.01	.00
☐	22 Bryan Clark	.03	.01	.00
☐	23 Keith Moreland	.06	.02	.00
☐	24 John Martin	.03	.01	.00
☐	25 Glenn Hubbard	.03	.01	.00
☐	26 Bud Black	.03	.01	.00
☐	27 Daryl Sconiers	.03	.01	.00
☐	28 Frank Viola	.07	.03	.01
☐	29 Danny Heep	.03	.01	.00
☐	30 Wade Boggs	4.50	1.80	.45
☐	31 Andy McGaffigan	.03	.01	.00
☐	32 Bobby Ramos	.03	.01	.00
☐	33 Tom Burgmeier	.03	.01	.00
☐	34 Eddie Milner	.03	.01	.00
☐	35 Don Sutton	.20	.08	.02
☐	36 Denny Walling	.03	.01	.00
☐	37 Texas Rangers TL Buddy Bell Rick Honeycutt	.08	.02	.00
☐	38 Luis DeLeon	.03	.01	.00
☐	39 Garth Iorg	.03	.01	.00
☐	40 Dusty Baker	.07	.03	.01
☐	41 Tony Bernazard	.05	.02	.00
☐	42 Johnny Grubb	.03	.01	.00
☐	43 Ron Reed	.03	.01	.00
☐	44 Jim Morrison	.03	.01	.00
☐	45 Jerry Mumphrey	.05	.02	.00
☐	46 Ray Smith	.03	.01	.00
☐	47 Rudy Law	.03	.01	.00
☐	48 Julio Franco	.25	.10	.02
☐	49 John Stuper	.03	.01	.00
☐	50 Chris Chambliss	.05	.02	.00
☐	51 Jim Frey MGR	.03	.01	.00
☐	52 Paul Splittorff	.05	.02	.00
☐	53 Juan Beniquez	.05	.02	.00
☐	54 Jesse Orosco	.06	.02	.00
☐	55 Dave Concepcion	.09	.04	.01
☐	56 Gary Allenson	.03	.01	.00
☐	57 Dan Schatzeder	.03	.01	.00
☐	58 Max Venable	.03	.01	.00
☐	59 Sammy Stewart	.03	.01	.00
☐	60 Paul Molitor	.10	.04	.01
☐	61 Chris Codiroli	.07	.03	.01
☐	62 Dave Hostetler	.03	.01	.00
☐	63 Ed VandeBerg	.05	.02	.00
☐	64 Mike Scioscia	.05	.02	.00
☐	65 Kirk Gibson	.25	.10	.02
☐	66 Houston Astros TL Jose Cruz Nolan Ryan	.12	.02	.00
☐	67 Gary Ward	.06	.02	.00
☐	68 Luis Salazar	.03	.01	.00

		MINT	VG-E	F-G
☐ 69	Rod Scurry	.03	.01	.00
☐ 70	Gary Matthews	.07	.03	.01
☐ 71	Leo Hernandez	.09	.04	.01
☐ 72	Mike Squires	.03	.01	.00
☐ 73	Jody Davis	.09	.04	.01
☐ 74	Jerry Martin	.03	.01	.00
☐ 75	Bob Forsch	.06	.02	.00
☐ 76	Alfredo Griffin	.05	.02	.00
☐ 77	Brett Butler	.08	.03	.01
☐ 78	Mike Torrez	.05	.02	.00
☐ 79	Rob Wilfong	.03	.01	.00
☐ 80	Steve Rogers	.07	.03	.01
☐ 81	Billy Martin MGR	.12	.05	.01
☐ 82	Doug Bird	.03	.01	.00
☐ 83	Richie Zisk	.05	.02	.00
☐ 84	Lenny Faedo	.03	.01	.00
☐ 85	Atlee Hammaker	.05	.02	.00
☐ 86	John Shelby	.08	.03	.01
☐ 87	Frank Pastore	.03	.01	.00
☐ 88	Rob Picciolo	.03	.01	.00
☐ 89	Mike Smithson	.10	.04	.01
☐ 90	Pedro Guerrero	.35	.14	.03
☐ 91	Dan Spillner	.03	.01	.00
☐ 92	Lloyd Moseby	.12	.05	.01
☐ 93	Bob Knepper	.08	.03	.01
☐ 94	Mario Ramirez	.05	.02	.00
☐ 95	Aurelio Lopez	.03	.01	.00
☐ 96	K.C. Royals TL	.08	.02	.00
	Hal McRae			
	Larry Gura			
☐ 97	LaMarr Hoyt	.08	.03	.01
☐ 98	Steve Nicosia	.03	.01	.00
☐ 99	Craig Lefferts	.12	.05	.01
☐ 100	Reggie Jackson	.50	.20	.05
☐ 101	Porfirio Altamirano	.03	.01	.00
☐ 102	Ken Oberkfell	.03	.01	.00
☐ 103	Dwayne Murphy	.06	.02	.00
☐ 104	Ken Dayley	.03	.01	.00
☐ 105	Tony Armas	.09	.04	.01
☐ 106	Tim Stoddard	.03	.01	.00
☐ 107	Ned Yost	.03	.01	.00
☐ 108	Randy Moffitt	.03	.01	.00
☐ 109	Brad Wellman	.05	.02	.00
☐ 110	Ron Guidry	.20	.08	.02
☐ 111	Bill Virdon MGR	.05	.02	.00
☐ 112	Tom Niedenfuer	.07	.03	.01
☐ 113	Kelly Paris	.09	.04	.01
☐ 114	Checklist 1-132	.08	.01	.00
☐ 115	Andre Thornton	.07	.03	.01
☐ 116	George Bjorkman	.03	.01	.00
☐ 117	Tom Veryzer	.03	.01	.00
☐ 118	Charlie Hough	.06	.02	.00
☐ 119	Johnny Wockenfuss	.03	.01	.00
☐ 120	Keith Hernandez	.35	.14	.03
☐ 121	Pat Sheridan	.12	.05	.01
☐ 122	Cecilio Guante	.05	.02	.00
☐ 123	Butch Wynegar	.05	.02	.00
☐ 124	Damaso Garcia	.09	.04	.01
☐ 125	Britt Burns	.07	.03	.01
☐ 126	Atlanta Braves TL	.15	.03	.00
	Dale Murphy			
	Craig McMurtry			
☐ 127	Mike Madden	.09	.04	.01
☐ 128	Rick Manning	.03	.01	.00
☐ 129	Bill Laskey	.03	.01	.00
☐ 130	Ozzie Smith	.15	.06	.01
☐ 131	Batting Leaders	.25	.10	.02
	Bill Madlock			
	Wade Boggs			
☐ 132	Home Run Leaders	.25	.10	.02
	Mike Schmidt			
	Jim Rice			
☐ 133	RBI Leaders	.25	.10	.02
	Dale Murphy			
	Cecil Cooper			
	Jim Rice			
☐ 134	Stolen Base Leaders	.25	.10	.02
	Tim Raines			
	Rickey Henderson			
☐ 135	Victory Leaders	.07	.03	.01
	John Denny			
	LaMarr Hoyt			
☐ 136	Strikeout Leaders	.15	.06	.01
	Steve Carlton			
	Jack Morris			
☐ 137	ERA Leaders	.06	.02	.00
	Atlee Hammaker			
	Rick Honeycutt			
☐ 138	Leading Firemen	.07	.03	.01
	Al Holland			
	Dan Quisenberry			
☐ 139	Bert Campaneris	.06	.02	.00
☐ 140	Storm Davis	.08	.03	.01
☐ 141	Pat Corrales MGR	.03	.01	.00
☐ 142	Rich Gale	.03	.01	.00
☐ 143	Jose Morales	.03	.01	.00
☐ 144	Brian Harper	.07	.03	.01
☐ 145	Gary Lavelle	.05	.02	.00
☐ 146	Ed Romero	.03	.01	.00
☐ 147	Dan Petry	.14	.06	.01
☐ 148	Joe Lefebvre	.03	.01	.00
☐ 149	Jon Matlack	.05	.02	.00
☐ 150	Dale Murphy	.75	.30	.07
☐ 151	Steve Trout	.05	.02	.00
☐ 152	Glenn Brummer	.03	.01	.00
☐ 153	Dick Tidrow	.03	.01	.00

	MINT	VG-E	F-G		MINT	VG-E	F-G
☐ 154 Dave Henderson	.07	.03	.01	☐ 203 Matt Keough	.03	.01	.00
☐ 155 Frank White	.07	.03	.01	☐ 204 Bobby Meacham	.20	.08	.02
☐ 156 Oakland A's TL	.12	.02	.00	☐ 205 Greg Minton	.05	.02	.00
Rickey Henderson				☐ 206 Andy Van Slyke	.50	.20	.05
Tim Conroy				☐ 207 Donnie Moore	.06	.02	.00
☐ 157 Gary Gaetti	.09	.04	.01	☐ 208 Jose Oquendo	.06	.02	.00
☐ 158 John Curtis	.03	.01	.00	☐ 209 Manny Sarmiento	.03	.01	.00
☐ 159 Darryl Cias	.05	.02	.00	☐ 210 Joe Morgan	.18	.08	.01
☐ 160 Mario Soto	.08	.03	.01	☐ 211 Rick Sweet	.03	.01	.00
☐ 161 Junior Ortiz	.05	.02	.00	☐ 212 Broderick Perkins	.03	.01	.00
☐ 162 Bob Ojeda	.09	.04	.01	☐ 213 Bruce Hurst	.08	.03	.01
☐ 163 Lorenzo Gray	.05	.02	.00	☐ 214 Paul Householder	.03	.01	.00
☐ 164 Scott Sanderson	.03	.01	.00	☐ 215 Tippy Martinez	.03	.01	.00
☐ 165 Ken Singleton	.08	.03	.01	☐ 216 White Sox TL	.08	.02	.00
☐ 166 Jamie Nelson	.08	.03	.01	Carlton Fisk			
☐ 167 Marshall Edwards	.03	.01	.00	Richard Dotson			
☐ 168 Juan Bonilla	.03	.01	.00	☐ 217 Alan Ashby	.03	.01	.00
☐ 169 Larry Parrish	.06	.02	.00	☐ 218 Rick Waits	.03	.01	.00
☐ 170 Jerry Reuss	.07	.03	.01	☐ 219 Joe Simpson	.03	.01	.00
☐ 171 Frank Robinson MGR	.14	.06	.01	☐ 220 Fernando Valenzuela	.35	.14	.03
☐ 172 Frank DiPino	.05	.02	.00	☐ 221 Cliff Johnson	.03	.01	.00
☐ 173 Marvell Wynne	.10	.04	.01	☐ 222 Rick Honeycutt	.05	.02	.00
☐ 174 Juan Berenguer	.03	.01	.00	☐ 223 Wayne Krenchicki	.03	.01	.00
☐ 175 Graig Nettles	.12	.05	.01	☐ 224 Sid Monge	.03	.01	.00
☐ 176 Lee Smith	.10	.04	.01	☐ 225 Lee Mazzilli	.05	.02	.00
☐ 177 Jerry Hairston	.03	.01	.00	☐ 226 Juan Eichelberger	.03	.01	.00
☐ 178 Bill Krueger	.07	.03	.01	☐ 227 Steve Braun	.03	.01	.00
☐ 179 Buck Martinez	.03	.01	.00	☐ 228 John Rabb	.10	.04	.01
☐ 180 Manny Trillo	.05	.02	.00	☐ 229 Paul Owens MGR	.03	.01	.00
☐ 181 Roy Thomas	.03	.01	.00	☐ 230 Rickey Henderson	.50	.20	.05
☐ 182 Darryl Strawberry	7.50	3.00	.75	☐ 231 Gary Woods	.03	.01	.00
☐ 183 Al Williams	.03	.01	.00	☐ 232 Tim Wallach	.09	.04	.01
☐ 184 Mike O'Berry	.03	.01	.00	☐ 233 Checklist 133-264	.08	.01	.00
☐ 185 Sixto Lezcano	.03	.01	.00	☐ 234 Rafael Ramirez	.03	.01	.00
☐ 186 Cardinal TL	.08	.02	.00	☐ 235 Matt Young	.09	.04	.01
Lonnie Smith				☐ 236 Ellis Valentine	.03	.01	.00
John Stuper				☐ 237 John Castino	.03	.01	.00
☐ 187 Luis Aponte	.03	.01	.00	☐ 238 Reid Nichols	.03	.01	.00
☐ 188 Bryan Little	.03	.01	.00	☐ 239 Jay Howell	.06	.02	.00
☐ 189 Tim Conroy	.06	.02	.00	☐ 240 Eddie Murray	.55	.22	.05
☐ 190 Ben Oglivie	.06	.02	.00	☐ 241 Billy Almon	.03	.01	.00
☐ 191 Mike Boddicker	.09	.04	.01	☐ 242 Alex Trevino	.03	.01	.00
☐ 192 Nick Esasky	.25	.10	.02	☐ 243 Pete Ladd	.03	.01	.00
☐ 193 Darrell Brown	.05	.02	.00	☐ 244 Candy Maldonado	.09	.04	.01
☐ 194 Domingo Ramos	.03	.01	.00	☐ 245 Rick Sutcliffe	.18	.08	.01
☐ 195 Jack Morris	.20	.08	.02	☐ 246 New York Mets TL	.12	.02	.00
☐ 196 Don Slaught	.05	.02	.00	Mookie Wilson			
☐ 197 Garry Hancock	.03	.01	.00	Tom Seaver			
☐ 198 Bill Doran	.65	.26	.06	☐ 247 Onix Concepcion	.03	.01	.00
☐ 199 Willie Hernandez	.25	.10	.02	☐ 248 Bill Dawley	.15	.06	.01
☐ 200 Andre Dawson	.25	.10	.02	☐ 249 Jay Johnstone	.05	.02	.00
☐ 201 Bruce Kison	.03	.01	.00	☐ 250 Bill Madlock	.14	.06	.01
☐ 202 Bobby Cox MGR	.03	.01	.00	☐ 251 Tony Gwynn	1.25	.50	.12

	MINT	VG-E	F-G
☐ 252 Larry Christenson	.03	.01	.00
☐ 253 Jim Wohlford	.03	.01	.00
☐ 254 Shane Rawley	.07	.03	.01
☐ 255 Bruce Benedict	.03	.01	.00
☐ 256 Dave Geisel	.03	.01	.00
☐ 257 Julio Cruz	.03	.01	.00
☐ 258 Luis Sanchez	.03	.01	.00
☐ 259 Sparky Anderson MGR	.06	.02	.00
☐ 260 Scott McGregor	.08	.03	.01
☐ 261 Bobby Brown	.03	.01	.00
☐ 262 Tom Candiotti	.15	.06	.01
☐ 263 Jack Fimple	.05	.02	.00
☐ 264 Doug Frobel	.07	.03	.01
☐ 265 Donnie Hill	.08	.03	.01
☐ 266 Steve Lubratich	.05	.02	.00
☐ 267 Carmelo Martinez	.25	.10	.02
☐ 268 Jack O'Connor	.03	.01	.00
☐ 269 Aurelio Rodriguez	.03	.01	.00
☐ 270 Jeff Russell	.06	.02	.00
☐ 271 Moose Haas	.05	.02	.00
☐ 272 Rick Dempsey	.05	.02	.00
☐ 273 Charlie Puleo	.03	.01	.00
☐ 274 Rick Monday	.05	.02	.00
☐ 275 Len Matuszek	.03	.01	.00
☐ 276 Angels TL	.12	.02	.00
Rod Carew			
Geoff Zahn			
☐ 277 Eddie Whitson	.06	.02	.00
☐ 278 Jorge Bell	.15	.06	.01
☐ 279 Ivan DeJesus	.03	.01	.00
☐ 280 Floyd Bannister	.07	.03	.01
☐ 281 Larry Milbourne	.03	.01	.00
☐ 282 Jim Barr	.03	.01	.00
☐ 283 Larry Biittner	.03	.01	.00
☐ 284 Howard Bailey	.03	.01	.00
☐ 285 Darrell Porter	.05	.02	.00
☐ 286 Lary Sorensen	.03	.01	.00
☐ 287 Warren Cromartie	.03	.01	.00
☐ 288 Jim Beattie	.03	.01	.00
☐ 289 Randy Johnson	.03	.01	.00
☐ 290 Dave Dravecky	.07	.03	.01
☐ 291 Chuck Tanner MGR	.05	.02	.00
☐ 292 Tony Scott	.03	.01	.00
☐ 293 Ed Lynch	.03	.01	.00
☐ 294 U.L. Washington	.03	.01	.00
☐ 295 Mike Flanagan	.07	.03	.01
☐ 296 Jeff Newman	.03	.01	.00
☐ 297 Bruce Berenyi	.03	.01	.00
☐ 298 Jim Gantner	.05	.02	.00
☐ 299 John Butcher	.03	.01	.00
☐ 300 Pete Rose	1.25	.50	.12
☐ 301 Frank LaCorte	.03	.01	.00
☐ 302 Barry Bonnell	.03	.01	.00

	MINT	VG-E	F-G
☐ 303 Marty Castillo	.03	.01	.00
☐ 304 Warren Brusstar	.03	.01	.00
☐ 305 Roy Smalley	.05	.02	.00
☐ 306 Dodgers TL	.10	.02	.00
Pedro Guerrero			
Bob Welch			
☐ 307 Bobby Mitchell	.03	.01	.00
☐ 308 Ron Hassey	.03	.01	.00
☐ 309 Tony Phillips	.06	.02	.00
☐ 310 Willie McGee	.30	.12	.03
☐ 311 Jerry Koosman	.08	.03	.01
☐ 312 Jorge Orta	.03	.01	.00
☐ 313 Mike Jorgensen	.03	.01	.00
☐ 314 Orlando Mercado	.05	.02	.00
☐ 315 Bob Grich	.07	.03	.01
☐ 316 Mark Bradley	.09	.04	.01
☐ 317 Greg Pryor	.03	.01	.00
☐ 318 Bill Gullickson	.05	.02	.00
☐ 319 Al Bumbry	.03	.01	.00
☐ 320 Bob Stanley	.05	.02	.00
☐ 321 Harvey Kuenn MGR	.05	.02	.00
☐ 322 Ken Schrom	.05	.02	.00
☐ 323 Alan Knicely	.03	.01	.00
☐ 324 Alejandro Pena	.20	.08	.02
☐ 325 Darrell Evans	.10	.04	.01
☐ 326 Bob Kearney	.03	.01	.00
☐ 327 Ruppert Jones	.03	.01	.00
☐ 328 Vern Ruhle	.03	.01	.00
☐ 329 Pat Tabler	.09	.04	.01
☐ 330 John Candelaria	.08	.03	.01
☐ 331 Bucky Dent	.08	.03	.01
☐ 332 Kevin Gross	.20	.08	.02
☐ 333 Larry Herndon	.05	.02	.00
☐ 334 Chuck Rainey	.03	.01	.00
☐ 335 Don Baylor	.12	.05	.01
☐ 336 Seattle Mariners TL	.08	.02	.00
Pat Putnam			
Matt Young			
☐ 337 Kevin Hagen	.07	.03	.01
☐ 338 Mike Warren	.10	.04	.01
☐ 339 Roy Lee Jackson	.03	.01	.00
☐ 340 Hal McRae	.06	.02	.00
☐ 341 Dave Tobik	.03	.01	.00
☐ 342 Tim Foli	.03	.01	.00
☐ 343 Mark Davis	.03	.01	.00
☐ 344 Rick Miller	.03	.01	.00
☐ 345 Kent Hrbek	.35	.14	.03
☐ 346 Kurt Bevacqua	.03	.01	.00
☐ 347 Allan Ramirez	.03	.01	.00
☐ 348 Toby Harrah	.05	.02	.00
☐ 349 Bob L. Gibson	.06	.02	.00
(Brewers Pitcher)			
☐ 350 George Foster	.14	.06	.01

		MINT	VG-E	F-G
☐ 351	Russ Nixon MGR	.03	.01	.00
☐ 352	Dave Stewart	.03	.01	.00
☐ 353	Jim Anderson	.03	.01	.00
☐ 354	Jeff Burroughs	.05	.02	.00
☐ 355	Jason Thompson	.07	.03	.01
☐ 356	Glenn Abbott	.03	.01	.00
☐ 357	Ron Cey	.10	.04	.01
☐ 358	Bob Dernier	.07	.03	.01
☐ 359	Jim Acker	.12	.05	.01
☐ 360	Willie Randolph	.06	.02	.00
☐ 361	Dave Smith	.07	.03	.01
☐ 362	David Green	.05	.02	.00
☐ 363	Tim Laudner	.03	.01	.00
☐ 364	Scott Fletcher	.05	.02	.00
☐ 365	Steve Bedrosian	.06	.02	.00
☐ 366	Padres TL	.08	.02	.00
	Terry Kennedy			
	Dave Dravecky			
☐ 367	Jamie Easterly	.03	.01	.00
☐ 368	Hubie Brooks	.10	.04	.01
☐ 369	Steve McCatty	.03	.01	.00
☐ 370	Tim Raines	.35	.14	.03
☐ 371	Dave Gumpert	.03	.01	.00
☐ 372	Gary Roenicke	.05	.02	.00
☐ 373	Bill Scherrer	.06	.02	.00
☐ 374	Don Money	.03	.01	.00
☐ 375	Dennis Leonard	.06	.02	.00
☐ 376	Dave Anderson	.09	.04	.01
☐ 377	Danny Darwin	.03	.01	.00
☐ 378	Bob Brenly	.07	.03	.01
☐ 379	Checklist 265-396	.08	.01	.00
☐ 380	Steve Garvey	.45	.18	.04
☐ 381	Ralph Houk MGR	.06	.02	.00
☐ 382	Chris Nyman	.05	.02	.00
☐ 383	Terry Puhl	.05	.02	.00
☐ 384	Lee Tunnell	.07	.03	.01
☐ 385	Tony Perez	.12	.05	.01
☐ 386	George Hendrick AS	.06	.02	.00
☐ 387	Johnny Ray AS	.07	.03	.01
☐ 388	Mike Schmidt AS	.30	.12	.03
☐ 389	Ozzie Smith AS	.08	.03	.01
☐ 390	Tim Raines AS	.20	.08	.02
☐ 391	Dale Murphy AS	.35	.14	.03
☐ 392	Andre Dawson AS	.15	.06	.01
☐ 393	Gary Carter AS	.25	.10	.02
☐ 394	Steve Rogers AS	.06	.02	.00
☐ 395	Steve Carlton AS	.30	.12	.03
☐ 396	Jesse Orosco AS	.06	.02	.00
☐ 397	Eddie Murray AS	.35	.14	.03
☐ 398	Lou Whitaker AS	.10	.04	.01
☐ 399	George Brett AS	.35	.14	.03
☐ 400	Cal Ripken AS	.35	.14	.03
☐ 401	Jim Rice AS	.25	.10	.02

		MINT	VG-E	F-G
☐ 402	Dave Winfield AS	.25	.10	.02
☐ 403	Lloyd Moseby AS	.10	.04	.01
☐ 404	Ted Simmons AS	.08	.03	.01
☐ 405	LaMarr Hoyt AS	.06	.02	.00
☐ 406	Ron Guidry AS	.12	.05	.01
☐ 407	Dan Quisenberry AS	.12	.05	.01
☐ 408	Lou Piniella	.08	.03	.01
☐ 409	Juan Agosto	.05	.02	.00
☐ 410	Claudell Washington	.06	.02	.00
☐ 411	Houston Jimenez	.07	.03	.01
☐ 412	Doug Rader MGR	.05	.02	.00
☐ 413	Spike Owen	.25	.10	.02
☐ 414	Mitchell Page	.03	.01	.00
☐ 415	Tommy John	.14	.06	.01
☐ 416	Dane Iorg	.03	.01	.00
☐ 417	Mike Armstrong	.03	.01	.00
☐ 418	Ron Hodges	.03	.01	.00
☐ 419	John Henry Johnson	.03	.01	.00
☐ 420	Cecil Cooper	.14	.06	.01
☐ 421	Charlie Lea	.05	.02	.00
☐ 422	Jose Cruz	.10	.04	.01
☐ 423	Mike Morgan	.03	.01	.00
☐ 424	Dann Bilardello	.03	.01	.00
☐ 425	Steve Howe	.05	.02	.00
☐ 426	Orioles TL	.15	.03	.00
	Cal Ripken			
	Mike Boddicker			
☐ 427	Rick Leach	.03	.01	.00
☐ 428	Fred Breining	.03	.01	.00
☐ 429	Randy Bush	.05	.02	.00
☐ 430	Rusty Staub	.09	.04	.01
☐ 431	Chris Bando	.03	.01	.00
☐ 432	Charlie Hudson	.15	.06	.01
☐ 433	Rich Hebner	.03	.01	.00
☐ 434	Harold Baines	.25	.10	.02
☐ 435	Neil Allen	.06	.02	.00
☐ 436	Rick Peters	.03	.01	.00
☐ 437	Mike Proly	.03	.01	.00
☐ 438	Biff Pocoroba	.03	.01	.00
☐ 439	Bob Stoddard	.03	.01	.00
☐ 440	Steve Kemp	.08	.03	.01
☐ 441	Bob Lillis MGR	.03	.01	.00
☐ 442	Byron McLaughlin	.03	.01	.00
☐ 443	Benny Ayala	.03	.01	.00
☐ 444	Steve Renko	.03	.01	.00
☐ 445	Jerry Remy	.03	.01	.00
☐ 446	Luis Pujols	.03	.01	.00
☐ 447	Tom Brunansky	.15	.06	.01
☐ 448	Ben Hayes	.03	.01	.00
☐ 449	Joe Pettini	.03	.01	.00
☐ 450	Gary Carter	.35	.14	.03
☐ 451	Bob Jones	.03	.01	.00
☐ 452	Chuck Porter	.03	.01	.00

	MINT	VG-E	F-G
☐ 453 Willie Upshaw	.08	.03	.01
☐ 454 Joe Beckwith	.03	.01	.00
☐ 455 Terry Kennedy	.08	.03	.01
☐ 456 Chicago Cubs TL	.10	.02	.00
Keith Moreland			
Fergie Jenkins			
☐ 457 Dave Rozema	.03	.01	.00
☐ 458 Kiko Garcia	.03	.01	.00
☐ 459 Kevin Hickey	.03	.01	.00
☐ 460 Dave Winfield	.40	.16	.04
☐ 461 Jim Maler	.03	.01	.00
☐ 462 Lee Lacy	.05	.02	.00
☐ 463 Dave Engle	.03	.01	.00
☐ 464 Jeff A. Jones	.05	.02	.00
(A's Pitcher)			
☐ 465 Mookie Wilson	.07	.03	.01
☐ 466 Gene Garber	.03	.01	.00
☐ 467 Mike Ramsey	.03	.01	.00
☐ 468 Geoff Zahn	.03	.01	.00
☐ 469 Tom O'Malley	.03	.01	.00
☐ 470 Nolan Ryan	.30	.12	.03
☐ 471 Dick Howser MGR	.05	.02	.00
☐ 472 Mike Brown	.06	.02	.00
(Red Sox Pitcher)			
☐ 473 Jim Dwyer	.03	.01	.00
☐ 474 Greg Bargar	.05	.02	.00
☐ 475 Gary Redus	.35	.14	.03
☐ 476 Tom Tellmann	.03	.01	.00
☐ 477 Rafael Landestoy	.03	.01	.00
☐ 478 Alan Bannister	.03	.01	.00
☐ 479 Frank Tanana	.05	.02	.00
☐ 480 Ron Kittle	.25	.10	.02
☐ 481 Mark Thurmond	.20	.08	.02
☐ 482 Enos Cabell	.03	.01	.00
☐ 483 Fergie Jenkins	.12	.05	.01
☐ 484 Ozzie Virgil	.06	.02	.00
☐ 485 Rick Rhoden	.08	.03	.01
☐ 486 N.Y. Yankees TL	.10	.02	.00
Don Baylor			
Ron Guidry			
☐ 487 Ricky Adams	.08	.03	.01
☐ 488 Jesse Barfield	.18	.08	.01
☐ 489 Dave Von Ohlen	.05	.02	.00
☐ 490 Cal Ripken	.65	.26	.06
☐ 491 Bobby Castillo	.03	.01	.00
☐ 492 Tucker Ashford	.03	.01	.00
☐ 493 Mike Norris	.05	.02	.00
☐ 494 Chili Davis	.09	.04	.01
☐ 495 Rollie Fingers	.18	.08	.01
☐ 496 Terry Francona	.05	.02	.00
☐ 497 Bud Anderson	.03	.01	.00
☐ 498 Rich Gedman	.10	.04	.01
☐ 499 Mike Witt	.10	.04	.01
☐ 500 George Brett	.55	.22	.05
☐ 501 Steve Henderson	.03	.01	.00
☐ 502 Joe Torre MGR	.07	.03	.01
☐ 503 Elias Sosa	.03	.01	.00
☐ 504 Mickey Rivers	.05	.02	.00
☐ 505 Pete Vuckovich	.07	.03	.01
☐ 506 Ernie Whitt	.03	.01	.00
☐ 507 Mike LaCoss	.03	.01	.00
☐ 508 Mel Hall	.12	.05	.01
☐ 509 Brad Havens	.03	.01	.00
☐ 510 Alan Trammell	.20	.08	.02
☐ 511 Marty Bystrom	.03	.01	.00
☐ 512 Oscar Gamble	.05	.02	.00
☐ 513 Dave Beard	.03	.01	.00
☐ 514 Floyd Rayford	.03	.01	.00
☐ 515 Gorman Thomas	.09	.04	.01
☐ 516 Montreal Expos TL	.10	.02	.00
Al Oliver			
Charlie Lea			
☐ 517 John Moses	.07	.03	.01
☐ 518 Greg Walker	.70	.28	.07
☐ 519 Ron Davis	.03	.01	.00
☐ 520 Bob Boone	.06	.02	.00
☐ 521 Pete Falcone	.03	.01	.00
☐ 522 Dave Bergman	.03	.01	.00
☐ 523 Glenn Hoffman	.03	.01	.00
☐ 524 Carlos Diaz	.03	.01	.00
☐ 525 Willie Wilson	.18	.08	.01
☐ 526 Ron Oester	.05	.02	.00
☐ 527 Checklist 397-528	.08	.01	.00
☐ 528 Mark Brouhard	.03	.01	.00
☐ 529 Keith Atherton	.06	.02	.00
☐ 530 Dan Ford	.03	.01	.00
☐ 531 Steve Boros MGR	.03	.01	.00
☐ 532 Eric Show	.03	.01	.00
☐ 533 Ken Landreaux	.05	.02	.00
☐ 534 Pete O'Brien	.75	.30	.07
☐ 535 Bo Diaz	.05	.02	.00
☐ 536 Doug Bair	.03	.01	.00
☐ 537 Johnny Ray	.10	.04	.01
☐ 538 Kevin Bass	.09	.04	.01
☐ 539 George Frazier	.03	.01	.00
☐ 540 George Hendrick	.08	.03	.01
☐ 541 Dennis Lamp	.03	.01	.00
☐ 542 Duane Kuiper	.03	.01	.00
☐ 543 Craig McMurtry	.09	.04	.01
☐ 544 Cesar Geronimo	.03	.01	.00
☐ 545 Bill Buckner	.09	.04	.01
☐ 546 Indians TL	.08	.02	.00
Mike Hargrove			
Lary Sorensen			
☐ 547 Mike Moore	.07	.03	.01
☐ 548 Ron Jackson	.03	.01	.00

	MINT	VG-E	F-G
☐ 549 Walt Terrell	.30	.12	.03
☐ 550 Jim Rice	.35	.14	.03
☐ 551 Scott Ullger	.05	.02	.00
☐ 552 Ray Burris	.03	.01	.00
☐ 553 Joe Nolan	.03	.01	.00
☐ 554 Ted Power	.07	.03	.01
☐ 555 Greg Brock	.08	.03	.01
☐ 556 Joey McLaughlin	.03	.01	.00
☐ 557 Wayne Tolleson	.05	.02	.00
☐ 558 Mike Davis	.07	.03	.01
☐ 559 Mike Scott	.15	.06	.01
☐ 560 Carlton Fisk	.14	.06	.01
☐ 561 Whitey Herzog MGR	.06	.02	.00
☐ 562 Manny Castillo	.03	.01	.00
☐ 563 Glenn Wilson	.10	.04	.01
☐ 564 Al Holland	.05	.02	.00
☐ 565 Leon Durham	.09	.04	.01
☐ 566 Jim Bibby	.05	.02	.00
☐ 567 Mike Heath	.03	.01	.00
☐ 568 Pete Filson	.05	.02	.00
☐ 569 Bake McBride	.03	.01	.00
☐ 570 Dan Quisenberry	.18	.08	.01
☐ 571 Bruce Bochy	.03	.01	.00
☐ 572 Jerry Royster	.03	.01	.00
☐ 573 Dave Kingman	.14	.06	.01
☐ 574 Brian Downing	.05	.02	.00
☐ 575 Jim Clancy	.05	.02	.00
☐ 576 Giants TL	.08	.02	.00
Jeff Leonard			
Atlee Hammaker			
☐ 577 Mark Clear	.03	.01	.00
☐ 578 Lenn Sakata	.03	.01	.00
☐ 579 Bob James	.15	.06	.01
☐ 580 Lonnie Smith	.07	.03	.01
☐ 581 Jose DeLeon	.25	.10	.02
☐ 582 Bob McClure	.03	.01	.00
☐ 583 Derrel Thomas	.03	.01	.00
☐ 584 Dave Schmidt	.03	.01	.00
☐ 585 Dan Driessen	.05	.02	.00
☐ 586 Joe Niekro	.08	.03	.01
☐ 587 Von Hayes	.15	.06	.01
☐ 588 Milt Wilcox	.03	.01	.00
☐ 589 Mike Easler	.07	.03	.01
☐ 590 Dave Stieb	.18	.08	.01
☐ 591 Tony LaRussa MGR	.05	.02	.00
☐ 592 Andre Robertson	.03	.01	.00
☐ 593 Jeff Lahti	.03	.01	.00
☐ 594 Gene Richards	.03	.01	.00
☐ 595 Jeff Reardon	.07	.03	.01
☐ 596 Ryne Sandberg	1.00	.40	.10
☐ 597 Rick Camp	.03	.01	.00
☐ 598 Rusty Kuntz	.03	.01	.00
☐ 599 Doug Sisk	.12	.05	.01

	MINT	VG-E	F-G
☐ 600 Rod Carew	.35	.14	.03
☐ 601 John Tudor	.20	.08	.01
☐ 602 John Wathan	.03	.01	.00
☐ 603 Renie Martin	.03	.01	.00
☐ 604 John Lowenstein	.03	.01	.00
☐ 605 Mike Caldwell	.05	.02	.00
☐ 606 Blue Jays TL	.10	.02	.00
Lloyd Moseby			
Dave Stieb			
☐ 607 Tom Hume	.03	.01	.00
☐ 608 Bobby Johnson	.03	.01	.00
☐ 609 Dan Meyer	.03	.01	.00
☐ 610 Steve Sax	.18	.08	.01
☐ 611 Chet Lemon	.06	.02	.00
☐ 612 Harry Spilman	.03	.01	.00
☐ 613 Greg Gross	.03	.01	.00
☐ 614 Len Barker	.05	.02	.00
☐ 615 Garry Templeton	.09	.04	.01
☐ 616 Don Robinson	.03	.01	.00
☐ 617 Rick Cerone	.03	.01	.00
☐ 618 Dickie Noles	.03	.01	.00
☐ 619 Jerry Dybzinski	.03	.01	.00
☐ 620 Al Oliver	.12	.05	.01
☐ 621 Frank Howard MGR	.05	.02	.00
☐ 622 Al Cowens	.05	.02	.00
☐ 623 Ron Washington	.03	.01	.00
☐ 624 Terry Harper	.03	.01	.00
☐ 625 Larry Gura	.05	.02	.00
☐ 626 Bob Clark	.03	.01	.00
☐ 627 Dave LaPoint	.05	.02	.00
☐ 628 Ed Jurak	.03	.01	.00
☐ 629 Rick Langford	.03	.01	.00
☐ 630 Ted Simmons	.10	.04	.01
☐ 631 Denny Martinez	.03	.01	.00
☐ 632 Tom Foley	.05	.02	.00
☐ 633 Mike Krukow	.07	.03	.01
☐ 634 Mike Marshall	.15	.06	.01
☐ 635 Dave Righetti	.15	.06	.01
☐ 636 Pat Putnam	.03	.01	.00
☐ 637 Phillies TL	.08	.02	.00
Gary Matthews			
John Denny			
☐ 638 George Vukovich	.03	.01	.00
☐ 639 Rick Lysander	.05	.02	.00
☐ 640 Lance Parrish	.25	.10	.02
☐ 641 Mike Richardt	.03	.01	.00
☐ 642 Tom Underwood	.03	.01	.00
☐ 643 Mike Brown	.25	.10	.02
(Angels OF)			
☐ 644 Tim Lollar	.03	.01	.00
☐ 645 Tony Pena	.12	.05	.01
☐ 646 Checklist 529-660	.08	.01	.00
☐ 647 Ron Roenicke	.03	.01	.00

		MINT	VG-E	F-G
☐ 648	Len Whitehouse	.03	.01	.00
☐ 649	Tom Herr	.09	.04	.01
☐ 650	Phil Niekro	.18	.08	.01
☐ 651	John McNamara MGR	.05	.02	.00
☐ 652	Rudy May	.03	.01	.00
☐ 653	Dave Stapleton	.03	.01	.00
☐ 654	Bob Bailor	.03	.01	.00
☐ 655	Amos Otis	.06	.02	.00
☐ 656	Bryn Smith	.05	.02	.00
☐ 657	Thad Bosley	.03	.01	.00
☐ 658	Jerry Augustine	.03	.01	.00
☐ 659	Duane Walker	.03	.01	.00
☐ 660	Ray Knight	.08	.03	.01
☐ 661	Steve Yeager	.05	.02	.00
☐ 662	Tom Brennan	.03	.01	.00
☐ 663	Johnnie LeMaster	.03	.01	.00
☐ 664	Dave Stegman	.03	.01	.00
☐ 665	Buddy Bell	.10	.04	.01
☐ 666	Detroit Tigers TL	.12	.02	.00
	Lou Whitaker			
	Jack Morris			
☐ 667	Vance Law	.03	.01	.00
☐ 668	Larry McWilliams	.05	.02	.00
☐ 669	Dave Lopes	.07	.03	.01
☐ 670	Rich Gossage	.18	.08	.01
☐ 671	Jamie Quirk	.03	.01	.00
☐ 672	Ricky Nelson	.08	.03	.01
☐ 673	Mike Walters	.08	.03	.01
☐ 674	Tim Flannery	.03	.01	.00
☐ 675	Pascual Perez	.05	.02	.00
☐ 676	Brian Giles	.03	.01	.00
☐ 677	Doyle Alexander	.05	.02	.00
☐ 678	Chris Speier	.03	.01	.00
☐ 679	Art Howe	.03	.01	.00
☐ 680	Fred Lynn	.20	.08	.02
☐ 681	Tom Lasorda MGR	.06	.02	.00
☐ 682	Dan Morogiello	.05	.02	.00
☐ 683	Marty Barrett	1.25	.50	.12
☐ 684	Bob Shirley	.03	.01	.00
☐ 685	Willie Aikens	.05	.02	.00
☐ 686	Joe Price	.03	.01	.00
☐ 687	Roy Howell	.03	.01	.00
☐ 688	George Wright	.03	.01	.00
☐ 689	Mike Fischlin	.03	.01	.00
☐ 690	Jack Clark	.12	.05	.01
☐ 691	Steve Lake	.05	.02	.00
☐ 692	Dickie Thon	.05	.02	.00
☐ 693	Alan Wiggins	.06	.02	.00
☐ 694	Mike Stanton	.03	.01	.00
☐ 695	Lou Whitaker	.15	.06	.01
☐ 696	Pirates TL	.10	.02	.00
	Bill Madlock			
	Rick Rhoden			

		MINT	VG-E	F-G
☐ 697	Dale Murray	.03	.01	.00
☐ 698	Marc Hill	.03	.01	.00
☐ 699	Dave Rucker	.03	.01	.00
☐ 700	Mike Schmidt	.45	.18	.04
☐ 701	NL Active Batting	.20	.08	.02
	Bill Madlock			
	Pete Rose			
	Dave Parker			
☐ 702	NL Active Hits	.20	.08	.02
	Pete Rose			
	Rusty Staub			
	Tony Perez			
☐ 703	NL Active Home Run	.18	.08	.01
	Mike Schmidt			
	Tony Perez			
	Dave Kingman			
☐ 704	NL Active RBI	.10	.04	.01
	Tony Perez			
	Rusty Staub			
	Al Oliver			
☐ 705	NL Active Steals	.10	.04	.01
	Joe Morgan			
	Cesar Cedeno			
	Larry Bowa			
☐ 706	NL Active Victory	.20	.08	.02
	Steve Carlton			
	Fergie Jenkins			
	Tom Seaver			
☐ 707	NL Active Strikeout	.20	.08	.02
	Steve Carlton			
	Nolan Ryan			
	Tom Seaver			
☐ 708	NL Active ERA	.18	.08	.01
	Tom Seaver			
	Steve Carlton			
	Steve Rogers			
☐ 709	NL Active Save	.08	.03	.01
	Bruce Sutter			
	Tug McGraw			
	Gene Garber			
☐ 710	AL Active Batting	.20	.08	.02
	Rod Carew			
	George Brett			
	Cecil Cooper			
☐ 711	AL Active Hits	.18	.08	.01
	Rod Carew			
	Bert Campaneris			
	Reggie Jackson			
☐ 712	AL Active Home Run	.18	.08	.01
	Reggie Jackson			
	Graig Nettles			
	Greg Luzinski			

		MINT	VG-E	F-G
☐ 713	AL Active RBI	.18	.08	.01
	Reggie Jackson			
	Ted Simmons			
	Graig Nettles			
☐ 714	AL Active Steals	.07	.03	.01
	Bert Campaneris			
	Dave Lopes			
	Omar Moreno			
☐ 715	AL Active Victory	.18	.08	.01
	Jim Palmer			
	Don Sutton			
	Tommy John			
☐ 716	AL Active Strikeout	.09	.04	.01
	Don Sutton			
	Bert Blyleven			
	Jerry Koosman			
☐ 717	AL Active ERA	.15	.06	.01
	Jim Palmer			
	Rollie Fingers			
	Ron Guidry			
☐ 718	AL Active Save	.15	.06	.01
	Rollie Fingers			
	Rich Gossage			
	Dan Quisenberry			
☐ 719	Andy Hassler	.03	.01	.00
☐ 720	Dwight Evans	.10	.04	.01
☐ 721	Del Crandall MGR	.03	.01	.00
☐ 722	Bob Welch	.06	.02	.00
☐ 723	Rich Dauer	.03	.01	.00
☐ 724	Eric Rasmussen	.03	.01	.00
☐ 725	Cesar Cedeno	.06	.02	.00
☐ 726	Brewers TL	.08	.02	.00
	Ted Simmons			
	Moose Haas			
☐ 727	Joel Youngblood	.03	.01	.00
☐ 728	Tug McGraw	.09	.04	.01
☐ 729	Gene Tenace	.03	.01	.00
☐ 730	Bruce Sutter	.15	.06	.01
☐ 731	Lynn Jones	.03	.01	.00
☐ 732	Terry Crowley	.03	.01	.00
☐ 733	Dave Collins	.05	.02	.00
☐ 734	Odell Jones	.03	.01	.00
☐ 735	Rick Burleson	.05	.02	.00
☐ 736	Dick Ruthven	.03	.01	.00
☐ 737	Jim Essian	.03	.01	.00
☐ 738	Bill Schroeder	.20	.08	.02
☐ 739	Bob Watson	.05	.02	.00
☐ 740	Tom Seaver	.40	.16	.04
☐ 741	Wayne Gross	.03	.01	.00
☐ 742	Dick Williams MGR	.03	.01	.00
☐ 743	Don Hood	.03	.01	.00
☐ 744	Jamie Allen	.10	.04	.01
☐ 745	Dennis Eckersley	.06	.02	.00

		MINT	VG-E	F-G
☐ 746	Mickey Hatcher	.03	.01	.00
☐ 747	Pat Zachry	.03	.01	.00
☐ 748	Jeff Leonard	.06	.02	.00
☐ 749	Doug Flynn	.03	.01	.00
☐ 750	Jim Palmer	.25	.10	.02
☐ 751	Charlie Moore	.03	.01	.00
☐ 752	Phil Garner	.05	.02	.00
☐ 753	Doug Gwosdz	.03	.01	.00
☐ 754	Kent Tekulve	.07	.03	.01
☐ 755	Garry Maddox	.05	.02	.00
☐ 756	Reds TL	.08	.02	.00
	Ron Oester			
	Mario Soto			
☐ 757	Larry Bowa	.09	.04	.01
☐ 758	Bill Stein	.03	.01	.00
☐ 759	Richard Dotson	.07	.03	.01
☐ 760	Bob Horner	.25	.10	.02
☐ 761	John Montefusco	.05	.02	.00
☐ 762	Rance Mulliniks	.03	.01	.00
☐ 763	Craig Swan	.03	.01	.00
☐ 764	Mike Hargrove	.05	.02	.00
☐ 765	Ken Forsch	.03	.01	.00
☐ 766	Mike Vail	.03	.01	.00
☐ 767	Carney Lansford	.09	.04	.01
☐ 768	Champ Summers	.03	.01	.00
☐ 769	Bill Caudill	.06	.02	.00
☐ 770	Ken Griffey	.07	.03	.01
☐ 771	Billy Gardner MGR	.03	.01	.00
☐ 772	Jim Slaton	.03	.01	.00
☐ 773	Todd Cruz	.03	.01	.00
☐ 774	Tom Gorman	.10	.04	.01
☐ 775	Dave Parker	.20	.08	.02
☐ 776	Craig Reynolds	.03	.01	.00
☐ 777	Tom Paciorek	.03	.01	.00
☐ 778	Andy Hawkins	.20	.08	.02
☐ 779	Jim Sundberg	.05	.02	.00
☐ 780	Steve Carlton	.35	.14	.03
☐ 781	Checklist 661-792	.08	.01	.00
☐ 782	Steve Balboni	.07	.03	.01
☐ 783	Luis Leal	.03	.01	.00
☐ 784	Leon Roberts	.03	.01	.00
☐ 785	Joaquin Andujar	.12	.05	.01
☐ 786	Red Sox TL	.25	.05	.01
	Wade Boggs			
	Bob Ojeda			
☐ 787	Bill Campbell	.03	.01	.00
☐ 788	Milt May	.03	.01	.00
☐ 789	Bert Blyleven	.12	.05	.01
☐ 790	Doug DeCinces	.09	.04	.01
☐ 791	Terry Forster	.08	.03	.01
☐ 792	Bill Russell	.06	.02	.00

1984 Topps Traded

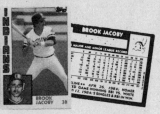

The cards in this 132-card set measure 2½" by 3½". In its now standard procedure, Topps issued its Traded (or extended) set for the fourth year in a row. Because all photos and statistics of its regular set for the year were developed during the fall and winter months of the preceding year, players who changed teams during the fall, winter, and spring months are portrayed with the teams they were with in 1983. The Traded set amends the shortcomings of the regular set by presenting the players with their proper teams for the current year. Rookies not contained in the regular set are also picked up in the Traded set. Again this year, the Topps affiliate in Ireland printed the cards, and the cards were available through hobby channels only.

	MINT	VG-E	F-G
Complete Set	75.00	30.00	7.50
Common Player	.10	.04	.01

		MINT	VG-E	F-G
1	T Willie Aikens	.15	.06	.01
2	T Luis Aponte	.10	.04	.01
3	T Mike Armstrong	.10	.04	.01
4	T Bob Bailor	.10	.04	.01
5	T Dusty Baker	.15	.06	.01
6	T Steve Balboni	.20	.08	.02
7	T Alan Bannister	.10	.04	.01
8	T Dave Beard	.10	.04	.01
9	T Joe Beckwith	.10	.04	.01
10	T Bruce Berenyi	.15	.06	.01
11	T Dave Bergman	.10	.04	.01
12	T Tony Bernazard	.15	.06	.01
13	T Yogi Berra	.30	.12	.03
14	T Barry Bonnell	.10	.04	.01
15	T Phil Bradley	4.00	1.60	.40
16	T Fred Breining	.10	.04	.01
17	T Bill Buckner	.35	.14	.03
18	T Ray Burris	.10	.04	.01
19	T John Butcher	.10	.04	.01
20	T Brett Butler	.35	.14	.03
21	T Enos Cabell	.10	.04	.01
22	T Bill Campbell	.15	.06	.01
23	T Bill Caudill	.15	.06	.01
24	T Bob Clark	.10	.04	.01
25	T Bryan Clark	.10	.04	.01
26	T Jaime Cocanower	.15	.06	.01
27	T Ron Darling	6.00	2.40	.60
28	T Alvin Davis	4.00	1.60	.40
29	T Ken Dayley	.15	.06	.01
30	T Jeff Dedmon	.15	.06	.01
31	T Bob Dernier	.15	.06	.01
32	T Carlos Diaz	.10	.04	.01
33	T Mike Easler	.15	.06	.01
34	T Dennis Eckersley	.15	.06	.01
35	T Jim Essian	.10	.04	.01
36	T Darrell Evans	.25	.10	.02
37	T Mike Fitzgerald	.15	.06	.01
38	T Tim Foli	.10	.04	.01
39	T George Frazier	.10	.04	.01
40	T Rich Gale	.10	.04	.01
41	T Barbaro Garbey	.20	.08	.02
42	T Dwight Gooden	40.00	16.00	4.00
43	T Rich Gossage	.35	.14	.03
44	T Wayne Gross	.10	.04	.01
45	T Mark Gubicza	.60	.24	.06
46	T Jackie Gutierrez	.25	.10	.02
47	T Mel Hall	.25	.10	.02
48	T Toby Harrah	.15	.06	.01
49	T Ron Hassey	.10	.04	.01
50	T Rich Hebner	.10	.04	.01
51	T Willie Hernandez	.35	.14	.03
52	T Ricky Horton	.35	.14	.03
53	T Art Howe	.10	.04	.01
54	T Dane Iorg	.10	.04	.01
55	T Brook Jacoby	1.50	.60	.15
56	T Mike Jeffcoat	.20	.08	.02
57	T Dave Johnson MGR	.20	.08	.02
58	T Lynn Jones	.10	.04	.01
59	T Ruppert Jones	.15	.06	.01
60	T Mike Jorgensen	.10	.04	.01
61	T Bob Kearney	.10	.04	.01
62	T Jimmy Key	1.00	.40	.10
63	T Dave Kingman	.50	.20	.05
64	T Jerry Koosman	.30	.12	.03
65	T Wayne Krenchicki	.10	.04	.01

			MINT	VG-E	F-G
☐	66	T Rusty Kuntz	.10	.04	.01
☐	67	T Rene Lachemann MGR	.10	.04	.01
☐	68	T Frank LaCorte	.10	.04	.01
☐	69	T Dennis Lamp	.10	.04	.01
☐	70	T Mark Langston	1.50	.60	.15
☐	71	T Rick Leach	.10	.04	.01
☐	72	T Craig Lefferts	.10	.04	.01
☐	73	T Gary Lucas	.10	.04	.01
☐	74	T Jerry Martin	.10	.04	.01
☐	75	T Carmelo Martinez	.30	.12	.03
☐	76	T Mike Mason	.30	.12	.03
☐	77	T Gary Matthews	.20	.08	.02
☐	78	T Andy McGaffigan	.10	.04	.01
☐	79	T Larry Milbourne	.10	.04	.01
☐	80	T Sid Monge	.10	.04	.01
☐	81	T Jackie Moore MGR	.10	.04	.01
☐	82	T Joe Morgan	1.00	.40	.10
☐	83	T Graig Nettles	.50	.20	.05
☐	84	T Phil Niekro	1.00	.40	.10
☐	85	T Ken Oberkfell	.15	.06	.01
☐	86	T Mike O'Berry	.10	.04	.01
☐	87	T Al Oliver	.25	.10	.02
☐	88	T Jorge Orta	.10	.04	.01
☐	89	T Amos Otis	.20	.08	.02
☐	90	T Dave Parker	1.00	.40	.10
☐	91	T Tony Perez	.45	.18	.04
☐	92	T Gerald Perry	.35	.14	.03
☐	93	T Gary Pettis	.60	.24	.06
☐	94	T Rob Picciolo	.10	.04	.01
☐	95	T Vern Rapp MGR	.10	.04	.01
☐	96	T Floyd Rayford	.10	.04	.01
☐	97	T Randy Ready	.25	.10	.02
☐	98	T Ron Reed	.10	.04	.01
☐	99	T Gene Richards	.10	.04	.01
☐	100	T Jose Rijo	.60	.24	.06
☐	101	T Jeff Robinson	.25	.10	.02
☐	102	T Ron Romanick	.75	.30	.07
☐	103	T Pete Rose	6.00	2.40	.60
☐	104	T Bret Saberhagen	3.00	1.20	.30
☐	105	T Juan Samuel	1.50	.60	.15
☐	106	T Scott Sanderson	.15	.06	.01
☐	107	T Dick Schofield	.75	.30	.07
☐	108	T Tom Seaver	1.25	.50	.12
☐	109	T Jim Slaton	.10	.04	.01
☐	110	T Mike Smithson	.10	.04	.01
☐	111	T Lary Sorensen	.10	.04	.01
☐	112	T Tim Stoddard	.10	.04	.01
☐	113	T Champ Summers	.10	.04	.01
☐	114	T Jim Sundberg	.15	.06	.01
☐	115	T Rick Sutcliffe	.50	.20	.05
☐	116	T Craig Swan	.10	.04	.01
☐	117	T Tim Teufel	.50	.20	.05

			MINT	VG-E	F-G
☐	118	T Derrel Thomas	.10	.04	.01
☐	119	T Gorman Thomas	.25	.10	.02
☐	120	T Alex Trevino	.10	.04	.01
☐	121	T Manny Trillo	.15	.06	.01
☐	122	T John Tudor	.40	.16	.04
☐	123	T Tom Underwood	.10	.04	.01
☐	124	T Mike Vail	.10	.04	.01
☐	125	T Tom Waddell	.25	.10	.02
☐	126	T Gary Ward	.15	.06	.01
☐	127	T Curt Wilkerson	.15	.06	.01
☐	128	T Frank Williams	.20	.08	.02
☐	129	T Glenn Wilson	.30	.12	.03
☐	130	T Johnny Wockenfuss	.10	.04	.01
☐	131	T Ned Yost	.10	.04	.01
☐	132	T Checklist: 1-132	.20	.02	.00

1985 Topps

The cards in this 792-card set measure 2½"
by 3½". The 1985 Topps set contains full col-
or cards. The fronts feature both the Topps
and team logos along with the team name,
player's name, and his position. The backs
feature player statistics with ink colors of light
green and maroon on a gray stock. A trivia
quiz is included on the lower portion of the
backs. The first ten cards (1-10) are Record
Breakers (RB), cards 131-143 are Father
and Son (FS) cards, and cards 701 to 722
portray All-Star selections (AS). Cards 271 to
282 represent "First Draft Picks" still active in
the Major Leagues and cards 389-404 feature the coach and players on the 1984 U.S.
Olympic Baseball Team. The manager cards
in the set are important in that they contain the
checklist of that team's players on the back.

		MINT	VG-E	F-G
	Complete Set	55.00	20.00	5.00
	Common Player	.03	.01	.00
☐ 1	Carlton Fisk RB	.15	.04	.01
	Longest game			
	by catcher			
☐ 2	Steve Garvey RB	.15	.06	.01
	Consecutive error-			
	less games, 1B			
☐ 3	Dwight Gooden RB	1.00	.40	.10
	Most strikeouts,			
	rookie, season			
☐ 4	Cliff Johnson RB	.05	.02	.00
	Most pinch homers,			
	lifetime			
☐ 5	Joe Morgan RB	.10	.04	.01
	Most homers,			
	2B, lifetime			
☐ 6	Pete Rose RB	.40	.16	.04
	Most singles,			
	lifetime			
☐ 7	Nolan Ryan RB	.15	.06	.01
	Most strikeouts,			
	lifetime			
☐ 8	Juan Samuel RB	.10	.04	.01
	Most stolen bases,			
	rookie, season			
☐ 9	Bruce Sutter RB	.08	.03	.01
	Most saves,			
	season, NL			
☐ 10	Don Sutton RB	.08	.03	.01
	Most seasons,			
	100 or more K's			
☐ 11	Ralph Houk MGR	.05	.02	.00
	(checklist back)			
☐ 12	Dave Lopes	.06	.02	.00
☐ 13	Tim Lollar	.03	.01	.00
☐ 14	Chris Bando	.03	.01	.00
☐ 15	Jerry Koosman	.07	.03	.01
☐ 16	Bobby Meacham	.03	.01	.00
☐ 17	Mike Scott	.15	.06	.01
☐ 18	Mickey Hatcher	.03	.01	.00
☐ 19	George Frazier	.03	.01	.00
☐ 20	Chet Lemon	.05	.02	.00
☐ 21	Lee Tunnell	.03	.01	.00
☐ 22	Duane Kuiper	.03	.01	.00
☐ 23	Bret Saberhagen	1.25	.50	.12
☐ 24	Jesse Barfield	.15	.06	.01
☐ 25	Steve Bedrosian	.06	.02	.00
☐ 26	Roy Smalley	.05	.02	.00
☐ 27	Bruce Berenyi	.03	.01	.00
☐ 28	Dann Bilardello	.03	.01	.00
☐ 29	Odell Jones	.03	.01	.00

		MINT	VG-E	F-G
☐ 30	Cal Ripken	.45	.18	.04
☐ 31	Terry Whitfield	.03	.01	.00
☐ 32	Chuck Porter	.03	.01	.00
☐ 33	Tito Landrum	.03	.01	.00
☐ 34	Ed Nunez	.08	.03	.01
☐ 35	Graig Nettles	.10	.04	.01
☐ 36	Fred Breining	.03	.01	.00
☐ 37	Reid Nichols	.03	.01	.00
☐ 38	Jackie Moore MGR	.05	.01	.00
	(checklist back)			
☐ 39	John Wockenfuss	.03	.01	.00
☐ 40	Phil Niekro	.15	.06	.01
☐ 41	Mike Fischlin	.03	.01	.00
☐ 42	Luis Sanchez	.03	.01	.00
☐ 43	Andre David	.09	.04	.01
☐ 44	Dickie Thon	.06	.02	.00
☐ 45	Greg Minton	.05	.02	.00
☐ 46	Gary Woods	.03	.01	.00
☐ 47	Dave Rozema	.03	.01	.00
☐ 48	Tony Fernandez	.35	.14	.03
☐ 49	Butch Davis	.06	.02	.00
☐ 50	John Candelaria	.07	.03	.01
☐ 51	Bob Watson	.05	.02	.00
☐ 52	Jerry Dybzinski	.03	.01	.00
☐ 53	Tom Gorman	.03	.01	.00
☐ 54	Cesar Cedeno	.06	.02	.00
☐ 55	Frank Tanana	.05	.02	.00
☐ 56	Jim Dwyer	.03	.01	.00
☐ 57	Pat Zachry	.03	.01	.00
☐ 58	Orlando Mercado	.03	.01	.00
☐ 59	Rick Waits	.03	.01	.00
☐ 60	George Hendrick	.06	.02	.00
☐ 61	Curt Kaufman	.08	.03	.01
☐ 62	Mike Ramsey	.03	.01	.00
☐ 63	Steve McCatty	.03	.01	.00
☐ 64	Mark Bailey	.09	.04	.01
☐ 65	Bill Buckner	.08	.03	.01
☐ 66	Dick Williams MGR	.05	.01	.00
	(checklist back)			
☐ 67	Rafael Santana	.09	.04	.01
☐ 68	Von Hayes	.12	.05	.01
☐ 69	Jim Winn	.07	.03	.01
☐ 70	Don Baylor	.10	.04	.01
☐ 71	Tim Laudner	.03	.01	.00
☐ 72	Rick Sutcliffe	.10	.04	.01
☐ 73	Rusty Kuntz	.03	.01	.00
☐ 74	Mike Krukow	.07	.03	.01
☐ 75	Willie Upshaw	.08	.03	.01
☐ 76	Alan Bannister	.03	.01	.00
☐ 77	Joe Beckwith	.03	.01	.00
☐ 78	Scott Fletcher	.05	.02	.00
☐ 79	Rick Mahler	.03	.01	.00
☐ 80	Keith Hernandez	.25	.10	.02

		MINT	VG-E	F-G
☐ 81	Lenn Sakata	.03	.01	.00
☐ 82	Joe Price	.03	.01	.00
☐ 83	Charlie Moore	.03	.01	.00
☐ 84	Spike Owen	.06	.02	.00
☐ 85	Mike Marshall	.12	.05	.01
☐ 86	Don Aase	.05	.02	.00
☐ 87	David Green	.05	.02	.00
☐ 88	Bryn Smith	.03	.01	.00
☐ 89	Jackie Gutierrez	.08	.03	.01
☐ 90	Rich Gossage	.12	.05	.01
☐ 91	Jeff Burroughs	.03	.01	.00
☐ 92	Paul Owens MGR (checklist back)	.05	.01	.00
☐ 93	Don Schulze	.07	.03	.01
☐ 94	Toby Harrah	.05	.02	.00
☐ 95	Jose Cruz	.09	.04	.01
☐ 96	Johnny Ray	.09	.04	.01
☐ 97	Pete Filson	.03	.01	.00
☐ 98	Steve Lake	.03	.01	.00
☐ 99	Milt Wilcox	.03	.01	.00
☐ 100	George Brett	.45	.18	.04
☐ 101	Jim Acker	.03	.01	.00
☐ 102	Tommy Dunbar	.05	.02	.00
☐ 103	Randy Lerch	.03	.01	.00
☐ 104	Mike Fitzgerald	.05	.02	.00
☐ 105	Ron Kittle	.12	.05	.01
☐ 106	Pascual Perez	.03	.01	.00
☐ 107	Tom Foley	.03	.01	.00
☐ 108	Darnell Coles	.15	.06	.01
☐ 109	Gary Roenicke	.05	.02	.00
☐ 110	Alejandro Pena	.05	.02	.00
☐ 111	Doug DeCinces	.08	.03	.01
☐ 112	Tom Tellmann	.03	.01	.00
☐ 113	Tom Herr	.08	.03	.01
☐ 114	Bob James	.05	.02	.00
☐ 115	Rickey Henderson	.40	.16	.04
☐ 116	Dennis Boyd	.25	.10	.02
☐ 117	Greg Gross	.03	.01	.00
☐ 118	Eric Show	.05	.02	.00
☐ 119	Pat Corrales MGR (checklist back)	.05	.01	.00
☐ 120	Steve Kemp	.07	.03	.00
☐ 121	Checklist: 1-132	.07	.01	.00
☐ 122	Tom Brunansky	.12	.05	.01
☐ 123	Dave Smith	.07	.03	.01
☐ 124	Rich Hebner	.03	.01	.00
☐ 125	Kent Tekulve	.06	.02	.00
☐ 126	Ruppert Jones	.03	.01	.00
☐ 127	Mark Gubicza	.25	.10	.02
☐ 128	Ernie Whitt	.03	.01	.00
☐ 129	Gene Garber	.03	.01	.00
☐ 130	Al Oliver	.09	.04	.01
☐ 131	Buddy/Gus Bell FS	.07	.03	.01

		MINT	VG-E	F-G
☐ 132	Dale/Yogi Berra FS	.07	.03	.01
☐ 133	Bob/Ray Boone FS	.05	.02	.00
☐ 134	Terry/Tito Francona FS	.07	.03	.01
☐ 135	Terry/Bob Kennedy FS	.05	.02	.00
☐ 136	Jeff/Jim Kunkel FS	.05	.02	.00
☐ 137	Vance/Vern Law FS	.05	.02	.00
☐ 138	Dick/Dick Schofield FS	.05	.02	.00
☐ 139	Joel/Bob Skinner FS	.05	.02	.00
☐ 140	Roy/Roy Smalley FS	.05	.02	.00
☐ 141	Mike/D.Stenhouse FS	.05	.02	.00
☐ 142	Steve/Dizzy Trout FS	.05	.02	.00
☐ 143	Ozzie/Ozzie Virgil FS	.05	.02	.00
☐ 144	Ron Gardenhire	.03	.01	.00
☐ 145	Alvin Davis	1.50	.60	.15
☐ 146	Gary Redus	.06	.02	.00
☐ 147	Bill Swaggerty	.09	.04	.01
☐ 148	Steve Yeager	.05	.02	.00
☐ 149	Dickie Noles	.03	.01	.00
☐ 150	Jim Rice	.30	.12	.03
☐ 151	Moose Haas	.05	.02	.00
☐ 152	Steve Braun	.03	.01	.00
☐ 153	Frank LaCorte	.03	.01	.00
☐ 154	Argenis Salazar	.08	.03	.01
☐ 155	Yogi Berra MGR (checklist back)	.10	.03	.00
☐ 156	Craig Reynolds	.03	.01	.00
☐ 157	Tug McGraw	.07	.03	.01
☐ 158	Pat Tabler	.08	.03	.01
☐ 159	Carlos Diaz	.03	.01	.00
☐ 160	Lance Parrish	.20	.08	.02
☐ 161	Ken Schrom	.03	.01	.00
☐ 162	Benny Distefano	.10	.04	.01
☐ 163	Dennis Eckersley	.05	.02	.00
☐ 164	Jorge Orta	.03	.01	.00
☐ 165	Dusty Baker	.06	.02	.00
☐ 166	Keith Atherton	.03	.01	.00
☐ 167	Rufino Linares	.03	.01	.00
☐ 168	Garth Iorg	.03	.01	.00
☐ 169	Dan Spillner	.03	.01	.00
☐ 170	George Foster	.12	.05	.01
☐ 171	Bill Stein	.03	.01	.00
☐ 172	Jack Perconte	.03	.01	.00
☐ 173	Mike Young	.15	.06	.01
☐ 174	Rick Honeycutt	.05	.02	.00
☐ 175	Dave Parker	.15	.06	.01
☐ 176	Bill Schroeder	.03	.01	.00
☐ 177	Dave Von Ohlen	.03	.01	.00
☐ 178	Miguel Dilone	.03	.01	.00
☐ 179	Tommy John	.10	.04	.01
☐ 180	Dave Winfield	.30	.12	.03
☐ 181	Roger Clemens	8.00	3.25	.80
☐ 182	Tim Flannery	.03	.01	.00
☐ 183	Larry McWilliams	.05	.02	.00

		MINT	VG-E	F-G			MINT	VG-E	F-G
☐ 184	Carmen Castillo	.03	.01	.00	☐ 235	Garry Maddox	.05	.02	.00
☐ 185	Al Holland	.03	.01	.00	☐ 236	Mark Thurmond	.05	.02	.00
☐ 186	Bob Lillis MGR	.05	.01	.00	☐ 237	Julio Franco	.10	.04	.01
	(checklist back)				☐ 238	Jose Rijo	.25	.10	.02
☐ 187	Mike Walters	.05	.02	.00	☐ 239	Tim Teufel	.10	.04	.01
☐ 188	Greg Pryor	.03	.01	.00	☐ 240	Dave Stieb	.12	.05	.01
☐ 189	Warren Brusstar	.03	.01	.00	☐ 241	Jim Frey MGR	.05	.01	.00
☐ 190	Rusty Staub	.08	.03	.01		(checklist back)			
☐ 191	Steve Nicosia	.03	.01	.00	☐ 242	Greg Harris	.05	.02	.00
☐ 192	Howard Johnson	.03	.01	.00	☐ 243	Barbaro Garbey	.08	.03	.01
☐ 193	Jimmy Key	.35	.14	.03	☐ 244	Mike Jones	.05	.02	.00
☐ 194	Dave Stegman	.03	.01	.00	☐ 245	Chili Davis	.07	.03	.01
☐ 195	Glenn Hubbard	.03	.01	.00	☐ 246	Mike Norris	.03	.01	.00
☐ 196	Pete O'Brien	.08	.03	.01	☐ 247	Wayne Tolleson	.03	.01	.00
☐ 197	Mike Warren	.03	.01	.00	☐ 248	Terry Forster	.06	.02	.00
☐ 198	Eddie Milner	.03	.01	.00	☐ 249	Harold Baines	.15	.06	.01
☐ 199	Denny Martinez	.03	.01	.00	☐ 250	Jesse Orosco	.06	.02	.00
☐ 200	Reggie Jackson	.35	.14	.03	☐ 251	Brad Gulden	.03	.01	.00
☐ 201	Burt Hooton	.03	.01	.00	☐ 252	Dan Ford	.03	.01	.00
☐ 202	Gorman Thomas	.07	.03	.01	☐ 253	Sid Bream	.35	.14	.03
☐ 203	Bob McClure	.03	.01	.00	☐ 254	Pete Vuckovich	.06	.02	.00
☐ 204	Art Howe	.03	.01	.00	☐ 255	Lonnie Smith	.06	.02	.00
☐ 205	Steve Rogers	.06	.02	.00	☐ 256	Mike Stanton	.03	.01	.00
☐ 206	Phil Garner	.05	.02	.00	☐ 257	Bryan Little	.03	.01	.00
☐ 207	Mark Clear	.03	.01	.00	☐ 258	Mike Brown	.05	.02	.00
☐ 208	Champ Summers	.03	.01	.00		(Angels OF)			
☐ 209	Bill Campbell	.03	.01	.00	☐ 259	Gary Allenson	.03	.01	.00
☐ 210	Gary Matthews	.06	.02	.00	☐ 260	Dave Righetti	.12	.05	.01
☐ 211	Clay Christiansen	.09	.04	.01	☐ 261	Checklist: 133-264	.07	.01	.00
☐ 212	George Vukovich	.03	.01	.00	☐ 262	Greg Booker	.06	.02	.00
☐ 213	Billy Gardner MGR	.05	.01	.00	☐ 263	Mel Hall	.09	.04	.01
	(checklist back)				☐ 264	Joe Sambito	.05	.02	.00
☐ 214	John Tudor	.10	.04	.01	☐ 265	Juan Samuel	.35	.14	.03
☐ 215	Bob Brenly	.07	.03	.01	☐ 266	Frank Viola	.07	.03	.01
☐ 216	Jerry Don Gleaton	.03	.01	.00	☐ 267	Henry Cotto	.08	.03	.01
☐ 217	Leon Roberts	.03	.01	.00	☐ 268	Chuck Tanner MGR	.05	.01	.00
☐ 218	Doyle Alexander	.05	.02	.00		(checklist back)			
☐ 219	Gerald Perry	.05	.02	.00	☐ 269	Doug Baker	.06	.02	.00
☐ 220	Fred Lynn	.15	.06	.01	☐ 270	Dan Quisenberry	.12	.05	.01
☐ 221	Ron Reed	.03	.01	.00	☐ 271	Tim Foli FDP68	.03	.01	.00
☐ 222	Hubie Brooks	.09	.04	.01	☐ 272	Jeff Burroughs FDP69	.03	.01	.00
☐ 223	Tom Hume	.03	.01	.00	☐ 273	Bill Almon FDP74	.03	.01	.00
☐ 224	Al Cowens	.03	.01	.00	☐ 274	Floyd Bannister FDP76	.05	.02	.00
☐ 225	Mike Boddicker	.09	.04	.01	☐ 275	Harold Baines FDP77	.10	.04	.01
☐ 226	Juan Beniquez	.05	.02	.00	☐ 276	Bob Horner FDP78	.12	.05	.01
☐ 227	Danny Darwin	.03	.01	.00	☐ 277	Al Chambers FDP79	.05	.02	.00
☐ 228	Dion James	.09	.04	.01	☐ 278	D.Strawberry FDP80	.35	.14	.03
☐ 229	Dave LaPoint	.03	.01	.00	☐ 279	Mike Moore FDP81	.06	.02	.00
☐ 230	Gary Carter	.30	.12	.03	☐ 280	Shawon Dunston FDP82	.50	.20	.05
☐ 231	Dwayne Murphy	.06	.02	.00	☐ 281	Tim Belcher FDP83	.10	.04	.01
☐ 232	Dave Beard	.03	.01	.00	☐ 282	Shawn Abner FDP84	.35	.14	.03
☐ 233	Ed Jurak	.03	.01	.00	☐ 283	Fran Mullins	.03	.01	.00
☐ 234	Jerry Narron	.03	.01	.00	☐ 284	Marty Bystrom	.03	.01	.00

		MINT	VG-E	F-G
☐ 285	Dan Driessen	.03	.01	.00
☐ 286	Rudy Law	.03	.01	.00
☐ 287	Walt Terrell	.03	.01	.00
☐ 288	Jeff Kunkel	.08	.03	.01
☐ 289	Tom Underwood	.03	.01	.00
☐ 290	Cecil Cooper	.10	.04	.01
☐ 291	Bob Welch	.06	.02	.00
☐ 292	Brad Komminsk	.06	.02	.00
☐ 293	Curt Young	.08	.03	.01
☐ 294	Tom Nieto	.05	.02	.00
☐ 295	Joe Niekro	.07	.03	.01
☐ 296	Ricky Nelson	.05	.02	.00
☐ 297	Gary Lucas	.03	.01	.00
☐ 298	Marty Barrett	.09	.04	.01
☐ 299	Andy Hawkins	.06	.02	.00
☐ 300	Rod Carew	.35	.14	.03
☐ 301	John Montefusco	.05	.02	.00
☐ 302	Tim Corcoran	.03	.01	.00
☐ 303	Mike Jeffcoat	.05	.02	.00
☐ 304	Gary Gaetti	.08	.03	.01
☐ 305	Dale Berra	.05	.02	.00
☐ 306	Rick Reuschel	.05	.02	.00
☐ 307	Sparky Anderson MGR (checklist back)	.07	.02	.00
☐ 308	John Wathan	.03	.01	.00
☐ 309	Mike Witt	.10	.04	.01
☐ 310	Manny Trillo	.05	.02	.00
☐ 311	Jim Gott	.03	.01	.00
☐ 312	Marc Hill	.03	.01	.00
☐ 313	Dave Schmidt	.03	.01	.00
☐ 314	Ron Oester	.05	.02	.00
☐ 315	Doug Sisk	.05	.02	.00
☐ 316	John Lowenstein	.03	.01	.00
☐ 317	Jack Lazorko	.07	.03	.01
☐ 318	Ted Simmons	.09	.04	.01
☐ 319	Jeff Jones	.03	.01	.00
☐ 320	Dale Murphy	.50	.20	.05
☐ 321	Ricky Horton	.20	.08	.02
☐ 322	Dave Stapleton	.03	.01	.00
☐ 323	Andy McGaffigan	.03	.01	.00
☐ 324	Bruce Bochy	.03	.01	.00
☐ 325	John Denny	.06	.02	.00
☐ 326	Kevin Bass	.07	.03	.01
☐ 327	Brook Jacoby	.25	.10	.02
☐ 328	Bob Shirley	.03	.01	.00
☐ 329	Ron Washington	.03	.01	.00
☐ 330	Leon Durham	.08	.03	.01
☐ 331	Bill Laskey	.03	.01	.00
☐ 332	Brian Harper	.03	.01	.00
☐ 333	Willie Hernandez	.12	.05	.01
☐ 334	Dick Howser MGR (checklist back)	.05	.01	.00
☐ 335	Bruce Benedict	.03	.01	.00
☐ 336	Rance Mulliniks	.03	.01	.00
☐ 337	Billy Sample	.03	.01	.00
☐ 338	Britt Burns	.06	.02	.00
☐ 339	Danny Heep	.03	.01	.00
☐ 340	Robin Yount	.30	.12	.03
☐ 341	Floyd Rayford	.03	.01	.00
☐ 342	Ted Power	.07	.03	.01
☐ 343	Bill Russell	.05	.02	.00
☐ 344	Dave Henderson	.05	.02	.00
☐ 345	Charlie Lea	.05	.02	.00
☐ 346	Terry Pendleton	.25	.10	.02
☐ 347	Rick Langford	.03	.01	.00
☐ 348	Bob Boone	.05	.02	.00
☐ 349	Domingo Ramos	.03	.01	.00
☐ 350	Wade Boggs	3.00	1.20	.30
☐ 351	Juan Agosto	.03	.01	.00
☐ 352	Joe Morgan	.15	.06	.01
☐ 353	Julio Solano	.07	.03	.01
☐ 354	Andre Robertson	.03	.01	.00
☐ 355	Bert Blyleven	.08	.03	.01
☐ 356	Dave Meier	.09	.04	.01
☐ 357	Rich Bordi	.03	.01	.00
☐ 358	Tony Pena	.09	.04	.01
☐ 359	Pat Sheridan	.03	.01	.00
☐ 360	Steve Carlton	.30	.12	.03
☐ 361	Alfredo Griffin	.05	.02	.00
☐ 362	Craig McMurtry	.03	.01	.00
☐ 363	Ron Hodges	.03	.01	.00
☐ 364	Richard Dotson	.05	.02	.00
☐ 365	Danny Ozark MGR (checklist back)	.05	.01	.00
☐ 366	Todd Cruz	.03	.01	.00
☐ 367	Keefe Cato	.06	.02	.00
☐ 368	Dave Bergman	.03	.01	.00
☐ 369	R.J. Reynolds	.30	.12	.03
☐ 370	Bruce Sutter	.12	.05	.01
☐ 371	Mickey Rivers	.05	.02	.00
☐ 372	Roy Howell	.03	.01	.00
☐ 373	Mike Moore	.06	.02	.00
☐ 374	Brian Downing	.05	.02	.00
☐ 375	Jeff Reardon	.07	.03	.01
☐ 376	Jeff Newman	.03	.01	.00
☐ 377	Checklist: 265-396	.07	.01	.00
☐ 378	Alan Wiggins	.06	.02	.00
☐ 379	Charles Hudson	.06	.02	.00
☐ 380	Ken Griffey	.07	.03	.01
☐ 381	Roy Smith	.06	.02	.00
☐ 382	Denny Walling	.03	.01	.00
☐ 383	Rick Lysander	.03	.01	.00
☐ 384	Jody Davis	.08	.03	.01
☐ 385	Jose DeLeon	.05	.02	.00
☐ 386	Dan Gladden	.25	.10	.02
☐ 387	Buddy Biancalana	.08	.03	.01

	MINT	VG-E	F-G			MINT	VG-E	F-G
☐ 388 Bert Roberge	.03	.01	.00	☐ 439 Junior Ortiz	.03	.01	.00
☐ 389 Rod Dedeaux OLY COA	.03	.01	.00	☐ 440 Fernando Valenzuela	.30	.12	.03
☐ 390 Sid Akins OLY	.07	.03	.01	☐ 441 Duane Walker	.03	.01	.00
☐ 391 Flavio Alfaro OLY	.07	.03	.01	☐ 442 Ken Forsch	.03	.01	.00
☐ 392 Don August OLY	.07	.03	.01	☐ 443 George Wright	.03	.01	.00
☐ 393 Scott Bankhead OLY	.15	.06	.01	☐ 444 Tony Phillips	.03	.01	.00
☐ 394 Bob Caffrey OLY	.07	.03	.01	☐ 445 Tippy Martinez	.03	.01	.00
☐ 395 Mike Dunne OLY	.07	.03	.01	☐ 446 Jim Sundberg	.05	.02	.00
☐ 396 Gary Green OLY	.07	.03	.01	☐ 447 Jeff Lahti	.03	.01	.00
☐ 397 John Hoover OLY	.07	.03	.01	☐ 448 Derrel Thomas	.03	.01	.00
☐ 398 Shane Mack OLY	.25	.10	.02	☐ 449 Phil Bradley	1.25	.50	.12
☐ 399 John Marzano OLY	.10	.04	.01	☐ 450 Steve Garvey	.35	.14	.03
☐ 400 Oddibe McDowell OLY	1.50	.60	.15	☐ 451 Bruce Hurst	.07	.03	.01
☐ 401 Mark McGwire OLY	.50	.20	.05	☐ 452 John Castino	.03	.01	.00
☐ 402 Pat Pacillo OLY	.10	.04	.01	☐ 453 Tom Waddell	.12	.05	.01
☐ 403 Cory Snyder OLY	6.00	2.40	.60	☐ 454 Glenn Wilson	.10	.04	.01
☐ 404 Billy Swift OLY	.15	.06	.01	☐ 455 Bob Knepper	.08	.03	.01
☐ 405 Tom Veryzer	.03	.01	.00	☐ 456 Tim Foli	.03	.01	.00
☐ 406 Len Whitehouse	.03	.01	.00	☐ 457 Cecilio Guante	.03	.01	.00
☐ 407 Bobby Ramos	.03	.01	.00	☐ 458 Randy Johnson	.03	.01	.00
☐ 408 Sid Monge	.03	.01	.00	☐ 459 Charlie Leibrandt	.06	.02	.00
☐ 409 Brad Wellman	.03	.01	.00	☐ 460 Ryne Sandberg	.45	.18	.04
☐ 410 Bob Horner	.15	.06	.01	☐ 461 Marty Castillo	.03	.01	.00
☐ 411 Bobby Cox MGR	.05	.01	.00	☐ 462 Gary Lavelle	.05	.02	.00
(checklist back)				☐ 463 Dave Collins	.05	.02	.00
☐ 412 Bud Black	.03	.01	.00	☐ 464 Mike Mason	.10	.04	.01
☐ 413 Vance Law	.03	.01	.00	☐ 465 Bob Grich	.06	.02	.00
☐ 414 Gary Ward	.05	.02	.00	☐ 466 Tony LaRussa MGR	.05	.01	.00
☐ 415 Ron Darling	1.00	.40	.10	(checklist back)			
☐ 416 Wayne Gross	.03	.01	.00	☐ 467 Ed Lynch	.03	.01	.00
☐ 417 John Franco	.35	.14	.03	☐ 468 Wayne Krenchicki	.03	.01	.00
☐ 418 Ken Landreaux	.05	.02	.00	☐ 469 Sammy Stewart	.03	.01	.00
☐ 419 Mike Caldwell	.05	.02	.00	☐ 470 Steve Sax	.12	.05	.01
☐ 420 Andre Dawson	.20	.08	.02	☐ 471 Pete Ladd	.03	.01	.00
☐ 421 Dave Rucker	.03	.01	.00	☐ 472 Jim Essian	.03	.01	.00
☐ 422 Carney Lansford	.08	.03	.01	☐ 473 Tim Wallach	.07	.03	.01
☐ 423 Barry Bonnell	.03	.01	.00	☐ 474 Kurt Kepshire	.08	.03	.01
☐ 424 Al Nipper	.20	.08	.02	☐ 475 Andre Thornton	.07	.03	.01
☐ 425 Mike Hargrove	.05	.02	.00	☐ 476 Jeff Stone	.15	.06	.01
☐ 426 Vern Ruhle	.03	.01	.00	☐ 477 Bob Ojeda	.09	.04	.01
☐ 427 Mario Ramirez	.03	.01	.00	☐ 478 Kurt Bevacqua	.03	.01	.00
☐ 428 Larry Andersen	.03	.01	.00	☐ 479 Mike Madden	.03	.01	.00
☐ 429 Rick Cerone	.03	.01	.00	☐ 480 Lou Whitaker	.12	.05	.01
☐ 430 Ron Davis	.03	.01	.00	☐ 481 Dale Murray	.03	.01	.00
☐ 431 U.L. Washington	.03	.01	.00	☐ 482 Harry Spilman	.03	.01	.00
☐ 432 Thad Bosley	.03	.01	.00	☐ 483 Mike Smithson	.05	.02	.00
☐ 433 Jim Morrison	.03	.01	.00	☐ 484 Larry Bowa	.08	.03	.01
☐ 434 Gene Richards	.03	.01	.00	☐ 485 Matt Young	.05	.02	.00
☐ 435 Dan Petry	.09	.04	.01	☐ 486 Steve Balboni	.05	.02	.00
☐ 436 Willie Aikens	.05	.02	.00	☐ 487 Frank Williams	.10	.04	.01
☐ 437 Al Jones	.07	.03	.01	☐ 488 Joel Skinner	.07	.03	.01
☐ 438 Joe Torre MGR	.07	.02	.00	☐ 489 Bryan Clark	.03	.01	.00
(checklist back)				☐ 490 Jason Thompson	.05	.02	.00

	MINT	VG-E	F-G
☐ 491 Rick Camp	.03	.01	.00
☐ 492 Dave Johnson MGR (checklist back)	.07	.02	.00
☐ 493 Orel Hershiser	2.00	.80	.20
☐ 494 Rich Dauer	.03	.01	.00
☐ 495 Mario Soto	.07	.03	.01
☐ 496 Donnie Scott	.05	.02	.00
☐ 497 Gary Pettis (photo actually Gary's little brother, Lynn)	.35	.14	.03
☐ 498 Ed Romero	.03	.01	.00
☐ 499 Danny Cox	.15	.06	.01
☐ 500 Mike Schmidt	.35	.14	.03
☐ 501 Dan Schatzeder	.03	.01	.00
☐ 502 Rick Miller	.03	.01	.00
☐ 503 Tim Conroy	.03	.01	.00
☐ 504 Jerry Willard	.05	.02	.00
☐ 505 Jim Beattie	.03	.01	.00
☐ 506 Franklin Stubbs	1.00	.40	.10
☐ 507 Ray Fontenot	.03	.01	.00
☐ 508 John Shelby	.03	.01	.00
☐ 509 Milt May	.03	.01	.00
☐ 510 Kent Hrbek	.30	.12	.03
☐ 511 Lee Smith	.08	.03	.01
☐ 512 Tom Brookens	.03	.01	.00
☐ 513 Lynn Jones	.03	.01	.00
☐ 514 Jeff Cornell	.07	.03	.01
☐ 515 Dave Concepcion	.07	.03	.01
☐ 516 Roy Lee Jackson	.03	.01	.00
☐ 517 Jerry Martin	.03	.01	.00
☐ 518 Chris Chambliss	.05	.02	.00
☐ 519 Doug Rader MGR (checklist back)	.05	.01	.00
☐ 520 LaMarr Hoyt	.07	.03	.01
☐ 521 Rick Dempsey	.05	.02	.00
☐ 522 Paul Molitor	.09	.04	.01
☐ 523 Candy Maldonado	.07	.03	.01
☐ 524 Rob Wilfong	.03	.01	.00
☐ 525 Darrell Porter	.05	.02	.00
☐ 526 Dave Palmer	.05	.02	.00
☐ 527 Checklist: 397-528	.07	.01	.00
☐ 528 Bill Krueger	.03	.01	.00
☐ 529 Rich Gedman	.08	.03	.01
☐ 530 Dave Dravecky	.05	.02	.00
☐ 531 Joe Lefebvre	.03	.01	.00
☐ 532 Frank DiPino	.03	.01	.00
☐ 533 Tony Bernazard	.05	.02	.00
☐ 534 Brian Dayett	.06	.02	.00
☐ 535 Pat Putnam	.03	.01	.00
☐ 536 Kirby Puckett	6.00	2.40	.60
☐ 537 Don Robinson	.05	.02	.00
☐ 538 Keith Moreland	.06	.02	.00

	MINT	VG-E	F-G
☐ 539 Aurelio Lopez	.03	.01	.00
☐ 540 Claudell Washington	.06	.02	.00
☐ 541 Mark Davis	.03	.01	.00
☐ 542 Don Slaught	.03	.01	.00
☐ 543 Mike Squires	.03	.01	.00
☐ 544 Bruce Kison	.03	.01	.00
☐ 545 Lloyd Moseby	.10	.04	.01
☐ 546 Brent Gaff	.03	.01	.00
☐ 547 Pete Rose MGR (checklist back)	.45	.15	.03
☐ 548 Larry Parrish	.06	.02	.00
☐ 549 Mike Scioscia	.05	.02	.00
☐ 550 Scott McGregor	.06	.02	.00
☐ 551 Andy Van Slyke	.06	.02	.00
☐ 552 Chris Codiroli	.03	.01	.00
☐ 553 Bob Clark	.03	.01	.00
☐ 554 Doug Flynn	.03	.01	.00
☐ 555 Bob Stanley	.05	.02	.00
☐ 556 Sixto Lezcano	.03	.01	.00
☐ 557 Len Barker	.05	.02	.00
☐ 558 Carmelo Martinez	.07	.03	.01
☐ 559 Jay Howell	.06	.02	.00
☐ 560 Bill Madlock	.10	.04	.01
☐ 561 Darryl Motley	.03	.01	.00
☐ 562 Houston Jimenez	.03	.01	.00
☐ 563 Dick Ruthven	.03	.01	.00
☐ 564 Alan Ashby	.03	.01	.00
☐ 565 Kirk Gibson	.20	.08	.02
☐ 566 Ed VandeBerg	.03	.01	.00
☐ 567 Joel Youngblood	.03	.01	.00
☐ 568 Cliff Johnson	.03	.01	.00
☐ 569 Ken Oberkfell	.03	.01	.00
☐ 570 Darryl Strawberry	1.00	.40	.10
☐ 571 Charlie Hough	.06	.02	.00
☐ 572 Tom Paciorek	.03	.01	.00
☐ 573 Jay Tibbs	.20	.08	.02
☐ 574 Joe Altobelli MGR (checklist back)	.05	.01	.00
☐ 575 Pedro Guerrero	.20	.08	.02
☐ 576 Jaime Cocanower	.07	.03	.01
☐ 577 Chris Speier	.03	.01	.00
☐ 578 Terry Francona	.05	.02	.00
☐ 579 Ron Romanick	.25	.10	.02
☐ 580 Dwight Evans	.10	.04	.01
☐ 581 Mark Wagner	.03	.01	.00
☐ 582 Ken Phelps	.05	.02	.00
☐ 583 Bobby Brown	.03	.01	.00
☐ 584 Kevin Gross	.03	.01	.00
☐ 585 Butch Wynegar	.05	.02	.00
☐ 586 Bill Scherrer	.03	.01	.00
☐ 587 Doug Frobel	.05	.02	.00
☐ 588 Bobby Castillo	.03	.01	.00
☐ 589 Bob Dernier	.05	.02	.00

		MINT	VG-E	F-G			MINT	VG-E	F-G
☐ 590	Ray Knight	.07	.03	.01	☐ 641	Rod Scurry	.03	.01	.00
☐ 591	Larry Herndon	.05	.02	.00	☐ 642	Dave Owen	.06	.02	.00
☐ 592	Jeff Robinson	.10	.04	.01	☐ 643	Johnny Grubb	.03	.01	.00
☐ 593	Rick Leach	.03	.01	.00	☐ 644	Mark Huismann	.06	.02	.00
☐ 594	Curt Wilkerson	.05	.02	.00	☐ 645	Damaso Garcia	.07	.03	.01
☐ 595	Larry Gura	.05	.02	.00	☐ 646	Scot Thompson	.03	.01	.00
☐ 596	Jerry Hairston	.03	.01	.00	☐ 647	Rafael Ramirez	.03	.01	.00
☐ 597	Brad Lesley	.03	.01	.00	☐ 648	Bob Jones	.03	.01	.00
☐ 598	Jose Oquendo	.03	.01	.00	☐ 649	Sid Fernandez	1.00	.40	.10
☐ 599	Storm Davis	.06	.02	.00	☐ 650	Greg Luzinski	.09	.04	.01
☐ 600	Pete Rose	1.00	.40	.10	☐ 651	Jeff Russell	.03	.01	.00
☐ 601	Tom Lasorda MGR	.07	.02	.00	☐ 652	Joe Nolan	.03	.01	.00
	(checklist back)				☐ 653	Mark Brouhard	.03	.01	.00
☐ 602	Jeff Dedmon	.08	.03	.01	☐ 654	Dave Anderson	.03	.01	.00
☐ 603	Rick Manning	.03	.01	.00	☐ 655	Joaquin Andujar	.08	.03	.01
☐ 604	Daryl Sconiers	.03	.01	.00	☐ 656	Chuck Cottier MGR	.05	.01	.00
☐ 605	Ozzie Smith	.10	.04	.01		(checklist back)			
☐ 606	Rich Gale	.03	.01	.00	☐ 657	Jim Slaton	.03	.01	.00
☐ 607	Bill Almon	.03	.01	.00	☐ 658	Mike Stenhouse	.05	.02	.00
☐ 608	Craig Lefferts	.03	.01	.00	☐ 659	Checklist: 529-660	.07	.01	.00
☐ 609	Broderick Perkins	.03	.01	.00	☐ 660	Tony Gwynn	.40	.16	.04
☐ 610	Jack Morris	.15	.06	.01	☐ 661	Steve Crawford	.03	.01	.00
☐ 611	Ozzie Virgil	.06	.02	.00	☐ 662	Mike Heath	.03	.01	.00
☐ 612	Mike Armstrong	.05	.02	.00	☐ 663	Luis Aguayo	.03	.01	.00
☐ 613	Terry Puhl	.05	.02	.00	☐ 664	Steve Farr	.09	.04	.01
☐ 614	Al Williams	.03	.01	.00	☐ 665	Don Mattingly	8.00	3.25	.80
☐ 615	Marvell Wynne	.03	.01	.00	☐ 666	Mike LaCoss	.03	.01	.00
☐ 616	Scott Sanderson	.03	.01	.00	☐ 667	Dave Engle	.03	.01	.00
☐ 617	Willie Wilson	.15	.06	.01	☐ 668	Steve Trout	.03	.01	.00
☐ 618	Pete Falcone	.03	.01	.00	☐ 669	Lee Lacy	.05	.02	.00
☐ 619	Jeff Leonard	.06	.02	.00	☐ 670	Tom Seaver	.25	.10	.02
☐ 620	Dwight Gooden	8.00	3.25	.80	☐ 671	Dane Iorg	.03	.01	.00
☐ 621	Marvis Foley	.03	.01	.00	☐ 672	Juan Berenguer	.03	.01	.00
☐ 622	Luis Leal	.03	.01	.00	☐ 673	Buck Martinez	.03	.01	.00
☐ 623	Greg Walker	.10	.04	.01	☐ 674	Atlee Hammaker	.03	.01	.00
☐ 624	Benny Ayala	.03	.01	.00	☐ 675	Tony Perez	.10	.04	.01
☐ 625	Mark Langston	.40	.16	.04	☐ 676	Albert Hall	.08	.03	.01
☐ 626	German Rivera	.10	.04	.01	☐ 677	Wally Backman	.06	.02	.00
☐ 627	Eric Davis	7.00	2.80	.70	☐ 678	Joe McLaughlin	.03	.01	.00
☐ 628	Rene Lachemann MGR	.05	.01	.00	☐ 679	Bob Kearney	.03	.01	.00
	(checklist back)				☐ 680	Jerry Reuss	.05	.02	.00
☐ 629	Dick Schofield	.10	.04	.01	☐ 681	Ben Oglivie	.05	.02	.00
☐ 630	Tim Raines	.20	.08	.02	☐ 682	Doug Corbett	.03	.01	.00
☐ 631	Bob Forsch	.06	.02	.00	☐ 683	Whitey Herzog MGR	.05	.01	.00
☐ 632	Bruce Bochte	.05	.02	.00		(checklist back)			
☐ 633	Glenn Hoffman	.03	.01	.00	☐ 684	Bill Doran	.08	.03	.01
☐ 634	Bill Dawley	.03	.01	.00	☐ 685	Bill Caudill	.05	.02	.00
☐ 635	Terry Kennedy	.07	.03	.01	☐ 686	Mike Easler	.06	.02	.00
☐ 636	Shane Rawley	.06	.02	.00	☐ 687	Bill Gullickson	.05	.02	.00
☐ 637	Brett Butler	.08	.03	.01	☐ 688	Len Matuszek	.03	.01	.00
☐ 638	Mike Pagliarulo	1.50	.60	.15	☐ 689	Luis DeLeon	.03	.01	.00
☐ 639	Ed Hodge	.06	.02	.00	☐ 690	Alan Trammell	.15	.06	.01
☐ 640	Steve Henderson	.03	.01	.00	☐ 691	Dennis Rasmussen	.20	.08	.02

	MINT	VG-E	F-G
☐ 692 Randy Bush	.03	.01	.00
☐ 693 Tim Stoddard	.03	.01	.00
☐ 694 Joe Carter	1.25	.50	.12
☐ 695 Rick Rhoden	.07	.03	.01
☐ 696 John Rabb	.03	.01	.00
☐ 697 Onix Concepcion	.03	.01	.00
☐ 698 Jorge Bell	.12	.05	.01
☐ 699 Donnie Moore	.05	.02	.00
☐ 700 Eddie Murray	.40	.16	.04
☐ 701 Eddie Murray AS	.25	.10	.02
☐ 702 Damaso Garcia AS	.05	.02	.00
☐ 703 George Brett AS	.25	.10	.02
☐ 704 Cal Ripken AS	.25	.10	.02
☐ 705 Dave Winfield AS	.20	.08	.02
☐ 706 Rickey Henderson AS	.25	.10	.02
☐ 707 Tony Armas AS	.06	.02	.00
☐ 708 Lance Parrish AS	.12	.05	.01
☐ 709 Mike Boddicker AS	.06	.02	.00
☐ 710 Frank Viola AS	.06	.02	.00
☐ 711 Dan Quisenberry AS	.12	.05	.01
☐ 712 Keith Hernandez AS	.15	.06	.01
☐ 713 Ryne Sandberg AS	.20	.08	.02
☐ 714 Mike Schmidt AS	.25	.10	.02
☐ 715 Ozzie Smith AS	.07	.03	.01
☐ 716 Dale Murphy AS	.25	.10	.02
☐ 717 Tony Gwynn AS	.20	.08	.02
☐ 718 Jeff Leonard AS	.06	.02	.00
☐ 719 Gary Carter AS	.20	.08	.02
☐ 720 Rick Sutcliffe AS	.08	.03	.01
☐ 721 Bob Knepper AS	.06	.02	.00
☐ 722 Bruce Sutter AS	.09	.04	.01
☐ 723 Dave Stewart	.03	.01	.00
☐ 724 Oscar Gamble	.03	.01	.00
☐ 725 Floyd Bannister	.05	.02	.00
☐ 726 Al Bumbry	.03	.01	.00
☐ 727 Frank Pastore	.03	.01	.00
☐ 728 Bob Bailor	.03	.01	.00
☐ 729 Don Sutton	.15	.06	.01
☐ 730 Dave Kingman	.12	.05	.01
☐ 731 Neil Allen	.05	.02	.00
☐ 732 John McNamara MGR	.05	.01	.00
(checklist back)			
☐ 733 Tony Scott	.03	.01	.00
☐ 734 John Henry Johnson	.03	.01	.00
☐ 735 Garry Templeton	.08	.03	.01
☐ 736 Jerry Mumphrey	.05	.02	.00
☐ 737 Bo Diaz	.05	.02	.00
☐ 738 Omar Moreno	.03	.01	.00
☐ 739 Ernie Camacho	.03	.01	.00
☐ 740 Jack Clark	.10	.04	.01
☐ 741 John Butcher	.03	.01	.00
☐ 742 Ron Hassey	.03	.01	.00
☐ 743 Frank White	.06	.02	.00

	MINT	VG-E	F-G
☐ 744 Doug Bair	.03	.01	.00
☐ 745 Buddy Bell	.09	.04	.01
☐ 746 Jim Clancy	.03	.01	.00
☐ 747 Alex Trevino	.03	.01	.00
☐ 748 Lee Mazzilli	.05	.02	.00
☐ 749 Julio Cruz	.03	.01	.00
☐ 750 Rollie Fingers	.15	.06	.01
☐ 751 Kelvin Chapman	.08	.03	.01
☐ 752 Bob Owchinko	.03	.01	.00
☐ 753 Greg Brock	.06	.02	.00
☐ 754 Larry Milbourne	.03	.01	.00
☐ 755 Ken Singleton	.08	.03	.01
☐ 756 Rob Picciolo	.03	.01	.00
☐ 757 Willie McGee	.35	.14	.03
☐ 758 Ray Burris	.03	.01	.00
☐ 759 Jim Fanning MGR	.05	.01	.00
(checklist back)			
☐ 760 Nolan Ryan	.35	.14	.03
☐ 761 Jerry Remy	.03	.01	.00
☐ 762 Eddie Whitson	.05	.02	.00
☐ 763 Kiko Garcia	.03	.01	.00
☐ 764 Jamie Easterly	.03	.01	.00
☐ 765 Willie Randolph	.05	.02	.00
☐ 766 Paul Mirabella	.03	.01	.00
☐ 767 Darrell Brown	.03	.01	.00
☐ 768 Ron Cey	.08	.03	.01
☐ 769 Joe Cowley	.05	.02	.00
☐ 770 Carlton Fisk	.12	.05	.01
☐ 771 Geoff Zahn	.03	.01	.00
☐ 772 Johnnie LeMaster	.03	.01	.00
☐ 773 Hal McRae	.05	.02	.00
☐ 774 Dennis Lamp	.03	.01	.00
☐ 775 Mookie Wilson	.06	.02	.00
☐ 776 Jerry Royster	.03	.01	.00
☐ 777 Ned Yost	.03	.01	.00
☐ 778 Mike Davis	.06	.02	.00
☐ 779 Nick Esasky	.06	.02	.00
☐ 780 Mike Flanagan	.07	.03	.01
☐ 781 Jim Gantner	.05	.02	.00
☐ 782 Tom Niedenfuer	.06	.02	.00
☐ 783 Mike Jorgensen	.03	.01	.00
☐ 784 Checklist: 661-792	.07	.01	.00
☐ 785 Tony Armas	.09	.04	.01
☐ 786 Enos Cabell	.03	.01	.00
☐ 787 Jim Wohlford	.03	.01	.00
☐ 788 Steve Comer	.03	.01	.00
☐ 789 Luis Salazar	.03	.01	.00
☐ 790 Ron Guidry	.15	.06	.01
☐ 791 Ivan DeJesus	.03	.01	.00
☐ 792 Darrell Evans	.12	.05	.01

1985 Topps Traded

*The cards in this 132-card set measure 2½"
by 3½". In its now standard procedure,
Topps issued its Traded (or extended) set for
the fifth year in a row. Because all photos and
statistics of its regular set were
developed during the fall and winter months
of the preceding year, players who changed
teams during the fall, winter, and spring
months are portrayed in the 1985 regular issue set with the teams they were with in 1984.
The Traded set amends the shortcomings of
the regular set by presenting the players with
their proper teams for the current year. Rookies not contained in the regular set are also
picked up in the Traded set. Again this year,
the Topps affiliate in Ireland printed the
cards, and the cards were available through
hobby channels only.*

		MINT	VG-E	F-G
	Complete Set	14.00	5.75	1.40
	Common Player	.06	.02	.00
☐	1 T Don Aase	.10	.04	.01
☐	2 T Bill Almon	.06	.02	.00
☐	3 T Benny Ayala	.06	.02	.00
☐	4 T Dusty Baker	.10	.04	.01
☐	5 T G.Bamberger MGR	.10	.04	.01
☐	6 T Dale Berra	.10	.04	.01
☐	7 T Rich Bordi	.06	.02	.00
☐	8 T Daryl Boston	.25	.10	.02
☐	9 T Hubie Brooks	.25	.10	.02
☐	10 T Chris Brown	2.25	.90	.22
☐	11 T Tom Browning	.75	.30	.07
☐	12 T Al Bumbry	.06	.02	.00

		MINT	VG-E	F-G
☐	13 T Ray Burris	.06	.02	.00
☐	14 T Jeff Burroughs	.06	.02	.00
☐	15 T Bill Campbell	.06	.02	.00
☐	16 T Don Carman	.35	.14	.03
☐	17 T Gary Carter	.75	.30	.07
☐	18 T Bobby Castillo	.06	.02	.00
☐	19 T Bill Caudill	.10	.04	.01
☐	20 T Rick Cerone	.06	.02	.00
☐	21 T Bryan Clark	.06	.02	.00
☐	22 T Jack Clark	.25	.10	.02
☐	23 T Pat Clements	.25	.10	.02
☐	24 T Vince Coleman	4.50	1.80	.45
☐	25 T Dave Collins	.10	.04	.01
☐	26 T Danny Darwin	.06	.02	.00
☐	27 T Jim Davenport MGR	.06	.02	.00
☐	28 T Jerry Davis	.15	.06	.01
☐	29 T Brian Dayett	.06	.02	.00
☐	30 T Ivan DeJesus	.06	.02	.00
☐	31 T Ken Dixon	.25	.10	.02
☐	32 T Mariano Duncan	.75	.30	.07
☐	33 T John Felske MGR	.06	.02	.00
☐	34 T Mike Fitzgerald	.06	.02	.00
☐	35 T Ray Fontenot	.06	.02	.00
☐	36 T Greg Gagne	.20	.08	.02
☐	37 T Oscar Gamble	.10	.04	.01
☐	38 T Scott Garrelts	.35	.14	.03
☐	39 T Bob L. Gibson	.06	.02	.00
☐	40 T Jim Gott	.06	.02	.00
☐	41 T David Green	.10	.04	.01
☐	42 T Alfredo Griffin	.10	.04	.01
☐	43 T Ozzie Guillen	.75	.30	.07
☐	44 T Eddie Haas MGR	.06	.02	.00
☐	45 T Terry Harper	.06	.02	.00
☐	46 T Toby Harrah	.10	.04	.01
☐	47 T Greg Harris	.10	.04	.01
☐	48 T Ron Hassey	.06	.02	.00
☐	49 T Rickey Henderson	1.00	.40	.10
☐	50 T Steve Henderson	.06	.02	.00
☐	51 T George Hendrick	.10	.04	.01
☐	52 T Joe Hesketh	.30	.12	.03
☐	53 T Teddy Higuera	2.00	.80	.20
☐	54 T Donnie Hill	.10	.04	.01
☐	55 T Al Holland	.10	.04	.01
☐	56 T Burt Hooton	.06	.02	.00
☐	57 T Jay Howell	.10	.04	.01
☐	58 T Ken Howell	.25	.10	.02
☐	59 T LaMarr Hoyt	.15	.06	.01
☐	60 T Tim Hulett	.20	.08	.02
☐	61 T Bob James	.10	.04	.01
☐	62 T Steve Jeltz	.15	.06	.01
☐	63 T Cliff Johnson	.06	.02	.00
☐	64 T Howard Johnson	.10	.04	.01
☐	65 T Ruppert Jones	.10	.04	.01

	MINT	VG-E	F-G
☐ 66 T Steve Kemp	.10	.04	.01
☐ 67 T Bruce Kison	.06	.02	.00
☐ 68 T Alan Knicely	.06	.02	.00
☐ 69 T Mike LaCoss	.06	.02	.00
☐ 70 T Lee Lacy	.10	.04	.01
☐ 71 T Dave LaPoint	.06	.02	.00
☐ 72 T Gary Lavelle	.10	.04	.01
☐ 73 T Vance Law	.06	.02	.00
☐ 74 T Johnnie LeMaster	.06	.02	.00
☐ 75 T Sixto Lezcano	.06	.02	.00
☐ 76 T Tim Lollar	.06	.02	.00
☐ 77 T Fred Lynn	.25	.10	.02
☐ 78 T Billy Martin MGR	.15	.06	.01
☐ 79 T Ron Mathis	.15	.06	.01
☐ 80 T Len Matuszek	.06	.02	.00
☐ 81 T Gene Mauch MGR	.10	.04	.01
☐ 82 T Oddibe McDowell	1.00	.40	.10
☐ 83 T Roger McDowell	1.00	.40	.10
☐ 84 T John McNamara MGR	.10	.04	.01
☐ 85 T Donnie Moore	.10	.04	.01
☐ 86 T Gene Nelson	.06	.02	.00
☐ 87 T Steve Nicosia	.06	.02	.00
☐ 88 T Al Oliver	.20	.08	.02
☐ 89 T Joe Orsulak	.30	.12	.03
☐ 90 T Rob Picciolo	.06	.02	.00
☐ 91 T Chris Pittaro	.15	.06	.01
☐ 92 T Jim Presley	2.00	.80	.20
☐ 93 T Rick Reuschel	.10	.04	.01
☐ 94 T Bert Roberge	.06	.02	.00
☐ 95 T Bob Rodgers MGR	.06	.02	.00
☐ 96 T Jerry Royster	.06	.02	.00
☐ 97 T Dave Rozema	.06	.02	.00
☐ 98 T Dave Rucker	.06	.02	.00
☐ 99 T Vern Ruhle	.06	.02	.00
☐ 100 T Paul Runge	.15	.06	.01
☐ 101 T Mark Salas	.30	.12	.03
☐ 102 T Luis Salazar	.06	.02	.00
☐ 103 T Joe Sambito	.10	.04	.01
☐ 104 T Rick Schu	.25	.10	.02
☐ 105 T Donnie Scott	.06	.02	.00
☐ 106 T Larry Sheets	.50	.20	.05
☐ 107 T Don Slaught	.10	.04	.01
☐ 108 T Roy Smalley	.10	.04	.01
☐ 109 T Lonnie Smith	.10	.04	.01
☐ 110 T Nate Snell	.15	.06	.01
☐ 111 T Chris Speier	.06	.02	.00
☐ 112 T Mike Stenhouse	.10	.04	.01
☐ 113 T Tim Stoddard	.06	.02	.00
☐ 114 T Jim Sundberg	.10	.04	.01
☐ 115 T Bruce Sutter	.25	.10	.02
☐ 116 T Don Sutton	.50	.20	.05
☐ 117 T Kent Tekulve	.10	.04	.01
☐ 118 T Tom Tellman	.06	.02	.00

	MINT	VG-E	F-G
☐ 119 T Walt Terrell	.10	.04	.01
☐ 120 T Mickey Tettleton	.10	.04	.01
☐ 121 T Derrel Thomas	.06	.02	.00
☐ 122 T Rich Thompson	.10	.04	.01
☐ 123 T Alex Trevino	.06	.02	.00
☐ 124 T John Tudor	.20	.08	.02
☐ 125 T Jose Uribe	.10	.04	.01
☐ 126 T Bobby Valentine MGR	.15	.06	.01
☐ 127 T Dave Von Ohlen	.06	.02	.00
☐ 128 T U.L. Washington	.06	.02	.00
☐ 129 T Earl Weaver MGR	.15	.06	.01
☐ 130 T Eddie Whitson	.10	.04	.01
☐ 131 T Herm Winningham	.20	.08	.02
☐ 132 T Checklist 1-132	.10	.02	.00

1986 Topps

The cards in this 792-card set are standard size (2½" by 3½"). The first seven cards are a tribute to Pete Rose and his career. Cards 2-7 show small photos of Pete's Topps cards of the given years on the front with biographical information pertaining to those years on the back. The team leader cards were done differently with a simple player action shot on a white background; the player pictured is dubbed the "Dean" of that team, i.e., the player with the longest continuous service with that team. Topps again features a "Turn Back the Clock" series (401-405). Record breakers of the previous year are acknowledged on cards 201 to 207. Cards 701-722 feature All-Star selections from each league. Manager cards feature the team checklist on the reverse. Ryne Sandberg (#690) is the only player card in the set without a Topps

logo on the front of the card; this omission
was never corrected by Topps. There are two
other uncorrected errors involving misnum-
bered cards; see card numbers 51, 57, 141,
and 171 in the checklist below. The backs of
all the cards have a distinctive red background. Topps also printed cards on the bot-
toms of their wax pack boxes; there are four
different boxes, each with four cards. These
sixteen cards ("numbered" A through P) are
listed at the end of the checklist below but are
not considered an integral part of the set and
are not included in the complete set price
below.

	MINT	VG-E	F-G
Complete Set	24.00	10.00	2.40
Common Player	.03	.01	.00
1 Pete Rose	.85	.20	.04
2 Rose Special: '63-'66	.25	.10	.02
3 Rose Special: '67-'70	.25	.10	.02
4 Rose Special: '71-'74	.25	.10	.02
5 Rose Special: '75-'78	.25	.10	.02
6 Rose Special: '79-'82	.25	.10	.02
7 Rose Special: '83-'85	.25	.10	.02
8 Dwayne Murphy	.05	.02	.00
9 Roy Smith	.03	.01	.00
10 Tony Gwynn	.25	.10	.02
11 Bob Ojeda	.08	.03	.01
12 Jose Uribe	.08	.03	.01
13 Bob Kearney	.03	.01	.00
14 Julio Cruz	.03	.01	.00
15 Eddie Whitson	.05	.02	.00
16 Rick Schu	.06	.02	.00
17 Mike Stenhouse	.03	.01	.00
18 Brent Gaff	.03	.01	.00
19 Rich Hebner	.03	.01	.00
20 Lou Whitaker	.12	.05	.01
21 G.Bamberger MGR (checklist back)	.05	.01	.00
22 Duane Walker	.03	.01	.00
23 Manny Lee	.10	.04	.01
24 Len Barker	.05	.02	.00
25 Willie Wilson	.15	.06	.01
26 Frank DiPino	.03	.01	.00
27 Ray Knight	.08	.03	.01
28 Eric Davis	1.00	.40	.10
29 Tony Phillips	.03	.01	.00
30 Eddie Murray	.35	.14	.03
31 Jamie Easterly	.03	.01	.00
32 Steve Yeager	.05	.02	.00
33 Jeff Lahti	.03	.01	.00
34 Ken Phelps	.03	.01	.00
35 Jeff Reardon	.06	.02	.00
36 Tigers Leaders Lance Parrish	.12	.05	.01
37 Mark Thurmond	.05	.02	.00
38 Glenn Hoffman	.03	.01	.00
39 Dave Rucker	.03	.01	.00
40 Ken Griffey	.06	.02	.00
41 Brad Wellman	.03	.01	.00
42 Geoff Zahn	.03	.01	.00
43 Dave Engle	.03	.01	.00
44 Lance McCullers	.25	.10	.02
45 Damaso Garcia	.07	.03	.01
46 Billy Hatcher	.06	.02	.00
47 Juan Berenguer	.03	.01	.00
48 Bill Almon	.03	.01	.00
49 Rick Manning	.03	.01	.00
50 Dan Quisenberry	.14	.06	.01
51 Bobby Wine MGR ERR (checklist back) (number of card on back is actually 57)	.08	.02	.00
52 Chris Welsh	.03	.01	.00
53 Len Dykstra	1.50	.60	.15
54 John Franco	.09	.04	.01
55 Fred Lynn	.15	.06	.01
56 Tom Niedenfuer	.06	.02	.00
57 Bill Doran (see also 51)	.10	.04	.01
58 Bill Krueger	.03	.01	.00
59 Andre Thornton	.06	.02	.00
60 Dwight Evans	.10	.04	.01
61 Karl Best	.10	.04	.01
62 Bob Boone	.05	.02	.50
63 Ron Roenicke	.03	.01	.00
64 Floyd Bannister	.06	.02	.00
65 Dan Driessen	.03	.01	.00
66 Cardinals Leaders Bob Forsch	.05	.02	.00
67 Carmelo Martinez	.05	.02	.00
68 Ed Lynch	.03	.01	.00
69 Luis Aguayo	.03	.01	.00
70 Dave Winfield	.30	.12	.03
71 Ken Schrom	.05	.02	.00
72 Shawon Dunston	.10	.04	.01
73 Randy O'Neal	.05	.02	.00
74 Rance Mulliniks	.03	.01	.00
75 Jose DeLeon	.05	.02	.00
76 Dion James	.05	.02	.00
77 Charlie Leibrandt	.06	.02	.00
78 Bruce Benedict	.03	.01	.00
79 Dave Schmidt	.03	.01	.00

		MINT	VG-E	F-G
☐ 80	Darryl Strawberry	.40	.16	.04
☐ 81	Gene Mauch MGR	.05	.01	.00
	(checklist back)			
☐ 82	Tippy Martinez	.03	.01	.00
☐ 83	Phil Garner	.05	.02	.00
☐ 84	Curt Young	.03	.01	.00
☐ 85	Tony Perez	.10	.04	.01
☐ 86	Tom Waddell	.03	.01	.00
☐ 87	Candy Maldonado	.07	.03	.01
☐ 88	Tom Nieto	.03	.01	.00
☐ 89	Randy St.Claire	.05	.02	.00
☐ 90	Garry Templeton	.08	.03	.01
☐ 91	Steve Crawford	.03	.01	.00
☐ 92	Al Cowens	.05	.02	.00
☐ 93	Scot Thompson	.03	.01	.00
☐ 94	Rich Bordi	.03	.01	.00
☐ 95	Ozzie Virgil	.05	.02	.00
☐ 96	Blue Jays Leaders	.05	.02	.00
	Jim Clancy			
☐ 97	Gary Gaetti	.08	.03	.01
☐ 98	Dick Ruthven	.03	.01	.00
☐ 99	Buddy Biancalana	.03	.01	.00
☐ 100	Nolan Ryan	.35	.14	.03
☐ 101	Dave Bergman	.03	.01	.00
☐ 102	Joe Orsulak	.25	.10	.02
☐ 103	Luis Salazar	.03	.01	.00
☐ 104	Sid Fernandez	.20	.08	.02
☐ 105	Gary Ward	.06	.02	.00
☐ 106	Ray Burris	.03	.01	.00
☐ 107	Rafael Ramirez	.03	.01	.00
☐ 108	Ted Power	.07	.03	.01
☐ 109	Len Matuszek	.03	.01	.00
☐ 110	Scott McGregor	.07	.03	.01
☐ 111	Roger Craig MGR	.05	.01	.00
	(checklist back)			
☐ 112	Bill Campbell	.03	.01	.00
☐ 113	U.L. Washington	.03	.01	.00
☐ 114	Mike Brown	.03	.01	.00
☐ 115	Jay Howell	.05	.02	.00
☐ 116	Brook Jacoby	.10	.04	.01
☐ 117	Bruce Kison	.03	.01	.00
☐ 118	Jerry Royster	.03	.01	.00
☐ 119	Barry Bonnell	.03	.01	.00
☐ 120	Steve Carlton	.30	.12	.03
☐ 121	Nelson Simmons	.15	.06	.01
☐ 122	Pete Filson	.03	.01	.00
☐ 123	Greg Walker	.10	.04	.01
☐ 124	Luis Sanchez	.03	.01	.00
☐ 125	Dave Lopes	.06	.02	.00
☐ 126	Mets Leaders	.05	.02	.00
	Mookie Wilson			
☐ 127	Jack Howell	.35	.14	.03
☐ 128	John Wathan	.03	.01	.00
☐ 129	Jeff Dedmon	.03	.01	.00
☐ 130	Alan Trammell	.15	.06	.01
☐ 131	Checklist: 1-132	.06	.01	.00
☐ 132	Razor Shines	.06	.02	.00
☐ 133	Andy McGaffigan	.03	.01	.00
☐ 134	Carney Lansford	.09	.04	.01
☐ 135	Joe Niekro	.07	.03	.01
☐ 136	Mike Hargrove	.05	.02	.00
☐ 137	Charlie Moore	.03	.01	.00
☐ 138	Mark Davis	.03	.01	.00
☐ 139	Daryl Boston	.08	.03	.01
☐ 140	John Candelaria	.07	.03	.01
☐ 141	Chuck Cottier MGR	.08	.03	.01
	(checklist back)			
	(see also 171)			
☐ 142	Bob Jones	.03	.01	.00
☐ 143	Dave Van Gorder	.03	.01	.00
☐ 144	Doug Sisk	.03	.01	.00
☐ 145	Pedro Guerrero	.20	.08	.02
☐ 146	Jack Perconte	.03	.01	.00
☐ 147	Larry Sheets	.10	.04	.01
☐ 148	Mike Heath	.03	.01	.00
☐ 149	Brett Butler	.09	.04	.01
☐ 150	Joaquin Andujar	.08	.03	.01
☐ 151	Dave Stapleton	.03	.01	.00
☐ 152	Mike Morgan	.03	.01	.00
☐ 153	Ricky Adams	.03	.01	.00
☐ 154	Bert Roberge	.03	.01	.00
☐ 155	Bob Grich	.06	.02	.00
☐ 156	White Sox Leaders	.05	.02	.00
	Richard Dotson			
☐ 157	Ron Hassey	.03	.01	.00
☐ 158	Derrel Thomas	.03	.01	.00
☐ 159	Orel Hershiser	.35	.14	.03
☐ 160	Chet Lemon	.05	.02	.00
☐ 161	Lee Tunnell	.03	.01	.00
☐ 162	Greg Gagne	.05	.02	.00
☐ 163	Pete Ladd	.03	.01	.00
☐ 164	Steve Balboni	.06	.02	.00
☐ 165	Mike Davis	.06	.02	.00
☐ 166	Dickie Thon	.05	.02	.00
☐ 167	Zane Smith	.06	.02	.00
☐ 168	Jeff Burroughs	.03	.01	.00
☐ 169	George Wright	.03	.01	.00
☐ 170	Gary Carter	.30	.12	.03
☐ 171	Bob Rodgers MGR ERR	.10	.04	.01
	(checklist back)			
	(number of card on			
	back actually 141)			
☐ 172	Jerry Reed	.09	.04	.01
☐ 173	Wayne Gross	.03	.01	.00
☐ 174	Brian Snyder	.10	.04	.01
☐ 175	Steve Sax	.12	.05	.01

	MINT	VG-E	F-G
☐ 176 Jay Tibbs	.03	.01	.00
☐ 177 Joel Youngblood	.03	.01	.00
☐ 178 Ivan DeJesus	.03	.01	.00
☐ 179 Stu Cliburn	.15	.06	.01
☐ 180 Don Mattingly	3.50	1.50	.30
☐ 181 Al Nipper	.03	.01	.00
☐ 182 Bobby Brown	.03	.01	.00
☐ 183 Larry Andersen	.03	.01	.00
☐ 184 Tim Laudner	.03	.01	.00
☐ 185 Rollie Fingers	.15	.06	.01
☐ 186 Astros Leaders	.07	.03	.01
Jose Cruz			
☐ 187 Scott Fletcher	.05	.02	.00
☐ 188 Bob Dernier	.03	.01	.00
☐ 189 Mike Mason	.03	.01	.00
☐ 190 George Hendrick	.06	.02	.00
☐ 191 Wally Backman	.06	.02	.00
☐ 192 Milt Wilcox	.03	.01	.00
☐ 193 Daryl Sconiers	.03	.01	.00
☐ 194 Craig McMurtry	.03	.01	.00
☐ 195 Dave Concepcion	.07	.03	.01
☐ 196 Doyle Alexander	.05	.02	.00
☐ 197 Enos Cabell	.03	.01	.00
☐ 198 Ken Dixon	.06	.02	.00
☐ 199 Dick Howser MGR	.05	.01	.00
(checklist back)			
☐ 200 Mike Schmidt	.40	.16	.04
☐ 201 RB: Vince Coleman	.25	.10	.02
Most stolen bases,			
season, rookie			
☐ 202 RB: Dwight Gooden	.50	.20	.05
Youngest 20 game			
winner			
☐ 203 RB: Keith Hernandez	.15	.06	.01
Most game winning			
RBI's			
☐ 204 RB: Phil Niekro	.12	.05	.01
Oldest shutout			
pitcher			
☐ 205 RB: Tony Perez	.08	.03	.01
Oldest grand slammer			
☐ 206 RB: Pete Rose	.40	.16	.04
Most hits, lifetime			
☐ 207 RB: Fern.Valenzuela	.15	.06	.01
Most cons. innings,			
start of season,			
no earned runs			
☐ 208 Ramon Romero	.08	.03	.01
☐ 209 Randy Ready	.06	.02	.00
☐ 210 Calvin Schiraldi	.15	.06	.01
☐ 211 Ed Wojna	.10	.04	.01
☐ 212 Chris Speier	.03	.01	.00
☐ 213 Bob Shirley	.03	.01	.00

	MINT	VG-E	F-G
☐ 214 Randy Bush	.03	.01	.00
☐ 215 Frank White	.06	.02	.00
☐ 216 A's Leaders	.05	.02	.00
Dwayne Murphy			
☐ 217 Bill Scherrer	.03	.01	.00
☐ 218 Randy Hunt	.08	.03	.01
☐ 219 Dennis Lamp	.03	.01	.00
☐ 220 Bob Horner	.15	.06	.01
☐ 221 Dave Henderson	.06	.02	.00
☐ 222 Craig Gerber	.08	.03	.01
☐ 223 Atlee Hammaker	.05	.02	.00
☐ 224 Cesar Cedeno	.06	.02	.00
☐ 225 Ron Darling	.20	.08	.02
☐ 226 Lee Lacy	.06	.02	.00
☐ 227 Al Jones	.03	.01	.00
☐ 228 Tom Lawless	.03	.01	.00
☐ 229 Bill Gullickson	.05	.02	.00
☐ 230 Terry Kennedy	.06	.02	.00
☐ 231 Jim Frey MGR	.05	.01	.00
(checklist back)			
☐ 232 Rick Rhoden	.07	.03	.01
☐ 233 Steve Lyons	.07	.03	.01
☐ 234 Doug Corbett	.03	.01	.00
☐ 235 Butch Wynegar	.05	.02	.00
☐ 236 Frank Eufemia	.08	.03	.01
☐ 237 Ted Simmons	.10	.04	.01
☐ 238 Larry Parrish	.06	.02	.00
☐ 239 Joel Skinner	.05	.02	.00
☐ 240 Tommy John	.10	.04	.01
☐ 241 Tony Fernandez	.10	.04	.01
☐ 242 Rich Thompson	.08	.03	.01
☐ 243 Johnny Grubb	.03	.01	.00
☐ 244 Craig Lefferts	.03	.01	.00
☐ 245 Jim Sundberg	.05	.02	.00
☐ 246 Phillies Leaders	.15	.06	.01
Steve Carlton			
☐ 247 Terry Harper	.03	.01	.00
☐ 248 Spike Owen	.05	.02	.00
☐ 249 Rob Deer	.45	.18	.04
☐ 250 Dwight Gooden	2.50	1.00	.25
☐ 251 Rich Dauer	.03	.01	.00
☐ 252 Bobby Castillo	.03	.01	.00
☐ 253 Dann Bilardello	.03	.01	.00
☐ 254 Ozzie Guillen	.45	.18	.04
☐ 255 Tony Armas	.09	.04	.01
☐ 256 Kurt Kepshire	.03	.01	.00
☐ 257 Doug DeCinces	.08	.03	.01
☐ 258 Tim Burke	.20	.08	.02
☐ 259 Dan Pasqua	.50	.20	.05
☐ 260 Tony Pena	.10	.04	.01
☐ 261 Bobby Valentine MGR	.05	.01	.00
(checklist back)			
☐ 262 Mario Ramirez	.03	.01	.00

	MINT	VG-E	F-G
☐ 263 Checklist: 133-264	.06	.01	.00
☐ 264 Darren Daulton	.20	.08	.02
☐ 265 Ron Davis	.03	.01	.00
☐ 266 Keith Moreland	.06	.02	.00
☐ 267 Paul Molitor	.09	.04	.01
☐ 268 Mike Scott	.25	.10	.02
☐ 269 Dane Iorg	.03	.01	.00
☐ 270 Jack Morris	.15	.06	.01
☐ 271 Dave Collins	.05	.02	.00
☐ 272 Tim Tolman	.08	.03	.01
☐ 273 Jerry Willard	.03	.01	.00
☐ 274 Ron Gardenhire	.03	.01	.00
☐ 275 Charlie Hough	.06	.02	.00
☐ 276 Yankees Leaders	.06	.02	.00
Willie Randolph			
☐ 277 Jaime Cocanower	.03	.01	.00
☐ 278 Sixto Lezcano	.03	.01	.00
☐ 279 Al Pardo	.10	.04	.01
☐ 280 Tim Raines	.20	.08	.02
☐ 281 Steve Mura	.03	.01	.00
☐ 282 Jerry Mumphrey	.05	.02	.00
☐ 283 Mike Fischlin	.03	.01	.00
☐ 284 Brian Dayett	.03	.01	.00
☐ 285 Buddy Bell	.09	.04	.01
☐ 286 Luis DeLeon	.03	.01	.00
☐ 287 John Christensen	.07	.03	.01
☐ 288 Don Aase	.05	.02	.00
☐ 289 Johnnie LeMaster	.03	.01	.00
☐ 290 Carlton Fisk	.12	.05	.01
☐ 291 Tom Lasorda MGR	.10	.02	.00
(checklist back)			
☐ 292 Chuck Porter	.03	.01	.00
☐ 293 Chris Chambliss	.05	.02	.00
☐ 294 Danny Cox	.09	.04	.01
☐ 295 Kirk Gibson	.20	.08	.02
☐ 296 Geno Petralli	.03	.01	.00
☐ 297 Tim Lollar	.03	.01	.00
☐ 298 Craig Reynolds	.03	.01	.00
☐ 299 Bryn Smith	.05	.02	.00
☐ 300 George Brett	.40	.16	.04
☐ 301 Dennis Rasmussen	.08	.03	.01
☐ 302 Greg Gross	.03	.01	.00
☐ 303 Curt Wardle	.08	.03	.01
☐ 304 Mike Gallego	.08	.03	.01
☐ 305 Phil Bradley	.20	.08	.02
☐ 306 Padres Leaders	.05	.02	.00
Terry Kennedy			
☐ 307 Dave Sax	.03	.01	.00
☐ 308 Ray Fontenot	.03	.01	.00
☐ 309 John Shelby	.03	.01	.00
☐ 310 Greg Minton	.05	.02	.00
☐ 311 Dick Schofield	.06	.02	.00
☐ 312 Tom Filer	.05	.02	.00

	MINT	VG-E	F-G
☐ 313 Joe DeSa	.06	.02	.00
☐ 314 Frank Pastore	.03	.01	.00
☐ 315 Mookie Wilson	.06	.02	.00
☐ 316 Sammy Khalifa	.10	.04	.01
☐ 317 Ed Romero	.03	.01	.00
☐ 318 Terry Whitfield	.03	.01	.00
☐ 319 Rick Camp	.03	.01	.00
☐ 320 Jim Rice	.30	.12	.03
☐ 321 Earl Weaver MGR	.08	.02	.00
(checklist back)			
☐ 322 Bob Forsch	.06	.02	.00
☐ 323 Jerry Davis	.06	.02	.00
☐ 324 Dan Schatzeder	.03	.01	.00
☐ 325 Juan Beniquez	.05	.02	.00
☐ 326 Kent Tekulve	.05	.02	.00
☐ 327 Mike Pagliarulo	.25	.10	.02
☐ 328 Pete O'Brien	.09	.04	.01
☐ 329 Kirby Puckett	.40	.16	.04
☐ 330 Rick Sutcliffe	.10	.04	.01
☐ 331 Alan Ashby	.03	.01	.00
☐ 332 Darryl Motley	.03	.01	.00
☐ 333 Tom Henke	.06	.02	.00
☐ 334 Ken Oberkfell	.03	.01	.00
☐ 335 Don Sutton	.15	.06	.01
☐ 336 Indians Leaders	.05	.02	.00
Andre Thornton			
☐ 337 Darnell Coles	.08	.03	.01
☐ 338 Jorge Bell	.15	.06	.01
☐ 339 Bruce Berenyi	.03	.01	.00
☐ 340 Cal Ripken	.40	.16	.04
☐ 341 Frank Williams	.03	.01	.00
☐ 342 Gary Redus	.05	.02	.00
☐ 343 Carlos Diaz	.03	.01	.00
☐ 344 Jim Wohlford	.03	.01	.00
☐ 345 Donnie Moore	.05	.02	.00
☐ 346 Bryan Little	.03	.01	.00
☐ 347 Teddy Higuera	.90	.36	.09
☐ 348 Cliff Johnson	.03	.01	.00
☐ 349 Mark Clear	.03	.01	.00
☐ 350 Jack Clark	.12	.05	.01
☐ 351 Chuck Tanner MGR	.05	.01	.00
(checklist back)			
☐ 352 Harry Spilman	.03	.01	.00
☐ 353 Keith Atherton	.03	.01	.00
☐ 354 Tony Bernazard	.05	.02	.00
☐ 355 Lee Smith	.07	.03	.01
☐ 356 Mickey Hatcher	.03	.01	.00
☐ 357 Ed VandeBerg	.03	.01	.00
☐ 358 Rick Dempsey	.05	.02	.00
☐ 359 Mike LaCoss	.03	.01	.00
☐ 360 Lloyd Moseby	.12	.05	.01
☐ 361 Shane Rawley	.07	.03	.01
☐ 362 Tom Paciorek	.03	.01	.00

	MINT	VG-E	F-G		MINT	VG-E	F-G
☐ 363 Terry Forster	.07	.03	.01	☐ 408 Dave Smith	.06	.02	.00
☐ 364 Reid Nichols	.03	.01	.00	☐ 409 Paul Runge	.09	.04	.01
☐ 365 Mike Flanagan	.07	.03	.01	☐ 410 Dave Kingman	.10	.04	.01
☐ 366 Reds Leaders	.06	.02	.00	☐ 411 Sparky Anderson MGR	.08	.02	.00
Dave Concepcion				(checklist back)			
☐ 367 Aurelio Lopez	.03	.01	.00	☐ 412 Jim Clancy	.03	.01	.00
☐ 368 Greg Brock	.06	.02	.00	☐ 413 Tim Flannery	.03	.01	.00
☐ 369 Al Holland	.03	.01	.00	☐ 414 Tom Gorman	.03	.01	.00
☐ 370 Vince Coleman	2.00	.80	.20	☐ 415 Hal McRae	.05	.02	.00
☐ 371 Bill Stein	.03	.01	.00	☐ 416 Denny Martinez	.03	.01	.00
☐ 372 Ben Oglivie	.06	.02	.00	☐ 417 R.J. Reynolds	.05	.02	.00
☐ 373 Urbano Lugo	.08	.03	.01	☐ 418 Alan Knicely	.03	.01	.00
☐ 374 Terry Francona	.05	.02	.00	☐ 419 Frank Wills	.08	.03	.01
☐ 375 Rich Gedman	.08	.03	.01	☐ 420 Von Hayes	.10	.04	.01
☐ 376 Bill Dawley	.03	.01	.00	☐ 421 Dave Palmer	.05	.02	.00
☐ 377 Joe Carter	.25	.10	.02	☐ 422 Mike Jorgensen	.03	.01	.00
☐ 378 Bruce Bochte	.05	.02	.00	☐ 423 Dan Spillner	.03	.01	.00
☐ 379 Bobby Meacham	.03	.01	.00	☐ 424 Rick Miller	.03	.01	.00
☐ 380 LaMarr Hoyt	.07	.03	.01	☐ 425 Larry McWilliams	.03	.01	.00
☐ 381 Ray Miller MGR	.05	.01	.00	☐ 426 Brewers Leaders	.05	.02	.00
(checklist back)				Charlie Moore			
☐ 382 Ivan Calderon	.25	.10	.02	☐ 427 Joe Cowley	.05	.02	.00
☐ 383 Chris Brown	1.25	.50	.12	☐ 428 Max Venable	.03	.01	.00
☐ 384 Steve Trout	.03	.01	.00	☐ 429 Greg Booker	.03	.01	.00
☐ 385 Cecil Cooper	.10	.04	.01	☐ 430 Kent Hrbek	.15	.06	.01
☐ 386 Cecil Fielder	.25	.10	.02	☐ 431 George Frazier	.03	.01	.00
☐ 387 Steve Kemp	.07	.03	.01	☐ 432 Mark Bailey	.03	.01	.00
☐ 388 Dickie Noles	.03	.01	.00	☐ 433 Chris Codiroli	.03	.01	.00
☐ 389 Glenn Davis	1.50	.60	.15	☐ 434 Curt Wilkerson	.03	.01	.00
☐ 390 Tom Seaver	.30	.12	.03	☐ 435 Bill Caudill	.05	.02	.00
☐ 391 Julio Franco	.09	.04	.01	☐ 436 Doug Flynn	.03	.01	.00
☐ 392 John Russell	.05	.02	.00	☐ 437 Rick Mahler	.03	.01	.00
☐ 393 Chris Pittaro	.08	.03	.01	☐ 438 Clint Hurdle	.03	.01	.00
☐ 394 Checklist: 265-396	.06	.01	.00	☐ 439 Rick Honeycutt	.05	.02	.00
☐ 395 Scott Garrelts	.05	.02	.00	☐ 440 Alvin Davis	.20	.08	.02
☐ 396 Red Sox Leaders	.07	.03	.01	☐ 441 Whitey Herzog MGR	.07	.01	.00
Dwight Evans				(checklist back)			
☐ 397 Steve Buechele	.25	.10	.02	☐ 442 Ron Robinson	.03	.01	.00
☐ 398 Earnie Riles	.40	.16	.04	☐ 443 Bill Buckner	.08	.03	.01
☐ 399 Bill Swift	.05	.02	.00	☐ 444 Alex Trevino	.03	.01	.00
☐ 400 Rod Carew	.30	.12	.03	☐ 445 Bert Blyleven	.09	.04	.01
☐ 401 Turn Back 5 Years	.15	.06	.01	☐ 446 Lenn Sakata	.03	.01	.00
Fern.Valenzuela '81				☐ 447 Jerry Don Gleaton	.03	.01	.00
☐ 402 Turn Back 10 Years	.15	.06	.01	☐ 448 Herm Winningham	.15	.06	.01
Tom Seaver '76				☐ 449 Rod Scurry	.03	.01	.00
☐ 403 Turn Back 15 Years	.15	.06	.01	☐ 450 Graig Nettles	.12	.05	.01
Willie Mays '71				☐ 451 Mark Brown	.08	.03	.01
☐ 404 Turn Back 20 Years	.10	.04	.01	☐ 452 Bob Clark	.06	.02	.00
Frank Robinson '66				☐ 453 Steve Jeltz	.06	.02	.00
☐ 405 Turn Back 25 Years	.15	.06	.01	☐ 454 Burt Hooton	.03	.01	.00
Roger Maris '61				☐ 455 Willie Randolph	.06	.02	.00
☐ 406 Scott Sanderson	.03	.01	.00	☐ 456 Braves Leaders	.25	.10	.02
☐ 407 Sal Butera	.03	.01	.00	Dale Murphy			

		MINT	VG-E	F-G
☐ 457	Mickey Tettleton	.09	.04	.01
☐ 458	Kevin Bass	.07	.03	.01
☐ 459	Luis Leal	.03	.01	.00
☐ 460	Leon Durham	.08	.03	.01
☐ 461	Walt Terrell	.03	.01	.00
☐ 462	Domingo Ramos	.03	.01	.00
☐ 463	Jim Gott	.03	.01	.00
☐ 464	Ruppert Jones	.03	.01	.00
☐ 465	Jesse Orosco	.05	.02	.00
☐ 466	Tom Foley	.03	.01	.00
☐ 467	Bob James	.05	.02	.00
☐ 468	Mike Scioscia	.05	.02	.00
☐ 469	Storm Davis	.07	.03	.01
☐ 470	Bill Madlock	.10	.04	.01
☐ 471	Bobby Cox MGR	.05	.01	.00
	(checklist back)			
☐ 472	Joe Hesketh	.10	.04	.01
☐ 473	Mark Brouhard	.03	.01	.00
☐ 474	John Tudor	.10	.04	.01
☐ 475	Juan Samuel	.12	.05	.01
☐ 476	Ron Mathis	.10	.04	.01
☐ 477	Mike Easler	.06	.02	.00
☐ 478	Andy Hawkins	.06	.02	.00
☐ 479	Bob Melvin	.09	.04	.01
☐ 480	Oddibe McDowell	.35	.14	.03
☐ 481	Scott Bradley	.10	.04	.01
☐ 482	Rick Lysander	.03	.01	.00
☐ 483	George Vukovich	.03	.01	.00
☐ 484	Donnie Hill	.03	.01	.00
☐ 485	Gary Matthews	.06	.02	.00
☐ 486	Angels Leaders	.05	.02	.00
	Bobby Grich			
☐ 487	Bret Saberhagen	.25	.10	.02
☐ 488	Lou Thornton	.10	.04	.01
☐ 489	Jim Winn	.03	.01	.00
☐ 490	Jeff Leonard	.06	.02	.00
☐ 491	Pascual Perez	.03	.01	.00
☐ 492	Kelvin Chapman	.03	.01	.00
☐ 493	Gene Nelson	.03	.01	.00
☐ 494	Gary Roenicke	.05	.02	.00
☐ 495	Mark Langston	.06	.02	.00
☐ 496	Jay Johnstone	.05	.02	.00
☐ 497	John Stuper	.03	.01	.00
☐ 498	Tito Landrum	.03	.01	.00
☐ 499	Bob L. Gibson	.03	.01	.00
☐ 500	Rickey Henderson	.35	.14	.03
☐ 501	Dave Johnson MGR	.08	.02	.00
	(checklist back)			
☐ 502	Glen Cook	.10	.04	.01
☐ 503	Mike Fitzgerald	.03	.01	.00
☐ 504	Denny Walling	.03	.01	.00
☐ 505	Jerry Koosman	.07	.03	.01
☐ 506	Bill Russell	.05	.02	.00

		MINT	VG-E	F-G
☐ 507	Steve Ontiveros	.20	.08	.02
☐ 508	Alan Wiggins	.06	.02	.00
☐ 509	Ernie Camacho	.03	.01	.00
☐ 510	Wade Boggs	1.50	.60	.15
☐ 511	Ed Nunez	.05	.02	.00
☐ 512	Thad Bosley	.03	.01	.00
☐ 513	Ron Washington	.03	.01	.00
☐ 514	Mike Jones	.03	.01	.00
☐ 515	Darrell Evans	.08	.03	.01
☐ 516	Giants Leaders	.05	.02	.00
	Greg Minton			
☐ 517	Milt Thompson	.20	.08	.02
☐ 518	Buck Martinez	.03	.01	.00
☐ 519	Danny Darwin	.03	.01	.00
☐ 520	Keith Hernandez	.25	.10	.02
☐ 521	Nate Snell	.10	.04	.01
☐ 522	Bob Bailor	.03	.01	.00
☐ 523	Joe Price	.03	.01	.00
☐ 524	Darrell Miller	.07	.03	.01
☐ 525	Marvell Wynne	.03	.01	.00
☐ 526	Charlie Lea	.05	.02	.00
☐ 527	Checklist: 397-528	.06	.01	.00
☐ 528	Terry Pendleton	.05	.02	.00
☐ 529	Marc Sullivan	.08	.03	.01
☐ 530	Rich Gossage	.12	.05	.01
☐ 531	Tony LaRussa MGR	.05	.01	.00
	(checklist back)			
☐ 532	Don Carman	.25	.10	.02
☐ 533	Billy Sample	.03	.01	.00
☐ 534	Jeff Calhoun	.08	.03	.01
☐ 535	Toby Harrah	.05	.02	.00
☐ 536	Jose Rijo	.07	.03	.01
☐ 537	Mark Salas	.06	.02	.00
☐ 538	Dennis Eckersley	.06	.02	.00
☐ 539	Glenn Hubbard	.03	.01	.00
☐ 540	Dan Petry	.10	.04	.01
☐ 541	Jorge Orta	.03	.01	.00
☐ 542	Don Schulze	.03	.01	.00
☐ 543	Jerry Narron	.03	.01	.00
☐ 544	Eddie Milner	.05	.02	.00
☐ 545	Jimmy Key	.10	.04	.01
☐ 546	Mariners Leaders	.05	.02	.00
	Dave Henderson			
☐ 547	Roger McDowell	.40	.16	.04
☐ 548	Mike Young	.10	.04	.01
☐ 549	Bob Welch	.06	.02	.00
☐ 550	Tom Herr	.08	.03	.01
☐ 551	Dave LaPoint	.03	.01	.00
☐ 552	Marc Hill	.03	.01	.00
☐ 553	Jim Morrison	.03	.01	.00
☐ 554	Paul Householder	.03	.01	.00
☐ 555	Hubie Brooks	.10	.04	.01
☐ 556	John Denny	.07	.03	.01

		MINT	VG-E	F-G
☐ 557	Gerald Perry	.05	.02	.00
☐ 558	Tim Stoddard	.03	.01	.00
☐ 559	Tommy Dunbar	.03	.01	.00
☐ 560	Dave Righetti	.14	.06	.01
☐ 561	Bob Lillis MGR	.05	.01	.00
	(checklist back)			
☐ 562	Joe Beckwith	.03	.01	.00
☐ 563	Alejandro Sanchez	.05	.02	.00
☐ 564	Warren Brusstar	.03	.01	.00
☐ 565	Tom Brunansky	.10	.04	.01
☐ 566	Alfredo Griffin	.05	.02	.00
☐ 567	Jeff Barkley	.08	.03	.01
☐ 568	Donnie Scott	.03	.01	.00
☐ 569	Jim Acker	.03	.01	.00
☐ 570	Rusty Staub	.08	.03	.01
☐ 571	Mike Jeffcoat	.03	.01	.00
☐ 572	Paul Zuvella	.07	.03	.01
☐ 573	Tom Hume	.03	.01	.00
☐ 574	Ron Kittle	.10	.04	.01
☐ 575	Mike Boddicker	.09	.04	.01
☐ 576	Expos Leaders	.12	.05	.01
	Andre Dawson			
☐ 577	Jerry Reuss	.06	.02	.00
☐ 578	Lee Mazzilli	.05	.02	.00
☐ 579	Jim Slaton	.03	.01	.00
☐ 580	Willie McGee	.20	.08	.02
☐ 581	Bruce Hurst	.07	.03	.01
☐ 582	Jim Gantner	.05	.02	.00
☐ 583	Al Bumbry	.03	.01	.00
☐ 584	Brian Fisher	.25	.10	.02
☐ 585	Garry Maddox	.05	.02	.00
☐ 586	Greg Harris	.05	.02	.00
☐ 587	Rafael Santana	.03	.01	.00
☐ 588	Steve Lake	.03	.01	.00
☐ 589	Sid Bream	.06	.02	.00
☐ 590	Bob Knepper	.07	.03	.01
☐ 591	Jackie Moore MGR	.05	.01	.00
	(checklist back)			
☐ 592	Frank Tanana	.05	.02	.00
☐ 593	Jesse Barfield	.15	.06	.01
☐ 594	Chris Bando	.03	.01	.00
☐ 595	Dave Parker	.20	.08	.02
☐ 596	Onix Concepcion	.03	.01	.00
☐ 597	Sammy Stewart	.03	.01	.00
☐ 598	Jim Presley	.75	.30	.07
☐ 599	Rick Aguilera	.30	.12	.03
☐ 600	Dale Murphy	.45	.18	.04
☐ 601	Gary Lucas	.03	.01	.00
☐ 602	Mariano Duncan	.45	.18	.04
☐ 603	Bill Laskey	.03	.01	.00
☐ 604	Gary Pettis	.08	.03	.01
☐ 605	Dennis Boyd	.08	.03	.01

		MINT	VG-E	F-G
☐ 606	Royals Leaders	.05	.02	.00
	Hal McRae			
☐ 607	Ken Dayley	.03	.01	.00
☐ 608	Bruce Bochy	.03	.01	.00
☐ 609	Barbaro Garbey	.03	.01	.00
☐ 610	Ron Guidry	.15	.06	.01
☐ 611	Gary Woods	.03	.01	.00
☐ 612	Richard Dotson	.06	.02	.00
☐ 613	Roy Smalley	.05	.02	.00
☐ 614	Rick Waits	.03	.01	.00
☐ 615	Johnny Ray	.09	.04	.01
☐ 616	Glenn Brummer	.03	.01	.00
☐ 617	Lonnie Smith	.06	.02	.00
☐ 618	Jim Pankovits	.05	.02	.00
☐ 619	Danny Heep	.03	.01	.00
☐ 620	Bruce Sutter	.12	.05	.01
☐ 621	John Felske MGR	.05	.01	.00
	(checklist back)			
☐ 622	Gary Lavelle	.05	.02	.00
☐ 623	Floyd Rayford	.03	.01	.00
☐ 624	Steve McCatty	.03	.01	.00
☐ 625	Bob Brenly	.05	.02	.00
☐ 626	Roy Thomas	.03	.01	.00
☐ 627	Ron Oester	.05	.02	.00
☐ 628	Kirk McCaskill	.75	.30	.07
☐ 629	Mitch Webster	.75	.30	.07
☐ 630	Fernando Valenzuela	.30	.12	.03
☐ 631	Steve Braun	.03	.01	.00
☐ 632	Dave Von Ohlen	.03	.01	.00
☐ 633	Jackie Gutierrez	.03	.01	.00
☐ 634	Roy Lee Jackson	.03	.01	.00
☐ 635	Jason Thompson	.06	.02	.00
☐ 636	Cubs Leaders	.06	.02	.00
	Lee Smith			
☐ 637	Rudy Law	.03	.01	.00
☐ 638	John Butcher	.03	.01	.00
☐ 639	Bo Diaz	.05	.02	.00
☐ 640	Jose Cruz	.09	.04	.01
☐ 641	Wayne Tolleson	.03	.01	.00
☐ 642	Ray Searage	.03	.01	.00
☐ 643	Tom Brookens	.03	.01	.00
☐ 644	Mark Gubicza	.07	.03	.01
☐ 645	Dusty Baker	.06	.02	.00
☐ 646	Mike Moore	.05	.02	.00
☐ 647	Mel Hall	.08	.03	.01
☐ 648	Steve Bedrosian	.06	.02	.00
☐ 649	Ronn Reynolds	.08	.03	.01
☐ 650	Dave Stieb	.12	.05	.01
☐ 651	Billy Martin MGR	.08	.02	.00
	(checklist back)			
☐ 652	Tom Browning	.25	.10	.02
☐ 653	Jim Dwyer	.03	.01	.00
☐ 654	Ken Howell	.08	.03	.01

		MINT	VG-E	F-G
☐ 655	Manny Trillo	.05	.02	.00
☐ 656	Brian Harper	.03	.01	.00
☐ 657	Juan Agosto	.03	.01	.00
☐ 658	Rob Wilfong	.03	.01	.00
☐ 659	Checklist: 529-660	.06	.01	.00
☐ 660	Steve Garvey	.35	.14	.03
☐ 661	Roger Clemens	2.00	.80	.20
☐ 662	Bill Schroeder	.03	.01	.00
☐ 663	Neil Allen	.05	.02	.00
☐ 664	Tim Corcoran	.03	.01	.00
☐ 665	Alejandro Pena	.06	.02	.00
☐ 666	Rangers Leaders	.05	.02	.00
	Charlie Hough			
☐ 667	Tim Teufel	.07	.03	.01
☐ 668	Cecilio Guante	.03	.01	.00
☐ 669	Ron Cey	.09	.04	.01
☐ 670	Willie Hernandez	.10	.04	.01
☐ 671	Lynn Jones	.03	.01	.00
☐ 672	Rob Picciolo	.03	.01	.00
☐ 673	Ernie Whitt	.03	.01	.00
☐ 674	Pat Tabler	.08	.03	.01
☐ 675	Claudell Washington	.06	.02	.00
☐ 676	Matt Young	.05	.02	.00
☐ 677	Nick Esasky	.05	.02	.00
☐ 678	Dan Gladden	.05	.02	.00
☐ 679	Britt Burns	.06	.02	.00
☐ 680	George Foster	.12	.05	.01
☐ 681	Dick Williams MGR	.05	.01	.00
	(checklist back)			
☐ 682	Junior Ortiz	.03	.01	.00
☐ 683	Andy Van Slyke	.06	.02	.00
☐ 684	Bob McClure	.03	.01	.00
☐ 685	Tim Wallach	.07	.03	.01
☐ 686	Jeff Stone	.06	.02	.00
☐ 687	Mike Trujillo	.08	.03	.01
☐ 688	Larry Herndon	.03	.01	.00
☐ 689	Dave Stewart	.03	.01	.00
☐ 690	Ryne Sandberg	.45	.18	.04
	(no Topps logo			
	on front)			
☐ 691	Mike Madden	.03	.01	.00
☐ 692	Dale Berra	.03	.01	.00
☐ 693	Tom Tellmann	.03	.01	.00
☐ 694	Garth Iorg	.03	.01	.00
☐ 695	Mike Smithson	.03	.01	.00
☐ 696	Dodgers Leaders	.05	.02	.00
	Bill Russell			
☐ 697	Bud Black	.03	.01	.00
☐ 698	Brad Komminsk	.06	.02	.00
☐ 699	Pat Corrales MGR	.05	.01	.00
	(checklist back)			
☐ 700	Reggie Jackson	.35	.14	.03
☐ 701	Keith Hernandez AS	.15	.06	.01
☐ 702	Tom Herr AS	.06	.02	.00
☐ 703	Tim Wallach AS	.06	.02	.00
☐ 704	Ozzie Smith AS	.08	.03	.01
☐ 705	Dale Murphy AS	.25	.10	.02
☐ 706	Pedro Guerrero AS	.15	.06	.01
☐ 707	Willie McGee AS	.12	.05	.01
☐ 708	Gary Carter AS	.20	.08	.02
☐ 709	Dwight Gooden AS	.50	.20	.05
☐ 710	John Tudor AS	.06	.02	.00
☐ 711	Jeff Reardon AS	.06	.02	.00
☐ 712	Don Mattingly AS	.50	.20	.05
☐ 713	Damaso Garcia AS	.06	.02	.00
☐ 714	George Brett AS	.30	.12	.03
☐ 715	Cal Ripken AS	.25	.10	.02
☐ 716	Rickey Henderson AS	.25	.10	.02
☐ 717	Dave Winfield AS	.20	.08	.02
☐ 718	Jorge Bell AS	.10	.04	.01
☐ 719	Carlton Fisk AS	.10	.04	.01
☐ 720	Bret Saberhagen AS	.12	.05	.01
☐ 721	Ron Guidry AS	.12	.05	.01
☐ 722	Dan Quisenberry AS	.10	.04	.01
☐ 723	Marty Bystrom	.03	.01	.00
☐ 724	Tim Hulett	.07	.03	.01
☐ 725	Mario Soto	.08	.03	.01
☐ 726	Orioles Leaders	.05	.02	.00
	Rick Dempsey			
☐ 727	David Green	.03	.01	.00
☐ 728	Mike Marshall	.12	.05	.01
☐ 729	Jim Beattie	.03	.01	.00
☐ 730	Ozzie Smith	.10	.04	.01
☐ 731	Don Robinson	.03	.01	.00
☐ 732	Floyd Youmans	1.00	.40	.10
☐ 733	Ron Romanick	.05	.02	.00
☐ 734	Marty Barrett	.10	.04	.01
☐ 735	Dave Dravecky	.06	.02	.00
☐ 736	Glenn Wilson	.09	.04	.01
☐ 737	Pete Vuckovich	.05	.02	.00
☐ 738	Andre Robertson	.03	.01	.00
☐ 739	Dave Rozema	.03	.01	.00
☐ 740	Lance Parrish	.20	.08	.02
☐ 741	Pete Rose MGR	.35	.10	.02
	(checklist back)			
☐ 742	Frank Viola	.05	.02	.00
☐ 743	Pat Sheridan	.03	.01	.00
☐ 744	Lary Sorensen	.03	.01	.00
☐ 745	Willie Upshaw	.07	.03	.01
☐ 746	Denny Gonzalez	.07	.03	.01
☐ 747	Rick Cerone	.03	.01	.00
☐ 748	Steve Henderson	.03	.01	.00
☐ 749	Ed Jurak	.03	.01	.00
☐ 750	Gorman Thomas	.07	.03	.00
☐ 751	Howard Johnson	.03	.01	.00
☐ 752	Mike Krukow	.07	.03	.01

		MINT	VG-E	F-G
☐ 753	Dan Ford	.03	.01	.00
☐ 754	Pat Clements	.20	.08	.02
☐ 755	Harold Baines	.20	.08	.02
☐ 756	Pirates Leaders	.05	.02	.00
	Rick Rhoden			
☐ 757	Darrell Porter	.05	.02	.00
☐ 758	Dave Anderson	.03	.01	.00
☐ 759	Moose Haas	.05	.02	.00
☐ 760	Andre Dawson	.20	.08	.02
☐ 761	Don Slaught	.03	.01	.00
☐ 762	Eric Show	.03	.01	.00
☐ 763	Terry Puhl	.05	.02	.00
☐ 764	Kevin Gross	.03	.01	.00
☐ 765	Don Baylor	.10	.04	.01
☐ 766	Rick Langford	.03	.01	.00
☐ 767	Jody Davis	.08	.03	.01
☐ 768	Vern Ruhle	.03	.01	.00
☐ 769	Harold Reynolds	.12	.05	.01
☐ 770	Vida Blue	.08	.03	.01
☐ 771	John McNamara MGR	.05	.01	.00
	(checklist back)			
☐ 772	Brian Downing	.05	.02	.00
☐ 773	Greg Pryor	.03	.01	.00
☐ 774	Terry Leach	.03	.01	.00
☐ 775	Al Oliver	.10	.04	.01
☐ 776	Gene Garber	.03	.01	.00
☐ 777	Wayne Krenchicki	.03	.01	.00
☐ 778	Jerry Hairston	.03	.01	.00
☐ 779	Rick Reuschel	.05	.02	.00
☐ 780	Robin Yount	.25	.10	.02
☐ 781	Joe Nolan	.03	.01	.00
☐ 782	Ken Landreaux	.05	.02	.00
☐ 783	Ricky Horton	.03	.01	.00
☐ 784	Alan Bannister	.03	.01	.00
☐ 785	Bob Stanley	.05	.02	.00
☐ 786	Twins Leaders	.05	.02	.00
	Mickey Hatcher			
☐ 787	Vance Law	.03	.01	.00
☐ 788	Marty Castillo	.03	.01	.00
☐ 789	Kurt Bevacqua	.03	.01	.00
☐ 790	Phil Niekro	.15	.06	.01
☐ 791	Checklist: 661-792	.06	.01	.00
☐ 792	Charles Hudson	.06	.02	.00
☐ A	Jorge Bell	.15	.06	.01
	(wax pack box card)			
☐ B	Wade Boggs	1.50	.60	.15
	(wax pack box card)			
☐ C	George Brett	.75	.30	.07
	(wax pack box card)			
☐ D	Vince Coleman	1.00	.40	.10
	(wax pack box card)			
☐ E	Carlton Fisk	.15	.06	.01
	(wax pack box card)			

		MINT	VG-E	F-G
☐ F	Dwight Gooden	1.50	.60	.15
	(wax pack box card)			
☐ G	Pedro Guerrero	.25	.10	.02
	(wax pack box card)			
☐ H	Ron Guidry	.20	.08	.02
	(wax pack box card)			
☐ I	Reggie Jackson	.60	.24	.06
	(wax pack box card)			
☐ J	Don Mattingly	2.00	.80	.20
	(wax pack box card)			
☐ K	Oddibe McDowell	.35	.14	.03
	(wax pack box card)			
☐ L	Willie McGee	.25	.10	.02
	(wax pack box card)			
☐ M	Dale Murphy	1.00	.40	.10
	(wax pack box card)			
☐ N	Pete Rose	1.25	.50	.12
	(wax pack box card)			
☐ O	Bret Saberhagen	.25	.10	.02
	(wax pack box card)			
☐ P	Fernando Valenzuela	.25	.10	.02
	(wax pack box card)			

1986 Topps Traded

This 132-card extended set was distributed by Topps to dealers in a special red and white box as a complete set. The card fronts are identical in style to the Topps regular issue and are also 2½" by 3½". The backs are printed in red and black on white card stock. Cards are numbered (with a T suffix) alphabetically according to the name of the player.

		MINT	VG-E	F-G
	Complete Set	13.00	5.00	1.00
	Common Player	.06	.02	.00
☐ 1	T Andy Allanson	.20	.08	.02
☐ 2	T Neil Allen	.06	.02	.00
☐ 3	T Joaquin Andujar	.10	.04	.01
☐ 4	T Paul Assenmacher	.20	.08	.02
☐ 5	T Scott Bailes	.20	.08	.02
☐ 6	T Don Baylor	.15	.06	.01
☐ 7	T Steve Bedrosian	.10	.04	.01
☐ 8	T Juan Beniquez	.10	.04	.01
☐ 9	T Juan Berenguer	.06	.02	.00
☐ 10	T Mike Bielecki	.10	.04	.01
☐ 11	T Barry Bonds	.75	.30	.07
☐ 12	T Bobby Bonilla	.20	.08	.02
☐ 13	T Juan Bonilla	.06	.02	.00
☐ 14	T Rich Bordi	.06	.02	.00
☐ 15	T Steve Boros MGR	.06	.02	.00
☐ 16	T Rick Burleson	.10	.04	.01
☐ 17	T Bill Campbell	.06	.02	.00
☐ 18	T Tom Candiotti	.10	.04	.01
☐ 19	T John Cangelosi	.35	.14	.03
☐ 20	T Jose Canseco	3.50	1.40	.35
☐ 21	T Carmen Castillo	.10	.04	.01
☐ 22	T Rick Cerone	.06	.02	.00
☐ 23	T John Cerutti	.35	.14	.03
☐ 24	T Will Clark	1.25	.50	.12
☐ 25	T Mark Clear	.06	.02	.00
☐ 26	T Darnell Coles	.15	.06	.01
☐ 27	T Dave Collins	.10	.04	.01
☐ 28	T Tim Conroy	.06	.02	.00
☐ 29	T Joe Cowley	.10	.04	.01
☐ 30	T Joel Davis	.20	.08	.02
☐ 31	T Rob Deer	.40	.16	.04
☐ 32	T John Denny	.10	.04	.01
☐ 33	T Mike Easler	.10	.04	.01
☐ 34	T Mark Eichhorn	.50	.20	.05
☐ 35	T Steve Farr	.06	.02	.00
☐ 36	T Scott Fletcher	.10	.04	.01
☐ 37	T Terry Forster	.10	.04	.01
☐ 38	T Terry Francona	.06	.02	.00
☐ 39	T Jim Fregosi MGR	.10	.04	.01
☐ 40	T Andres Galarraga	.25	.10	.02
☐ 41	T Ken Griffey	.10	.04	.01
☐ 42	T Bill Gullickson	.10	.04	.01
☐ 43	T Jose Guzman	.20	.08	.02
☐ 44	T Moose Haas	.10	.04	.01
☐ 45	T Billy Hatcher	.10	.04	.01
☐ 46	T Mike Heath	.06	.02	.00
☐ 47	T Tom Hume	.06	.02	.00
☐ 48	T Pete Incaviglia	2.00	.80	.20
☐ 49	T Dane Iorg	.06	.02	.00
☐ 50	T Bo Jackson	2.00	.80	.20

		MINT	VG-E	F-G
☐ 51	T Wally Joyner	3.50	1.40	.35
☐ 52	T Charlie Kerfeld	.35	.14	.03
☐ 53	T Eric King	.35	.14	.03
☐ 54	T Bob Kipper	.06	.02	.00
☐ 55	T Wayne Krenchicki	.06	.02	.00
☐ 56	T John Kruk	.30	.12	.03
☐ 57	T Mike LaCoss	.06	.02	.00
☐ 58	T Pete Ladd	.06	.02	.00
☐ 59	T Mike Laga	.10	.04	.01
☐ 60	T Hal Lanier MGR	.10	.04	.01
☐ 61	T Dave LaPoint	.06	.02	.00
☐ 62	T Rudy Law	.06	.02	.00
☐ 63	T Rick Leach	.06	.02	.00
☐ 64	T Tim Leary	.10	.04	.01
☐ 65	T Dennis Leonard	.10	.04	.01
☐ 66	T Jim Leyland MGR	.06	.02	.00
☐ 67	T Steve Lyons	.06	.02	.00
☐ 68	T Mickey Mahler	.06	.02	.00
☐ 69	T Candy Maldonado	.10	.04	.01
☐ 70	T Roger Mason	.15	.06	.01
☐ 71	T Bob McClure	.06	.02	.00
☐ 72	T Andy McGaffigan	.06	.02	.00
☐ 73	T Gene Michael MGR	.06	.02	.00
☐ 74	T Kevin Mitchell	.75	.30	.07
☐ 75	T Omar Moreno	.06	.02	.00
☐ 76	T Jerry Mumphrey	.06	.02	.00
☐ 77	T Phil Niekro	.25	.10	.02
☐ 78	T Randy Niemann	.06	.02	.00
☐ 79	T Juan Nieves	.20	.08	.02
☐ 80	T Otis Nixon	.15	.06	.01
☐ 81	T Bob Ojeda	.15	.06	.01
☐ 82	T Jose Oquendo	.06	.02	.00
☐ 83	T Tom Paciorek	.06	.02	.00
☐ 84	T Dave Palmer	.06	.02	.00
☐ 85	T Frank Pastore	.06	.02	.00
☐ 86	T Lou Piniella MGR	.10	.04	.01
☐ 87	T Dan Plesac	.20	.08	.02
☐ 88	T Darrell Porter	.10	.04	.01
☐ 89	T Rey Quinones	.20	.08	.02
☐ 90	T Gary Redus	.10	.04	.01
☐ 91	T Bip Roberts	.15	.06	.01
☐ 92	T Billy Jo Robidoux	.35	.14	.03
☐ 93	T Jeff Robinson	.10	.04	.01
☐ 94	T Gary Roenicke	.10	.04	.01
☐ 95	T Ed Romero	.06	.02	.00
☐ 96	T Argenis Salazar	.06	.02	.00
☐ 97	T Joe Sambito	.10	.04	.01
☐ 98	T Billy Sample	.06	.02	.00
☐ 99	T Dave Schmidt	.06	.02	.00
☐ 100	T Ken Schrom	.10	.04	.01
☐ 101	T Tom Seaver	.45	.18	.04
☐ 102	T Ted Simmons	.15	.06	.01
☐ 103	T Sammy Stewart	.06	.02	.00

			MINT	VG-E	F-G
☐ 104	T Kurt Stillwell	....	.15	.06	.01
☐ 105	T Franklin Stubbs	....	.15	.06	.01
☐ 106	T Dale Sveum	....	.20	.08	.02
☐ 107	T Chuck Tanner MGR	..	.10	.04	.01
☐ 108	T Danny Tartabull	....	.75	.30	.07
☐ 109	T Tim Teufel	....	.10	.04	.01
☐ 110	T Bob Tewksbury	......	.35	.14	.03
☐ 111	T Andres Thomas	......	.35	.14	.03
☐ 112	T Milt Thompson	......	.10	.04	.01
☐ 113	T Robby Thompson	......	.40	.16	.04
☐ 114	T Jay Tibbs	....	.06	.02	.00
☐ 115	T Wayne Tolleson	......	.06	.02	.00
☐ 116	T Alex Trevino	....	.06	.02	.00
☐ 117	T Manny Trillo	....	.06	.02	.00
☐ 118	T Ed VandeBerg	......	.06	.02	.00
☐ 119	T Ozzie Virgil	....	.06	.02	.00
☐ 120	T Bob Walk	....	.06	.02	.00
☐ 121	T Gene Walter	....	.15	.06	.01
☐ 122	T Claudell Washington	..	.10	.04	.01
☐ 123	T Bill Wegman	....	.20	.08	.02
☐ 124	T Dick Williams MGR	...	.06	.02	.00
☐ 125	T Mitch Williams	......	.30	.12	.03
☐ 126	T Bobby Witt	....	.50	.20	.05
☐ 127	T Todd Worrell	....	1.00	.40	.10
☐ 128	T George Wright	....	.06	.02	.00
☐ 129	T Ricky Wright	....	.06	.02	.00
☐ 130	T Steve Yeager	....	.06	.02	.00
☐ 131	T Paul Zuvella	....	.06	.02	.00
☐ 132	T Checklist card	....	.10	.01	.00

1987 Topps

This 792-card set is reminiscent of the 1962 Topps baseball cards with their simulated wood grain borders. The backs are printed in yellow and blue on gray card stock. The manager cards contain a checklist of the respec-

tive team's players on the back. Subsets in the set include Record Breakers (1-7), Turn Back the Clock (311-315), and All-Star selections (595-616). The Team Leader cards typically show players conferring on the mound inside a white cloud. The wax pack wrapper gives details of ''Spring Fever Baseball'' where a lucky collector can win a trip for four to Spring Training. Four different sets of two smaller (2⅛" by 3") cards were printed on the side of the wax pack box; these eight cards are lettered A through H and listed at the end of the checklist below.

		MINT	VG-E	F-G
	Complete Set	22.00	9.00	2.20
	Common Player	.03	.01	.00
☐ 1	RB: Roger Clemens .... Most strikeouts, 9 inning game	.35	.14	.03
☐ 2	RB: Jim Deshaies ...... Most cons. K's, start of game	.10	.04	.01
☐ 3	RB: Dwight Evans ...... Earliest home run, season	.08	.03	.01
☐ 4	RB: Davey Lopes ...... Most steals, season 40-year-old	.06	.02	.00
☐ 5	RB: Dave Righetti ...... Most saves, season	.10	.04	.01
☐ 6	RB: Ruben Sierra ...... Youngest player to switch hit homers in game	.15	.06	.01
☐ 7	RB: Todd Worrell ...... Most saves, season, rookie	.15	.06	.01
☐ 8	Terry Pendleton	.05	.02	.00
☐ 9	Jay Tibbs	.03	.01	.00
☐ 10	Cecil Cooper	.09	.04	.01
☐ 11	Indians Team .... (mound conference)	.03	.01	.00
☐ 12	Jeff Sellers	.12	.05	.01
☐ 13	Nick Esasky	.03	.01	.00
☐ 14	Dave Stewart	.03	.01	.00
☐ 15	Claudell Washington ...	.05	.02	.00
☐ 16	Pat Clements	.05	.02	.00
☐ 17	Pete O'Brien	.08	.03	.01
☐ 18	Dick Howser MGR ...... (checklist back)	.06	.01	.00

	MINT	VG-E	F-G
☐ 19 Matt Young	.03	.01	.00
☐ 20 Gary Carter	.25	.10	.02
☐ 21 Mark Davis	.03	.01	.00
☐ 22 Doug DeCinces	.07	.03	.01
☐ 23 Lee Smith	.07	.03	.01
☐ 24 Tony Walker	.12	.05	.01
☐ 25 Bert Blyleven	.09	.04	.01
☐ 26 Greg Brock	.05	.02	.00
☐ 27 Joe Cowley	.05	.02	.00
☐ 28 Rick Dempsey	.05	.02	.00
☐ 29 Jimmy Key	.07	.03	.01
☐ 30 Tim Raines	.25	.10	.02
☐ 31 Braves Team	.03	.01	.00
(Hubbard/Ramirez)			
☐ 32 Tim Leary	.03	.01	.00
☐ 33 Andy Van Slyke	.05	.02	.00
☐ 34 Jose Rijo	.05	.02	.00
☐ 35 Sid Bream	.05	.02	.00
☐ 36 Eric King	.25	.10	.02
☐ 37 Marvell Wynne	.03	.01	.00
☐ 38 Dennis Leonard	.05	.02	.00
☐ 39 Marty Barrett	.10	.04	.01
☐ 40 Dave Righetti	.12	.05	.01
☐ 41 Bo Diaz	.05	.02	.00
☐ 42 Gary Redus	.05	.02	.00
☐ 43 Gene Michael MGR	.06	.01	.00
(checklist back)			
☐ 44 Greg Harris	.05	.02	.00
☐ 45 Jim Presley	.20	.08	.02
☐ 46 Dan Gladden	.05	.02	.00
☐ 47 Dennis Powell	.08	.03	.01
☐ 48 Wally Backman	.07	.03	.01
☐ 49 Terry Harper	.03	.01	.00
☐ 50 Dave Smith	.06	.02	.00
☐ 51 Mel Hall	.07	.03	.01
☐ 52 Keith Atherton	.03	.01	.00
☐ 53 Ruppert Jones	.03	.01	.00
☐ 54 Bill Dawley	.03	.01	.00
☐ 55 Tim Wallach	.07	.03	.01
☐ 56 Brewers Team	.03	.01	.00
(mound conference)			
☐ 57 Scott Nielsen	.15	.06	.01
☐ 58 Thad Bosley	.03	.01	.00
☐ 59 Ken Dayley	.03	.01	.00
☐ 60 Tony Pena	.10	.04	.01
☐ 61 Bobby Thigpen	.20	.08	.02
☐ 62 Bobby Meacham	.03	.01	.00
☐ 63 Fred Toliver	.05	.02	.00
☐ 64 Harry Spilman	.03	.01	.00
☐ 65 Tom Browning	.08	.03	.01
☐ 66 Marc Sullivan	.03	.01	.00
☐ 67 Bill Swift	.03	.01	.00

	MINT	VG-E	F-G
☐ 68 Tony LaRussa MGR	.06	.01	.00
(checklist back)			
☐ 69 Lonnie Smith	.05	.02	.00
☐ 70 Charlie Hough	.05	.02	.00
☐ 71 Mike Aldrete	.12	.05	.01
☐ 72 Walt Terrell	.03	.01	.00
☐ 73 Dave Anderson	.03	.01	.00
☐ 74 Dan Pasqua	.15	.06	.01
☐ 75 Ron Darling	.20	.08	.02
☐ 76 Rafael Ramirez	.03	.01	.00
☐ 77 Bryan Oelkers	.03	.01	.00
☐ 78 Tom Foley	.03	.01	.00
☐ 79 Juan Nieves	.06	.02	.00
☐ 80 Wally Joyner	2.00	.80	.20
☐ 81 Padres Team	.03	.01	.00
(Hawkins/Kennedy)			
☐ 82 Rob Murphy	.15	.06	.01
☐ 83 Mike Davis	.05	.02	.00
☐ 84 Steve Lake	.03	.01	.00
☐ 85 Kevin Bass	.07	.03	.01
☐ 86 Nate Snell	.03	.01	.00
☐ 87 Mark Salas	.03	.01	.00
☐ 88 Ed Wojna	.03	.01	.00
☐ 89 Ozzie Guillen	.10	.04	.01
☐ 90 Dave Stieb	.10	.04	.01
☐ 91 Harold Reynolds	.03	.01	.00
☐ 92 Urbano Lugo	.03	.01	.00
☐ 93 Jim Leyland MGR	.06	.01	.00
(checklist back)			
☐ 94 Calvin Schiraldi	.09	.04	.01
☐ 95 Oddibe McDowell	.20	.08	.02
☐ 96 Frank Williams	.03	.01	.00
☐ 97 Glenn Wilson	.08	.03	.01
☐ 98 Bill Scherrer	.03	.01	.00
☐ 99 Darryl Motley	.03	.01	.00
☐ 100 Steve Garvey	.30	.12	.03
☐ 101 Carl Willis	.10	.04	.01
☐ 102 Paul Zuvella	.03	.01	.00
☐ 103 Rick Aguilera	.05	.02	.00
☐ 104 Billy Sample	.03	.01	.00
☐ 105 Floyd Youmans	.10	.04	.01
☐ 106 Blue Jays Team	.10	.04	.01
(Bell/Barfield)			
☐ 107 John Butcher	.03	.01	.00
☐ 108 Jim Gantner	.03	.01	.00
(Brewers logo			
reversed)			
☐ 109 R.J. Reynolds	.05	.02	.00
☐ 110 John Tudor	.09	.04	.01
☐ 111 Alfredo Griffin	.05	.02	.00
☐ 112 Alan Ashby	.03	.01	.00
☐ 113 Neil Allen	.05	.02	.00
☐ 114 Billy Beane	.05	.02	.00

		MINT	VG-E	F-G
☐ 115	Donnie Moore	.05	.02	.00
☐ 116	Bill Russell	.05	.02	.00
☐ 117	Jim Beattie	.03	.01	.00
☐ 118	Bobby Valentine MGR (checklist back)	.06	.01	.00
☐ 119	Ron Robinson	.05	.02	.00
☐ 120	Eddie Murray	.30	.12	.03
☐ 121	Kevin Romine	.12	.05	.01
☐ 122	Jim Clancy	.03	.01	.00
☐ 123	John Kruk	.25	.10	.02
☐ 124	Ray Fontenot	.03	.01	.00
☐ 125	Bob Brenly	.05	.02	.00
☐ 126	Mike Loynd	.25	.10	.02
☐ 127	Vance Law	.03	.01	.00
☐ 128	Checklist 1-132	.06	.01	.00
☐ 129	Rick Cerone	.03	.01	.00
☐ 130	Dwight Gooden	1.00	.40	.10
☐ 131	Pirates Team (Bream/Pena)	.05	.02	.00
☐ 132	Paul Assenmacher	.10	.04	.01
☐ 133	Jose Oquendo	.03	.01	.00
☐ 134	Rich Yett	.05	.02	.00
☐ 135	Mike Easler	.06	.02	.00
☐ 136	Ron Romanick	.05	.02	.00
☐ 137	Jerry Willard	.03	.01	.00
☐ 138	Roy Lee Jackson	.03	.01	.00
☐ 139	Devon White	.30	.12	.03
☐ 140	Bret Saberhagen	.15	.06	.01
☐ 141	Herm Winningham	.03	.01	.00
☐ 142	Rick Sutcliffe	.10	.04	.01
☐ 143	Steve Boros MGR (checklist back)	.06	.01	.00
☐ 144	Mike Scioscia	.05	.02	.00
☐ 145	Charlie Kerfeld	.10	.04	.01
☐ 146	Tracy Jones	.25	.10	.02
☐ 147	Randy Niemann	.03	.01	.00
☐ 148	Dave Collins	.05	.02	.00
☐ 149	Ray Searage	.03	.01	.00
☐ 150	Wade Boggs	1.00	.40	.10
☐ 151	Mike LaCoss	.03	.01	.00
☐ 152	Toby Harrah	.03	.01	.00
☐ 153	Duane Ward	.12	.05	.01
☐ 154	Tom O'Malley	.03	.01	.00
☐ 155	Eddie Whitson	.05	.02	.00
☐ 156	Mariners Team (mound conference)	.03	.01	.00
☐ 157	Danny Darwin	.03	.01	.00
☐ 158	Tim Teufel	.05	.02	.00
☐ 159	Ed Olwine	.12	.05	.01
☐ 160	Julio Franco	.09	.04	.01
☐ 161	Steve Ontiveros	.03	.01	.00
☐ 162	Mike Lavalliere	.09	.04	.01
☐ 163	Kevin Gross	.03	.01	.00

		MINT	VG-E	F-G
☐ 164	Sammy Khalifa	.03	.01	.00
☐ 165	Jeff Reardon	.06	.02	.00
☐ 166	Bob Boone	.05	.02	.00
☐ 167	Jim Deshaies	.25	.10	.02
☐ 168	Lou Piniella MGR (checklist back)	.07	.01	.00
☐ 169	Ron Washington	.03	.01	.00
☐ 170	Bo Jackson	1.00	.40	.10
☐ 171	Chuck Cary	.15	.06	.01
☐ 172	Ron Oester	.03	.01	.00
☐ 173	Alex Trevino	.03	.01	.00
☐ 174	Henry Cotto	.03	.01	.00
☐ 175	Bob Stanley	.05	.02	.00
☐ 176	Steve Buechele	.03	.01	.00
☐ 177	Keith Moreland	.05	.02	.00
☐ 178	Cecil Fielder	.07	.03	.01
☐ 179	Bill Wegman	.07	.03	.01
☐ 180	Chris Brown	.15	.06	.01
☐ 181	Cardinals Team (mound conference)	.03	.01	.00
☐ 182	Lee Lacy	.03	.01	.00
☐ 183	Andy Hawkins	.03	.01	.00
☐ 184	Bobby Bonilla	.15	.06	.01
☐ 185	Roger McDowell	.10	.04	.01
☐ 186	Bruce Benedict	.03	.01	.00
☐ 187	Mark Huismann	.03	.01	.00
☐ 188	Tony Phillips	.03	.01	.00
☐ 189	Joe Hesketh	.05	.02	.00
☐ 190	Jim Sundberg	.05	.02	.00
☐ 191	Charles Hudson	.05	.02	.00
☐ 192	Cory Snyder	.60	.24	.06
☐ 193	Roger Craig MGR (checklist back)	.06	.01	.00
☐ 194	Kirk McCaskill	.10	.04	.01
☐ 195	Mike Pagliarulo	.15	.06	.01
☐ 196	Randy O'Neal	.03	.01	.00
☐ 197	Mark Bailey	.03	.01	.00
☐ 198	Lee Mazzilli	.03	.01	.00
☐ 199	Mariano Duncan	.08	.03	.01
☐ 200	Pete Rose	.60	.24	.06
☐ 201	John Cangelosi	.25	.10	.02
☐ 202	Ricky Wright	.03	.01	.00
☐ 203	Mike Kingery	.20	.08	.02
☐ 204	Sammy Stewart	.03	.01	.00
☐ 205	Graig Nettles	.10	.04	.01
☐ 206	Twins Team (mound conference)	.03	.01	.00
☐ 207	George Frazier	.03	.01	.00
☐ 208	John Shelby	.03	.01	.00
☐ 209	Rick Schu	.03	.01	.00
☐ 210	Lloyd Moseby	.10	.04	.01
☐ 211	John Morris	.03	.01	.00
☐ 212	Mike Fitzgerald	.03	.01	.00

		MINT	VG-E	F-G
☐ 213	Randy Myers	.45	.18	.04
☐ 214	Omar Moreno	.03	.01	.00
☐ 215	Mark Langston	.06	.02	.00
☐ 216	B.J. Surhoff	.50	.20	.05
☐ 217	Chris Codiroli	.03	.01	.00
☐ 218	Sparky Anderson MGR (checklist back)	.06	.01	.00
☐ 219	Cecilio Guante	.03	.01	.00
☐ 220	Joe Carter	.20	.08	.02
☐ 221	Vern Ruhle	.03	.01	.00
☐ 222	Denny Walling	.03	.01	.00
☐ 223	Charlie Leibrandt	.05	.02	.00
☐ 224	Wayne Tolleson	.03	.01	.00
☐ 225	Mike Smithson	.03	.01	.00
☐ 226	Max Venable	.03	.01	.00
☐ 227	Jamie Moyer	.15	.06	.01
☐ 228	Curt Wilkerson	.03	.01	.00
☐ 229	Mike Birkbeck	.12	.05	.01
☐ 230	Don Baylor	.10	.04	.01
☐ 231	Giants Team (mound conference)	.03	.01	.00
☐ 232	Reggie Williams	.15	.06	.01
☐ 233	Russ Morman	.20	.08	.02
☐ 234	Pat Sheridan	.03	.01	.00
☐ 235	Alvin Davis	.12	.05	.01
☐ 236	Tommy John	.10	.04	.01
☐ 237	Jim Morrison	.03	.01	.00
☐ 238	Bill Krueger	.03	.01	.00
☐ 239	Juan Espino	.03	.01	.00
☐ 240	Steve Balboni	.05	.02	.00
☐ 241	Danny Heep	.03	.01	.00
☐ 242	Rick Mahler	.03	.01	.00
☐ 243	Whitey Herzog MGR (checklist back)	.06	.01	.00
☐ 244	Dickie Noles	.03	.01	.00
☐ 245	Willie Upshaw	.07	.03	.01
☐ 246	Jim Dwyer	.03	.01	.00
☐ 247	Jeff Reed	.03	.01	.00
☐ 248	Gene Walter	.05	.02	.00
☐ 249	Jim Pankovits	.03	.01	.00
☐ 250	Teddy Higuera	.15	.06	.01
☐ 251	Rob Wilfong	.03	.01	.00
☐ 252	Denny Martinez	.03	.01	.00
☐ 253	Eddie Milner	.05	.02	.00
☐ 254	Bob Tewksbury	.20	.08	.02
☐ 255	Juan Samuel	.10	.04	.01
☐ 256	Royals Team (Brett/F.White)	.10	.04	.01
☐ 257	Bob Forsch	.05	.02	.00
☐ 258	Steve Yeager	.05	.02	.00
☐ 259	Mike Greenwell	.15	.06	.01
☐ 260	Vida Blue	.07	.03	.01
☐ 261	Ruben Sierra	1.00	.40	.10
☐ 262	Jim Winn	.03	.01	.00
☐ 263	Stan Javier	.07	.03	.01
☐ 264	Checklist 133-264	.06	.01	.00
☐ 265	Darrell Evans	.07	.03	.01
☐ 266	Jeff Hamilton	.15	.06	.01
☐ 267	Howard Johnson	.03	.01	.00
☐ 268	Pat Corrales MGR (checklist back)	.06	.01	.00
☐ 269	Cliff Speck	.08	.03	.01
☐ 270	Jody Davis	.07	.03	.01
☐ 271	Mike Brown (Mariners P)	.03	.01	.00
☐ 272	Andres Galarraga	.08	.03	.01
☐ 273	Gene Nelson	.03	.01	.00
☐ 274	Jeff Hearron	.10	.04	.01
☐ 275	LaMarr Hoyt	.06	.02	.00
☐ 276	Jackie Gutierrez	.03	.01	.00
☐ 277	Juan Agosto	.03	.01	.00
☐ 278	Gary Pettis	.07	.03	.01
☐ 279	Dan Plesac	.20	.08	.02
☐ 280	Jeff Leonard	.06	.02	.00
☐ 281	Reds Team (Rose conference)	.10	.04	.01
☐ 282	Jeff Calhoun	.09	.04	.01
☐ 283	Doug Drabek	.15	.06	.01
☐ 284	John Moses	.15	.06	.01
☐ 285	Dennis Boyd	.08	.03	.01
☐ 286	Mike Woodard	.05	.02	.00
☐ 287	Dave Von Ohlen	.03	.01	.00
☐ 288	Tito Landrum	.03	.01	.00
☐ 289	Bob Kipper	.03	.01	.00
☐ 290	Leon Durham	.07	.03	.01
☐ 291	Mitch Williams	.20	.08	.02
☐ 292	Franklin Stubbs	.10	.04	.01
☐ 293	Bob Rodgers MGR (checklist back)	.06	.01	.00
☐ 294	Steve Jeltz	.03	.01	.00
☐ 295	Len Dykstra	.20	.08	.02
☐ 296	Andres Thomas	.25	.10	.02
☐ 297	Don Schulze	.03	.01	.00
☐ 298	Larry Herndon	.03	.01	.00
☐ 299	Joel Davis	.10	.04	.01
☐ 300	Reggie Jackson	.30	.12	.03
☐ 301	Luis Aquino	.09	.04	.01
☐ 302	Bill Schroeder	.03	.01	.00
☐ 303	Juan Berenguer	.03	.01	.00
☐ 304	Phil Garner	.05	.02	.00
☐ 305	John Franco	.08	.03	.01
☐ 306	Red Sox Team (mound conference)	.05	.02	.00
☐ 307	Lee Guetterman	.12	.05	.01
☐ 308	Don Slaught	.03	.01	.00
☐ 309	Mike Young	.07	.03	.01

		MINT	VG-E	F-G
☐ 310	Frank Viola	.05	.02	.00
☐ 311	Turn Back 1982 Rickey Henderson	.12	.05	-.01
☐ 312	Turn Back 1977 Reggie Jackson	.12	.05	.01
☐ 313	Turn Back 1972 Roberto Clemente	.12	.05	.01
☐ 314	Turn Back 1967 Carl Yastrzemski	.12	.05	.01
☐ 315	Turn Back 1962 Maury Wills	.06	.02	.00
☐ 316	Brian Fisher	.05	.02	.00
☐ 317	Clint Hurdle	.03	.01	.00
☐ 318	Jim Fregosi MGR (checklist back)	.06	.01	.00
☐ 319	Greg Swindell	.45	.18	.04
☐ 320	Barry Bonds	.35	.14	.03
☐ 321	Mike Laga	.03	.01	.00
☐ 322	Chris Bando	.03	.01	.00
☐ 323	Al Newman	.10	.04	.01
☐ 324	Dave Palmer	.05	.02	.00
☐ 325	Garry Templeton	.07	.03	.01
☐ 326	Mark Gubicza	.06	.02	.00
☐ 327	Dale Sveum	.15	.06	.01
☐ 328	Bob Welch	.06	.02	.00
☐ 329	Ron Roenicke	.03	.01	.00
☐ 330	Mike Scott	.15	.06	.01
☐ 331	Mets Team (Carter/Strawberry)	.12	.05	.01
☐ 332	Joe Price	.03	.01	.00
☐ 333	Ken Phelps	.03	.01	.00
☐ 334	Ed Correa	.35	.14	.03
☐ 335	Candy Maldonado	.08	.03	.01
☐ 336	Allan Anderson	.15	.06	.01
☐ 337	Darrell Miller	.03	.01	.00
☐ 338	Tim Conroy	.03	.01	.00
☐ 339	Donnie Hill	.03	.01	.00
☐ 340	Roger Clemens	1.00	.40	.10
☐ 341	Mike Brown (Pirates OF)	.03	.01	.00
☐ 342	Bob James	.03	.01	.00
☐ 343	Hal Lanier MGR (checklist back)	.06	.01	.00
☐ 344	Joe Niekro	.07	.03	.01
☐ 345	Andre Dawson	.16	.07	.01
☐ 346	Shawon Dunston	.10	.04	.01
☐ 347	Mickey Brantley	.10	.04	.01
☐ 348	Carmelo Martinez	.05	.02	.00
☐ 349	Storm Davis	.07	.03	.01
☐ 350	Keith Hernandez	.20	.08	.02
☐ 351	Gene Garber	.03	.01	.00
☐ 352	Mike Felder	.10	.04	.01
☐ 353	Ernie Camacho	.03	.01	.00

		MINT	VG-E	F-G
☐ 354	Jamie Quirk	.03	.01	.00
☐ 355	Don Carman	.05	.02	.00
☐ 356	White Sox Team (mound conference)	.03	.01	.00
☐ 357	Steve Fireovid	.10	.04	.01
☐ 358	Sal Butera	.03	.01	.00
☐ 359	Doug Corbett	.03	.01	.00
☐ 360	Pedro Guerrero	.20	.08	.02
☐ 361	Mark Thurmond	.03	.01	.00
☐ 362	Luis Quinones	.10	.04	.01
☐ 363	Jose Guzman	.10	.04	.01
☐ 364	Randy Bush	.03	.01	.00
☐ 365	Rick Rhoden	.05	.02	.00
☐ 366	Mark McGwire	.10	.04	.01
☐ 367	Jeff Lahti	.03	.01	.00
☐ 368	John McNamara MGR (checklist back)	.06	.01	.00
☐ 369	Brian Dayett	.03	.01	.00
☐ 370	Fred Lynn	.15	.06	.01
☐ 371	Mark Eichhorn	.35	.14	.03
☐ 372	Jerry Mumphrey	.05	.02	.00
☐ 373	Jeff Dedmon	.03	.01	.00
☐ 374	Glenn Hoffman	.03	.01	.00
☐ 375	Ron Guidry	.15	.06	.01
☐ 376	Scott Bradley	.05	.02	.00
☐ 377	John Henry Johnson	.03	.01	.00
☐ 378	Rafael Santana	.03	.01	.00
☐ 379	John Russell	.03	.01	.00
☐ 380	Rich Gossage	.12	.05	.01
☐ 381	Expos Team (mound conference)	.03	.01	.00
☐ 382	Rudy Law	.03	.01	.00
☐ 383	Ron Davis	.03	.01	.00
☐ 384	Johnny Grubb	.03	.01	.00
☐ 385	Orel Hershiser	.15	.06	.01
☐ 386	Dickie Thon	.05	.02	.00
☐ 387	T.R. Bryden	.12	.05	.01
☐ 388	Geno Petralli	.03	.01	.00
☐ 389	Jeff Robinson	.03	.01	.00
☐ 390	Gary Matthews	.05	.02	.00
☐ 391	Jay Howell	.05	.02	.00
☐ 392	Checklist 265-396	.06	.01	.00
☐ 393	Pete Rose MGR (checklist back)	.35	.10	.02
☐ 394	Mike Bielecki	.06	.02	.00
☐ 395	Damaso Garcia	.07	.03	.01
☐ 396	Tim Lollar	.03	.01	.00
☐ 397	Greg Walker	.10	.04	.01
☐ 398	Brad Havens	.03	.01	.00
☐ 399	Curt Ford	.20	.08	.02
☐ 400	George Brett	.30	.12	.03
☐ 401	Billy Jo Robidoux	.10	.04	.01
☐ 402	Mike Trujillo	.03	.01	.00

		MINT	VG-E	F-G
☐ 403	Jerry Royster	.03	.01	.00
☐ 404	Doug Sisk	.03	.01	.00
☐ 405	Brook Jacoby	.09	.04	.01
☐ 406	Yankees Team (Henderson/Mattingly)	.25	.10	.02
☐ 407	Jim Acker	.03	.01	.00
☐ 408	John Mizerock	.03	.01	.00
☐ 409	Milt Thompson	.03	.01	.00
☐ 410	Fernando Valenzuela	.25	.10	.02
☐ 411	Darnell Coles	.09	.04	.01
☐ 412	Eric Davis	.50	.20	.05
☐ 413	Moose Haas	.05	.02	.00
☐ 414	Joe Orsulak	.05	.02	.00
☐ 415	Bobby Witt	.40	.16	.04
☐ 416	Tom Nieto	.03	.01	.00
☐ 417	Pat Perry	.07	.03	.01
☐ 418	Dick Williams MGR (checklist back)	.06	.01	.00
☐ 419	Mark Portugal	.10	.04	.01
☐ 420	Will Clark	.60	.24	.06
☐ 421	Jose DeLeon	.05	.02	.00
☐ 422	Jack Howell	.05	.02	.00
☐ 423	Jaime Cocanower	.03	.01	.00
☐ 424	Chris Speier	.03	.01	.00
☐ 425	Tom Seaver	.25	.10	.02
☐ 426	Floyd Rayford	.03	.01	.00
☐ 427	Ed Nunez	.03	.01	.00
☐ 428	Bruce Bochy	.03	.01	.00
☐ 429	Tim Pyznarski	.15	.06	.01
☐ 430	Mike Schmidt	.30	.12	.03
☐ 431	Dodgers Team (mound conference)	.05	.02	.00
☐ 432	Jim Slaton	.03	.01	.00
☐ 433	Ed Hearn	.10	.04	.01
☐ 434	Mike Fischlin	.03	.01	.00
☐ 435	Bruce Sutter	.12	.05	.01
☐ 436	Andy Allanson	.15	.06	.01
☐ 437	Ted Power	.06	.02	.00
☐ 438	Kelly Downs	.12	.05	.01
☐ 439	Karl Best	.03	.01	.00
☐ 440	Willie McGee	.15	.06	.01
☐ 441	Dave Leiper	.10	.04	.01
☐ 442	Mitch Webster	.09	.04	.01
☐ 443	John Felske MGR (checklist back)	.06	.01	.00
☐ 444	Jeff Russell	.03	.01	.00
☐ 445	Dave Lopes	.06	.02	.00
☐ 446	Chuck Finley	.12	.05	.01
☐ 447	Bill Almon	.03	.01	.00
☐ 448	Chris Bosio	.10	.04	.01
☐ 449	Pat Dodson	.20	.08	.02
☐ 450	Kirby Puckett	.30	.12	.03
☐ 451	Joe Sambito	.05	.02	.00

		MINT	VG-E	F-G
☐ 452	Dave Henderson	.05	.02	.00
☐ 453	Scott Terry	.10	.04	.01
☐ 454	Luis Salazar	.03	.01	.00
☐ 455	Mike Boddicker	.07	.03	.01
☐ 456	A's Team (mound conference)	.03	.01	.00
☐ 457	Len Matuszek	.03	.01	.00
☐ 458	Kelly Gruber	.03	.01	.00
☐ 459	Dennis Eckersley	.05	.02	.00
☐ 460	Darryl Strawberry	.30	.12	.03
☐ 461	Craig McMurtry	.03	.01	.00
☐ 462	Scott Fletcher	.05	.02	.00
☐ 463	Tom Candiotti	.05	.02	.00
☐ 464	Butch Wynegar	.05	.02	.00
☐ 465	Todd Worrell	.35	.14	.03
☐ 466	Kal Daniels	.15	.06	.01
☐ 467	Randy St.Claire	.03	.01	.00
☐ 468	George Bamberger MGR (checklist back)	.06	.01	.00
☐ 469	Mike Diaz	.20	.08	.02
☐ 470	Dave Dravecky	.06	.02	.00
☐ 471	Ronn Reynolds	.03	.01	.00
☐ 472	Bill Doran	.09	.04	.01
☐ 473	Steve Farr	.03	.01	.00
☐ 474	Jerry Narron	.03	.01	.00
☐ 475	Scott Garrelts	.05	.02	.00
☐ 476	Danny Tartabull	.25	.10	.02
☐ 477	Ken Howell	.05	.02	.00
☐ 478	Tim Laudner	.03	.01	.00
☐ 479	Bob Sebra	.10	.04	.01
☐ 480	Jim Rice	.25	.10	.02
☐ 481	Phillies Team (cage conference)	.05	.02	.00
☐ 482	Daryl Boston	.05	.02	.00
☐ 483	Dwight Lowry	.15	.06	.01
☐ 484	Jim Traber	.09	.04	.01
☐ 485	Tony Fernandez	.09	.04	.01
☐ 486	Otis Nixon	.15	.06	.01
☐ 487	Dave Gumpert	.03	.01	.00
☐ 488	Ray Knight	.07	.03	.01
☐ 489	Bill Gullickson	.05	.02	.00
☐ 490	Dale Murphy	.35	.14	.03
☐ 491	Ron Karkovice	.25	.10	.02
☐ 492	Mike Heath	.03	.01	.00
☐ 493	Tom Lasorda MGR (checklist back)	.07	.01	.00
☐ 494	Barry Jones	.10	.04	.01
☐ 495	Gorman Thomas	.08	.03	.01
☐ 496	Bruce Bochte	.05	.02	.00
☐ 497	Dale Mohorcic	.15	.06	.01
☐ 498	Bob Kearney	.03	.01	.00
☐ 499	Bruce Ruffin	.30	.12	.03
☐ 500	Don Mattingly	2.00	.80	.20

	MINT	VG-E	F-G
☐ 501 Craig Lefferts	.03	.01	.00
☐ 502 Dick Schofield	.05	.02	.00
☐ 503 Larry Andersen	.03	.01	.00
☐ 504 Mickey Hatcher	.03	.01	.00
☐ 505 Bryn Smith	.03	.01	.00
☐ 506 Orioles Team	.05	.02	.00
(mound conference)			
☐ 507 Dave Stapleton	.03	.01	.00
☐ 508 Scott Bankhead	.05	.02	.00
☐ 509 Enos Cabell	.03	.01	.00
☐ 510 Tom Henke	.06	.02	.00
☐ 511 Steve Lyons	.03	.01	.00
☐ 512 Dave Magadan	.60	.24	.06
☐ 513 Carmen Castillo	.03	.01	.00
☐ 514 Orlando Mercado	.03	.01	.00
☐ 515 Willie Hernandez	.09	.04	.01
☐ 516 Ted Simmons	.09	.04	.01
☐ 517 Mario Soto	.07	.03	.01
☐ 518 Gene Mauch MGR	.06	.01	.00
(checklist back)			
☐ 519 Curt Young	.03	.01	.00
☐ 520 Jack Clark	.10	.04	.01
☐ 521 Rick Reuschel	.05	.02	.00
☐ 522 Checklist 397-528	.06	.01	.00
☐ 523 Earnie Riles	.07	.03	.01
☐ 524 Bob Shirley	.03	.01	.00
☐ 525 Phil Bradley	.18	.08	.01
☐ 526 Roger Mason	.07	.03	.01
☐ 527 Jim Wohlford	.03	.01	.00
☐ 528 Ken Dixon	.05	.02	.00
☐ 529 Alvaro Espinoza	.09	.04	.01
☐ 530 Tony Gwynn	.30	.12	.03
☐ 531 Astros Team	.07	.03	.01
(Y.Berra conference)			
☐ 532 Jeff Stone	.05	.02	.00
☐ 533 Argenis Salazar	.03	.01	.00
☐ 534 Scott Sanderson	.03	.01	.00
☐ 535 Tony Armas	.09	.04	.01
☐ 536 Terry Mulholland	.10	.04	.01
☐ 537 Rance Mulliniks	.03	.01	.00
☐ 538 Tom Niedenfuer	.06	.02	.00
☐ 539 Reid Nichols	.03	.01	.00
☐ 540 Terry Kennedy	.06	.02	.00
☐ 541 Rafael Belliard	.10	.04	.01
☐ 542 Ricky Horton	.03	.01	.00
☐ 543 Dave Johnson MGR	.08	.01	.00
(checklist back)			
☐ 544 Zane Smith	.03	.01	.00
☐ 545 Buddy Bell	.09	.04	.01
☐ 546 Mike Morgan	.03	.01	.00
☐ 547 Rob Deer	.15	.06	.01
☐ 548 Bill Mooneyham	.10	.04	.01
☐ 549 Bob Melvin	.03	.01	.00

	MINT	VG-E	F-G
☐ 550 Pete Incaviglia	1.00	.40	.10
☐ 551 Frank Wills	.03	.01	.00
☐ 552 Larry Sheets	.05	.02	.00
☐ 553 Mike Maddux	.10	.04	.01
☐ 554 Buddy Biancalana	.03	.01	.00
☐ 555 Dennis Rasmussen	.06	.02	.00
☐ 556 Angels Team	.05	.02	.00
(mound conference)			
☐ 557 John Cerutti	.20	.08	.02
☐ 558 Greg Gagne	.05	.02	.00
☐ 559 Lance McCullers	.05	.02	.00
☐ 560 Glenn Davis	.30	.12	.03
☐ 561 Rey Quinones	.10	.04	.01
☐ 562 Bryan Clutterbuck	.10	.04	.01
☐ 563 John Stefero	.03	.01	.00
☐ 564 Larry McWilliams	.03	.01	.00
☐ 565 Dusty Baker	.06	.02	.00
☐ 566 Tim Hulett	.05	.02	.00
☐ 567 Greg Mathews	.25	.10	.02
☐ 568 Earl Weaver MGR	.08	.01	.00
(checklist back)			
☐ 569 Wade Rowdon	.10	.04	.01
☐ 570 Sid Fernandez	.20	.08	.02
☐ 571 Ozzie Virgil	.05	.02	.00
☐ 572 Pete Ladd	.03	.01	.00
☐ 573 Hal McRae	.05	.02	.00
☐ 574 Manny Lee	.05	.02	.00
☐ 575 Pat Tabler	.07	.03	.01
☐ 576 Frank Pastore	.03	.01	.00
☐ 577 Dann Bilardello	.03	.01	.00
☐ 578 Billy Hatcher	.05	.02	.00
☐ 579 Rick Burleson	.06	.02	.00
☐ 580 Mike Krukow	.07	.03	.01
☐ 581 Cubs Team	.05	.02	.00
(Cey/Trout)			
☐ 582 Bruce Berenyi	.03	.01	.00
☐ 583 Junior Ortiz	.03	.01	.00
☐ 584 Ron Kittle	.09	.04	.01
☐ 585 Scott Bailes	.10	.04	.01
☐ 586 Ben Oglivie	.06	.02	.00
☐ 587 Eric Plunk	.08	.03	.01
☐ 588 Wallace Johnson	.03	.01	.00
☐ 589 Steve Crawford	.03	.01	.00
☐ 590 Vince Coleman	.35	.14	.03
☐ 591 Spike Owen	.05	.02	.00
☐ 592 Chris Welsh	.03	.01	.00
☐ 593 Chuck Tanner MGR	.06	.01	.00
(checklist back)			
☐ 594 Rick Anderson	.03	.01	.00
☐ 595 Keith Hernandez AS	.10	.04	.01
☐ 596 Steve Sax AS	.07	.03	.01
☐ 597 Mike Schmidt AS	.20	.08	.02
☐ 598 Ozzie Smith AS	.07	.03	.01

		MINT	VG-E	F-G
☐ 599	Tony Gwynn AS	.12	.05	.01
☐ 600	Dave Parker AS	.09	.04	.01
☐ 601	Darryl Strawberry AS	.15	.06	.01
☐ 602	Gary Carter AS	.12	.05	.01
☐ 603	Dwight Gooden AS	.25	.10	.02
☐ 604	Fern. Valenzuela AS	.12	.05	.01
☐ 605	Todd Worrell AS	.09	.04	.01
☐ 606	Don Mattingly AS	.35	.14	.03
☐ 607	Tony Bernazard AS	.05	.02	.00
☐ 608	Wade Boggs AS	.25	.10	.02
☐ 609	Cal Ripken AS	.12	.05	.01
☐ 610	Jim Rice AS	.12	.05	.01
☐ 611	Kirby Puckett AS	.12	.05	.01
☐ 612	George Bell AS	.08	.03	.01
☐ 613	Lance Parrish AS	.08	.03	.01
☐ 614	Roger Clemens AS	.25	.10	.02
☐ 615	Teddy Higuera AS	.07	.03	.01
☐ 616	Dave Righetti AS	.07	.03	.01
☐ 617	Al Nipper	.03	.01	.00
☐ 618	Tom Kelly MGR	.06	.01	.00
	(checklist back)			
☐ 619	Jerry Reed	.03	.01	.00
☐ 620	Jose Canseco	2.00	.80	.20
☐ 621	Danny Cox	.05	.02	.00
☐ 622	Glenn Braggs	.40	.16	.04
☐ 623	Kurt Stillwell	.15	.06	.01
☐ 624	Tim Burke	.05	.02	.00
☐ 625	Mookie Wilson	.05	.02	.00
☐ 626	Joel Skinner	.05	.02	.00
☐ 627	Ken Oberkfell	.03	.01	.00
☐ 628	Bob Walk	.03	.01	.00
☐ 629	Larry Parrish	.05	.02	.00
☐ 630	John Candelaria	.07	.03	.01
☐ 631	Tigers Team	.05	.02	.00
	(mound conference)			
☐ 632	Rob Woodward	.10	.04	.01
☐ 633	Jose Uribe	.03	.01	.00
☐ 634	Rafael Palmeiro	.30	.12	.03
☐ 635	Ken Schrom	.05	.02	.00
☐ 636	Darren Daulton	.09	.04	.01
☐ 637	Bip Roberts	.09	.04	.01
☐ 638	Rich Bordi	.03	.01	.00
☐ 639	Gerald Perry	.03	.01	.00
☐ 640	Mark Clear	.03	.01	.00
☐ 641	Domingo Ramos	.03	.01	.00
☐ 642	Al Pulido	.03	.01	.00
☐ 643	Ron Shepherd	.05	.02	.00
☐ 644	John Denny	.06	.02	.00
☐ 645	Dwight Evans	.09	.04	.01
☐ 646	Mike Mason	.03	.01	.00
☐ 647	Tom Lawless	.03	.01	.00
☐ 648	Barry Larkin	.45	.18	.04
☐ 649	Mickey Tettleton	.03	.01	.00

		MINT	VG-E	F-G
☐ 650	Hubie Brooks	.09	.04	.01
☐ 651	Benny Distefano	.05	.02	.00
☐ 652	Terry Forster	.05	.02	.00
☐ 653	Kevin Mitchell	.35	.14	.03
☐ 654	Checklist 529-660	.06	.01	.00
☐ 655	Jesse Barfield	.15	.06	.01
☐ 656	Rangers Team	.05	.02	.00
	(Valentine/R.Wright)			
☐ 657	Tom Waddell	.03	.01	.00
☐ 658	Robby Thompson	.30	.12	.03
☐ 659	Aurelio Lopez	.03	.01	.00
☐ 660	Bob Horner	.15	.06	.01
☐ 661	Lou Whitaker	.10	.04	.01
☐ 662	Frank DiPino	.03	.01	.00
☐ 663	Cliff Johnson	.03	.01	.00
☐ 664	Mike Marshall	.10	.04	.01
☐ 665	Rod Scurry	.03	.01	.00
☐ 666	Von Hayes	.12	.05	.01
☐ 667	Ron Hassey	.03	.01	.00
☐ 668	Juan Bonilla	.03	.01	.00
☐ 669	Bud Black	.03	.01	.00
☐ 670	Jose Cruz	.09	.04	.01
☐ 671	Ray Soff	.09	.04	.01
☐ 672	Chili Davis	.07	.03	.01
☐ 673	Don Sutton	.12	.05	.01
☐ 674	Bill Campbell	.03	.01	.00
☐ 675	Ed Romero	.03	.01	.00
☐ 676	Charlie Moore	.03	.01	.00
☐ 677	Bob Grich	.05	.02	.00
☐ 678	Carney Lansford	.07	.03	.01
☐ 679	Kent Hrbek	.15	.06	.01
☐ 680	Ryne Sandberg	.25	.10	.02
☐ 681	George Bell	.15	.06	.01
☐ 682	Jerry Reuss	.05	.02	.00
☐ 683	Gary Roenicke	.05	.02	.00
☐ 684	Kent Tekulve	.05	.02	.00
☐ 685	Jerry Hairston	.03	.01	.00
☐ 686	Doyle Alexander	.05	.02	.00
☐ 687	Alan Trammell	.12	.05	.01
☐ 688	Juan Beniquez	.05	.02	.00
☐ 689	Darrell Porter	.05	.02	.00
☐ 690	Dane Iorg	.03	.01	.00
☐ 691	Dave Parker	.15	.06	.01
☐ 692	Frank White	.06	.02	.00
☐ 693	Terry Puhl	.05	.02	.00
☐ 694	Phil Niekro	.15	.06	.01
☐ 695	Chico Walker	.15	.06	.01
☐ 696	Gary Lucas	.03	.01	.00
☐ 697	Ed Lynch	.03	.01	.00
☐ 698	Ernie Whitt	.03	.01	.00
☐ 699	Ken Landreaux	.05	.02	.00
☐ 700	Dave Bergman	.03	.01	.00
☐ 701	Willie Randolph	.06	.02	.00

	MINT	VG-E	F-G
☐ 702 Greg Gross	.03	.01	.00
☐ 703 Dave Schmidt	.03	.01	.00
☐ 704 Jesse Orosco	.05	.02	.00
☐ 705 Bruce Hurst	.07	.03	.01
☐ 706 Rick Manning	.03	.01	.00
☐ 707 Bob McClure	.03	.01	.00
☐ 708 Scott McGregor	.07	.03	.01
☐ 709 Dave Kingman	.10	.04	.01
☐ 710 Gary Gaetti	.09	.04	.01
☐ 711 Ken Griffey	.06	.02	.00
☐ 712 Don Robinson	.03	.01	.00
☐ 713 Tom Brookens	.03	.01	.00
☐ 714 Dan Quisenberry	.10	.04	.01
☐ 715 Bob Dernier	.05	.02	.00
☐ 716 Rick Leach	.03	.01	.00
☐ 717 Ed VandeBerg	.03	.01	.00
☐ 718 Steve Carlton	.25	.10	.02
☐ 719 Tom Hume	.03	.01	.00
☐ 720 Richard Dotson	.05	.02	.00
☐ 721 Tom Herr	.07	.03	.01
☐ 722 Bob Knepper	.07	.03	.01
☐ 723 Brett Butler	.08	.03	.01
☐ 724 Greg Minton	.05	.02	.00
☐ 725 George Hendrick	.05	.02	.00
☐ 726 Frank Tanana	.05	.02	.00
☐ 727 Mike Moore	.05	.02	.00
☐ 728 Tippy Martinez	.03	.01	.00
☐ 729 Tom Paciorek	.03	.01	.00
☐ 730 Eric Show	.03	.01	.00
☐ 731 Dave Concepcion	.08	.03	.01
☐ 732 Manny Trillo	.05	.02	.00
☐ 733 Bill Caudill	.05	.02	.00
☐ 734 Bill Madlock	.10	.04	.01
☐ 735 Rickey Henderson	.30	.12	.03
☐ 736 Steve Bedrosian	.05	.02	.00
☐ 737 Floyd Bannister	.05	.02	.00
☐ 738 Jorge Orta	.03	.01	.00
☐ 739 Chet Lemon	.05	.02	.00
☐ 740 Rich Gedman	.08	.03	.01
☐ 741 Paul Molitor	.08	.03	.01
☐ 742 Andy McGaffigan	.03	.01	.00
☐ 743 Dwayne Murphy	.05	.02	.00
☐ 744 Roy Smalley	.05	.02	.00
☐ 745 Glenn Hubbard	.03	.01	.00
☐ 746 Bob Ojeda	.08	.03	.01
☐ 747 Johnny Ray	.08	.03	.01
☐ 748 Mike Flanagan	.07	.03	.01
☐ 749 Ozzie Smith	.12	.05	.01
☐ 750 Steve Trout	.05	.02	.00
☐ 751 Garth Iorg	.03	.01	.00
☐ 752 Dan Petry	.09	.04	.01
☐ 753 Rick Honeycutt	.05	.02	.00
☐ 754 Dave LaPoint	.03	.01	.00

	MINT	VG-E	F-G
☐ 755 Luis Aguayo	.03	.01	.00
☐ 756 Carlton Fisk	.12	.05	.01
☐ 757 Nolan Ryan	.30	.12	.03
☐ 758 Tony Bernazard	.05	.02	.00
☐ 759 Joel Youngblood	.03	.01	.00
☐ 760 Mike Witt	.10	.04	.01
☐ 761 Greg Pryor	.03	.01	.00
☐ 762 Gary Ward	.05	.02	.00
☐ 763 Tim Flannery	.03	.01	.00
☐ 764 Bill Buckner	.08	.03	.01
☐ 765 Kirk Gibson	.20	.08	.02
☐ 766 Don Aase	.05	.02	.00
☐ 767 Ron Cey	.07	.03	.01
☐ 768 Dennis Lamp	.03	.01	.00
☐ 769 Steve Sax	.12	.05	.01
☐ 770 Dave Winfield	.25	.10	.02
☐ 771 Shane Rawley	.07	.03	.01
☐ 772 Harold Baines	.15	.06	.01
☐ 773 Robin Yount	.25	.10	.02
☐ 774 Wayne Krenchicki	.03	.01	.00
☐ 775 Joaquin Andujar	.08	.03	.01
☐ 776 Tom Brunansky	.09	.04	.01
☐ 777 Chris Chambliss	.05	.02	.00
☐ 778 Jack Morris	.15	.06	.01
☐ 779 Craig Reynolds	.03	.01	.00
☐ 780 Andre Thornton	.05	.02	.00
☐ 781 Atlee Hammaker	.05	.02	.00
☐ 782 Brian Downing	.05	.02	.00
☐ 783 Willie Wilson	.12	.05	.01
☐ 784 Cal Ripken	.25	.10	.02
☐ 785 Terry Francona	.03	.01	.00
☐ 786 Jimy Williams MGR	.06	.01	.00
(checklist back)			
☐ 787 Alejandro Pena	.05	.02	.00
☐ 788 Tim Stoddard	.03	.01	.00
☐ 789 Dan Schatzeder	.03	.01	.00
☐ 790 Julio Cruz	.03	.01	.00
☐ 791 Lance Parrish	.20	.08	.02
☐ 792 Checklist 661-792	.06	.01	.00
☐ A Don Baylor	.15	.06	.01
(wax pack box card)			
☐ B Steve Carlton	.30	.12	.03
(wax pack box card)			
☐ C Ron Cey	.10	.04	.01
(wax pack box card)			
☐ D Cecil Cooper	.10	.04	.01
(wax pack box card)			
☐ E Rickey Henderson	.50	.20	.05
(wax pack box card)			
☐ F Jim Rice	.30	.12	.03
(wax pack box card)			
☐ G Don Sutton	.20	.08	.02
(wax pack box card)			

	MINT	VG-E	F-G
☐ **H** Dave Winfield	.30	.12	.03
(wax pack box card)			

1981 Donruss

DAVE PARKER OUTFIELD

*The cards in this 605-card set measure 2½″
by 3½″. In 1981 Donruss launched itself into
the baseball card market with a set containing 600 numbered cards and five unnumbered checklists. Even though the five
checklist cards are unnumbered they are
numbered below (601-605) for convenience
in reference. The cards are printed on thin
stock and more than one pose exists for several popular players. The numerous errors of
the first print run were later corrected by the
company. These are marked P1 and P2 in
the checklist.*

	MINT	VG-E	F-G
Complete Set	22.00	9.00	2.20
Common Player (1-605)	.03	.01	.00

		MINT	VG-E	F-G
☐	1 Ozzie Smith	.35	.14	.03
☐	2 Rollie Fingers	.30	.12	.03
☐	3 Rick Wise	.06	.02	.00
☐	4 Gene Richards	.03	.01	.00
☐	5 Alan Trammell	.30	.12	.03
☐	6 Tom Brookens	.03	.01	.00
☐	7 A Duffy Dyer P1	.06	.02	.00
	1980 batting average			
	has decimal point			
☐	7 B Duffy Dyer P2	.06	.02	.00
	1980 batting average			
	has no decimal point			
☐	8 Mark Fidrych	.10	.04	.01
☐	9 Dave Rozema	.03	.01	.00

		MINT	VG-E	F-G
☐	10 Ricky Peters	.03	.01	.00
☐	11 Mike Schmidt	1.00	.40	.00
☐	12 Willie Stargell	.30	.12	.03
☐	13 Tim Foli	.03	.01	.00
☐	14 Manny Sanguillen	.06	.02	.00
☐	15 Grant Jackson	.03	.01	.00
☐	16 Eddie Solomon	.03	.01	.00
☐	17 Omar Moreno	.03	.01	.00
☐	18 Joe Morgan	.30	.12	.03
☐	19 Rafael Landestoy	.03	.01	.00
☐	20 Bruce Bochy	.03	.01	.00
☐	21 Joe Sambito	.06	.02	.00
☐	22 Manny Trillo	.06	.02	.00
☐	23 A Dave Smith P1	.25	.10	.02
	Line box around stats			
	is not complete			
☐	23 B Dave Smith P2	.25	.10	.02
	Box totally encloses			
	stats at top			
☐	24 Terry Puhl	.06	.02	.00
☐	25 Bump Wills	.03	.01	.00
☐	26 A John Ellis P1 ERR	.50	.20	.05
	Photo on front			
	shows Danny Walton			
☐	26 B John Ellis P2 COR ...	.10	.04	.01
☐	27 Jim Kern	.03	.01	.00
☐	28 Richie Zisk	.06	.02	.00
☐	29 John Mayberry	.06	.02	.00
☐	30 Bob Davis	.03	.01	.00
☐	31 Jackson Todd	.03	.01	.00
☐	32 Al Woods	.03	.01	.00
☐	33 Steve Carlton	.60	.24	.06
☐	34 Lee Mazzilli	.06	.02	.00
☐	35 John Stearns	.03	.01	.00
☐	36 Roy Lee Jackson	.06	.02	.00
☐	37 Mike Scott	.30	.12	.03
☐	38 Lamar Johnson	.03	.01	.00
☐	39 Kevin Bell	.03	.01	.00
☐	40 Ed Farmer	.03	.01	.00
☐	41 Ross Baumgarten	.03	.01	.00
☐	42 Leo Sutherland	.03	.01	.00
☐	43 Dan Meyer	.03	.01	.00
☐	44 Ron Reed	.03	.01	.00
☐	45 Mario Mendoza	.03	.01	.00
☐	46 Rick Honeycutt	.06	.02	.00
☐	47 Glenn Abbott	.03	.01	.00
☐	48 Leon Roberts	.03	.01	.00
☐	49 Rod Carew	.60	.24	.06
☐	50 Bert Campaneris	.06	.02	.00
☐	51 A Tom Donahue P1 ERR	.10	.04	.01
	Name on front			
	misspelled Donahue			
☐	51 B Tom Donohue P2 COR	.10	.04	.01

		MINT	VG-E	F-G
☐ 52	Dave Frost	.03	.01	.00
☐ 53	Ed Halicki	.03	.01	.00
☐ 54	Dan Ford	.06	.02	.00
☐ 55	Garry Maddox	.06	.02	.00
☐ 56 A	Steve Garvey P1 "Surpassed 25 HR"	.60	.24	.06
☐ 56 B	Steve Garvey P2 "Surpassed 21 HR"	.60	.24	.06
☐ 57	Bill Russell	.06	.02	.00
☐ 58	Don Sutton	.30	.12	.03
☐ 59	Reggie Smith	.10	.04	.01
☐ 60	Rick Monday	.06	.02	.00
☐ 61	Ray Knight	.10	.04	.01
☐ 62	Johnny Bench	.50	.20	.05
☐ 63	Mario Soto	.10	.04	.01
☐ 64	Doug Bair	.03	.01	.00
☐ 65	George Foster	.20	.08	.02
☐ 66	Jeff Burroughs	.06	.02	.00
☐ 67	Keith Hernandez	.35	.14	.03
☐ 68	Tom Herr	.10	.04	.01
☐ 69	Bob Forsch	.06	.02	.00
☐ 70	John Fulgham	.03	.01	.00
☐ 71 A	Bobby Bonds P1 ERR 986 lifetime HR	.25	.10	.02
☐ 71 B	Bobby Bonds P2 COR 326 lifetime HR	.10	.04	.01
☐ 72 A	Rennie Stennett P1 "breaking broke leg"	.06	.02	.00
☐ 72 B	Rennie Stennett P2 Word "broke" deleted	.06	.02	.00
☐ 73	Joe Strain	.03	.01	.00
☐ 74	Ed Whitson	.06	.02	.00
☐ 75	Tom Griffin	.03	.01	.00
☐ 76	Billy North	.03	.01	.00
☐ 77	Gene Garber	.03	.01	.00
☐ 78	Mike Hargrove	.06	.02	.00
☐ 79	Dave Rosello	.03	.01	.00
☐ 80	Ron Hassey	.03	.01	.00
☐ 81	Sid Monge	.03	.01	.00
☐ 82 A	Joe Charboneau P1 '78 highlights, "For some reason"	.15	.06	.01
☐ 82 B	Joe Charboneau P2 phrase "For some reason" deleted	.10	.04	.01
☐ 83	Cecil Cooper	.18	.08	.01
☐ 84	Sal Bando	.06	.02	.00
☐ 85	Moose Haas	.06	.02	.00
☐ 86	Mike Caldwell	.06	.02	.00
☐ 87 A	Larry Hisle P1 77 highlights, line ends with "28 RBI"	.12	.05	.01
☐ 87 B	Larry Hisle P2 correct line "28 HR"	.10	.04	.01
☐ 88	Luis Gomez	.03	.01	.00
☐ 89	Larry Parrish	.06	.02	.00
☐ 90	Gary Carter	.60	.24	.06
☐ 91	Bill Gullickson	.25	.10	.02
☐ 92	Fred Norman	.03	.01	.00
☐ 93	Tommy Hutton	.03	.01	.00
☐ 94	Carl Yastrzemski	.80	.32	.08
☐ 95	Glenn Hoffman	.06	.02	.00
☐ 96	Dennis Eckersley	.06	.02	.00
☐ 97 A	Tom Burgmeier P1 ERR Throws: Right	.06	.02	.00
☐ 97 B	Tom Burgmeier P2 COR Throws: Left	.06	.02	.00
☐ 98	Win Remmerswaal	.03	.01	.00
☐ 99	Bob Horner	.25	.10	.02
☐ 100	George Brett	.80	.32	.08
☐ 101	Dave Chalk	.03	.01	.00
☐ 102	Dennis Leonard	.06	.02	.00
☐ 103	Renie Martin	.03	.01	.00
☐ 104	Amos Otis	.06	.02	.00
☐ 105	Graig Nettles	.15	.06	.01
☐ 106	Eric Soderholm	.03	.01	.00
☐ 107	Tommy John	.15	.06	.01
☐ 108	Tom Underwood	.03	.01	.00
☐ 109	Lou Piniella	.12	.05	.01
☐ 110	Mickey Klutts	.03	.01	.00
☐ 111	Bobby Murcer	.10	.04	.01
☐ 112	Eddie Murray	.80	.32	.08
☐ 113	Rick Dempsey	.06	.02	.00
☐ 114	Scott McGregor	.10	.04	.01
☐ 115	Ken Singleton	.10	.04	.01
☐ 116	Gary Roenicke	.06	.02	.00
☐ 117	Dave Revering	.03	.01	.00
☐ 118	Mike Norris	.03	.01	.00
☐ 119	Rickey Henderson	.70	.28	.07
☐ 120	Mike Heath	.03	.01	.00
☐ 121	Dave Cash	.03	.01	.00
☐ 122	Randy Jones	.06	.02	.00
☐ 123	Eric Rasmussen	.03	.01	.00
☐ 124	Jerry Mumphrey	.06	.02	.00
☐ 125	Richie Hebner	.03	.01	.00
☐ 126	Mark Wagner	.03	.01	.00
☐ 127	Jack Morris	.30	.12	.03
☐ 128	Dan Petry	.15	.06	.01
☐ 129	Bruce Robbins	.03	.01	.00
☐ 130	Champ Summers	.03	.01	.00
☐ 131 A	Pete Rose P1 last line ends with "see card 251"	1.25	.50	.12

		MINT	VG-E	F-G
☐ 131	**B** Pete Rose P2 .... last line corrected "see card 371"	1.25	.50	.12
☐ 132	Willie Stargell	.30	.12	.03
☐ 133	Ed Ott....................	.03	.01	.00
☐ 134	Jim Bibby	.06	.02	.00
☐ 135	Bert Blyleven	.15	.06	.01
☐ 136	Dave Parker	.30	.12	.03
☐ 137	Bill Robinson	.03	.01	.00
☐ 138	Enos Cabell	.03	.01	.00
☐ 139	Dave Bergman	.03	.01	.00
☐ 140	J.R. Richard	.10	.04	.01
☐ 141	Ken Forsch	.06	.02	.00
☐ 142	Larry Bowa	.12	.05	.01
☐ 143	Frank LaCorte	.03	.01	.00
☐ 144	Dennis Walling	.03	.01	.00
☐ 145	Buddy Bell	.15	.06	.01
☐ 146	Ferguson Jenkins	.18	.08	.01
☐ 147	Dannny Darwin	.06	.02	.00
☐ 148	John Grubb	.03	.01	.00
☐ 149	Alfredo Griffin	.10	.04	.01
☐ 150	Jerry Garvin	.03	.01	.00
☐ 151	Paul Mirabella	.03	.01	.00
☐ 152	Rick Bosetti	.03	.01	.00
☐ 153	Dick Ruthven	.03	.01	.00
☐ 154	Frank Taveras	.03	.01	.00
☐ 155	Craig Swan	.03	.01	.00
☐ 156	Jeff Reardon	.40	.16	.04
☐ 157	Steve Henderson	.03	.01	.00
☐ 158	Jim Morrison	.03	.01	.00
☐ 159	Glenn Borgmann	.03	.01	.00
☐ 160	LaMarr Hoyt	.40	.16	.04
☐ 161	Rich Wortham	.03	.01	.00
☐ 162	Thad Bosley	.03	.01	.00
☐ 163	Julio Cruz	.03	.01	.00
☐ 164	**A** Del Unser P1 .... no "3B" heading	.06	.02	.00
☐ 164	**B** Del Unser P2 .... Batting record on back corrected ("3B")	.06	.02	.00
☐ 165	Jim Anderson	.03	.01	.00
☐ 166	Jim Beattie	.03	.01	.00
☐ 167	Shane Rawley	.10	.04	.01
☐ 168	Joe Simpson	.03	.01	.00
☐ 169	Rod Carew	.60	.24	.06
☐ 170	Fred Patek	.03	.01	.00
☐ 171	Frank Tanana	.06	.02	.00
☐ 172	Alfredo Martinez	.03	.01	.00
☐ 173	Chris Knapp	.03	.01	.00
☐ 174	Joe Rudi	.06	.02	.00
☐ 175	Greg Luzinski	.15	.06	.01
☐ 176	Steve Garvey	.60	.24	.06
☐ 177	Joe Ferguson	.03	.01	.00
☐ 178	Bob Welch	.10	.04	.01
☐ 179	Dusty Baker	.10	.04	.01
☐ 180	Rudy Law	.03	.01	.00
☐ 181	Dave Concepcion	.15	.06	.01
☐ 182	Johnny Bench	.50	.20	.05
☐ 183	Mike LaCoss	.03	.01	.00
☐ 184	Ken Griffey	.10	.04	.01
☐ 185	Dave Collins	.06	.02	.00
☐ 186	Brian Asselstine	.03	.01	.00
☐ 187	Garry Templeton	.10	.04	.01
☐ 188	Mike Phillips	.03	.01	.00
☐ 189	Pete Vuckovich	.06	.02	.00
☐ 190	John Urrea	.03	.01	.00
☐ 191	Tony Scott	.03	.01	.00
☐ 192	Darrell Evans	.12	.05	.01
☐ 193	Milt May	.03	.01	.00
☐ 194	Bob Knepper	.12	.05	.01
☐ 195	Randy Moffitt	.03	.01	.00
☐ 196	Larry Herndon	.03	.01	.00
☐ 197	Rick Camp	.03	.01	.00
☐ 198	Andre Thornton	.10	.04	.01
☐ 199	Tom Veryzer	.03	.01	.00
☐ 200	Gary Alexander	.03	.01	.00
☐ 201	Rick Waits	.03	.01	.00
☐ 202	Rick Manning	.03	.01	.00
☐ 203	Paul Molitor	.15	.06	.01
☐ 204	Jim Gantner	.06	.02	.00
☐ 205	Paul Mitchell	.03	.01	.00
☐ 206	Reggie Cleveland	.03	.01	.00
☐ 207	Sixto Lezcano	.03	.01	.00
☐ 208	Bruce Benedict	.03	.01	.00
☐ 209	Rodney Scott	.03	.01	.00
☐ 210	John Tamargo	.03	.01	.00
☐ 211	Bill Lee	.06	.02	.00
☐ 212	Andre Dawson	.25	.10	.02
☐ 213	Rowland Office	.03	.01	.00
☐ 214	Carl Yastrzemski	.80	.32	.08
☐ 215	Jerry Remy	.06	.02	.00
☐ 216	Mike Torrez	.06	.02	.00
☐ 217	Skip Lockwood	.03	.01	.00
☐ 218	Fred Lynn	.25	.10	.02
☐ 219	Chris Chambliss	.06	.02	.00
☐ 220	Willie Aikens	.06	.02	.00
☐ 221	John Wathan	.03	.01	.00
☐ 222	Dan Quisenberry	.25	.10	.02
☐ 223	Willie Wilson	.20	.08	.02
☐ 224	Clint Hurdle	.03	.01	.00
☐ 225	Bob Watson	.06	.02	.00
☐ 226	Jim Spencer	.03	.01	.00
☐ 227	Ron Guidry	.30	.12	.03
☐ 228	Reggie Jackson	.80	.32	.08
☐ 229	Oscar Gamble	.06	.02	.00
☐ 230	Jeff Cox	.03	.01	.00

	MINT	VG-E	F-G
☐ 231 Luis Tiant	.10	.04	.01
☐ 232 Rich Dauer	.03	.01	.00
☐ 233 Dan Graham	.03	.01	.00
☐ 234 Mike Flanagan	.10	.04	.01
☐ 235 John Lowenstein	.03	.01	.00
☐ 236 Benny Ayala	.03	.01	.00
☐ 237 Wayne Gross	.03	.01	.00
☐ 238 Rick Langford	.03	.01	.00
☐ 239 Tony Armas	.12	.05	.01
☐ 240 A Bob Lacy P1 ERR	.12	.05	.01
Name misspelled Bob "Lacy"			
☐ 240 B Bob Lacey P2 COR	.08	.03	.01
☐ 241 Gene Tenace	.03	.01	.00
☐ 242 Bob Shirley	.03	.01	.00
☐ 243 Gary Lucas	.10	.04	.01
☐ 244 Jerry Turner	.03	.01	.00
☐ 245 John Wockenfuss	.03	.01	.00
☐ 246 Stan Papi	.03	.01	.00
☐ 247 Milt Wilcox	.03	.01	.00
☐ 248 Dan Schatzeder	.03	.01	.00
☐ 249 Steve Kemp	.10	.04	.01
☐ 250 Jim Lentine	.03	.01	.00
☐ 251 Pete Rose	1.25	.50	.12
☐ 252 Bill Madlock	.20	.08	.02
☐ 253 Dale Berra	.06	.02	.00
☐ 254 Kent Tekulve	.06	.02	.00
☐ 255 Enrique Romo	.03	.01	.00
☐ 256 Mike Easler	.06	.02	.00
☐ 257 Chuck Tanner MGR	.06	.02	.00
☐ 258 Art Howe	.03	.01	.00
☐ 259 Alan Ashby	.03	.01	.00
☐ 260 Nolan Ryan	.50	.20	.05
☐ 261 A Vern Ruhle P1 ERR	.50	.20	.05
Photo on front actually Ken Forsch			
☐ 261 B Vern Ruhle P2 COR	.10	.04	.01
☐ 262 Bob Boone	.06	.02	.00
☐ 263 Cesar Cedeno	.10	.04	.01
☐ 264 Jeff Leonard	.10	.04	.01
☐ 265 Pat Putnam	.03	.01	.00
☐ 266 Jon Matlack	.06	.02	.00
☐ 267 Dave Rajsich	.03	.01	.00
☐ 268 Bill Sample	.03	.01	.00
☐ 269 Damaso Garcia	.50	.20	.05
☐ 270 Tom Buskey	.03	.01	.00
☐ 271 Joey McLaughlin	.03	.01	.00
☐ 272 Barry Bonnell	.03	.01	.00
☐ 273 Tug McGraw	.10	.04	.01
☐ 274 Mike Jorgensen	.03	.01	.00
☐ 275 Pat Zachry	.03	.01	.00
☐ 276 Neil Allen	.06	.02	.00
☐ 277 Joel Youngblood	.03	.01	.00
☐ 278 Greg Pryor	.03	.01	.00
☐ 279 Britt Burns	.30	.12	.03
☐ 280 Rich Dotson	.25	.10	.02
☐ 281 Chet Lemon	.10	.04	.01
☐ 282 Rusty Kuntz	.03	.01	.00
☐ 283 Ted Cox	.03	.01	.00
☐ 284 Sparky Lyle	.12	.05	.01
☐ 285 Larry Cox	.03	.01	.00
☐ 286 Floyd Bannister	.06	.02	.00
☐ 287 Byron McLaughlin	.03	.01	.00
☐ 288 Rodney Craig	.03	.01	.00
☐ 289 Bobby Grich	.10	.04	.01
☐ 290 Dickie Thon	.10	.04	.01
☐ 291 Mark Clear	.06	.02	.00
☐ 292 Dave Lemanczyk	.03	.01	.00
☐ 293 Jason Thompson	.06	.02	.00
☐ 294 Rick Miller	.03	.01	.00
☐ 295 Lonnie Smith	.06	.02	.00
☐ 296 Ron Cey	.15	.06	.01
☐ 297 Steve Yeager	.06	.02	.00
☐ 298 Bobby Castillo	.03	.01	.00
☐ 299 Manny Mota	.06	.02	.00
☐ 300 Jay Johnstone	.06	.02	.00
☐ 301 Dan Driessen	.06	.02	.00
☐ 302 Joe Nolan	.03	.01	.00
☐ 303 Paul Householder	.06	.02	.00
☐ 304 Harry Spilman	.03	.01	.00
☐ 305 Cesar Geronimo	.03	.01	.00
☐ 306 A Gary Mathews P1 ERR	.15	.06	.01
Name misspelled			
☐ 306 B Gary Matthews P2 COR	.10	.04	.01
☐ 307 Ken Reitz	.03	.01	.00
☐ 308 Ted Simmons	.15	.06	.01
☐ 309 John Littlefield	.06	.02	.00
☐ 310 George Frazier	.03	.01	.00
☐ 311 Dane Iorg	.03	.01	.00
☐ 312 Mike Ivie	.03	.01	.00
☐ 313 Dennis Littlejohn	.03	.01	.00
☐ 314 Gary Lavelle	.06	.02	.00
☐ 315 Jack Clark	.15	.06	.01
☐ 316 Jim Wohlford	.03	.01	.00
☐ 317 Rick Matula	.03	.01	.00
☐ 318 Toby Harrah	.06	.02	.00
☐ 319 A Dwane Kuiper P1 ERR	.12	.05	.01
Name misspelled			
☐ 319 B Duane Kuiper P2 COR	.08	.03	.01
☐ 320 Len Barker	.06	.02	.00
☐ 321 Victor Cruz	.03	.01	.00
☐ 322 Dell Alston	.03	.01	.00
☐ 323 Robin Yount	.50	.20	.05
☐ 324 Charlie Moore	.03	.01	.00
☐ 325 Lary Sorensen	.03	.01	.00

	MINT	VG-E	F-G
☐ 326 A Gorman Thomas P1 .. 2nd line on back: "30 HR mark 4th"	.15	.06	.01
☐ 326 B Gorman Thomas P2 .. "30 HR mark 3rd"	.10	.04	.01
☐ 327 Bob Rodgers MGR	.03	.01	.00
☐ 328 Phil Niekro	.25	.10	.02
☐ 329 Chris Speier	.03	.01	.00
☐ 330 A Steve Rodgers P1 ERR .... Name misspelled	.15	.06	.01
☐ 330 B Steve Rogers P2 COR	.10	.04	.01
☐ 331 Woodie Fryman	.03	.01	.00
☐ 332 Warren Cromartie	.03	.01	.00
☐ 333 Jerry White	.03	.01	.00
☐ 334 Tony Perez	.15	.06	.01
☐ 335 Carlton Fisk	.20	.08	.02
☐ 336 Dick Drago	.03	.01	.00
☐ 337 Steve Renko	.03	.01	.00
☐ 338 Jim Rice	.60	.24	.06
☐ 339 Jerry Royster	.03	.01	.00
☐ 340 Frank White	.10	.04	.01
☐ 341 Jamie Quirk	.03	.01	.00
☐ 342 A Paul Spittorff P1 ERR . Name misspelled	.10	.04	.01
☐ 342 B Paul Spittorff P2 COR	.08	.03	.01
☐ 343 Marty Pattin	.03	.01	.00
☐ 344 Pete LaCock	.03	.01	.00
☐ 345 Willie Randolph	.10	.04	.01
☐ 346 Rick Cerone	.06	.02	.00
☐ 347 Rich Gossage	.20	.08	.02
☐ 348 Reggie Jackson	.75	.30	.07
☐ 349 Ruppert Jones	.06	.02	.00
☐ 350 Dave McKay	.03	.01	.00
☐ 351 Yogi Berra MGR	.20	.08	.02
☐ 352 Doug DeCinces	.10	.04	.01
☐ 353 Jim Palmer	.35	.14	.03
☐ 354 Tippy Martinez	.06	.02	.00
☐ 355 Al Bumbry	.03	.01	.00
☐ 356 Earl Weaver MGR	.10	.04	.01
☐ 357 A Bob Picciolo P1 ERR . Name misspelled	.06	.02	.00
☐ 357 B Rob Picciolo P2 COR .	.06	.02	.00
☐ 358 Matt Keough	.03	.01	.00
☐ 359 Dwayne Murphy	.06	.02	.00
☐ 360 Brian Kingman	.03	.01	.00
☐ 361 Bill Fahey	.03	.01	.00
☐ 362 Steve Mura	.03	.01	.00
☐ 363 Dennis Kinney	.03	.01	.00
☐ 364 Dave Winfield	.50	.20	.05
☐ 365 Lou Whitaker	.20	.08	.02
☐ 366 Lance Parrish	.35	.14	.03

	MINT	VG-E	F-G
☐ 367 Tim Corcoran	.03	.01	.00
☐ 368 Pat Underwood	.03	.01	.00
☐ 369 Al Cowens	.06	.02	.00
☐ 370 Sparky Anderson MGR .	.06	.02	.00
☐ 371 Pete Rose	1.25	.50	.12
☐ 372 Phil Gamer	.06	.02	.00
☐ 373 Steve Nicosia	.03	.01	.00
☐ 374 John Candelaria	.06	.02	.00
☐ 375 Don Robinson	.06	.02	.00
☐ 376 Lee Lacy	.06	.02	.00
☐ 377 John Milner	.03	.01	.00
☐ 378 Craig Reynolds	.03	.01	.00
☐ 379 A Luis Pujols P1 ERR ... Name misspelled	.10	.04	.01
☐ 379 B Luis Pujols P2 COR ..	.06	.02	.00
☐ 380 Joe Niekro	.06	.02	.00
☐ 381 Joaquin Andujar	.15	.06	.01
☐ 382 Keith Moreland	.45	.18	.04
☐ 383 Jose Cruz	.15	.06	.01
☐ 384 Bill Virdon MGR	.06	.02	.00
☐ 385 Jim Sundberg	.06	.02	.00
☐ 386 Doc Medich	.03	.01	.00
☐ 387 Al Oliver	.15	.06	.01
☐ 388 Jim Norris	.03	.01	.00
☐ 389 Bob Bailor	.03	.01	.00
☐ 390 Ernie Whitt	.03	.01	.00
☐ 391 Otto Velez	.03	.01	.00
☐ 392 Roy Howell	.03	.01	.00
☐ 393 Bob Walk	.06	.02	.00
☐ 394 Doug Flynn	.03	.01	.00
☐ 395 Pete Falcone	.03	.01	.00
☐ 396 Tom Hausman	.03	.01	.00
☐ 397 Elliott Maddox	.03	.01	.00
☐ 398 Mike Squires	.03	.01	.00
☐ 399 Marvis Foley	.03	.01	.00
☐ 400 Steve Trout	.06	.02	.00
☐ 401 Wayne Nordhagen	.03	.01	.00
☐ 402 Tony LaRussa MGR	.06	.02	.00
☐ 403 Bruce Bochte	.06	.02	.00
☐ 404 Bake McBride	.06	.02	.00
☐ 405 Jerry Narron	.03	.01	.00
☐ 406 Rob Dressler	.03	.01	.00
☐ 407 Dave Heaverlo	.03	.01	.00
☐ 408 Tom Paciorek	.03	.01	.00
☐ 409 Carney Lansford	.15	.06	.01
☐ 410 Brian Downing	.06	.02	.00
☐ 411 Don Aase	.06	.02	.00
☐ 412 Jim Barr	.03	.01	.00
☐ 413 Don Baylor	.20	.08	.02
☐ 414 Jim Fregosi	.06	.02	.00
☐ 415 Dallas Green MGR	.06	.02	.00
☐ 416 Dave Lopes	.10	.04	.01
☐ 417 Jerry Reuss	.06	.02	.00

		MINT	VG-E	F-G			MINT	VG-E	F-G
☐ 418	Rick Sutcliffe	.15	.06	.01	☐ 466	Dennis Werth	.03	.01	.00
☐ 419	Derrel Thomas	.03	.01	.00	☐ 467	Ron Davis	.03	.01	.00
☐ 420	Tommy Lasorda MGR	.10	.04	.01	☐ 468	Reggie Jackson	.75	.30	.07
☐ 421	Charles Leibrandt	.35	.14	.03	☐ 469	Bobby Brown	.03	.01	.00
☐ 422	Tom Seaver	.50	.20	.05	☐ 470	Mike Davis	.30	.12	.03
☐ 423	Ron Oester	.06	.02	.00	☐ 471	Gaylord Perry	.30	.12	.03
☐ 424	Junior Kennedy	.03	.01	.00	☐ 472	Mark Belanger	.06	.02	.00
☐ 425	Tom Seaver	.50	.20	.05	☐ 473	Jim Palmer	.35	.14	.03
☐ 426	Bobby Cox MGR	.03	.01	.00	☐ 474	Sammy Stewart	.03	.01	.00
☐ 427	Leon Durham	.50	.20	.05	☐ 475	Tim Stoddard	.03	.01	.00
☐ 428	Terry Kennedy	.12	.05	.01	☐ 476	Steve Stone	.06	.02	.00
☐ 429	Silvio Martinez	.03	.01	.00	☐ 477	Jeff Newman	.03	.01	.00
☐ 430	George Hendrick	.10	.04	.01	☐ 478	Steve McCatty	.03	.01	.00
☐ 431	Red Schoendienst MGR	.06	.02	.00	☐ 479	Billy Martin MGR	.15	.06	.01
☐ 432	Johnnie LeMaster	.03	.01	.00	☐ 480	Mitchell Page	.03	.01	.00
☐ 433	Vida Blue	.10	.04	.01	☐ 481	Cy Young Winner 1980	.30	.12	.03
☐ 434	John Montefusco	.06	.02	.00		Steve Carlton			
☐ 435	Terry Whitfield	.03	.01	.00	☐ 482	Bill Buckner	.15	.06	.01
☐ 436	Dave Bristol MGR	.03	.01	.00	☐ 483 A	Ivan DeJesus P1 ERR	.06	.02	.00
☐ 437	Dale Murphy	1.25	.50	.12		lifetime hits "702"			
☐ 438	Jerry Dybzinski	.03	.01	.00	☐ 483 B	Ivan DeJesus P2 COR	.06	.02	.00
☐ 439	Jorge Orta	.03	.01	.00		lifetime hits "642"			
☐ 440	Wayne Garland	.03	.01	.00	☐ 484	Cliff Johnson	.03	.01	.00
☐ 441	Miguel Dilone	.03	.01	.00	☐ 485	Lenny Randle	.03	.01	.00
☐ 442	Dave Garcia MGR	.03	.01	.00	☐ 486	Larry Milbourne	.03	.01	.00
☐ 443	Don Money	.03	.01	.00	☐ 487	Roy Smalley	.06	.02	.00
☐ 444 A	Buck Martinez P1 ERR	.12	.05	.01	☐ 488	John Castino	.06	.02	.00
	reverse negative				☐ 489	Ron Jackson	.03	.01	.00
☐ 444 B	Buck Martinez P2 COR	.08	.03	.01	☐ 490 A	Dave Roberts P1	.06	.02	.00
☐ 445	Jerry Augustine	.03	.01	.00		Career Highlights:			
☐ 446	Ben Oglivie	.06	.02	.00		"Showed pop in"			
☐ 447	Jim Slaton	.06	.02	.00	☐ 490 B	Dave Roberts P2	.06	.02	.00
☐ 448	Doyle Alexander	.06	.02	.00		"Declared himself"			
☐ 449	Tony Bernazard	.06	.02	.00	☐ 491	MVP: George Brett	.50	.20	.05
☐ 450	Scott Sanderson	.03	.01	.00	☐ 492	Mike Cubbage	.03	.01	.00
☐ 451	Dave Palmer	.06	.02	.00	☐ 493	Rob Wilfong	.03	.01	.00
☐ 452	Stan Bahnsen	.03	.01	.00	☐ 494	Danny Goodwin	.03	.01	.00
☐ 453	Dick Williams MGR	.06	.02	.00	☐ 495	Jose Morales	.03	.01	.00
☐ 454	Rick Burleson	.06	.02	.00	☐ 496	Mickey Rivers	.06	.02	.00
☐ 455	Gary Allenson	.03	.01	.00	☐ 497	Mike Edwards	.03	.01	.00
☐ 456	Bob Stanley	.06	.02	.00	☐ 498	Mike Sadek	.03	.01	.00
☐ 457 A	John Tudor P1 ERR	1.00	.40	.10	☐ 499	Lenn Sakata	.03	.01	.00
	lifetime W-L "9.7"				☐ 500	Gene Michael MGR	.06	.02	.00
☐ 457 B	John Tudor P2 COR	1.00	.40	.10	☐ 501	Dave Roberts	.03	.01	.00
	corrected "9-7"				☐ 502	Steve Dillard	.03	.01	.00
☐ 458	Dwight Evans	.15	.06	.01	☐ 503	Jim Essian	.03	.01	.00
☐ 459	Glenn Hubbard	.03	.01	.00	☐ 504	Rance Mulliniks	.03	.01	.00
☐ 460	U.L. Washington	.03	.01	.00	☐ 505	Darrell Porter	.06	.02	.00
☐ 461	Larry Gura	.06	.02	.00	☐ 506	Joe Torre MGR	.10	.04	.01
☐ 462	Rich Gale	.03	.01	.00	☐ 507	Terry Crowley	.03	.01	.00
☐ 463	Hal McRae	.06	.02	.00	☐ 508	Bill Travers	.03	.01	.00
☐ 464	Jim Frey MGR	.03	.01	.00	☐ 509	Nelson Norman	.03	.01	.00
☐ 465	Bucky Dent	.10	.04	.01	☐ 510	Bob McClure	.03	.01	.00

		MINT	VG-E	F-G
☐ 511	Steve Howe	.15	.06	.01
☐ 512	Dave Rader	.03	.01	.00
☐ 513	Mick Kelleher	.03	.01	.00
☐ 514	Kiko Garcia	.03	.01	.00
☐ 515	Larry Biittner	.03	.01	.00
☐ 516 A	Willie Norwood P1 .... Career Highlights: "Spent most of"	.06	.02	.00
☐ 516 B	Willie Norwood P2 ... "Traded to Seattle"	.06	.02	.00
☐ 517	Bo Diaz	.06	.02	.00
☐ 518	Juan Beniquez	.06	.02	.00
☐ 519	Scot Thompson	.03	.01	.00
☐ 520	Jim Tracy	.03	.01	.00
☐ 521	Carlos Lezcano	.03	.01	.00
☐ 522	Joe Amalfitano MGR ...	.03	.01	.00
☐ 523	Preston Hanna	.03	.01	.00
☐ 524 A	Ray Burris P1 .... Career Highlights: "Went on ..."	.06	.02	.00
☐ 524 B	Ray Burris P2 .... "Drafted by ..."	.06	.02	.00
☐ 525	Broderick Perkins	.03	.01	.00
☐ 526	Mickey Hatcher	.03	.01	.00
☐ 527	John Goryl MGR	.03	.01	.00
☐ 528	Dick Davis	.03	.01	.00
☐ 529	Butch Wynegar	.06	.02	.00
☐ 530	Sal Butera	.03	.01	.00
☐ 531	Jerry Koosman	.10	.04	.01
☐ 532 A	Geoff Zahn P1 .... Career Highlights: "Was 2nd in"	.06	.02	.00
☐ 532 B	Geoff Zahn P2 .... "Signed a 3 year"	.06	.02	.00
☐ 533	Dennis Martinez	.03	.01	.00
☐ 534	Gary Thomasson	.03	.01	.00
☐ 535	Steve Macko	.03	.01	.00
☐ 536	Jim Kaat	.15	.06	.01
☐ 537	Best Hitters George Brett Rod Carew	1.00	.40	.10
☐ 538	Tim Raines	4.00	1.60	.40
☐ 539	Keith Smith	.03	.01	.00
☐ 540	Ken Macha	.03	.01	.00
☐ 541	Burt Hooton	.03	.01	.00
☐ 542	Butch Hobson	.03	.01	.00
☐ 543	Bill Stein	.03	.01	.00
☐ 544	Dave Stapleton	.06	.02	.00
☐ 545	Bob Pate	.03	.01	.00
☐ 546	Doug Corbett	.10	.04	.01
☐ 547	Darrell Jackson	.03	.01	.00
☐ 548	Pete Redfern	.03	.01	.00
☐ 549	Roger Erickson	.03	.01	.00

		MINT	VG-E	F-G
☐ 550	Al Hrabosky	.06	.02	.00
☐ 551	Dick Tidrow	.03	.01	.00
☐ 552	Dave Ford	.03	.01	.00
☐ 553	Dave Kingman	.15	.06	.01
☐ 554 A	Mike Vail P1 .... Career Highlights: "After two ..."	.06	.02	.00
☐ 554 B	Mike Vail P2 .... "Traded to ..."	.06	.02	.00
☐ 555 A	Jerry Martin P1 .... Career Highlights: "Overcame a ..."	.06	.02	.00
☐ 555 B	Jerry Martin P2 .... "Traded to ..."	.06	.02	.00
☐ 556 A	Jesus Figueroa P1 .... Career Highlights: "Had an ..."	.06	.02	.00
☐ 556 B	Jesus Figueroa P2 ... "Traded to ..."	.06	.02	.00
☐ 557	Don Stanhouse	.03	.01	.00
☐ 558	Barry Foote	.03	.01	.00
☐ 559	Tim Blackwell	.03	.01	.00
☐ 560	Bruce Sutter	.20	.08	.02
☐ 561	Rick Reuschel	.06	.02	.00
☐ 562	Lynn McGlothen	.03	.01	.00
☐ 563 A	Bob Owchinko P1 .... Career Highlights: "Traded to ..."	.06	.02	.00
☐ 563 B	Bob Owchinko P2 ... "Involved in a ..."	.06	.02	.00
☐ 564	John Verhoeven	.03	.01	.00
☐ 565	Ken Landreaux	.06	.02	.00
☐ 566 A	Glen Adams P1 ERR Name misspelled	.10	.04	.01
☐ 566 B	Glenn Adams P2 COR	.06	.02	.00
☐ 567	Hosken Powell	.03	.01	.00
☐ 568	Dick Noles	.03	.01	.00
☐ 569	Danny Ainge	.25	.10	.02
☐ 570	Bobby Mattick MGR ...	.03	.01	.00
☐ 571	Joe Lefebvre	.06	.02	.00
☐ 572	Bobby Clark	.03	.01	.00
☐ 573	Dennis Lamp	.03	.01	.00
☐ 574	Randy Lerch	.03	.01	.00
☐ 575	Mookie Wilson	.35	.14	.03
☐ 576	Ron LeFlore	.06	.02	.00
☐ 577	Jim Dwyer	.03	.01	.00
☐ 578	Bill Castro	.03	.01	.00
☐ 579	Greg Minton	.06	.02	.00
☐ 580	Mark Littell	.03	.01	.00
☐ 581	Andy Hassler	.03	.01	.00
☐ 582	Dave Stieb	.30	.12	.03
☐ 583	Ken Oberkfell	.06	.02	.00
☐ 584	Larry Bradford	.03	.01	.00

		MINT	VG-E	F-G
☐ 585	Fred Stanley	.03	.01	.00
☐ 586	Bill Caudill	.06	.02	.00
☐ 587	Doug Capilla	.03	.01	.00
☐ 588	George Riley	.03	.01	.00
☐ 589	Willie Hernandez	.15	.06	.01
☐ 590	MVP: Mike Schmidt	.45	.18	.04
☐ 591	Cy Young Winner 1980: Steve Stone	.06	.02	.00
☐ 592	Rick Sofield	.03	.01	.00
☐ 593	Bombo Rivera	.03	.01	.00
☐ 594	Gary Ward	.10	.04	.01
☐ 595	A Dave Edwards P1 Career Highlights: "Sidelined the"	.06	.02	.00
☐ 595	B Dave Edwards P2 "Traded to ..."	.06	.02	.00
☐ 596	Mike Proly	.03	.01	.00
☐ 597	Tommy Boggs	.03	.01	.00
☐ 598	Greg Gross	.03	.01	.00
☐ 599	Elias Sosa	.03	.01	.00
☐ 600	Pat Kelly	.03	.01	.00
☐ 601	A Checklist 1 P1 ERR unnumbered (51 Donahue)	.10	.01	.00
☐ 601	B Checklist 1 P2 COR unnumbered (51 Donohue)	.75	.07	.00
☐ 602	Checklist 2 unnumbered	.10	.01	.00
☐ 603	A Checklist 3 P1 ERR unnumbered (306 Mathews)	.10	.01	.00
☐ 603	B Checklist 3 P2 COR unnumbered (306 Matthews)	.10	.01	.00
☐ 604	A Checklist 4 P1 ERR unnumbered (379 Pujois)	.10	.01	.00
☐ 604	B Checklist 4 P2 COR unnumbered (379 Pujols)	.10	.01	.00
☐ 605	A Checklist 5 P1 ERR unnumbered (566 Glen Adams)	.10	.01	.00
☐ 605	B Checklist 5 P2 COR unnumbered (566 Glenn Adams)	.10	.01	.00

1982 Donruss

The 1982 Donruss set contains 653 numbered cards and the seven unnumbered checklists; each card measures 2½" by 3½". The first 26 cards of this set are entitled Donruss Diamond Kings (DK) and feature the artwork of Dick Perez of Perez-Steele Galleries. The set was marketed with puzzle pieces rather than with bubble gum. There are 63 pieces to the puzzle, which when put together make a collage of Babe Ruth entitled "Hall of Fame Diamond King." The card stock in this year's Donruss cards is considerably thicker than that of the 1981 cards. The seven unnumbered checklist cards are arbitrarily assigned numbers 654 through 660 and are listed at the end of the list below.

		MINT	VG-E	F-G
	Complete Set	22.00	9.00	2.20
	Common Player (1-660)	.03	.01	.00
☐ 1	Pete Rose DK	1.50	.60	.15
☐ 2	Gary Carter DK	.50	.20	.05
☐ 3	Steve Garvey DK	.50	.20	.05
☐ 4	Vida Blue DK	.10	.04	.01
☐ 5	A Alan Trammell DK ERR (name misspelled)	.60	.24	.06
☐ 5	B Alan Trammell DK COR	.30	.12	.03
☐ 6	Len Barker DK	.06	.02	.00
☐ 7	Dwight Evans DK	.12	.05	.01
☐ 8	Rod Carew DK	.50	.20	.05

		MINT	VG-E	F-G
☐ 9	George Hendrick DK	.08	.03	.01
☐ 10	Phil Niekro DK	.30	.12	.03
☐ 11	Richie Zisk DK	.06	.02	.00
☐ 12	Dave Parker DK	.30	.12	.03
☐ 13	Nolan Ryan DK	.50	.20	.05
☐ 14	Ivan DeJesus DK	.06	.02	.00
☐ 15	George Brett DK	.75	.30	.07
☐ 16	Tom Seaver DK	.50	.20	.05
☐ 17	Dave Kingman DK	.12	.05	.01
☐ 18	Dave Winfield DK	.45	.18	.04
☐ 19	Mike Norris DK	.06	.02	.00
☐ 20	Carlton Fisk DK	.20	.08	.02
☐ 21	Ozzie Smith DK	.15	.06	.01
☐ 22	Roy Smalley DK	.06	.02	.00
☐ 23	Buddy Bell DK	.10	.04	.01
☐ 24	Ken Singleton DK	.10	.04	.01
☐ 25	John Mayberry DK	.06	.02	.00
☐ 26	Gorman Thomas DK	.10	.04	.01
☐ 27	Earl Weaver MGR	.08	.03	.01
☐ 28	Rollie Fingers	.20	.08	.02
☐ 29	Sparky Anderson MGR	.08	.03	.01
☐ 30	Dennis Eckersley	.06	.02	.00
☐ 31	Dave Winfield	.45	.18	.04
☐ 32	Burt Hooton	.03	.01	.00
☐ 33	Rick Waits	.03	.01	.00
☐ 34	George Brett	.65	.26	.06
☐ 35	Steve McCatty	.03	.01	.00
☐ 36	Steve Rogers	.06	.02	.00
☐ 37	Bill Stein	.03	.01	.00
☐ 38	Steve Renko	.03	.01	.00
☐ 39	Mike Squires	.03	.01	.00
☐ 40	George Hendrick	.08	.03	.01
☐ 41	Bob Knepper	.10	.04	.01
☐ 42	Steve Carlton	.50	.20	.05
☐ 43	Larry Bittner	.03	.01	.00
☐ 44	Chris Welsh	.06	.02	.00
☐ 45	Steve Nicosia	.03	.01	.00
☐ 46	Jack Clark	.15	.06	.01
☐ 47	Chris Chambliss	.06	.02	.00
☐ 48	Ivan DeJesus	.03	.01	.00
☐ 49	Lee Mazzilli	.06	.02	.00
☐ 50	Julio Cruz	.03	.01	.00
☐ 51	Pete Redfern	.03	.01	.00
☐ 52	Dave Stieb	.20	.08	.02
☐ 53	Doug Corbett	.03	.01	.00
☐ 54	Jorge Bell	1.50	.60	.15
☐ 55	Joe Simpson	.03	.01	.00
☐ 56	Rusty Staub	.10	.04	.01
☐ 57	Hector Cruz	.03	.01	.00
☐ 58	Claudell Washington	.08	.03	.01
☐ 59	Enrique Romo	.03	.01	.00
☐ 60	Gary Lavelle	.06	.02	.00
☐ 61	Tim Flannery	.03	.01	.00

		MINT	VG-E	F-G
☐ 62	Joe Nolan	.03	.01	.00
☐ 63	Larry Bowa	.12	.05	.01
☐ 64	Sixto Lezcano	.03	.01	.00
☐ 65	Joe Sambito	.06	.02	.00
☐ 66	Bruce Kison	.03	.01	.00
☐ 67	Wayne Nordhagen	.03	.01	.00
☐ 68	Woodie Fryman	.03	.01	.00
☐ 69	Billy Sample	.03	.01	.00
☐ 70	Amos Otis	.08	.03	.01
☐ 71	Matt Keough	.03	.01	.00
☐ 72	Toby Harrah	.06	.02	.00
☐ 73	Dave Righetti	1.25	.50	.12
☐ 74	Carl Yastrzemski	.70	.28	.07
☐ 75	Bob Welch	.08	.03	.01
☐ 76	A Alan Trammel ERR	.60	.24	.06
	(name misspelled)			
☐ 76	B Alan Trammell CORR	.25	.10	.02
☐ 77	Rick Dempsey	.06	.02	.00
☐ 78	Paul Molitor	.12	.05	.01
☐ 79	Dennis Martinez	.03	.01	.00
☐ 80	Jim Slaton	.03	.01	.00
☐ 81	Champ Summers	.03	.01	.00
☐ 82	Carney Lansford	.12	.05	.01
☐ 83	Barry Foote	.03	.01	.00
☐ 84	Steve Garvey	.50	.20	.05
☐ 85	Rick Manning	.03	.01	.00
☐ 86	John Wathan	.03	.01	.00
☐ 87	Brian Kingman	.03	.01	.00
☐ 88	Andre Dawson	.25	.10	.02
☐ 89	Jim Kern	.03	.01	.00
☐ 90	Bobby Grich	.08	.03	.01
☐ 91	Bob Forsch	.06	.02	.00
☐ 92	Art Howe	.03	.01	.00
☐ 93	Marty Bystrom	.03	.01	.00
☐ 94	Ozzie Smith	.15	.06	.01
☐ 95	Dave Parker	.25	.10	.02
☐ 96	Doyle Alexander	.06	.02	.00
☐ 97	Al Hrabosky	.06	.02	.00
☐ 98	Frank Taveras	.03	.01	.00
☐ 99	Tim Blackwell	.03	.01	.00
☐ 100	Floyd Bannister	.06	.02	.00
☐ 101	Alfredo Griffin	.06	.02	.00
☐ 102	Dave Engle	.03	.01	.00
☐ 103	Mario Soto	.10	.04	.01
☐ 104	Ross Baumgarten	.03	.01	.00
☐ 105	Ken Singleton	.10	.04	.01
☐ 106	Ted Simmons	.15	.06	.01
☐ 107	Jack Morris	.25	.10	.02
☐ 108	Bob Watson	.06	.02	.00
☐ 109	Dwight Evans	.15	.06	.01
☐ 110	Tom Lasorda MGR	.10	.04	.01
☐ 111	Bert Blyleven	.15	.06	.01
☐ 112	Dan Quisenberry	.20	.08	.02

		MINT	VG-E	F-G
☐ 113	Rickey Henderson	.60	.24	.06
☐ 114	Gary Carter	.50	.20	.05
☐ 115	Brian Downing	.06	.02	.00
☐ 116	Al Oliver	.15	.06	.01
☐ 117	LaMarr Hoyt	.10	.04	.01
☐ 118	Cesar Cedeno	.08	.03	.01
☐ 119	Keith Moreland	.08	.03	.01
☐ 120	Bob Shirley	.03	.01	.00
☐ 121	Terry Kennedy	.08	.03	.01
☐ 122	Frank Pastore	.03	.01	.00
☐ 123	Gene Garber	.03	.01	.00
☐ 124	Tony Pena	.15	.06	.01
☐ 125	Allen Ripley	.03	.01	.00
☐ 126	Randy Martz	.03	.01	.00
☐ 127	Richie Zisk	.06	.02	.00
☐ 128	Mike Scott	.25	.10	.02
☐ 129	Lloyd Moseby	.15	.06	.01
☐ 130	Rob Wilfong	.03	.01	.00
☐ 131	Tim Stoddard	.03	.01	.00
☐ 132	Gorman Thomas	.12	.05	.01
☐ 133	Dan Petry	.15	.06	.01
☐ 134	Bob Stanley	.06	.02	.00
☐ 135	Lou Piniella	.10	.04	.01
☐ 136	Pedro Guerrero	.35	.14	.03
☐ 137	Len Barker	.06	.02	.00
☐ 138	Rich Gale	.03	.01	.00
☐ 139	Wayne Gross	.03	.01	.00
☐ 140	Tim Wallach	.45	.18	.04
☐ 141	Gene Mauch MGR	.06	.02	.00
☐ 142	Doc Medich	.03	.01	.00
☐ 143	Tony Bernazard	.06	.02	.00
☐ 144	Bill Virdon MGR	.06	.02	.00
☐ 145	John Littlefield	.03	.01	.00
☐ 146	Dave Bergman	.03	.01	.00
☐ 147	Dick Davis	.03	.01	.00
☐ 148	Tom Seaver	.40	.16	.04
☐ 149	Matt Sinatro	.03	.01	.00
☐ 150	Chuck Tanner MGR	.06	.02	.00
☐ 151	Leon Durham	.15	.06	.01
☐ 152	Gene Tenace	.03	.01	.00
☐ 153	Al Bumbry	.03	.01	.00
☐ 154	Mark Brouhard	.03	.01	.00
☐ 155	Rick Peters	.03	.01	.00
☐ 156	Jerry Remy	.03	.01	.00
☐ 157	Rick Reuschel	.06	.02	.00
☐ 158	Steve Howe	.06	.02	.00
☐ 159	Alan Bannister	.03	.01	.00
☐ 160	U.L. Washington	.03	.01	.00
☐ 161	Rick Langford	.03	.01	.00
☐ 162	Bill Gullickson	.06	.02	.00
☐ 163	Mark Wagner	.03	.01	.00
☐ 164	Geoff Zahn	.03	.01	.00
☐ 165	Ron LeFlore	.06	.02	.00
☐ 166	Dane Iorg	.03	.01	.00
☐ 167	Joe Niekro	.08	.03	.01
☐ 168	Pete Rose	1.25	.50	.12
☐ 169	Dave Collins	.06	.02	.00
☐ 170	Rick Wise	.06	.02	.00
☐ 171	Jim Bibby	.06	.02	.00
☐ 172	Larry Herndon	.06	.02	.00
☐ 173	Bob Horner	.25	.10	.02
☐ 174	Steve Dillard	.03	.01	.00
☐ 175	Mookie Wilson	.10	.04	.01
☐ 176	Dan Meyer	.03	.01	.00
☐ 177	Fernando Arroyo	.03	.01	.00
☐ 178	Jackson Todd	.03	.01	.00
☐ 179	Darrell Jackson	.03	.01	.00
☐ 180	Al Woods	.03	.01	.00
☐ 181	Jim Anderson	.03	.01	.00
☐ 182	Dave Kingman	.15	.06	.01
☐ 183	Steve Henderson	.03	.01	.00
☐ 184	Brian Asselstine	.03	.01	.00
☐ 185	Rod Scurry	.03	.01	.00
☐ 186	Fred Breining	.08	.03	.01
☐ 187	Danny Boone	.03	.01	.00
☐ 188	Junior Kennedy	.03	.01	.00
☐ 189	Sparky Lyle	.12	.05	.01
☐ 190	Whitey Herzog MGR	.06	.02	.00
☐ 191	Dave Smith	.06	.02	.00
☐ 192	Ed Ott	.03	.01	.00
☐ 193	Greg Luzinski	.12	.05	.01
☐ 194	Bill Lee	.06	.02	.00
☐ 195	Don Zimmer MGR	.03	.01	.00
☐ 196	Hal McRae	.06	.02	.00
☐ 197	Mike Norris	.06	.02	.00
☐ 198	Duane Kuiper	.03	.01	.00
☐ 199	Rick Cerone	.03	.01	.00
☐ 200	Jim Rice	.45	.18	.04
☐ 201	Steve Yeager	.06	.02	.00
☐ 202	Tom Brookens	.03	.01	.00
☐ 203	Jose Morales	.03	.01	.00
☐ 204	Roy Howell	.03	.01	.00
☐ 205	Tippy Martinez	.03	.01	.00
☐ 206	Moose Haas	.06	.02	.00
☐ 207	Al Cowens	.06	.02	.00
☐ 208	Dave Stapleton	.03	.01	.00
☐ 209	Bucky Dent	.08	.03	.01
☐ 210	Ron Cey	.10	.04	.01
☐ 211	Jorge Orta	.03	.01	.00
☐ 212	Jamie Quirk	.03	.01	.00
☐ 213	Jeff Jones	.03	.01	.00
☐ 214	Tim Raines	.50	.20	.05
☐ 215	Jon Matlack	.06	.02	.00
☐ 216	Rod Carew	.50	.20	.05
☐ 217	Jim Kaat	.15	.06	.01
☐ 218	Joe Pittman	.03	.01	.00

		MINT	VG-E	F-G
☐ 219	Larry Christenson	.03	.01	.00
☐ 220	Juan Bonilla	.06	.02	.00
☐ 221	Mike Easler	.08	.03	.01
☐ 222	Vida Blue	.08	.03	.01
☐ 223	Rick Camp	.03	.01	.00
☐ 224	Mike Jorgensen	.03	.01	.00
☐ 225	Jody Davis	.50	.20	.05
☐ 226	Mike Parrott	.03	.01	.00
☐ 227	Jim Clancy	.06	.02	.00
☐ 228	Hosken Powell	.03	.01	.00
☐ 229	Tom Hume	.03	.01	.00
☐ 230	Britt Burns	.08	.03	.01
☐ 231	Jim Palmer	.30	.12	.03
☐ 232	Bob Rodgers MGR	.03	.01	.00
☐ 233	Milt Wilcox	.03	.01	.00
☐ 234	Dave Revering	.03	.01	.00
☐ 235	Mike Torrez	.06	.02	.00
☐ 236	Robert Castillo	.03	.01	.00
☐ 237	Von Hayes	1.00	.40	.10
☐ 238	Renie Martin	.03	.01	.00
☐ 239	Dwayne Murphy	.06	.02	.00
☐ 240	Rodney Scott	.03	.01	.00
☐ 241	Fred Patek	.03	.01	.00
☐ 242	Mickey Rivers	.06	.02	.00
☐ 243	Steve Trout	.06	.02	.00
☐ 244	Jose Cruz	.12	.05	.01
☐ 245	Manny Trillo	.06	.02	.00
☐ 246	Lary Sorensen	.03	.01	.00
☐ 247	Dave Edwards	.03	.01	.00
☐ 248	Dan Driessen	.03	.01	.00
☐ 249	Tommy Boggs	.03	.01	.00
☐ 250	Dale Berra	.06	.02	.00
☐ 251	Ed Whitson	.06	.02	.00
☐ 252	Lee Smith	.50	.20	.05
☐ 253	Tom Paciorek	.03	.01	.00
☐ 254	Pat Zachry	.03	.01	.00
☐ 255	Luis Leal	.03	.01	.00
☐ 256	John Castino	.03	.01	.00
☐ 257	Rich Dauer	.03	.01	.00
☐ 258	Cecil Cooper	.15	.06	.01
☐ 259	Dave Rozema	.03	.01	.00
☐ 260	John Tudor	.15	.06	.01
☐ 261	Jerry Mumphrey	.06	.02	.00
☐ 262	Jay Johnstone	.06	.02	.00
☐ 263	Bo Diaz	.06	.02	.00
☐ 264	Dennis Leonard	.06	.02	.00
☐ 265	Jim Spencer	.03	.01	.00
☐ 266	John Milner	.03	.01	.00
☐ 267	Don Aase	.06	.02	.00
☐ 268	Jim Sundberg	.06	.02	.00
☐ 269	Lamar Johnson	.03	.01	.00
☐ 270	Frank LaCorte	.03	.01	.00
☐ 271	Barry Evans	.03	.01	.00

		MINT	VG-E	F-G
☐ 272	Enos Cabell	.03	.01	.00
☐ 273	Del Unser	.03	.01	.00
☐ 274	George Foster	.15	.06	.01
☐ 275	Brett Butler	.60	.24	.06
☐ 276	Lee Lacy	.06	.02	.00
☐ 277	Ken Reitz	.03	.01	.00
☐ 278	Keith Hernandez	.30	.12	.03
☐ 279	Doug DeCinces	.10	.04	.01
☐ 280	Charlie Moore	.03	.01	.00
☐ 281	Lance Parrish	.30	.12	.03
☐ 282	Ralph Houk MGR	.06	.02	.00
☐ 283	Rich Gossage	.20	.08	.02
☐ 284	Jerry Reuss	.06	.02	.00
☐ 285	Mike Stanton	.03	.01	.00
☐ 286	Frank White	.08	.03	.01
☐ 287	Bob Owchinko	.03	.01	.00
☐ 288	Scott Sanderson	.03	.01	.00
☐ 289	Bump Wills	.03	.01	.00
☐ 290	Dave Frost	.03	.01	.00
☐ 291	Chet Lemon	.06	.02	.00
☐ 292	Tito Landrum	.03	.01	.00
☐ 293	Vern Ruhle	.03	.01	.00
☐ 294	Mike Schmidt	.60	.24	.06
☐ 295	Sam Mejias	.03	.01	.00
☐ 296	Gary Lucas	.03	.01	.00
☐ 297	John Candelaria	.08	.03	.01
☐ 298	Jerry Martin	.03	.01	.00
☐ 299	Dale Murphy	.90	.36	.09
☐ 300	Mike Lum	.03	.01	.00
☐ 301	Tom Hausman	.03	.01	.00
☐ 302	Glenn Abbott	.03	.01	.00
☐ 303	Roger Erickson	.03	.01	.00
☐ 304	Otto Velez	.03	.01	.00
☐ 305	Danny Goodwin	.03	.01	.00
☐ 306	John Mayberry	.06	.02	.00
☐ 307	Lenny Randle	.03	.01	.00
☐ 308	Bob Bailor	.03	.01	.00
☐ 309	Jerry Morales	.03	.01	.00
☐ 310	Rufino Linares	.03	.01	.00
☐ 311	Kent Tekulve	.06	.02	.00
☐ 312	Joe Morgan	.25	.10	.02
☐ 313	John Urrea	.03	.01	.00
☐ 314	Paul Householder	.03	.01	.00
☐ 315	Garry Maddox	.06	.02	.00
☐ 316	Mike Ramsey	.03	.01	.00
☐ 317	Alan Ashby	.03	.01	.00
☐ 318	Bob Clark	.03	.01	.00
☐ 319	Tony LaRussa MGR	.06	.02	.00
☐ 320	Charlie Lea	.06	.02	.00
☐ 321	Danny Darwin	.03	.01	.00
☐ 322	Cesar Geronimo	.03	.01	.00
☐ 323	Tom Underwood	.03	.01	.00
☐ 324	Andre Thornton	.08	.03	.01

	MINT	VG-E	F-G			MINT	VG-E	F-G
☐ 325 Rudy May	.03	.01	.00	☐ 375 Bruce Benedict	.03	.01	.00
☐ 326 Frank Tanana	.06	.02	.00	☐ 376 Tim Foli	.03	.01	.00
☐ 327 Davey Lopes	.08	.03	.01	☐ 377 Al Holland	.06	.02	.00
☐ 328 Richie Hebner	.03	.01	.00	☐ 378 Ken Kravec	.03	.01	.00
☐ 329 Mike Flanagan	.08	.03	.01	☐ 379 Jeff Burroughs	.06	.02	.00
☐ 330 Mike Caldwell	.06	.02	.00	☐ 380 Pete Falcone	.03	.01	.00
☐ 331 Scott McGregor	.08	.03	.01	☐ 381 Ernie Whitt	.03	.01	.00
☐ 332 Jerry Augustine	.03	.01	.00	☐ 382 Brad Havens	.06	.02	.00
☐ 333 Stan Papi	.03	.01	.00	☐ 383 Terry Crowley	.03	.01	.00
☐ 334 Rick Miller	.03	.01	.00	☐ 384 Don Money	.03	.01	.00
☐ 335 Graig Nettles	.15	.06	.01	☐ 385 Dan Schatzeder	.03	.01	.00
☐ 336 Dusty Baker	.08	.03	.01	☐ 386 Gary Allenson	.03	.01	.00
☐ 337 Dave Garcia MGR	.03	.01	.00	☐ 387 Yogi Berra MGR	.15	.06	.01
☐ 338 Larry Gura	.06	.02	.00	☐ 388 Ken Landreaux	.06	.02	.00
☐ 339 Cliff Johnson	.03	.01	.00	☐ 389 Mike Hargrove	.06	.02	.00
☐ 340 Warren Cromartie	.03	.01	.00	☐ 390 Darryl Motley	.12	.05	.01
☐ 341 Steve Comer	.03	.01	.00	☐ 391 Dave McKay	.03	.01	.00
☐ 342 Rick Burleson	.06	.02	.00	☐ 392 Stan Bahnsen	.03	.01	.00
☐ 343 John Martin	.03	.01	.00	☐ 393 Ken Forsch	.03	.01	.00
☐ 344 Craig Reynolds	.03	.01	.00	☐ 394 Mario Mendoza	.03	.01	.00
☐ 345 Mike Proly	.03	.01	.00	☐ 395 Jim Morrison	.03	.01	.00
☐ 346 Ruppert Jones	.03	.01	.00	☐ 396 Mike Ivie	.03	.01	.00
☐ 347 Omar Moreno	.03	.01	.00	☐ 397 Broderick Perkins	.03	.01	.00
☐ 348 Greg Minton	.06	.02	.00	☐ 398 Darrell Evans	.12	.05	.01
☐ 349 Rick Mahler	.20	.08	.02	☐ 399 Ron Reed	.03	.01	.00
☐ 350 Alex Trevino	.03	.01	.00	☐ 400 Johnny Bench	.40	.16	.04
☐ 351 Mike Krukow	.08	.03	.01	☐ 401 Steve Bedrosian	.30	.12	.03
☐ 352 A Shane Rawley ERR	.60	.24	.06	☐ 402 Bill Robinson	.03	.01	.00
(photo actually				☐ 403 Bill Buckner	.12	.05	.01
Jim Anderson)				☐ 404 Ken Oberkfell	.03	.01	.00
☐ 352 B Shane Rawley COR	.10	.04	.01	☐ 405 Cal Ripken Jr.	5.00	2.00	.50
☐ 353 Garth Iorg	.03	.01	.00	☐ 406 Jim Gantner	.06	.02	.00
☐ 354 Pete Mackanin	.03	.01	.00	☐ 407 Kirk Gibson	.35	.14	.03
☐ 355 Paul Moskau	.03	.01	.00	☐ 408 Tony Perez	.15	.06	.01
☐ 356 Richard Dotson	.08	.03	.01	☐ 409 Tommy John	.18	.08	.01
☐ 357 Steve Stone	.06	.02	.00	☐ 410 Dave Stewart	.15	.06	.01
☐ 358 Larry Hisle	.06	.02	.00	☐ 411 Dan Spillner	.03	.01	.00
☐ 359 Aurelio Lopez	.03	.01	.00	☐ 412 Willie Aikens	.06	.02	.00
☐ 360 Oscar Gamble	.06	.02	.00	☐ 413 Mike Heath	.03	.01	.00
☐ 361 Tom Burgmeier	.03	.01	.00	☐ 414 Ray Burris	.03	.01	.00
☐ 362 Terry Forster	.08	.03	.01	☐ 415 Leon Roberts	.03	.01	.00
☐ 363 Joe Charboneau	.06	.02	.00	☐ 416 Mike Witt	1.00	.40	.10
☐ 364 Ken Brett	.03	.01	.00	☐ 417 Bob Molinaro	.03	.01	.00
☐ 365 Tony Armas	.12	.05	.01	☐ 418 Steve Braun	.03	.01	.00
☐ 366 Chris Speier	.03	.01	.00	☐ 419 Nolan Ryan	.40	.16	.04
☐ 367 Fred Lynn	.20	.08	.02	☐ 420 Tug McGraw	.10	.04	.01
☐ 368 Buddy Bell	.12	.05	.01	☐ 421 Dave Concepcion	.12	.05	.01
☐ 369 Jim Essian	.03	.01	.00	☐ 422 A Juan Eichelberger			
☐ 370 Terry Puhl	.06	.02	.00	ERR	.60	.24	.06
☐ 371 Greg Gross	.03	.01	.00	(photo actually			
☐ 372 Bruce Sutter	.20	.08	.02	Gary Lucas)			
☐ 373 Joe Lefebvre	.03	.01	.00	☐ 422 B Juan Eichelberger	.08	.03	.01
☐ 374 Ray Knight	.08	.03	.01	COR			

		MINT	VG-E	F-G
☐ 423	Rick Rhoden	.08	.03	.01
☐ 424	Frank Robinson MGR	.15	.06	.01
☐ 425	Eddie Miller	.03	.01	.00
☐ 426	Bill Caudill	.06	.02	.00
☐ 427	Doug Flynn	.03	.01	.00
☐ 428	Larry Andersen	.03	.01	.00
☐ 429	Al Williams	.03	.01	.00
☐ 430	Jerry Garvin	.03	.01	.00
☐ 431	Glenn Adams	.03	.01	.00
☐ 432	Barry Bonnell	.03	.01	.00
☐ 433	Jerry Narron	.03	.01	.00
☐ 434	John Stearns	.03	.01	.00
☐ 435	Mike Tyson	.03	.01	.00
☐ 436	Glenn Hubbard	.03	.01	.00
☐ 437	Eddie Solomon	.03	.01	.00
☐ 438	Jeff Leonard	.06	.02	.00
☐ 439	Randy Bass	.03	.01	.00
☐ 440	Mike LaCoss	.03	.01	.00
☐ 441	Gary Matthews	.08	.03	.01
☐ 442	Mark Littell	.03	.01	.00
☐ 443	Don Sutton	.25	.10	.02
☐ 444	John Harris	.03	.01	.00
☐ 445	Vada Pinson CO	.08	.03	.01
☐ 446	Elias Sosa	.03	.01	.00
☐ 447	Charlie Hough	.08	.03	.01
☐ 448	Willie Wilson	.20	.08	.02
☐ 449	Fred Stanley	.03	.01	.00
☐ 450	Tom Veryzer	.03	.01	.00
☐ 451	Ron Davis	.03	.01	.00
☐ 452	Mark Clear	.03	.01	.00
☐ 453	Bill Russell	.06	.02	.00
☐ 454	Lou Whitaker	.15	.06	.01
☐ 455	Dan Graham	.03	.01	.00
☐ 456	Reggie Cleveland	.03	.01	.00
☐ 457	Sammy Stewart	.03	.01	.00
☐ 458	Pete Vuckovich	.10	.04	.01
☐ 459	John Wockenfuss	.03	.01	.00
☐ 460	Glen Hoffman	.03	.01	.00
☐ 461	Willie Randolph	.08	.03	.01
☐ 462	Fernando Valenzuela	.50	.20	.05
☐ 463	Ron Hassey	.03	.01	.00
☐ 464	Paul Splittorff	.06	.02	.00
☐ 465	Rob Picciolo	.03	.01	.00
☐ 466	Larry Parrish	.06	.02	.00
☐ 467	Johnny Grubb	.03	.01	.00
☐ 468	Dan Ford	.03	.01	.00
☐ 469	Silvio Martinez	.03	.01	.00
☐ 470	Kiko Garcia	.03	.01	.00
☐ 471	Bob Boone	.06	.02	.00
☐ 472	Luis Salazar	.03	.01	.00
☐ 473	Randy Niemann	.03	.01	.00
☐ 474	Tom Griffin	.03	.01	.00
☐ 475	Phil Niekro	.20	.08	.02
☐ 476	Hubie Brooks	.15	.06	.01
☐ 477	Dick Tidrow	.03	.01	.00
☐ 478	Jim Beattie	.03	.01	.00
☐ 479	Damaso Garcia	.10	.04	.01
☐ 480	Mickey Hatcher	.03	.01	.00
☐ 481	Joe Price	.03	.01	.00
☐ 482	Ed Farmer	.03	.01	.00
☐ 483	Eddie Murray	.65	.26	.06
☐ 484	Ben Oglivie	.08	.03	.01
☐ 485	Kevin Saucier	.03	.01	.00
☐ 486	Bobby Murcer	.10	.04	.01
☐ 487	Bill Campbell	.06	.02	.00
☐ 488	Reggie Smith	.10	.04	.01
☐ 489	Wayne Garland	.03	.01	.00
☐ 490	Jim Wright	.03	.01	.00
☐ 491	Billy Martin MGR	.15	.06	.01
☐ 492	Jim Fanning MGR	.03	.01	.00
☐ 493	Don Baylor	.15	.06	.01
☐ 494	Rick Honeycutt	.06	.02	.00
☐ 495	Carlton Fisk	.18	.08	.01
☐ 496	Denny Walling	.03	.01	.00
☐ 497	Bake McBride	.03	.01	.00
☐ 498	Darrell Porter	.06	.02	.00
☐ 499	Gene Richards	.03	.01	.00
☐ 500	Ron Oester	.06	.02	.00
☐ 501	Ken Dayley	.20	.08	.02
☐ 502	Jason Thompson	.06	.02	.00
☐ 503	Milt May	.03	.01	.00
☐ 504	Doug Bird	.03	.01	.00
☐ 505	Bruce Bochte	.06	.02	.00
☐ 506	Neil Allen	.06	.02	.00
☐ 507	Joey McLaughlin	.03	.01	.00
☐ 508	Butch Wynegar	.06	.02	.00
☐ 509	Gary Roenicke	.06	.02	.00
☐ 510	Robin Yount	.50	.20	.05
☐ 511	Dave Tobik	.03	.01	.00
☐ 512	Rich Gedman	.75	.30	.07
☐ 513	Gene Nelson	.10	.04	.01
☐ 514	Rick Monday	.06	.02	.00
☐ 515	Miguel Dilone	.03	.01	.00
☐ 516	Clint Hurdle	.03	.01	.00
☐ 517	Jeff Newman	.03	.01	.00
☐ 518	Grant Jackson	.03	.01	.00
☐ 519	Andy Hassler	.03	.01	.00
☐ 520	Pat Putnam	.03	.01	.00
☐ 521	Greg Pryor	.03	.01	.00
☐ 522	Tony Scott	.03	.01	.00
☐ 523	Steve Mura	.03	.01	.00
☐ 524	Johnnie LeMaster	.03	.01	.00
☐ 525	Dick Ruthven	.03	.01	.00
☐ 526	John McNamara MGR	.03	.01	.00
☐ 527	Larry McWilliams	.06	.02	.00
☐ 528	Johnny Ray	.75	.30	.07

	MINT	VG-E	F-G
☐ 529 Pat Tabler	.75	.30	.07
☐ 530 Tom Herr	.10	.04	.01
☐ 531 A San Diego Chicken (with TM)	.90	.36	.09
☐ 531 B San Diego Chicken (without TM)	.90	.36	.09
☐ 532 Sal Butera	.03	.01	.00
☐ 533 Mike Griffin	.03	.01	.00
☐ 534 Kelvin Moore	.06	.02	.00
☐ 535 Reggie Jackson	.50	.20	.05
☐ 536 Ed Romero	.03	.01	.00
☐ 537 Derrel Thomas	.03	.01	.00
☐ 538 Mike O'Berry	.03	.01	.00
☐ 539 Jack O'Connor	.03	.01	.00
☐ 540 Bob Ojeda	.75	.30	.07
☐ 541 Roy Lee Jackson	.03	.01	.00
☐ 542 Lynn Jones	.03	.01	.00
☐ 543 Gaylord Perry	.25	.10	.02
☐ 544 A Phil Garner ERR (reverse negative)	.50	.20	.05
☐ 544 B Phil Garner COR	.08	.03	.01
☐ 545 Garry Templeton	.10	.04	.01
☐ 546 Rafael Ramirez	.03	.01	.00
☐ 547 Jeff Reardon	.08	.03	.01
☐ 548 Ron Guidry	.20	.08	.02
☐ 549 Tim Laudner	.08	.03	.01
☐ 550 John Henry Johnson	.03	.01	.00
☐ 551 Chris Bando	.03	.01	.00
☐ 552 Bobby Brown	.03	.01	.00
☐ 553 Larry Bradford	.03	.01	.00
☐ 554 Scott Fletcher	.30	.12	.03
☐ 555 Jerry Royster	.03	.01	.00
☐ 556 Shooty Babitt	.03	.01	.00
☐ 557 Kent Hrbek	2.50	1.00	.25
☐ 558 Yankee Winners Ron Guidry Tommy John	.15	.06	.01
☐ 559 Mark Bomback	.03	.01	.00
☐ 560 Julio Valdez	.03	.01	.00
☐ 561 Buck Martinez	.03	.01	.00
☐ 562 Mike Marshall (Dodger hitter)	1.25	.50	.12
☐ 563 Rennie Stennett	.03	.01	.00
☐ 564 Steve Crawford	.06	.02	.00
☐ 565 Bob Babcock	.03	.01	.00
☐ 566 Johnny Podres CO	.06	.02	.00
☐ 567 Paul Serna	.06	.02	.00
☐ 568 Harold Baines	.35	.14	.03
☐ 569 Dave LaRoche	.03	.01	.00
☐ 570 Lee May	.06	.02	.00
☐ 571 Gary Ward	.06	.02	.00
☐ 572 John Denny	.08	.03	.01
☐ 573 Roy Smalley	.06	.02	.00

	MINT	VG-E	F-G
☐ 574 Bob Brenly	.35	.14	.03
☐ 575 Bronx Bombers Reggie Jackson Dave Winfield	.40	.16	.04
☐ 576 Luis Pujols	.03	.01	.00
☐ 577 Butch Hobson	.03	.01	.00
☐ 578 Harvey Kuenn MGR	.06	.02	.00
☐ 579 Cal Ripken Sr. (Orioles coach)	.10	.04	.01
☐ 580 Juan Berenguer	.03	.01	.00
☐ 581 Benny Ayala	.03	.01	.00
☐ 582 Vance Law	.03	.01	.00
☐ 583 Rick Leach	.06	.02	.00
☐ 584 George Frazier	.03	.01	.00
☐ 585 Phillies Finest Pete Rose Mike Schmidt	.75	.30	.07
☐ 586 Joe Rudi	.06	.02	.00
☐ 587 Juan Beniquez	.06	.02	.00
☐ 588 Luis DeLeon	.10	.04	.01
☐ 589 Craig Swan	.03	.01	.00
☐ 590 Dave Chalk	.03	.01	.00
☐ 591 Billy Gardner	.03	.01	.00
☐ 592 Sal Bando	.06	.02	.00
☐ 593 Bert Campaneris	.08	.03	.01
☐ 594 Steve Kemp	.08	.03	.01
☐ 595 A Randy Lerch ERR (Braves)	.50	.20	.05
☐ 595 B Randy Lerch COR (Brewers)	.08	.03	.01
☐ 596 Bryan Clark	.03	.01	.00
☐ 597 David Ford	.03	.01	.00
☐ 598 Mike Scioscia	.06	.02	.00
☐ 599 John Lowenstein	.03	.01	.00
☐ 600 Rene Lachemann MGR	.03	.01	.00
☐ 601 Mick Kelleher	.03	.01	.00
☐ 602 Ron Jackson	.03	.01	.00
☐ 603 Jerry Koosman	.08	.03	.01
☐ 604 Dave Goltz	.03	.01	.00
☐ 605 Ellis Valentine	.03	.01	.00
☐ 606 Lonnie Smith	.08	.03	.01
☐ 607 Joaquin Andujar	.12	.05	.01
☐ 608 Garry Hancock	.03	.01	.00
☐ 609 Jerry Turner	.03	.01	.00
☐ 610 Bob Bonner	.03	.01	.00
☐ 611 Jim Dwyer	.03	.01	.00
☐ 612 Terry Bulling	.03	.01	.00
☐ 613 Joel Youngblood	.03	.01	.00
☐ 614 Larry Milbourne	.03	.01	.00
☐ 615 Gene Roof (name on front is Phil Roof)	.10	.04	.01
☐ 616 Keith Drumright	.03	.01	.00

		MINT	VG-E	F-G
☐ 617	Dave Rosello	.03	.01	.00
☐ 618	Rickey Keeton	.03	.01	.00
☐ 619	Dennis Lamp	.03	.01	.00
☐ 620	Sid Monge	.03	.01	.00
☐ 621	Jerry White	.03	.01	.00
☐ 622	Luis Aguayo	.03	.01	.00
☐ 623	Jamie Easterly	.03	.01	.00
☐ 624	Steve Sax	1.25	.50	.12
☐ 625	Dave Roberts	.03	.01	.00
☐ 626	Rick Bosetti	.03	.01	.00
☐ 627	Terry Francona	.20	.08	.02
☐ 628	Pride of Reds	.35	.14	.03
	Tom Seaver			
	Johnny Bench			
☐ 629	Paul Mirabella	.03	.01	.00
☐ 630	Rance Mulliniks	.03	.01	.00
☐ 631	Kevin Hickey	.06	.02	.00
☐ 632	Reid Nichols	.03	.01	.00
☐ 633	Dave Geisel	.03	.01	.00
☐ 634	Ken Griffey	.08	.03	.01
☐ 635	Bob Lemon MGR	.10	.04	.01
☐ 636	Orlando Sanchez	.03	.01	.00
☐ 637	Bill Almon	.03	.01	.00
☐ 638	Danny Ainge	.08	.03	.01
☐ 639	Willie Stargell	.25	.10	.02
☐ 640	Bob Sykes	.03	.01	.00
☐ 641	Ed Lynch	.10	.04	.01
☐ 642	John Ellis	.03	.01	.00
☐ 643	Ferguson Jenkins	.15	.06	.01
☐ 644	Lenn Sakata	.03	.01	.00
☐ 645	Julio Gonzalez	.03	.01	.00
☐ 646	Jesse Orosco	.08	.03	.01
☐ 647	Jerry Dybzinski	.03	.01	.00
☐ 648	Tommy Davis	.06	.02	.00
☐ 649	Ron Gardenhire	.08	.03	.01
☐ 650	Felipe Alou	.06	.02	.00
☐ 651	Harvey Haddix	.06	.02	.00
☐ 652	Willie Upshaw	.08	.03	.01
☐ 653	Bill Madlock	.15	.06	.01
☐ 654 A	DK Checklist	.15	.02	.00
	(unnumbered)			
	(with Trammel)			
☐ 654 B	DK Checklist	.12	.02	.00
	(unnumbered)			
	(with Trammel)			
☐ 655	Checklist 1	.07	.01	.00
	(unnumbered)			
☐ 656	Checklist 2	.07	.01	.00
	(unnumbered)			
☐ 657	Checklist 3	.07	.01	.00
	(unnumbered)			
☐ 658	Checklist 4	.07	.01	.00
	(unnumbered)			

		MINT	VG-E	F-G
☐ 659	Checklist 5	.07	.01	.00
	(unnumbered)			
☐ 660	Checklist 6	.07	.01	.00
	(unnumbered)			

1983 Donruss

The cards in this 660-card set measure 2½"
by 3½". The 1983 Donruss baseball set, issued with a 63-piece Diamond King puzzle,
again leads off with a 26-card Diamond
Kings (DK) series. Of the remaining 634
cards, two are combination cards, one portrays the San Diego Chicken, one shows the
completed Ty Cobb puzzle, and seven are
unnumbered checklist cards. The seven unnumbered checklist cards are arbitrarily assigned numbers 654 through 660 and are
listed at the end of the list below. The Donruss
logo and the year of issue are shown in the
upper left corner of the obverse. The card
backs have black print on yellow and white
and are numbered on a small ball design.
The complete set price below includes only
the more common of each variation pair.

	MINT	VG-E	F-G
Complete Set (660)	27.00	11.00	2.70
Common Player (1-660)	.03	.01	.00

		MINT	VG-E	F-G
☐ 1	Fernando Valenzuela DK	.50	.20	.05
☐ 2	Rollie Fingers DK	.25	.10	.02
☐ 3	Reggie Jackson DK	.50	.20	.05
☐ 4	Jim Palmer DK	.35	.14	.03
☐ 5	Jack Morris DK	.30	.12	.03

	MINT	VG-E	F-G			MINT	VG-E	F-G
☐ 6 George Foster DK	.15	.06	.01	☐ 59 Tony Pena	.15	.06	.01
☐ 7 Jim Sundberg DK	.06	.02	.00	☐ 60 Gary Lavelle	.05	.02	.00
☐ 8 Willie Stargell DK	.25	.10	.02	☐ 61 Tim Lollar	.03	.01	.00
☐ 9 Dave Stieb DK	.20	.08	.02	☐ 62 Frank Pastore	.03	.01	.00
☐ 10 Joe Niekro DK	.08	.03	.01	☐ 63 Garry Maddox	.05	.02	.00
☐ 11 Rickey Henderson DK	.50	.20	.05	☐ 64 Bob Forsch	.05	.02	.00
☐ 12 Dale Murphy DK	.75	.30	.07	☐ 65 Harry Spilman	.03	.01	.00
☐ 13 Toby Harrah DK	.06	.02	.00	☐ 66 Geoff Zahn	.03	.01	.00
☐ 14 Bill Buckner DK	.12	.05	.01	☐ 67 Salome Barojas	.03	.01	.00
☐ 15 Willie Wilson DK	.20	.08	.02	☐ 68 David Palmer	.05	.02	.00
☐ 16 Steve Carlton DK	.40	.16	.04	☐ 69 Charlie Hough	.07	.03	.01
☐ 17 Ron Guidry DK	.25	.10	.02	☐ 70 Dan Quisenberry	.18	.08	.01
☐ 18 Steve Rogers DK	.06	.02	.00	☐ 71 Tony Armas	.10	.04	.01
☐ 19 Kent Hrbek DK	.30	.12	.03	☐ 72 Rick Sutcliffe	.15	.06	.01
☐ 20 Keith Hernandez DK	.30	.12	.03	☐ 73 Steve Balboni	.07	.03	.01
☐ 21 Floyd Bannister DK	.06	.02	.00	☐ 74 Jerry Remy	.03	.01	.00
☐ 22 John Bench DK	.40	.16	.04	☐ 75 Mike Scioscia	.05	.02	.00
☐ 23 Britt Burns DK	.06	.02	.00	☐ 76 John Wockenfuss	.03	.01	.00
☐ 24 Joe Morgan DK	.25	.10	.02	☐ 77 Jim Palmer	.25	.10	.02
☐ 25 Carl Yastrzemski DK	.75	.30	.07	☐ 78 Rollie Fingers	.20	.08	.02
☐ 26 Terry Kennedy DK	.08	.03	.01	☐ 79 Joe Nolan	.03	.01	.00
☐ 27 Gary Roenicke	.06	.02	.00	☐ 80 Pete Vuckovich	.07	.03	.01
☐ 28 Dwight Bernard	.03	.01	.00	☐ 81 Rick Leach	.03	.01	.00
☐ 29 Pat Underwood	.03	.01	.00	☐ 82 Rick Miller	.03	.01	.00
☐ 30 Gary Allenson	.03	.01	.00	☐ 83 Graig Nettles	.14	.06	.01
☐ 31 Ron Guidry	.20	.08	.02	☐ 84 Ron Cey	.10	.04	.01
☐ 32 Burt Hooton	.03	.01	.00	☐ 85 Miguel Dilone	.03	.01	.00
☐ 33 Chris Bando	.03	.01	.00	☐ 86 John Wathan	.03	.01	.00
☐ 34 Vida Blue	.08	.03	.01	☐ 87 Kelvin Moore	.03	.01	.00
☐ 35 Rickey Henderson	.45	.18	.04	☐ 88 A Byrn Smith ERR	.15	.06	.01
☐ 36 Ray Burris	.03	.01	.00	(sic, Bryn)			
☐ 37 John Butcher	.03	.01	.00	☐ 88 B Bryn Smith COR	.75	.30	.07
☐ 38 Don Aase	.05	.02	.00	☐ 89 Dave Hostetler	.05	.02	.00
☐ 39 Jerry Koosman	.07	.03	.01	☐ 90 Rod Carew	.40	.16	.04
☐ 40 Bruce Sutter	.15	.06	.01	☐ 91 Lonnie Smith	.07	.03	.01
☐ 41 Jose Cruz	.10	.04	.01	☐ 92 Bob Knepper	.09	.04	.01
☐ 42 Pete Rose	1.00	.40	.10	☐ 93 Marty Bystrom	.03	.01	.00
☐ 43 Cesar Cedeno	.07	.03	.01	☐ 94 Chris Welsh	.03	.01	.00
☐ 44 Floyd Chiffer	.05	.02	.00	☐ 95 Jason Thompson	.05	.02	.00
☐ 45 Larry McWilliams	.03	.01	.00	☐ 96 Tom O'Malley	.05	.02	.00
☐ 46 Alan Fowlkes	.03	.01	.00	☐ 97 Phil Niekro	.20	.08	.02
☐ 47 Dale Murphy	.75	.30	.07	☐ 98 Neil Allen	.05	.02	.00
☐ 48 Doug Bird	.03	.01	.00	☐ 99 Bill Buckner	.10	.04	.01
☐ 49 Hubie Brooks	.10	.04	.01	☐ 100 Ed VandeBerg	.03	.03	.01
☐ 50 Floyd Bannister	.06	.02	.00	☐ 101 Jim Clancy	.03	.01	.00
☐ 51 Jack O'Connor	.03	.01	.00	☐ 102 Robert Castillo	.03	.01	.00
☐ 52 Steve Senteney	.03	.01	.00	☐ 103 Bruce Berenyi	.03	.01	.00
☐ 53 Gary Gaetti	.75	.30	.07	☐ 104 Carlton Fisk	.15	.06	.01
☐ 54 Damaso Garcia	.09	.04	.01	☐ 105 Mike Flanagan	.07	.03	.01
☐ 55 Gene Nelson	.03	.01	.00	☐ 106 Cecil Cooper	.15	.06	.01
☐ 56 Mookie Wilson	.08	.03	.01	☐ 107 Jack Morris	.20	.08	.02
☐ 57 Allen Ripley	.03	.01	.00	☐ 108 Mike Morgan	.03	.01	.00
☐ 58 Bob Horner	.20	.08	.02	☐ 109 Luis Aponte	.05	.02	.00

		MINT	VG-E	F-G
☐ 110	Pedro Guerrero	.30	.12	.03
☐ 111	Len Barker	.05	.02	.00
☐ 112	Willie Wilson	.20	.08	.02
☐ 113	Dave Beard	.03	.01	.00
☐ 114	Mike Gates	.03	.01	.00
☐ 115	Reggie Jackson	.40	.16	.04
☐ 116	George Wright	.08	.03	.01
☐ 117	Vance Law	.03	.01	.00
☐ 118	Nolan Ryan	.35	.14	.03
☐ 119	Mike Krukow	.08	.03	.01
☐ 120	Ozzie Smith	.15	.06	.01
☐ 121	Broderick Perkins	.03	.01	.00
☐ 122	Tom Seaver	.35	.14	.03
☐ 123	Chris Chambliss	.05	.02	.00
☐ 124	Chuck Tanner MGR	.03	.01	.00
☐ 125	Johnnie LeMaster	.03	.01	.00
☐ 126	Mel Hall	.75	.30	.07
☐ 127	Bruce Bochte	.05	.02	.00
☐ 128	Charlie Puleo	.03	.01	.00
☐ 129	Luis Leal	.03	.01	.00
☐ 130	John Pacella	.03	.01	.00
☐ 131	Glenn Gulliver	.03	.01	.00
☐ 132	Don Money	.03	.01	.00
☐ 133	Dave Rozema	.03	.01	.00
☐ 134	Bruce Hurst	.09	.04	.01
☐ 135	Rudy May	.03	.01	.00
☐ 136	Tom Lasorda MGR	.07	.03	.01
☐ 137	Dan Spillner	.10	.04	.01
	(photo actually			
	Ed Whitson)			
☐ 138	Jerry Martin	.03	.01	.00
☐ 139	Mike Norris	.05	.02	.00
☐ 140	Al Oliver	.12	.05	.01
☐ 141	Daryl Sconiers	.03	.01	.00
☐ 142	Lamar Johnson	.03	.01	.00
☐ 143	Harold Baines	.25	.10	.02
☐ 144	Alan Ashby	.03	.01	.00
☐ 145	Garry Templeton	.10	.04	.01
☐ 146	Al Holland	.05	.02	.00
☐ 147	Bo Diaz	.05	.02	.00
☐ 148	Dave Concepcion	.10	.04	.01
☐ 149	Rick Camp	.03	.01	.00
☐ 150	Jim Morrison	.03	.01	.00
☐ 151	Randy Martz	.03	.01	.00
☐ 152	Keith Hernandez	.30	.12	.03
☐ 153	John Lowenstein	.03	.01	.00
☐ 154	Mike Caldwell	.05	.02	.00
☐ 155	Milt Wilcox	.03	.01	.00
☐ 156	Rich Gedman	.12	.05	.01
☐ 157	Rich Gossage	.18	.08	.01
☐ 158	Jerry Reuss	.06	.02	.00
☐ 159	Ron Hassey	.03	.01	.00
☐ 160	Larry Gura	.05	.02	.00
☐ 161	Dwayne Murphy	.06	.02	.00
☐ 162	Woodie Fryman	.03	.01	.00
☐ 163	Steve Comer	.03	.01	.00
☐ 164	Ken Forsch	.03	.01	.00
☐ 165	Dennis Lamp	.03	.01	.00
☐ 166	David Green	.08	.03	.01
☐ 167	Terry Puhl	.05	.02	.00
☐ 168	Mike Schmidt	.50	.20	.05
☐ 169	Eddie Milner	.15	.06	.01
☐ 170	John Curtis	.03	.01	.00
☐ 171	Don Robinson	.03	.01	.00
☐ 172	Rich Gale	.03	.01	.00
☐ 173	Steve Bedrosian	.07	.03	.01
☐ 174	Willie Hernandez	.15	.06	.01
☐ 175	Ron Gardenhire	.03	.01	.00
☐ 176	Jim Beattie	.03	.01	.00
☐ 177	Tim Laudner	.03	.01	.00
☐ 178	Buck Martinez	.03	.01	.00
☐ 179	Kent Hrbek	.35	.14	.03
☐ 180	Alfredo Griffin	.05	.02	.00
☐ 181	Larry Andersen	.03	.01	.00
☐ 182	Pete Falcone	.03	.01	.00
☐ 183	Jody Davis	.08	.03	.01
☐ 184	Glen Hubbard	.03	.01	.00
☐ 185	Dale Berra	.05	.02	.00
☐ 186	Greg Minton	.05	.02	.00
☐ 187	Gary Lucas	.03	.01	.00
☐ 188	Dave Van Gorder	.03	.01	.00
☐ 189	Bob Dernier	.06	.02	.00
☐ 190	Willie McGee	1.25	.50	.12
☐ 191	Dickie Thon	.05	.02	.00
☐ 192	Bob Boone	.05	.02	.00
☐ 193	Britt Burns	.05	.02	.00
☐ 194	Jeff Reardon	.07	.03	.01
☐ 195	Jon Matlack	.05	.02	.00
☐ 196	Don Slaught	.25	.10	.02
☐ 197	Fred Stanley	.03	.01	.00
☐ 198	Rick Manning	.03	.01	.00
☐ 199	Dave Righetti	.15	.06	.01
☐ 200	Dave Stapleton	.03	.01	.00
☐ 201	Steve Yeager	.03	.01	.00
☐ 202	Enos Cabell	.03	.01	.00
☐ 203	Sammy Stewart	.03	.01	.00
☐ 204	Moose Haas	.03	.01	.00
☐ 205	Lenn Sakata	.03	.01	.00
☐ 206	Charlie Moore	.03	.01	.00
☐ 207	Alan Trammell	.15	.06	.01
☐ 208	Jim Rice	.35	.14	.03
☐ 209	Roy Smalley	.05	.02	.00
☐ 210	Bill Russell	.05	.02	.00
☐ 211	Andre Thornton	.07	.03	.01
☐ 212	Willie Aikens	.05	.02	.00
☐ 213	Dave McKay	.03	.01	.00

		MINT	VG-E	F-G
☐ 214	Tim Blackwell	.03	.01	.00
☐ 215	Buddy Bell	.10	.04	.01
☐ 216	Doug DeCinces	.10	.04	.01
☐ 217	Tom Herr	.08	.03	.01
☐ 218	Frank LaCorte	.03	.01	.00
☐ 219	Steve Carlton	.35	.14	.03
☐ 220	Terry Kennedy	.08	.03	.01
☐ 221	Mike Easler	.06	.02	.00
☐ 222	Jack Clark	.14	.06	.01
☐ 223	Gene Garber	.03	.01	.00
☐ 224	Scott Holman	.05	.02	.00
☐ 225	Mike Proly	.03	.01	.00
☐ 226	Terry Bulling	.03	.01	.00
☐ 227	Jerry Garvin	.03	.01	.00
☐ 228	Ron Davis	.03	.01	.00
☐ 229	Tom Hume	.03	.01	.00
☐ 230	Marc Hill	.03	.01	.00
☐ 231	Dennis Martinez	.03	.01	.00
☐ 232	Jim Gantner	.05	.02	.00
☐ 233	Larry Pashnick	.03	.01	.00
☐ 234	Dave Collins	.05	.02	.00
☐ 235	Tom Burgmeier	.03	.01	.00
☐ 236	Ken Landreaux	.05	.02	.00
☐ 237	John Denny	.08	.03	.01
☐ 238	Hal McRae	.06	.02	.00
☐ 239	Matt Keough	.03	.01	.00
☐ 240	Doug Flynn	.03	.01	.00
☐ 241	Fred Lynn	.20	.08	.02
☐ 242	Billy Sample	.03	.01	.00
☐ 243	Tom Paciorek	.03	.01	.00
☐ 244	Joe Sambito	.05	.02	.00
☐ 245	Sid Monge	.03	.01	.00
☐ 246	Ken Oberkfell	.03	.01	.00
☐ 247	Joe Pittman	.10	.04	.01
	(photo actually			
	Juan Eichelberger)			
☐ 248	Mario Soto	.07	.03	.01
☐ 249	Claudell Washington	.07	.03	.01
☐ 250	Rick Rhoden	.07	.03	.01
☐ 251	Darrell Evans	.09	.04	.01
☐ 252	Steve Henderson	.03	.01	.00
☐ 253	Manny Castillo	.03	.01	.00
☐ 254	Craig Swan	.03	.01	.00
☐ 255	Joey McLaughlin	.03	.01	.00
☐ 256	Pete Redfern	.03	.01	.00
☐ 257	Ken Singleton	.08	.03	.01
☐ 258	Robin Yount	.30	.12	.03
☐ 259	Elias Sosa	.03	.01	.00
☐ 260	Bob Ojeda	.12	.05	.01
☐ 261	Bobby Murcer	.09	.04	.01
☐ 262	Candy Maldonado	.35	.14	.03
☐ 263	Rick Waits	.03	.01	.00
☐ 264	Greg Pryor	.03	.01	.00
☐ 265	Bob Owchinko	.03	.01	.00
☐ 266	Chris Speier	.03	.01	.00
☐ 267	Bruce Kison	.03	.01	.00
☐ 268	Mark Wagner	.03	.01	.00
☐ 269	Steve Kemp	.07	.03	.01
☐ 270	Phil Garner	.05	.02	.00
☐ 271	Gene Richards	.03	.01	.00
☐ 272	Renie Martin	.03	.01	.00
☐ 273	Dave Roberts	.03	.01	.00
☐ 274	Dan Driessen	.05	.02	.00
☐ 275	Rufino Linares	.03	.01	.00
☐ 276	Lee Lacy	.05	.02	.00
☐ 277	Ryne Sandberg	3.50	1.40	.35
☐ 278	Darrell Porter	.05	.02	.00
☐ 279	Cal Ripken	.75	.30	.07
☐ 280	Jamie Easterly	.03	.01	.00
☐ 281	Bill Fahey	.03	.01	.00
☐ 282	Glenn Hoffman	.03	.01	.00
☐ 283	Willie Randolph	.06	.02	.00
☐ 284	Fernando Valenzuela	.35	.14	.03
☐ 285	Alan Bannister	.03	.01	.00
☐ 286	Paul Splittorff	.03	.01	.00
☐ 287	Joe Rudi	.05	.02	.00
☐ 288	Bill Gullickson	.03	.01	.00
☐ 289	Danny Darwin	.03	.01	.00
☐ 290	Andy Hassler	.03	.01	.00
☐ 291	Ernesto Escarrega	.03	.01	.00
☐ 292	Steve Mura	.03	.01	.00
☐ 293	Tony Scott	.03	.01	.00
☐ 294	Manny Trillo	.05	.02	.00
☐ 295	Greg Harris	.05	.02	.00
☐ 296	Luis DeLeon	.03	.01	.00
☐ 297	Kent Tekulve	.07	.03	.01
☐ 298	Atlee Hammaker	.05	.02	.00
☐ 299	Bruce Benedict	.03	.01	.00
☐ 300	Fergie Jenkins	.12	.05	.01
☐ 301	Dave Kingman	.12	.05	.01
☐ 302	Bill Caudill	.05	.02	.00
☐ 303	John Castino	.03	.01	.00
☐ 304	Ernie Whitt	.03	.01	.00
☐ 305	Randy Johnson	.05	.02	.00
☐ 306	Garth Iorg	.03	.01	.00
☐ 307	Gaylord Perry	.20	.08	.02
☐ 308	Ed Lynch	.03	.01	.00
☐ 309	Keith Moreland	.07	.03	.01
☐ 310	Rafael Ramirez	.03	.01	.00
☐ 311	Bill Madlock	.15	.06	.01
☐ 312	Milt May	.03	.01	.00
☐ 313	John Montefusco	.05	.02	.00
☐ 314	Wayne Krenchicki	.03	.01	.00
☐ 315	George Vukovich	.03	.01	.00
☐ 316	Joaquin Andujar	.10	.04	.01
☐ 317	Craig Reynolds	.03	.01	.00

	MINT	VG-E	F-G			MINT	VG-E	F-G
☐ 318 Rick Burleson	.06	.02	.00	☐ 366 Brad Mills	.03	.01	.00
☐ 319 Richard Dotson	.06	.02	.00	☐ 367 Brian Downing	.03	.01	.00
☐ 320 Steve Rogers	.06	.02	.00	☐ 368 Mike Richardt	.03	.01	.00
☐ 321 Dave Schmidt	.03	.01	.00	☐ 369 Aurelio Rodriguez	.03	.01	.00
☐ 322 Bud Black	.20	.08	.02	☐ 370 Dave Smith	.06	.02	.00
☐ 323 Jeff Burroughs	.05	.02	.00	☐ 371 Tug McGraw	.09	.04	.01
☐ 324 Von Hayes	.18	.08	.01	☐ 372 Doug Bair	.03	.01	.00
☐ 325 Butch Wynegar	.05	.02	.00	☐ 373 Ruppert Jones	.03	.01	.00
☐ 326 Carl Yastrzemski	.50	.20	.05	☐ 374 Alex Trevino	.03	.01	.00
☐ 327 Ron Roenicke	.03	.01	.00	☐ 375 Ken Dayley	.03	.01	.00
☐ 328 Howard Johnson	.12	.05	.01	☐ 376 Rod Scurry	.03	.01	.00
☐ 329 Rick Dempsey	.05	.02	.00	☐ 377 Bob Brenly	.07	.03	.01
☐ 330 A Jim Slaton	.07	.03	.01	☐ 378 Scot Thompson	.03	.01	.00
(bio printed				☐ 379 Julio Cruz	.03	.01	.00
black on white)				☐ 380 John Stearns	.03	.01	.00
☐ 330 B Jim Slaton	.07	.03	.01	☐ 381 Dale Murray	.03	.01	.00
(bio printed				☐ 382 Frank Viola	.45	.18	.04
black on yellow)				☐ 383 Al Bumbry	.03	.01	.00
☐ 331 Benny Ayala	.03	.01	.00	☐ 384 Ben Oglivie	.07	.03	.01
☐ 332 Ted Simmons	.12	.05	.01	☐ 385 Dave Tobik	.03	.01	.00
☐ 333 Lou Whitaker	.15	.06	.01	☐ 386 Bob Stanley	.05	.02	.00
☐ 334 Chuck Rainey	.03	.01	.00	☐ 387 Andre Robertson	.03	.01	.00
☐ 335 Lou Piniella	.10	.04	.01	☐ 388 Jorge Orta	.03	.01	.00
☐ 336 Steve Sax	.18	.08	.01	☐ 389 Ed Whitson	.05	.02	.00
☐ 337 Toby Harrah	.06	.02	.00	☐ 390 Don Hood	.03	.01	.00
☐ 338 George Brett	.45	.18	.04	☐ 391 Tom Underwood	.03	.01	.00
☐ 339 Davey Lopes	.07	.03	.01	☐ 392 Tim Wallach	.08	.03	.01
☐ 340 Gary Carter	.35	.14	.03	☐ 393 Steve Renko	.03	.01	.00
☐ 341 John Grubb	.03	.01	.00	☐ 394 Mickey Rivers	.06	.02	.00
☐ 342 Tim Foli	.03	.01	.00	☐ 395 Greg Luzinski	.10	.04	.01
☐ 343 Jim Kaat	.10	.04	.01	☐ 396 Art Howe	.03	.01	.00
☐ 344 Mike LaCoss	.03	.01	.00	☐ 397 Alan Wiggins	.15	.06	.01
☐ 345 Larry Christenson	.03	.01	.00	☐ 398 Jim Barr	.03	.01	.00
☐ 346 Juan Bonilla	.03	.01	.00	☐ 399 Ivan DeJesus	.03	.01	.00
☐ 347 Omar Moreno	.03	.01	.00	☐ 400 Tom Lawless	.05	.02	.00
☐ 348 Chili Davis	.12	.05	.01	☐ 401 Bob Walk	.03	.01	.00
☐ 349 Tommy Boggs	.03	.01	.00	☐ 402 Jimmy Smith	.03	.01	.00
☐ 350 Rusty Staub	.10	.04	.01	☐ 403 Lee Smith	.09	.04	.01
☐ 351 Bump Wills	.03	.01	.00	☐ 404 George Hendrick	.07	.03	.01
☐ 352 Rick Sweet	.03	.01	.00	☐ 405 Eddie Murray	.50	.20	.05
☐ 353 Jim Gott	.09	.04	.01	☐ 406 Marshall Edwards	.03	.01	.00
☐ 354 Terry Felton	.03	.01	.00	☐ 407 Lance Parrish	.30	.12	.03
☐ 355 Jim Kern	.03	.01	.00	☐ 408 Carney Lansford	.10	.04	.01
☐ 356 Bill Almon	.03	.01	.00	☐ 409 Dave Winfield	.35	.14	.03
☐ 357 Tippy Martinez	.03	.01	.00	☐ 410 Bob Welch	.07	.03	.01
☐ 358 Roy Howell	.03	.01	.00	☐ 411 Larry Milbourne	.03	.01	.00
☐ 359 Dan Petry	.12	.05	.01	☐ 412 Dennis Leonard	.05	.02	.00
☐ 360 Jerry Mumphrey	.05	.02	.00	☐ 413 Dan Meyer	.03	.01	.00
☐ 361 Mark Clear	.03	.01	.00	☐ 414 Charlie Lea	.05	.02	.00
☐ 362 Mike Marshall	.20	.08	.02	☐ 415 Rick Honeycutt	.05	.02	.00
☐ 363 Lary Sorenson	.03	.01	.00	☐ 416 Mike Witt	.10	.04	.01
☐ 364 Amos Otis	.07	.03	.01	☐ 417 Steve Trout	.05	.02	.00
☐ 365 Rick Langford	.03	.01	.00	☐ 418 Glenn Brummer	.03	.01	.00

		MINT	VG-E	F-G
☐ 419	Denny Walling	.03	.01	.00
☐ 420	Gary Matthews	.08	.03	.01
☐ 421	Charlie Leibrandt (Liebrandt on front of card)	.06	.02	.00
☐ 422	Juan Eichelberger (photo actually Joe Pittman)	.07	.03	.01
☐ 423	Matt Guante	.10	.04	.01
☐ 424	Bill Laskey	.10	.04	.01
☐ 425	Jerry Royster	.03	.01	.00
☐ 426	Dickie Noles	.03	.01	.00
☐ 427	George Foster	.15	.06	.01
☐ 428	Mike Moore	.25	.10	.02
☐ 429	Gary Ward	.06	.02	.00
☐ 430	Barry Bonnell	.05	.02	.00
☐ 431	Ron Washington	.05	.02	.00
☐ 432	Rance Mulliniks	.03	.01	.00
☐ 433	Mike Stanton	.03	.01	.00
☐ 434	Jesse Orosco	.08	.03	.01
☐ 435	Larry Bowa	.10	.04	.01
☐ 436	Biff Pocoroba	.03	.01	.00
☐ 437	Johnny Ray	.12	.05	.01
☐ 438	Joe Morgan	.25	.10	.02
☐ 439	Eric Show	.12	.05	.01
☐ 440	Larry Biittner	.03	.01	.00
☐ 441	Greg Gross	.03	.01	.00
☐ 442	Gene Tenace	.03	.01	.00
☐ 443	Danny Heep	.03	.01	.00
☐ 444	Bobby Clark	.03	.01	.00
☐ 445	Kevin Hickey	.03	.01	.00
☐ 446	Scott Sanderson	.03	.01	.00
☐ 447	Frank Tanana	.06	.02	.00
☐ 448	Cesar Geronimo	.03	.01	.00
☐ 449	Jimmy Sexton	.03	.01	.00
☐ 450	Mike Hargrove	.05	.02	.00
☐ 451	Doyle Alexander	.05	.02	.00
☐ 452	Dwight Evans	.12	.05	.01
☐ 453	Terry Forster	.07	.03	.01
☐ 454	Tom Brookens	.03	.01	.00
☐ 455	Rich Dauer	.03	.01	.00
☐ 456	Rob Picciolo	.03	.01	.00
☐ 457	Terry Crowley	.03	.01	.00
☐ 458	Ned Yost	.03	.01	.00
☐ 459	Kirk Gibson	.25	.10	.02
☐ 460	Reid Nichols	.03	.01	.00
☐ 461	Oscar Gamble	.06	.02	.00
☐ 462	Dusty Baker	.07	.03	.01
☐ 463	Jack Perconte	.03	.01	.00
☐ 464	Frank White	.07	.03	.01
☐ 465	Mickey Klutts	.03	.01	.00
☐ 466	Warren Cromartie	.03	.01	.00
☐ 467	Larry Parrish	.06	.02	.00
☐ 468	Bobby Grich	.08	.03	.01
☐ 469	Dane Iorg	.03	.01	.00
☐ 470	Joe Niekro	.08	.03	.01
☐ 471	Ed Farmer	.03	.01	.00
☐ 472	Tim Flannery	.03	.01	.00
☐ 473	Dave Parker	.25	.10	.02
☐ 474	Jeff Leonard	.07	.03	.01
☐ 475	Al Hrabosky	.05	.02	.00
☐ 476	Ron Hodges	.03	.01	.00
☐ 477	Leon Durham	.09	.04	.01
☐ 478	Jim Essian	.03	.01	.00
☐ 479	Roy Lee Jackson	.03	.01	.00
☐ 480	Brad Havens	.03	.01	.00
☐ 481	Joe Price	.03	.01	.00
☐ 482	Tony Bernazard	.05	.02	.00
☐ 483	Scott McGregor	.08	.03	.01
☐ 484	Paul Molitor	.12	.05	.01
☐ 485	Mike Ivie	.03	.01	.00
☐ 486	Ken Griffey	.09	.04	.01
☐ 487	Dennis Eckersley	.06	.02	.00
☐ 488	Steve Garvey	.40	.16	.04
☐ 489	Mike Fischlin	.03	.01	.00
☐ 490	U.L. Washington	.03	.01	.00
☐ 491	Steve McCatty	.03	.01	.00
☐ 492	Roy Johnson	.03	.01	.00
☐ 493	Don Baylor	.12	.05	.01
☐ 494	Bobby Johnson	.03	.01	.00
☐ 495	Mike Squires	.03	.01	.00
☐ 496	Bert Roberge	.03	.01	.00
☐ 497	Dick Ruthven	.03	.01	.00
☐ 498	Tito Landrum	.03	.01	.00
☐ 499	Sixto Lezcano	.03	.01	.00
☐ 500	Johnny Bench	.35	.14	.03
☐ 501	Larry Whisenton	.03	.01	.00
☐ 502	Manny Sarmiento	.03	.01	.00
☐ 503	Fred Breining	.03	.01	.00
☐ 504	Bill Campbell	.03	.01	.00
☐ 505	Todd Cruz	.03	.01	.00
☐ 506	Bob Bailor	.03	.01	.00
☐ 507	Dave Stieb	.18	.08	.01
☐ 508	Al Williams	.03	.01	.00
☐ 509	Dan Ford	.03	.01	.00
☐ 510	Gorman Thomas	.10	.04	.01
☐ 511	Chet Lemon	.06	.02	.00
☐ 512	Mike Torrez	.05	.02	.00
☐ 513	Shane Rawley	.06	.02	.00
☐ 514	Mark Belanger	.05	.02	.00
☐ 515	Rodney Craig	.03	.01	.00
☐ 516	Onix Concepcion	.05	.02	.00
☐ 517	Mike Heath	.03	.01	.00
☐ 518	Andre Dawson	.20	.08	.02
☐ 519	Luis Sanchez	.03	.01	.00
☐ 520	Terry Bogener	.03	.01	.00

	MINT	VG-E	F-G
☐ 521 Rudy Law	.03	.01	.00
☐ 522 Ray Knight	.08	.03	.01
☐ 523 Joe Lefebvre	.03	.01	.00
☐ 524 Jim Wohlford	.03	.01	.00
☐ 525 Julio Franco	1.25	.50	.12
☐ 526 Ron Oester	.05	.02	.00
☐ 527 Rick Mahler	.05	.02	.00
☐ 528 Steve Nicosia	.03	.01	.00
☐ 529 Junior Kennedy	.03	.01	.00
☐ 530 A Whitey Herzog MGR	.10	.04	.01
(bio printed black on white)			
☐ 530 B Whitey Herzog MGR	.10	.04	.01
(bio printed black on yellow)			
☐ 531 A Don Sutton	.35	.14	.03
(blue border on photo)			
☐ 531 B Don Sutton	.35	.14	.03
(green border on photo)			
☐ 532 Mark Brouhard	.03	.01	.00
☐ 533 A Sparky Anderson MGR	.10	.04	.01
(bio printed black on white)			
☐ 533 B Sparky Anderson MGR	.10	.04	.01
(bio printed black on yellow)			
☐ 534 Roger LaFrancois	.03	.01	.00
☐ 535 George Frazier	.03	.01	.00
☐ 536 Tom Niedenfuer	.08	.03	.01
☐ 537 Ed Glynn	.03	.01	.00
☐ 538 Lee May	.06	.02	.00
☐ 539 Bob Kearney	.08	.03	.01
☐ 540 Tim Raines	.30	.12	.03
☐ 541 Paul Mirabella	.03	.01	.00
☐ 542 Luis Tiant	.08	.03	.01
☐ 543 Ron LeFlore	.05	.02	.00
☐ 544 Dave LaPoint	.12	.05	.01
☐ 545 Randy Moffitt	.03	.01	.00
☐ 546 Luis Aguayo	.03	.01	.00
☐ 547 Brad Lesley	.06	.02	.00
☐ 548 Luis Salazar	.03	.01	.00
☐ 549 John Candelaria	.08	.03	.01
☐ 550 Dave Bergman	.03	.01	.00
☐ 551 Bob Watson	.06	.02	.00
☐ 552 Pat Tabler	.12	.05	.01
☐ 553 Brent Gaff	.03	.01	.00
☐ 554 Al Cowens	.03	.01	.00
☐ 555 Tom Brunansky	.20	.08	.02
☐ 556 Lloyd Moseby	.14	.06	.01
☐ 557 A Pascual Perez ERR	2.00	.80	.20
(Twins in glove)			
☐ 557 B Pascual Perez COR	.10	.04	.01
(Braves in glove)			
☐ 558 Willie Upshaw	.08	.03	.01
☐ 559 Richie Zisk	.05	.02	.00
☐ 560 Pat Zachry	.03	.01	.00
☐ 561 Jay Johnstone	.05	.02	.00
☐ 562 Carlos Diaz	.10	.04	.01
☐ 563 John Tudor	.12	.05	.01
☐ 564 Frank Robinson MGR	.14	.06	.01
☐ 565 Dave Edwards	.03	.01	.00
☐ 566 Paul Householder	.03	.01	.00
☐ 567 Ron Reed	.03	.01	.00
☐ 568 Mike Ramsey	.03	.01	.00
☐ 569 Kiko Garcia	.03	.01	.00
☐ 570 Tommy John	.12	.05	.01
☐ 571 Tony LaRussa MGR	.05	.02	.00
☐ 572 Joel Youngblood	.03	.01	.00
☐ 573 Wayne Tolleson	.06	.02	.00
☐ 574 Keith Creel	.03	.01	.00
☐ 575 Billy Martin MGR	.12	.05	.01
☐ 576 Jerry Dybzinski	.03	.01	.00
☐ 577 Rick Cerone	.03	.01	.00
☐ 578 Tony Perez	.12	.05	.01
☐ 579 Greg Brock	.35	.14	.03
☐ 580 Glen Wilson	.60	.24	.06
☐ 581 Tim Stoddard	.03	.01	.00
☐ 582 Bob McClure	.03	.01	.00
☐ 583 Jim Dwyer	.03	.01	.00
☐ 584 Ed Romero	.03	.01	.00
☐ 585 Larry Herndon	.03	.01	.00
☐ 586 Wade Boggs	12.00	5.00	1.20
☐ 587 Jay Howell	.06	.02	.00
☐ 588 Dave Stewart	.03	.01	.00
☐ 589 Bert Blyleven	.12	.05	.01
☐ 590 Dick Howser MGR	.05	.02	.00
☐ 591 Wayne Gross	.03	.01	.00
☐ 592 Terry Francona	.05	.02	.00
☐ 593 Don Werner	.03	.01	.00
☐ 594 Bill Stein	.03	.01	.00
☐ 595 Jesse Barfield	.25	.10	.02
☐ 596 Bobby Molinaro	.03	.01	.00
☐ 597 Mike Vail	.03	.01	.00
☐ 598 Tony Gwynn	4.50	1.80	.45
☐ 599 Gary Rajsich	.05	.02	.00
☐ 600 Jerry Ujdur	.03	.01	.00
☐ 601 Cliff Johnson	.03	.01	.00
☐ 602 Jerry White	.03	.01	.00
☐ 603 Bryan Clark	.03	.01	.00
☐ 604 Joe Ferguson	.03	.01	.00
☐ 605 Guy Sularz	.03	.01	.00
☐ 606 A Ozzie Virgil	.10	.04	.01
(green border on photo)			

		MINT	VG-E	F-G
☐ 606	B Ozzie Virgil	.10	.04	.01
	(orange border on photo)			
☐ 607	Terry Harper	.03	.01	.00
☐ 608	Harvey Kuenn MGR	.05	.02	.00
☐ 609	Jim Sundberg	.05	.02	.00
☐ 610	Willie Stargell	.20	.08	.02
☐ 611	Reggie Smith	.08	.03	.01
☐ 612	Rob Wilfong	.03	.01	.00
☐ 613	The Niekro Brothers	.12	.05	.01
	Joe Niekro Phil Niekro			
☐ 614	Lee Elia MGR	.03	.01	.00
☐ 615	Mickey Hatcher	.03	.01	.00
☐ 616	Jerry Hairston	.03	.01	.00
☐ 617	John Martin	.03	.01	.00
☐ 618	Wally Backman	.08	.03	.01
☐ 619	Storm Davis	.45	.18	.04
☐ 620	Alan Knicely	.03	.01	.00
☐ 621	John Stuper	.08	.03	.01
☐ 622	Matt Sinatro	.03	.01	.00
☐ 623	Gene Petralli	.03	.01	.00
☐ 624	Duane Walker	.06	.02	.00
☐ 625	Dick Williams MGR	.03	.01	.00
☐ 626	Pat Corrales MGR	.03	.01	.00
☐ 627	Vern Ruhle	.03	.01	.00
☐ 628	Joe Torre MGR	.07	.03	.01
☐ 629	Anthony Johnson	.05	.02	.00
☐ 630	Steve Howe	.05	.02	.00
☐ 631	Gary Woods	.03	.01	.00
☐ 632	LaMarr Hoyt	.07	.03	.01
☐ 633	Steve Swisher	.03	.01	.00
☐ 634	Terry Leach	.03	.01	.00
☐ 635	Jeff Newman	.03	.01	.00
☐ 636	Brett Butler	.10	.04	.01
☐ 637	Gary Gray	.03	.01	.00
☐ 638	Lee Mazzilli	.05	.02	.00
☐ 639	A Ron Jackson ERR	10.00	4.00	1.00
	(A's in glove)			
☐ 639	B Ron Jackson COR	.15	.06	.01
	(Angels in glove, red border on photo)			
☐ 639	C Ron Jackson COR	.50	.20	.05
	(Angels in glove, green border on photo)			
☐ 640	Juan Beniquez	.05	.02	.00
☐ 641	Dave Rucker	.03	.01	.00
☐ 642	Luis Pujols	.03	.01	.00
☐ 643	Rick Monday	.05	.02	.00
☐ 644	Hosken Powell	.03	.01	.00
☐ 645	The Chicken	.25	.10	.02

		MINT	VG-E	F-G
☐ 646	Dave Engle	.03	.01	.00
☐ 647	Dick Davis	.03	.01	.00
☐ 648	Frank Robinson	.12	.05	.01
	Vida Blue Joe Morgan			
☐ 649	Al Chambers	.08	.03	.01
☐ 650	Jesus Vega	.05	.02	.00
☐ 651	Jeff Jones	.03	.01	.00
☐ 652	Marvis Foley	.03	.01	.00
☐ 653	Ty Cobb Puzzle Card	.05	.02	.00
☐ 654	A Dick Perez/Diamond King Checklist (unnumbered) (word "checklist" omitted from back)	.15	.02	.00
☐ 654	B Dick Perez/Diamond King Checklist (unnumbered) (word "checklist" is on back)	.15	.02	.00
☐ 655	Checklist 1 (unnumbered)	.07	.01	.00
☐ 656	Checklist 2 (unnumbered)	.07	.01	.00
☐ 657	Checklist 3 (unnumbered)	.07	.01	.00
☐ 658	Checklist 4 (unnumbered)	.07	.01	.00
☐ 659	Checklist 5 (unnumbered)	.07	.01	.00
☐ 660	Checklist 6 (unnumbered)	.07	.01	.00

1984 Donruss

The 1984 Donruss set contains a total of 660 cards, each measuring 2½" by 3½"; however, only 658 are numbered. The first 26 cards in the set are again Diamond Kings (DK), although the drawings this year were styled differently and are easily differentiated from other DK issues. A new feature, Rated Rookies (RR), was introduced with this set with Bill Madden's 20 selections comprising numbers 27 through 46. Two "Living Legend" cards designated A (featuring Gaylord Perry and Rollie Fingers) and B (featuring Johnny Bench and Carl Yastrzemski) were issued as bonus cards in wax packs, but were not issued in the vending sets sold to hobby dealers. The seven unnumbered checklist cards are arbitrarily assigned numbers 652 through 658 and are listed at the end of the list below. The designs on the fronts of the Donruss cards changed considerably from the past two years. The backs contain statistics and are printed in green and black ink. The cards were distributed with a 63-piece puzzle of Duke Snider.

	MINT	VG-E	F-G
Complete Set (658)	225.00	90.00	22.00
Common Player (1-660)	.07	.03	.01

		MINT	VG-E	F-G
☐	1 Robin Yount DK	.75	.30	.07
☐	2 Dave Concepcion DK ..	.12	.05	.01
☐	3 Dwayne Murphy DK ...	.09	.04	.01
☐	4 John Castino DK	.09	.04	.01
☐	5 Leon Durham DK	.12	.05	.01
☐	6 Rusty Staub DK	.12	.05	.01
☐	7 Jack Clark DK	.15	.06	.01
☐	8 Dave Dravecky DK ...	.09	.04	.01
☐	9 Al Oliver DK	.15	.06	.01
☐	10 Dave Righetti DK	.20	.08	.02
☐	11 Hal McRae DK	.09	.04	.01
☐	12 Ray Knight DK	.12	.05	.01
☐	13 Bruce Sutter DK	.15	.06	.01
☐	14 Bob Horner DK	.25	.10	.02
☐	15 Lance Parrish DK	.30	.12	.03
☐	16 Matt Young DK	.09	.04	.01
☐	17 Fred Lynn DK	.20	.08	.02
☐	18 Ron Kittle DK	.20	.08	.02
☐	19 Jim Clancy DK	.09	.04	.01
☐	20 Bill Madlock DK	.15	.06	.01
☐	21 Larry Parrish DK	.12	.05	.01
☐	22 Eddie Murray DK	.75	.30	.07
☐	23 Mike Schmidt DK	.90	.36	.09
☐	24 Pedro Guerrero DK ...	.35	.14	.03
☐	25 Andre Thornton DK ...	.12	.05	.01
☐	26 Wade Boggs DK........	2.50	1.00	.25

		MINT	VG-E	F-G
☐	27 Joel Skinner RR	.20	.08	.02
☐	28 Tommy Dunbar RR	.10	.04	.01
☐	29 A Mike Stenhouse RR ..	.20	.08	.02
	ERR (no back number)			
☐	29 B Mike Stenhouse RR ..	1.50	.60	.15
	COR			
☐	30 A Ron Darling RR ERR	6.00	2.40	.60
	(no number on back)			
☐	30 B Ron Darling RR COR .	9.00	3.75	.90
☐	31 Dion James RR	.25	.10	.02
☐	32 Tony Fernandez RR ...	3.00	1.20	.30
☐	33 Angel Salazar RR	.10	.04	.01
☐	34 Kevin McReynolds RR .	4.00	1.60	.40
☐	35 Dick Schofield RR	1.25	.50	.12
☐	36 Brad Komminsk RR ...	.25	.10	.02
☐	37 Tim Teufel RR	.50	.20	.05
☐	38 Doug Frobel RR	.15	.06	.01
☐	39 Greg Gagne RR	.35	.14	.03
☐	40 Mike Fuentes RR	.10	.04	.01
☐	41 Joe Carter RR	6.00	2.40	.60
☐	42 Mike Brown RR OF ...	.35	.14	.03
☐	43 Mike Jeffcoat RR	.15	.06	.01
☐	44 Sid Fernandez RR	6.00	2.40	.60
☐	45 Brian Dayett RR	.15	.06	.01
☐	46 Chris Smith RR	.10	.04	.01
☐	47 Eddie Murray	.75	.30	.07
☐	48 Robin Yount	.50	.20	.05
☐	49 Lance Parrish	.35	.14	.03
☐	50 Jim Rice	.60	.24	.06
☐	51 Dave Winfield	.45	.18	.04
☐	52 Fernando Valenzuela ...	.45	.18	.04
☐	53 George Brett	.75	.30	.07
☐	54 Rickey Henderson	.70	.28	.07
☐	55 Gary Carter	.60	.24	.06
☐	56 Buddy Bell	.12	.05	.01
☐	57 Reggie Jackson	.75	.30	.07
☐	58 Harold Baines	.25	.10	.02
☐	59 Ozzie Smith	.20	.08	.02
☐	60 Nolan Ryan	.60	.24	.06
☐	61 Pete Rose	2.00	.80	.20
☐	62 Ron Oester	.07	.03	.01
☐	63 Steve Garvey	.55	.22	.05
☐	64 Jason Thompson	.09	.04	.01
☐	65 Jack Clark	.15	.06	.01
☐	66 Dale Murphy	1.25	.50	.12
☐	67 Leon Durham	.20	.08	.02
☐	68 Darryl Strawberry	10.00	4.00	1.00
☐	69 Richie Zisk	.07	.03	.01
☐	70 Kent Hrbek	.40	.16	.04
☐	71 Dave Stieb	.25	.10	.02
☐	72 Ken Schrom	.10	.04	.01
☐	73 George Bell	.25	.10	.02
☐	74 John Moses	.10	.04	.01

			MINT	VG-E	F-G
☐	75	Ed Lynch	.07	.03	.01
☐	76	Chuck Rainey	.07	.03	.01
☐	77	Biff Pocoroba	.07	.03	.01
☐	78	Cecilio Guante	.07	.03	.01
☐	79	Jim Barr	.07	.03	.01
☐	80	Kurt Bevacqua	.07	.03	.01
☐	81	Tom Foley	.08	.03	.01
☐	82	Joe Lefebvre	.07	.03	.01
☐	83	Andy Van Slyke	.50	.20	.05
☐	84	Bob Lillis MGR	.07	.03	.01
☐	85	Rick Adams	.09	.04	.01
☐	86	Jerry Hairston	.07	.03	.01
☐	87	Bob James	.20	.08	.02
☐	88	Joe Altobelli MGR	.07	.03	.01
☐	89	Ed Romero	.07	.03	.01
☐	90	John Grubb	.07	.03	.01
☐	91	John Henry Johnson	.07	.03	.01
☐	92	Juan Espino	.08	.03	.01
☐	93	Candy Maldonado	.10	.04	.01
☐	94	Andre Thornton	.10	.04	.01
☐	95	Onix Concepcion	.07	.03	.01
☐	96	Don Hill	.10	.04	.01
☐	97	Andre Dawson	.25	.10	.02
☐	98	Frank Tanana	.10	.04	.01
☐	99	Curt Wilkerson	.10	.04	.01
☐	100	Larry Gura	.10	.04	.01
☐	101	Dwayne Murphy	.10	.04	.01
☐	102	Tom Brennan	.07	.03	.01
☐	103	Dave Righetti	.25	.10	.02
☐	104	Steve Sax	.25	.10	.02
☐	105	Dan Petry	.20	.08	.02
☐	106	Cal Ripken	.75	.30	.07
☐	107	Paul Molitor	.15	.06	.01
☐	108	Fred Lynn	.25	.10	.02
☐	109	Neil Allen	.10	.04	.01
☐	110	Joe Niekro	.10	.04	.01
☐	111	Steve Carlton	.50	.20	.05
☐	112	Terry Kennedy	.10	.04	.01
☐	113	Bill Madlock	.15	.06	.01
☐	114	Chili Davis	.10	.04	.01
☐	115	Jim Gantner	.10	.04	.01
☐	116	Tom Seaver	.50	.20	.05
☐	117	Bill Buckner	.15	.06	.01
☐	118	Bill Caudill	.10	.04	.01
☐	119	Jim Clancy	.07	.03	.01
☐	120	John Castino	.07	.03	.01
☐	121	Dave Concepcion	.10	.04	.01
☐	122	Greg Luzinski	.15	.06	.01
☐	123	Mike Boddicker	.15	.06	.01
☐	124	Pete Ladd	.07	.03	.01
☐	125	Juan Berenguer	.07	.03	.01
☐	126	John Montefusco	.07	.03	.01
☐	127	Ed Jurak	.07	.03	.01

			MINT	VG-E	F-G
☐	128	Tom Niedenfuer	.10	.04	.01
☐	129	Bert Blyleven	.15	.06	.01
☐	130	Bud Black	.07	.03	.01
☐	131	Gorman Heimueller	.07	.03	.01
☐	132	Dan Schatzeder	.07	.03	.01
☐	133	Ron Jackson	.07	.03	.01
☐	134	Tom Henke	.50	.20	.05
☐	135	Kevin Hickey	.07	.03	.01
☐	136	Mike Scott	.30	.12	.03
☐	137	Bo Diaz	.10	.04	.01
☐	138	Glenn Brummer	.07	.03	.01
☐	139	Sid Monge	.07	.03	.01
☐	140	Rich Gale	.07	.03	.01
☐	141	Brett Butler	.15	.06	.01
☐	142	Brian Harper	.10	.04	.01
☐	143	John Rabb	.10	.04	.01
☐	144	Gary Woods	.07	.03	.01
☐	145	Pat Putnam	.07	.03	.01
☐	146	Jim Acker	.20	.08	.02
☐	147	Mickey Hatcher	.07	.03	.01
☐	148	Todd Cruz	.07	.03	.01
☐	149	Tom Tellmann	.07	.03	.01
☐	150	John Wockenfuss	.07	.03	.01
☐	151	Wade Boggs	8.00	3.25	.80
☐	152	Don Baylor	.15	.06	.01
☐	153	Bob Welch	.10	.04	.01
☐	154	Alan Bannister	.07	.03	.01
☐	155	Willie Aikens	.10	.04	.01
☐	156	Jeff Burroughs	.07	.03	.01
☐	157	Bryan Little	.07	.03	.01
☐	158	Bob Boone	.10	.04	.01
☐	159	Dave Hostetler	.07	.03	.01
☐	160	Jerry Dybzinski	.07	.03	.01
☐	161	Mike Madden	.15	.06	.01
☐	162	Luis DeLeon	.07	.03	.01
☐	163	Willie Hernandez	.30	.12	.03
☐	164	Frank Pastore	.07	.03	.01
☐	165	Rick Camp	.07	.03	.01
☐	166	Lee Mazzilli	.20	.08	.02
☐	167	Scot Thompson	.07	.03	.01
☐	168	Bob Forsch	.10	.04	.01
☐	169	Mike Flanagan	.10	.04	.01
☐	170	Rick Manning	.07	.03	.01
☐	171	Chet Lemon	.10	.04	.01
☐	172	Jerry Remy	.07	.03	.01
☐	173	Ron Guidry	.25	.10	.02
☐	174	Pedro Guerrero	.40	.16	.04
☐	175	Willie Wilson	.25	.10	.02
☐	176	Carney Lansford	.15	.06	.01
☐	177	Al Oliver	.20	.08	.02
☐	178	Jim Sundberg	.10	.04	.01
☐	179	Bobby Grich	.12	.05	.01
☐	180	Rich Dotson	.10	.04	.01

		MINT	VG-E	F-G
☐ 181	Joaquin Andujar	.15	.06	.01
☐ 182	Jose Cruz	.15	.06	.01
☐ 183	Mike Schmidt	1.00	.40	.10
☐ 184	Gary Redus	.35	.14	.03
☐ 185	Garry Templeton	.15	.06	.01
☐ 186	Tony Pena	.20	.08	.02
☐ 187	Greg Minton	.10	.04	.01
☐ 188	Phil Niekro	.30	.12	.03
☐ 189	Ferguson Jenkins	.20	.08	.02
☐ 190	Mookie Wilson	.10	.04	.01
☐ 191	Jim Beattie	.07	.03	.01
☐ 192	Gary Ward	.10	.04	.01
☐ 193	Jesse Barfield	.30	.12	.03
☐ 194	Pete Filson	.07	.03	.01
☐ 195	Roy Lee Jackson	.07	.03	.01
☐ 196	Rick Sweet	.07	.03	.01
☐ 197	Jesse Orosco	.10	.04	.01
☐ 198	Steve Lake	.07	.03	.01
☐ 199	Ken Dayley	.07	.03	.01
☐ 200	Manny Sarmiento	.07	.03	.01
☐ 201	Mark Davis	.07	.03	.01
☐ 202	Tim Flannery	.07	.03	.01
☐ 203	Bill Scherrer	.10	.04	.01
☐ 204	Al Holland	.07	.03	.01
☐ 205	Dave Von Ohlen	.07	.03	.01
☐ 206	Mike LaCoss	.07	.03	.01
☐ 207	Juan Beniquez	.07	.03	.01
☐ 208	Juan Agosto	.07	.03	.01
☐ 209	Bobby Ramos	.07	.03	.01
☐ 210	Al Bumbry	.07	.03	.01
☐ 211	Mark Brouhard	.07	.03	.01
☐ 212	Howard Bailey	.07	.03	.01
☐ 213	Bruce Hurst	.15	.06	.01
☐ 214	Bob Shirley	.07	.03	.01
☐ 215	Pat Zachry	.07	.03	.01
☐ 216	Julio Franco	.20	.08	.02
☐ 217	Mike Armstrong	.07	.03	.01
☐ 218	Dave Beard	.07	.03	.01
☐ 219	Steve Rogers	.10	.04	.01
☐ 220	John Butcher	.07	.03	.01
☐ 221	Mike Smithson	.15	.06	.01
☐ 222	Frank White	.15	.06	.01
☐ 223	Mike Heath	.07	.03	.01
☐ 224	Chris Bando	.07	.03	.01
☐ 225	Roy Smalley	.10	.04	.01
☐ 226	Dusty Baker	.10	.04	.01
☐ 227	Lou Whitaker	.25	.10	.02
☐ 228	John Lowenstein	.07	.03	.01
☐ 229	Ben Oglivie	.10	.04	.01
☐ 230	Doug DeCinces	.15	.06	.01
☐ 231	Lonnie Smith	.10	.04	.01
☐ 232	Ray Knight	.15	.06	.01
☐ 233	Gary Matthews	.10	.04	.01
☐ 234	Juan Bonilla	.07	.03	.01
☐ 235	Rod Scurry	.07	.03	.01
☐ 236	Atlee Hammaker	.07	.03	.01
☐ 237	Mike Caldwell	.07	.03	.01
☐ 238	Keith Hernandez	.35	.14	.03
☐ 239	Larry Bowa	.15	.06	.01
☐ 240	Tony Bernazard	.10	.04	.01
☐ 241	Damaso Garcia	.15	.06	.01
☐ 242	Tom Brunansky	.25	.10	.02
☐ 243	Dan Driessen	.07	.03	.01
☐ 244	Ron Kittle	.25	.10	.02
☐ 245	Tim Stoddard	.07	.03	.01
☐ 246	Bob L. Gibson	.10	.04	.01
	(Brewers Pitcher)			
☐ 247	Marty Castillo	.07	.03	.01
☐ 248	Don Mattingly	90.00	30.00	6.00
☐ 249	Jeff Newman	.07	.03	.01
☐ 250	Alejandro Pena	.25	.10	.02
☐ 251	Toby Harrah	.07	.03	.01
☐ 252	Cesar Geronimo	.07	.03	.01
☐ 253	Tom Underwood	.07	.03	.01
☐ 254	Doug Flynn	.07	.03	.01
☐ 255	Andy Hassler	.07	.03	.01
☐ 256	Odell Jones	.07	.03	.01
☐ 257	Rudy Law	.07	.03	.01
☐ 258	Harry Spilman	.07	.03	.01
☐ 259	Marty Bystrom	.07	.03	.01
☐ 260	Dave Rucker	.07	.03	.01
☐ 261	Ruppert Jones	.07	.03	.01
☐ 262	Jeff R. Jones	.10	.04	.01
	(Reds OF)			
☐ 263	Gerald Perry	.25	.10	.02
☐ 264	Gene Tenace	.07	.03	.01
☐ 265	Brad Wellman	.10	.04	.01
☐ 266	Dickie Noles	.07	.03	.01
☐ 267	Jamie Allen	.10	.04	.01
☐ 268	Jim Gott	.07	.03	.01
☐ 269	Ron Davis	.07	.03	.01
☐ 270	Benny Ayala	.07	.03	.01
☐ 271	Ned Yost	.07	.03	.01
☐ 272	Dave Rozema	.07	.03	.01
☐ 273	Dave Stapleton	.07	.03	.01
☐ 274	Lou Piniella	.10	.04	.01
☐ 275	Jose Morales	.07	.03	.01
☐ 276	Brod Perkins	.07	.03	.01
☐ 277	Butch Davis	.10	.04	.01
☐ 278	Tony Phillips	.10	.04	.01
☐ 279	Jeff Reardon	.10	.04	.01
☐ 280	Ken Forsch	.07	.03	.01
☐ 281	Pete O'Brien	1.50	.60	.15
☐ 282	Tom Paciorek	.07	.03	.01
☐ 283	Frank LaCorte	.07	.03	.01
☐ 284	Tim Lollar	.07	.03	.01

		MINT	VG-E	F-G			MINT	VG-E	F-G
☐ 285	Greg Gross	.07	.03	.01	☐ 338	Rick Sutcliffe	.20	.08	.02
☐ 286	Alex Trevino	.07	.03	.01	☐ 339	Mark Huismann	.15	.06	.01
☐ 287	Gene Garber	.07	.03	.01	☐ 340	Tim Conroy	.15	.06	.01
☐ 288	Dave Parker	.30	.12	.03	☐ 341	Scott Sanderson	.07	.03	.01
☐ 289	Lee Smith	.15	.06	.01	☐ 342	Larry Biittner	.07	.03	.01
☐ 290	Dave LaPoint	.07	.03	.01	☐ 343	Dave Stewart	.07	.03	.01
☐ 291	John Shelby	.10	.04	.01	☐ 344	Darryl Motley	.07	.03	.01
☐ 292	Charlie Moore	.07	.03	.01	☐ 345	Chris Codiroli	.10	.04	.01
☐ 293	Alan Trammell	.25	.10	.02	☐ 346	Rich Behenna	.10	.04	.01
☐ 294	Tony Armas	.15	.06	.01	☐ 347	Andre Robertson	.07	.03	.01
☐ 295	Shane Rawley	.10	.04	.01	☐ 348	Mike Marshall	.20	.08	.02
☐ 296	Greg Brock	.10	.04	.01	☐ 349	Larry Herndon	.07	.03	.01
☐ 297	Hal McRae	.10	.04	.01	☐ 350	Rich Dauer	.07	.03	.01
☐ 298	Mike Davis	.15	.06	.01	☐ 351	Cecil Cooper	.20	.08	.02
☐ 299	Tim Raines	.35	.14	.03	☐ 352	Rod Carew	.50	.20	.05
☐ 300	Bucky Dent	.10	.04	.01	☐ 353	Willie McGee	.30	.12	.03
☐ 301	Tommy John	.20	.08	.02	☐ 354	Phil Garner	.10	.04	.01
☐ 302	Carlton Fisk	.20	.08	.02	☐ 355	Joe Morgan	.25	.10	.02
☐ 303	Darrell Porter	.10	.04	.01	☐ 356	Luis Salazar	.07	.03	.01
☐ 304	Dickie Thon	.10	.04	.01	☐ 357	John Candelaria	.10	.04	.01
☐ 305	Garry Maddox	.10	.04	.01	☐ 358	Bill Laskey	.07	.03	.01
☐ 306	Cesar Cedeno	.10	.04	.01	☐ 359	Bob McClure	.07	.03	.01
☐ 307	Gary Lucas	.07	.03	.01	☐ 360	Dave Kingman	.20	.08	.02
☐ 308	Johnny Ray	.15	.06	.01	☐ 361	Ron Cey	.15	.06	.01
☐ 309	Andy McGaffigan	.07	.03	.01	☐ 362	Matt Young	.15	.06	.01
☐ 310	Claudell Washington	.10	.04	.01	☐ 363	Lloyd Moseby	.20	.08	.02
☐ 311	Ryne Sandberg	1.75	.70	.17	☐ 364	Frank Viola	.15	.06	.01
☐ 312	George Foster	.25	.10	.02	☐ 365	Eddie Milner	.10	.04	.01
☐ 313	Spike Owen	.35	.14	.03	☐ 366	Floyd Bannister	.10	.04	.01
☐ 314	Gary Gaetti	.15	.06	.01	☐ 367	Dan Ford	.07	.03	.01
☐ 315	Willie Upshaw	.15	.06	.01	☐ 368	Moose Haas	.07	.03	.01
☐ 316	Al Williams	.07	.03	.01	☐ 369	Doug Bair	.07	.03	.01
☐ 317	Jorge Orta	.07	.03	.01	☐ 370	Ray Fontenot	.10	.04	.01
☐ 318	Orlando Mercado	.07	.03	.01	☐ 371	Luis Aponte	.07	.03	.01
☐ 319	Junior Ortiz	.07	.03	.01	☐ 372	Jack Fimple	.07	.03	.01
☐ 320	Mike Proly	.07	.03	.01	☐ 373	Neal Heaton	.15	.06	.01
☐ 321	Randy Johnson	.07	.03	.01	☐ 374	Greg Pryor	.07	.03	.01
☐ 322	Jim Morrison	.07	.03	.01	☐ 375	Wayne Gross	.07	.03	.01
☐ 323	Max Venable	.07	.03	.01	☐ 376	Charlie Lea	.07	.03	.01
☐ 324	Tony Gwynn	1.75	.70	.17	☐ 377	Steve Lubratich	.07	.03	.01
☐ 325	Duane Walker	.07	.03	.01	☐ 378	Jon Matlack	.10	.04	.01
☐ 326	Ozzie Virgil	.07	.03	.01	☐ 379	Julio Cruz	.07	.03	.01
☐ 327	Jeff Lahti	.07	.03	.01	☐ 380	John Mizerock	.07	.03	.01
☐ 328	Bill Dawley	.15	.06	.01	☐ 381	Kevin Gross	.25	.10	.02
☐ 329	Rob Wilfong	.07	.03	.01	☐ 382	Mike Ramsey	.07	.03	.01
☐ 330	Marc Hill	.07	.03	.01	☐ 383	Doug Gwosdz	.07	.03	.01
☐ 331	Ray Burris	.07	.03	.01	☐ 384	Kelly Paris	.10	.04	.01
☐ 332	Allan Ramirez	.10	.04	.01	☐ 385	Pete Falcone	.07	.03	.01
☐ 333	Chuck Porter	.07	.03	.01	☐ 386	Milt May	.07	.03	.01
☐ 334	Wayne Krenchicki	.07	.03	.01	☐ 387	Fred Breining	.07	.03	.01
☐ 335	Gary Allenson	.07	.03	.01	☐ 388	Craig Lefferts	.15	.06	.01
☐ 336	Bobby Meacham	.25	.10	.02	☐ 389	Steve Henderson	.07	.03	.01
☐ 337	Joe Beckwith	.07	.03	.01	☐ 390	Randy Moffitt	.07	.03	.01

		MINT	VG-E	F-G			MINT	VG-E	F-G
☐ 391	Ron Washington	.07	.03	.01	☐ 444	Mike Easler	.10	.04	.01
☐ 392	Gary Roenicke	.07	.03	.01	☐ 445	Renie Martin	.07	.03	.01
☐ 393	Tom Candiotti	.25	.10	.02	☐ 446	Dennis Rasmussen	.75	.30	.07
☐ 394	Larry Pashnick	.07	.03	.01	☐ 447	Ted Power	.15	.06	.01
☐ 395	Dwight Evans	.15	.06	.01	☐ 448	Charlie Hudson	.15	.06	.01
☐ 396	Goose Gossage	.20	.08	.02	☐ 449	Danny Cox	.40	.16	.04
☐ 397	Derrel Thomas	.07	.03	.01	☐ 450	Kevin Bass	.15	.06	.01
☐ 398	Juan Eichelberger	.07	.03	.01	☐ 451	Daryl Sconiers	.07	.03	.01
☐ 399	Leon Roberts	.07	.03	.01	☐ 452	Scott Fletcher	.10	.04	.01
☐ 400	Davey Lopes	.10	.04	.01	☐ 453	Bryn Smith	.07	.03	.01
☐ 401	Bill Gullickson	.10	.04	.01	☐ 454	Jim Dwyer	.07	.03	.01
☐ 402	Geoff Zahn	.07	.03	.01	☐ 455	Rob Picciolo	.07	.03	.01
☐ 403	Billy Sample	.07	.03	.01	☐ 456	Enos Cabell	.07	.03	.01
☐ 404	Mike Squires	.07	.03	.01	☐ 457	Dennis Boyd	1.50	.60	.15
☐ 405	Craig Reynolds	.07	.03	.01	☐ 458	Butch Wynegar	.07	.03	.01
☐ 406	Eric Show	.07	.03	.01	☐ 459	Burt Hooton	.07	.03	.01
☐ 407	John Denny	.10	.04	.01	☐ 460	Ron Hassey	.07	.03	.01
☐ 408	Dann Bilardello	.07	.03	.01	☐ 461	Danny Jackson	.75	.30	.07
☐ 409	Bruce Benedict	.07	.03	.01	☐ 462	Bob Kearney	.07	.03	.01
☐ 410	Kent Tekulve	.10	.04	.01	☐ 463	Terry Francona	.10	.04	.01
☐ 411	Mel Hall	.15	.06	.01	☐ 464	Wayne Tolleson	.07	.03	.01
☐ 412	John Stuper	.07	.03	.01	☐ 465	Mickey Rivers	.10	.04	.01
☐ 413	Rick Dempsey	.10	.04	.01	☐ 466	John Wathan	.07	.03	.01
☐ 414	Don Sutton	.30	.12	.03	☐ 467	Bill Almon	.07	.03	.01
☐ 415	Jack Morris	.30	.12	.03	☐ 468	George Vukovich	.07	.03	.01
☐ 416	John Tudor	.20	.08	.02	☐ 469	Steve Kemp	.10	.04	.01
☐ 417	Willie Randolph	.10	.04	.01	☐ 470	Ken Landreaux	.07	.03	.01
☐ 418	Jerry Reuss	.10	.04	.01	☐ 471	Milt Wilcox	.07	.03	.01
☐ 419	Don Slaught	.10	.04	.01	☐ 472	Tippy Martinez	.07	.03	.01
☐ 420	Steve McCatty	.07	.03	.01	☐ 473	Ted Simmons	.15	.06	.01
☐ 421	Tim Wallach	.15	.06	.01	☐ 474	Tim Foli	.07	.03	.01
☐ 422	Larry Parrish	.10	.04	.01	☐ 475	George Hendrick	.10	.04	.01
☐ 423	Brian Downing	.10	.04	.01	☐ 476	Terry Puhl	.10	.04	.01
☐ 424	Britt Burns	.10	.04	.01	☐ 477	Von Hayes	.25	.10	.02
☐ 425	David Green	.10	.04	.01	☐ 478	Bobby Brown	.07	.03	.01
☐ 426	Jerry Mumphrey	.10	.04	.01	☐ 479	Lee Lacy	.10	.04	.01
☐ 427	Ivan DeJesus	.07	.03	.01	☐ 480	Joel Youngblood	.07	.03	.01
☐ 428	Mario Soto	.10	.04	.01	☐ 481	Jim Slaton	.07	.03	.01
☐ 429	Gene Richards	.07	.03	.01	☐ 482	Mike Fitzgerald	.10	.04	.01
☐ 430	Dale Berra	.10	.04	.01	☐ 483	Keith Moreland	.15	.06	.01
☐ 431	Darrell Evans	.15	.06	.01	☐ 484	Ron Roenicke	.07	.03	.01
☐ 432	Glenn Hubbard	.07	.03	.01	☐ 485	Luis Leal	.07	.03	.01
☐ 433	Jody Davis	.15	.06	.01	☐ 486	Bryan Oelkers	.10	.04	.01
☐ 434	Danny Heep	.07	.03	.01	☐ 487	Bruce Berenyi	.07	.03	.01
☐ 435	Ed Nunez	.30	.12	.03	☐ 488	LaMarr Hoyt	.15	.06	.01
☐ 436	Bobby Castillo	.07	.03	.01	☐ 489	Joe Nolan	.07	.03	.01
☐ 437	Ernie Whitt	.07	.03	.01	☐ 490	Marshall Edwards	.07	.03	.01
☐ 438	Scott Ulger	.07	.03	.01	☐ 491	Mike Laga	.10	.04	.01
☐ 439	Doyle Alexander	.07	.03	.01	☐ 492	Rick Cerone	.07	.03	.01
☐ 440	Domingo Ramos	.07	.03	.01	☐ 493	Rick Miller	.10	.04	.01
☐ 441	Craig Swan	.07	.03	.01		(listed as Mike			
☐ 442	Warren Brusstar	.07	.03	.01		on card front)			
☐ 443	Len Barker	.07	.03	.01	☐ 494	Rick Honeycutt	.10	.04	.01

	MINT	VG-E	F-G		MINT	VG-E	F-G
☐ 495 Mike Hargrove	.10	.04	.01	☐ 547 Tug McGraw	.15	.06	.01
☐ 496 Joe Simpson	.07	.03	.01	☐ 548 Dave Smith	.10	.04	.01
☐ 497 Keith Atherton	.07	.03	.01	☐ 549 Len Matuszek	.07	.03	.01
☐ 498 Chris Welsh	.07	.03	.01	☐ 550 Tom Hume	.07	.03	.01
☐ 499 Bruce Kison	.07	.03	.01	☐ 551 Dave Dravecky	.10	.04	.01
☐ 500 Bobby Johnson	.07	.03	.01	☐ 552 Rick Rhoden	.10	.04	.01
☐ 501 Jerry Koosman	.10	.04	.01	☐ 553 Duane Kuiper	.07	.03	.01
☐ 502 Frank DiPino	.07	.03	.01	☐ 554 Rusty Staub	.10	.04	.01
☐ 503 Tony Perez	.15	.06	.01	☐ 555 Bill Campbell	.07	.03	.01
☐ 504 Ken Oberkfell	.07	.03	.01	☐ 556 Mike Torrez	.10	.04	.01
☐ 505 Mark Thurmond	.20	.08	.02	☐ 557 Dave Henderson	.10	.04	.01
☐ 506 Joe Price	.07	.03	.01	☐ 558 Len Whitehouse	.07	.03	.01
☐ 507 Pascual Perez	.07	.03	.01	☐ 559 Barry Bonnell	.07	.03	.01
☐ 508 Marvell Wynne	.15	.06	.01	☐ 560 Rick Lysander	.07	.03	.01
☐ 509 Mike Krukow	.15	.06	.01	☐ 561 Garth Iorg	.07	.03	.01
☐ 510 Dick Ruthven	.07	.03	.01	☐ 562 Bryan Clark	.07	.03	.01
☐ 511 Al Cowens	.07	.03	.01	☐ 563 Brian Giles	.07	.03	.01
☐ 512 Cliff Johnson	.07	.03	.01	☐ 564 Vern Ruhle	.07	.03	.01
☐ 513 Randy Bush	.07	.03	.01	☐ 565 Steve Bedrosian	.10	.04	.01
☐ 514 Sammy Stewart	.07	.03	.01	☐ 566 Larry McWilliams	.07	.03	.01
☐ 515 Bill Schroeder	.20	.08	.02	☐ 567 Jeff Leonard	.07	.03	.01
☐ 516 Aurelio Lopez	.07	.03	.01	☐ 568 Alan Wiggins	.10	.04	.01
☐ 517 Mike Brown	.10	.04	.01	☐ 569 Jeff Russell	.10	.04	.01
(Red Sox pitcher)				☐ 570 Salome Barojas	.07	.03	.01
☐ 518 Graig Nettles	.15	.06	.01	☐ 571 Dane Iorg	.07	.03	.01
☐ 519 Dave Sax	.07	.03	.01	☐ 572 Bob Knepper	.15	.06	.01
☐ 520 Gerry Willard	.15	.06	.01	☐ 573 Gary Lavelle	.10	.04	.01
☐ 521 Paul Splittorff	.07	.03	.01	☐ 574 Gorman Thomas	.15	.06	.01
☐ 522 Tom Burgmeier	.07	.03	.01	☐ 575 Manny Trillo	.10	.04	.01
☐ 523 Chris Speier	.07	.03	.01	☐ 576 Jim Palmer	.35	.14	.03
☐ 524 Bobby Clark	.07	.03	.01	☐ 577 Dale Murray	.07	.03	.01
☐ 525 George Wright	.07	.03	.01	☐ 578 Tom Brookens	.07	.03	.01
☐ 526 Dennis Lamp	.07	.03	.01	☐ 579 Rich Gedman	.15	.06	.01
☐ 527 Tony Scott	.07	.03	.01	☐ 580 Bill Doran	.30	.12	.03
☐ 528 Ed Whitson	.10	.04	.01	☐ 581 Steve Yeager	.07	.03	.01
☐ 529 Ron Reed	.07	.03	.01	☐ 582 Dan Spilner	.07	.03	.01
☐ 530 Charlie Puleo	.07	.03	.01	☐ 583 Dan Quisenberry	.20	.08	.02
☐ 531 Jerry Royster	.07	.03	.01	☐ 584 Rance Mulliniks	.07	.03	.01
☐ 532 Don Robinson	.07	.03	.01	☐ 585 Storm Davis	.15	.06	.01
☐ 533 Steve Trout	.07	.03	.01	☐ 586 Dave Schmidt	.07	.03	.01
☐ 534 Bruce Sutter	.20	.08	.02	☐ 587 Bill Russell	.10	.04	.01
☐ 535 Bob Horner	.25	.10	.02	☐ 588 Pat Sheridan	.15	.06	.01
☐ 536 Pat Tabler	.15	.06	.01	☐ 589 Rafael Ramirez	.07	.03	.01
☐ 537 Chris Chambliss	.10	.04	.01	(A's on front)			
☐ 538 Bob Ojeda	.15	.06	.01	☐ 590 Bud Anderson	.07	.03	.01
☐ 539 Alan Ashby	.07	.03	.01	☐ 591 George Frazier	.07	.03	.01
☐ 540 Jay Johnstone	.07	.03	.01	☐ 592 Lee Tunnell	.10	.04	.01
☐ 541 Bob Dernier	.10	.04	.01	☐ 593 Kirk Gibson	.30	.12	.03
☐ 542 Brook Jacoby	2.00	.80	.20	☐ 594 Scott McGregor	.10	.04	.01
☐ 543 U.L. Washington	.07	.03	.01	☐ 595 Bob Bailor	.07	.03	.01
☐ 544 Danny Darwin	.07	.03	.01	☐ 596 Tommy Herr	.10	.04	.01
☐ 545 Kiko Garcia	.07	.03	.01	☐ 597 Luis Sanchez	.07	.03	.01
☐ 546 Vance Law	.07	.03	.01	☐ 598 Dave Engle	.07	.03	.01

		MINT	VG-E	F-G
☐ 599	Craig McMurtry	.10	.04	.01
☐ 600	Carlos Diaz	.07	.03	.01
☐ 601	Tom O'Malley	.07	.03	.01
☐ 602	Nick Esasky	.30	.12	.03
☐ 603	Ron Hodges	.07	.03	.01
☐ 604	Ed VandeBerg	.07	.03	.01
☐ 605	Alfredo Griffin	.07	.03	.01
☐ 606	Glen Hoffman	.07	.03	.01
☐ 607	Hubie Brooks	.15	.06	.01
☐ 608	Richard Barnes	.07	.03	.01
☐ 609	Greg Walker	1.25	.50	.12
☐ 610	Ken Singleton	.10	.04	.01
☐ 611	Mark Clear	.07	.03	.01
☐ 612	Buck Martinez	.07	.03	.01
☐ 613	Ken Griffey	.10	.04	.01
☐ 614	Reid Nichols	.07	.03	.01
☐ 615	Doug Sisk	.10	.04	.01
☐ 616	Bob Brenly	.10	.04	.01
☐ 617	Joey McLaughlin	.07	.03	.01
☐ 618	Glenn Wilson	.15	.06	.01
☐ 619	Bob Stoddard	.07	.03	.01
☐ 620	Lenn Sakata	.07	.03	.01
☐ 621	Mike Young	1.00	.40	.10
☐ 622	John Stefero	.10	.04	.01
☐ 623	Carmelo Martinez	.30	.12	.03
☐ 624	Dave Bergman	.07	.03	.01
☐ 625	Runnin' Reds	.20	.08	.02
	(sic, Redbirds)			
	David Green			
	Willie McGee			
	Lonnie Smith			
	Ozzie Smith			
☐ 626	Rudy May	.07	.03	.01
☐ 627	Matt Keough	.07	.03	.01
☐ 628	Jose DeLeon	.25	.10	.02
☐ 629	Jim Essian	.07	.03	.01
☐ 630	Darnell Coles	1.00	.40	.10
☐ 631	Mike Warren	.15	.06	.01
☐ 632	Del Crandall MGR	.07	.03	.01
☐ 633	Dennis Martinez	.07	.03	.01
☐ 634	Mike Moore	.10	.04	.01
☐ 635	Lary Sorensen	.07	.03	.01
☐ 636	Rick Nelson	.10	.04	.01
☐ 637	Omar Moreno	.07	.03	.01
☐ 638	Charlie Hough	.10	.04	.01
☐ 639	Dennis Eckersley	.10	.04	.01
☐ 640	Walt Terrell	.35	.14	.03
☐ 641	Denny Walling	.07	.03	.01
☐ 642	Dave Anderson	.15	.06	.01
☐ 643	Jose Oquendo	.10	.04	.01
☐ 644	Bob Stanley	.10	.04	.01
☐ 645	Dave Geisel	.07	.03	.01
☐ 646	Scott Garrelts	.50	.20	.05

		MINT	VG-E	F-G
☐ 647	Gary Pettis	1.00	.40	.10
☐ 648	Duke Snider	.07	.03	.01
	Puzzle Card			
☐ 649	Johnnie LeMaster	.07	.03	.01
☐ 650	Dave Collins	.10	.04	.01
☐ 651	The Chicken	.25	.10	.02
☐ 652	DK Checklist	.10	.01	.00
	(unnumbered)			
☐ 653	Checklist 1-130	.08	.01	.00
	(unnumbered)			
☐ 654	Checklist 131-234	.08	.01	.00
	(unnumbered)			
☐ 655	Checklist 235-338	.08	.01	.00
	(unnumbered)			
☐ 656	Checklist 339-442	.08	.01	.00
	(unnumbered)			
☐ 657	Checklist 443-546	.08	.01	.00
	(unnumbered)			
☐ 658	Checklist 547-651	.08	.01	.00
	(unnumbered)			
☐ A	Living Legends A:	2.50	1.00	.25
	Gaylord Perry			
	Rollie Fingers			
☐ B	Living Legends B:	3.50	1.40	.35
	Carl Yastrzemski			
	Johnny Bench			

1985 Donruss

*The cards in this 660-card set measure 2½"
by 3½". The 1985 Donruss regular issue
cards have fronts that feature jet black borders on which orange lines have been
placed. The fronts contain the standard team
logo, player's name, position, and Donruss
logo. The cards were distributed with puzzle
pieces from a Dick Perez rendition of Lou*

Gehrig. The first 26 cards of the set feature Diamond Kings (DK), for the fourth year in a row; the artwork on the Diamond Kings was again produced by the Perez-Steele Galleries. Cards 27-46 feature Rated Rookies (RR). The unnumbered checklist cards are arbitrarily numbered below as numbers 654 through 660. The boxes in which the wax packs were contained feature four baseball cards, with backs. The price of the set below does not include these cards; however, these cards are priced at the end of the list below.

	MINT	VG-E	F-G
Complete Set	80.00	32.00	8.00
Common Player	.04	.02	.00

		MINT	VG-E	F-G
☐	1 Ryne Sandberg DK	.50	.20	.05
☐	2 Doug DeCinces DK	.08	.03	.01
☐	3 Richard Dotson DK	.06	.02	.00
☐	4 Bert Blyleven DK	.10	.04	.01
☐	5 Lou Whitaker DK	.15	.06	.01
☐	6 Dan Quisenberry DK	.15	.06	.01
☐	7 Don Mattingly DK	4.00	1.60	.40
☐	8 Carney Lansford DK	.08	.03	.01
☐	9 Frank Tanana DK	.06	.02	.00
☐	10 Willie Upshaw DK	.08	.03	.01
☐	11 Claudell Washington DK	.08	.03	.01
☐	12 Mike Marshall DK	.15	.06	.01
☐	13 Joaquin Andujar DK	.10	.04	.01
☐	14 Cal Ripken DK	.45	.18	.04
☐	15 Jim Rice DK	.35	.14	.03
☐	16 Don Sutton DK	.15	.06	.01
☐	17 Frank Viola DK	.08	.03	.01
☐	18 Alvin Davis DK	.50	.20	.05
☐	19 Mario Soto DK	.08	.03	.01
☐	20 Jose Cruz DK	.10	.04	.01
☐	21 Charlie Lea DK	.06	.02	.00
☐	22 Jesse Orosco DK	.08	.03	.01
☐	23 Juan Samuel DK	.20	.08	.02
☐	24 Tony Pena DK	.12	.05	.01
☐	25 Tony Gwynn DK	.45	.18	.04
☐	26 Bob Brenly DK	.08	.03	.01
☐	27 Danny Tartabull RR	3.50	1.40	.35
☐	28 Mike Bielecki RR	.10	.04	.01
☐	29 Steve Lyons RR	.15	.06	.01
☐	30 Jeff Reed RR	.10	.04	.01
☐	31 Tony Brewer RR	.10	.04	.01
☐	32 John Morris RR	.15	.06	.01
☐	33 Daryl Boston RR	.35	.14	.03
☐	34 Alfonso Pulido RR	.10	.04	.01

		MINT	VG-E	F-G
☐	35 Steve Kiefer RR	.10	.04	.01
☐	36 Larry Sheets RR	.50	.20	.05
☐	37 Scott Bradley RR	.30	.12	.03
☐	38 Calvin Schiraldi RR	1.00	.40	.10
☐	39 Shawon Dunston RR	1.50	.60	.15
☐	40 Charlie Mitchell RR	.10	.04	.01
☐	41 Billy Hatcher RR	.35	.14	.03
☐	42 Russ Stephans RR	.10	.04	.01
☐	43 Alejandro Sanchez RR	.10	.04	.01
☐	44 Steve Jeltz RR	.15	.06	.01
☐	45 Jim Traber RR	1.00	.40	.10
☐	46 Doug Loman RR	.20	.08	.02
☐	47 Eddie Murray	.40	.16	.04
☐	48 Robin Yount	.25	.10	.02
☐	49 Lance Parrish	.20	.08	.02
☐	50 Jim Rice	.35	.14	.03
☐	51 Dave Winfield	.30	.12	.03
☐	52 Fernando Valenzuela	.30	.12	.03
☐	53 George Brett	.50	.20	.05
☐	54 Dave Kingman	.12	.05	.01
☐	55 Gary Carter	.35	.14	.03
☐	56 Buddy Bell	.10	.04	.01
☐	57 Reggie Jackson	.40	.16	.04
☐	58 Harold Baines	.20	.08	.02
☐	59 Ozzie Smith	.10	.04	.01
☐	60 Nolan Ryan	.35	.14	.03
☐	61 Mike Schmidt	.45	.18	.04
☐	62 Dave Parker	.20	.08	.02
☐	63 Tony Gwynn	.45	.18	.04
☐	64 Tony Pena	.12	.05	.01
☐	65 Jack Clark	.12	.05	.01
☐	66 Dale Murphy	.60	.24	.06
☐	67 Ryne Sandberg	.45	.18	.04
☐	68 Keith Hernandez	.25	.10	.02
☐	69 Alvin Davis	2.25	.90	.22
☐	70 Kent Hrbek	.30	.12	.03
☐	71 Willie Upshaw	.10	.04	.01
☐	72 Dave Engle	.04	.02	.00
☐	73 Alfredo Griffin	.06	.02	.00
☐	74 A Jack Perconte	.15	.04	.01
	(Career Highlights four lines)			
☐	74 B Jack Perconte	.15	.06	.01
	(Career Highlights three lines)			
☐	75 Jesse Orosco	.08	.03	.01
☐	76 Jody Davis	.10	.04	.01
☐	77 Bob Horner	.15	.06	.01
☐	78 Larry McWilliams	.04	.02	.00
☐	79 Joel Youngblood	.04	.02	.00
☐	80 Alan Wiggins	.04	.02	.00
☐	81 Ron Oester	.04	.02	.00
☐	82 Ozzie Virgil	.04	.02	.00

		MINT	VG-E	F-G
☐ 83	Ricky Horton	.15	.06	.01
☐ 84	Bill Doran	.08	.03	.01
☐ 85	Rod Carew	.35	.14	.03
☐ 86	LaMarr Hoyt	.10	.04	.01
☐ 87	Tim Wallach	.08	.03	.01
☐ 88	Mike Flanagan	.08	.03	.01
☐ 89	Jim Sundberg	.06	.02	.00
☐ 90	Chet Lemon	.06	.02	.00
☐ 91	Bob Stanley	.06	.02	.00
☐ 92	Willie Randolph	.06	.02	.00
☐ 93	Bill Russell	.06	.02	.00
☐ 94	Julio Franco	.12	.05	.01
☐ 95	Dan Quisenberry	.15	.06	.01
☐ 96	Bill Caudill	.06	.02	.00
☐ 97	Bill Gullickson	.06	.02	.00
☐ 98	Danny Darwin	.04	.02	.00
☐ 99	Curtis Wilkerson	.04	.02	.00
☐ 100	Bud Black	.04	.02	.00
☐ 101	Tony Phillips	.04	.02	.00
☐ 102	Tony Bernazard	.06	.02	.00
☐ 103	Jay Howell	.06	.02	.00
☐ 104	Burt Hooton	.04	.02	.00
☐ 105	Milt Wilcox	.04	.02	.00
☐ 106	Rich Dauer	.04	.02	.00
☐ 107	Don Sutton	.15	.06	.01
☐ 108	Mike Witt	.12	.05	.01
☐ 109	Bruce Sutter	.15	.06	.01
☐ 110	Enos Cabell	.04	.02	.00
☐ 111	John Denny	.06	.02	.00
☐ 112	Dave Dravecky	.06	.02	.00
☐ 113	Marvell Wynne	.04	.02	.00
☐ 114	Johnnie LeMaster	.04	.02	.00
☐ 115	Chuck Porter	.04	.02	.00
☐ 116	John Gibbons	.08	.03	.01
☐ 117	Keith Moreland	.06	.02	.00
☐ 118	Darnell Coles	.10	.04	.01
☐ 119	Dennis Lamp	.04	.02	.00
☐ 120	Ron Davis	.04	.02	.00
☐ 121	Nick Esasky	.06	.02	.00
☐ 122	Vance Law	.04	.02	.00
☐ 123	Gary Roenicke	.04	.02	.00
☐ 124	Bill Schroeder	.04	.02	.00
☐ 125	Dave Rozema	.04	.02	.00
☐ 126	Bobby Meacham	.04	.02	.00
☐ 127	Marty Barrett	.12	.05	.01
☐ 128	R.J. Reynolds	.30	.12	.03
☐ 129	Ernie Camacho (photo actually Rich Thompson)	.06	.02	.00
☐ 130	Jorge Orta	.04	.02	.00
☐ 131	Lary Sorensen	.04	.02	.00
☐ 132	Terry Francona	.06	.02	.00
☐ 133	Fred Lynn	.15	.06	.01
☐ 134	Bob Jones	.04	.02	.00
☐ 135	Jerry Hairston	.04	.02	.00
☐ 136	Kevin Bass	.08	.03	.01
☐ 137	Garry Maddox	.06	.02	.00
☐ 138	Dave LaPoint	.04	.02	.00
☐ 139	Kevin McReynolds	.15	.06	.01
☐ 140	Wayne Krenchicki	.04	.02	.00
☐ 141	Rafael Ramirez	.04	.02	.00
☐ 142	Rod Scurry	.04	.02	.00
☐ 143	Greg Minton	.06	.02	.00
☐ 144	Tim Stoddard	.04	.02	.00
☐ 145	Steve Henderson	.04	.02	.00
☐ 146	George Bell	.15	.06	.01
☐ 147	Dave Meier	.04	.02	.00
☐ 148	Sammy Stewart	.04	.02	.00
☐ 149	Mark Brouhard	.04	.02	.00
☐ 150	Larry Herndon	.04	.02	.00
☐ 151	Oil Can Boyd	.12	.05	.01
☐ 152	Brian Dayett	.04	.02	.00
☐ 153	Tom Niedenfuer	.06	.02	.00
☐ 154	Brook Jacoby	.10	.04	.01
☐ 155	Onix Concepcion	.04	.02	.00
☐ 156	Tim Conroy	.04	.02	.00
☐ 157	Joe Hesketh	.25	.10	.02
☐ 158	Brian Downing	.06	.02	.00
☐ 159	Tommy Dunbar	.04	.02	.00
☐ 160	Marc Hill	.04	.02	.00
☐ 161	Phil Garner	.04	.02	.00
☐ 162	Jerry Davis	.10	.04	.01
☐ 163	Bill Campbell	.04	.02	.00
☐ 164	John Franco	.35	.14	.03
☐ 165	Len Barker	.04	.02	.00
☐ 166	Benny Distefano	.10	.04	.01
☐ 167	George Frazier	.04	.02	.00
☐ 168	Tito Landrum	.04	.02	.00
☐ 169	Cal Ripken	.40	.16	.04
☐ 170	Cecil Cooper	.12	.05	.01
☐ 171	Alan Trammell	.15	.06	.01
☐ 172	Wade Boggs	4.00	1.60	.40
☐ 173	Don Baylor	.12	.05	.01
☐ 174	Pedro Guerrero	.25	.10	.02
☐ 175	Frank White	.08	.03	.01
☐ 176	Rickey Henderson	.45	.18	.04
☐ 177	Charlie Lea	.06	.02	.00
☐ 178	Pete O'Brien	.08	.03	.01
☐ 179	Doug DeCinces	.08	.03	.01
☐ 180	Ron Kittle	.15	.06	.01
☐ 181	George Hendrick	.06	.02	.00
☐ 182	Joe Niekro	.08	.03	.01
☐ 183	Juan Samuel	.20	.08	.02
☐ 184	Mario Soto	.08	.03	.01
☐ 185	Goose Gossage	.15	.06	.01
☐ 186	Johnny Ray	.10	.04	.01

		MINT	VG-E	F-G
☐ 187	Bob Brenly	.08	.03	.01
☐ 188	Craig McMurtry	.04	.02	.00
☐ 189	Leon Durham	.10	.04	.01
☐ 190	Dwight Gooden	10.00	4.00	1.00
☐ 191	Barry Bonnell	.04	.02	.00
☐ 192	Tim Teufel	.06	.02	.00
☐ 193	Dave Stieb	.15	.06	.01
☐ 194	Mickey Hatcher	.04	.02	.00
☐ 195	Jesse Barfield	.15	.06	.01
☐ 196	Al Cowens	.04	.02	.00
☐ 197	Hubie Brooks	.10	.04	.01
☐ 198	Steve Trout	.04	.02	.00
☐ 199	Glenn Hubbard	.04	.02	.00
☐ 200	Bill Madlock	.10	.04	.01
☐ 201	Jeff Robinson	.10	.04	.01
☐ 202	Eric Show	.04	.02	.00
☐ 203	Dave Concepcion	.08	.03	.01
☐ 204	Ivan DeJesus	.04	.02	.00
☐ 205	Neil Allen	.06	.02	.00
☐ 206	Jerry Mumphrey	.06	.02	.00
☐ 207	Mike Brown	.06	.02	.00
	(Angels OF)			
☐ 208	Carlton Fisk	.15	.06	.01
☐ 209	Bryn Smith	.06	.02	.00
☐ 210	Tippy Martinez	.04	.02	.00
☐ 211	Dion James	.06	.02	.00
☐ 212	Willie Hernandez	.12	.05	.01
☐ 213	Mike Easler	.06	.02	.00
☐ 214	Ron Guidry	.20	.08	.02
☐ 215	Rick Honeycutt	.06	.02	.00
☐ 216	Brett Butler	.10	.04	.01
☐ 217	Larry Gura	.06	.02	.00
☐ 218	Ray Burris	.04	.02	.00
☐ 219	Steve Rogers	.06	.02	.00
☐ 220	Frank Tanana	.06	.02	.00
☐ 221	Ned Yost	.04	.02	.00
☐ 222	Bret Saberhagen	1.50	.60	.15
☐ 223	Mike Davis	.06	.02	.00
☐ 224	Bert Blyleven	.10	.04	.01
☐ 225	Steve Kemp	.08	.03	.01
☐ 226	Jerry Reuss	.06	.02	.00
☐ 227	Darrell Evans	.10	.04	.01
☐ 228	Wayne Gross	.04	.02	.00
☐ 229	Jim Gantner	.06	.02	.00
☐ 230	Bob Boone	.06	.02	.00
☐ 231	Lonnie Smith	.06	.02	.00
☐ 232	Frank DiPino	.04	.02	.00
☐ 233	Jerry Koosman	.06	.02	.00
☐ 234	Graig Nettles	.12	.05	.01
☐ 235	John Tudor	.12	.05	.01
☐ 236	John Rabb	.06	.02	.00
☐ 237	Rick Manning	.04	.02	.00
☐ 238	Mike Fitzgerald	.06	.02	.00
☐ 239	Gary Matthews	.06	.02	.00
☐ 240	Jim Presley	2.00	.80	.20
☐ 241	Dave Collins	.06	.02	.00
☐ 242	Gary Gaetti	.10	.04	.01
☐ 243	Dann Bilardello	.04	.02	.00
☐ 244	Rudy Law	.04	.02	.00
☐ 245	John Lowenstein	.04	.02	.00
☐ 246	Tom Tellman	.04	.02	.00
☐ 247	Howard Johnson	.04	.02	.00
☐ 248	Ray Fontenot	.04	.02	.00
☐ 249	Tony Armas	.10	.04	.01
☐ 250	Candy Maldonado	.08	.03	.01
☐ 251	Mike Jeffcoat	.06	.02	.00
☐ 252	Dane Iorg	.04	.02	.00
☐ 253	Bruce Bochte	.06	.02	.00
☐ 254	Pete Rose	1.50	.60	.15
☐ 255	Don Aase	.06	.02	.00
☐ 256	George Wright	.04	.02	.00
☐ 257	Britt Burns	.06	.02	.00
☐ 258	Mike Scott	.15	.06	.01
☐ 259	Len Matuszek	.04	.02	.00
☐ 260	Dave Rucker	.04	.02	.00
☐ 261	Craig Lefferts	.04	.02	.00
☐ 262	Jay Tibbs	.20	.08	.02
☐ 263	Bruce Benedict	.04	.02	.00
☐ 264	Don Robinson	.06	.02	.00
☐ 265	Gary Lavelle	.06	.02	.00
☐ 266	Scott Sanderson	.04	.02	.00
☐ 267	Matt Young	.04	.02	.00
☐ 268	Ernie Whitt	.06	.02	.00
☐ 269	Houston Jimenez	.04	.02	.00
☐ 270	Ken Dixon	.25	.10	.02
☐ 271	Peter Ladd	.04	.02	.00
☐ 272	Juan Berenguer	.04	.02	.00
☐ 273	Roger Clemens	10.00	4.00	1.00
☐ 274	Rick Cerone	.04	.02	.00
☐ 275	Dave Anderson	.04	.02	.00
☐ 276	George Vukovich	.04	.02	.00
☐ 277	Greg Pryor	.04	.02	.00
☐ 278	Mike Warren	.04	.02	.00
☐ 279	Bob James	.04	.02	.00
☐ 280	Bobby Grich	.08	.03	.01
☐ 281	Mike Mason	.10	.04	.01
☐ 282	Ron Reed	.04	.02	.00
☐ 283	Alan Ashby	.04	.02	.00
☐ 284	Mark Thurmond	.04	.02	.00
☐ 285	Joe Lefebvre	.04	.02	.00
☐ 286	Ted Power	.08	.03	.01
☐ 287	Chris Chambliss	.06	.02	.00
☐ 288	Lee Tunnell	.04	.02	.00
☐ 289	Rich Bordi	.04	.02	.00
☐ 290	Glenn Brummer	.04	.02	.00
☐ 291	Mike Boddicker	.10	.04	.01

	MINT	VG-E	F-G		MINT	VG-E	F-G
☐ 292 Rollie Fingers	.15	.06	.01	☐ 345 Carney Lansford	.10	.04	.01
☐ 293 Lou Whitaker	.15	.06	.01	☐ 346 Jerry Willard	.04	.02	.00
☐ 294 Dwight Evans	.10	.04	.01	☐ 347 Ken Griffey	.08	.03	.00
☐ 295 Don Mattingly	12.50	5.00	1.25	☐ 348 Franklin Stubbs	1.00	.40	.10
☐ 296 Mike Marshall	.15	.06	.01	☐ 349 Aurelio Lopez	.04	.02	.00
☐ 297 Willie Wilson	.15	.06	.01	☐ 350 Al Bumbry	.04	.02	.00
☐ 298 Mike Heath	.04	.02	.00	☐ 351 Charlie Moore	.04	.02	.00
☐ 299 Tim Raines	.25	.10	.02	☐ 352 Luis Sanchez	.04	.02	.00
☐ 300 Larry Parrish	.06	.02	.00	☐ 353 Darrell Porter	.06	.02	.00
☐ 301 Geoff Zahn	.04	.02	.00	☐ 354 Bill Dawley	.04	.02	.00
☐ 302 Rich Dotson	.06	.02	.00	☐ 355 Charles Hudson	.06	.02	.00
☐ 303 David Green	.04	.02	.00	☐ 356 Garry Templeton	.10	.04	.01
☐ 304 Jose Cruz	.10	.04	.01	☐ 357 Cecilio Guante	.04	.02	.00
☐ 305 Steve Carlton	.35	.14	.03	☐ 358 Jeff Leonard	.06	.02	.00
☐ 306 Gary Redus	.06	.02	.00	☐ 359 Paul Molitor	.10	.04	.01
☐ 307 Steve Garvey	.35	.14	.03	☐ 360 Ron Gardenhire	.04	.02	.00
☐ 308 Jose DeLeon	.06	.02	.00	☐ 361 Larry Bowa	.08	.03	.01
☐ 309 Randy Lerch	.04	.02	.00	☐ 362 Bob Kearney	.04	.02	.00
☐ 310 Claudell Washington	.06	.02	.00	☐ 363 Garth Iorg	.04	.02	.00
☐ 311 Lee Smith	.08	.03	.01	☐ 364 Tom Brunansky	.12	.05	.01
☐ 312 Darryl Strawberry	1.50	.60	.15	☐ 365 Brad Gulden	.04	.02	.00
☐ 313 Jim Beattie	.04	.02	.00	☐ 366 Greg Walker	.10	.04	.01
☐ 314 John Butcher	.04	.02	.00	☐ 367 Mike Young	.12	.05	.01
☐ 315 Damaso Garcia	.08	.03	.01	☐ 368 Rick Waits	.04	.02	.00
☐ 316 Mike Smithson	.04	.02	.00	☐ 369 Doug Bair	.04	.02	.00
☐ 317 Luis Leal	.04	.02	.00	☐ 370 Bob Shirley	.04	.02	.00
☐ 318 Ken Phelps	.06	.02	.00	☐ 371 Bob Ojeda	.08	.03	.01
☐ 319 Wally Backman	.08	.03	.01	☐ 372 Bob Welch	.08	.03	.01
☐ 320 Ron Cey	.10	.04	.01	☐ 373 Neal Heaton	.06	.02	.00
☐ 321 Brad Komminsk	.08	.03	.01	☐ 374 Danny Jackson	.08	.03	.01
☐ 322 Jason Thompson	.06	.02	.00	☐ 375 Donnie Hill	.04	.02	.00
☐ 323 Frank Williams	.10	.04	.01	☐ 376 Mike Stenhouse	.06	.02	.00
☐ 324 Tim Lollar	.04	.02	.00	☐ 377 Bruce Kison	.04	.02	.00
☐ 325 Eric Davis	8.00	3.25	.80	☐ 378 Wayne Tolleson	.04	.02	.00
☐ 326 Von Hayes	.12	.05	.01	☐ 379 Floyd Bannister	.06	.02	.00
☐ 327 Andy Van Slyke	.08	.03	.01	☐ 380 Vern Ruhle	.04	.02	.00
☐ 328 Craig Reynolds	.04	.02	.00	☐ 381 Tim Corcoran	.04	.02	.00
☐ 329 Dick Schofield	.08	.03	.01	☐ 382 Kurt Kepshire	.08	.03	.01
☐ 330 Scott Fletcher	.06	.02	.00	☐ 383 Bobby Brown	.04	.02	.00
☐ 331 Jeff Reardon	.08	.03	.01	☐ 384 Dave Van Gorder	.04	.02	.00
☐ 332 Rick Dempsey	.06	.02	.00	☐ 385 Rick Mahler	.04	.02	.00
☐ 333 Ben Oglivie	.06	.02	.00	☐ 386 Lee Mazzilli	.06	.02	.00
☐ 334 Dan Petry	.12	.05	.01	☐ 387 Bill Laskey	.04	.02	.00
☐ 335 Jackie Gutierrez	.08	.03	.01	☐ 388 Thad Bosley	.04	.02	.00
☐ 336 Dave Righetti	.15	.06	.01	☐ 389 Al Chambers	.04	.02	.00
☐ 337 Alejandro Pena	.06	.02	.00	☐ 390 Tony Fernandez	.12	.05	.01
☐ 338 Mel Hall	.08	.03	.01	☐ 391 Ron Washington	.04	.02	.00
☐ 339 Pat Sheridan	.04	.02	.00	☐ 392 Bill Swaggerty	.10	.04	.01
☐ 340 Keith Atherton	.04	.02	.00	☐ 393 Bob L. Gibson	.04	.02	.00
☐ 341 David Palmer	.06	.02	.00	☐ 394 Marty Castillo	.04	.02	.00
☐ 342 Gary Ward	.06	.02	.00	☐ 395 Steve Crawford	.04	.02	.00
☐ 343 Dave Stewart	.04	.02	.00	☐ 396 Clay Christiansen	.12	.05	.01
☐ 344 Mark Gubicza	.35	.14	.03	☐ 397 Bob Bailor	.04	.02	.00

		MINT	VG-E	F-G
☐ 398	Mike Hargrove	.06	.02	.00
☐ 399	Charlie Leibrandt	.06	.02	.00
☐ 400	Tom Burgmeier	.04	.02	.00
☐ 401	Razor Shines	.10	.04	.01
☐ 402	Rob Wilfong	.04	.02	.00
☐ 403	Tom Henke	.08	.03	.01
☐ 404	Al Jones	.10	.04	.01
☐ 405	Mike LaCoss	.04	.02	.00
☐ 406	Luis DeLeon	.04	.02	.00
☐ 407	Greg Gross	.04	.02	.00
☐ 408	Tom Hume	.04	.02	.00
☐ 409	Rick Camp	.04	.02	.00
☐ 410	Milt May	.04	.02	.00
☐ 411	Henry Cotto	.08	.03	.01
☐ 412	David Von Ohlen	.04	.02	.00
☐ 413	Scott McGregor	.08	.03	.01
☐ 414	Ted Simmons	.10	.04	.01
☐ 415	Jack Morris	.15	.06	.01
☐ 416	Bill Buckner	.08	.03	.01
☐ 417	Butch Wynegar	.06	.02	.00
☐ 418	Steve Sax	.12	.05	.01
☐ 419	Steve Balboni	.06	.02	.00
☐ 420	Dwayne Murphy	.06	.02	.00
☐ 421	Andre Dawson	.20	.08	.02
☐ 422	Charlie Hough	.08	.03	.01
☐ 423	Tommy John	.12	.05	.01
☐ 424 A	Tom Seaver ERR (photo actually Floyd Bannister)	1.25	.50	.12
☐ 424 B	Tom Seaver COR	6.00	2.40	.60
☐ 425	Tommy Herr	.10	.04	.01
☐ 426	Terry Puhl	.06	.02	.00
☐ 427	Al Holland	.04	.02	.00
☐ 428	Eddie Milner	.04	.02	.00
☐ 429	Terry Kennedy	.08	.03	.01
☐ 430	John Candelaria	.08	.03	.01
☐ 431	Manny Trillo	.06	.02	.00
☐ 432	Ken Oberkfell	.04	.02	.00
☐ 433	Rick Sutcliffe	.10	.04	.01
☐ 434	Ron Darling	1.00	.40	.10
☐ 435	Spike Owen	.06	.02	.00
☐ 436	Frank Viola	.08	.03	.01
☐ 437	Lloyd Moseby	.10	.04	.01
☐ 438	Kirby Puckett	6.50	2.60	.65
☐ 439	Jim Clancy	.04	.02	.00
☐ 440	Mike Moore	.06	.02	.00
☐ 441	Doug Sisk	.06	.02	.00
☐ 442	Dennis Eckersley	.06	.02	.00
☐ 443	Gerald Perry	.06	.02	.00
☐ 444	Dale Berra	.06	.02	.00
☐ 445	Dusty Baker	.06	.02	.00
☐ 446	Ed Whitson	.06	.02	.00
☐ 447	Cesar Cedeno	.08	.03	.01
☐ 448	Rick Schu	.20	.08	.02
☐ 449	Joaquin Andujar	.10	.04	.01
☐ 450	Mark Bailey	.10	.04	.01
☐ 451	Ron Romanick	.20	.08	.02
☐ 452	Julio Cruz	.04	.02	.00
☐ 453	Miguel Dilone	.04	.02	.00
☐ 454	Storm Davis	.08	.03	.01
☐ 455	Jaime Cocanower	.08	.03	.01
☐ 456	Barbaro Garbey	.08	.03	.01
☐ 457	Rich Gedman	.08	.03	.01
☐ 458	Phil Niekro	.15	.06	.01
☐ 459	Mike Scioscia	.06	.02	.00
☐ 460	Pat Tabler	.08	.03	.01
☐ 461	Darryl Motley	.04	.02	.00
☐ 462	Chris Codiroli	.04	.02	.00
☐ 463	Doug Flynn	.04	.02	.00
☐ 464	Billy Sample	.04	.02	.00
☐ 465	Mickey Rivers	.06	.02	.00
☐ 466	John Wathan	.04	.02	.00
☐ 467	Bill Krueger	.04	.02	.00
☐ 468	Andre Thornton	.06	.02	.00
☐ 469	Rex Hudler	.10	.04	.01
☐ 470	Sid Bream	.35	.14	.03
☐ 471	Kirk Gibson	.20	.08	.02
☐ 472	John Shelby	.04	.02	.00
☐ 473	Moose Haas	.06	.02	.00
☐ 474	Doug Corbett	.04	.02	.00
☐ 475	Willie McGee	.35	.14	.03
☐ 476	Bob Knepper	.08	.03	.01
☐ 477	Kevin Gross	.04	.02	.00
☐ 478	Carmelo Martinez	.08	.03	.01
☐ 479	Kent Tekulve	.06	.02	.00
☐ 480	Chili Davis	.08	.03	.01
☐ 481	Bobby Clark	.04	.02	.00
☐ 482	Mookie Wilson	.06	.02	.00
☐ 483	Dave Owen	.08	.03	.01
☐ 484	Ed Nunez	.06	.02	.00
☐ 485	Rance Mulliniks	.04	.02	.00
☐ 486	Ken Schrom	.04	.02	.00
☐ 487	Jeff Russell	.04	.02	.00
☐ 488	Tom Paciorek	.04	.02	.00
☐ 489	Dan Ford	.04	.02	.00
☐ 490	Mike Caldwell	.06	.02	.00
☐ 491	Scottie Earl	.08	.03	.01
☐ 492	Jose Rijo	.30	.12	.03
☐ 493	Bruce Hurst	.08	.03	.01
☐ 494	Ken Landreaux	.06	.02	.00
☐ 495	Mike Fischlin	.04	.02	.00
☐ 496	Don Slaught	.04	.02	.00
☐ 497	Steve McCatty	.04	.02	.00
☐ 498	Gary Lucas	.04	.02	.00
☐ 499	Gary Pettis	.08	.03	.01
☐ 500	Marvis Foley	.04	.02	.00

	MINT	VG-E	F-G
☐ 501 Mike Squires	.04	.02	.00
☐ 502 Jim Pankovitz	.08	.03	.01
☐ 503 Luis Aguayo	.04	.02	.00
☐ 504 Ralph Citarella	.08	.03	.01
☐ 505 Bruce Bochy	.04	.02	.00
☐ 506 Bob Owchinko	.04	.02	.00
☐ 507 Pascual Perez	.04	.02	.00
☐ 508 Lee Lacy	.06	.02	.00
☐ 509 Atlee Hammaker	.06	.02	.00
☐ 510 Bob Dernier	.06	.02	.00
☐ 511 Ed VandeBerg	.04	.02	.00
☐ 512 Cliff Johnson	.04	.02	.00
☐ 513 Len Whitehouse	.04	.02	.00
☐ 514 Dennis Martinez	.04	.02	.00
☐ 515 Ed Romero	.04	.02	.00
☐ 516 Rusty Kuntz	.04	.02	.00
☐ 517 Rick Miller	.04	.02	.00
☐ 518 Dennis Rasmussen	.08	.03	.01
☐ 519 Steve Yeager	.06	.02	.00
☐ 520 Chris Bando	.04	.02	.00
☐ 521 U.L. Washington	.04	.02	.00
☐ 522 Curt Young	.08	.03	.01
☐ 523 Angel Salazar	.06	.02	.00
☐ 524 Curt Kaufman	.08	.03	.01
☐ 525 Odell Jones	.04	.02	.00
☐ 526 Juan Agosto	.04	.02	.00
☐ 527 Denny Walling	.04	.02	.00
☐ 528 Andy Hawkins	.06	.02	.00
☐ 529 Sixto Lezcano	.04	.02	.00
☐ 530 Skeeter Barnes	.06	.02	.00
☐ 531 Randy Johnson	.04	.02	.00
☐ 532 Jim Morrison	.04	.02	.00
☐ 533 Warren Brusstar	.04	.02	.00
☐ 534 A Jeff Pendleton ERR (wrong first name)	.30	.12	.03
☐ 534 B Terry Pendleton COR	2.25	.90	.22
☐ 535 Vic Rodriguez	.10	.04	.01
☐ 536 Bob McClure	.04	.02	.00
☐ 537 Dave Bergman	.04	.02	.00
☐ 538 Mark Clear	.04	.02	.00
☐ 539 Mike Pagliarulo	2.00	.80	.20
☐ 540 Terry Whitfield	.04	.02	.00
☐ 541 Joe Beckwith	.04	.02	.00
☐ 542 Jeff Burroughs	.04	.02	.00
☐ 543 Dan Schatzeder	.04	.02	.00
☐ 544 Donnie Scott	.06	.02	.00
☐ 545 Jim Slaton	.04	.02	.00
☐ 546 Greg Luzinski	.10	.04	.01
☐ 547 Mark Salas	.25	.10	.02
☐ 548 Dave Smith	.08	.03	.01
☐ 549 John Wockenfuss	.04	.02	.00
☐ 550 Frank Pastore	.04	.02	.00
☐ 551 Tim Flannery	.04	.02	.00
☐ 552 Rick Rhoden	.08	.03	.01
☐ 553 Mark Davis	.06	.02	.00
☐ 554 Jeff Dedmon	.08	.03	.01
☐ 555 Gary Woods	.04	.02	.00
☐ 556 Danny Heep	.04	.02	.00
☐ 557 Mark Langston	.45	.18	.04
☐ 558 Darrell Brown	.04	.02	.00
☐ 559 Jimmy Key	.45	.18	.04
☐ 560 Rick Lysander	.04	.02	.00
☐ 561 Doyle Alexander	.06	.02	.00
☐ 562 Mike Stanton	.04	.02	.00
☐ 563 Sid Fernandez	1.00	.40	.10
☐ 564 Richie Hebner	.04	.02	.00
☐ 565 Alex Trevino	.04	.02	.00
☐ 566 Brian Harper	.04	.02	.00
☐ 567 Dan Gladden	.25	.10	.02
☐ 568 Luis Salazar	.04	.02	.00
☐ 569 Tom Foley	.04	.02	.00
☐ 570 Larry Andersen	.04	.02	.00
☐ 571 Danny Cox	.08	.03	.01
☐ 572 Joe Sambito	.06	.02	.00
☐ 573 Juan Beniquez	.06	.02	.00
☐ 574 Joel Skinner	.06	.02	.00
☐ 575 Randy St.Claire	.10	.04	.01
☐ 576 Floyd Rayford	.04	.02	.00
☐ 577 Roy Howell	.04	.02	.00
☐ 578 John Grubb	.04	.02	.00
☐ 579 Ed Jurak	.04	.02	.00
☐ 580 John Montefusco	.06	.02	.00
☐ 581 Orel Hershiser	2.50	1.00	.25
☐ 582 Tom Waddell	.10	.04	.01
☐ 583 Mark Huismann	.04	.02	.00
☐ 584 Joe Morgan	.15	.06	.01
☐ 585 Jim Wohlford	.04	.02	.00
☐ 586 Dave Schmidt	.04	.02	.00
☐ 587 Jeff Kunkel	.08	.03	.01
☐ 588 Hal McRae	.06	.02	.00
☐ 589 Bill Almon	.04	.02	.00
☐ 590 Carmen Castillo	.04	.02	.00
☐ 591 Omar Moreno	.04	.02	.00
☐ 592 Ken Howell	.25	.10	.02
☐ 593 Tom Brookens	.04	.02	.00
☐ 594 Joe Nolan	.04	.02	.00
☐ 595 Willie Lozado	.10	.04	.01
☐ 596 Tom Nieto	.06	.02	.00
☐ 597 Walt Terrell	.04	.02	.00
☐ 598 Al Oliver	.10	.04	.01
☐ 599 Shane Rawley	.06	.02	.00
☐ 600 Denny Gonzalez	.08	.03	.01
☐ 601 Mark Grant	.08	.03	.01
☐ 602 Mike Armstrong	.04	.02	.00
☐ 603 George Foster	.12	.05	.01
☐ 604 Davey Lopes	.06	.02	.00

	MINT	VG-E	F-G
☐ 605 Salome Barojas	.04	.02	.00
☐ 606 Roy Lee Jackson	.04	.02	.00
☐ 607 Pete Filson	.04	.02	.00
☐ 608 Duane Walker	.04	.02	.00
☐ 609 Glenn Wilson	.08	.03	.01
☐ 610 Rafael Santana	.08	.03	.01
☐ 611 Roy Smith	.08	.03	.01
☐ 612 Ruppert Jones	.04	.02	.00
☐ 613 Joe Cowley	.06	.02	.00
☐ 614 Al Nipper	.25	.10	.02
(photo actually			
Mike Brown)			
☐ 615 Gene Nelson	.04	.02	.00
☐ 616 Joe Carter	.75	.30	.07
☐ 617 Ray Knight	.10	.04	.01
☐ 618 Chuck Rainey	.04	.02	.00
☐ 619 Dan Driessen	.04	.02	.00
☐ 620 Daryl Sconiers	.04	.02	.00
☐ 621 Bill Stein	.04	.02	.00
☐ 622 Roy Smalley	.06	.02	.00
☐ 623 Ed Lynch	.04	.02	.00
☐ 624 Jeff Stone	.25	.10	.02
☐ 625 Bruce Berenyi	.04	.02	.00
☐ 626 Kelvin Chapman	.08	.03	.01
☐ 627 Joe Price	.04	.02	.00
☐ 628 Steve Bedrosian	.06	.02	.00
☐ 629 Vic Mata	.10	.04	.01
☐ 630 Mike Krukow	.08	.03	.01
☐ 631 Phil Bradley	1.75	.70	.17
☐ 632 Jim Gott	.04	.02	.00
☐ 633 Randy Bush	.04	.02	.00
☐ 634 Tom Browning	1.00	.40	.10
☐ 635 Lou Gehrig	.06	.02	.00
Puzzle Card			
☐ 636 Reid Nichols	.04	.02	.00
☐ 637 Dan Pasqua	2.50	1.00	.25
☐ 638 German Rivera	.10	.04	.01
☐ 639 Don Schulze	.08	.03	.01
☐ 640 A Mike Jones	.15	.06	.01
(Career Highlights,			
five lines)			
☐ 640 B Mike Jones	.15	.06	.01
(Career Highlights,			
four lines)			
☐ 641 Pete Rose	1.00	.40	.10
☐ 642 Wade Rowdon	.10	.04	.01
☐ 643 Jerry Narron	.04	.02	.00
☐ 644 Darrell Miller	.15	.06	.01
☐ 645 Tim Hulett	.20	.08	.02
☐ 646 Andy McGaffigan	.04	.02	.00
☐ 647 Kurt Bevacqua	.04	.02	.00
☐ 648 John Russell	.20	.08	.02
☐ 649 Ron Robinson	.20	.08	.02

	MINT	VG-E	F-G
☐ 650 Donnie Moore	.06	.02	.00
☐ 651 A Two for the Title	2.50	1.00	.25
Dave Winfield			
Don Mattingly			
(yellow letters)			
☐ 651 B Two for the Title	6.00	2.40	.60
Dave Winfield			
Don Mattingly			
(white letters)			
☐ 652 Tim Laudner	.04	.02	.00
☐ 653 Steve Farr	.10	.04	.01
☐ 654 DK Checklist 1-26	.09	.01	.00
(unnumbered)			
☐ 655 Checklist 27-130	.07	.01	.00
(unnumbered)			
☐ 656 Checklist 131-234	.07	.01	.00
(unnumbered)			
☐ 657 Checklist 235-338	.07	.01	.00
(unnumbered)			
☐ 658 Checklist 339-442	.07	.01	.00
(unnumbered)			
☐ 659 Checklist 443-546	.07	.01	.00
(unnumbered)			
☐ 660 Checklist 547-653	.07	.01	.00
(unnumbered)			
☐ PC1 Dwight Gooden	4.00	1.60	.40
(wax pack box card)			
☐ PC2 Ryne Sandberg	.50	.20	.05
(wax pack box card)			
☐ PC3 Ron Kittle	.20	.08	.02
(wax pack box card)			
☐ PUZ Lou Gehrig	.06	.02	.00
Puzzle Card			
(wax pack box card)			

1985 Donruss Highlights

This 56-card set features the players and pitchers of the month for each league as well as a number of highlight cards commemorating the 1985 season. The Donruss Company dedicated the last two cards to their own selections for Rookies of the Year (ROY). This set proved to be much more popular than the Donruss Company had predicted, as their first and only print run was exhausted even before card dealers' initial orders were filled.

	MINT	VG-E	F-G
Complete Set	20.00	8.00	2.00
Common Player	.10	.04	.01
☐ 1 Tom Seaver: Sets Opening Day Record	.50	.20	.05
☐ 2 Rollie Fingers: Sets AL Save Mark	.20	.08	.02
☐ 3 Mike Davis: AL Player April	.10	.04	.01
☐ 4 Charlie Leibrandt: AL Pitcher April	.10	.04	.01
☐ 5 Dale Murphy: NL Player April	1.00	.40	.10
☐ 6 Fernando Valenzuela: NL Pitcher April	.50	.20	.05
☐ 7 Larry Bowa: NL Shortstop Record	.15	.06	.01
☐ 8 Dave Concepcion: Joins Reds' 2000 Hit Club	.10	.04	.01
☐ 9 Tony Perez: Eldest Grand Slammer	.20	.08	.02
☐ 10 Pete Rose: NL Career Run Leader	2.00	.80	.20
☐ 11 George Brett: AL Player May	1.00	.40	.10
☐ 12 Dave Stieb: AL Pitcher May	.20	.08	.02
☐ 13 Dave Parker: NL Player May	.30	.12	.03
☐ 14 Andy Hawkins: NL Pitcher May	.10	.04	.01
☐ 15 Andy Hawkins: Records 11th Straight Win	.10	.04	.01
☐ 16 Von Hayes: Two Homers in First Inning	.20	.08	.02
☐ 17 Rickey Henderson: AL Player June	1.00	.40	.10
☐ 18 Jay Howell: AL Pitcher June	.10	.04	.01
☐ 19 Pedro Guerrero: NL Player June	.30	.12	.03
☐ 20 John Tudor: NL Pitcher June	.20	.08	.02
☐ 21 Hernandez/Carter: Marathon Game Iron Men	.50	.20	.05
☐ 22 Nolan Ryan: Records 4000th K	.60	.24	.06
☐ 23 LaMarr Hoyt: All-Star Game MVP	.10	.04	.01
☐ 24 Oddibe McDowell: 1st Ranger to Hit for Cycle	.90	.36	.09
☐ 25 George Brett: AL Player July	1.00	.40	.10
☐ 26 Bret Saberhagen: AL Pitcher July	.60	.24	.06
☐ 27 Keith Hernandez: NL Player July	.40	.16	.04
☐ 28 Fernando Valenzuela: NL Pitcher July	.50	.20	.05
☐ 29 McGee/Coleman: Record Setting Base Stealers	1.25	.50	.12
☐ 30 Tom Seaver: Notches 300th Career Win	.50	.20	.05
☐ 31 Rod Carew: Strokes 3000th Hit	.50	.20	.05
☐ 32 Dwight Gooden: Establishes Met Record	2.50	1.00	.25
☐ 33 Dwight Gooden: Achieves Strikeout Milestone	2.50	1.00	.25
☐ 34 Eddie Murray: Explodes for 9 RBI	1.00	.40	.10
☐ 35 Don Baylor: AL Career HBP Leader	.20	.08	.02
☐ 36 Don Mattingly: AL Player August	3.00	1.20	.30
☐ 37 Dave Righetti: AL Pitcher August	.20	.08	.02
☐ 38 Willie McGee: NL Player August	.30	.12	.03
☐ 39 Shane Rawley: NL Pitcher August	.10	.04	.01
☐ 40 Pete Rose: Ty-Breaking Hit	2.00	.80	.20
☐ 41 Andre Dawson: Hits 3 HR's Drives in 8 Runs	.30	.12	.03
☐ 42 Rickey Henderson: Sets Yankee Theft Mark	1.00	.40	.10
☐ 43 Tom Browning: 20 Wins in Rookie Season	.30	.12	.03

		MINT	VG-E	F-G
☐ 44	Don Mattingly: Yankee Milestone for Hits	3.00	1.20	.30
☐ 45	Don Mattingly: AL Player September	3.00	1.20	.30
☐ 46	Charlie Leibrandt: AL Pitcher September	.10	.04	.01
☐ 47	Gary Carter: NL Player September	.50	.20	.05
☐ 48	Dwight Gooden: NL Pitcher September	2.50	1.00	.25
☐ 49	Wade Boggs: Major League Record Setter	2.50	1.00	.25
☐ 50	Phil Niekro: Hurls Shutout for 300th Win	.30	.12	.03
☐ 51	Darrell Evans: Venerable HR King	.10	.04	.01
☐ 52	Willie McGee: NL Switch-Hitting Record	.30	.12	.03
☐ 53	Dave Winfield: Equals DiMaggio Feat	.50	.20	.05
☐ 54	Vince Coleman: Donruss NL ROY	3.00	1.20	.30
☐ 55	Ozzie Guillen: Donruss AL ROY	.50	.20	.05
☐ 56	Checklist card (unnumbered)	.10	.01	.00

1986 Donruss

The cards in this 660-card set measure 2½"
by 3½". The 1986 Donruss regular issue
cards have fronts that feature blue borders.
The fronts contain the standard team logo,
player's name, position, and Donruss logo.
The cards were distributed with puzzle
pieces from a Dick Perez rendition of Hank

Aaron. The first 26 cards of the set are Diamond Kings (DK), for the fifth year in a row;
the artwork on the Diamond Kings was again
produced by the Perez-Steele Galleries.
Cards 27-46 again feature Rated Rookies
(RR); Danny Tartabull is included in this subset for the second year in a row. The unnumbered checklist cards are arbitrarily
numbered below as numbers 654 through
660. The boxes in which the wax packs were
contained feature four baseball cards, with
backs. The price of the set below does not
include these cards; however, these cards
are priced at the end of the list below.

		MINT	VG-E	F-G
	Complete Set	40.00	16.00	4.00
	Common Player	.03	.01	.00
☐ 1	Kirk Gibson DK	.25	.10	.02
☐ 2	Goose Gossage DK	.15	.06	.01
☐ 3	Willie McGee DK	.20	.08	.02
☐ 4	George Bell DK	.15	.06	.01
☐ 5	Tony Armas DK	.10	.04	.01
☐ 6	Chili Davis DK	.08	.03	.01
☐ 7	Cecil Cooper DK	.12	.05	.01
☐ 8	Mike Boddicker DK	.10	.04	.01
☐ 9	Davey Lopes DK	.08	.03	.01
☐ 10	Bill Doran DK	.10	.04	.01
☐ 11	Bret Saberhagen DK	.25	.10	.02
☐ 12	Brett Butler DK	.10	.04	.01
☐ 13	Harold Baines DK	.20	.08	.02
☐ 14	Mike Davis DK	.10	.04	.01
☐ 15	Tony Perez DK	.12	.05	.01
☐ 16	Willie Randolph DK	.08	.03	.01
☐ 17	Bob Boone DK	.08	.03	.01
☐ 18	Orel Hershiser DK	.30	.12	.03
☐ 19	Johnny Ray DK	.10	.04	.01
☐ 20	Gary Ward DK	.08	.03	.01
☐ 21	Rick Mahler DK	.06	.02	.00
☐ 22	Phil Bradley DK	.25	.10	.02
☐ 23	Jerry Koosman DK	.08	.03	.01
☐ 24	Tom Brunansky DK	.12	.05	.01
☐ 25	Andre Dawson DK	.20	.08	.02
☐ 26	Dwight Gooden DK	1.25	.50	.12
☐ 27	Kal Daniels RR	.50	.20	.05
☐ 28	Fred McGriff RR	.10	.04	.01
☐ 29	Cory Snyder RR	2.00	.80	.20
☐ 30	Jose Guzman RR	.25	.10	.02
☐ 31	Ty Gainey RR	.20	.08	.02
☐ 32	Johnny Abrego RR	.10	.04	.01
☐ 33	Andres Galarraga RR	.35	.14	.03

		MINT	VG-E	F-G			MINT	VG-E	F-G
☐ 34	Dave Shipanoff RR	.15	.06	.01	☐ 87	Andre Dawson	.20	.08	.02
☐ 35	Mark McLemore RR	.15	.06	.01	☐ 88	Eddie Murray	.40	.16	.04
☐ 36	Marty Clary RR	.10	.04	.01	☐ 89	Dion James	.05	.02	.00
☐ 37	Paul O'Neill RR	.20	.08	.02	☐ 90	Chet Lemon	.05	.02	.00
☐ 38	Danny Tartabull RR	.60	.24	.06	☐ 91	Bob Stanley	.05	.02	.00
☐ 39	Jose Canseco RR	9.00	3.75	.90	☐ 92	Willie Randolph	.05	.02	.00
☐ 40	Juan Nieves RR	.35	.14	.03	☐ 93	Mike Scioscia	.05	.02	.00
☐ 41	Lance McCullers RR	.25	.10	.02	☐ 94	Tom Waddell	.03	.01	.00
☐ 42	Rick Surhoff RR	.10	.04	.01	☐ 95	Danny Jackson	.06	.02	.00
☐ 43	Todd Worrell RR	1.25	.50	.12	☐ 96	Mike Davis	.07	.03	.01
☐ 44	Bob Kipper RR	.20	.08	.02	☐ 97	Mike Fitzgerald	.03	.01	.00
☐ 45	John Habyan RR	.15	.06	.01	☐ 98	Gary Ward	.05	.02	.00
☐ 46	Mike Woodard RR	.10	.04	.01	☐ 99	Pete O'Brien	.08	.03	.01
☐ 47	Mike Boddicker	.08	.03	.01	☐ 100	Bret Saberhagen	.25	.10	.02
☐ 48	Robin Yount	.25	.10	.02	☐ 101	Alfredo Griffin	.05	.02	.00
☐ 49	Lou Whitaker	.15	.06	.01	☐ 102	Brett Butler	.08	.03	.01
☐ 50	Oil Can Boyd	.08	.03	.01	☐ 103	Ron Guidry	.15	.06	.01
☐ 51	Rickey Henderson	.35	.14	.03	☐ 104	Jerry Reuss	.05	.02	.00
☐ 52	Mike Marshall	.12	.05	.01	☐ 105	Jack Morris	.15	.06	.01
☐ 53	George Brett	.40	.16	.04	☐ 106	Rick Dempsey	.05	.02	.00
☐ 54	Dave Kingman	.12	.05	.01	☐ 107	Ray Burris	.03	.01	.00
☐ 55	Hubie Brooks	.10	.04	.01	☐ 108	Brian Downing	.05	.02	.00
☐ 56	Oddibe McDowell	.45	.18	.04	☐ 109	Willie McGee	.15	.06	.01
☐ 57	Doug DeCinces	.08	.03	.01	☐ 110	Bill Doran	.08	.03	.01
☐ 58	Britt Burns	.06	.02	.00	☐ 111	Kent Tekulve	.05	.02	.00
☐ 59	Ozzie Smith	.10	.04	.01	☐ 112	Tony Gwynn	.25	.10	.02
☐ 60	Jose Cruz	.10	.04	.01	☐ 113	Marvell Wynne	.03	.01	.00
☐ 61	Mike Schmidt	.50	.20	.05	☐ 114	David Green	.03	.01	.00
☐ 62	Pete Rose	1.00	.40	.10	☐ 115	Jim Gantner	.05	.02	.00
☐ 63	Steve Garvey	.35	.14	.03	☐ 116	George Foster	.12	.05	.01
☐ 64	Tony Pena	.10	.04	.01	☐ 117	Steve Trout	.03	.01	.00
☐ 65	Chili Davis	.08	.03	.01	☐ 118	Mark Langston	.07	.03	.01
☐ 66	Dale Murphy	.60	.24	.06	☐ 119	Tony Fernandez	.10	.04	.01
☐ 67	Ryne Sandberg	.35	.14	.03	☐ 120	John Butcher	.03	.01	.00
☐ 68	Gary Carter	.30	.12	.03	☐ 121	Ron Robinson	.03	.01	.00
☐ 69	Alvin Davis	.12	.05	.01	☐ 122	Dan Spillner	.03	.01	.00
☐ 70	Kent Hrbek	.15	.06	.01	☐ 123	Mike Young	.10	.04	.01
☐ 71	George Bell	.15	.06	.01	☐ 124	Paul Molitor	.10	.04	.01
☐ 72	Kirby Puckett	.60	.24	.06	☐ 125	Kirk Gibson	.15	.06	.01
☐ 73	Lloyd Moseby	.12	.05	.01	☐ 126	Ken Griffey	.05	.02	.00
☐ 74	Bob Kearney	.03	.01	.00	☐ 127	Tony Armas	.09	.04	.01
☐ 75	Dwight Gooden	2.50	1.00	.25	☐ 128	Mariano Duncan	.40	.16	.04
☐ 76	Gary Matthews	.06	.02	.00	☐ 129	Pat Tabler	.08	.03	.01
☐ 77	Rick Mahler	.03	.01	.00	☐ 130	Frank White	.06	.02	.00
☐ 78	Benny Distefano	.03	.01	.00	☐ 131	Carney Lansford	.09	.04	.01
☐ 79	Jeff Leonard	.05	.02	.00	☐ 132	Vance Law	.03	.01	.00
☐ 80	Kevin McReynolds	.10	.04	.01	☐ 133	Dick Schofield	.06	.02	.00
☐ 81	Ron Oester	.05	.02	.00	☐ 134	Wayne Tolleson	.03	.01	.00
☐ 82	John Russell	.03	.01	.00	☐ 135	Greg Walker	.10	.04	.01
☐ 83	Tommy Herr	.07	.03	.01	☐ 136	Denny Walling	.03	.01	.00
☐ 84	Jerry Mumphrey	.05	.02	.00	☐ 137	Ozzie Virgil	.03	.01	.00
☐ 85	Ron Romanick	.03	.01	.00	☐ 138	Ricky Horton	.03	.01	.00
☐ 86	Daryl Boston	.05	.02	.00	☐ 139	LaMarr Hoyt	.07	.03	.01

		MINT	VG-E	F-G
☐ 140	Wayne Krenchicki	.03	.01	.00
☐ 141	Glenn Hubbard	.03	.01	.00
☐ 142	Cecilio Guante	.03	.01	.00
☐ 143	Mike Krukow	.07	.03	.01
☐ 144	Lee Smith	.08	.03	.01
☐ 145	Edwin Nunez	.05	.02	.00
☐ 146	Dave Stieb	.12	.05	.01
☐ 147	Mike Smithson	.03	.01	.00
☐ 148	Ken Dixon	.05	.02	.00
☐ 149	Danny Darwin	.03	.01	.00
☐ 150	Chris Pittaro	.08	.03	.01
☐ 151	Bill Buckner	.08	.03	.01
☐ 152	Mike Pagliarulo	.25	.10	.02
☐ 153	Bill Russell	.05	.02	.00
☐ 154	Brook Jacoby	.10	.04	.01
☐ 155	Pat Sheridan	.03	.01	.00
☐ 156	Mike Gallego	.08	.03	.01
☐ 157	Jim Wohlford	.03	.01	.00
☐ 158	Gary Pettis	.08	.03	.01
☐ 159	Toby Harrah	.05	.02	.00
☐ 160	Richard Dotson	.05	.02	.00
☐ 161	Bob Knepper	.08	.03	.01
☐ 162	Dave Dravecky	.06	.02	.00
☐ 163	Greg Gross	.03	.01	.00
☐ 164	Eric Davis	1.25	.50	.12
☐ 165	Gerald Perry	.05	.02	.00
☐ 166	Rick Rhoden	.07	.03	.01
☐ 167	Keith Moreland	.06	.02	.00
☐ 168	Jack Clark	.12	.05	.01
☐ 169	Storm Davis	.07	.03	.01
☐ 170	Cecil Cooper	.12	.05	.01
☐ 171	Alan Trammell	.15	.06	.01
☐ 172	Roger Clemens	2.50	1.00	.25
☐ 173	Don Mattingly	5.00	2.00	.50
☐ 174	Pedro Guerrero	.25	.10	.02
☐ 175	Willie Wilson	.15	.06	.01
☐ 176	Dwayne Murphy	.06	.02	.00
☐ 177	Tim Raines	.20	.08	.02
☐ 178	Larry Parrish	.06	.02	.00
☐ 179	Mike Witt	.10	.04	.01
☐ 180	Harold Baines	.20	.08	.02
☐ 181	Vince Coleman	2.50	1.00	.25
	(BA 2.67 on back)			
☐ 182	Jeff Heathcock	.08	.03	.01
☐ 183	Steve Carlton	.30	.12	.03
☐ 184	Mario Soto	.08	.03	.01
☐ 185	Goose Gossage	.14	.06	.01
☐ 186	Johnny Ray	.10	.04	.01
☐ 187	Dan Gladden	.06	.02	.00
☐ 188	Bob Horner	.15	.06	.01
☐ 189	Rick Sutcliffe	.10	.04	.01
☐ 190	Keith Hernandez	.25	.10	.02
☐ 191	Phil Bradley	.20	.08	.02
☐ 192	Tom Brunansky	.10	.04	.01
☐ 193	Jesse Barfield	.15	.06	.01
☐ 194	Frank Viola	.07	.03	.01
☐ 195	Willie Upshaw	.08	.03	.01
☐ 196	Jim Beattie	.03	.01	.00
☐ 197	Darryl Strawberry	.60	.24	.06
☐ 198	Ron Cey	.08	.03	.01
☐ 199	Steve Bedrosian	.05	.02	.00
☐ 200	Steve Kemp	.06	.02	.00
☐ 201	Manny Trillo	.05	.02	.00
☐ 202	Garry Templeton	.08	.03	.01
☐ 203	Dave Parker	.18	.08	.01
☐ 204	John Denny	.06	.02	.00
☐ 205	Terry Pendleton	.06	.02	.00
☐ 206	Terry Puhl	.05	.02	.00
☐ 207	Bobby Grich	.06	.02	.00
☐ 208	Ozzie Guillen	.50	.20	.05
☐ 209	Jeff Reardon	.07	.03	.01
☐ 210	Cal Ripken	.35	.14	.03
☐ 211	Bill Schroeder	.05	.02	.00
☐ 212	Dan Petry	.10	.04	.01
☐ 213	Jim Rice	.35	.14	.03
☐ 214	Dave Righetti	.14	.06	.01
☐ 215	Fernando Valenzuela	.30	.12	.03
☐ 216	Julio Franco	.10	.04	.01
☐ 217	Darryl Motley	.03	.01	.00
☐ 218	Dave Collins	.05	.02	.00
☐ 219	Tim Wallach	.07	.03	.01
☐ 220	George Wright	.03	.01	.00
☐ 221	Tommy Dunbar	.03	.01	.00
☐ 222	Steve Balboni	.05	.02	.00
☐ 223	Jay Howell	.05	.02	.00
☐ 224	Joe Carter	.30	.12	.03
☐ 225	Ed Whitson	.05	.02	.00
☐ 226	Orel Hershiser	.30	.12	.03
☐ 227	Willie Hernandez	.12	.05	.01
☐ 228	Lee Lacy	.05	.02	.00
☐ 229	Rollie Fingers	.15	.06	.01
☐ 230	Bob Boone	.05	.02	.00
☐ 231	Joaquin Andujar	.08	.03	.01
☐ 232	Craig Reynolds	.05	.02	.00
☐ 233	Shane Rawley	.06	.02	.00
☐ 234	Eric Show	.05	.02	.00
☐ 235	Jose DeLeon	.05	.02	.00
☐ 236	Jose Uribe	.08	.03	.01
☐ 237	Moose Haas	.05	.02	.00
☐ 238	Wally Backman	.07	.03	.01
☐ 239	Dennis Eckersley	.05	.02	.00
☐ 240	Mike Moore	.06	.02	.00
☐ 241	Damaso Garcia	.06	.02	.00
☐ 242	Tim Teufel	.06	.02	.00
☐ 243	Dave Concepcion	.08	.03	.01
☐ 244	Floyd Bannister	.06	.02	.00

	MINT	VG-E	F-G		MINT	VG-E	F-G
☐ 245 Fred Lynn	.15	.06	.01	☐ 295 Dale Berra	.05	.02	.00
☐ 246 Charlie Moore	.03	.01	.00	☐ 296 Greg Brock	.06	.02	.00
☐ 247 Walt Terrell	.03	.01	.00	☐ 297 Charlie Leibrandt	.06	.02	.00
☐ 248 Dave Winfield	.25	.10	.02	☐ 298 Bill Krueger	.03	.01	.00
☐ 249 Dwight Evans	.10	.04	.01	☐ 299 Bryn Smith	.05	.02	.00
☐ 250 Dennis Powell	.12	.05	.01	☐ 300 Burt Hooton	.03	.01	.00
☐ 251 Andre Thornton	.06	.02	.00	☐ 301 Stu Cliburn	.15	.06	.01
☐ 252 Onix Concepcion	.03	.01	.00	☐ 302 Luis Salazar	.03	.01	.00
☐ 253 Mike Heath	.03	.01	.00	☐ 303 Ken Dayley	.03	.01	.00
☐ 254 A David Palmer ERR	.10	.04	.01	☐ 304 Frank DiPino	.03	.01	.00
(position 2B)				☐ 305 Von Hayes	.12	.05	.01
☐ 254 B David Palmer COR	.50	.20	.05	☐ 306 Gary Redus	.05	.02	.00
(position P)				☐ 307 Craig Lefferts	.03	.01	.00
☐ 255 Donnie Moore	.05	.02	.00	☐ 308 Sammy Khalifa	.09	.04	.01
☐ 256 Curtis Wilkerson	.03	.01	.00	☐ 309 Scott Garrelts	.05	.02	.00
☐ 257 Julio Cruz	.03	.01	.00	☐ 310 Rick Cerone	.03	.01	.00
☐ 258 Nolan Ryan	.30	.12	.03	☐ 311 Shawon Dunston	.10	.04	.01
☐ 259 Jeff Stone	.06	.02	.00	☐ 312 Howard Johnson	.03	.01	.00
☐ 260 John Tudor	.12	.05	.01	☐ 313 Jim Presley	.50	.20	.05
☐ 261 Mark Thurmond	.05	.02	.00	☐ 314 Gary Gaetti	.10	.04	.01
☐ 262 Jay Tibbs	.03	.01	.00	☐ 315 Luis Leal	.03	.01	.00
☐ 263 Rafael Ramirez	.03	.01	.00	☐ 316 Mark Salas	.06	.02	.00
☐ 264 Larry McWilliams	.03	.01	.00	☐ 317 Bill Caudill	.05	.02	.00
☐ 265 Mark Davis	.03	.01	.00	☐ 318 Dave Henderson	.06	.02	.00
☐ 266 Bob Dernier	.03	.01	.00	☐ 319 Rafael Santana	.03	.01	.00
☐ 267 Matt Young	.03	.01	.00	☐ 320 Leon Durham	.08	.03	.01
☐ 268 Jim Clancy	.03	.01	.00	☐ 321 Bruce Sutter	.12	.05	.01
☐ 269 Mickey Hatcher	.03	.01	.00	☐ 322 Jason Thompson	.05	.02	.00
☐ 270 Sammy Stewart	.03	.01	.00	☐ 323 Bob Brenly	.05	.02	.00
☐ 271 Bob L. Gibson	.03	.01	.00	☐ 324 Carmelo Martinez	.05	.02	.00
☐ 272 Nelson Simmons	.15	.06	.01	☐ 325 Eddie Milner	.05	.02	.00
☐ 273 Rich Gedman	.09	.04	.01	☐ 326 Juan Samuel	.12	.05	.01
☐ 274 Butch Wynegar	.05	.02	.00	☐ 327 Tom Nieto	.03	.01	.00
☐ 275 Ken Howell	.06	.02	.00	☐ 328 Dave Smith	.06	.02	.00
☐ 276 Mel Hall	.08	.03	.01	☐ 329 Urbano Lugo	.08	.03	.01
☐ 277 Jim Sundberg	.05	.02	.00	☐ 330 Joel Skinner	.05	.02	.00
☐ 278 Chris Codiroli	.03	.01	.00	☐ 331 Bill Gullickson	.05	.02	.00
☐ 279 Herman Winningham	.15	.06	.01	☐ 332 Floyd Rayford	.03	.01	.00
☐ 280 Rod Carew	.30	.12	.03	☐ 333 Ben Oglivie	.05	.02	.00
☐ 281 Don Slaught	.03	.01	.00	☐ 334 Lance Parrish	.18	.08	.01
☐ 282 Scott Fletcher	.05	.02	.00	☐ 335 Jackie Gutierrez	.03	.01	.00
☐ 283 Bill Dawley	.03	.01	.00	☐ 336 Dennis Rasmussen	.06	.02	.00
☐ 284 Andy Hawkins	.06	.02	.00	☐ 337 Terry Whitfield	.03	.01	.00
☐ 285 Glenn Wilson	.10	.04	.01	☐ 338 Neal Heaton	.03	.01	.00
☐ 286 Nick Esasky	.06	.02	.00	☐ 339 Jorge Orta	.03	.01	.00
☐ 287 Claudell Washington	.06	.02	.00	☐ 340 Donnie Hill	.03	.01	.00
☐ 288 Lee Mazzilli	.05	.02	.00	☐ 341 Joe Hesketh	.07	.03	.01
☐ 289 Jody Davis	.08	.03	.01	☐ 342 Charlie Hough	.06	.02	.00
☐ 290 Darrell Porter	.05	.02	.00	☐ 343 Dave Rozema	.03	.01	.00
☐ 291 Scott McGregor	.07	.03	.01	☐ 344 Greg Pryor	.03	.01	.00
☐ 292 Ted Simmons	.10	.04	.01	☐ 345 Mickey Tettleton	.07	.03	.01
☐ 293 Aurelio Lopez	.03	.01	.00	☐ 346 George Vukovich	.03	.01	.00
☐ 294 Marty Barrett	.12	.05	.01	☐ 347 Don Baylor	.10	.04	.01

		MINT	VG-E	F-G			MINT	VG-E	F-G
☐ 348	Carlos Diaz	.03	.01	.00	☐ 401	Terry Francona	.05	.02	.00
☐ 349	Barbaro Garbey	.03	.01	.00	☐ 402	Jim Slaton	.03	.01	.00
☐ 350	Larry Sheets	.10	.04	.01	☐ 403	Bill Stein	.03	.01	.00
☐ 351	Ted Higuera	1.00	.40	.10	☐ 404	Tim Hulett	.06	.02	.00
☐ 352	Juan Beniquez	.05	.02	.00	☐ 405	Alan Ashby	.03	.01	.00
☐ 353	Bob Forsch	.06	.02	.00	☐ 406	Tim Stoddard	.03	.01	.00
☐ 354	Mark Bailey	.03	.01	.00	☐ 407	Garry Maddox	.05	.02	.00
☐ 355	Larry Andersen	.03	.01	.00	☐ 408	Ted Power	.07	.03	.01
☐ 356	Terry Kennedy	.07	.03	.01	☐ 409	Len Barker	.06	.02	.00
☐ 357	Don Robinson	.03	.01	.00	☐ 410	Denny Gonzalez	.05	.02	.00
☐ 358	Jim Gott	.03	.01	.00	☐ 411	George Frazier	.03	.01	.00
☐ 359	Earnie Riles	.50	.20	.05	☐ 412	Andy Van Slyke	.06	.02	.00
☐ 360	John Christensen	.07	.03	.01	☐ 413	Jim Dwyer	.03	.01	.00
☐ 361	Ray Fontenot	.03	.01	.00	☐ 414	Paul Householder	.03	.01	.00
☐ 362	Spike Owen	.06	.02	.00	☐ 415	Alejandro Sanchez	.05	.02	.00
☐ 363	Jim Acker	.03	.01	.00	☐ 416	Steve Crawford	.03	.01	.00
☐ 364	Ron Davis	.03	.01	.00	☐ 417	Dan Pasqua	.20	.08	.02
☐ 365	Tom Hume	.03	.01	.00	☐ 418	Enos Cabell	.03	.01	.00
☐ 366	Carlton Fisk	.15	.06	.01	☐ 419	Mike Jones	.03	.01	.00
☐ 367	Nate Snell	.10	.04	.01	☐ 420	Steve Kiefer	.03	.01	.00
☐ 368	Rick Manning	.03	.01	.00	☐ 421	Tim Burke	.25	.10	.02
☐ 369	Darrell Evans	.10	.04	.01	☐ 422	Mike Mason	.03	.01	.00
☐ 370	Ron Hassey	.03	.01	.00	☐ 423	Ruppert Jones	.03	.01	.00
☐ 371	Wade Boggs	2.00	.80	.20	☐ 424	Jerry Hairston	.03	.01	.00
☐ 372	Rick Honeycutt	.05	.02	.00	☐ 425	Tito Landrum	.03	.01	.00
☐ 373	Chris Bando	.03	.01	.00	☐ 426	Jeff Calhoun	.08	.03	.01
☐ 374	Bud Black	.03	.01	.00	☐ 427	Don Carman	.25	.10	.02
☐ 375	Steve Henderson	.03	.01	.00	☐ 428	Tony Perez	.12	.05	.01
☐ 376	Charlie Lea	.03	.01	.00	☐ 429	Jerry Davis	.03	.01	.00
☐ 377	Reggie Jackson	.35	.14	.03	☐ 430	Bob Walk	.03	.01	.00
☐ 378	Dave Schmidt	.03	.01	.00	☐ 431	Brad Wellman	.03	.01	.00
☐ 379	Bob James	.03	.01	.00	☐ 432	Terry Forster	.06	.02	.00
☐ 380	Glenn Davis	1.50	.60	.15	☐ 433	Billy Hatcher	.06	.02	.00
☐ 381	Tim Corcoran	.03	.01	.00	☐ 434	Clint Hurdle	.03	.01	.00
☐ 382	Danny Cox	.07	.03	.01	☐ 435	Ivan Calderon	.25	.10	.02
☐ 383	Tim Flannery	.03	.01	.00	☐ 436	Pete Filson	.03	.01	.00
☐ 384	Tom Browning	.15	.06	.01	☐ 437	Tom Henke	.07	.03	.01
☐ 385	Rick Camp	.03	.01	.00	☐ 438	Dave Engle	.03	.01	.00
☐ 386	Jim Morrison	.03	.01	.00	☐ 439	Tom Filer	.05	.02	.00
☐ 387	Dave LaPoint	.03	.01	.00	☐ 440	Gorman Thomas	.08	.03	.01
☐ 388	Davey Lopes	.06	.02	.00	☐ 441	Rick Aguilera	.25	.10	.02
☐ 389	Al Cowens	.05	.02	.00	☐ 442	Scott Sanderson	.03	.01	.00
☐ 390	Doyle Alexander	.05	.02	.00	☐ 443	Jeff Dedmon	.03	.01	.00
☐ 391	Tim Laudner	.03	.01	.00	☐ 444	Joe Orsulak	.25	.10	.02
☐ 392	Don Aase	.05	.02	.00	☐ 445	Atlee Hammaker	.05	.02	.00
☐ 393	Jaime Cocanower	.03	.01	.00	☐ 446	Jerry Royster	.03	.01	.00
☐ 394	Randy O'Neal	.05	.02	.00	☐ 447	Buddy Bell	.09	.04	.01
☐ 395	Mike Easler	.05	.02	.00	☐ 448	Dave Rucker	.03	.01	.00
☐ 396	Scott Bradley	.05	.02	.00	☐ 449	Ivan DeJesus	.03	.01	.00
☐ 397	Tom Niedenfuer	.06	.02	.00	☐ 450	Jim Pankovits	.03	.01	.00
☐ 398	Jerry Willard	.03	.01	.00	☐ 451	Jerry Narron	.03	.01	.00
☐ 399	Lonnie Smith	.06	.02	.00	☐ 452	Bryan Little	.03	.01	.00
☐ 400	Bruce Bochte	.05	.02	.00	☐ 453	Gary Lucas	.03	.01	.00

		MINT	VG-E	F-G
☐ 454	Dennis Martinez	.03	.01	.00
☐ 455	Ed Romero	.03	.01	.00
☐ 456	Bob Melvin	.08	.03	.01
☐ 457	Glenn Hoffman	.03	.01	.00
☐ 458	Bob Shirley	.03	.01	.00
☐ 459	Bob Welch	.06	.02	.00
☐ 460	Carmen Castillo	.03	.01	.00
☐ 461	Dave Leiper	.08	.03	.01
☐ 462	Tim Birtsas	.15	.06	.01
☐ 463	Randy St.Claire	.03	.01	.00
☐ 464	Chris Welsh	.03	.01	.00
☐ 465	Greg Harris	.05	.02	.00
☐ 466	Lynn Jones	.03	.01	.00
☐ 467	Dusty Baker	.06	.02	.00
☐ 468	Roy Smith	.03	.01	.00
☐ 469	Andre Robertson	.03	.01	.00
☐ 470	Ken Landreaux	.05	.02	.00
☐ 471	Dave Bergman	.03	.01	.00
☐ 472	Gary Roenicke	.05	.02	.00
☐ 473	Pete Vuckovich	.05	.02	.00
☐ 474	Kirk McCaskill	1.00	.40	.10
☐ 475	Jeff Lahti	.03	.01	.00
☐ 476	Mike Scott	.25	.10	.02
☐ 477	Darren Daulton	.25	.10	.02
☐ 478	Graig Nettles	.12	.05	.01
☐ 479	Bill Almon	.03	.01	.00
☐ 480	Greg Minton	.05	.02	.00
☐ 481	Randy Ready	.03	.01	.00
☐ 482	Lenny Dykstra	1.50	.60	.15
☐ 483	Thad Bosley	.03	.01	.00
☐ 484	Harold Reynolds	.15	.06	.01
☐ 485	Al Oliver	.10	.04	.01
☐ 486	Roy Smalley	.05	.02	.00
☐ 487	John Franco	.10	.04	.01
☐ 488	Juan Agosto	.03	.01	.00
☐ 489	Al Pardo	.10	.04	.01
☐ 490	Bill Wegman	.15	.06	.01
☐ 491	Frank Tanana	.06	.02	.00
☐ 492	Brian Fisher	.30	.12	.03
☐ 493	Mark Clear	.03	.01	.00
☐ 494	Len Matuszek	.03	.01	.00
☐ 495	Ramon Romero	.08	.03	.01
☐ 496	John Wathan	.03	.01	.00
☐ 497	Rob Picciolo	.03	.01	.00
☐ 498	U.L. Washington	.03	.01	.00
☐ 499	John Candelaria	.07	.03	.01
☐ 500	Duane Walker	.03	.01	.00
☐ 501	Gene Nelson	.03	.01	.00
☐ 502	John Mizerock	.03	.01	.00
☐ 503	Luis Aguayo	.03	.01	.00
☐ 504	Kurt Kepshire	.03	.01	.00
☐ 505	Ed Wojna	.10	.04	.01
☐ 506	Joe Price	.03	.01	.00
☐ 507	Milt Thompson	.20	.08	.02
☐ 508	Junior Ortiz	.03	.01	.00
☐ 509	Vida Blue	.07	.03	.01
☐ 510	Steve Engel	.08	.03	.01
☐ 511	Karl Best	.08	.03	.01
☐ 512	Cecil Fielder	.25	.10	.02
☐ 513	Frank Eufemia	.10	.04	.01
☐ 514	Tippy Martinez	.03	.01	.00
☐ 515	Billy Robidoux	.35	.14	.03
☐ 516	Bill Scherrer	.03	.01	.00
☐ 517	Bruce Hurst	.07	.03	.01
☐ 518	Rich Bordi	.03	.01	.00
☐ 519	Steve Yeager	.05	.02	.00
☐ 520	Tony Bernazard	.05	.02	.00
☐ 521	Hal McRae	.06	.02	.00
☐ 522	Jose Rijo	.08	.03	.01
☐ 523	Mitch Webster	.75	.30	.07
☐ 524	Jack Howell	.35	.14	.03
☐ 525	Alan Bannister	.03	.01	.00
☐ 526	Ron Kittle	.10	.04	.01
☐ 527	Phil Garner	.05	.02	.00
☐ 528	Kurt Bevacqua	.03	.01	.00
☐ 529	Kevin Gross	.03	.01	.00
☐ 530	Bo Diaz	.05	.02	.00
☐ 531	Ken Oberkfell	.03	.01	.00
☐ 532	Rick Reuschel	.05	.02	.00
☐ 533	Ron Meridith	.10	.04	.01
☐ 534	Steve Braun	.03	.01	.00
☐ 535	Wayne Gross	.03	.01	.00
☐ 536	Ray Searage	.03	.01	.00
☐ 537	Tom Brookens	.03	.01	.00
☐ 538	Al Nipper	.05	.02	.00
☐ 539	Billy Sample	.03	.01	.00
☐ 540	Steve Sax	.12	.05	.01
☐ 541	Dan Quisenberry	.12	.05	.01
☐ 542	Tony Phillips	.03	.01	.00
☐ 543	Floyd Youmans	1.00	.40	.10
☐ 544	Steve Buechele	.25	.10	.02
☐ 545	Craig Gerber	.08	.03	.01
☐ 546	Joe DeSa	.07	.03	.01
☐ 547	Brian Harper	.03	.01	.00
☐ 548	Kevin Bass	.07	.03	.01
☐ 549	Tom Foley	.03	.01	.00
☐ 550	Dave Van Gorder	.03	.01	.00
☐ 551	Bruce Bochy	.03	.01	.00
☐ 552	R.J. Reynolds	.05	.02	.00
☐ 553	Chris Brown	1.25	.50	.12
☐ 554	Bruce Benedict	.03	.01	.00
☐ 555	Warren Brusstar	.03	.01	.00
☐ 556	Danny Heep	.03	.01	.00
☐ 557	Darnell Coles	.08	.03	.01
☐ 558	Greg Gagne	.05	.02	.00
☐ 559	Ernie Whitt	.03	.01	.00

	MINT	VG-E	F-G
☐ 560 Ron Washington	.03	.01	.00
☐ 561 Jimmy Key	.10	.04	.01
☐ 562 Billy Swift	.06	.02	.00
☐ 563 Ron Darling	.25	.10	.02
☐ 564 Dick Ruthven	.03	.01	.00
☐ 565 Zane Smith	.06	.02	.00
☐ 566 Sid Bream	.06	.02	.00
☐ 567 A Joel Youngblood ERR (position P)	.10	.04	.01
☐ 567 B Joel Youngblood COR (position IF)	.50	.20	.05
☐ 568 Mario Ramirez	.03	.01	.00
☐ 569 Tom Runnells	.10	.04	.01
☐ 570 Rick Schu	.06	.02	.00
☐ 571 Bill Campbell	.03	.01	.00
☐ 572 Dickie Thon	.05	.02	.00
☐ 573 Al Holland	.03	.01	.00
☐ 574 Reid Nichols	.03	.01	.00
☐ 575 Bert Roberge	.03	.01	.00
☐ 576 Mike Flanagan	.07	.03	.01
☐ 577 Tim Leary	.03	.01	.00
☐ 578 Mike Laga	.05	.02	.00
☐ 579 Steve Lyons	.05	.02	.00
☐ 580 Phil Niekro	.15	.06	.01
☐ 581 Gilberto Reyes	.15	.06	.01
☐ 582 Jamie Easterly	.03	.01	.00
☐ 583 Mark Gubicza	.07	.03	.01
☐ 584 Stan Javier	.20	.08	.02
☐ 585 Bill Laskey	.03	.01	.00
☐ 586 Jeff Russell	.03	.01	.00
☐ 587 Dickie Noles	.03	.01	.00
☐ 588 Steve Farr	.03	.01	.00
☐ 589 Steve Ontiveros	.20	.08	.02
☐ 590 Mike Hargrove	.05	.02	.00
☐ 591 Marty Bystrom	.03	.01	.00
☐ 592 Franklin Stubbs	.10	.04	.01
☐ 593 Larry Herndon	.03	.01	.00
☐ 594 Bill Swaggerty	.03	.01	.00
☐ 595 Carlos Ponce	.07	.03	.01
☐ 596 Pat Perry	.07	.03	.01
☐ 597 Ray Knight	.08	.03	.01
☐ 598 Steve Lombardozzi	.15	.06	.01
☐ 599 Brad Havens	.03	.01	.00
☐ 600 Pat Clements	.15	.06	.01
☐ 601 Joe Niekro	.08	.03	.01
☐ 602 Hank Aaron Puzzle Card	.10	.04	.01
☐ 603 Dwayne Henry	.08	.03	.01
☐ 604 Mookie Wilson	.06	.02	.00
☐ 605 Buddy Biancalana	.05	.02	.00
☐ 606 Rance Mulliniks	.03	.01	.00
☐ 607 Alan Wiggins	.06	.02	.00
☐ 608 Joe Cowley	.05	.02	.00

	MINT	VG-E	F-G
☐ 609 A Tom Seaver (green borders on name)	.35	.14	.03
☐ 609 B Tom Seaver (yellow borders on name)	1.00	.40	.10
☐ 610 Neil Allen	.05	.02	.00
☐ 611 Don Sutton	.18	.08	.01
☐ 612 Fred Toliver	.15	.06	.01
☐ 613 Jay Baller	.10	.04	.01
☐ 614 Marc Sullivan	.08	.03	.01
☐ 615 John Grubb	.03	.01	.00
☐ 616 Bruce Kison	.03	.01	.00
☐ 617 Bill Madlock	.10	.04	.01
☐ 618 Chris Chambliss	.06	.02	.00
☐ 619 Dave Stewart	.03	.01	.00
☐ 620 Tim Lollar	.03	.01	.00
☐ 621 Gary Lavelle	.05	.02	.00
☐ 622 Charlie Hudson	.05	.02	.00
☐ 623 Joel Davis	.20	.08	.02
☐ 624 Joe Johnson	.20	.08	.02
☐ 625 Sid Fernandez	.20	.08	.02
☐ 626 Dennis Lamp	.03	.01	.00
☐ 627 Terry Harper	.03	.01	.00
☐ 628 Jack Lazorko	.03	.01	.00
☐ 629 Roger McDowell	.50	.20	.05
☐ 630 Mark Funderburk	.15	.06	.01
☐ 631 Ed Lynch	.03	.01	.00
☐ 632 Rudy Law	.03	.01	.00
☐ 633 Roger Mason	.15	.06	.01
☐ 634 Mike Felder	.20	.08	.02
☐ 635 Ken Schrom	.05	.02	.00
☐ 636 Bob Ojeda	.08	.03	.01
☐ 637 Ed VandeBerg	.03	.01	.00
☐ 638 Bobby Meacham	.03	.01	.00
☐ 639 Cliff Johnson	.03	.01	.00
☐ 640 Garth Iorg	.03	.01	.00
☐ 641 Dan Driessen	.03	.01	.00
☐ 642 Mike Brown OF	.05	.02	.00
☐ 643 John Shelby	.03	.01	.00
☐ 644 Pete Rose (Ty-Breaking)	.30	.12	.03
☐ 645 The Knuckle Brothers Phil Niekro Joe Niekro	.10	.04	.01
☐ 646 Jesse Orosco	.06	.02	.00
☐ 647 Billy Beane	.20	.08	.02
☐ 648 Cesar Cedeno	.06	.02	.00
☐ 649 Bert Blyleven	.10	.04	.01
☐ 650 Max Venable	.03	.01	.00
☐ 651 Fleet Feet Vince Coleman Willie McGee	.30	.12	.03

		MINT	VG-E	F-G
☐ 652	Calvin Schiraldi	.09	.04	.01
☐ 653	King of Kings	.75	.30	.07
	Pete Rose			
☐ 654	CL: Diamond Kings	.08	.01	.00
	(unnumbered)			
☐ 655 A	CL 1: 27-130	.10	.01	.00
	(unnumbered)			
	(45 Beane ERR)			
☐ 655 B	CL 1: 27-130	.50	.05	.01
	(unnumbered)			
	(45 Habyan COR)			
☐ 656	CL 2: 131-234	.06	.01	.00
	(unnumbered)			
☐ 657	CL 3: 235-338	.06	.01	.00
	(unnumbered)			
☐ 658	CL 4: 339-442	.06	.01	.00
	(unnumbered)			
☐ 659	CL 5: 443-546	.06	.01	.00
	(unnumbered)			
☐ 660	CL 6: 547-653	.06	.01	.00
	(unnumbered)			
☐ PC4	Kirk Gibson	.35	.14	.03
	(wax pack box card)			
☐ PC5	Willie Hernandez	.15	.06	.01
	(wax pack box card)			
☐ PC6	Doug DeCinces	.10	.04	.01
	(wax pack box card)			
☐ PUZ	Hank Aaron	.06	.02	.00
	Puzzle Card			
	(wax pack box card)			
☐ PC7	Wade Boggs	2.00	.80	.20
	(all star box card)			
☐ PC8	Lee Smith	.10	.04	.01
	(all star box card)			
☐ PC9	Cecil Cooper	.10	.04	.01
	(all star box card)			
☐ PUZ	Hank Aaron	.06	.02	.00
	Puzzle Card			
	(all star box card)			

1986 Donruss Rookies

The 1986 Donruss ''The Rookies'' set features 56 cards plus a 15-piece puzzle of Hank Aaron. Cards are in full color and are standard size, 2½" by 3½". The set was distributed in a small green box with gold lettering. Although the set was wrapped in cellophane, the top card was #1 Joyner resulting in a percentage of (Joyner) cards arriving in less than perfect condition. Card fronts are similar in design to the 1986 Donruss regular issue except for the presence of ''The Rookies'' logo in the lower left corner and a bluish green border instead of a blue border.

		MINT	VG-E	F-G
	Complete Set	21.00	7.50	1.75
	Common Player	.06	.02	.00
☐ 1	Wally Joyner	5.00	1.50	.30
☐ 2	Tracy Jones	.40	.16	.04
☐ 3	Allan Anderson	.20	.08	.02
☐ 4	Ed Correa	.40	.16	.04
☐ 5	Reggie Williams	.25	.10	.02
☐ 6	Charlie Kerfeld	.30	.12	.03
☐ 7	Andres Galarraga	.20	.08	.02
☐ 8	Bob Tewksbury	.30	.12	.03
☐ 9	Al Newman	.20	.08	.02
☐ 10	Andres Thomas	.40	.16	.04
☐ 11	Barry Bonds	.90	.36	.09
☐ 12	Juan Nieves	.10	.04	.01
☐ 13	Mark Eichhorn	.60	.24	.06
☐ 14	Dan Plesac	.25	.10	.02
☐ 15	Cory Snyder	1.75	.70	.17
☐ 16	Kelly Gruber	.20	.08	.02
☐ 17	Kevin Mitchell	.75	.30	.07

		MINT	VG-E	F-G
☐ 18	Steve Lombardozzi	.10	.04	.01
☐ 19	Mitch Williams	.35	.14	.03
☐ 20	John Cerutti	.35	.14	.03
☐ 21	Todd Worrell	.75	.30	.07
☐ 22	Jose Canseco	3.50	1.40	.35
☐ 23	Pete Incaviglia	2.25	.90	.22
☐ 24	Jose Guzman	.10	.04	.01
☐ 25	Scott Bailes	.20	.08	.02
☐ 26	Greg Mathews	.50	.20	.05
☐ 27	Eric King	.50	.20	.05
☐ 28	Paul Assenmacher	.20	.08	.02
☐ 29	Jeff Sellers	.20	.08	.02
☐ 30	Bobby Bonilla	.20	.08	.02
☐ 31	Doug Drabek	.20	.08	.02
☐ 32	Will Clark	1.25	.50	.12
☐ 33	Leon "Bip" Roberts	.20	.08	.02
☐ 34	Jim Deshaies	.60	.24	.06
☐ 35	Mike Lavalliere	.20	.08	.02
☐ 36	Scott Bankhead	.20	.08	.02
☐ 37	Dale Sveum	.20	.08	.02
☐ 38	Bo Jackson	2.25	.90	.22
☐ 39	Rob Thompson	.50	.20	.05
☐ 40	Eric Plunk	.20	.08	.02
☐ 41	Bill Bathe	.20	.08	.02
☐ 42	John Kruk	.40	.16	.04
☐ 43	Andy Allanson	.20	.08	.02
☐ 44	Mark Portugal	.20	.08	.02
☐ 45	Danny Tartabull	.75	.30	.07
☐ 46	Bob Kipper	.06	.02	.00
☐ 47	Gene Walter	.20	.08	.02
☐ 48	Rey Quinones	.20	.08	.02
☐ 49	Bobby Witt	.60	.24	.06
☐ 50	Bill Mooneyham	.20	.08	.02
☐ 51	John Cangelosi	.50	.20	.05
☐ 52	Ruben Sierra	1.75	.70	.17
☐ 53	Rob Woodward	.20	.08	.02
☐ 54	Ed Hearn	.20	.08	.02
☐ 55	Joel McKeon	.20	.08	.02
☐ 56	Checklist card	.20	.02	.00

1986 Donruss Highlights

Donruss' second edition of Highlights was released late in 1986. The cards are standard size measuring 2½" by 3½" and are glossy in appearance. Cards commemorate events during the 1986 season, as well as players and pitchers of the month from each league. The set was distributed in its own red, white, blue, and gold box along with a small Hank Aaron puzzle. Card fronts are similar to the regular 1986 Donruss issue except that the Highlights logo is positioned in the lower left-hand corner and the borders are in gold instead of blue. The backs are printed in black and gold on white card stock.

		MINT	VG-E	F-G
	Complete Set	9.00	3.00	.75
	Common Player	.06	.02	.00
☐ 1	Will Clark Homers in First At-Bat	.35	.14	.03
☐ 2	Jose Rijo Oakland Milestone for Strikeouts	.10	.04	.01
☐ 3	George Brett Royals' All-Time Hit Man	.35	.14	.03
☐ 4	Mike Schmidt Phillies RBI Leader	.45	.18	.04
☐ 5	Roger Clemens KKKKKKKKKK KKKKKKKKKK	.75	.30	.07
☐ 6	Roger Clemens AL Pitcher April	.75	.30	.07

		MINT	VG-E	F-G			MINT	VG-E	F-G
☐ 7	Kirby Puckett AL Player April	.30	.12	.03	☐ 30	Eric Davis NL Player July	.40	.16	.04
☐ 8	Dwight Gooden NL Pitcher April	.75	.30	.07	☐ 31	Bert Blyleven Records 3000th Strikeout	.10	.04	.01
☐ 9	Johnny Ray NL Player April	.06	.02	.00	☐ 32	Bobby Doerr '86 HOF Inductee	.15	.06	.01
☐ 10	Reggie Jackson Eclipses Mantle HR Record	.50	.20	.05	☐ 33	Ernie Lombardi '86 HOF Inductee	.15	.06	.01
☐ 11	Wade Boggs First Five Hit Game of Career	.75	.30	.07	☐ 34	Willie McCovey '86 HOF Inductee	.20	.08	.02
☐ 12	Don Aase AL Pitcher May	.05	.02	.00	☐ 35	Steve Carlton Notches 4000th K	.30	.12	.03
☐ 13	Wade Boggs AL Player May	.75	.30	.07	☐ 36	Mike Schmidt Surpasses DiMaggio Record	.45	.18	.04
☐ 14	Jeff Reardon NL Pitcher May	.05	.02	.00	☐ 37	Juan Samuel Records 3rd "Quadruple Double"	.10	.04	.01
☐ 15	Hubie Brooks NL Player May	.10	.04	.01	☐ 38	Mike Witt AL Pitcher August	.10	.04	.01
☐ 16	Don Sutton Notches 300th	.20	.08	.02	☐ 39	Doug DeCinces AL Player August	.05	.02	.00
☐ 17	Roger Clemens Starts 14-0	.75	.30	.07	☐ 40	Bill Gullickson NL Pitcher August	.05	.02	.00
☐ 18	Roger Clemens AL Pitcher June	.75	.30	.07	☐ 41	Dale Murphy NL Player August	.40	.16	.04
☐ 19	Kent Hrbek AL Player June	.20	.08	.02	☐ 42	Joe Carter Sets Tribe Offensive Record	.20	.08	.02
☐ 20	Rick Rhoden NL Pitcher June	.05	.02	.00	☐ 43	Bo Jackson Longest HR in Royals Stadium	.40	.16	.04
☐ 21	Kevin Bass NL Player June	.15	.06	.01	☐ 44	Joe Cowley Majors 1st No-Hitter in 2 Years	.05	.02	.00
☐ 22	Bob Horner Blasts 4 HRs in 1 Game	.15	.06	.01	☐ 45	Jim Deshaies Sets ML Strikeout Record	.15	.06	.01
☐ 23	Wally Joyner Starting All Star Rookie	.75	.30	.07	☐ 46	Mike Scott No Hitter Clinches Division	.20	.08	.02
☐ 24	Darryl Strawberry Starts 3rd Straight All Star Game	.45	.18	.04	☐ 47	Bruce Hurst AL Pitcher September	.10	.04	.01
☐ 25	Fernando Valenzuela Ties All Star Game Record	.30	.12	.03	☐ 48	Don Mattingly AL Player September	1.00	.40	.10
☐ 26	Roger Clemens All Star Game MVP	.75	.30	.07	☐ 49	Mike Krukow NL Pitcher September	.10	.04	.01
☐ 27	Jack Morris AL Pitcher July	.15	.06	.01	☐ 50	Steve Sax NL Player September	.20	.08	.02
☐ 28	Scott Fletcher AL Player July	.05	.02	.00	☐ 51	John Cangelosi AL Rookie Steals Record	.20	.08	.02
☐ 29	Todd Worrell NL Pitcher July	.20	.08	.02					

		MINT	VG-E	F-G
☐ 52	Dave Righetti .... ML Save Mark	.15	.06	.01
☐ 53	Don Mattingly .... Yankee Record for Hits and Doubles	1.00	.40	.10
☐ 54	Todd Worrell .... Donruss NL ROY	.30	.12	.03
☐ 55	Jose Canseco .... Donruss AL ROY	1.00	.40	.10
☐ 56	Checklist card	.10	.01	.00

1987 Donruss

This 660-card set was distributed along with a puzzle of Roberto Clemente. The checklist cards are numbered throughout the set as multiples of 100. The wax pack boxes contain four cards printed on the bottom of the box. Cards measure 2½" by 3½" and feature a black and gold border on the front; the backs are also done in black and gold on white card stock. The popular Diamond King subset returns for the sixth consecutive year. Some of the Diamond King (1-26) selections are repeats from prior years; Perez-Steele Galleries has indicated that a five-year rotation will be maintained in order to avoid depleting the pool of available worthy ''kings'' on some of the teams.

		MINT	VG-E	F-G
	Complete Set	25.00	10.00	2.50
	Common Player	.03	.01	.00
☐ 1	Wally Joyner DK	1.25	.30	.06
☐ 2	Roger Clemens DK	.60	.24	.06
☐ 3	Dale Murphy DK	.40	.16	.04

		MINT	VG-E	F-G
☐ 4	Darryl Strawberry DK ...	.40	.16	.04
☐ 5	Ozzie Smith DK	.10	.04	.01
☐ 6	Jose Canseco DK	1.00	.40	.10
☐ 7	Charlie Hough DK	.06	.02	.00
☐ 8	Brook Jacoby DK	.09	.04	.01
☐ 9	Fred Lynn DK	.15	.06	.01
☐ 10	Rick Rhoden DK	.06	.02	.00
☐ 11	Chris Brown DK	.15	.06	.01
☐ 12	Von Hayes DK	.12	.05	.01
☐ 13	Jack Morris DK	.15	.06	.01
☐ 14	Kevin McReynolds DK ..	.12	.05	.01
☐ 15	George Brett DK	.35	.14	.03
☐ 16	Ted Higuera DK	.15	.06	.01
☐ 17	Hubie Brooks DK	.10	.04	.01
☐ 18	Mike Scott DK	.18	.08	.01
☐ 19	Kirby Puckett DK	.25	.10	.02
☐ 20	Dave Winfield DK	.25	.10	.02
☐ 21	Lloyd Moseby DK	.10	.04	.01
☐ 22	Eric Davis DK	.50	.20	.05
☐ 23	Jim Presley DK	.25	.10	.02
☐ 24	Keith Moreland DK	.08	.03	.01
☐ 25	Greg Walker DK	.10	.04	.01
☐ 26	Steve Sax DK	.15	.06	.01
☐ 27	DK Checklist 1-26	.06	.01	.00
☐ 28	B.J. Surhoff RR	.60	.24	.06
☐ 29	Randy Myers RR	.45	.18	.04
☐ 30	Ken Gerhart RR	.25	.10	.02
☐ 31	Benito Santiago RR	.25	.10	.02
☐ 32	Greg Swindell RR	.45	.18	.04
☐ 33	Mike Birkbeck RR	.12	.05	.01
☐ 34	Terry Steinbach RR	.35	.14	.03
☐ 35	Bo Jackson RR	1.25	.50	.12
☐ 36	Greg Maddux RR	.10	.04	.01
☐ 37	Jim Lindeman RR	.20	.08	.01
☐ 38	Devon White RR	.30	.12	.03
☐ 39	Eric Bell RR	.25	.10	.02
☐ 40	Will Fraser RR	.12	.05	.01
☐ 41	Jerry Browne RR	.12	.05	.01
☐ 42	Chris James RR	.20	.08	.02
☐ 43	Rafael Palmeiro RR	.40	.12	.03
☐ 44	Pat Dodson RR	.25	.10	.02
☐ 45	Duane Ward RR	.10	.04	.01
☐ 46	Mark McGwire RR	.10	.04	.01
☐ 47	Bruce Fields RR	.10	.04	.01
☐ 48	Eddie Murray	.25	.10	.02
☐ 49	Ted Higuera	.15	.06	.01
☐ 50	Kirk Gibson	.20	.08	.02
☐ 51	Oil Can Boyd	.08	.03	.01
☐ 52	Don Mattingly	2.00	.80	.20
☐ 53	Pedro Guerrero	.20	.08	.02
☐ 54	George Brett	.30	.12	.03
☐ 55	Jose Rijo	.08	.03	.01
☐ 56	Tim Raines	.25	.10	.02

		MINT	VG-E	F-G			MINT	VG-E	F-G
☐	57 Ed Correa	.35	.14	.03	☐	110 Donnie Moore	.05	.02	.00
☐	58 Mike Witt	.10	.04	.01	☐	111 Jack Clark	.09	.04	.01
☐	59 Greg Walker	.10	.04	.01	☐	112 Bob Knepper	.08	.03	.01
☐	60 Ozzie Smith	.10	.04	.01	☐	113 Von Hayes	.12	.05	.01
☐	61 Glenn Davis	.25	.10	.02	☐	114 Leon"Bip" Roberts	.09	.04	.01
☐	62 Glenn Wilson	.10	.04	.01	☐	115 Tony Pena	.09	.04	.01
☐	63 Tom Browning	.10	.04	.01	☐	116 Scott Garrelts	.05	.02	.00
☐	64 Tony Gwynn	.30	.12	.03	☐	117 Paul Molitor	.08	.03	.01
☐	65 R.J. Reynolds	.06	.02	.00	☐	118 Darryl Strawberry	.30	.12	.03
☐	66 Will Clark	.60	.24	.06	☐	119 Shawon Dunston	.09	.04	.01
☐	67 Ozzie Virgil	.05	.02	.00	☐	120 Jim Presley	.18	.08	.01
☐	68 Rick Sutcliffe	.10	.04	.01	☐	121 Jesse Barfield	.15	.06	.01
☐	69 Gary Carter	.25	.10	.02	☐	122 Gary Gaetti	.09	.04	.01
☐	70 Mike Moore	.05	.02	.00	☐	123 Kurt Stillwell	.12	.05	.01
☐	71 Bert Blyleven	.08	.03	.01	☐	124 Joel Davis	.12	.05	.01
☐	72 Tony Fernandez	.09	.04	.01	☐	125 Mike Boddicker	.08	.03	.01
☐	73 Kent Hrbek	.15	.06	.01	☐	126 Robin Yount	.25	.10	.02
☐	74 Lloyd Moseby	.10	.04	.01	☐	127 Alan Trammell	.15	.06	.01
☐	75 Alvin Davis	.10	.04	.01	☐	128 Dave Righetti	.12	.05	.01
☐	76 Keith Hernandez	.20	.08	.02	☐	129 Dwight Evans	.09	.04	.01
☐	77 Ryne Sandberg	.25	.10	.02	☐	130 Mike Scioscia	.05	.02	.00
☐	78 Dale Murphy	.40	.16	.04	☐	131 Julio Franco	.09	.04	.01
☐	79 Sid Bream	.06	.02	.00	☐	132 Bret Saberhagen	.15	.06	.01
☐	80 Chris Brown	.15	.06	.01	☐	133 Mike Davis	.06	.02	.00
☐	81 Steve Garvey	.30	.12	.03	☐	134 Joe Hesketh	.05	.02	.00
☐	82 Mario Soto	.08	.03	.01	☐	135 Wally Joyner	2.00	.80	.20
☐	83 Shane Rawley	.07	.03	.01	☐	136 Don Slaught	.03	.01	.00
☐	84 Willie McGee	.15	.06	.01	☐	137 Daryl Boston	.05	.02	.00
☐	85 Jose Cruz	.09	.04	.01	☐	138 Nolan Ryan	.30	.12	.03
☐	86 Brian Downing	.05	.02	.00	☐	139 Mike Schmidt	.35	.14	.03
☐	87 Ozzie Guillen	.10	.04	.01	☐	140 Tommy Herr	.08	.03	.01
☐	88 Hubie Brooks	.10	.04	.01	☐	141 Garry Templeton	.07	.03	.01
☐	89 Cal Ripken	.25	.10	.02	☐	142 Kal Daniels	.12	.05	.01
☐	90 Juan Nieves	.07	.03	.01	☐	143 Billy Sample	.03	.01	.00
☐	91 Lance Parrish	.20	.08	.02	☐	144 Johnny Ray	.09	.04	.01
☐	92 Jim Rice	.25	.10	.02	☐	145 Rob Thompson	.30	.12	.03
☐	93 Ron Guidry	.15	.06	.01	☐	146 Bob Dernier	.05	.02	.00
☐	94 Fernando Valenzuela	.25	.10	.02	☐	147 Danny Tartabull	.25	.10	.02
☐	95 Andy Allanson	.12	.05	.01	☐	148 Ernie Whitt	.03	.01	.00
☐	96 Willie Wilson	.12	.05	.01	☐	149 Kirby Puckett	.25	.10	.02
☐	97 Jose Canseco	1.25	.50	.12	☐	150 Mike Young	.09	.04	.01
☐	98 Jeff Reardon	.06	.02	.00	☐	151 Ernest Riles	.07	.03	.01
☐	99 Bobby Witt	.40	.16	.04	☐	152 Frank Tanana	.05	.02	.00
☐	100 Checklist	.06	.01	.00	☐	153 Rich Gedman	.08	.03	.01
☐	101 Jose Guzman	.06	.02	.00	☐	154 Willie Randolph	.06	.02	.00
☐	102 Steve Balboni	.05	.02	.00	☐	155 Bill Madlock	.09	.04	.01
☐	103 Tony Phillips	.03	.01	.00	☐	156 Joe Carter	.18	.08	.01
☐	104 Brook Jacoby	.08	.03	.01	☐	157 Danny Jackson	.06	.02	.00
☐	105 Dave Winfield	.25	.10	.02	☐	158 Carney Lansford	.09	.04	.01
☐	106 Orel Hershiser	.15	.06	.01	☐	159 Bryn Smith	.05	.02	.00
☐	107 Lou Whitaker	.10	.04	.01	☐	160 Gary Pettis	.05	.02	.00
☐	108 Fred Lynn	.15	.06	.01	☐	161 Oddibe McDowell	.20	.08	.02
☐	109 Bill Wegman	.03	.01	.00	☐	162 John Cangelosi	.25	.10	.02

		MINT	VG-E	F-G			MINT	VG-E	F-G
☐ 163	Mike Scott	.15	.06	.01	☐ 216	Bob Stanley	.05	.02	.00
☐ 164	Eric Show	.03	.01	.00	☐ 217	Joe Niekro	.07	.03	.01
☐ 165	Juan Samuel	.10	.04	.01	☐ 218	Tom Niedenfuer	.06	.02	.00
☐ 166	Nick Esasky	.03	.01	.00	☐ 219	Brett Butler	.08	.03	.01
☐ 167	Zane Smith	.03	.01	.00	☐ 220	Charlie Leibrandt	.05	.02	.00
☐ 168	Mike Brown	.03	.01	.00	☐ 221	Steve Ontiveros	.05	.02	.00
☐ 169	Keith Moreland	.05	.02	.00	☐ 222	Tim Burke	.05	.02	.00
☐ 170	John Tudor	.08	.03	.01	☐ 223	Curtis Wilkerson	.03	.01	.00
☐ 171	Ken Dixon	.05	.02	.00	☐ 224	Pete Incaviglia	1.00	.40	.10
☐ 172	Jim Gantner	.05	.02	.00	☐ 225	Lonnie Smith	.06	.02	.00
☐ 173	Jack Morris	.15	.06	.01	☐ 226	Chris Codiroli	.03	.01	.00
☐ 174	Bruce Hurst	.08	.03	.01	☐ 227	Scott Bailes	.10	.04	.01
☐ 175	Dennis Rasmussen	.06	.02	.00	☐ 228	Rickey Henderson	.30	.12	.03
☐ 176	Mike Marshall	.10	.04	.01	☐ 229	Ken Howell	.06	.02	.00
☐ 177	Dan Quisenberry	.12	.05	.01	☐ 230	Darnell Coles	.10	.04	.01
☐ 178	Eric Plunk	.10	.04	.01	☐ 231	Don Aase	.05	.02	.00
☐ 179	Tim Wallach	.08	.03	.01	☐ 232	Tim Leary	.03	.01	.00
☐ 180	Steve Buechele	.05	.02	.00	☐ 233	Bob Boone	.05	.02	.00
☐ 181	Don Sutton	.12	.05	.01	☐ 234	Ricky Horton	.03	.01	.00
☐ 182	Dave Schmidt	.03	.01	.00	☐ 235	Mark Bailey	.03	.01	.00
☐ 183	Terry Pendleton	.05	.02	.00	☐ 236	Kevin Gross	.03	.01	.00
☐ 184	Jim Deshaies	.20	.08	.02	☐ 237	Lance McCullers	.05	.02	.00
☐ 185	Steve Bedrosian	.05	.02	.00	☐ 238	Cecilio Guante	.03	.01	.00
☐ 186	Pete Rose	.60	.24	.06	☐ 239	Bob Melvin	.03	.01	.00
☐ 187	Dave Dravecky	.06	.02	.00	☐ 240	Billy Jo Robidoux	.05	.02	.00
☐ 188	Rick Reuschel	.05	.02	.00	☐ 241	Roger McDowell	.10	.04	.01
☐ 189	Dan Gladden	.05	.02	.00	☐ 242	Leon Durham	.08	.03	.01
☐ 190	Rick Mahler	.03	.01	.00	☐ 243	Ed Nunez	.03	.01	.00
☐ 191	Thad Bosley	.03	.01	.00	☐ 244	Jimmy Key	.08	.03	.01
☐ 192	Ron Darling	.20	.08	.02	☐ 245	Mike Smithson	.03	.01	.00
☐ 193	Matt Young	.03	.01	.00	☐ 246	Bo Diaz	.05	.02	.00
☐ 194	Tom Brunansky	.09	.04	.01	☐ 247	Carlton Fisk	.10	.04	.01
☐ 195	Dave Stieb	.10	.04	.01	☐ 248	Larry Sheets	.05	.02	.00
☐ 196	Frank Viola	.05	.02	.00	☐ 249	Juan Castillo	.03	.01	.00
☐ 197	Tom Henke	.05	.02	.00	☐ 250	Eric King	.25	.10	.02
☐ 198	Karl Best	.03	.01	.00	☐ 251	Doug Drabek	.20	.08	.02
☐ 199	Dwight Gooden	1.00	.40	.10	☐ 252	Wade Boggs	1.00	.40	.10
☐ 200	Checklist	.06	.01	.00	☐ 253	Mariano Duncan	.08	.03	.01
☐ 201	Steve Trout	.03	.01	.00	☐ 254	Pat Tabler	.08	.03	.01
☐ 202	Rafael Ramirez	.03	.01	.00	☐ 255	Frank White	.06	.02	.00
☐ 203	Bob Walk	.03	.01	.00	☐ 256	Alfredo Griffin	.05	.02	.00
☐ 204	Roger Mason	.05	.02	.00	☐ 257	Floyd Youmans	.10	.04	.01
☐ 205	Terry Kennedy	.06	.02	.00	☐ 258	Rob Wilfong	.03	.01	.00
☐ 206	Ron Oester	.05	.02	.00	☐ 259	Pete O'Brien	.08	.03	.01
☐ 207	John Russell	.03	.01	.00	☐ 260	Tim Hulett	.05	.02	.00
☐ 208	Greg Mathews	.20	.08	.02	☐ 261	Dickie Thon	.05	.02	.00
☐ 209	Charlie Kerfeld	.10	.04	.01	☐ 262	Darren Daulton	.05	.02	.00
☐ 210	Reggie Jackson	.30	.12	.03	☐ 263	Vince Coleman	.30	.12	.03
☐ 211	Floyd Bannister	.05	.02	.00	☐ 264	Andy Hawkins	.03	.01	.00
☐ 212	Vance Law	.03	.01	.00	☐ 265	Eric Davis	.50	.20	.05
☐ 213	Rich Bordi	.03	.01	.00	☐ 266	Andres Thomas	.30	.12	.03
☐ 214	Dan Plesac	.20	.08	.02	☐ 267	Mike Diaz	.25	.10	.02
☐ 215	Dave Collins	.05	.02	.00	☐ 268	Chili Davis	.08	.03	.01

		MINT	VG-E	F-G			MINT	VG-E	F-G
☐ 269	Jody Davis	.07	.03	.01	☐ 322	Lee Guetterman	.12	.05	.01
☐ 270	Phil Bradley	.15	.06	.01	☐ 323	Sid Fernandez	.18	.08	.01
☐ 271	George Bell	.15	.06	.01	☐ 324	Jerry Mumphrey	.05	.02	.00
☐ 272	Keith Atherton	.03	.01	.00	☐ 325	David Palmer	.05	.02	.00
☐ 273	Storm Davis	.07	.03	.01	☐ 326	Bill Almon	.03	.01	.00
☐ 274	Rob Deer	.15	.06	.01	☐ 327	Candy Maldonado	.06	.02	.00
☐ 275	Walt Terrell	.03	.01	.00	☐ 328	John Kruk	.25	.10	.02
☐ 276	Roger Clemens	1.00	.40	.10	☐ 329	John Denny	.06	.02	.00
☐ 277	Mike Easler	.06	.02	.00	☐ 330	Milt Thompson	.05	.02	.00
☐ 278	Steve Sax	.12	.05	.01	☐ 331	Mike Lavalliere	.10	.04	.01
☐ 279	Andre Thornton	.06	.02	.00	☐ 332	Alan Ashby	.03	.01	.00
☐ 280	Jim Sundberg	.05	.02	.00	☐ 333	Doug Corbett	.03	.01	.00
☐ 281	Bill Bathe	.10	.04	.01	☐ 334	Ron Karkovice	.25	.10	.02
☐ 282	Jay Tibbs	.03	.01	.00	☐ 335	Mitch Webster	.08	.03	.01
☐ 283	Dick Schofield	.05	.02	.00	☐ 336	Lee Lacy	.05	.02	.00
☐ 284	Mike Mason	.03	.01	.00	☐ 337	Glenn Braggs	.45	.18	.04
☐ 285	Jerry Hairston	.03	.01	.00	☐ 338	Dwight Lowry	.15	.06	.01
☐ 286	Bill Doran	.07	.03	.01	☐ 339	Don Baylor	.10	.04	.01
☐ 287	Tim Flannery	.03	.01	.00	☐ 340	Brian Fisher	.05	.02	.00
☐ 288	Gary Redus	.05	.02	.00	☐ 341	Reggie Williams	.20	.08	.02
☐ 289	John Franco	.09	.04	.01	☐ 342	Tom Candiotti	.05	.02	.00
☐ 290	Paul Assenmacher	.10	.04	.01	☐ 343	Rudy Law	.03	.01	.00
☐ 291	Joe Orsulak	.03	.01	.00	☐ 344	Curt Young	.03	.01	.00
☐ 292	Lee Smith	.07	.03	.01	☐ 345	Mike Fitzgerald	.03	.01	.00
☐ 293	Mike Laga	.03	.01	.00	☐ 346	Ruben Sierra	1.00	.40	.10
☐ 294	Rick Dempsey	.05	.02	.00	☐ 347	Mitch Williams	.25	.10	.02
☐ 295	Mike Felder	.06	.02	.00	☐ 348	Jorge Orta	.03	.01	.00
☐ 296	Tom Brookens	.03	.01	.00	☐ 349	Mickey Tettleton	.03	.01	.00
☐ 297	Al Nipper	.03	.01	.00	☐ 350	Ernie Camacho	.03	.01	.00
☐ 298	Mike Pagliarulo	.15	.06	.01	☐ 351	Ron Kittle	.08	.03	.01
☐ 299	Franklin Stubbs	.10	.04	.01	☐ 352	Ken Landreaux	.03	.01	.00
☐ 300	Checklist	.06	.01	.00	☐ 353	Chet Lemon	.05	.02	.00
☐ 301	Steve Farr	.03	.01	.00	☐ 354	John Shelby	.03	.01	.00
☐ 302	Bill Mooneyham	.10	.04	.01	☐ 355	Mark Clear	.03	.01	.00
☐ 303	Andres Galarraga	.08	.03	.01	☐ 356	Doug DeCinces	.07	.03	.01
☐ 304	Scott Fletcher	.05	.02	.00	☐ 357	Ken Dayley	.03	.01	.00
☐ 305	Jack Howell	.05	.02	.00	☐ 358	Phil Garner	.05	.02	.00
☐ 306	Russ Morman	.25	.10	.02	☐ 359	Steve Jeltz	.03	.01	.00
☐ 307	Todd Worrell	.20	.08	.02	☐ 360	Ed Whitson	.03	.01	.00
☐ 308	Dave Smith	.06	.02	.00	☐ 361	Barry Bonds	.35	.14	.03
☐ 309	Jeff Stone	.05	.02	.00	☐ 362	Vida Blue	.07	.03	.01
☐ 310	Ron Robinson	.03	.01	.00	☐ 363	Cecil Cooper	.09	.04	.01
☐ 311	Bruce Bochy	.03	.01	.00	☐ 364	Bob Ojeda	.08	.03	.01
☐ 312	Jim Winn	.03	.01	.00	☐ 365	Dennis Eckersley	.05	.02	.00
☐ 313	Mark Davis	.03	.01	.00	☐ 366	Mike Morgan	.03	.01	.00
☐ 314	Jeff Dedmon	.03	.01	.00	☐ 367	Willie Upshaw	.07	.03	.01
☐ 315	Jamie Moyer	.15	.06	.01	☐ 368	Allan Anderson	.15	.06	.01
☐ 316	Wally Backman	.07	.03	.01	☐ 369	Bob Gullickson	.05	.02	.00
☐ 317	Ken Phelps	.05	.02	.00	☐ 370	Bobby Thigpen	.18	.08	.01
☐ 318	Steve Lombardozzi	.06	.02	.00	☐ 371	Juan Beniquez	.05	.02	.00
☐ 319	Rance Mulliniks	.03	.01	.00	☐ 372	Charlie Moore	.03	.01	.00
☐ 320	Tim Laudner	.03	.01	.00	☐ 373	Dan Petry	.09	.04	.01
☐ 321	Mark Eichhorn	.30	.12	.03	☐ 374	Rod Scurry	.03	.01	.00

		MINT	VG-E	F-G			MINT	VG-E	F-G
☐ 375	Tom Seaver	.25	.10	.02	☐ 428	Ruppert Jones	.03	.01	.00
☐ 376	Ed VandeBerg	.03	.01	.00	☐ 429	Harold Baines	.15	.06	.01
☐ 377	Tony Bernazard	.05	.02	.00	☐ 430	Pat Perry	.03	.01	.00
☐ 378	Greg Pryor	.03	.01	.00	☐ 431	Terry Puhl	.05	.02	.00
☐ 379	Dwayne Murphy	.05	.02	.00	☐ 432	Don Carman	.05	.02	.00
☐ 380	Andy McGaffigan	.03	.01	.00	☐ 433	Eddie Milner	.05	.02	.00
☐ 381	Kirk McCaskill	.10	.04	.01	☐ 434	LaMarr Hoyt	.05	.02	.00
☐ 382	Greg Harris	.05	.02	.00	☐ 435	Rick Rhoden	.06	.02	.00
☐ 383	Rich Dotson	.05	.02	.00	☐ 436	Jose Uribe	.03	.01	.00
☐ 384	Craig Reynolds	.03	.01	.00	☐ 437	Ken Oberkfell	.03	.01	.00
☐ 385	Greg Gross	.03	.01	.00	☐ 438	Ron Davis	.03	.01	.00
☐ 386	Tito Landrum	.03	.01	.00	☐ 439	Jesse Orosco	.05	.02	.00
☐ 387	Craig Lefferts	.03	.01	.00	☐ 440	Scott Bradley	.06	.02	.00
☐ 388	Dave Parker	.15	.06	.01	☐ 441	Randy Bush	.03	.01	.00
☐ 389	Bob Horner	.15	.06	.01	☐ 442	John Cerutti	.20	.08	.02
☐ 390	Pat Clements	.03	.01	.00	☐ 443	Roy Smalley	.05	.02	.00
☐ 391	Jeff Leonard	.06	.02	.00	☐ 444	Kelly Gruber	.03	.01	.00
☐ 392	Chris Speier	.03	.01	.00	☐ 445	Bob Kearney	.03	.01	.00
☐ 393	John Moses	.15	.06	.01	☐ 446	Ed Hearn	.10	.04	.01
☐ 394	Garth Iorg	.03	.01	.00	☐ 447	Scott Sanderson	.03	.01	.00
☐ 395	Greg Gagne	.05	.02	.00	☐ 448	Bruce Benedict	.03	.01	.00
☐ 396	Nate Snell	.03	.01	.00	☐ 449	Junior Ortiz	.03	.01	.00
☐ 397	Bryan Clutterbuck	.10	.04	.01	☐ 450	Mike Aldrete	.12	.05	.01
☐ 398	Darrell Evans	.08	.03	.01	☐ 451	Kevin McReynolds	.12	.05	.01
☐ 399	Steve Crawford	.03	.01	.00	☐ 452	Rob Murphy	.15	.06	.01
☐ 400	Checklist	.06	.01	.00	☐ 453	Kent Tekulve	.05	.02	.00
☐ 401	Phil Lombardi	.25	.10	.02	☐ 454	Curt Ford	.25	.10	.02
☐ 402	Rick Honeycutt	.05	.02	.00	☐ 455	Davey Lopes	.06	.02	.00
☐ 403	Ken Schrom	.05	.02	.00	☐ 456	Bobby Grich	.06	.02	.00
☐ 404	Bud Black	.03	.01	.00	☐ 457	Jose DeLeon	.05	.02	.00
☐ 405	Donnie Hill	.03	.01	.00	☐ 458	Andre Dawson	.15	.06	.01
☐ 406	Wayne Krenchicki	.03	.01	.00	☐ 459	Mike Flanagan	.07	.03	.01
☐ 407	Chuck Finley	.10	.04	.01	☐ 460	Joey Meyer	.25	.10	.02
☐ 408	Toby Harrah	.05	.02	.00	☐ 461	Chuck Cary	.20	.08	.02
☐ 409	Steve Lyons	.03	.01	.00	☐ 462	Bill Buckner	.08	.03	.01
☐ 410	Kevin Bass	.07	.03	.01	☐ 463	Bob Shirley	.03	.01	.00
☐ 411	Marvell Wynne	.03	.01	.00	☐ 464	Jeff Hamilton	.15	.06	.01
☐ 412	Ron Roenicke	.03	.01	.00	☐ 465	Phil Niekro	.15	.06	.01
☐ 413	Tracy Jones	.25	.10	.02	☐ 466	Mark Gubicza	.06	.02	.00
☐ 414	Gene Garber	.03	.01	.00	☐ 467	Jerry Willard	.03	.01	.00
☐ 415	Mike Bielecki	.03	.01	.00	☐ 468	Bob Sebra	.10	.04	.01
☐ 416	Frank DiPino	.03	.01	.00	☐ 469	Larry Parrish	.05	.02	.00
☐ 417	Andy Van Slyke	.05	.02	.00	☐ 470	Charlie Hough	.06	.02	.00
☐ 418	Jim Dwyer	.03	.01	.00	☐ 471	Hal McRae	.05	.02	.00
☐ 419	Ben Oglivie	.06	.02	.00	☐ 472	Dave Leiper	.05	.02	.00
☐ 420	Dave Bergman	.03	.01	.00	☐ 473	Mel Hall	.07	.03	.01
☐ 421	Joe Sambito	.05	.02	.00	☐ 474	Dan Pasqua	.12	.05	.01
☐ 422	Bob Tewksbury	.20	.08	.02	☐ 475	Bob Welch	.06	.02	.00
☐ 423	Len Matuszek	.03	.01	.00	☐ 476	Johnny Grubb	.03	.01	.00
☐ 424	Mike Kingery	.15	.06	.01	☐ 477	Jim Traber	.09	.04	.01
☐ 425	Dave Kingman	.10	.04	.01	☐ 478	Chris Bosio	.10	.04	.01
☐ 426	Al Newman	.10	.04	.01	☐ 479	Mark McLemore	.06	.02	.00
☐ 427	Gary Ward	.06	.02	.00	☐ 480	John Morris	.03	.01	.00

		MINT	VG-E	F-G			MINT	VG-E	F-G
☐ 481	Billy Hatcher	.05	.02	.00	☐ 534	Jerry Royster	.03	.01	.00
☐ 482	Dan Schatzeder	.03	.01	.00	☐ 535	Mike Maddux	.07	.03	.01
☐ 483	Rich Gossage	.12	.05	.01	☐ 536	Ted Power	.07	.03	.01
☐ 484	Jim Morrison	.03	.01	.00	☐ 537	Ted Simmons	.09	.04	.01
☐ 485	Bob Brenly	.05	.02	.00	☐ 538	Rafael Belliard	.10	.04	.01
☐ 486	Bill Schroeder	.03	.01	.00	☐ 539	Chico Walker	.15	.06	.01
☐ 487	Mookie Wilson	.06	.02	.00	☐ 540	Bob Forsch	.05	.02	.00
☐ 488	Dave Martinez	.18	.08	.01	☐ 541	John Stefero	.03	.01	.00
☐ 489	Harold Reynolds	.03	.01	.00	☐ 542	Dale Sveum	.12	.05	.01
☐ 490	Jeff Hearron	.10	.04	.01	☐ 543	Mark Thurmond	.03	.01	.00
☐ 491	Mickey Hatcher	.03	.01	.00	☐ 544	Jeff Sellers	.12	.05	.01
☐ 492	Barry Larkin	.50	.20	.05	☐ 545	Joel Skinner	.05	.02	.00
☐ 493	Bob James	.03	.01	.00	☐ 546	Alex Trevino	.03	.01	.00
☐ 494	John Habyan	.03	.01	.00	☐ 547	Randy Kutcher	.10	.04	.01
☐ 495	Jim Adduci	.15	.06	.01	☐ 548	Joaquin Andujar	.08	.03	.01
☐ 496	Mike Heath	.03	.01	.00	☐ 549	Casey Candaele	.10	.04	.01
☐ 497	Tim Stoddard	.03	.01	.00	☐ 550	Jeff Russell	.03	.01	.00
☐ 498	Tony Armas	.08	.03	.01	☐ 551	John Candelaria	.07	.03	.01
☐ 499	Dennis Powell	.10	.04	.01	☐ 552	Joe Cowley	.05	.02	.00
☐ 500	Checklist	.06	.01	.00	☐ 553	Danny Cox	.05	.02	.00
☐ 501	Chris Bando	.03	.01	.00	☐ 554	Denny Walling	.03	.01	.00
☐ 502	Dave Cone	.10	.04	.01	☐ 555	Bruce Ruffin	.30	.12	.03
☐ 503	Jay Howell	.05	.02	.00	☐ 556	Buddy Bell	.09	.04	.01
☐ 504	Tom Foley	.03	.01	.00	☐ 557	Jimmy Jones	.20	.08	.02
☐ 505	Ray Chadwick	.10	.04	.01	☐ 558	Bobby Bonilla	.15	.06	.01
☐ 506	Mike Loynd	.25	.10	.02	☐ 559	Jeff Robinson	.03	.01	.00
☐ 507	Neil Allen	.05	.02	.00	☐ 560	Ed Olwine	.10	.04	.01
☐ 508	Danny Darwin	.03	.01	.00	☐ 561	Glenallen Hill	.35	.14	.03
☐ 509	Rick Schu	.03	.01	.00	☐ 562	Lee Mazzilli	.05	.02	.00
☐ 510	Jose Oquendo	.03	.01	.00	☐ 563	Mike Brown	.03	.01	.00
☐ 511	Gene Walter	.05	.02	.00	☐ 564	George Frazier	.03	.01	.00
☐ 512	Terry McGriff	.10	.04	.01	☐ 565	Mike Sharperson	.10	.04	.01
☐ 513	Ken Griffey	.06	.02	.00	☐ 566	Mark Portugal	.10	.04	.01
☐ 514	Benny Distefano	.03	.01	.00	☐ 567	Rick Leach	.03	.01	.00
☐ 515	Terry Mulholland	.10	.04	.01	☐ 568	Mark Langston	.07	.03	.01
☐ 516	Ed Lynch	.03	.01	.00	☐ 569	Rafael Santana	.03	.01	.00
☐ 517	Bill Swift	.03	.01	.00	☐ 570	Manny Trillo	.05	.02	.00
☐ 518	Manny Lee	.05	.02	.00	☐ 571	Cliff Speck	.09	.04	.01
☐ 519	Andre David	.03	.01	.00	☐ 572	Bob Kipper	.03	.01	.00
☐ 520	Scott McGregor	.07	.03	.01	☐ 573	Kelly Downs	.10	.04	.01
☐ 521	Rick Manning	.03	.01	.00	☐ 574	Randy Asadoor	.15	.06	.01
☐ 522	Willie Hernandez	.09	.04	.01	☐ 575	Dave Magadan	.50	.20	.05
☐ 523	Marty Barrett	.10	.04	.01	☐ 576	Marvin Freeman	.25	.10	.02
☐ 524	Wayne Tolleson	.03	.01	.00	☐ 577	Jeff Lahti	.03	.01	.00
☐ 525	Jose Gonzalez	.30	.12	.03	☐ 578	Jeff Calhoun	.05	.02	.00
☐ 526	Cory Snyder	.60	.24	.06	☐ 579	Gus Polidor	.08	.03	.01
☐ 527	Buddy Biancalana	.03	.01	.00	☐ 580	Gene Nelson	.03	.01	.00
☐ 528	Moose Haas	.03	.01	.00	☐ 581	Tim Teufel	.05	.02	.00
☐ 529	Wilfredo Tejada	.10	.04	.01	☐ 582	Odell Jones	.03	.01	.00
☐ 530	Stu Cliburn	.03	.01	.00	☐ 583	Mark Ryal	.10	.04	.01
☐ 531	Dale Mohorcic	.15	.06	.01	☐ 584	Randy O'Neal	.03	.01	.00
☐ 532	Ron Hassey	.03	.01	.00	☐ 585	Mike Greenwell	.15	.06	.01
☐ 533	Ty Gainey	.03	.01	.00	☐ 586	Ray Knight	.07	.03	.01

		MINT	VG-E	F-G
☐ 587	Ralph Bryant	.25	.10	.02
☐ 588	Carmen Castillo	.03	.01	.00
☐ 589	Ed Wojna	.03	.01	.00
☐ 590	Stan Javier	.05	.02	.00
☐ 591	Jeff Musselman	.10	.04	.01
☐ 592	Mike Stanley	.10	.04	.01
☐ 593	Darrell Porter	.05	.02	.00
☐ 594	Drew Hall	.12	.05	.01
☐ 595	Rob Nelson	.15	.06	.01
☐ 596	Bryan Oelkers	.03	.01	.00
☐ 597	Scott Nielsen	.15	.06	.01
☐ 598	Brian Holton	.10	.04	.01
☐ 599	Kevin Mitchell	.35	.14	.03
☐ 600	Checklist	.06	.01	.00
☐ 601	Jackie Gutierrez	.03	.01	.00
☐ 602	Barry Jones	.12	.05	.01
☐ 603	Jerry Narron	.03	.01	.00
☐ 604	Steve Lake	.03	.01	.00
☐ 605	Jim Pankovits	.03	.01	.00
☐ 606	Ed Romero	.03	.01	.00
☐ 607	Dave LaPoint	.03	.01	.00
☐ 608	Don Robinson	.03	.01	.00
☐ 609	Mike Krukow	.07	.03	.01
☐ 610	Dave Valle	.03	.01	.00
☐ 611	Len Dykstra	.20	.08	.02
☐ 612	Roberto Clemente	.07	.03	.01
	Puzzle Card			
☐ 613	Mike Trujillo	.05	.02	.00
☐ 614	Damaso Garcia	.06	.02	.00
☐ 615	Neal Heaton	.03	.01	.00
☐ 616	Juan Berenguer	.03	.01	.00
☐ 617	Steve Carlton	.25	.10	.02
☐ 618	Gary Lucas	.03	.01	.00
☐ 619	Geno Petralli	.03	.01	.00
☐ 620	Rick Aguilera	.05	.02	.00
☐ 621	Fred McGriff	.10	.04	.01
☐ 622	Dave Henderson	.06	.02	.00
☐ 623	Dave Clark	.20	.08	.02
☐ 624	Angel Salazar	.03	.01	.00
☐ 625	Randy Hunt	.03	.01	.00
☐ 626	John Gibbons	.03	.01	.00
☐ 627	Kevin Brown	.20	.08	.02
☐ 628	Bill Dawley	.03	.01	.00
☐ 629	Aurelio Lopez	.03	.01	.00
☐ 630	Charlie Hudson	.05	.02	.00
☐ 631	Ray Soff	.09	.04	.01
☐ 632	Ray Hayward	.10	.04	.01
☐ 633	Spike Owen	.05	.02	.00
☐ 634	Glenn Hubbard	.03	.01	.00
☐ 635	Kevin Elster	.20	.08	.02
☐ 636	Mike LaCoss	.03	.01	.00
☐ 637	Dwayne Henry	.10	.04	.01
☐ 638	Rey Quinones	.10	.04	.01

		MINT	VG-E	F-G
☐ 639	Jim Clancy	.03	.01	.00
☐ 640	Larry Andersen	.03	.01	.00
☐ 641	Calvin Schiraldi	.08	.03	.01
☐ 642	Stan Jefferson	.15	.06	.01
☐ 643	Marc Sullivan	.03	.01	.00
☐ 644	Mark Grant	.03	.01	.00
☐ 645	Cliff Johnson	.03	.01	.00
☐ 646	Howard Johnson	.03	.01	.00
☐ 647	Dave Sax	.03	.01	.00
☐ 648	Dave Stewart	.03	.01	.00
☐ 649	Danny Heep	.03	.01	.00
☐ 650	Joe Johnson	.03	.01	.00
☐ 651	Bob Brower	.25	.10	.02
☐ 652	Rob Woodward	.05	.02	.00
☐ 653	John Mizerock	.03	.01	.00
☐ 654	Tim Pyznarski	.18	.08	.01
☐ 655	Luis Aquino	.09	.04	.01
☐ 656	Mickey Brantley	.12	.05	.01
☐ 657	Doyle Alexander	.05	.02	.00
☐ 658	Sammy Stewart	.03	.01	.00
☐ 659	Jim Acker	.03	.01	.00
☐ 660	Pete Ladd	.03	.01	.00
☐ PC	10 Dale Murphy	.50	.20	.05
	(wax box card)			
☐ PC	11 Jeff Reardon	.10	.04	.01
	(wax box card)			
☐ PC	12 Jose Canseco	.75	.30	.07
	(wax box card)			
☐ PUZ	Clemente Puzzle	.08	.03	.01
	(wax box card)			

1959 Fleer

The cards in this 80-card set measure 2¹/₂" by 3¹/₂". The 1959 Fleer set, designated as R418-1 in the ACC, portrays the life of Ted

Williams. The wording of the wrapper, "Baseball's Greatest Series," has led to speculation that Fleer contemplated similar sets honoring other baseball immortals, but chose to develop instead the format of the 1960 and 1961 issues. Card number 68, which was withdrawn early in production, is considered scarce and has even been counterfeited; the fake has a rosy coloration and a cross-hatch pattern visible over the picture area.

		MINT	VG-E	F-G
	Complete Set	175.00	70.00	18.00
	Common Cards	.90	.36	.09
☐ 1	The Early Years	5.00	1.00	.20
☐ 2	Ted's Idol Babe Ruth	3.00	1.20	.30
☐ 3	Practice Makes Perfect .	.90	.36	.09
☐ 4	Learns Fine Points	.90	.36	.09
☐ 5	Ted's Fame Spreads	.90	.36	.09
☐ 6	Ted Turns Pro	.90	.36	.09
☐ 7	From Mound to Plate ...	.90	.36	.09
☐ 8	1937 First Full Season .	.90	.36	.09
☐ 9	First Step to Majors	.90	.36	.09
☐ 10	Gunning as Pasttime ...	.90	.36	.09
☐ 11	First Spring Training .... (with Jimmie Foxx)	1.50	.60	.15
☐ 12	Burning Up Minors	.90	.36	.09
☐ 13	1939 Shows Will Stay ...	.90	.36	.09
☐ 14	Outstanding Rookie '39 .	.90	.36	.09
☐ 15	Licks Sophomore Jinx ..	.90	.36	.09
☐ 16	1941 Greatest Year	.90	.36	.09
☐ 17	How Ted Hit .400	.90	.36	.09
☐ 18	1941 All Star Hero	.90	.36	.09
☐ 19	Ted Wins Triple Crown ..	.90	.36	.09
☐ 20	On to Naval Training ...	.90	.36	.09
☐ 21	Honors for Williams	.90	.36	.09
☐ 22	1944 Ted Solos	.90	.36	.09
☐ 23	Williams Wins Wings	.90	.36	.09
☐ 24	1945 Sharpshooter	.90	.36	.09
☐ 25	1945 Ted Discharged ...	.90	.36	.09
☐ 26	Off to Flying Start	.90	.36	.09
☐ 27	7/9/46 One Man Show ..	.90	.36	.09
☐ 28	The Williams Shift	.90	.36	.09
☐ 29	Ted Hits for Cycle	.90	.36	.09
☐ 30	Beating Williams Shift ..	.90	.36	.09
☐ 31	Sox Lose Series	.90	.36	.09
☐ 32	Most Valuable Player ...	.90	.36	.09
☐ 33	Another Triple Crown ...	.90	.36	.09
☐ 34	Runs Scored Record ...	.90	.36	.09
☐ 35	Sox Miss Pennant	.90	.36	.09

		MINT	VG-E	F-G
☐ 36	Banner Year for Ted	.90	.36	.09
☐ 37	1949 Sox Miss Again ...	.90	.36	.09
☐ 38	1949 Power Rampage .	.90	.36	.09
☐ 39	1950 Great Start	.90	.36	.09
☐ 40	Ted Crashes into Wall ...	.90	.36	.09
☐ 41	1950 Ted Recovers	.90	.36	.09
☐ 42	Slowed by Injury	.90	.36	.09
☐ 43	Double Play Lead	.90	.36	.09
☐ 44	Back to Marines	.90	.36	.09
☐ 45	Farewell to Baseball? ..	.90	.36	.09
☐ 46	Ready for Combat	.90	.36	.09
☐ 47	Ted Crash Lands Jet ...	.90	.36	.09
☐ 48	1953 Ted Returns	.90	.36	.09
☐ 49	Smash Return	.90	.36	.09
☐ 50	1954 Spring Injury	.90	.36	.09
☐ 51	Ted is Patched Up	.90	.36	.09
☐ 52	1954 Ted's Comeback .	.90	.36	.09
☐ 53	Comeback is Success ..	.90	.36	.09
☐ 54	Ted Hooks Big One	.90	.36	.09
☐ 55	Retirement "No Go"	.90	.36	.09
☐ 56	2000th Hit	.90	.36	.09
☐ 57	400th Homer	.90	.36	.09
☐ 58	Williams Hits .388	.90	.36	.09
☐ 59	Hot September for Ted .	.90	.36	.09
☐ 60	More Records for Ted ...	.90	.36	.09
☐ 61	1957 Outfielder Ted	.90	.36	.09
☐ 62	1958 6th Batting Title ...	.90	.36	.09
☐ 63	Ted's All-Star Record ...	.90	.36	.09
☐ 64	Daughter and Daddy	.90	.36	.09
☐ 65	1958 August 30	.90	.36	.09
☐ 66	1958 Powerhouse	.90	.36	.09
☐ 67	Two Famous Fishermen	1.50	.60	.15
☐ 68	Ted Signs for 1959	120.00	50.00	12.00
☐ 69	A Future Ted Williams? .	.90	.36	.09
☐ 70	Williams and Thorpe ...	2.00	.80	.20
☐ 71	Hitting Fund. 1	.90	.36	.09
☐ 72	Hitting Fund. 2	.90	.36	.09
☐ 73	Hitting Fund. 3	.90	.36	.09
☐ 74	Here's How	.90	.36	.09
☐ 75	Williams' Value to Sox ..	.90	.36	.09
☐ 76	On Base Record	.90	.36	.09
☐ 77	Ted Relaxes	.90	.36	.09
☐ 78	Honors for Williams	.90	.36	.09
☐ 79	Where Ted Stands	.90	.36	.09
☐ 80	Ted's Goals for 1959	1.50	.50	.10

1960 Fleer

The cards in this 79-card set measure 2¹/₂" by 3¹/₂". The cards from the 1960 Fleer series of Baseball Greats are sometimes mistaken for 1930s cards by collectors not familiar with this set. The cards each contain a tinted photo of a baseball immortal, and were issued in one series. There are no known scarcities, although a number 80 card (Pepper Martin reverse with either a Tinker, Collins, or Grove obverse) exists (this is not considered part of the set). The catalog designation for 1960 Fleer is R418-2.

	MINT	VG-E	F-G
Complete Set (79)	120.00	50.00	12.00
Common Player (1-79) ..	.80	.32	.08

		MINT	VG-E	F-G
☐ 1	Napoleon Lajoie	5.00	.60	.10
☐ 2	Christy Mathewson	2.50	1.00	.25
☐ 3	George H. Ruth	15.00	6.00	1.50
☐ 4	Carl Hubbell	1.25	.50	.12
☐ 5	Grover Alexander	1.50	.60	.15
☐ 6	Walter P. Johnson	3.00	1.20	.30
☐ 7	Charles A. Bender	.80	.32	.08
☐ 8	Roger P. Bresnahan	.80	.32	.08
☐ 9	Mordecai P. Brown	.80	.32	.08
☐ 10	Tristram Speaker	1.50	.60	.15
☐ 11	Joseph (Arky) Vaughan ..	.80	.32	.08
☐ 12	Zachariah Wheat	.80	.32	.08
☐ 13	George Sisler	1.00	.40	.10
☐ 14	Connie Mack	1.25	.50	.12
☐ 15	Clark C. Griffith	.80	.32	.08
☐ 16	Louis Boudreau	1.25	.50	.12
☐ 17	Ernest Lombardi	.80	.32	.08

		MINT	VG-E	F-G
☐ 18	Henry Manush	.80	.32	.08
☐ 19	Martin Marion	.80	.32	.08
☐ 20	Edward Collins	.80	.32	.08
☐ 21	James Maranville	.80	.32	.08
☐ 22	Joseph Medwick	.80	.32	.08
☐ 23	Edward Barrow	.80	.32	.08
☐ 24	Gordon Cochrane	1.00	.40	.10
☐ 25	James J. Collins	.80	.32	.08
☐ 26	Robert Feller	3.50	1.40	.35
☐ 27	Lucius Appling	1.25	.50	.12
☐ 28	Lou Gehrig	8.00	3.25	.80
☐ 29	Charles Hartnett	.80	.32	.08
☐ 30	Charles Klein	.80	.32	.08
☐ 31	Anthony Lazzeri	.80	.32	.08
☐ 32	Aloysius Simmons	.80	.32	.08
☐ 33	Wilbert Robinson	.80	.32	.08
☐ 34	Edgar Rice	.80	.32	.08
☐ 35	Herbert Pennock	.80	.32	.08
☐ 36	Melvin Ott	1.25	.50	.12
☐ 37	Frank O'Doul	.80	.32	.08
☐ 38	John Mize	1.25	.50	.12
☐ 39	Edmund Miller	.80	.32	.08
☐ 40	Joseph Tinker	.80	.32	.08
☐ 41	John Baker	.80	.32	.08
☐ 42	Tyrus Cobb	9.00	3.75	.90
☐ 43	Paul Derringer	.80	.32	.08
☐ 44	Adrian Anson	1.00	.40	.10
☐ 45	James Bottomley	.80	.32	.08
☐ 46	Edward S. Plank	1.00	.40	.10
☐ 47	Denton (Cy) Young ...	2.00	.80	.20
☐ 48	Hack Wilson	1.00	.40	.10
☐ 49	Edward Walsh	.80	.32	.08
☐ 50	Frank Chance	.80	.32	.08
☐ 51	Arthur Vance	.80	.32	.08
☐ 52	William Terry	1.00	.40	.10
☐ 53	James Foxx	2.00	.80	.20
☐ 54	Vernon Gomez	1.25	.50	.12
☐ 55	Branch Rickey	.80	.32	.08
☐ 56	Raymond Schalk	.80	.32	.08
☐ 57	John Evers	.80	.32	.08
☐ 58	Charles Gehringer	1.00	.40	.10
☐ 59	Burleigh Grimes	.80	.32	.08
☐ 60	Robert (Lefty) Grove ..	1.50	.60	.15
☐ 61	George Waddell	.80	.32	.08
☐ 62	John (Honus) Wagner ..	3.00	1.20	.30
☐ 63	Charles (Red) Ruffing ...	.80	.32	.08
☐ 64	Kenesaw M. Landis ...	.80	.32	.08
☐ 65	Harry Heilmann	.80	.32	.08
☐ 66	John McGraw	1.00	.40	.10
☐ 67	Hugh Jennings	.80	.32	.08
☐ 68	Harold Newhouser	.80	.32	.08
☐ 69	Waite Hoyt	.80	.32	.08
☐ 70	Louis (Bobo) Newsom ..	.80	.32	.08

		MINT	VG-E	F-G
☐ 71	Howard (Earl) Averill ...	.80	.32	.08
☐ 72	Theodore Williams	9.00	3.75	.90
☐ 73	Warren Giles	.80	.32	.08
☐ 74	Ford Frick	.80	.32	.08
☐ 75	Hazen (Kiki) Cuyler	.80	.32	.08
☐ 76	Paul Waner	.80	.32	.08
☐ 77	Harold (Pie) Traynor	1.00	.40	.10
☐ 78	Lloyd Waner	.80	.32	.08
☐ 79	Ralph Kiner	1.50	.60	.15
☐ 80	Pepper Martin *	75.00	30.00	7.50
	(Collins, Tinker or Grove pictured)			

1961 Fleer

The cards in this 154-card set measure 2½"
by 3½". In 1961, Fleer continued its Baseball
Greats format by issuing this series of cards.
The set was released in two distinct series, 1-
88 and 89-154 (of which the last is more difficult to obtain). The players within each series
are conveniently numbered in alphabetical
order. It appears that this set continued to be
issued the following year by Fleer. The catalog number is F418-3.

		MINT	VG-E	F-G
	Complete Set	275.00	110.00	27.00
	Common Player (1-88) ..	.80	.32	.08
	Common Player (89-154)	2.00	.80	.20
☐ 1	Baker/Cobb/Wheat ..... (checklist back)	7.50	1.00	.20
☐ 2	Grover C. Alexander ...	1.25	.50	.12
☐ 3	Nick Altrock	.80	.32	.08
☐ 4	Cap Anson	1.00	.40	.10

		MINT	VG-E	F-G
☐ 5	Earl Averill	.80	.32	.08
☐ 6	Frank Baker	.80	.32	.08
☐ 7	Dave Bancroft	.80	.32	.08
☐ 8	Chief Bender	.80	.32	.08
☐ 9	Jim Bottomley	.80	.32	.08
☐ 10	Roger Bresnahan	.80	.32	.08
☐ 11	Mordecai Brown	.80	.32	.08
☐ 12	Max Carey	.80	.32	.08
☐ 13	Jack Chesbro	.80	.32	.08
☐ 14	Ty Cobb	9.00	3.75	.90
☐ 15	Mickey Cochrane	1.00	.40	.10
☐ 16	Eddie Collins	.80	.32	.08
☐ 17	Earle Combs	.80	.32	.08
☐ 18	Charles Comiskey	.80	.32	.08
☐ 19	Kiki Cuyler	.80	.32	.08
☐ 20	Paul Derringer	.80	.32	.08
☐ 21	Howard Ehmke	.80	.32	.08
☐ 22	W. Evans	.80	.32	.08
☐ 23	Johnny Evers	.80	.32	.08
☐ 24	Urban Faber	.80	.32	.08
☐ 25	Bob Feller	3.50	1.40	.35
☐ 26	Wes Ferrell	.80	.32	.08
☐ 27	Lew Fonseca	.80	.32	.08
☐ 28	Jimmy Foxx	2.00	.80	.20
☐ 29	Ford Frick	.80	.32	.08
☐ 30	Frank Frisch	1.00	.40	.10
☐ 31	Lou Gehrig	8.00	3.25	.80
☐ 32	Charlie Gehringer	1.00	.40	.10
☐ 33	Warren Giles	.80	.32	.08
☐ 34	Lefty Gomez	1.25	.50	.12
☐ 35	Goose Goslin	.80	.32	.08
☐ 36	Clark Griffith	.80	.32	.08
☐ 37	Burleigh Grimes	.80	.32	.08
☐ 38	Lefty Grove	1.50	.60	.15
☐ 39	Chick Haley	.80	.32	.08
☐ 40	Jesse Haines	.80	.32	.08
☐ 41	Gabby Hartnett	.80	.32	.08
☐ 42	Harry Heilmann	.80	.32	.08
☐ 43	Rogers Hornsby	2.00	.80	.20
☐ 44	Waite Hoyt	.80	.32	.08
☐ 45	Carl Hubbell	1.25	.50	.12
☐ 46	Miller Huggins	.80	.32	.08
☐ 47	Hugh Jennings	.80	.32	.08
☐ 48	Ban Johnson	.80	.32	.08
☐ 49	Walter Johnson	3.00	1.20	.30
☐ 50	Ralph Kiner	1.50	.60	.15
☐ 51	Chuck Klein	.80	.32	.08
☐ 52	Johnny Kling	.80	.32	.08
☐ 53	K.M. Landis	.80	.32	.08
☐ 54	Tony Lazzeri	.80	.32	.08
☐ 55	Ernie Lombardi	.80	.32	.08
☐ 56	Dolf Luque	.80	.32	.08
☐ 57	Heine Manush	.80	.32	.08

		MINT	VG-E	F-G
☐ 58	Marty Marion	.80	.32	.08
☐ 59	Christy Mathewson	2.50	1.00	.25
☐ 60	John McGraw	1.00	.40	.10
☐ 61	Joe Medwick	.80	.32	.08
☐ 62	E. (Bing) Miller	.80	.32	.08
☐ 63	Johnny Mize	1.50	.60	.15
☐ 64	John Mostil	.80	.32	.08
☐ 65	Art Nehf	.80	.32	.08
☐ 66	Hal Newhouser	.80	.32	.08
☐ 67	D. (Bobo) Newsom	.80	.32	.08
☐ 68	Mel Ott	1.25	.50	.12
☐ 69	Allie Reynolds	.80	.32	.08
☐ 70	Sam Rice	.80	.32	.08
☐ 71	Eppa Rixey	.80	.32	.08
☐ 72	Edd Roush	.80	.32	.08
☐ 73	Schoolboy Rowe	.80	.32	.08
☐ 74	Red Ruffing	.80	.32	.08
☐ 75	Babe Ruth	15.00	6.00	1.50
☐ 76	Joe Sewell	.80	.32	.08
☐ 77	Al Simmons	.80	.32	.08
☐ 78	George Sisler	1.00	.40	.10
☐ 79	Tris Speaker	1.50	.60	.15
☐ 80	Fred Toney	.80	.32	.08
☐ 81	Dazzy Vance	.80	.32	.08
☐ 82	Jim Vaughn	.80	.32	.08
☐ 83	Ed Walsh	.80	.32	.08
☐ 84	Lloyd Waner	.80	.32	.08
☐ 85	Paul Waner	.80	.32	.08
☐ 86	Zack Wheat	.80	.32	.08
☐ 87	Hack Wilson	1.00	.40	.10
☐ 88	Jimmy Wilson	.80	.32	.08
☐ 89	Sisler and Traynor (checklist back)	7.50	1.00	.20
☐ 90	Babe Adams	2.00	.80	.20
☐ 91	Dale Alexander	2.00	.80	.20
☐ 92	Jim Bagby	2.00	.80	.20
☐ 93	Ossie Bluege	2.00	.80	.20
☐ 94	Lou Boudreau	3.50	1.40	.35
☐ 95	Tom Bridges	2.00	.80	.20
☐ 96	Donie Bush	2.00	.80	.20
☐ 97	Dolph Camilli	2.00	.80	.20
☐ 98	Frank Chance	3.00	1.20	.30
☐ 99	Jimmy Collins	3.00	1.20	.30
☐ 100	Stan Coveleskie	3.00	1.20	.30
☐ 101	Hugh Critz	2.00	.80	.20
☐ 102	Alvin Crowder	2.00	.80	.20
☐ 103	Joe Dugan	2.00	.80	.20
☐ 104	Bibb Falk	2.00	.80	.20
☐ 105	Rick Ferrell	3.00	1.20	.30
☐ 106	Art Fletcher	2.00	.80	.20
☐ 107	Dennis Galehouse	2.00	.80	.20
☐ 108	Chick Galloway	2.00	.80	.20
☐ 109	Mule Haas	2.00	.80	.20
☐ 110	Stan Hack	2.00	.80	.20
☐ 111	Bump Hadley	2.00	.80	.20
☐ 112	Billy B. Hamilton	3.00	1.20	.30
☐ 113	Joe Hauser	2.00	.80	.20
☐ 114	Babe Herman	2.00	.80	.20
☐ 115	Travis Jackson	3.00	1.20	.30
☐ 116	Eddie Joost	2.00	.80	.20
☐ 117	Addie Joss	3.50	1.40	.35
☐ 118	Joe Judge	2.00	.80	.20
☐ 119	Joe Kuhel	2.00	.80	.20
☐ 120	Napoleon Lajoie	6.00	2.40	.60
☐ 121	Dutch Leonard	2.00	.80	.20
☐ 122	Ted Lyons	3.00	1.20	.30
☐ 123	Connie Mack	6.00	2.40	.60
☐ 124	Rabbit Maranville	3.00	1.20	.30
☐ 125	Fred Marberry	2.00	.80	.20
☐ 126	Joe McGinnity	4.00	1.60	.40
☐ 127	Oscar Melillo	2.00	.80	.20
☐ 128	Ray Mueller	2.00	.80	.20
☐ 129	Kid Nichols	3.50	1.40	.35
☐ 130	Lefty O'Doul	2.00	.80	.20
☐ 131	Bob O'Farrell	2.00	.80	.20
☐ 132	Roger Peckinpaugh	2.00	.80	.20
☐ 133	Herb Pennock	3.00	1.20	.30
☐ 134	George Pipgras	2.00	.80	.20
☐ 135	Eddie Plank	3.50	1.40	.35
☐ 136	Ray Schalk	3.00	1.20	.30
☐ 137	Hal Schumacher	2.00	.80	.20
☐ 138	Luke Sewell	2.00	.80	.20
☐ 139	Bob Shawkey	2.00	.80	.20
☐ 140	Riggs Stephenson	2.00	.80	.20
☐ 141	Billy Sullivan	2.00	.80	.20
☐ 142	Bill Terry	5.00	2.00	.50
☐ 143	Joe Tinker	3.00	1.20	.30
☐ 144	Pie Traynor	4.00	1.60	.40
☐ 145	Hal Trosky	2.00	.80	.20
☐ 146	George Uhle	2.00	.80	.20
☐ 147	Johnny VanderMeer	2.50	1.00	.25
☐ 148	Arky Vaughan	3.00	1.20	.30
☐ 149	Rube Waddell	3.00	1.20	.30
☐ 150	Honus Wagner	9.00	3.75	.90
☐ 151	Dixie Walker	2.00	.80	.20
☐ 152	Ted Williams	15.00	6.00	1.50
☐ 153	Cy Young	7.50	3.00	.75
☐ 154	Ross Young	4.00	1.60	.40

1963 Fleer

The cards in this 66-card set measure 2½" by 3½". The Fleer set of current baseball players was marketed in 1963 in a gum card style waxed wrapper package which contained a cherry cookie instead of gum. The cards were printed in sheets of 66 with the scarce card of Adcock apparently being replaced by the unnumbered checklist card for the final press run. The complete set price includes the checklist card. The catalog designation is R418-4.

		MINT	VG-E	F-G
	Complete Set	200.00	80.00	20.00
	Common Player (1-66)	.90	.36	.09
1	Steve Barber	2.00	.50	.10
2	Ron Hansen	.90	.36	.09
3	Milt Pappas	1.25	.50	.12
4	Brooks Robinson	9.00	3.75	.90
5	Willie Mays	15.00	6.00	1.50
6	Lou Clinton	.90	.36	.09
7	Bill Monbouquette	.90	.36	.09
8	Carl Yastrzemski	18.00	7.25	1.80
9	Ray Herbert	.90	.36	.09
10	Jim Landis	.90	.36	.09
11	Dick Donovan	.90	.36	.09
12	Tito Francona	.90	.36	.09
13	Jerry Kindall	.90	.36	.09
14	Frank Lary	1.25	.50	.12
15	Dick Howser	1.25	.50	.12
16	Jerry Lumpe	.90	.36	.09
17	Norm Siebern	.90	.36	.09
18	Don Lee	.90	.36	.09
19	Albie Pearson	.90	.36	.09
20	Bob Rodgers	.90	.36	.09

		MINT	VG-E	F-G
21	Leon Wagner	.90	.36	.09
22	Jim Kaat	2.50	1.00	.25
23	Vic Power	.90	.36	.09
24	Rich Rollins	.90	.36	.09
25	Bobby Richardson	1.75	.70	.17
26	Ralph Terry	1.25	.50	.12
27	Tom Cheney	.90	.36	.09
28	Chuck Cottier	.90	.36	.09
29	Jim Piersall	1.25	.50	.12
30	Dave Stenhouse	.90	.36	.09
31	Glen Hobbie	.90	.36	.09
32	Ron Santo	1.50	.60	.15
33	Gene Freese	.90	.36	.09
34	Vada Pinson	1.50	.60	.15
35	Bob Purkey	.90	.36	.09
36	Joe Amalfitano	.90	.36	.09
37	Bob Aspromonte	.90	.36	.09
38	Dick Farrell	.90	.36	.09
39	Al Spangler	.90	.36	.09
40	Tommy Davis	1.25	.50	.12
41	Don Drysdale	6.00	2.40	.60
42	Sandy Koufax	15.00	6.00	1.50
43	Maury Wills	12.50	5.00	1.25
44	Frank Bolling	.90	.36	.09
45	Warren Spahn	6.00	2.40	.60
46	Joe Adcock SP	40.00	16.00	4.00
47	Roger Craig	1.50	.60	.15
48	Al Jackson	.90	.36	.09
49	Rod Kanehl	.90	.36	.09
50	Ruben Amaro	.90	.36	.09
51	John Callison	1.25	.50	.12
52	Clay Dalrymple	.90	.36	.09
53	Don Demeter	.90	.36	.09
54	Art Mahaffey	.90	.36	.09
55	Smokey Burgess	1.25	.50	.12
56	Roberto Clemente	15.00	6.00	1.50
57	Roy Face	1.25	.50	.12
58	Vernon Law	1.25	.50	.12
59	Bill Mazeroski	1.75	.70	.17
60	Ken Boyer	1.75	.70	.17
61	Bob Gibson	6.00	2.40	.60
62	Gene Oliver	.90	.36	.09
63	Bill White	1.25	.50	.12
64	Orlando Cepeda	1.75	.70	.17
65	Jim Davenport	1.25	.50	.12
66	Bill O'Dell	1.50	.50	.10
67	Checklist card (unnumbered)	50.00	10.00	2.00

1981 Fleer

The cards in this 660-card set measure 2½"
by 3½". This issue of cards marks Fleer's first
entry into the current player baseball card
market since 1963. Players from the same
team are conveniently grouped together by
number in the set. The teams are ordered (by
1980 standings) as follows: Philadelphia (1-
27), Kansas City (28-50), Houston (51-78),
New York Yankees (79-109), Los Angeles
(110-141), Montreal (142-168), Baltimore
(169-195), Cincinnati (196-220), Boston
(221-241), Atlanta (242-267), California (268-
290), Chicago Cubs (291-315), New York
Mets (316-338), Chicago White Sox (339-
359), Pittsburgh (360-386), Cleveland (387-
408), Toronto (409-431), San Francisco (432-
458), Detroit (459-483), San Diego (484-
506), Milwaukee (507-527), St. Louis (528-
550), Minnesota (551-571), Oakland (572-
594), Seattle (595-616), and Texas (617-
637). Cards 638-660 feature specials and
checklists. There were three distinct printings: the two following the primary run were
designed to correct numerous errors. The
variations caused by these multiple printings
are noted in the checklist below (P1, P2, or
P3).

	MINT	VG-E	F-G
Complete Set (660)	22.00	9.00	2.20
Common Player (1-660)	.03	.01	.00

		MINT	VG-E	F-G
☐ 1	Pete Rose	1.75	.70	.17
☐ 2	Larry Bowa	.12	.05	.01
☐ 3	Manny Trillo	.06	.02	.00

		MINT	VG-E	F-G
☐ 4	Bob Boone	.06	.02	.00
☐ 5	Mike Schmidt............ See 640A	.80	.32	.08
☐ 6 A	Steve Carlton P1 ..... Pitcher of Year See also 660A Back "1066 Cardinals"	.60	.24	.06
☐ 6 B	Steve Carlton P2 ..... Pitcher of Year Back "1066 Cardinals"	.60	.24	.06
☐ 6 C	Steve Carlton P3 ..... "1966 Cardinals"	1.75	.70	.17
☐ 7	Tug McGraw .... See 657A	.10	.04	.01
☐ 8	Larry Christenson........	.03	.01	.00
☐ 9	Bake McBride	.06	.02	.00
☐ 10	Greg Luzinski	.12	.05	.01
☐ 11	Ron Reed	.03	.01	.00
☐ 12	Dickie Noles	.03	.01	.00
☐ 13	Keith Moreland	.45	.18	.04
☐ 14	Bob Walk	.06	.02	.00
☐ 15	Lonnie Smith	.08	.03	.01
☐ 16	Dick Ruthven	.03	.01	.00
☐ 17	Sparky Lyle	.12	.05	.01
☐ 18	Greg Gross	.03	.01	.00
☐ 19	Garry Maddox	.06	.02	.00
☐ 20	Nino Espinosa	.03	.01	.00
☐ 21	George Vukovich	.03	.01	.00
☐ 22	John Vukovich	.03	.01	.00
☐ 23	Ramon Aviles	.03	.01	.00
☐ 24 A	Ken Saucier P1 .... Name on front "Ken"	.06	.02	.00
☐ 24 B	Ken Saucier P2 .... Name on front "Ken"	.06	.02	.00
☐ 24 C	Kevin Saucier P3 ...... Name on front "Kevin"	.35	.14	.03
☐ 25	Randy Lerch	.03	.01	.00
☐ 26	Del Unser	.03	.01	.00
☐ 27	Tim McCarver	.06	.02	.00
☐ 28	George Brett .... See 655A	.80	.32	.08
☐ 29	Willie Wilson .... See 653A	.20	.08	.02
☐ 30	Paul Splittorff	.06	.02	.00
☐ 31	Dan Quisenberry	.20	.08	.02
☐ 32 A	Amos Otis P1 ...... Batting Pose "Outfield" (32 on back)	.10	.04	.01
☐ 32 B	Amos Otis P2 ...... "Series Starter" (483 on back)	.10	.04	.01
☐ 33	Steve Busby	.06	.02	.00

		MINT	VG-E	F-G
☐ 34	U.L. Washington	.03	.01	.00
☐ 35	Dave Chalk	.03	.01	.00
☐ 36	Darrell Porter	.06	.02	.00
☐ 37	Marty Pattin	.03	.01	.00
☐ 38	Larry Gura	.06	.02	.00
☐ 39	Renie Martin	.03	.01	.00
☐ 40	Rich Gale	.03	.01	.00
☐ 41	A Hal McRae P1 "Royals" on front in black letters	.50	.20	.05
☐ 41	B Hal McRae P2 "Royals" on front in blue letters	.10	.04	.01
☐ 42	Dennis Leonard	.06	.02	.00
☐ 43	Willie Aikens	.06	.02	.00
☐ 44	Frank White	.10	.04	.01
☐ 45	Clint Hurdle	.03	.01	.00
☐ 46	John Wathan	.03	.01	.00
☐ 47	Pete LaCock	.03	.01	.00
☐ 48	Rance Mulliniks	.03	.01	.00
☐ 49	Jeff Twitty	.03	.01	.00
☐ 50	Jamie Quirk	.03	.01	.00
☐ 51	Art Howe	.03	.01	.00
☐ 52	Ken Forsch	.03	.01	.00
☐ 53	Vern Ruhle	.03	.01	.00
☐ 54	Joe Niekro	.10	.04	.01
☐ 55	Frank LaCorte	.03	.01	.00
☐ 56	J.R. Richard	.10	.04	.01
☐ 57	Nolan Ryan	.45	.18	.04
☐ 58	Enos Cabell	.03	.01	.00
☐ 59	Cesar Cedeno	.10	.04	.01
☐ 60	Jose Cruz	.15	.06	.01
☐ 61	Bill Virdon MGR	.06	.02	.00
☐ 62	Terry Puhl	.06	.02	.00
☐ 63	Joaquin Andujar	.12	.05	.01
☐ 64	Alan Ashby	.03	.01	.00
☐ 65	Joe Sambito	.06	.02	.00
☐ 66	Denny Walling	.03	.01	.00
☐ 67	Jeff Leonard	.10	.04	.01
☐ 68	Luis Pujols	.03	.01	.00
☐ 69	Bruce Bochy	.03	.01	.00
☐ 70	Rafael Landestoy	.03	.01	.00
☐ 71	Dave Smith	.25	.10	.02
☐ 72	Danny Heep	.15	.06	.01
☐ 73	Julio Gonzalez	.03	.01	.00
☐ 74	Craig Reynolds	.03	.01	.00
☐ 75	Gary Woods	.03	.01	.00
☐ 76	Dave Bergman	.03	.01	.00
☐ 77	Randy Niemann	.03	.01	.00
☐ 78	Joe Morgan	.30	.12	.03
☐ 79	Reggie Jackson See 650A	.75	.30	.07
☐ 80	Bucky Dent	.10	.04	.01

		MINT	VG-E	F-G
☐ 81	Tommy John	.15	.06	.01
☐ 82	Luis Tiant	.10	.04	.01
☐ 83	Rick Cerone	.06	.02	.00
☐ 84	Dick Howser MGR	.10	.04	.01
☐ 85	Lou Piniella	.10	.04	.01
☐ 86	Ron Davis	.03	.01	.00
☐ 87	A Craig Nettles P1 ERR Name on back misspelled "Craig"	11.00	4.50	1.10
☐ 87	B Graig Nettles P2 COR "Graig"	.30	.12	.03
☐ 88	Ron Guidry	.25	.10	.02
☐ 89	Rich Gossage	.20	.08	.02
☐ 90	Rudy May	.03	.01	.00
☐ 91	Gaylord Perry	.25	.10	.02
☐ 92	Eric Soderholm	.03	.01	.00
☐ 93	Bob Watson	.06	.02	.00
☐ 94	Bobby Murcer	.10	.04	.01
☐ 95	Bobby Brown	.03	.01	.00
☐ 96	Jim Spencer	.03	.01	.00
☐ 97	Tom Underwood	.03	.01	.00
☐ 98	Oscar Gamble	.06	.02	.00
☐ 99	Johnny Oates	.03	.01	.00
☐ 100	Fred Stanley	.03	.01	.00
☐ 101	Ruppert Jones	.03	.01	.00
☐ 102	Dennis Werth	.03	.01	.00
☐ 103	Joe Lefebvre	.06	.02	.00
☐ 104	Brian Doyle	.06	.02	.00
☐ 105	Aurelio Rodriguez	.03	.01	.00
☐ 106	Doug Bird	.03	.01	.00
☐ 107	Mike Griffin	.03	.01	.00
☐ 108	Tim Lollar	.10	.04	.01
☐ 109	Willie Randolph	.10	.04	.01
☐ 110	Steve Garvey	.50	.20	.05
☐ 111	Reggie Smith	.10	.04	.01
☐ 112	Don Sutton	.25	.10	.02
☐ 113	Burt Hooton	.03	.01	.00
☐ 114	A Dave Lopes P1 small hand on back	.50	.20	.05
☐ 114	B Dave Lopes P2 no hand	.10	.04	.01
☐ 115	Dusty Baker	.08	.03	.01
☐ 116	Tom Lasorda MGR	.08	.03	.01
☐ 117	Bill Russell	.06	.02	.00
☐ 118	Jerry Reuss	.06	.02	.00
☐ 119	Terry Forster	.06	.02	.00
☐ 120	A Bob Welch P1 Name on back Bob	.15	.06	.01
☐ 120	B Bob Welch P1 Name on back Robert	.15	.06	.01
☐ 121	Don Stanhouse	.03	.01	.00
☐ 122	Rick Monday	.06	.02	.00
☐ 123	Derrel Thomas	.03	.01	.00

		MINT	VG-E	F-G
☐ 124	Joe Ferguson	.03	.01	.00
☐ 125	Rick Sutcliffe	.15	.06	.01
☐ 126	A Ron Cey P1 small hand on back	.50	.20	.05
☐ 126	B Ron Cey P2 no hand	.15	.06	.01
☐ 127	Dave Goltz	.03	.01	.00
☐ 128	Jay Johnstone	.06	.02	.00
☐ 129	Steve Yeager	.03	.01	.00
☐ 130	Gary Weiss	.03	.01	.00
☐ 131	Mike Scioscia	.35	.14	.03
☐ 132	Vic Davalillo	.03	.01	.00
☐ 133	Doug Rau	.03	.01	.00
☐ 134	Pepe Frias	.03	.01	.00
☐ 135	Mickey Hatcher	.03	.01	.00
☐ 136	Steve Howe	.15	.06	.01
☐ 137	Robert Castillo	.03	.01	.00
☐ 138	Gary Thomasson	.03	.01	.00
☐ 139	Rudy Law	.03	.01	.00
☐ 140	Fernand Valenzuela (sic, Fernando)	5.00	2.00	.50
☐ 141	Manny Mota	.06	.02	.00
☐ 142	Gary Carter	.50	.20	.05
☐ 143	Steve Rogers	.08	.03	.01
☐ 144	Warren Cromartie	.03	.01	.00
☐ 145	Andre Dawson	.25	.10	.02
☐ 146	Larry Parrish	.06	.02	.00
☐ 147	Rowland Office	.03	.01	.00
☐ 148	Ellis Valentine	.06	.02	.00
☐ 149	Dick Williams MGR	.03	.01	.00
☐ 150	Bill Gullickson	.25	.10	.02
☐ 151	Elias Sosa	.03	.01	.00
☐ 152	John Tamargo	.03	.01	.00
☐ 153	Chris Speier	.03	.01	.00
☐ 154	Ron LeFlore	.06	.02	.00
☐ 155	Rodney Scott	.03	.01	.00
☐ 156	Stan Bahnsen	.03	.01	.00
☐ 157	Bill Lee	.06	.02	.00
☐ 158	Fred Norman	.03	.01	.00
☐ 159	Woodie Fryman	.03	.01	.00
☐ 160	Dave Palmer	.06	.02	.00
☐ 161	Jerry White	.03	.01	.00
☐ 162	Roberto Ramos	.03	.01	.00
☐ 163	John D'Acquisto	.03	.01	.00
☐ 164	Tommy Hutton	.03	.01	.00
☐ 165	Charlie Lea	.20	.08	.02
☐ 166	Scott Sanderson	.03	.01	.00
☐ 167	Ken Macha	.03	.01	.00
☐ 168	Tony Bernazard	.06	.02	.00
☐ 169	Jim Palmer	.30	.12	.03
☐ 170	Steve Stone	.06	.02	.00
☐ 171	Mike Flanagan	.10	.04	.01
☐ 172	Al Bumbry	.03	.01	.00
☐ 173	Doug DeCinces	.10	.04	.01
☐ 174	Scott McGregor	.10	.04	.01
☐ 175	Mark Belanger	.06	.02	.00
☐ 176	Tim Stoddard	.03	.01	.00
☐ 177	A Rick Dempsey P1 small hand on front	.50	.20	.05
☐ 177	B Rick Dempsey P2 no hand	.10	.04	.01
☐ 178	Earl Weaver MGR	.08	.03	.01
☐ 179	Tippy Martinez	.06	.02	.00
☐ 180	Dennis Martinez	.03	.01	.00
☐ 181	Sammy Stewart	.03	.01	.00
☐ 182	Rich Dauer	.03	.01	.00
☐ 183	Lee May	.06	.02	.00
☐ 184	Eddie Murray	.75	.30	.07
☐ 185	Benny Ayala	.03	.01	.00
☐ 186	John Lowenstein	.03	.01	.00
☐ 187	Gary Roenicke	.06	.02	.00
☐ 188	Ken Singleton	.10	.04	.01
☐ 189	Dan Graham	.03	.01	.00
☐ 190	Terry Crowley	.03	.01	.00
☐ 191	Kiko Garcia	.03	.01	.00
☐ 192	Dave Ford	.03	.01	.00
☐ 193	Mark Corey	.03	.01	.00
☐ 194	Lenn Sakata	.03	.01	.00
☐ 195	Doug DeCinces	.10	.04	.01
☐ 196	Johnny Bench	.50	.20	.05
☐ 197	Dave Concepcion	.12	.05	.01
☐ 198	Ray Knight	.10	.04	.01
☐ 199	Ken Griffey	.08	.03	.01
☐ 200	Tom Seaver	.50	.20	.05
☐ 201	Dave Collins	.06	.02	.00
☐ 202	A George Foster P1 Slugger number on back 216	.20	.08	.02
☐ 202	B George Foster P2 Slugger number on back 202	.20	.08	.02
☐ 203	Junior Kennedy	.03	.01	.00
☐ 204	Frank Pastore	.03	.01	.00
☐ 205	Dan Driessen	.06	.02	.00
☐ 206	Hector Cruz	.03	.01	.00
☐ 207	Paul Moskau	.03	.01	.00
☐ 208	Charlie Leibrandt	.30	.12	.03
☐ 209	Harry Spilman	.03	.01	.00
☐ 210	Joe Price	.06	.02	.00
☐ 211	Tom Hume	.03	.01	.00
☐ 212	Joe Nolan	.03	.01	.00
☐ 213	Doug Bair	.03	.01	.00
☐ 214	Mario Soto	.10	.04	.01
☐ 215	A Bill Bonham P1 small hand on back	.50	.20	.05

		MINT	VG-E	F-G
☐ 215	B Bill Bonham P2 no hand	.06	.02	.00
☐ 216	George Foster See 202	.20	.08	.02
☐ 217	Paul Householder	.08	.03	.01
☐ 218	Ron Oester	.06	.02	.00
☐ 219	Sam Mejias	.03	.01	.00
☐ 220	Sheldon Burnside	.03	.01	.00
☐ 221	Carl Yastrzemski	.75	.30	.07
☐ 222	Jim Rice	.50	.20	.05
☐ 223	Fred Lynn	.25	.10	.02
☐ 224	Carlton Fisk	.20	.08	.02
☐ 225	Rick Burleson	.06	.02	.00
☐ 226	Dennis Eckersley	.06	.02	.00
☐ 227	Butch Hobson	.03	.01	.00
☐ 228	Tom Burgmeier	.03	.01	.00
☐ 229	Garry Hancock	.03	.01	.00
☐ 230	Don Zimmer MGR	.03	.01	.00
☐ 231	Steve Renko	.03	.01	.00
☐ 232	Dwight Evans	.12	.05	.01
☐ 233	Mike Torrez	.06	.02	.00
☐ 234	Bob Stanley	.06	.02	.00
☐ 235	Jim Dwyer	.03	.01	.00
☐ 236	Dave Stapleton	.06	.02	.00
☐ 237	Glen Hoffman	.06	.02	.00
☐ 238	Jerry Remy	.06	.02	.00
☐ 239	Dick Drago	.03	.01	.00
☐ 240	Bill Campbell	.06	.02	.00
☐ 241	Tony Perez	.15	.06	.01
☐ 242	Phil Niekro	.25	.10	.02
☐ 243	Dale Murphy	1.25	.50	.12
☐ 244	Bob Horner	.25	.10	.02
☐ 245	Jeff Burroughs	.06	.02	.00
☐ 246	Rick Camp	.03	.01	.00
☐ 247	Bob Cox MGR	.03	.01	.00
☐ 248	Bruce Benedict	.03	.01	.00
☐ 249	Gene Garber	.03	.01	.00
☐ 250	Jerry Royster	.03	.01	.00
☐ 251	A Gary Matthews P1 small hand on back	.50	.20	.05
☐ 251	B Gary Matthews P2 no hand	.10	.04	.01
☐ 252	Chris Chambliss	.06	.02	.00
☐ 253	Luis Gomez	.03	.01	.00
☐ 254	Bill Nahorodny	.03	.01	.00
☐ 255	Doyle Alexander	.06	.02	.00
☐ 256	Brian Asselstine	.03	.01	.00
☐ 257	Biff Pocoroba	.03	.01	.00
☐ 258	Mike Lum	.03	.01	.00
☐ 259	Charlie Spikes	.03	.01	.00
☐ 260	Glen Hubbard	.03	.01	.00
☐ 261	Tommy Boggs	.03	.01	.00
☐ 262	Al Hrabosky	.06	.02	.00

		MINT	VG-E	F-G
☐ 263	Rick Matula	.03	.01	.00
☐ 264	Preston Hanna	.03	.01	.00
☐ 265	Larry Bradford	.03	.01	.00
☐ 266	Rafael Ramirez	.20	.08	.02
☐ 267	Larry McWilliams	.03	.01	.00
☐ 268	Rod Carew	.50	.20	.05
☐ 269	Bobby Grich	.10	.04	.01
☐ 270	Carney Lansford	.15	.06	.01
☐ 271	Don Baylor	.20	.08	.02
☐ 272	Joe Rudi	.06	.02	.00
☐ 273	Dan Ford	.03	.01	.00
☐ 274	Jim Fregosi	.06	.02	.00
☐ 275	Dave Frost	.03	.01	.00
☐ 276	Frank Tanana	.06	.02	.00
☐ 277	Dickie Thon	.08	.03	.01
☐ 278	Jason Thompson	.06	.02	.00
☐ 279	Rick Miller	.03	.01	.00
☐ 280	Bert Campaneris	.08	.03	.01
☐ 281	Tom Donohue	.03	.01	.00
☐ 282	Brian Downing	.06	.02	.00
☐ 283	Fred Patek	.03	.01	.00
☐ 284	Bruce Kison	.03	.01	.00
☐ 285	Dave LaRoche	.03	.01	.00
☐ 286	Don Aase	.06	.02	.00
☐ 287	Jim Barr	.03	.01	.00
☐ 288	Alfredo Martinez	.03	.01	.00
☐ 289	Larry Harlow	.03	.01	.00
☐ 290	Andy Hassler	.03	.01	.00
☐ 291	Dave Kingman	.15	.06	.01
☐ 292	Bill Buckner	.12	.05	.01
☐ 293	Rick Reuschel	.06	.02	.00
☐ 294	Bruce Sutter	.20	.08	.02
☐ 295	Jerry Martin	.03	.01	.00
☐ 296	Scot Thompson	.03	.01	.00
☐ 297	Ivan DeJesus	.03	.01	.00
☐ 298	Steve Dillard	.03	.01	.00
☐ 299	Dick Tidrow	.03	.01	.00
☐ 300	Randy Martz	.03	.01	.00
☐ 301	Lenny Randle	.03	.01	.00
☐ 302	Lynn McGlothen	.03	.01	.00
☐ 303	Cliff Johnson	.03	.01	.00
☐ 304	Tim Blackwell	.03	.01	.00
☐ 305	Dennis Lamp	.03	.01	.00
☐ 306	Bill Caudill	.06	.02	.00
☐ 307	Carlos Lezcano	.03	.01	.00
☐ 308	Jim Tracy	.03	.01	.00
☐ 309	Doug Capilla	.03	.01	.00
☐ 310	Willie Hernandez	.15	.06	.01
☐ 311	Mike Vail	.03	.01	.00
☐ 312	Mike Krukow	.10	.04	.01
☐ 313	Barry Foote	.03	.01	.00
☐ 314	Larry Biittner	.03	.01	.00
☐ 315	Mike Tyson	.03	.01	.00

		MINT	VG-E	F-G
☐ 316	Lee Mazzilli	.06	.02	.00
☐ 317	John Stearns	.03	.01	.00
☐ 318	Alex Trevino	.03	.01	.00
☐ 319	Craig Swan	.03	.01	.00
☐ 320	Frank Taveras	.03	.01	.00
☐ 321	Steve Henderson	.03	.01	.00
☐ 322	Neil Allen	.06	.02	.00
☐ 323	Mark Bomback	.03	.01	.00
☐ 324	Mike Jorgensen	.03	.01	.00
☐ 325	Joe Torre MGR	.10	.04	.01
☐ 326	Elliott Maddox	.03	.01	.00
☐ 327	Pete Falcone	.03	.01	.00
☐ 328	Ray Burris	.03	.01	.00
☐ 329	Claudell Washington	.06	.02	.00
☐ 330	Doug Flynn	.03	.01	.00
☐ 331	Joel Youngblood	.03	.01	.00
☐ 332	Bill Almon	.03	.01	.00
☐ 333	Tom Hausman	.03	.01	.00
☐ 334	Pat Zachry	.03	.01	.00
☐ 335	Jeff Reardon	.35	.14	.03
☐ 336	Wally Backman	.50	.20	.05
☐ 337	Dan Norman	.03	.01	.00
☐ 338	Jerry Morales	.03	.01	.00
☐ 339	Ed Farmer	.03	.01	.00
☐ 340	Bob Molinaro	.03	.01	.00
☐ 341	Todd Cruz	.03	.01	.00
☐ 342 A	Britt Burns P1 small hand on front	.50	.20	.05
☐ 342 B	Britt Burns P2 no hand	.30	.12	.03
☐ 343	Kevin Bell	.03	.01	.00
☐ 344	Tony LaRussa MGR	.06	.02	.00
☐ 345	Steve Trout	.06	.02	.00
☐ 346	Harold Baines	2.00	.80	.20
☐ 347	Richard Wortham	.03	.01	.00
☐ 348	Wayne Nordhagen	.03	.01	.00
☐ 349	Mike Squires	.03	.01	.00
☐ 350	Lamar Johnson	.03	.01	.00
☐ 351	Rickey Henderson	.70	.28	.07
☐ 352	Francisco Barrios	.03	.01	.00
☐ 353	Thad Bosley	.03	.01	.00
☐ 354	Chet Lemon	.06	.02	.00
☐ 355	Bruce Kimm	.03	.01	.00
☐ 356	Richard Dotson	.25	.10	.02
☐ 357	Jim Morrison	.03	.01	.00
☐ 358	Mike Proly	.03	.01	.00
☐ 359	Greg Pryor	.03	.01	.00
☐ 360	Dave Parker	.30	.12	.03
☐ 361	Omar Moreno	.03	.01	.00
☐ 362 A	Kent Tekulve P1 Back "1071 Waterbury" and "1078 Pirates"	.12	.05	.01
☐ 362 B	Kent Tekulve P2 "1971 Waterbury" and "1978 Pirates"	.08	.03	.01
☐ 363	Willie Stargell	.30	.12	.03
☐ 364	Phil Garner	.06	.02	.00
☐ 365	Ed Ott	.03	.01	.00
☐ 366	Don Robinson	.03	.01	.00
☐ 367	Chuck Tanner MGR	.03	.01	.00
☐ 368	Jim Rooker	.03	.01	.00
☐ 369	Dale Berra	.06	.02	.00
☐ 370	Jim Bibby	.03	.01	.00
☐ 371	Steve Nicosia	.03	.01	.00
☐ 372	Mike Easler	.08	.03	.01
☐ 373	Bill Robinson	.03	.01	.00
☐ 374	Lee Lacy	.06	.02	.00
☐ 375	John Candelaria	.08	.03	.01
☐ 376	Manny Sanguillen	.06	.02	.00
☐ 377	Rick Rhoden	.08	.03	.01
☐ 378	Grant Jackson	.03	.01	.00
☐ 379	Tim Foli	.03	.01	.00
☐ 380	Rod Scurry	.12	.05	.01
☐ 381	Bill Madlock	.15	.06	.01
☐ 382 A	Kurt Bevacqua P1 ERR P on cap backwards	.20	.08	.02
☐ 382 B	Kurt Bevacqua P2 COR	.06	.02	.00
☐ 383	Bert Blyleven	.12	.05	.01
☐ 384	Eddie Solomon	.03	.01	.00
☐ 385	Enrique Romo	.03	.01	.00
☐ 386	John Milner	.03	.01	.00
☐ 387	Mike Hargrove	.06	.02	.00
☐ 388	Jorge Orta	.03	.01	.00
☐ 389	Toby Harrah	.06	.02	.00
☐ 390	Tom Veryzer	.03	.01	.00
☐ 391	Miguel Dilone	.03	.01	.00
☐ 392	Dan Spillner	.03	.01	.00
☐ 393	Jack Brohamer	.03	.01	.00
☐ 394	Wayne Garland	.03	.01	.00
☐ 395	Sid Monge	.03	.01	.00
☐ 396	Rick Waits	.03	.01	.00
☐ 397	Joe Charboneau	.10	.04	.01
☐ 398	Gary Alexander	.03	.01	.00
☐ 399	Jerry Dybzinski	.03	.01	.00
☐ 400	Mike Stanton	.03	.01	.00
☐ 401	Mike Paxton	.03	.01	.00
☐ 402	Gary Gray	.06	.02	.00
☐ 403	Rick Manning	.03	.01	.00
☐ 404	Bo Diaz	.06	.02	.00
☐ 405	Ron Hassey	.03	.01	.00
☐ 406	Ross Grimsley	.03	.01	.00
☐ 407	Victor Cruz	.03	.01	.00
☐ 408	Len Barker	.06	.02	.00
☐ 409	Bob Bailor	.03	.01	.00

		MINT	VG-E	F-G
☐ 410	Otto Velez	.03	.01	.00
☐ 411	Ernie Whitt	.03	.01	.00
☐ 412	Jim Clancy	.03	.01	.00
☐ 413	Barry Bonnell	.03	.01	.00
☐ 414	Dave Stieb	.20	.08	.02
☐ 415	Damaso Garcia	.45	.18	.04
☐ 416	John Mayberry	.06	.02	.00
☐ 417	Roy Howell	.03	.01	.00
☐ 418	Dan Ainge	.20	.08	.02
☐ 419 A	Jesse Jefferson P1	.06	.02	.00
	Back says Pirates			
☐ 419 B	Jesse Jefferson P2	.06	.02	.00
	Back says Pirates			
☐ 419 C	Jesse Jefferson P3	.35	.14	.03
	Back says Blue Jays			
☐ 420	Joey McLaughlin	.03	.01	.00
☐ 421	Lloyd Moseby	1.00	.40	.10
☐ 422	Al Woods	.03	.01	.00
☐ 423	Garth Iorg	.03	.01	.00
☐ 424	Doug Ault	.03	.01	.00
☐ 425	Ken Schrom	.15	.06	.01
☐ 426	Mike Willis	.03	.01	.00
☐ 427	Steve Braun	.03	.01	.00
☐ 428	Bob Davis	.03	.01	.00
☐ 429	Jerry Garvin	.03	.01	.00
☐ 430	Alfredo Griffin	.06	.02	.00
☐ 431	Bob Mattick MGR	.03	.01	.00
☐ 432	Vida Blue	.08	.03	.01
☐ 433	Jack Clark	.12	.05	.01
☐ 434	Willie McCovey	.30	.12	.03
☐ 435	Mike Ivie	.03	.01	.00
☐ 436 A	Darrel Evans P1 ERR	.30	.12	.03
	Name on front "Darrel"			
☐ 436 B	Darrell Evans P2	.12	.05	.01
	Name on front "Darrell"			
☐ 437	Terry Whitfield	.03	.01	.00
☐ 438	Rennie Stennett	.03	.01	.00
☐ 439	John Montefusco	.06	.02	.00
☐ 440	Jim Wohlford	.03	.01	.00
☐ 441	Bill North	.03	.01	.00
☐ 442	Milt May	.03	.01	.00
☐ 443	Max Venable	.03	.01	.00
☐ 444	Ed Whitson	.06	.02	.00
☐ 445	Al Holland	.12	.05	.01
☐ 446	Randy Moffitt	.03	.01	.00
☐ 447	Bob Knepper	.12	.05	.01
☐ 448	Gary Lavelle	.06	.02	.00
☐ 449	Greg Minton	.06	.02	.00
☐ 450	Johnnie LeMaster	.03	.01	.00
☐ 451	Larry Herndon	.03	.01	.00
☐ 452	Rich Murray	.03	.01	.00
☐ 453	Joe Pettini	.03	.01	.00
☐ 454	Allen Ripley	.03	.01	.00
☐ 455	Dennis Littlejohn	.03	.01	.00
☐ 456	Tom Griffin	.03	.01	.00
☐ 457	Alan Hargesheimer	.03	.01	.00
☐ 458	Joe Strain	.03	.01	.00
☐ 459	Steve Kemp	.08	.03	.01
☐ 460	Sparky Anderson MGR	.08	.03	.01
☐ 461	Alan Trammell	.20	.08	.02
☐ 462	Mark Fidrych	.10	.04	.01
☐ 463	Lou Whitaker	.15	.06	.01
☐ 464	Dave Rozema	.03	.01	.00
☐ 465	Milt Wilcox	.03	.01	.00
☐ 466	Champ Summers	.03	.01	.00
☐ 467	Lance Parrish	.35	.14	.03
☐ 468	Dan Petry	.12	.05	.01
☐ 469	Pat Underwood	.03	.01	.00
☐ 470	Rick Peters	.03	.01	.00
☐ 471	Al Cowens	.03	.01	.00
☐ 472	John Wockenfuss	.03	.01	.00
☐ 473	Tom Brookens	.03	.01	.00
☐ 474	Richie Hebner	.03	.01	.00
☐ 475	Jack Morris	.35	.14	.03
☐ 476	Jim Lentine	.03	.01	.00
☐ 477	Bruce Robbins	.03	.01	.00
☐ 478	Mark Wagner	.03	.01	.00
☐ 479	Tim Corcoran	.03	.01	.00
☐ 480 A	Stan Papi P1	.15	.06	.01
	Front as Pitcher			
☐ 480 B	Stan Papi P2	.10	.04	.01
	Front as Shortstop			
☐ 481	Kirk Gibson	2.00	.80	.20
☐ 482	Dan Schatzeder	.03	.01	.00
☐ 483 A	Amos Otis P1	.10	.04	.01
	See card 32			
☐ 483 B	Amos Otis P2	.10	.04	.01
	See card 32			
☐ 484	Dave Winfield	.45	.18	.04
☐ 485	Rollie Fingers	.25	.10	.02
☐ 486	Gene Richards	.03	.01	.00
☐ 487	Randy Jones	.06	.02	.00
☐ 488	Ozzie Smith	.25	.10	.02
☐ 489	Gene Tenace	.03	.01	.00
☐ 490	Bill Fahey	.03	.01	.00
☐ 491	John Curtis	.03	.01	.00
☐ 492	Dave Cash	.03	.01	.00
☐ 493 A	Tim Flannery P1	.12	.05	.01
	Batting right			
☐ 493 B	Tim Flannery P2	.08	.03	.01
	Batting left			
☐ 494	Jerry Mumphrey	.06	.02	.00
☐ 495	Bob Shirley	.03	.01	.00
☐ 496	Steve Mura	.03	.01	.00
☐ 497	Eric Rasmussen	.03	.01	.00
☐ 498	Broderick Perkins	.03	.01	.00

		MINT	VG-E	F-G
☐ 499	Barry Evans	.03	.01	.00
☐ 500	Chuck Baker	.03	.01	.00
☐ 501	Luis Salazar	.06	.02	.00
☐ 502	Gary Lucas	.10	.04	.01
☐ 503	Mike Armstrong	.10	.04	.01
☐ 504	Jerry Turner	.03	.01	.00
☐ 505	Dennis Kinney	.03	.01	.00
☐ 506	Willie Montanez	.03	.01	.00
☐ 507	Gorman Thomas	.10	.04	.01
☐ 508	Ben Oglivie	.08	.03	.01
☐ 509	Larry Hisle	.06	.02	.00
☐ 510	Sal Bando	.06	.02	.00
☐ 511	Robin Yount	.45	.18	.04
☐ 512	Mike Caldwell	.06	.02	.00
☐ 513	Sixto Lezcano	.03	.01	.00
☐ 514 A	Bill Travers P1 ERR .. "Jerry Augustine" with Augustine back	.15	.06	.01
☐ 514 B	Bill Travers P2 COR .	.10	.04	.01
☐ 515	Paul Molitor	.12	.05	.01
☐ 516	Moose Haas	.06	.02	.00
☐ 517	Bill Castro	.03	.01	.00
☐ 518	Jim Slaton	.06	.02	.00
☐ 519	Lary Sorensen	.03	.01	.00
☐ 520	Bob McClure	.03	.01	.00
☐ 521	Charlie Moore	.03	.01	.00
☐ 522	Jim Gantner	.06	.02	.00
☐ 523	Reggie Cleveland	.03	.01	.00
☐ 524	Don Money	.03	.01	.00
☐ 525	Bill Travers	.03	.01	.00
☐ 526	Buck Martinez	.03	.01	.00
☐ 527	Dick Davis	.03	.01	.00
☐ 528	Ted Simmons	.15	.06	.01
☐ 529	Garry Templeton	.10	.04	.01
☐ 530	Ken Reitz	.03	.01	.00
☐ 531	Tony Scott	.03	.01	.00
☐ 532	Ken Oberkfell	.03	.01	.00
☐ 533	Bob Sykes	.03	.01	.00
☐ 534	Keith Smith	.03	.01	.00
☐ 535	John Littlefield	.03	.01	.00
☐ 536	Jim Kaat	.15	.06	.01
☐ 537	Bob Forsch	.06	.02	.00
☐ 538	Mike Phillips	.03	.01	.00
☐ 539	Terry Landrum	.08	.03	.01
☐ 540	Leon Durham	.50	.20	.05
☐ 541	Terry Kennedy	.10	.04	.01
☐ 542	George Hendrick	.08	.03	.01
☐ 543	Dane Iorg	.03	.01	.00
☐ 544	Mark Littell	.03	.01	.00
☐ 545	Keith Hernandez	.30	.12	.03
☐ 546	Silvio Martinez	.03	.01	.00
☐ 547 A	Don Hood P1 ERR ... "Pete Vuckovich" with Vuckovich back	.20	.08	.02
☐ 547 B	Don Hood P2 COR ...	.10	.04	.01
☐ 548	Bobby Bonds	.10	.04	.01
☐ 549	Mike Ramsey	.03	.01	.00
☐ 550	Tom Herr	.10	.04	.01
☐ 551	Roy Smalley	.06	.02	.00
☐ 552	Jerry Koosman	.08	.03	.01
☐ 553	Ken Landreaux	.06	.02	.00
☐ 554	John Castino	.06	.02	.00
☐ 555	Doug Corbett	.08	.03	.01
☐ 556	Bombo Rivera	.03	.01	.00
☐ 557	Ron Jackson	.03	.01	.00
☐ 558	Butch Wynegar	.06	.02	.00
☐ 559	Hosken Powell	.03	.01	.00
☐ 560	Pete Redfern	.03	.01	.00
☐ 561	Roger Erickson	.03	.01	.00
☐ 562	Glenn Adams	.03	.01	.00
☐ 563	Rick Sofield	.03	.01	.00
☐ 564	Geoff Zahn	.03	.01	.00
☐ 565	Pete Mackanin	.03	.01	.00
☐ 566	Mike Cubbage	.03	.01	.00
☐ 567	Darrell Jackson	.03	.01	.00
☐ 568	Dave Edwards	.03	.01	.00
☐ 569	Rob Wilfong	.03	.01	.00
☐ 570	Sal Butera	.03	.01	.00
☐ 571	Jose Morales	.03	.01	.00
☐ 572	Rick Langford	.03	.01	.00
☐ 573	Mike Norris	.06	.02	.00
☐ 574	Rickey Henderson	.70	.28	.07
☐ 575	Tony Armas	.10	.04	.01
☐ 576	Dave Revering	.03	.01	.00
☐ 577	Jeff Newman	.03	.01	.00
☐ 578	Bob Lacey	.03	.01	.00
☐ 579	Brian Kingman	.03	.01	.00
☐ 580	Mitchell Page	.03	.01	.00
☐ 581	Billy Martin MGR	.10	.04	.01
☐ 582	Rob Picciolo	.03	.01	.00
☐ 583	Mike Heath	.03	.01	.00
☐ 584	Mickey Klutts	.03	.01	.00
☐ 585	Orlando Gonzalez	.03	.01	.00
☐ 586	Mike Davis	.30	.12	.03
☐ 587	Wayne Gross	.03	.01	.00
☐ 588	Matt Keough	.03	.01	.00
☐ 589	Steve McCatty	.03	.01	.00
☐ 590	Dwayne Murphy	.06	.02	.00
☐ 591	Mario Guerrero	.03	.01	.00
☐ 592	Dave McKay	.03	.01	.00
☐ 593	Jim Essian	.03	.01	.00
☐ 594	Dave Heaverlo	.03	.01	.00
☐ 595	Maury Wills MGR	.08	.03	.01
☐ 596	Juan Beniquez	.06	.02	.00

		MINT	VG-E	F-G
☐ 597	Rodney Craig	.03	.01	.00
☐ 598	Jim Anderson	.03	.01	.00
☐ 599	Floyd Bannister	.06	.02	.00
☐ 600	Bruce Bochte	.06	.02	.00
☐ 601	Julio Cruz	.06	.02	.00
☐ 602	Ted Cox	.03	.01	.00
☐ 603	Dan Meyer	.03	.01	.00
☐ 604	Larry Cox	.03	.01	.00
☐ 605	Bill Stein	.03	.01	.00
☐ 606	Steve Garvey	.50	.20	.05
☐ 607	Dave Roberts	.03	.01	.00
☐ 608	Leon Roberts	.03	.01	.00
☐ 609	Reggie Walton	.03	.01	.00
☐ 610	Dave Edler	.03	.01	.00
☐ 611	Larry Milbourne	.03	.01	.00
☐ 612	Kim Allen	.03	.01	.00
☐ 613	Mario Mendoza	.03	.01	.00
☐ 614	Tom Paciorek	.03	.01	.00
☐ 615	Glenn Abbott	.03	.01	.00
☐ 616	Joe Simpson	.03	.01	.00
☐ 617	Mickey Rivers	.06	.02	.00
☐ 618	Jim Kern	.03	.01	.00
☐ 619	Jim Sundberg	.06	.02	.00
☐ 620	Richie Zisk	.06	.02	.00
☐ 621	Jon Matlack	.06	.02	.00
☐ 622	Ferguson Jenkins	.15	.06	.01
☐ 623	Pat Corrales MGR	.06	.02	.00
☐ 624	Ed Figueroa	.03	.01	.00
☐ 625	Buddy Bell	.12	.05	.01
☐ 626	Al Oliver	.12	.05	.01
☐ 627	Doc Medich	.03	.01	.00
☐ 628	Bump Wills	.03	.01	.00
☐ 629	Rusty Staub	.10	.04	.01
☐ 630	Pat Putnam	.03	.01	.00
☐ 631	John Grubb	.03	.01	.00
☐ 632	Danny Darwin	.03	.01	.00
☐ 633	Ken Clay	.03	.01	.00
☐ 634	Jim Norris	.03	.01	.00
☐ 635	John Butcher	.15	.06	.01
☐ 636	Dave Roberts	.03	.01	.00
☐ 637	Billy Sample	.03	.01	.00
☐ 638	Carl Yastrzemski	.75	.30	.07
☐ 639	Cecil Cooper	.18	.08	.01
☐ 640 A	Mike Schmidt P1 (Portrait) "Third Base" (number on back 5)	1.00	.40	.10
☐ 640 B	Mike Schmidt P2 "1980 Home Run King" (640 on back)	1.00	.40	.10
☐ 641 A	CL: Phils/Royals P1 41 is Hal McRae	.07	.01	.00

		MINT	VG-E	F-G
☐ 641 B	CL: Phils/Royals P2 41 is Hal McRae& Double Threat	.07	.01	.00
☐ 642	CL: Astros/Yankees	.07	.01	.00
☐ 643	CL: Expos/Dodgers	.07	.01	.00
☐ 644 A	CL: Reds/Orioles P1 202 is George Foster	.07	.01	.00
☐ 644 B	CL: Reds/Orioles P2 202 is Foster Slugger	.07	.01	.00
☐ 645 A	Rose/Bowa/Schmidt Triple Threat P1 (No number on back)	2.00	.80	.20
☐ 645 B	Rose/Bowa/Schmidt Triple Threat P2 (Back numbered 645)	1.00	.40	.10
☐ 646	CL: Braves/Red Sox	.07	.01	.00
☐ 647	CL: Cubs/Angels	.07	.01	.00
☐ 648	CL: Mets/White Sox	.07	.01	.00
☐ 649	CL: Indians/Pirates	.07	.01	.00
☐ 650 A	Reggie Jackson Mr. Baseball P1 Number on back 79	.80	.32	.08
☐ 650 B	Reggie Jackson Mr. Baseball P2 Number on back 650	.70	.28	.07
☐ 651	CL: Giants/Blue Jays	.07	.01	.00
☐ 652 A	CL: Tigers/Padres P1 483 is listed	.07	.01	.00
☐ 652 B	CL: Tigers/Padres P2 483 is deleted	.07	.01	.00
☐ 653 A	Willie Wilson P1 Most Hits Most Runs Number on back 29	.25	.10	.02
☐ 653 B	Willie Wilson P2 Most Hits Most Runs Number on back 653	.25	.10	.02
☐ 654 A	CL: Brewers/Cards P1 514 Jerry Augustine 547 Pete Vuckovich	.07	.01	.00
☐ 654 B	CL: Brewers/Cards P2 514 Billy Travers 547 Don Hood	.07	.01	.00
☐ 655 A	George Brett P1 .390 Average Number on back 28	.75	.30	.07
☐ 655 B	George Brett P2 .390 Average Number on back 655	.75	.30	.07
☐ 656	CL: Twins/Oakland A's	.07	.01	.00
☐ 657 A	Tug McGraw P1 Game Saver Number on back 7	.10	.04	.01

	MINT	VG-E	F-G
☐ 657 B Tug McGraw P2 ...... Game Saver Number on back 657	.10	.04	.01
☐ 658 CL: Rangers/Mariners ...	.07	.01	.00
☐ 659 A Checklist P1 .... of Special Cards Last lines on front Wilson Most Hits	.07	.01	.00
☐ 659 B Checklist P2 .... of Special Cards Last lines on front Otis Series Starter	.07	.01	.00
☐ 660 A Steve Carlton P1 ..... Golden Arm Back "1066 Cardinals" Number on back 6	.60	.24	.06
☐ 660 B Steve Carlton P2 ..... Golden Arm Number on back 660 Back "1066 Cardinals"	.60	.24	.06
☐ 660 C Steve Carlton P3 ..... Golden Arm "1966 Cardinals"	2.00	.80	.20

1982 Fleer

The cards in this 660-card set measure 2½ by 3½". The 1982 Fleer set is again ordered by teams; in fact the players within each team are listed in alphabetical order. The teams are ordered (by 1981 standings) as follows: Los Angeles (1-29), New York Yankees (30-56), Cincinnati (57-84), Oakland (85-109), St. Louis (110-132), Milwaukee (133-156), Baltimore (157-182), Montreal (183-211), Houston (212-237), Philadelphia (238-262),

Detroit (263-286), Boston (287-312), Texas (313-334), Chicago White Sox (335-358), Cleveland (359-382), San Francisco (383-403), Kansas City (404-427), Atlanta (428-449), California (450-474), Pittsburgh (475-501), Seattle (502-519), New York Mets (520-544), Minnesota (545-565), San Diego (566-585), Chicago Cubs (586-607), and Toronto (608-627). Cards numbered 628 through 646 are special cards highlighting some of the stars and leaders of the 1981 season. The last 14 cards in the set (647-660) are checklist cards. The backs feature player statistics and a full color team logo in the upper right-hand corner of each card.

	MINT	VG-E	F-G
Complete Set	21.00	8.50	2.10
Common Player (1-660)	.03	.01	.00

		MINT	VG-E	F-G
☐	1 Dusty Baker	.12	.05	.01
☐	2 Robert Castillo	.03	.01	.00
☐	3 Ron Cey	.10	.04	.01
☐	4 Terry Forster	.06	.02	.00
☐	5 Steve Garvey	.40	.16	.04
☐	6 Dave Goltz	.03	.01	.00
☐	7 Pedro Guerrero	.30	.12	.03
☐	8 Burt Hooton	.03	.01	.00
☐	9 Steve Howe	.06	.02	.00
☐	10 Jay Johnstone	.06	.02	.00
☐	11 Ken Landreaux	.06	.02	.00
☐	12 Davey Lopes	.08	.03	.01
☐	13 Mike Marshall	1.25	.50	.12
☐	14 Bobby Mitchell	.06	.02	.00
☐	15 Rick Monday	.06	.02	.00
☐	16 Tom Niedenfuer	.45	.18	.04
☐	17 Ted Power	.40	.16	.04
☐	18 Jerry Reuss	.06	.02	.00
☐	19 Ron Roenicke	.06	.02	.00
☐	20 Bill Russell	.06	.02	.00
☐	21 Steve Sax	1.25	.50	.12
☐	22 Mike Scioscia	.03	.01	.00
☐	23 Reggie Smith	.08	.03	.01
☐	24 Dave Stewart	.15	.06	.01
☐	25 Rick Sutcliffe	.15	.06	.01
☐	26 Derrel Thomas	.03	.01	.00
☐	27 Fernando Valenzuela ...	.50	.20	.05
☐	28 Bob Welch	.08	.03	.01
☐	29 Steve Yeager	.06	.02	.00
☐	30 Bobby Brown	.03	.01	.00
☐	31 Rick Cerone	.03	.01	.00
☐	32 Ron Davis	.03	.01	.00

		MINT	VG-E	F-G			MINT	VG-E	F-G
☐ 33	Bucky Dent	.08	.03	.01	☐ 86	Shooty Babitt	.03	.01	.00
☐ 34	Barry Foote	.03	.01	.00	☐ 87	Dave Beard	.03	.01	.00
☐ 35	George Frazier	.03	.01	.00	☐ 88	Rick Bosetti	.03	.01	.00
☐ 36	Oscar Gamble	.06	.02	.00	☐ 89	Keith Drumright	.03	.01	.00
☐ 37	Rich Gossage	.20	.08	.02	☐ 90	Wayne Gross	.03	.01	.00
☐ 38	Ron Guidry	.20	.08	.02	☐ 91	Mike Heath	.03	.01	.00
☐ 39	Reggie Jackson	.50	.20	.05	☐ 92	Rickey Henderson	.50	.20	.05
☐ 40	Tommy John	.15	.06	.01	☐ 93	Cliff Johnson	.03	.01	.00
☐ 41	Rudy May	.03	.01	.00	☐ 94	Jeff Jones	.03	.01	.00
☐ 42	Larry Milbourne	.03	.01	.00	☐ 95	Matt Keough	.03	.01	.00
☐ 43	Jerry Mumphrey	.06	.02	.00	☐ 96	Brian Kingman	.03	.01	.00
☐ 44	Bobby Murcer	.10	.04	.01	☐ 97	Mickey Klutts	.03	.01	.00
☐ 45	Gene Nelson	.10	.04	.01	☐ 98	Rick Langford	.03	.01	.00
☐ 46	Graig Nettles	.15	.06	.01	☐ 99	Steve McCatty	.03	.01	.00
☐ 47	Johnny Oates	.03	.01	.00	☐ 100	Dave McKay	.03	.01	.00
☐ 48	Lou Piniella	.10	.04	.01	☐ 101	Dwayne Murphy	.06	.02	.00
☐ 49	Willie Randolph	.08	.03	.01	☐ 102	Jeff Newman	.03	.01	.00
☐ 50	Rick Reuschel	.06	.02	.00	☐ 103	Mike Norris	.06	.02	.00
☐ 51	Dave Revering	.03	.01	.00	☐ 104	Bob Owchinko	.03	.01	.00
☐ 52	Dave Righetti	1.25	.50	.12	☐ 105	Mitchell Page	.03	.01	.00
☐ 53	Aurelio Rodriguez	.03	.01	.00	☐ 106	Rob Picciolo	.03	.01	.00
☐ 54	Bob Watson	.06	.02	.00	☐ 107	Jim Spencer	.03	.01	.00
☐ 55	Dennis Werth	.03	.01	.00	☐ 108	Fred Stanley	.03	.01	.00
☐ 56	Dave Winfield	.40	.16	.04	☐ 109	Tom Underwood	.03	.01	.00
☐ 57	Johnny Bench	.40	.16	.04	☐ 110	Joaquin Andujar	.12	.05	.01
☐ 58	Bruce Berenyi	.03	.01	.00	☐ 111	Steve Braun	.03	.01	.00
☐ 59	Larry Biittner	.03	.01	.00	☐ 112	Bob Forsch	.06	.02	.00
☐ 60	Scott Brown	.03	.01	.00	☐ 113	George Hendrick	.08	.03	.01
☐ 61	Dave Collins	.06	.02	.00	☐ 114	Keith Hernandez	.30	.12	.03
☐ 62	Geoff Combe	.03	.01	.00	☐ 115	Tom Herr	.08	.03	.01
☐ 63	Dave Concepcion	.10	.04	.01	☐ 116	Dane Iorg	.03	.01	.00
☐ 64	Dan Driessen	.03	.01	.00	☐ 117	Jim Kaat	.15	.06	.01
☐ 65	Joe Edelen	.03	.01	.00	☐ 118	Tito Landrum	.03	.01	.00
☐ 66	George Foster	.15	.06	.01	☐ 119	Sixto Lezcano	.03	.01	.00
☐ 67	Ken Griffey	.10	.04	.01	☐ 120	Mark Littell	.03	.01	.00
☐ 68	Paul Householder	.03	.01	.00	☐ 121	John Martin	.03	.01	.00
☐ 69	Tom Hume	.03	.01	.00	☐ 122	Silvio Martinez	.03	.01	.00
☐ 70	Junior Kennedy	.03	.01	.00	☐ 123	Ken Oberkfell	.03	.01	.00
☐ 71	Ray Knight	.10	.04	.01	☐ 124	Darrell Porter	.06	.02	.00
☐ 72	Mike LaCoss	.03	.01	.00	☐ 125	Mike Ramsey	.03	.01	.00
☐ 73	Rafael Landestoy	.03	.01	.00	☐ 126	Orlando Sanchez	.03	.01	.00
☐ 74	Charlie Leibrandt	.06	.02	.00	☐ 127	Bob Shirley	.03	.01	.00
☐ 75	Sam Mejias	.03	.01	.00	☐ 128	Lary Sorensen	.03	.01	.00
☐ 76	Paul Moskau	.03	.01	.00	☐ 129	Bruce Sutter	.20	.08	.02
☐ 77	Joe Nolan	.03	.01	.00	☐ 130	Bob Sykes	.03	.01	.00
☐ 78	Mike O'Berry	.03	.01	.00	☐ 131	Garry Templeton	.10	.04	.01
☐ 79	Ron Oester	.06	.02	.00	☐ 132	Gene Tenace	.03	.01	.00
☐ 80	Frank Pastore	.03	.01	.00	☐ 133	Jerry Augustine	.03	.01	.00
☐ 81	Joe Price	.03	.01	.00	☐ 134	Sal Bando	.06	.02	.00
☐ 82	Tom Seaver	.40	.16	.04	☐ 135	Mark Brouhard	.03	.01	.00
☐ 83	Mario Soto	.10	.04	.01	☐ 136	Mike Caldwell	.03	.01	.00
☐ 84	Mike Vail	.03	.01	.00	☐ 137	Reggie Cleveland	.03	.01	.00
☐ 85	Tony Armas	.10	.04	.01	☐ 138	Cecil Cooper	.15	.06	.01

		MINT	VG-E	F-G
☐ 139	Jamie Easterly	.03	.01	.00
☐ 140	Marshall Edwards	.03	.01	.00
☐ 141	Rollie Fingers	.20	.08	.02
☐ 142	Jim Gantner	.06	.02	.00
☐ 143	Moose Haas	.06	.02	.00
☐ 144	Larry Hisle	.06	.02	.00
☐ 145	Roy Howell	.03	.01	.00
☐ 146	Rickey Keeton	.03	.01	.00
☐ 147	Randy Lerch	.03	.01	.00
☐ 148	Paul Molitor	.10	.04	.01
☐ 149	Don Money	.03	.01	.00
☐ 150	Charlie Moore	.03	.01	.00
☐ 151	Ben Oglivie	.06	.02	.00
☐ 152	Ted Simmons	.12	.05	.01
☐ 153	Jim Slaton	.06	.02	.00
☐ 154	Gorman Thomas	.10	.04	.01
☐ 155	Robin Yount	.50	.20	.05
☐ 156	Pete Vuckovich	.10	.04	.01
☐ 157	Benny Ayala	.03	.01	.00
☐ 158	Mark Belanger	.06	.02	.00
☐ 159	Al Bumbry	.03	.01	.00
☐ 160	Terry Crowley	.03	.01	.00
☐ 161	Rich Dauer	.03	.01	.00
☐ 162	Doug DeCinces	.10	.04	.01
☐ 163	Rick Dempsey	.06	.02	.00
☐ 164	Jim Dwyer	.03	.01	.00
☐ 165	Mike Flanagan	.08	.03	.01
☐ 166	Dave Ford	.03	.01	.00
☐ 167	Dan Graham	.03	.01	.00
☐ 168	Wayne Krenchicki	.03	.01	.00
☐ 169	John Lowenstein	.03	.01	.00
☐ 170	Dennis Martinez	.03	.01	.00
☐ 171	Tippy Martinez	.03	.01	.00
☐ 172	Scott McGregor	.08	.03	.01
☐ 173	Jose Morales	.03	.01	.00
☐ 174	Eddie Murray	.60	.24	.06
☐ 175	Jim Palmer	.30	.12	.03
☐ 176	Cal Ripken	5.00	2.00	.50
☐ 177	Gary Roenicke	.03	.01	.00
☐ 178	Lenn Sakata	.03	.01	.00
☐ 179	Ken Singleton	.10	.04	.01
☐ 180	Sammy Stewart	.03	.01	.00
☐ 181	Tim Stoddard	.03	.01	.00
☐ 182	Steve Stone	.06	.02	.00
☐ 183	Stan Bahnsen	.03	.01	.00
☐ 184	Ray Burris	.03	.01	.00
☐ 185	Gary Carter	.50	.20	.05
☐ 186	Warren Cromartie	.03	.01	.00
☐ 187	Andre Dawson	.25	.10	.02
☐ 188	Terry Francona	.20	.08	.02
☐ 189	Woodie Fryman	.03	.01	.00
☐ 190	Bill Gullickson	.06	.02	.00
☐ 191	Grant Jackson	.03	.01	.00

		MINT	VG-E	F-G
☐ 192	Wallace Johnson	.06	.02	.00
☐ 193	Charlie Lea	.06	.02	.00
☐ 194	Bill Lee	.06	.02	.00
☐ 195	Jerry Manuel	.03	.01	.00
☐ 196	Brad Mills	.06	.02	.00
☐ 197	John Milner	.03	.01	.00
☐ 198	Rowland Office	.03	.01	.00
☐ 199	David Palmer	.06	.02	.00
☐ 200	Larry Parrish	.06	.02	.00
☐ 201	Mike Phillips	.03	.01	.00
☐ 202	Tim Raines	.50	.20	.05
☐ 203	Bobby Ramos	.03	.01	.00
☐ 204	Jeff Reardon	.10	.04	.01
☐ 205	Steve Rogers	.08	.03	.01
☐ 206	Scott Sanderson	.03	.01	.00
☐ 207	Rodney Scott	.03	.01	.00
☐ 208	Elias Sosa	.03	.01	.00
☐ 209	Chris Speier	.03	.01	.00
☐ 210	Tim Wallach	.45	.18	.04
☐ 211	Jerry White	.03	.01	.00
☐ 212	Alan Ashby	.03	.01	.00
☐ 213	Cesar Cedeno	.08	.03	.01
☐ 214	Jose Cruz	.12	.05	.01
☐ 215	Kiko Garcia	.03	.01	.00
☐ 216	Phil Garner	.06	.02	.00
☐ 217	Danny Heep	.03	.01	.00
☐ 218	Art Howe	.03	.01	.00
☐ 219	Bob Knepper	.10	.04	.01
☐ 220	Frank LaCorte	.03	.01	.00
☐ 221	Joe Niekro	.10	.04	.01
☐ 222	Joe Pittman	.03	.01	.00
☐ 223	Terry Puhl	.06	.02	.00
☐ 224	Luis Pujols	.03	.01	.00
☐ 225	Craig Reynolds	.03	.01	.00
☐ 226	J.R. Richard	.10	.04	.01
☐ 227	Dave Roberts	.03	.01	.00
☐ 228	Vern Ruhle	.03	.01	.00
☐ 229	Nolan Ryan	.45	.18	.04
☐ 230	Joe Sambito	.06	.02	.00
☐ 231	Tony Scott	.03	.01	.00
☐ 232	Dave Smith	.06	.02	.00
☐ 233	Harry Spilman	.03	.01	.00
☐ 234	Don Sutton	.30	.12	.03
☐ 235	Dickie Thon	.08	.03	.01
☐ 236	Denny Walling	.03	.01	.00
☐ 237	Gary Woods	.03	.01	.00
☐ 238	Luis Aguayo	.03	.01	.00
☐ 239	Ramon Aviles	.03	.01	.00
☐ 240	Bob Boone	.06	.02	.00
☐ 241	Larry Bowa	.12	.05	.01
☐ 242	Warren Brusstar	.03	.01	.00
☐ 243	Steve Carlton	.50	.20	.05
☐ 244	Larry Christenson	.03	.01	.00

	MINT	VG-E	F-G		MINT	VG-E	F-G
☐ 245 Dick Davis	.03	.01	.00	☐ 298 Carney Lansford	.12	.05	.01
☐ 246 Greg Gross	.03	.01	.00	☐ 299 Rick Miller	.03	.01	.00
☐ 247 Sparky Lyle	.12	.05	.01	☐ 300 Reid Nichols	.03	.01	.00
☐ 248 Garry Maddox	.06	.02	.00	☐ 301 Bob Ojeda	.75	.30	.07
☐ 249 Gary Matthews	.08	.03	.01	☐ 302 Tony Perez	.15	.06	.01
☐ 250 Bake McBride	.06	.02	.00	☐ 303 Chuck Rainey	.03	.01	.00
☐ 251 Tug McGraw	.10	.04	.01	☐ 304 Jerry Remy	.05	.02	.00
☐ 252 Keith Moreland	.08	.03	.01	☐ 305 Jim Rice	.50	.20	.05
☐ 253 Dickie Noles	.03	.01	.00	☐ 306 Joe Rudi	.06	.02	.00
☐ 254 Mike Proly	.03	.01	.00	☐ 307 Bob Stanley	.06	.02	.00
☐ 255 Ron Reed	.03	.01	.00	☐ 308 Dave Stapleton	.03	.01	.00
☐ 256 Pete Rose	1.25	.50	.12	☐ 309 Frank Tanana	.06	.02	.00
☐ 257 Dick Ruthven	.03	.01	.00	☐ 310 Mike Torrez	.06	.02	.00
☐ 258 Mike Schmidt	.70	.28	.07	☐ 311 John Tudor	.15	.06	.01
☐ 259 Lonnie Smith	.08	.03	.01	☐ 312 Carl Yastrzemski	.70	.28	.07
☐ 260 Manny Trillo	.06	.02	.00	☐ 313 Buddy Bell	.12	.05	.01
☐ 261 Del Unser	.03	.01	.00	☐ 314 Steve Comer	.03	.01	.00
☐ 262 George Vukovich	.03	.01	.00	☐ 315 Danny Darwin	.03	.01	.00
☐ 263 Tom Brookens	.03	.01	.00	☐ 316 John Ellis	.03	.01	.00
☐ 264 George Cappuzzello	.03	.01	.00	☐ 317 John Grubb	.03	.01	.00
☐ 265 Marty Castillo	.06	.02	.00	☐ 318 Rick Honeycutt	.06	.02	.00
☐ 266 Al Cowens	.03	.01	.00	☐ 319 Charlie Hough	.08	.03	.01
☐ 267 Kirk Gibson	.40	.16	.04	☐ 320 Ferguson Jenkins	.15	.06	.01
☐ 268 Richie Hebner	.03	.01	.00	☐ 321 John Henry Johnson	.03	.01	.00
☐ 269 Ron Jackson	.03	.01	.00	☐ 322 Jim Kern	.03	.01	.00
☐ 270 Lynn Jones	.03	.01	.00	☐ 323 Jon Matlack	.06	.02	.00
☐ 271 Steve Kemp	.08	.03	.01	☐ 324 Doc Medich	.03	.01	.00
☐ 272 Rick Leach	.06	.02	.00	☐ 325 Mario Mendoza	.03	.01	.00
☐ 273 Aurelio Lopez	.03	.01	.00	☐ 326 Al Oliver	.15	.06	.01
☐ 274 Jack Morris	.30	.12	.03	☐ 327 Pat Putnam	.03	.01	.00
☐ 275 Kevin Saucier	.03	.01	.00	☐ 328 Mickey Rivers	.06	.02	.00
☐ 276 Lance Parrish	.35	.14	.03	☐ 329 Leon Roberts	.03	.01	.00
☐ 277 Rick Peters	.03	.01	.00	☐ 330 Billy Sample	.03	.01	.00
☐ 278 Dan Petry	.12	.05	.01	☐ 331 Bill Stein	.03	.01	.00
☐ 279 David Rozema	.03	.01	.00	☐ 332 Jim Sundberg	.06	.02	.00
☐ 280 Stan Papi	.03	.01	.00	☐ 333 Mark Wagner	.03	.01	.00
☐ 281 Dan Schatzeder	.03	.01	.00	☐ 334 Bump Wills	.03	.01	.00
☐ 282 Champ Summers	.03	.01	.00	☐ 335 Bill Almon	.03	.01	.00
☐ 283 Alan Trammell	.20	.08	.02	☐ 336 Harold Baines	.35	.14	.03
☐ 284 Lou Whitaker	.15	.06	.01	☐ 337 Ross Baumgarten	.03	.01	.00
☐ 285 Milt Wilcox	.03	.01	.00	☐ 338 Tony Bernazard	.06	.02	.00
☐ 286 John Wockenfuss	.03	.01	.00	☐ 339 Britt Burns	.08	.03	.01
☐ 287 Gary Allenson	.03	.01	.00	☐ 340 Richard Dotson	.08	.03	.01
☐ 288 Tom Burgmeier	.03	.01	.00	☐ 341 Jim Essian	.03	.01	.00
☐ 289 Bill Campbell	.03	.01	.00	☐ 342 Ed Farmer	.03	.01	.00
☐ 290 Mark Clear	.03	.01	.00	☐ 343 Carlton Fisk	.18	.08	.01
☐ 291 Steve Crawford	.06	.02	.00	☐ 344 Kevin Hickey	.06	.02	.00
☐ 292 Dennis Eckersley	.06	.02	.00	☐ 345 LaMarr Hoyt	.10	.04	.01
☐ 293 Dwight Evans	.12	.05	.01	☐ 346 Lamar Johnson	.03	.01	.00
☐ 294 Rich Gedman	.75	.30	.07	☐ 347 Jerry Koosman	.08	.03	.01
☐ 295 Garry Hancock	.03	.01	.00	☐ 348 Rusty Kuntz	.03	.01	.00
☐ 296 Glenn Hoffman	.03	.01	.00	☐ 349 Dennis Lamp	.03	.01	.00
☐ 297 Bruce Hurst	.10	.04	.01	☐ 350 Ron LeFlore	.06	.02	.00

		MINT	VG-E	F-G
☐ 351	Chet Lemon	.08	.03	.01
☐ 352	Greg Luzinski	.12	.05	.01
☐ 353	Bob Molinaro	.03	.01	.00
☐ 354	Jim Morrison	.03	.01	.00
☐ 355	Wayne Nordhagen	.03	.01	.00
☐ 356	Greg Pryor	.03	.01	.00
☐ 357	Mike Squires	.03	.01	.00
☐ 358	Steve Trout	.06	.02	.00
☐ 359	Alan Bannister	.03	.01	.00
☐ 360	Len Barker	.08	.03	.01
☐ 361	Bert Blyleven	.12	.05	.01
☐ 362	Joe Charboneau	.06	.02	.00
☐ 363	John Denny	.10	.04	.01
☐ 364	Bo Diaz	.06	.02	.00
☐ 365	Miguel Dilone	.03	.01	.00
☐ 366	Jerry Dybzinski	.03	.01	.00
☐ 367	Wayne Garland	.03	.01	.00
☐ 368	Mike Hargrove	.06	.02	.00
☐ 369	Toby Harrah	.06	.02	.00
☐ 370	Ron Hassey	.03	.01	.00
☐ 371	Von Hayes	1.00	.40	.10
☐ 372	Pat Kelly	.03	.01	.00
☐ 373	Duane Kuiper	.03	.01	.00
☐ 374	Rick Manning	.03	.01	.00
☐ 375	Sid Monge	.03	.01	.00
☐ 376	Jorge Orta	.03	.01	.00
☐ 377	Dave Rosello	.03	.01	.00
☐ 378	Dan Spillner	.03	.01	.00
☐ 379	Mike Stanton	.03	.01	.00
☐ 380	Andre Thornton	.08	.03	.01
☐ 381	Tom Veryzer	.03	.01	.00
☐ 382	Rick Waits	.03	.01	.00
☐ 383	Doyle Alexander	.06	.02	.00
☐ 384	Vida Blue	.08	.03	.01
☐ 385	Fred Breining	.08	.03	.01
☐ 386	Enos Cabell	.03	.01	.00
☐ 387	Jack Clark	.12	.05	.01
☐ 388	Darrell Evans	.10	.04	.01
☐ 389	Tom Griffin	.03	.01	.00
☐ 390	Larry Herndon	.03	.01	.00
☐ 391	Al Holland	.06	.02	.00
☐ 392	Gary Lavelle	.06	.02	.00
☐ 393	Johnnie LeMaster	.03	.01	.00
☐ 394	Jerry Martin	.03	.01	.00
☐ 395	Milt May	.03	.01	.00
☐ 396	Greg Minton	.06	.02	.00
☐ 397	Joe Morgan	.25	.10	.02
☐ 398	Joe Pettini	.03	.01	.00
☐ 399	Alan Ripley	.03	.01	.00
☐ 400	Billy Smith	.03	.01	.00
☐ 401	Rennie Stennett	.03	.01	.00
☐ 402	Ed Whitson	.06	.02	.00
☐ 403	Jim Wohlford	.03	.01	.00

		MINT	VG-E	F-G
☐ 404	Willie Aikens	.06	.02	.00
☐ 405	George Brett	.70	.28	.07
☐ 406	Ken Brett	.06	.02	.00
☐ 407	Dave Chalk	.03	.01	.00
☐ 408	Rich Gale	.03	.01	.00
☐ 409	Cesar Geronimo	.03	.01	.00
☐ 410	Larry Gura	.06	.02	.00
☐ 411	Clint Hurdle	.03	.01	.00
☐ 412	Mike Jones	.03	.01	.00
☐ 413	Dennis Leonard	.06	.02	.00
☐ 414	Renie Martin	.03	.01	.00
☐ 415	Lee May	.06	.02	.00
☐ 416	Hal McRae	.06	.02	.00
☐ 417	Darryl Motley	.12	.05	.01
☐ 418	Rance Mulliniks	.03	.01	.00
☐ 419	Amos Otis	.08	.03	.01
☐ 420	Ken Phelps	.30	.12	.03
☐ 421	Jamie Quirk	.03	.01	.00
☐ 422	Dan Quisenberry	.20	.08	.02
☐ 423	Paul Splittorff	.06	.02	.00
☐ 424	U.L. Washington	.03	.01	.00
☐ 425	John Wathan	.03	.01	.00
☐ 426	Frank White	.08	.03	.01
☐ 427	Willie Wilson	.20	.08	.02
☐ 428	Brian Asselstine	.03	.01	.00
☐ 429	Bruce Benedict	.03	.01	.00
☐ 430	Tom Boggs	.03	.01	.00
☐ 431	Larry Bradford	.03	.01	.00
☐ 432	Rick Camp	.03	.01	.00
☐ 433	Chris Chambliss	.06	.02	.00
☐ 434	Gene Garber	.03	.01	.00
☐ 435	Preston Hanna	.03	.01	.00
☐ 436	Bob Horner	.25	.10	.02
☐ 437	Glenn Hubbard	.03	.01	.00
☐ 438	A Al Hrabosky (height 5'1")	15.00	6.00	1.50
☐ 438	B Al Hrabosky (height 5'1")	.75	.30	.07
☐ 438	C Al Hrabosky (height 5'10")	.10	.04	.01
☐ 439	Rufino Linares	.05	.02	.00
☐ 440	Rick Mahler	.20	.08	.02
☐ 441	Ed Miller	.03	.01	.00
☐ 442	John Montefusco	.06	.02	.00
☐ 443	Dale Murphy	.90	.36	.09
☐ 444	Phil Niekro	.20	.08	.02
☐ 445	Gaylord Perry	.20	.08	.02
☐ 446	Biff Pocoroba	.03	.01	.00
☐ 447	Rafael Ramirez	.03	.01	.00
☐ 448	Jerry Royster	.03	.01	.00
☐ 449	Claudell Washington	.08	.03	.01
☐ 450	Don Aase	.06	.02	.00
☐ 451	Don Baylor	.15	.06	.01

	MINT	VG-E	F-G
☐ 452 Juan Beniquez	.06	.02	.00
☐ 453 Rick Burleson	.06	.02	.00
☐ 454 Bert Campaneris	.08	.03	.01
☐ 455 Rod Carew	.50	.20	.05
☐ 456 Bob Clark	.03	.01	.00
☐ 457 Brian Downing	.06	.02	.00
☐ 458 Dan Ford	.03	.01	.00
☐ 459 Ken Forsch	.03	.01	.00
☐ 460 A Dave Frost (5 mm space before ERA)	.35	.14	.03
☐ 460 B Dave Frost (1 mm space)	.05	.02	.00
☐ 461 Bobby Grich	.08	.03	.01
☐ 462 Larry Harlow	.03	.01	.00
☐ 463 John Harris	.03	.01	.00
☐ 464 Andy Hassler	.03	.01	.00
☐ 465 Butch Hobson	.03	.01	.00
☐ 466 Jesse Jefferson	.03	.01	.00
☐ 467 Bruce Kison	.03	.01	.00
☐ 468 Fred Lynn	.25	.10	.02
☐ 469 Angel Moreno	.03	.01	.00
☐ 470 Ed Ott	.03	.01	.00
☐ 471 Fred Patek	.03	.01	.00
☐ 472 Steve Renko	.03	.01	.00
☐ 473 Mike Witt	1.00	.40	.10
☐ 474 Geoff Zahn	.03	.01	.00
☐ 475 Gary Alexander	.03	.01	.00
☐ 476 Dale Berra	.06	.02	.00
☐ 477 Kurt Bevacqua	.03	.01	.00
☐ 478 Jim Bibby	.06	.02	.00
☐ 479 John Candelaria	.08	.03	.01
☐ 480 Victor Cruz	.03	.01	.00
☐ 481 Mike Easler	.08	.03	.01
☐ 482 Tim Foli	.03	.01	.00
☐ 483 Lee Lacy	.08	.03	.01
☐ 484 Vance Law	.03	.01	.00
☐ 485 Bill Madlock	.15	.06	.01
☐ 486 Willie Montanez	.03	.01	.00
☐ 487 Omar Moreno	.03	.01	.00
☐ 488 Steve Nicosia	.03	.01	.00
☐ 489 Dave Parker	.25	.10	.02
☐ 490 Tony Pena	.15	.06	.01
☐ 491 Pascual Perez	.06	.02	.00
☐ 492 Johnny Ray	.60	.24	.06
☐ 493 Rick Rhoden	.08	.03	.01
☐ 494 Bill Robinson	.03	.01	.00
☐ 495 Don Robinson	.03	.01	.00
☐ 496 Enrique Romo	.03	.01	.00
☐ 497 Rod Scurry	.03	.01	.00
☐ 498 Eddie Solomon	.03	.01	.00
☐ 499 Willie Stargell	.25	.10	.02
☐ 500 Kent Tekulve	.08	.03	.01
☐ 501 Jason Thompson	.06	.02	.00

	MINT	VG-E	F-G
☐ 502 Glenn Abbott	.03	.01	.00
☐ 503 Jim Anderson	.03	.01	.00
☐ 504 Floyd Bannister	.06	.02	.00
☐ 505 Bruce Bochte	.06	.02	.00
☐ 506 Jeff Burroughs	.06	.02	.00
☐ 507 Bryan Clark	.03	.01	.00
☐ 508 Ken Clay	.03	.01	.00
☐ 509 Julio Cruz	.03	.01	.00
☐ 510 Dick Drago	.03	.01	.00
☐ 511 Gary Gray	.03	.01	.00
☐ 512 Dan Meyer	.03	.01	.00
☐ 513 Jerry Narron	.03	.01	.00
☐ 514 Tom Paciorek	.03	.01	.00
☐ 515 Casey Parsons	.03	.01	.00
☐ 516 Lenny Randle	.03	.01	.00
☐ 517 Shane Rawley	.08	.03	.01
☐ 518 Joe Simpson	.03	.01	.00
☐ 519 Richie Zisk	.06	.02	.00
☐ 520 Neil Allen	.06	.02	.00
☐ 521 Bob Bailor	.03	.01	.00
☐ 522 Hubie Brooks	.15	.06	.01
☐ 523 Mike Cubbage	.03	.01	.00
☐ 524 Pete Falcone	.03	.01	.00
☐ 525 Doug Flynn	.03	.01	.00
☐ 526 Tom Hausman	.03	.01	.00
☐ 527 Ron Hodges	.03	.01	.00
☐ 528 Randy Jones	.06	.02	.00
☐ 529 Mike Jorgensen	.03	.01	.00
☐ 530 Dave Kingman	.15	.06	.01
☐ 531 Ed Lynch	.10	.04	.01
☐ 532 Mike Marshall (screwball pitcher)	.06	.02	.00
☐ 533 Lee Mazzilli	.06	.02	.00
☐ 534 Dyar Miller	.03	.01	.00
☐ 535 Mike Scott	.25	.10	.02
☐ 536 Rusty Staub	.10	.04	.01
☐ 537 John Stearns	.03	.01	.00
☐ 538 Craig Swan	.03	.01	.00
☐ 539 Frank Taveras	.03	.01	.00
☐ 540 Alex Trevino	.03	.01	.00
☐ 541 Ellis Valentine	.03	.01	.00
☐ 542 Mookie Wilson	.08	.03	.01
☐ 543 Joel Youngblood	.03	.01	.00
☐ 544 Pat Zachry	.03	.01	.00
☐ 545 Glenn Adams	.03	.01	.00
☐ 546 Fernando Arroyo	.03	.01	.00
☐ 547 John Verhoeven	.03	.01	.00
☐ 548 Sal Butera	.03	.01	.00
☐ 549 John Castino	.03	.01	.00
☐ 550 Don Cooper	.03	.01	.00
☐ 551 Doug Corbett	.03	.01	.00
☐ 552 Dave Engle	.03	.01	.00
☐ 553 Roger Erickson	.03	.01	.00

	MINT	VG-E	F-G
☐ 554 Danny Goodwin	.03	.01	.00
☐ 555 A Darrell Jackson (black hat)	1.25	.50	.12
☐ 555 B Darrell Jackson (red hat)	.08	.03	.01
☐ 556 Pete Mackanin	.03	.01	.00
☐ 557 Jack O'Connor	.03	.01	.00
☐ 558 Hosken Powell	.03	.01	.00
☐ 559 Pete Redfern	.03	.01	.00
☐ 560 Roy Smalley	.06	.02	.00
☐ 561 Chuck Baker	.03	.01	.00
☐ 562 Gary Ward	.06	.02	.00
☐ 563 Rob Wilfong	.03	.01	.00
☐ 564 Al Williams	.03	.01	.00
☐ 565 Butch Wynegar	.06	.02	.00
☐ 566 Randy Bass	.03	.01	.00
☐ 567 Juan Bonilla	.03	.01	.00
☐ 568 Danny Boone	.03	.01	.00
☐ 569 John Curtis	.03	.01	.00
☐ 570 Juan Eichelberger	.03	.01	.00
☐ 571 Barry Evans	.03	.01	.00
☐ 572 Tim Flannery	.03	.01	.00
☐ 573 Ruppert Jones	.03	.01	.00
☐ 574 Terry Kennedy	.08	.03	.01
☐ 575 Joe Lefebvre	.03	.01	.00
☐ 576 A John Littlefield ERR (left handed)	50.00	20.00	5.00
☐ 576 B John Littlefield COR (right handed)	.08	.03	.01
☐ 577 Gary Lucas	.03	.01	.00
☐ 578 Steve Mura	.03	.01	.00
☐ 579 Broderick Perkins	.03	.01	.00
☐ 580 Gene Richards	.03	.01	.00
☐ 581 Luis Salazar	.03	.01	.00
☐ 582 Ozzie Smith	.18	.08	.01
☐ 583 John Urrea	.03	.01	.00
☐ 584 Chris Welsh	.06	.02	.00
☐ 585 Rick Wise	.06	.02	.00
☐ 586 Doug Bird	.03	.01	.00
☐ 587 Tim Blackwell	.03	.01	.00
☐ 588 Bobby Bonds	.08	.03	.01
☐ 589 Bill Buckner	.12	.05	.01
☐ 590 Bill Caudill	.06	.02	.00
☐ 591 Hector Cruz	.03	.01	.00
☐ 592 Jody Davis	.45	.18	.04
☐ 593 Ivan DeJesus	.03	.01	.00
☐ 594 Steve Dillard	.03	.01	.00
☐ 595 Leon Durham	.10	.04	.01
☐ 596 Rawly Eastwick	.03	.01	.00
☐ 597 Steve Henderson	.03	.01	.00
☐ 598 Mike Krukow	.08	.03	.01
☐ 599 Mike Lum	.03	.01	.00
☐ 600 Randy Martz	.03	.01	.00

	MINT	VG-E	F-G
☐ 601 Jerry Morales	.03	.01	.00
☐ 602 Ken Reitz	.03	.01	.00
☐ 603 A Lee Smith ERR (Cubs logo reversed)	.90	.36	.09
☐ 603 B Lee Smith COR	.60	.24	.06
☐ 604 Dick Tidrow	.03	.01	.00
☐ 605 Jim Tracy	.03	.01	.00
☐ 606 Mike Tyson	.03	.01	.00
☐ 607 Ty Waller	.06	.02	.00
☐ 608 Danny Ainge	.08	.03	.01
☐ 609 Jorge Bell	1.50	.60	.15
☐ 610 Mark Bomback	.03	.01	.00
☐ 611 Barry Bonnell	.03	.01	.00
☐ 612 Jim Clancy	.06	.02	.00
☐ 613 Damaso Garcia	.10	.04	.01
☐ 614 Jerry Garvin	.03	.01	.00
☐ 615 Alfredo Griffin	.06	.02	.00
☐ 616 Garth Iorg	.03	.01	.00
☐ 617 Luis Leal	.03	.01	.00
☐ 618 Ken Macha	.03	.01	.00
☐ 619 John Mayberry	.06	.02	.00
☐ 620 Joey McLaughlin	.03	.01	.00
☐ 621 Lloyd Moseby	.15	.06	.01
☐ 622 Dave Stieb	.15	.06	.01
☐ 623 Jackson Todd	.03	.01	.00
☐ 624 Willie Upshaw	.08	.03	.01
☐ 625 Otto Velez	.03	.01	.00
☐ 626 Ernie Whitt	.03	.01	.00
☐ 627 Al Woods	.03	.01	.00
☐ 628 All Star Game Cleveland, Ohio	.06	.02	.00
☐ 629 All Star Infielders Frank White and Bucky Dent	.06	.02	.00
☐ 630 Big Red Machine Dan Driessen Dave Concepcion George Foster	.08	.03	.01
☐ 631 Bruce Sutter Top NL Relief Pitcher	.10	.04	.01
☐ 632 "Steve and Carlton" Steve Carlton and Carlton Fisk	.20	.08	.02
☐ 633 Carl Yastrzemski 3000th Game	.30	.12	.03
☐ 634 Dynamic Duo Johnny Bench and Tom Seaver	.25	.10	.02
☐ 635 West Meets East Fernando Valenzuela and Gary Carter	.30	.12	.03
☐ 636 A Fernando Valenzuela: NL SO King ("he" NL)	.35	.14	.03

	MINT	VG-E	F-G
☐ 636 **B** Fernando Valenzuela: NL SO King ("the" NL)	.30	.12	.03
☐ 637 Mike Schmidt .... Home Run King	.35	.14	.03
☐ 638 NL All Stars .... Gary Carter and Dave Parker	.20	.08	.02
☐ 639 Perfect Game .... Len Barker and Bo Diaz (catcher actually Ron Hassey)	.08	.03	.01
☐ 640 Pete and Re-Pete .... Pete Rose and Son	1.25	.50	.12
☐ 641 Phillies Finest .... Lonnie Smith Mike Schmidt Steve Carlton	.30	.12	.03
☐ 642 Red Sox Reunion .... Fred Lynn and Dwight Evans	.10	.04	.01
☐ 643 Rickey Henderson ..... Most Hits and Runs	.30	.12	.03
☐ 644 Rollie Fingers........... Most Saves AL	.10	.04	.01
☐ 645 Tom Seaver .... Most 1981 Wins	.20	.08	.02
☐ 646 **A** Yankee Powerhouse . Reggie Jackson and Dave Winfield (comma on back after outfielder)	.50	.20	.05
☐ 646 **B** Yankee Powerhouse . Reggie Jackson and Dave Winfield (no comma)	.40	.16	.04
☐ 647 CL: Yankees/Dodgers ..	.08	.01	.00
☐ 648 CL: A's/Reds	.07	.01	.00
☐ 649 CL: Cards/Brewers	.07	.01	.00
☐ 650 CL: Expos/Orioles	.07	.01	.00
☐ 651 CL: Astros/Phillies	.07	.01	.00
☐ 652 CL: Tigers/Red Sox	.07	.01	.00
☐ 653 CL: Rangers/White Sox ..	.07	.01	.00
☐ 654 CL: Giants/Indians	.07	.01	.00
☐ 655 CL: Royals/Braves	.07	.01	.00
☐ 656 CL: Angels/Pirates	.07	.01	.00
☐ 657 CL: Mariners/Mets	.07	.01	.00
☐ 658 CL: Padres/Twins	.07	.01	.00
☐ 659 CL: Blue Jays/Cubs	.07	.01	.00
☐ 660 Specials Checklist	.10	.01	.00

1983 Fleer

The cards in this 660-card set measure 2½" by 3½". In 1983, for the third straight year, Fleer has produced a baseball series numbering 660 cards. Of these, 1-628 are player cards, 629-646 are special cards, and 647-660 are checklist cards. The player cards are again ordered alphabetically within team. The team order relates back to each team's on-field performance during the previous year, i.e., World Champion Cardinals (1-25), AL Champion Brewers (26-51), Baltimore (52-75), California (76-103), Kansas City (104-128), Atlanta (129-152), Philadelphia (153-176), Boston (177-200), Los Angeles (201-227), Chicago White Sox (228-251), San Francisco (252-276), Montreal (277-301), Pittsburgh (302-326), Detroit (327-351), San Diego (352-375), New York Yankees (376-399), Cleveland (400-423), Toronto (424-444), Houston (445-469), Seattle (470-489), Chicago Cubs (490-512), Oakland (513-535), New York Mets (536-561), Texas (562-583), Cincinnati (584-606), and Minnesota (607-628). The front of each card has a colorful team logo at bottom left and the player's name and position at lower right. The reverses are done in shades of brown on white. The cards are numbered on the back next to a small black and white photo of the player.

		MINT	VG-E	F-G
	Complete Set	25.00	10.00	2.50
	Common Player (1-660)	.03	.01	.00
☐ 1	Joaquin Andujar	.12	.05	.01
☐ 2	Doug Bair	.03	.01	.00
☐ 3	Steve Braun	.03	.01	.00
☐ 4	Glenn Brummer	.03	.01	.00
☐ 5	Bob Forsch	.06	.02	.00
☐ 6	David Green	.08	.03	.01
☐ 7	George Hendrick	.07	.03	.01
☐ 8	Keith Hernandez	.30	.12	.03
☐ 9	Tom Herr	.08	.03	.01
☐ 10	Dane Iorg	.03	.01	.00
☐ 11	Jim Kaat	.12	.05	.01
☐ 12	Jeff Lahti	.06	.02	.00
☐ 13	Tito Landrum	.03	.01	.00
☐ 14	Dave LaPoint	.12	.05	.01
☐ 15	Willie McGee	1.25	.50	.12
☐ 16	Steve Mura	.03	.01	.00
☐ 17	Ken Oberkfell	.03	.01	.00
☐ 18	Darrell Porter	.05	.02	.00
☐ 19	Mike Ramsey	.03	.01	.00
☐ 20	Gene Roof	.05	.02	.00
☐ 21	Lonnie Smith	.07	.03	.01
☐ 22	Ozzie Smith	.15	.06	.01
☐ 23	John Stuper	.07	.03	.01
☐ 24	Bruce Sutter	.15	.06	.01
☐ 25	Gene Tenace	.03	.01	.00
☐ 26	Jerry Augustine	.03	.01	.00
☐ 27	Dwight Bernard	.03	.01	.00
☐ 28	Mark Brouhard	.03	.01	.00
☐ 29	Mike Caldwell	.05	.02	.00
☐ 30	Cecil Cooper	.14	.06	.01
☐ 31	Jamie Easterly	.03	.01	.00
☐ 32	Marshall Edwards	.03	.01	.00
☐ 33	Rollie Fingers	.18	.08	.01
☐ 34	Jim Gantner	.05	.02	.00
☐ 35	Moose Haas	.03	.01	.00
☐ 36	Roy Howell	.03	.01	.00
☐ 37	Peter Ladd	.03	.01	.00
☐ 38	Bob McClure	.03	.01	.00
☐ 39	Doc Medich	.03	.01	.00
☐ 40	Paul Molitor	.10	.04	.01
☐ 41	Don Money	.03	.01	.00
☐ 42	Charlie Moore	.03	.01	.00
☐ 43	Ben Oglivie	.07	.03	.01
☐ 44	Ed Romero	.03	.01	.00
☐ 45	Ted Simmons	.12	.05	.01
☐ 46	Jim Slaton	.03	.01	.00
☐ 47	Don Sutton	.25	.10	.02
☐ 48	Gorman Thomas	.10	.04	.01
☐ 49	Pete Vuckovich	.07	.03	.01
☐ 50	Ned Yost	.03	.01	.00
☐ 51	Robin Yount	.30	.12	.03
☐ 52	Benny Ayala	.03	.01	.00
☐ 53	Bob Bonner	.03	.01	.00
☐ 54	Al Bumbry	.03	.01	.00
☐ 55	Terry Crowley	.03	.01	.00
☐ 56	Storm Davis	.45	.18	.04
☐ 57	Rich Dauer	.03	.01	.00
☐ 58	Rick Dempsey	.05	.02	.00
☐ 59	Jim Dwyer	.03	.01	.00
☐ 60	Mike Flanagan	.08	.03	.01
☐ 61	Dan Ford	.03	.01	.00
☐ 62	Glenn Gulliver	.03	.01	.00
☐ 63	John Lowenstein	.03	.01	.00
☐ 64	Dennis Martinez	.03	.01	.00
☐ 65	Tippy Martinez	.03	.01	.00
☐ 66	Scott McGregor	.08	.03	.01
☐ 67	Eddie Murray	.55	.22	.05
☐ 68	Joe Nolan	.03	.01	.00
☐ 69	Jim Palmer	.30	.12	.03
☐ 70	Cal Ripken Jr.	.70	.28	.07
☐ 71	Gary Roenicke	.05	.02	.00
☐ 72	Lenn Sakata	.03	.01	.00
☐ 73	Ken Singleton	.08	.03	.01
☐ 74	Sammy Stewart	.03	.01	.00
☐ 75	Tim Stoddard	.03	.01	.00
☐ 76	Don Aase	.05	.02	.00
☐ 77	Don Baylor	.12	.05	.01
☐ 78	Juan Beniquez	.05	.02	.00
☐ 79	Bob Boone	.05	.02	.00
☐ 80	Rick Burleson	.06	.02	.00
☐ 81	Rod Carew	.40	.16	.04
☐ 82	Bobby Clark	.03	.01	.00
☐ 83	Doug Corbett	.03	.01	.00
☐ 84	John Curtis	.03	.01	.00
☐ 85	Doug DeCinces	.09	.04	.01
☐ 86	Brian Downing	.05	.02	.00
☐ 87	Joe Ferguson	.03	.01	.00
☐ 88	Tim Foli	.03	.01	.00
☐ 89	Ken Forsch	.03	.01	.00
☐ 90	Dave Goltz	.03	.01	.00
☐ 91	Bobby Grich	.07	.03	.01
☐ 92	Andy Hassler	.03	.01	.00
☐ 93	Reggie Jackson	.45	.18	.04
☐ 94	Ron Jackson	.03	.01	.00
☐ 95	Tommy John	.15	.06	.01
☐ 96	Bruce Kison	.03	.01	.00
☐ 97	Fred Lynn	.18	.08	.01
☐ 98	Ed Ott	.03	.01	.00
☐ 99	Steve Renko	.03	.01	.00
☐ 100	Luis Sanchez	.03	.01	.00
☐ 101	Rob Wilfong	.03	.01	.00
☐ 102	Mike Witt	.12	.05	.01
☐ 103	Geoff Zahn	.03	.01	.00

		MINT	VG-E	F-G
☐ 104	Willie Aikens	.03	.01	.00
☐ 105	Mike Armstrong	.03	.01	.00
☐ 106	Vida Blue	.08	.03	.01
☐ 107	Bud Black	.20	.08	.02
☐ 108	George Brett	.50	.20	.05
☐ 109	Bill Castro	.03	.01	.00
☐ 110	Onix Concepcion	.06	.02	.00
☐ 111	Dave Frost	.03	.01	.00
☐ 112	Cesar Geronimo	.03	.01	.00
☐ 113	Larry Gura	.05	.02	.00
☐ 114	Steve Hammond	.05	.02	.00
☐ 115	Don Hood	.03	.01	.00
☐ 116	Dennis Leonard	.05	.02	.00
☐ 117	Jerry Martin	.03	.01	.00
☐ 118	Lee May	.05	.02	.00
☐ 119	Hal McRae	.06	.02	.00
☐ 120	Amos Otis	.06	.02	.00
☐ 121	Greg Pryor	.03	.01	.00
☐ 122	Dan Quisenberry	.15	.06	.01
☐ 123	Don Slaught	.20	.08	.02
☐ 124	Paul Splittorff	.05	.02	.00
☐ 125	U.L. Washington	.03	.01	.00
☐ 126	John Wathan	.03	.01	.00
☐ 127	Frank White	.07	.03	.01
☐ 128	Willie Wilson	.18	.08	.01
☐ 129	Steve Bedrosian	.06	.02	.00
☐ 130	Bruce Benedict	.03	.01	.00
☐ 131	Tommy Boggs	.03	.01	.00
☐ 132	Brett Butler	.09	.04	.01
☐ 133	Rick Camp	.03	.01	.00
☐ 134	Chris Chambliss	.05	.02	.00
☐ 135	Ken Dayley	.03	.01	.00
☐ 136	Gene Garber	.03	.01	.00
☐ 137	Terry Harper	.03	.01	.00
☐ 138	Bob Horner	.20	.08	.02
☐ 139	Glenn Hubbard	.03	.01	.00
☐ 140	Rufino Linares	.03	.01	.00
☐ 141	Rick Mahler	.05	.02	.00
☐ 142	Dale Murphy	.75	.30	.07
☐ 143	Phil Niekro	.20	.08	.02
☐ 144	Pascual Perez	.05	.02	.00
☐ 145	Biff Pocoroba	.03	.01	.00
☐ 146	Rafael Ramirez	.03	.01	.00
☐ 147	Jerry Royster	.03	.01	.00
☐ 148	Ken Smith	.03	.01	.00
☐ 149	Bob Walk	.03	.01	.00
☐ 150	Claudell Washington	.06	.02	.00
☐ 151	Bob Watson	.06	.02	.00
☐ 152	Larry Whisenton	.03	.01	.00
☐ 153	Porfirio Altamirano	.03	.01	.00
☐ 154	Marty Bystrom	.03	.01	.00
☐ 155	Steve Carlton	.35	.14	.03
☐ 156	Larry Christenson	.03	.01	.00

		MINT	VG-E	F-G
☐ 157	Ivan DeJesus	.03	.01	.00
☐ 158	John Denny	.08	.03	.01
☐ 159	Bob Dernier	.07	.03	.01
☐ 160	Bo Diaz	.05	.02	.00
☐ 161	Ed Farmer	.03	.01	.00
☐ 162	Greg Gross	.03	.01	.00
☐ 163	Mike Krukow	.08	.03	.01
☐ 164	Garry Maddox	.05	.02	.00
☐ 165	Gary Matthews	.08	.03	.01
☐ 166	Tug McGraw	.09	.04	.01
☐ 167	Bob Molinaro	.03	.01	.00
☐ 168	Sid Monge	.03	.01	.00
☐ 169	Ron Reed	.03	.01	.00
☐ 170	Bill Robinson	.03	.01	.00
☐ 171	Pete Rose	1.00	.40	.10
☐ 172	Dick Ruthven	.03	.01	.00
☐ 173	Mike Schmidt	.50	.20	.05
☐ 174	Manny Trillo	.05	.02	.00
☐ 175	Ozzie Virgil	.06	.02	.00
☐ 176	George Vuckovich	.03	.01	.00
☐ 177	Gary Allenson	.03	.01	.00
☐ 178	Luis Aponte	.05	.02	.00
☐ 179	Wade Boggs	12.00	5.00	1.20
☐ 180	Tom Burgmeier	.03	.01	.00
☐ 181	Mark Clear	.03	.01	.00
☐ 182	Dennis Eckersley	.05	.02	.00
☐ 183	Dwight Evans	.12	.05	.01
☐ 184	Rich Gedman	.10	.04	.01
☐ 185	Glenn Hoffman	.03	.01	.00
☐ 186	Bruce Hurst	.09	.04	.01
☐ 187	Carney Lansford	.10	.04	.01
☐ 188	Rick Miller	.03	.01	.00
☐ 189	Reid Nichols	.03	.01	.00
☐ 190	Bob Ojeda	.09	.04	.01
☐ 191	Tony Perez	.12	.05	.01
☐ 192	Chuck Rainey	.03	.01	.00
☐ 193	Jerry Remy	.03	.01	.00
☐ 194	Jim Rice	.30	.12	.03
☐ 195	Bob Stanley	.05	.02	.00
☐ 196	Dave Stapleton	.03	.01	.00
☐ 197	Mike Torrez	.05	.02	.00
☐ 198	John Tudor	.12	.05	.01
☐ 199	Julio Valdez	.03	.01	.00
☐ 200	Carl Yastrzemski	.55	.22	.05
☐ 201	Dusty Baker	.07	.03	.01
☐ 202	Joe Beckwith	.03	.01	.00
☐ 203	Greg Brock	.35	.14	.03
☐ 204	Ron Cey	.10	.04	.01
☐ 205	Terry Forster	.07	.03	.01
☐ 206	Steve Garvey	.40	.16	.04
☐ 207	Pedro Guerrero	.30	.12	.03
☐ 208	Burt Hooton	.03	.01	.00
☐ 209	Steve Howe	.05	.02	.00

	MINT	VG-E	F-G			MINT	VG-E	F-G
☐ 210 Ken Landreaux	.05	.02	.00	☐ 263 Duane Kuiper	.03	.01	.00
☐ 211 Mike Marshall	.20	.08	.02	☐ 264 Bill Laskey	.08	.03	.01
☐ 212 Candy Maldonado	.35	.14	.03	☐ 265 Gary Lavelle	.05	.02	.00
☐ 213 Rick Monday	.05	.02	.00	☐ 266 Johnnie LeMaster	.03	.01	.00
☐ 214 Tom Niedenfuer	.07	.03	.01	☐ 267 Renie Martin	.03	.01	.00
☐ 215 Jorge Orta	.03	.01	.00	☐ 268 Milt May	.03	.01	.00
☐ 216 Jerry Reuss	.06	.02	.00	☐ 269 Greg Minton	.05	.02	.00
☐ 217 Ron Roenicke	.03	.01	.00	☐ 270 Joe Morgan	.20	.08	.02
☐ 218 Vicente Romo	.03	.01	.00	☐ 271 Tom O'Malley	.06	.02	.00
☐ 219 Bill Russell	.05	.02	.00	☐ 272 Reggie Smith	.09	.04	.01
☐ 220 Steve Sax	.18	.08	.01	☐ 273 Guy Sularz	.03	.01	.00
☐ 221 Mike Scioscia	.05	.02	.00	☐ 274 Champ Summers	.03	.01	.00
☐ 222 Dave Stewart	.03	.01	.00	☐ 275 Max Venable	.03	.01	.00
☐ 223 Derrel Thomas	.03	.01	.00	☐ 276 Jim Wohlford	.03	.01	.00
☐ 224 Fernando Valenzuela	.35	.14	.03	☐ 277 Ray Burris	.03	.01	.00
☐ 225 Bob Welch	.07	.03	.01	☐ 278 Gary Carter	.40	.16	.04
☐ 226 Ricky Wright	.06	.02	.00	☐ 279 Warren Cromartie	.03	.01	.00
☐ 227 Steve Yeager	.05	.02	.00	☐ 280 Andre Dawson	.25	.10	.02
☐ 228 Bill Almon	.03	.01	.00	☐ 281 Terry Francona	.05	.02	.00
☐ 229 Harold Baines	.25	.10	.02	☐ 282 Doug Flynn	.03	.01	.00
☐ 230 Salome Barojas	.03	.01	.00	☐ 283 Woody Fryman	.03	.01	.00
☐ 231 Tony Bernazard	.05	.02	.00	☐ 284 Bill Gullickson	.05	.02	.00
☐ 232 Britt Burns	.07	.03	.01	☐ 285 Wallace Johnson	.05	.02	.00
☐ 233 Richard Dotson	.07	.03	.01	☐ 286 Charlie Lea	.05	.02	.00
☐ 234 Ernesto Escarrega	.03	.01	.00	☐ 287 Randy Lerch	.03	.01	.00
☐ 235 Carlton Fisk	.15	.06	.01	☐ 288 Brad Mills	.03	.01	.00
☐ 236 Jerry Hairston	.03	.01	.00	☐ 289 Dan Norman	.03	.01	.00
☐ 237 Kevin Hickey	.03	.01	.00	☐ 290 Al Oliver	.10	.04	.01
☐ 238 LaMarr Hoyt	.08	.03	.01	☐ 291 David Palmer	.06	.02	.00
☐ 239 Steve Kemp	.08	.03	.01	☐ 292 Tim Raines	.30	.12	.03
☐ 240 Jim Kern	.03	.01	.00	☐ 293 Jeff Reardon	.09	.04	.01
☐ 241 Ron Kittle	.70	.28	.07	☐ 294 Steve Rogers	.07	.03	.01
☐ 242 Jerry Koosman	.07	.03	.01	☐ 295 Scott Sanderson	.03	.01	.00
☐ 243 Dennis Lamp	.03	.01	.00	☐ 296 Dan Schatzeder	.03	.01	.00
☐ 244 Rudy Law	.03	.01	.00	☐ 297 Bryn Smith	.05	.02	.00
☐ 245 Vance Law	.03	.01	.00	☐ 298 Chris Speier	.03	.01	.00
☐ 246 Ron LeFlore	.05	.02	.00	☐ 299 Tim Wallach	.08	.03	.01
☐ 247 Greg Luzinski	.10	.04	.01	☐ 300 Jerry White	.03	.01	.00
☐ 248 Tom Paciorek	.03	.01	.00	☐ 301 Joel Youngblood	.03	.01	.00
☐ 249 Aurelio Rodriguez	.03	.01	.00	☐ 302 Ross Baumgarten	.03	.01	.00
☐ 250 Mike Squires	.03	.01	.00	☐ 303 Dale Berra	.05	.02	.00
☐ 251 Steve Trout	.05	.02	.00	☐ 304 John Candelaria	.07	.03	.01
☐ 252 Jim Barr	.03	.01	.00	☐ 305 Dick Davis	.03	.01	.00
☐ 253 Dave Bergman	.03	.01	.00	☐ 306 Mike Easler	.07	.03	.01
☐ 254 Fred Breining	.03	.01	.00	☐ 307 Richie Hebner	.03	.01	.00
☐ 255 Bob Brenly	.07	.03	.01	☐ 308 Lee Lacy	.06	.02	.00
☐ 256 Jack Clark	.14	.06	.01	☐ 309 Bill Madlock	.14	.06	.01
☐ 257 Chili Davis	.12	.05	.01	☐ 310 Larry McWilliams	.03	.01	.00
☐ 258 Darrell Evans	.09	.04	.01	☐ 311 John Milner	.03	.01	.00
☐ 259 Alan Fowlkes	.03	.01	.00	☐ 312 Omar Moreno	.03	.01	.00
☐ 260 Rich Gale	.03	.01	.00	☐ 313 Jim Morrison	.03	.01	.00
☐ 261 Atlee Hammaker	.05	.02	.00	☐ 314 Steve Nicosia	.03	.01	.00
☐ 262 Al Holland	.05	.02	.00	☐ 315 Dave Parker	.20	.08	.02

		MINT	VG-E	F-G
☐ 316	Tony Pena	.14	.06	.01
☐ 317	Johnny Ray	.12	.05	.01
☐ 318	Rick Rhoden	.08	.03	.01
☐ 319	Don Robinson	.03	.01	.00
☐ 320	Enrique Romo	.03	.01	.00
☐ 321	Manny Sarmiento	.03	.01	.00
☐ 322	Rod Scurry	.03	.01	.00
☐ 323	Jim Smith	.03	.01	.00
☐ 324	Willie Stargell	.20	.08	.02
☐ 325	Jason Thompson	.06	.02	.00
☐ 326	Kent Tekulve	.07	.03	.01
☐ 327	Tom Brookens	.03	.01	.00
☐ 328	Enos Cabell	.03	.01	.00
☐ 329	Kirk Gibson	.25	.10	.02
☐ 330	Larry Herndon	.03	.01	.00
☐ 331	Mike Ivie	.03	.01	.00
☐ 332	Howard Johnson	.12	.05	.01
☐ 333	Lynn Jones	.03	.01	.00
☐ 334	Rick Leach	.03	.01	.00
☐ 335	Chet Lemon	.06	.02	.00
☐ 336	Jack Morris	.20	.08	.02
☐ 337	Lance Parrish	.25	.10	.02
☐ 338	Larry Pashnick	.03	.01	.00
☐ 339	Dan Petry	.12	.05	.01
☐ 340	Dave Rozema	.03	.01	.00
☐ 341	Dave Rucker	.03	.01	.00
☐ 342	Elias Sosa	.03	.01	.00
☐ 343	Dave Tobik	.03	.01	.00
☐ 344	Alan Trammell	.20	.08	.02
☐ 345	Jerry Turner	.03	.01	.00
☐ 346	Jerry Ujdur	.03	.01	.00
☐ 347	Pat Underwood	.03	.01	.00
☐ 348	Lou Whitaker	.15	.06	.01
☐ 349	Milt Wilcox	.03	.01	.00
☐ 350	Glenn Wilson	.60	.24	.06
☐ 351	John Wockenfuss	.03	.01	.00
☐ 352	Kurt Bevacqua	.03	.01	.00
☐ 353	Juan Bonilla	.03	.01	.00
☐ 354	Floyd Chiffer	.03	.01	.00
☐ 355	Luis DeLeon	.03	.01	.00
☐ 356	Dave Dravecky	.40	.16	.04
☐ 357	Dave Edwards	.03	.01	.00
☐ 358	Juan Eichelberger	.03	.01	.00
☐ 359	Tim Flannery	.03	.01	.00
☐ 360	Tony Gwynn	4.50	1.80	.45
☐ 361	Ruppert Jones	.03	.01	.00
☐ 362	Terry Kennedy	.07	.03	.01
☐ 363	Joe Lefebvre	.03	.01	.00
☐ 364	Sixto Lezcano	.03	.01	.00
☐ 365	Tim Lollar	.03	.01	.00
☐ 366	Gary Lucas	.03	.01	.00
☐ 367	John Montefusco	.05	.02	.00
☐ 368	Broderick Perkins	.03	.01	.00
☐ 369	Joe Pittman	.03	.01	.00
☐ 370	Gene Richards	.03	.01	.00
☐ 371	Luis Salazar	.03	.01	.00
☐ 372	Eric Show	.12	.05	.01
☐ 373	Garry Templeton	.10	.04	.01
☐ 374	Chris Welsh	.03	.01	.00
☐ 375	Alan Wiggins	.20	.08	.02
☐ 376	Rick Cerone	.03	.01	.00
☐ 377	Dave Collins	.05	.02	.00
☐ 378	Roger Erickson	.03	.01	.00
☐ 379	George Frazier	.03	.01	.00
☐ 380	Oscar Gamble	.05	.02	.00
☐ 381	Goose Gossage	.18	.08	.01
☐ 382	Ken Griffey	.08	.03	.01
☐ 383	Ron Guidry	.20	.08	.02
☐ 384	Dave LaRoche	.03	.01	.00
☐ 385	Rudy May	.03	.01	.00
☐ 386	John Mayberry	.05	.02	.00
☐ 387	Lee Mazzilli	.05	.02	.00
☐ 388	Mike Morgan	.03	.01	.00
☐ 389	Jerry Mumphrey	.05	.02	.00
☐ 390	Bobby Murcer	.09	.04	.01
☐ 391	Graig Nettles	.14	.06	.01
☐ 392	Lou Piniella	.10	.04	.01
☐ 393	Willie Randolph	.06	.02	.00
☐ 394	Shane Rawley	.06	.02	.00
☐ 395	Dave Righetti	.15	.06	.01
☐ 396	Andre Robertson	.03	.01	.00
☐ 397	Roy Smalley	.05	.02	.00
☐ 398	Dave Winfield	.35	.14	.03
☐ 399	Butch Wynegar	.05	.02	.00
☐ 400	Chris Bando	.03	.01	.00
☐ 401	Alan Bannister	.03	.01	.00
☐ 402	Len Barker	.05	.02	.00
☐ 403	Tom Brennan	.03	.01	.00
☐ 404	Carmelo Castillo	.06	.02	.00
☐ 405	Miguel Dilone	.03	.01	.00
☐ 406	Jerry Dybzinski	.03	.01	.00
☐ 407	Mike Fischlin	.03	.01	.00
☐ 408	Ed Glynn	.06	.02	.00
	(photo actually			
	Bud Anderson)			
☐ 409	Mike Hargrove	.05	.02	.00
☐ 410	Toby Harrah	.05	.02	.00
☐ 411	Ron Hassey	.03	.01	.00
☐ 412	Von Hayes	.15	.06	.01
☐ 413	Rick Manning	.03	.01	.00
☐ 414	Bake McBride	.05	.02	.00
☐ 415	Larry Milbourne	.03	.01	.00
☐ 416	Bill Nahorodny	.03	.01	.00
☐ 417	Jack Perconte	.03	.01	.00
☐ 418	Lary Sorensen	.03	.01	.00
☐ 419	Dan Spillner	.03	.01	.00

		MINT	VG-E	F-G
☐ 420	Rick Sutcliffe	.15	.06	.01
☐ 421	Andre Thornton	.07	.03	.01
☐ 422	Rick Waits	.03	.01	.00
☐ 423	Eddie Whitson	.06	.02	.00
☐ 424	Jesse Barfield	.20	.08	.02
☐ 425	Barry Bonnell	.03	.01	.00
☐ 426	Jim Clancy	.03	.01	.00
☐ 427	Damaso Garcia	.08	.03	.01
☐ 428	Jerry Garvin	.03	.01	.00
☐ 429	Alfredo Griffin	.05	.02	.00
☐ 430	Garth Iorg	.03	.01	.00
☐ 431	Roy Lee Jackson	.03	.01	.00
☐ 432	Luis Leal	.03	.01	.00
☐ 433	Buck Martinez	.03	.01	.00
☐ 434	Joey McLaughlin	.03	.01	.00
☐ 435	Lloyd Moseby	.12	.05	.01
☐ 436	Rance Mulliniks	.03	.01	.00
☐ 437	Dale Murray	.03	.01	.00
☐ 438	Wayne Nordhagen	.03	.01	.00
☐ 439	Gene Petralli	.03	.01	.00
☐ 440	Hosken Powell	.03	.01	.00
☐ 441	Dave Stieb	.15	.06	.01
☐ 442	Willie Upshaw	.08	.03	.01
☐ 443	Ernie Whitt	.03	.01	.00
☐ 444	Al Woods	.03	.01	.00
☐ 445	Alan Ashby	.03	.01	.00
☐ 446	Jose Cruz	.10	.04	.01
☐ 447	Kiko Garcia	.03	.01	.00
☐ 448	Phil Garner	.05	.02	.00
☐ 449	Danny Heep	.03	.01	.00
☐ 450	Art Howe	.03	.01	.00
☐ 451	Bob Knepper	.09	.04	.01
☐ 452	Alan Knicely	.03	.01	.00
☐ 453	Ray Knight	.09	.04	.01
☐ 454	Frank LaCorte	.03	.01	.00
☐ 455	Mike LaCoss	.03	.01	.00
☐ 456	Randy Moffitt	.03	.01	.00
☐ 457	Joe Niekro	.08	.03	.01
☐ 458	Terry Puhl	.05	.02	.00
☐ 459	Luis Pujols	.03	.01	.00
☐ 460	Craig Reynolds	.03	.01	.00
☐ 461	Bert Roberge	.03	.01	.00
☐ 462	Vern Ruhle	.03	.01	.00
☐ 463	Nolan Ryan	.30	.12	.03
☐ 464	Joe Sambito	.05	.02	.00
☐ 465	Tony Scott	.03	.01	.00
☐ 466	Dave Smith	.07	.03	.01
☐ 467	Harry Spilman	.03	.01	.00
☐ 468	Dickie Thon	.06	.02	.00
☐ 469	Denny Walling	.03	.01	.00
☐ 470	Larry Andersen	.03	.01	.00
☐ 471	Floyd Bannister	.07	.03	.01
☐ 472	Jim Beattie	.03	.01	.00
☐ 473	Bruce Bochte	.05	.02	.00
☐ 474	Manny Castillo	.03	.01	.00
☐ 475	Bill Caudill	.05	.02	.00
☐ 476	Bryan Clark	.03	.01	.00
☐ 477	Al Cowens	.05	.02	.00
☐ 478	Julio Cruz	.03	.01	.00
☐ 479	Todd Cruz	.03	.01	.00
☐ 480	Gary Gray	.03	.01	.00
☐ 481	Dave Henderson	.08	.03	.01
☐ 482	Mike Moore	.25	.10	.02
☐ 483	Gaylord Perry	.20	.08	.02
☐ 484	Dave Revering	.03	.01	.00
☐ 485	Joe Simpson	.03	.01	.00
☐ 486	Mike Stanton	.03	.01	.00
☐ 487	Rick Sweet	.03	.01	.00
☐ 488	Ed VandeBerg	.08	.03	.01
☐ 489	Richie Zisk	.05	.02	.00
☐ 490	Doug Bird	.03	.01	.00
☐ 491	Larry Bowa	.10	.04	.01
☐ 492	Bill Buckner	.10	.04	.01
☐ 493	Bill Campbell	.03	.01	.00
☐ 494	Jody Davis	.08	.03	.01
☐ 495	Leon Durham	.08	.03	.01
☐ 496	Steve Henderson	.03	.01	.00
☐ 497	Willie Hernandez	.12	.05	.01
☐ 498	Ferguson Jenkins	.15	.06	.01
☐ 499	Jay Johnstone	.05	.02	.00
☐ 500	Junior Kennedy	.03	.01	.00
☐ 501	Randy Martz	.03	.01	.00
☐ 502	Jerry Morales	.03	.01	.00
☐ 503	Keith Moreland	.08	.03	.01
☐ 504	Dickie Noles	.03	.01	.00
☐ 505	Mike Proly	.03	.01	.00
☐ 506	Allen Ripley	.03	.01	.00
☐ 507	Ryne Sandberg	3.50	1.40	.35
☐ 508	Lee Smith	.10	.04	.01
☐ 509	Pat Tabler	.10	.04	.01
☐ 510	Dick Tidrow	.03	.01	.00
☐ 511	Bump Wills	.03	.01	.00
☐ 512	Gary Woods	.03	.01	.00
☐ 513	Tony Armas	.10	.04	.01
☐ 514	Dave Beard	.03	.01	.00
☐ 515	Jeff Burroughs	.05	.02	.00
☐ 516	John D'Acquisto	.03	.01	.00
☐ 517	Wayne Gross	.03	.01	.00
☐ 518	Mike Heath	.03	.01	.00
☐ 519	Rickey Henderson	.50	.20	.05
☐ 520	Cliff Johnson	.03	.01	.00
☐ 521	Matt Keough	.03	.01	.00
☐ 522	Brian Kingman	.03	.01	.00
☐ 523	Rick Langford	.03	.01	.00
☐ 524	Davey Lopes	.06	.02	.00
☐ 525	Steve McCatty	.03	.01	.00

	MINT	VG-E	F-G
☐ 526 Dave McKay	.03	.01	.00
☐ 527 Dan Meyer	.03	.01	.00
☐ 528 Dwayne Murphy	.06	.02	.00
☐ 529 Jeff Newman	.03	.01	.00
☐ 530 Mike Norris	.05	.02	.00
☐ 531 Bob Owchinko	.03	.01	.00
☐ 532 Joe Rudi	.06	.02	.00
☐ 533 Jimmy Sexton	.03	.01	.00
☐ 534 Fred Stanley	.03	.01	.00
☐ 535 Tom Underwood	.03	.01	.00
☐ 536 Neil Allen	.06	.02	.00
☐ 537 Wally Backman	.07	.03	.01
☐ 538 Bob Bailor	.03	.01	.00
☐ 539 Hubie Brooks	.12	.05	.01
☐ 540 Carlos Diaz	.10	.04	.01
☐ 541 Pete Falcone	.03	.01	.00
☐ 542 George Foster	.14	.06	.01
☐ 543 Ron Gardenhire	.03	.01	.00
☐ 544 Brian Giles	.03	.01	.00
☐ 545 Ron Hodges	.03	.01	.00
☐ 546 Randy Jones	.05	.02	.00
☐ 547 Mike Jorgensen	.03	.01	.00
☐ 548 Dave Kingman	.14	.06	.01
☐ 549 Ed Lynch	.03	.01	.00
☐ 550 Jesse Orosco	.07	.03	.01
☐ 551 Rick Ownbey	.06	.02	.00
☐ 552 Charlie Puleo	.03	.01	.00
☐ 553 Gary Rajsich	.03	.01	.00
☐ 554 Mike Scott	.20	.08	.02
☐ 555 Rusty Staub	.10	.04	.01
☐ 556 John Stearns	.03	.01	.00
☐ 557 Craig Swan	.03	.01	.00
☐ 558 Ellis Valentine	.03	.01	.00
☐ 559 Tom Veryzer	.03	.01	.00
☐ 560 Mookie Wilson	.07	.03	.01
☐ 561 Pat Zachry	.03	.01	.00
☐ 562 Buddy Bell	.10	.04	.01
☐ 563 John Butcher	.03	.01	.00
☐ 564 Steve Comer	.03	.01	.00
☐ 565 Danny Darwin	.03	.01	.00
☐ 566 Bucky Dent	.06	.02	.00
☐ 567 John Grubb	.03	.01	.00
☐ 568 Rick Honeycutt	.05	.02	.00
☐ 569 Dave Hostetler	.05	.02	.00
☐ 570 Charlie Hough	.06	.02	.00
☐ 571 Lamar Johnson	.03	.01	.00
☐ 572 Jon Matlack	.05	.02	.00
☐ 573 Paul Mirabella	.03	.01	.00
☐ 574 Larry Parrish	.06	.02	.00
☐ 575 Mike Richardt	.03	.01	.00
☐ 576 Mickey Rivers	.05	.02	.00
☐ 577 Billy Sample	.03	.01	.00
☐ 578 Dave Schmidt	.03	.01	.00
☐ 579 Bill Stein	.03	.01	.00
☐ 580 Jim Sundberg	.05	.02	.00
☐ 581 Frank Tanana	.06	.02	.00
☐ 582 Mark Wagner	.03	.01	.00
☐ 583 George Wright	.07	.03	.01
☐ 584 Johnny Bench	.35	.14	.03
☐ 585 Bruce Berenyi	.03	.01	.00
☐ 586 Larry Biittner	.03	.01	.00
☐ 587 Cesar Cedeno	.07	.03	.01
☐ 588 Dave Concepcion	.09	.04	.01
☐ 589 Dan Driessen	.05	.02	.00
☐ 590 Greg Harris	.06	.02	.00
☐ 591 Ben Hayes	.03	.01	.00
☐ 592 Paul Householder	.03	.01	.00
☐ 593 Tom Hume	.03	.01	.00
☐ 594 Wayne Krenchicki	.03	.01	.00
☐ 595 Rafael Landestoy	.03	.01	.00
☐ 596 Charlie Leibrandt	.06	.02	.00
☐ 597 Eddie Milner	.15	.06	.01
☐ 598 Ron Oester	.05	.02	.00
☐ 599 Frank Pastore	.03	.01	.00
☐ 600 Joe Price	.03	.01	.00
☐ 601 Tom Seaver	.35	.14	.03
☐ 602 Bob Shirley	.03	.01	.00
☐ 603 Mario Soto	.08	.03	.01
☐ 604 Alex Trevino	.03	.01	.00
☐ 605 Mike Vail	.03	.01	.00
☐ 606 Duane Walker	.06	.02	.00
☐ 607 Tom Brunansky	.15	.06	.01
☐ 608 Bobby Castillo	.03	.01	.00
☐ 609 John Castino	.03	.01	.00
☐ 610 Ron Davis	.03	.01	.00
☐ 611 Lenny Faedo	.03	.01	.00
☐ 612 Terry Felton	.03	.01	.00
☐ 613 Gary Gaetti	.60	.24	.06
☐ 614 Mickey Hatcher	.03	.01	.00
☐ 615 Brad Havens	.03	.01	.00
☐ 616 Kent Hrbek	.30	.12	.03
☐ 617 Randy Johnson	.03	.01	.00
☐ 618 Tim Laudner	.03	.01	.00
☐ 619 Jeff Little	.03	.01	.00
☐ 620 Bob Mitchell	.03	.01	.00
☐ 621 Jack O'Connor	.03	.01	.00
☐ 622 John Pacella	.03	.01	.00
☐ 623 Pete Redfern	.03	.01	.00
☐ 624 Jesus Vega	.03	.01	.00
☐ 625 Frank Viola	.45	.18	.04
☐ 626 Ron Washington	.05	.02	.00
☐ 627 Gary Ward	.06	.02	.00
☐ 628 Al Williams	.03	.01	.00

		MINT	VG-E	F-G
☐	629 Red Sox All-Stars	.18	.08	.01
	Carl Yastrzemski			
	Dennis Eckersley			
	Mark Clear			
☐	630 "300 Career Wins"	.12	.05	.01
	Gaylord Perry and			
	Terry Bulling 5/6/82			
☐	631 Pride of Venezuela ...	.06	.02	.00
	Dave Concepcion and			
	Manny Trillo			
☐	632 All-Star Infielders	.15	.06	.01
	Robin Yount and			
	Buddy Bell			
☐	633 Mr.Vet and Mr.Rookie ..	.20	.08	.02
	Dave Winfield and			
	Kent Hrbek			
☐	634 Fountain of Youth	.60	.24	.06
	Willie Stargell and			
	Pete Rose			
☐	635 Big Chiefs	.06	.02	.00
	Toby Harrah and			
	Andre Thornton			
☐	636 Smith Brothers	.08	.03	.01
	Ozzie and Lonnie			
☐	637 Base Stealers' Threat ..	.12	.05	.01
	Bo Diaz and			
	Gary Carter			
☐	638 All-Star Catchers	.15	.06	.01
	Carlton Fisk and			
	Gary Carter			
☐	639 The Silver Shoe	.30	.12	.03
	Rickey Henderson			
☐	640 Home Run Threats	.18	.08	.01
	Ben Oglivie and			
	Reggie Jackson			
☐	641 Two Teams Same Day ..	.06	.02	.00
	Joel Youngblood			
	August 4, 1982			
☐	642 Last Perfect Game	.06	.02	.00
	Ron Hassey and			
	Len Barker			
☐	643 Black and Blue	.06	.02	.00
	Bud Black			
☐	644 Black and Blue	.06	.02	.00
	Vida Blue			
☐	645 Speed and Power	.30	.12	.03
	Reggie Jackson			
☐	646 Speed and Power	.30	.12	.03
	Rickey Henderson			
☐	647 CL: Cards/Brewers	.07	.01	.00
☐	648 CL: Orioles/Angels	.07	.01	.00
☐	649 CL: Royals/Braves	.07	.01	.00
☐	650 CL: Phillies/Red Sox ...	.07	.01	.00

		MINT	VG-E	F-G
☐	651 CL: Dodgers/White Sox	.07	.01	.00
☐	652 CL: Giants/Expos	.07	.01	.00
☐	653 CL: Pirates/Tigers	.07	.01	.00
☐	654 CL: Padres/Yankees ...	.07	.01	.00
☐	655 CL: Indians/Blue Jays ...	.07	.01	.00
☐	656 CL: Astros/Mariners	.07	.01	.00
☐	657 CL: Cubs/A's	.07	.01	.00
☐	658 CL: Mets/Rangers	.07	.01	.00
☐	659 CL: Reds/Twins	.07	.01	.00
☐	660 CL: Specials/Teams	.09	.01	.00

1984 Fleer

The cards in this 660-card set measure 2½"
by 3½". The 1984 Fleer card set featured
fronts with full color team logos along with the
player's name and position and the Fleer
identification. The set features many imaginative photos, several multi-player cards,
and many more action shots than the 1983
card set. The backs are quite similar to the
1983 backs except that blue rather than
brown ink is used. The player cards are alphabetized within team and the teams are ordered by their 1983 season finish and won-
lost record, e.g., Baltimore (1-23),
Philadelphia (24-49), Chicago White Sox (50-
73), Detroit (74-95), Los Angeles (96-118),
New York Yankees (119-144), Toronto (145-
169), Atlanta (170-193), Milwaukee (194-
219), Houston (220-244), Pittsburgh (245-
269), Montreal (270-293), San Diego (294-
317), St. Louis (318-340), Kansas City (341-
364), San Francisco (365-387), Boston (388-
412), Texas (413-435), Oakland (436-461),
Cincinnati (462-485), Chicago (486-507),

California (508-532), Cleveland (533-555), Minnesota (556-579), New York Mets (580-603), and Seattle (604-625). Specials (626-646) and checklist cards (647-660) make up the end of the set.

	MINT	VG-E	F-G
Complete Set	48.00	18.00	4.50
Common Player (1-660)	.03	.01	.00

		MINT	VG-E	F-G
☐ 1	Mike Boddicker	.12	.05	.01
☐ 2	Al Bumbry	.03	.01	.00
☐ 3	Todd Cruz	.03	.01	.00
☐ 4	Rich Dauer	.03	.01	.00
☐ 5	Storm Davis	.07	.03	.01
☐ 6	Rick Dempsey	.05	.02	.00
☐ 7	Jim Dwyer	.03	.01	.00
☐ 8	Mike Flanagan	.07	.03	.01
☐ 9	Dan Ford	.03	.01	.00
☐ 10	John Lowenstein	.03	.01	.00
☐ 11	Dennis Martinez	.03	.01	.00
☐ 12	Tippy Martinez	.03	.01	.00
☐ 13	Scott McGregor	.07	.03	.01
☐ 14	Eddie Murray	.50	.20	.05
☐ 15	Joe Nolan	.03	.01	.00
☐ 16	Jim Palmer	.25	.10	.02
☐ 17	Cal Ripken	.60	.24	.06
☐ 18	Gary Roenicke	.05	.02	.00
☐ 19	Lenn Sakata	.03	.01	.00
☐ 20	John Shelby	.07	.03	.01
☐ 21	Ken Singleton	.09	.04	.01
☐ 22	Sammy Stewart	.03	.01	.00
☐ 23	Tim Stoddard	.03	.01	.00
☐ 24	Marty Bystrom	.03	.01	.00
☐ 25	Steve Carlton	.30	.12	.03
☐ 26	Ivan DeJesus	.03	.01	.00
☐ 27	John Denny	.07	.03	.01
☐ 28	Bob Dernier	.05	.02	.00
☐ 29	Bo Diaz	.05	.02	.00
☐ 30	Kiko Garcia	.03	.01	.00
☐ 31	Greg Gross	.03	.01	.00
☐ 32	Kevin Gross	.20	.08	.02
☐ 33	Von Hayes	.12	.05	.01
☐ 34	Willie Hernandez	.20	.08	.02
☐ 35	Al Holland	.05	.02	.00
☐ 36	Charles Hudson	.12	.05	.01
☐ 37	Joe Lefebvre	.03	.01	.00
☐ 38	Sixto Lezcano	.03	.01	.00
☐ 39	Garry Maddox	.05	.02	.00
☐ 40	Gary Matthews	.08	.03	.01
☐ 41	Len Matuszek	.03	.01	.00
☐ 42	Tug McGraw	.09	.04	.01
☐ 43	Joe Morgan	.18	.08	.01
☐ 44	Tony Perez	.12	.05	.01
☐ 45	Ron Reed	.03	.01	.00
☐ 46	Pete Rose	.75	.30	.07
☐ 47	Juan Samuel	1.50	.60	.15
☐ 48	Mike Schmidt	.40	.16	.04
☐ 49	Ozzie Virgil	.03	.01	.00
☐ 50	Juan Agosto	.05	.02	.00
☐ 51	Harold Baines	.20	.08	.02
☐ 52	Floyd Bannister	.06	.02	.00
☐ 53	Salome Barojas	.03	.01	.00
☐ 54	Britt Burns	.06	.02	.00
☐ 55	Julio Cruz	.03	.01	.00
☐ 56	Richard Dotson	.06	.02	.00
☐ 57	Jerry Dybzinski	.03	.01	.00
☐ 58	Carlton Fisk	.14	.06	.01
☐ 59	Scott Fletcher	.05	.02	.00
☐ 60	Jerry Hairston	.03	.01	.00
☐ 61	Kevin Hickey	.03	.01	.00
☐ 62	Marc Hill	.03	.01	.00
☐ 63	LaMarr Hoyt	.08	.03	.01
☐ 64	Ron Kittle	.15	.06	.01
☐ 65	Jerry Koosman	.07	.03	.01
☐ 66	Dennis Lamp	.03	.01	.00
☐ 67	Rudy Law	.03	.01	.00
☐ 68	Vance Law	.03	.01	.00
☐ 69	Greg Luzinski	.10	.04	.01
☐ 70	Tom Paciorek	.03	.01	.00
☐ 71	Mike Squires	.03	.01	.00
☐ 72	Dick Tidrow	.03	.01	.00
☐ 73	Greg Walker	.50	.20	.05
☐ 74	Glenn Abbott	.03	.01	.00
☐ 75	Howard Bailey	.03	.01	.00
☐ 76	Doug Bair	.03	.01	.00
☐ 77	Juan Berenguer	.03	.01	.00
☐ 78	Tom Brookens	.03	.01	.00
☐ 79	Enos Cabell	.03	.01	.00
☐ 80	Kirk Gibson	.25	.10	.02
☐ 81	John Grubb	.03	.01	.00
☐ 82	Larry Herndon	.03	.01	.00
☐ 83	Wayne Krenchicki	.03	.01	.00
☐ 84	Rick Leach	.03	.01	.00
☐ 85	Chet Lemon	.05	.02	.00
☐ 86	Aurelio Lopez	.03	.01	.00
☐ 87	Jack Morris	.20	.08	.02
☐ 88	Lance Parrish	.25	.10	.02
☐ 89	Dan Petry	.12	.05	.01
☐ 90	Dave Rozema	.03	.01	.00
☐ 91	Alan Trammell	.18	.08	.01
☐ 92	Lou Whitaker	.15	.06	.01
☐ 93	Milt Wilcox	.03	.01	.00
☐ 94	Glenn Wilson	.10	.04	.01
☐ 95	John Wockenfuss	.03	.01	.00
☐ 96	Dusty Baker	.05	.02	.00

		MINT	VG-E	F-G
☐ 97	Joe Beckwith	.03	.01	.00
☐ 98	Greg Brock	.05	.02	.00
☐ 99	Jack Fimple	.05	.02	.00
☐ 100	Pedro Guerrero	.25	.10	.02
☐ 101	Rick Honeycutt	.05	.02	.00
☐ 102	Burt Hooton	.03	.01	.00
☐ 103	Steve Howe	.05	.02	.00
☐ 104	Ken Landreaux	.05	.02	.00
☐ 105	Mike Marshall	.15	.06	.01
☐ 106	Rick Monday	.05	.02	.00
☐ 107	Jose Morales	.03	.01	.00
☐ 108	Tom Niedenfuer	.05	.02	.00
☐ 109	Alejandro Pena	.20	.08	.02
☐ 110	Jerry Reuss	.05	.02	.00
☐ 111	Bill Russell	.05	.02	.00
☐ 112	Steve Sax	.15	.06	.01
☐ 113	Mike Scioscia	.05	.02	.00
☐ 114	Derrel Thomas	.03	.01	.00
☐ 115	Fernando Valenzuela	.30	.12	.03
☐ 116	Bob Welch	.07	.03	.01
☐ 117	Steve Yeager	.05	.02	.00
☐ 118	Pat Zachry	.03	.01	.00
☐ 119	Don Baylor	.12	.05	.01
☐ 120	Bert Campaneris	.06	.02	.00
☐ 121	Rick Cerone	.03	.01	.00
☐ 122	Ray Fontenot	.07	.03	.01
☐ 123	George Frazier	.03	.01	.00
☐ 124	Oscar Gamble	.05	.02	.00
☐ 125	Goose Gossage	.14	.06	.01
☐ 126	Ken Griffey	.07	.03	.01
☐ 127	Ron Guidry	.14	.06	.01
☐ 128	Jay Howell	.06	.02	.00
☐ 129	Steve Kemp	.06	.02	.00
☐ 130	Matt Keough	.03	.01	.00
☐ 131	Don Mattingly	30.00	12.00	3.00
☐ 132	John Montefusco	.05	.02	.00
☐ 133	Omar Moreno	.03	.01	.00
☐ 134	Dale Murray	.03	.01	.00
☐ 135	Graig Nettles	.12	.05	.01
☐ 136	Lou Piniella	.09	.04	.01
☐ 137	Willie Randolph	.06	.02	.00
☐ 138	Shane Rawley	.06	.02	.00
☐ 139	Dave Righetti	.15	.06	.01
☐ 140	Andre Robertson	.03	.01	.00
☐ 141	Bob Shirley	.03	.01	.00
☐ 142	Roy Smalley	.05	.02	.00
☐ 143	Dave Winfield	.30	.12	.03
☐ 144	Butch Wynegar	.05	.02	.00
☐ 145	Jim Acker	.10	.04	.01
☐ 146	Doyle Alexander	.05	.02	.00
☐ 147	Jesse Barfield	.18	.08	.01
☐ 148	Jorge Bell	.15	.06	.01
☐ 149	Barry Bonnell	.03	.01	.00
☐ 150	Jim Clancy	.03	.01	.00
☐ 151	Dave Collins	.05	.02	.00
☐ 152	Tony Fernandez	1.50	.60	.15
☐ 153	Damaso Garcia	.08	.03	.01
☐ 154	Dave Geisel	.03	.01	.00
☐ 155	Jim Gott	.03	.01	.00
☐ 156	Alfredo Griffin	.05	.02	.00
☐ 157	Garth Iorg	.03	.01	.00
☐ 158	Roy Lee Jackson	.03	.01	.00
☐ 159	Cliff Johnson	.03	.01	.00
☐ 160	Luis Leal	.03	.01	.00
☐ 161	Buck Martinez	.03	.01	.00
☐ 162	Joey McLaughlin	.03	.01	.00
☐ 163	Randy Moffitt	.03	.01	.00
☐ 164	Lloyd Moseby	.12	.05	.01
☐ 165	Rance Mullinks	.03	.01	.00
☐ 166	Jorge Orta	.03	.01	.00
☐ 167	Dave Stieb	.15	.06	.01
☐ 168	Willie Upshaw	.08	.03	.01
☐ 169	Ernie Whitt	.03	.01	.00
☐ 170	Len Barker	.05	.02	.00
☐ 171	Steve Bedrosian	.05	.02	.00
☐ 172	Bruce Benedict	.03	.01	.00
☐ 173	Brett Butler	.09	.04	.01
☐ 174	Rick Camp	.03	.01	.00
☐ 175	Chris Chambliss	.05	.02	.00
☐ 176	Ken Dayley	.03	.01	.00
☐ 177	Pete Falcone	.03	.01	.00
☐ 178	Terry Forster	.07	.03	.01
☐ 179	Gene Garber	.03	.01	.00
☐ 180	Terry Harper	.03	.01	.00
☐ 181	Bob Horner	.20	.08	.02
☐ 182	Glenn Hubbard	.03	.01	.00
☐ 183	Randy Johnson	.03	.01	.00
☐ 184	Craig McMurtry	.08	.03	.01
☐ 185	Donnie Moore	.06	.02	.00
☐ 186	Dale Murphy	.60	.24	.06
☐ 187	Phil Niekro	.15	.06	.01
☐ 188	Pascual Perez	.05	.02	.00
☐ 189	Biff Pocoroba	.03	.01	.00
☐ 190	Rafael Ramirez	.03	.01	.00
☐ 191	Jerry Royster	.03	.01	.00
☐ 192	Claudell Washington	.05	.02	.00
☐ 193	Bob Watson	.05	.02	.00
☐ 194	Jerry Augustine	.03	.01	.00
☐ 195	Mark Brouhard	.03	.01	.00
☐ 196	Mike Caldwell	.05	.02	.00
☐ 197	Tom Candiotti	.15	.06	.01
☐ 198	Cecil Cooper	.14	.06	.01
☐ 199	Rollie Fingers	.15	.06	.01
☐ 200	Jim Gantner	.05	.02	.00
☐ 201	Bob L. Gibson	.06	.02	.00
☐ 202	Moose Haas	.05	.02	.00

	MINT	VG-E	F-G		MINT	VG-E	F-G
☐ 203 Roy Howell	.03	.01	.00	☐ 256 Larry McWilliams	.03	.01	.00
☐ 204 Pete Ladd	.03	.01	.00	☐ 257 Jim Morrison	.03	.01	.00
☐ 205 Rick Manning	.03	.01	.00	☐ 258 Dave Parker	.20	.08	.02
☐ 206 Bob McClure	.03	.01	.00	☐ 259 Tony Pena	.14	.06	.01
☐ 207 Paul Molitor	.10	.04	.01	☐ 260 Johnny Ray	.10	.04	.01
☐ 208 Don Money	.03	.01	.00	☐ 261 Rick Rhoden	.08	.03	.01
☐ 209 Charlie Moore	.03	.01	.00	☐ 262 Don Robinson	.03	.01	.00
☐ 210 Ben Oglivie	.06	.02	.00	☐ 263 Manny Sarmiento	.03	.01	.00
☐ 211 Chuck Porter	.03	.01	.00	☐ 264 Rod Scurry	.03	.01	.00
☐ 212 Ed Romero	.03	.01	.00	☐ 265 Kent Tekulve	.06	.02	.00
☐ 213 Ted Simmons	.10	.04	.01	☐ 266 Gene Tenace	.03	.01	.00
☐ 214 Jim Slaton	.03	.01	.00	☐ 267 Jason Thompson	.06	.02	.00
☐ 215 Don Sutton	.18	.08	.01	☐ 268 Lee Tunnell	.06	.02	.00
☐ 216 Tom Tellmann	.03	.01	.00	☐ 269 Marvell Wynne	.10	.04	.01
☐ 217 Pete Vuckovich	.07	.03	.01	☐ 270 Ray Burris	.03	.01	.00
☐ 218 Ned Yost	.03	.01	.00	☐ 271 Gary Carter	.35	.14	.03
☐ 219 Robin Yount	.30	.12	.03	☐ 272 Warren Cromartie	.03	.01	.00
☐ 220 Alan Ashby	.03	.01	.00	☐ 273 Andre Dawson	.20	.08	.02
☐ 221 Kevin Bass	.09	.04	.01	☐ 274 Doug Flynn	.03	.01	.00
☐ 222 Jose Cruz	.09	.04	.01	☐ 275 Terry Francona	.05	.02	.00
☐ 223 Bill Dawley	.09	.04	.01	☐ 276 Bill Gullickson	.05	.02	.00
☐ 224 Frank DiPino	.05	.02	.00	☐ 277 Bob James	.12	.05	.01
☐ 225 Bill Doran	.50	.20	.05	☐ 278 Charlie Lea	.05	.02	.00
☐ 226 Phil Garner	.05	.02	.00	☐ 279 Bryan Little	.03	.01	.00
☐ 227 Art Howe	.03	.01	.00	☐ 280 Al Oliver	.10	.04	.01
☐ 228 Bob Knepper	.08	.03	.01	☐ 281 Tim Raines	.25	.10	.02
☐ 229 Ray Knight	.08	.03	.01	☐ 282 Bobby Ramos	.03	.01	.00
☐ 230 Frank LaCorte	.03	.01	.00	☐ 283 Jeff Reardon	.08	.03	.01
☐ 231 Mike LaCoss	.03	.01	.00	☐ 284 Steve Rogers	.06	.02	.00
☐ 232 Mike Madden	.09	.04	.01	☐ 285 Scott Sanderson	.03	.01	.00
☐ 233 Jerry Mumphrey	.05	.02	.00	☐ 286 Dan Schatzeder	.03	.01	.00
☐ 234 Joe Niekro	.08	.03	.01	☐ 287 Bryn Smith	.03	.01	.00
☐ 235 Terry Puhl	.05	.02	.00	☐ 288 Chris Speier	.03	.01	.00
☐ 236 Luis Pujols	.03	.01	.00	☐ 289 Manny Trillo	.05	.02	.00
☐ 237 Craig Reynolds	.03	.01	.00	☐ 290 Mike Vail	.03	.01	.00
☐ 238 Vern Ruhle	.03	.01	.00	☐ 291 Tim Wallach	.08	.03	.01
☐ 239 Nolan Ryan	.25	.10	.02	☐ 292 Chris Welsh	.03	.01	.00
☐ 240 Mike Scott	.18	.08	.01	☐ 293 Jim Wohlford	.03	.01	.00
☐ 241 Tony Scott	.03	.01	.00	☐ 294 Kurt Bevacqua	.03	.01	.00
☐ 242 Dave Smith	.07	.03	.01	☐ 295 Juan Bonilla	.03	.01	.00
☐ 243 Dickie Thon	.06	.02	.00	☐ 296 Bobby Brown	.03	.01	.00
☐ 244 Denny Walling	.03	.01	.00	☐ 297 Luis DeLeon	.03	.01	.00
☐ 245 Dale Berra	.05	.02	.00	☐ 298 Dave Dravecky	.08	.03	.01
☐ 246 Jim Bibby	.05	.02	.00	☐ 299 Tim Flannery	.03	.01	.00
☐ 247 John Candelaria	.08	.03	.01	☐ 300 Steve Garvey	.40	.16	.04
☐ 248 Jose DeLeon	.20	.08	.02	☐ 301 Tony Gwynn	.90	.36	.09
☐ 249 Mike Easler	.07	.03	.01	☐ 302 Andy Hawkins	.20	.08	.02
☐ 250 Cecilio Guante	.03	.01	.00	☐ 303 Ruppert Jones	.03	.01	.00
☐ 251 Richie Hebner	.03	.01	.00	☐ 304 Terry Kennedy	.07	.03	.01
☐ 252 Lee Lacy	.06	.02	.00	☐ 305 Tim Lollar	.03	.01	.00
☐ 253 Bill Madlock	.12	.05	.01	☐ 306 Gary Lucas	.03	.01	.00
☐ 254 Milt May	.03	.01	.00	☐ 307 Kevin McReynolds	1.50	.60	.15
☐ 255 Lee Mazzilli	.05	.02	.00	☐ 308 Sid Monge	.03	.01	.00

		MINT	VG-E	F-G			MINT	VG-E	F-G
☐ 309	Mario Ramirez	.05	.02	.00	☐ 362	John Wathan	.03	.01	.00
☐ 310	Gene Richards	.03	.01	.00	☐ 363	Frank White	.07	.03	.01
☐ 311	Luis Salazar	.03	.01	.00	☐ 364	Willie Wilson	.15	.06	.01
☐ 312	Eric Show	.05	.02	.00	☐ 365	Jim Barr	.03	.01	.00
☐ 313	Elias Sosa	.03	.01	.00	☐ 366	Dave Bergman	.03	.01	.00
☐ 314	Garry Templeton	.08	.03	.01	☐ 367	Fred Breining	.03	.01	.00
☐ 315	Mark Thurmond	.12	.05	.01	☐ 368	Bob Brenly	.07	.03	.01
☐ 316	Ed Whitson	.06	.02	.00	☐ 369	Jack Clark	.12	.05	.01
☐ 317	Alan Wiggins	.06	.02	.00	☐ 370	Chili Davis	.10	.04	.01
☐ 318	Neil Allen	.06	.02	.00	☐ 371	Mark Davis	.03	.01	.00
☐ 319	Joaquin Andujar	.10	.04	.01	☐ 372	Darrell Evans	.09	.04	.01
☐ 320	Steve Braun	.03	.01	.00	☐ 373	Atlee Hammaker	.05	.02	.00
☐ 321	Glenn Brummer	.03	.01	.00	☐ 374	Mike Krukow	.07	.03	.01
☐ 322	Bob Forsch	.05	.02	.00	☐ 375	Duane Kuiper	.03	.01	.00
☐ 323	David Green	.05	.02	.00	☐ 376	Bill Laskey	.03	.01	.00
☐ 324	George Hendrick	.07	.03	.01	☐ 377	Gary Lavelle	.05	.02	.00
☐ 325	Tom Herr	.08	.03	.01	☐ 378	Johnnie LeMaster	.03	.01	.00
☐ 326	Dane Iorg	.03	.01	.00	☐ 379	Jeff Leonard	.08	.03	.01
☐ 327	Jeff Lahti	.03	.01	.00	☐ 380	Randy Lerch	.03	.01	.00
☐ 328	Dave LaPoint	.05	.02	.00	☐ 381	Renie Martin	.03	.01	.00
☐ 329	Willie McGee	.25	.10	.02	☐ 382	Andy McGaffigan	.03	.01	.00
☐ 330	Ken Oberkfell	.03	.01	.00	☐ 383	Greg Minton	.05	.02	.00
☐ 331	Darrell Porter	.05	.02	.00	☐ 384	Tom O'Malley	.03	.01	.00
☐ 332	Jamie Quirk	.03	.01	.00	☐ 385	Max Venable	.03	.01	.00
☐ 333	Mike Ramsey	.03	.01	.00	☐ 386	Brad Wellman	.05	.02	.00
☐ 334	Floyd Rayford	.03	.01	.00	☐ 387	Joel Youngblood	.03	.01	.00
☐ 335	Lonnie Smith	.07	.03	.01	☐ 388	Gary Allenson	.03	.01	.00
☐ 336	Ozzie Smith	.14	.06	.01	☐ 389	Luis Aponte	.03	.01	.00
☐ 337	John Stuper	.03	.01	.00	☐ 390	Tony Armas	.09	.04	.01
☐ 338	Bruce Sutter	.14	.06	.01	☐ 391	Doug Bird	.03	.01	.00
☐ 339	Andy Van Slyke	.35	.14	.03	☐ 392	Wade Boggs	4.00	1.60	.40
☐ 340	Dave Von Ohlen	.05	.02	.00	☐ 393	Dennis Boyd	.75	.30	.07
☐ 341	Willie Aikens	.05	.02	.00	☐ 394	Mike Brown	.05	.02	.00
☐ 342	Mike Armstrong	.03	.01	.00	☐ 395	Mark Clear	.03	.01	.00
☐ 343	Bud Black	.05	.02	.00	☐ 396	Dennis Eckersley	.05	.02	.00
☐ 344	George Brett	.45	.18	.04	☐ 397	Dwight Evans	.10	.04	.01
☐ 345	Onix Concepcion	.03	.01	.00	☐ 398	Rich Gedman	.09	.04	.01
☐ 346	Keith Creel	.03	.01	.00	☐ 399	Glenn Hoffman	.03	.01	.00
☐ 347	Larry Gura	.05	.02	.00	☐ 400	Bruce Hurst	.08	.03	.01
☐ 348	Don Hood	.03	.01	.00	☐ 401	John Henry Johnson	.03	.01	.00
☐ 349	Dennis Leonard	.06	.02	.00	☐ 402	Ed Jurak	.03	.01	.00
☐ 350	Hal McRae	.06	.02	.00	☐ 403	Rick Miller	.03	.01	.00
☐ 351	Amos Otis	.07	.03	.01	☐ 404	Jeff Newman	.03	.01	.00
☐ 352	Gaylord Perry	.15	.06	.01	☐ 405	Reid Nichols	.03	.01	.00
☐ 353	Greg Pryor	.03	.01	.00	☐ 406	Bob Ojeda	.09	.04	.01
☐ 354	Dan Quisenberry	.15	.06	.01	☐ 407	Jerry Remy	.03	.01	.00
☐ 355	Steve Renko	.03	.01	.00	☐ 408	Jim Rice	.35	.14	.03
☐ 356	Leon Roberts	.03	.01	.00	☐ 409	Bob Stanley	.05	.02	.00
☐ 357	Pat Sheridan	.10	.04	.01	☐ 410	Dave Stapleton	.03	.01	.00
☐ 358	Joe Simpson	.03	.01	.00	☐ 411	John Tudor	.15	.06	.01
☐ 359	Don Slaught	.05	.02	.00	☐ 412	Carl Yastrzemski	.45	.18	.04
☐ 360	Paul Splittorff	.05	.02	.00	☐ 413	Buddy Bell	.10	.04	.01
☐ 361	U.L. Washington	.03	.01	.00	☐ 414	Larry Biittner	.03	.01	.00

		MINT	VG-E	F-G
☐ 415	John Butcher	.03	.01	.00
☐ 416	Danny Darwin	.03	.01	.00
☐ 417	Bucky Dent	.06	.02	.00
☐ 418	Dave Hostetler	.03	.01	.00
☐ 419	Charlie Hough	.06	.02	.00
☐ 420	Bobby Johnson	.03	.01	.00
☐ 421	Odell Jones	.03	.01	.00
☐ 422	Jon Matlack	.05	.02	.00
☐ 423	Pete O'Brien	.50	.20	.05
☐ 424	Larry Parrish	.06	.02	.00
☐ 425	Mickey Rivers	.05	.02	.00
☐ 426	Billy Sample	.03	.01	.00
☐ 427	Dave Schmidt	.03	.01	.00
☐ 428	Mike Smithson	.10	.04	.01
☐ 429	Bill Stein	.03	.01	.00
☐ 430	Dave Stewart	.03	.01	.00
☐ 431	Jim Sundberg	.05	.02	.00
☐ 432	Frank Tanana	.06	.02	.00
☐ 433	Dave Tobik	.03	.01	.00
☐ 434	Wayne Tolleson	.03	.01	.00
☐ 435	George Wright	.03	.01	.00
☐ 436	Bill Almon	.03	.01	.00
☐ 437	Keith Atherton	.05	.02	.00
☐ 438	Dave Beard	.03	.01	.00
☐ 439	Tom Burgmeier	.03	.01	.00
☐ 440	Jeff Burroughs	.05	.02	.00
☐ 441	Chris Codiroli	.07	.03	.01
☐ 442	Tim Conroy	.07	.03	.01
☐ 443	Mike Davis	.08	.03	.01
☐ 444	Wayne Gross	.03	.01	.00
☐ 445	Garry Hancock	.03	.01	.00
☐ 446	Mike Heath	.03	.01	.00
☐ 447	Rickey Henderson	.45	.18	.04
☐ 448	Donnie Hill	.07	.03	.01
☐ 449	Bob Kearney	.03	.01	.00
☐ 450	Bill Krueger	.07	.03	.01
☐ 451	Rick Langford	.03	.01	.00
☐ 452	Carney Lansford	.09	.04	.01
☐ 453	Davey Lopes	.07	.03	.01
☐ 454	Steve McCatty	.03	.01	.00
☐ 455	Dan Meyer	.03	.01	.00
☐ 456	Dwayne Murphy	.06	.02	.00
☐ 457	Mike Norris	.05	.02	.00
☐ 458	Ricky Peters	.03	.01	.00
☐ 459	Tony Phillips	.07	.03	.01
☐ 460	Tom Underwood	.03	.01	.00
☐ 461	Mike Warren	.10	.04	.01
☐ 462	Johnny Bench	.40	.16	.04
☐ 463	Bruce Berenyi	.03	.01	.00
☐ 464	Dann Bilardello	.03	.01	.00
☐ 465	Cesar Cedeno	.07	.03	.01
☐ 466	Dave Concepcion	.09	.04	.01
☐ 467	Dan Driessen	.05	.02	.00
☐ 468	Nick Esasky	.25	.10	.02
☐ 469	Rich Gale	.03	.01	.00
☐ 470	Ben Hayes	.03	.01	.00
☐ 471	Paul Householder	.03	.01	.00
☐ 472	Tom Hume	.03	.01	.00
☐ 473	Alan Knicely	.03	.01	.00
☐ 474	Eddie Milner	.03	.01	.00
☐ 475	Ron Oester	.05	.02	.00
☐ 476	Kelly Paris	.07	.03	.01
☐ 477	Frank Pastore	.03	.01	.00
☐ 478	Ted Power	.07	.03	.01
☐ 479	Joe Price	.03	.01	.00
☐ 480	Charlie Puleo	.03	.01	.00
☐ 481	Gary Redus	.25	.10	.02
☐ 482	Bill Scherrer	.07	.03	.01
☐ 483	Mario Soto	.08	.03	.01
☐ 484	Alex Trevino	.03	.01	.00
☐ 485	Duane Walker	.03	.01	.00
☐ 486	Larry Bowa	.09	.04	.01
☐ 487	Warren Brusstar	.03	.01	.00
☐ 488	Bill Buckner	.09	.04	.01
☐ 489	Bill Campbell	.03	.01	.00
☐ 490	Ron Cey	.09	.04	.01
☐ 491	Jody Davis	.09	.04	.01
☐ 492	Leon Durham	.08	.03	.01
☐ 493	Mel Hall	.10	.04	.01
☐ 494	Ferguson Jenkins	.14	.06	.01
☐ 495	Jay Johnstone	.05	.02	.00
☐ 496	Craig Lefferts	.09	.04	.01
☐ 497	Carmelo Martinez	.20	.08	.02
☐ 498	Jerry Morales	.03	.01	.00
☐ 499	Keith Moreland	.07	.03	.01
☐ 500	Dickie Noles	.03	.01	.00
☐ 501	Mike Proly	.03	.01	.00
☐ 502	Chuck Rainey	.03	.01	.00
☐ 503	Dick Ruthven	.03	.01	.00
☐ 504	Ryne Sandberg	.75	.30	.07
☐ 505	Lee Smith	.09	.04	.01
☐ 506	Steve Trout	.05	.02	.00
☐ 507	Gary Woods	.03	.01	.00
☐ 508	Juan Beniquez	.05	.02	.00
☐ 509	Bob Boone	.06	.02	.00
☐ 510	Rick Burleson	.06	.02	.00
☐ 511	Rod Carew	.35	.14	.03
☐ 512	Bobby Clark	.03	.01	.00
☐ 513	John Curtis	.03	.01	.00
☐ 514	Doug DeCinces	.10	.04	.01
☐ 515	Brian Downing	.05	.02	.00
☐ 516	Tim Foli	.03	.01	.00
☐ 517	Ken Forsch	.03	.01	.00
☐ 518	Bobby Grich	.07	.03	.01
☐ 519	Andy Hassler	.03	.01	.00
☐ 520	Reggie Jackson	.45	.18	.04

		MINT	VG-E	F-G
☐ 521	Ron Jackson	.03	.01	.00
☐ 522	Tommy John	.15	.06	.01
☐ 523	Bruce Kison	.03	.01	.00
☐ 524	Steve Lubratich	.05	.02	.00
☐ 525	Fred Lynn	.18	.08	.01
☐ 526	Gary Pettis	.45	.18	.04
☐ 527	Luis Sanchez	.03	.01	.00
☐ 528	Daryl Sconiers	.03	.01	.00
☐ 529	Ellis Valentine	.03	.01	.00
☐ 530	Rob Wilfong	.03	.01	.00
☐ 531	Mike Witt	.10	.04	.01
☐ 532	Geoff Zahn	.03	.01	.00
☐ 533	Bud Anderson	.03	.01	.00
☐ 534	Chris Bando	.03	.01	.00
☐ 535	Alan Bannister	.03	.01	.00
☐ 536	Bert Blyleven	.11	.05	.01
☐ 537	Tom Brennan	.03	.01	.00
☐ 538	Jamie Easterly	.03	.01	.00
☐ 539	Juan Eichelberger	.03	.01	.00
☐ 540	Jim Essian	.03	.01	.00
☐ 541	Mike Fischlin	.03	.01	.00
☐ 542	Julio Franco	.12	.05	.01
☐ 543	Mike Hargrove	.05	.02	.00
☐ 544	Toby Harrah	.05	.02	.00
☐ 545	Ron Hassey	.03	.01	.00
☐ 546	Neal Heaton	.10	.04	.01
☐ 547	Bake McBride	.03	.01	.00
☐ 548	Broderick Perkins	.03	.01	.00
☐ 549	Lary Sorensen	.03	.01	.00
☐ 550	Dan Spillner	.03	.01	.00
☐ 551	Rick Sutcliffe	.12	.05	.01
☐ 552	Pat Tabler	.09	.04	.01
☐ 553	Gorman Thomas	.09	.04	.01
☐ 554	Andre Thornton	.07	.03	.01
☐ 555	George Vukovich	.03	.01	.00
☐ 556	Darrell Brown	.05	.02	.00
☐ 557	Tom Brunansky	.14	.06	.01
☐ 558	Randy Bush	.03	.01	.00
☐ 559	Bobby Castillo	.03	.01	.00
☐ 560	John Castino	.03	.01	.00
☐ 561	Ron Davis	.03	.01	.00
☐ 562	Dave Engle	.03	.01	.00
☐ 563	Lenny Faedo	.03	.01	.00
☐ 564	Pete Filson	.03	.01	.00
☐ 565	Gary Gaetti	.10	.04	.01
☐ 566	Mickey Hatcher	.03	.01	.00
☐ 567	Kent Hrbek	.30	.12	.03
☐ 568	Rusty Kuntz	.03	.01	.00
☐ 569	Tim Laudner	.03	.01	.00
☐ 570	Rick Lysander	.03	.01	.00
☐ 571	Bobby Mitchell	.03	.01	.00
☐ 572	Ken Schrom	.06	.02	.00
☐ 573	Ray Smith	.03	.01	.00
☐ 574	Tim Teufel	.35	.14	.03
☐ 575	Frank Viola	.07	.03	.01
☐ 576	Gary Ward	.06	.02	.00
☐ 577	Ron Washington	.03	.01	.00
☐ 578	Len Whitehouse	.03	.01	.00
☐ 579	Al Williams	.03	.01	.00
☐ 580	Bob Bailor	.03	.01	.00
☐ 581	Mark Bradley	.09	.04	.01
☐ 582	Hubie Brooks	.10	.04	.01
☐ 583	Carlos Diaz	.03	.01	.00
☐ 584	George Foster	.12	.05	.01
☐ 585	Brian Giles	.03	.01	.00
☐ 586	Danny Heep	.03	.01	.00
☐ 587	Keith Hernandez	.25	.10	.02
☐ 588	Ron Hodges	.03	.01	.00
☐ 589	Scott Holman	.03	.01	.00
☐ 590	Dave Kingman	.14	.06	.01
☐ 591	Ed Lynch	.03	.01	.00
☐ 592	Jose Oquendo	.06	.02	.00
☐ 593	Jesse Orosco	.07	.03	.01
☐ 594	Junior Ortiz	.05	.02	.00
☐ 595	Tom Seaver	.30	.12	.03
☐ 596	Doug Sisk	.10	.04	.01
☐ 597	Rusty Staub	.09	.04	.01
☐ 598	John Stearns	.03	.01	.00
☐ 599	Darryl Strawberry	7.50	3.00	.75
☐ 600	Craig Swan	.03	.01	.00
☐ 601	Walt Terrell	.25	.10	.02
☐ 602	Mike Torrez	.06	.02	.00
☐ 603	Mookie Wilson	.07	.03	.01
☐ 604	Jamie Allen	.07	.03	.01
☐ 605	Jim Beattie	.03	.01	.00
☐ 606	Tony Bernazard	.05	.02	.00
☐ 607	Manny Castillo	.03	.01	.00
☐ 608	Bill Caudill	.05	.02	.00
☐ 609	Bryan Clark	.03	.01	.00
☐ 610	Al Cowens	.05	.02	.00
☐ 611	Dave Henderson	.07	.03	.01
☐ 612	Steve Henderson	.03	.01	.00
☐ 613	Orlando Mercado	.05	.02	.00
☐ 614	Mike Moore	.07	.03	.01
☐ 615	Ricky Nelson	.07	.03	.01
☐ 616	Spike Owen	.20	.08	.02
☐ 617	Pat Putnam	.03	.01	.00
☐ 618	Ron Roenicke	.03	.01	.00
☐ 619	Mike Stanton	.03	.01	.00
☐ 620	Bob Stoddard	.03	.01	.00
☐ 621	Rick Sweet	.03	.01	.00
☐ 622	Roy Thomas	.03	.01	.00
☐ 623	Ed VandeBerg	.05	.02	.00
☐ 624	Matt Young	.12	.05	.01
☐ 625	Richie Zisk	.05	.02	.00

		MINT	VG-E	F-G
☐ 626	Fred Lynn 1982 AS Game RB	.10	.04	.01
☐ 627	Manny Trillo 1983 AS Game RB	.06	.02	.00
☐ 628	Steve Garvey NL Iron Man	.20	.08	.02
☐ 629	Rod Carew AL Batting Runner-Up	.20	.08	.02
☐ 630	Wade Boggs AL Batting Champion	.40	.16	.04
☐ 631	Tim Raines Letting Go The Raines	.16	.07	.01
☐ 632	Al Oliver Double Trouble	.10	.04	.01
☐ 633	Steve Sax AS Second Base	.10	.04	.01
☐ 634	Dickie Thon AS Shortstop	.06	.02	.00
☐ 635	Ace Firemen Dan Quisenberry and Tippy Martinez	.06	.02	.00
☐ 636	Reds Reunited Joe Morgan Pete Rose Tony Perez	.40	.16	.04
☐ 637	Backstop Stars Lance Parrish Bob Boone	.08	.03	.01
☐ 638	Geo.Brett and G.Perry Pine Tar 7/24/83	.25	.10	.02
☐ 639	1983 No Hitters Dave Righetti Mike Warren Bob Forsch	.08	.03	.01
☐ 640	Bench and Yaz Retiring Superstars	.25	.10	.02
☐ 641	Gaylord Perry Going Out In Style	.10	.04	.01
☐ 642	Steve Carlton 300 Club and Strikeout Record	.20	.08	.02
☐ 643	Altobelli and Owens WS Managers	.05	.02	.00
☐ 644	Rick Dempsey World Series MVP	.05	.02	.00
☐ 645	Mike Boddicker WS Rookie Winner	.07	.03	.01
☐ 646	Scott McGregor WS Clincher	.05	.02	.00
☐ 647	CL: Orioles/Royals	.08	.01	.00
☐ 648	CL: Phillies/Giants	.07	.01	.00
☐ 649	CL: White Sox/Red Sox	.07	.01	.00
☐ 650	CL: Tigers/Rangers	.07	.01	.00

		MINT	VG-E	F-G
☐ 651	CL: Dodgers/A's	.07	.01	.00
☐ 652	CL: Yankees/Reds	.07	.01	.00
☐ 653	CL: Blue Jays/Cubs	.07	.01	.00
☐ 654	CL: Braves/Angels	.07	.01	.00
☐ 655	CL: Brewers/Indians	.07	.01	.00
☐ 656	CL: Astros/Twins	.07	.01	.00
☐ 657	CL: Pirates/Mets	.07	.01	.00
☐ 658	CL: Expos/Mariners	.07	.01	.00
☐ 659	CL: Padres/Specials	.07	.01	.00
☐ 660	CL: Cardinals/Teams	.08	.01	.00

1984 Fleer Update

The cards in this 132-card set measure 2½"
by 3½". For the first time, the Fleer Gum Company issued a traded, extended, or update
set. The purpose of the set was the same as
the traded sets issued by Topps over the past
four years, i.e., to portray players with their
proper team for the current year and to portray rookies who were not in their regular issue. Like the Topps Traded sets of the past
four years, the Fleer Update sets were distributed through hobby channels only. The
set was quite popular with collectors, and apparently, the print run was relatively short, as
the set was quickly in short supply and exhib-
ited a rapid and dramatic price increase. The
cards are numbered on the back with a U
prefix; the order corresponds to the alphabetical order of the subjects' names.

	MINT	VG-E	F-G
Complete Set	250.00	100.00	25.00
Common Player	.20	.08	.02

		MINT	VG-E	F-G
☐ 1 U	Willie Aikens	.25	.10	.02

		MINT	VG-E	F-G
☐	2 U Luis Aponte	.20	.08	.02
☐	3 U Mark Bailey	.25	.10	.02
☐	4 U Bob Bailor	.20	.08	.02
☐	5 U Dusty Baker	.25	.10	.02
☐	6 U Steve Balboni	.25	.10	.02
☐	7 U Alan Bannister	.20	.08	.02
☐	8 U Marty Barrett	4.00	1.60	.40
☐	9 U Dave Beard	.20	.08	.02
☐	10 U Joe Beckwith	.20	.08	.02
☐	11 U Dave Bergman	.20	.08	.02
☐	12 U Tony Bernazard	.25	.10	.02
☐	13 U Bruce Bochte	.25	.10	.02
☐	14 U Barry Bonnell	.20	.08	.02
☐	15 U Phil Bradley	9.00	3.75	.90
☐	16 U Fred Breining	.20	.08	.02
☐	17 U Mike Brown	.25	.10	.02
☐	18 U Bill Buckner	.35	.14	.03
☐	19 U Ray Burris	.20	.08	.02
☐	20 U John Butcher	.20	.08	.02
☐	21 U Brett Butler	.35	.14	.03
☐	22 U Enos Cabell	.20	.08	.02
☐	23 U Bill Campbell	.20	.08	.02
☐	24 U Bill Caudill	.25	.10	.02
☐	25 U Bobby Clark	.20	.08	.02
☐	26 U Bryan Clark	.20	.08	.02
☐	27 U Roger Clemens	75.00	30.00	7.50
☐	28 U Jaime Cocanower	.25	.10	.02
☐	29 U Ron Darling	12.00	5.00	1.20
☐	30 U Alvin Davis	8.00	3.25	.80
☐	31 U Bob Dernier	.25	.10	.02
☐	32 U Carlos Diaz	.20	.08	.02
☐	33 U Mike Easler	.25	.10	.02
☐	34 U Dennis Eckersley	.25	.10	.02
☐	35 U Jim Essian	.20	.08	.02
☐	36 U Darrell Evans	.35	.14	.03
☐	37 U Mike Fitzgerald	.25	.10	.02
☐	38 U Tim Foli	.20	.08	.02
☐	39 U John Franco	2.00	.80	.20
☐	40 U George Frazier	.20	.08	.02
☐	41 U Rich Gale	.20	.08	.02
☐	42 U Barbaro Garbey	.35	.14	.03
☐	43 U Dwight Gooden	75.00	30.00	6.00
☐	44 U Goose Gossage	1.00	.40	.10
☐	45 U Wayne Gross	.20	.08	.02
☐	46 U Mark Gubicza	1.00	.40	.10
☐	47 U Jackie Gutierrez	.35	.14	.03
☐	48 U Toby Harrah	.25	.10	.02
☐	49 U Ron Hassey	.20	.08	.02
☐	50 U Richie Hebner	.20	.08	.02
☐	51 U Willie Hernandez	.75	.30	.07
☐	52 U Ed Hodge	.25	.10	.02
☐	53 U Ricky Horton	.60	.24	.06
☐	54 U Art Howe	.20	.08	.02
☐	55 U Dane Iorg	.20	.08	.02
☐	56 U Brook Jacoby	4.00	1.60	.40
☐	57 U Dion James	.60	.24	.06
☐	58 U Mike Jeffcoat	.25	.10	.02
☐	59 U Ruppert Jones	.25	.10	.02
☐	60 U Bob Kearney	.20	.08	.02
☐	61 U Jimmy Key	2.00	.80	.20
☐	62 U Dave Kingman	.50	.20	.05
☐	63 U Brad Komminsk	.50	.20	.05
☐	64 U Jerry Koosman	.25	.10	.02
☐	65 U Wayne Krenchicki	.20	.08	.02
☐	66 U Rusty Kuntz	.20	.08	.02
☐	67 U Frank LaCorte	.20	.08	.02
☐	68 U Dennis Lamp	.20	.08	.02
☐	69 U Tito Landrum	.20	.08	.02
☐	70 U Mark Langston	3.00	1.20	.30
☐	71 U Rick Leach	.20	.08	.02
☐	72 U Craig Lefferts	.20	.08	.02
☐	73 U Gary Lucas	.20	.08	.02
☐	74 U Jerry Martin	.20	.08	.02
☐	75 U Carmelo Martinez	.25	.10	.02
☐	76 U Mike Mason	.50	.20	.05
☐	77 U Gary Matthews	.25	.10	.02
☐	78 U Andy McGaffigan	.20	.08	.02
☐	79 U Joey McLaughlin	.20	.08	.02
☐	80 U Joe Morgan	3.00	1.20	.30
☐	81 U Darryl Motley	.25	.10	.02
☐	82 U Graig Nettles	1.00	.40	.10
☐	83 U Phil Niekro	3.00	1.20	.30
☐	84 U Ken Oberkfell	.20	.08	.02
☐	85 U Al Oliver	.50	.20	.05
☐	86 U Jorge Orta	.20	.08	.02
☐	87 U Amos Otis	.25	.10	.02
☐	88 U Bob Owchinko	.20	.08	.02
☐	89 U Dave Parker	3.00	1.20	.30
☐	90 U Jack Perconte	.20	.08	.02
☐	91 U Tony Perez	.75	.30	.07
☐	92 U Gerald Perry	.35	.14	.03
☐	93 U Kirby Puckett	40.00	16.00	4.00
☐	94 U Shane Rawley	.35	.14	.03
☐	95 U Floyd Rayford	.25	.10	.02
☐	96 U Ron Reed	.20	.08	.02
☐	97 U R.J. Reynolds	1.50	.60	.15
☐	98 U Gene Richards	.20	.08	.02
☐	99 U Jose Rijo	1.00	.40	.10
☐	100 U Jeff Robinson	.25	.10	.02
☐	101 U Ron Romanick	1.50	.60	.15
☐	102 U Pete Rose	25.00	10.00	2.50
☐	103 U Bret Saberhagen	6.00	2.40	.60
☐	104 U Scott Sanderson	.25	.10	.02
☐	105 U Dick Schofield	2.00	.80	.20
☐	106 U Tom Seaver	8.00	3.25	.80
☐	107 U Jim Slaton	.25	.10	.02

			MINT	VG-E	F-G
☐	108 U	Mike Smithson	.20	.08	.02
☐	109 U	Lary Sorensen	.20	.08	.02
☐	110 U	Tim Stoddard	.20	.08	.02
☐	111 U	Jeff Stone	1.00	.40	.10
☐	112 U	Champ Summers	.20	.08	.02
☐	113 U	Jim Sundberg	.25	.10	.02
☐	114 U	Rick Sutcliffe	.75	.30	.07
☐	115 U	Craig Swan	.20	.08	.02
☐	116 U	Derrel Thomas	.20	.08	.02
☐	117 U	Gorman Thomas	.30	.12	.03
☐	118 U	Alex Trevino	.20	.08	.02
☐	119 U	Manny Trillo	.25	.10	.02
☐	120 U	John Tudor	.50	.20	.05
☐	121 U	Tom Underwood	.20	.08	.02
☐	122 U	Mike Vail	.20	.08	.02
☐	123 U	Tom Waddell	.25	.10	.02
☐	124 U	Gary Ward	.25	.10	.02
☐	125 U	Terry Whitfield	.20	.08	.02
☐	126 U	Curtis Wilkerson	.25	.10	.02
☐	127 U	Frank Williams	.35	.14	.03
☐	128 U	Glenn Wilson	.35	.14	.03
☐	129 U	John Wockenfuss	.20	.08	.02
☐	130 U	Ned Yost	.20	.08	.02
☐	131 U	Mike Young	2.00	.80	.20
☐	132 U	Checklist: 1-132	.25	.02	.00

number, and statistics format that Fleer has been using over the past few years. The cards are ordered alphabetically within team. The teams are ordered based on their respective performance during the prior year, e.g., World Champion Detroit Tigers (1-25), NL Champion San Diego (26-48), Chicago Cubs (49-71), New York Mets (72-95), Toronto (96-119), New York Yankees (120-147), Boston (148-169), Baltimore (170-195), Kansas City (196-218), St. Louis (219-243), Philadelphia (244-269), Minnesota (270-292), California (293-317), Atlanta (318-342), Houston (343-365), Los Angeles (366-391), Montreal (392-413), Oakland (414-436), Cleveland (437-460), Pittsburgh (461-481), Seattle (482-505), Chicago White Sox (506-530), Cincinnati (531-554), Texas (555-575), Milwaukee (576-601), and San Francisco (602-625). Specials (626-643), Rookie pairs (644-653), and checklist cards (654-660) complete the set. The black and white photo on the reverse is included for the third straight year.

1985 Fleer

The cards in this 660-card set measure 2½" by 3½". The 1985 Fleer set features fronts which contain the team logo along with the player's name and position. The borders enclosing the photo are color coded to correspond to the player's team. In each case, the color is one of the standard colors of that team, e.g., orange for Baltimore, red for St. Louis, etc. The backs feature the same name,

			MINT	VG-E	F-G
		Complete Set	45.00	18.00	4.50
		Common Player (1-660)	.03	.01	.00
☐	1	Doug Bair	.05	.02	.00
☐	2	Juan Berenguer	.03	.01	.00
☐	3	Dave Bergman	.03	.01	.00
☐	4	Tom Brookens	.03	.01	.00
☐	5	Marty Castillo	.03	.01	.00
☐	6	Darrell Evans	.08	.03	.01
☐	7	Barbaro Garbey	.08	.03	.01
☐	8	Kirk Gibson	.20	.08	.02
☐	9	John Grubb	.03	.01	.00
☐	10	Willie Hernandez	.15	.06	.01
☐	11	Larry Herndon	.03	.01	.00
☐	12	Howard Johnson	.03	.01	.00
☐	13	Ruppert Jones	.03	.01	.00
☐	14	Rusty Kuntz	.03	.01	.00
☐	15	Chet Lemon	.05	.02	.00
☐	16	Aurelio Lopez	.03	.01	.00
☐	17	Sid Monge	.03	.01	.00
☐	18	Jack Morris	.15	.06	.01
☐	19	Lance Parrish	.20	.08	.02
☐	20	Dan Petry	.10	.04	.01
☐	21	Dave Rozema	.03	.01	.00
☐	22	Bill Scherrer	.03	.01	.00

		MINT	VG-E	F-G
☐ 23	Alan Trammell	.15	.06	.01
☐ 24	Lou Whitaker	.12	.05	.01
☐ 25	Milt Wilcox	.03	.01	.00
☐ 26	Kurt Bevacqua	.03	.01	.00
☐ 27	Greg Booker	.05	.02	.00
☐ 28	Bobby Brown	.03	.01	.00
☐ 29	Luis DeLeon	.03	.01	.00
☐ 30	Dave Dravecky	.05	.02	.00
☐ 31	Tim Flannery	.03	.01	.00
☐ 32	Steve Garvey	.35	.14	.03
☐ 33	Goose Gossage	.12	.05	.01
☐ 34	Tony Gwynn	.40	.16	.04
☐ 35	Greg Harris	.05	.02	.00
☐ 36	Andy Hawkins	.05	.02	.00
☐ 37	Terry Kennedy	.07	.03	.01
☐ 38	Craig Lefferts	.03	.01	.00
☐ 39	Tim Lollar	.03	.01	.00
☐ 40	Carmelo Martinez	.05	.02	.00
☐ 41	Kevin McReynolds	.15	.06	.01
☐ 42	Graig Nettles	.12	.05	.01
☐ 43	Luis Salazar	.03	.01	.00
☐ 44	Eric Show	.03	.01	.00
☐ 45	Garry Templeton	.07	.03	.01
☐ 46	Mark Thurmond	.05	.02	.00
☐ 47	Ed Whitson	.05	.02	.00
☐ 48	Alan Wiggins	.06	.02	.00
☐ 49	Rich Bordi	.03	.01	.00
☐ 50	Larry Bowa	.07	.03	.01
☐ 51	Warren Brusstar	.03	.01	.00
☐ 52	Ron Cey	.09	.04	.01
☐ 53	Henry Cotto	.09	.04	.01
☐ 54	Jody Davis	.08	.03	.01
☐ 55	Bob Dernier	.05	.02	.00
☐ 56	Leon Durham	.08	.03	.01
☐ 57	Dennis Eckersley	.05	.02	.00
☐ 58	George Frazier	.03	.01	.00
☐ 59	Richie Hebner	.03	.01	.00
☐ 60	Dave Lopes	.06	.02	.00
☐ 61	Gary Matthews	.07	.03	.01
☐ 62	Keith Moreland	.08	.03	.01
☐ 63	Rick Reuschel	.05	.02	.00
☐ 64	Dick Ruthven	.03	.01	.00
☐ 65	Ryne Sandberg	.40	.16	.04
☐ 66	Scott Sanderson	.03	.01	.00
☐ 67	Lee Smith	.07	.03	.01
☐ 68	Tim Stoddard	.03	.01	.00
☐ 69	Rick Sutcliffe	.10	.04	.01
☐ 70	Steve Trout	.03	.01	.00
☐ 71	Gary Woods	.03	.01	.00
☐ 72	Wally Backman	.07	.03	.01
☐ 73	Bruce Berenyi	.03	.01	.00
☐ 74	Hubie Brooks	.10	.04	.01
☐ 75	Kelvin Chapman	.09	.04	.01
☐ 76	Ron Darling	.50	.20	.05
☐ 77	Sid Fernandez	.50	.20	.05
☐ 78	Mike Fitzgerald	.03	.01	.00
☐ 79	George Foster	.12	.05	.01
☐ 80	Brent Gaff	.03	.01	.00
☐ 81	Ron Gardenhire	.03	.01	.00
☐ 82	Dwight Gooden	7.50	3.00	.75
☐ 83	Tom Gorman	.03	.01	.00
☐ 84	Danny Heep	.03	.01	.00
☐ 85	Keith Hernandez	.25	.10	.02
☐ 86	Ray Knight	.07	.03	.01
☐ 87	Ed Lynch	.03	.01	.00
☐ 88	Jose Oquendo	.03	.01	.00
☐ 89	Jesse Orosco	.05	.02	.00
☐ 90	Rafael Santana	.08	.03	.01
☐ 91	Doug Sisk	.03	.01	.00
☐ 92	Rusty Staub	.07	.03	.01
☐ 93	Darryl Strawberry	.90	.36	.09
☐ 94	Walt Terrell	.05	.02	.00
☐ 95	Mookie Wilson	.07	.03	.01
☐ 96	Jim Acker	.03	.01	.00
☐ 97	Willie Aikens	.05	.02	.00
☐ 98	Doyle Alexander	.05	.02	.00
☐ 99	Jesse Barfield	.15	.06	.01
☐ 100	George Bell	.15	.06	.01
☐ 101	Jim Clancy	.05	.02	.00
☐ 102	Dave Collins	.05	.02	.00
☐ 103	Tony Fernandez	.10	.04	.01
☐ 104	Damaso Garcia	.08	.03	.01
☐ 105	Jim Gott	.03	.01	.00
☐ 106	Alfredo Griffin	.05	.02	.00
☐ 107	Garth Iorg	.03	.01	.00
☐ 108	Roy Lee Jackson	.03	.01	.00
☐ 109	Cliff Johnson	.03	.01	.00
☐ 110	Jimmy Key	.35	.14	.03
☐ 111	Dennis Lamp	.03	.01	.00
☐ 112	Rick Leach	.03	.01	.00
☐ 113	Luis Leal	.03	.01	.00
☐ 114	Buck Martinez	.03	.01	.00
☐ 115	Lloyd Moseby	.10	.04	.01
☐ 116	Rance Mulliniks	.03	.01	.00
☐ 117	Dave Stieb	.12	.05	.01
☐ 118	Willie Upshaw	.08	.03	.01
☐ 119	Ernie Whitt	.03	.01	.00
☐ 120	Mike Armstrong	.03	.01	.00
☐ 121	Don Baylor	.12	.05	.01
☐ 122	Marty Bystrom	.03	.01	.00
☐ 123	Rick Cerone	.03	.01	.00
☐ 124	Joe Cowley	.03	.01	.00
☐ 125	Brian Dayett	.03	.01	.00
☐ 126	Tim Foli	.03	.01	.00
☐ 127	Ray Fontenot	.03	.01	.00
☐ 128	Ken Griffey	.07	.03	.01

	MINT	VG-E	F-G		MINT	VG-E	F-G
☐ 129 Ron Guidry	.15	.06	.01	☐ 182 Tippy Martinez	.03	.01	.00
☐ 130 Toby Harrah	.05	.02	.00	☐ 183 Scott McGregor	.07	.03	.01
☐ 131 Jay Howell	.06	.02	.00	☐ 184 Eddie Murray	.40	.16	.04
☐ 132 Steve Kemp	.08	.03	.01	☐ 185 Joe Nolan	.03	.01	.00
☐ 133 Don Mattingly	7.50	3.00	.75	☐ 186 Floyd Rayford	.03	.01	.00
☐ 134 Bobby Meacham	.03	.01	.00	☐ 187 Cal Ripken	.40	.16	.04
☐ 135 John Montefusco	.05	.02	.00	☐ 188 Gary Roenicke	.05	.02	.00
☐ 136 Omar Moreno	.03	.01	.00	☐ 189 Lenn Sakata	.03	.01	.00
☐ 137 Dale Murray	.03	.01	.00	☐ 190 John Shelby	.03	.01	.00
☐ 138 Phil Niekro	.15	.06	.01	☐ 191 Ken Singleton	.07	.03	.01
☐ 139 Mike Pagliarulo	1.25	.50	.12	☐ 192 Sammy Stewart	.03	.01	.00
☐ 140 Willie Randolph	.06	.02	.00	☐ 193 Bill Swaggerty	.09	.04	.01
☐ 141 Dennis Rasmussen	.07	.03	.01	☐ 194 Tom Underwood	.03	.01	.00
☐ 142 Dave Righetti	.15	.06	.01	☐ 195 Mike Young	.15	.06	.01
☐ 143 Jose Rijo	.30	.12	.03	☐ 196 Steve Balboni	.07	.03	.01
☐ 144 Andre Robertson	.03	.01	.00	☐ 197 Joe Beckwith	.03	.01	.00
☐ 145 Bob Shirley	.03	.01	.00	☐ 198 Bud Black	.03	.01	.00
☐ 146 Dave Winfield	.35	.14	.03	☐ 199 George Brett	.40	.16	.04
☐ 147 Butch Wynegar	.05	.02	.00	☐ 200 Onix Concepcion	.03	.01	.00
☐ 148 Gary Allenson	.03	.01	.00	☐ 201 Mark Gubicza	.25	.10	.02
☐ 149 Tony Armas	.09	.04	.01	☐ 202 Larry Gura	.05	.02	.00
☐ 150 Marty Barrett	.12	.05	.01	☐ 203 Mark Huismann	.05	.02	.00
☐ 151 Wade Boggs	2.50	1.00	.25	☐ 204 Dane Iorg	.03	.01	.00
☐ 152 Dennis Boyd	.08	.03	.01	☐ 205 Danny Jackson	.06	.02	.00
☐ 153 Bill Buckner	.08	.03	.01	☐ 206 Charlie Leibrandt	.06	.02	.00
☐ 154 Mark Clear	.03	.01	.00	☐ 207 Hal McRae	.06	.02	.00
☐ 155 Roger Clemens	7.50	3.00	.75	☐ 208 Darryl Motley	.03	.01	.00
☐ 156 Steve Crawford	.03	.01	.00	☐ 209 Jorge Orta	.03	.01	.00
☐ 157 Mike Easler	.06	.02	.00	☐ 210 Greg Pryor	.03	.01	.00
☐ 158 Dwight Evans	.10	.04	.01	☐ 211 Dan Quisenberry	.12	.05	.01
☐ 159 Rich Gedman	.09	.04	.01	☐ 212 Bret Saberhagen	1.00	.40	.10
☐ 160 Jackie Gutierrez	.07	.03	.01	☐ 213 Pat Sheridan	.03	.01	.00
☐ 161 Bruce Hurst	.07	.03	.01	☐ 214 Don Slaught	.03	.01	.00
☐ 162 John Henry Johnson	.03	.01	.00	☐ 215 U.L. Washington	.03	.01	.00
☐ 163 Rick Miller	.03	.01	.00	☐ 216 John Wathan	.03	.01	.00
☐ 164 Reid Nichols	.03	.01	.00	☐ 217 Frank White	.06	.02	.00
☐ 165 Al Nipper	.15	.06	.01	☐ 218 Willie Wilson	.12	.05	.01
☐ 166 Bob Ojeda	.09	.04	.01	☐ 219 Neil Allen	.05	.02	.00
☐ 167 Jerry Remy	.03	.01	.00	☐ 220 Joaquin Andujar	.08	.03	.01
☐ 168 Jim Rice	.35	.14	.03	☐ 221 Steve Braun	.03	.01	.00
☐ 169 Bob Stanley	.05	.02	.00	☐ 222 Danny Cox	.08	.03	.01
☐ 170 Mike Boddicker	.06	.02	.00	☐ 223 Bob Forsch	.06	.02	.00
☐ 171 Al Bumbry	.03	.01	.00	☐ 224 David Green	.05	.02	.00
☐ 172 Todd Cruz	.03	.01	.00	☐ 225 George Hendrick	.06	.02	.00
☐ 173 Rich Dauer	.03	.01	.00	☐ 226 Tom Herr	.08	.03	.01
☐ 174 Storm Davis	.07	.03	.01	☐ 227 Ricky Horton	.15	.06	.01
☐ 175 Rick Dempsey	.05	.02	.00	☐ 228 Art Howe	.03	.01	.00
☐ 176 Jim Dwyer	.03	.01	.00	☐ 229 Mike Jorgensen	.03	.01	.00
☐ 177 Mike Flanagan	.06	.02	.00	☐ 230 Kurt Kepshire	.08	.03	.01
☐ 178 Dan Ford	.03	.01	.00	☐ 231 Jeff Lahti	.03	.01	.00
☐ 179 Wayne Gross	.03	.01	.00	☐ 232 Tito Landrum	.03	.01	.00
☐ 180 John Lowenstein	.03	.01	.00	☐ 233 Dave LaPoint	.03	.01	.00
☐ 181 Dennis Martinez	.03	.01	.00	☐ 234 Willie McGee	.25	.10	.02

		MINT	VG-E	F-G			MINT	VG-E	F-G
☐ 235	Tom Nieto	.05	.02	.00	☐ 288	Ken Schrom	.06	.02	.00
☐ 236	Terry Pendleton	.35	.14	.03	☐ 289	Mike Smithson	.05	.02	.00
☐ 237	Darrell Porter	.05	.02	.00	☐ 290	Tim Teufel	.06	.02	.00
☐ 238	Dave Rucker	.03	.01	.00	☐ 291	Frank Viola	.08	.03	.01
☐ 239	Lonnie Smith	.06	.02	.00	☐ 292	Ron Washington	.03	.01	.00
☐ 240	Ozzie Smith	.10	.04	.01	☐ 293	Don Aase	.05	.02	.00
☐ 241	Bruce Sutter	.12	.05	.01	☐ 294	Juan Beniquez	.05	.02	.00
☐ 242	Andy Van Slyke	.07	.03	.01	☐ 295	Bob Boone	.05	.02	.00
☐ 243	Dave Von Ohlen	.03	.01	.00	☐ 296	Mike Brown	.05	.02	.00
☐ 244	Larry Andersen	.03	.01	.00		(Angels OF)			
☐ 245	Bill Campbell	.03	.01	.00	☐ 297	Rod Carew	.30	.12	.03
☐ 246	Steve Carlton	.30	.12	.03	☐ 298	Doug Corbett	.03	.01	.00
☐ 247	Tim Corcoran	.03	.01	.00	☐ 299	Doug DeCinces	.08	.03	.01
☐ 248	Ivan DeJesus	.03	.01	.00	☐ 300	Brian Downing	.05	.02	.00
☐ 249	John Denny	.06	.02	.00	☐ 301	Ken Forsch	.03	.01	.00
☐ 250	Bo Diaz	.05	.02	.00	☐ 302	Bobby Grich	.06	.02	.00
☐ 251	Greg Gross	.03	.01	.00	☐ 303	Reggie Jackson	.35	.14	.03
☐ 252	Kevin Gross	.03	.01	.00	☐ 304	Tommy John	.10	.04	.01
☐ 253	Von Hayes	.12	.05	.01	☐ 305	Curt Kaufman	.08	.03	.01
☐ 254	Al Holland	.03	.01	.00	☐ 306	Bruce Kison	.03	.01	.00
☐ 255	Charles Hudson	.05	.02	.00	☐ 307	Fred Lynn	.15	.06	.01
☐ 256	Jerry Koosman	.07	.03	.01	☐ 308	Gary Pettis	.08	.03	.01
☐ 257	Joe Lefebvre	.03	.01	.00	☐ 309	Ron Romanick	.25	.10	.02
☐ 258	Sixto Lezcano	.03	.01	.00	☐ 310	Luis Sanchez	.03	.01	.00
☐ 259	Garry Maddox	.05	.02	.00	☐ 311	Dick Schofield	.07	.03	.01
☐ 260	Len Matuszek	.03	.01	.00	☐ 312	Daryl Sconiers	.03	.01	.00
☐ 261	Tug McGraw	.08	.03	.01	☐ 313	Jim Slaton	.03	.01	.00
☐ 262	Al Oliver	.10	.04	.01	☐ 314	Derrel Thomas	.03	.01	.00
☐ 263	Shane Rawley	.07	.03	.01	☐ 315	Rob Wilfong	.03	.01	.00
☐ 264	Juan Samuel	.20	.08	.02	☐ 316	Mike Witt	.10	.04	.01
☐ 265	Mike Schmidt	.35	.14	.03	☐ 317	Geoff Zahn	.03	.01	.00
☐ 266	Jeff Stone	.20	.08	.02	☐ 318	Len Barker	.03	.01	.00
☐ 267	Ozzie Virgil	.06	.02	.00	☐ 319	Steve Bedrosian	.06	.02	.00
☐ 268	Glenn Wilson	.08	.03	.01	☐ 320	Bruce Benedict	.03	.01	.00
☐ 269	John Wockenfuss	.03	.01	.00	☐ 321	Rick Camp	.03	.01	.00
☐ 270	Darrell Brown	.03	.01	.00	☐ 322	Chris Chambliss	.05	.02	.00
☐ 271	Tom Brunansky	.10	.04	.01	☐ 323	Jeff Dedmon	.07	.03	.01
☐ 272	Randy Bush	.03	.01	.00	☐ 324	Terry Forster	.06	.02	.00
☐ 273	John Butcher	.03	.01	.00	☐ 325	Gene Garber	.03	.01	.00
☐ 274	Bobby Castillo	.03	.01	.00	☐ 326	Albert Hall	.08	.03	.01
☐ 275	Ron Davis	.03	.01	.00	☐ 327	Terry Harper	.03	.01	.00
☐ 276	Dave Engle	.03	.01	.00	☐ 328	Bob Horner	.15	.06	.01
☐ 277	Pete Filson	.03	.01	.00	☐ 329	Glenn Hubbard	.03	.01	.00
☐ 278	Gary Gaetti	.09	.04	.01	☐ 330	Randy Johnson	.03	.01	.00
☐ 279	Mickey Hatcher	.03	.01	.00	☐ 331	Brad Komminsk	.06	.02	.00
☐ 280	Ed Hodge	.06	.02	.00	☐ 332	Rick Mahler	.03	.01	.00
☐ 281	Kent Hrbek	.25	.10	.02	☐ 333	Craig McMurtry	.03	.01	.00
☐ 282	Houston Jimenez	.03	.01	.00	☐ 334	Donnie Moore	.05	.02	.00
☐ 283	Tim Laudner	.03	.01	.00	☐ 335	Dale Murphy	.50	.20	.05
☐ 284	Rick Lysander	.03	.01	.00	☐ 336	Ken Oberkfell	.03	.01	.00
☐ 285	Dave Meier	.09	.04	.01	☐ 337	Pascual Perez	.03	.01	.00
☐ 286	Kirby Puckett	5.00	2.00	.50	☐ 338	Gerald Perry	.05	.02	.00
☐ 287	Pat Putnam	.03	.01	.00	☐ 339	Rafael Ramirez	.03	.01	.00

		MINT	VG-E	F-G
☐ 340	Jerry Royster	.03	.01	.00
☐ 341	Alex Trevino	.03	.01	.00
☐ 342	Claudell Washington	.06	.02	.00
☐ 343	Alan Ashby	.03	.01	.00
☐ 344	Mark Bailey	.07	.03	.01
☐ 345	Kevin Bass	.07	.03	.01
☐ 346	Enos Cabell	.03	.01	.00
☐ 347	Jose Cruz	.10	.04	.01
☐ 348	Bill Dawley	.03	.01	.00
☐ 349	Frank DiPino	.03	.01	.00
☐ 350	Bill Doran	.07	.03	.01
☐ 351	Phil Garner	.05	.02	.00
☐ 352	Bob Knepper	.08	.03	.01
☐ 353	Mike LaCoss	.03	.01	.00
☐ 354	Jerry Mumphrey	.05	.02	.00
☐ 355	Joe Niekro	.08	.03	.01
☐ 356	Terry Puhl	.05	.02	.00
☐ 357	Craig Reynolds	.03	.01	.00
☐ 358	Vern Ruhle	.03	.01	.00
☐ 359	Nolan Ryan	.30	.12	.03
☐ 360	Joe Sambito	.05	.02	.00
☐ 361	Mike Scott	.15	.06	.01
☐ 362	Dave Smith	.07	.03	.01
☐ 363	Julio Solano	.07	.03	.01
☐ 364	Dickie Thon	.05	.02	.00
☐ 365	Denny Walling	.03	.01	.00
☐ 366	Dave Anderson	.03	.01	.00
☐ 367	Bob Bailor	.03	.01	.00
☐ 368	Greg Brock	.05	.02	.00
☐ 369	Carlos Diaz	.03	.01	.00
☐ 370	Pedro Guerrero	.25	.10	.02
☐ 371	Orel Hershiser	1.50	.60	.15
☐ 372	Rick Honeycutt	.05	.02	.00
☐ 373	Burt Hooton	.03	.01	.00
☐ 374	Ken Howell	.20	.08	.02
☐ 375	Ken Landreaux	.05	.02	.00
☐ 376	Candy Maldonado	.06	.02	.00
☐ 377	Mike Marshall	.12	.05	.01
☐ 378	Tom Niedenfuer	.06	.02	.00
☐ 379	Alejandro Pena	.05	.02	.00
☐ 380	Jerry Reuss	.05	.02	.00
☐ 381	R.J. Reynolds	.25	.10	.02
☐ 382	German Rivera	.10	.04	.01
☐ 383	Bill Russell	.05	.02	.00
☐ 384	Steve Sax	.15	.06	.01
☐ 385	Mike Scioscia	.05	.02	.00
☐ 386	Franklin Stubbs	.60	.24	.06
☐ 387	Fernando Valenzuela	.30	.12	.03
☐ 388	Bob Welch	.06	.02	.00
☐ 389	Terry Whitfield	.03	.01	.00
☐ 390	Steve Yeager	.05	.02	.00
☐ 391	Pat Zachry	.03	.01	.00
☐ 392	Fred Breining	.03	.01	.00
☐ 393	Gary Carter	.30	.12	.03
☐ 394	Andre Dawson	.20	.08	.02
☐ 395	Miguel Dilone	.03	.01	.00
☐ 396	Dan Driessen	.05	.02	.00
☐ 397	Doug Flynn	.03	.01	.00
☐ 398	Terry Francona	.05	.02	.00
☐ 399	Bill Gullickson	.05	.02	.00
☐ 400	Bob James	.05	.02	.00
☐ 401	Charlie Lea	.05	.02	.00
☐ 402	Bryan Little	.03	.01	.00
☐ 403	Gary Lucas	.03	.01	.00
☐ 404	David Palmer	.05	.02	.00
☐ 405	Tim Raines	.20	.08	.02
☐ 406	Mike Ramsey	.03	.01	.00
☐ 407	Jeff Reardon	.06	.02	.00
☐ 408	Steve Rogers	.06	.02	.00
☐ 409	Dan Schatzeder	.03	.01	.00
☐ 410	Bryn Smith	.05	.02	.00
☐ 411	Mike Stenhouse	.03	.01	.00
☐ 412	Tim Wallach	.08	.03	.01
☐ 413	Jim Wohlford	.03	.01	.00
☐ 414	Bill Almon	.03	.01	.00
☐ 415	Keith Atherton	.03	.01	.00
☐ 416	Bruce Bochte	.05	.02	.00
☐ 417	Tom Burgmeier	.03	.01	.00
☐ 418	Ray Burris	.03	.01	.00
☐ 419	Bill Caudill	.05	.02	.00
☐ 420	Chris Codiroli	.03	.01	.00
☐ 421	Tim Conroy	.03	.01	.00
☐ 422	Mike Heath	.03	.01	.00
☐ 423	Jim Essian	.03	.01	.00
☐ 424	Mike Heath	.03	.01	.00
☐ 425	Rickey Henderson	.40	.16	.04
☐ 426	Donnie Hill	.03	.01	.00
☐ 427	Dave Kingman	.09	.04	.01
☐ 428	Bill Krueger	.03	.01	.00
☐ 429	Carney Lansford	.08	.03	.01
☐ 430	Steve McCatty	.03	.01	.00
☐ 431	Joe Morgan	.15	.06	.01
☐ 432	Dwayne Murphy	.06	.02	.00
☐ 433	Tony Phillips	.03	.01	.00
☐ 434	Lary Sorensen	.03	.01	.00
☐ 435	Mike Warren	.05	.02	.00
☐ 436	Curt Young	.09	.04	.01
☐ 437	Luis Aponte	.03	.01	.00
☐ 438	Chris Bando	.03	.01	.00
☐ 439	Tony Bernazard	.05	.02	.00
☐ 440	Bert Blyleven	.09	.04	.01
☐ 441	Brett Butler	.09	.04	.01
☐ 442	Ernie Camacho	.03	.01	.00
☐ 443	Joe Carter	.25	.10	.02
☐ 444	Carmelo Castillo	.03	.01	.00
☐ 445	Jamie Easterly	.03	.01	.00

		MINT	VG-E	F-G
☐ 446	Steve Farr	.09	.04	.01
☐ 447	Mike Fischlin	.03	.01	.00
☐ 448	Julio Franco	.10	.04	.01
☐ 449	Mel Hall	.08	.03	.01
☐ 450	Mike Hargrove	.05	.02	.00
☐ 451	Neal Heaton	.05	.02	.00
☐ 452	Brook Jacoby	.12	.05	.01
☐ 453	Mike Jeffcoat	.05	.02	.00
☐ 454	Don Schulze	.07	.03	.01
☐ 455	Roy Smith	.07	.03	.01
☐ 456	Pat Tabler	.08	.03	.01
☐ 457	Andre Thornton	.07	.03	.01
☐ 458	George Vukovich	.03	.01	.00
☐ 459	Tom Waddell	.10	.04	.01
☐ 460	Jerry Willard	.03	.01	.00
☐ 461	Dale Berra	.05	.02	.00
☐ 462	John Candelaria	.07	.03	.01
☐ 463	Jose DeLeon	.05	.02	.00
☐ 464	Doug Frobel	.03	.01	.00
☐ 465	Cecilio Guante	.03	.01	.00
☐ 466	Brian Harper	.03	.01	.00
☐ 467	Lee Lacy	.05	.02	.00
☐ 468	Bill Madlock	.12	.05	.01
☐ 469	Lee Mazzilli	.05	.02	.00
☐ 470	Larry McWilliams	.05	.02	.00
☐ 471	Jim Morrison	.03	.01	.00
☐ 472	Tony Pena	.12	.05	.01
☐ 473	Johnny Ray	.09	.04	.01
☐ 474	Rick Rhoden	.07	.03	.01
☐ 475	Don Robinson	.03	.01	.00
☐ 476	Rod Scurry	.03	.01	.00
☐ 477	Kent Tekulve	.06	.02	.00
☐ 478	Jason Thompson	.06	.02	.00
☐ 479	John Tudor	.15	.06	.01
☐ 480	Lee Tunnell	.03	.01	.00
☐ 481	Marvell Wynne	.03	.01	.00
☐ 482	Salome Barojas	.03	.01	.00
☐ 483	Dave Beard	.03	.01	.00
☐ 484	Jim Beattie	.03	.01	.00
☐ 485	Barry Bonnell	.03	.01	.00
☐ 486	Phil Bradley	1.25	.50	.12
☐ 487	Al Cowens	.05	.02	.00
☐ 488	Alvin Davis	1.25	.50	.12
☐ 489	Dave Henderson	.07	.03	.01
☐ 490	Steve Henderson	.03	.01	.00
☐ 491	Bob Kearney	.03	.01	.00
☐ 492	Mark Langston	.50	.20	.05
☐ 493	Larry Milbourne	.03	.01	.00
☐ 494	Paul Mirabella	.03	.01	.00
☐ 495	Mike Moore	.06	.02	.00
☐ 496	Edwin Nunez	.05	.02	.00
☐ 497	Spike Owen	.05	.02	.00
☐ 498	Jack Perconte	.03	.01	.00
☐ 499	Ken Phelps	.05	.02	.00
☐ 500	Jim Presley	1.50	.60	.15
☐ 501	Mike Stanton	.03	.01	.00
☐ 502	Bob Stoddard	.03	.01	.00
☐ 503	Gorman Thomas	.09	.04	.01
☐ 504	Ed VandeBerg	.03	.01	.00
☐ 505	Matt Young	.03	.01	.00
☐ 506	Juan Agosto	.03	.01	.00
☐ 507	Harold Baines	.20	.08	.02
☐ 508	Floyd Bannister	.05	.02	.00
☐ 509	Britt Burns	.06	.02	.00
☐ 510	Julio Cruz	.03	.01	.00
☐ 511	Richard Dotson	.06	.02	.00
☐ 512	Jerry Dybzinski	.03	.01	.00
☐ 513	Carlton Fisk	.12	.05	.01
☐ 514	Scott Fletcher	.05	.02	.00
☐ 515	Jerry Hairston	.03	.01	.00
☐ 516	Marc Hill	.03	.01	.00
☐ 517	LaMarr Hoyt	.06	.02	.00
☐ 518	Ron Kittle	.12	.05	.01
☐ 519	Rudy Law	.03	.01	.00
☐ 520	Vance Law	.03	.01	.00
☐ 521	Greg Luzinski	.09	.04	.01
☐ 522	Gene Nelson	.03	.01	.00
☐ 523	Tom Paciorek	.03	.01	.00
☐ 524	Ron Reed	.03	.01	.00
☐ 525	Bert Roberge	.03	.01	.00
☐ 526	Tom Seaver	.25	.10	.02
☐ 527	Roy Smalley	.05	.02	.00
☐ 528	Dan Spillner	.03	.01	.00
☐ 529	Mike Squires	.03	.01	.00
☐ 530	Greg Walker	.12	.05	.01
☐ 531	Cesar Cedeno	.07	.03	.01
☐ 532	Dave Concepcion	.08	.03	.01
☐ 533	Eric Davis	6.00	2.40	.60
☐ 534	Nick Esasky	.05	.02	.00
☐ 535	Tom Foley	.03	.01	.00
☐ 536	John Franco	.40	.16	.04
☐ 537	Brad Gulden	.03	.01	.00
☐ 538	Tom Hume	.03	.01	.00
☐ 539	Wayne Krenchicki	.03	.01	.00
☐ 540	Andy McGaffigan	.03	.01	.00
☐ 541	Eddie Milner	.05	.02	.00
☐ 542	Ron Oester	.05	.02	.00
☐ 543	Bob Owchinko	.03	.01	.00
☐ 544	Dave Parker	.15	.06	.01
☐ 545	Frank Pastore	.03	.01	.00
☐ 546	Tony Perez	.12	.05	.01
☐ 547	Ted Power	.07	.03	.01
☐ 548	Joe Price	.03	.01	.00
☐ 549	Gary Redus	.06	.02	.00
☐ 550	Pete Rose	.75	.30	.07
☐ 551	Jeff Russell	.03	.01	.00

	MINT	VG-E	F-G		MINT	VG-E	F-G
☐ 552 Mario Soto	.06	.02	.00	☐ 605 Chili Davis	.07	.03	.01
☐ 553 Jay Tibbs	.15	.06	.01	☐ 606 Mark Davis	.03	.01	.00
☐ 554 Duane Walker	.03	.01	.00	☐ 607 Dan Gladden	.20	.08	.02
☐ 555 Alan Bannister	.03	.01	.00	☐ 608 Atlee Hammaker	.05	.02	.00
☐ 556 Buddy Bell	.09	.04	.01	☐ 609 Mike Krukow	.07	.03	.01
☐ 557 Danny Darwin	.03	.01	.00	☐ 610 Duane Kuiper	.03	.01	.00
☐ 558 Charlie Hough	.07	.03	.01	☐ 611 Bob Lacey	.03	.01	.00
☐ 559 Bobby Jones	.03	.01	.00	☐ 612 Bill Laskey	.03	.01	.00
☐ 560 Odell Jones	.03	.01	.00	☐ 613 Gary Lavelle	.05	.02	.00
☐ 561 Jeff Kunkel	.09	.04	.01	☐ 614 Johnnie LeMaster	.03	.01	.00
☐ 562 Mike Mason	.09	.04	.01	☐ 615 Jeff Leonard	.06	.02	.00
☐ 563 Pete O'Brien	.08	.03	.01	☐ 616 Randy Lerch	.03	.01	.00
☐ 564 Larry Parrish	.06	.02	.00	☐ 617 Greg Minton	.05	.02	.00
☐ 565 Mickey Rivers	.05	.02	.00	☐ 618 Steve Nicosia	.03	.01	.00
☐ 566 Billy Sample	.03	.01	.00	☐ 619 Gene Richards	.03	.01	.00
☐ 567 Dave Schmidt	.03	.01	.00	☐ 620 Jeff Robinson	.10	.04	.01
☐ 568 Donnie Scott	.05	.02	.00	☐ 621 Scot Thompson	.03	.01	.00
☐ 569 Dave Stewart	.03	.01	.00	☐ 622 Manny Trillo	.05	.02	.00
☐ 570 Frank Tanana	.05	.02	.00	☐ 623 Brad Wellman	.03	.01	.00
☐ 571 Wayne Tolleson	.03	.01	.00	☐ 624 Frank Williams	.10	.04	.01
☐ 572 Gary Ward	.06	.02	.00	☐ 625 Joel Youngblood	.03	.01	.00
☐ 573 Curtis Wilkerson	.05	.02	.00	☐ 626 Cal Ripken IA	.25	.10	.02
☐ 574 George Wright	.03	.01	.00	☐ 627 Mike Schmidt IA	.25	.10	.02
☐ 575 Ned Yost	.03	.01	.00	☐ 628 Giving The Signs	.05	.02	.00
☐ 576 Mark Brouhard	.03	.01	.00	Sparky Anderson			
☐ 577 Mike Caldwell	.05	.02	.00	☐ 629 AL Pitcher's Nightmare	.25	.10	.02
☐ 578 Bobby Clark	.03	.01	.00	Dave Winfield			
☐ 579 Jaime Cocanower	.05	.02	.00	Rickey Henderson			
☐ 580 Cecil Cooper	.10	.04	.01	☐ 630 NL Pitcher's Nightmare	.25	.10	.02
☐ 581 Rollie Fingers	.15	.06	.01	Mike Schmidt			
☐ 582 Jim Gantner	.05	.02	.00	Ryne Sandberg			
☐ 583 Moose Haas	.05	.02	.00	☐ 631 NL All-Stars	.25	.10	.02
☐ 584 Dion James	.06	.02	.00	Darryl Strawberry			
☐ 585 Pete Ladd	.03	.01	.00	Gary Carter			
☐ 586 Rick Manning	.03	.01	.00	Steve Garvey			
☐ 587 Bob McClure	.03	.01	.00	Ozzie Smith			
☐ 588 Paul Molitor	.09	.04	.01	☐ 632 A-S Winning Battery	.08	.03	.01
☐ 589 Charlie Moore	.03	.01	.00	Gary Carter			
☐ 590 Ben Oglivie	.06	.02	.00	Charlie Lea			
☐ 591 Chuck Porter	.03	.01	.00	☐ 633 NL Pennant Clinchers	.12	.05	.01
☐ 592 Randy Ready	.10	.04	.01	Steve Garvey			
☐ 593 Ed Romero	.03	.01	.00	Goose Gossage			
☐ 594 Bill Schroeder	.03	.01	.00	☐ 634 NL Rookie Phenoms	1.00	.40	.10
☐ 595 Ray Searage	.03	.01	.00	Dwight Gooden			
☐ 596 Ted Simmons	.09	.04	.01	Juan Samuel			
☐ 597 Jim Sundberg	.05	.02	.00	☐ 635 Toronto's Big Guns	.07	.03	.01
☐ 598 Don Sutton	.15	.06	.01	Willie Upshaw			
☐ 599 Tom Tellmann	.03	.01	.00	☐ 636 Toronto's Big Guns	.07	.03	.01
☐ 600 Rick Waits	.03	.01	.00	Lloyd Moseby			
☐ 601 Robin Yount	.25	.10	.02	☐ 637 HOLLAND: Al Holland	.05	.02	.00
☐ 602 Dusty Baker	.05	.02	.00	☐ 638 TUNNELL: Lee Tunnell	.05	.02	.00
☐ 603 Bob Brenly	.07	.03	.01	☐ 639 500th Homer	.25	.10	.02
☐ 604 Jack Clark	.09	.04	.01	Reggie Jackson			

		MINT	VG-E	F-G
☐ 640	4000th Hit .... Pete Rose	.35	.14	.03
☐ 641	Father and Son .... Cal Ripken Jr. and Sr.	.25	.10	.02
☐ 642	Cubs: Division Champs .	.05	.02	.00
☐ 643	Two Perfect Games and One No-Hitter: Mike Witt David Palmer Jack Morris	.07	.03	.01
☐ 644	Willie Lozado and .... Vic Mata	.10	.04	.01
☐ 645	Kelly Gruber and .... Randy O'Neal	.15	.06	.01
☐ 646	Jose Roman and .... Joel Skinner	.12	.05	.01
☐ 647	Steve Kiefer and .... Danny Tartabull	2.25	.90	.22
☐ 648	Rob Deer and .... Alejandro Sanchez	1.50	.60	.15
☐ 649	Bill Hatcher and .... Shawon Dunston	1.00	.40	.10
☐ 650	Ron Robinson and ...... Mike Bielecki	.15	.06	.01
☐ 651	Zane Smith and .... Paul Zuvella	.15	.06	.01
☐ 652	Joe Hesketh and .... Glenn Davis	4.50	1.80	.45
☐ 653	John Russell and .... Steve Jeltz	.20	.08	.02
☐ 654	CL: Tigers/Padres and Cubs/Mets	.07	.01	.00
☐ 655	CL: Blue Jays/Yankees . and Red Sox/Orioles	.07	.01	.00
☐ 656	CL: Royals/Cardinals . and Phillies/Twins	.07	.01	.00
☐ 657	CL: Angels/Braves and Astros/Dodgers	.07	.01	.00
☐ 658	CL: Expos/A's .... and Indians/Pirates	.07	.01	.00
☐ 659	CL: Mariners/White Sox . and Reds/Rangers	.07	.01	.00
☐ 660	CL: Brewers/Giants and Special Cards	.07	.01	.00

1985 Fleer Update

This 132-card set was issued late in the collecting year and features new players and players on new teams compared to the 1985 Fleer regular issue cards. Cards measure 2½" by 3½" and were distributed together as a complete set within a special box. The cards are numbered with a U prefix and are ordered alphabetically by the player's name.

		MINT	VG-E	F-G
	Complete Set	15.00	6.00	1.50
	Common Player (1-132)	.05	.02	.00
☐ U1	Don Aase	.10	.04	.01
☐ U2	Bill Almon	.05	.02	.00
☐ U3	Dusty Baker	.10	.04	.01
☐ U4	Dale Berra	.10	.04	.01
☐ U5	Karl Best	.15	.06	.01
☐ U6	Tim Birtsas	.35	.14	.03
☐ U7	Vida Blue	.10	.04	.01
☐ U8	Rich Bordi	.05	.02	.00
☐ U9	Daryl Boston	.25	.10	.02
☐ U10	Hubie Brooks	.25	.10	.02
☐ U11	Chris Brown	2.25	.90	.22
☐ U12	Tom Browning	.75	.30	.07
☐ U13	Al Bumbry	.05	.02	.00
☐ U14	Tim Burke	.35	.14	.03
☐ U15	Ray Burris	.05	.02	.00
☐ U16	Jeff Burroughs	.05	.02	.00
☐ U17	Ivan Calderon	.25	.10	.02
☐ U18	Jeff Calhoun	.15	.06	.01
☐ U19	Bill Campbell	.05	.02	.00
☐ U20	Don Carman	.35	.14	.03
☐ U21	Gary Carter	.75	.30	.07
☐ U22	Bobby Castillo	.05	.02	.00
☐ U23	Bill Caudill	.10	.04	.01

		MINT	VG-E	F-G
☐ U24	Rick Cerone	.05	.02	.00
☐ U25	Jack Clark	.25	.10	.02
☐ U26	Pat Clements	.25	.10	.02
☐ U27	Stewart Cliburn	.25	.10	.02
☐ U28	Vince Coleman	4.50	1.80	.45
☐ U29	Dave Collins	.10	.04	.01
☐ U30	Fritz Connally	.15	.06	.01
☐ U31	Henry Cotto	.05	.02	.00
☐ U32	Danny Darwin	.05	.02	.00
☐ U33	Darren Daulton	.25	.10	.02
☐ U34	Jerry Davis	.15	.06	.01
☐ U35	Brian Dayett	.10	.04	.01
☐ U36	Ken Dixon	.20	.08	.02
☐ U37	Tommy Dunbar	.10	.04	.01
☐ U38	Mariano Duncan	.75	.30	.07
☐ U39	Bob Fallon	.10	.04	.01
☐ U40	Brian Fisher	.35	.14	.03
☐ U41	Mike Fitzgerald	.05	.02	.00
☐ U42	Ray Fontenot	.05	.02	.00
☐ U43	Greg Gagne	.10	.04	.01
☐ U44	Oscar Gamble	.10	.04	.01
☐ U45	Jim Gott	.05	.02	.00
☐ U46	David Green	.05	.02	.00
☐ U47	Alfredo Griffin	.05	.02	.00
☐ U48	Ozzie Guillen	.75	.30	.07
☐ U49	Toby Harrah	.10	.04	.01
☐ U50	Ron Hassey	.05	.02	.00
☐ U51	Rickey Henderson	1.00	.40	.10
☐ U52	Steve Henderson	.05	.02	.00
☐ U53	George Hendrick	.10	.04	.01
☐ U54	Teddy Higuera	2.00	.80	.20
☐ U55	Al Holland	.10	.04	.01
☐ U56	Burt Hooton	.05	.02	.00
☐ U57	Jay Howell	.15	.06	.01
☐ U58	LaMarr Hoyt	.15	.06	.01
☐ U59	Tim Hulett	.15	.06	.01
☐ U60	Bob James	.10	.04	.01
☐ U61	Cliff Johnson	.05	.02	.00
☐ U62	Howard Johnson	.10	.04	.01
☐ U63	Ruppert Jones	.10	.04	.01
☐ U64	Steve Kemp	.10	.04	.01
☐ U65	Bruce Kison	.05	.02	.00
☐ U66	Mike LaCoss	.05	.02	.00
☐ U67	Lee Lacy	.10	.04	.01
☐ U68	Dave LaPoint	.05	.02	.00
☐ U69	Gary Lavelle	.10	.04	.01
☐ U70	Vance Law	.05	.02	.00
☐ U71	Manny Lee	.15	.06	.01
☐ U72	Sixto Lezcano	.05	.02	.00
☐ U73	Tim Lollar	.05	.02	.00
☐ U74	Urbano Lugo	.10	.04	.01
☐ U75	Fred Lynn	.25	.10	.02
☐ U76	Steve Lyons	.25	.10	.02
☐ U77	Mickey Mahler	.05	.02	.00
☐ U78	Ron Mathis	.15	.06	.01
☐ U79	Len Matuszek	.10	.04	.01
☐ U80	Oddibe McDowell (part of bio actually Roger's)	1.50	.60	.15
☐ U81	Roger McDowell	1.00	.40	.10
☐ U82	Donnie Moore	.10	.04	.01
☐ U83	Ron Musselman	.10	.04	.01
☐ U84	Al Oliver	.25	.10	.02
☐ U85	Joe Orsulak	.25	.10	.02
☐ U86	Dan Pasqua	1.50	.60	.15
☐ U87	Chris Pittaro	.15	.06	.01
☐ U88	Rick Reuschel	.10	.04	.01
☐ U89	Earnie Riles	.75	.30	.07
☐ U90	Jerry Royster	.05	.02	.00
☐ U91	Dave Rozema	.05	.02	.00
☐ U92	Dave Rucker	.05	.02	.00
☐ U93	Vern Ruhle	.05	.02	.00
☐ U94	Mark Salas	.35	.14	.03
☐ U95	Luis Salazar	.05	.02	.00
☐ U96	Joe Sambito	.10	.04	.01
☐ U97	Billy Sample	.05	.02	.00
☐ U98	Alex Sanchez	.10	.04	.01
☐ U99	Calvin Schiraldi	.75	.30	.07
☐ U100	Rick Schu	.25	.10	.02
☐ U101	Larry Sheets	.50	.20	.05
☐ U102	Ron Shephard	.10	.04	.01
☐ U103	Nelson Simmons	.15	.06	.01
☐ U104	Don Slaught	.10	.04	.01
☐ U105	Roy Smalley	.10	.04	.01
☐ U106	Lonnie Smith	.10	.04	.01
☐ U107	Nate Snell	.15	.06	.01
☐ U108	Lary Sorensen	.05	.02	.00
☐ U109	Chris Speier	.05	.02	.00
☐ U110	Mike Stenhouse	.10	.04	.01
☐ U111	Tim Stoddard	.05	.02	.00
☐ U112	John Stuper	.05	.02	.00
☐ U113	Jim Sundberg	.10	.04	.01
☐ U114	Bruce Sutter	.25	.10	.02
☐ U115	Don Sutton	.50	.20	.05
☐ U116	Bruce Tanner	.15	.06	.01
☐ U117	Kent Tekulve	.10	.04	.01
☐ U118	Walt Terrell	.10	.04	.01
☐ U119	Mickey Tettleton	.10	.04	.01
☐ U120	Rich Thompson	.10	.04	.01
☐ U121	Louis Thornton	.10	.04	.01
☐ U122	Alex Trevino	.05	.02	.00
☐ U123	John Tudor	.20	.08	.02
☐ U124	Jose Uribe	.10	.04	.01
☐ U125	Dave Valle	.10	.04	.01
☐ U126	Dave Von Ohlen	.05	.02	.00
☐ U127	Curt Wardle	.10	.04	.01

	MINT	VG-E	F-G
☐ U128 U.L. Washington	.05	.02	.00
☐ U129 Ed Whitson	.10	.04	.01
☐ U130 Herm Winningham ..	.20	.08	.02
☐ U131 Rich Yett	.10	.04	.01
☐ U132 Checklist U1-U132 ..	.05	.01	.00

1986 Fleer

The cards in this 660-card set measure 2½"
by 3½". The 1986 Fleer set features fronts
which contain the team logo along with the
player's name and position. The player cards
are alphabetized within team and the teams
are ordered by their 1985 season finish and
won-lost record, e.g., Kansas City (1-25), St.
Louis (26-49), Toronto (50-73), New York
Mets (74-97), New York Yankees (98-122),
Los Angeles (123-147), California (148-171),
Cincinnati (172-196), Chicago White Sox
(197-220), Detroit (221-243), Montreal (244-
267), Baltimore (268-291), Houston (292-
314), San Diego (315-338), Boston (339-
360), Chicago Cubs (361-385), Minnesota
(386-409), Oakland (410-432), Philadelphia
(433-457), Seattle (458-481), Milwaukee
(482-506), Atlanta (507-532), San Francisco
(533-555), Texas (556-578), Cleveland (579-
601), and Pittsburgh (602-625). Specials
(626-643), Rookie pairs (644-653), and
checklist cards (654-660) complete the set.
The Dennis and Tippy Martinez cards were
apparently switched in the set numbering as
their adjacent numbers (279 and 280) were
reversed on the Orioles checklist card. The

border enclosing the photo is dark blue. The
backs feature the same name, number, and
statistics format that Fleer has been using
over the past few years. Wax pack and cello
pack boxes contained a four-card panel on
the bottom; these cards were numbered C-1
through C-8 and are listed at the end of the list
of regular issue cards below. The set is considered complete without the box bottom
cards.

		MINT	VG-E	F-G
	Complete Set	27.00	11.00	2.70
	Common Player	.03	.01	.00
☐	1 Steve Balboni	.05	.02	.00
☐	2 Joe Beckwith	.03	.01	.00
☐	3 Buddy Biancalana	.03	.01	.00
☐	4 Bud Black	.03	.01	.00
☐	5 George Brett	.35	.14	.03
☐	6 Onix Concepcion	.03	.01	.00
☐	7 Steve Farr	.03	.01	.00
☐	8 Mark Gubicza	.06	.02	.00
☐	9 Dane Iorg	.03	.01	.00
☐	10 Danny Jackson	.06	.02	.00
☐	11 Lynn Jones	.03	.01	.00
☐	12 Mike Jones	.03	.01	.00
☐	13 Charlie Leibrandt	.05	.02	.00
☐	14 Hal McRae	.05	.02	.00
☐	15 Omar Moreno	.03	.01	.00
☐	16 Darryl Motley	.03	.01	.00
☐	17 Jorge Orta	.03	.01	.00
☐	18 Dan Quisenberry	.12	.05	.01
☐	19 Bret Saberhagen	.25	.10	.02
☐	20 Pat Sheridan	.03	.01	.00
☐	21 Lonnie Smith	.06	.02	.00
☐	22 Jim Sundberg	.05	.02	.00
☐	23 John Wathan	.03	.01	.00
☐	24 Frank White	.06	.02	.00
☐	25 Willie Wilson	.15	.06	.01
☐	26 Joaquin Andujar	.08	.03	.01
☐	27 Steve Braun	.03	.01	.00
☐	28 Bill Campbell	.03	.01	.00
☐	29 Cesar Cedeno	.06	.02	.00
☐	30 Jack Clark	.12	.05	.01
☐	31 Vince Coleman	1.50	.60	.15
☐	32 Danny Cox	.07	.03	.01
☐	33 Ken Dayley	.03	.01	.00
☐	34 Ivan DeJesus	.03	.01	.00
☐	35 Bob Forsch	.05	.02	.00
☐	36 Brian Harper	.03	.01	.00
☐	37 Tom Herr	.08	.03	.01

		MINT	VG-E	F-G
☐ 38	Ricky Horton	.05	.02	.00
☐ 39	Kurt Kepshire	.03	.01	.00
☐ 40	Jeff Lahti	.03	.01	.00
☐ 41	Tito Landrum	.03	.01	.00
☐ 42	Willie McGee	.15	.06	.01
☐ 43	Tom Nieto	.03	.01	.00
☐ 44	Terry Pendleton	.05	.02	.00
☐ 45	Darrell Porter	.05	.02	.00
☐ 46	Ozzie Smith	.10	.04	.01
☐ 47	John Tudor	.10	.04	.01
☐ 48	Andy Van Slyke	.06	.02	.00
☐ 49	Todd Worrell	1.00	.40	.10
☐ 50	Jim Acker	.03	.01	.00
☐ 51	Doyle Alexander	.05	.02	.00
☐ 52	Jesse Barfield	.15	.06	.01
☐ 53	George Bell	.15	.06	.01
☐ 54	Jeff Burroughs	.03	.01	.00
☐ 55	Bill Caudill	.05	.02	.00
☐ 56	Jim Clancy	.03	.01	.00
☐ 57	Tony Fernandez	.10	.04	.01
☐ 58	Tom Filer	.05	.02	.00
☐ 59	Damaso Garcia	.07	.03	.01
☐ 60	Tom Henke	.06	.02	.00
☐ 61	Garth Iorg	.03	.01	.00
☐ 62	Cliff Johnson	.03	.01	.00
☐ 63	Jimmy Key	.08	.03	.01
☐ 64	Dennis Lamp	.03	.01	.00
☐ 65	Gary Lavelle	.05	.02	.00
☐ 66	Buck Martinez	.03	.01	.00
☐ 67	Lloyd Moseby	.10	.04	.01
☐ 68	Rance Mulliniks	.03	.01	.00
☐ 69	Al Oliver	.10	.04	.01
☐ 70	Dave Stieb	.10	.04	.01
☐ 71	Louis Thornton	.10	.04	.01
☐ 72	Willie Upshaw	.07	.03	.01
☐ 73	Ernie Whitt	.03	.01	.00
☐ 74	Rick Aguilera	.25	.10	.02
☐ 75	Wally Backman	.07	.03	.01
☐ 76	Gary Carter	.35	.14	.03
☐ 77	Ron Darling	.20	.08	.02
☐ 78	Len Dykstra	1.00	.40	.10
☐ 79	Sid Fernandez	.20	.08	.02
☐ 80	George Foster	.12	.05	.01
☐ 81	Dwight Gooden	2.00	.80	.20
☐ 82	Tom Gorman	.03	.01	.00
☐ 83	Danny Heep	.03	.01	.00
☐ 84	Keith Hernandez	.25	.10	.02
☐ 85	Howard Johnson	.03	.01	.00
☐ 86	Ray Knight	.07	.03	.01
☐ 87	Terry Leach	.03	.01	.00
☐ 88	Ed Lynch	.03	.01	.00
☐ 89	Roger McDowell	.50	.20	.05
☐ 90	Jesse Orosco	.06	.02	.00
☐ 91	Tom Paciorek	.03	.01	.00
☐ 92	Ronn Reynolds	.08	.03	.01
☐ 93	Rafael Santana	.03	.01	.00
☐ 94	Doug Sisk	.03	.01	.00
☐ 95	Rusty Staub	.07	.03	.01
☐ 96	Darryl Strawberry	.35	.14	.03
☐ 97	Mookie Wilson	.06	.02	.00
☐ 98	Neil Allen	.05	.02	.00
☐ 99	Don Baylor	.10	.04	.01
☐ 100	Dale Berra	.05	.02	.00
☐ 101	Rich Bordi	.03	.01	.00
☐ 102	Marty Bystrom	.03	.01	.00
☐ 103	Joe Cowley	.03	.01	.00
☐ 104	Brian Fisher	.25	.10	.02
☐ 105	Ken Griffey	.06	.02	.00
☐ 106	Ron Guidry	.15	.06	.01
☐ 107	Ron Hassey	.03	.01	.00
☐ 108	Rickey Henderson	.35	.14	.03
☐ 109	Don Mattingly	3.50	1.40	.35
☐ 110	Bobby Meacham	.03	.01	.00
☐ 111	John Montefusco	.05	.02	.00
☐ 112	Phil Niekro	.15	.06	.01
☐ 113	Mike Pagliarulo	.25	.10	.02
☐ 114	Dan Pasqua	.20	.08	.02
☐ 115	Willie Randolph	.06	.02	.00
☐ 116	Dave Righetti	.15	.06	.01
☐ 117	Andre Robertson	.03	.01	.00
☐ 118	Billy Sample	.03	.01	.00
☐ 119	Bob Shirley	.03	.01	.00
☐ 120	Ed Whitson	.05	.02	.00
☐ 121	Dave Winfield	.30	.12	.03
☐ 122	Butch Wynegar	.05	.02	.00
☐ 123	Dave Anderson	.03	.01	.00
☐ 124	Bob Bailor	.03	.01	.00
☐ 125	Greg Brock	.05	.02	.00
☐ 126	Enos Cabell	.03	.01	.00
☐ 127	Bobby Castillo	.03	.01	.00
☐ 128	Carlos Diaz	.03	.01	.00
☐ 129	Mariano Duncan	.35	.14	.03
☐ 130	Pedro Guerrero	.25	.10	.02
☐ 131	Orel Hershiser	.30	.12	.03
☐ 132	Rick Honeycutt	.05	.02	.00
☐ 133	Ken Howell	.05	.02	.00
☐ 134	Ken Landreaux	.05	.02	.00
☐ 135	Bill Madlock	.10	.04	.01
☐ 136	Candy Maldonado	.06	.02	.00
☐ 137	Mike Marshall	.12	.05	.01
☐ 138	Len Matuszek	.03	.01	.00
☐ 139	Tom Niedenfuer	.06	.02	.00
☐ 140	Alejandro Pena	.05	.02	.00
☐ 141	Jerry Reuss	.06	.02	.00
☐ 142	Bill Russell	.05	.02	.00
☐ 143	Steve Sax	.12	.05	.01

		MINT	VG-E	F-G
☐ 144	Mike Scioscia	.05	.02	.00
☐ 145	Fernando Valenzuela	.30	.12	.03
☐ 146	Bob Welch	.06	.02	.00
☐ 147	Terry Whitfield	.03	.01	.00
☐ 148	Juan Beniquez	.05	.02	.00
☐ 149	Bob Boone	.05	.02	.00
☐ 150	John Candelaria	.07	.03	.01
☐ 151	Rod Carew	.30	.12	.03
☐ 152	Stewart Cliburn	.15	.06	.01
☐ 153	Doug DeCinces	.08	.03	.01
☐ 154	Brian Downing	.05	.02	.00
☐ 155	Ken Forsch	.03	.01	.00
☐ 156	Craig Gerber	.08	.03	.01
☐ 157	Bobby Grich	.07	.03	.01
☐ 158	George Hendrick	.06	.02	.00
☐ 159	Al Holland	.03	.01	.00
☐ 160	Reggie Jackson	.35	.14	.03
☐ 161	Ruppert Jones	.05	.02	.00
☐ 162	Urbano Lugo	.08	.03	.01
☐ 163	Kirk McCaskill	.60	.24	.06
☐ 164	Donnie Moore	.05	.02	.00
☐ 165	Gary Pettis	.08	.03	.01
☐ 166	Ron Romanick	.05	.02	.00
☐ 167	Dick Schofield	.07	.03	.01
☐ 168	Daryl Sconiers	.03	.01	.00
☐ 169	Jim Slaton	.03	.01	.00
☐ 170	Don Sutton	.15	.06	.01
☐ 171	Mike Witt	.10	.04	.01
☐ 172	Buddy Bell	.09	.04	.01
☐ 173	Tom Browning	.15	.06	.01
☐ 174	Dave Concepcion	.08	.03	.01
☐ 175	Eric Davis	1.00	.40	.10
☐ 176	Bo Diaz	.05	.02	.00
☐ 177	Nick Esasky	.06	.02	.00
☐ 178	John Franco	.10	.04	.01
☐ 179	Tom Hume	.03	.01	.00
☐ 180	Wayne Krenchicki	.03	.01	.00
☐ 181	Andy McGaffigan	.03	.01	.00
☐ 182	Eddie Milner	.05	.02	.00
☐ 183	Ron Oester	.05	.02	.00
☐ 184	Dave Parker	.15	.06	.01
☐ 185	Frank Pastore	.03	.01	.00
☐ 186	Tony Perez	.10	.04	.01
☐ 187	Ted Power	.07	.03	.01
☐ 188	Joe Price	.03	.01	.00
☐ 189	Gary Redus	.05	.02	.00
☐ 190	Ron Robinson	.03	.01	.00
☐ 191	Pete Rose	.60	.24	.06
☐ 192	Mario Soto	.08	.03	.01
☐ 193	John Stuper	.03	.01	.00
☐ 194	Jay Tibbs	.03	.01	.00
☐ 195	Dave Van Gorder	.03	.01	.00
☐ 196	Max Venable	.03	.01	.00
☐ 197	Juan Agosto	.03	.01	.00
☐ 198	Harold Baines	.15	.06	.01
☐ 199	Floyd Bannister	.05	.02	.00
☐ 200	Britt Burns	.05	.02	.00
☐ 201	Julio Cruz	.03	.01	.00
☐ 202	Joel Davis	.20	.08	.02
☐ 203	Richard Dotson	.05	.02	.00
☐ 204	Carlton Fisk	.12	.05	.01
☐ 205	Scott Fletcher	.05	.02	.00
☐ 206	Ozzie Guillen	.40	.16	.04
☐ 207	Jerry Hairston	.03	.01	.00
☐ 208	Tim Hulett	.05	.02	.00
☐ 209	Bob James	.05	.02	.00
☐ 210	Ron Kittle	.10	.04	.01
☐ 211	Rudy Law	.03	.01	.00
☐ 212	Bryan Little	.03	.01	.00
☐ 213	Gene Nelson	.03	.01	.00
☐ 214	Reid Nichols	.03	.01	.00
☐ 215	Luis Salazar	.03	.01	.00
☐ 216	Tom Seaver	.25	.10	.02
☐ 217	Dan Spillner	.03	.01	.00
☐ 218	Bruce Tanner	.10	.04	.01
☐ 219	Greg Walker	.10	.04	.01
☐ 220	Dave Wehrmeister	.03	.01	.00
☐ 221	Juan Berenguer	.03	.01	.00
☐ 222	Dave Bergman	.03	.01	.00
☐ 223	Tom Brookens	.03	.01	.00
☐ 224	Darrell Evans	.09	.04	.01
☐ 225	Barbaro Garbey	.03	.01	.00
☐ 226	Kirk Gibson	.15	.06	.01
☐ 227	John Grubb	.03	.01	.00
☐ 228	Willie Hernandez	.12	.05	.01
☐ 229	Larry Herndon	.03	.01	.00
☐ 230	Chet Lemon	.05	.02	.00
☐ 231	Aurelio Lopez	.03	.01	.00
☐ 232	Jack Morris	.15	.06	.01
☐ 233	Randy O'Neal	.03	.01	.00
☐ 234	Lance Parrish	.18	.08	.01
☐ 235	Dan Petry	.10	.04	.01
☐ 236	Alex Sanchez	.03	.01	.00
☐ 237	Bill Scherrer	.03	.01	.00
☐ 238	Nelson Simmons	.15	.06	.01
☐ 239	Frank Tanana	.05	.02	.00
☐ 240	Walt Terrell	.03	.01	.00
☐ 241	Alan Trammell	.15	.06	.01
☐ 242	Lou Whitaker	.12	.05	.01
☐ 243	Milt Wilcox	.03	.01	.00
☐ 244	Hubie Brooks	.10	.04	.01
☐ 245	Tim Burke	.20	.08	.02
☐ 246	Andre Dawson	.20	.08	.02
☐ 247	Mike Fitzgerald	.03	.01	.00
☐ 248	Terry Francona	.05	.02	.00
☐ 249	Bill Gullickson	.05	.02	.00

	MINT	VG-E	F-G		MINT	VG-E	F-G
☐ 250 Joe Hesketh	.07	.03	.01	☐ 303 Charlie Kerfeld	.30	.12	.03
☐ 251 Bill Laskey	.03	.01	.00	☐ 304 Bob Knepper	.07	.03	.01
☐ 252 Vance Law	.03	.01	.00	☐ 305 Ron Mathis	.10	.04	.01
☐ 253 Charlie Lea	.03	.01	.00	☐ 306 Jerry Mumphrey	.05	.02	.00
☐ 254 Gary Lucas	.03	.01	.00	☐ 307 Jim Pankovits	.03	.01	.00
☐ 255 David Palmer	.05	.02	.00	☐ 308 Terry Puhl	.05	.02	.00
☐ 256 Tim Raines	.20	.08	.02	☐ 309 Craig Reynolds	.03	.01	.00
☐ 257 Jeff Reardon	.07	.03	.01	☐ 310 Nolan Ryan	.30	.12	.03
☐ 258 Bert Roberge	.03	.01	.00	☐ 311 Mike Scott	.20	.08	.02
☐ 259 Dan Schatzeder	.03	.01	.00	☐ 312 Dave Smith	.07	.03	.01
☐ 260 Bryn Smith	.05	.02	.00	☐ 313 Dickie Thon	.05	.02	.00
☐ 261 Randy St.Claire	.03	.01	.00	☐ 314 Denny Walling	.03	.01	.00
☐ 262 Scot Thompson	.03	.01	.00	☐ 315 Kurt Bevacqua	.03	.01	.00
☐ 263 Tim Wallach	.08	.03	.01	☐ 316 Al Bumbry	.03	.01	.00
☐ 264 U.L. Washington	.03	.01	.00	☐ 317 Jerry Davis	.03	.01	.00
☐ 265 Mitch Webster	.50	.20	.05	☐ 318 Luis DeLeon	.03	.01	.00
☐ 266 Herm Winningham	.15	.06	.01	☐ 319 Dave Dravecky	.06	.02	.00
☐ 267 Floyd Youmans	.65	.26	.06	☐ 320 Tim Flannery	.03	.01	.00
☐ 268 Don Aase	.05	.02	.00	☐ 321 Steve Garvey	.35	.14	.03
☐ 269 Mike Boddicker	.08	.03	.01	☐ 322 Goose Gossage	.14	.06	.01
☐ 270 Rich Dauer	.03	.01	.00	☐ 323 Tony Gwynn	.30	.12	.03
☐ 271 Storm Davis	.07	.03	.01	☐ 324 Andy Hawkins	.06	.02	.00
☐ 272 Rick Dempsey	.05	.02	.00	☐ 325 LaMarr Hoyt	.07	.03	.01
☐ 273 Ken Dixon	.06	.02	.00	☐ 326 Roy Lee Jackson	.03	.01	.00
☐ 274 Jim Dwyer	.03	.01	.00	☐ 327 Terry Kennedy	.07	.03	.01
☐ 275 Mike Flanagan	.07	.03	.01	☐ 328 Craig Lefferts	.03	.01	.00
☐ 276 Wayne Gross	.03	.01	.00	☐ 329 Carmelo Martinez	.05	.02	.00
☐ 277 Lee Lacy	.06	.02	.00	☐ 330 Lance McCullers	.25	.10	.02
☐ 278 Fred Lynn	.15	.06	.01	☐ 331 Kevin McReynolds	.10	.04	.01
☐ 279 Tippy Martinez	.05	.01	.00	☐ 332 Graig Nettles	.12	.05	.01
☐ 280 Dennis Martinez	.05	.01	.00	☐ 333 Jerry Royster	.03	.01	.00
☐ 281 Scott McGregor	.07	.03	.01	☐ 334 Eric Show	.03	.01	.00
☐ 282 Eddie Murray	.35	.14	.03	☐ 335 Tim Stoddard	.03	.01	.00
☐ 283 Floyd Rayford	.03	.01	.00	☐ 336 Garry Templeton	.07	.03	.01
☐ 284 Cal Ripken	.35	.14	.03	☐ 337 Mark Thurmond	.05	.02	.00
☐ 285 Gary Roenicke	.05	.02	.00	☐ 338 Ed Wojna	.10	.04	.01
☐ 286 Larry Sheets	.08	.03	.01	☐ 339 Tony Armas	.09	.04	.01
☐ 287 John Shelby	.03	.01	.00	☐ 340 Marty Barrett	.12	.05	.01
☐ 288 Nate Snell	.10	.04	.01	☐ 341 Wade Boggs	1.50	.60	.15
☐ 289 Sammy Stewart	.03	.01	.00	☐ 342 Dennis Boyd	.08	.03	.01
☐ 290 Alan Wiggins	.06	.02	.00	☐ 343 Bill Buckner	.08	.03	.01
☐ 291 Mike Young	.10	.04	.01	☐ 344 Mark Clear	.03	.01	.00
☐ 292 Alan Ashby	.03	.01	.00	☐ 345 Roger Clemens	1.50	.60	.15
☐ 293 Mark Bailey	.03	.01	.00	☐ 346 Steve Crawford	.03	.01	.00
☐ 294 Kevin Bass	.07	.03	.01	☐ 347 Mike Easler	.05	.02	.00
☐ 295 Jeff Calhoun	.08	.03	.01	☐ 348 Dwight Evans	.10	.04	.01
☐ 296 Jose Cruz	.10	.04	.01	☐ 349 Rich Gedman	.09	.04	.01
☐ 297 Glenn Davis	.75	.30	.07	☐ 350 Jackie Gutierrez	.03	.01	.00
☐ 298 Bill Dawley	.03	.01	.00	☐ 351 Glenn Hoffman	.03	.01	.00
☐ 299 Frank DiPino	.03	.01	.00	☐ 352 Bruce Hurst	.07	.03	.01
☐ 300 Bill Doran	.07	.03	.01	☐ 353 Bruce Kison	.03	.01	.00
☐ 301 Phil Garner	.05	.02	.00	☐ 354 Tim Lollar	.03	.01	.00
☐ 302 Jeff Heathcock	.08	.03	.01	☐ 355 Steve Lyons	.03	.01	.00

		MINT	VG-E	F-G
☐ 356	Al Nipper	.03	.01	.00
☐ 357	Bob Ojeda	.08	.03	.01
☐ 358	Jim Rice	.30	.12	.03
☐ 359	Bob Stanley	.05	.02	.00
☐ 360	Mike Trujillo	.08	.03	.01
☐ 361	Thad Bosley	.03	.01	.00
☐ 362	Warren Brusstar	.03	.01	.00
☐ 363	Ron Cey	.08	.03	.01
☐ 364	Jody Davis	.08	.03	.01
☐ 365	Bob Dernier	.03	.01	.00
☐ 366	Shawon Dunston	.09	.04	.01
☐ 367	Leon Durham	.08	.03	.01
☐ 368	Dennis Eckersley	.05	.02	.00
☐ 369	Ray Fontenot	.03	.01	.00
☐ 370	George Frazier	.03	.01	.00
☐ 371	Bill Hatcher	.06	.02	.00
☐ 372	Dave Lopes	.06	.02	.00
☐ 373	Gary Matthews	.06	.02	.00
☐ 374	Ron Meredith	.09	.04	.01
☐ 375	Keith Moreland	.06	.02	.00
☐ 376	Reggie Patterson	.03	.01	.00
☐ 377	Dick Ruthven	.03	.01	.00
☐ 378	Ryne Sandberg	.30	.12	.03
☐ 379	Scott Sanderson	.03	.01	.00
☐ 380	Lee Smith	.07	.03	.01
☐ 381	Lary Sorensen	.03	.01	.00
☐ 382	Chris Speier	.03	.01	.00
☐ 383	Rick Sutcliffe	.10	.04	.01
☐ 384	Steve Trout	.03	.01	.00
☐ 385	Gary Woods	.03	.01	.00
☐ 386	Bert Blyleven	.10	.04	.01
☐ 387	Tom Brunansky	.10	.04	.01
☐ 388	Randy Bush	.03	.01	.00
☐ 389	John Butcher	.03	.01	.00
☐ 390	Ron Davis	.03	.01	.00
☐ 391	Dave Engle	.03	.01	.00
☐ 392	Frank Eufemia	.10	.04	.01
☐ 393	Pete Filson	.03	.01	.00
☐ 394	Gary Gaetti	.09	.04	.01
☐ 395	Greg Gagne	.05	.02	.00
☐ 396	Mickey Hatcher	.03	.01	.00
☐ 397	Kent Hrbek	.15	.06	.01
☐ 398	Tim Laudner	.03	.01	.00
☐ 399	Rick Lysander	.03	.01	.00
☐ 400	Dave Meier	.03	.01	.00
☐ 401	Kirby Puckett	.60	.24	.06
☐ 402	Mark Salas	.06	.02	.00
☐ 403	Ken Schrom	.05	.02	.00
☐ 404	Roy Smalley	.05	.02	.00
☐ 405	Mike Smithson	.05	.02	.00
☐ 406	Mike Stenhouse	.05	.02	.00
☐ 407	Tim Teufel	.06	.02	.00
☐ 408	Frank Viola	.07	.03	.01
☐ 409	Ron Washington	.03	.01	.00
☐ 410	Keith Atherton	.03	.01	.00
☐ 411	Dusty Baker	.06	.02	.00
☐ 412	Tim Birtsas	.20	.08	.02
☐ 413	Bruce Bochte	.05	.02	.00
☐ 414	Chris Codiroli	.03	.01	.00
☐ 415	Dave Collins	.05	.02	.00
☐ 416	Mike Davis	.06	.02	.00
☐ 417	Alfredo Griffin	.05	.02	.00
☐ 418	Mike Heath	.03	.01	.00
☐ 419	Steve Henderson	.03	.01	.00
☐ 420	Donnie Hill	.03	.01	.00
☐ 421	Jay Howell	.05	.02	.00
☐ 422	Tommy John	.10	.04	.01
☐ 423	Dave Kingman	.10	.04	.01
☐ 424	Bill Krueger	.03	.01	.00
☐ 425	Rick Langford	.03	.01	.00
☐ 426	Carney Lansford	.08	.03	.01
☐ 427	Steve McCatty	.03	.01	.00
☐ 428	Dwayne Murphy	.06	.02	.00
☐ 429	Steve Ontiveros	.20	.08	.02
☐ 430	Tony Phillips	.03	.01	.00
☐ 431	Jose Rijo	.08	.03	.01
☐ 432	Mickey Tettleton	.10	.04	.01
☐ 433	Luis Aguayo	.03	.01	.00
☐ 434	Larry Andersen	.03	.01	.00
☐ 435	Steve Carlton	.30	.12	.03
☐ 436	Don Carman	.25	.10	.02
☐ 437	Tim Corcoran	.03	.01	.00
☐ 438	Darren Daulton	.20	.08	.02
☐ 439	John Denny	.06	.02	.00
☐ 440	Tom Foley	.03	.01	.00
☐ 441	Greg Gross	.03	.01	.00
☐ 442	Kevin Gross	.03	.01	.00
☐ 443	Von Hayes	.12	.05	.01
☐ 444	Charles Hudson	.05	.02	.00
☐ 445	Garry Maddox	.05	.02	.00
☐ 446	Shane Rawley	.06	.02	.00
☐ 447	Dave Rucker	.03	.01	.00
☐ 448	John Russell	.05	.02	.00
☐ 449	Juan Samuel	.10	.04	.01
☐ 450	Mike Schmidt	.40	.16	.04
☐ 451	Rick Schu	.06	.02	.00
☐ 452	Dave Shipanoff	.15	.06	.01
☐ 453	Dave Stewart	.03	.01	.00
☐ 454	Jeff Stone	.05	.02	.00
☐ 455	Kent Tekulve	.05	.02	.00
☐ 456	Ozzie Virgil	.06	.02	.00
☐ 457	Glenn Wilson	.10	.04	.01
☐ 458	Jim Beattie	.03	.01	.00
☐ 459	Karl Best	.08	.03	.01
☐ 460	Barry Bonnell	.03	.01	.00
☐ 461	Phil Bradley	.20	.08	.02

		MINT	VG-E	F-G
☐ 462	Ivan Calderon	.20	.08	.02
☐ 463	Al Cowens	.05	.02	.00
☐ 464	Alvin Davis	.20	.08	.02
☐ 465	Dave Henderson	.06	.02	.00
☐ 466	Bob Kearney	.03	.01	.00
☐ 467	Mark Langston	.07	.03	.01
☐ 468	Bob Long	.03	.01	.00
☐ 469	Mike Moore	.06	.02	.00
☐ 470	Edwin Nunez	.05	.02	.00
☐ 471	Spike Owen	.06	.02	.00
☐ 472	Jack Perconte	.03	.01	.00
☐ 473	Jim Presley	.30	.12	.03
☐ 474	Donnie Scott	.03	.01	.00
☐ 475	Bill Swift	.05	.02	.00
☐ 476	Danny Tartabull	.25	.10	.02
☐ 477	Gorman Thomas	.08	.03	.01
☐ 478	Roy Thomas	.03	.01	.00
☐ 479	Ed VandeBerg	.03	.01	.00
☐ 480	Frank Wills	.10	.04	.01
☐ 481	Matt Young	.03	.01	.00
☐ 482	Ray Burris	.03	.01	.00
☐ 483	Jaime Cocanower	.03	.01	.00
☐ 484	Cecil Cooper	.10	.04	.01
☐ 485	Danny Darwin	.03	.01	.00
☐ 486	Rollie Fingers	.15	.06	.01
☐ 487	Jim Gantner	.05	.02	.00
☐ 488	Bob L. Gibson	.03	.01	.00
☐ 489	Moose Haas	.05	.02	.00
☐ 490	Teddy Higuera	.65	.26	.06
☐ 491	Paul Householder	.03	.01	.00
☐ 492	Pete Ladd	.03	.01	.00
☐ 493	Rick Manning	.03	.01	.00
☐ 494	Bob McClure	.03	.01	.00
☐ 495	Paul Molitor	.09	.04	.01
☐ 496	Charlie Moore	.03	.01	.00
☐ 497	Ben Oglivie	.06	.02	.00
☐ 498	Randy Ready	.05	.02	.00
☐ 499	Earnie Riles	.35	.14	.03
☐ 500	Ed Romero	.03	.01	.00
☐ 501	Bill Schroeder	.03	.01	.00
☐ 502	Ray Searage	.03	.01	.00
☐ 503	Ted Simmons	.10	.04	.01
☐ 504	Pete Vuckovich	.05	.02	.00
☐ 505	Rick Waits	.03	.01	.00
☐ 506	Robin Yount	.25	.10	.02
☐ 507	Len Barker	.05	.02	.00
☐ 508	Steve Bedrosian	.05	.02	.00
☐ 509	Bruce Benedict	.03	.01	.00
☐ 510	Rick Camp	.03	.01	.00
☐ 511	Rick Cerone	.03	.01	.00
☐ 512	Chris Chambliss	.05	.02	.00
☐ 513	Jeff Dedmon	.03	.01	.00
☐ 514	Terry Forster	.06	.02	.00
☐ 515	Gene Garber	.03	.01	.00
☐ 516	Terry Harper	.03	.01	.00
☐ 517	Bob Horner	.15	.06	.01
☐ 518	Glenn Hubbard	.03	.01	.00
☐ 519	Joe Johnson	.20	.08	.02
☐ 520	Brad Komminsk	.06	.02	.00
☐ 521	Rick Mahler	.03	.01	.00
☐ 522	Dale Murphy	.45	.18	.04
☐ 523	Ken Oberkfell	.03	.01	.00
☐ 524	Pascual Perez	.03	.01	.00
☐ 525	Gerald Perry	.03	.01	.00
☐ 526	Rafael Ramirez	.03	.01	.00
☐ 527	Steve Shields	.08	.03	.01
☐ 528	Zane Smith	.05	.02	.00
☐ 529	Bruce Sutter	.12	.05	.01
☐ 530	Milt Thompson	.20	.08	.02
☐ 531	Claudell Washington	.06	.02	.00
☐ 532	Paul Zuvella	.05	.02	.00
☐ 533	Vida Blue	.07	.03	.01
☐ 534	Bob Brenly	.05	.02	.00
☐ 535	Chris Brown	.90	.36	.09
☐ 536	Chili Davis	.08	.03	.01
☐ 537	Mark Davis	.03	.01	.00
☐ 538	Rob Deer	.25	.10	.02
☐ 539	Dan Driessen	.03	.01	.00
☐ 540	Scott Garrelts	.06	.02	.00
☐ 541	Dan Gladden	.06	.02	.00
☐ 542	Jim Gott	.03	.01	.00
☐ 543	David Green	.05	.02	.00
☐ 544	Atlee Hammaker	.05	.02	.00
☐ 545	Mike Jeffcoat	.03	.01	.00
☐ 546	Mike Krukow	.07	.03	.01
☐ 547	Dave LaPoint	.03	.01	.00
☐ 548	Jeff Leonard	.05	.02	.00
☐ 549	Greg Minton	.05	.02	.00
☐ 550	Alex Trevino	.03	.01	.00
☐ 551	Manny Trillo	.05	.02	.00
☐ 552	Jose Uribe	.08	.03	.01
☐ 553	Brad Wellman	.03	.01	.00
☐ 554	Frank Williams	.03	.01	.00
☐ 555	Joel Youngblood	.03	.01	.00
☐ 556	Alan Bannister	.03	.01	.00
☐ 557	Glenn Brummer	.03	.01	.00
☐ 558	Steve Buechele	.25	.10	.02
☐ 559	Jose Guzman	.25	.10	.02
☐ 560	Toby Harrah	.05	.02	.00
☐ 561	Greg Harris	.05	.02	.00
☐ 562	Dwayne Henry	.10	.04	.01
☐ 563	Burt Hooton	.03	.01	.00
☐ 564	Charlie Hough	.06	.02	.00
☐ 565	Mike Mason	.03	.01	.00
☐ 566	Oddibe McDowell	.30	.12	.03
☐ 567	Dickie Noles	.03	.01	.00

	MINT	VG-E	F-G
☐ 568 Pete O'Brien	.08	.03	.01
☐ 569 Larry Parrish	.06	.02	.00
☐ 570 Dave Rozema	.03	.01	.00
☐ 571 Dave Schmidt	.03	.01	.00
☐ 572 Don Slaught	.03	.01	.00
☐ 573 Wayne Tolleson	.03	.01	.00
☐ 574 Duane Walker	.03	.01	.00
☐ 575 Gary Ward	.06	.02	.00
☐ 576 Chris Welsh	.03	.01	.00
☐ 577 Curtis Wilkerson	.03	.01	.00
☐ 578 George Wright	.03	.01	.00
☐ 579 Chris Bando	.03	.01	.00
☐ 580 Tony Bernazard	.05	.02	.00
☐ 581 Brett Butler	.08	.03	.01
☐ 582 Ernie Camacho	.03	.01	.00
☐ 583 Joe Carter	.25	.10	.02
☐ 584 Carmen Castillo	.03	.01	.00
☐ 585 Jamie Easterly	.03	.01	.00
☐ 586 Julio Franco	.10	.04	.01
☐ 587 Mel Hall	.08	.03	.01
☐ 588 Mike Hargrove	.05	.02	.00
☐ 589 Neal Heaton	.03	.01	.00
☐ 590 Brook Jacoby	.10	.04	.01
☐ 591 Otis Nixon	.20	.08	.02
☐ 592 Jerry Reed	.08	.03	.01
☐ 593 Vern Ruhle	.03	.01	.00
☐ 594 Pat Tabler	.08	.03	.01
☐ 595 Rich Thompson	.07	.03	.01
☐ 596 Andre Thornton	.06	.02	.00
☐ 597 Dave Von Ohlen	.03	.01	.00
☐ 598 George Vukovich	.03	.01	.00
☐ 599 Tom Waddell	.03	.01	.00
☐ 600 Curt Wardle	.08	.03	.01
☐ 601 Jerry Willard	.03	.01	.00
☐ 602 Bill Almon	.03	.01	.00
☐ 603 Mike Bielecki	.05	.02	.00
☐ 604 Sid Bream	.07	.03	.01
☐ 605 Mike Brown	.05	.02	.00
☐ 606 Pat Clements	.20	.08	.02
☐ 607 Jose DeLeon	.05	.02	.00
☐ 608 Denny Gonzalez	.05	.02	.00
☐ 609 Cecilio Guante	.03	.01	.00
☐ 610 Steve Kemp	.06	.02	.00
☐ 611 Sam Khalifa	.10	.04	.01
☐ 612 Lee Mazzilli	.05	.02	.00
☐ 613 Larry McWilliams	.03	.01	.00
☐ 614 Jim Morrison	.03	.01	.00
☐ 615 Joe Orsulak	.25	.10	.02
☐ 616 Tony Pena	.12	.05	.01
☐ 617 Johnny Ray	.10	.04	.01
☐ 618 Rick Reuschel	.05	.02	.00
☐ 619 R.J. Reynolds	.06	.02	.00
☐ 620 Rick Rhoden	.06	.02	.00

	MINT	VG-E	F-G
☐ 621 Don Robinson	.03	.01	.00
☐ 622 Jason Thompson	.06	.02	.00
☐ 623 Lee Tunnell	.03	.01	.00
☐ 624 Jim Winn	.03	.01	.00
☐ 625 Marvell Wynne	.03	.01	.00
☐ 626 Dwight Gooden IA	.50	.20	.05
☐ 627 Don Mattingly IA	.90	.36	.09
☐ 628 4192 (Pete Rose)	.40	.16	.04
☐ 629 3000 Career Hits	.20	.08	.02
Rod Carew			
☐ 630 300 Career Wins	.15	.06	.01
Tom Seaver			
Phil Niekro			
☐ 631 Ouch (Don Baylor)	.07	.03	.01
☐ 632 Instant Offense	.20	.08	.02
Darryl Strawberry			
Tim Raines			
☐ 633 Shortstops Supreme	.15	.06	.01
Cal Ripken			
Alan Trammell			
☐ 634 Boggs and "Hero"	.50	.20	.05
Wade Boggs			
George Brett			
☐ 635 Braves Dynamic Duo	.25	.10	.02
Bob Horner			
Dale Murphy			
☐ 636 Cardinal Ignitors	.35	.14	.03
Willie McGee			
Vince Coleman			
☐ 637 Terror on Basepaths	.35	.14	.03
Vince Coleman			
☐ 638 Charlie Hustle / Dr.K	1.00	.40	.10
Pete Rose			
Dwight Gooden			
☐ 639 1984 and 1985 AL	1.50	.60	.15
Batting Champs			
Wade Boggs			
Don Mattingly			
☐ 640 NL West Sluggers	.25	.10	.02
Dale Murphy			
Steve Garvey			
Dave Parker			
☐ 641 Staff Aces	.50	.20	.05
Fernando Valenzuela			
Dwight Gooden			
☐ 642 Blue Jay Stoppers	.07	.03	.01
Jimmy Key			
Dave Stieb			
☐ 643 AL All-Star Backstops	.07	.03	.01
Carlton Fisk			
Rich Gedman			
☐ 644 Gene Walter and	.25	.10	.02
Benito Santiago			

		MINT	VG-E	F-G
☐ 645	Mike Woodard and Collin Ward	.12	.05	.01
☐ 646	Kal Daniels and Paul O'Neill	.40	.16	.04
☐ 647	Andres Galarraga and Fred Toliver	.35	.14	.03
☐ 648	Bob Kipper and Curt Ford	.20	.08	.02
☐ 649	Jose Canseco and Eric Plunk	6.50	2.60	.65
☐ 650	Mark McLemore and Gus Polidor	.15	.06	.01
☐ 651	Rob Woodward and Mickey Brantley	.25	.10	.02
☐ 652	Billy Jo Robidoux and Mark Funderburk	.25	.10	.02
☐ 653	Cecil Fielder and Cory Snyder	2.00	.80	.20
☐ 654	CL: Royals/Cardinals Blue Jays/Mets	.07	.01	.00
☐ 655	CL: Yankees/Dodgers Angels/Reds	.07	.01	.00
☐ 656	CL: White Sox/Tigers Expos/Orioles (279 Dennis, 280 Tippy)	.07	.01	.00
☐ 657	CL: Astros/Padres Red Sox/Cubs	.07	.01	.00
☐ 658	CL: Twins/A's Phillies/Mariners	.07	.01	.00
☐ 659	CL: Brewers/Braves Giants/Rangers	.07	.01	.00
☐ 660	CL: Indians/Pirates Special Cards	.07	.01	.00
☐ C1	Royals Logo (wax pack box card)	.05	.02	.00
☐ C2	George Brett (wax pack box card)	.60	.24	.06
☐ C3	Ozzie Guillen (wax pack box card)	.25	.10	.02
☐ C4	Dale Murphy (wax pack box card)	.90	.36	.09
☐ C5	Cardinals Logo (wax pack box card)	.05	.02	.00
☐ C6	Tom Browning (wax pack box card)	.15	.06	.01
☐ C7	Gary Carter (wax pack box card)	.35	.14	.03
☐ C8	Carlton Fisk (wax pack box card)	.15	.06	.01

1986 Fleer Update

This 132-card set was distributed by Fleer to dealers as a complete set within a custom box. In addition to the complete set of 132 cards, the box also contains 25 Team Logo Stickers. The card fronts look very similar to the 1986 Fleer regular issue. The cards are numbered (with a U prefix) alphabetically according to player's last name. Cards measure the standard size, 2½" by 3½".

		MINT	VG-E	F-G
	Complete Set	15.00	6.00	1.50
	Common Player	.06	.02	.00
☐ U1	Mike Aldrete	.20	.08	.02
☐ U2	Andy Allanson	.20	.08	.02
☐ U3	Neil Allen	.06	.02	.00
☐ U4	Joaquin Andujar	.10	.04	.01
☐ U5	Paul Assenmacher	.20	.08	.02
☐ U6	Scott Bailes	.20	.08	.02
☐ U7	Jay Baller	.10	.04	.01
☐ U8	Scott Bankhead	.20	.08	.02
☐ U9	Bill Bathe	.15	.06	.01
☐ U10	Don Baylor	.15	.06	.01
☐ U11	Billy Beane	.15	.06	.01
☐ U12	Steve Bedrosian	.10	.04	.01
☐ U13	Juan Beniquez	.10	.04	.01
☐ U14	Barry Bonds	.75	.30	.07
☐ U15	Bobby Bonilla	.20	.08	.02
☐ U16	Rich Bordi	.06	.02	.00
☐ U17	Bill Campbell	.06	.02	.00
☐ U18	Tom Candiotti	.10	.04	.01
☐ U19	John Cangelosi	.35	.14	.03
☐ U20	Jose Canseco (headings on back for a pitcher)	3.00	1.20	.30

		MINT	VG-E	F-G
☐ U21	Chuck Cary	.20	.08	.02
☐ U22	Juan Castillo	.15	.06	.01
☐ U23	Rick Cerone	.06	.02	.00
☐ U24	John Cerutti	.30	.12	.03
☐ U25	Will Clark	1.25	.50	.12
☐ U26	Mark Clear	.06	.02	.00
☐ U27	Darnell Coles	.20	.08	.02
☐ U28	Dave Collins	.06	.02	.00
☐ U29	Tim Conroy	.06	.02	.00
☐ U30	Ed Correa	.35	.14	.03
☐ U31	Joe Cowley	.10	.04	.01
☐ U32	Bill Dawley	.06	.02	.00
☐ U33	Rob Deer	.40	.16	.04
☐ U34	John Denny	.10	.04	.01
☐ U35	Jim Deshaies	.50	.20	.05
☐ U36	Doug Drabek	.20	.08	.02
☐ U37	Mike Easler	.10	.04	.01
☐ U38	Mark Eichhorn	.50	.20	.05
☐ U39	Dave Engle	.06	.02	.00
☐ U40	Mike Fischlin	.06	.02	.00
☐ U41	Scott Fletcher	.10	.04	.01
☐ U42	Terry Forster	.10	.04	.01
☐ U43	Terry Francona	.06	.02	.00
☐ U44	Andres Galarraga	.20	.08	.02
☐ U45	Lee Guetterman	.20	.08	.02
☐ U46	Bill Gullickson	.10	.04	.01
☐ U47	Jackie Gutierrez	.06	.02	.00
☐ U48	Moose Haas	.10	.04	.01
☐ U49	Billy Hatcher	.10	.04	.01
☐ U50	Mike Heath	.06	.02	.00
☐ U51	Guy Hoffman	.06	.02	.00
☐ U52	Tom Hume	.06	.02	.00
☐ U53	Pete Incaviglia	2.00	.80	.20
☐ U54	Dane Iorg	.06	.02	.00
☐ U55	Chris James	.35	.14	.03
☐ U56	Stan Javier	.20	.08	.02
☐ U57	Tommy John	.15	.06	.01
☐ U58	Tracy Jones	.30	.12	.03
☐ U59	Wally Joyner	3.50	1.40	.35
☐ U60	Wayne Krenchicki	.06	.02	.00
☐ U61	John Kruk	.30	.12	.03
☐ U62	Mike LaCoss	.06	.02	.00
☐ U63	Pete Ladd	.06	.02	.00
☐ U64	Dave LaPoint	.06	.02	.00
☐ U65	Mike Lavalliere	.15	.06	.01
☐ U66	Rudy Law	.06	.02	.00
☐ U67	Dennis Leonard	.10	.04	.01
☐ U68	Steve Lombardozzi	.15	.06	.01
☐ U69	Aurelio Lopez	.06	.02	.00
☐ U70	Mickey Mahler	.06	.02	.00
☐ U71	Candy Maldonado	.10	.04	.01
☐ U72	Roger Mason	.15	.06	.01
☐ U73	Greg Mathews	.35	.14	.03
☐ U74	Andy McGaffigan	.06	.02	.00
☐ U75	Joel McKeon	.20	.08	.02
☐ U76	Kevin Mitchell	.60	.24	.06
☐ U77	Bill Mooneyham	.15	.06	.01
☐ U78	Omar Moreno	.06	.02	.00
☐ U79	Jerry Mumphrey	.06	.02	.00
☐ U80	Al Newman	.15	.06	.01
☐ U81	Phil Niekro	.25	.10	.02
☐ U82	Randy Niemann	.06	.02	.00
☐ U83	Juan Nieves	.10	.04	.01
☐ U84	Bob Ojeda	.15	.06	.01
☐ U85	Rick Ownbey	.06	.02	.00
☐ U86	Tom Paciorek	.06	.02	.00
☐ U87	David Palmer	.06	.02	.00
☐ U88	Jeff Parrett	.15	.06	.01
☐ U89	Pat Perry	.15	.06	.01
☐ U90	Dan Plesac	.20	.08	.02
☐ U91	Darrell Porter	.10	.04	.01
☐ U92	Luis Quinones	.15	.06	.01
☐ U93	Rey Quinones	.20	.08	.02
☐ U94	Gary Redus	.10	.04	.01
☐ U95	Jeff Reed	.15	.06	.01
☐ U96	Bip Roberts	.15	.06	.01
☐ U97	Billy Joe Robidoux	.20	.08	.02
☐ U98	Gary Roenicke	.10	.04	.01
☐ U99	Ron Roenicke	.06	.02	.00
☐ U100	Angel Salazar	.06	.02	.00
☐ U101	Joe Sambito	.10	.04	.01
☐ U102	Billy Sample	.06	.02	.00
☐ U103	Dave Schmidt	.06	.02	.00
☐ U104	Ken Schrom	.10	.04	.01
☐ U105	Ruben Sierra	1.50	.60	.15
☐ U106	Ted Simmons	.15	.06	.01
☐ U107	Sammy Stewart	.06	.02	.00
☐ U108	Kurt Stillwell	.15	.06	.01
☐ U109	Dale Sveum	.15	.06	.01
☐ U110	Tim Teufel	.10	.04	.01
☐ U111	Bob Tewksbury	.35	.14	.03
☐ U112	Andres Thomas	.35	.14	.03
☐ U113	Jason Thompson	.06	.02	.00
☐ U114	Milt Thompson	.10	.04	.01
☐ U115	Rob Thompson	.40	.16	.04
☐ U116	Jay Tibbs	.06	.02	.00
☐ U117	Fred Toliver	.10	.04	.01
☐ U118	Wayne Tolleson	.06	.02	.00
☐ U119	Alex Trevino	.06	.02	.00
☐ U120	Manny Trillo	.06	.02	.00
☐ U121	Ed VandeBerg	.06	.02	.00
☐ U122	Ozzie Virgil	.06	.02	.00
☐ U123	Tony Walker	.25	.10	.02
☐ U124	Gene Walter	.10	.04	.01
☐ U125	Duane Ward	.20	.08	.02
☐ U126	Jerry Willard	.06	.02	.00

		MINT	VG-E	F-G
☐ U127	Mitch Williams	.30	.12	.03
☐ U128	Reggie Williams	.30	.12	.03
☐ U129	Bobby Witt	.45	.18	.04
☐ U130	Marvell Wynne	.06	.02	.00
☐ U131	Steve Yeager	.06	.02	.00
☐ U132	Checklist card	.10	.01	.00

1987 Fleer

This 660-card set features a distinctive blue border which fades to white on the card fronts. The backs are printed in blue, red, and pink on white card stock. The bottom of the card back shows an innovative graph of the player's ability, e.g., "He's got the stuff" for pitchers and "How he's hitting 'em," for hitters. Cards are numbered on the back and are again the standard 2½" by 3½". Cards are again organized numerically by teams, i.e., World Champion Mets (1-25), Boston Red Sox (26-48), Houston Astros (49-72), California Angels (73-95), New York Yankees (96-120), Texas Rangers (121-143), Detroit Tigers (144-168), Philadelphia Phillies (169-192), Cincinnati Reds (193-218), Toronto Blue Jays (219-240), Cleveland Indians (241-263), San Francisco Giants (264-288), St. Louis Cardinals (289-312), Montreal Expos (313-337), Milwaukee Brewers (338-361), Kansas City Royals (362-384), Oakland A's (385-410), San Diego Padres (411-435), Los Angeles Dodgers (436-460), Baltimore Orioles (461-483), Chicago White Sox (484-508), Atlanta Braves (509-532), Minnesota Twins (533-554), Chicago Cubs (555-578),

Seattle Mariners (579-600), and Pittsburgh Pirates (601-624). The last 36 cards in the set consist of Specials (625-643), Rookie Pairs (644-653), and checklists (654-660).

		MINT	VG-E	F-G
	Complete Set	25.00	10.00	2.50
	Common Player	.03	.01	.00
☐ 1	Rick Aguilera	.06	.02	.00
☐ 2	Richard Anderson	.03	.01	.00
☐ 3	Wally Backman	.06	.02	.00
☐ 4	Gary Carter	.25	.10	.02
☐ 5	Ron Darling	.20	.08	.02
☐ 6	Len Dykstra	.20	.08	.02
☐ 7	Kevin Elster	.20	.08	.02
☐ 8	Sid Fernandez	.18	.08	.01
☐ 9	Dwight Gooden	1.00	.40	.10
☐ 10	Ed Hearn	.10	.04	.01
☐ 11	Danny Heep	.03	.01	.00
☐ 12	Keith Hernandez	.20	.08	.02
☐ 13	Howard Johnson	.03	.01	.00
☐ 14	Ray Knight	.07	.03	.01
☐ 15	Lee Mazzilli	.05	.02	.00
☐ 16	Roger McDowell	.10	.04	.01
☐ 17	Kevin Mitchell	.35	.14	.03
☐ 18	Randy Niemann	.03	.01	.00
☐ 19	Bob Ojeda	.08	.03	.01
☐ 20	Jesse Orosco	.05	.02	.00
☐ 21	Rafael Santana	.03	.01	.00
☐ 22	Doug Sisk	.03	.01	.00
☐ 23	Darryl Strawberry	.30	.12	.03
☐ 24	Tim Teufel	.05	.02	.00
☐ 25	Mookie Wilson	.05	.02	.00
☐ 26	Tony Armas	.08	.03	.01
☐ 27	Marty Barrett	.10	.04	.01
☐ 28	Don Baylor	.10	.04	.01
☐ 29	Wade Boggs	1.00	.40	.10
☐ 30	Oil Can Boyd	.08	.03	.01
☐ 31	Bill Buckner	.08	.03	.01
☐ 32	Roger Clemens	1.00	.40	.10
☐ 33	Steve Crawford	.03	.01	.00
☐ 34	Dwight Evans	.08	.03	.01
☐ 35	Rich Gedman	.08	.03	.01
☐ 36	Dave Henderson	.06	.02	.00
☐ 37	Bruce Hurst	.08	.03	.01
☐ 38	Tim Lollar	.03	.01	.00
☐ 39	Al Nipper	.03	.01	.00
☐ 40	Spike Owen	.05	.02	.00
☐ 41	Jim Rice	.25	.10	.02
☐ 42	Ed Romero	.03	.01	.00
☐ 43	Joe Sambito	.05	.02	.00
☐ 44	Calvin Schiraldi	.08	.03	.01

			MINT	VG-E	F-G
☐	45	Tom Seaver	.25	.10	.02
☐	46	Jeff Sellers	.12	.05	.01
☐	47	Bob Stanley	.05	.02	.00
☐	48	Sammy Stewart	.03	.01	.00
☐	49	Larry Andersen	.03	.01	.00
☐	50	Alan Ashby	.03	.01	.00
☐	51	Kevin Bass	.07	.03	.01
☐	52	Jeff Calhoun	.05	.02	.00
☐	53	Jose Cruz	.09	.04	.01
☐	54	Danny Darwin	.03	.01	.00
☐	55	Glenn Davis	.25	.10	.02
☐	56	Jim Deshaies	.25	.10	.02
☐	57	Bill Doran	.08	.03	.01
☐	58	Phil Garner	.05	.02	.00
☐	59	Billy Hatcher	.05	.02	.00
☐	60	Charlie Kerfeld	.08	.03	.01
☐	61	Bob Knepper	.08	.03	.01
☐	62	Dave Lopes	.06	.02	.00
☐	63	Aurelio Lopez	.03	.01	.00
☐	64	Jim Pankovits	.03	.01	.00
☐	65	Terry Puhl	.05	.02	.00
☐	66	Craig Reynolds	.03	.01	.00
☐	67	Nolan Ryan	.30	.12	.03
☐	68	Mike Scott	.16	.07	.01
☐	69	Dave Smith	.06	.02	.00
☐	70	Dickie Thon	.05	.02	.00
☐	71	Tony Walker	.15	.06	.01
☐	72	Denny Walling	.03	.01	.00
☐	73	Bob Boone	.05	.02	.00
☐	74	Rick Burleson	.06	.02	.00
☐	75	John Candelaria	.07	.03	.01
☐	76	Doug Corbett	.03	.01	.00
☐	77	Doug DeCinces	.07	.03	.01
☐	78	Brian Downing	.05	.02	.00
☐	79	Chuck Finley	.10	.04	.01
☐	80	Terry Forster	.06	.02	.00
☐	81	Bob Grich	.06	.02	.00
☐	82	George Hendrick	.06	.02	.00
☐	83	Jack Howell	.05	.02	.00
☐	84	Reggie Jackson	.30	.12	.03
☐	85	Ruppert Jones	.03	.01	.00
☐	86	Wally Joyner	2.00	.80	.20
☐	87	Gary Lucas	.03	.01	.00
☐	88	Kirk McCaskill	.10	.04	.01
☐	89	Donnie Moore	.05	.02	.00
☐	90	Gary Pettis	.07	.03	.01
☐	91	Vern Ruhle	.03	.01	.00
☐	92	Dick Schofield	.05	.02	.00
☐	93	Don Sutton	.12	.05	.01
☐	94	Rob Wilfong	.03	.01	.00
☐	95	Mike Witt	.10	.04	.01
☐	96	Doug Drabek	.20	.08	.02
☐	97	Mike Easler	.06	.02	.00
☐	98	Mike Fischlin	.03	.01	.00
☐	99	Brian Fisher	.05	.02	.00
☐	100	Ron Guidry	.15	.06	.01
☐	101	Rickey Henderson	.30	.12	.03
☐	102	Tommy John	.10	.04	.01
☐	103	Ron Kittle	.09	.04	.01
☐	104	Don Mattingly	2.00	.80	.20
☐	105	Bobby Meacham	.03	.01	.00
☐	106	Joe Niekro	.07	.03	.01
☐	107	Mike Pagliarulo	.15	.06	.01
☐	108	Dan Pasqua	.12	.05	.01
☐	109	Willie Randolph	.06	.02	.00
☐	110	Dennis Rasmussen	.07	.03	.01
☐	111	Dave Righetti	.12	.05	.01
☐	112	Gary Roenicke	.05	.02	.00
☐	113	Rod Scurry	.03	.01	.00
☐	114	Bob Shirley	.03	.01	.00
☐	115	Joel Skinner	.05	.02	.00
☐	116	Tim Stoddard	.03	.01	.00
☐	117	Bob Tewksbury	.20	.08	.02
☐	118	Wayne Tolleson	.03	.01	.00
☐	119	Claudell Washington	.05	.02	.00
☐	120	Dave Winfield	.25	.10	.02
☐	121	Steve Buechele	.05	.02	.00
☐	122	Ed Correa	.35	.14	.03
☐	123	Scott Fletcher	.05	.02	.00
☐	124	Jose Guzman	.06	.02	.00
☐	125	Toby Harrah	.05	.02	.00
☐	126	Greg Harris	.05	.02	.00
☐	127	Charlie Hough	.05	.02	.00
☐	128	Pete Incaviglia	1.00	.40	.10
☐	129	Mike Mason	.05	.02	.00
☐	130	Oddibe McDowell	.20	.08	.02
☐	131	Dave Mohorcic	.15	.06	.01
☐	132	Pete O'Brien	.09	.04	.01
☐	133	Tom Paciorek	.03	.01	.00
☐	134	Larry Parrish	.05	.02	.00
☐	135	Geno Petralli	.03	.01	.00
☐	136	Darrell Porter	.05	.02	.00
☐	137	Jeff Russell	.03	.01	.00
☐	138	Ruben Sierra	1.00	.40	.10
☐	139	Don Slaught	.03	.01	.00
☐	140	Gary Ward	.05	.02	.00
☐	141	Curtis Wilkerson	.03	.01	.00
☐	142	Mitch Williams	.25	.10	.02
☐	143	Bobby Witt	.40	.16	.04
☐	144	Dave Bergman	.03	.01	.00
☐	145	Tom Brookens	.03	.01	.00
☐	146	Bill Campbell	.03	.01	.00
☐	147	Chuck Cary	.20	.08	.02
☐	148	Darnell Coles	.09	.04	.01
☐	149	Dave Collins	.05	.02	.00
☐	150	Darrell Evans	.08	.03	.01

	MINT	VG-E	F-G		MINT	VG-E	F-G
☐ 151 Kirk Gibson	.20	.08	.02	☐ 204 Barry Larkin	.45	.18	.04
☐ 152 John Grubb	.03	.01	.00	☐ 205 Eddie Milner	.05	.02	.00
☐ 153 Willie Hernandez	.09	.04	.01	☐ 206 Rob Murphy	.15	.06	.01
☐ 154 Larry Herndon	.03	.01	.00	☐ 207 Ron Oester	.05	.02	.00
☐ 155 Eric King	.25	.10	.02	☐ 208 Dave Parker	.15	.06	.01
☐ 156 Chet Lemon	.05	.02	.00	☐ 209 Tony Perez	.10	.04	.01
☐ 157 Dwight Lowry	.15	.06	.01	☐ 210 Ted Power	.07	.03	.01
☐ 158 Jack Morris	.15	.06	.01	☐ 211 Joe Price	.03	.01	.00
☐ 159 Randy O'Neal	.03	.01	.00	☐ 212 Ron Robinson	.03	.01	.00
☐ 160 Lance Parrish	.20	.08	.02	☐ 213 Pete Rose	.60	.24	.06
☐ 161 Dan Petry	.09	.04	.01	☐ 214 Mario Soto	.08	.03	.01
☐ 162 Pat Sheridan	.03	.01	.00	☐ 215 Kurt Stillwell	.15	.06	.01
☐ 163 Jim Slaton	.03	.01	.00	☐ 216 Max Venable	.03	.01	.00
☐ 164 Frank Tanana	.05	.02	.00	☐ 217 Chris Welsh	.03	.01	.00
☐ 165 Walt Terrell	.03	.01	.00	☐ 218 Carl Willis	.12	.05	.01
☐ 166 Mark Thurmond	.03	.01	.00	☐ 219 Jesse Barfield	.15	.06	.01
☐ 167 Alan Trammell	.12	.05	.01	☐ 220 George Bell	.15	.06	.01
☐ 168 Lou Whitaker	.10	.04	.01	☐ 221 Bill Caudill	.05	.02	.00
☐ 169 Luis Aguayo	.03	.01	.00	☐ 222 John Cerutti	.25	.10	.02
☐ 170 Steve Bedrosian	.05	.02	.00	☐ 223 Jim Clancy	.03	.01	.00
☐ 171 Don Carman	.05	.02	.00	☐ 224 Mark Eichhorn	.30	.12	.03
☐ 172 Darren Daulton	.03	.01	.00	☐ 225 Tony Fernandez	.09	.04	.01
☐ 173 Greg Gross	.03	.01	.00	☐ 226 Damaso Garcia	.07	.03	.01
☐ 174 Kevin Gross	.03	.01	.00	☐ 227 Kelly Gruber	.03	.01	.00
☐ 175 Von Hayes	.12	.05	.01	☐ 228 Tom Henke	.05	.02	.00
☐ 176 Charles Hudson	.05	.02	.00	☐ 229 Garth Iorg	.03	.01	.00
☐ 177 Tom Hume	.03	.01	.00	☐ 230 Cliff Johnson	.03	.01	.00
☐ 178 Steve Jeltz	.03	.01	.00	☐ 231 Joe Johnson	.03	.01	.00
☐ 179 Mike Maddux	.09	.04	.01	☐ 232 Jimmy Key	.08	.03	.01
☐ 180 Shane Rawley	.07	.03	.01	☐ 233 Dennis Lamp	.03	.01	.00
☐ 181 Gary Redus	.05	.02	.00	☐ 234 Rick Leach	.03	.01	.00
☐ 182 Ron Roenicke	.03	.01	.00	☐ 235 Buck Martinez	.03	.01	.00
☐ 183 Bruce Ruffin	.30	.12	.03	☐ 236 Lloyd Moseby	.10	.04	.01
☐ 184 John Russell	.03	.01	.00	☐ 237 Rance Mulliniks	.03	.01	.00
☐ 185 Juan Samuel	.10	.04	.01	☐ 238 Dave Stieb	.10	.04	.01
☐ 186 Dan Schatzeder	.03	.01	.00	☐ 239 Willie Upshaw	.07	.03	.01
☐ 187 Mike Schmidt	.30	.12	.03	☐ 240 Ernie Whitt	.03	.01	.00
☐ 188 Rick Schu	.03	.01	.00	☐ 241 Andy Allanson	.12	.05	.01
☐ 189 Jeff Stone	.05	.02	.00	☐ 242 Scott Bailes	.10	.04	.01
☐ 190 Kent Tekulve	.05	.02	.00	☐ 243 Chris Bando	.03	.01	.00
☐ 191 Milt Thompson	.05	.02	.00	☐ 244 Tony Bernazard	.05	.02	.00
☐ 192 Glenn Wilson	.09	.04	.01	☐ 245 John Butcher	.03	.01	.00
☐ 193 Buddy Bell	.09	.04	.01	☐ 246 Brett Butler	.08	.03	.01
☐ 194 Tom Browning	.09	.04	.01	☐ 247 Ernie Camacho	.03	.01	.00
☐ 195 Sal Butera	.03	.01	.00	☐ 248 Tom Candiotti	.03	.01	.00
☐ 196 Dave Concepcion	.08	.03	.01	☐ 249 Joe Carter	.18	.08	.01
☐ 197 Kal Daniels	.12	.05	.01	☐ 250 Carmen Castillo	.03	.01	.00
☐ 198 Eric Davis	.45	.18	.04	☐ 251 Julio Franco	.08	.03	.01
☐ 199 John Denny	.06	.02	.00	☐ 252 Mel Hall	.08	.03	.01
☐ 200 Bo Diaz	.05	.02	.00	☐ 253 Brook Jacoby	.08	.03	.01
☐ 201 Nick Esasky	.03	.01	.00	☐ 254 Phil Niekro	.15	.06	.01
☐ 202 John Franco	.08	.03	.01	☐ 255 Otis Nixon	.15	.06	.01
☐ 203 Bill Gullickson	.05	.02	.00	☐ 256 Dickie Noles	.03	.01	.00

		MINT	VG-E	F-G
☐ 257	Bryan Oelkers	.03	.01	.00
☐ 258	Ken Schrom	.05	.02	.00
☐ 259	Don Schulze	.03	.01	.00
☐ 260	Cory Snyder	.60	.24	.06
☐ 261	Pat Tabler	.08	.03	.01
☐ 262	Andre Thornton	.06	.02	.00
☐ 263	Rich Yett	.03	.01	.00
☐ 264	Mike Aldrete	.12	.05	.01
☐ 265	Juan Berenguer	.03	.01	.00
☐ 266	Vida Blue	.07	.03	.01
☐ 267	Bob Brenly	.05	.02	.00
☐ 268	Chris Brown	.15	.06	.01
☐ 269	Will Clark	.60	.24	.06
☐ 270	Chili Davis	.08	.03	.01
☐ 271	Mark Davis	.03	.01	.00
☐ 272	Kelly Downs	.10	.04	.01
☐ 273	Scott Garrelts	.05	.02	.00
☐ 274	Dan Gladden	.05	.02	.00
☐ 275	Mike Krukow	.07	.03	.01
☐ 276	Randy Kutcher	.15	.06	.01
☐ 277	Mike LaCoss	.03	.01	.00
☐ 278	Jeff Leonard	.05	.02	.00
☐ 279	Candy Maldonado	.06	.02	.00
☐ 280	Roger Mason	.05	.02	.00
☐ 281	Bob Melvin	.03	.01	.00
☐ 282	Greg Minton	.05	.02	.00
☐ 283	Jeff Robinson	.03	.01	.00
☐ 284	Harry Spilman	.03	.01	.00
☐ 285	Robby Thompson	.30	.12	.03
☐ 286	Jose Uribe	.03	.01	.00
☐ 287	Frank Williams	.03	.01	.00
☐ 288	Joel Youngblood	.03	.01	.00
☐ 289	Jack Clark	.10	.04	.01
☐ 290	Vince Coleman	.35	.14	.03
☐ 291	Tom Conroy	.03	.01	.00
☐ 292	Danny Cox	.05	.02	.00
☐ 293	Ken Dayley	.03	.01	.00
☐ 294	Curt Ford	.25	.10	.02
☐ 295	Bob Forsch	.05	.02	.00
☐ 296	Tom Herr	.07	.03	.01
☐ 297	Ricky Horton	.03	.01	.00
☐ 298	Clint Hurdle	.03	.01	.00
☐ 299	Jeff Lahti	.03	.01	.00
☐ 300	Steve Lake	.03	.01	.00
☐ 301	Tito Landrum	.03	.01	.00
☐ 302	Mike Lavalliere	.03	.01	.00
☐ 303	Greg Mathews	.20	.08	.02
☐ 304	Willie McGee	.15	.06	.01
☐ 305	Jose Oquendo	.03	.01	.00
☐ 306	Terry Pendleton	.05	.02	.00
☐ 307	Pat Perry	.07	.03	.01
☐ 308	Ozzie Smith	.12	.05	.01
☐ 309	Ray Soff	.09	.04	.01
☐ 310	John Tudor	.09	.04	.01
☐ 311	Andy Van Slyke	.06	.02	.00
☐ 312	Todd Worrell	.20	.08	.02
☐ 313	Dann Bilardello	.03	.01	.00
☐ 314	Hubie Brooks	.09	.04	.01
☐ 315	Tim Burke	.05	.02	.00
☐ 316	Andre Dawson	.16	.07	.01
☐ 317	Mike Fitzgerald	.03	.01	.00
☐ 318	Tom Foley	.03	.01	.00
☐ 319	Andres Galarraga	.08	.03	.01
☐ 320	Joe Hesketh	.05	.02	.00
☐ 321	Wallace Johnson	.03	.01	.00
☐ 322	Wayne Krenchicki	.03	.01	.00
☐ 323	Vance Law	.03	.01	.00
☐ 324	Dennis Martinez	.03	.01	.00
☐ 325	Bob McClure	.03	.01	.00
☐ 326	Andy McGaffigan	.03	.01	.00
☐ 327	Al Newman	.10	.04	.01
☐ 328	Tim Raines	.25	.10	.02
☐ 329	Jeff Reardon	.06	.02	.00
☐ 330	Luis Rivera	.10	.04	.01
☐ 331	Bob Sebra	.10	.04	.01
☐ 332	Bryn Smith	.05	.02	.00
☐ 333	Jay Tibbs	.03	.01	.00
☐ 334	Tim Wallach	.08	.03	.01
☐ 335	Mitch Webster	.07	.03	.01
☐ 336	Jim Wohlford	.03	.01	.00
☐ 337	Floyd Youmans	.16	.07	.01
☐ 338	Chris Bosio	.10	.04	.01
☐ 339	Glenn Braggs	.40	.16	.04
☐ 340	Rick Cerone	.03	.01	.00
☐ 341	Mark Clear	.03	.01	.00
☐ 342	Bryan Clutterbuck	.10	.04	.01
☐ 343	Cecil Cooper	.09	.04	.01
☐ 344	Rob Deer	.15	.06	.01
☐ 345	Jim Gantner	.05	.02	.00
☐ 346	Ted Higuera	.15	.06	.01
☐ 347	John H. Johnson	.03	.01	.00
☐ 348	Tim Leary	.03	.01	.00
☐ 349	Rick Manning	.03	.01	.00
☐ 350	Paul Molitor	.08	.03	.01
☐ 351	Charlie Moore	.03	.01	.00
☐ 352	Juan Nieves	.07	.03	.01
☐ 353	Ben Oglivie	.06	.02	.00
☐ 354	Dan Plesac	.20	.08	.02
☐ 355	Ernest Riles	.07	.03	.01
☐ 356	Billy Joe Robidoux	.09	.04	.01
☐ 357	Bill Schroeder	.03	.01	.00
☐ 358	Dale Sveum	.10	.04	.01
☐ 359	Gorman Thomas	.08	.03	.01
☐ 360	Bill Wegman	.06	.02	.00
☐ 361	Robin Yount	.25	.10	.02
☐ 362	Steve Balboni	.05	.02	.00

		MINT	VG-E	F-G
☐ 363	Scott Bankhead	.06	.02	.00
☐ 364	Buddy Biancalana	.03	.01	.00
☐ 365	Bud Black	.03	.01	.00
☐ 366	George Brett	.30	.12	.03
☐ 367	Steve Farr	.03	.01	.00
☐ 368	Mark Gubicza	.06	.02	.00
☐ 369	Bo Jackson	1.00	.40	.10
☐ 370	Danny Jackson	.06	.02	.00
☐ 371	Mike Kingery	.20	.08	.02
☐ 372	Rudy Law	.03	.01	.00
☐ 373	Charlie Leibrandt	.05	.02	.00
☐ 374	Dennis Leonard	.05	.02	.00
☐ 375	Hal McRae	.05	.02	.00
☐ 376	Jorge Orta	.03	.01	.00
☐ 377	Jamie Quirk	.03	.01	.00
☐ 378	Dan Quisenberry	.12	.05	.01
☐ 379	Bret Saberhagen	.15	.06	.01
☐ 380	Angel Salazar	.03	.01	.00
☐ 381	Lonnie Smith	.05	.02	.00
☐ 382	Jim Sundberg	.05	.02	.00
☐ 383	Frank White	.06	.02	.00
☐ 384	Willie Wilson	.12	.05	.01
☐ 385	Joaquin Andujar	.08	.03	.01
☐ 386	Doug Bair	.05	.02	.00
☐ 387	Dusty Baker	.06	.02	.00
☐ 388	Bruce Bochte	.05	.02	.00
☐ 389	Jose Canseco	1.25	.50	.12
☐ 390	Chris Codiroli	.03	.01	.00
☐ 391	Mike Davis	.05	.02	.00
☐ 392	Alfredo Griffin	.05	.02	.00
☐ 393	Moose Haas	.03	.01	.00
☐ 394	Donnie Hill	.03	.01	.00
☐ 395	Jay Howell	.05	.02	.00
☐ 396	Dave Kingman	.10	.04	.01
☐ 397	Carney Lansford	.09	.04	.01
☐ 398	Dave Leiper	.07	.03	.01
☐ 399	Bill Mooneyham	.10	.04	.01
☐ 400	Dwayne Murphy	.05	.02	.00
☐ 401	Steve Ontiveros	.05	.02	.00
☐ 402	Tony Phillips	.03	.01	.00
☐ 403	Eric Plunk	.05	.02	.00
☐ 404	Jose Rijo	.08	.03	.01
☐ 405	Terry Steinbach	.35	.14	.03
☐ 406	Dave Stewart	.03	.01	.00
☐ 407	Mickey Tettleton	.03	.01	.00
☐ 408	Dave Von Ohlen	.03	.01	.00
☐ 409	Jerry Willard	.03	.01	.00
☐ 410	Curt Young	.03	.01	.00
☐ 411	Bruce Bochy	.03	.01	.00
☐ 412	Dave Dravecky	.05	.02	.00
☐ 413	Tim Flannery	.03	.01	.00
☐ 414	Steve Garvey	.25	.10	.02
☐ 415	Goose Gossage	.12	.05	.01
☐ 416	Tony Gwynn	.25	.10	.02
☐ 417	Andy Hawkins	.05	.02	.00
☐ 418	LaMarr Hoyt	.06	.02	.00
☐ 419	Terry Kennedy	.06	.02	.00
☐ 420	John Kruk	.25	.10	.02
☐ 421	Dave LaPoint	.03	.01	.00
☐ 422	Craig Lefferts	.03	.01	.00
☐ 423	Carmelo Martinez	.05	.02	.00
☐ 424	Lance McCullers	.05	.02	.00
☐ 425	Kevin McReynolds	.12	.05	.01
☐ 426	Graig Nettles	.12	.05	.01
☐ 427	Bip Roberts	.09	.04	.01
☐ 428	Jerry Royster	.03	.01	.00
☐ 429	Benito Santiago	.25	.10	.02
☐ 430	Eric Show	.03	.01	.00
☐ 431	Bob Stoddard	.03	.01	.00
☐ 432	Garry Templeton	.07	.03	.01
☐ 433	Gene Walter	.05	.02	.00
☐ 434	Ed Whitson	.03	.01	.00
☐ 435	Marvell Wynne	.03	.01	.00
☐ 436	Dave Anderson	.03	.01	.00
☐ 437	Greg Brock	.05	.02	.00
☐ 438	Enos Cabell	.03	.01	.00
☐ 439	Mariano Duncan	.08	.03	.01
☐ 440	Pedro Guerrero	.20	.08	.02
☐ 441	Orel Hershiser	.16	.07	.01
☐ 442	Rick Honeycutt	.03	.01	.00
☐ 443	Ken Howell	.03	.01	.00
☐ 444	Ken Landreaux	.03	.01	.00
☐ 445	Bill Madlock	.09	.04	.01
☐ 446	Mike Marshall	.12	.05	.01
☐ 447	Len Matuszek	.03	.01	.00
☐ 448	Tom Niedenfuer	.06	.02	.00
☐ 449	Alejandro Pena	.05	.02	.00
☐ 450	Dennis Powell	.09	.04	.01
☐ 451	Jerry Reuss	.05	.02	.00
☐ 452	Bill Russell	.05	.02	.00
☐ 453	Steve Sax	.12	.05	.01
☐ 454	Mike Scioscia	.05	.02	.00
☐ 455	Franklin Stubbs	.09	.04	.01
☐ 456	Alex Trevino	.03	.01	.00
☐ 457	Fernando Valenzuela	.25	.10	.02
☐ 458	Ed VandeBerg	.03	.01	.00
☐ 459	Bob Welch	.06	.02	.00
☐ 460	Reggie Williams	.18	.08	.01
☐ 461	Don Aase	.05	.02	.00
☐ 462	Juan Beniquez	.05	.02	.00
☐ 463	Mike Boddicker	.07	.03	.01
☐ 464	Juan Bonilla	.03	.01	.00
☐ 465	Rich Bordi	.03	.01	.00
☐ 466	Storm Davis	.07	.03	.01
☐ 467	Rick Dempsey	.05	.02	.00
☐ 468	Ken Dixon	.05	.02	.00

	MINT	VG-E	F-G
☐ 469 Jim Dwyer	.03	.01	.00
☐ 470 Mike Flanagan	.07	.03	.01
☐ 471 Jackie Gutierrez	.03	.01	.00
☐ 472 Brad Havens	.03	.01	.00
☐ 473 Lee Lacy	.05	.02	.00
☐ 474 Fred Lynn	.15	.06	.01
☐ 475 Scott McGregor	.07	.03	.01
☐ 476 Eddie Murray	.25	.10	.02
☐ 477 Tom O'Malley	.03	.01	.00
☐ 478 Cal Ripken Jr.	.25	.10	.02
☐ 479 Larry Sheets	.06	.02	.00
☐ 480 John Shelby	.03	.01	.00
☐ 481 Nate Snell	.03	.01	.00
☐ 482 Jim Traber	.09	.04	.01
☐ 483 Mike Young	.07	.03	.01
☐ 484 Neil Allen	.05	.02	.00
☐ 485 Harold Baines	.15	.06	.01
☐ 486 Floyd Bannister	.05	.02	.00
☐ 487 Daryl Boston	.05	.02	.00
☐ 488 Ivan Calderon	.15	.06	.01
☐ 489 John Cangelosi	.25	.10	.02
☐ 490 Steve Carlton	.25	.10	.02
☐ 491 Joe Cowley	.05	.02	.00
☐ 492 Julio Cruz	.03	.01	.00
☐ 493 Bill Dawley	.03	.01	.00
☐ 494 Jose DeLeon	.05	.02	.00
☐ 495 Richard Dotson	.05	.02	.00
☐ 496 Carlton Fisk	.12	.05	.01
☐ 497 Ozzie Guillen	.10	.04	.01
☐ 498 Jerry Hairston	.03	.01	.00
☐ 499 Ron Hassey	.03	.01	.00
☐ 500 Tim Hulett	.05	.02	.00
☐ 501 Bob James	.03	.01	.00
☐ 502 Steve Lyons	.03	.01	.00
☐ 503 Joel McKeon	.20	.08	.02
☐ 504 Gene Nelson	.03	.01	.00
☐ 505 Dave Schmidt	.03	.01	.00
☐ 506 Ray Searage	.03	.01	.00
☐ 507 Bobby Thigpen	.18	.08	.01
☐ 508 Greg Walker	.10	.04	.01
☐ 509 Jim Acker	.03	.01	.00
☐ 510 Doyle Alexander	.05	.02	.00
☐ 511 Paul Assenmacher	.10	.04	.01
☐ 512 Bruce Benedict	.03	.01	.00
☐ 513 Chris Chambliss	.05	.02	.00
☐ 514 Jeff Dedmon	.03	.01	.00
☐ 515 Gene Garber	.03	.01	.00
☐ 516 Ken Griffey	.06	.02	.00
☐ 517 Terry Harper	.03	.01	.00
☐ 518 Bob Horner	.15	.06	.01
☐ 519 Glenn Hubbard	.03	.01	.00
☐ 520 Rick Mahler	.03	.01	.00
☐ 521 Omar Moreno	.03	.01	.00
☐ 522 Dale Murphy	.45	.18	.04
☐ 523 Ken Oberkfell	.03	.01	.00
☐ 524 Ed Olwine	.10	.04	.01
☐ 525 David Palmer	.05	.02	.00
☐ 526 Rafael Ramirez	.03	.01	.00
☐ 527 Billy Sample	.03	.01	.00
☐ 528 Ted Simmons	.09	.04	.01
☐ 529 Zane Smith	.03	.01	.00
☐ 530 Bruce Sutter	.10	.04	.01
☐ 531 Andres Thomas	.25	.10	.02
☐ 532 Ozzie Virgil	.05	.02	.00
☐ 533 Allan Anderson	.15	.06	.01
☐ 534 Keith Atherton	.03	.01	.00
☐ 535 Billy Beane	.06	.02	.00
☐ 536 Bert Blyleven	.09	.04	.01
☐ 537 Tom Brunansky	.09	.04	.01
☐ 538 Randy Bush	.03	.01	.00
☐ 539 George Frazier	.03	.01	.00
☐ 540 Gary Gaetti	.08	.03	.01
☐ 541 Greg Gagne	.05	.02	.00
☐ 542 Mickey Hatcher	.03	.01	.00
☐ 543 Neal Heaton	.03	.01	.00
☐ 544 Kent Hrbek	.15	.06	.01
☐ 545 Roy Lee Jackson	.03	.01	.00
☐ 546 Tim Laudner	.03	.01	.00
☐ 547 Steve Lombardozzi	.07	.03	.01
☐ 548 Mark Portugal	.10	.04	.01
☐ 549 Kirby Puckett	.25	.10	.02
☐ 550 Jeff Reed	.03	.01	.00
☐ 551 Mark Salas	.03	.01	.00
☐ 552 Roy Smalley	.05	.02	.00
☐ 553 Mike Smithson	.03	.01	.00
☐ 554 Frank Viola	.05	.02	.00
☐ 555 Thad Bosley	.03	.01	.00
☐ 556 Ron Cey	.07	.03	.01
☐ 557 Jody Davis	.07	.03	.01
☐ 558 Ron Davis	.03	.01	.00
☐ 559 Bob Dernier	.05	.02	.00
☐ 560 Frank DiPino	.03	.01	.00
☐ 561 Shawon Dunston	.09	.04	.01
☐ 562 Leon Durham	.08	.03	.01
☐ 563 Dennis Eckersley	.05	.02	.00
☐ 564 Terry Francona	.03	.01	.00
☐ 565 Dave Gumpert	.03	.01	.00
☐ 566 Guy Hoffman	.03	.01	.00
☐ 567 Ed Lynch	.03	.01	.00
☐ 568 Gary Matthews	.05	.02	.00
☐ 569 Keith Moreland	.07	.03	.01
☐ 570 Jamie Moyer	.15	.06	.01
☐ 571 Jerry Mumphrey	.05	.02	.00
☐ 572 Ryne Sandberg	.25	.10	.02
☐ 573 Scott Sanderson	.03	.01	.00
☐ 574 Lee Smith	.07	.03	.01

		MINT	VG-E	F-G
☐ 575	Chris Speier	.03	.01	.00
☐ 576	Rick Sutcliffe	.10	.04	.01
☐ 577	Manny Trillo	.05	.02	.00
☐ 578	Steve Trout	.05	.02	.00
☐ 579	Karl Best	.03	.01	.00
☐ 580	Phil Bradley	.20	.08	.02
☐ 581	Scott Bradley	.06	.02	.00
☐ 582	Mickey Brantley	.20	.08	.02
☐ 583	Mike Brown	.03	.01	.00
☐ 584	Alvin Davis	.10	.04	.01
☐ 585	Lee Guetterman	.12	.05	.01
☐ 586	Mark Huismann	.05	.02	.00
☐ 587	Bob Kearney	.03	.01	.00
☐ 588	Pete Ladd	.03	.01	.00
☐ 589	Mark Langston	.07	.03	.01
☐ 590	Mike Moore	.06	.02	.00
☐ 591	Mike Morgan	.03	.01	.00
☐ 592	John Moses	.10	.04	.01
☐ 593	Ken Phelps	.05	.02	.00
☐ 594	Jim Presley	.15	.06	.01
☐ 595	Rey Quinones	.10	.04	.01
☐ 596	Harold Reynolds	.03	.01	.00
☐ 597	Billy Swift	.03	.01	.00
☐ 598	Danny Tartabull	.25	.10	.02
☐ 599	Steve Yeager	.05	.02	.00
☐ 600	Matt Young	.03	.01	.00
☐ 601	Bill Almon	.03	.01	.00
☐ 602	Rafael Belliard	.10	.04	.01
☐ 603	Mike Bielecki	.03	.01	.00
☐ 604	Barry Bonds	.35	.14	.03
☐ 605	Bobby Bonilla	.15	.06	.01
☐ 606	Sid Bream	.05	.02	.00
☐ 607	Mike Brown	.03	.01	.00
☐ 608	Pat Clements	.05	.02	.00
☐ 609	Mike Diaz	.25	.10	.02
☐ 610	Cecilio Guante	.03	.01	.00
☐ 611	Barry Jones	.15	.06	.01
☐ 612	Bob Kipper	.03	.01	.00
☐ 613	Larry McWilliams	.03	.01	.00
☐ 614	Jim Morrison	.03	.01	.00
☐ 615	Joe Orsulak	.03	.01	.00
☐ 616	Junior Ortiz	.03	.01	.00
☐ 617	Tony Pena	.10	.04	.01
☐ 618	Johnny Ray	.09	.04	.01
☐ 619	Rick Reuschel	.05	.02	.00
☐ 620	R.J. Reynolds	.06	.02	.00
☐ 621	Rick Rhoden	.06	.02	.00
☐ 622	Don Robinson	.03	.01	.00
☐ 623	Bob Walk	.03	.01	.00
☐ 624	Jim Winn	.03	.01	.00
☐ 625	Youthful Power	.40	.16	.04
	Pete Incaviglia			
	Jose Canseco			

		MINT	VG-E	F-G
☐ 626	300 Game Winners	.10	.04	.01
	Don Sutton			
	Phil Niekro			
☐ 627	AL Firemen	.08	.03	.01
	Dave Righetti			
	Don Aase			
☐ 628	Rookie All-Stars	.90	.36	.09
	Wally Joyner			
	Jose Canseco			
☐ 629	Magic Mets	.75	.30	.07
	Gary Carter			
	Sid Fernandez			
	Dwight Gooden			
	Keith Hernandez			
	Darryl Strawberry			
☐ 630	NL Best Righties	.08	.03	.01
	Mike Scott			
	Mike Krukow			
☐ 631	Sensational Southpaws	.12	.05	.01
	Fernando Valenzuela			
	John Franco			
☐ 632	Count 'Em	.08	.03	.01
	Bob Horner			
☐ 633	AL Pitcher's Nightmare	.40	.16	.04
	Jose Canseco			
	Jim Rice			
	Kirby Puckett			
☐ 634	All Star Battery	.75	.30	.07
	Gary Carter			
	Roger Clemens			
☐ 635	4000 Strikeouts	.15	.06	.01
	Steve Carlton			
☐ 636	Big Bats at First	.15	.06	.01
	Glenn Davis			
	Eddie Murray			
☐ 637	On Base	.40	.16	.04
	Wade Boggs			
	Keith Hernandez			
☐ 638	Sluggers Left Side	.90	.36	.09
	Don Mattingly			
	Darryl Strawberry			
☐ 639	Former MVP's	.15	.06	.01
	Dave Parker			
	Ryne Sandberg			
☐ 640	Dr. K & Super K	.90	.36	.09
	Dwight Gooden			
	Roger Clemens			
☐ 641	AL West Stoppers	.08	.03	.01
	Mike Witt			
	Charlie Hough			
☐ 642	Doubles and Triples	.08	.03	.01
	Juan Samuel			
	Tim Raines			

	MINT	VG-E	F-G
☐ 643 Outfielders with Punch Harold Baines Jesse Barfield	.08	.03	.01
☐ 644 Dave Clark and Greg Swindell	.60	.24	.06
☐ 645 Ron Karkovice and Russ Morman	.35	.14	.03
☐ 646 Devon White and Willie Fraser	.35	.14	.03
☐ 647 Mike Stanley and Jerry Browne	.25	.10	.02
☐ 648 Dave Magadan and Phil Lombardi	.75	.30	.07
☐ 649 Jose Gonzalez and Ralph Bryant	.60	.24	.06
☐ 650 Jimmy Jones and Randy Asadoor	.35	.14	.03
☐ 651 Tracy Jones and Marvin Freeman	.35	.14	.03
☐ 652 John Stefero and Kevin Seitzer	.20	.08	.02
☐ 653 Rob Nelson and Steve Fireovid	.20	.08	.02
☐ 654 CL: Mets/Red Sox Astros/Angels	.06	.01	.00
☐ 655 CL: Yankees/Rangers Tigers/Phillies	.06	.01	.00
☐ 656 CL: Reds/Blue Jays Indians/Giants	.06	.01	.00
☐ 657 CL: Cardinals/Expos Brewers/Royals	.06	.01	.00
☐ 658 CL: A's/Padres Dodgers/Orioles	.06	.01	.00
☐ 659 CL: White Sox/Braves Twins/Cubs	.06	.01	.00
☐ 660 CL: Mariners/Pirates Special Cards	.06	.01	.00
☐ C1 Mets Logo (wax box card)	.08	.03	.01
☐ C2 Jesse Barfield (wax box card)	.15	.06	.01
☐ C3 George Brett (wax box card)	.50	.20	.05
☐ C4 Dwight Gooden (wax box card)	.75	.30	.07
☐ C5 Boston Logo (wax box card)	.08	.03	.01
☐ C6 Keith Hernandez (wax box card)	.25	.10	.02
☐ C7 Wally Joyner (wax box card)	1.00	.40	.10
☐ C8 Dale Murphy (wax box card)	.60	.24	.06

	MINT	VG-E	F-G
☐ C9 Astros Logo (wax box card)	.08	.03	.01
☐ C10 Dave Parker (wax box card)	.20	.08	.02
☐ C11 Kirby Puckett (wax box card)	.40	.16	.04
☐ C12 Dave Righetti (wax box card)	.20	.08	.02
☐ C13 Angels Logo (wax box card)	.08	.03	.01
☐ C14 Ryne Sandberg (wax box card)	.30	.12	.03
☐ C15 Mike Schmidt (wax box card)	.50	.20	.05
☐ C16 Robin Yount (wax box card)	.30	.12	.03

1948 Bowman

The 48-card Bowman set of 1948 was the first major set of the post-war period. Each 2¹/₁₆" by 2½" card had a black and white photo of a current player, with his biographical information printed in black ink on a gray back. Due to the printing process and the 36-card sheet size upon which Bowman was then printing, the 12 cards marked with an SP in the checklist are scarcer numerically, as they were removed from the printing sheet in order to make room for the 12 high numbers (37-48). Many cards are found with overprinted, transposed, or blank backs.

	MINT	VG-E	F-G
Complete Set	700.00	280.00	70.00
Common Player (1-36)	5.00	2.00	.50

	MINT	VG-E	F-G
Common Player (37-48)	9.00	3.75	.90
Common Player SP	12.50	5.00	1.25

☐	1	Bob Elliott	20.00	5.00	1.00
☐	2	Ewell Blackwell	6.50	2.60	.65
☐	3	Ralph Kiner	20.00	8.00	2.00
☐	4	Johnny Mize	16.00	6.50	1.60
☐	5	Bob Feller	35.00	14.00	3.50
☐	6	Yogi Berra	75.00	30.00	7.50
☐	7	Peter Reiser SP	15.00	6.00	1.50
☐	8	Phil Rizzuto SP	50.00	20.00	5.00
☐	9	Walker Cooper	5.00	2.00	.50
☐	10	Buddy Rosar	5.00	2.00	.50
☐	11	Johnny Lindell	5.00	2.00	.50
☐	12	Johnny Sain	9.00	3.75	.90
☐	13	Willard Marshall SP	12.50	5.00	1.25
☐	14	Allie Reynolds	9.00	3.75	.90
☐	15	Eddie Joost	5.00	2.00	.50
☐	16	Jack Lohrke SP	12.50	5.00	1.25
☐	17	Enos Slaughter	16.00	6.50	1.60
☐	18	Warren Spahn	35.00	14.00	3.50
☐	19	Tommy Henrich	7.00	2.80	.70
☐	20	Buddy Kerr SP	12.50	5.00	1.25
☐	21	Ferris Fain	6.00	2.40	.60
☐	22	Floyd Bevens SP	12.50	5.00	1.25
☐	23	Larry Jansen	5.00	2.00	.50
☐	24	Dutch Leonard SP	12.50	5.00	1.25
☐	25	Barney McCosky	5.00	2.00	.50
☐	26	Frank Shea SP	12.50	5.00	1.25
☐	27	Sid Gordon	5.00	2.00	.50
☐	28	Emil Verban SP	12.50	5.00	1.25
☐	29	Joe Page SP	13.50	5.50	1.00
☐	30	Whitey Lockman SP	12.50	5.00	1.25
☐	31	Bill McCahan	5.00	2.00	.50
☐	32	Bill Rigney	5.00	2.00	.50
☐	33	Bill Johnson	5.00	2.00	.50
☐	34	Sheldon Jones SP	12.50	5.00	1.25
☐	35	Snuffy Stirnweiss	5.00	2.00	.50
☐	36	Stan Musial	150.00	60.00	15.00
☐	37	Clint Hartung	9.00	3.75	.90
☐	38	Red Schoendienst	12.00	5.00	1.20
☐	39	Augie Galan	9.00	3.75	.90
☐	40	Marty Marion	12.00	5.00	1.20
☐	41	Rex Barney	9.00	3.75	.90
☐	42	Ray Poat	9.00	3.75	.90
☐	43	Bruce Edwards	9.00	3.75	.90
☐	44	Johnny Wyrostek	9.00	3.75	.9S
☐	45	Hank Sauer	10.00	4.00	1.00
☐	46	Herman Wehmeier	9.00	3.75	.90
☐	47	Bobby Thomson	12.00	5.00	1.20
☐	48	Dave Koslo	12.00	4.00	.80

1949 Bowman

No. 207 of a Series of 240
JOHNNY "Hippity" HOPP
First Base—Outfield—Pittsburgh Pirate
Born: Hastings, Neb., July 19, 1916
Bats: Left Throws: Left Ht. 5.10 Wt.
Johnny came to the majors at the end of th
campaign with the St. Louis Cardinals an
seasons in the minors. He remained w
Redbirds until sold to the Boston Braves
At the end of the 1947 season the Brov
him to the Pirates. In 120 games for
last year he hit .278. He hat .333 for th
in 1946.

#201—BASEBALL GAME AND
Get this original exciting game. It is
size plastic baseball. Complete with
ers and directions. Lots of fun. Can
bank. A swell item.
den. Big bargain. Do
and 5 Baseball wra
BASEBALL P G
PANTUCK

(Not valid where contrary
Offer expires 12/31/49) ©Bowm

JOHNNY "Hippity" HOPP

*The cards in this 240-card set measure 2¹/₁₆"
by 2½". In 1949 Bowman took an intermediate step between black and white and full
color with this set of tinted photos on colored
backgrounds. Collectors should note the series price variations which reflect some in-
consistencies in the printing process. There
are four major varieties in name printing
which are noted in the checklist below: NOF:
name on front; NNOF: no name on front; PR:
printed name on back; and SCR: script name
on back. These variations resulted when
Bowman used twelve of the lower numbers
to fill out the last press sheet of 36 cards add-
ing to numbers 217-240.*

	MINT	VG-E	F-G
Complete Set	4000.00	1600.00	500.00
Common Card			
(1-3/5-36/73)	5.00	2.00	.50
Common Card (37-72) .	5.50	2.20	.55
Common Card			
(4/74-108)	4.50	1.80	.45
Common Card (109-144)	3.50	1.40	.35
Common Card (145-180)	27.00	11.00	2.70
Common Card (181-216)	22.00	9.00	2.20
Common Card (217-240)	22.00	9.00	2.20

☐	1	Vern Bickford	20.00	3.00	.60
☐	2	Whitey Lockman	5.00	2.00	.50
☐	3	Bob Porterfield	5.00	2.00	.50
☐	4	A Jerry Priddy NNOF ...	5.00	2.00	.50
☐	4	B Jerry Priddy NOF	18.00	7.25	1.80
☐	5	Hank Sauer	6.00	2.40	.60
☐	6	Phil Cavarretta	6.00	2.40	.60

		MINT	VG-E	F-G
☐	7 Joe Dobson	5.00	2.00	.50
☐	8 Murray Dickson	5.00	2.00	.50
☐	9 Ferris Fain	6.00	2.40	.60
☐	10 Ted Gray	5.00	2.00	.50
☐	11 Lou Boudreau	12.50	5.00	1.25
☐	12 Cass Michaels	5.00	2.00	.50
☐	13 Bob Chesnes	5.00	2.00	.50
☐	14 Curt Simmons	7.50	3.00	.75
☐	15 Ned Garver	5.00	2.00	.50
☐	16 Al Kozar	5.00	2.00	.50
☐	17 Earl Torgeson	5.00	2.00	.50
☐	18 Bobby Thomson	6.00	2.40	.60
☐	19 Bobby Brown	9.00	3.75	.90
☐	20 Gene Hermanski	5.00	2.00	.50
☐	21 Frank Baumholtz	5.00	2.00	.50
☐	22 Peanuts Lowrey	5.00	2.00	.50
☐	23 Bobby Doerr	12.50	5.00	1.25
☐	24 Stan Musial	120.00	50.00	12.00
☐	25 Carl Scheib	5.00	2.00	.50
☐	26 George Kell	12.50	5.00	1.25
☐	27 Bob Feller	32.00	13.00	3.20
☐	28 Don Kolloway	5.00	2.00	.50
☐	29 Ralph Kiner	15.00	6.00	1.50
☐	30 Andy Seminick	5.00	2.00	.50
☐	31 Dick Kokos	5.00	2.00	.50
☐	32 Eddie Yost	5.00	2.00	.50
☐	33 Warren Spahn	27.00	11.00	2.70
☐	34 Dave Koslo	5.00	2.00	.50
☐	35 Vic Raschi	7.00	2.80	.70
☐	36 Pee Wee Reese	27.00	11.00	2.70
☐	37 John Wyrostek	5.50	2.20	.55
☐	38 Emil Verban	5.50	2.20	.55
☐	39 Billy Goodman	6.50	2.60	.65
☐	40 Red Munger	5.50	2.20	.55
☐	41 Lou Brissie	5.50	2.20	.55
☐	42 Hoot Evers	5.50	2.20	.55
☐	43 Dale Mitchell	6.50	2.60	.65
☐	44 Dave Philley	5.50	2.20	.55
☐	45 Wally Westlake	5.50	2.20	.55
☐	46 Robin Roberts	40.00	16.00	4.00
☐	47 Johnny Sain	7.00	2.80	.70
☐	48 Willard Marshall	5.50	2.20	.55
☐	49 Frank Shea	5.50	2.20	.55
☐	50 Jackie Robinson	120.00	50.00	12.00
☐	51 Herman Wehmeier	5.50	2.20	.55
☐	52 Johnny Schmitz	5.50	2.20	.55
☐	53 Jack Kramer	5.50	2.20	.55
☐	54 Marty Marion	7.50	3.00	.75
☐	55 Eddie Joost	5.50	2.20	.55
☐	56 Pat Mullin	5.50	2.20	.55
☐	57 Gene Bearden	5.50	2.20	.55
☐	58 Bob Elliott	6.50	2.60	.65
☐	59 Jack Lohrke	5.50	2.20	.55

		MINT	VG-E	F-G
☐	60 Yogi Berra	50.00	20.00	5.00
☐	61 Rex Barney	5.50	2.20	.55
☐	62 Grady Hatton	5.50	2.20	.55
☐	63 Andy Pafko	5.50	2.20	.55
☐	64 Dom DiMaggio	7.50	3.00	.75
☐	65 Enos Slaughter	12.50	5.00	1.25
☐	66 Elmer Valo	5.50	2.20	.55
☐	67 Alvin Dark	7.50	3.00	.75
☐	68 Sheldon Jones	5.50	2.20	.55
☐	69 Tommy Henrich	7.50	3.00	.75
☐	70 Carl Furillo	10.00	4.00	1.00
☐	71 Vern Stephens	6.50	2.60	.65
☐	72 Tommy Holmes	6.50	2.60	.65
☐	73 Billy Cox	6.50	2.60	.65
☐	74 Tom McBride	4.50	1.80	.45
☐	75 Eddie Mayo	4.50	1.80	.45
☐	76 Bill Nicholson	4.50	1.80	.45
☐	77 Ernie Bonham	4.50	1.80	.45
☐	78 A Sam Zoldak NNOF	4.50	1.80	.45
☐	78 B Sam Zoldak NOF	18.00	7.25	1.80
☐	79 Ron Northey	4.50	1.80	.45
☐	80 Bill McCahan	4.50	1.80	.45
☐	81 Virgil Stallcup	4.50	1.80	.45
☐	82 Joe Page	6.50	2.60	.65
☐	83 A Bob Scheffing NNOF	4.50	1.80	.45
☐	83 B Bob Scheffing NOF	18.00	7.25	1.80
☐	84 Roy Campanella	100.00	40.00	10.00
☐	85 A Johnny Mize NNOF	16.00	6.50	1.60
☐	85 B Johnny Mize NOF	40.00	16.00	4.00
☐	86 Johnny Pesky	5.00	2.00	.50
☐	87 Randy Gumpert	4.50	1.80	.45
☐	88 A Bill Salkeld NNOF	4.50	1.80	.45
☐	88 B Bill Salkeld NOF	18.00	7.25	1.80
☐	89 Mizell Platt	4.50	1.80	.45
☐	90 Gil Coan	4.50	1.80	.45
☐	91 Dick Wakefield	4.50	1.80	.45
☐	92 Willie Jones	4.50	1.80	.45
☐	93 Ed Stevens	4.50	1.80	.45
☐	94 Mickey Vernon	7.50	3.00	.75
☐	95 Howie Pollet	4.50	1.80	.45
☐	96 Taft Wright	4.50	1.80	.45
☐	97 Danny Litwhiler	4.50	1.80	.45
☐	98 A Phil Rizzuto NNOF	18.00	7.25	1.80
☐	98 B Phil Rizzuto NOF	40.00	16.00	4.00
☐	99 Frank Gustine	4.50	1.80	.45
☐	100 Gil Hodges	35.00	14.00	3.50
☐	101 Sid Gordon	4.50	1.80	.45
☐	102 Stan Spence	4.50	1.80	.45
☐	103 Joe Tipton	4.50	1.80	.45
☐	104 Ed Stanky	5.50	2.20	.55
☐	105 Bill Kennedy	4.50	1.80	.45
☐	106 Jake Early	4.50	1.80	.45
☐	107 Eddie Lake	4.50	1.80	.45

	MINT	VG-E	F-G			MINT	VG-E	F-G
☐ 108 Ken Heintzelman	4.50	1.80	.45	☐ 155 Mickey Guerra	27.00	11.00	2.70
☐ 109 A Ed Fitzgerald SCR	4.00	1.60	.40	☐ 156 Al Zarilla	27.00	11.00	2.70
☐ 109 B Ed Fitzgerald PR	15.00	6.00	1.50	☐ 157 Walt Masterson	27.00	11.00	2.70
☐ 110 Early Wynn	30.00	12.00	3.00	☐ 158 Harry Brecheen	30.00	12.00	3.00
☐ 111 Red Schoendienst	6.00	2.40	.60	☐ 159 Glen Moulder	27.00	11.00	2.70
☐ 112 Sam Chapman	3.50	1.40	.35	☐ 160 Jim Blackburn	27.00	11.00	2.70
☐ 113 Ray LaManno	3.50	1.40	.35	☐ 161 Jocko Thompson	27.00	11.00	2.70
☐ 114 Allie Reynolds	7.50	3.00	.75	☐ 162 Preacher Roe	36.00	15.00	3.60
☐ 115 Dutch Leonard	3.50	1.40	.35	☐ 163 Clyde McCullough	27.00	11.00	2.70
☐ 116 Joe Hatton	3.50	1.40	.35	☐ 164 Vic Wertz	30.00	12.00	3.00
☐ 117 Walker Cooper	3.50	1.40	.35	☐ 165 Snuffy Stirnweiss	30.00	12.00	3.00
☐ 118 Sam Mele	3.50	1.40	.35	☐ 166 Mike Tresh	27.00	11.00	2.70
☐ 119 Floyd Baker	3.50	1.40	.35	☐ 167 Babe Martin	27.00	11.00	2.70
☐ 120 Cliff Fannin	3.50	1.40	.35	☐ 168 Doyle Lade	27.00	11.00	2.70
☐ 121 Mark Christman	3.50	1.40	.35	☐ 169 Jeff Heath	27.00	11.00	2.70
☐ 122 George Vico	3.50	1.40	.35	☐ 170 Bill Rigney	27.00	11.00	2.70
☐ 123 Johnny Blatnick	3.50	1.40	.35	☐ 171 Dick Fowler	27.00	11.00	2.70
☐ 124 A Danny Murtaugh SCR	4.00	1.60	.40	☐ 172 Eddie Pellagrini	27.00	11.00	2.70
☐ 124 B Danny Murtaugh PR	15.00	6.00	1.50	☐ 173 Eddie Stewart	27.00	11.00	2.70
☐ 125 Ken Keltner	4.00	1.60	.40	☐ 174 Terry Moore	30.00	12.00	3.00
☐ 126 A Al Brazle SCR	4.00	1.60	.40	☐ 175 Luke Appling	40.00	16.00	4.00
☐ 126 B Al Brazle PR	15.00	6.00	1.50	☐ 176 Ken Raffensberger	27.00	11.00	2.70
☐ 127 A Hank Majeski SCR	4.00	1.60	.40	☐ 177 Stan Lopata	27.00	11.00	2.70
☐ 127 B Hank Majeski PR	15.00	6.00	1.50	☐ 178 Tom Brown	27.00	11.00	2.70
☐ 128 Johnny VanderMeer	6.00	2.40	.60	☐ 179 Hugh Casey	30.00	12.00	3.00
☐ 129 Bill Johnson	4.00	1.60	.40	☐ 180 Connie Berry	27.00	11.00	2.70
☐ 130 Harry Walker	4.00	1.60	.40	☐ 181 Gus Niarhos	22.00	9.00	2.20
☐ 131 Paul Lehner	3.50	1.40	.35	☐ 182 Hall Peck	22.00	9.00	2.20
☐ 132 A Al Evans SCR	4.00	1.60	.40	☐ 183 Lou Stringer	22.00	9.00	2.20
☐ 132 B Al Evans PR	15.00	6.00	1.50	☐ 184 Bob Chipman	22.00	9.00	2.20
☐ 133 Aaron Robinson	3.50	1.40	.35	☐ 185 Pete Reiser	25.00	10.00	2.50
☐ 134 Hank Borowy	3.50	1.40	.35	☐ 186 Buddy Kerr	22.00	9.00	2.20
☐ 135 Stan Rojek	3.50	1.40	.35	☐ 187 Phil Marchildon	22.00	9.00	2.20
☐ 136 Hank Edwards	3.50	1.40	.35	☐ 188 Karl Drews	22.00	9.00	2.20
☐ 137 Ted Wilks	3.50	1.40	.35	☐ 189 Earl Wooten	22.00	9.00	2.20
☐ 138 Buddy Rosar	3.50	1.40	.35	☐ 190 Jim Hearn	22.00	9.00	2.20
☐ 139 Hank Arft	3.50	1.40	.35	☐ 191 Joe Haynes	22.00	9.00	2.20
☐ 140 Ray Scarborough	3.50	1.40	.35	☐ 192 Harry Gumbert	22.00	9.00	2.20
☐ 141 Ulysses Lupien	3.50	1.40	.35	☐ 193 Ken Trinkle	22.00	9.00	2.20
☐ 142 Eddie Waitkus	3.50	1.40	.35	☐ 194 Ralph Branca	25.00	10.00	2.50
☐ 143 A Bob Dillinger SCR	4.00	1.60	.40	☐ 195 Eddie Bockman	22.00	9.00	2.20
☐ 143 B Bob Dillinger PR	15.00	6.00	1.50	☐ 196 Fred Hutchinson	25.00	10.00	2.50
☐ 144 Mickey Haefner	3.50	1.40	.35	☐ 197 Johnny Lindell	22.00	9.00	2.20
☐ 145 Sylvester Donnelly	27.00	11.00	2.70	☐ 198 Steve Gromek	22.00	9.00	2.20
☐ 146 Mike McCormick	27.00	11.00	2.70	☐ 199 Tex Hughson	22.00	9.00	2.20
☐ 147 Bert Singleton	27.00	11.00	2.70	☐ 200 Jess Dobernic	22.00	9.00	2.20
☐ 148 Bob Swift	27.00	11.00	2.70	☐ 201 Sibby Sisti	22.00	9.00	2.20
☐ 149 Roy Partee	27.00	11.00	2.70	☐ 202 Larry Jansen	22.00	9.00	2.20
☐ 150 Allie Clark	27.00	11.00	2.70	☐ 203 Barney McCosky	22.00	9.00	2.20
☐ 151 Mickey Harris	27.00	11.00	2.70	☐ 204 Bob Savage	22.00	9.00	2.20
☐ 152 Clarence Maddern	27.00	11.00	2.70	☐ 205 Dick Sisler	22.00	9.00	2.20
☐ 153 Phil Masi	27.00	11.00	2.70	☐ 206 Bruce Edwards	22.00	9.00	2.20
☐ 154 Clint Hartung	27.00	11.00	2.70	☐ 207 Johnny Hopp	25.00	10.00	2.50

		MINT	VG-E	F-G
☐ 208	Dizzy Trout	25.00	10.00	2.50
☐ 209	Charlie Keller	30.00	12.00	3.00
☐ 210	Joe Gordon	30.00	12.00	3.00
☐ 211	Boo Ferriss	22.00	9.00	2.20
☐ 212	Ralph Hamner	22.00	9.00	2.20
☐ 213	Red Barrett	22.00	9.00	2.20
☐ 214	Richie Ashburn	75.00	30.00	7.50
☐ 215	Kirby Higbe	22.00	9.00	2.20
☐ 216	Schoolboy Rowe	25.00	10.00	2.50
☐ 217	Marino Pieretti	22.00	9.00	2.20
☐ 218	Dick Kryhoski	22.00	9.00	2.20
☐ 219	Virgil "Fire" Trucks	25.00	10.00	2.50
☐ 220	Johnny McCarthy	22.00	9.00	2.20
☐ 221	Bob Muncrief	22.00	9.00	2.20
☐ 222	Alex Kellner	22.00	9.00	2.20
☐ 223	Bobby Hofman	22.00	9.00	2.20
☐ 224	Satchell Paige	500.00	200.00	50.00
☐ 225	Gerry Coleman	30.00	12.00	3.00
☐ 226	Duke Snider	325.00	130.00	32.00
☐ 227	Fritz Ostermueller	22.00	9.00	2.20
☐ 228	Jackie Mayo	22.00	9.00	2.20
☐ 229	Ed Lopat	40.00	16.00	4.00
☐ 230	Augie Galan	22.00	9.00	2.20
☐ 231	Earl Johnson	22.00	9.00	2.20
☐ 232	George McQuinn	22.00	9.00	2.20
☐ 233	Larry Doby	40.00	16.00	4.00
☐ 234	Rip Sewell	22.00	9.00	2.20
☐ 235	Jim Russell	22.00	9.00	2.20
☐ 236	Fred Sanford	22.00	9.00	2.20
☐ 237	Monte Kennedy	22.00	9.00	2.20
☐ 238	Bob Lemon	90.00	36.00	9.00
☐ 239	Frank McCormick	22.00	9.00	2.20
☐ 240	Babe Young (photo actually Bobby Young)	30.00	12.00	3.00

1950 Bowman

The cards in this 252-card set measure 2 1/16" by 2 1/2". This set, marketed in 1950 by Bowman, represented a major improvement in terms of quality over their previous efforts. Each card was a beautifully colored line drawing developed from a simple photograph. The first 72 cards are the scarcest in the set while the final 72 cards may be found with or without the copyright line. This was the only Bowman sports set to carry the famous "5-Star" logo.

		MINT	VG-E	F-G
	Complete Set	2000.00	800.00	250.00
	Common Player (1-72)	10.00	4.00	1.00
	Common Player (73-252)	4.00	1.60	.40
☐ 1	Mel Parnell	36.00	6.00	1.00
☐ 2	Vern Stephens	11.00	4.50	1.10
☐ 3	Dom DiMaggio	15.00	6.00	1.50
☐ 4	Gus Zernial	12.00	5.00	1.20
☐ 5	Bob Kuzava	10.00	4.00	1.00
☐ 6	Bob Feller	45.00	18.00	4.50
☐ 7	Jim Hegan	11.00	4.50	1.10
☐ 8	George Kell	20.00	8.00	2.00
☐ 9	Vic Wertz	11.00	4.50	1.10
☐ 10	Tommy Henrich	12.00	5.00	1.20
☐ 11	Phil Rizzuto	35.00	14.00	3.50
☐ 12	Joe Page	12.00	5.00	1.20
☐ 13	Ferris Fain	12.00	5.00	1.20
☐ 14	Alex Kellner	10.00	4.00	1.00
☐ 15	Al Kozar	10.00	4.00	1.00
☐ 16	Roy Sievers	12.00	5.00	1.20
☐ 17	Sid Hudson	10.00	4.00	1.00
☐ 18	Eddie Robinson	10.00	4.00	1.00
☐ 19	Warren Spahn	40.00	16.00	4.00
☐ 20	Bob Elliott	12.00	5.00	1.20
☐ 21	Pee Wee Reese	35.00	14.00	3.50
☐ 22	Jackie Robinson	120.00	50.00	12.00
☐ 23	Don Newcombe	16.00	6.50	1.60
☐ 24	Johnny Schmitz	10.00	4.00	1.00
☐ 25	Hank Sauer	11.00	4.50	1.10
☐ 26	Grady Hatton	10.00	4.00	1.00
☐ 27	Herman Wehmeier	10.00	4.00	1.00
☐ 28	Bobby Thomson	12.00	5.00	1.20
☐ 29	Eddie Stanky	11.00	4.50	1.10
☐ 30	Eddie Waitkus	11.00	4.50	1.10
☐ 31	Del Ennis	11.00	4.50	1.10
☐ 32	Robin Roberts	25.00	10.00	2.50
☐ 33	Ralph Kiner	20.00	8.00	2.00
☐ 34	Murry Dickson	10.00	4.00	1.00
☐ 35	Enos Slaughter	20.00	8.00	2.00

		MINT	VG-E	F-G
☐ 36	Eddie Kazak	10.00	4.00	1.00
☐ 37	Luke Appling	16.00	6.50	1.60
☐ 38	Bill Wight	10.00	4.00	1.00
☐ 39	Larry Doby	12.00	5.00	1.20
☐ 40	Bob Lemon	20.00	8.00	2.00
☐ 41	Hoot Evers	10.00	4.00	1.00
☐ 42	Art Houtteman	10.00	4.00	1.00
☐ 43	Bobby Doerr	20.00	8.00	2.00
☐ 44	Joe Dobson	10.00	4.00	1.00
☐ 45	Al Zarilla	10.00	4.00	1.00
☐ 46	Yogi Berra	80.00	32.00	8.00
☐ 47	Jerry Coleman	12.00	5.00	1.20
☐ 48	Lou Brissie	10.00	4.00	1.00
☐ 49	Elmer Valo	10.00	4.00	1.00
☐ 50	Dick Kokos	10.00	4.00	1.00
☐ 51	Ned Garver	10.00	4.00	1.00
☐ 52	Sam Mele	10.00	4.00	1.00
☐ 53	Clyde Vollmer	10.00	4.00	1.00
☐ 54	Gil Coan	10.00	4.00	1.00
☐ 55	Buddy Kerr	10.00	4.00	1.00
☐ 56	Del Crandall	12.00	5.00	1.20
☐ 57	Vern Bickford	10.00	4.00	1.00
☐ 58	Carl Furillo	15.00	6.00	1.50
☐ 59	Ralph Branca	12.00	5.00	1.20
☐ 60	Andy Pafko	10.00	4.00	1.00
☐ 61	Bob Rush	10.00	4.00	1.00
☐ 62	Ted Kluszewski	15.00	6.00	1.50
☐ 63	Ewell Blackwell	11.00	4.50	1.10
☐ 64	Al Dark	12.00	5.00	1.20
☐ 65	Dave Koslo	10.00	4.00	1.00
☐ 66	Larry Jansen	10.00	4.00	1.00
☐ 67	Willie Jones	10.00	4.00	1.00
☐ 68	Curt Simmons	11.00	4.50	1.10
☐ 69	Wally Westlake	10.00	4.00	1.00
☐ 70	Bob Chesnes	10.00	4.00	1.00
☐ 71	Red Schoendienst	12.00	5.00	1.20
☐ 72	Howie Pollet	10.00	4.00	1.00
☐ 73	Willard Marshall	4.00	1.60	.40
☐ 74	Johnny Antonelli	5.00	2.00	.50
☐ 75	Roy Campanella	65.00	26.00	6.50
☐ 76	Rex Barney	4.00	1.60	.40
☐ 77	Duke Snider	50.00	20.00	5.00
☐ 78	Mickey Owen	4.00	1.60	.40
☐ 79	Johnny VanderMeer	5.00	2.00	.50
☐ 80	Howard Fox	4.00	1.60	.40
☐ 81	Ron Northey	4.00	1.60	.40
☐ 82	Whitey Lockman	4.00	1.60	.40
☐ 83	Sheldon Jones	4.00	1.60	.40
☐ 84	Richie Ashburn	12.00	5.00	1.20
☐ 85	Ken Heintzelman	4.00	1.60	.40
☐ 86	Stan Rojek	4.00	1.60	.40
☐ 87	Bill Werle	4.00	1.60	.40
☐ 88	Marty Marion	6.00	2.40	.60
☐ 89	Red Munger	4.00	1.60	.40
☐ 90	Harry Brecheen	4.00	1.60	.40
☐ 91	Cass Michaels	4.00	1.60	.40
☐ 92	Hank Majeski	4.00	1.60	.40
☐ 93	Gene Bearden	4.00	1.60	.40
☐ 94	Lou Boudreau	11.00	4.50	1.10
☐ 95	Aaron Robinson	4.00	1.60	.40
☐ 96	Virgil Trucks	4.00	1.60	.40
☐ 97	Maurice McDermott	4.00	1.60	.40
☐ 98	Ted Williams	150.00	60.00	15.00
☐ 99	Billy Goodman	4.50	1.80	.45
☐ 100	Vic Raschi	5.50	2.20	.55
☐ 101	Bobby Brown	6.50	2.60	.65
☐ 102	Billy Johnson	4.50	1.80	.45
☐ 103	Eddie Joost	4.00	1.60	.40
☐ 104	Sam Chapman	4.00	1.60	.40
☐ 105	Bob Dillinger	4.00	1.60	.40
☐ 106	Cliff Fannin	4.00	1.60	.40
☐ 107	Sam Dente	4.00	1.60	.40
☐ 108	Ray Scarborough	4.00	1.60	.40
☐ 109	Sid Gordon	4.00	1.60	.40
☐ 110	Tommy Holmes	5.00	2.00	.50
☐ 111	Walker Cooper	4.00	1.60	.40
☐ 112	Gil Hodges	20.00	8.00	2.00
☐ 113	Gene Hermanski	4.00	1.60	.40
☐ 114	Wayne Terwilliger	4.00	1.60	.40
☐ 115	Roy Smalley	4.00	1.60	.40
☐ 116	Virgil Stallcup	4.00	1.60	.40
☐ 117	Bill Rigney	4.00	1.60	.40
☐ 118	Clint Hartung	4.00	1.60	.40
☐ 119	Dick Sisler	4.00	1.60	.40
☐ 120	John Thompson	4.00	1.60	.40
☐ 121	Andy Seminick	4.00	1.60	.40
☐ 122	Johnny Hopp	4.50	1.80	.45
☐ 123	Dino Restelli	4.00	1.60	.40
☐ 124	Clyde McCullough	4.00	1.60	.40
☐ 125	Del Rice	4.00	1.60	.40
☐ 126	Al Brazle	4.00	1.60	.40
☐ 127	Dave Philley	4.00	1.60	.40
☐ 128	Phil Masi	4.00	1.60	.40
☐ 129	Joe Gordon	5.00	2.00	.50
☐ 130	Dale Mitchell	4.50	1.80	.45
☐ 131	Steve Gromek	4.00	1.60	.40
☐ 132	James "Mickey" Vernon	5.50	2.20	.55
☐ 133	Don Kolloway	4.00	1.60	.40
☐ 134	Paul Trout	4.00	1.60	.40
☐ 135	Pat Mullin	4.00	1.60	.40
☐ 136	Warren Rosar	4.00	1.60	.40
☐ 137	Johnny Pesky	4.50	1.80	.45
☐ 138	Allie Reynolds	6.50	2.60	.65
☐ 139	Johnny Mize	12.00	5.00	1.20
☐ 140	Pete Suder	4.00	1.60	.40
☐ 141	Joe Coleman	4.00	1.60	.40

		MINT	VG-E	F-G
☐ 142	Sherman Lollar	5.00	2.00	.50
☐ 143	Eddie Stewart	4.00	1.60	.40
☐ 144	Al Evans	4.00	1.60	.40
☐ 145	Jack Graham	4.00	1.60	.40
☐ 146	Floyd Baker	4.00	1.60	.40
☐ 147	Mike Garcia	5.00	2.00	.50
☐ 148	Early Wynn	12.00	5.00	1.20
☐ 149	Bob Swift	4.00	1.60	.40
☐ 150	George Vico	4.00	1.60	.40
☐ 151	Fred Hutchinson	5.00	2.00	.50
☐ 152	Ellis Kinder	4.00	1.60	.40
☐ 153	Walt Masterson	4.00	1.60	.40
☐ 154	Gus Niarhos	4.00	1.60	.40
☐ 155	Frank Shea	4.00	1.60	.40
☐ 156	Fred Sanford	4.00	1.60	.40
☐ 157	Mike Guerra	4.00	1.60	.40
☐ 158	Paul Lehner	4.00	1.60	.40
☐ 159	Joe Tipton	4.00	1.60	.40
☐ 160	Mickey Harris	4.00	1.60	.40
☐ 161	Sherry Robertson	4.00	1.60	.40
☐ 162	Eddie Yost	4.00	1.60	.40
☐ 163	Earl Torgeson	4.00	1.60	.40
☐ 164	Sibby Sisti	4.00	1.60	.40
☐ 165	Bruce Edwards	4.00	1.60	.40
☐ 166	Joe Hatton	4.00	1.60	.40
☐ 167	Preacher Roe	6.00	2.40	.60
☐ 168	Bob Scheffing	4.00	1.60	.40
☐ 169	Hank Edwards	4.00	1.60	.40
☐ 170	Dutch Leonard	4.00	1.60	.40
☐ 171	Harry Gumbert	4.00	1.60	.40
☐ 172	Peanuts Lowrey	4.00	1.60	.40
☐ 173	Lloyd Merriman	4.00	1.60	.40
☐ 174	Hank Thompson	4.50	1.80	.45
☐ 175	Monte Kennedy	4.00	1.60	.40
☐ 176	Sylvester Donnelly	4.00	1.60	.40
☐ 177	Hank Borowy	4.00	1.60	.40
☐ 178	Eddie Fitzgerald	4.00	1.60	.40
☐ 179	Chuck Diering	4.00	1.60	.40
☐ 180	Harry Walker	4.00	1.60	.40
☐ 181	Marino Pieretti	4.00	1.60	.40
☐ 182	Sam Zoldak	4.00	1.60	.40
☐ 183	Mickey Haefner	4.00	1.60	.40
☐ 184	Randy Gumpert	4.00	1.60	.40
☐ 185	Howie Judson	4.00	1.60	.40
☐ 186	Ken Keltner	4.50	1.80	.45
☐ 187	Lou Stringer	4.00	1.60	.40
☐ 188	Earl Johnson	4.00	1.60	.40
☐ 189	Owen Friend	4.00	1.60	.40
☐ 190	Ken Wood	4.00	1.60	.40
☐ 191	Dick Starr	4.00	1.60	.40
☐ 192	Bob Chipman	4.00	1.60	.40
☐ 193	Pete Reiser	5.00	2.00	.50
☐ 194	Billy Cox	4.50	1.80	.45
☐ 195	Phil Cavarretta	4.50	1.80	.45
☐ 196	Doyle Lade	4.00	1.60	.40
☐ 197	Johnny Wyrostek	4.00	1.60	.40
☐ 198	Danny Litwhiler	4.00	1.60	.40
☐ 199	Jack Kramer	4.00	1.60	.40
☐ 200	Kirby Higbe	4.00	1.60	.40
☐ 201	Pete Castiglione	4.00	1.60	.40
☐ 202	Cliff Chambers	4.00	1.60	.40
☐ 203	Danny Murtaugh	4.50	1.80	.45
☐ 204	Granny Hamner	4.00	1.60	.40
☐ 205	Mike Goliat	4.00	1.60	.40
☐ 206	Stan Lopata	4.00	1.60	.40
☐ 207	Max Lanier	4.00	1.60	.40
☐ 208	Jim Hearn	4.00	1.60	.40
☐ 209	Johnny Lindell	4.00	1.60	.40
☐ 210	Ted Gray	4.00	1.60	.40
☐ 211	Charley Keller	4.50	1.80	.45
☐ 212	Gerry Priddy	4.00	1.60	.40
☐ 213	Carl Scheib	4.00	1.60	.40
☐ 214	Dick Fowler	4.00	1.60	.40
☐ 215	Ed Lopat	6.50	2.60	.65
☐ 216	Bob Porterfield	4.00	1.60	.40
☐ 217	Casey Stengel MGR	32.00	13.00	3.20
☐ 218	Cliff Mapes	4.00	1.60	.40
☐ 219	Hank Bauer	12.00	5.00	1.20
☐ 220	Leo Durocher MGR	12.00	5.00	1.20
☐ 221	Don Mueller	5.00	2.00	.50
☐ 222	Bobby Morgan	4.00	1.60	.40
☐ 223	Jim Russell	4.00	1.60	.40
☐ 224	Jack Banta	4.00	1.60	.40
☐ 225	Eddie Sawyer MGR	4.00	1.60	.40
☐ 226	Jim Konstanty	7.00	2.80	.70
☐ 227	Bob Miller	4.00	1.60	.40
☐ 228	Bill Nicholson	4.00	1.60	.40
☐ 229	Frank Frisch	15.00	6.00	1.50
☐ 230	Bill Serena	4.00	1.60	.40
☐ 231	Preston Ward	4.00	1.60	.40
☐ 232	Al Rosen	12.00	5.00	1.20
☐ 233	Allie Clark	4.00	1.60	.40
☐ 234	Bobby Shantz	7.50	3.00	.75
☐ 235	Harold Gilbert	4.00	1.60	.40
☐ 236	Bob Cain	4.00	1.60	.40
☐ 237	Bill Salkeld	4.00	1.60	.40
☐ 238	Vernal Jones	4.00	1.60	.40
☐ 239	Bill Howerton	4.00	1.60	.40
☐ 240	Eddie Lake	4.00	1.60	.40
☐ 241	Neil Berry	4.00	1.60	.40
☐ 242	Dick Kryhoski	4.00	1.60	.40
☐ 243	Johnny Groth	4.00	1.60	.40
☐ 244	Dale Coogan	4.00	1.60	.40
☐ 245	Al Papai	4.00	1.60	.40
☐ 246	Walt Dropo	5.00	2.00	.50
☐ 247	Irv Noren	4.50	1.80	.45

	MINT	VG-E	F-G
☐ 248 Sam Jethroe	4.50	1.80	.45
☐ 249 Snuffy Stimweiss	4.00	1.60	.40
☐ 250 Ray Coleman	4.00	1.60	.40
☐ 251 John Moss	4.00	1.60	.40
☐ 252 Billy DeMars	12.50	2.00	.40

1951 Bowman

The cards in this 324-card set measure 2¹/₁₆" by 3¹/₈". Many of the obverses of the cards appearing in the 1951 Bowman set are enlargements of those appearing in the previous year. The high number series (253-324) is highly valued and contains the Rookie cards of Mickey Mantle and Willie Mays. Card number 195 depicts Paul Richards in caricature. George Kell's card (#46) incorrectly lists him as being in the "1941" Bowman series. Player names are found printed in a panel on the front of the card. These cards were also sold in sheets in variety stores in the Philadelphia area.

	MINT	VG-E	F-G
Complete Set	3300.00	1500.00	350.00
Common Player (1-36)	5.00	2.00	.50
Common Player (37-72)	4.50	1.80	.45
Common Player (73-252)	4.00	1.60	.40
Common Player (253-324)	12.50	5.00	1.25
☐ 1 Whitey Ford	200.00	20.00	4.00
☐ 2 Yogi Berra	65.00	26.00	6.50
☐ 3 Robin Roberts	16.00	6.50	1.60
☐ 4 Del Ennis	5.50	2.20	.55
☐ 5 Dale Mitchell	5.50	2.20	.55

	MINT	VG-E	F-G
☐ 6 Don Newcombe	7.50	3.00	.75
☐ 7 Gil Hodges	18.00	7.25	1.80
☐ 8 Paul Lehner	5.00	2.00	.50
☐ 9 Sam Chapman	5.00	2.00	.50
☐ 10 Red Schoendienst	6.50	2.60	.65
☐ 11 Red Munger	5.00	2.00	.50
☐ 12 Hank Majeski	5.00	2.00	.50
☐ 13 Eddie Stanky	5.50	2.20	.55
☐ 14 Al Dark	6.00	2.40	.60
☐ 15 Johnny Pesky	5.50	2.20	.55
☐ 16 Maurice McDermott	5.00	2.00	.50
☐ 17 Pete Castiglione	5.00	2.00	.50
☐ 18 Gil Coan	5.00	2.00	.50
☐ 19 Sid Gordon	5.00	2.00	.50
☐ 20 Del Crandell (sic, Crandall)	5.50	2.20	.55
☐ 21 Snuffy Stimweiss	5.00	2.00	.50
☐ 22 Hank Sauer	5.50	2.20	.55
☐ 23 Hoot Evers	5.00	2.00	.50
☐ 24 Ewell Blackwell	5.50	2.20	.55
☐ 25 Vic Raschi	6.00	2.40	.60
☐ 26 Phil Rizzuto	18.00	7.25	1.80
☐ 27 Jim Konstanty	5.50	2.20	.55
☐ 28 Eddie Waitkus	5.00	2.00	.50
☐ 29 Allie Clark	5.00	2.00	.50
☐ 30 Bob Feller	27.00	11.00	2.70
☐ 31 Roy Campanella	50.00	20.00	5.00
☐ 32 Duke Snider	36.00	15.00	3.60
☐ 33 Bob Hooper	5.00	2.00	.50
☐ 34 Marty Marion	6.00	2.40	.60
☐ 35 Al Zarilla	5.00	2.00	.50
☐ 36 Joe Dobson	5.00	2.00	.50
☐ 37 Whitey Lockman	4.50	1.80	.45
☐ 38 Al Evans	4.50	1.80	.45
☐ 39 Ray Scarborough	4.50	1.80	.45
☐ 40 Gus Bell	5.50	2.20	.55
☐ 41 Eddie Yost	4.50	1.80	.45
☐ 42 Vern Bickford	4.50	1.80	.45
☐ 43 Billy DeMars	4.50	1.80	.45
☐ 44 Roy Smalley	4.50	1.80	.45
☐ 45 Art Houtteman	4.50	1.80	.45
☐ 46 George Kell 1941	14.00	5.75	1.40
☐ 47 Grady Hatton	4.50	1.80	.45
☐ 48 Ken Raffensberger	4.50	1.80	.45
☐ 49 Jerry Coleman	5.00	2.00	.50
☐ 50 Johnny Mize	12.00	5.00	1.20
☐ 51 Andy Seminick	4.50	1.80	.45
☐ 52 Dick Sisler	4.50	1.80	.45
☐ 53 Bob Lemon	12.00	5.00	1.20
☐ 54 Ray Boone	5.00	2.00	.50
☐ 55 Gene Hermanski	4.50	1.80	.45
☐ 56 Ralph Branca	5.00	2.00	.50
☐ 57 Alex Kellner	4.50	1.80	.45

		MINT	VG-E	F-G
☐	58 Enos Slaughter	12.00	5.00	1.20
☐	59 Randy Gumpert	4.50	1.80	.45
☐	60 Chico Carrasquel	4.50	1.80	.45
☐	61 Jim Hearn	4.50	1.80	.45
☐	62 Lou Boudreau	10.00	4.00	1.00
☐	63 Bob Dillinger	4.50	1.80	.45
☐	64 Bill Werle	4.50	1.80	.45
☐	65 Mickey Vernon	5.00	2.00	.50
☐	66 Bob Elliott	5.00	2.00	.50
☐	67 Roy Sievers	5.00	2.00	.50
☐	68 Dick Kokos	4.50	1.80	.45
☐	69 Johnny Schmitz	4.50	1.80	.45
☐	70 Ron Northey	4.50	1.80	.45
☐	71 Jerry Priddy	4.50	1.80	.45
☐	72 Lloyd Merriman	4.50	1.80	.45
☐	73 Tommy Byrne	4.50	1.80	.45
☐	74 Billy Johnson	4.50	1.80	.45
☐	75 Russ Meyer	4.00	1.60	.40
☐	76 Stan Lopata	4.00	1.60	.40
☐	77 Mike Goliat	4.00	1.60	.40
☐	78 Early Wynn	12.00	5.00	1.20
☐	79 Jim Hegan	4.00	1.60	.40
☐	80 Pee Wee Reese	20.00	8.00	2.00
☐	81 Carl Furillo	7.00	2.80	.70
☐	82 Joe Tipton	4.00	1.60	.40
☐	83 Carl Scheib	4.00	1.60	.40
☐	84 Barney McCosky	4.00	1.60	.40
☐	85 Eddie Kazak	4.00	1.60	.40
☐	86 Harry Brecheen	4.00	1.60	.40
☐	87 Floyd Baker	4.00	1.60	.40
☐	88 Eddie Robinson	4.00	1.60	.40
☐	89 Hank Thompson	4.50	1.80	.45
☐	90 Dave Koslo	4.00	1.60	.40
☐	91 Clyde Vollmer	4.00	1.60	.40
☐	92 Vern Stephens	4.50	1.80	.45
☐	93 Danny O'Connell	4.00	1.60	.40
☐	94 Clyde McCullough	4.00	1.60	.40
☐	95 Sherry Robertson	4.00	1.60	.40
☐	96 Sandy Consuegra	4.00	1.60	.40
☐	97 Bob Kuzava	4.00	1.60	.40
☐	98 Willard Marshall	4.00	1.60	.40
☐	99 Earl Torgeson	4.00	1.60	.40
☐	100 Sherm Lollar	4.50	1.80	.45
☐	101 Owen Friend	4.00	1.60	.40
☐	102 Dutch Leonard	4.00	1.60	.40
☐	103 Andy Pafko	4.00	1.60	.40
☐	104 Virgil Trucks	4.00	1.60	.40
☐	105 Don Kolloway	4.00	1.60	.40
☐	106 Pat Mullin	4.00	1.60	.40
☐	107 Johnny Wyrostek	4.00	1.60	.40
☐	108 Virgil Stallcup	4.00	1.60	.40
☐	109 Allie Reynolds	6.50	2.60	.65
☐	110 Bobby Brown	6.00	2.40	.60

		MINT	VG-E	F-G
☐	111 Curt Simmons	5.00	2.00	.50
☐	112 Willie Jones	4.00	1.60	.40
☐	113 Bill Nicholson	4.00	1.60	.40
☐	114 Sam Zoldak	4.00	1.60	.40
☐	115 Steve Gromek	4.00	1.60	.40
☐	116 Bruce Edwards	4.00	1.60	.40
☐	117 Eddie Miksis	4.00	1.60	.40
☐	118 Preacher Roe	6.00	2.40	.60
☐	119 Eddie Joost	4.00	1.60	.40
☐	120 Joe Coleman	4.00	1.60	.40
☐	121 Gerry Staley	4.00	1.60	.40
☐	122 Joe Garagiola	20.00	8.00	2.00
☐	123 Howie Judson	4.00	1.60	.40
☐	124 Gus Niarhos	4.00	1.60	.40
☐	125 Bill Rigney	4.00	1.60	.40
☐	126 Bobby Thomson	6.00	2.40	.60
☐	127 Sal Maglie	7.50	3.00	.75
☐	128 Ellis Kinder	4.00	1.60	.40
☐	129 Matt Batts	4.00	1.60	.40
☐	130 Tom Saffell	4.00	1.60	.40
☐	131 Cliff Chambers	4.00	1.60	.40
☐	132 Cass Michaels	4.00	1.60	.40
☐	133 Sam Dente	4.00	1.60	.40
☐	134 Warren Spahn	21.00	8.50	2.10
☐	135 Walker Cooper	4.00	1.60	.40
☐	136 Ray Coleman	4.00	1.60	.40
☐	137 Dick Starr	4.00	1.60	.40
☐	138 Phil Cavarretta	4.50	1.80	.45
☐	139 Doyle Lade	4.00	1.60	.40
☐	140 Eddie Lake	4.00	1.60	.40
☐	141 Fred Hutchinson	4.50	1.80	.45
☐	142 Aaron Robinson	4.00	1.60	.40
☐	143 Ted Kluszewski	6.50	2.60	.65
☐	144 Herman Wehmeier	4.00	1.60	.40
☐	145 Fred Sanford	4.00	1.60	.40
☐	146 Johnny Hopp	4.00	1.60	.40
☐	147 Ken Heintzelman	4.00	1.60	.40
☐	148 Granny Hamner	4.00	1.60	.40
☐	149 Bubba Church	4.00	1.60	.40
☐	150 Mike Garcia	5.00	2.00	.50
☐	151 Larry Doby	6.50	2.60	.65
☐	152 Cal Abrams	4.00	1.60	.40
☐	153 Rex Barney	4.00	1.60	.40
☐	154 Pete Suder	4.00	1.60	.40
☐	155 Lou Brissie	4.00	1.60	.40
☐	156 Del Rice	4.00	1.60	.40
☐	157 Al Brazle	4.00	1.60	.40
☐	158 Chuck Diering	4.00	1.60	.40
☐	159 Eddie Stewart	4.00	1.60	.40
☐	160 Phil Masi	4.00	1.60	.40
☐	161 Wes Westrum	4.00	1.60	.40
☐	162 Larry Jansen	4.00	1.60	.40
☐	163 Monte Kennedy	4.00	1.60	.40

	MINT	VG-E	F-G
☐ 164 Bill Wight	4.00	1.60	.40
☐ 165 Ted Williams	120.00	50.00	12.00
☐ 166 Stan Rojek	4.00	1.60	.40
☐ 167 Murry Dickson	4.00	1.60	.40
☐ 168 Sam Mele	4.00	1.60	.40
☐ 169 Sid Hudson	4.00	1.60	.40
☐ 170 Sibby Sisti	4.00	1.60	.40
☐ 171 Buddy Kerr	4.00	1.60	.40
☐ 172 Ned Garver	4.00	1.60	.40
☐ 173 Hank Arft	4.00	1.60	.40
☐ 174 Mickey Owen	4.00	1.60	.40
☐ 175 Wayne Terwilliger	4.00	1.60	.40
☐ 176 Vic Wertz	4.00	1.60	.40
☐ 177 Charlie Keller	4.50	1.80	.45
☐ 178 Ted Gray	4.00	1.60	.40
☐ 179 Danny Litwhiler	4.00	1.60	.40
☐ 180 Howie Fox	4.00	1.60	.40
☐ 181 Casey Stengel	25.00	10.00	2.50
☐ 182 Tom Ferrick	4.00	1.60	.40
☐ 183 Hank Bauer	6.00	2.40	.60
☐ 184 Eddie Sawyer	4.00	1.60	.40
☐ 185 Jimmy Bloodworth	4.00	1.60	.40
☐ 186 Richie Ashburn	8.00	3.25	.80
☐ 187 Al Rosen	6.50	2.60	.65
☐ 188 Bobby Avila	4.50	1.80	.45
☐ 189 Erv Palica	4.00	1.60	.40
☐ 190 Joe Hatton	4.00	1.60	.40
☐ 191 Billy Hitchcock	4.00	1.60	.40
☐ 192 Hank Wyse	4.00	1.60	.40
☐ 193 Ted Wilks	4.00	1.60	.40
☐ 194 Peanuts Lowrey	4.00	1.60	.40
☐ 195 Paul Richards (caricature)	6.00	2.40	.60
☐ 196 Billy Pierce	6.50	2.60	.65
☐ 197 Bob Cain	4.00	1.60	.40
☐ 198 Monte Irvin	21.00	8.50	2.10
☐ 199 Sheldon Jones	4.00	1.60	.40
☐ 200 Jack Kramer	4.00	1.60	.40
☐ 201 Steve O'Neill	4.00	1.60	.40
☐ 202 Mike Guerra	4.00	1.60	.40
☐ 203 Vernon Law	6.00	2.40	.60
☐ 204 Vic Lombardi	4.00	1.60	.40
☐ 205 Mickey Grasso	4.00	1.60	.40
☐ 206 Conrado Marrero	4.00	1.60	.40
☐ 207 Billy Southworth	4.00	1.60	.40
☐ 208 Blix Donnelly	4.00	1.60	.40
☐ 209 Ken Wood	4.00	1.60	.40
☐ 210 Les Moss	4.00	1.60	.40
☐ 211 Hal Jeffcoat	4.00	1.60	.40
☐ 212 Bob Rush	4.00	1.60	.40
☐ 213 Neil Berry	4.00	1.60	.40
☐ 214 Bob Swift	4.00	1.60	.40
☐ 215 Ken Peterson	4.00	1.60	.40
☐ 216 Connie Ryan	4.00	1.60	.40
☐ 217 Joe Page	5.00	2.00	.50
☐ 218 Ed Lopat	6.00	2.40	.60
☐ 219 Gene Woodling	6.00	2.40	.60
☐ 220 Bob Miller	4.00	1.60	.40
☐ 221 Dick Whitman	4.00	1.60	.40
☐ 222 Thurman Tucker	4.00	1.60	.40
☐ 223 Johnny VanderMeer	5.00	2.00	.50
☐ 224 Billy Cox	4.50	1.80	.45
☐ 225 Dan Bankhead	4.00	1.60	.40
☐ 226 Jimmy Dykes	4.00	1.60	.40
☐ 227 Bobby Schantz (sic, Shantz)	5.00	2.00	.50
☐ 228 Cloyd Boyer	4.50	1.80	.45
☐ 229 Bill Howerton	4.00	1.60	.40
☐ 230 Max Lanier	4.00	1.60	.40
☐ 231 Luis Aloma	4.00	1.60	.40
☐ 232 Nelson Fox	18.00	7.25	1.80
☐ 233 Leo Durocher MGR	10.00	4.00	1.00
☐ 234 Clint Hartung	4.00	1.60	.40
☐ 235 Jack Lohrke	4.00	1.60	.40
☐ 236 Warren Rosar	4.00	1.60	.40
☐ 237 Billy Goodman	4.50	1.80	.45
☐ 238 Peter Reiser	5.00	2.00	.50
☐ 239 Bill MacDonald	4.00	1.60	.40
☐ 240 Joe Haynes	4.00	1.60	.40
☐ 241 Irv Noren	4.00	1.60	.40
☐ 242 Sam Jethroe	4.00	1.60	.40
☐ 243 Johnny Antonelli	4.50	1.80	.45
☐ 244 Cliff Fannin	4.00	1.60	.40
☐ 245 John Berardino	4.50	1.80	.45
☐ 246 Bill Serena	4.00	1.60	.40
☐ 247 Bob Ramazotti	4.00	1.60	.40
☐ 248 Johnny Klippstein	4.00	1.60	.40
☐ 249 Johnny Groth	4.00	1.60	.40
☐ 250 Hank Borowy	4.00	1.60	.40
☐ 251 Willard Ramsdell	4.00	1.60	.40
☐ 252 Dixie Howell	4.00	1.60	.40
☐ 253 Mickey Mantle	800.00	320.00	80.00
☐ 254 Jackie Jensen	21.00	8.50	2.10
☐ 255 Milo Candini	12.50	5.00	1.25
☐ 256 Ken Sylvestri	12.50	5.00	1.25
☐ 257 Birdie Tebbetts	12.50	5.00	1.25
☐ 258 Luke Easter	14.00	5.75	1.40
☐ 259 Chuck Dressen MGR	14.00	5.75	1.40
☐ 260 Carl Erskine	21.00	8.50	2.10
☐ 261 Wally Moses	12.50	5.00	1.25
☐ 262 Gus Zernial	12.50	5.00	1.25
☐ 263 Howie Pollet	12.50	5.00	1.25
☐ 264 Don Richmond	12.50	5.00	1.25
☐ 265 Steve Bilko	12.50	5.00	1.25
☐ 266 Harry Dorish	12.50	5.00	1.25
☐ 267 Ken Holcomb	12.50	5.00	1.25

		MINT	VG-E	F-G
☐ 268	Don Mueller	14.00	5.75	1.40
☐ 269	Ray Noble	12.50	5.00	1.25
☐ 270	Willard Nixon	12.50	5.00	1.25
☐ 271	Tommy Wright	12.50	5.00	1.25
☐ 272	Billy Meyer MGR	12.50	5.00	1.25
☐ 273	Danny Murtaugh	12.50	5.00	1.25
☐ 274	George Metkovich	12.50	5.00	1.25
☐ 275	Bucky Harris MGR	18.00	7.25	1.80
☐ 276	Frank Quinn	12.50	5.00	1.25
☐ 277	Roy Hartsfield	12.50	5.00	1.25
☐ 278	Norman Roy	12.50	5.00	1.25
☐ 279	Jim Delsing	12.50	5.00	1.25
☐ 280	Frank Overmire	12.50	5.00	1.25
☐ 281	Al Widmar	12.50	5.00	1.25
☐ 282	Frank Frisch	21.00	8.50	2.10
☐ 283	Walt Dubiel	12.50	5.00	1.25
☐ 284	Gene Bearden	12.50	5.00	1.25
☐ 285	Johnny Lipon	12.50	5.00	1.25
☐ 286	Bob Usher	12.50	5.00	1.25
☐ 287	Jim Blackburn	12.50	5.00	1.25
☐ 288	Bobby Adams	12.50	5.00	1.25
☐ 289	Cliff Mapes	12.50	5.00	1.25
☐ 290	Bill Dickey	45.00	18.00	4.50
☐ 291	Tommy Henrich	18.00	7.25	1.80
☐ 292	Eddie Pellegrini	12.50	5.00	1.25
☐ 293	Ken Johnson	12.50	5.00	1.25
☐ 294	Jocko Thompson	12.50	5.00	1.25
☐ 295	Al Lopez MGR	25.00	10.00	2.50
☐ 296	Bob Kennedy	12.50	5.00	1.25
☐ 297	Dave Philley	12.50	5.00	1.25
☐ 298	Joe Astroth	12.50	5.00	1.25
☐ 299	Clyde King	12.50	5.00	1.25
☐ 300	Hal Rice	12.50	5.00	1.25
☐ 301	Tommy Glaviano	12.50	5.00	1.25
☐ 302	Jim Busby	12.50	5.00	1.25
☐ 303	Marv Rotblatt	12.50	5.00	1.25
☐ 304	Al Gettell	12.50	5.00	1.25
☐ 305	Willie Mays	500.00	200.00	50.00
☐ 306	Jim Piersall	21.00	8.50	2.10
☐ 307	Walt Masterson	12.50	5.00	1.25
☐ 308	Ted Beard	12.50	5.00	1.25
☐ 309	Mel Queen	12.50	5.00	1.25
☐ 310	Erv Dusak	12.50	5.00	1.25
☐ 311	Mickey Harris	12.50	5.00	1.25
☐ 312	Gene Mauch	18.00	7.25	1.80
☐ 313	Ray Mueller	12.50	5.00	1.25
☐ 314	Johnny Sain	18.00	7.25	1.80
☐ 315	Zack Taylor	12.50	5.00	1.25
☐ 316	Duane Pillette	12.50	5.00	1.25
☐ 317	Smokey Burgess	15.00	6.00	1.50
☐ 318	Warren Hacker	12.50	5.00	1.25
☐ 319	Red Rolfe	14.00	5.75	1.40
☐ 320	Hal White	12.50	5.00	1.25

		MINT	VG-E	F-G
☐ 321	Earl Johnson	12.50	5.00	1.25
☐ 322	Luke Sewell	14.00	5.75	1.40
☐ 323	Joe Adcock	18.00	7.25	1.80
☐ 324	Johnny Pramesa	20.00	6.00	1.00

1952 Bowman

The cards in this 252-card set measure 2 1/16"
by 3 1/8". While the Bowman set of 1952 re-
tained the card size introduced in 1951, it em-
ployed a modification of color tones from the
two preceding years. The cards also appeared with a facsimile autograph on the
front and, for the first time since 1949, premium advertising on the back. The 1952 set
was sold in sheets as well as in gum packs.
Artwork for 15 cards that were never issued
was recently discovered.

		MINT	VG-E	F-G
	Complete Set	2000.00	800.00	250.00
	Common Player (1-36)	4.50	1.80	.45
	Common Player (37-180)	4.00	1.60	.40
	Common Player (181-216)	3.50	1.40	.35
	Common Player (217-252)	7.00	2.80	.70
☐ 1	Yogi Berra	125.00	20.00	4.00
☐ 2	Bobby Thomson	6.00	2.40	.60
☐ 3	Fred Hutchinson	5.00	2.00	.50
☐ 4	Robin Roberts	16.00	6.50	1.60
☐ 5	Minnie Minoso	9.00	3.75	.90
☐ 6	Virgil Stallcup	4.50	1.80	.45
☐ 7	Mike Garcia	5.00	2.00	.50
☐ 8	Pee Wee Reese	20.00	8.00	2.00

		MINT	VG-E	F-G
☐ 9	Vern Stephens	5.00	2.00	.50
☐ 10	Bob Hooper	4.50	1.80	.45
☐ 11	Ralph Kiner	16.00	6.50	1.60
☐ 12	Max Surkont	4.50	1.80	.45
☐ 13	Cliff Mapes	4.50	1.80	.45
☐ 14	Cliff Chambers	4.50	1.80	.45
☐ 15	Sam Mele	4.50	1.80	.45
☐ 16	Turk Lown	4.50	1.80	.45
☐ 17	Ed Lopat	6.50	2.60	.65
☐ 18	Don Mueller	5.00	2.00	.50
☐ 19	Bob Cain	4.50	1.80	.45
☐ 20	Willie Jones	4.50	1.80	.45
☐ 21	Nelson Fox	7.50	3.00	.75
☐ 22	Willard Ramsdell	4.50	1.80	.45
☐ 23	Bob Lemon	12.50	5.00	1.25
☐ 24	Carl Furillo	6.50	2.60	.65
☐ 25	Mickey McDermott	4.50	1.80	.45
☐ 26	Eddie Joost	4.50	1.80	.45
☐ 27	Joe Garagiola	15.00	6.00	1.50
☐ 28	Ray Hartsfield	4.50	1.80	.45
☐ 29	Ned Garver	4.50	1.80	.45
☐ 30	Red Schoendienst	6.00	2.40	.60
☐ 31	Eddie Yost	4.50	1.80	.45
☐ 32	Eddie Miksis	4.50	1.80	.45
☐ 33	Gil McDougald	9.00	3.75	.90
☐ 34	Alvin Dark	5.50	2.20	.55
☐ 35	Granny Hamner	4.50	1.80	.45
☐ 36	Cass Michaels	4.50	1.80	.45
☐ 37	Vic Raschi	5.50	2.20	.55
☐ 38	Whitey Lockman	4.50	1.80	.45
☐ 39	Vic Wertz	4.50	1.80	.45
☐ 40	Bubba Church	4.00	1.60	.40
☐ 41	Chico Carrasquel	4.00	1.60	.40
☐ 42	Johnny Wyrostek	4.00	1.60	.40
☐ 43	Bob Feller	27.00	11.00	2.70
☐ 44	Roy Campanella	50.00	20.00	5.00
☐ 45	Johnny Pesky	4.50	1.80	.45
☐ 46	Carl Scheib	4.00	1.60	.40
☐ 47	Pete Castiglione	4.00	1.60	.40
☐ 48	Vern Bickford	4.00	1.60	.40
☐ 49	Jim Hearn	4.00	1.60	.40
☐ 50	Gerry Staley	4.00	1.60	.40
☐ 51	Gil Coan	4.00	1.60	.40
☐ 52	Phil Rizzuto	18.00	7.25	1.80
☐ 53	Richie Ashburn	8.00	3.25	.80
☐ 54	Billy Pierce	5.00	2.00	.50
☐ 55	Ken Raffensberger	4.00	1.60	.40
☐ 56	Clyde King	4.00	1.60	.40
☐ 57	Clyde Vollmer	4.00	1.60	.40
☐ 58	Hank Majeski	4.00	1.60	.40
☐ 59	Murry Dickson	4.00	1.60	.40
☐ 60	Sid Gordon	4.00	1.60	.40
☐ 61	Tommy Byrne	4.00	1.60	.40
☐ 62	Joe Presko	4.00	1.60	.40
☐ 63	Irv Noren	4.00	1.60	.40
☐ 64	Roy Smalley	4.00	1.60	.40
☐ 65	Hank Bauer	6.00	2.40	.60
☐ 66	Sal Maglie	6.00	2.40	.60
☐ 67	Johnny Groth	4.00	1.60	.40
☐ 68	Jim Busby	4.00	1.60	.40
☐ 69	Joe Adcock	5.00	2.00	.50
☐ 70	Carl Erskine	6.00	2.40	.60
☐ 71	Vernon Law	5.00	2.00	.50
☐ 72	Earl Torgeson	4.00	1.60	.40
☐ 73	Gerry Coleman	4.50	1.80	.45
☐ 74	Wes Westrum	4.00	1.60	.40
☐ 75	George Kell	10.00	4.00	1.00
☐ 76	Del Ennis	4.50	1.80	.45
☐ 77	Eddie Robinson	4.00	1.60	.40
☐ 78	Lloyd Merriman	4.00	1.60	.40
☐ 79	Lou Brissie	4.00	1.60	.40
☐ 80	Gil Hodges	15.00	6.00	1.50
☐ 81	Billy Goodman	4.50	1.80	.45
☐ 82	Gus Zernial	4.00	1.60	.40
☐ 83	Howie Pollet	4.00	1.60	.40
☐ 84	Sam Jethroe	4.00	1.60	.40
☐ 85	Marty Marion	5.00	2.00	.50
☐ 86	Cal Abrams	4.00	1.60	.40
☐ 87	Mickey Vernon	4.50	1.80	.45
☐ 88	Bruce Edwards	4.00	1.60	.40
☐ 89	Billy Hitchcock	4.00	1.60	.40
☐ 90	Larry Jansen	4.00	1.60	.40
☐ 91	Don Kolloway	4.00	1.60	.40
☐ 92	Eddie Waitkus	4.00	1.60	.40
☐ 93	Paul Richards	4.00	1.60	.40
☐ 94	Luke Sewell	4.00	1.60	.40
☐ 95	Luke Easter	4.00	1.60	.40
☐ 96	Ralph Branca	4.50	1.80	.45
☐ 97	Willard Marshall	4.00	1.60	.40
☐ 98	Jimmy Dykes	4.00	1.60	.40
☐ 99	Clyde McCullough	4.00	1.60	.40
☐ 100	Sibby Sisti	4.00	1.60	.40
☐ 101	Mickey Mantle	400.00	160.00	40.00
☐ 102	Peanuts Lowrey	4.00	1.60	.40
☐ 103	Joe Haynes	4.00	1.60	.40
☐ 104	Hal Jeffcoat	4.00	1.60	.40
☐ 105	Bobby Brown	6.00	2.40	.60
☐ 106	Randy Gumpert	4.00	1.60	.40
☐ 107	Del Rice	4.00	1.60	.40
☐ 108	George Metkovich	4.00	1.60	.40
☐ 109	Tom Morgan	4.00	1.60	.40
☐ 110	Max Lanier	4.00	1.60	.40
☐ 111	Hoot Evers	4.00	1.60	.40
☐ 112	Smokey Burgess	4.50	1.80	.45
☐ 113	Al Zarilla	4.00	1.60	.40
☐ 114	Frank Hiller	4.00	1.60	.40

	MINT	VG-E	F-G			MINT	VG-E	F-G
☐ 115 Larry Doby	6.00	2.40	.60	☐ 168 Preacher Roe	6.00	2.40	.60
☐ 116 Duke Snider	36.00	15.00	3.60	☐ 169 Walt Dropo	4.00	1.60	.40
☐ 117 Bill Wight	4.00	1.60	.40	☐ 170 Joe Astroth	4.00	1.60	.40
☐ 118 Ray Murray	4.00	1.60	.40	☐ 171 Mel Queen	4.00	1.60	.40
☐ 119 Bill Howerton	4.00	1.60	.40	☐ 172 Ebba St.Claire	4.00	1.60	.40
☐ 120 Chet Nichols	4.00	1.60	.40	☐ 173 Gene Bearden	4.00	1.60	.40
☐ 121 Al Corwin	4.00	1.60	.40	☐ 174 Mickey Grasso	4.00	1.60	.40
☐ 122 Billy Johnson	4.00	1.60	.40	☐ 175 Ransom Jackson	4.00	1.60	.40
☐ 123 Sid Hudson	4.00	1.60	.40	☐ 176 Harry Brecheen	4.00	1.60	.40
☐ 124 Birdie Tebbetts	4.00	1.60	.40	☐ 177 Gene Woodling	5.00	2.00	.50
☐ 125 Howie Fox	4.00	1.60	.40	☐ 178 Dave Williams	4.50	1.80	.45
☐ 126 Phil Cavarretta	4.50	1.80	.45	☐ 179 Pete Suder	4.00	1.60	.40
☐ 127 Dick Sisler	4.00	1.60	.40	☐ 180 Eddie Fitzgerald	4.00	1.60	.40
☐ 128 Don Newcombe	6.00	2.40	.60	☐ 181 Joe Collins	4.00	1.60	.40
☐ 129 Gus Niarhos	4.00	1.60	.40	☐ 182 Dave Koslo	3.50	1.40	.35
☐ 130 Allie Clark	4.00	1.60	.40	☐ 183 Pat Mullin	3.50	1.40	.35
☐ 131 Bob Swift	4.00	1.60	.40	☐ 184 Curt Simmons	4.00	1.60	.40
☐ 132 Dave Cole	4.00	1.60	.40	☐ 185 Eddie Stewart	3.50	1.40	.35
☐ 133 Dick Kryhoski	4.00	1.60	.40	☐ 186 Frank Smith	3.50	1.40	.35
☐ 134 Al Brazle	4.00	1.60	.40	☐ 187 Jim Hegan	3.50	1.40	.35
☐ 135 Mickey Harris	4.00	1.60	.40	☐ 188 Charlie Dressen MGR	4.00	1.60	.40
☐ 136 Gene Hermanski	4.00	1.60	.40	☐ 189 Jim Piersall	5.00	2.00	.50
☐ 137 Stan Rojek	4.00	1.60	.40	☐ 190 Dick Fowler	3.50	1.40	.35
☐ 138 Ted Wilks	4.00	1.60	.40	☐ 191 Bob Friend	5.00	2.00	.50
☐ 139 Jerry Priddy	4.00	1.60	.40	☐ 192 John Cusick	3.50	1.40	.35
☐ 140 Ray Scarborough	4.00	1.60	.40	☐ 193 Bobby Young	3.50	1.40	.35
☐ 141 Hank Edwards	4.00	1.60	.40	☐ 194 Bob Porterfield	3.50	1.40	.35
☐ 142 Early Wynn	11.00	4.50	1.10	☐ 195 Frank Baumholtz	3.50	1.40	.35
☐ 143 Sandy Consuegra	4.00	1.60	.40	☐ 196 Stan Musial	125.00	50.00	12.50
☐ 144 Joe Hatton	4.00	1.60	.40	☐ 197 Charlie Silvera	3.50	1.40	.35
☐ 145 Johnny Mize	12.00	5.00	1.20	☐ 198 Chuck Diering	3.50	1.40	.35
☐ 146 Leo Durocher MGR	9.00	3.75	.90	☐ 199 Ted Gray	3.50	1.40	.35
☐ 147 Marlin Stuart	4.00	1.60	.40	☐ 200 Ken Silvestri	3.50	1.40	.35
☐ 148 Ken Heintzelman	4.00	1.60	.40	☐ 201 Ray Coleman	3.50	1.40	.35
☐ 149 Howie Judson	4.00	1.60	.40	☐ 202 Harry Perkowski	3.50	1.40	.35
☐ 150 Herman Wehmeier	4.00	1.60	.40	☐ 203 Steve Gromek	3.50	1.40	.35
☐ 151 Al Rosen	6.50	2.60	.65	☐ 204 Andy Pafko	3.50	1.40	.35
☐ 152 Billy Cox	4.50	1.80	.45	☐ 205 Walt Masterson	3.50	1.40	.35
☐ 153 Fred Hatfield	4.00	1.60	.40	☐ 206 Elmer Valo	3.50	1.40	.35
☐ 154 Ferris Fain	4.50	1.80	.45	☐ 207 George Strickland	3.50	1.40	.35
☐ 155 Billy Meyer	4.00	1.60	.40	☐ 208 Walker Cooper	3.50	1.40	.35
☐ 156 Warren Spahn	18.00	7.25	1.80	☐ 209 Dick Littlefield	3.50	1.40	.35
☐ 157 Jim Delsing	4.00	1.60	.40	☐ 210 Archie Wilson	3.50	1.40	.35
☐ 158 Bucky Harris MGR	7.50	3.00	.75	☐ 211 Paul Minner	3.50	1.40	.35
☐ 159 Dutch Leonard	4.00	1.60	.40	☐ 212 Solly Hemus	3.50	1.40	.35
☐ 160 Eddie Stanky	4.50	1.80	.45	☐ 213 Monte Kennedy	3.50	1.40	.35
☐ 161 Jackie Jensen	6.00	2.40	.60	☐ 214 Ray Boone	3.50	1.40	.35
☐ 162 Monte Irvin	10.00	4.00	1.00	☐ 215 Sheldon Jones	3.50	1.40	.35
☐ 163 Johnny Lipon	4.00	1.60	.40	☐ 216 Matt Batts	3.50	1.40	.35
☐ 164 Connie Ryan	4.00	1.60	.40	☐ 217 Casey Stengel	30.00	12.00	3.00
☐ 165 Saul Rogovin	4.00	1.60	.40	☐ 218 Willie Mays	300.00	120.00	30.00
☐ 166 Bobby Adams	4.00	1.60	.40	☐ 219 Neil Berry	7.00	2.80	.70
☐ 167 Bobby Avila	4.50	1.80	.45	☐ 220 Russ Meyer	7.00	2.80	.70

		MINT	VG-E	F-G
☐ 221	Lou Kretlow	7.00	2.80	.70
☐ 222	Dixie Howell	7.00	2.80	.70
☐ 223	Harry Simpson	7.00	2.80	.70
☐ 224	Johnny Schmitz	7.00	2.80	.70
☐ 225	Del Wilber	7.00	2.80	.70
☐ 226	Alex Kellner	7.00	2.80	.70
☐ 227	Clyde Sukeforth	7.00	2.80	.70
☐ 228	Bob Chipman	7.00	2.80	.70
☐ 229	Hank Arft	7.00	2.80	.70
☐ 230	Frank Shea	7.00	2.80	.70
☐ 231	Dee Fondy	7.00	2.80	.70
☐ 232	Enos Slaughter	21.00	8.50	2.10
☐ 233	Bob Kuzava	7.00	2.80	.70
☐ 234	Fred Fitzsimmons	7.00	2.80	.70
☐ 235	Steve Souchock	7.00	2.80	.70
☐ 236	Tommy Brown	7.00	2.80	.70
☐ 237	Sherman Lollar	8.00	3.25	.80
☐ 238	Roy McMillan	7.00	2.80	.70
☐ 239	Dale Mitchell	8.00	3.25	.80
☐ 240	Billy Loes	8.00	3.25	.80
☐ 241	Mel Parnell	8.00	3.25	.80
☐ 242	Everett Kell	7.00	2.80	.70
☐ 243	Red Munger	7.00	2.80	.70
☐ 244	Lew Burdette	16.00	6.50	1.60
☐ 245	George Schmees	7.00	2.80	.70
☐ 246	Jerry Snyder	7.00	2.80	.70
☐ 247	John Pramesa	7.00	2.80	.70
☐ 248	Bill Werle	7.00	2.80	.70
☐ 249	Hank Thompson	8.00	3.25	.80
☐ 250	Ivan Delock	7.00	2.80	.70
☐ 251	Jack Lohrke	7.00	2.80	.70
☐ 252	Frank Crosetti	30.00	5.00	1.00

1953 Bowman Color

The cards in this 160-card set measure 2½" by 3¾". The 1953 Bowman Color set, consid-ered by many to be the best looking set of the modern era, contains Kodachrome photo-graphs with no names or facsimile auto-graphs on the face. Numbers 113 to 160 are somewhat more difficult to obtain. There are two cards of Al Corwin (126 and 149). Card number 159 is actually a picture of Floyd Baker.

		MINT	VG-E	F-G
	Complete Set	2750.00	1200.00	300.00
	Common Player (1-96)	7.00	2.80	.70
	Common Player (97-112)	8.00	3.25	.80
	Common Player (113-128)	18.00	7.25	1.80
	Common Player (129-160)	12.00	5.00	1.20
☐ 1	Dave Williams	30.00	4.00	.80
☐ 2	Vic Wertz	7.00	2.80	.70
☐ 3	Sam Jethroe	7.00	2.80	.70
☐ 4	Art Houtteman	7.00	2.80	.70
☐ 5	Sid Gordon	7.00	2.80	.70
☐ 6	Joe Ginsberg	7.00	2.80	.70
☐ 7	Harry Chiti	7.00	2.80	.70
☐ 8	Al Rosen	10.00	4.00	1.00
☐ 9	Phil Rizzuto	27.00	11.00	2.70
☐ 10	Richie Ashburn	12.50	5.00	1.25
☐ 11	Bobby Shantz	8.00	3.25	.80
☐ 12	Carl Erskine	10.00	4.00	1.00
☐ 13	Gus Zernial	7.00	2.80	.70
☐ 14	Billy Loes	8.00	3.25	.80
☐ 15	Jim Busby	7.00	2.80	.70
☐ 16	Bob Friend	8.00	3.25	.80
☐ 17	Jerry Staley	7.00	2.80	.70
☐ 18	Nelson Fox	12.50	5.00	1.25
☐ 19	Alvin Dark	8.00	3.25	.80
☐ 20	Don Lenhardt	7.00	2.80	.70
☐ 21	Joe Garagiola	18.00	7.25	1.80
☐ 22	Bob Porterfield	7.00	2.80	.70
☐ 23	Herman Wehmeier	7.00	2.80	.70
☐ 24	Jackie Jensen	9.00	3.75	.90
☐ 25	Hoot Evers	7.00	2.80	.70
☐ 26	Roy McMillan	7.00	2.80	.70
☐ 27	Vic Raschi	9.00	3.75	.90
☐ 28	Smokey Burgess	8.00	3.25	.80
☐ 29	Bobby Avila	8.00	3.25	.80
☐ 30	Phil Cavarretta	8.00	3.25	.80
☐ 31	Jimmy Dykes	8.00	3.25	.80
☐ 32	Stan Musial	150.00	60.00	15.00
☐ 33	Pee Wee Reese HOR	40.00	16.00	4.00
☐ 34	Gil Coan	7.00	2.80	.70
☐ 35	Maurice McDermott	7.00	2.80	.70

		MINT	VG-E	F-G
☐ 36	Minnie Minoso	10.00	4.00	1.00
☐ 37	Jim Wilson	7.00	2.80	.70
☐ 38	Harry Byrd	7.00	2.80	.70
☐ 39	Paul Richards MGR	7.00	2.80	.70
☐ 40	Larry Doby	9.00	3.75	.90
☐ 41	Sammy White	7.00	2.80	.70
☐ 42	Tommy Brown	7.00	2.80	.70
☐ 43	Mike Garcia	8.00	3.25	.80
☐ 44	Berra/Bauer/Mantle	120.00	50.00	12.00
☐ 45	Walt Dropo	7.00	2.80	.70
☐ 46	Roy Campanella	80.00	32.00	8.00
☐ 47	Ned Garver	7.00	2.80	.70
☐ 48	Hank Sauer	8.00	3.25	.80
☐ 49	Eddie Stanky	8.00	3.25	.80
☐ 50	Lou Kretlow	7.00	2.80	.70
☐ 51	Monte Irvin	15.00	6.00	1.50
☐ 52	Marty Marion	9.00	3.75	.90
☐ 53	Del Rice	7.00	2.80	.70
☐ 54	Chico Carrasquel	7.00	2.80	.70
☐ 55	Leo Durocher MGR	11.00	4.50	1.10
☐ 56	Bob Cain	7.00	2.80	.70
☐ 57	Lou Boudreau MGR	14.00	5.75	1.40
☐ 58	Willard Marshall	7.00	2.80	.70
☐ 59	Mickey Mantle	400.00	160.00	40.00
☐ 60	Granny Hamner	7.00	2.80	.70
☐ 61	George Kell	16.00	6.50	1.60
☐ 62	Ted Kluszewski	11.00	4.50	1.10
☐ 63	Gil McDougald	10.00	4.00	1.00
☐ 64	Curt Simmons	8.00	3.25	.80
☐ 65	Robin Roberts	20.00	8.00	2.00
☐ 66	Mel Parnell	7.00	2.80	.70
☐ 67	Mel Clark	7.00	2.80	.70
☐ 68	Allie Reynolds	11.00	4.50	1.10
☐ 69	Charley Grimm MGR	7.00	2.80	.70
☐ 70	Clint Courtney	7.00	2.80	.70
☐ 71	Paul Minner	7.00	2.80	.70
☐ 72	Ted Gray	7.00	2.80	.70
☐ 73	Billy Pierce	9.00	3.75	.90
☐ 74	Don Mueller	7.00	2.80	.70
☐ 75	Saul Rogovin	7.00	2.80	.70
☐ 76	Jim Hearn	7.00	2.80	.70
☐ 77	Mickey Grasso	7.00	2.80	.70
☐ 78	Carl Furillo	11.00	4.50	1.10
☐ 79	Ray Boone	7.00	2.80	.70
☐ 80	Ralph Kiner	16.00	6.50	1.60
☐ 81	Enos Slaughter	16.00	6.50	1.60
☐ 82	Joe Astroth	7.00	2.80	.70
☐ 83	Jack Daniels	7.00	2.80	.70
☐ 84	Hank Bauer	9.00	3.75	.90
☐ 85	Solly Hemus	7.00	2.80	.70
☐ 86	Harry Simpson	7.00	2.80	.70
☐ 87	Harry Perkowski	7.00	2.80	.70
☐ 88	Joe Dobson	7.00	2.80	.70
☐ 89	Sandy Consuegra	7.00	2.80	.70
☐ 90	Joe Nuxhall	8.00	3.25	.80
☐ 91	Steve Souchock	7.00	2.80	.70
☐ 92	Gil Hodges	27.00	11.00	2.70
☐ 93	Phil Rizzuto and Billy Martin	65.00	26.00	6.50
☐ 94	Bob Addis	7.00	2.80	.70
☐ 95	Wally Moses	7.00	2.80	.70
☐ 96	Sal Maglie	10.00	4.00	1.00
☐ 97	Ed Mathews	30.00	12.00	3.00
☐ 98	Hector Rodriguez	8.00	3.25	.80
☐ 99	Warren Spahn	30.00	12.00	3.00
☐ 100	Bill Wight	8.00	3.25	.80
☐ 101	Red Schoendienst	12.00	5.00	1.20
☐ 102	Jim Hegan	8.00	3.25	.80
☐ 103	Del Ennis	9.00	3.75	.90
☐ 104	Luke Easter	9.00	3.75	.90
☐ 105	Eddie Joost	8.00	3.25	.80
☐ 106	Ken Raffensberger	8.00	3.25	.80
☐ 107	Alex Kellner	8.00	3.25	.80
☐ 108	Bobby Adams	8.00	3.25	.80
☐ 109	Ken Wood	8.00	3.25	.80
☐ 110	Bob Rush	8.00	3.25	.80
☐ 111	Jim Dyck	8.00	3.25	.80
☐ 112	Toby Atwell	8.00	3.25	.80
☐ 113	Karl Drews	18.00	7.25	1.80
☐ 114	Bob Feller	120.00	50.00	12.00
☐ 115	Cloyd Boyer	21.00	8.50	2.10
☐ 116	Eddie Yost	18.00	7.25	1.80
☐ 117	Duke Snider	250.00	100.00	25.00
☐ 118	Billy Martin	90.00	36.00	9.00
☐ 119	Dale Mitchell	21.00	8.50	2.10
☐ 120	Marlin Stuart	18.00	7.25	1.80
☐ 121	Yogi Berra	200.00	80.00	20.00
☐ 122	Bill Serena	18.00	7.25	1.80
☐ 123	Johnny Lipon	18.00	7.25	1.80
☐ 124	Charlie Dressen MGR	21.00	8.50	2.10
☐ 125	Fred Hatfield	18.00	7.25	1.80
☐ 126	Al Corwin	18.00	7.25	1.80
☐ 127	Dick Kryhoski	18.00	7.25	1.80
☐ 128	Whitey Lockman	18.00	7.25	1.80
☐ 129	Russ Meyer	12.00	5.00	1.20
☐ 130	Cass Michaels	12.00	5.00	1.20
☐ 131	Connie Ryan	12.00	5.00	1.20
☐ 132	Fred Hutchinson	16.00	6.50	1.60
☐ 133	Willie Jones	12.00	5.00	1.20
☐ 134	Johnny Pesky	12.00	5.00	1.20
☐ 135	Bobby Morgan	12.00	5.00	1.20
☐ 136	Jim Brideweser	12.00	5.00	1.20
☐ 137	Sam Dente	12.00	5.00	1.20
☐ 138	Bubba Church	12.00	5.00	1.20
☐ 139	Pete Runnels	16.00	6.50	1.60
☐ 140	Al Brazle	12.00	5.00	1.20

		MINT	VG-E	F-G
☐ 141	Frank Shea	12.00	5.00	1.20
☐ 142	Larry Miggins	12.00	5.00	1.20
☐ 143	Al Lopez MGR	21.00	8.50	2.10
☐ 144	Warren Hacker	12.00	5.00	1.20
☐ 145	George Shuba	12.00	5.00	1.20
☐ 146	Early Wynn	50.00	20.00	5.00
☐ 147	Clem Koshorek	12.00	5.00	1.20
☐ 148	Billy Goodman	12.00	5.00	1.20
☐ 149	Al Corwin	12.00	5.00	1.20
☐ 150	Carl Scheib	12.00	5.00	1.20
☐ 151	Joe Adcock	15.00	6.00	1.50
☐ 152	Clyde Vollmer	12.00	5.00	1.20
☐ 153	Whitey Ford	150.00	60.00	15.00
☐ 154	Turk Lown	12.00	5.00	1.20
☐ 155	Allie Clark	12.00	5.00	1.20
☐ 156	Max Surkont	12.00	5.00	1.20
☐ 157	Sherman Lollar	12.00	5.00	1.20
☐ 158	Howard Fox	12.00	5.00	1.20
☐ 159	Mickey Vernon (photo actually Floyd Baker)	16.00	6.50	1.60
☐ 160	Cal Abrams	18.00	6.00	1.00

1953 Bowman BW

The cards in this 64-card set measure 2½" by 3¾". Some collectors believe that the high cost of producing the 1953 color series forced Bowman to issue this set in black and white, since the two sets are identical in design except for the element of color. This set was also produced in fewer numbers than its color counterpart, and is popular among collectors for the challenge involved in completing it.

	MINT	VG-E	F-G
Complete Set	1000.00	400.00	125.00
Common Player (1-64)	13.00	5.25	1.30

		MINT	VG-E	F-G
☐ 1	Gus Bell	40.00	8.00	1.50
☐ 2	Willard Nixon	13.00	5.25	1.30
☐ 3	Bill Rigney	13.00	5.25	1.30
☐ 4	Pat Mullin	13.00	5.25	1.30
☐ 5	Dee Fondy	13.00	5.25	1.30
☐ 6	Ray Murray	13.00	5.25	1.30
☐ 7	Andy Seminick	13.00	5.25	1.30
☐ 8	Pete Suder	13.00	5.25	1.30
☐ 9	Walt Masterson	13.00	5.25	1.30
☐ 10	Dick Sisler	13.00	5.25	1.30
☐ 11	Dick Gernert	13.00	5.25	1.30
☐ 12	Randy Jackson	13.00	5.25	1.30
☐ 13	Joe Tipton	13.00	5.25	1.30
☐ 14	Bill Nicholson	13.00	5.25	1.30
☐ 15	Johnny Mize	45.00	18.00	4.50
☐ 16	Stu Miller	13.00	5.25	1.30
☐ 17	Virgil Trucks	15.00	6.00	1.50
☐ 18	Billy Hoeft	13.00	5.25	1.30
☐ 19	Paul LaPalme	13.00	5.25	1.30
☐ 20	Eddie Robinson	13.00	5.25	1.30
☐ 21	Clarence Podbielan	13.00	5.25	1.30
☐ 22	Matt Batts	13.00	5.25	1.30
☐ 23	Wilmer Mizell	15.00	6.00	1.50
☐ 24	Del Wilber	13.00	5.25	1.30
☐ 25	Johnny Sain	25.00	10.00	2.50
☐ 26	Preacher Roe	25.00	10.00	2.50
☐ 27	Bob Lemon	45.00	18.00	4.50
☐ 28	Hoyt Wilhelm	45.00	18.00	4.50
☐ 29	Sid Hudson	13.00	5.25	1.30
☐ 30	Walker Cooper	13.00	5.25	1.30
☐ 31	Gene Woodling	18.00	7.25	1.80
☐ 32	Rocky Bridges	13.00	5.25	1.30
☐ 33	Bob Kuzava	13.00	5.25	1.30
☐ 34	Ebba St.Claire	13.00	5.25	1.30
☐ 35	Johnny Wyrostek	13.00	5.25	1.30
☐ 36	Jim Piersall	21.00	8.50	2.10
☐ 37	Hal Jeffcoat	13.00	5.25	1.30
☐ 38	Dave Cole	13.00	5.25	1.30
☐ 39	Casey Stengel	150.00	60.00	15.00
☐ 40	Larry Jansen	13.00	5.25	1.30
☐ 41	Bob Ramazotti	13.00	5.25	1.30
☐ 42	Howie Judson	13.00	5.25	1.30
☐ 43	Hal Bevan	13.00	5.25	1.30
☐ 44	Jim Delsing	13.00	5.25	1.30
☐ 45	Irv Noren	13.00	5.25	1.30
☐ 46	Bucky Harris	25.00	10.00	2.50
☐ 47	Jack Lohrke	13.00	5.25	1.30
☐ 48	Steve Ridzik	13.00	5.25	1.30
☐ 49	Floyd Baker	13.00	5.25	1.30
☐ 50	Dutch Leonard	13.00	5.25	1.30
☐ 51	Lou Burdette	20.00	8.00	2.00
☐ 52	Ralph Branca	16.00	6.50	1.60
☐ 53	Morris Martin	13.00	5.25	1.30

		MINT	VG-E	F-G
☐ 54	Bill Miller	13.00	5.25	1.30
☐ 55	Don Johnson	13.00	5.25	1.30
☐ 56	Roy Smalley	13.00	5.25	1.30
☐ 57	Andy Pafko	13.00	5.25	1.30
☐ 58	Jim Konstanty	15.00	6.00	1.50
☐ 59	Duane Pillette	13.00	5.25	1.30
☐ 60	Billy Cox	15.00	6.00	1.50
☐ 61	Tom Gorman	13.00	5.25	1.30
☐ 62	Keith Thomas	13.00	5.25	1.30
☐ 63	Steve Gromek	13.00	5.25	1.30
☐ 64	Andy Hansen	18.00	6.00	1.25

1954 Bowman

*The cards in this 224-card set measure 2½"
by 3¾". A contractual problem apparently resulted in the deletion of the number 66 Ted
Williams card from this Bowman set, thereby
creating a scarcity which is highly valued
among collectors. The set price below does
NOT include number 66 Williams. Many errors in players' statistics exist (and some
were corrected) while a few players' names
were printed on the front, instead of appearing as a facsimile autograph.*

		MINT	VG-E	F-G
	Complete Set	950.00	400.00	95.00
	Common Player (1-128)	1.75	.70	.17
	Common Player (129-224)	2.25	.90	.22
☐ 1	Phil Rizzuto	60.00	10.00	2.50
☐ 2	Jackie Jensen	3.00	1.20	.30
☐ 3	Marion Fricano	1.75	.70	.17
☐ 4	Bob Hooper	1.75	.70	.17
☐ 5	Bill Hunter	1.75	.70	.17

		MINT	VG-E	F-G
☐ 6	Nelson Fox	4.50	1.80	.45
☐ 7	Walt Dropo	1.75	.70	.17
☐ 8	Jim Busby	1.75	.70	.17
☐ 9	Davey Williams	2.25	.90	.22
☐ 10	Carl Erskine	3.50	1.40	.35
☐ 11	Sid Gordon	1.75	.70	.17
☐ 12	Roy McMillan	1.75	.70	.17
☐ 13	Paul Minner	1.75	.70	.17
☐ 14	Gerry Staley	1.75	.70	.17
☐ 15	Richie Ashburn	5.00	2.00	.50
☐ 16	Jim Wilson	1.75	.70	.17
☐ 17	Tom Gorman	1.75	.70	.17
☐ 18	Hoot Evers	1.75	.70	.17
☐ 19	Bobby Shantz	2.25	.90	.22
☐ 20	Art Houtteman	1.75	.70	.17
☐ 21	Vic Wertz	1.75	.70	.17
☐ 22	Sam Mele	1.75	.70	.17
☐ 23	Harvey Kuenn	6.00	2.40	.60
☐ 24	Bob Porterfield	1.75	.70	.17
☐ 25	Wes Westrum	1.75	.70	.17
☐ 26	Billy Cox	2.25	.90	.22
☐ 27	Dick Cole	1.75	.70	.17
☐ 28	Jim Greengrass	1.75	.70	.17
☐ 29	Johnny Klippstein	1.75	.70	.17
☐ 30	Del Rice	1.75	.70	.17
☐ 31	Smoky Burgess	2.25	.90	.22
☐ 32	Del Crandall	2.25	.90	.22
☐ 33 A	Vic Raschi (no mention of trade on back)	2.75	1.10	.27
☐ 33 B	Vic Raschi (traded to St.Louis)	12.00	5.00	1.20
☐ 34	Sammy White	1.75	.70	.17
☐ 35	Eddie Joost	1.75	.70	.17
☐ 36	George Strickland	1.75	.70	.17
☐ 37	Dick Kokos	1.75	.70	.17
☐ 38	Minnie Minoso	3.50	1.40	.35
☐ 39	Ned Garver	1.75	.70	.17
☐ 40	Gil Coan	1.75	.70	.17
☐ 41	Alvin Dark	2.25	.90	.22
☐ 42	Billy Loes	1.75	.70	.17
☐ 43	Bob Friend	2.25	.90	.22
☐ 44	Harry Perkowski	1.75	.70	.17
☐ 45	Ralph Kiner	11.00	4.50	1.10
☐ 46	Rip Repulski	1.75	.70	.17
☐ 47	Granny Hamner	1.75	.70	.17
☐ 48	Jack Dittmer	1.75	.70	.17
☐ 49	Harry Byrd	1.75	.70	.17
☐ 50	George Kell	8.00	3.25	.80
☐ 51	Alex Kellner	1.75	.70	.17
☐ 52	Joe Ginsberg	1.75	.70	.17
☐ 53	Don Lenhardt	1.75	.70	.17
☐ 54	Chico Carrasquel	1.75	.70	.17

		MINT	VG-E	F-G			MINT	VG-E	F-G
☐	55 Jim Delsing	1.75	.70	.17	☐	107 Paul LaPalme	1.75	.70	.17
☐	56 Maurice McDermott	1.75	.70	.17	☐	108 Bobby Adams	1.75	.70	.17
☐	57 Hoyt Wilhelm	8.00	3.25	.80	☐	109 Roy Smalley	1.75	.70	.17
☐	58 Pee Wee Reese	14.00	5.75	1.40	☐	110 Red Schoendienst	2.75	1.10	.27
☐	59 Bob Schultz	1.75	.70	.17	☐	111 Murry Dickson	1.75	.70	.17
☐	60 Fred Baczewski	1.75	.70	.17	☐	112 Andy Pafko	1.75	.70	.17
☐	61 Eddie Miksis	1.75	.70	.17	☐	113 Allie Reynolds	3.50	1.40	.35
☐	62 Enos Slaughter	8.00	3.25	.80	☐	114 Willard Nixon	1.75	.70	.17
☐	63 Earl Torgeson	1.75	.70	.17	☐	115 Don Bollweg	1.75	.70	.17
☐	64 Eddie Mathews	11.00	4.50	1.10	☐	116 Luke Easter	1.75	.70	.17
☐	65 Mickey Mantle	200.00	80.00	20.00	☐	117 Dick Kryhoski	1.75	.70	.17
☐	66 A Jim Piersall	60.00	24.00	6.00	☐	118 Bob Boyd	1.75	.70	.17
☐	66 B Ted Williams	900.00	360.00	90.00	☐	119 Fred Hatfield	1.75	.70	.17
☐	67 Carl Scheib	1.75	.70	.17	☐	120 Mel Hoderlein	1.75	.70	.17
☐	68 Bobby Avila	1.75	.70	.17	☐	121 Ray Katt	1.75	.70	.17
☐	69 Clint Courtney	1.75	.70	.17	☐	122 Carl Furillo	3.50	1.40	.35
☐	70 Willard Marshall	1.75	.70	.17	☐	123 Toby Atwell	1.75	.70	.17
☐	71 Ted Gray	1.75	.70	.17	☐	124 Gus Bell	1.75	.70	.17
☐	72 Eddie Yost	1.75	.70	.17	☐	125 Warren Hacker	1.75	.70	.17
☐	73 Don Mueller	2.25	.90	.22	☐	126 Cliff Chambers	1.75	.70	.17
☐	74 Jim Gilliam	3.50	1.40	.35	☐	127 Del Ennis	1.75	.70	.17
☐	75 Max Surkont	1.75	.70	.17	☐	128 Ebba St.Claire	2.25	.90	.22
☐	76 Joe Nuxhall	2.25	.90	.22	☐	129 Hank Bauer	3.50	1.40	.35
☐	77 Bob Rush	1.75	.70	.17	☐	130 Milt Bolling	2.25	.90	.22
☐	78 Sal Yvars	1.75	.70	.17	☐	131 Joe Astroth	2.25	.90	.22
☐	79 Curt Simmons	2.25	.90	.22	☐	132 Bob Feller	20.00	8.00	2.00
☐	80 Johnny Logan	2.25	.90	.22	☐	133 Duane Pillette	2.25	.90	.22
☐	81 Jerry Coleman	2.25	.90	.22	☐	134 Luis Aloma	2.25	.90	.22
☐	82 Billy Goodman	1.75	.70	.17	☐	135 Johnny Pesky	2.25	.90	.22
☐	83 Ray Murray	1.75	.70	.17	☐	136 Clyde Vollmer	2.25	.90	.22
☐	84 Larry Doby	3.50	1.40	.35	☐	137 Al Corwin	2.25	.90	.22
☐	85 Jim Dyck	1.75	.70	.17	☐	138 Gil Hodges	14.00	5.75	1.40
☐	86 Harry Dorish	1.75	.70	.17	☐	139 Preston Ward	2.25	.90	.22
☐	87 Don Lund	1.75	.70	.17	☐	140 Saul Rogovin	2.25	.90	.22
☐	88 Tom Umphlett	1.75	.70	.17	☐	141 Joe Garagiola	12.50	5.00	1.25
☐	89 Willie Mays	100.00	40.00	10.00	☐	142 Al Brazle	2.25	.90	.22
☐	90 Roy Campanella	36.00	15.00	3.60	☐	143 Willie Jones	2.25	.90	.22
☐	91 Cal Abrams	1.75	.70	.17	☐	144 Ernie Johnson	2.25	.90	.22
☐	92 Ken Raffensberger	1.75	.70	.17	☐	145 Billy Martin	15.00	6.00	1.50
☐	93 Bill Serena	1.75	.70	.17	☐	146 Dick Gernert	2.25	.90	.22
☐	94 Solly Hemus	1.75	.70	.17	☐	147 Joe DeMaestri	2.25	.90	.22
☐	95 Robin Roberts	9.00	3.75	.90	☐	148 Dale Mitchell	2.75	1.10	.27
☐	96 Joe Adcock	2.25	.90	.22	☐	149 Bob Young	2.25	.90	.22
☐	97 Gil McDougald	3.00	1.20	.30	☐	150 Cass Michaels	2.25	.90	.22
☐	98 Ellis Kinder	1.75	.70	.17	☐	151 Pat Mullin	2.25	.90	.22
☐	99 Pete Suder	1.75	.70	.17	☐	152 Mickey Vernon	2.75	1.10	.27
☐	100 Mike Garcia	2.25	.90	.22	☐	153 Whitey Lockman	2.25	.90	.22
☐	101 Don Larsen	5.00	2.00	.50	☐	154 Don Newcombe	3.50	1.40	.35
☐	102 Billy Pierce	2.50	1.00	.25	☐	155 Frank Thomas	2.75	1.10	.27
☐	103 Steve Souchock	1.75	.70	.17	☐	156 Rocky Bridges	2.25	.90	.22
☐	104 Frank Shea	1.75	.70	.17	☐	157 Turk Lown	2.25	.90	.22
☐	105 Sal Maglie	2.75	1.10	.27	☐	158 Stu Miller	2.25	.90	.22
☐	106 Clem Labine	2.25	.90	.22	☐	159 Johnny Lindell	2.25	.90	.22

	MINT	VG-E	F-G
☐ 160 Danny O'Connell	2.25	.90	.22
☐ 161 Yogi Berra	35.00	14.00	3.50
☐ 162 Ted Lepcio	2.25	.90	.22
☐ 163 A Dave Philley	2.75	1.10	.27
(no mention of			
trade on back)			
☐ 163 B Dave Philley	12.00	5.00	1.20
(traded to			
Cleveland)			
☐ 164 Early Wynn	10.00	4.00	1.00
☐ 165 Johnny Groth	2.25	.90	.22
☐ 166 Sandy Consuegra	2.25	.90	.22
☐ 167 Billy Hoeft	2.25	.90	.22
☐ 168 Ed Fitzgerald	2.25	.90	.22
☐ 169 Larry Jansen	2.25	.90	.22
☐ 170 Duke Snider	35.00	14.00	3.50
☐ 171 Carlos Bernier	2.25	.90	.22
☐ 172 Andy Seminick	2.25	.90	.22
☐ 173 Dee Fondy	2.25	.90	.22
☐ 174 Pete Castiglione	2.25	.90	.22
☐ 175 Mel Clark	2.25	.90	.22
☐ 176 Vern Bickford	2.25	.90	.22
☐ 177 Whitey Ford	21.00	8.50	2.10
☐ 178 Del Wilber	2.25	.90	.22
☐ 179 Morris Martin	2.25	.90	.22
☐ 180 Joe Tipton	2.25	.90	.22
☐ 181 Les Moss	2.25	.90	.22
☐ 182 Sherman Lollar	2.75	1.10	.27
☐ 183 Matt Batts	2.25	.90	.22
☐ 184 Mickey Grasso	2.25	.90	.22
☐ 185 Daryl Spencer	2.25	.90	.22
☐ 186 Russ Meyer	2.25	.90	.22
☐ 187 Vernon Law	2.75	1.10	.27
☐ 188 Frank Smith	2.25	.90	.22
☐ 189 Randy Jackson	2.25	.90	.22
☐ 190 Joe Presko	2.25	.90	.22
☐ 191 Karl Drews	2.25	.90	.22
☐ 192 Lou Burdette	3.50	1.40	.35
☐ 193 Eddie Robinson	2.25	.90	.22
☐ 194 Sid Hudson	2.25	.90	.22
☐ 195 Bob Cain	2.25	.90	.22
☐ 196 Bob Lemon	10.00	4.00	1.00
☐ 197 Lou Kretlow	2.25	.90	.22
☐ 198 Virgil Trucks	2.75	1.10	.27
☐ 199 Steve Gromek	2.25	.90	.22
☐ 200 Conrado Marrero	2.25	.90	.22
☐ 201 Bobby Thomson	3.50	1.40	.35
☐ 202 George Shuba	2.75	1.10	.27
☐ 203 Vic Janowicz	2.75	1.10	.27
☐ 204 Jackie Collum	2.25	.90	.22
☐ 205 Hal Jeffcoat	2.25	.90	.22
☐ 206 Steve Bilko	2.25	.90	.22
☐ 207 Stan Lopata	2.25	.90	.22

	MINT	VG-E	F-G
☐ 208 Johnny Antonelli	2.75	1.10	.27
☐ 209 Gene Woodling	3.00	1.20	.30
☐ 210 Jim Piersall	3.50	1.40	.35
☐ 211 Al Robertson	2.25	.90	.22
☐ 212 Owen Friend	2.25	.90	.22
☐ 213 Dick Littlefield	2.25	.90	.22
☐ 214 Ferris Fain	2.75	1.10	.27
☐ 215 Johnny Bucha	2.25	.90	.22
☐ 216 Jerry Snyder	2.25	.90	.22
☐ 217 Henry Thompson	2.75	1.10	.27
☐ 218 Preacher Roe	3.50	1.40	.35
☐ 219 Hal Rice	2.25	.90	.22
☐ 220 Hobie Landrith	2.25	.90	.22
☐ 221 Frank Baumholtz	2.25	.90	.22
☐ 222 Memo Luna	2.25	.90	.22
☐ 223 Steve Ridzik	2.25	.90	.22
☐ 224 Bill Bruton	4.00	1.00	.27

1955 Bowman

The cards in this 320-card set measure 2½"
by 3¾". The Bowman set of 1955 is known as
the "TV set" because each player photograph is cleverly shown within a television set
design. The set contains umpire cards, some
transposed pictures (e.g., Johnsons and
Bollings), an incorrect spelling for Harvey
Kuenn, and a traded line for Palica (all of
which are noted in the checklist below).
Some three-card advertising strips exist.

	MINT	VG-E	F-G
Complete Set	1000.00	400.00	125.00
Common Player (1-96)	1.25	.50	.12
Common Player (97-224)	.90	.36	.09
Common Player			
(225-320)	3.50	1.40	.35

		MINT	VG-E	F-G
	Common Umpires (225-320)	6.00	2.40	.60
☐	1 Hoyt Wilhelm	30.00	5.00	1.00
☐	2 Alvin Dark	1.75	.70	.17
☐	3 Joe Coleman	1.25	.50	.12
☐	4 Eddie Waitkus	1.25	.50	.12
☐	5 Jim Robertson	1.25	.50	.12
☐	6 Pete Suder	1.25	.50	.12
☐	7 Gene Baker	1.25	.50	.12
☐	8 Warren Hacker	1.25	.50	.12
☐	9 Gil McDougald	2.50	1.00	.25
☐	10 Phil Rizzuto	13.00	5.25	1.30
☐	11 Billy Bruton	1.25	.50	.12
☐	12 Andy Pafko	1.25	.50	.12
☐	13 Clyde Vollmer	1.25	.50	.12
☐	14 Gus Keriazakos	1.25	.50	.12
☐	15 Frank Sullivan	1.25	.50	.12
☐	16 Jim Piersall	2.00	.80	.20
☐	17 Del Ennis	1.50	.60	.15
☐	18 Stan Lopata	1.25	.50	.12
☐	19 Bobby Avila	1.25	.50	.12
☐	20 Al Smith	1.25	.50	.12
☐	21 Don Hoak	1.25	.50	.12
☐	22 Roy Campanella	27.00	11.00	2.70
☐	23 Al Kaline	16.00	6.50	1.60
☐	24 Al Aber	1.25	.50	.12
☐	25 Minnie Minoso	2.50	1.00	.25
☐	26 Virgil Trucks	1.25	.50	.12
☐	27 Preston Ward	1.25	.50	.12
☐	28 Dick Cole	1.25	.50	.12
☐	29 Red Schoendienst	2.00	.80	.20
☐	30 Bill Sarni	1.25	.50	.12
☐	31 Johnny Temple	1.50	.60	.15
☐	32 Wally Post	1.25	.50	.12
☐	33 Nelson Fox	3.50	1.40	.35
☐	34 Clint Courtney	1.25	.50	.12
☐	35 Bill Tuttle	1.25	.50	.12
☐	36 Wayne Belardi	1.25	.50	.12
☐	37 Pee Wee Reese	16.00	6.50	1.60
☐	38 Early Wynn	7.50	3.00	.75
☐	39 Bob Darnell	1.25	.50	.12
☐	40 Vic Wertz	1.25	.50	.12
☐	41 Mel Clark	1.25	.50	.12
☐	42 Bob Greenwood	1.25	.50	.12
☐	43 Bob Buhl	1.25	.50	.12
☐	44 Danny O'Connell	1.25	.50	.12
☐	45 Tom Umphlett	1.25	.50	.12
☐	46 Mickey Vernon	1.50	.60	.15
☐	47 Sammy White	1.25	.50	.12
☐	48 A Milt Bolling ERR (photo actually Frank Bolling)	1.50	.60	.15

		MINT	VG-E	F-G
☐	48 B Milt Bolling COR	6.00	2.40	.60
☐	49 Jim Greengrass	1.25	.50	.12
☐	50 Hobie Landrith	1.25	.50	.12
☐	51 Elvin Tappe	1.25	.50	.12
☐	52 Hal Rice	1.25	.50	.12
☐	53 Alex Kellner	1.25	.50	.12
☐	54 Don Bollweg	1.25	.50	.12
☐	55 Cal Abrams	1.25	.50	.12
☐	56 Billy Cox	1.50	.60	.15
☐	57 Bob Friend	1.50	.60	.15
☐	58 Frank Thomas	1.50	.60	.15
☐	59 Whitey Ford	14.00	5.75	1.40
☐	60 Enos Slaughter	7.50	3.00	.75
☐	61 Paul LaPalme	1.25	.50	.12
☐	62 Royce Lint	1.25	.50	.12
☐	63 Irv Noren	1.25	.50	.12
☐	64 Curt Simmons	1.50	.60	.15
☐	65 Don Zimmer	2.00	.80	.20
☐	66 George Shuba	1.50	.60	.15
☐	67 Don Larsen	2.50	1.00	.25
☐	68 Elston Howard	6.00	2.40	.60
☐	69 Bill Hunter	1.25	.50	.12
☐	70 Lou Burdette	2.00	.80	.20
☐	71 Dave Jolly	1.25	.50	.12
☐	72 Chet Nichols	1.25	.50	.12
☐	73 Eddie Yost	1.25	.50	.12
☐	74 Jerry Snyder	1.25	.50	.12
☐	75 Brooks Lawrence	1.25	.50	.12
☐	76 Tom Poholsky	1.25	.50	.12
☐	77 Jim McDonald	1.25	.50	.12
☐	78 Gil Coan	1.25	.50	.12
☐	79 Willie Miranda	1.25	.50	.12
☐	80 Lou Limmer	1.25	.50	.12
☐	81 Bob Morgan	1.25	.50	.12
☐	82 Lee Walls	1.25	.50	.12
☐	83 Max Surkont	1.25	.50	.12
☐	84 George Freese	1.25	.50	.12
☐	85 Cass Michaels	1.25	.50	.12
☐	86 Ted Gray	1.25	.50	.12
☐	87 Randy Jackson	1.25	.50	.12
☐	88 Steve Bilko	1.25	.50	.12
☐	89 Lou Boudreau MGR	7.00	2.80	.70
☐	90 Art Dittmar	1.25	.50	.12
☐	91 Dick Marlowe	1.25	.50	.12
☐	92 George Zuverink	1.25	.50	.12
☐	93 Andy Seminick	1.25	.50	.12
☐	94 Hank Thompson	1.50	.60	.15
☐	95 Sal Maglie	2.00	.80	.20
☐	96 Ray Narleski	1.25	.50	.12
☐	97 Johnny Podres	2.50	1.00	.25
☐	98 Jim Gilliam	2.50	1.00	.25
☐	99 Jerry Coleman	1.25	.50	.12
☐	100 Tom Morgan	.90	.36	.09

	MINT	VG-E	F-G
☐ 101 **A** Don Johnson ERR ...	1.00	.40	.10
(photo actually			
Ernie Johnson)			
☐ 101 **B** Don Johnson COR ..	4.50	1.80	.45
☐ 102 Bobby Thomson	2.50	1.00	.25
☐ 103 Eddie Mathews	8.50	3.50	.85
☐ 104 Bob Porterfield	.90	.36	.09
☐ 105 Johnny Schmitz	.90	.36	.09
☐ 106 Del Rice	.90	.36	.09
☐ 107 Solly Hemus	.90	.36	.09
☐ 108 Lou Kretlow	.90	.36	.09
☐ 109 Vern Stephens	1.00	.40	.10
☐ 110 Bob Miller	.90	.36	.09
☐ 111 Steve Ridzik	.90	.36	.09
☐ 112 Granny Hamner	.90	.36	.09
☐ 113 Bob Hall	.90	.36	.09
☐ 114 Vic Janowicz	1.00	.40	.10
☐ 115 Roger Bowman	.90	.36	.09
☐ 116 Sandy Consuegra	.90	.36	.09
☐ 117 Johnny Groth	.90	.36	.09
☐ 118 Bobby Adams	.90	.36	.09
☐ 119 Joe Astroth	.90	.36	.09
☐ 120 Ed Burtschy	.90	.36	.09
☐ 121 Rufus Crawford	.90	.36	.09
☐ 122 Al Corwin	.90	.36	.09
☐ 123 Marv Grissom	.90	.36	.09
☐ 124 Johnny Antonelli	1.00	.40	.10
☐ 125 Paul Giel	.90	.36	.09
☐ 126 Billy Goodman	1.00	.40	.10
☐ 127 Hank Majeski	.90	.36	.09
☐ 128 Mike Garcia	1.00	.40	.10
☐ 129 Hal Naragon	.90	.36	.09
☐ 130 Richie Ashburn	3.50	1.40	.35
☐ 131 Willard Marshall	.90	.36	.09
☐ 132 **A** Harvey Kueen ERR ..	2.00	.80	.20
(sic, Kuenn)			
☐ 132 **B** Harvey Kuenn COR ..	6.00	2.40	.60
☐ 133 Charles King	.90	.36	.09
☐ 134 Bob Feller	18.00	7.25	1.80
☐ 135 Lloyd Merriman	.90	.36	.09
☐ 136 Rocky Bridges	.90	.36	.09
☐ 137 Bob Talbot	.90	.36	.09
☐ 138 Davey Williams	1.00	.40	.10
☐ 139 Shantz Brothers	1.75	.70	.17
Wilmer and Bobby			
☐ 140 Bobby Shantz	1.50	.60	.15
☐ 141 Wes Westrum	.90	.36	.09
☐ 142 Rudy Regalado	.90	.36	.09
☐ 143 Don Newcombe	3.50	1.40	.35
☐ 144 Art Houtteman	.90	.36	.09
☐ 145 Bob Nieman	.90	.36	.09
☐ 146 Don Liddle	.90	.36	.09
☐ 147 Sam Mele	.90	.36	.09

	MINT	VG-E	F-G
☐ 148 Bob Chakales	.90	.36	.09
☐ 149 Cloyd Boyer	1.00	.40	.10
☐ 150 Bill Klaus	.90	.36	.09
☐ 151 Jim Brideweser	.90	.36	.09
☐ 152 Johnny Klippstein	.90	.36	.09
☐ 153 Eddie Robinson	.90	.36	.09
☐ 154 Frank Lary	1.25	.50	.12
☐ 155 Gerry Staley	.90	.36	.09
☐ 156 Jim Hughes	.90	.36	.09
☐ 157 **A** Ernie Johnson ERR ..	1.00	.40	.10
(photo actually			
Don Johnson)			
☐ 157 **B** Ernie Johnson COR ..	4.50	1.80	.45
☐ 158 Gil Hodges	9.00	3.75	.90
☐ 159 Harry Byrd	.90	.36	.09
☐ 160 Bill Skowron	2.50	1.00	.25
☐ 161 Matt Batts	.90	.36	.09
☐ 162 Charlie Maxwell	.90	.36	.09
☐ 163 Sid Gordon	.90	.36	.09
☐ 164 Toby Atwell	.90	.36	.09
☐ 165 Maurice McDermott	.90	.36	.09
☐ 166 Jim Busby	.90	.36	.09
☐ 167 Bob Grim	1.25	.50	.12
☐ 168 Yogi Berra	25.00	10.00	2.50
☐ 169 Carl Furillo	3.00	1.20	.30
☐ 170 Carl Erskine	2.50	1.00	.25
☐ 171 Robin Roberts	7.00	2.80	.70
☐ 172 Willie Jones	.90	.36	.09
☐ 173 Chico Carrasquel	.90	.36	.09
☐ 174 Sherman Lollar	1.00	.40	.10
☐ 175 Wilmer Shantz	.90	.36	.09
☐ 176 Joe DeMaestri	.90	.36	.09
☐ 177 Willard Nixon	.90	.36	.09
☐ 178 Tom Brewer	.90	.36	.09
☐ 179 Hank Aaron	50.00	20.00	5.00
☐ 180 Johnny Logan	1.00	.40	.10
☐ 181 Eddie Miksis	.90	.36	.09
☐ 182 Bob Rush	.90	.36	.09
☐ 183 Ray Katt	.90	.36	.09
☐ 184 Willie Mays	50.00	20.00	5.00
☐ 185 Vic Raschi	1.50	.60	.15
☐ 186 Alex Grammas	.90	.36	.09
☐ 187 Fred Hatfield	.90	.36	.09
☐ 188 Ned Garver	.90	.36	.09
☐ 189 Jack Collum	.90	.36	.09
☐ 190 Fred Baczewski	.90	.36	.09
☐ 191 Bob Lemon	7.50	3.00	.75
☐ 192 George Strickland	.90	.36	.09
☐ 193 Howie Judson	.90	.36	.09
☐ 194 Joe Nuxhall	1.00	.40	.10
☐ 195 **A** Erv Palica	1.00	.40	.10
(without trade)			

	MINT	VG-E	F-G
☐ 195 **B** Erv Palica (with trade)	8.00	3.25	.80
☐ 196 Russ Meyer	.90	.36	.09
☐ 197 Ralph Kiner	8.00	3.25	.80
☐ 198 Dave Pope	.90	.36	.09
☐ 199 Vernon Law	1.00	.40	.10
☐ 200 Dick Littlefield	.90	.36	.09
☐ 201 Allie Reynolds	3.00	1.20	.30
☐ 202 Mickey Mantle	120.00	50.00	12.00
☐ 203 Steve Gromek	.90	.36	.09
☐ 204 **A** Frank Bolling ERR (photo actually Milt Bolling)	1.00	.40	.10
☐ 204 **B** Frank Bolling COR	4.50	1.80	.45
☐ 205 Rip Repulski	.90	.36	.09
☐ 206 Ralph Beard	.90	.36	.09
☐ 207 Frank Shea	.90	.36	.09
☐ 208 Eddy Fitzgerald	.90	.36	.09
☐ 209 Smokey Burgess	1.00	.40	.10
☐ 210 Earl Torgeson	.90	.36	.09
☐ 211 Sonny Dixon	.90	.36	.09
☐ 212 Jack Dittmer	.90	.36	.09
☐ 213 George Kell	6.50	2.60	.65
☐ 214 Billy Pierce	1.50	.60	.15
☐ 215 Bob Kuzava	.90	.36	.09
☐ 216 Preacher Roe	2.00	.80	.20
☐ 217 Del Crandall	1.00	.40	.10
☐ 218 Joe Adcock	1.50	.60	.15
☐ 219 Whitey Lockman	1.00	.40	.10
☐ 220 Jim Hearn	.90	.36	.09
☐ 221 Hector Brown	.90	.36	.09
☐ 222 Russ Kemmerer	.90	.36	.09
☐ 223 Hal Jeffcoat	.90	.36	.09
☐ 224 Dee Fondy	.90	.36	.09
☐ 225 Paul Richards	4.00	1.60	.40
☐ 226 W. McKinley UMP	6.00	2.40	.60
☐ 227 Frank Baumholtz	3.50	1.40	.35
☐ 228 John Phillips	3.50	1.40	.35
☐ 229 Jim Brosnan	4.00	1.60	.40
☐ 230 Al Brazle	3.50	1.40	.35
☐ 231 Jim Konstanty	4.00	1.60	.40
☐ 232 Birdie Tebbetts	4.00	1.60	.40
☐ 233 Bill Serena	3.50	1.40	.35
☐ 234 Dick Bartell	3.50	1.40	.35
☐ 235 J. Paparella UMP	6.00	2.40	.60
☐ 236 Murry Dickson	3.50	1.40	.35
☐ 237 Johnny Wyrostek	3.50	1.40	.35
☐ 238 Eddie Stanky	5.00	2.00	.50
☐ 239 Edwin Rommel UMP	6.00	2.40	.60
☐ 240 Billy Loes	5.00	2.00	.50
☐ 241 Johnny Pesky	4.00	1.60	.40
☐ 242 Ernie Banks	80.00	32.00	8.00
☐ 243 Gus Bell	4.00	1.60	.40

	MINT	VG-E	F-G
☐ 244 Duane Pillette	3.50	1.40	.35
☐ 245 Bill Miller	3.50	1.40	.35
☐ 246 Hank Bauer	8.50	3.50	.85
☐ 247 Dutch Leonard	3.50	1.40	.35
☐ 248 Harry Dorish	3.50	1.40	.35
☐ 249 Billy Gardner	4.50	1.80	.45
☐ 250 Larry Napp UMP	6.00	2.40	.60
☐ 251 Stan Jok	3.50	1.40	.35
☐ 252 Roy Smalley	3.50	1.40	.35
☐ 253 Jim Wilson	3.50	1.40	.35
☐ 254 Bennett Flowers	3.50	1.40	.35
☐ 255 Pete Runnels	4.00	1.60	.40
☐ 256 Owen Friend	3.50	1.40	.35
☐ 257 Tom Alston	3.50	1.40	.35
☐ 258 John Stevens UMP	6.00	2.40	.60
☐ 259 Don Mossi	5.00	2.00	.50
☐ 260 Edwin Hurley UMP	6.00	2.40	.60
☐ 261 Walt Moryn	3.50	1.40	.35
☐ 262 Jim Lemon	4.00	1.60	.40
☐ 263 Eddie Joost	3.50	1.40	.35
☐ 264 Bill Henry	3.50	1.40	.35
☐ 265 Albert Barlick UMP	6.00	2.40	.60
☐ 266 Mike Fornieles	3.50	1.40	.35
☐ 267 Jim Honochick UMP	18.00	7.25	1.80
☐ 268 Roy Lee Hawes	3.50	1.40	.35
☐ 269 Joe Amalfitano	3.50	1.40	.35
☐ 270 Chico Fernandez	3.50	1.40	.35
☐ 271 Bob Hooper	3.50	1.40	.35
☐ 272 John Flaherty UMP	6.00	2.40	.60
☐ 273 Bubba Church	3.50	1.40	.35
☐ 274 Jim Delsing	3.50	1.40	.35
☐ 275 William Grieve UMP	6.00	2.40	.60
☐ 276 Ike Delock	3.50	1.40	.35
☐ 277 Ed Runge UMP	6.00	2.40	.60
☐ 278 Charles Neal	4.50	1.80	.45
☐ 279 Hank Soar UMP	6.00	2.40	.60
☐ 280 Clyde McCullough	3.50	1.40	.35
☐ 281 Charles Berry UMP	6.00	2.40	.60
☐ 282 Phil Cavarretta	4.00	1.60	.40
☐ 283 Nestor Chylak UMP	6.00	2.40	.60
☐ 284 Bill Jackowski UMP	6.00	2.40	.60
☐ 285 Walt Dropo	4.00	1.60	.40
☐ 286 Frank Secory UMP	6.00	2.40	.60
☐ 287 Ron Mrozinski	3.50	1.40	.35
☐ 288 Dick Smith	3.50	1.40	.35
☐ 289 Arthur Gore UMP	6.00	2.40	.60
☐ 290 Hershell Freeman	3.50	1.40	.35
☐ 291 Frank Dascoli UMP	6.00	2.40	.60
☐ 292 Marv Blaylock	3.50	1.40	.35
☐ 293 Thomas Gorman UMP	6.00	2.40	.60
☐ 294 Wally Moses	4.00	1.60	.40
☐ 295 Lee Ballanfant UMP	6.00	2.40	.60
☐ 296 Bill Virdon	12.00	5.00	1.20

		MINT	VG-E	F-G
☐ 297	Dusty Boggess UMP	6.00	2.40	.60
☐ 298	Charlie Grimm	4.50	1.80	.45
☐ 299	Lon Warneke UMP	6.00	2.40	.60
☐ 300	Tommy Byrne	4.00	1.60	.40
☐ 301	William Engeln UMP ...	6.00	2.40	.60
☐ 302	Frank Malzone	5.00	2.00	.50
☐ 303	Jocko Conlan UMP	18.00	7.25	1.80
☐ 304	Harry Chiti	3.50	1.40	.35
☐ 305	Frank Umont UMP	6.00	2.40	.60
☐ 306	Bob Cerv	4.50	1.80	.45
☐ 307	Babe Pinelli UMP	7.50	3.00	.75
☐ 308	Al Lopez MGR	12.00	5.00	1.20
☐ 309	Hal Dixon UMP	6.00	2.40	.60
☐ 310	Ken Lehman	3.50	1.40	.35
☐ 311	Lawrence Goetz UMP ...	6.00	2.40	.60
☐ 312	Bill Wight	3.50	1.40	.35
☐ 313	Augie Donatelli UMP ...	9.00	3.75	.90
☐ 314	Dale Mitchell	4.50	1.80	.45
☐ 315	Cal Hubbard UMP	18.00	7.25	1.80
☐ 316	Marion Fricano	3.50	1.40	.35
☐ 317	William Summers UMP ..	6.00	2.40	.60
☐ 318	Sid Hudson	3.50	1.40	.35
☐ 319	Albert Schroll	3.50	1.40	.35
☐ 320	George Susce Jr.	6.00	1.50	.30

1970 Kellogg's

The cards in this 75-card set measure 2¼" by 3½". The 1970 Kellogg's set was Kellogg's first venture into the baseball card producing field. The design incorporates a brilliant color photo of the player set against an indistinct background, which is then covered with a layer of plastic to simulate a 3-D look. Cards 16-30 seem to be in shorter supply than the other cards in the set.

		MINT	VG-E	F-G
	Complete Set	65.00	25.00	6.00
	Common Player (1-15) ..	.60	.24	.06
	Common Player (16-30) .	.75	.30	.07
	Common Player (31-75) .	.60	.24	.06
☐ 1	Ed Kranepool	.60	.24	.06
☐ 2	Pete Rose	10.00	4.00	1.00
☐ 3	Cleon Jones	.60	.24	.06
☐ 4	Willie McCovey	2.50	1.00	.25
☐ 5	Mel Stottlemyre	.75	.30	.07
☐ 6	Frank Howard	.75	.30	.07
☐ 7	Tom Seaver	4.00	1.60	.40
☐ 8	Don Sutton	1.50	.60	.15
☐ 9	Jim Wynn	.75	.30	.07
☐ 10	Jim Maloney	.75	.30	.07
☐ 11	Tommie Agee	.60	.24	.06
☐ 12	Willie Mays	5.00	2.00	.50
☐ 13	Juan Marichal	2.50	1.00	.25
☐ 14	Dave McNally	.75	.30	.07
☐ 15	Frank Robinson	3.00	1.20	.30
☐ 16	Carlos May	.75	.30	.07
☐ 17	Bill Singer	.75	.30	.07
☐ 18	Rick Reichardt	.75	.30	.07
☐ 19	Boog Powell	1.00	.40	.10
☐ 20	Gaylord Perry	2.50	1.00	.25
☐ 21	Brooks Robinson	4.00	1.60	.40
☐ 22	Luis Aparicio	3.00	1.20	.30
☐ 23	Joel Horlen	.75	.30	.07
☐ 24	Mike Epstein	.75	.30	.07
☐ 25	Tom Haller	.75	.30	.07
☐ 26	Willie Crawford	.75	.30	.07
☐ 27	Roberto Clemente	6.00	2.40	.60
☐ 28	Matty Alou	.75	.30	.07
☐ 29	Willie Stargell	2.50	1.00	.25
☐ 30	Tim Cullen	.75	.30	.07
☐ 31	Randy Hundley	.50	.20	.05
☐ 32	Reggie Jackson	5.00	2.00	.50
☐ 33	Rich Allen	.75	.30	.07
☐ 34	Tim McCarver	.75	.30	.07
☐ 35	Ray Culp	.50	.20	.05
☐ 36	Jim Fregosi	.75	.30	.07
☐ 37	Billy Williams	2.50	1.00	.25
☐ 38	Johnny Odom	.60	.24	.06
☐ 39	Bert Campaneris	.75	.30	.07
☐ 40	Ernie Banks	3.00	1.20	.30
☐ 41	Chris Short	.60	.24	.06
☐ 42	Ron Santo	.90	.36	.09
☐ 43	Glenn Beckert	.60	.24	.06
☐ 44	Lou Brock	3.00	1.20	.30
☐ 45	Larry Hisle	.75	.30	.07
☐ 46	Reggie Smith	.75	.30	.07
☐ 47	Rod Carew	3.00	1.20	.30
☐ 48	Curt Flood	.75	.30	.07

		MINT	VG-E	F-G
☐ 49	Jim Lonborg	.75	.30	.07
☐ 50	Sam McDowell	.75	.30	.07
☐ 51	Sal Bando	.75	.30	.07
☐ 52	Al Kaline	3.00	1.20	.30
☐ 53	Gary Nolan	.60	.24	.06
☐ 54	Rico Petrocelli	.60	.24	.06
☐ 55	Ollie Brown	.60	.24	.06
☐ 56	Luis Tiant	.75	.30	.07
☐ 57	Bill Freehan	.75	.30	.07
☐ 58	Johnny Bench	3.50	1.40	.35
☐ 59	Joe Pepitone	.75	.30	.07
☐ 60	Bobby Murcer	.90	.36	.09
☐ 61	Harmon Killebrew	2.50	1.00	.25
☐ 62	Don Wilson	.60	.24	.06
☐ 63	Tony Oliva	.90	.36	.09
☐ 64	Jim Perry	.75	.30	.07
☐ 65	Mickey Lolich	.90	.36	.09
☐ 66	Jose Laboy	.60	.24	.06
☐ 67	Dean Chance	.60	.24	.06
☐ 68	Bud Harrelson	.60	.24	.06
☐ 69	Willie Horton	.75	.30	.07
☐ 70	Wally Bunker	.60	.24	.06
☐ 71	Bob Gibson	2.50	1.00	.25
☐ 72	Joe Morgan	2.50	1.00	.25
☐ 73	Denny McLain	.90	.36	.09
☐ 74	Tommy Harper	.60	.24	.06
☐ 75	Don Mincher	.60	.24	.06

1971 Kellogg's

The cards in this 75-card set measure 2¼" by 3½". The 1971 set of 3-D cards marketed by the Kellogg Company is the scarcest of all that company's issues. It was distributed as single cards, one in each package of cereal, without the usual complete set mail-in offer. In addition, card dealers were unable to ob-

tain this set in quantity, as they have in other years. All the cards are available with and without the copyright notice on the back; the version without carries a slight premium for most numbers. Prices listed below are for the more common variety with copyright.

		MINT	VG-E	F-G
	Complete Set	400.00	160.00	40.00
	Common Player (1-75)	3.25	1.30	.32
☐ 1	Wayne Simpson	3.25	1.30	.32
☐ 2	Tom Seaver	15.00	6.00	1.50
☐ 3	Jim Perry	3.75	1.50	.37
☐ 4	Bob Robertson	3.25	1.30	.32
☐ 5	Roberto Clemente	18.00	7.25	1.80
☐ 6	Gaylord Perry	7.50	3.00	.75
☐ 7	Felipe Alou	3.75	1.50	.37
☐ 8	Denis Menke	3.25	1.30	.32
☐ 9	Don Kessinger	3.25	1.30	.32
☐ 10	Willie Mays	18.00	7.25	1.80
☐ 11	Jim Hickman	3.25	1.30	.32
☐ 12	Tony Oliva	5.00	2.00	.50
☐ 13	Manny Sanguillen	3.75	1.50	.37
☐ 14	Frank Howard	3.75	1.50	.37
☐ 15	Frank Robinson	9.00	3.75	.90
☐ 16	Willie Davis	3.75	1.50	.37
☐ 17	Lou Brock	10.00	4.00	1.00
☐ 18	Cesar Tovar	3.25	1.30	.32
☐ 19	Luis Aparicio	7.50	3.00	.75
☐ 20	Boog Powell	5.00	2.00	.50
☐ 21	Dick Selma	3.25	1.30	.32
☐ 22	Danny Walton	3.25	1.30	.32
☐ 23	Carl Morton	3.25	1.30	.32
☐ 24	Sonny Siebert	3.25	1.30	.32
☐ 25	Jim Merritt	3.25	1.30	.32
☐ 26	Jose Cardenal	3.25	1.30	.32
☐ 27	Don Mincher	3.25	1.30	.32
☐ 28	Clyde Wright	3.25	1.30	.32
☐ 29	Les Cain	3.25	1.30	.32
☐ 30	Danny Cater	3.25	1.30	.32
☐ 31	Don Sutton	7.50	3.00	.75
☐ 32	Chuck Dobson	3.25	1.30	.32
☐ 33	Willie McCovey	10.00	4.00	1.00
☐ 34	Mike Epstein	3.25	1.30	.32
☐ 35	Paul Blair	3.75	1.50	.37
☐ 36	Gary Nolan	3.25	1.30	.32
☐ 37	Sam McDowell	3.75	1.50	.37
☐ 38	Amos Otis	3.75	1.50	.37
☐ 39	Ray Fosse	3.25	1.30	.32
☐ 40	Mel Stottlemyre	3.75	1.50	.37
☐ 41	Clarence Gaston	3.25	1.30	.32

		MINT	VG-E	F-G
☐ 42	Dick Dietz	3.25	1.30	.32
☐ 43	Roy White	3.75	1.50	.37
☐ 44	Al Kaline	12.00	5.00	1.20
☐ 45	Carlos May	3.25	1.30	.32
☐ 46	Tommie Agee	3.25	1.30	.32
☐ 47	Tommy Harper	3.25	1.30	.32
☐ 48	Larry Dierker	3.25	1.30	.32
☐ 49	Mike Cuellar	3.75	1.50	.37
☐ 50	Ernie Banks	10.00	4.00	1.00
☐ 51	Bob Gibson	9.00	3.75	.90
☐ 52	Reggie Smith	3.75	1.50	.37
☐ 53	Matty Alou	3.75	1.50	.37
☐ 54	Alex Johnson	3.25	1.30	.32
☐ 55	Harmon Killebrew	9.00	3.75	.90
☐ 56	Bill Grabarkewitz	3.25	1.30	.32
☐ 57	Richie Allen	5.00	2.00	.50
☐ 58	Tony Perez	6.00	2.40	.60
☐ 59	Dave McNally	3.75	1.50	.37
☐ 60	Jim Palmer	9.00	3.75	.90
☐ 61	Billy Williams	9.00	3.75	.90
☐ 62	Joe Torre	5.00	2.00	.50
☐ 63	Jim Northrup	3.25	1.30	.32
☐ 64	Jim Fregosi	3.75	1.50	.37
☐ 65	Pete Rose	40.00	16.00	4.00
☐ 66	Bud Harrelson	3.25	1.30	.32
☐ 67	Tony Taylor	3.25	1.30	.32
☐ 68	Willie Stargell	9.00	3.75	.90
☐ 69	Tony Horton	3.25	1.30	.32
☐ 70	Claude Osteen	3.25	1.30	.32
☐ 71	Glenn Beckert	3.25	1.30	.32
☐ 72	Nate Colbert	3.25	1.30	.32
☐ 73	Rick Monday	3.75	1.50	.37
☐ 74	Tommy John	6.00	2.40	.60
☐ 75	Chris Short	3.25	1.30	.32

1972 Kellogg's

The cards in this 54-card set measure 2⅛" by 3¼". The dimensions of the cards in the 1972 Kellogg's set were reduced in comparison to those of the 1971 series. In addition, the length of the set was set at 54 cards rather than the 75 of the previous year. The cards of this Kellogg's set are characterized by the diagonal bands found on the obverse.

		MINT	VG-E	F-G
	Complete Set	40.00	16.00	4.00
	Common Player (1-54)	.40	.16	.04
☐ 1	Tom Seaver	4.00	1.60	.40
☐ 2	Amos Otis	.60	.24	.06
☐ 3	Willie Davis	.50	.20	.05
☐ 4	Wilbur Wood	.50	.20	.05
☐ 5	Bill Parsons	.40	.16	.04
☐ 6	Pete Rose	9.00	3.75	.90
☐ 7	Willie McCovey	2.50	1.00	.25
☐ 8	Ferguson Jenkins	.75	.30	.07
☐ 9	Vida Blue	.50	.20	.05
☐ 10	Joe Torre	.75	.30	.07
☐ 11	Merv Rettenmund	.40	.16	.04
☐ 12	Bill Melton	.40	.16	.04
☐ 13	Jim Palmer	2.50	1.00	.25
☐ 14	Doug Rader	.40	.16	.04
☐ 15	Dave Roberts	.40	.16	.04
☐ 16	Bobby Murcer	.50	.20	.05
☐ 17	Wes Parker	.40	.16	.04
☐ 18	Joe Coleman	.40	.16	.04
☐ 19	Manny Sanguillen	.50	.20	.05
☐ 20	Reggie Jackson	4.50	1.80	.45
☐ 21	Ralph Garr	.40	.16	.04
☐ 22	Jim Hunter	2.00	.80	.20
☐ 23	Rick Wise	.40	.16	.04
☐ 24	Glenn Beckert	.40	.16	.04
☐ 25	Tony Oliva	.75	.30	.07
☐ 26	Bob Gibson	2.00	.80	.20
☐ 27	Mike Cuellar	.50	.20	.05
☐ 28	Chris Speier	.40	.16	.04
☐ 29	Dave McNally	.50	.20	.05
☐ 30	Leo Cardenas	.40	.16	.04
☐ 31	Bill Freehan	.50	.20	.05
☐ 32	Bud Harrelson	.40	.16	.04
☐ 33	Sam McDowell	.50	.20	.05
☐ 34	Claude Osteen	.40	.16	.04
☐ 35	Reggie Smith	.50	.20	.05
☐ 36	Sonny Siebert	.40	.16	.04
☐ 37	Lee May	.50	.20	.05
☐ 38	Mickey Lolich	.60	.24	.06
☐ 39	Cookie Rojas	.40	.16	.04

		MINT	VG-E	F-G
☐ 40	Dick Drago	.40	.16	.04
☐ 41	Nate Colbert	.40	.16	.04
☐ 42	Andy Messersmith	.50	.20	.05
☐ 43	Dave Johnson	.50	.20	.05
☐ 44	Steve Blass	.40	.16	.04
☐ 45	Bob Robertson	.40	.16	.04
☐ 46	Billy Williams	2.00	.80	.20
☐ 47	Juan Marichal	2.00	.80	.20
☐ 48	Lou Brock	2.50	1.00	.25
☐ 49	Roberto Clemente	4.50	1.80	.45
☐ 50	Mel Stottlemyre	.50	.20	.05
☐ 51	Don Wilson	.40	.16	.04
☐ 52	Sal Bando	.50	.20	.05
☐ 53	Willie Stargell	2.00	.80	.20
☐ 54	Willie Mays	4.50	1.80	.45

		MINT	VG-E	F-G
☐ 8	Pie Traynor	.40	.16	.04
☐ 9	Honus Wagner	1.00	.40	.10
☐ 10	Eddie Collins	.40	.16	.04
☐ 11	Tris Speaker	.60	.24	.06
☐ 12	Cy Young	.60	.24	.06
☐ 13	Lou Gehrig	1.25	.50	.12
☐ 14	Babe Ruth	2.00	.80	.20
☐ 15	Ty Cobb	1.25	.50	.12

1973 Kellogg's 2D

The cards in this 54-card set measure 2¼" by 3½". The 1973 Kellogg's set is the only non 3-D set produced by the Kellogg Company. Apparently Kellogg's decided to have the cards produced through Visual Panographics rather than by Xograph as in the other years. The complete set could be obtained from the company through a box top redemption procedure. The card size is slightly larger than the previous year.

1972 Kellogg's ATG

The cards in this 15-card set measure 2¼" by 3½". The 1972 All-Time Greats 3-D set was issued with Kellogg's Danish Go Rounds. The set is a reissue of a 1970 set issued by Rold Gold Pretzels to commemorate baseball's first 100 years. The set contains two different cards of Babe Ruth.

		MINT	VG-E	F-G
	Complete Set	10.00	4.00	1.00
	Common Player (1-15)	.40	.16	.04
☐ 1	Walter Johnson	1.00	.40	.10
☐ 2	Rogers Hornsby	.60	.24	.06
☐ 3	John McGraw	.40	.16	.04
☐ 4	Mickey Cochrane	.50	.20	.05
☐ 5	George Sisler	.50	.20	.05
☐ 6	Babe Ruth	2.00	.80	.20
☐ 7	Lefty Grove	.60	.24	.06

		MINT	VG-E	F-G
	Complete Set	35.00	14.00	3.50
	Common Player (1-54)	.40	.16	.04
☐ 1	Amos Otis	.60	.24	.06
☐ 2	Ellie Rodriguez	.40	.16	.04
☐ 3	Mickey Lolich	.60	.24	.06
☐ 4	Tony Oliva	.60	.24	.06
☐ 5	Don Sutton	1.50	.60	.15
☐ 6	Pete Rose	9.00	3.75	.90
☐ 7	Steve Carlton	3.50	1.40	.35
☐ 8	Bobby Bonds	.60	.24	.06
☐ 9	Wilbur Wood	.50	.20	.05
☐ 10	Billy Williams	2.00	.80	.20
☐ 11	Steve Blass	.40	.16	.04

		MINT	VG-E	F-G
☐ 12	Jon Matlack	.50	.20	.05
☐ 13	Cesar Cedeno	.50	.20	.05
☐ 14	Bob Gibson	2.00	.80	.20
☐ 15	Sparky Lyle	.60	.24	.06
☐ 16	Nolan Ryan	3.00	1.20	.30
☐ 17	Jim Palmer	2.00	.80	.20
☐ 18	Ray Fosse	.40	.16	.04
☐ 19	Bobby Murcer	.60	.24	.06
☐ 20	Jim Hunter	2.00	.80	.20
☐ 21	Tom McCraw	.40	.16	.04
☐ 22	Reggie Jackson	4.00	1.60	.40
☐ 23	Bill Stoneman	.40	.16	.04
☐ 24	Lou Piniella	.60	.24	.06
☐ 25	Willie Stargell	2.00	.80	.20
☐ 26	Dick Allen	.60	.24	.06
☐ 27	Carlton Fisk	1.25	.50	.12
☐ 28	Ferguson Jenkins	.75	.30	.07
☐ 29	Phil Niekro	2.00	.80	.20
☐ 30	Gary Nolan	.40	.16	.04
☐ 31	Joe Torre	.60	.24	.06
☐ 32	Bobby Tolan	.40	.16	.04
☐ 33	Nate Colbert	.40	.16	.04
☐ 34	Joe Morgan	2.00	.80	.20
☐ 35	Bert Blyleven	.60	.24	.06
☐ 36	Joe Rudi	.50	.20	.05
☐ 37	Ralph Garr	.40	.16	.04
☐ 38	Gaylord Perry	1.50	.60	.15
☐ 39	Bobby Grich	.50	.20	.05
☐ 40	Lou Brock	2.00	.80	.20
☐ 41	Pete Broberg	.40	.16	.04
☐ 42	Manny Sanguillen	.50	.20	.05
☐ 43	Willie Davis	.50	.20	.05
☐ 44	Dave Kingman	.75	.30	.07
☐ 45	Carlos May	.40	.16	.04
☐ 46	Tom Seaver	3.00	1.20	.30
☐ 47	Mike Cuellar	.50	.20	.05
☐ 48	Joe Coleman	.40	.16	.04
☐ 49	Claude Osteen	.50	.20	.05
☐ 50	Steve Kline	.40	.16	.04
☐ 51	Rod Carew	3.00	1.20	.30
☐ 52	Al Kaline	2.50	1.00	.25
☐ 53	Larry Dierker	.40	.16	.04
☐ 54	Ron Santo	.60	.24	.06

1974 Kellogg's

The cards in this 54-card set measure 2⅛" by 3¼". In 1974 the Kellogg's set returned to its 3-D format; it also returned to the smaller-size card. Complete sets could be obtained from the company through a box top offer.

		MINT	VG-E	F-G
	Complete Set	35.00	14.00	3.50
	Common Player (1-54)	.30	.12	.03
☐ 1	Bob Gibson	2.00	.80	.20
☐ 2	Rick Monday	.40	.16	.04
☐ 3	Joe Coleman	.30	.12	.03
☐ 4	Bert Campaneris	.40	.16	.04
☐ 5	Carlton Fisk	.90	.36	.09
☐ 6	Jim Palmer	2.00	.80	.20
☐ 7	Ron Santo	.50	.20	.05
☐ 8	Nolan Ryan	3.00	1.20	.30
☐ 9	Greg Luzinski	.60	.24	.06
☐ 10	Buddy Bell	.60	.24	.06
☐ 11	Bob Watson	.40	.16	.04
☐ 12	Bill Singer	.30	.12	.03
☐ 13	Dave May	.30	.12	.03
☐ 14	Jim Brower	.30	.12	.03
☐ 15	Manny Sanguillen	.40	.16	.04
☐ 16	Jeff Burroughs	.40	.16	.04
☐ 17	Amos Otis	.40	.16	.04
☐ 18	Ed Goodson	.30	.12	.03
☐ 19	Nate Colbert	.30	.12	.03
☐ 20	Reggie Jackson	4.00	1.60	.40
☐ 21	Ted Simmons	.75	.30	.07
☐ 22	Bobby Murcer	.50	.20	.05
☐ 23	Willie Horton	.40	.16	.04
☐ 24	Orlando Cepeda	.60	.24	.06
☐ 25	Ron Hunt	.30	.12	.03
☐ 26	Wayne Twitchell	.30	.12	.03

		MINT	VG-E	F-G
☐ 27	Ron Fairly	.30	.12	.03
☐ 28	Johnny Bench	3.00	1.20	.30
☐ 29	John Mayberry	.30	.12	.03
☐ 30	Rod Carew	3.00	1.20	.30
☐ 31	Ken Holtzman	.40	.16	.04
☐ 32	Billy Williams	1.50	.60	.15
☐ 33	Dick Allen	.60	.24	.06
☐ 34	Wilbur Wood	.40	.16	.04
☐ 35	Danny Thompson	.30	.12	.03
☐ 36	Joe Morgan	2.00	.80	.20
☐ 37	Willie Stargell	1.50	.60	.15
☐ 38	Pete Rose	8.00	3.25	.80
☐ 39	Bobby Bonds	.50	.20	.05
☐ 40	Chris Speier	.30	.12	.03
☐ 41	Sparky Lyle	.50	.20	.05
☐ 42	Cookie Rojas	.30	.12	.03
☐ 43	Tommy Davis	.40	.16	.04
☐ 44	Jim Hunter	1.50	.60	.15
☐ 45	Willie Davis	.40	.16	.04
☐ 46	Bert Blyleven	.50	.20	.05
☐ 47	Pat Kelly	.30	.12	.03
☐ 48	Ken Singleton	.40	.16	.04
☐ 49	Manny Mota	.40	.16	.04
☐ 50	Dave Johnson	.40	.16	.04
☐ 51	Sal Bando	.40	.16	.04
☐ 52	Tom Seaver	3.00	1.20	.30
☐ 53	Felix Millan	.30	.12	.03
☐ 54	Ron Blomberg	.30	.12	.03

1975 Kellogg's

The cards in this 57-card set measure 2⅛" by 3¼". The 1975 Kellogg's 3-D set could be obtained card by card in cereal boxes or as a set from a box top offer from the company. Card number 44 Jim Hunter exists with the A's emblem or the Yankee's emblem on the back of the card.

		MINT	VG-E	F-G
	Complete Set	90.00	36.00	9.00
	Common Player (1-57)	.50	.20	.05
☐ 1	Roy White	.60	.24	.06
☐ 2	Ross Grimsley	.50	.20	.05
☐ 3	Reggie Smith	.60	.24	.06
☐ 4	Bob Grich	.60	.24	.06
☐ 5	Greg Gross	.50	.20	.05
☐ 6	Bob Watson	.60	.24	.06
☐ 7	Johnny Bench	5.00	2.00	.50
☐ 8	Jeff Burroughs	.60	.24	.06
☐ 9	Elliott Maddox	.50	.20	.05
☐ 10	Jon Matlack	.60	.24	.06
☐ 11	Pete Rose	12.50	5.00	1.25
☐ 12	Lee Stanton	.50	.20	.05
☐ 13	Bake McBride	.50	.20	.05
☐ 14	Jorge Orta	.50	.20	.05
☐ 15	Al Oliver	1.25	.50	.12
☐ 16	John Briggs	.50	.20	.05
☐ 17	Steve Garvey	5.00	2.00	.50
☐ 18	Brooks Robinson	4.00	1.60	.40
☐ 19	John Hiller	.60	.24	.06
☐ 20	Lynn McGlothlen	.50	.20	.05
☐ 21	Cleon Jones	.50	.20	.05
☐ 22	Fergie Jenkins	1.00	.40	.10
☐ 23	Bill North	.50	.20	.05
☐ 24	Steve Busby	.60	.24	.06
☐ 25	Richie Zisk	.60	.24	.06
☐ 26	Nolan Ryan	5.00	2.00	.50
☐ 27	Joe Morgan	3.00	1.20	.30
☐ 28	Joe Rudi	.60	.24	.06
☐ 29	Jose Cardenal	.50	.20	.05
☐ 30	Andy Messersmith	.60	.24	.06
☐ 31	Willie Montanez	.50	.20	.05
☐ 32	Bill Buckner	.90	.36	.09
☐ 33	Rod Carew	5.00	2.00	.50
☐ 34	Lou Piniella	.75	.30	.07
☐ 35	Ralph Garr	.60	.24	.06
☐ 36	Mike Marshall	.60	.24	.06
☐ 37	Garry Maddox	.60	.24	.06
☐ 38	Dwight Evans	1.00	.40	.10
☐ 39	Lou Brock	4.00	1.60	.40
☐ 40	Ken Singleton	.80	.32	.08
☐ 41	Steve Braun	.50	.20	.05
☐ 42	Rich Allen	.90	.36	.09
☐ 43	John Grubb	.50	.20	.05
☐ 44	Jim Hunter (2)	3.00	1.20	.30
☐ 45	Gaylord Perry	2.00	.80	.20
☐ 46	George Hendrick	.80	.32	.08
☐ 47	Sparky Lyle	.90	.36	.09
☐ 48	Dave Cash	.50	.20	.05
☐ 49	Luis Tiant	.75	.30	.07
☐ 50	Cesar Geronimo	.50	.20	.05

		MINT	VG-E	F-G
☐ 51	Carl Yastrzemski	8.00	3.25	.80
☐ 52	Ken Brett	.50	.20	.05
☐ 53	Hal McRae	.80	.32	.08
☐ 54	Reggie Jackson	6.00	2.40	.60
☐ 55	Rollie Fingers	2.00	.80	.20
☐ 56	Mike Schmidt	8.00	3.25	.80
☐ 57	Richie Hebner	.50	.20	.05

1976 Kellogg's

The cards in this 57-card set measure 2⅛" by 3¼". The 1976 Kellogg's 3-D set could be obtained card by card in cereal boxes or as a set from the company for box tops. Card number 6, that of Clay Carroll, exists with both a Reds or White Sox emblem on the back. Cards 1-3 (marked in the checklist below with SP) were apparently printed apart from the other 54 and are in shorter supply.

		MINT	VG-E	F-G
	Complete Set	45.00	18.00	4.50
	Common Player (1-3) SP	6.00	2.40	.60
	Common Player (4-57)	.30	.12	.03
☐ 1	Steve Hargan SP	6.00	2.40	.60
☐ 2	Claudell Washington SP	6.00	2.40	.60
☐ 3	Don Gullett SP	6.00	2.40	.60
☐ 4	Randy Jones	.40	.16	.04
☐ 5	Jim Hunter	1.50	.60	.15
☐ 6	Clay Carroll (2)	.60	.24	.06
☐ 7	Joe Rudi	.40	.16	.04
☐ 8	Reggie Jackson	3.50	1.40	.35
☐ 9	Felix Millan	.30	.12	.03
☐ 10	Jim Rice	2.50	1.00	.25
☐ 11	Bert Blyleven	.50	.20	.05
☐ 12	Ken Singleton	.40	.16	.04

		MINT	VG-E	F-G
☐ 13	Don Sutton	1.25	.50	.12
☐ 14	Joe Morgan	2.00	.80	.20
☐ 15	Dave Parker	1.50	.60	.15
☐ 16	Dave Cash	.30	.12	.03
☐ 17	Ron LeFlore	.40	.16	.04
☐ 18	Greg Luzinski	.60	.24	.06
☐ 19	Dennis Eckersley	.40	.16	.04
☐ 20	Bill Madlock	.90	.36	.09
☐ 21	George Scott	.30	.12	.03
☐ 22	Willie Stargell	1.25	.50	.12
☐ 23	Al Hrabosky	.40	.16	.04
☐ 24	Carl Yastrzemski	4.00	1.60	.40
☐ 25	Jim Kaat	.75	.30	.07
☐ 26	Marty Perez	.30	.12	.03
☐ 27	Bob Watson	.30	.12	.03
☐ 28	Eric Soderholm	.30	.12	.03
☐ 29	Bill Lee	.30	.12	.03
☐ 30	Frank Tanana	.40	.16	.04
☐ 31	Fred Lynn	1.50	.60	.15
☐ 32	Tom Seaver	3.00	1.20	.30
☐ 33	Steve Busby	.40	.16	.04
☐ 34	Gary Carter	3.50	1.40	.35
☐ 35	Rick Wise	.30	.12	.03
☐ 36	Johnny Bench	2.50	1.00	.25
☐ 37	Jim Palmer	1.50	.60	.15
☐ 38	Bobby Murcer	.50	.20	.05
☐ 39	Von Joshua	.30	.12	.03
☐ 40	Lou Brock	2.00	.80	.20
☐ 41	Mickey Rivers (2)	.40	.16	.04
☐ 42	Manny Sanguillen	.40	.16	.04
☐ 43	Jerry Reuss	.40	.16	.04
☐ 44	Ken Griffey	.40	.16	.04
☐ 45	Jorge Orta	.30	.12	.03
☐ 46	John Mayberry	.30	.12	.03
☐ 47	Vida Blue (2)	.40	.16	.04
☐ 48	Rod Carew	2.50	1.00	.25
☐ 49	Jon Matlack	.40	.16	.04
☐ 50	Boog Powell	.50	.20	.05
☐ 51	Mike Hargrove	.50	.20	.05
☐ 52	Paul Lindblad	.30	.12	.03
☐ 53	Thurman Munson	2.50	1.00	.25
☐ 54	Steve Garvey	3.00	1.20	.30
☐ 55	Pete Rose	7.50	3.00	.75
☐ 56	Greg Gross	.30	.12	.03
☐ 57	Ted Simmons	.75	.30	.07

1977 Kellogg's

The cards in this 57-card set measure 2⅛" by 3¼". The 1977 Kellogg's series of 3-D Baseball player cards could be obtained card by card from cereal boxes or by sending in box tops and money. Each player's picture appears in miniature form on the reverse, an idea begun in 1971 and replaced in subsequent years by the use of a picture of the Kellogg's mascot.

	MINT	VG-E	F-G
Complete Set	32.00	13.00	3.20
Common Player (1-57)	.25	.10	.02

		MINT	VG-E	F-G
☐ 1	George Foster	.90	.36	.09
☐ 2	Bert Campaneris	.30	.12	.03
☐ 3	Fergie Jenkins	.60	.24	.06
☐ 4	Dock Ellis	.25	.10	.02
☐ 5	John Montefusco	.25	.10	.02
☐ 6	George Brett	5.00	2.00	.50
☐ 7	John Candelaria	.35	.14	.03
☐ 8	Fred Norman	.25	.10	.02
☐ 9	Bill Travers	.25	.10	.02
☐ 10	Hal McRae	.30	.12	.03
☐ 11	Doug Rau	.25	.10	.02
☐ 12	Greg Luzinski	.60	.24	.06
☐ 13	Ralph Garr	.30	.12	.03
☐ 14	Steve Garvey	3.00	1.20	.30
☐ 15	Rick Manning	.25	.10	.02
☐ 16	Lyman Bostock	.35	.14	.03
☐ 17	Randy Jones	.30	.12	.03
☐ 18	Ron Cey	.50	.20	.05
☐ 19	Dave Parker	1.00	.40	.10
☐ 20	Pete Rose	6.50	2.60	.65
☐ 21	Wayne Garland	.25	.10	.02
☐ 22	Bill North	.25	.10	.02
☐ 23	Thurman Munson	2.00	.80	.20
☐ 24	Tom Poquette	.25	.10	.02
☐ 25	Ron LeFlore	.30	.12	.03
☐ 26	Mark Fidrych	.35	.14	.03
☐ 27	Sixto Lezcano	.25	.10	.02
☐ 28	Dave Winfield	2.50	1.00	.25
☐ 29	Jerry Koosman	.35	.14	.03
☐ 30	Mike Hargrove	.30	.12	.03
☐ 31	Willie Montanez	.25	.10	.02
☐ 32	Don Stanhouse	.25	.10	.02
☐ 33	Jay Johnstone	.25	.10	.02
☐ 34	Bake McBride	.25	.10	.02
☐ 35	Dave Kingman	.60	.24	.06
☐ 36	Fred Patek	.25	.10	.02
☐ 37	Garry Maddox	.30	.12	.03
☐ 38	Ken Reitz	.25	.10	.02
☐ 39	Bobby Grich	.30	.12	.03
☐ 40	Cesar Geronimo	.25	.10	.02
☐ 41	Jim Lonborg	.30	.12	.03
☐ 42	Ed Figueroa	.25	.10	.02
☐ 43	Bill Madlock	.80	.32	.08
☐ 44	Jerry Remy	.25	.10	.02
☐ 45	Frank Tanana	.30	.12	.03
☐ 46	Al Oliver	.80	.32	.08
☐ 47	Charlie Hough	.35	.14	.03
☐ 48	Lou Piniella	.50	.20	.05
☐ 49	Ken Griffey	.35	.14	.03
☐ 50	Jose Cruz	.60	.24	.06
☐ 51	Rollie Fingers	1.00	.40	.10
☐ 52	Chris Chambliss	.30	.12	.03
☐ 53	Rod Carew	2.50	1.00	.25
☐ 54	Andy Messersmith	.35	.14	.03
☐ 55	Mickey Rivers	.30	.12	.03
☐ 56	Butch Wynegar	.30	.12	.03
☐ 57	Steve Carlton	2.50	1.00	.25

1978 Kellogg's

The cards in this 57-card set measure 2¹⁄₈" by 3¹⁄₄". This 1978 3-D Kellogg's series marks the first year in which Tony the Tiger appears on the reverse of each card next to the team and MLB logos. Once again the set could be obtained as individually wrapped cards in cereal boxes or as a set via a mail-in offer.

		MINT	VG-E	F-G
	Complete Set	25.00	10.00	2.50
	Common Player (1-57)	.20	.08	.02
☐ 1	Steve Carlton	2.00	.80	.20
☐ 2	Bucky Dent	.25	.10	.02
☐ 3	Mike Schmidt	3.00	1.20	.30
☐ 4	Ken Griffey	.25	.10	.02
☐ 5	Al Cowens	.20	.08	.02
☐ 6	George Brett	3.00	1.20	.30
☐ 7	Lou Brock	1.50	.60	.15
☐ 8	Rich Gossage	.65	.26	.06
☐ 9	Tom Johnson	.20	.08	.02
☐ 10	George Foster	.65	.26	.06
☐ 11	Dave Winfield	2.00	.80	.20
☐ 12	Dan Meyer	.20	.08	.02
☐ 13	Chris Chambliss	.25	.10	.02
☐ 14	Paul Dade	.20	.08	.02
☐ 15	Jeff Burroughs	.25	.10	.02
☐ 16	Jose Cruz	.35	.14	.03
☐ 17	Mickey Rivers	.25	.10	.02
☐ 18	John Candelaria	.25	.10	.02
☐ 19	Ellis Valentine	.20	.08	.02
☐ 20	Hal McRae	.25	.10	.02
☐ 21	Dave Rozema	.20	.08	.02
☐ 22	Lenny Randle	.20	.08	.02
☐ 23	Willie McCovey	1.50	.60	.15
☐ 24	Ron Cey	.50	.20	.05
☐ 25	Eddie Murray	5.00	2.00	.50
☐ 26	Larry Bowa	.35	.14	.03
☐ 27	Tom Seaver	2.00	.80	.20
☐ 28	Garry Maddox	.25	.10	.02
☐ 29	Rod Carew	2.00	.80	.20
☐ 30	Thurman Munson	1.50	.60	.15
☐ 31	Gary Templeton	.50	.20	.05
☐ 32	Eric Soderholm	.20	.08	.02
☐ 33	Greg Luzinski	.50	.20	.05
☐ 34	Reggie Smith	.25	.10	.02
☐ 35	Dave Goltz	.20	.08	.02
☐ 36	Tommy John	.60	.24	.06
☐ 37	Ralph Garr	.25	.10	.02
☐ 38	Alan Bannister	.20	.08	.02
☐ 39	Bob Bailor	.20	.08	.02
☐ 40	Reggie Jackson	3.00	1.20	.30
☐ 41	Cecil Cooper	.60	.24	.06
☐ 42	Burt Hooton	.20	.08	.02
☐ 43	Sparky Lyle	.40	.16	.04
☐ 44	Steve Ontiveros	.20	.08	.02
☐ 45	Rick Reuschel	.25	.10	.02
☐ 46	Lyman Bostock	.25	.10	.02
☐ 47	Mitchell Page	.20	.08	.02
☐ 48	Bruce Sutter	.75	.30	.07
☐ 49	Jim Rice	2.00	.80	.20
☐ 50	Ken Forsch	.25	.10	.02
☐ 51	Nolan Ryan	2.00	.80	.20
☐ 52	Dave Parker	1.00	.40	.10
☐ 53	Bert Blyleven	.40	.16	.04
☐ 54	Frank Tanana	.25	.10	.02
☐ 55	Ken Singleton	.35	.14	.03
☐ 56	Mike Hargrove	.25	.10	.02
☐ 57	Don Sutton	1.00	.40	.10

1979 Kellogg's

The cards in this 60-card set measure 1¹⁵⁄₁₆" by 3¹⁄₄". The 1979 edition of Kellogg's 3-D baseball cards have a ³⁄₁₆" reduced width from the previous year; a nicely designed curved panel above the picture gives this set a distinctive appearance. The set contains the largest number of cards issued in a Kellogg's set since the 1971 series.

		MINT	VG-E	F-G
	Complete Set	20.00	8.00	2.00
	Common Player (1-60)	.15	.06	.01
☐ 1	Bruce Sutter	.60	.24	.06
☐ 2	Ted Simmons	.40	.16	.04
☐ 3	Ross Grimsley	.15	.06	.01
☐ 4	Wayne Nordhagen	.15	.06	.01
☐ 5	Jim Palmer	1.25	.50	.12

		MINT	VG-E	F-G
☐ 6	John Henry Johnson	.15	.06	.01
☐ 7	Jason Thompson	.25	.10	.02
☐ 8	Pat Zachry	.15	.06	.01
☐ 9	Dennis Eckersley	.20	.08	.02
☐ 10	Paul Splittorff	.15	.06	.01
☐ 11	Ron Guidry	1.00	.40	.10
☐ 12	Jeff Burroughs	.15	.06	.01
☐ 13	Rod Carew	2.00	.80	.20
☐ 14	Buddy Bell	.30	.12	.03
☐ 15	Jim Rice	2.00	.80	.20
☐ 16	Garry Maddox	.20	.08	.02
☐ 17	Willie McCovey	1.50	.60	.15
☐ 18	Steve Carlton	2.00	.80	.20
☐ 19	J.R. Richard	.25	.10	.02
☐ 20	Paul Molitor	.40	.16	.04
☐ 21	Dave Parker	.75	.30	.07
☐ 22	Pete Rose	5.00	2.00	.50
☐ 23	Vida Blue	.25	.10	.02
☐ 24	Richie Zisk	.20	.08	.02
☐ 25	Darrell Porter	.15	.06	.01
☐ 26	Dan Driessen	.15	.06	.01
☐ 27	Geoff Zahn	.15	.06	.01
☐ 28	Phil Niekro	1.00	.40	.10
☐ 29	Tom Seaver	2.00	.80	.20
☐ 30	Fred Lynn	.75	.30	.07
☐ 31	Bill Bonham	.15	.06	.01
☐ 32	George Foster	.60	.24	.06
☐ 33	Terry Puhl	.20	.08	.02
☐ 34	John Candelaria	.20	.08	.02
☐ 35	Bob Knepper	.30	.12	.03
☐ 36	Fred Patek	.15	.06	.01
☐ 37	Chris Chambliss	.20	.08	.02
☐ 38	Bob Forsch	.20	.08	.02
☐ 39	Ken Griffey	.25	.10	.02
☐ 40	Jack Clark	.75	.30	.07
☐ 41	Dwight Evans	.50	.20	.05
☐ 42	Lee Mazzilli	.20	.08	.02
☐ 43	Mario Guerrero	.15	.06	.01
☐ 44	Larry Bowa	.35	.14	.03
☐ 45	Carl Yastrzemski	3.00	1.20	.30
☐ 46	Reggie Jackson	2.50	1.00	.25
☐ 47	Rick Reuschel	.20	.08	.02
☐ 48	Mike Flanagan	.25	.10	.02
☐ 49	Gaylord Perry	.75	.30	.07
☐ 50	George Brett	3.00	1.20	.30
☐ 51	Craig Reynolds	.15	.06	.01
☐ 52	Dave Lopes	.25	.10	.02
☐ 53	Bill Almon	.15	.06	.01
☐ 54	Roy Howell	.15	.06	.01
☐ 55	Frank Tanana	.20	.08	.02
☐ 56	Doug Rau	.15	.06	.01
☐ 57	Rick Monday	.20	.08	.02
☐ 58	Jon Matlack	.20	.08	.02

		MINT	VG-E	F-G
☐ 59	Ron Jackson	.15	.06	.01
☐ 60	Jim Sundberg	.20	.08	.02

1980 Kellogg's

The cards in this 60-card set measure 1⅞" by 3¼". The 1980 Kellogg's 3-D set is quite similar to, but smaller (narrower) than, the other recent Kellogg's issues. Sets could be obtained card by card from cereal boxes or as a set from a box top offer from the company.

	MINT	VG-E	F-G
Complete Set	16.00	6.50	1.60
Common Player (1-60)	.15	.06	.01

		MINT	VG-E	F-G
☐ 1	Ross Grimsley	.15	.06	.01
☐ 2	Mike Schmidt	2.00	.80	.20
☐ 3	Mike Flanagan	.20	.08	.02
☐ 4	Ron Guidry	.80	.32	.08
☐ 5	Bert Blyleven	.30	.12	.03
☐ 6	Dave Kingman	.35	.14	.03
☐ 7	Jeff Newman	.15	.06	.01
☐ 8	Steve Rogers	.25	.10	.02
☐ 9	George Brett	2.00	.80	.20
☐ 10	Bruce Sutter	.60	.24	.06
☐ 11	Gorman Thomas	.30	.12	.03
☐ 12	Darrell Porter	.15	.06	.01
☐ 13	Roy Smalley	.15	.06	.01
☐ 14	Steve Carlton	1.50	.60	.15
☐ 15	Jim Palmer	1.00	.40	.10
☐ 16	Bob Bailor	.15	.06	.01
☐ 17	Jason Thompson	.15	.06	.01
☐ 18	Graig Nettles	.35	.14	.03
☐ 19	Ron Cey	.30	.12	.03
☐ 20	Nolan Ryan	1.50	.60	.15
☐ 21	Ellis Valentine	.15	.06	.01
☐ 22	Larry Hisle	.20	.08	.02

		MINT	VG-E	F-G
☐ 23	Dave Parker	.75	.30	.07
☐ 24	Eddie Murray	2.00	.80	.20
☐ 25	Willie Stargell	.75	.30	.07
☐ 26	Reggie Jackson	2.00	.80	.20
☐ 27	Carl Yastrzemski	2.00	.80	.20
☐ 28	Andre Thorton	.25	.10	.02
☐ 29	Dave Lopes	.20	.08	.02
☐ 30	Ken Singleton	.25	.10	.02
☐ 31	Steve Garvey	1.50	.60	.15
☐ 32	Dave Winfield	1.50	.60	.15
☐ 33	Steve Kemp	.20	.08	.02
☐ 34	Claudell Washington	.20	.08	.02
☐ 35	Pete Rose	4.00	1.60	.40
☐ 36	Cesar Cedeno	.20	.08	.02
☐ 37	John Stearns	.15	.06	.01
☐ 38	Lee Mazzilli	.15	.06	.01
☐ 39	Larry Bowa	.30	.12	.03
☐ 40	Fred Lynn	.60	.24	.06
☐ 41	Carlton Fisk	.60	.24	.06
☐ 42	Vida Blue	.25	.10	.02
☐ 43	Keith Hernandez	1.00	.40	.10
☐ 44	Ted Simmons	.40	.16	.04
☐ 45	Chet Lemon	.20	.08	.02
☐ 46	Jim Rice	1.50	.60	.15
☐ 47	Ferguson Jenkins	.35	.14	.03
☐ 48	Gary Matthews	.20	.08	.02
☐ 49	Tom Seaver	1.50	.60	.15
☐ 50	George Foster	.60	.24	.06
☐ 51	Phil Niekro	1.00	.40	.10
☐ 52	Johnny Bench	1.50	.60	.15
☐ 53	Buddy Bell	.30	.12	.03
☐ 54	Lance Parrish	1.00	.40	.10
☐ 55	Joaquin Andujar	.25	.10	.02
☐ 56	Don Baylor	.35	.14	.03
☐ 57	Jack Clark	.60	.24	.06
☐ 58	J.R. Richard	.25	.10	.02
☐ 59	Bruce Bochte	.20	.08	.02
☐ 60	Rod Carew	1.50	.60	.15

1981 Kellogg's

The cards in this 66-card set measure 2½" by 3½". The 1981 Kellogg's set witnessed an increase in both the size of the card and the size of the set. For the first time, cards were not packed in cereal sizes but available only by mail-in procedure. The offer for the card set was advertised on boxes of Kellogg's Corn Flakes. The cards were printed on a different stock than in previous years, presumably to prevent the cracking problem which has plagued all Kellogg's 3-D issues. At the end of the promotion, the remainder of the sets not distributed (to cereal-eaters) were "sold" into the organized hobby, thus creating a situation where the set is relatively plentiful compared to other years of Kellogg's.

		MINT	VG-E	F-G
	Complete Set	5.00	2.00	.50
	Common Player	.06	.02	.00
☐ 1	George Foster	.15	.06	.01
☐ 2	Jim Palmer	.25	.10	.02
☐ 3	Reggie Jackson	.75	.30	.07
☐ 4	Al Oliver	.10	.04	.01
☐ 5	Mike Schmidt	.75	.30	.07
☐ 6	Nolan Ryan	.35	.14	.03
☐ 7	Bucky Dent	.07	.03	.01
☐ 8	George Brett	.75	.30	.07
☐ 9	Jim Rice	.35	.14	.03
☐ 10	Steve Garvey	.45	.18	.04
☐ 11	Willie Stargell	.25	.10	.02
☐ 12	Phil Niekro	.25	.10	.02
☐ 13	Dave Parker	.25	.10	.02
☐ 14	Cesar Cedeno	.07	.03	.01

		MINT	VG-E	F-G
☐ 15	Don Baylor	.08	.03	.01
☐ 16	J.R. Richard	.07	.03	.01
☐ 17	Tony Perez	.10	.04	.01
☐ 18	Eddie Murray	.75	.30	.07
☐ 19	Chet Lemon	.08	.03	.01
☐ 20	Ben Oglivie	.07	.03	.01
☐ 21	Dave Winfield	.45	.18	.04
☐ 22	Joe Morgan	.25	.10	.02
☐ 23	Vida Blue	.07	.03	.01
☐ 24	Willie Wilson	.10	.04	.01
☐ 25	Steve Henderson	.06	.02	.00
☐ 26	Rod Carew	.45	.18	.04
☐ 27	Garry Templeton	.10	.04	.01
☐ 28	Dave Concepcion	.10	.04	.01
☐ 29	Dave Lopes	.07	.03	.01
☐ 30	Ken Landreaux	.06	.02	.00
☐ 31	Keith Hernandez	.30	.12	.03
☐ 32	Cecil Cooper	.10	.04	.01
☐ 33	Rickey Henderson	.50	.20	.05
☐ 34	Frank White	.08	.03	.01
☐ 35	George Hendrick	.08	.03	.01
☐ 36	Reggie Smith	.07	.03	.01
☐ 37	Tug McGraw	.06	.02	.00
☐ 38	Tom Seaver	.45	.18	.04
☐ 39	Ken Singleton	.09	.04	.01
☐ 40	Fred Lynn	.15	.06	.01
☐ 41	Rich Gossage	.15	.06	.01
☐ 42	Terry Puhl	.06	.02	.00
☐ 43	Larry Bowa	.10	.04	.01
☐ 44	Phil Garner	.06	.02	.00
☐ 45	Ron Guidry	.20	.08	.02
☐ 46	Lee Mazzilli	.06	.02	.00
☐ 47	Dave Kingman	.10	.04	.01
☐ 48	Carl Yastrzemski	.75	.30	.07
☐ 49	Rick Burleson	.07	.03	.01
☐ 50	Steve Carlton	.45	.18	.04
☐ 51	Alan Trammell	.20	.08	.02
☐ 52	Tommy John	.15	.06	.01
☐ 53	Paul Molitor	.10	.04	.01
☐ 54	Joe Charbonneau	.06	.02	.00
☐ 55	Rick Langford	.06	.02	.00
☐ 56	Bruce Sutter	.10	.04	.01
☐ 57	Robin Yount	.25	.10	.02
☐ 58	Steve Stone	.06	.02	.00
☐ 59	Larry Gura	.06	.02	.00
☐ 60	Mike Flanagan	.07	.03	.01
☐ 61	Bob Horner	.25	.10	.02
☐ 62	Bruce Bochte	.06	.02	.00
☐ 63	Pete Rose	1.00	.40	.10
☐ 64	Buddy Bell	.10	.04	.01
☐ 65	Johnny Bench	.35	.14	.03
☐ 66	Mike Hargrove	.06	.02	.00

1982 Kellogg's

The cards in this 64-card set measure 2⅛" by 3¼". The 1982 version of 3-D cards prepared for the Kellogg Company by Visual Panographics, Inc., is not only smaller in physical dimensions from the 1981 series (which was standard card size at 2½" by 3½") but is also two cards shorter in length (64 in '82 and 66 in '81). In addition, while retaining the policy of not inserting single cards into cereal packages and offering the sets through box top mail-ins only, the Kellogg Company accepted box tops from four types of cereals, as opposed to only one type the previous year. Each card features a color 3-D ballplayer picture with a vertical line of white stars on each side set upon a blue background. The player's name and the word Kellogg's are printed in red on the obverse, and the card number is found on the bottom right of the reverse.

		MINT	VG-E	F-G
Complete Set		10.00	4.00	1.00
Common Player		.06	.02	.00
☐ 1	Richie Zisk	.06	.02	.00
☐ 2	Bill Buckner	.10	.04	.01
☐ 3	George Brett	.75	.30	.07
☐ 4	Rickey Henderson	.60	.24	.06
☐ 5	Jack Morris	.15	.06	.01
☐ 6	Ozzie Smith	.15	.06	.01
☐ 7	Rollie Fingers	.15	.06	.01
☐ 8	Tom Seaver	.45	.18	.04
☐ 9	Fernando Valenzuela	.45	.18	.04
☐ 10	Hubie Brooks	.10	.04	.01
☐ 11	Nolan Ryan	.45	.18	.04

		MINT	VG-E	F-G
☐ 12	Dave Winfield	.35	.14	.03
☐ 13	Bob Horner	.20	.08	.02
☐ 14	Reggie Jackson	.60	.24	.06
☐ 15	Burt Hooton	.06	.02	.00
☐ 16	Mike Schmidt	.75	.30	.07
☐ 17	Bruce Sutter	.15	.06	.01
☐ 18	Pete Rose	1.00	.40	.10
☐ 19	Dave Kingman	.12	.05	.01
☐ 20	Neil Allen	.06	.02	.00
☐ 21	Don Sutton	.25	.10	.02
☐ 22	Dave Concepcion	.10	.04	.01
☐ 23	Keith Hernandez	.25	.10	.02
☐ 24	Gary Carter	.45	.18	.04
☐ 25	Carlton Fisk	.20	.08	.02
☐ 26	Ron Guidry	.20	.08	.02
☐ 27	Steve Carlton	.35	.14	.03
☐ 28	Robin Yount	.35	.14	.03
☐ 29	Dan Castino	.07	.03	.01
☐ 30	Johnny Bench	.35	.14	.03
☐ 31	Bob Knepper	.10	.04	.01
☐ 32	Rich Gossage	.15	.06	.01
☐ 33	Buddy Bell	.10	.04	.01
☐ 34	Art Howe	.06	.02	.00
☐ 35	Tony Armas	.10	.04	.01
☐ 36	Phil Niekro	.25	.10	.02
☐ 37	Len Barker	.08	.03	.01
☐ 38	Bob Grich	.09	.04	.01
☐ 39	Steve Kemp	.08	.03	.01
☐ 40	Kirk Gibson	.25	.10	.02
☐ 41	Carney Lansford	.10	.04	.01
☐ 42	Jim Palmer	.25	.10	.02
☐ 43	Carl Yastrzemski	.60	.24	.06
☐ 44	Rick Burleson	.07	.03	.01
☐ 45	Dwight Evans	.10	.04	.01
☐ 46	Ron Cey	.10	.04	.01
☐ 47	Steve Garvey	.45	.18	.04
☐ 48	Dave Parker	.20	.08	.02
☐ 49	Mike Easler	.07	.03	.01
☐ 50	Dusty Baker	.08	.03	.01
☐ 51	Rod Carew	.40	.16	.04
☐ 52	Chris Chambliss	.07	.03	.01
☐ 53	Tim Raines	.35	.14	.03
☐ 54	Chet Lemon	.08	.03	.01
☐ 55	Bill Madlock	.15	.06	.01
☐ 56	George Foster	.15	.06	.01
☐ 57	Dwayne Murphy	.07	.03	.01
☐ 58	Ken Singleton	.10	.04	.01
☐ 59	Mike Norris	.06	.02	.00
☐ 60	Cecil Cooper	.12	.05	.01
☐ 61	Al Oliver	.15	.06	.01
☐ 62	Willie Wilson	.12	.05	.01
☐ 63	Vida Blue	.08	.03	.01
☐ 64	Eddie Murray	.60	.24	.06

1983 Kellogg's

The cards in this 60-card set measure 1⅞" by 3¼". For the 14th year in a row, the Kellogg Company issued a card set of Major League players. The set of 3-D cards contains the photo, player's autograph, Kellogg's logo, and name and position of the player on the front of the card. The backs feature the player's team logo, career statistics, player biography, and a narrative on the player's career.

		MINT	VG-E	F-G
	Complete Set	10.00	4.00	1.00
	Common Player	.06	.02	.00
☐ 1	Rod Carew	.40	.16	.04
☐ 2	Rollie Fingers	.20	.08	.02
☐ 3	Reggie Jackson	.60	.24	.06
☐ 4	George Brett	.75	.30	.07
☐ 5	Hal McRae	.08	.03	.01
☐ 6	Pete Rose	1.00	.40	.10
☐ 7	Fernando Valenzuela	.35	.14	.03
☐ 8	Rickey Henderson	.60	.24	.06
☐ 9	Carl Yastrzemski	.60	.24	.06
☐ 10	Rich Gossage	.15	.06	.01
☐ 11	Eddie Murray	.60	.24	.06
☐ 12	Buddy Bell	.10	.04	.01
☐ 13	Jim Rice	.45	.18	.04
☐ 14	Robin Yount	.35	.14	.03
☐ 15	Dave Winfield	.35	.14	.03
☐ 16	Harold Baines	.25	.10	.02
☐ 17	Garry Templeton	.08	.03	.01
☐ 18	Bill Madlock	.15	.06	.01
☐ 19	Pete Vuckovich	.08	.03	.01
☐ 20	Pedro Guerrero	.25	.10	.02
☐ 21	Ozzie Smith	.15	.06	.01

		MINT	VG-E	F-G
☐ 22	George Foster	.12	.05	.01
☐ 23	Willie Wilson	.12	.05	.01
☐ 24	Johnny Ray	.10	.04	.01
☐ 25	George Hendrick	.08	.03	.01
☐ 26	Andre Thornton	.10	.04	.01
☐ 27	Leon Durham	.10	.04	.01
☐ 28	Cecil Cooper	.12	.05	.01
☐ 29	Don Baylor	.10	.04	.01
☐ 30	Lonnie Smith	.08	.03	.01
☐ 31	Nolan Ryan	.35	.14	.03
☐ 32	Dan Quisenberry	.12	.05	.01
☐ 33	Len Barker	.08	.03	.01
☐ 34	Neil Allen	.08	.03	.01
☐ 35	Jack Morris	.25	.10	.02
☐ 36	Dave Stieb	.12	.05	.01
☐ 37	Bruce Sutter	.12	.05	.01
☐ 38	Jim Sundberg	.06	.02	.00
☐ 39	Jim Palmer	.25	.10	.02
☐ 40	Lance Parrish	.25	.10	.02
☐ 41	Floyd Bannister	.08	.03	.01
☐ 42	Larry Gura	.06	.02	.00
☐ 43	Britt Burns	.08	.03	.01
☐ 44	Toby Harrah	.08	.03	.01
☐ 45	Steve Carlton	.35	.14	.03
☐ 46	Greg Minton	.06	.02	.00
☐ 47	Gorman Thomas	.08	.03	.01
☐ 48	Jack Clark	.15	.06	.01
☐ 49	Keith Hernandez	.25	.10	.02
☐ 50	Greg Luzinski	.10	.04	.01
☐ 51	Fred Lynn	.15	.06	.01
☐ 52	Dale Murphy	.75	.30	.07
☐ 53	Kent Hrbek	.35	.14	.03
☐ 54	Bob Horner	.20	.08	.02
☐ 55	Gary Carter	.45	.18	.04
☐ 56	Carlton Fisk	.15	.06	.01
☐ 57	Dave Concepcion	.10	.04	.01
☐ 58	Mike Schmidt	.75	.30	.07
☐ 59	Bill Buckner	.10	.04	.01
☐ 60	Bob Grich	.08	.03	.01

1975 Hostess

DON SUTTON
PITCHER
Los Angeles DODGERS

*The cards in this 150-card set measure 2¼"
by 3¼" individually or 3¼" by 7¼" as panels
of three. The 1975 Hostess set was issued in
panels of three cards each on the backs of
family-size packages of Hostess cakes. Card
number 125, Bill Madlock, was listed correctly as an infielder and incorrectly as a pitcher.
Number 11, Burt Hooton, and number 89,
Doug Rader, are spelled two different ways.
Some panels are more scarce than others as
they were issued only on the backs of less
popular Hostess products. These scarcer
panels are shown with asterisks in the checklist. Although complete panel prices are not
explicitly listed, they would generally have a
value 25% greater than the sum of the values
of the individual players on that panel.*

		MINT	VG-E	F-G
	Complete Indiv. Set	120.00	50.00	12.00
	Common Player	.30	.12	.03

		MINT	VG-E	F-G
☐ 1	Bob Tolan	.30	.12	.03
☐ 2	Cookie Rojas	.30	.12	.03
☐ 3	Darrell Evans	.50	.20	.05
☐ 4	Sal Bando	.40	.16	.04
☐ 5	Joe Morgan	2.00	.80	.20
☐ 6	Mickey Lolich	.50	.20	.05
☐ 7	Don Sutton	1.50	.60	.15
☐ 8	Bill Melton	.30	.12	.03
☐ 9	Tim Foli	.30	.12	.03
☐ 10	Joe LaHoud	.30	.12	.03
☐ 11 A	Bert Hooten (sic)	1.00	.40	.10
☐ 11 B	Burt Hooton	1.00	.40	.10
☐ 12	Paul Blair	.30	.12	.03

		MINT	VG-E	F-G
☐	13 Jim Barr	.30	.12	.03
☐	14 Toby Harrah	.40	.16	.04
☐	15 John Milner	.30	.12	.03
☐	16 Ken Holtzman	.40	.16	.04
☐	17 Cesar Cedeno	.40	.16	.04
☐	18 Dwight Evans	.60	.24	.06
☐	19 Willie McCovey	2.50	1.00	.25
☐	20 Tony Oliva	.60	.24	.06
☐	21 Manny Sanguillen	.40	.16	.04
☐	22 Mickey Rivers	.40	.16	.04
☐	23 Lou Brock	2.50	1.00	.25
☐	24 Graig Nettles	1.50	.60	.15
	(Craig on front)			
☐	25 Jim Wynn	.40	.16	.04
☐	26 George Scott	.30	.12	.03
☐	27 Greg Luzinski	.50	.20	.05
☐	28 Bert Campaneris	.40	.16	.04
☐	29 Pete Rose	9.00	3.75	.90
☐	30 Buddy Bell	.50	.20	.05
☐	31 Gary Matthews	.40	.16	.04
☐	32 Freddie Patek	.30	.12	.03
☐	33 Mike Lum	.30	.12	.03
☐	34 Ellie Rodriguez	.30	.12	.03
☐	35 Milt May	.50	.20	.05
	(photo actually			
	Lee May)			
☐	36 Willie Horton	.40	.16	.04
☐	37 Dave Winfield	3.00	1.20	.30
☐	38 Tom Grieve	.40	.16	.04
☐	39 Barry Foote	.30	.12	.03
☐	40 Joe Rudi	.40	.16	.04
☐	41 Bake McBride	.30	.12	.03
☐	42 Mike Cuellar	.40	.16	.04
☐	43 Garry Maddox	.40	.16	.04
☐	44 Carlos May	.30	.12	.03
☐	45 Bud Harrelson	.30	.12	.03
☐	46 Dave Chalk	.30	.12	.03
☐	47 Dave Concepcion	.50	.20	.05
☐	48 Carl Yastrzemski	6.00	2.40	.60
☐	49 Steve Garvey	4.00	1.60	.40
☐	50 Amos Otis	.40	.16	.04
☐	51 Rick Reuschel	.40	.16	.04
☐	52 Rollie Fingers	1.00	.40	.10
☐	53 Bob Watson	.40	.16	.04
☐	54 John Ellis	.30	.12	.03
☐	55 Bob Bailey	.30	.12	.03
☐	56 Rod Carew	4.00	1.60	.40
☐	57 Rich Hebner	.30	.12	.03
☐	58 Nolan Ryan	4.00	1.60	.40
☐	59 Reggie Smith	.50	.20	.05
☐	60 Joe Coleman	.30	.12	.03
☐	61 Ron Cey	.50	.20	.05
☐	62 Darrell Porter	.40	.16	.04

		MINT	VG-E	F-G
☐	63 Steve Carlton	4.00	1.60	.40
☐	64 Gene Tenace	.30	.12	.03
☐	65 Jose Cardenal	.30	.12	.03
☐	66 Bill Lee	.30	.12	.03
☐	67 Dave Lopes	.40	.16	.04
☐	68 Wilbur Wood	.40	.16	.04
☐	69 Steve Renko	.30	.12	.03
☐	70 Joe Torre	.50	.20	.05
☐	71 Ted Sizemore	.30	.12	.03
☐	72 Bobby Grich	.40	.16	.04
☐	73 Chris Speier	.30	.12	.03
☐	74 Bert Blyleven	.60	.24	.06
☐	75 Tom Seaver	4.00	1.60	.40
☐	76 Nate Colbert	.30	.12	.03
☐	77 Don Kessinger	.40	.16	.04
☐	78 George Medich	.30	.12	.03
☐	79 Andy Messersmith *	.50	.20	.05
☐	80 Robin Yount *	7.50	3.00	.75
☐	81 Al Oliver *	1.00	.40	.10
☐	82 Bill Singer *	.40	.16	.04
☐	83 Johnny Bench *	4.00	1.60	.40
☐	84 Gaylord Perry *	2.00	.80	.20
☐	85 Dave Kingman *	1.00	.40	.10
☐	86 Ed Herrmann *	.40	.16	.04
☐	87 Ralph Garr *	.40	.16	.04
☐	88 Reggie Jackson *	6.00	2.40	.60
☐	89 A Doug Radar ERR *	1.00	.40	.10
	(sic, Rader)			
☐	89 B Doug Rader COR *	2.00	.80	.20
☐	90 Elliott Maddox *	.40	.16	.04
☐	91 Bill Russell *	.50	.20	.05
☐	92 John Mayberry *	.40	.16	.04
☐	93 Dave Cash *	.40	.16	.04
☐	94 Jeff Burroughs *	.40	.16	.04
☐	95 Ted Simmons *	1.00	.40	.10
☐	96 Joe Decker *	.40	.16	.04
☐	97 Bill Buckner *	1.00	.40	.10
☐	98 Bobby Darwin *	.40	.16	.04
☐	99 Phil Niekro *	2.50	1.00	.25
☐	100 Jim Sundberg	.40	.16	.04
☐	101 Greg Gross	.30	.12	.03
☐	102 Luis Tiant	.50	.20	.05
☐	103 Glenn Beckert	.30	.12	.03
☐	104 Hal McRae	.40	.16	.04
☐	105 Mike Jorgensen	.30	.12	.03
☐	106 Mike Hargrove	.40	.16	.04
☐	107 Don Gullett	.40	.16	.04
☐	108 Tito Fuentes	.30	.12	.03
☐	109 John Grubb	.30	.12	.03
☐	110 Jim Kaat	.75	.30	.07
☐	111 Felix Millan	.30	.12	.03
☐	112 Don Money	.30	.12	.03
☐	113 Rick Monday	.40	.16	.04

		MINT	VG-E	F-G
☐ 114	Dick Bosman	.30	.12	.03
☐ 115	Roger Metzger	.30	.12	.03
☐ 116	Fergie Jenkins	.75	.30	.07
☐ 117	Dusty Baker	.50	.20	.05
☐ 118	Billy Champion *	.40	.16	.04
☐ 119	Bob Gibson *	3.00	1.20	.30
☐ 120	Bill Freehan *	.50	.20	.05
☐ 121	Cesar Geronimo	.30	.12	.03
☐ 122	Jorge Orta	.30	.12	.03
☐ 123	Cleon Jones	.30	.12	.03
☐ 124	Steve Busby	.40	.16	.04
☐ 125 A	Bill Madlock ERR (pitcher)	1.50	.60	.15
☐ 125 B	Bill Madlock COR (infielder)	1.50	.60	.15
☐ 126	Jim Palmer	2.50	1.00	.25
☐ 127	Tony Perez	.75	.30	.07
☐ 128	Larry Hisle	.40	.16	.04
☐ 129	Rusty Staub	.50	.20	.05
☐ 130	Hank Aaron *	6.00	2.40	.60
☐ 131	Rennie Stennett *	.40	.16	.04
☐ 132	Rico Petrocelli *	.50	.20	.05
☐ 133	Mike Schmidt	5.00	2.00	.50
☐ 134	Sparky Lyle	.50	.20	.05
☐ 135	Willie Stargell	2.00	.80	.20
☐ 136	Ken Henderson	.30	.12	.03
☐ 137	Willie Montanez	.30	.12	.03
☐ 138	Thurman Munson	3.00	1.20	.30
☐ 139	Richie Zisk	.40	.16	.04
☐ 140	George Hendrick	.40	.16	.04
☐ 141	Bobby Murcer	.50	.20	.05
☐ 142	Lee May	.40	.16	.04
☐ 143	Carlton Fisk	.75	.30	.07
☐ 144	Brooks Robinson	3.00	1.20	.30
☐ 145	Bobby Bonds	.40	.16	.04
☐ 146	Gary Sutherland	.30	.12	.03
☐ 147	Oscar Gamble	.30	.12	.03
☐ 148	Jim Hunter	2.00	.80	.20
☐ 149	Tug McGraw	.50	.20	.05
☐ 150	Dave McNally	.40	.16	.04

1976 Hostess

The cards in this 150-card set measure 2¼" by 3¼" individually or 3¼" by 7¼" as panels of three. The 1976 Hostess set contains color, numbered cards issued in panels of three cards each on family-size packages of Hostess cakes. Scarcer panels (those only found on less popular Hostess products) are listed in the checklist below with asterisks. Complete panels of three have a value 25% more than the sum of the individual cards on the panel. Ten additional numbers (151-160) were apparently planned but never actually issued. These exist as proof cards and are quite scarce, e.g., 151 Ferguson Jenkins, 152 Mike Cuellar, 153 Tom Murphy, 155 Barry Foote, 157 Richie Zisk, 158 Ken Holtzman, and 159 Cliff Johnson.

		MINT	VG-E	F-G
	Complete Indiv. Set (150)	120.00	50.00	12.00
	Common Player (1-150)	.30	.12	.03
☐ 1	Fred Lynn	1.50	.60	.15
☐ 2	Joe Morgan	2.00	.80	.20
☐ 3	Phil Niekro	2.00	.80	.20
☐ 4	Gaylord Perry	1.50	.60	.15
☐ 5	Bob Watson	.40	.16	.04
☐ 6	Bill Freehan	.40	.16	.04
☐ 7	Lou Brock	2.50	1.00	.25
☐ 8	Al Fitzmorris	.30	.12	.03
☐ 9	Rennie Stennett	.30	.12	.03
☐ 10	Tony Oliva	.60	.24	.06
☐ 11	Robin Yount	3.00	1.20	.30
☐ 12	Rick Manning	.30	.12	.03
☐ 13	Bobby Grich	.40	.16	.04
☐ 14	Terry Forster	.40	.16	.04

		MINT	VG-E	F-G
☐ 15	Dave Kingman	.60	.24	.06
☐ 16	Thurman Munson	3.00	1.20	.30
☐ 17	Rick Reuschel	.40	.16	.04
☐ 18	Bobby Bonds	.40	.16	.04
☐ 19	Steve Garvey	4.00	1.60	.40
☐ 20	Vida Blue	.40	.16	.04
☐ 21	Dave Rader	.30	.12	.03
☐ 22	Johnny Bench	3.00	1.20	.30
☐ 23	Luis Tiant	.50	.20	.05
☐ 24	Darrell Evans	.50	.20	.05
☐ 25	Larry Dierker	.30	.12	.03
☐ 26	Willie Horton	.40	.16	.04
☐ 27	John Ellis	.30	.12	.03
☐ 28	Al Cowens	.40	.16	.04
☐ 29	Jerry Reuss	.40	.16	.04
☐ 30	Reggie Smith	.50	.20	.05
☐ 31	Bobby Darwin *	.40	.16	.04
☐ 32	Fritz Peterson *	.40	.16	.04
☐ 33	Rod Carew *	4.00	1.60	.40
☐ 34	Carlos May *	.40	.16	.04
☐ 35	Tom Seaver *	4.00	1.60	.40
☐ 36	Brooks Robinson *	4.00	1.60	.40
☐ 37	Jose Cardenal	.30	.12	.03
☐ 38	Ron Blomberg	.30	.12	.03
☐ 39	Leroy Stanton	.30	.12	.03
☐ 40	Dave Cash	.30	.12	.03
☐ 41	John Montefusco	.40	.16	.04
☐ 42	Bob Tolan	.30	.12	.03
☐ 43	Carl Morton	.30	.12	.03
☐ 44	Rick Burleson	.50	.20	.05
☐ 45	Don Gullett	.40	.16	.04
☐ 46	Vern Ruhle	.30	.12	.03
☐ 47	Cesar Cedeno	.40	.16	.04
☐ 48	Toby Harrah	.40	.16	.04
☐ 49	Willie Stargell	2.00	.80	.20
☐ 50	Al Hrabosky *	.40	.16	.04
☐ 51	Amos Otis	.40	.16	.04
☐ 52	Bud Harrelson	.30	.12	.03
☐ 53	Jim Hughes	.30	.12	.03
☐ 54	George Scott	.30	.12	.03
☐ 55	Mike Vail *	.40	.16	.04
☐ 56	Jim Palmer *	3.00	1.20	.30
☐ 57	Jorge Orta *	.40	.16	.04
☐ 58	Chris Chambliss *	.50	.20	.05
☐ 59	Dave Chalk *	.40	.16	.04
☐ 60	Ray Burris *	.40	.16	.04
☐ 61	Bert Campaneris *	.50	.20	.05
☐ 62	Gary Carter *	5.00	2.00	.50
☐ 63	Ron Cey *	.75	.30	.07
☐ 64	Carlton Fisk *	1.00	.40	.10
☐ 65	Marty Perez *	.40	.16	.04
☐ 66	Pete Rose *	9.00	3.75	.90
☐ 67	Roger Metzger *	.40	.16	.04
☐ 68	Jim Sundberg *	.40	.16	.04
☐ 69	Ron LeFlore *	.40	.16	.04
☐ 70	Ted Sizemore *	.40	.16	.04
☐ 71	Steve Busby *	.50	.20	.05
☐ 72	Manny Sanguillen *	.50	.20	.05
☐ 73	Larry Hisle *	.40	.16	.04
☐ 74	Pete Broberg *	.40	.16	.04
☐ 75	Boog Powell *	.75	.30	.07
☐ 76	Ken Singleton *	.75	.30	.07
☐ 77	Rich Gossage *	1.50	.60	.15
☐ 78	Jerry Grote *	.40	.16	.04
☐ 79	Nolan Ryan *	4.00	1.60	.40
☐ 80	Rick Monday *	.50	.20	.05
☐ 81	Graig Nettles *	.75	.30	.07
☐ 82	Chris Speier *	.30	.12	.03
☐ 83	Dave Winfield *	3.00	1.20	.30
☐ 84	Mike Schmidt *	5.00	2.00	.50
☐ 85	Buzz Capra *	.30	.12	.03
☐ 86	Tony Perez *	.75	.30	.07
☐ 87	Dwight Evans *	.60	.24	.06
☐ 88	Mike Hargrove *	.30	.12	.03
☐ 89	Joe Coleman *	.30	.12	.03
☐ 90	Greg Gross *	.30	.12	.03
☐ 91	John Mayberry *	.40	.16	.04
☐ 92	John Candelaria *	.50	.20	.05
☐ 93	Bake McBride *	.30	.12	.03
☐ 94	Hank Aaron *	5.00	2.00	.50
☐ 95	Buddy Bell *	.50	.20	.05
☐ 96	Steve Braun *	.30	.12	.03
☐ 97	Jon Matlack *	.40	.16	.04
☐ 98	Lee May *	.40	.16	.04
☐ 99	Wilbur Wood *	.40	.16	.04
☐ 100	Bill Madlock *	.75	.30	.07
☐ 101	Frank Tanana *	.40	.16	.04
☐ 102	Mickey Rivers *	.40	.16	.04
☐ 103	Mike Ivie *	.30	.12	.03
☐ 104	Rollie Fingers *	1.00	.40	.10
☐ 105	Dave Lopes *	.40	.16	.04
☐ 106	George Foster *	1.00	.40	.10
☐ 107	Denny Doyle *	.30	.12	.03
☐ 108	Earl Williams *	.30	.12	.03
☐ 109	Tom Veryzer *	.30	.12	.03
☐ 110	J.R. Richard *	.40	.16	.04
☐ 111	Jeff Burroughs *	.30	.12	.03
☐ 112	Al Oliver *	.80	.32	.08
☐ 113	Ted Simmons *	.75	.30	.07
☐ 114	George Brett *	6.00	2.40	.60
☐ 115	Frank Duffy *	.30	.12	.03
☐ 116	Bert Blyleven *	.50	.20	.05
☐ 117	Darrell Porter *	.30	.12	.03
☐ 118	Don Baylor *	.50	.20	.05
☐ 119	Bucky Dent *	.40	.16	.04
☐ 120	Felix Millan *	.30	.12	.03

		MINT	VG-E	F-G
☐ 121	Mike Cuellar	.40	.16	.04
☐ 122	Gene Tenace	.30	.12	.03
☐ 123	Bobby Murcer	.50	.20	.05
☐ 124	Willie McCovey	2.00	.80	.20
☐ 125	Greg Luzinski	.50	.20	.05
☐ 126	Larry Parrish	.60	.24	.06
☐ 127	Jim Rice	4.00	1.60	.40
☐ 128	Dave Concepcion	.50	.20	.05
☐ 129	Jim Wynn	.40	.16	.04
☐ 130	Tom Grieve	.40	.16	.04
☐ 131	Mike Cosgrove	.30	.12	.03
☐ 132	Dan Meyer	.30	.12	.03
☐ 133	Dave Parker	2.00	.80	.20
☐ 134	Don Kessinger	.40	.16	.04
☐ 135	Hal McRae	.40	.16	.04
☐ 136	Don Money	.30	.12	.03
☐ 137	Dennis Eckersley	.40	.16	.04
☐ 138	Fergie Jenkins	.60	.24	.06
☐ 139	Mike Torrez	.40	.16	.04
☐ 140	Jerry Morales	.30	.12	.03
☐ 141	Jim Hunter	2.00	.80	.20
☐ 142	Gary Matthews	.40	.16	.04
☐ 143	Randy Jones	.40	.16	.04
☐ 144	Mike Jorgensen	.30	.12	.03
☐ 145	Larry Bowa	.40	.16	.04
☐ 146	Reggie Jackson	4.00	1.60	.40
☐ 147	Steve Yeager	.30	.12	.03
☐ 148	Dave May	.30	.12	.03
☐ 149	Carl Yastrzemski	5.00	2.00	.50
☐ 150	Cesar Geronimo	.30	.12	.03

1977 Hostess

*The cards in this 150-card set measure 2¼"
by 3¼" individually or 3¼" by 7¼" as panels
of three. The 1977 Hostess set contains color,
numbered cards issued in panels of three
cards each with Hostess family-size cake*

*products. Scarcer panels are listed in the
checklist below with asterisks. Although
complete panel prices are not explicitly listed
below, they would generally have a value
25% greater than the sum of the individual
players on the panel.*

		MINT	VG-E	F-G
	Complete Indiv. Set	120.00	50.00	12.00
	Common Player	.30	.12	.03
☐ 1	Jim Palmer	2.50	1.00	.25
☐ 2	Joe Morgan	2.00	.80	.20
☐ 3	Reggie Jackson	4.00	1.60	.40
☐ 4	Carl Yastrzemski	5.00	2.00	.50
☐ 5	Thurman Munson	3.00	1.20	.30
☐ 6	Johnny Bench	3.00	1.20	.30
☐ 7	Tom Seaver	3.50	1.40	.35
☐ 8	Pete Rose	8.00	3.25	.80
☐ 9	Rod Carew	3.50	1.40	.35
☐ 10	Luis Tiant	.40	.16	.04
☐ 11	Phil Garner	.30	.12	.03
☐ 12	Sixto Lezcano	.30	.12	.03
☐ 13	Mike Torrez	.30	.12	.03
☐ 14	Dave Lopes	.40	.16	.04
☐ 15	Doug DeCinces	.50	.20	.05
☐ 16	Jim Spencer	.30	.12	.03
☐ 17	Hal McRae	.40	.16	.04
☐ 18	Mike Hargrove	.30	.12	.03
☐ 19	Willie Montanez *	.40	.16	.04
☐ 20	Roger Metzger *	.40	.16	.04
☐ 21	Dwight Evans *	1.00	.40	.10
☐ 22	Steve Rogers *	1.00	.40	.10
☐ 23	Jim Rice *	4.00	1.60	.40
☐ 24	Pete Falcone *	.40	.16	.04
☐ 25	Greg Luzinski *	1.00	.40	.10
☐ 26	Randy Jones *	.50	.20	.05
☐ 27	Willie Stargell *	2.00	.80	.20
☐ 28	John Hiller *	.40	.16	.04
☐ 29	Bobby Murcer *	.50	.20	.05
☐ 30	Rick Monday *	.50	.20	.05
☐ 31	John Montefusco *	.40	.16	.04
☐ 32	Lou Brock *	3.00	1.20	.30
☐ 33	Bill North *	.40	.16	.04
☐ 34	Robin Yount *	3.00	1.20	.30
☐ 35	Steve Garvey *	5.00	2.00	.50
☐ 36	George Brett *	6.00	2.40	.60
☐ 37	Toby Harrah *	.50	.20	.05
☐ 38	Jerry Royster *	.40	.16	.04
☐ 39	Bob Watson *	.40	.16	.04
☐ 40	George Foster	1.00	.40	.10
☐ 41	Gary Carter	3.50	1.40	.35
☐ 42	John Denny	.50	.20	.05

		MINT	VG-E	F-G
☐	43 Mike Schmidt	4.50	1.80	.45
☐	44 Dave Winfield	3.00	1.20	.30
☐	45 Al Oliver	.80	.32	.08
☐	46 Mark Fidrych	.50	.20	.05
☐	47 Larry Herndon	.30	.12	.03
☐	48 Dave Goltz	.30	.12	.03
☐	49 Jerry Morales	.30	.12	.03
☐	50 Ron LeFlore	.40	.16	.04
☐	51 Fred Lynn	1.50	.60	.15
☐	52 Vida Blue	.40	.16	.04
☐	53 Rick Manning	.30	.12	.03
☐	54 Bill Buckner	.60	.24	.06
☐	55 Lee May	.40	.16	.04
☐	56 John Mayberry	.40	.16	.04
☐	57 Darrell Chaney	.30	.12	.03
☐	58 Cesar Cedeno	.40	.16	.04
☐	59 Ken Griffey	.40	.16	.04
☐	60 Dave Kingman	.60	.24	.06
☐	61 Ted Simmons	.75	.30	.07
☐	62 Larry Bowa	.50	.20	.05
☐	63 Frank Tanana	.40	.16	.04
☐	64 Jason Thompson	.40	.16	.04
☐	65 Ken Brett	.30	.12	.03
☐	66 Roy Smalley	.40	.16	.04
☐	67 Ray Burris	.30	.12	.03
☐	68 Rick Burleson	.50	.20	.05
☐	69 Buddy Bell	.50	.20	.05
☐	70 Don Sutton	1.50	.60	.15
☐	71 Mark Belanger	.40	.16	.04
☐	72 Dennis Leonard	.40	.16	.04
☐	73 Gaylord Perry	1.50	.60	.15
☐	74 Dick Ruthven	.30	.12	.03
☐	75 Jose Cruz	.50	.20	.05
☐	76 Cesar Geronimo	.30	.12	.03
☐	77 Jerry Koosman	.50	.20	.05
☐	78 Garry Templeton	1.00	.40	.10
☐	79 Jim Hunter	2.00	.80	.20
☐	80 John Candelaria	.50	.20	.05
☐	81 Nolan Ryan	3.50	1.40	.35
☐	82 Rusty Staub	.50	.20	.05
☐	83 Jim Barr	.30	.12	.03
☐	84 Butch Wynegar	.40	.16	.04
☐	85 Jose Cardenal	.30	.12	.03
☐	86 Claudell Washington	.40	.16	.04
☐	87 Bill Travers	.30	.12	.03
☐	88 Rick Waits	.30	.12	.03
☐	89 Ron Cey	.50	.20	.05
☐	90 Al Bumbry	.30	.12	.03
☐	91 Bucky Dent	.40	.16	.04
☐	92 Amos Otis	.40	.16	.04
☐	93 Tom Grieve	.40	.16	.04
☐	94 Enos Cabell	.30	.12	.03
☐	95 Dave Concepcion	.40	.16	.04
☐	96 Felix Millan	.30	.12	.03
☐	97 Bake McBride	.30	.12	.03
☐	98 Chris Chambliss	.40	.16	.04
☐	99 Butch Metzger	.30	.12	.03
☐	100 Rennie Stennett	.30	.12	.03
☐	101 Dave Roberts	.30	.12	.03
☐	102 Lyman Bostock	.40	.16	.04
☐	103 Rick Reuschel	.40	.16	.04
☐	104 Carlton Fisk	.75	.30	.07
☐	105 Jim Slaton	.30	.12	.03
☐	106 Dennis Eckersley	.40	.16	.04
☐	107 Ken Singleton	.50	.20	.05
☐	108 Ralph Garr	.30	.12	.03
☐	109 Freddie Patek	.40	.16	.04
☐	110 Jim Sundberg *	.40	.16	.04
☐	111 Phil Niekro *	2.00	.80	.20
☐	112 J.R. Richard *	.50	.20	.05
☐	113 Gary Nolan *	.40	.16	.04
☐	114 Jon Matlack *	.50	.20	.05
☐	115 Keith Hernandez *	3.00	1.20	.30
☐	116 Graig Nettles *	1.00	.40	.10
☐	117 Steve Carlton *	3.50	1.40	.35
☐	118 Bill Madlock *	1.50	.60	.15
☐	119 Jerry Reuss *	.60	.24	.06
☐	120 Aurelio Rodriguez *	.40	.16	.04
☐	121 Dan Ford *	.40	.16	.04
☐	122 Ray Fosse *	.40	.16	.04
☐	123 George Hendrick *	.50	.20	.05
☐	124 Alan Ashby *	.30	.12	.03
☐	125 Joe Lis	.30	.12	.03
☐	126 Sal Bando	.40	.16	.04
☐	127 Richie Zisk	.30	.12	.03
☐	128 Rich Gossage	.80	.32	.08
☐	129 Don Baylor	.50	.20	.05
☐	130 Dave McKay	.30	.12	.03
☐	131 Bob Grich	.40	.16	.04
☐	132 Dave Pagan	.30	.12	.03
☐	133 Dave Cash	.30	.12	.03
☐	123 Steve Braun	.30	.12	.03
☐	135 Dan Meyer	.30	.12	.03
☐	136 Bill Stein	.30	.12	.03
☐	137 Rollie Fingers	1.25	.50	.12
☐	138 Brian Downing	.50	.20	.05
☐	139 Bill Singer	.30	.12	.03
☐	140 Doyle Alexander	.40	.16	.04
☐	141 Gene Tenace	.30	.12	.03
☐	142 Gary Matthews	.40	.16	.04
☐	143 Don Gullett	.40	.16	.04
☐	144 Wayne Garland	.30	.12	.03
☐	145 Pete Broberg	.30	.12	.03
☐	146 Joe Rudi	.40	.16	.04
☐	147 Glenn Abbott	.30	.12	.03
☐	148 George Scott	.30	.12	.03

		MINT	VG-E	F-G
☐ 149	Bert Campaneris	.40	.16	.04
☐ 150	Andy Messersmith	.40	.16	.04

1978 Hostess

Joe Leonard Morgan

87

JOE MORGAN
CINCINNATI REDS   2b

The cards in this 150-card set measure 2¼"
by 3¼" individually or 3¼" by 7¼" as panels
of three. The 1978 Hostess set contains full
color, numbered cards issued in panels of
three each on family packages of Hostess cake products. Scarcer panels are listed
in the checklist with asterisks. The 1978 Hostess panels are considered by some collectors to be somewhat more difficult to obtain
than Hostess panels of other years. Although
complete panel prices are not explicitly listed
below, they would generally have a value
25% greater than the sum of the individual
players on the panel.

		MINT	VG-E	F-G
	Complete Indiv. Set	120.00	50.00	12.00
	Common Player	.30	.12	.03
☐ 1	Butch Hobson	.30	.12	.03
☐ 2	George Foster	1.00	.40	.10
☐ 3	Bob Forsch	.40	.16	.04
☐ 4	Tony Perez	.75	.30	.07
☐ 5	Bruce Sutter	1.00	.40	.10
☐ 6	Hal McRae	.40	.16	.04
☐ 7	Tommy John	.75	.30	.07
☐ 8	Greg Luzinski	.50	.20	.05
☐ 9	Enos Cabell	.30	.12	.03
☐ 10	Doug DeCinces	.50	.20	.05
☐ 11	Willie Stargell	1.50	.60	.15
☐ 12	Ed Halicki	.30	.12	.03
☐ 13	Larry Hisle	.40	.16	.04

		MINT	VG-E	F-G
☐ 14	Jim Slaton	.30	.12	.03
☐ 15	Buddy Bell	.50	.20	.05
☐ 16	Earl Williams	.30	.12	.03
☐ 17	Glenn Abbott	.30	.12	.03
☐ 18	Dan Ford	.30	.12	.03
☐ 19	Gary Matthews	.40	.16	.04
☐ 20	Eric Soderholm	.30	.12	.03
☐ 21	Bump Wills	.30	.12	.03
☐ 22	Keith Hernandez	2.50	1.00	.25
☐ 23	Dave Cash	.30	.12	.03
☐ 24	George Scott	.30	.12	.03
☐ 25	Ron Guidry	1.50	.60	.15
☐ 26	Dave Kingman	.60	.24	.06
☐ 27	George Brett	5.00	2.00	.50
☐ 28	Bob Watson *	.40	.16	.04
☐ 29	Bob Boone *	.50	.20	.05
☐ 30	Reggie Smith *	.60	.24	.06
☐ 31	Eddie Murray *	9.00	3.75	.90
☐ 32	Gary Lavelle *	.40	.16	.04
☐ 33	Rennie Stennett *	.40	.16	.04
☐ 34	Duane Kuiper *	.40	.16	.04
☐ 35	Sixto Lezcano *	.40	.16	.04
☐ 36	Dave Rozema *	.40	.16	.04
☐ 37	Butch Wynegar *	.50	.20	.05
☐ 38	Mitchell Page *	.40	.16	.04
☐ 39	Bill Stein *	.40	.16	.04
☐ 40	Elliott Maddox *	.30	.12	.03
☐ 41	Mike Hargrove *	.40	.16	.04
☐ 42	Bobby Bonds	.50	.20	.05
☐ 43	Garry Templeton	.60	.24	.06
☐ 44	Johnny Bench	3.50	1.40	.35
☐ 45	Jim Rice	3.50	1.40	.35
☐ 46	Bill Buckner	.60	.24	.06
☐ 47	Reggie Jackson	4.00	1.60	.40
☐ 48	Freddie Patek	.30	.12	.03
☐ 49	Steve Carlton	3.50	1.40	.35
☐ 50	Cesar Cedeno	.40	.16	.04
☐ 51	Steve Yeager	.30	.12	.03
☐ 52	Phil Garner	.30	.12	.03
☐ 53	Lee May	.40	.16	.04
☐ 54	Darrell Evans	.50	.20	.05
☐ 55	Steve Kemp	.50	.20	.05
☐ 56	Dusty Baker	.50	.20	.05
☐ 57	Ray Fosse	.30	.12	.03
☐ 58	Manny Sanguillen	.40	.16	.04
☐ 59	Tom Johnson	.30	.12	.03
☐ 60	Lee Stanton	.30	.12	.03
☐ 61	Jeff Burroughs	.40	.16	.04
☐ 62	Bobby Grich	.40	.16	.04
☐ 63	Dave Winfield	3.00	1.20	.30
☐ 64	Dan Driessen	.30	.12	.03
☐ 65	Ted Simmons	.75	.30	.07
☐ 66	Jerry Remy	.30	.12	.03

		MINT	VG-E	F-G
☐ 67	Al Cowens	.40	.16	.04
☐ 68	Sparky Lyle	.60	.24	.06
☐ 69	Manny Trillo	.40	.16	.04
☐ 70	Don Sutton	1.50	.60	.15
☐ 71	Larry Bowa	.50	.20	.05
☐ 72	Jose Cruz	.50	.20	.05
☐ 73	Willie McCovey	2.00	.80	.20
☐ 74	Bert Blyleven	.60	.24	.06
☐ 75	Ken Singleton	.50	.20	.05
☐ 76	Bill North	.30	.12	.03
☐ 77	Jason Thompson	.40	.16	.04
☐ 78	Dennis Eckersley	.40	.16	.04
☐ 79	Jim Sundberg	.40	.16	.04
☐ 80	Jerry Koosman	.50	.20	.05
☐ 81	Bruce Bochte	.30	.12	.03
☐ 82	George Hendrick	.40	.16	.04
☐ 83	Nolan Ryan	3.00	1.20	.30
☐ 84	Roy Howell	.30	.12	.03
☐ 85	Roger Metzger	.30	.12	.03
☐ 86	Doc Medich	.30	.12	.03
☐ 87	Joe Morgan	2.00	.80	.20
☐ 88	Dennis Leonard	.40	.16	.04
☐ 89	Willie Randolph	.40	.16	.04
☐ 90	Bobby Murcer	.50	.20	.05
☐ 91	Rick Manning	.30	.12	.03
☐ 92	J.R. Richard	.40	.16	.04
☐ 93	Ron Cey	.50	.20	.05
☐ 94	Sal Bando	.40	.16	.04
☐ 95	Ron LeFlore	.40	.16	.04
☐ 96	Dave Goltz	.30	.12	.03
☐ 97	Dan Meyer	.30	.12	.03
☐ 98	Chris Chambliss	.40	.16	.04
☐ 99	Biff Pocoroba	.30	.12	.03
☐ 100	Oscar Gamble	.40	.16	.04
☐ 101	Frank Tanana	.40	.16	.04
☐ 102	Len Randle	.30	.12	.03
☐ 103	Tommy Hutton	.30	.12	.03
☐ 104	John Candelaria	.50	.20	.05
☐ 105	George Orta	.30	.12	.03
☐ 106	Ken Reitz	.30	.12	.03
☐ 107	Bill Campbell	.30	.12	.03
☐ 108	Dave Concepcion	.50	.20	.05
☐ 109	Joe Ferguson	.30	.12	.03
☐ 110	Mickey Rivers	.40	.16	.04
☐ 111	Paul Splittorff	.30	.12	.03
☐ 112	Dave Lopes	.40	.16	.04
☐ 113	Mike Schmidt	4.50	1.80	.45
☐ 114	Joe Rudi	.40	.16	.04
☐ 115	Milt May	.30	.12	.03
☐ 116	Jim Palmer	2.00	.80	.20
☐ 117	Bill Madlock	1.00	.40	.10
☐ 118	Roy Smalley	.40	.16	.04
☐ 119	Cecil Cooper	.90	.36	.09

		MINT	VG-E	F-G
☐ 120	Rick Langford	.30	.12	.03
☐ 121	Ruppert Jones	.40	.16	.04
☐ 122	Phil Niekro	1.50	.60	.15
☐ 123	Toby Harrah	.40	.16	.04
☐ 124	Chet Lemon	.40	.16	.04
☐ 125	Gene Tenace	.30	.12	.03
☐ 126	Steve Henderson	.30	.12	.03
☐ 127	Mike Torrez	.30	.12	.03
☐ 128	Pete Rose	8.00	3.25	.80
☐ 129	John Denny	.50	.20	.05
☐ 130	Darrell Porter	.40	.16	.04
☐ 131	Rick Reuschel	.40	.16	.04
☐ 132	Graig Nettles	.75	.30	.07
☐ 133	Garry Maddox	.40	.16	.04
☐ 134	Mike Flanagan	.40	.16	.04
☐ 135	Dave Parker	2.00	.80	.20
☐ 136	Terry Whitfield	.30	.12	.03
☐ 137	Wayne Garland	.30	.12	.03
☐ 138	Robin Yount	3.00	1.20	.30
☐ 139	Gaylord Perry	1.50	.60	.15
☐ 140	Rod Carew	3.00	1.20	.30
☐ 141	Greg Gross	.30	.12	.03
☐ 142	Barry Bonnell	.30	.12	.03
☐ 143	Willie Montanez	.30	.12	.03
☐ 144	Rollie Fingers	1.25	.50	.12
☐ 145	Lyman Bostock	.40	.16	.04
☐ 146	Gary Carter	3.50	1.40	.35
☐ 147	Ron Blomberg	.30	.12	.03
☐ 148	Bob Bailor	.30	.12	.03
☐ 149	Tom Seaver	3.50	1.40	.35
☐ 150	Thurman Munson	3.00	1.20	.30

1979 Hostess

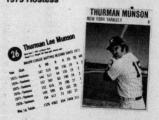

*The cards in this 150-card set measure 3¼"
by 7¼" as panels of three. The 1979 Hostess
set contains full color, numbered cards issued in panels of three cards each on the*

backs of family-size Hostess cake products. Scarcer panels are listed in the checklist below with asterisks. Although complete panel prices are not explicitly listed below they would generally have a value 25% greater than the sum of the individual players on the panel.

		MINT	VG-E	F-G
	Complete Indiv. Set	120.00	50.00	12.00
	Common Player	.30	.12	.03

		MINT	VG-E	F-G
☐ 1	John Denny	.40	.16	.04
☐ 2	Jim Rice	3.50	1.40	.35
☐ 3	Doug Bair	.30	.12	.03
☐ 4	Darrell Porter	.40	.16	.04
☐ 5	Ross Grimsley	.30	.12	.03
☐ 6	Bobby Murcer	.50	.20	.05
☐ 7	Lee Mazzilli	.30	.12	.03
☐ 8	Steve Garvey	3.50	1.40	.35
☐ 9	Mike Schmidt	4.50	1.80	.45
☐ 10	Terry Whitfield	.30	.12	.03
☐ 11	Jim Palmer	2.50	1.00	.25
☐ 12	Omar Moreno	.30	.12	.03
☐ 13	Duane Kuiper	.30	.12	.03
☐ 14	Mike Caldwell	.40	.16	.04
☐ 15	Steve Kemp	.50	.20	.05
☐ 16	Dave Goltz	.30	.12	.03
☐ 17	Mitchell Page	.30	.12	.03
☐ 18	Bill Stein	.30	.12	.03
☐ 19	Gene Tenace	.30	.12	.03
☐ 20	Jeff Burroughs	.40	.16	.04
☐ 21	Francisco Barrios	.30	.12	.03
☐ 22	Mike Torrez	.30	.12	.03
☐ 23	Ken Reitz	.30	.12	.03
☐ 24	Gary Carter	3.50	1.40	.35
☐ 25	Al Hrabosky	.40	.16	.04
☐ 26	Thurman Munson	3.00	1.20	.30
☐ 27	Bill Buckner	.60	.24	.06
☐ 28	Ron Cey *	.60	.24	.06
☐ 29	J.R. Richard *	.50	.20	.05
☐ 30	Greg Luzinski *	1.00	.40	.10
☐ 31	Ed Ott *	.40	.16	.04
☐ 32	Dennis Martinez *	.40	.16	.04
☐ 33	Darrell Evans *	.60	.24	.06
☐ 34	Ron LeFlore *	.40	.16	.04
☐ 35	Rick Waits	.30	.12	.03
☐ 36	Cecil Cooper	.80	.32	.08
☐ 37	Leon Roberts	.30	.12	.03
☐ 38	Rod Carew	3.00	1.20	.30
☐ 39	John Henry Johnson	.30	.12	.03
☐ 40	Chet Lemon	.40	.16	.04
☐ 41	Craig Swan	.30	.12	.03
☐ 42	Gary Matthews	.40	.16	.04
☐ 43	Lamar Johnson	.30	.12	.03
☐ 44	Ted Simmons	.75	.30	.07
☐ 45	Ken Griffey	.50	.20	.05
☐ 46	Fred Patek	.30	.12	.03
☐ 47	Frank Tanana	.40	.16	.04
☐ 48	Goose Gossage	1.00	.40	.10
☐ 49	Burt Hooton	.30	.12	.03
☐ 50	Ellis Valentine	.30	.12	.03
☐ 51	Ken Forsch	.30	.12	.03
☐ 52	Bob Knepper	.60	.24	.06
☐ 53	Dave Parker	2.00	.80	.20
☐ 54	Doug DeCinces	.50	.20	.05
☐ 55	Robin Yount	3.00	1.20	.30
☐ 56	Rusty Staub	.50	.20	.05
☐ 57	Gary Alexander	.30	.12	.03
☐ 58	Julio Cruz	.30	.12	.03
☐ 59	Matt Keough	.30	.12	.03
☐ 60	Roy Smalley	.40	.16	.04
☐ 61	Joe Morgan	2.00	.80	.20
☐ 62	Phil Niekro	2.00	.80	.20
☐ 63	Don Baylor	.50	.20	.05
☐ 64	Dwight Evans	.50	.20	.05
☐ 65	Tom Seaver	3.00	1.20	.30
☐ 66	George Hendrick	.40	.16	.04
☐ 67	Rick Reuschel	.40	.16	.04
☐ 68	George Brett	5.00	2.00	.50
☐ 69	Lou Piniella	.50	.20	.05
☐ 70	Enos Cabell	.30	.12	.03
☐ 71	Steve Carlton	3.00	1.20	.30
☐ 72	Reggie Smith	.50	.20	.05
☐ 73	Rick Dempsey *	.50	.20	.05
☐ 74	Vida Blue *	.50	.20	.05
☐ 75	Phil Garner *	.40	.16	.04
☐ 76	Rick Manning *	.40	.16	.04
☐ 77	Mark Fidrych *	.50	.20	.05
☐ 78	Mario Guerrero *	.40	.16	.04
☐ 79	Bob Stinson *	.40	.16	.04
☐ 80	Al Oliver *	1.00	.40	.10
☐ 81	Doug Flynn *	.40	.16	.04
☐ 82	John Mayberry *	.40	.16	.04
☐ 83	Gaylord Perry *	1.50	.60	.15
☐ 84	Joe Rudi	.40	.16	.04
☐ 85	Dave Concepcion	.50	.20	.05
☐ 86	John Candelaria	.40	.16	.04
☐ 87	Pete Vuckovich	.40	.16	.04
☐ 88	Ivan DeJesus	.30	.12	.03
☐ 89	Ron Guidry	1.50	.60	.15
☐ 90	Hal McRae	.40	.16	.04
☐ 91	Cesar Cedeno	.40	.16	.04
☐ 92	Don Sutton	1.50	.60	.15
☐ 93	Andre Thornton	.50	.20	.05

		MINT	VG-E	F-G
☐ 94	Roger Erickson	.30	.12	.03
☐ 95	Larry Hisle	.40	.16	.04
☐ 96	Jason Thompson	.40	.16	.04
☐ 97	Jim Sundberg	.40	.16	.04
☐ 98	Bob Horner	3.00	1.20	.30
☐ 99	Ruppert Jones	.40	.16	.04
☐ 100	Willie Montanez	.30	.12	.03
☐ 101	Nolan Ryan	3.00	1.20	.30
☐ 102	Ozzie Smith	1.00	.40	.10
☐ 103	Eric Soderholm	.30	.12	.03
☐ 104	Willie Stargell	1.50	.60	.15
☐ 105 A	Bob Bailor ERR (reverse negative)	.50	.20	.05
☐ 105 B	Bob Bailor COR	.75	.30	.07
☐ 106	Carlton Fisk	.90	.36	.09
☐ 107	George Foster	1.00	.40	.10
☐ 108	Keith Hernandez	2.50	1.00	.25
☐ 109	Dennis Leonard	.40	.16	.04
☐ 110	Graig Nettles	.80	.32	.08
☐ 111	Jose Cruz	.50	.20	.05
☐ 112	Bobby Grich	.40	.16	.04
☐ 113	Bob Boone	.40	.16	.04
☐ 114	Dave Lopes	.40	.16	.04
☐ 115	Eddie Murray	4.50	1.80	.45
☐ 116	Jack Clark	1.25	.50	.12
☐ 117	Lou Whitaker	1.00	.40	.10
☐ 118	Miguel Dilone	.30	.12	.03
☐ 119	Sal Bando	.40	.16	.04
☐ 120	Reggie Jackson	4.00	1.60	.40
☐ 121	Dale Murphy	8.00	3.25	.80
☐ 122	Jon Matlack	.40	.16	.04
☐ 123	Bruce Bochte	.30	.12	.03
☐ 124	John Stearns	.30	.12	.03
☐ 125	Dave Winfield	3.00	1.20	.30
☐ 126	Jorge Orta	.30	.12	.03
☐ 127	Garry Templeton	.50	.20	.05
☐ 128	Johnny Bench	3.00	1.20	.30
☐ 129	Butch Hobson	.30	.12	.03
☐ 130	Bruce Sutter	1.00	.40	.10
☐ 131	Bucky Dent	.40	.16	.04
☐ 132	Amos Otis	.40	.16	.04
☐ 133	Bert Blyleven	.50	.20	.05
☐ 134	Larry Bowa	.50	.20	.05
☐ 135	Ken Singleton	.50	.20	.05
☐ 136	Sixto Lezcano	.30	.12	.03
☐ 137	Roy Howell	.30	.12	.03
☐ 138	Bill Madlock	.90	.36	.09
☐ 139	Dave Revering	.30	.12	.03
☐ 140	Richie Zisk	.40	.16	.04
☐ 141	Butch Wynegar	.40	.16	.04
☐ 142	Alan Ashby	.30	.12	.03
☐ 143	Sparky Lyle	.50	.20	.05
☐ 144	Pete Rose	8.00	3.25	.80

		MINT	VG-E	F-G
☐ 145	Dennis Eckersley	.40	.16	.04
☐ 146	Dave Kingman	.60	.24	.06
☐ 147	Buddy Bell	.50	.20	.05
☐ 148	Mike Hargrove	.40	.16	.04
☐ 149	Jerry Koosman	.50	.20	.05
☐ 150	Toby Harrah	.40	.16	.04

1986 Sportflics

This 200-card set was marketed with 133 small trivia cards. This inaugural set for Sportflics was well received by the public. Sportflics was distributed by Major League Marketing; the company is also affiliated with Wrigley and Amurol. The set features 139 single player "magic motion" cards (which can be tilted to show three different pictures of the same player), 50 "Tri-Stars" (which show three different players), 10 "Big Six" cards (which show six players who share similar achievements), and one World Champs card featuring 12 members of the victorious Kansas City Royals. All cards measure 2½" by 3½"

	MINT	VG-E	F-G
Complete Set	40.00	16.00	4.00
Common Player	.15	.06	.01

		MINT	VG-E	F-G
☐ 1	George Brett	1.50	.60	.15
☐ 2	Don Mattingly	4.00	1.60	.40
☐ 3	Wade Boggs	2.50	1.00	.25
☐ 4	Eddie Murray	1.25	.50	.12
☐ 5	Dale Murphy	1.50	.60	.15
☐ 6	Rickey Henderson	1.25	.50	.12
☐ 7	Harold Baines	.40	.16	.04
☐ 8	Cal Ripken	1.00	.40	.10

		MINT	VG-E	F-G
☐ 9	Orel Hershiser	.50	.20	.05
☐ 10	Bret Saberhagen	.40	.16	.04
☐ 11	Tim Raines	.60	.24	.06
☐ 12	Fernando Valenzuela	.50	.20	.05
☐ 13	Tony Gwynn	.60	.24	.06
☐ 14	Pedro Guerrero	.40	.16	.04
☐ 15	Keith Hernandez	.40	.16	.04
☐ 16	Ernie Riles	.35	.14	.03
☐ 17	Jim Rice	.50	.20	.05
☐ 18	Ron Guidry	.40	.16	.04
☐ 19	Willie McGee	.50	.20	.05
☐ 20	Ryne Sandberg	.75	.30	.07
☐ 21	Kirk Gibson	.45	.18	.04
☐ 22	Ozzie Guillen	.65	.26	.06
☐ 23	Dave Parker	.45	.18	.04
☐ 24	Vince Coleman	2.00	.80	.20
☐ 25	Tom Seaver	.75	.30	.07
☐ 26	Brett Butler	.25	.10	.02
☐ 27	Steve Carlton	.75	.30	.07
☐ 28	Gary Carter	.75	.30	.07
☐ 29	Cecil Cooper	.30	.12	.03
☐ 30	Jose Cruz	.25	.10	.02
☐ 31	Alvin Davis	.25	.10	.02
☐ 32	Dwight Evans	.25	.10	.02
☐ 33	Julio Franco	.25	.10	.02
☐ 34	Damaso Garcia	.20	.08	.02
☐ 35	Steve Garvey	1.00	.40	.10
☐ 36	Kent Hrbek	.40	.16	.04
☐ 37	Reggie Jackson	1.00	.40	.10
☐ 38	Fred Lynn	.35	.14	.03
☐ 39	Paul Molitor	.25	.10	.02
☐ 40	Jim Presley	.50	.20	.05
☐ 41	Dave Righetti	.35	.14	.03
☐ 42	Robin Yount	.50	.20	.05
☐ 43	Nolan Ryan	.75	.30	.07
☐ 44	Mike Schmidt	1.25	.50	.12
☐ 45	Lee Smith	.25	.10	.02
☐ 46	Rick Sutcliffe	.25	.10	.02
☐ 47	Bruce Sutter	.30	.12	.03
☐ 48	Lou Whitaker	.30	.12	.03
☐ 49	Dave Winfield	.65	.26	.06
☐ 50	Pete Rose	2.50	1.00	.25
☐ 51	NL MVP's	1.00	.40	.10
	Ryne Sandberg			
	Steve Garvey			
	Pete Rose			
☐ 52	Slugging Stars	.75	.30	.07
	George Brett			
	Harold Baines			
	Jim Rice			

		MINT	VG-E	F-G
☐ 53	No-Hitters	.25	.10	.02
	Phil Niekro			
	Jerry Reuss			
	Mike Witt			
☐ 54	Big Hitters	1.25	.50	.12
	Don Mattingly			
	Cal Ripken			
	Robin Yount			
☐ 55	Bullpen Aces	.25	.10	.02
	Dan Quisenberry			
	Goose Gossage			
	Lee Smith			
☐ 56	Rookies of The Year	1.25	.50	.12
	Darryl Strawberry			
	Steve Sax			
	Pete Rose			
☐ 57	AL MVP's	.60	.24	.06
	Cal Ripken			
	Don Baylor			
	Reggie Jackson			
☐ 58	Repeat Batting Champs	1.00	.40	.10
	Dave Parker			
	Bill Madlock			
	Pete Rose			
☐ 59	Cy Young Winners	.25	.10	.02
	LaMarr Hoyt			
	Mike Flanagan			
	Ron Guidry			
☐ 60	Double Award Winners	.35	.14	.03
	Fernando Valenzuela			
	Rick Sutcliffe			
	Tom Seaver			
☐ 61	Home Run Champs	.75	.30	.07
	Reggie Jackson			
	Jim Rice			
	Tony Armas			
☐ 62	NL MVP's	1.00	.40	.10
	Keith Hernandez			
	Dale Murphy			
	Mike Schmidt			
☐ 63	AL MVP's	.60	.24	.06
	Robin Yount			
	George Brett			
	Fred Lynn			
☐ 64	Comeback Players	.20	.08	.02
	Bert Blyleven			
	Jerry Koosman			
	John Denny			
☐ 65	Cy Young Relievers	.25	.10	.02
	Willie Hernandez			
	Rollie Fingers			
	Bruce Sutter			

			MINT	VG-E	F-G
☐	66	Rookies of The Year ... Bob Horner Andre Dawson Gary Matthews	.25	.10	.02
☐	67	Rookies of The Year ... Ron Kittle Carlton Fisk Tom Seaver	.35	.14	.03
☐	68	Home Run Champs .... Mike Schmidt George Foster Dave Kingman	.35	.14	.03
☐	69	Double Award Winners . Cal Ripken Rod Carew Pete Rose	1.25	.50	.12
☐	70	Cy Young Winners ..... Rick Sutcliffe Steve Carlton Tom Seaver	.45	.18	.04
☐	71	Top Sluggers .... Reggie Jackson Fred Lynn Robin Yount	.45	.18	.04
☐	72	Rookies of The Year ... Dave Righetti Fernando Valenzuela Rick Sutcliffe	.35	.14	.03
☐	73	Rookies of The Year ... Fred Lynn Eddie Murray Cal Ripken	.75	.30	.07
☐	74	Rookies of The Year ... Alvin Davis Lou Whitaker Rod Carew	.35	.14	.03
☐	75	Batting Champs .... Don Mattingly Wade Boggs Carney Lansford	1.50	.60	.15
☐	76	Jesse Barfield	.45	.18	.04
☐	77	Phil Bradley	.45	.18	.04
☐	78	Chris Brown	.75	.30	.07
☐	79	Tom Browning	.35	.14	.03
☐	80	Tom Brunansky	.25	.10	.02
☐	81	Bill Buckner	.20	.08	.02
☐	82	Chili Davis	.20	.08	.02
☐	83	Mike Davis	.20	.08	.02
☐	84	Rich Gedman	.25	.10	.02
☐	85	Willie Hernandez	.25	.10	.02
☐	86	Ron Kittle	.25	.10	.02
☐	87	Lee Lacy	.15	.06	.01
☐	88	Bill Madlock	.25	.10	.02

			MINT	VG-E	F-G
☐	89	Mike Marshall	.25	.10	.02
☐	90	Keith Moreland	.15	.06	.01
☐	91	Graig Nettles	.25	.10	.02
☐	92	Lance Parrish	.35	.14	.03
☐	93	Kirby Puckett	.75	.30	.07
☐	94	Juan Samuel	.25	.10	.02
☐	95	Steve Sax	.30	.12	.03
☐	96	Dave Stieb	.30	.12	.03
☐	97	Darryl Strawberry	1.25	.50	.12
☐	98	Willie Upshaw	.20	.08	.02
☐	99	Frank Viola	.20	.08	.02
☐	100	Dwight Gooden	3.50	1.40	.35
☐	101	Joaquin Andujar	.25	.10	.02
☐	102	George Bell	.35	.14	.03
☐	103	Bert Blyleven	.20	.08	.02
☐	104	Mike Boddicker	.20	.08	.02
☐	105	Britt Burns	.20	.08	.02
☐	106	Rod Carew	.75	.30	.07
☐	107	Jack Clark	.30	.12	.03
☐	108	Danny Cox	.25	.10	.02
☐	109	Ron Darling	.50	.20	.05
☐	110	Andre Dawson	.45	.18	.04
☐	111	Leon Durham	.25	.10	.02
☐	112	Tony Fernandez	.30	.12	.03
☐	113	Tommy Herr	.20	.08	.02
☐	114	Teddy Higuera	.60	.24	.06
☐	115	Bob Horner	.35	.14	.03
☐	116	Dave Kingman	.25	.10	.02
☐	117	Jack Morris	.35	.14	.03
☐	118	Dan Quisenberry	.35	.14	.03
☐	119	Jeff Reardon	.25	.10	.02
☐	120	Bryn Smith	.15	.06	.01
☐	121	Ozzie Smith	.25	.10	.02
☐	122	John Tudor	.25	.10	.02
☐	123	Tim Wallach	.25	.10	.02
☐	124	Willie Wilson	.30	.12	.03
☐	125	Carlton Fisk	.35	.14	.03
☐	126	RBI Sluggers .... Gary Carter Al Oliver George Foster	.35	.14	.03
☐	127	Run Scorers .... Tim Raines Ryne Sandberg Keith Hernandez	.60	.24	.06
☐	128	Run Scorers .... Paul Molitor Cal Ripken Willie Wilson	.60	.24	.06
☐	129	No-Hitters .... John Candelaria Dennis Eckersley Bob Forsch	.20	.08	.02

		MINT	VG-E	F-G
☐ 130	World Series MVP's Pete Rose Ron Cey Rollie Fingers	.75	.30	.07
☐ 131	All-Star Game MVPs Dave Concepcion George Foster Bill Madlock	.20	.08	.02
☐ 132	Cy Young Winners John Denny Fernando Valenzuela Vida Blue	.25	.10	.02
☐ 133	Comeback Players Rich Dotson Joaquin Andujar Doyle Alexander	.20	.08	.02
☐ 134	Big Winners Rick Sutcliffe Tom Seaver John Denny	.45	.18	.04
☐ 135	Veteran Pitchers Tom Seaver Phil Niekro Don Sutton	.50	.20	.05
☐ 136	Rookies of The Year Dwight Gooden Vince Coleman Alfredo Griffin	1.50	.60	.15
☐ 137	All-Star Game MVPs Gary Carter Fred Lynn Steve Garvey	.50	.20	.05
☐ 138	Veteran Hitters Tony Perez Rusty Staub Pete Rose	.75	.30	.07
☐ 139	Power Hitters Mike Schmidt Jim Rice George Foster	.60	.24	.06
☐ 140	Batting Champs Tony Gwynn Al Oliver Bill Buckner	.35	.14	.03
☐ 141	No-Hitters Nolan Ryan Jack Morris Dave Righetti	.40	.16	.04
☐ 142	No-Hitters Tom Seaver Bert Blyleven Vida Blue	.35	.14	.03

		MINT	VG-E	F-G
☐ 143	Strikeout Kings Nolan Ryan Fernando Valenzuela Dwight Gooden	1.50	.60	.15
☐ 144	Base Stealers Tim Raines Willie Wilson Davey Lopes	.45	.18	.04
☐ 145	RBI Sluggers Tony Armas Cecil Cooper Eddie Murray	.40	.16	.04
☐ 146	AL MVP's Rod Carew Jim Rice Rollie Fingers	.50	.20	.05
☐ 147	World Series MVP's Alan Trammell Rick Dempsey Reggie Jackson	.45	.18	.04
☐ 148	World Series MVP's Darrell Porter Pedro Guerrero Mike Schmidt	.45	.18	.04
☐ 149	ERA Leaders Mike Boddicker Rick Sutcliffe Ron Guidry	.25	.10	.02
☐ 150	Comeback Players Reggie Jackson Dave Kingman Fred Lynn	.45	.18	.04
☐ 151	Buddy Bell	.20	.08	.02
☐ 152	Dennis Boyd	.20	.08	.02
☐ 153	Dave Concepcion	.20	.08	.02
☐ 154	Brian Downing	.15	.06	.01
☐ 155	Shawon Dunston	.25	.10	.02
☐ 156	John Franco	.25	.10	.02
☐ 157	Scott Garrelts	.20	.08	.02
☐ 158	Bob James	.15	.06	.01
☐ 159	Charlie Leibrandt	.20	.08	.02
☐ 160	Oddibe McDowell	.75	.30	.07
☐ 161	Roger McDowell	.50	.20	.05
☐ 162	Mike Moore	.20	.08	.02
☐ 163	Phil Niekro	.50	.20	.05
☐ 164	Al Oliver	.25	.10	.02
☐ 165	Tony Pena	.25	.10	.02
☐ 166	Ted Power	.20	.08	.02
☐ 167	Mike Scioscia	.15	.06	.01
☐ 168	Mario Soto	.20	.08	.02
☐ 169	Bob Stanley	.20	.08	.02
☐ 170	Gary Templeton	.20	.08	.02
☐ 171	Andre Thornton	.20	.08	.02

		MINT	VG-E	F-G
☐ 172	Alan Trammell	.30	.12	.03
☐ 173	Doug DeCinces	.25	.10	.02
☐ 174	Greg Walker	.25	.10	.02
☐ 175	Don Sutton	.40	.16	.04
☐ 176	1985 Award Winners	1.50	.60	.15
	Ozzie Guillen			
	Bret Saberhagen			
	Don Mattingly			
	Vince Coleman			
	Dwight Gooden			
	Willie McGee			
☐ 177	1985 Hot Rookies	.50	.20	.05
	Stew Cliburn			
	Brian Fisher			
	Joe Hesketh			
	Joe Orsulak			
	Mark Salas			
	Larry Sheets			
☐ 178	1986 Rookies To Watch	6.00	2.40	.60
	Jose Canseco			
	Mark Funderburk			
	Mike Greenwell			
	Steve Lombardozzi			
	Billy Joe Robidoux			
	Dan Tartabull			
☐ 179	1985 Gold Glovers	1.00	.40	.10
	George Brett			
	Ron Guidry			
	Keith Hernandez			
	Don Mattingly			
	Willie McGee			
	Dale Murphy			
☐ 180	Active Lifetime .300	1.00	.40	.10
	Wade Boggs			
	George Brett			
	Rod Carew			
	Cecil Cooper			
	Don Mattingly			
	Willie Wilson			
☐ 181	Active Lifetime .300	1.00	.40	.10
	Tony Gwynn			
	Bill Madlock			
	Pedro Guerrero			
	Dave Parker			
	Pete Rose			
	Keith Hernandez			
☐ 182	1985 Milestones	1.00	.40	.10
	Rod Carew			
	Phil Niekro			
	Pete Rose			
	Nolan Ryan			
	Tom Seaver			
	Matt Tallman (fan)			

		MINT	VG-E	F-G
☐ 183	1985 Triple Crown	1.00	.40	.10
	Wade Boggs			
	Darrell Evans			
	Don Mattingly			
	Willie McGee			
	Dale Murphy			
	Dave Parker			
☐ 184	1985 Highlights	2.00	.80	.20
	Wade Boggs			
	Dwight Gooden			
	Rickey Henderson			
	Don Mattingly			
	Willie McGee			
	John Tudor			
☐ 185	1985 20 Game Winners .	1.25	.50	.12
	Dwight Gooden			
	Ron Guidry			
	John Tudor			
	Joaquin Andujar			
	Bret Saberhagen			
	Tom Browning			
☐ 186	World Series Champs ...	.50	.20	.05
	L. Smith, Dane Iorg			
	W. Wilson, Leibrandt			
	G. Brett, Saberhagen			
	D. Motley, Quisenberry			
	D. Jackson, Sundberg			
	S. Balboni, F. White			
☐ 187	Hubie Brooks	.25	.10	.02
☐ 188	Glenn Davis	.75	.30	.07
☐ 189	Darrell Evans	.25	.10	.02
☐ 190	Rich Gossage	.35	.14	.03
☐ 191	Andy Hawkins	.20	.08	.02
☐ 192	Jay Howell	.20	.08	.02
☐ 193	LaMarr Hoyt	.25	.10	.02
☐ 194	Davey Lopes	.20	.08	.02
☐ 195	Mike Scott	.35	.14	.03
☐ 196	Ted Simmons	.25	.10	.02
☐ 197	Gary Ward	.15	.06	.01
☐ 198	Bob Welch	.20	.08	.02
☐ 199	Mike Young	.25	.10	.02
☐ 200	Buddy Biancalana	.15	.06	.01

1986 Sportflics Decade Greats

This set of 75 three-phase "animated" cards was produced by Sportflics and manufactured by Opti-Graphics of Arlington, Texas. Cards are standard size, 2½" by 3½", and feature both sepia (players of the '30s and '40s) and full color cards. The concept of the set was that the best players at each position for each decade (from the '30s to the '80s) were chosen. The bios were written by Les Woodcock. Also included with the set in the specially designed collector box are 51 trivia cards with historical questions about the six decades of All-Star games.

	MINT	VG-E	F-G
Complete Set	16.00	6.50	1.60
Common Player (1-75)	.15	.06	.01

		MINT	VG-E	F-G
☐ 1	Babe Ruth	2.00	.80	.20
☐ 2	Jimmie Foxx	.35	.14	.03
☐ 3	Lefty Grove	.35	.14	.03
☐ 4	Hank Greenberg	.35	.14	.03
☐ 5	Al Simmons	.25	.10	.02
☐ 6	Carl Hubbell	.25	.10	.02
☐ 7	Joe Cronin	.25	.10	.02
☐ 8	Mel Ott	.25	.10	.02
☐ 9	Lefty Gomez	.25	.10	.02
☐ 10	Lou Gehrig	1.00	.40	.10
	(Best '30s Player)			
☐ 11	Pie Traynor	.25	.10	.02
☐ 12	Charlie Gehringer	.25	.10	.02
☐ 13	Best '30s Catchers	.25	.10	.02
	Bill Dickey			
	Mickey Cochrane			
	Gabby Hartnett			
☐ 14	Best '30s Pitchers	.35	.14	.03
	Dizzy Dean			
	Red Ruffing			
	Paul Derringer			
☐ 15	Best '30s Outfielders	.25	.10	.02
	Paul Waner			
	Joe Medwick			
	Earl Averill			
☐ 16	Bob Feller	.75	.30	.07
☐ 17	Lou Boudreau	.25	.10	.02
☐ 18	Enos Slaughter	.25	.10	.02
☐ 19	Hal Newhouser	.15	.06	.01
☐ 20	Joe DiMaggio	1.25	.50	.12
☐ 21	Pee Wee Reese	.35	.14	.03
☐ 22	Phil Rizzuto	.25	.10	.02
☐ 23	Ernie Lombardi	.25	.10	.02
☐ 24	Best '40s Infielders	.25	.10	.02
	Johnny Mize			
	Joe Gordon			
	George Kell			
☐ 25	Ted Williams	1.00	.40	.10
	(Best '40s Player)			
☐ 26	Mickey Mantle	2.00	.80	.20
☐ 27	Warren Spahn	.25	.10	.02
☐ 28	Jackie Robinson	.50	.20	.05
☐ 29	Ernie Banks	.35	.14	.03
☐ 30	Stan Musial	.50	.20	.05
	(Best '50s Player)			
☐ 31	Yogi Berra	.50	.20	.05
☐ 32	Duke Snider	.75	.30	.07
☐ 33	Roy Campanella	.75	.30	.07
☐ 34	Eddie Mathews	.35	.14	.03
☐ 35	Ralph Kiner	.25	.10	.02
☐ 36	Early Wynn	.25	.10	.02
☐ 37	Double Play Duo	.25	.10	.02
	Nellie Fox			
	Luis Aparicio			
☐ 38	Best '50s First Base	.25	.10	.02
	Gil Hodges			
	Ted Kluszewski			
	Mickey Vernon			
☐ 39	Best '50s Pitchers	.25	.10	.02
	Bob Lemon			
	Don Newcombe			
	Robin Roberts			
☐ 40	Henry Aaron	1.00	.40	.10
☐ 41	Frank Robinson	.35	.14	.03
☐ 42	Bob Gibson	.35	.14	.03
☐ 43	Roberto Clemente	1.00	.40	.10
☐ 44	Whitey Ford	.35	.14	.03
☐ 45	Brooks Robinson	.50	.20	.05
☐ 46	Juan Marichal	.35	.14	.03
☐ 47	Carl Yastrzemski	1.00	.40	.10

		MINT	VG-E	F-G
☐ 48	Best '60s First Base	.35	.14	.03
	Willie McCovey			
	Harmon Killebrew			
	Orlando Cepeda			
☐ 49	Best '60s Catchers	.15	.06	.01
	Joe Torre			
	Elston Howard			
	Bill Freehan			
☐ 50	Willie Mays	1.00	.40	.10
	(Best '50s Player)			
☐ 51	Best '60s Outfielders	.25	.10	.02
	Al Kaline			
	Tony Oliva			
	Billy Williams			
☐ 52	Tom Seaver	.75	.30	.07
☐ 53	Reggie Jackson	1.00	.40	.10
☐ 54	Steve Carlton	.75	.30	.07
☐ 55	Mike Schmidt	1.00	.40	.10
☐ 56	Joe Morgan	.35	.14	.03
☐ 57	Jim Rice	.50	.20	.05
☐ 58	Jim Palmer	.35	.14	.03
☐ 59	Lou Brock	.35	.14	.03
☐ 60	Pete Rose	1.25	.50	.12
	(Best '70s Player)			
☐ 61	Steve Garvey	.75	.30	.07
☐ 62	Best '70s Catchers	.25	.10	.02
	Thurman Munson			
	Carlton Fisk			
	Ted Simmons			
☐ 63	Best '70s Pitchers	.25	.10	.02
	Vida Blue			
	Catfish Hunter			
	Nolan Ryan			
☐ 64	George Brett	1.00	.40	.10
☐ 65	Don Mattingly	2.00	.80	.20
☐ 66	Fernando Valenzuela ...	.35	.14	.03
☐ 67	Dale Murphy	1.00	.40	.10
☐ 68	Wade Boggs	1.25	.50	.12
☐ 69	Rickey Henderson	1.00	.40	.10
☐ 70	Eddie Murray	.75	.30	.07
	(Best '80s Player)			
☐ 71	Ron Guidry	.25	.10	.02
☐ 72	Best '80s Catchers	.25	.10	.02
	Gary Carter			
	Lance Parrish			
	Tony Pena			
☐ 73	Best '80s Infielders	.25	.10	.02
	Cal Ripken			
	Lou Whitaker			
	Robin Yount			

		MINT	VG-E	F-G
☐ 74	Best '80s Outfielders	.25	.10	.02
	Pedro Guerrero			
	Tim Raines			
	Dave Winfield			
☐ 75	Dwight Gooden	1.25	.50	.12

1986 Sportflics Rookies

This set of 50 three-phase "animated" cards features top rookies of 1986 as well as a few outstanding rookies from the past. These "Magic Motion" cards are standard size 2½" by 3½" and feature a distinctive light blue border on the front of the card. Cards were distributed in a light blue box which also contained 34 trivia cards, each measuring 1¾" by 2". There are 47 single player cards along with two Tri-Stars and one Big Six.

		MINT	VG-E	F-G
	Complete Set (50)	15.00	6.00	1.50
	Common Player (1-50) ..	.10	.04	.01
☐ 1	John Kruk	.30	.12	.03
☐ 2	Edwin Correa...........	.40	.16	.04
☐ 3	Pete Incaviglia	1.50	.60	.15
☐ 4	Dale Sveum	.20	.08	.02
☐ 5	Juan Nieves	.30	.12	.03
☐ 6	Will Clark	.75	.30	.07
☐ 7	Wally Joyner	3.00	1.20	.30
☐ 8	Lance McCullers	.20	.08	.02
☐ 9	Scott Bailes	.20	.08	.02
☐ 10	Dan Plesac	.20	.08	.02
☐ 11	Jose Canseco	2.00	.80	.20
☐ 12	Bobby Witt	.50	.20	.05
☐ 13	Barry Bonds	.75	.30	.07
☐ 14	Andres Thomas	.40	.16	.04

		MINT	VG-E	F-G
☐ 15	Jim Deshaies	.50	.20	.05
☐ 16	Ruben Sierra	1.50	.60	.15
☐ 17	Steve Lombardozzi	.10	.04	.01
☐ 18	Cory Snyder	1.25	.50	.12
☐ 19	Reggie Williams	.20	.08	.02
☐ 20	Mitch Williams	.30	.12	.03
☐ 21	Glenn Braggs	.60	.24	.06
☐ 22	Danny Tartabull	.50	.20	.05
☐ 23	Charlie Kerfeld	.30	.12	.03
☐ 24	Paul Assenmacher	.20	.08	.02
☐ 25	Robby Thompson	.50	.20	.05
☐ 26	Bobby Bonilla	.20	.08	.02
☐ 27	Andres Galarraga	.30	.12	.03
☐ 28	Billy Jo Robidoux	.20	.08	.02
☐ 29	Bruce Ruffin	.40	.16	.04
☐ 30	Greg Swindell	.60	.24	.06
☐ 31	John Cangelosi	.30	.12	.03
☐ 32	Jim Traber	.20	.08	.02
☐ 33	Russ Morman	.35	.14	.03
☐ 34	Barry Larkin	.60	.24	.06
☐ 35	Todd Worrell	.60	.24	.06
☐ 36	John Cerutti	.30	.12	.03
☐ 37	Mike Kingery	.25	.10	.02
☐ 38	Mark Eichhorn	.50	.20	.05
☐ 39	Scott Bankhead	.15	.06	.01
☐ 40	Bo Jackson	1.50	.60	.15
☐ 41	Greg Mathews	.40	.16	.04
☐ 42	Eric King	.40	.16	.04
☐ 43	Kal Daniels	.25	.10	.02
☐ 44	Calvin Schiraldi	.20	.08	.02
☐ 45	Mickey Brantley	.30	.12	.03
☐ 46	Tri-Stars	.60	.24	.06
	Willie Mays			
	Pete Rose			
	Fred Lynn			
☐ 47	Tri-Stars	.60	.24	.06
	Tom Seaver			
	Fern. Valenzuela			
	Dwight Gooden			
☐ 48	Big Six	.60	.24	.06
	Eddie Murray			
	Lou Whitaker			
	Dave Righetti			
	Steve Sax			
	Cal Ripken Jr.			
	Darryl Strawberry			
☐ 49	Kevin Mitchell	.50	.20	.05
☐ 50	Mike Diaz	.40	.16	.04

1987 Sportflics

This 200-card set was produced by Sportflics and again features three sequence action pictures on each card. Cards measure
2½" by 3½" and are in full color. Also included with the cards were 136 small team logo
and trivia cards. The set includes 165 individual
players, 20 Tri-Stars (the top three players in
each league at each position), and 15 other
miscellaneous multi-player cards. The cards
feature a red border on the front. A full-color
face shot of the player is printed on the back
of the card. Cards are numbered on the back
in the upper right corner.

		MINT	VG-E	F-G
	Complete Set	35.00	14.00	3.50
	Common Player	.15	.06	.01
☐ 1	Don Mattingly	2.50	1.00	.25
☐ 2	Wade Boggs	1.25	.50	.12
☐ 3	Dale Murphy	.90	.36	.09
☐ 4	Rickey Henderson	.75	.30	.07
☐ 5	George Brett	.75	.30	.07
☐ 6	Eddie Murray	.60	.24	.06
☐ 7	Kirby Puckett	.50	.20	.05
☐ 8	Ryne Sandberg	.50	.20	.05
☐ 9	Cal Ripken Jr.	.50	.20	.05
☐ 10	Roger Clemens	1.25	.50	.12
☐ 11	Ted Higuera	.25	.10	.02
☐ 12	Steve Sax	.25	.10	.02
☐ 13	Chris Brown	.25	.10	.02
☐ 14	Jesse Barfield	.35	.14	.03
☐ 15	Kent Hrbek	.25	.10	.02
☐ 16	Robin Yount	.45	.18	.04
☐ 17	Glenn Davis	.60	.24	.06
☐ 18	Hubie Brooks	.25	.10	.02

		MINT	VG-E	F-G
☐ 19	Mike Scott	.30	.12	.03
☐ 20	Darryl Strawberry	.75	.30	.07
☐ 21	Alvin Davis	.25	.10	.02
☐ 22	Eric Davis	.75	.30	.07
☐ 23	Danny Tartabull	.50	.20	.05
☐ 24	Cory Snyder	.75	.30	.07
☐ 25	Pete Rose	1.25	.50	.12
☐ 26	Wally Joyner	2.50	1.00	.25
☐ 27	Pedro Guerrero	.35	.14	.03
☐ 28	Tom Seaver	.75	.30	.07
☐ 29	Bob Knepper	.20	.08	.02
☐ 30	Mike Schmidt	1.00	.40	.10
☐ 31	Tony Gwynn	.60	.24	.06
☐ 32	Don Slaught	.15	.06	.01
☐ 33	Todd Worrell	.35	.14	.03
☐ 34	Tim Raines	.35	.14	.03
☐ 35	Dave Parker	.35	.14	.03
☐ 36	Bob Ojeda	.25	.10	.02
☐ 37	Pete Incaviglia	1.00	.40	.10
☐ 38	Bruce Hurst	.25	.10	.02
☐ 39	Bobby Witt	.50	.20	.05
☐ 40	Steve Garvey	.60	.24	.06
☐ 41	Dave Winfield	.50	.20	.05
☐ 42	Jose Cruz	.20	.08	.02
☐ 43	Orel Hershiser	.25	.10	.02
☐ 44	Reggie Jackson	1.00	.40	.10
☐ 45	Chili Davis	.20	.08	.02
☐ 46	Robby Thompson	.35	.14	.03
☐ 47	Dennis Boyd	.25	.10	.02
☐ 48	Kirk Gibson	.35	.14	.03
☐ 49	Fred Lynn	.25	.10	.02
☐ 50	Gary Carter	.60	.24	.06
☐ 51	George Bell	.30	.12	.03
☐ 52	Pete O'Brien	.25	.10	.02
☐ 53	Ron Darling	.35	.14	.03
☐ 54	Paul Molitor	.20	.08	.02
☐ 55	Mike Pagliarulo	.25	.10	.02
☐ 56	Mike Boddicker	.20	.08	.02
☐ 57	Dave Righetti	.25	.10	.02
☐ 58	Len Dykstra	.35	.14	.03
☐ 59	Mike Witt	.25	.10	.02
☐ 60	Tony Bernazard	.15	.06	.01
☐ 61	John Kruk	.30	.12	.03
☐ 62	Mike Krukow	.20	.08	.02
☐ 63	Sid Fernandez	.35	.14	.03
☐ 64	Gary Gaetti	.25	.10	.02
☐ 65	Vince Coleman	.60	.24	.06
☐ 66	Pat Tabler	.25	.10	.02
☐ 67	Mike Scioscia	.15	.06	.01
☐ 68	Scott Garrelts	.15	.06	.01
☐ 69	Brett Butler	.25	.10	.02
☐ 70	Bill Buckner	.20	.08	.02
☐ 71	Dennis Rasmussen	.20	.08	.02

		MINT	VG-E	F-G
☐ 72	Tim Wallach	.20	.08	.02
☐ 73	Bob Horner	.30	.12	.03
☐ 74	Willie McGee	.30	.12	.03
☐ 75	Tri-Stars	1.50	.60	.15
	Don Mattingly			
	Wally Joyner			
	Eddie Murray			
☐ 76	Jesse Orosco	.15	.06	.01
☐ 77	Tri-Stars	.25	.10	.02
	Todd Worrell			
	Jeff Reardon			
	Lee Smith			
☐ 78	Candy Maldonado	.25	.10	.02
☐ 79	Tri-Stars	.25	.10	.02
	Ozzie Smith			
	Hubie Brooks			
	Shawon Dunston			
☐ 80	Tri-Stars	1.00	.40	.10
	George Bell			
	Jose Canseco			
	Jim Rice			
☐ 81	Bert Blyleven	.25	.10	.02
☐ 82	Mike Marshall	.25	.10	.02
☐ 83	Ron Guidry	.25	.10	.02
☐ 84	Julio Franco	.20	.08	.02
☐ 85	Willie Wilson	.25	.10	.02
☐ 86	Lee Lacy	.15	.06	.01
☐ 87	Jack Morris	.30	.12	.03
☐ 88	Ray Knight	.25	.10	.02
☐ 89	Phil Bradley	.35	.14	.03
☐ 90	Jose Canseco	2.00	.80	.20
☐ 91	Gary Ward	.20	.08	.02
☐ 92	Mike Easler	.20	.08	.02
☐ 93	Tony Pena	.25	.10	.02
☐ 94	Dave Smith	.20	.08	.02
☐ 95	Will Clark	.75	.30	.07
☐ 96	Lloyd Moseby	.20	.08	.02
☐ 97	Jim Rice	.50	.20	.05
☐ 98	Shawon Dunston	.25	.10	.02
☐ 99	Don Sutton	.35	.14	.03
☐ 100	Dwight Gooden	1.25	.50	.12
☐ 101	Lance Parrish	.35	.14	.03
☐ 102	Mark Langston	.25	.10	.02
☐ 103	Floyd Youmans	.30	.12	.03
☐ 104	Lee Smith	.25	.10	.02
☐ 105	Willie Hernandez	.25	.10	.02
☐ 106	Doug DeCinces	.20	.08	.02
☐ 107	Ken Schrom	.15	.06	.01
☐ 108	Don Carman	.15	.06	.01
☐ 109	Brook Jacoby	.25	.10	.02
☐ 110	Steve Bedrosian	.15	.06	.01

	MINT	VG-E	F-G
☐ 111 Tri-Stars	.75	.30	.07
Roger Clemens			
Jack Morris			
Ted Higuera			
☐ 112 Tri-Stars	.20	.08	.02
Marty Barrett			
Tony Bernazard			
Lou Whitaker			
☐ 113 Tri-Stars	.35	.14	.03
Cal Ripken			
Scott Fletcher			
Tony Fernandez			
☐ 114 Tri-Stars	1.00	.40	.10
Wade Boggs			
George Brett			
Gary Gaetti			
☐ 115 Tri-Stars	.50	.20	.05
Mike Schmidt			
Chris Brown			
Tim Wallach			
☐ 116 Tri-Stars	.35	.14	.03
Ryne Sandberg			
Johnny Ray			
Bill Doran			
☐ 117 Tri-Stars	.35	.14	.03
Dave Parker			
Tony Gwynn			
Kevin Bass			
☐ 118 Big Six Rookies	2.00	.80	.20
Ty Gainey			
Terry Steinbach			
David Clark			
Pat Dodson			
Phil Lombardi			
Benito Santiago			
☐ 119 Hi-Lite Tri-Stars	.50	.20	.05
Dave Righetti			
Fernando Valenzuela			
Mike Scott			
☐ 120 Tri-Stars	1.00	.40	.10
Fernando Valenzuela			
Mike Scott			
Dwight Gooden			
☐ 121 Johnny Ray	.20	.08	.02
☐ 122 Keith Moreland	.20	.08	.02
☐ 123 Juan Samuel	.25	.10	.02
☐ 124 Wally Backman	.20	.08	.02
☐ 125 Nolan Ryan	.60	.24	.06
☐ 126 Greg Harris	.20	.08	.02
☐ 127 Kirk McCaskill	.30	.12	.03
☐ 128 Dwight Evans	.25	.10	.02
☐ 129 Rick Rhoden	.20	.08	.02
☐ 130 Bill Madlock	.25	.10	.02

	MINT	VG-E	F-G
☐ 131 Oddibe McDowell	.35	.14	.03
☐ 132 Darrell Evans	.20	.08	.02
☐ 133 Keith Hernandez	.35	.14	.03
☐ 134 Tom Brunansky	.20	.08	.02
☐ 135 Kevin McReynolds	.30	.12	.03
☐ 136 Scott Fletcher	.20	.08	.02
☐ 137 Lou Whitaker	.25	.10	.02
☐ 138 Carney Lansford	.25	.10	.02
☐ 139 Andre Dawson	.30	.12	.03
☐ 140 Carlton Fisk	.25	.10	.02
☐ 141 Buddy Bell	.20	.08	.02
☐ 142 Ozzie Smith	.25	.10	.02
☐ 143 Dan Pasqua	.30	.12	.03
☐ 144 Kevin Mitchell	.35	.14	.03
☐ 145 Bret Saberhagen	.25	.10	.02
☐ 146 Charlie Kerfeld	.25	.10	.02
☐ 147 Phil Niekro	.30	.12	.03
☐ 148 John Candelaria	.20	.08	.02
☐ 149 Rich Gedman	.25	.10	.02
☐ 150 Fernando Valenzuela	.50	.20	.05
☐ 151 Tri-Stars	.35	.14	.03
Gary Carter			
Mike Scioscia			
Tony Pena			
☐ 152 Tri-Stars	.60	.24	.06
Tim Raines			
Jose Cruz			
Vince Coleman			
☐ 153 Tri-Stars	.35	.14	.03
Jesse Barfield			
Harold Baines			
Dave Winfield			
☐ 154 Tri-Stars	.35	.14	.03
Lance Parrish			
Don Slaught			
Rich Gedman			
☐ 155 Tri-Stars	.75	.30	.07
Dale Murphy			
Kevin McReynolds			
Eric Davis			
☐ 156 Hi-Lite Tri-Stars	.50	.20	.05
Don Sutton			
Mike Schmidt			
Jim Deshaies			
☐ 157 Speedburners	.45	.18	.04
Rickey Henderson			
John Cangelosi			
Gary Pettis			

	MINT	VG-E	F-G
☐ 158 Big Six Rookies	2.00	.80	.20
Randy Asadoor			
Casey Candaele			
Kevin Seitzer			
Rafael Palmeiro			
Tim Pyznarski			
Dave Cochrane			
☐ 159 Big Six	2.50	1.00	.25
Don Mattingly			
Rickey Henderson			
Roger Clemens			
Dale Murphy			
Eddie Murray			
Dwight Gooden			
☐ 160 Roger McDowell	.25	.10	.02
☐ 161 Brian Downing	.15	.06	.01
☐ 162 Bill Doran	.25	.10	.02
☐ 163 Don Baylor	.25	.10	.02
☐ 164 Alfredo Griffin	.15	.06	.01
☐ 165 Don Aase	.15	.06	.01
☐ 166 Glenn Wilson	.25	.10	.02
☐ 167 Dan Quisenberry	.25	.10	.02
☐ 168 Frank White	.20	.08	.02
☐ 169 Cecil Cooper	.25	.10	.02
☐ 170 Jody Davis	.25	.10	.02
☐ 171 Harold Baines	.35	.14	.03
☐ 172 Rob Deer	.35	.14	.03
☐ 173 John Tudor	.25	.10	.02
☐ 174 Larry Parrish	.20	.08	.02
☐ 175 Kevin Bass	.25	.10	.02
☐ 176 Joe Carter	.45	.18	.04
☐ 177 Mitch Webster	.25	.10	.02
☐ 178 Dave Kingman	.30	.12	.03
☐ 179 Jim Presley	.40	.16	.04
☐ 180 Mel Hall	.25	.10	.02
☐ 181 Shane Rawley	.20	.08	.02
☐ 182 Marty Barrett	.30	.12	.03
☐ 183 Damaso Garcia	.20	.08	.02
☐ 184 Bobby Grich	.20	.08	.02
☐ 185 Leon Durham	.20	.08	.02
☐ 186 Ozzie Guillen	.25	.10	.02
☐ 187 Tony Fernandez	.25	.10	.02
☐ 188 Alan Trammell	.25	.10	.02
☐ 189 Jim Clancy	.15	.06	.01
☐ 190 Bo Jackson	1.25	.50	.12
☐ 191 Bob Forsch	.20	.08	.02
☐ 192 John Franco	.25	.10	.02
☐ 193 Von Hayes	.35	.14	.03

	MINT	VG-E	F-G
☐ 194 Tri-Stars	.25	.10	.02
Don Aase			
Dave Righetti			
Mark Eichhorn			
☐ 195 Tri-Stars	.35	.14	.03
Keith Hernandez			
Jack Clark			
Glenn Davis			
☐ 196 Hi-Lite Tri-Stars	.75	.30	.07
Roger Clemens			
Joe Cowley			
Bob Horner			
☐ 197 Big Six	1.00	.40	.10
George Brett			
Hubie Brooks			
Tony Gwynn			
Ryne Sandberg			
Tim Raines			
Wade Boggs			
☐ 198 Tri-Stars	.50	.20	.05
Kirby Puckett			
Rickey Henderson			
Fred Lynn			
☐ 199 Speedburners	1.00	.40	.10
Tim Raines			
Vince Coleman			
Eric Davis			
☐ 200 Steve Carlton	.50	.20	.05

The HOUSE OF COLLECTIBLES Series

☐ *Please send me the following price guides –*
☐ *I would like the most current edition of the books listed below.*

THE OFFICIAL PRICE GUIDES TO:

☐ 199-3	**American Silver & Silver Plate** 5th Ed.	$11.95
☐ 513-1	**Antique Clocks** 3rd Ed.	10.95
☐ 283-3	**Antique & Modern Dolls** 3rd Ed.	10.95
☐ 287-6	**Antique & Modern Firearms** 6th Ed.	11.95
☐ 738-X	**Antiques & Collectibles** 8th Ed.	10.95
☐ 289-2	**Antique Jewelry** 5th Ed.	11.95
☐ 539-5	**Beer Cans & Collectibles** 4th Ed.	7.95
☐ 521-2	**Bottles Old & New** 10th Ed.	10.95
☐ 532-8	**Carnival Glass** 2nd Ed.	10.95
☐ 295-7	**Collectible Cameras** 2nd Ed.	10.95
☐ 548-4	**Collectibles of the '50s & '60s** 1st Ed.	9.95
☐ 740-1	**Collectible Toys** 4th Ed.	10.95
☐ 531-X	**Collector Cars** 7th Ed.	12.95
☐ 538-7	**Collector Handguns** 4th Ed.	14.95
☐ 290-6	**Collector Knives** 8th Ed.	11.95
☐ 518-2	**Collector Plates** 4th Ed.	11.95
☐ 296-5	**Collector Prints** 7th Ed.	12.95
☐ 001-6	**Depression Glass** 2nd Ed.	9.95
☐ 589-1	**Fine Art** 1st Ed.	19.95
☐ 311-2	**Glassware** 3rd Ed.	10.95
☐ 243-4	**Hummel Figurines & Plates** 6th Ed.	10.95
☐ 523-9	**Kitchen Collectibles** 2nd Ed.	10.95
☐ 291-4	**Military Collectibles** 5th Ed.	11.95
☐ 525-5	**Music Collectibles** 6th Ed.	11.95
☐ 313-9	**Old Books & Autographs** 7th Ed.	11.95
☐ 298-1	**Oriental Collectibles** 3rd Ed.	11.95
☐ 746-0	**Overstreet Comic Book** 17th Ed.	11.95
☐ 522-0	**Paperbacks & Magazines** 1st Ed.	10.95
☐ 297-3	**Paper Collectibles** 5th Ed.	10.95
☐ 529-8	**Pottery & Porcelain** 6th Ed.	11.95
☐ 524-7	**Radio, TV & Movie Memorabilia** 3rd Ed.	11.95
☐ 288-4	**Records** 7th Ed.	10.95
☐ 247-7	**Royal Doulton** 5th Ed.	11.95
☐ 280-9	**Science Fiction & Fantasy Collectibles** 2nd Ed.	10.95
☐ 299-X	**Star Trek/Star Wars Collectibles** 1st Ed.	7.95
☐ 248-5	**Wicker** 3rd Ed.	10.95

THE OFFICIAL:

☐ 445-3	**Collector's Journal** 1st Ed.	4.95
☐ 549-2	**Directory to U.S. Flea Markets** 1st Ed.	4.95
☐ 365-1	**Encyclopedia of Antiques** 1st Ed.	9.95
☐ 369-4	**Guide to Buying and Selling Antiques** 1st Ed.	9.95
☐ 414-3	**Identification Guide to Early American Furniture** 1st Ed.	9.95

☐ 413-5 **Identification Guide to Glassware** 1st Ed. $9.95
☐ 448-8 **Identification Guide to Gunmarks** 2nd Ed. 9.95
☐ 412-7 **Identification Guide to Pottery & Porcelain** 1st Ed. 9.95
☐ 415-1 **Identification Guide to Victorian Furniture** 1st Ed. 9.95

THE OFFICIAL (SMALL SIZE) PRICE GUIDES TO:
☐ 309-0 **Antiques & Flea Markets** 4th Ed. 4.95
☐ 269-8 **Antique Jewelry** 3rd Ed. 4.95
☐ 737-1 **Baseball Cards** 7th Ed. 4.95
☐ 488-7 **Bottles** 2nd Ed. 4.95
☐ 544-1 **Cars & Trucks** 3rd Ed. 5.95
☐ 519-0 **Collectible Americana** 2nd Ed. 4.95
☐ 294-9 **Collectible Records** 3rd Ed. 4.95
☐ 306-6 **Dolls** 4th Ed. 4.95
☐ 520-4 **Football Cards** 6th Ed. 4.95
☐ 540-9 **Glassware** 3rd Ed. 4.95
☐ 526-3 **Hummels** 4th Ed. 4.95
☐ 279-5 **Military Collectibles** 3rd Ed. 4.95
☐ 278-7 **Pocket Knives** 3rd Ed. 4.95
☐ 527-1 **Scouting Collectibles** 4th Ed. 4.95
☐ 494-1 **Star Trek/Star Wars Collectibles** 3rd Ed. 3.95
☐ 307-4 **Toys** 4th Ed. 4.95

THE OFFICIAL BLACKBOOK PRICE GUIDES OF:
☐ 743-6 **U.S. Coins** 26th Ed. 3.95
☐ 742-8 **U.S. Paper Money** 20th Ed. 3.95
☐ 741-X **U.S. Postage Stamps** 10th Ed. 3.95

THE OFFICIAL NUMISMATIC GUIDE SERIES:
☐ 254-X **The Official Guide to Detecting Counterfeit Money** 2nd Ed. 7.95
☐ 257-4 **The Official Guide to Mint Errors** 4th Ed. 7.95

THE OFFICIAL INVESTORS GUIDE TO BUYING & SELLING:
☐ 534-4 **Gold, Silver & Diamonds** 2nd Ed. 12.95
☐ 535-2 **Gold Coins** 2nd Ed. 12.95
☐ 536-0 **Silver Coins** 2nd Ed. 12.95
☐ 537-9 **Silver Dollars** 2nd Ed. 12.95

SPECIAL INTEREST SERIES:
☐ 506-9 **From Hearth to Cookstove** 3rd Ed. 17.95
☐ 530-1 **Lucky Number Lottery Guide** 1st Ed. 4.95
☐ 504-2 **On Method Acting** 8th Printing 6.95

TOTAL	

SEE FOLLOWING PAGE FOR ORDERING INSTRUCTIONS

BILL HENDERSON'S CARDS
"King of the Commons"

2320 RUGER AVE. - PG9
JANESVILLE, WISCONSIN 53545
1-608-755-0922

"ALWAYS BUYING" Call or Write for Quote

"ALWAYS BUYING" Call or Write for Quote

	HI NOS.	COMMONS EACH	EX/MT TO MINT CONDITION		GROUP LOTS FOR SALE			VG Condition		
				50 Diff.	100 Diff.	300 Asst.	500 Asst.	50 Different	100	200
1948 BOWMAN		4.00								
1949 BOWMAN		4.00								
50-51 BOWMAN	12.00	3.50	51 (2-72) 4.00	165.				100.		
1952 TOPPS	75.00	7.00	(2-80) 10.00	315.				190.		
1952 BOWMAN	7.00	3.50	(2-72) 3.75	165.				100.		
1953 TOPPS	14.00	4.00		185.				110.		
1953 BOWMAN	10.00	7.50	(113-128) 18.00	340.				200.		
1954 TOPPS		2.00	(51-75) 4.00	95.	180.			58.		
1954 BOWMAN		1.50	(129-224) 2.00	70.	135.			45.		
1955 TOPPS	4.50	1.50	(151-160) 3.50	70.	135.	390.		45.		
1955 BOWMAN	4.00-6. Umps	.75	(2-96) 1.00	35.	68.	200.		20.	40.	
1956 TOPPS		1.50	(181-260) 2.50	70.	135.	390.		40.	75.	
1957 TOPPS	4.50	1.00	(353-407) 1.25	45.	85.	245.		28.	50.	
1958 TOPPS		.65	(1-110) .85	30.	58.	170.		40.		
1959 TOPPS		.45	(1-110) .60	20.	40.	115.	185.	24.	46.	
1960 TOPPS	(553-572 2.50) .60	.40	(441-506) .60	20.	38.	110.	175.	24.	46.	
1961 TOPPS	6.50-8.50 S.N.	.40	(371-522) .40	17.	32.	92.	150.	20.	38.	
1962 TOPPS	2.00-5.00 RKS.	.60	(371-522) .60	17.	32.	92.	150.	20.	38.	
1963 TOPPS	2.00	.30	(197-446) .50	14.	28.	80.		20.		
1964 TOPPS	1.00	.30	(371-522) .50	14.	28.	80.	130.	18.	35.	
1965 TOPPS	(447-522 .50) .85	.30	(199-446) .35	14.	28.	80.	130.	18.	35.	
1966 TOPPS	5.00	.30	(447-522) .60	14.	28.	80.	130.	18.	35.	
1967 TOPPS	3.00	.30	(458-533) 1.00	14.	28.	80.	130.	18.	35.	
1968 TOPPS	(13-110 .25) .40	.25	(458-533) .30	12.	24.	*70.	110.	15.	28.	
1969 TOPPS		.25	(219-327) .40		24.	*70.	110.	15.	28.	
1970 TOPPS	1.00	.25	(553-636) .50		24.	*70.	110.	15.	28.	
1971 TOPPS	1.00	.25	(524-643) .50		24.	*70.	110.	15.	28.	
1972 TOPPS	(395-525 .25) 1.00	.25	(526-656) .50		24.	*70.	110.	15.	28.	
1973 TOPPS	.75	.20	(397-528) .25		18.	*52.	85.	10.	19.	
1974 TOPPS		.20			18.	*52.	*85.	10.	19.	
1975 TOPPS	(8-132 .25)	.20			18.	*52.	*85.	10.	19.	
1976-77		.15			14.	*42.	*68.	9.	16.	
1978-1980		.10			8.	*22.	*35.	5.	9.	
1981 thru 1987 Topps, Fleer or Donrus Specify Year & Company		.10			5. Per Yr.	*14. Per Yr.	*20. Per Yr.	3.	6.	
1984 DONRUS		.25		12.	24.	*70.	*110.			

SPECIAL IN VG CONDITION-POSTPAID

250	58-62	60.00
500	58-62	115.00
250	60-69	45.00
500	60-69	90.00
1000	60-69	175.00
250	70-79	20.00
500	70-79	40.00
1000	70-79	75.00
250	80-84	10.00
500	80-84	17.00
1000	80-84	30.00

*These lots are all different.

Special 1 Different from each year 1950-86 from above $30.00 postpaid.
Special 100 Different from each year 1956-86 from above $725.00 postpaid.
Special 10 Different from each year 1956-86 from above $75.00 postpaid.
All lot groups are my choice only.

All assorted lots will contain as many different as possible.
Please list alternates whenever possible.
Send your want list and I will fill them at the above price for commons. High numbers, specials, scarce series, and stars extra.

Minimum order $7.50 - Postage and handling .50 per 100 cards (minimum $1.75)

Have thousands of star and super star cards. Call or send for star list.
Also interested in purchasing your collection.
*Groups include various years of my choice.

SETS AVAILABLE
POSTAGE 2.50 PER SET

1979 Topps	$95.00
1980 Topps	90.00
1981 Topps	55.00
1981 Topps	17.00
1981 Fleer	14.00
1982 Topps	55.00
1982 Donrus	14.00
1983 Topps	55.00
1984 Topps	55.00
1985 Topps	55.00
1986 Topps	25.00
1987 Topps	18.00

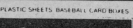

San Diego Sports Collectibles

THE WEST COAST'S LARGEST BASEBALL CARD STORE

SUPER CARD LOTS

We have good quantities of all lots listed below. This is an excellent way of obtaining major portions of sets at low prices.

1. TOPPS 1959-1965
1500 different cards, approximately 80 each year, including: Aaron, Allen, Alston, Aparicio, Banks, Bauer, Boyer, Brock, Bunning, Burdette, Carew, Cash, Cepeda, Clemente, Dark, Davis, Drysdale, Face, Flood, Ford, Gibson, Gilliam, Groat, Hodges, Houk, E. Howard, F. Howard, Jenkins, John, Kaat, Kaline, Killebrew, Koufax, Kubek, Kuenn, Larsen, Lopez, Mantle, Maris, Martin, Mathews, Mays, Mazeroski, McCovey, McGraw, McLain, Minoso, Moon, Morgan, Murcer, Niekro, Oliva, Perez, Perry, Pierce, Piniella, Piersall, Pinson, Podres, Powell, B. Robby, F. Robby, Rose, Santo, Schoendienst, Score, Shantz, Skowron, Spahn, Stargell, Staub, Sutton, Tiant, Torre, Turley, Virdon, Wilhelm, Wills, Zimmer and Yaz. Very Good to Excellent condition.
$295.00

2. TOPPS 1959-1965
150 different cards including Clemente, Mays, Aaron, Drysdale, Ford, Killebrew, Wynn, Hodges, Spahn, Banks, Mathews, Roberts, Aparicio, Fox, Minoso and many more. Very Good to Excellent condition.
$89.00

3. TOPPS 1964-1974
150 different cards including: Aaron, Banks, Clemente, Drysdale, Ford, Gibson, Hodges, Kaline, Killebrew, Koufax, Mathews, Mays, McCovey, Morgan, Roberts, F. Robby, Aparicio, Hunter and many more. Very Good to Excellent condition.
$89.00

4. TOPPS 1976-1983
200 different; including Rose, Henderson, Bench, Carlton, Schmidt, Lynn, Rice, Winfield, Garvey, Palmer, Brett, Seaver, Jackson, Carew, Murphy, Murray, Guerrero, Perry, Hunter, Stargell, Parker, Foster, Jenkins, McCovey, Sutton, Bowa, Tiant, Cooper, Blue. Excellent to Mint condition.**$39.00**

5. TOPPS/FLEER/DONRUSS 1981-1987
800 assorted including Valenzuela, Rose, Henderson, Schmidt, Carlton, Seaver, Bench, Murphy, Carew, Ripken, Palmer, Brett, Winfield, Rice, Jackson, Guerrero, Garvey, Carter, Morgan, Perry, Dawson, Murray, Lynn, Strawberry, and Yaz. Excellent to Mint condition.**$19.95**

COMPLETE MINT SETS

Donruss Highlights 1986 (60)	$ 8.95	Star Co. Garvey (36)	$ 6.95
Donruss Highlights 1985 (60)	34.50	Star Co. Strawberry (36)	6.95
Sportflic Rookies 1986 (50)	13.95	Star Co. Yaz (24)	6.95
Topps 1987 (792)	19.95	Star Co. Jackson (36)	6.95
Topps 1986 (792)	24.50	Star Co. Carew (36)	6.95
Topps Glossy Stars 1984 (22)	5.95	Star Co. Murphy (36)	6.95
Topps Glossy Stars 1985 (22)	4.95	Star Co. Seaver (24)	6.95
Topps Glossy Stars 1986 (22)	3.50	Star Co. Ryan (24)	6.95
Topps Record Holders 1986 (44)	5.95	Star Co. Raines (24)	6.95
Topps Mini Set 1986 (66)	7.95	Star Co. Clemens (24)	6.95
Fleer Sluggers & Pitchers 1986 (44)	8.95	Ralston 1984 (33)	4.95
Star Co. Mattingly (24)	6.95	**FOOTBALL**	
Star Co. Canseco (15)	6.95	Topps 1985 (396)	9.95
Star Co. Joyner (15)	6.95	Topps 1984 (396)	12.95
Star Co. Rice (24)	6.95	Topps 1983 (396)	9.95
Star Co. Boggs (24)	6.95	Topps 1982 (528)	10.95
Star Co. Brett (24)	6.95	Topps 1981 (528)	12.95

San Diego Sports Collectibles

THE WEST COAST'S LARGEST BASEBALL CARD STORE

TOPPS HALL OF FAMER LOTS

Over the years we have built a large inventory of these popular **regular issue** Topps cards. All cards are in very good condition or better and are **guaranteed** originals. All cards are our choice but we will do our best to send your **three** preferences.

PLAYER	YEARS	3 DIFF.	PLAYER	YEARS	3 DIFF.	PLAYER	YEARS	3 DIFF.
Henry Aaron	1962-1967	$21.95	Willie Mays	1969-1973	14.95	Pete Rose	1966-1969	59.00
Henry Aaron	1968-1972	14.95	Willie McCovey	1967-1971	6.95	Pete Rose	1977-1980	8.25
Henry Aaron	1973-1976	9.95	Willie McCovey	1972-1976	2.95	Nolan Ryan	1973-1976	3.75
Ernie Banks	1966-1971	8.95	Willie McCovey	1977-1980	1.95	Nolan Ryan	1977-1980	1.95
Johnny Bench	1973-1976	6.50	Joe Morgan	1966-1970	3.75	Mike Schmidt	1977-1980	5.50
Johnny Bench	1977-1980	3.25	Joe Morgan	1971-1975	2.50	Mike Schmidt	1981-1986	1.45
Lou Brock	1966-1971	8.00	Joe Morgan	1976-1980	1.50	Tom Seaver	1968-1970	19.95
Lou Brock	1972-1977	3.00	Thurman Munson	1976-1979	2.50	Tom Seaver	1976-1980	2.95
Rod Carew	1968-1971	14.95	Jim Palmer	1967-1971	8.95	Willie Stargell	1964-1969	7.95
Rod Carew	1973-1977	6.50	Jim Palmer	1972-1976	2.25	Willie Stargell	1970-1975	2.95
Rod Carew	1978-1980	3.00	Jim Palmer	1977-1980	1.75	Willie Stargell	1976-1980	1.75
Steve Carlton	1967-1970	24.95	Gaylord Perry	1967-1971	5.75	Dave Winfield	1975-1977	4.95
Steve Carlton	1971-1976	8.25	Gaylord Perry	1972-1976	2.75	Dave Winfield	1978-1980	2.95
Steve Carlton	1977-1980	2.75	Gaylord Perry	1977-1980	1.45	Dave Winfield	1981-1986	1.45
Roberto Clemente	1965-1968	18.25	Robin Roberts	1959-1965	4.75	Early Wynn	1959-1962	6.25
Roberto Clemente	1968-1973	12.95	Brooks Robinson	1964-1969	7.50	Carl Yastrzemski	1964-1969	34.50
Don Drysdale	1959-1964	9.95	Brooks Robinson	1970-1973	5.95	Carl Yastrzemski	1970-1973	12.95
Don Drysdale	1965-1969	7.25	Brooks Robinson	1974-1977	2.50	Carl Yastrzemski	1974-1977	7.75
Steve Garvey	1973-1976	7.95	Frank Robinson	1959-1964	10.50	Carl Yastrzemski	1978-1980	2.95
Steve Garvey	1977-1980	4.50	Frank Robinson	1965-1971	8.50	Robin Yount	1976-1980	2.75
Bob Gibson	1965-1969	6.25	Frank Robinson	1972-1975	3.25			
Bob Gibson	1970-1975	3.95						
Gil Hodges	1959-1966	6.25						
Gil Hodges	1967-1972	2.95						
Catfish Hunter	1966-1970	3.95						
Catfish Hunter	1971-1975	1.95						
Catfish Hunter	1976-1979	1.00						
Reggie Jackson	1971-1975	9.50						
Reggie Jackson	1976-1980	3.70						
Al Kaline	1964-1969	6.00						
Al Kaline	1971-1975	3.75						
Harmon Killebrew	1960-1965	8.25						
Harmon Killebrew	1966-1971	5.95						
Harmon Killebrew	1972-1975	2.20						
Sandy Koufax	1959-1966	24.95						
Fred Lynn	1976-1980	2.25						
Mickey Mantle	1959-1963	99.00						
Mickey Mantle	1964-1969	75.00						
Juan Marichal	1962-1966	6.50						
Juan Marichal	1967-1970	5.50						
Juan Marichal	1971-1974	2.75						
Ed Mathews	1959-1964	6.95						
Ed Mathews	1965-1968	5.50						
Willie Mays	1959-1963	29.75						
Willie Mays	1964-1968	24.50						

San Diego Sports Collectibles Catalogue

MICKEY MANTLE

FREE!

Please send send stamps to receive a listing of thousands of old baseball cards from the early 1900's to present. Includes Topps Sets, Singles and Stars as well as Bowman, Fleer, Donruss, Goudey, Tobacco, Leaf and many other regional and miscellaneous issues. Also featured are Football Cards and Sports Collectibles of all types. Issued 3 times yearly.

MAIL ORDER INSTRUCTIONS

CREDIT CARD HOLDERS FOR INSTANT SERVICE MON.-SAT. Call Toll Free 1-800-621-0852 Ext. 561 orders only. All other inquiries call (619) 282-0143.

SHIPPING & INSURANCE

1-25 cards	$1.25
26-100 cards	2.50
101-180 cards	4.95
801 or more	9.95

Complete Sets $2.50
California residents please add 6% sales tax.

Send Payment To
S.D. Sports Collectibles
5043 Westminster Terr., Dept. V
San Diego, CA 92116

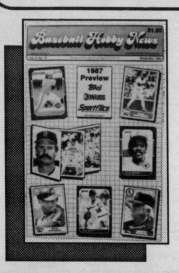

See for yourself why baseball card collectors have proclaimed Baseball Hobby News the bible of their hobby. Take advantage of this special introductory offer for only $1.00 per issue. The cover price of each monthly issue is $1.95, so you are being offered a substantial savings. You can also add $3.00 to our regular rates and receive three extra issues.

Each issue of Baseball Hobby News contains: Rookies and Superstars Price Poll •Investing tips •News about Topps, Fleer and Donruss cards •Calendar of baseball card shows •How to start or build a collection •Nostalgic stories about retired players •Articles about collectors •How to sell your cards or buy more •Player autograph address lists •Display advertising and classifieds from hundreds of leading dealers.

FIRST BASE

We have a large mail order catalog; just send us $2.00 for postage and handling for the catalog. Below is a partial list of special offers we have for sale. Include $2.00 for postage and handling per order. All inquiries require a self-addressed stamped envelope. We have most Topps, Donruss, Fleer, etc. Sets and Singles for sale. These are listed in our catalog that we will send you. Better yet, why don't you stop in some time and see for yourself.

COMPLETE SETS

1986 Rangers Performance (28)	6.95
1985 Rangers Performance (28)	6.95
1984 Rangers Jarvis (28)	5.95
1983 Rangers Affiliated (28)	4.95
1984 Ralston Baseball (33)	4.95
1983 Seven-Eleven 3D Coins (12)	12.95
1983 Fleer Stamps (224)	3.95
1983 Seven-Eleven 3D Coins (12)	12.95
1982 K-Mart Baseball (33)	1.50
1981 Topps 5x7 Dodgers/Angels (18)	6.95
1978 Tucson Toros (24)	3.95
1980 Tucson Toros (24)	3.95
1983 Police Cowboys (28)	9.95
1981 Police Cowboys (14)	7.95
1980 Police Cowboys (14)	9.95
1979 Police Cowboys (15)	13.95
1986 McDonalds Cowboys (25)	9.95
1986 McDonalds All-Stars (24)	4.95

BASEBALL CARD LOTS

1958 Topps 25 diff (f-vg)	7.95
1959 Topps 25 diff (f-vg)	6.95
1960 Topps 25 diff (f-vg)	4.95
1961 Topps 25 diff (f-vg)	4.50
1962 Topps 25 diff (f-vg)	4.50
1963 Topps 25 diff (f-vg)	3.95
1964 Topps 25 diff (f-vg)	3.50
1965 Topps 25 diff (f-vg)	3.50
1966 Topps 25 diff (f-vg)	2.95
1967 Topps 25 diff (f-vg)	2.95
1968 Topps 25 diff (f-vg)	2.95
1969 Topps 25 diff (f-vg)	2.95
1970 Topps 25 diff (f-vg)	2.50
1971 Topps 25 diff (f-vg)	2.25
1972 Topps 25 diff (f-vg)	1.95
1973 Topps 25 diff (f-vg)	1.75
1974 Topps 25 diff (f-vg)	1.75

SPECIAL OFFERS

#1: Type Set: One card from each year of Topps baseball 1952 through 1987, our choice of cards, 36 cards for 12.95.

#2: Baseball cigarette card from 1910, our choice 5.95.

#3: 500 assorted (mostly different) baseball cards from 1978 to 1984 in excellent condition for 19.95.

#4: Dallas Cowboy Weekly: 20 different back issues, our choice, for 14.95. We also have most single issues from 1977 to date available from 1.00 to 2.00 each. Send your want list. Some older issues also available.

#5: Poster: Robert Redford as "The Natural" plus free Bucky Dent poster, 6.95 postpaid.

#6: 1978 Topps baseball cards 50 different in excellent to mint condition, 3.95.

#7: 1979 Topps baseball cards 50 different in excellent to mint condition including some stars, 3.95.

#8: 1980 Topps baseball cards 50 different in excellent to mint condition including some stars, 3.95.

#9: 1981 Topps baseball cards 50 different in excellent to mint condition including some stars, 3.95.

#10: 89 different 1984-85 Topps hockey cards in excellent to mint condition including some stars, 2.95.

#11: 66 different 1981-82 Topps basketball cards in excellent to mint condition including stars, 3.95.

#12: 115 different 1983 Topps football cards in excellent to mint condition including many stars, 2.95.

#13: Super Bowl XX game program, 5.00.

#14: 1979 Scottsdale Dodge Arizona Convention postcard set of 9 including Jocko Conlon, Charlie Grimm, etc. for 3.50.

#15: Dallas Cowboy Media Guide (not issued to the public): 1986 edition 5.00, 1985 edition 5.00. Dallas Cowboy Bluebook: 1986 edition 13.95, 1985 edition 13.95.

FIRST BASE

231 Webb Chapel Village
Dallas, Texas 75229
(214) 243-5271

COMPLETE MINT

BASEBALL CARD SETS

1987 TOPPS (792)	$22.00
1987 FLEER (660 + WORLD SERIES)	$28.00
1987 DONRUSS (660)	P.O.R.
1987 SPORTFLICS (200 + TRIVIA)	$38.00
1987 SPORTFLICS (26 + 5 ROOKIES)	$12.00
1987 TOPPS GLOSSY ALL-STAR (22)	$5.00
1987 DONRUSS DIAMOND KINGS 5 × 7	$9.00
1987 DONRUSS/LEAF CANADIAN (264)	$14.00
1986 TOPPS (792)	$24.00
1986 FLEER (660)	$28.00
1986 DONRUSS (660)	P.O.R.
1986 TOPPS TRADED (132)	$14.00
1986 FLEER UPDATE (132)	$16.00
1986 DONRUSS ROOKIES (56)	$22.00
1986 SPORTFLICS ROOKIES (50)	$15.00
1986 DONRUSS HIGHLIGHTS (56)	$10.00
1986 TOPPS GLOSSY ALL-STAR (22)	$5.00
1986 TOPPS GLOSSY MINIS (66)	$7.00
1986 TOPPS SUPERS (5 × 7) (60)	$8.00
1986 DONRUSS ALL-STARS (60)	$5.00
1986 DONRUSS ALL-STARS POP-UPS (18)	$9.00
1986 DONRUSS DIAMOND KINGS (5 × 7) (28)	$14.00
1986 DONRUSS/LEAF CANADIAN (264)	$12.00
1986 FLEER GLOSSY MINIATURES (120)	$18.00
1986 SPORTFLICS DECADE GREATS (75)	$60.00
1985 TOPPS (792)	$13.00
1985 TOPPS TRADED (132)	$14.00
1985 FLEER UPDATED (132)	

1985 TOPPS GLOSSY ALL-STAR (22)	$6.00
1985 TOPPS GLOSSIES (40)	$12.00
1985 TOPPS PETE ROSE SET (120)	$16.00
1985 TOPPS HOME RUN KINGS (33)	$5.00
1985 TOPPS DONRUSS DIAMOND KINGS (5 × 7) (28)	$8.00
1985 DONRUSS HIGHLIGHTS (56)	$28.00
1984 TOPPS GLOSSY ALL-STAR (22)	$6.00
1984 O.P.C. (396)	$35.00
1984 TOPPS (792)	$70.00
1982 TOPPS TRADED (132)	$20.00
1982 TOPPS STICKERS (260 + ALBUM)	$10.00
1982 FLEER STAMPS (Box of 600 unopened)	$10.00
1981 TOPPS STICKERS (262 + ALBUM)	$10.00
1990 TOPPS SUPERS (60 - gray backs)	$8.00

SPORTFLICS 4 1/2" MAGIC MOTION DISCS
Mickey Mantle, Wade Boggs, Roger Clemens, Pete Rose,
Jose Canseco, Bo Jackson, Mike Schmidt, Gary Carter
$6.00 each or all 8 for $40.00

BILL DODGE
P.O. 40154
Bay Village, OH 44140

CLASSIFIED ADVERTISING

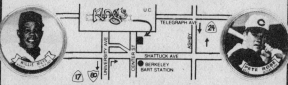

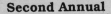

COMPLETE SETS FOR SALE (NR MT-MT)

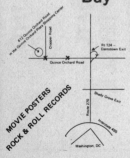

$2.50

BASEBALL CARD
MONTHLY

FLEER
ALL
STAR
TEAM

Dwight Gooden
METS • RIGHT HAND PITCHER

1986 Cards Here!

Current
Price Guide

Who's Hot
& Who's Not

Now! Get
BECKETT
BASEBALL
CARD
MONTHLY
for up to
½ OFF
the cover price!

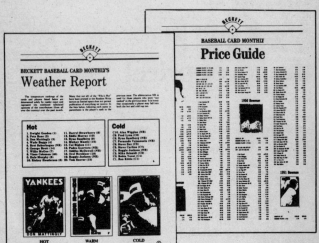